CORPORATE FINANCE

First Canadian Edition

CORPORATE FINANCE

Stephen A. Ross
Yale University

Randolph W. Westerfield
University of Southern California

Jeffrey F. Jaffe
The Wharton School
University of Pennsylvania

Gordon S. Roberts
York University

Represented in Canada by:

**Times Mirror
Professional Publishing Ltd.**

IRWIN

Toronto • Chicago • Bogotá • Boston • Buenos Aires
Caracas • London • Madrid • Mexico City • Sydney

*To our parents, family, and friends
with love and gratitude*

IRWIN
Concerned About Our Environment
    In recognition of the fact that our company is a large end-user of
fragile yet replenishable resources, we at IRWIN can assure you that
every effort is made to meet or exceed Environmental Protection Agency (EPA)
recommendations and requirements for a "greener" workplace.
    To preserve these natural assets, a number of environmental policies, both
companywide and department-specific, have been implemented. From the use
of 50% recycled paper in our textbooks to the printing of promotional materials
with recycled stock and soy inks to our office paper recycling program, we are
committed to reducing waste and replacing environmentally unsafe products
with safer alternatives.

Sponsoring editor: Evelyn Veitch
Product manager: Murray Moman
Project editor: Karen M. Smith
Designer: Larry J. Cope
Cover designer: Joshua Paul Carr
Cover photographer: Westlight, Inc.
Art coordinator: Heather Burbridge
Compositor: Carlisle Communications, Ltd.
Typeface: 10/12 Times Roman
Printer: R. R. Donnelley & Sons Company

Library of Congress Catalog Card No. 94-79192
ISBN 0-256-15491-0

Printed in the United States of America
 2 3 4 5 6 7 8 9 0 DO 2 1 0 9 8 7 6

ABOUT THE AUTHORS

Stephen A. Ross holds the position of Sterling Professor of Economics and Finance, Yale University. One of the most widely published authors in finance and economics, Professor Ross is recognized for his work in developing the Arbitrage Pricing Theory. He has also made substantial contributions to the discipline through his research in signalling, agency theory, options, and the theory of the term structure of interest rates. Previously the president of the American Finance Association, he serves as an associate editor of the *Journal of Finance* and the *Journal of Economic Theory.* He is co-chairman of Roll and Ross Asset Management Corporation.

Randolph W. Westerfield is Chairman of the Finance and Business Economics Department and Charles B. Thornton Professor of Finance at the University of Southern California. At the Wharton School, University of Pennsylvania, the Student Committee on Undergraduate Teaching Evaluation repeatedly awarded him the highest score for teaching undergraduate finance. His research interests are in corporate financial policy, investment management and analysis, mergers and acquisitions, and pension fund management. Dr. Westerfield has been a consultant to a number of corporations and government organizations. He is Associate Editor of the *Journal of Banking and Finance* and the *Financial Review.*

Jeffrey F. Jaffe has been a frequent contributor to finance and economic literature. His best known work concerns insider trading. He has also made contributions concerning initial public offerings, regulation of utilities, the behavior of marketmakers, the fluctuation of gold prices, the theoretical effect of inflation on the interest rate, the empirical effect of inflation on capital asset prices, the relationship between small capitalization stocks and the January effect, and the capital structure decision.

Gordon S. Roberts is Director, Financial Services Program, and Canadian Imperial Bank of Commerce Professor of Finance, at York University. His extensive teaching experience includes finance classes for undergraduate and MBA students, managers, and bankers under the auspices of the Institute of Canadian Bankers. Professor Roberts conducts research on duration models for bond portfolio management, corporate finance and banking. He has served on the editorial boards of *The Financial Review, Journal of Financial Research, Canadian Investment Review* and *Canadian Journal of Administrative Sciences.*

PREFACE

The teaching and the practice of corporate finance in Canada have become more challenging than ever before. The last 15 years have seen fundamental changes in financial markets and financial instruments. Scarcely a day goes by without an announcement in the financial press about such matters as takeovers, financial restructuring, and leveraged buyouts. Both the theory and practice of corporate finance have been moving ahead with uncommon speed, and our teaching must keep pace.

These developments place new burdens on the teaching of corporate finance. On one hand, the changing world of finance makes it more difficult to keep materials up to date. On the other, the teacher must distinguish the permanent from the temporary and avoid the temptation to follow fads. Our solution to this problem is to emphasize the modern fundamentals of the theory of finance and to make the theory come to life with contemporary, Canadian examples. All too often the beginning student views corporate finance as a collection of unrelated topics that are unified largely because they are bound together between the covers of one book. Our aim is to present corporate finance as the working of a small number of integrated and powerful intuitions.

The Intended Audience of This Book

This book has been written for the introductory courses in corporate finance at the MBA level and for intermediate courses in many undergraduate programs. Some instructors will find our text appropriate for the introductory course at the undergraduate level as well.

We assume that most students either will have taken or will be concurrently enrolled in courses in accounting, statistics, and economics. This exposure will help students understand some of the more difficult material. However, the book is self-contained, and a prior knowledge of these areas is not essential. The only mathematics prerequisite is basic algebra.

Coverage

Corporate Finance, First Canadian Edition contains innovative coverage on a wide variety of topics. For example, Chapter 8, Strategy and Analysis in Using Net Present Value presents approaches for identifying sources of positive net present value. Chapter 30, Financial Distress, describes financial distress and the restructuring decisions that financially distressed firms must make in the 1990s. The chapter discusses recent changes in Canadian laws such as the Bankruptcy and Insolvency Act (1993) that have encouraged private workouts instead of liquidations. Chapter 19, on issuing equity securities, contains a modern, up-to-date discussion of IPOs and the costs of going public in Canada.

This is just a sampling. Because *Corporate Finance* is not a "me-too" book, we have taken a very close look at what is likely to be relevant in the second half of the 1990s. Because we are writing first for the student (as opposed to the instructor) we have opted for detailed explanation of key topics over maximizing the number of secondary issues covered.

Clearly, there is no topic in finance more important than risk and return, and many new developments have occurred in this area. We incorporate these developments in four chapters: Chapter 9, Capital Market Theory: An Overview; Chapter 10, Return and Risk: The Capital Asset Pricing Model (CAPM); Chapter 11, An Alternative View of Risk and Return: The Arbitrage Pricing Theory; and Chapter 12, Risk, Return, and Capital Budgeting.

Important features include material in Chapter 9 that provides a complete overview of risk and return. This chapter is self-contained and allows instructors to bypass Chapters 10 and 11 if they choose. Many instructors find this desirable if their students have had prior exposure to risk concepts or if the material is not needed. Chapter 10 is a self-contained chapter on the CAPM, and Chapter 11 remains a self-contained treatment of the Arbitrage Pricing Theory.

Almost every firm must make a number of key financial decisions during its life. The text identifies many of these decisions and how they were made by well-known Canadian and U.S. firms. For example, we illustrate the discussion of financial distress with material on Olympia & York.

Attention to Pedagogy

We see three keys to good pedagogy in a corporate finance text: (1) extensive examples, questions, and problems; (2) consistency in the level of difficulty; and (3) conceptual coherence.

There is room for both easy and difficult textbooks in corporate finance. Of course, good textbooks should not shift haphazardly from difficult to easy, and vice versa. Our objective is to write a text that is consistently moderate in difficulty. Our book is designed for two audiences—the MBA and the intermediate undergraduate. Therefore our objective has been to write a book with sufficient flexibility to be taught to both of these audiences. We have written the core material on value, risk, capital budgeting, and capital structure at a consistently moderate level of difficulty. Some chapters can be omitted without loss of continuity for a more introductory-level treatment. More specialized chapters, such as those on options, warrants and convertibles, and mergers and acquisitions, may be covered in more advanced courses.

We have found that many textbooks lack conceptual coherence. We attempt to use consistently the intuitions of arbitrage, net present value, efficient markets, and options throughout the book. However, we have also attempted to enliven some of the conceptual material by including the recent results of modern financial research. This research has at times raised more questions than answers; therefore we have presented some of the puzzles, anomalies, and unresolved questions of corporate finance. We hope that this will pique the curiosity of the students and motivate them to work harder to grasp the complexities of modern corporate finance.

Study Features

Getting the theory and concepts current and up-to-date is only one phase of developing a corporate finance text. To be an effective teaching tool, the text must present the theory and concepts in a coherent way that can be easily learned. With this is mind, we have included several study features:

1. *Concept Questions.* After each major section in a chapter is a unique learning tool called "Concept Questions." Concept Questions point to essential material and allow students to test their recall and comprehension periodically.
2. *Key Terms.* Students will note that important words are highlighted in boldface type the first time they appear. They are also listed at the end of the chapter along with the page number on which they first appear. New words appear in *italics* when they are first mentioned. Both key terms and new words are defined in the glossary at the end of the text.
3. *Demonstration Problems.* Throughout the text we have provided worked-out examples to give students a clear understanding of the logic and structure of the solution process.
4. *Boxed Material.* Interesting concepts and topics are examined and expanded in boxes.
5. *Equations.* Key equations are highlighted for easy reference.
6. *Problem Sets.* These are graded for difficulty, moving from easier problems intended to build confidence and skill to more difficult problems designed to challenge the enthusiastic student. Problems have been grouped according to the concepts they test on. Additionally, we have tried to make the problems in the critical "concept" chapters, such as those on value, risk, and capital structure, especially challenging and interesting. We provide answers to selected problems at the end of the book.
7. *Enumerated Chapter Summaries.* At the end of each chapter a numbered summary provides a quick review of key concepts in the chapter.
8. *Suggested Readings.* Each chapter is followed by a short, annotated list of books and articles to which interested students can refer for additional information.

Supplements

As with the text, developing supplements of extraordinary quality and utility was the primary objective. Each component in the supplements package underwent extensive review and revision.

Instructor's Manual

Part I of the Instructor's Manual contains lecture notes with ideas and comments on each chapter. Also featured are selected equations along with handouts and transparencies to accompany lectures. Part II of the Instructor's Manual consists of detailed answers to Concept Questions and Text Problems.

Software

Provided free to adopters, *Spreadsheet Models for Corporate Finance* consists of 20 Lotus 1-2-3 spreadsheets. Developed by Delvin D. Hawley of the University of Mississippi, the software provides additional review of concepts and refines students' spreadsheet techniques and skills for constructing simple models.

Acetates

Over 100 acetates provide numerous worked-out solutions to problems and highlight key charts and tables.

Acknowledgments

Many people have contributed their time and expertise to the development and writing of this text. We extend our thanks once again for their assistance and countless insights.

For the first Canadian Edition, we thank the following reviewers:

Iraj Fooladi, *Dalhousie University*

David Fowler, *York University*

Sumon C. Mazumdar, *McGill University*

David A. Stangeland, *University of Manitoba*

Kirk Vandezande, *Simon Fraser University*

Brice Scheschuk was the research assistant for this project, and Linda Hendry provided the solutions for the questions and problems. Lillian Brown, Lorraine Colpitts, and Rebecca Roberts provided valuable typing and editorial assistance.

Much credit must go to a first-class group of people at Irwin and Times Mirror Professional Publishing who worked on this First Canadian Edition. Especially important were Rod Banister, Publisher; Mike Junior, Publisher; and Evelyn Veitch, Sponsoring Editor. With hands-on responsibility for the present edition, Evelyn Veitch guided its development with much appreciated tact and flexibility. Finally, Milton Vacon, Times Mirror Senior Publisher's Representative, provided guidance and moral support.

Through the development of this edition, we have taken great care to discover and eliminate errors. Our goal is to provide the best Canadian textbook available on this subject. Please write and tell us how to make this a better text. Forward your comments to:

Professor Gordon S. Roberts
Faculty of Administrative Studies, Finance Area
4700 Keele Street
York University
North York, Ontario M3J 1R7

Stephen A. Ross
Randolph W. Westerfield
Jeffrey F. Jaffe
Gordon S. Roberts

NOTE TO THE STUDENT

"Why are textbook prices so high?"

This is, by far, the most frequently-asked question heard in the publishing industry. There are many factors that influence the price of your new textbook. Here are just a few:

- **Author Royalties:** Authors are paid based on a percentage of new book sales and **do not** receive royalties on the sale of a used book. They are also deprived of their rightful royalties when their books are illegally photocopied.

- **The Cost of Instructor Support Materials:** Your instructor may be making use of teaching supplements, many of which are provided by the publisher. Teaching supplements include videos, colour transparencies, instructor's manuals, software, computerized testing materials and more. These supplements are designed as part of a learning package to enhance your educational experience.

- **Developmental Costs:** These are costs associated with the extensive development of your textbook. Expenses include permissions fees, manuscript review costs, artwork, typesetting, printing and binding costs, and more.

- **Marketing Costs:** Instructors need to be made aware of new textbooks. Marketing costs include academic conventions, remuneration of the publisher's representatives, promotional advertising pieces, and the provision of instructor's examination copies.

- **Book Store Markups:** In order to stay in business, your local book store must cover its costs. A textbook is a commodity, just like any other item your bookstore may sell, and bookstores are the most effective way to get the textbook from the publisher to you.

- **Publisher Profits:** In order to continue to supply students with quality textbooks, publishers must make a profit to stay in business. Like the authors, publishers **do not** receive any compensation from the sale of a used book or the illegal photocopying of their textbooks.

We at Irwin Dorsey/Times Mirror Professional Publishing hope you will find this information useful and that it addresses some of your concerns. We also thank you for your purchase of this new textbook. If you have any questions that we can answer, please write to us at:

Times Mirror Professional Publishing
College Division
130 Flaska Drive
Markham, Ontario   L6G 1B8

CONTENTS IN BRIEF

CONTENTS

PART ONE
OVERVIEW

To engage in business, the financial managers of a corporation must find answers to three kinds of important questions. First, what long-term investments should the firm take on? This is the capital budgeting decision. Second, how can cash be raised for the required investments? We call this the financing decision. Third, what short-term investments should the firm take on and how should they be financed? These decisions involve short-term finance.

In Chapter 1 we discuss these important questions, briefly introducing the basic ideas of this book and describing the nature of the modern corporation and why it has emerged as the leading form of the business firm. Using a perspective that views the firm as a set of contracts, the chapter discusses the goals of the modern corporation. Though the goals of shareholders and managers may not always be the same, conflicts usually will be resolved in favor of the shareholders. Finally, the chapter reviews some salient features of modern financial markets. This preliminary material will be familiar to students who have some background in accounting, finance, and economics.

Chapter 2 examines the basic accounting statements. It is review material for students with an accounting background. We describe the balance sheet and the income statement. The point of the chapter is to show the ways of converting data from accounting statements into cash flow. Understanding how to identify cash flow from accounting statements is especially important for later chapters on capital budgeting.

CHAPTER 1

Introduction to Corporate Finance

The Canadian Video Product Company designs and manufactures popular software for video game consoles. The company was started in 1992, and soon thereafter its game Gadfly made the cover of *Entertainment Canada* magazine. Company sales in 1994 were over $10 million. Initially, Canadian Video Product borrowed $500,000 from the Canadian Enterprise Opportunities Agency (a venture capital lender) and put up its warehouse for collateral against the loan. Now the financial management of Canadian Video Product realizes that its initial financing was too small. In the long run Canadian Video Product would like to expand its design activity to the education and business areas. However, at present the company has a short-run cash flow problem and cannot buy even $50,000 of materials to fill its holiday orders.

Canadian Video Product's experience illustrates the basic concerns of corporate finance (discussed in Section 1.1).

1. What long-term investment strategy should a company take on?
2. How can cash be raised for the required investments?
3. How much short-term cash flow does a company need to pay its bills?

These are not the only questions of corporate finance. They are, however, among the most important questions and, taken in order, they provide a rough outline of our book.

One way that companies raise cash to finance their investment activities is by selling or "issuing" securities. The securities, sometimes called *financial instruments* or *claims,* may be roughly classified as *equity* or *debt,* loosely called *stocks* or *bonds.* The difference between equity and debt is a basic distinction in the modern theory of finance. All securities of a firm are claims that depend on or are contingent on the value of the firm.[1] In Section 1.2 we show how debt and equity securities depend on the firm's value, and we describe them as different contingent claims.

In Section 1.3 we discuss different organizational forms and the pros and cons of the decision to become a corporation.

In Section 1.4 we take a close look at the goals of the corporation and discuss why maximizing shareholder wealth is likely to be its primary goal. Throughout the rest of the book, we assume that the firm's performance depends on the value it creates for its shareholders. Shareholders are made better off when the value of their shares is increased by the firm's decisions.

---

[1]We tend to use the words *firm, company,* and *business* interchangably. However, there is a difference between a firm and a corporation. We discuss this difference in Section 1.3.

A company raises cash by issuing securities in the financial markets. In Section 1.5 we describe some of the basic features of the financial markets. Roughly speaking, there are two types of financial markets: money markets and capital markets.

Section 1.6 covers trends in financial markets and management, and the last section of this chapter (1.7) outlines the rest of the book.

1.1   What Is Corporate Finance?

Suppose you decide to start a firm to make tennis balls. To do this, you hire managers to buy raw materials, and you assemble a work force that will produce and sell finished tennis balls. In the language of finance, you make an investment in assets such as inventory, machinery, land, and labour. The amount of cash you invest in assets must be matched by an equal amount of cash raised by financing. When you begin to sell tennis balls, your firm will generate cash. This is the basis of value creation. The purpose of the firm is to create value for you, the owner. The value is reflected in the framework of the simple balance-sheet model of the firm.

The Balance-Sheet Model of the Firm

Suppose we take a financial snapshot of the firm and its activities at a single point in time. Figure 1.1, a graphic conceptualization of the balance sheet, will help introduce you to corporate finance.

Figure 1.1
The balance-sheet model of the firm

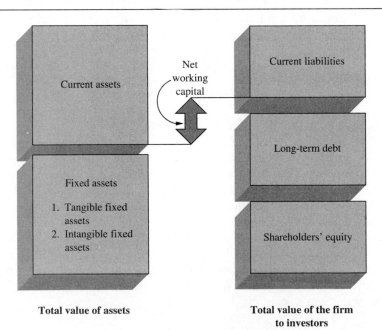

Total value of assets   **Total value of the firm to investors**

Left side: total value of assets. Right side: total value of the firm to investors, which determines how the value is distributed.

The assets of the firm are on the left side of the balance sheet. These assets can be thought of as current and fixed. *Fixed assets* are those that will last a long time, such as a building. Some fixed assets are tangible, such as machinery and equipment. Other fixed assets are intangible, such as patents, trademarks, and the quality of management. The other category of assets, *current assets,* comprises those that have short lives, such as inventory. The tennis balls that your firm has made but has not yet sold are part of its inventory. Unless you have overproduced, they will leave the firm shortly.

Before a company can invest in an asset, it must obtain financing, which means that it must raise the money to pay for the investment. The forms of financing are represented on the right side of the balance sheet. A firm will issue (sell) pieces of paper called *debt* (loan agreements) or *equity shares* (share certificates). Just as assets are classified as long-lived or short-lived, so too are liabilities. A short-term debt is called a *current liability.* Short-term debt represents loans and other obligations that must be repaid within one year. Long-term debt is debt that does not have to be repaid within one year. Shareholders' equity represents the difference between the value of the assets and the debt of the firm. In this sense it is a residual claim on the firm's assets.

From the balance-sheet model of the firm it is easy to see why finance can be thought of as the study of the following three questions:

1. In what long-lived assets should the firm invest? This question concerns the left side of the balance sheet. Of course, the type and proportions of assets the firm needs tend to be set by the nature of the business. We use the terms **capital budgeting** and *capital expenditure* to describe the process of making and managing expenditures on long-lived assets.

2. How can the firm raise cash for required capital expenditures? This question concerns the right side of the balance sheet. The answer involves the firm's **capital structure,** which represents the proportions of the firm's financing from current and long-term debt and equity.

3. How should short-term operating cash flows be managed? This question concerns the upper portion of the balance sheet. There is a mismatch between the timing of cash inflows and cash outflows during operating activities. Furthermore, the amount and timing of operating cash flows are not known with certainty. The financial managers must attempt to manage the gaps in cash flow. From an accounting perspective, short-term management of cash flow is associated with a firm's **net working capital.** Net working capital is defined as current assets minus current liabilities. From a financial perspective, the short-term cash flow problem comes from the mismatching of cash inflows and outflows. It is the subject of short-term finance.

Capital Structure

Financing arrangements determine how the value of the firm is sliced up like a pie. The persons or institutions that buy debt from the firm are called *creditors.*[2] The holders of equity shares are called *shareholders.*

---

[2] We tend to use the words *creditors, debtholders,* and *bondholders* interchangably. In later chapters we examine the differences among the kinds of creditors.

Figure 1.2
Two pie models of
the firm

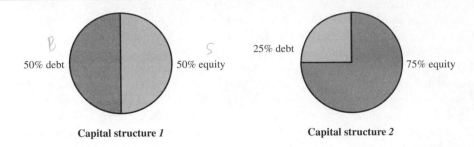

50% debt   50% equity   25% debt   75% equity

Capital structure *1*   Capital structure *2*

Sometimes it is useful to think of the firm as a pie. Initially, the size of the pie will depend on how well the firm has made its investment decisions. After a firm has made its investment decisions, it determines the value of its assets (e.g., its buildings, land, and inventories).

The firm can then determine its capital structure. It might initially have raised the cash to invest in its assets by issuing more debt than equity; now it can consider changing that mix by issuing more equity and using the proceeds to buy back some of its debt. Financing decisions like this can be made independently of the original investment decisions. The decisions to issue debt and equity affect how the pie is sliced.

The pie we are thinking of is depicted in Figure 1.2. The size of the pie is the value of the firm in the financial markets. We can write the value of the firm, V, as

$$V = B + S$$

where B is the value of the debt and S is the value of the equity. The pie diagram considers two ways of slicing the pie: 50 percent debt and 50 percent equity, and 25 percent debt and 75 percent equity. The way the pie is sliced could affect its value. If so, the goal of the financial manager will be to choose the ratio of debt to equity that makes the value of the pie—that is, the value of the firm, V—as large as it can be.

The Financial Manager

In large firms the finance activity is usually associated with a senior officer of the firm (such as a vice president of finance) and some lesser officers. Figure 1.3 depicts a general organizational structure emphasizing the finance activity within the firm. Reporting to the vice president of finance are the treasurer and controller. The treasurer is responsible for handling cash flows, deciding on capital expenditures, and making financial plans. The controller handles the accounting function, which includes taxes, cost and financial accounting, and information systems. Our discussion of corporate finance is much more relevant to the treasurer's function.

We think that a financial manger's most important job is to create value from the firm's capital budgeting, financing, and liquidity activities. How do financial managers create value?

1. The firm should try to buy assets that generate more cash than they cost.
2. The firm should sell bonds, shares, and other financial instruments that raise more cash than they cost.

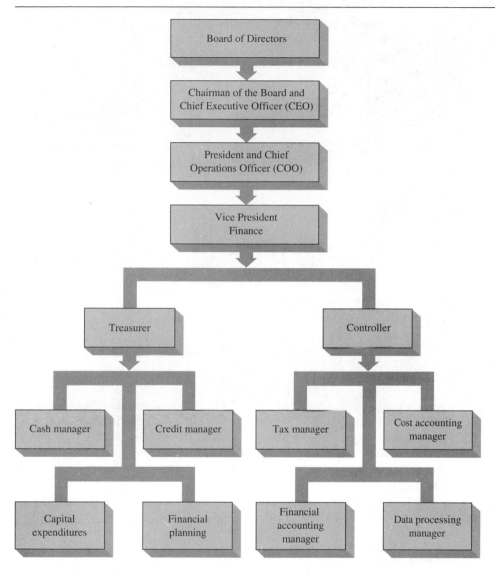

Figure 1.3
Hypothetical organization chart

Thus, the firm must create more cash flow than it uses. The cash flow paid to bondholders and shareholders of the firm should be higher than the cash flows put into the firm by the bondholders and shareholders. To see how this is done, we can trace the cash flows from the firm to the financial markets and back again.

The interplay of the firm's finance with the financial markets is illustrated in Figure 1.4. The arrows in the figure trace cash flow from the firm to the financial markets and back again. Suppose we begin with the firm's investment activities. These include generating the working capital necessary to produce and sell goods and services, and the purchase of fixed assets (*A*). To finance its investment the firm sells debt and equity shares to participants in the financial markets. The resulting cash flows

Figure 1.4
Cash flows
between the
firm and the
financial markets

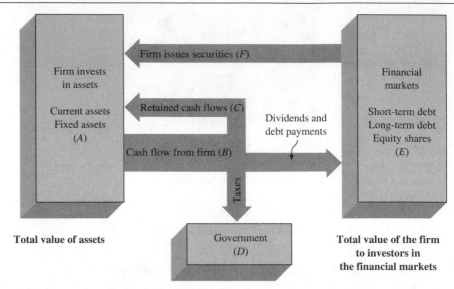

A. Firm invests in assets (capital budgeting).
B. Firms's operations generate cash flow.
C. Retained cash flows are reinvested in firm.
D. Cash is paid to government as taxes.
E. Cash is paid out to investors in the form of interest and dividends.
F. Firm issues securities to raise cash (the financing decision).

from the financial markets to the firm (*F*). This cash is invested in the investment activities of the firm (*A*) by the firm's management. The cash generated by the firm (*B*) is paid to shareholders and bondholders (*E*). Shareholders receive cash in the form of dividends; bondholders who lent funds to the firm receive interest and, when the initial loan is repaid, principal. Not all of the firm's cash is paid out. Some is retained (*C*), and some is paid to governments as taxes (*D*).

Over time, if the cash paid to shareholders and bondholders (*E*) is greater than the cash raised in the financial markets (*F*), value will be created.

Identification of Cash Flows

Unfortunately, it is not all that easy to observe cash flows directly. Much of the information we obtain is in the form of accounting statements, and much of the work of financial analysis is to extract cash flow information from accounting statements. The following example illustrates how this is done.

▪ *Example*

The Midland Company refines and trades gold. At the end of the year it sold some gold for $1 million. The company had acquired the gold for $900,000 at the beginning of the year. The company paid cash for the gold when it was purchased. Unfortunately, it has yet to collect from the customer to whom the gold was sold. The following is a standard accounting of Midland's financial circumstances at year-end:

THE MIDLAND COMPANY
Accounting View
Income Statement
Year Ended December 31

Sales	$1,000,000
Costs	− 900,000
Profit	$ 100,000

By generally accepted accounting principles (GAAP), the sale is recorded even though the customer has yet to pay. It is assumed that the customer will pay soon. From the accounting perspective, Midland seems to be profitable. The perspective of corporate finance is different. It focuses on cash flows:

THE MIDLAND COMPANY
Corporate Finance View
Income Statement
Year Ended December 31

Cash inflow	0
Cash outflow	−$900,000
	−$900,000

The perspective of corporate finance examines whether cash flows are being created by the gold trading operations of Midland. Value creation depends on cash flows. For Midland, value creation depends on whether and when it actually receives $1 million. ■

Timing of Cash Flows

The value of an investment made by the firm depends on the timing of cash flows. One of the most important assumptions of finance is that individuals prefer to receive cash flows earlier rather than later. One dollar received today is worth more than one dollar received next year. This time preference plays a role in stock and bond prices.

■ *Example*

The Midland Company is attempting to choose between two proposals for new products. Both proposals will provide cash flows over a four-year period and will initially cost $10,000. The cash flows from the proposals are as follows:

Year	New product A	New product B
1	0	$ 4,000
2	0	4,000
3	0	4,000
4	$20,000	4,000
Total	$20,000	$16,000

At first it appears that new product A would be best. However, the cash flows from proposal B come earlier than those of A. Without more information we cannot decide which set of cash flows would create greater value. It depends on whether the value of getting cash from B up front outweighs the extra total cash from A. Bond and stock prices reflect this preference for earlier cash, and we will see how to use them to decide between A and B.

Risk of Cash Flows

The firm must consider risk. The amount and timing of cash flows are not usually known with certainty. Most investors have an aversion to risk.

■ *Example*

The Midland Company is considering expanding operations overseas. It is evaluating Europe and Japan as possible sites. Europe is considered to be relatively safe, whereas Japan is seen as very risky. In both cases the company would close down operations after one year.

After doing a complete financial analysis, Midland has come up with the following cash flows of the alternative plans for expansion under three equally likely scenarios: pessimistic, most likely, and optimistic:

	Pessimistic	Most likely	Optimistic
Europe	$75,000	$100,000	$125,000
Japan	0	150,000	200,000

If we ignore the pessimistic scenario, perhaps Japan is the better alternative. When we take the pessimistic scenario into account, the choice is unclear. Japan appears to be riskier, but it also offers a higher expected level of cash flow. What is risk and how can it be defined? We must try to answer this important question. Corporate finance cannot avoid coping with risky alternatives, and much of our book is devoted to developing methods for evaluating risky opportunities. ■

CONCEPT QUESTIONS

- ■ What are three basic questions of corporate finance?
- ■ Describe capital structure.
- ■ List three reasons why value creation is difficult.

1.2   Corporate Securities as Contingent Claims on Total Firm Value

What is the essential difference between debt and equity? The answer can be found by thinking about what happens to the payoffs to debt and equity when the value of the firm changes.

The basic feature of debt is that it is a promise by the borrowing firm to repay a fixed dollar amount by a certain date.

■ *Example*

The Canadian Corporation promises to pay $100 to the True North Insurance Company at the end of one year. This is a debt of the Canadian Corporation. Holders of the Canadian Corporation's debt will receive $100 if the value of the Canadian Corporation's assets is equal to or more than $100 at the end of the year.

Formally, the debtholders have been promised an amount F at the end of the year. If the value of the firm, X, is equal to or greater than F at year end, debtholders will get

contingency → a chance or possible event

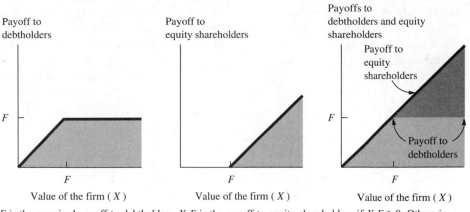

Figure 1.5
Debt and equity as
contingent claims

F is the promised payoff to debtholders. X-F is the payoff to equity shareholders if X-F >0. Otherwise the payoff is 0.

F. Of course, if the firm does not have enough to pay off the promised amount, the firm will be "broke." It may be forced to liquidate its assets for whatever they are worth, and bondholders will receive X. Mathematically this means that the debtholders have a claim to X or F, whichever is smaller. Figure 1.5 illustrates the general nature of the payoff structure to debtholders.

Suppose at year end the Canadian Corporation's value is $100. The firm has promised to pay the True North Insurance Company $100, so the debtholders will get $100.

Now suppose the Canadian Corporation's value is $200 at year end and the debtholders are promised $100. How much will the debtholders receive? It should be clear that they will receive the same amount as when the Canadian Corporation was worth $100.

Suppose the firm's value is $75 at year end and debtholders are promised $100. How much will the debtholders receive? In this case the debtholders will get $75. ∎

The shareholders' claim on firm value at the end of the period is the amount that remains after the debtholders are paid. Of course, shareholders get nothing if the firm's value is equal to or less than the amount promised to the debtholders.

∎ *Example*

The Canadian Corporation will sell its assets for $200 at year end. The firm has promised to pay the insurance company $100 at that time. The shareholders will get the residual value of $100. ∎

Algebraically, the shareholders' claim is $X - F$ if $X > F$ and zero if $X \leq F$. This is depicted in Figure 1.5. The sum of the debtholders' claim and the shareholders' claim is always the value of the firm at the end of the period.

The debt and equity securities issued by a firm derive their value from the total value of the firm. In the words of finance theory, debt and equity securities are **contingent claims** on the total firm value.

When the value of the firm exceeds the amount promised to debtholders, the shareholders obtain the residual of the firm's value over the amount promised the debtholders, and the debtholders obtain the amount promised. When the value of the firm is less than the amount promised the debtholders, the shareholders receive nothing and the debtholders get the value of the firm.

CONCEPT QUESTIONS

- What is a contingent claim?
- Describe equity and debt as contingent claims.

1.3   The Corporate Firm

The firm is a way of organizing the economic activity of many individuals. There are many reasons why so much economic activity is carried out by firms and not by individuals. The theory of firms, however, does not tell us much about why most large firms are corporations rather than any of the other legal forms that firms can assume.

A basic problem of the firm is how to raise cash. The corporate form of business (that is, organizing the firm as a corporation) is the standard method for solving problems encountered in raising large amounts of cash. However, business can take other forms. In this section we consider the three basic legal forms of organizing firms (sole proprietorship, partnership, and corporation) and we see how firms go about the task of raising large amounts of money under each form.

The Sole Proprietorship

A **sole proprietorship** is a business owned by one person. Suppose you decide to start a business to produce mousetraps. Going into business is simple: You announce to all who will listen, "Today I am going to build a better mousetrap."

Most large cities require that you obtain a business license. Afterward, you can try to hire as many people as you need and borrow whatever money you need. At year end all the profits and the losses will be yours.

Here are some important factors in considering a sole proprietorship:

1. The sole proprietorship is the cheapest type of corporation to form. No formal charter is required, and few government regulations must be satisfied.
2. A sole proprietorship pays no corporate income taxes. All profits of the business are taxed as individual income.
3. The sole proprietorship has unlimited liability for business debts and obligations. No distinction is made between personal and business assets.
4. The life of the sole proprietorship is limited by the life of the sole proprietor.
5. Because the only money invested in the firm is the proprietor's, the equity money that can be raised by the sole proprietor is limited to the proprietor's personal wealth.

The Partnership

Any two or more persons can get together and form a **partnership.** Partnerships fall into two categories: general partnerships and limited partnerships.

In a *general partnership* all partners agree to provide some fraction of the work and cash and to share the profits and losses. Each partner is liable for the debts of the partnership. A partnership agreement specifies the nature of the arrangement. The partnership agreement may be an oral agreement or a formal document setting forth the understanding.

Limited partnerships permit the liability of some of the partners to be limited to the amount of cash each has contributed to the partnership. Limited partnerships usually require that (1) at least one partner be a general partner and (2) the limited partners do not participate in managing the business.

Here are some points that are important when considering a partnership:

1. Partnerships are usually inexpensive and easy to form. In complicated arrangements, including general and limited partnerships, written documents are required. Business licenses and filing fees may be necessary.
2. General partners have unlimited liability for all debts. The liability of limited partners is usually limited to the contribution each has made to the partnership. If one general partner is unable to meet his or her commitment, the shortfall must be made up by the other general partners.
3. The general partnership is terminated when a general partner dies or withdraws (but this is not so for a limited partner). It is difficult for a partnership to transfer ownership without dissolving. Usually, all general partners must agree. However, limited partners may sell their interest in a business.
4. It is difficult for a partnership to raise large amounts of cash. Equity contributions are limited to a partner's ability and desire to contribute to the partnership. Many companies start life as a proprietorship or partnership, but at some point they need to convert to corporate form.
5. Income from a partnership is taxed as personal income to the partners.
6. Management control resides with the general partners. Usually a majority vote is required on important matters, such as the amount of profit to be retained in the business.

It is very difficult for large business organizations to exist as sole proprietorships or partnerships. The main advantage is the cost of getting started. Afterward, the disadvantages, which may become severe, are (1) unlimited liability, (2) limited life of the enterprise, and (3) difficulty of transferring ownership. These three advantages lead to (4) the difficulty of raising cash.

The Corporation

Of the many forms of business enterprise, the **corporation** is by far the most important. Most large Canadian firms, such as Bank of Montreal and Northern Telecom, are organized as corporations. As a distinct legal entity, a corporation can have a name and enjoy many of the legal powers of natural persons. For example,

A Comparison of Partnership and Corporations

	Corporation	Partnership
Liquidity and marketability	Common stock can be listed on stock exchange.	Units are subject to substantial restrictions on transferability. There is no established trading market for partnership units.
Voting rights	Usually each share of common stock entitles each holder to one vote per share on matters requiring a vote and on the election of the directors. Directors determine top management.	Some voting rights by limited partners. However, general partner has exclusive control and management of operations.
Taxation	Corporate income is taxable. Dividends to shareholders are also taxable, but Revenue Canada attempts to avoid double taxation through use of the dividend tax credit.	Partnerships are not taxable. Partners pay taxes on distributed shares of partnership.
Reinvestment and dividend payout	Corporations have broad latitude on dividend payout decisions.	Partnerships are generally prohibited from reinvesting partnership cash flow. All net cash flow is distributed to partners.
Liability	Shareholders are not personally liable for obligations of the corporation.	Limited partners are not liable for obligations of partnerships. General partners may have unlimited liability.
Continuity of existence	Corporations have perpetual life.	Partnerships have a limited life.

corporations can acquire and exchange property. Corporations may enter into contracts and may sue and be sued. For jurisdictional purposes, the corporation is a citizen of its province of incorporation. (It cannot vote, however.)

Starting a corporation is more complicated than starting a proprietorship or partnership. The incorporators must prepare articles of incorporation and a set of bylaws. The articles of incorporation must include

1. Name of the corporation.
2. Intended life of the corporation. (It may be forever.)
3. Business purpose.
4. Number of shares that the corporation is authorized to issue, with a statement of limitations and rights of different classes of shares.
5. Nature of the rights granted to shareholders.
6. Number of members of the initial board of directors.

The bylaws (the rules to be used by the corporation to regulate its own existence) concern its shareholders, directors, and officers. Bylaws range from the briefest possible statement of rules for the corporation's management to hundreds of pages of text.

In its simplest form, the corporation comprises three sets of distinct interests: the shareholders (the owners), the directors, and the corporation officers (the top management). Traditionally, the shareholders control the corporation's direction, policies, and activities. The shareholders elect a board of directors, who in turn select top management. Top management serves as corporate officers and manages the operation of the corporation in the best interests of the shareholders.

The separation of ownership from management gives the corporation several advantages over proprietorships and partnerships:

1. Because ownership in a corporation is represented by shares, ownership can be readily transferred to new owners. Because the corporation exists independently of those who own its shares, there is no limit to the transferability of shares as there is in partnerships.

2. The corporation has unlimited life. Because the corporation is separate from its owners, the death or withdrawal of an owner does not affect its existence. The corporation can continue on after the original owners have withdrawn.

3. The shareholders' liability is limited to the amount invested in the ownership shares. For example, if a shareholder purchased $1,000 in shares of a corporation, the potential loss would be $1,000. In a partnership, a general partner with a $1,000 contribution could lose the $1,000 plus any other indebtedness of the partnership.

Limited liability, ease of ownership transfer, and perpetual succession are the major advantages of the corporate form of business organization. These give the corporation an enhanced ability to raise cash.

There is, however, one great disadvantage to incorporation. Federal and provincial governments tax corporate income. Corporate dividends received by shareholders are also taxable. The dividend tax credit for individual shareholders and a corporate dividend exclusion reduce the bite of double taxation for Canadian corporations. These tax provisions are discussed in the appendix to this chapter.

CONCEPT QUESTIONS

- Define a proprietorship, a partnership, and a corporation.
- What are the advantages of the corporate form of business organization?

Goals of the Corporate Firm   1.4

What is the primary goal of the corporation? It is impossible to give a definitive answer to this important question because the corporation is an artificial being, not a natural person. It exists "as a legal entity, separate and distinct from the individual members of the company."[3]

---

[3]From *Salomon* v. *Salomon & Co., Ltd.* [1987] A.C. 22 (U.K. H.L.) ([1895–99] All E.R. Rep. 33) (4 Mans. 89). This is the classic case of the inviolability of the corporation as a separate entity. The decision rendered in this case has been used as consideration in numerous British and Canadian cases.

It is necessary to identify precisely who controls the corporation. We shall consider the **set-of-contracts viewpoint** which suggests that the corporate firm will attempt to maximize the shareholders' wealth in the firm.

Agency Costs and the Set-of-Contracts Perspective

The corporation can be viewed as a complicated set of contracting relationships among individuals—a legal contrivance that serves as the nexus for the contracting relationships. The corporate firm is not an individual; it is a way of bringing the conflicting objectives of individuals into an equilibrium within a legal framework of contracts.

This is the set-of-contracts theory of the firm.[4] The firm is viewed as nothing more than a set of contracts. One of the contract claims is a residual claim (equity) on the firm's assets and cash flows. The equity contract can be defined as a principal–agent relationship. The members of the management team are the agents, and the equity investors (shareholders) are the principals. This discussion focuses on conflict between shareholders and managers. It is assumed that the two groups, left alone, will each attempt to act in its own self-interest. We also assume that shareholders are unanimous in defining their self-interest; we explain how perfect markets make this happen in Chapter 3.

The shareholders, however, can discourage the managers from diverging from the shareholders' interests by devising appropriate incentives for managers and then monitoring their behavior. Doing so, unfortunately, is complicated and costly. The costs of resolving the conflicts of interest between managers and shareholders are special types of costs called **agency costs.** These costs include the monitoring costs of the shareholders and the incentive fee paid to the managers. It can be expected that contracts will be devised that will provide the managers with appropriate incentives to maximize the shareholders' wealth. Thus, agency problems do not mean that the corporate firm will not act in the best interests of shareholders, only that it is costly to make it do so. However, agency problems can never be perfectly solved, and managers may not always act in the best interests of shareholders. *Residual losses* are the lost wealth of the shareholders due to divergent behavior of the managers.

Managerial Goals

Managerial goals are different from those of shareholders. What will managers maximize if they are left to pursue their own goals rather than shareholders' goals?

Williamson proposes the notion of *expense preference.*[5] He argues that managers obtain value from certain kinds of expenses. In particular, company cars, office furniture, office location, and funds for discretionary investment have value to managers beyond that which comes from their productivity.

---

[4]M. C. Jensen and W. Meckling, "Theory of the Firm: Managerial Behavior, Agency Costs and Ownership Structure," *Journal of Financial Economics* 3 (1976).

[5]O. Williamson, "Managerial Discretion and Business Behavior," *American Economic Review* 53 (1963).

	Number of shareholders	Listed shares outstanding (millions)	Market value ($ millions)	
BCE Inc.	260,747	306.294	13,592	
Royal Bank of Canada	150,000	313.886	8,948	
Imperial Oil	22,468	193.841	9,062	
Northern Telecom	10,492	249.215	10,903	
The Seagram Co. Ltd.	7,400	373.773	13,689	

Table 1.1
The largest Canadian corporations

Source: *Report on Business Magazine, The Globe and Mail,* July 1992, and *The TSE Review,* 1992. The table does not include Canadian subsidiaries of foreign companies.

Donaldson conducted a series of interviews with chief executives of several large companies.[6] He concluded that managers are influenced by three underlying motivations in defining the corporate mission:

1. *Survival.* Organizational survival means that management must always command sufficient resources to support the firm's activities.
2. *Independence.* This is the freedom to make decisions and take action without encountering external parties or depending on outside financial markets.
3. *Self-sufficiency.* Managers do not want to depend on external parties.

These motivations lead to what Donaldson concludes is the basic financial objective of managers: the maximization of corporate wealth. Corporate wealth is that wealth over which management has effective control; it is closely associated with corporate growth and corporate size. Corporate wealth is not necessarily shareholder wealth. Corporate wealth tends to lead to increased growth by providing funds for growth and limiting the extent to which equity is raised. Increased growth and size are not necessarily the same thing as increased shareholder wealth.

Separation of Ownership and Control

Some people argue that shareholders do not control the corporation. They argue that shareholder ownership is too diffuse and fragmented for effective control of management. A striking feature of the modern large corporation is the diffusion of ownership among thousands of investors. For example, Table 1.1 shows that over 260,000 persons and institutions own shares of Bell Canada Enterprises, Inc. (BCE) stock. While this argument is certainly worth considering, it is less true in Canada than in the United States. In 1991 over 70 percent of U.S. corporations were widely held compared to only 15 percent in Canada. Many domestically owned Canadian corporations have controlling shareholders.[7] Still, controlling agency costs through

[6]G. Donaldson, *Managing Corporate Wealth: The Operations of a Comprehensive Financial Goals System* (New York: Praeger, 1984).

[7]Important exceptions are chartered banks. The Bank Act prohibits any one interest from owning more than 10 percent of the shares. The data on widely held corporations are from D. H. Thain and D. S. R. Leighton, "Ownership Structure and the Board," *Canadian Investment Review,* Fall 1991, pp. 61–66.

reexamining the rules of corporate governance is of considerable interest in corporate Canada.[8]

As we discussed earlier, one of the most important advantages of the corporate form of business organization is that it allows ownership of shares to be transferred. The resulting diffuse ownership, however, brings with it the separation of ownership and control of the large corporation. The possible separation of ownership and control raises an important question: Who controls the firm?

Do Shareholders Control Managerial Behavior?

The claim that managers can ignore the interests of shareholders is deduced from the fact that ownership in large corporations is widely dispersed. As a consequence, it is often claimed that individual shareholders cannot control management. There is some merit in this argument, but it is too simplistic.

The extent to which shareholders can control managers depends on (1) the costs of monitoring management, (2) the costs of implementing the control devices, and (3) the benefits of control.

When a conflict of interest exists between management and shareholders, who wins? Does management or the shareholders control the firm? Ownership in large corporations is diffuse compared to the closely held corporation. However, shareholders have several control devices (some more effective than others) to bond management to the self-interest of shareholders.

1. Shareholders determine the membership of the board of directors by voting. Thus, shareholders control the directors, who in turn select the management team.

2. Contracts with management and arrangements for compensation, such as stock option plans, can be made so that management has an incentive to pursue shareholders' goals. Similarly, management may be given loans to buy the firm's shares.

3. If the price of a firm's stock drops too low because of poor management, the firm may be acquired by a group of shareholders, by another firm, or by an individual. This is called a takeover. In a takeover, top management of the acquired firm may find itself out of a job. This pressures management to make decisions in the shareholders' interests. Fear of a takeover gives managers incentive to take actions that will maximize stock prices.

4. Competition in the managerial labour market may force managers to perform in the best interest of shareholders. Otherwise they will be replaced. Firms willing to pay the most will lure good managers. These are likely to be firms that compensate managers based on the value they create.

The available evidence and theory are consistent with the idea of shareholder control. However, there can be no doubt that, at times, corporations pursue managerial goals at the expense of shareholders.

---

[8]At least one well-known researcher believes that "like fads and fashions in economic markets, the current tendency to attribute all of the failings of the American and Canadian economies to infirmities in the corporate governance system is grossly overstated." See Ronald J. Daniels, "The 'Crisis' in Canadian Corporate Governance," *Director* 51 (Toronto: Institute of Corporate Directors, August 1993).

- What are two types of agency costs?
- How are managers bonded to shareholders?
- Can you recall some managerial goals?
- What is the set-of-contracts perspective?

Financial Institutions, Financial Markets, and the Corporation

1.5

We have seen that the primary advantages of the corporate form of organization are that (1) ownership can be transferred more quickly and easily than with other forms and (2) money can be raised more readily. Both advantages are significantly enhanced by the existence of financial institutions and markets. Financial markets play an extremely important role in corporate finance.

Financial Institutions

Financial institutions act as intermediaries between investors (funds suppliers) and firms raising funds. (Federal and provincial governments and individuals also raise funds in financial markets but our examples will focus on firms.) Financial institutions justify their existence by providing a variety of services that promote efficient allocation of funds. Canadian financial institutions include chartered banks and other depository institutions (trust companies and credit unions) as well as nondepository institutions (investment dealers, insurance companies, pension funds, and mutual funds).[9]

Table 1.2 ranks Canada's top 10 financial institutions by total assets. They include the "Big Six" domestically owned chartered banks, one credit union (Caisses populaires), a pension fund (Caisse de depot), and two financial holding companies (CT Financial and Power Financial).

Because they are allowed to diversify by operating in all provinces, Canada's chartered banks are good-sized on an international scale. Table 1.2 shows that the chartered banks also hold the top slots domestically, but pension funds and financial holding companies offering one-stop financial shopping are gaining on the banks.

Chartered banks operate under federal regulation, accepting deposits from suppliers of funds and making commercial loans to mid-sized businesses, corporate loans to large companies, and personal loans and mortgages to individuals. Banks make the majority of their income from the spread between the interest paid on deposits and the higher rate earned on loans. This process is called indirect finance because banks receive funds in the form of deposits and engage in a separate lending contract with funds demanders. Figure 1.6's top panel illustrates indirect finance.

Chartered banks also provide other services that generate fees instead of spread income. For example, a large corporate customer seeking short-term debt funding can borrow directly from another large corporation with funds to supply through a bankers acceptance. This is an interest-bearing IOU which is stamped by a bank guaranteeing

---

[9]Our discussion of Canadian financial institutions draws on L. Kryzanowski and G. S. Roberts, "Bank Structure in Canada," in *Banking Structure in Major Countries*, ed. G. G. Kaufman (Boston: Kluwer, 1992).

Table 1.2 The largest financial institutions in Canada, 1992

Rank by assets	Assets ($ thousands)	Company (head office)	Rank by revenue	Revenue ($ thousands)	Rank by net income	Net income ($ thousands)	Return on assets	Return on shareholders equity	Employees	Major shareholders
1	$138,293,000	Royal Bank of Canada (Montreal), October 1992	1	$12,199,000	7	$107,000	0.08%	1.40%	50,893	Wide distribution
2	$132,212,000	Canadian Imperial Bank of Commerce (Toronto), October 1992	2	$11,468,461	23	$11,590	0.01%	0.17%	34,426	Wide distribution
3	$109,035,275	Bank of Montreal (Montreal), October 1992	3	$8,847,196	2	$639,621	0.62%	13.17%	32,126	Wide distribution
4	$97,660,809	Bank of Nova Scotia (Toronto), October 1992	4	$8,420,179	1	$676,224	0.73%	13.93%	29,888	Wide distribution
5	$74,133,000	Toronto Dominion Bank (Toronto), October 1992	6	$6,138,000	3	$408,000	0.57%	8.25%	23,514	Wide distribution
6	$56,529,000	Confederation caisses populaires Desjardins (Quebec City), December 1992	5	$6,469,900	4	$287,700	0.53%	9.29%	38,490	Members
7	$44,264,510	CT Financial Services Inc. (London, Ont.), December 1992	9	$4,047,961	5	$193,227	0.45%	10.25%	17,019	Imasco 98%
8	$41,307,000	Caisse de depot et placement du Quebec (Montreal), December 1992	11	$2,969,000	n.a.	n.a.	n.a.	n.a.	353	Quebec government 100%
9	$40,044,740	National Bank of Canada (Montreal), October 1992	10	$3,713,168*	66	$1,016	0.00%	0.06%	11,962	Wide distribution
10	$26,094,046	Power Financial Corp (Montreal), December 1992	7	$5,867,451	6	$184,884	0.74%	10.48%	7,600	Power 69% Caisse de depot 12%

Source: *The Financial Post Magazine*, May 1993.

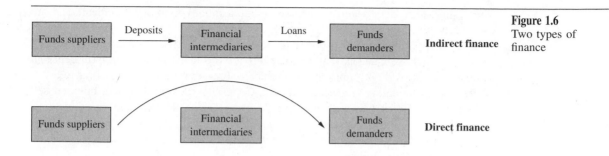

Figure 1.6
Two types of finance

the borrower's credit. Instead of spread income, the bank receives a stamping fee. Bankers acceptances are an example of direct finance as illustrated in Figure 1.6's lower panel. Notice that the key difference between direct finance and indirect finance is that in direct finance funds do not pass through the bank's balance sheet in the form of a deposit and loan. Often called securitization because a security (the bankers acceptance) is created, direct finance is growing rapidly.

Trust companies also accept deposits and make loans. In addition, trust companies engage in fiduciary activities—managing assets for estates, registered retirement savings plans, and so on. The current Bank Act allows banks to own trust companies, and the trust company sector is undergoing restructuring. Like trust companies, credit unions also accept deposits and make loans.

Investment dealers are nondepository institutions that assist firms in issuing new securities in exchange for fee income. Investment dealers also aid investors in buying and selling securities. Chartered banks own majority stakes in five of Canada's top investment dealers.

Insurance companies include property and casualty insurance and health and life insurance companies. Life insurance companies engage in indirect finance by accepting funds in a form similar to deposits and making loans.

Pension funds invest contributions from employers and employees in securities offered by financial markets. Mutual funds pool individual investments to purchase a diversified portfolio of securities.

We base this survey of the principal activities of financial institutions on their main activities today. Recent deregulation now allows chartered banks, trust companies, insurance companies, and investment dealers to engage in most activities of the others with one exception: Chartered banks are not allowed to sell life insurance through their branch networks. Although not every institution plans to become a one-stop financial supermarket, the different types of institutions will likely continue to become more alike.

Like financial institutions, financial markets differ. Principal differences concern the types of securities that are traded, how trading is conducted, and who the buyers and sellers are. Some of these differences are discussed next.

Money versus Capital Markets

Financial markets can be classified as either money markets or capital markets. Short-term debt securities of many varieties are bought and sold in **money markets.**

These short-term debt securities are often called money-market instruments and are essentially IOUs. For example, a bankers acceptance represents short-term borrowing by large corporations and is a money-market instrument. Treasury bills are an IOU of the Government of Canada. **Capital markets** are the markets for long-term debt and shares of stock so the Toronto Stock Exchange, for example, is a capital market.

The money market is a dealer market. Generally speaking, dealers buy and sell something for themselves at their own risk. A car dealer, for example, buys and sells automobiles. In contrast, brokers and agents match buyers and sellers, but they do not actually own the commodity. A real estate agent or broker, for example, does not normally buy and sell houses.

The largest money-market dealers are chartered banks and investment dealers. Their trading facilities, along with other market participants, are connected electronically via telephone and computer linkages so the money market has no actual physical location.

Primary versus Secondary Markets

Financial markets function as both primary and secondary markets for debt and equity securities. The term *primary market* refers to the original sale of securities by governments and corporations. The secondary markets are where these securities are bought and sold after the original sale. Equities are, of course, issued solely by corporations. Debt securities are issued by both governments and corporations. The following discussion focuses on corporate securities only.

Primary Markets

In a primary market transaction, the corporation is the seller and raises money through the transaction. Corporations engage in two types of primary market transactions: public offerings and private placements. A public offering, as the name suggests, involves selling securities to the general public, while a private placement is a negotiated sale involving a specific buyer. These topics are detailed in Chapters 19 and 20 so we only introduce the bare essentials here.

Most publicly offered debt and equity securities are underwritten. In Canada, underwriting is conducted by investment dealers specializing in marketing securities. In 1990, Canada's three largest underwriters were RBC Dominion, ScotiaMcLeod, and Wood Gundy.

When a public offering is underwritten, an investment dealer or a group of investment dealers (called a *syndicate*) typically purchases the securities from the firm and markets them to the public. The underwriters hope to profit by reselling the securities to investors at a higher price than they paid the firm for them.

By law, public offerings of debt and equity must be registered with provincial authorities, the most important being the Ontario Securities Commission (OSC). Registration requires the firm to disclose a great deal of information before selling any securities. The accounting, legal, and underwriting costs of public offerings can be considerable.

1. Tokyo	$1,403,887.0
2. New York	1,325,332.4
3. Taiwan	787,845.7
4. London	587,808.1
5. Germany	554,208.1
6. Zurich	400,253.2
7. Osaka	266,463.2
8. Paris	127,019.3
9. Korea	74,616.0
10. Midwest	71,304.4
11. Vienna	59,313.3
12. Toronto	55,179.8
13. Basel	55,005.8
14. Italy	44,859.5
15. Amsterdam	44,101.8
16. Pacific	41,418.4
17. Australia	39,765.8
18. Madrid	38,248.9
19. American	37,415.0
20. Hong Kong	34,683.7

Table 1.3
Top 20 world exchange equity trading summary, 1990 (in millions of U.S. dollars)

Source: *TSE Review,* August 1991, p. 11.

Partly to avoid the various regulatory requirements and the expense of public offerings, debt and equity arc often sold privately to large financial institutions such as life insurance companies or pension funds. Such private placements do not have to be registered with the OSC and do not require the involvement of underwriters.

Secondary Markets

A secondary market transaction involves one owner or creditor selling to another. It is therefore the secondary markets that provide the means for transferring ownership of corporate securities. There are two kinds of secondary markets: auction markets and dealer markets.

Dealer markets in stocks and long-term debt are called over-the-counter (OTC) markets. Trading in debt securities take place over the counter. The expression *over the counter* refers to days of old when securities were literally bought and sold at counters in offices around the country. Today, like the money market, a significant fraction of the market for stocks and all of the market for long-term debt have no central location; the many dealers are connected electronically.

The equity shares of most large firms in Canada trade in organized auction and dealer markets. The largest stock market in Canada is the Toronto Stock Exchange (TSE). Table 1.3 shows the top 20 stock exchanges in the world in 1990. The TSE ranked twelfth. Smaller stock exchanges in Canada include the Montreal Stock Exchange and Vancouver Stock Exchange.

Auction markets differ from dealer markets in two ways. First, an auction market or exchange, unlike a dealer market, has a physical location (like Bay Street or Wall Street). Second, in a dealer market, most buying and selling is done by the dealer. The primary purpose of an auction market, on the other hand, is to match those who wish

Table 1.4
End-of-year
market value of
selected TSE listed
securities,
1985–92

	Number of companies	Number of issues	Number of shares outstanding	Market value
1992	1119	1492	40.7	703.1
1991	1138	1538	38.6	703.5
1990	1193	1593	37.8	703.3
1989	1214	1632	36.8	804.4
1988	1214	1656	33.3	727.5
1987	1208	1695	30.6	737.7
1986	1085	1570	23.4	608.9
1985	966	1438	19.7	585.2

Source: *The TSE Review,* 1992.

to sell with those who wish to buy. Dealers play a limited role. For example, the TSE is computerizing its floor trading, replacing the trading floor with a wide-area computer network. This technological shift makes the TSE a hybrid of auction and dealer markets.[10]

Listing

Stocks that trade on an organized exchange are said to be listed on that exchange. To be listed, firms must meet certain minimum criteria concerning, for example, asset size and number of shareholders. These criteria differ for different exchanges. To be listed on the TSE, a company is expected to satisfy certain minimum requirements concerning finances and public distribution.[11] There are three financial requirements:

1. Net tangible assets of $1,000,000.
2. Adequate working capital and capitalization to carry on the business.
3. Evidence satisfactory to the Exchange, indicating a likelihood of future profitability.

or

1. Earnings of at least $100,000, before taxes and extraordinary items, in the fiscal year immediately preceding the filing of the listing application.
2. Pretax cash flow of $400,000 in the fiscal year immediately preceding the filing of the listing application.
3. Adequate working capital and capitalization to carry on the business.

At least 1,000,000 freely tradable shares having an aggregate market value of $1,000,000 must be held by at least 300 public holders, each holding one board lot [100 shares] or more. Table 1.4 gives the market values of selected TSE-listed securities.

---

[10]S. McHale, "TSE Votes to Computerize Floor Trading," *The Globe and Mail,* February 13, 1992, p. B7.

[11]*TSE Members' Manual,* 1992.

- Distinguish between money markets and capital markets.
- What is listing?
- What is the difference between a primary market and a secondary market?
- What are the principal financial institutions in Canada? What is the principal role of each?
- What are direct and indirect finance? How do they differ?
- What is a dealer market? How do dealer and auction markets differ?
- What is the largest auction market in Canada?

Trends in Financial Markets and Management   1.6

Like all markets, financial markets are experiencing rapid globalization. At the same time, interest rates, foreign exchange rates, and other macroeconomic variables have become more volatile. The toolkit of available financial management techniques has expanded rapidly in response to a need to control increased risk from volatility and to track complexities arising from dealings in many countries. Improved computer technology makes new financial engineering applications practical.

When financial managers or investment dealers design new securities or financial processes, their efforts are referred to as financial engineering. Successful financial engineering reduces and controls risk and minimizes taxes. Financial engineering creates a variety of debt securities and reinforces the trend toward securitization of credit introduced earlier. A controversial example is the invention of junk bonds in the United States, which allowed smaller firms to take over much larger ones through leveraged buyouts. In addition, options and optionlike securities are becoming important in controlling risk.

Financial engineering also seeks to reduce financing costs of issuing securities as well as the costs of complying with rules laid down by regulatory authorities. An example is the Prompt Offering Prospectus (POP) which allows firms that frequently issue new equity to bypass repetitive OSC registration requirements.

In addition to financial engineering, advances in computer technology also create opportunities to combine different types of financial institutions to take advantage of economies of scale and scope. Large institutions operate in all provinces and internationally, enjoying more lax regulations in some jurisdictions than in others. Financial institutions pressure authorities to deregulate in a push–pull process called the regulatory dialectic.

For example, in the mid-1980s Quebec removed almost all restrictions on combining different types of financial institutions. As a result, Quebec-based institutions grew much faster than their competitors outside the province. At that time Quebec was the only province that allowed chartered banks to own investment dealers. Quebec's example pressured regulators to allow chartered banks this power in other provinces.

More broadly, the regulatory dialectic has produced Canada's current regulations which allow financial institutions almost unlimited scope to enter each others' traditional businesses.[12]

These trends have made financial management a much more complex and technical activity. For this reason, many business students find introductory finance one of their most challenging subjects. The trends we reviewed have also increased the stakes. In the face of increased competition globally, the payoff for good financial management is great. The finance function is also becoming important in corporate strategic planning. The good news is that career opportunities (and compensation) in financial positions are highly competitive.

CONCEPT QUESTION

■ How do key trends in financial markets affect Canadian financial institutions?

1.7   Outline of the Text

Now that we have taken the quick tour through all of corporate finance, we can take a closer look at this book. The book is divided into seven parts. The long-term investment decision is covered first. Financing decisions and working capital are covered next. Finally, a series of special topics is covered. Here are the seven parts:

Part 1: Overview

Part 2: Value and Capital Budgeting

Part 3: Risk

Part 4: Capital Structure and Dividend Policy

Part 5: Long-Term Financing

Part 6: Financial Planning and Short-Term Finance

Part 7: Special Topics

Part 2 describes how investment opportunities are valued in financial markets. This part contains the basic theory. Because finance is a subject that builds understanding from the ground up, the material is very important. The most important concept in Part 2 is net present value. We develop the net-present-value rule into a tool for valuing investment alternatives. We discuss general formulas and apply them to a variety of different financial instruments.

Part 3 introduces basic measures of risk. The capital asset pricing model (CAPM) and the arbitrage pricing theory (APT) are used to devise methods for incorporating risk in valuation. As part of this discussion, we describe the famous beta coefficient. Finally, we use the preceding pricing models to handle capital budgeting under risk.

Part 4 examines two interrelated topics: capital structure and dividend policy. Capital structure is the extent to which the firm relies on debt. It cannot be separated from the amount of cash dividends the firm decides to pay out to its equity shareholders.

---

[12]This discussion draws on L. Kryzanowski and G. S. Roberts, "Bank Structure in Canada."

Part 5 concerns long-term financing. We describe the securities that corporations issue to raise cash as well as the mechanics of offering securities for public sale. Here we discuss call provisions, warrants, convertibles, and leasing.

Part 6 is devoted to financial planning and short-term finance. The first chapter describes financial planning. Next we focus on managing the firm's current assets and current liabilities. We describe aspects of the firm's short-term financial management. Separate chapters on cash management and credit management are included.

Part 7 covers two important special topics: mergers and international corporate finance.

Key Terms

Capital budgeting 5

Capital structure 5

Net working capital 5

Contingent claims 11

Sole proprietorship 12

Partnership 13

Corporation 13

Set-of-contracts viewpoint 16

Agency costs 16

Money markets 21

Capital markets 22

Suggested Readings

A survey of trends affecting chartered banks and other Canadian financial institutions is found in:

L. Kryzanowski and G. S. Roberts, "Bank Structure in Canada." In G. G. Kaufman, ed., *Banking Structure in Major Countries.* Boston: Kluwer, 1992.

Two nontechnical discussions of financial engineering and trends are:

J. D. Finnerty. "Financial Engineering in Corporate Finance: An Overview." In C. W. Smith and C.W. Smithson, eds., *The Handbook of Financial Engineering* (Grand Rapids: Harper Business, 1990).

D. R. Lessard. "Global Competition and Corporate Finance in the 1990s." *Journal of Applied Corporate Finance,* Winter 1991, pp. 59–72.

Questions and Problems

1.1 Suppose you were the financial manager of an incorporated business. What kinds of goals do you think would be appropriate? Suppose that you changed jobs to become financial manager of a not-for-profit organization. How would this change your answer?

1.2 Can our goal of maximizing the value of the shareholders' wealth conflict with other goals such as avoiding unethical or illegal behavior? In particular, do you think that topics such as customer and employee safety, the environment, and the general good of society fit into this framwork? Think of some specific scenarios to illustrate your answer.

1.3   What are the major types of financial institutions and financial markets in Canada?

1.4   Distinguish between direct and indirect finance. Give an example of each.

1.5   What are some major trends in Canadian financial markets? Explain how these trends affect the practice of financial management in Canada.

Taxes

Taxes are very important since cash flows are measured after taxes. In this section, we examine corporate and personal tax rates and how taxes are calculated. We apply this knowledge to see how different types of income are taxed in the hands of individuals and corporations.

The size of the tax bill is determined through tax laws and regulations in the annual budgets of the federal government (administered by Revenue Canada) and provincial governments. If the various rules of taxation seem a little bizarre or convoluted to you, keep in mind that tax law is the result of political forces as well as economic forces. The tax law is continually evolving so our discussion cannot make you a tax expert. Rather, it will give you an understanding of the tax principles important for financial management along with the ability to ask the right questions when consulting a tax expert.

Individual Tax Rates

Individual tax rates in effect for federal and provincial taxes for 1992 are shown in Table 1A.1. These rates apply to income from employment (wages and salary) and from unincorporated businesses. Investment income is also taxable. Interest income is taxed at the same rates as employment income, but special provisions reduce the taxes payable on dividends and capital gains. We discuss these in detail later in the appendix.

In making financial decisions it is frequently important to distinguish between average and marginal tax rates. The percentage rates shown in Table 1A.1 are all marginal rates.

With the exception of Quebec residents, taxpayers file one tax return. In computing your tax, you first find the federal tax and then calculate the provincial tax as a percentage of the federal tax. Table 1A.2 gives these percentages.

Taxes on Investment Income

When introducing the topic of taxes, we warned that tax laws are not always logical. The treatment of dividends in Canada is at least a partial exception because there are two clear goals. First, corporations pay dividends from after-tax income so tax laws shelter dividends from full tax in the hands of shareholders to avoid double taxation. Second, tax shelters for dividends apply only to dividends paid by Canadian

Taxable income	Tax	Rate on excess	**Table 1A.1** Individual income tax rates, 1992*
Federal			
$ 1	$ —	17%	
29,590	5,030	26	
59,180	12,724	29	
Quebec			
$ 1	$ —	16	
7,000	1,120	19	
14,000	2,450	21	
23,000	4,340	23	
50,000	10,550	24	

* Actual rates are higher, as this table does not include surcharges that apply in the higher bracket.

Source: 1992 Income Tax Act.

		Table 1A.2 Provincial tax as a percentage of basic federal tax
Alberta	46.0%	
British Columbia	52.0	
Manitoba	52.0	
New Brunswick	60.0	
Newfoundland	64.5	
Nova Scotia	59.5	
Ontario	54.5	
Prince Edward Island	59.5	
Saskatchewan	50.0	
Northwest Territories	44.0	
Yukon Territory	45.0	
Nonresidents	52.0	

* Actual rates are higher, as this table does not include surcharges that apply in the higher bracket.

Source: 1992 Income Tax Act.

corporations. This is to encourage Canadian investors to invest in Canadian companies as opposed to foreign ones.[13]

To see how dividends are taxed we start with common shares held by individual investors. Table 1A.3 shows how the dividend tax credit reduces the effective tax rate on dividends for investors in each federal tax bracket. The steps follow the instructions on federal tax returns. Actual dividends are grossed up by 25 percent and federal tax is calculated on the grossed-up figure. A dividend tax credit of 16 2/3 percent of the actual dividend is subtracted from the federal tax to get the federal tax payable. The provincial tax (for Ontario in this example) is calculated and added.

Capital gains arise when an investment increases in value above its purchase price. Before the 1994 Federal Budget was released, each individual was entitled to

---

[13]Evidence that the dividend tax credit causes investors to favour Canadian stocks is provided in L. Booth, "The Dividend Tax Credit and Canadian Ownership Objectives," *Canadian Journal of Economics* 20 (May 1987).

Table 1A.3
Dividend tax credit
for Ontario
residents, 1992

	Federal tax rate		
	17 Percent	26 Percent	29 Percent
Dividends	$1,000	$1,000	$1,000
Gross-up at 25%	250	250	250
Grossed-up dividends	1,250.00	1,250.00	1,250.00
Federal tax	212.50	325.00	362.50
Less dividend tax credit (.1667 × $1,000)	(166.70)	(166.70)	(166.70)
Federal tax payable	45.80	158.30	195.80
Provincial tax at 54.5% of federal tax	24.96	86.27	106.71
Total tax	70.76	244.57	302.51
Effective combined tax rates			
Dividends	7.08%	24.46%	30.23%
Ordinary income	26.27%	40.17%	44.81%

Table 1A.4
Corporate tax
rates, 1993

	Federal	Ontario	Combined
Basic corporations	28%	15.5%	43.5%
Manufacturing and processing companies	22	14.5	36.5
All small corporations (taxable income below $200,000)	12	10	22.0

Source: *Canadian Tax News,* October-November 1993; *Ontario Tax Reporter,* 1993; and Federal Budget, 1993.

receive a lifetime capital gains tax exemption of $100,000. This limit was calculated net of any capital losses.[14] However, the 1994 Federal Budget eliminated the lifetime exemption, and taxes apply at 75 percent of the applicable marginal rate. For example, individuals in the highest bracket in Table 1A.3 would pay taxes on capital gains at a nominal rate of 44.81% × .75 = 33.61%.

In practice, capital gains are lightly taxed since individuals only pay taxes on realized capital gains when shares are sold. Since many individuals hold shares for a long time (have unrealized capital gains), the time value of money dramatically reduces the effective tax rate on capital gains.[15]

Corporate Taxes

Canadian corporations, like individuals, are subject to corporate taxes levied by the federal and provincial governments. Table 1A.4 shows corporate tax rates using Ontario as an example. You can see from the table that small corporations (income under $200,000) and, to a lesser degree, manufacturing and processing companies, receive a tax break in the form of lower rates.

---

[14]A higher limit of $500,000 still applies to certain capital gains generated in farm property and small businesses. All gains (without limit) on the sale of a principal residence are tax-free.

[15]L. D. Booth and D. J. Johnston, "The Ex-Dividend Day Behavior of Canadian Stock Prices: Tax Changes and Clientele Effects," *Journal of Finance* 39 (June 1984), pp. 457–76. Booth and Johnston find a "very low effective tax rate on capital gains" in the 1970s prior to the introduction of the current lifetime exemption. They compare their results with a U.S. study that found an effective tax rate on capital gains under 7 percent.

Comparing the rates in Table 1A.4 with the personal tax rates in Table 1A.1 appears to reveal a tax advantage for small businesses and professionals in forming a corporation. The tax rate on corporate income of, say, $150,000 is less than the personal tax rate assessed on income of unincorporated businesses. But this is oversimplified because dividends paid to the owners are also taxed as we saw earlier.

Taxable Income

Interest and dividends are treated differently in calculating corporate tax. Interest paid is deducted from EBIT (earnings before interest and taxes) in calculating taxable income, but dividends paid are not. Because interest is a tax-deductible expense, debt financing has a tax advantage over financing with common stock.

The tables are turned when we contrast interest and dividends earned by the firm. Interest earned is fully taxable just like any other form of ordinary income. Dividends on common shares received from other Canadian corporations qualify for a 100-percent exemption and are received tax-free.

Capital Gains, Carryforward, and Carryback

If a firm disposes of an asset for more than it paid originally, the difference is a capital gain. As with individuals, firms receive favourable tax treatment on capital gains which are taxed at 75 percent of the marginal tax rate.

When calculating capital gains for tax purposes, a firm nets out all capital losses in the same year. If capital losses exceed capital gains, the net capital loss may be carried back to reduce taxable capital gains in the three prior years. Under the carryback feature, a firm files a revised tax return and receives a refund of prior years' taxes.

A similar carryback and carryforward provision applies to operating losses. In this case, the carryback period is three years and carryforward is allowed for up to seven years.

Investment Tax Credits

An investment tax credit is intended to promote investment in certain regions of the country—presently Atlantic Canada but applied more broadly in past years. An investment tax credit allows a qualified firm to subtract a set percentage of an investment directly from taxes payable.

Appendix Questions and Problems

1.A1 Distinguish between an average tax rate and a marginal tax rate.

1.A2 How does tax treatment of investment income differ among interest, dividends, and capital gains?

1.A3 Explain how carryback/carryforward provisions and investment tax credits reduce corporate taxes.

Accounting Statements and Cash Flow

Chapter 2 describes the basic accounting statements used for reporting corporate activity. It focuses on practical details of cash flow. It will become obvious in the next several chapters that knowing how to determine cash flow helps the financial manager make better decisions. Students who have had accounting courses will not find the material new and can think of it as a review with an emphasis on finance. We discuss cash flow further in later chapters.

The Balance Sheet 2.1

The **balance sheet** is an accountant's snapshot of the firm's accounting value on a particular date, as though the firm stood momentarily still. The balance sheet has two sides: On the left are the *assets* and on the right the *liabilities* and *shareholders' equity*. The balance sheet states what the firm owns and how it is financed. The accounting definition that underlies the balance sheet and describes the balance is

Assets ≡ Liabilities + Shareholders' equity

We have put a three-line equality in the balance equation to indicate that it must always hold, by definition. In fact, the shareholders' equity is defined to be the difference between the assets and the liabilities of the firm. In principle, equity is what the shareholders would have remaining after the firm discharged its obligations.

Table 2.1 gives the 19X2 and 19X1 balance sheet for the fictitious Canadian Composite Corporation. The assets in the balance sheet are listed in order by the length of time it normally takes a going concern to convert them to cash. The asset side depends on the nature of the business and how management chooses to conduct it. Management must make decisions about cash versus marketable securities, credit versus cash sales, whether to make or buy commodities, whether to lease or purchase items, the types of business in which to engage, and so on. The liabilities and the shareholders' equity are listed in the order in which they must be paid.

The liability and shareholders' equity side reflects the types and proportions of financing, which depend on management's choice of capital structure, as between debt and equity and between current debt and long-term debt.

When analyzing a balance sheet, the financial manager should be aware of three concerns: accounting measures of liquidity, debt versus equity, and value versus cost.

Table 2.1 Balance sheet of the Canadian Composite Corporation

CANADIAN COMPOSITE CORPORATION
Balance Sheet
19X2 and 19X1
(in $ millions)

Assets	19X2	19X1	Liabilities (debt) and Stockholders' Equity	19X2	19X1
Current assets:			Current liabilities:		
Cash and equivalents	$ 140	$ 107	Accounts payable	$213	$197
Accounts receivable	294	270	Notes payable	50	53
Inventories	269	280	Accrued expenses	223	205
Other	58	50	Total current liabilities	486	455
Total current assets	761	707	Long-term liabilities:		
Long-term assets:			Deferred taxes	117	104
Property, plant, and equipment	1,423	1,274	Long-term debt	471	458
Less accumulated depreciation	(550)	(460)	Total long-term liabilities	588	562
Net property, plant, and equipment	873	814	Stockholders' equity:		
Intangible assets and others	245	221	Preferred stock	39	39
			Common stock	55	32
			Accumulated retained earnings	390	347
Total long-term assets	1,118	1,035	Total equity	805	725
Total assets	$1,879	$1,742	Total liabilities and stockholders' equity	$1,879	$1,742

Liquidity

Liquidity refers to the ease and speed with which assets can be converted to cash. Current assets are the most liquid and include cash and those assets that will be turned into cash within a year from the date of the balance sheet. Accounts receivable are the amount not yet collected from customers for goods or services sold to them (after adjustment for potential bad debts). Inventory is composed of raw materials to be used in production, work in process, and finished goods. Fixed assets are the least liquid kind of asset. Tangible fixed assets include property, plant, and equipment. These assets do not convert to cash from normal business activity, and they are not usually used to pay expenses, such as payroll.

Some fixed assets are not tangible. Intangible assets have no physical existence but can be very valuable. Examples of intangible assets are the value of a trademark, the value of a patent, and the value of customer recognition. The more liquid a firm's assets, the less likely the firm is to experience problems meeting short-term obligations. Thus, the probability that a firm will avoid financial distress can be linked to its liquidity. Unfortunately, liquid assets frequently have lower rates of return than fixed assets; for example, cash generates no investment income. To the extent to which a firm invests in liquid assets, it sacrifices an opportunity to invest in more profitable investment vehicles.

Debt versus Equity

Liabilities are obligations of the firm that require a payout of cash within a stipulated time period. Many liabilities involve contractual obligations to repay a stated amount with interest over a period. Thus, liabilities are debts and are frequently associated with nominally fixed cash burdens, called *debt service,* that put the firm in default of a contract if they are not paid. *Shareholders' equity* is a claim against the firm's assets that is residual and not fixed. In general terms, when the firm borrows, it gives the bondholders first claim on the firm's cash flow.[1] Bondholders can sue if the firm defaults on its bond contracts. This may lead the firm to declare itself bankrupt. Shareholders' equity is the residual difference between assets and liabilities:

$$\text{Assets} - \text{Liabilities} \equiv \text{Shareholders' equity}$$

This is the shareholders' share in the firm stated in accounting terms. The accounting value of shareholders' equity increases when retained earnings are added. This occurs when the firm retains part of its earnings instead of paying them out as dividends.

Value versus Cost

The accounting value of a firm's assets is frequently referred to as the *carrying value* or the *book value* of the assets.[2] Under **generally accepted accounting principles (GAAP),** audited financial statements of firms in Canada carry the assets at historical cost adjusted for depreciation. Thus the terms *carrying value* and *book value* are unfortunate. They specifically say "value," when in fact the accounting numbers are based on cost. This misleads many readers of financial statements into thinking that the firm's assets are recorded at true market values. *Market value* is the price at which willing buyers and sellers trade the assets. It would be only a coincidence if accounting value and market value were the same. In fact, management's job is to create a value for the firm that is higher than its cost.

There are many users of a firm's balance sheet and each may seek different information from it. A banker may look at a balance sheet for evidence of liquidity and working capital. A supplier may also note the size of accounts payable which reflects the general promptness of payments. Many users of financial statements, including managers and investors, want to know the value of the firm, not its cost. This is not found on the balance sheet. In fact, many of a firm's true resources (good management, proprietary assets, and so on) do not appear on the balance sheet.

CONCEPT QUESTIONS

- What is the balance-sheet equation?
- What three things should be kept in mind when looking at a balance sheet?

---

[1]Bondholders are investors in the firm's debt. They are creditors of the firm. In this discussion, the term *bondholder* means the same thing as *creditor.*

[2]Confusion often arises because many financial accounting terms have the same meaning. This presents a problem with jargon for the reader of financial statements. For example, the following terms usually refer to the same thing: *assets minus liabilities, net worth, shareholders' equity, owner's equity,* and *equity capitalization.*

2.2

The Income Statement

The **income statement** measures performance over a specific period of time (say, a year). The accounting definition of income is

Revenue − Expenses ≡ Income

If the balance sheet is like a snapshot, the income statement is like a video recording of what happened between two snapshots. Table 2.2 gives the income statement for the Canadian Composite Corporation for 19X2.

The income statement usually includes several sections. The operations section reports the firm's revenues and expenses from principal operations. Among other things, the nonoperating section of the income statement includes all financing costs, such as interest expense. Usually a second section reports as a separate item the amount of taxes levied on income. The last item on the income statement is the bottom line, or net income. Net income is frequently expressed per share of common stock, that is, earnings per share.

When analyzing an income statement, the financial manager should keep in mind GAAP, noncash items, time, and costs.

Generally Accepted Accounting Principles (GAAP)

Revenue is recognized on an income statement when the earnings process is virtually completed and an exchange of goods or services has occurred. Therefore, the unrealized appreciation in owning property will not be recognized as income. This provides a device for smoothing income by selling appreciated property at convenient

---

Table 2.2
Income statement
of the Canadian
Composite
Corporation

CANADIAN COMPOSITE CORPORATION
Income Statement
19X2
(in $ millions)

Total operating revenues	$ 2,262
Cost of goods sold	(1,655)
Selling, general, and administrative expenses	(327)
Depreciation	(90)
Operating income	190
Other income	29
Earnings before interest and taxes	219
Interest expense	(49)
Pretax Income	170
Taxes	(84)
Current: $71	
Deferred: $13	
Net income	$ 86
Retained earnings: $43	
Dividends: $43	

times. For example, if the firm owns a tree farm that has doubled in value, then in a year when its earnings from other businesses are down, it can raise overall earnings by selling some trees. The matching principle of GAAP dictates that revenues be matched with expenses. Thus, income is reported when it is earned or accrued, even though no cash flow has necessarily occurred. (For example, when goods are sold for credit, sales and profits are reported.)

Noncash Items

The economic value of assets is intimately connected to their future incremental cash flows. However, cash flow does not appear on an income statement. There are several **noncash items** that are expenses against revenues, but do not affect cash flow directly.[3] The most important of these is *depreciation.* Depreciation reflects the accountant's estimate of the cost of equipment used up in the production process. For example, suppose an asset with a five-year life and no resale value is purchased for $1,000. According to accountants, the $1,000 cost must be expensed over the useful life of the asset. If straight-line depreciation is used, there will be five equal installments and $200 of depreciation expense will be incurred each year. From a finance perspective, the cost of the asset is the actual negative cash flow incurred when the asset is acquired (that is, $1,000, not the accountant's smoothed $200-per-year depreciation expense).

Another noncash expense is *deferred taxes.* Deferred taxes result from differences between accounting income and true taxable income.[4] Notice that the accounting tax shown on the income statement for the Canadian Composite Corporation is $84 million. It can be broken down as current taxes and deferred taxes. The current tax portion is actually sent to the tax authorities (for example, Revenue Canada). The deferred tax portion is not. However, the theory is that if taxable income is less than accounting income in the current year, it will be more than accounting income later. Consequently, taxes that are not paid today will have to be paid in the future, and they represent a liability of the firm. It shows up on the balance sheet as deferred tax liability. From the cash flow perspective, though, deferred tax is not a cash outflow.

Time and Costs

It is often useful to think of the future as having two distinct parts: the *short run* and the *long run.* The short run is that period in which certain equipment, resources, and commitments of the firm are fixed; but it is long enough for the firm to vary its output by using more labour and raw materials. The short run is not a precise period of time that will be the same for all industries. However, all firms making decisions in the short run have some fixed costs, that is, costs that will not change because of the fixed

---

[3]Although it is a noncash expense, depreciation has tax implications (discussed later) that affect cash flow.

[4]One situation in which taxable income may be lower than accounting income is when the firm uses capital cost allowance (CCA) depreciation expense procedures for Revenue Canada but uses straight-line procedures allowed by GAAP for reporting purposes. We discuss CCA in Chapter 7.

commitments. In real business activity, examples of fixed costs are bond interest, overhead, and property taxes. Costs that are not fixed are variable. Variable costs change as the output of the firm changes; some examples are raw materials and wages for production line workers. In the long run, all costs are variable.[5]

Financial accountants do not distinguish between variable costs and fixed costs. Instead, accounting costs usually fit into a classification that distinguishes product costs from period costs. Product costs are the total production costs (raw materials, direct labour, and manufacturing overhead) incurred during a period and are reported on the income statement as the cost of goods sold. Both variable and fixed costs are included in product costs. Period costs are costs that are allocated to a time period; they are called *selling, general,* and *administrative expenses.* One period cost would be the company president's salary.

CONCEPT QUESTIONS

- What is the income statement equation?
- What are three things to keep in mind when looking at an income statement?
- What are noncash expenses?

2.3   Net Working Capital

Net working capital is current assets minus current liabilities. Net working capital is positive when current assets are greater than current liabilities. This means the cash that will become available over the next 12 months is greater than the cash that must be paid out. The net working capital of the Canadian Composite Corporation is $275 million in 19X2 and $252 million in 19X1:

	Current assets ($ millions)	–	Current liabilities ($ millions)	=	Net working capital ($ millions)
19X2	$761	–	$486	=	$275
19X1	$707	–	$455	=	$252

In addition to investing in fixed assets (capital spending), a firm can invest in net working capital. This is called the *change in net working capital.* The **change in net working capital** in 19X2 is the difference between the net working capital in 19X2 and 19X1; that is, $275 million – $252 million = $23 million. The change in net working capital is usually positive in a growing firm.

CONCEPT QUESTIONS

- What is net working capital?
- What is the change in net working capital?

---

[5]When one famous economist was asked about the difference between the long run and the short run, he said, "In the long run we are all dead."

Financial Cash Flow   2.4

Perhaps the most important item that can be extracted from financial statements is the actual **cash flow.** There is an accounting statement called the *statement of changes in financial position.* This statement helps to explain the change in accounting cash and equivalents, which for Canadian Composite is $33 million in 19X2. Notice in Table 2.1 that cash and equivalents increases from $107 million in 19X1 to $140 million in 19X2. However, we will look at cash flow from a different perspective, the perspective of finance.

The first point we should mention is that cash flow is not the same as net working capital. For example, increasing inventory requires using cash. Because both inventories and cash are current assets, this does not affect net working capital. In this case, an increase in a particular net working capital account, such as inventory, is associated with decreasing cash flow.

Just as we established that the value of a firm's assets is always equal to the value of the liabilities plus the value of the equity, the cash flows from the firm's assets generated by its operating activities, CF(A), must equal the cash flows to the firm's creditors, CF(B), and equity investors, CF(S):

$$CF(A) = CF(B) + CF(S)$$

The first step in determining a firm's cash flows is to figure out the *cash flow from operations.* Table 2.3 shows, operating cash flow is the cash flow generated by business activities, including sales of goods and services. Operating cash flow reflects tax payments, but not financing, capital spending, or changes in net working capital.[6]

	(in $ millions)
Earnings before interest and taxes	$ 219
Depreciation	90
Current taxes	(71)
Operating cash flow	$ 238

Another important component of cash flow involves *changes in long-term assets.*[7] The net change in long-term assets equals sales of long-term assets minus the acquisition of long-term assets. The result is the cash flow used for capital spending:

Acquisition of long-term assets	$ 198
Sales of fixed assets	(25)
Capital spending	$ 173

In this example, cash flow for capital spending is positive because the Canadian Composite Corporation is growing and acquired more long-term assets than it sold. If the firm were downsizing, asset sales would exceed acquisitions making long-term assets a source of cash. Cash flows are also used for making investments in net

---

[6]It is important to note that operating cash flow is measured from the financial, not the accounting, point of view. Accountants view operating activities to include changes in net working capital (excluding cash and cash equivalents).

[7]This is equivalent to the accountant's investing activities.

Table 2.3
Financial cash flow
of the Canadian
Composite
Corporation

CANADIAN COMPOSITE CORPORATION
Financial Cash Flow 19X2
(in $ millions)

Cash flow of the firm	
Operating cash flow	$ 238
(Earnings before interest and taxes plus depreciation minus taxes)	
Capital spending	(173)
(Acquisitions of long-term assets minus sales of long-term assets)	
Additions to net working capital	(23)
Total	$ 42
Cash flow to investors in the firm	
Debt	$ 36
(Interest plus retirement of debt minus long-term debt financing)	
Equity	6
(Dividends plus repurchase of equity minus new equity financing)	
Total	$ 42

working capital.[8] In the Canadian Composite Corporation in 19X2, *additions to net working capital* are

Additions to net working capital	$23

Total cash flows generated by the firm's assets are the sum of

Operating cash flow	$ 238
Capital spending	(173)
Additions to net working capital	(23)
Total cash flow of the firm	$ 42

The total outgoing cash flow of the firm can be separated into cash flows paid to creditors and cash flows paid to shareholders.[9] The cash flow paid to creditors represents a regrouping of the data in Table 2.3 and an explicit recording of interest expense. Creditors are paid an amount generally referred to as *debt service*. Debt service is interest payments plus repayments of principal (that is, retirement of debt).

An important source of cash flow comes from selling new debt. Thus, an increase in long-term debt is the net effect of new borrowing and repayment of maturing obligations plus interest expense.

Cash flow paid to creditors
($ millions)

Interest	$ 49
Retirement of debt	73
Debt service	122
Proceeds from long-term debt sales	(86)
Total	$ 36

---

[8]As stated earlier, an accountant would include the changes in net working capital (excluding cash and cash equivalents) in operating activities.

[9]An accountant would call these financing activities. The one key difference in this section is that interest payments would not be financing. They are considered an operating activity by accountants.

Cash flow of the firm also is paid to the shareholders. It is the net effect of paying dividends plus repurchasing outstanding shares of stock and issuing new shares of stock.

Cash flow to shareholders
($ millions)

Dividends	$ 43
Repurchase of stock	6
Cash to shareholders	49
Proceeds from new stock issue	(43)
Total	$ 6

Some important observations can be drawn from our discussion of cash flow:

1. Several types of cash flow are relevant to understanding the financial situation of the firm. **Operating cash flow,** defined as earnings before interest and depreciation minus taxes, measures the cash generated from operations not counting capital spending or working capital requirements. It should usually be positive; a firm is in trouble if operating cash flow is negative for a long time because the firm is not generating enough cash to pay operating costs.

Total cash flow of the firm includes adjustments for capital spending and additions to net working capital. It will frequently be negative. When a firm is growing at a rapid rate, spending on inventory and fixed assets can be higher than cash flow from sales. On the other hand, positive total cash flow is not always a sign of financial health. An unprofitable firm with negative cash flow from operations could show positive total cash flow temporarily by selling assets. This was a common occurrence in the airline industry in the early 1990s.

2. Net income is not cash flow. The net income of the Canadian Composite Corporation in 19X2 was $86 million, whereas cash flow was $42 million. The two numbers are not usually the same. In determining the economic and financial condition of a firm, cash flow is more revealing.

CONCEPT QUESTIONS

- How is cash flow different from changes in net working capital?
- What is the difference between operating cash flow and total cash flow of the firm?

Summary and Conclusions · 2.5

Besides introducing you to corporate accounting, the purpose of this chapter has been to teach you how to determine cash flow from the accounting statements of a typical company.

1. Cash flow is generated by the firm and paid to creditors and shareholders. It can be classified as
   a. Cash flow from operations.
   b. Cash flow from changes in fixed assets.
   c. Cash flow from changes in working capital.

2. There is a cash flow identity that says that cash flow from assets equals cash flow to bondholders and shareholders.

3. Calculations of cash flow are not difficult, but they require care and particular attention to detail in properly accounting for noncash expenses such as depreciation and deferred taxes. It is especially important that you do not confuse cash flow with changes in net working capital and net income.

Key Terms

Balance sheet 33	Change in net working
Generally accepted accounting	capital 38
principles (GAAP) 35	Cash flow 39
Income statement 36	Operating cash flow 41
Noncash items 37	Total cash flow of the firm 41

Suggested Reading

There are many excellent textbooks on accounting. One that we have found helpful is:

R. H. Garrison, G. R. Chesley, and R. F. Carroll. *Managerial Accounting Concepts for Planning, Control, Decision Making,* 2d Canadian ed. Homewood Ill: Richard D. Irwin, 1993.

Questions and Problems

The Balance Sheet

2.1 Prepare a December 31 balance sheet using the following data:

Cash	$ 4,000
Patents	82,000
Accounts payable	6,000
Accounts receivable	8,000
Taxes payable	2,000
Machinery	34,000
Bonds payable	7,000
Accumulated retained earnings	6,000
Common stock	107,000

2.2 The following table presents the long-term liabilities and shareholders' equity of Information Control Corp. of one year ago:

Long-term debt	$ 50,000,000
Preferred stock	30,000,000
Common stock	100,000,000
Retained earnings	20,000,000

During the past year, Information Control issued $10 million of new common stock. The firm generated $5 million of net income and paid $3 million of dividends. Construct today's balance sheet that reflects the changes that occurred at Information Control Corp. during the year.

The Income Statement

2.3 Prepare an income statement using the following data:

Sales	$500,000
Cost of goods sold	200,000
Administrative expenses	100,000
Interest expense	50,000

The firm's tax rate is 40 percent.

2.4 The Flying Lion Corporation reported the following data on the income statement of one of its divisions. Flying Lion Corporation has other profitable divisions.

	19X2	19X1
Net sales	$800,000	$500,000
Cost of goods sold	560,000	320,000
Operating expenses	75,000	56,000
Depreciation	300,000	200,000
Tax rate	40%	40%

a. Prepare an income statement for each year.

b. Determine the cash flow during each year.

Financial Cash Flow

2.5 What are the differences between accounting profit and cash flow?

2.6 During 1992, the True North Tire Company had gross sales of $1 million. The firm's cost of goods sold and selling expenses were $300,000 and $200,000, respectively. These figures do not include depreciation. True North also had notes payable of $1 million. These notes carried an interest rate of 10 percent. Depreciation was $100,000. True North's tax rate in 1992 was 40 percent.

a. What was True North's net operating income?

b. What were the firm's earnings before taxes?

c. What was True North's net income?

d. What was True North's cash flow from operations?

2.7 The Beacon Corporation provided the following current information:

Proceeds from short-term borrowing	$ 6,000
Proceeds from long-term borrowing	20,000
Proceeds from the sale of common stock	1,000
Purchases of fixed assets	1,000
Purchases of inventories	4,000
Payment of dividends	22,000

Prepare a cash flow statement for Beacon Corporation.

2.8 Burnside Corporation's accountants prepared the following financial statements for year-end 19X2:

BURNSIDE CORPORATION
Income Statement
19X2

Revenue	$400
Expenses	250
Depreciation	50
Net income	$100
Dividends	$ 50

BURNSIDE CORPORATION
Balance Sheets
December 31

	19X2	19X1
Assets		
Current assets	$ 150	$ 100
Net fixed assets	200	100
Total assets	$ 350	$ 200
Liabilities and equity		
Current liabilities	$ 75	$ 50
Long-term debt	75	0
Shareholders' equity	200	150
Total liabilities and equity	$ 350	$ 200

a. Determine the change in net working capital in 19X2.

b. Determine the cash flow during the year 19X2.

APPENDIX   **Financial Statement Analysis**

This appendix shows how to rearrange data from financial statements into financial ratios that provide information about five areas of financial performance:

1. *Short-term solvency*—the firm's ability to meet its short-run obligations.
2. *Activity*—the firm's ability to control its investment in assets.
3. *Financial leverage*—the extent to which a firm relies on debt financing.
4. *Profitability*—the extent to which a firm is profitable.
5. *Value*—the value of the firm.

This appendix also discusses the interpretation, uses, and shortcomings of financial ratios.

Our discussion covers a representative sampling of ratios chosen to be consistent with the practice of experienced financial analysts and the output of commercially available financial analysis software.

For each of the ratios discussed, several questions are important:

1. How is the ratio calculated?
2. What is it intended to measure, and why might we be interested?

3. What might a high or low value be telling us? How might such values be misleading?

4. How could this measure be improved?

We consider each question in turn. The Canadian Composite Corporation financial statements in Tables 2.1, 2.2, and 2.3 provide inputs for the examples that follow. (Monetary values are given in $ millions.)

Short-Term Solvency

Ratios of short-term solvency measure the firm's ability to meet recurring financial obligations (that is, to pay its bills). To the extent that a firm has sufficient cash flow, it can avoid defaulting on its financial obligations and thus avoid financial distress. Liquidity measures short-term solvency and is often associated with net working capital, the difference between current assets and current liabilities. Recall that current liabilities are debts due within one year from the date of the balance sheet. One source from which to pay these debts is current assets.

The most widely used measures of liquidity are the current ratio and the quick ratio.

Current Ratio

To find the current ratio, divide current assets by current liabilities. For the Canadian Composite Corporation, the figure for 19X2 is

$$\text{Current ratio} = \frac{\text{Total current assets}}{\text{Total current liabilities}} = \frac{761}{486} = 1.57$$

If a firm is having financial difficulty, it may not be able to pay its bills (accounts payable) on time or it may need to extend its bank credit (notes payable). As a consequence, current liabilities may rise faster than current assets and the current ratio may fall. This could be the first sign of financial trouble. Of course, a firm's current ratio should be calculated over several years for historical perspective, and it should be compared to the current ratios of other firms with similar operating activities.

While a higher current ratio generally indicates greater liquidity, it is possible for the current ratio to be too high. A current ratio far above the industry average could indicate excessive inventory or difficulty in collecting accounts receivable.

Quick Ratio

The quick ratio is computed by subtracting inventories from current assets and dividing the difference (called *quick assets*) by current liabilities:

$$\text{Quick ratio} = \frac{\text{Quick assets}}{\text{Total current liabilities}} = \frac{492}{486} = 1.01$$

Quick assets are those current assets that are quickly convertible into cash. Inventories are the least liquid current assets. Many financial analysts believe it is important to determine a firm's ability to pay off current liabilities without relying on the sale of inventories. Comparing the quick ratio to the industry average may help to detect cases in which a high current ratio reflects excessive inventory.

Activity

Activity ratios are constructed to measure how effectively the firm's assets are being managed. The level of a firm's investment in assets depends on many factors. For example, Kiddie City might have a large stock of toys at the peak of the Christmas season; yet that same inventory in January would be undesirable. How can the appropriate level of investment in assets be measured? One logical starting point is to compare assets with sales for the year to arrive at turnover. The idea is to find out how quickly assets are used to generate sales.

Total Asset Turnover

The total asset turnover ratio is determined by dividing total operating revenues for the accounting period by the average of total assets. The total asset turnover ratio for the Canadian Composite Corporation for 19X2 is

$$\text{Total asset turnover} = \frac{\text{Total operating revenues}}{\text{Average total assets}} = \frac{2,262}{1,810.5} = 1.25$$

$$\text{Average total assets} = \frac{1,879 + 1,742}{2} = 1,810.5$$

This ratio is intended to indicate how effectively a firm is using its assets. If the asset turnover ratio is high, the firm is presumably using its assets effectively in generating sales. If the ratio is low, the firm is not using its assets up to their capacity and must either increase sales or dispose of some of the assets. Total asset turnover differs across industries. Firms with relatively small investments in fixed assets, such as retail and wholesale trade firms, tend to have high ratios of total asset turnover when compared with firms that require a large investment in fixed assets, such as manufacturing firms. One problem in interpreting this ratio is that it is maximized by using older assets because their accounting value is lower than newer assets.

Receivables Turnover

The receivables turnover ratio is calculated by dividing sales by average receivables during the accounting period. If the number of days in the year (365) is divided by the receivables turnover ratio, the average collection period can be determined. Net receivables are used for these calculations.[10] The average receivables, receivables turnover ratio, and average collection period for the Canadian Composite Corporation are

---

[10]Net receivables are determined after an allowance for potential bad debts.

$$\text{Average receivables} = \frac{294 + 270}{2} = 282$$

$$\text{Receivables turnover} = \frac{\text{Total operating revenues}}{\text{Average receivables}} = \frac{2{,}262}{282} = 8.02$$

$$\text{Average collection period} = \frac{\text{Days in period}}{\text{Receivables turnover}} = \frac{365}{8.02} = 45.5 \text{ days}$$

The receivables turnover ratio and the average collection period provide some information on the success of the firm in managing its investment in accounts receivable. The actual value of these ratios reflects the firm's credit policy. If a firm has a liberal credit policy, the amount of its receivables will be higher than under a restrictive credit policy. One common rule of thumb that financial analysts use is that the average collection period of a firm should not exceed the time allowed for payment in the credit terms by more than 10 days.

Inventory Turnover

The ratio of inventory turnover is calculated by dividing the cost of goods sold by average inventory. Because inventory is always stated in terms of historical cost, it must be divided by cost of goods sold instead of sales. (Sales include a margin for profit and are not commensurate with inventory.) The number of days in the year divided by the inventory turnover ratio yields the *days in inventory ratio* (the number of days it takes to get goods produced and sold). It is called *shelf life* for retail and wholesale trade firms. The inventory ratios for the Canadian Composite Corporation are

$$\text{Average inventory} = \frac{269 + 280}{2} = 274.5$$

$$\text{Inventory turnover} = \frac{\text{Cost of goods sold}}{\text{Average inventory}} = \frac{1{,}655}{274.5} = 6.03$$

$$\text{Days in inventory} = \frac{\text{Days in period}}{\text{Inventory turnover}} = \frac{365}{6.03} = 60.5 \text{ days}$$

The inventory ratios measure how quickly inventory is produced and sold. They are significantly affected by the production technology of goods being manufactured. It takes longer to produce a gas turbine engine than a loaf of bread. The ratios are also affected by the perishability of the finished goods. A large increase in the ratio of days in inventory could suggest either an ominously high inventory of unsold finished goods or a change in the firm's product mix to goods with longer production periods.

The method of inventory valuation can materially affect the computed inventory ratios. Thus, financial analysts should be aware of the different inventory valuation methods and how they might affect the ratios.

Financial Leverage

Financial leverage measures the extent to which a firm relies on debt financing rather than equity. Measures of financial leverage are tools in determining the probability that the firm will default on its debt contracts. The more debt a firm has, the more likely it is that the firm will become unable to fulfill its contractual obligations. In other words, too much debt can lead to a higher probability of insolvency and financial distress.

On the positive side, debt is an important form of financing, and provides a significant tax advantage because interest payments are tax deductible. If a firm uses debt, creditors and equity investors may have conflicts of interest. Creditors may want the firm to invest in less risky ventures than those the equity investors prefer.

Debt Ratio

The debt ratio is calculated by dividing total debt by total assets. We can also use several other ways to express the extent to which a firm uses debt, such as the debt-equity ratio and the equity multiplier (that is, total assets divided by equity). The debt ratios for the Canadian Composite Corporation for 19X2 are

$$\text{Debt ratio} = \frac{\text{Total debt}}{\text{Total assets}} = \frac{1{,}074}{1{,}879} = 0.57$$

$$\text{Debt-equity ratio} = \frac{\text{Total debt}}{\text{Total equity}} = \frac{1{,}074}{805} = 1.33$$

$$\text{Equity multiplier} = \frac{\text{Total assets}}{\text{Total equity}} = \frac{1{,}879}{805} = 2.33$$

Debt ratios provide information about protection of creditors from insolvency and the ability of firms to obtain additional financing for potentially attractive investment opportunities. However, debt is carried on the balance sheet simply as the unpaid balance. Consequently, no adjustment is made for the current level of interest rates (which may be higher or lower than when the debt was originally issued) or risk. Thus, the accounting value of debt may differ substantially from its market value.

Interest Coverage

The interest coverage ratio is calculated by dividing earnings (before interest and taxes) by interest. This ratio emphasizes the ability of the firm to generate enough income to cover interest expense. For the Canadian Composite Corporation, this ratio is

$$\text{Interest coverage} = \frac{\text{Earnings before interest and taxes}}{\text{Interest expense}} = \frac{219}{49} = 4.5$$

Interest expense is an obstacle that a firm must surmount if it is to avoid default. The interest coverage ratio is directly connected to the firm's ability to pay interest. However, since interest is paid in cash, it would probably make sense to add back depreciation (a noncash expense) to income in computing this ratio and to include other financing expenses paid in cash, such as payments of principal and lease payments.

A large debt burden is a problem only if the firm's cash flow is insufficient to make the required debt service payments. This is related to the uncertainty of future cash flows. Firms with predictable cash flows are frequently said to have more *debt capacity* than firms with highly uncertain cash flows. Therefore, it makes sense to compute the variability of the firm's cash flows. One possible way to do this is to calculate the standard deviation of cash flows relative to the average cash flow.

Profitability

One of the most difficult attributes of a firm to conceptualize and to measure is profitability. In a general sense, accounting profits are the difference between revenues and costs. Unfortunately, there is no completely unambiguous way to know when a firm is profitable. At best, a financial analyst can measure current or past accounting profitability. Many business opportunities, however, involve sacrificing current profits for future profits. For example, all new products require large start-up costs and, as a consequence, produce low initial profits. Thus, current profits can be a poor reflection of true future profitability.

Different industries employ different amounts of capital and differ in risk. For this reason, benchmark measures of profitability differ among industries.

Profit Margin

Profit margins are computed by dividing profits by total operating revenue. Thus, they express profits as a percentage of total operating revenue. The most important margin is the net profit margin. The net profit margin for the Canadian Composite Corporation is

$$\text{Net profit margin} = \frac{\text{Net income}}{\text{Total operating revenue}} = \frac{86}{2{,}262} = 0.038\ (3.8\%)$$

$$\text{Gross profit margin} = \frac{\text{Earnings before interest and taxes}}{\text{Total operating revenues}} = \frac{219}{2{,}262} = 0.097\ (9.7\%)$$

In general, profit margins reflect the firm's ability to produce a project or service at a low cost or to sell it at a high price. Profit margins are not direct measures of profitability because they are based on total operating revenue, not on the investment made in assets by the firm or the equity investors. Trade firms tend to have low margins and service firms tend to have high margins.

Return on Assets

One common measure of managerial performance is the ratio of income to average total assets, both before tax and after tax. These ratios for the Canadian Composite Corporation for 19X2 are

$$\text{Net return on assets} = \frac{\text{Net income}}{\text{Average total assets}} = \frac{86}{1{,}810.5} = 0.0475\ (4.75\%)$$

$$\text{Gross return on assets} = \frac{\text{Earnings before interest and taxes}}{\text{Average total assets}} = \frac{219}{1{,}810.5} = 0.121\ (12.1\%)$$

One of the most interesting aspects of return on assets (ROA) is how some financial ratios can be linked together to compute ROA in the *DuPont system of financial control.* This system expresses ROA in terms of the profit margin and asset turnover. The basic components of the system are as follows:

$$ROA = \text{Profit margin} \times \text{Asset turnover}$$

$$ROA \text{ (net)} = \frac{\text{Net income}}{\text{Total operating revenue}} \times \frac{\text{Total operating revenue}}{\text{Average total assets}}$$

$$0.0475 = 0.038 \times 1.25$$

$$ROA(\text{gross}) = \frac{\text{Earnings before interest and taxes}}{\text{Total operating revenue}} \times \frac{\text{Total operating revenue}}{\text{Average total assets}}$$

$$0.121 = 0.097 \times 1.25$$

Firms can increase ROA by increasing profit margins or asset turnover. Of course, competition limits their ability to do so simultaneously. Thus, firms tend to face a trade-off between turnover and margin. In retail trade, for example, mail-order companies have low margins and high turnover whereas high-quality jewelry stores have high margins and low turnover.

It is often useful to describe financial strategies in terms of margins and turnover. Suppose a firm selling pneumatic equipment is thinking about providing customers with more liberal credit terms. This will probably decrease asset turnover (because receivables would increase more than sales). Thus, the margins will have to go up to keep ROA from falling.

Return on Equity

This ratio (ROE) is defined as net income after interest and taxes divided by average common shareholders' equity, which for the Canadian Composite Corporation is

$$ROE = \frac{\text{Net income}}{\text{Average shareholders' equity}} = \frac{86}{765} = 0.11 \ (11\%)$$

$$\text{Average shareholders' equity} = \frac{805 + 725}{2} = 765$$

The difference between ROA and ROE is due to financial leverage. To see this, consider the following breakdown of ROE expanding the DuPont equation:

$$ROE = \text{Profit margin} \times \text{Asset turnover} \times \text{Equity multiplier}$$

$$= \frac{\text{Net income}}{\text{Total operating revenue}} \times \frac{\text{Total operating revenue}}{\text{Average total assets}} \times \frac{\text{Average total assets}}{\text{Average shareholders' equity}}$$

$$0.11 = 0.038 \times 1.25 \times 2.36$$

From the preceding numbers, it would appear that financial leverage always magnifies ROE. Actually, this occurs only when ROA (gross) is greater than the interest rate on debt.

Payout Ratio

The *payout ratio* is the proportion of net income paid out in cash dividends. For the Canadian Composite Corporation,

$$\text{Payout ratio} = \frac{\text{Cash dividends}}{\text{Net income}} = \frac{43}{86} = 0.5$$

The *retention ratio* is the proportion of net income added to retained earnings. For the Canadian Composite Corporation this ratio is

$$\text{Retention ratio} = \frac{\text{Retained earnings}}{\text{Net income}} = \frac{43}{86} = 0.5$$

Retained earnings = Net income − Dividends

Market-Value Ratios

We can learn many things from a close examination of balance sheets and income statements. However, one very important characteristic of a firm that cannot be found on an accounting statement is its market value.

Market Price

The market price of a share of common stock is the price that buyers and sellers establish when they trade the stock. The market value of the common equity of a firm is the market price of a share of common stock multiplied by the number of shares outstanding.

Sometimes the words *fair market value* are used to describe market prices. Fair market value is the price at which common stock would change hands between a willing buyer and a willing seller, both having knowledge of the relevant facts. Thus, market prices give guesses about the true worth of the assets of a firm. In an efficient stock market, market prices reflect all relevant facts about firms, and thus reveal the true value of the firm's underlying assets.

The market value of Imperial Oil is many times greater than that of Rio Alta. This may suggest nothing more than the fact that Imperial Oil is a bigger firm than Rio Alta (hardly a surprising revelation). Financial analysts construct ratios to extract information that is independent of a firm's size.

Price-Earnings (P/E) Ratio

One way to calculate the P/E ratio is to divide the current market price by the earnings per share of common stock for the latest year. The 1993 P/E ratios of the largest firms in Canada, the United States, Japan, and Germany are as follows:

United States	Japan	Germany	Canada
Exxon 17	Nippon Telegraph & Telephone 155.2	Allianz Holding 79.2	BCE 11.1
General Electric 17	Toyota Motor 14	Daimler Benz 18.5	Seagram 21.9
Philip Morris 9	Tokyo Electric Power 94.2	Siemens 14.1	Imperial Oil 39.8

As can be seen, some firms have high P/E ratios (Tokyo Electric Power, for example) and some firms have low ones (BCE). Since the P/E ratio measures how much investors are willing to pay per dollar of current earnings, higher P/Es are often taken to mean that the firm has significant prospects for future growth. Of course, if a firm had no or almost no earnings, its P/E would probably be quite large; so, as always, care is needed in interpreting this ratio.

Dividend Yield

The dividend yield is calculated by annualizing the last observed dividend payment of a firm and dividing by the current market price:

$$\text{Dividend yield} = \frac{\text{Dividend per share}}{\text{Market price per share}}$$

The 1993 dividend yields (in percent) for the largest firms in Canada, the United States, Japan, and Germany are:

United States	Japan	Germany	Canada
Exxon 4.5	Nippon Telegraph & Telephone .5	Allianz Holding .6	BCE 5.95
General Electric 2.7	Toyota Motor 1.1	Daimler Benz 2.3	Seagram 4.11
Philip Morris 4.9	Tokyo Electric Power 1.3	Siemens 2.0	Imperial Oil 3.83

Like P/E ratios, dividend yields are related to the market's perception of future growth prospects for firms. Firms with high growth prospects will generally have lower dividend yields.

Market-to-Book (M/B) Value and the Q Ratio

The market-to-book value ratio is calculated by dividing the market price per share by the book value per share. Since book value per share is an accounting number, it reflects historical costs. In a loose sense, the market-to-book ratio therefore compares the market value of the firm's investments to their cost. A value less than 1 could mean that the firm has not been successful overall in creating value for its shareholders.

There is another ratio, called *Tobin's* Q, that is very much like the M/B ratio. Tobin's Q ratio divides the market value of all of the firm's debt plus equity by the replacement value of the firm's assets. The Q ratios for several firms are:[11]

High Qs	
Coca-Cola	4.2
IBM	4.2
Low Qs	
National Steel	0.53
U.S. Steel	0.61

The Q ratio differs from the M/B ratio in that the Q ratio uses market value of the debt plus equity. It also uses the replacement value of all assets and not the historical cost value.

---

[11]E. B. Lindberg and S. Ross, "Tobin's Q and Industrial Organization," *Journal of Business* 54 (January 1981).

If a firm has a Q ratio above 1 it has an incentive to invest that is probably greater than for a firm with a Q ratio below 1. Firms with high Q ratios tend to be those firms with attractive investment opportunities or a significant competitive advantage.

Using Financial Ratios

Financial ratios have a variety of uses within a firm. Among the most important is performance evaluation. For example, managers are frequently evaluated and compensated on the basis of accounting measures of performance such as profit margin and return on equity. Also, firms with multiple divisions frequently compare their performance using financial statement information. Another important internal use is planning for the future. Historical financial statement information is very useful for generating projections about the future and for checking the realism of assumptions made in those projections.

Financial statements are useful to parties outside the firm, including short-term and long-term creditors and potential investors. For example, such information is quite useful in deciding whether or not to grant credit to a new customer.[12] When firms borrow from chartered banks, loan agreements almost always require that financial statements be submitted periodically. Most bankers use computer software to prepare common-size statements and to calculate ratios for their accounts. More advanced software uses expert system technology to generate a preliminary diagnosis of the borrower by comparing the company's ratios against benchmark parameters selected by the banker.

Choosing a Benchmark

The firm's historical ratios are standard benchmarks for financial ratio analysis. Historical benchmarks are used to establish a trend. Another means of establishing a benchmark is to identify firms that are similar in the sense that they compete in the same markets, have similar assets, and operate in similar ways. In practice, establishing such a peer group involves judgment on the part of the analyst since no two companies are identical.

Various benchmarks are available.[13] Statistics Canada publications include typical balance sheets, income statements, and selected ratios for firms in around 180 industries. Dun & Bradstreet Canada provides key business ratios for Canadian corporations. Other sources of benchmarks for Canadian companies include financial databases available from *The Financial Post* and *InfoGlobe*.[14] Several financial institutions gather their own financial ratio databases by compiling information on their loan customers. In this way, they seek to obtain more current, industry-specific information than is available from services like Statistics Canada and Dun & Bradstreet.

---

[12]Chapter 28 shows how statistical models based on ratios are used to predict insolvency.

[13]This discussion draws on L. Kryzanowski, M. To, and R. Seguin, *Business Solvency Risk Analysis* (Institute of Canadian Bankers, 1990), Chapter 3.

[14]Analysts examining U.S. companies will find comparable information available from Robert Morris Associates.

Obtaining current information is not the only challenge facing the financial analyst. Most large Canadian corporations do business in several industries so the analyst often compares the company against several industry averages. Further, it is necessary to recognize that the industry average is not necessarily optimal. For example, agricultural analysts know that farmers are suffering with painfully low average profitability coupled with excessive debt. Despite these shortcomings, the industry average is a useful benchmark for ratio analysis.

Potential Pitfalls of Financial Ratio Analysis

Financial ratio analysis is not based on any underlying theory to help identify which quantities to examine and to guide in establishing benchmarks. For this reason, individual judgment guided by experience plays an important role. Recognizing this, chartered banks are investing in expert system technology to pool the experience of many individual lenders and to standardize judgment.

Several other general problems frequently crop up. Different firms end their fiscal years at different times. For firms in seasonal businesses (such as a retailer with a large Christmas season), this can lead to difficulties in comparing balance sheets because of fluctuations in accounts during the year. For any particular firm, unusual or transient events, such as a one-time profit from an asset sale, may affect financial performance. In comparing firms, such events can give misleading signals.

Summary and Conclusions

Much research indicates that accounting statements provide important information about the value of the firm. Financial analysts and managers learn how to rearrange financial statements to squeeze out the maximum amount of information. In particular, analysts and managers use financial ratios to summarize the firm's liquidity, activity, financial leverage, and profitability. When possible, they also use market values. This appendix describes the most popular financial ratios. The following points should be kept in mind when trying to interpret financial statements:

1. Measures of profitability such as return on equity suffer from several potential deficiencies as indicators of performance. They do not take into account the risk or timing of cash flows.

2. Financial ratios are linked to one another. For example, return on equity is determined from the profit margins, the asset turnover ratio, and the financial leverage.

3. Financial ratio analysis seldom looks at ratios in isolation. As we have illustrated, financial analysts compare a firm's present ratios against historical ratios and industry averages.

4. Because ratio analysis is based on experience rather than on theory, special care must be taken to achieve consistent interpretations. Since financial ratios are based on accounting numbers, ratios may be misleading if management engages in accounting window dressing to improve reported performance. The hardest performance measures for management to manipulate are those based on market values because the market can usually see through attempts to manipulate accounting numbers.

Appendix Questions and Problems

2.A1 What effect would the following actions have on a firm's current ratio? Assume that net working capital is positive.

a. Inventory is purchased for cash.

b. A supplier is paid.

c. A bank loan is repaid.

d. A long-term debt matures and is paid.

e. A customer pays off an account.

f. Inventory is sold.

2.A2 If a company reports a 5 percent profit margin, a total asset turnover of 2, and a total debt ratio of .50, what are its ROA and ROE?

2.A3 Consider the following information for the PVI Corporation:

Credit sales	$5,885
Cost of goods sold	4,021
Accounts receivable	880
Accounts payable	642

How long does it take PVI to collect on its sales? How long does PVI take to pay its suppliers?

Use the following financial statement information for Stowe Enterprises to work Problems 2.A4 through 2.A6.

STOWE ENTERPRISES
1994 Income Statement

Sales	$1,400
Cost of goods sold	700
Depreciation	200
Earnings before interest and taxes	$ 500
Interest paid	150
Taxable income	$ 350
Taxes	119
Net income	$ 231
Addition to retained earnings	$ 62
Dividends	169

STOWE ENTERPRISES
Abbreviated Balance Sheets, 1993–1994

Assets	1993	1994	Liabilities and owners' equity	1993	1994
Current assets			Current liabilities		
Cash	$ 200	$ 503	Accounts payable	$ 500	$ 530
Accounts			Notes payable	543	460
receivable	650	688	Other	214	183
Inventory	1,045	700	Long-term debt	1,097	1,184
Fixed assets			Owners' equity		
Net plant and			Common stock	190	240
equipment	1,490	1,689	Capital surplus	400	480
			Accumulated retained		
			earnings	441	503
			Total liabilities and		
Total assets	$3,385	$3,580	owners' equity	$3,385	$3,580

2.A4 Compute the following ratios for Stowe Enterprises for 1993 and 1994:

Short-term solvency ratios	Asset management ratios	Long-term solvency ratios	Profitability ratios
Current ratio	Total asset turnover	Debt ratio	Profit margin
Quick ratio	Inventory turnover	Debt-to-equity ratio	Return on assets
Cash ratio	Receivables turnover	Equity multiplier	Return on equity
		Times interest earned	
		Cash coverage ratio	

2.A5 Construct the DuPont identity for Stowe Enterprises for 1994.

2.A6 Prepare a statement of cash flows for Stowe.

2.A7 For how many days in 1994 could Stowe continue to operate if its production were suspended?

2.A8 Stowe has 60 shares outstanding in 1994. The price per share is $40. What are the P/E ratio and market-to-book ratio?

2.A9 In response to complaints about high prices, a grocery chain runs the following advertising campaign: "If you pay your child 25 cents to go buy $10 worth of groceries, then your child makes twice as much on the trip as we do." You've collected the following information from the grocery chain's financial statements:

Sales	$114 million
Net income	1.42 million
Total assets	8 million
Total debt	3 million

Evaluate the claim. What is the basis for the statement? Is this claim misleading? Why or why not?

2.A10 Select an industry featured in recent financial news. Then obtain annual reports on two companies in that industry and conduct a ratio analysis for the most recent two years. Make the relevant comparisons between the companies and against industry norms. Based on your ratio analysis, how do the two companies differ? Compare your comments against recent newspaper articles on the industry. (Note: This question is much easier using ratio analysis software.)

PART TWO
VALUE AND CAPITAL BUDGETING

Firms and individuals invest in a large variety of assets. Some are real assets such as machinery and land, and some are financial assets such as stocks and bonds. The objective of the investment is to maximize value. In the simplest terms, this means to find assets that add more value to the firm than they cost. To do this we need a theory of value. Developing such a theory is the goal of Part Two.

Finance is the study of markets and instruments that deal with cash flows over time. In Chapter 3 we describe how financial markets allow us to determine the values of financial instruments. We study some stylized examples and show why financial markets and financial instruments are created. We introduce the basic principles of rational decision-making and apply these principles to a two-period investment. Here, we introduce one of the most important ideas in finance: net present value (NPV). We show why net present value is useful and the conditions that make it applicable.

In Chapter 4 we extend the concept of net present value to more than one time period. The mathematics of compounding and discounting is presented. In Chapter 5 we apply net present value to bonds and stocks. This is a very important chapter because net present value can be used to determine the value of a wide variety of financial instruments.

Although we have made a strong case for using the NPV rule in Chapters 3 and 4, Chapter 6 presents four other rules: the payback rule, the accounting-rate-of-return rule, the internal rate of return (IRR), and the profitability index. Each of these alternatives has some redeeming features, but they are not sufficient to replace the NPV rule.

In Chapter 7 we analyze how to estimate the cash flows required for capital budgeting. We start the chapter with a discussion of the concept of incremental cash flows—the difference between the cash flows for the firm with and without the project. Chapter 8 focuses on assessing the reliability and reasonableness of estimates of NPV. The chapter introduces techniques for dealing with uncertain incremental cash flows in capital budgeting, including break-even analysis, decision trees, and sensitivity analysis.

CHAPTER **3**

Financial Markets
and Net Present
Value: First
Principles of Finance
(Advanced)

CHAPTER **4**

Net Present Value

CHAPTER **5**

How to Value Bonds
and Stocks

CHAPTER **6**

Some Alternative
Investment Rules

CHAPTER **7**

New Present Value
and Capital
Budgeting

CHAPTER **8**

Strategy and Analysis
in Using Net Present
Value

Financial Markets and Net Present Value: First Principles of Finance (Advanced)

Finance refers to the process by which special markets deal with cash flows over time. These markets are called *financial markets*. Making investment and financing decisions requires an understanding of the basic economic principles of financial markets. This introductory chapter describes a financial market as one that makes it possible for individuals and corporations to borrow and lend. As a consequence, financial markets can be used by individuals to adjust their patterns of consumption over time and by corporations to adjust their patterns of investment spending over time. The main point of this chapter is that individuals and corporations can use the financial markets to help them make investment decisions. We introduce one of the most important ideas in finance: net present value.

By far the most important economic decisions are those that involve investments in real assets. We don't mean savings decisions, which are decisions not to consume some of this year's income, but decisions regarding actual investments: building a machine or a whole factory or a McDonald's, for example. These decisions determine the economic future for a society. Economists use the word *capital* to describe the total stock of machines and equipment that a society possesses and uses to produce goods and services. Investment decisions are decisions about whether or not to increase this stock of capital.

The investment decisions made today determine how much additional capital the society will add to its current stock of capital. That capital then can be used in the future to produce goods and services for the society. Some of the forms that capital takes are obvious, like steel mills and computers. But many kinds of capital are things that you probably never would have considered as part of a country's capital stock. Public roads, for example, are a form of capital, and the decisions to build them are investment decisions. Perhaps most important, the decision you are making to invest in an education is no different in principle from these other investment decisions. Your decision to invest in education is a decision to build your human capital, just as a company's decision to build a new factory is a decision to invest in physical capital.[1]

---

[1] If you have any doubt about the importance of human capital as part of a country's wealth, think about the conditions of Germany and Japan at the end of World War II. The physical capital of these countries had been destroyed, and even the basic social capital like roads, sewer systems, and factories was in rubble. Even though these countries might have appeared to be economically crippled beyond repair, a look below the surface would have revealed a different picture. A huge part of the wealth of these countries consisted of the human capital inherent in their literate and skilled populations. Building on this substantial base of capital by a long-term policy of investment has brought Germany and Japan to a very high standard of living.

The total of all the capital possessed by a society is a measure of its wealth. The purpose of this chapter is to develop the basic principles that guide rational investment decision-making. We show that a particular investment decision should be made if it is superior to available alternatives in the financial markets.

3.1   The Financial Market Economy

Financial markets develop to facilitate borrowing and lending between individuals. Here we talk about how this happens. Suppose we describe the economic circumstances of two people: Tom and Leslie. Both Tom and Leslie have current income of $100,000. Tom is a very patient person, and some people call him a miser. He wants to consume only $50,000 of current income and save the rest. Leslie is a very impatient person, and some people call her extravagant. She wants to consume $150,000 this year. Tom and Leslie have different intertemporal consumption preferences.

Such preferences are personal matters and have more to do with psychology than with finance. However, it seems that Tom and Leslie could strike a deal: Tom could give up some of his income this year in exchange for future income that Leslie can promise to give him. Tom can *lend* $50,000 to Leslie, and Leslie can *borrow* $50,000 from Tom.

Suppose that they do strike this deal, with Tom giving up $50,000 this year in exchange for $55,000 next year. This is illustrated in Figure 3.1 with the basic cash flow time chart, a representation of the timing and amount of the cash flows. The cash flows that are received are represented by an arrow pointing up from the point on the time line at which the cash flow occurs. The cash flows paid out are represented by an arrow pointing down. In other words, for each dollar Tom trades away or lends, he gets a commitment to get it back as well as to receive 10 percent more.

In the language of finance, 10 percent is the annual rate of interest on the loan. When a dollar is lent out, the repayment of $1.10 can be thought of as being made up

---

Figure 3.1
Tom's and
Leslie's cash flows

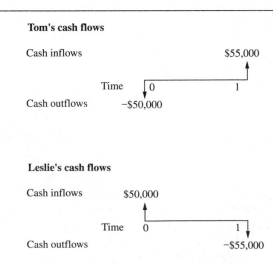

of two parts. First, the lender gets the dollar back; that is the *principal repayment.* Second, the lender receives an *interest payment,* which is $0.10 in this example.

Now, not only have Tom and Leslie struck a deal, but as a by-product of their bargain they have created a financial instrument, the IOU. This piece of paper entitles whoever receives it to present it to Leslie next year and redeem it for $55,000. Financial instruments that entitle whoever possesses them to receive payment are called *bearer instruments* because whoever bears them can use them. Presumably there could be more such IOUs in the economy written by many different lenders and borrowers like Tom and Leslie.

Of course, if you have lent some money this year and expect to be repaid next year, you are indifferent to who pays you back, as long as you get your money. In a completely honest society where people borrow only when they are certain that they will be able to repay the loan, lenders can be assured that the IOUs they hold will be repaid. Similarly, if the society is not entirely peopled by honest folks, governments can impose penalties to discourage individuals from borrowing when they do not have the ability to repay their loans. In either of these worlds, however, if the lenders are sure that the loans will be repaid, it follows that the lenders will not care whose loans they actually are holding.

Even in a virtuous society, people can make honest mistakes. Individuals may borrow in the full expectation that they will be able to fulfill the terms of their contracts, but circumstances may prevent them from doing so. More importantly, both the lender and the borrower may recognize there is some possibility that the loan will not be repaid. In this case there must be provisions in the contract to cover such a possibility. We defer our discussion of these possibilities until later in the book. For the present we assume that we are dealing with risk-free bonds, that is, IOUs or bonds that are sure to be repaid.

The Anonymous Market

If the borrower does not care whom she has to pay back, and if the lender does not care whose IOUs he is holding, we could just as well drop Tom's and Leslie's names from their contract. All we need is a record book, in which we could record the fact that Tom has lent $50,000 and Leslie has borrowed $50,000 and that the terms of the loan, the interest rate, are 10 percent. Perhaps another person could keep the records for borrowers and lenders—for a fee, of course. In fact—and this is one of the virtues of such an arrangement—Tom and Leslie wouldn't even need to meet. Instead of needing to find and trade with each other, they could each trade with the record keeper. The record keeper could deal with thousands of such borrowers and lenders, none of whom would need to meet the other.

Institutions that perform this sort of market function, matching borrowers and lenders or traders, are called **financial intermediaries.** Chartered banks are modern examples of financial intermediaries. A bank's depositors lend the bank money, and the bank makes loans from the funds it has on deposit. In essence, the bank is an intermediary between the depositors and the ultimate borrowers. To make the market work, we must be certain that the market clears. By *market clearing* we mean that the total amount that people like Tom wish to lend to the market, say $11 million, equals the total amount that people like Leslie wish to borrow.

Market Clearing

If the lenders wish to lend more than the borrowers want to borrow, then presumably the interest rate is too high. Because there would not be enough borrowing for all of the lenders at, say, 15 percent, there are really only two ways that the market could be made to clear. One is to ration the lenders. For example, if the lenders wish to lend $20 million when interest rates are at 15 percent and the borrowers wish to borrow only $8 million, the market could take, say, 8/20 of each dollar, or $0.40, from each of the lenders and distribute it to the borrowers. This is one possible scheme for making the market clear, but it is not one that would be sustainable in a free and competitive marketplace. Why not?

To answer this important question, we return to our lender, Tom. Tom sees that interest rates are 15 percent and, not surprisingly, rather than simply lending the $50,000 that he was willing to lend when rates were 10 percent, Tom decides that at the higher rates he would like to lend more, say, $80,000. But since the lenders want to lend more money than the borrowers want to borrow, the record keepers tell Tom that they won't be able to take all of his $80,000; rather, they will take only 40 percent of it, or $32,000. With the interest rate at 15 percent, people are not willing to borrow enough to match up with all of the loans that are available at that rate.

Tom is not very pleased with that state of affairs, but he can do something to improve his situation. Suppose that he knows that Leslie is borrowing $20,000 in the market at the 15-percent interest rate. That means that Leslie must repay $20,000 on her loan next year plus the interest of 15 percent of $20,000, or $0.15 × $20,000 = $3,000. Suppose that Tom goes to Leslie and offers to lend her the $20,000 for 14 percent. Leslie is happy because she will save 1 percent on the deal and will need to pay back only $2,800 in interest next year. This is $200 less than if she had borrowed from the record keepers. Tom is happy, too, because he has found a way to lend some of the money that the record keepers would not take. The net result of this transaction is that the record keepers have lost Leslie as a customer. Why should she borrow from them when Tom will lend her the money at a lower interest rate?

Tom and Leslie are not the only ones cutting side deals in the marketplace, and it is clear that the record keepers will not be able to maintain the 15-percent rate. The interest rate must fall if they are to stay in business.

Suppose, then, that the market clears at the rate of 10 percent. At this rate the amount of money that the lenders wish to lend, $11 million, is exactly equal to the amount that the borrowers desire. We refer to the interest rate that clears the market, 10 percent in our example, as the **equilibrium rate of interest.**

In this section we have shown that, in the market for loans, bonds or IOUs are traded. These are *financial instruments.* The interest rate on these loans is set so that the total demand for such loans by borrowers equals the total supply of loans by lenders. At a higher interest rate, lenders wish to supply more loans than are demanded, and if the interest rate is lower than this equilibrium level, borrowers demand more loans than lenders are willing to supply.

CONCEPT QUESTIONS

- What is an interest rate?
- What do we mean when we say a market clears?
- What is an equilibrium rate of interest?

Making Consumption Choices   3.2

Figure 3.2 illustrates the situation faced by an individual in the financial market. This person is assumed to have an income of $50,000 this year and an income of $60,000 next year. The market allows him not only to consume $50,000 worth of goods this year and $60,000 next year, but also to borrow and lend at the equilibrium interest rate. The line *AB* in Figure 3.2 shows all of the consumption possibilities open to the person through borrowing or lending, and the shaded area contains all of the feasible choices. Looking at this figure more closely reveals exactly why points in the shaded area are available.

We will use the letter r to denote the interest rate—the equilibrium rate—in this market. The rate is risk-free because we assume that no default can take place. Look at point *A* on the vertical axis of Figure 3.2. Point *A* represents consumption next year (on the vertical axis) of

$$A = \$60,000 + \$50,000 \times (1 + r)$$

For example, if the rate of interest is 10 percent, then point *A* is

$$A = \$60,000 + \$50,000 \times (1 + 0.1)$$
$$= \$60,000 + \$55,000$$
$$= \$115,000$$

Point *A* is the maximum amount of wealth that this person can spend in the second year. He gets to point *A* by lending the full income that is available this year, $50,000, and consuming none of it. In the second year, then, he will have the second year's income of $60,000 plus the proceeds from the loan that he made in the first year, $55,000, for a total of $115,000.

Following the same logic, Point *B* is a distance of

$$B = \$50,000 + \$60,000/(1 + r)$$

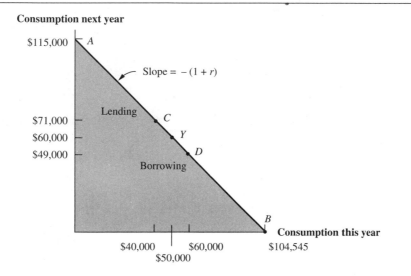

Consumption next year

$115,000 — *A*

Slope = − (1 + *r*)

Lending   *C*

$71,000
$60,000 — *Y*
$49,000 — *D*

Borrowing

B

Consumption this year

$40,000 $60,000 $104,545
$50,000

Figure 3.2
Intertemporal consumption opportunities

along the horizontal axis. If the interest rate is 10 percent, point B will be

$$B = \$50,000 + \$60,000/(1 + 0.1)$$
$$= \$50,000 + \$54,545$$
$$= \$104,545 \quad \text{(rounded off to the nearest dollar)}$$

Why do we divide next year's income of $60,000 by $(1 + r)$ or 1.1 in the preceding computation? Point B represents the maximum amount available for this person to consume this year. To achieve that maximum he would borrow as much as possible and repay the loan from the income, $60,000, that he was going to receive next year. Because $60,000 will be available to repay the loan next year, we are asking how much he could borrow this year at an interest rate of r and still be able to repay the loan. The answer is

$$\$60,000/(1 + r)$$

because if he borrows this amount, he must repay it next year with interest. Thus, next year he must repay

$$[\$60,000/(1 + r)] \times (1 + r) = \$60,000$$

no matter what the interest rate, r, is. In our example we found that he could borrow $54,545 and, sure enough,

$$\$54,545 \times 1.1 = \$60,000$$

(after rounding off to the nearest dollar).

Furthermore, by borrowing and lending different amounts, the person can achieve any point on the line AB. For example, at point C he has chosen to lend $10,000 of today's income. This means that at point C he will have

Consumption this year at point $C = \$50,000 - \$10,000 = \$40,000$

and

Consumption next year at point $C = \$60,000 + \$10,000 \times (1 + r) = \$71,000$

when the interest rate is 10 percent.

Similarly, at point D, the individual has decided to borrow $10,000 and repay the loan next year. At point D, then,

Consumption this year at point $C = \$50,000 + \$10,000 = \$60,000$

and

Consumption next year at point $D = \$60,000 - \$10,000 \times (1 + r) = \$49,000$

at an interest rate of 10 percent.

In fact, this person can consume at any point on the line AB. This line has a slope of $-(1 + r)$, which means that, for each dollar that is added to the x coordinate along the line, $(1 + r)$ dollars are subtracted from the y coordinate. Moving along the line from point A, the initial point of $50,000 this year and $60,000 next year, toward point B gives the person more consumption today and less next year. In other words, moving toward point B is borrowing. Similarly, moving up toward point A, he is consuming

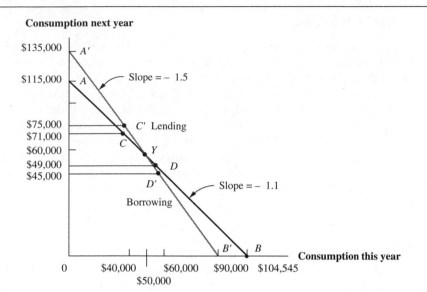

Figure 3.3
The effect of different interest rates on consumption opportunities

less today and more next year and he is lending. The line is a straight line because the individual has no effect on the interest rate. This is one of the assumptions of perfectly competitive financial markets.

Where in Figure 3.2 will the person actually be? The answer to that question depends on the individual's tastes and personal situation, just as it did before there was a market. If the person is impatient, he might wish to borrow money at a point such as *D,* and if he is patient, he might wish to lend some of this year's income and enjoy more consumption next year at, for example, a point such as *C.*

Notice that whether we think of someone as patient or impatient depends on the interest rate he or she faces in the market. Suppose that our individual was impatient and chose to borrow $10,000 and move to point *D.* Now suppose that we raise the interest rate to 20 percent or even 50 percent. Suddenly our impatient person may become very patient and might prefer to lend some of this year's income to take advantage of the very high interest rate. The general result is depicted in Figure 3.3. We can see that lending at point *C'* yields much greater future income and consumption possibilities than before.[2]

CONCEPT QUESTIONS

■ How does an individual change consumption across periods through borrowing and lending?

■ How do interest rate changes affect one's degree of impatience?

---

[2]Those familiar with consumer theory might be aware of the surprising case where raising the interest rate actually makes people borrow more or lowering the rate makes them lend more. The latter case might occur, for example, if the decline in the interest rate made the lenders have so little consumption next year that they have no choice but to lend out even more than they were before, just to subsist. Nothing we do depends on excluding such cases, but it is much easier to ignore them, and the resulting analysis fits the real markets much more closely.

3.3   The Competitive Market

In the previous analysis we assumed the individual moves freely along the line *AB,* and we ignored—and assumed that the individual ignores—any effect his borrowing or lending decisions might have on the equilibrium interest rate itself. What would happen, though, if the total amount of loans outstanding in the market when the person was doing no borrowing or lending was $10 million, and if our person then decided to lend, say, $5 million? His lending would be half as much as the rest of the market put together, and it would not be unreasonable to think that the equilibrium interest rate would fall to induce more borrowers into the market to take his additional loans. In such a situation the person has some power in the market to influence the equilibrium rate significantly, and he would take this power into consideration in making his decisions.

In modern financial markets, however, the total amount of borrowing and lending is not $10 million; rather, as we say in Chapter 1, it is far higher. In such a huge market no one investor or even any single company can have a significant effect (although a government might). We assume, then, in all of our subsequent discussions and analyses that the financial market is perfectly competitive. By that we mean no individuals or firms think they have any effect whatsoever on the interest rates that they face no matter how much borrowing, lending, or investing they do. In the language of economics, individuals who respond to rates and prices by acting as though they have no influence on them are called *price takers,* and this assumption is sometimes called the *price-taking assumption.* It is the condition of **perfectly competitive financial markets** (or, more simply, *perfect markets*). The following conditions characterize perfect financial markets:

1. Trading is costless. Access to the financial markets is free.
2. Information about borrowing and lending opportunities is readily available.
3. There are many traders, and no single trader can have a significant impact on market prices.

How Many Interest Rates Are There in a Competitive Market?

An important point about this one-year market where no defaults can take place is that only one interest rate can be quoted in the market at any one time. Suppose that some competing record keepers decide to set up a rival market. To attract customers, their business plan is to offer lower interest rates, say, 9 percent, to attract borrowers away from the first market and soon have all of the business.

Their business plan will work, but it will do so beyond their wildest expectations. They will indeed attract the borrowers, all $11 million worth of them! But the matter doesn't stop there. By offering to borrow and lend at 9 percent when another market is offering 10 percent, they have created the proverbial money machine.

The world of finance is populated by sharp-eyed inhabitants who would not let this opportunity slip by them. Any one of these, whether a borrower or a lender, would go to the new market and borrow everything he could at the 9-percent rate. At the same time he was borrowing in the new market, he would also be striking a deal to lend in the old market at the 10-percent rate. If he could borrow $100 million at 9 percent and lend it at 10 percent, he could net 1 percent, or $1 million, next year. He would repay the $109 million he owed to the new market from the $110 million he would receive when the 10-percent loan he had made in the original market was repaid, pocketing $1 million.

This process of striking a deal in one market and an offsetting deal in another simultaneously and at more favourable terms is called *arbitrage;* the individuals who do it are called *arbitrageurs.* Of course, someone must be paying for all of this free money, and it must be the record keepers because the borrowers and the lenders are all making money. Our intrepid, entrepreneurial record keepers will lose their proverbial shirts and go out of business. The moral of this is clear: As soon as different interest rates are offered for essentially the same risk-free loans, arbitrageurs will take advantage of the situation by borrowing at the low rate and lending at the high rate. The gap between the two rates will be closed quickly, and for all practical purposes there will be only one rate available in the market.

CONCEPT QUESTIONS

- What is the most important feature of a competitive financial market?
- What conditions are likely to lead to this?
- What is arbitrage and why does it result in one rate for riskless loans?

The Basic Principle 3.4

We have already shown how people use the financial markets to adjust their patterns of consumption over time to fit their particular preferences. By borrowing and lending, they can greatly expand their range of choices. They need only to have access to a market with an interest rate at which they can borrow and lend.

In the previous section we saw how these savings and consumption decisions depend on the interest rate. The financial markets also provide a benchmark against which proposed investments can be compared, and the interest rate is the basis for a test that any proposed investment must pass. The financial markets give the individual, the corporation, or even the government a standard of comparison for economic decisions. This benchmark is critical when investment decisions are being made.

The way we use the financial markets to aid us in making investment decisions is a direct consequence of our basic assumption that individuals can never be made worse off by increasing the range of choices open to them. People always can make use of the financial markets to adjust their savings and consumption by borrowing or lending. An investment project is worth undertaking only if it increases the range of choices in the financial markets. To do this, the project must be at least as desirable as what is available in the financial markets.[3] If it were not as desirable as what the financial markets have to offer, people could simply use the financial markets instead of undertaking the investment. This point will govern us in all of our investment decisions. It is the *first principle of investment decision-making,* and it is the foundation on which all of our rules are built.

CONCEPT QUESTION

- Describe the basic financial principle of investment decision-making.

---

[3]You might wonder what to do if an investment is exactly as desirable as an alternative in the financial markets. In principle, if there is a tie, it doesn't matter whether or not we take on the investment. In practice, we've never seen an exact tie.

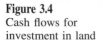

Figure 3.4
Cash flows for
investment in land

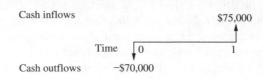

3.5   Practicing the Principle

Let us apply the basic principle of investment decision-making to some concrete situations.

A Lending Example

Consider a person who is concerned only about this year and next. She has an income of $100,000 this year and expects to make the same amount next year. The interest rate is 10 percent. This individual is thinking about investing in a piece of land that costs $70,000. She is certain that next year the land will be worth $75,000, a sure $5,000 gain. Should she undertake the investment? This situation is described in Figure 3.4 with the cash flow time chart.

A moment's thought should be all it takes to convince her that this is not an attractive business deal. By investing $70,000 in the land, she will have $75,000 available next year. Suppose, instead, that she puts the same $70,000 into a loan in the financial market. At the 10 percent rate of interest this $70,000 would grow to

$$(1 + 0.1) \times \$70,000 = \$77,000$$

next year.

It would be foolish to buy the land when the same $70,000 investment in the financial market would beat it by $2,000 (that is, $77,000 from the loan minus $75,000 from the land investment).

Figure 3.5 illustrates this situation. Notice that the $70,000 loan gives no less income today and $2,000 more next year. This example illustrates some amazing features of the financial markets. It is remarkable to consider all of the information that we did *not* use when arriving at the decision not to invest in the land. We did not need to know how much income the person has this year or next year. We also did not need to know whether the person preferred more income this year or next.

We did not need to know any of these other facts, and, more importantly, the person making the decision did not need to know them either. She only needed to be able to compare the investment with a relevant alternative available in the financial market. When the proposed investment fell short of that standard—by $2,000 in the previous example—regardless of what the individual wanted to do, she knew that she should not buy the land.

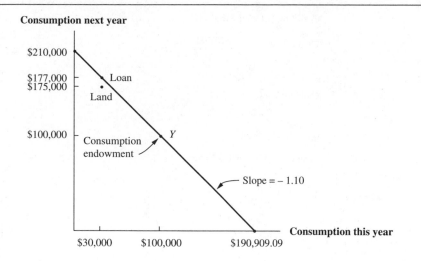

Figure 3.5
Consumption
opportunities with
borrowing and
lending

A Borrowing Example

Let us sweeten the deal a bit. Suppose that instead of being worth $75,000 next year, the land will be worth $80,000. What should our investor do now? This case is a bit more difficult. After all, even if the land seems like a good deal, this person's income this year is $100,000. Does she really want to make a $70,000 investment this year? Won't that leave only $30,000 for consumption?

The answers to these questions are yes, the individual should buy the land; yes, she does want to make a $70,000 investment this year; and, most surprising of all, even though her income is $100,000, making the $70,000 investment will not leave her with $30,000 to consume this year! Now let us see how finance lets us get around the basic laws of arithmetic.

The financial markets are the key to solving our problem. First, the financial markets can be used as a standard of comparison against which any investment project must measure up. Second, they can be used as a tool to help the individual actually undertake investments. These twin features of the financial markets enable us to make the right investment decision.

Suppose that the person borrows the $70,000 initial investment that is needed to purchase the land. Next year she must repay this loan. Because the interest rate is 10 percent, she will owe the financial market $77,000 next year. This is depicted in Figure 3.6. Because the land will be worth $80,000 next year, she will be able to sell it, pay off her debt of $77,000, and have $3,000 extra cash.

If she wishes, this person can now consume an extra $3,000 worth of goods and services next year. This possibility is illustrated in Figure 3.7. In fact, even if she wants to do all of her consuming this year, she is still better off taking the investment. All she must do is take out a loan this year and repay it from the proceeds of the land next year and profit by $3,000.

Furthermore, instead of borrowing just the $70,000 that she needed to purchase the land, she could have borrowed $72,727.27. She could have used $70,000 to buy

Figure 3.6
Cash flows of
borrowing to
purchase the land

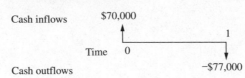

Cash flows of borrowing

Cash inflows $70,000

Time   0   1

Cash outflows   −$77,000

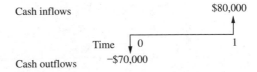

Cash flows of investing in land

Cash inflows $80,000

Time   0   1

Cash outflows   −$70,000

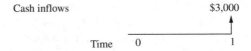

Cash flows of borrowing and investing in land

Cash inflows $3,000

Time   0   1

Figure 3.7
Consumption
opportunities with
investment
opportunity and
borrowing and
lending

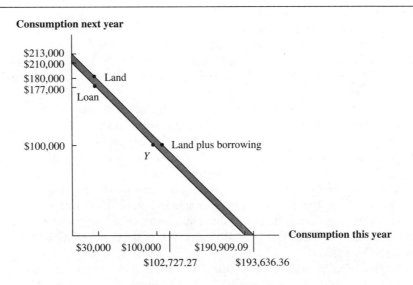

Consumption next year

$213,000
$210,000
$180,000 — • Land
$177,000
        Loan

$100,000 — • Land plus borrowing
              Y

Consumption this year

$30,000 $100,000 $190,909.09
          $102,727.27 $193,636.36

the land and consumed the remaining \$2,727.27. We will call \$2,727.27 the net present value of the transaction. Notice that it is equal to \$3,000 × 1/1.1. How did we figure out that this was the exact amount that she could borrow? It was easy: If \$72,727.27 is the amount that she borrows, then, because the interest rate is 10 percent, she must repay

$$\$72,727.27 \times (1 + 0.1) = \$80,000$$

next year, and that is exactly what the land will be worth. The line through the investment position in Figure 3.7 illustrates this borrowing possibility.

The amazing thing about both of these cases, one where the land is worth \$75,000 next year and the other where it is worth \$80,000 next year, is that we needed only to compare the investment with the financial markets to decide whether it was worth undertaking or not. This is one of the more important points in all of finance. It is true regardless of the consumption preferences of the individual. This is one of a number of *separation theorems* in finance. It states that the value of an investment to an individual is not dependent on consumption preferences. In our examples we showed that the person's decision to invest in land was not affected by consumption preferences. However, these preferences dictated whether the person borrowed or lent.

CONCEPT QUESTIONS

- Describe how the financial markets can be used to evaluate investment alternatives.
- What is the separation theorem? Why is it important?

Illustrating the Investment Decision   3.6

Figure 3.2, discussed earlier, describes the possibilities open to a person who has an income of \$50,000 this year and \$60,000 next year and faces a financial market in which the interest rate is 10 percent. But, at that moment, the person has no investment possibilities beyond the 10 percent borrowing and lending that is available in the financial market.

Suppose that we give this person the chance to undertake an investment project that will require a \$30,000 outlay of cash this year and that will return \$40,000 to the investor next year. Refer to Figure 3.2 and determine how you could include this new possibility in that figure and how you could use the figure to help you decide whether to undertake the investment.

Now look at Figure 3.8. In Figure 3.8 we have labeled the original point with \$50,000 this year and \$60,000 next year as point *A*. We have also added a new point *B*, with \$20,000 available for consumption this year and \$100,000 next year. The difference between point *A* and point *B* is that at point *A* the person is just where we started him off, and at point *B* the person has also decided to undertake the investment project. As a result of this decision, the person at point *B* has

$$\$50,000 - \$30,000 = \$20,000$$

left for consumption this year, and

$60,000 + $40,000 = $100,000

available next year. These are the coordinates of point *B*.

We must use our knowledge of the individual's borrowing and lending opportunities in order to decide whether to accept or reject the investment. This is illustrated in Figure 3.9. Figure 3.9 is similar to Figure 3.8, but in it we have drawn a line through point *A* that shows the possibilities open to the person if he stays at point *A* and does not take the investment. This line is exactly the same as the one in Figure 3.2. We have also drawn a parallel line through point *B* that shows the new possibilities that are available to the person if he undertakes the investment. The two lines are parallel

Figure 3.8
Consumption choices with investment but no financial markets

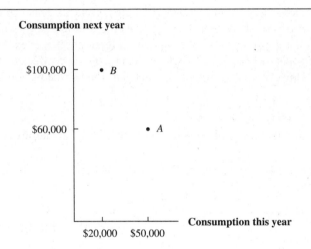

Figure 3.9
Consumption choices with investment opportunities and financial markets

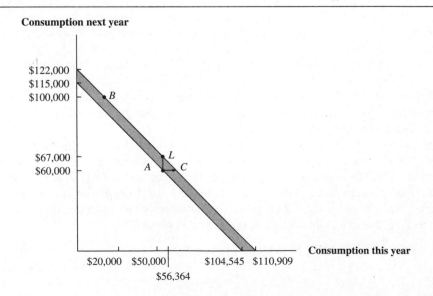

because the slope of each is determined by the same interest rate, 10 percent. It does not matter whether the person takes the investment and goes to point B or does not and stays at point A; in the financial market, each dollar of lending is a dollar less available for consumption this year and moves him to the left by a dollar along the x-axis. Because the interest rate is 10 percent, the $1 loan repays $1.10 and it moves him up by $1.10 along the y-axis.

It is easy to see from Figure 3.9 that the investment has made the person better off. The line through point B is higher than the line through point A. Thus, no matter what pattern of consumption this person wanted this year and next, he could have more in each year if he undertook the investment.

For example, suppose that our individual wanted to consume everything this year. If he did not take the investment, the point where the line through point A intersected the x-axis would give the maximum amount of consumption he could enjoy this year—$104,545. To recall how we found this figure, review the analysis of Figure 3.2. But in Figure 3.9 the line that goes through point B intersects the x-axis at a higher point than the line that goes through point A. Along this line the person can have the $20,000 that is left after investing $30,000, plus all that he can borrow and repay with both next year's income and the proceeds from the investment. The total amount available to consume today is therefore

$50,000 − $30,000 + ($60,000 + $40,000)/(1 + 0.1)

= $20,000 + $100,000/(1.1)

= $110,909

The additional consumption available this year from undertaking the investment and using the financial market is the difference on the x-axis between the points where these two lines intersect:

$110,909 − $104,545 = $6,364

This difference is an important measure of what the investment is worth to the person. It answers a variety of questions. For example, it is the answer to the question: How much money would we need to give the investor this year to make him just as well off as he is with the investment?

Because the line through point B is parallel to the line through point A but has been moved over by $6,364, we know that if we were to add this amount to the investor's current income this year at point A and take away the investment, he would wind up on the line through point B and with the same possibilities. If we do this, the person will have $56,364 this year and $60,000 next year, which is the situation of the point on the line through point B that lies to the right of point A in Figure 3.9. This is point C.

We could also ask a different question: How much money would we need to give the investor next year to make him just as well off as he is with the investment?

This is the same as asking how much higher the line through point B is than the line through point A. In other words, what is the difference in Figure 3.9 between the point where the line through A intercepts the y-axis and the point where the line through B intercepts the y-axis?

The point where the line through A intercepts the y-axis shows the maximum amount the person could consume next year if all of his current income were lent out and the proceeds of the loan were consumed along with next year's income.

As we showed in our analysis of Figure 3.2, this amount is $115,000. How does this compare with what the person can have next year if he takes the investment? By taking the investment we saw that the person would be at point *B* where he has $20,000 left this year and would have $100,000 next year. By lending the $20,000 that is left this year and adding the proceeds of this loan to the $100,000, we find the line through *B* intercepts the *y*-axis at

$$\$20,000 \times (1.1) + \$100,000 = \$122,000$$

The difference between this amount and $115,000 is

$$\$122,000 - \$115,000 = \$7,000$$

which is the answer to the question of how much we would need to give the person next year to make him as well off as he is with the investment.

There is a simple relationship between these two numbers. If we multiply $6,364 by 1.1 we get $7,000! Consider why this must be so. The $6,364 is the amount of extra cash we must give the person this year to substitute for having the investment. In a financial market with a 10 percent rate of interest, however, $1 this year is worth exactly the same as $1.10 next year. Thus, $6,364 this year is the same as $6,364 × 1.1 next year. In other words, the person does not care whether he has the investment, $6,364, this year or $6,364 × 1.1 next year. But we already showed that the investor is equally willing to have the investment and to have $7,000 next year. This must mean that

$$\$6,364 \times 1.1 = \$7,000$$

You can also verify this relationship between these two variables by using Figure 3.9. Because the lines through *A* and *B* have the same slope of −1.1, the difference of $7,000 between where they intersect on the *y*-axis and $6,364 between where they intersect on the *x*-axis must be in the ratio of 1.1 to 1.

Now we can show you how to evaluate the investment opportunity on a stand-alone basis. Here are the relevant facts: The individual must give up $30,000 this year to get $40,000 next year. These cash flows are illustrated in Figure 3.10.

The investment rule that follows from the previous analysis is the net present value (NPV) rule. Here we convert all consumption values to the present and add them up:

$$
\begin{aligned}
\text{Net present value} &= -\$30,000 + \$40,000 \times (1/1.1) \\
&= -\$30,000 + \$36,364 \\
&= \$6,364
\end{aligned}
$$

The future amount, $40,000, is called the *future value (FV)*.

Figure 3.10
Case flows for the investment project

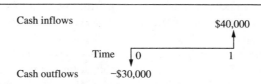

The net present value of an investment is a simple criterion for deciding whether or not to undertake it. NPV answers the question of how much cash an investor would need to have today as a substitute for making the investment. If the net present value is positive, the investment is worth taking on because doing so is essentially the same as receiving a cash payment equal to the net present value. If the net present value is negative, taking on the investment today is equivalent to giving up some cash today, and the investment should be rejected.

We use the term *net present value* to emphasize that we are already including the current cost of the investment in determining its value and not simply measuring what it will return. For example, if the interest rate is 10 percent and an investment of $30,000 today will produce a total cash return of $40,000 in one year's time, the *present value* of the $40,000 by itself is

$40,000/1.1 = $36,364

but the *net present value* of the investment is $36,364 minus the original investment:

Net present value = $36,364 − $30,000 = $6,364

The present value of a future cash flow is the value of that cash flow after considering the appropriate market interest rate. The net present value of an investment is the present value of the investment's future cash flows, minus the initial cost of the investment. We have just decided that our investment is a good opportunity. It has a positive net present value because it is worth more than it costs.

In general, the above can be stated in terms of the **net present value rule:**

An investment is worth making if it has a positive NPV. If an investment's NPV is negative, it should be rejected.

CONCEPT QUESTIONS

- Give the definitions of net present value, future value, and present value.
- What information does a person need to compute an investment's net present value?

Corporate Investment Decision-Making   3.7

Up to now, everything we have done has been from the perspective of the individual investor. How do corporations and firms make investment decisions? Are their decisions governed by a much more complicated set of rules and principles than the simple NPV rule that we have developed for individuals?

We return to questions of corporate decision-making and corporate governance later in the book, but it is remarkable how well our central ideas and the NPV rule hold up even when applied to corporations.

We may view firms as ways in which many investors can pool their resources to make large-scale business decisions. Suppose, for example, that you own 1 percent of some firm. Now suppose further that this firm is considering whether or not to undertake some investment. If that investment passes the NPV rule, that is, if it has a

Figure 3.11
Consumption
choices, the NPV
rule, and the
corporation

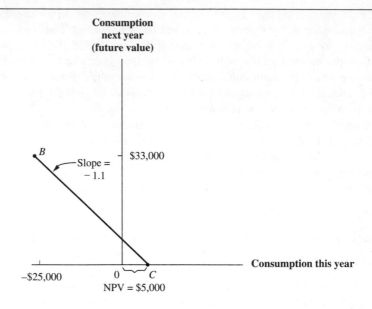

positive NPV, then 1 percent of the NPV belongs to you. If the firm takes on this investment, the value of the whole firm will rise by the NPV and your investment in the firm will rise by 1 percent of the NPV of the investment. Similarly, the other shareholders in the firm will profit by having the firm take on the positive NPV project because the value of their shares in the firm will also increase. This means that the shareholders in the firm will be unanimous in wanting the firm to increase its value by taking on the positive NPV project. If you follow this line of reasoning, you will also be able to see why the shareholders would oppose the firm's taking on any projects with a negative NPV because this would lower the value of their shares.

One difference between the firm and the individual is that the firm has no consumption endowment. In terms of our one-period consumption diagram, the firm starts at the origin. Figure 3.11 illustrates the situation of a firm with investment opportunity B. B is an investment that has a future value of $33,000 and will cost $25,000 now. If the interest rate is 10 percent, the NPV of B can be determined using the NPV rule. This is marked as point C in Figure 3.11. The cash flows of this investment are depicted in Figure 3.12.

One common objection to this line of reasoning is that people differ in their tastes and that they won't necessarily agree to take on or reject investments by the NPV rule. For instance, suppose that you and we each own some shares in a company. Further suppose that we are older than you and might be anxious to spend our money. Being younger, you might be more patient than we are and more willing to wait for a good long-term investment to pay off.

Because of the financial markets we all agree that the company should take on investments with positive NPVs and reject those with negative NPVs. If there were no financial markets, then, being impatient, we might want the company to do little or no investing so that we could have as much money as possible to consume now, and,

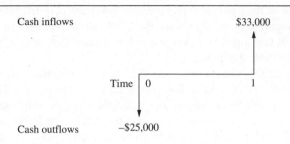

Figure 3.12
Corporate investment cash flows

being patient, you might prefer the company to make some investments. With financial markets, we are both satisfied by having the company follow the NPV rule.

To see why this is so, suppose that the company takes on a positive NPV investment. Let us assume that this investment has a net payoff of $1 million next year. That means that the value of the company will increase by $1 million next year; consequently, if you own 1 percent of the company's shares, the value of your shares will increase by 1 percent of $1 million, or $10,000, next year. Because you are patient, you might be prepared to wait for your $10,000 until next year. Being impatient, we do not want to wait—and with financial markets, we do not need to wait. We can simply borrow against the extra $10,000 we will have tomorrow and use the loan to consume more today.

In fact, if there is also a market for the firm's shares, we do not even need to borrow. After the company takes on a positive NPV investment, our shares in the company increase in value today. This is because owning the shares today entitles investors to their portion of the extra $1 million the company will have next year. This means that the shares would rise in value today by the present value of $1 million. Because you want to delay your consumption, you could wait until next year and sell your shares then to have extra consumption next year. Being impatient, we might sell our shares now and use the money to consume more today. If we owned 1 percent of the company's shares, we could sell our shares for an extra amount equal to the present value of $10,000.

In reality, shareholders in big companies do not vote on every investment decision, and their managers must have rules to follow. We have seen that all shareholders in a company will be made better off—no matter what their levels of patience or impatience—if managers follow the NPV rule. This is a marvelous result because it makes it possible for many different owners to delegate decision-making powers to the managers. They need only to tell the managers to follow the NPV rule, and if the managers do so, they will be doing exactly what the shareholders want them to do. Sometimes this form of the NPV rule is stated as having the managers maximize the value of the company. As we argued, the current value of the shares of the company will increase by the NPV of any investments that the company undertakes. This means that the managers of the company can make the shareholders as well off as possible by taking on all positive NPV projects and rejecting projects with negative NPVs.

Separating investment decision-making from the owners is a basic requirement of the modern large firm. The **separation theorem** in financial markets says that all investors will want to accept or reject the same investment projects by using the NPV rule, regardless of their personal preferences. Investors can delegate the operations of the firm and require that managers use the NPV rule. Of course, much remains for us to discuss about this topic. For example, what ensures that managers will actually do what is best for their shareholders?

We discussed this interesting topic in Chapter 1, and we take it up again later in the book. For now, though, we will no longer consider our perspective to be that of the lone investor. Instead, thanks to the separation theorem, we will use the NPV rule for companies as well as for investors. Our justification of the NPV rule depends on the conditions necessary to derive the separation theorem. These conditions are the ones that result in competitive financial markets. The analysis we have presented has been restricted to risk-free cash flows in one time period. However, the separation theorem also can be derived for risky cash flows that extend beyond one period.

For the reader interested in studying further about the separation theorem, we include several suggested readings at the end of this chapter that build on the material we have presented.

CONCEPT QUESTION

- In terms of the net present value rule, what is the essential difference between the individual and the corporation?

3.8   Summary and Conclusions

Finance is a subject that builds understanding from the ground up. Whenever you encounter a new problem or issue in finance, you can always return to the basic principles of this chapter for guidance.

1. Financial markets exist because people want to adjust their consumption over time. They do so by borrowing and lending.

2. Financial markets provide the key test for investment decision-making. Whether a particular investment decision should or should not be taken depends only on this test: If there is a superior alternative in the financial markets, the investment should be rejected; if not, the investment is worth taking. The most important thing about this principle is that the investor need not use his preferences to decide whether the investment should be taken. Regardless of the individual's preference for consumption this year versus next, regardless of how patient or impatient the individual is, making the proper investment decision depends only on comparing it with the alternatives in the financial markets.

3. The net present value of an investment helps us make the comparison between the investment and the financial market. If the NPV is positive, our rule tells us to undertake the investment. This illustrates the second major feature of the financial markets and investment. Not only does the NPV rule tell us which investments to accept and which to reject, the financial markets also provide us with the tools for acquiring the funds to make the investments. In short, we use the financial markets to decide both what to do and how to do it.

4. The NPV rule can be applied to corporations as well as to individuals. The separation theorem developed in this chapter says that all of the owners of the firm would agree that the firm should use the NPV rule even though each might differ in personal tastes for consumption and savings.

In the next chapter we learn more about the NPV rule by using it to examine a wide array of problems in finance.

Key Terms

Financial intermediaries 61
Equilibrium rate of interest 62
Perfectly competitive financial
  market 66

Net present value rule 75
Separation theorem 77

Suggested Readings

Two books that have good discussions of the consumption and savings decisions of individuals and the beginnings of financial markets are:

E. F. Fama and M. H. Miller. *The Theory of Finance.* Chap. 1. New York: Holt, Rinehart & Winston, 1971.

J. Hirshleifer. *Investment, Interest and Capital.* Chap. 1. Englewood Cliffs, N.J.: Prentice Hall, 1970.

The seminal work on the net present value rule is:

J. G. Fisher. *The Theory of Interest.* New York: Augustus M. Kelly, 1965. (This is a reprint of the 1930 edition.)

A rigorous treatment of the net present value rule along the lines of Irving Fisher can be found in:

J. Hirshleifer. "On the Theory of Optimal Investment Decision." *Journal of Political Economy* 66 (August 1958).

Questions and Problems

Making Consumption Choices

3.1 Currently, Jean Boudreau makes $100,000. Next year his income will be $120,000. Jean is a big spender and he wants to consume $150,000 this year. The equilibrium interest rate is 10 percent. What will be Jean's consumption potential next year if he consumes $150,000 this year?

3.2 Rich Atkinson is a miser. His current income is $50,000; next year he will earn $40,000. He plans to consume only $20,000 this year. The current interest rate is 12 percent. What will Rich's consumption potential be next year?

The Competitive Financial Market

3.3 What is the basic reason that financial markets develop?

3.4 Suppose that the equilibrium interest rate is 10 percent. What would happen in the market if a group of financial intermediaries attempts to control interest rates at 6 percent?

Illustrating the Investment Decision

3.5 The following figure depicts the financial situation of Ms. J. Fawn. In period 0 her labour income and current consumption are $40; later, in period 1, her labour income and consumption will be $22. She has an opportunity to make the investment represented by point D. By borrowing and lending, she will be able to reach any point along the line EDF.

   a. What is the market rate of interest? (Hint: The new market interest rate line EF is parallel to AH.)

   b. What is the NPV of point D?

   c. If Ms. Fawn wishes to consume the same quantity in each period, how much should she borrow in period 0?

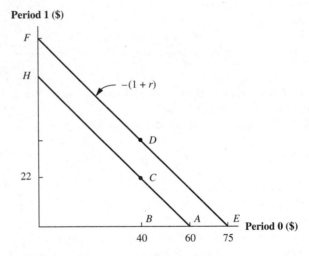

3.6 Harry Hernandez has $60,000 this year. He faces the investment opportunities represented by point B in the following figure.

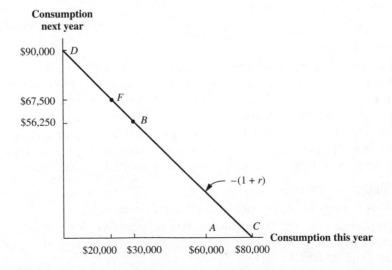

He wants to consume $20,000 this year and $67,500 next year. This pattern of consumption is represented by point *F*.

a. What is the market interest rate?

b. How much must Harry invest in financial assets and productive assets today if he follows an optimum strategy?

c. What is the NPV of his investment in nonfinancial assets?

3.7 Suppose that the person in the land-investment example in the text wants to consume $60,000 this year.

a. Detail a plan of investment and borrowing or lending that would permit her to consume $60,000 if the land investment is worth $75,000 next year.

b. Detail a plan of investment and borrowing or lending that would permit her to consume $60,000 if the land investment is worth $80,000 next year.

c. In which of these cases should she invest in the land? In each of these cases, how much will she be able to consume next year?

Corporate Investment Decision-Making

3.8 *a.* Briefly explain why, from the shareholders' perspective, it is desirable for corporations to maximize NPV.

b. What assumptions are necessary for this argument to be correct?

3.9 Consider a one-year world with perfect capital markets in which the interest rate is 10 percent. Suppose a firm has $12 million in cash. The firm invests $7 million today, and $5 million is paid to shareholders. The NPV of the firm's investment is $3 million. All shareholders are identical.

a. How much cash will the firm receive next year from its investment?

b. Suppose shareholders plan to spend $10 million today.

(i) How can they do this?

(ii) How much money will they have available to spend next year if they follow your plan?

3.10 To answer this question, refer to the figure on the next page. The Badvest Corporation is an all-equity firm with *BD* in cash on hand. It has an investment opportunity at point *C,* and it plans to invest *AD* in real assets today. Thus, the firm will need to raise *AB* by a new issue of equity.

a. What is the present value of the investment?

b. What is the rate of return on the old equity? Measure this rate of return from before the investment plans are announced to afterwards.

c. What is the rate of return on the new equity?

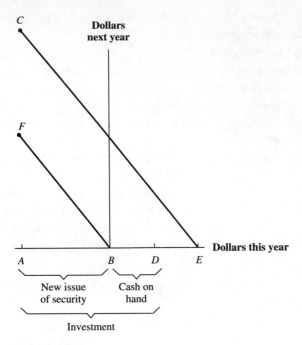

CHAPTER 4

Net Present Value

We now examine one of the most important concepts in all of corporate finance, the relationship between $1 today and $1 in the future. Consider the following example: A firm is contemplating investing $1 million in a project that is expected to pay out $200,000 per year for nine years. Should the firm accept the project? One might say yes at first glance, since the total inflows of $1.8 million (= $200,000 × 9) are greater than the $1 million outflow. However, the $1 million is paid out *immediately,* whereas the $200,000 per year is received in the future. Also, the immediate payment is known with certainty, whereas the later inflows can only be estimated. Thus, we need to know the relationship between a dollar today and a (possibly uncertain) dollar in the future before deciding on the project.

This relationship is called the *time-value-of-money concept.* It is important in such areas as capital budgeting, lease-versus-buy decisions, accounts receivable analysis, financing arrangements, mergers, and pension funding.

The basics are presented in this chapter. We begin by discussing two fundamental concepts: future value and present value. Next, we treat simplifying formulas such as perpetuities and annuities.

The One-Period Case   4.1

■ *Example*

Antony Robart is trying to sell a piece of raw land in Saskatchewan. Yesterday, he was offered $10,000 for the property. He was ready to accept the offer when another individual offered him $11,424. However, the second offer was to be paid a year from now. Antony has satisfied himself that both buyers are honest, so he has no fear that the offer he selects will fall through. These two offers are pictured as cash flows in Figure 4.1. Which offer should Mr. Robart choose?

Cynthia Titos, Antony's financial adviser, points out that if Antony takes the first offer, he could invest the $10,000 in the bank at 12 percent. At the end of one year, he would have

$$\underset{\substack{\text{Return of}\\ \text{principal}}}{\$10,000} + \underset{\text{Interest}}{0.12 \times \$10,000} = \$10,000 \times 1.12 = \$11,200$$

Figure 4.1
Cash flow for Mr.
Robart's sale

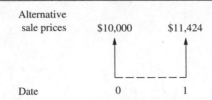

Because this is less than the $11,424 Antony could receive from the second offer, Ms. Titos recommends that he take the latter. This analysis uses the concept of **future value** or **compound value,** which is the value of a sum after investing over one or more periods. Here the compound or future value of $10,000 is $11,200. ∎

An alternative method employs the concept of **present value.** One can determine present value by asking the following question: How much money must Antony put in the bank today so that he will have $11,424 next year? We can write this algebraically as

$$PV \times 1.12 = \$11,424 \qquad (4.1)$$

We want to solve for present value (PV), the amount of money that yields $11,424 if invested at 12 percent today. Solving for PV, we have

$$PV = \frac{\$11,424}{1.12} = \$10,200$$

The formula for PV can be written as

Present Value of Investment:

$$PV = \frac{C_1}{1 + r}$$

where C_1 is cash flow at date 1 and r is the interest rate.

Present value analysis tells us that a payment of $11,424 to be received next year has a present value of $10,200 today. In other words, at a 12-percent interest rate, Mr. Robart should be indifferent to whether you give him $10,200 today or $11,424 next year. If you give him $10,200 today, he can put it in the bank and receive $11,424 next year.

Because the second offer has a present value of $10,200, whereas the first offer is for only $10,000, present value analysis also indicates that Mr. Robart should take the second offer. In other words, both future value analysis and present value analysis lead to the same decision. As it turns out, present value analysis and future value analysis must always lead to the same decision.

As simple as this example is, it contains the basic principles that we will be working with over the next few chapters. We now use another example to develop the concept of net present value.

∎ *Example*

Genevieve Gagnon is thinking about investing in a piece of land that costs $85,000. She is certain that next year the land will be worth $91,000, a sure $6,000 gain. Given

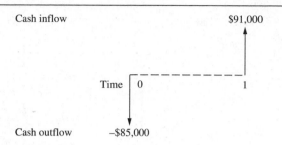

Figure 4.2
Cash flows for
land investment

that the interest rate in the bank is 10 percent, should she undertake the investment in land? Ms. Gagnon's choice is described in Figure 4.2 with the cash flow time chart.

A moment's thought should be all it takes to convince her that this is not an attractive business deal. By investing $85,000 in the land, she will have $91,000 available next year. Suppose, instead, that she puts the same $85,000 into the bank. At the interest rate of 10 percent, this $85,000 would grow to

$$(1 + 0.10) \times \$85,000 = \$93,500$$

next year.

It would be foolish to buy the land when investing the same $85,000 in the financial market would produce an extra $2,500 (that is, $93,500 from the bank minus $91,000 from the land investment). This is a future-value calculation.

Alternatively, she could calculate the present value of the sale price next year as

$$\text{Present value} = \frac{\$91,000}{1.10} = \$82,727.27$$

Since the present value of next year's sales price is less than this year's purchase price of $85,000, present value analysis also indicates that she should not purchase the property. ∎

Frequently, business people want to determine the exact *cost* or *benefit* of a decision. The decision to buy this year and sell next year can be evaluated as

Net Present Value of Investment:

$$-\$2,273 = -\$85,000 \quad + \quad \frac{\$91,000}{1.10} \tag{4.2}$$

Cost of   Present value of
land today   next year's sales price

Equation (4.2) says that the value of the investment is −$2,273, after stating all the benefits and all the costs as of date 0. We say that −$2,273 is the **net present value (NPV)** of the investment. That is, NPV is the present value of future cash flows minus the present value of the cost of the investment. Because the net present value is negative, Genevieve Gagnon should not purchase the land.

Both the Robart and the Gagnon examples deal with perfect certainty. That is, Antony Robart knows with perfect certainty that he could sell his land for $11,424 next year. Similarly, Genevieve Gagnon knows with perfect certainty that she could

Figure 4.3
Cash flows for
investment in
painting

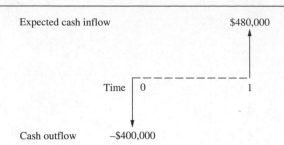

receive $91,000 for selling her land. Unfortunately, business people frequently do not know future cash flows. This uncertainty is treated in the next example.

■ *Example*

Atkinson Art, Inc., is a firm that speculates in modern paintings. The manager is thinking of buying an original Picasso for $400,000 with the intention of selling it at the end of one year. The manager *expects* that the painting will be worth $480,000 in one year. The relevant cash flows are depicted in Figure 4.3.

Of course, this is only an expectation—the painting could be worth more or less than $480,000. Suppose the interest rate granted by banks is 10 percent. Should the firm purchase the piece of art?

Our first thought might be to discount at the interest rate, yielding

$$\frac{\$480,000}{1.10} = \$436,364$$

Since $436,364 is greater than $400,000, it looks at first glance as if the painting should be purchased. However, 10 percent is the return one can earn on a riskless investment. Because the painting is quite risky, a higher *discount rate* is called for. The manager chooses a rate of 25 percent to reflect this risk. In other words, he argues that a 25-percent expected return is fair compensation for an investment as risky as this painting.

The present value of the painting becomes

$$\frac{\$480,000}{1.25} = \$384,000$$

Thus, the manager believes that the painting is currently overpriced at $400,000 and does not make the purchase. ■

The above analysis is typical of decision-making in today's corporations, though real-world examples are, of course, much more complex. Unfortunately, any example with risk poses a problem not faced by a riskless example. In an example with riskless cash flows, the appropriate interest rate can be determined by simply checking with a few banks.[1] The selection of the discount rate for a risky investment is quite a difficult task. We simply do not know at this point whether the discount rate on the painting should be 11 percent, 25 percent, 52 percent, or some other percentage.

---

[1] In Chapter 9, we discuss estimation of the riskless rate in more detail.

Because the choice of a discount rate is so difficult, we merely wanted to broach the subject here. The rest of the chapter will revert back to examples under perfect certainty. We must wait until the specific material on risk and return is covered in later chapters before a risk-adjusted analysis can be presented.

CONCEPT QUESTIONS

■ Define future value and present value.
■ How does one use net present value when making an investment decision?

The Multiperiod Case   4.2

The previous section presented the calculation of future value and present value for one period only. We will now perform the calculations for the multiperiod case.

Future Value and Compounding

Suppose an individual were to make a loan of $1. At the end of the first year, the borrower would owe the lender the principal amount of $1 plus the interest on the loan at the interest rate of r. For the specific case where the interest rate is, say, 9 percent, the borrower owes the lender

$$\$1 \times (1 + r) = \$1 \times 1.09 = \$1.09$$

At the end of the year, though, the lender has two choices. He or she can either take the $1.09—or, more generally, $(1 + r)$—out of the capital market, or leave it in and lend it again for a second year. The process of leaving the money in the capital market and lending it for another year is called **compounding**.

Suppose that the lender decides to compound the loan for another year by taking the proceeds from the first one-year loan, $1.09, and lending this amount for the next year. At the end of next year, then, the borrower will owe

$$\$1 \times (1 + r) \times (1 + r) = \$1 \times (1 + r)^2 = 1 + 2r + r^2$$
$$\$1 \times (1.09) \times (1.09) = \$1 + \$0.18 + 0.0081 = \$1.1881$$

This is the total the lender will receive two years from now by compounding the loan.

In other words, by providing a ready opportunity for lending, the capital market enables the investor to transform $1 today into $1.1881 at the end of two years. At the end of three years, the cash will be $1 \times (1.09)^3 = \$1.2950$. The shaded area indicates the difference between compound and simple interest. The difference is substantial over a period of many years or decades, as shown in Figure 4.4.

The most important point to notice is that the total amount that the lender receives is not just the $1 lent out plus two years' worth of interest on $1:

$$2 \times r = 2 \times \$0.09 = \$0.18$$

The lender also gets back an amount r^2, which is the interest in the second year on the interest that was earned in the first year. The term, $2 \times r$, represents **simple interest**

Figure 4.4
Simple and
compound interest

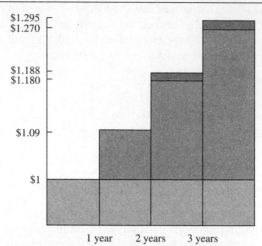

The shaded area indicates the difference between compound
and simple interest. The difference is substantial over a period
of many years or decades.

over the two years, and the term, r^2, is referred to as the *interest on interest*. In our
example this latter amount is exactly

$$r^2 = (\$0.09)^2 = \$0.0081$$

When cash is invested at **compound interest,** each interest payment is reinvested. With
simple interest, the interest is not reinvested. Benjamin Franklin's statement, "Money
makes money and the money that money makes makes more money," is a colourful way
of explaining compound interest. The difference between compound interest and simple
interest is also illustrated in Figure 4.4. In this example the difference does not amount
to much because the loan is for $1. If the loan were for $1 million, the lender would
receive $1,188,100 in two years' time. Of this amount, $8,100 is interest on interest. The
lesson is that those small numbers beyond the decimal point can add up to significant
dollar amounts when the transactions are for large amounts. In addition, the longer-
lasting the loan, the more important interest on interest becomes.

The general formula for an investment over many periods can be written as

Future Value of an Investment:

$$FV = C_0 \times (1 + r)^T$$

where C_0 is the cash to be invested at date 0, r is the interest rate, and T is the number
of periods over which the cash is invested.

■ *Example*

Irene Lau has put $500 in a savings account at the Home Bank of Canada. The account
earns 7 percent, compounded annually. How much will Ms. Lau have at the end of
three years?

$$\$500 \times 1.07 \times 1.07 \times 1.07 = \$500 \times (1.07)^3 = \$612.52$$

Figure 4.5 illustrates the growth of Ms. Lau's account. ■

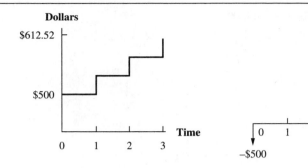

Figure 4.5
Mrs. Lau's savings
account

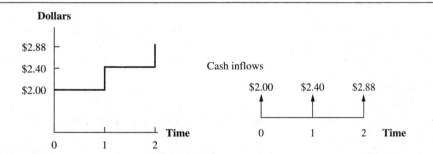

Figure 4.6
The growth of
dividends

■ *Example*
Heather Courtney invested $1,000 in the stock of the BMH Company. The company pays a current dividend of $2 per share, which is expected to grow by 20 percent per year for the next two years. What will the dividend of the BMH Company be after two years?

$$\$2 \times (1.20)^2 = \$2.88$$

Figure 4.6 illustrates the increasing value of BMH's dividends. ■

The two previous examples can be calculated in any one of three ways: by hand, by calculator, or with the help of a table. The appropriate table is Table A.3, which appears in the back of the text. This table presents *future values of $1 at the end of* T *periods.* The table is used by locating the appropriate interest rate on the horizontal and the appropriate number of periods on the vertical.

For example, Irene Lau would look at the following portion of Table A.3:

	Interest rate		
Period	6%	7%	8%
1	1.0600	1.0700	1.0800
2	1.1236	1.1449	1.1664
3	1.1910	1.2250	1.2597
4	1.2625	1.3108	1.3605

Figure 4.7
Cash flows for
purchase of a car

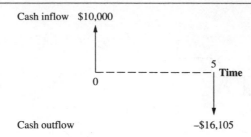

She could calculate the future value of her $500 as

$500   ×   1.2250   = $612.50
Initial   Future value
investment   of $1

In the example concerning Irene Lau, we gave you both the initial investment and the interest rate and then asked you to calculate the future value. Alternatively, the interest rate could have been unknown, as shown in the following example.

▪ *Example*

Raghu Venugopal, who recently won $10,000 in a lottery, wants to buy a car in five years. Raghu estimates that the car will cost $16,105 at that time. His cash flows are displayed in Figure 4.7.

What interest rate must he earn to be able to afford the car? The ratio of purchase price to initial cash is

$$\frac{\$16,105}{\$10,000} = 1.6105$$

Thus, he must earn an interest rate that allows $1 to become $1.6105 in five years. Table A.3 tells us that an interest rate of 10 percent will allow him to purchase the car. One can express the problem algebraically as

$$\$10,000 \times (1 + r)^5 = \$16,105$$

where r is the interest rate needed to purchase the car. Because $16,105/$10,000 = 1.6105, we have

$$(1 + r)^5 = 1.6105$$

Either the table or any sophisticated hand calculator solves[2] for r. ▪

The Power of Compounding: A Digression

Most people who have had any experience with compounding are impressed with its power over long periods of time. Take the stock market, for example. In Chapter 9, we use data collected by the Alexander Group to calculate that the average Canadian

---

[2]Conceptually, we are taking the fifth roots of both sides of the equation. That is,

$$r = \sqrt[5]{1.605} - 1$$

common stock had approximately a 13-percent rate of return per year from 1948 through 1992. A return of this magnitude may not appear to be anything special over, say, a one-year period. However, $1 placed in these stocks at the beginning of 1948 would have been worth $123.41 at the end of 1992.

The example illustrates the great difference between compound and simple interest. At 13 percent, simple interest on $1 is 13 cents a year. Simple interest over 44 years is $5.72 (44 × $0.13). That is, an individual withdrawing 13 cents every year would have withdrawn $5.72 over 44 years. This is quite a bit below the $123.41 that was obtained by reinvestment of all principal and interest.

The results are more impressive over even longer periods of time. A person with no experience in compounding might think that the value of $1 at the end of 88 years would be twice the value of $1 at the end of 44 years, if the yearly rate of return stayed the same. Actually the value of $1 at the end of 88 years would be the *square* of the value of $1 at the end of 44 years. That is, if the annual rate of return remained the same, a $1 investment in common stocks should be worth $15,230.03 [or $1 × (123.41 × 123.41)].

A few years ago an archaeologist unearthed a relic stating that Julius Caesar lent the Roman equivalent of one penny to someone. Since there was no record of the penny ever being repaid, the archaeologist wondered what the interest and principal would be if a descendant of Caesar tried to collect from a descendant of the borrower in the 20th century. The archaeologist felt that a rate of 6 percent might be appropriate. To his surprise, the principal and interest due after more than 2,000 years was far greater than the entire wealth on earth.

The power of compounding can explain one reason why the parents of well-to-do families frequently bequeath wealth to their grandchildren rather than to their children.[3] That is, they skip a generation. The parents would rather make the grandchildren very rich than make the children moderately rich. We have found that in these families the grandchildren have a more positive view of the power of compounding than do the children.

Present Value and Discounting

We now know that an annual interest rate of 9 percent enables the investor to transform $1 today into $1.1881 two years from now. In addition, we would like to know:

> How much would an investor need to lend today to make it possible to receive $1 two years from today?

Algebraically, we can write this as

$$PV \times (1.09)^2 = \$1 \tag{4.3}$$

In (4.3), PV stands for present value, the amount of money we must lend today in order to receive $1 in two years' time. Solving for PV in (4.3), we have

$$PV = \frac{\$1}{1.1881} = \$0.84$$

---

[3]Tax avoidance is likely another reason.

Figure 4.8
Compounding and
discounting

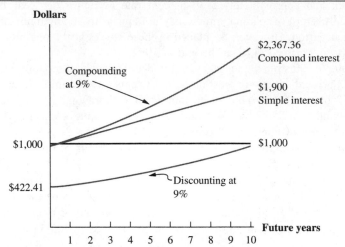

The top line shows the growth of $1,000 at compound interest with the funds invested at 9 percent: $1,000 × (1.09)^{10} = $2,367.36. Simple interest is shown on the next line. It is $1,000 + 10 × ($1,000 × 0.09) = $1,900. The bottom line shows the discounted value of $1,000 if the interest rate is 9 percent.

This process of calculating the present value of a future cash flow is called **discounting.** It is the opposite of compounding. The difference between compounding and discounting is illustrated in Figure 4.8.

To be certain that $0.84 is in fact the present value of $1 to be received in two years, we must check whether or not, if we loaned out $0.84 and rolled over the loan for two years, we would get exactly $1 back. If this were the case, the capital markets would be saying that $1 received in two years' time is equivalent to having $0.84 today. Checking with the exact numbers, we get

$0.84168 × 1.09 × 1.09 = $1

In other words, when we have capital markets with a sure interest rate of 9 percent, we are indifferent between receiving $0.84 today or $1 in two years. We have no reason to treat these two choices differently from each other, because if we had $0.84 today and loaned it out for two years, it would return $1 to us at the end of that time. The value 0.84 $[1/(1.09)^2]$ is called the **present value factor.** It is the factor used to calculate the present value of a future cash flow.

■ *Example*

Pat Song will receive $10,000 three years from now. Pat can earn 8 percent on his investments. What is the present value of his future cash flow?

$$PV = \$10,000 \times (1/1.08)^3$$
$$= \$10,000 \times 0.7938$$
$$= \$7,938$$

Figure 4.9 illustrates the application of the present value factor to Pat's investment.

When his investments grow at an 8-percent rate of interest, Pat Song is equally inclined toward receiving $7,938 now or receiving $10,000 in three years' time. After

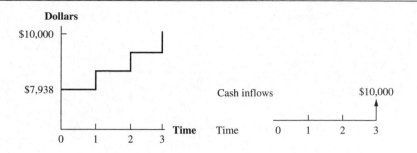

Figure 4.9
Discounting Pat
Song's opportunity

all, he could convert the $7,938 he receives today into $10,000 in three years by lending it at an interest rate of 8 percent.

Pat Song could have reached his present value calculation in one of three ways. The computation could have been done by hand, by calculator, or with the help of Table A.1, which appears in the back of the text. This table presents *present value of $1 to be received after* T *periods.* The table is used by locating the appropriate interest rate on the horizontal and the appropriate number of periods on the vertical. For example, Pat Song would look at the following portion of Table A.1:

		Interest rate	
Period	7%	8%	9%
1	0.9346	0.9529	0.9174
2	0.8734	0.8573	0.8417
3	0.8163	0.7938	0.7722
4	0.7629	0.7350	0.7084

The appropriate present value factor is 0.7938. ∎

In the above example, we gave both the interest rate and the future cash flow. Alternatively, the interest rate could have been unknown.

∎ *Example*

A customer of the Cristall Corp. wants to buy a tugboat today. Rather than paying immediately, he will pay $50,000 in three years. It will cost the Cristall Corp. $38,610 to build the tugboat immediately. The relevant cash flows to Cristall Corp. are displayed in Figure 4.10. By charging what interest rate would the Cristall Corp. neither gain nor lose on the sale? The ratio of construction cost to sale price is

$$\frac{\$36,810}{\$50,000} = 0.7722$$

We must determine the interest rate that allows $1 to be received in three years to have a present value of $0.7722. Table A.1 tells us that 9 percent is that interest rate.[4] ∎

---

[4]Algebraically, we are solving for r in the equation

$$\frac{\$50,000}{(1 + r)^3} = \$38,610 \quad \text{or, equivalently,} \quad \frac{\$1}{(1 + r)^3} = \$0.7722$$

Figure 4.10
Cash flows for
tugboat

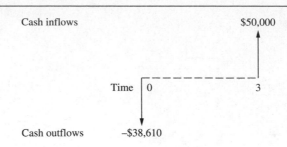

Frequently, an investor or a business will receive more than one cash flow. The present value of the set of cash flows is simply the sum of the present values of the individual cash flows. This is illustrated in the following example.

■ *Example*

Terence Chiu has won a lottery and will receive the following set of cash flows over the next two years:

Year	Cash flow
1	$2,000
2	$5,000

Terence can currently earn 6 percent in his passbook savings account. The present value of the cash flows is

Year	Cash flow × Present value factor = Present value		
1	$2,000	$\times \dfrac{1}{1.06} = 0.943$	= $1,887
2	$5,000	$\times 1/(1.06)^2 = 0.890$	= $4,450
		Total	$6,337

In other words, Terence is equally inclined toward receiving $6,337 today and receiving $2,000 and $5,000 over the next two years. ■

The Algebraic Formula

To derive an algebraic formula for net present value of a cash flow, recall that the PV of receiving a cash flow one year from now is

$$PV = C_1/(1 + r)$$

and the PV of receiving a cash flow two years from now is

$$PV = C_2/(1 + r)^2$$

We can write the NPV of a T-period project as

$$NPV = -C_0 + \frac{C_1}{1 + r} + \frac{C_2}{(1 + r)^2} + \ldots + \frac{C_T}{(1 + r)^T} = -C_0 + \sum_{t=1}^{T} \frac{C_i}{(1 + r)^t}$$

The initial flow, $-C_0$, is assumed to be negative because it represents an investment. The term $\sum$ is shorthand for the sum of the series.[5]

CONCEPT QUESTIONS

- What is the difference between simple interest and compound interest?
- What is the formula for the net present value of a project?

Compounding Periods 4.3

So far we have assumed that compounding and discounting occur yearly. Sometimes compounding may occur more frequently than just once a year. For example, imagine that a bank pays a 10-percent interest rate "compounded semiannually." This means that a $1,000 deposit in the bank would be worth $1,000 \times 1.05 = \$1,050$ after six months, and $\$1,050 \times 1.05 = \$1,102.50$ at the end of the year. The end-of-the-year wealth can be written as[6]

$$\$1,000 \,(1 + 0.10/2)^2 = \$1,000 \times (1.05)^2 = \$1,102.50$$

Of course, a $1,000 deposit would be worth $1,100 (or $1,000 \times 1.10$) with yearly compounding. Note that the future value at the end of one year is greater with semiannual compounding than with yearly compounding. With yearly compounding, the original $1,000 remains the investment base for the full year. The original $1,000 is the investment base only for the first six months with semiannual compounding. The base over the second six months is $1,050. Hence, one gets *interest on interest* with semiannual compounding.

Because $\$1,000 \times 1.1025 = \$1,102.50$, 10 percent compounded semiannually is the same as 10.25 percent compounded annually. In other words, a rational investor will be indifferent between a rate of 10 percent compounded semiannually, or a rate of 10.25 percent compounded annually.

Quarterly compounding at 10 percent yields wealth at the end of one year of

$$\$1,000 \,(1 + 0.10/4)^4 = \$1,103.81$$

More generally, compounding an investment m times a year provides end-of-year wealth of

$$C_0(1 + r/m)^m \tag{4.4}$$

where C_0 is one's initial investment and r is the **stated annual interest rate.** The stated annual interest rate is the annual interest rate without consideration of compounding.

---

[5]In Chapter 6 we apply the NPV formula to investments that have a cash inflow in year 0 and outflows in later years. For these investments, the term, $-C_0$, is replaced by $-PV$ (outflows).

[6]In addition to using a calculator, one can still use Table A.3 when the compounding period is less than a year. Here, one sets the interest rate at 5 percent and the number of periods at two.

■ *Example*

What is the end-of-year wealth if Julie Andrew receives a 24-percent rate of interest compounded monthly on a $1 investment? Using (4.4), her wealth is

$$\$1(1 + 0.24/12)^{12} = \$1 \times (1.02)^{12}$$
$$= \$1.2682$$

The annual rate of return is 26.82 percent. This annual rate of return is called the **effective annual interest rate.** Due to compounding, the effective annual interest rate is greater than the stated annual interest rate of 24 percent. Algebraically, we can rewrite the effective annual interest rate as

Effective Annual Interest Rate:

$$(1 + r/m)^m - 1 \qquad\qquad (4.5)$$

Students are often bothered by the subtraction of 1 in (4.5). Note that end-of-year wealth is composed of both the interest earned over the year and the original principal. We remove the original principal by subtracting one in (4.5). ■

■ *Example*

If the stated annual rate of interest, 8 percent, is compounded quarterly, what is the effective annual rate of interest? Using (4.5), we have

$$(1 + r/m)^m - 1 = (1 + 0.08/4)^4 - 1 = 0.0824 = 8.24\%$$

Referring back to our original example where $C_0 = \$1,000$ and $r = 10\%$, we can generate the following table:

C^0	Compounding frequency (m)	C_1	Effective annual interest rate = $(1 + r/m)^m - 1$
$1,000	Yearly ($m = 1$)	$1,100.00	0.10
1,000	Semiannually ($m = 2$)	1,102.50	0.1025
1,000	Quarterly ($m = 4$)	1,103.81	0.10381
1,000	Daily ($m = 365$)	1,105.16	0.10516 ■

Compounding over Many Years

Formula (4.4) applies for an investment over one year. For an investment over one or more (T) years, the formula becomes

Future Value with Compounding:

$$FV = C_0 (1 + r/m)^{mT} \qquad\qquad (4.6)$$

■ *Example*

Margaret Cortes is investing $5,000 at 12 percent per year, compounded quarterly for five years. What is her wealth at the end of five years? Using (4.6), her wealth is

$$\$5,000 \times (1 + .12/4)^{4 \times 5} = \$5,000 \times (1.03)^{20}$$
$$= \$5,000 \times 1.8061 = \$9,030.50 \;\blacksquare$$

Cost of Borrowing Disclosure regulations (part of the Bank Act) in Canada require that lenders disclose an annual percentage rate on virtually all consumer loans. This rate must be displayed on a loan document in a prominent and unambiguous way. Unfortunately, this does not tell the borrower the effective annual rate on the loan.

■ *Example*

Suppose that a credit card agreement quotes an annual percentage rate of 18 percent. Monthly payments are required. Based on our discussion, an annual percentage rate of 18 percent with monthly payments is really .18/12 = .015 or 1.5 percent per month. The effective annual rate is thus

$$\text{Effective annual rate} = [1 + .18/12]^{12} - 1$$
$$= 1.015^{12} - 1$$
$$= 1.1956 - 1$$
$$= 19.56\% \quad ■$$

The difference between an annual percentage rate and an effective annual rate probably will not be great, but it is somewhat ironic that cost-of-borrowing disclosure regulations sometimes require lenders to be untruthful about the actual rate on a loan.

■ *Example*

The Alberta Treasury Branch offers one-year Guaranteed Investment Certificates (GICs) at 7 percent per year compounded semiannually. Canada Trust offers one-year GICs at 7.25 percent compounded annually. Which would you prefer?

The effective annual rate at Canada Trust is 7.25 percent since the compounding is annual. To find the effective annual rate offered by the Alberta Treasury Branch, use Equation 4.5:

$$\text{Effective annual interest rate} = (1+r/m)^m - 1$$
$$= (1+.07/2)^2 - 1$$
$$= 7.1225\%$$

You would prefer the Canada Trust GIC since it offers a higher effective annual rate.

Continuous Compounding (Advanced)

The previous discussion shows that one can compound much more frequently than once a year. One could compound semiannually, quarterly, monthly, daily, hourly, each minute, or even more often. The limiting case would be to compound every infinitesimal instant, which is commonly called **continuous compounding.**

Though the idea of compounding this rapidly may boggle the mind, a simple formula is involved. With continuous compounding, the value at the end of *T* years is expressed as

$$C_0 \times e^{rT} \qquad\qquad\qquad (4.7)$$

where C_0 is the initial investment, *r* is the stated annual interest rate, and *T* is the number of years over which the investment runs. The number e is a constant and is approximately equal to 2.718. It is not an unknown like C_0, *r*, and *T*.

■ *Example*

John MacDonald invested $1,000 at a continuously compounded rate of 10 percent for one year. What is the value of his wealth at the end of one year?

From formula (4.7) we have

$$\$1,000 \times e^{.10} = \$1,000 \times 1.1052 = \$1,105.20$$

This number can easily be read from our Table A.5. One merely sets r, the value on the horizontal dimension, to 10 percent and sets T, the value on the vertical dimension, to 1. For this problem, the relevant portion of the table is

Period	Continuously compounded rate (r)		
	9%	10%	11%
1	1.0942	1.1052	1.1163
2	1.1972	1.2214	1.2461
3	1.3100	1.3499	1.3910

Note that a continuously compounded rate of 10 percent is equivalent to an annually compounded rate of 10.52 percent. In other words, John MacDonald would not care whether his bank quoted a continuously compounded rate of 10 percent or a 10.52 percent rate, compounded annually. ■

■ *Example*

John MacDonald's brother, Robert, invested $1,000 at a continuously compounded rate of 10 percent for two years.

The appropriate formula here is

$$\$1,000 \times e^{.10 \times .2} = \$1,000 \times e^{.20} = \$1,221.40$$

Using the portion of the table of continuously compounded rates reproduced above, we find the value to be 1.2214. ■

Figure 4.11 illustrates the relationship among annual, semiannual, and continuous compounding. Semiannual compounding gives rise to both a smoother curve and a higher ending value than does annual compounding. Continuous compounding has both the smoothest curve and the highest ending value of all.

■ *Example*

The Ontario provincial lottery is going to pay you $1,000 at the end of four years. If the annual continuously compounded rate of interest is 8 percent, what is the present value of this payment?

$$\$1,000 \times \frac{1}{e^{.08 \times 4}} = \$1,000 \times \frac{1}{1.3771} = \$726.16 \quad ■$$

CONCEPT QUESTIONS

- What is a stated annual interest rate?
- What is an effective annual interest rate?
- What is the relationship between the stated annual interest rate and the effective annual interest rate?
- Define continuous compounding.

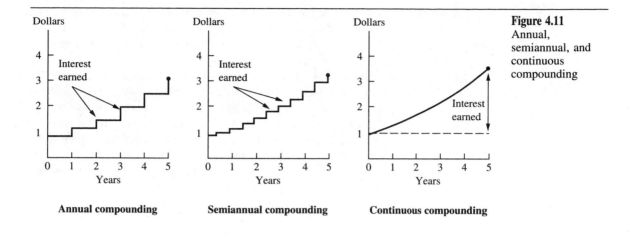

Figure 4.11
Annual,
semiannual, and
continuous
compounding

Annual compounding   **Semiannual compounding**   **Continuous compounding**

Simplifications   4.4

The first part of this chapter has examined the concepts of future value and present value. Although these concepts allow one to answer a host of problems concerning the time value of money, the human effort involved can frequently be excessive. For example, consider a bank calculating the present value on a 20-year monthly mortgage. Because this mortgage has 240 (or 20 × 12) payments, a lot of time is needed to perform a conceptually simple task.

Because many basic finance problems are potentially so time-consuming, we search out simplifications in this section. We provide simplifying formulas for four classes of cash flow streams:

Perpetuity

Growing perpetuity

Annuity

Growing annuity.

Perpetuity

A **perpetuity** is a constant stream of cash flows without end. If you are thinking that perpetuities have no relevance to reality, it will surprise you that there is a well-known case of an unending cash flow stream: the British bonds called *consols*. An investor purchasing a consol is entitled to receive yearly interest from the British government forever.

How can the price of a consol be determined? Consider a consol that pays a coupon of C dollars each year and will do so forever. Simply applying the PV formula gives us

$$PV = \frac{C}{1 + r} + \frac{C}{(1 + r)^2} + \frac{C}{(1 + r)^3} + \cdots$$

where the dots at the end of the formula stand for the infinite string of terms that continues the formula. Series like the preceding one are called *geometric series.* It is well known that even though they have an infinite number of terms, the whole series has a finite sum because each term is only a fraction of the preceding term. Before turning to a calculus book, though, it is worth going back to our original principles to see if a bit of financial intuition can help us find the PV.

The present value of the consol is the present value of all of its future coupons. In other words, it is an amount of money that, if an investor had it today, would make it possible to achieve the same pattern of expenditures that the consol and its coupons would. Suppose that an investor wanted to spend exactly C dollars each year. If our investor owned the consol, this spending pattern would be possible. How much money must the investor have today to spend the same amount? Clearly the amount needed is exactly enough so that the interest on the money would be C dollars per year. If the investor had any more, spending could be more than C dollars each year. If the amount were any less, the investor would eventually run out of money spending C dollars per year.

The amount that will give the investor C dollars each year, and therefore the present value of the consol, is simply

$$PV = \frac{C}{r} \tag{4.8}$$

To confirm that this is the right answer, notice that if we lend the amount C/r, the interest it earns each year will be

$$\text{Interest} = \frac{C}{r} \times r = C$$

which is exactly the consol payment.[7] To sum up, we have shown that for a consol

Formula for Present Value of Perpetuity:

$$PV = \frac{C}{1+r} + \frac{C}{(1+r)^2} + \frac{C}{(1+r)^3} + \ldots$$
$$= C/r$$

It is comforting to know how easily we can use a bit of financial intuition to solve this mathematical problem.

■ *Example*

Consider a perpetuity paying $100 a year. If the interest rate is 8 percent, what is the value of the consol? Using (4.8), we have

---

[7]We can prove this by looking at the PV equation:

$$PV = C/(1+r) + C/(1+r)^2 + \ldots$$

Let $C/(1+r) = a$ and $1/(1+r) = x$. We now have

$$PV = a(1 + x + x^2 \ldots) \tag{1}$$

Next we can multiply by x:

$$xPV = ax + ax^2 + \ldots \tag{2}$$

Subtracting (2) from (1) gives

$$PV(1 - x) = a$$

Now we substitute for a and x and rearrange:

$$PV = C/r$$

$$PV = \frac{\$100}{0.08} = \$1,250$$

Now suppose that interest rates fall to 6 percent. Using (4.8), the value of the perpetuity is

$$PV = \frac{\$100}{0.06} = \$1,666.67$$

Note that the value of the perpetuity rises with a drop in the interest rate. Conversely, the value of the perpetuity falls with a rise in the interest rate. ∎

Growing Perpetuity

Imagine an apartment building where cash flows to the landlord after expenses will be $100,000 next year. These cash flows are expected to rise at 5 percent per year. If one assumes that this rise will continue indefinitely, the cash flow stream is termed a **growing perpetuity.** Positing an 11-percent discount rate, the present value of the cash flows can be represented as

$$PV = \frac{\$100,000}{1.11} + \frac{\$100,000(1.05)}{(1.11)^2} + \frac{\$100,000(1.05)^2}{(1.11)^3} + \ldots$$

$$+ \frac{100,000(1.05)^{N-1}}{(1.11)^N} + \ldots$$

Algebraically, we can write the formula as

$$PV = \frac{C}{1+r} + \frac{C \times (1+g)}{(1+r)^2} + \frac{C \times (1+g)^2}{((1+r)^3} + \ldots \qquad (4.9)$$

$$+ \frac{C \times (1+g)^{N-1}}{(1+r)^N} + \ldots$$

where C is the cash flow to be received one period hence, g is the rate of growth per period, expressed as a percentage, and r is the interest rate.

Fortunately, (4.9) reduces to the following simplification:[8]

Formula for Present Value of Growing Perpetuity:

$$PV = \frac{C}{r-g} \qquad (4.10)$$

---

[8]PV is the sum of an infinite geometric series:

$$PV = a(1 + x + x^2 + \ldots)$$

where $a = C/(1+r)$ and $x = (1+g)/(1+r)$. Previously we showed that the sum of an infinite geometric series is $a/(1-x)$. Using this result and substituting for a and x, we find

$$PV = C/(r-g)$$

Note that this geometric series converges to a finite sum only when x is less than 1. This implies that the growth rate, g, must be less than the interest rate, r.

From (4.10), the present value of the cash flows from the apartment building is

$$\frac{\$100,000}{0.11 - 0.05} = \$1,666,667$$

There are three important points concerning the growing perpetuity formula:

1. *The Numerator.* The numerator in (4.10) is the cash flow one period hence, not at date 0. Consider the following example:

■ *Example*

Hoffstein Corporation is just about to pay a dividend of $3.00 per share. Investors anticipate that the annual dividend will rise by 6 percent a year forever. The applicable interest rate is 11 percent. What is the price of the stock today?

The numerator in formula (4.10) is the cash flow to be received next period. Since the growth rate is 6 percent, the dividend next year is $3.18 (or $3.00 × 1.06). The price of the stock today is

$$\underset{\substack{\text{Imminent}\\\text{dividend}}}{\$66.60 \quad = \quad \$3.00} \quad + \quad \underset{\substack{\text{Present value}\\\text{of all dividends}\\\text{beginning a year}\\\text{from now}}}{\frac{\$3.18}{0.11 - 0.06}}$$

The price of $66.60 includes both the dividend to be received immediately and the present value of all dividends beginning a year from now. Formula (4.10) only makes it possible to calculate the present value of all dividends beginning a year from now. Be sure you understand this example; test questions on this subject always seem to trip up a few of our students. ■

2. *The Interest Rate and the Growth Rate.* The interest rate r must be greater than the growth rate g for the growing perpetuity formula to work. Consider the case in which the growth rate approaches the interest rate in magnitude. Then the denominator in the growing perpetuity formula gets infinitesimally small and the present value grows infinitely large. The present value is in fact undefined when r is less than g.

3. *The Timing Assumption.* Cash generally flows into and out of real-world firms both randomly and nearly continuously. However, formula (4.10) assumes that cash flows are received and disbursed at regular and discrete points in time. In the example of the apartment, we assumed that the net cash flows of $100,000 only occurred once a year. In reality, rent cheques are commonly received every month. Payments for maintenance and other expenses may occur anytime within the year.

The growing perpetuity formula of (4.10) can be applied only by assuming a regular and discrete pattern of cash flow. Although this assumption is sensible because the formula saves so much time, the user should never forget that it is an assumption. This point will be mentioned again in the chapters ahead.

A few words should be said about terminology. Authors of financial textbooks generally use one of two conventions to refer to time. A minority of financial writers treat cash flows as being received on exact *dates,* for example date 0, date 1, and so forth. Under this convention, date 0 represents the present time. However, because a year is an interval, not a specific moment in time, the great majority of authors refer to cash flows that occur at the end of a year (or, alternatively, at the end of a period). Under this *end-of-the-year* convention, the end of year 0 is the present, the end of year 1 occurs one period hence, and so on.[9] (The beginning of year 0 has already passed and is not generally referred to.)

The interchangability of the two conventions can be seen from the following chart:

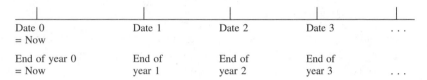

Date 0	Date 1	Date 2	Date 3	. . .
= Now				
End of year 0	End of	End of	End of	
= Now	year 1	year 2	year 3	. . .

We strongly believe that the *dates convention* reduces ambiguity. However, we use both conventions because you are likely to see the *end-of-year convention* in later courses. In fact, both conventions may appear in the same example for the sake of practice.

Annuity

An **annuity** is a level stream of regular payments that lasts for a fixed number of periods. Not surprisingly, annuities are among the most common kinds of financial instruments. The pensions that people receive when they retire are often in the form of an annuity. Leases, mortgages, and pension plans are also annuities.

To figure out the present value of an annuity we need to evaluate the following equation:

$$\frac{C}{1 + r} + \frac{C}{(1 + r)^2} + \frac{C}{(1 + r)^3} + \ldots + \frac{C}{(1 + r)^T}$$

The present value of receiving only the coupons for T periods must be less than the present value of a consol, but how much less? To answer this we have to look at consols a bit more closely. Consider the following time chart:

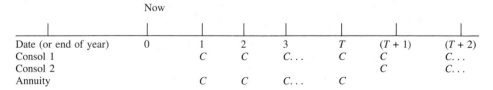

	Now						
Date (or end of year)	0	1	2	3	T	$(T + 1)$	$(T + 2)$
Consol 1		C	C	$C\ldots$	C	C	$C\ldots$
Consol 2						C	$C\ldots$
Annuity		C	C	$C\ldots$	C		

Consol 1 is a normal consol with its first payment at date 1. The first payment of consol 2 occurs at date $T + 1$.

---

[9]Sometimes financial writers merely speak of a cash flow in year *x*. Although this terminology is ambiguous, such writers generally mean the end of year *x*.

The present value of having a cash flow of C at each of T dates is equal to the present value of consol 1 minus the present value of consol 2. The present value of consol 1 is given by

$$PV = \frac{C}{r} \tag{4.11}$$

Consol 2 is just a consol with its first payment at date $T + 1$. From the perpetuity formula, this consol will be worth C/r at date T.[10] However, we do not want the value at date T. We want the value now (in other words, the present value at date 0). We must discount C/r back by T periods. Therefore, the present value of consol 2 is

$$PV = C/r \times 1/(1 + r)^T \tag{4.12}$$

The present value of having cash flows for T years is the present value of a consol with its first payment at date 1 minus the present value of a consol with its first payment at date $T + 1$. Thus, the present value of an annuity is formula (4.11) minus formula (4.12). This can be written as

$$C/r - C/r\,[1/(1 + r)^T]$$

This simplifies to

Formula for Present Value of Annuity:[11,12]

$$PV = C\left[\frac{1}{r} - \frac{1}{r(1 + r)^T}\right] \tag{4.13}$$

■ *Example*

Andrea Mullings has just won a lottery, paying $50,000 a year for 20 years. She is to receive her first payment a year from now. The lottery advertisements bill this as the Million Dollar Lottery because $1,000,000 = $50,000 \times 20$. If the interest rate is 8 percent, what is the true value of the prize?

Formula (4.13) yields

$$\begin{array}{ll}
\text{Present value of} \\
\text{Million Dollar Lottery}
\end{array} = \quad \$50{,}000 \times [1/0.08 - 1/0.08\,(1.08)^{20}]$$

$$\begin{array}{ccc}
\text{Periodic payment} & & \text{Annuity factor} \\
= \$\ 50{,}000 & \times & 9.8181 \\
= \$490{,}905
\end{array}$$

Rather than being overjoyed at winning, Ms. Mullings sues the lottery authorities for misrepresentation and fraud. Her legal brief states that she was promised $1 million but received only $490,905. ■

The term we use to compute the value of the stream of level payments, C, for T years is called an **annuity factor.** The annuity factor in the current example is 9.8181.

---

[10]Students frequently think that C/r is the present value at date $T + 1$ because the consol's first payment is at date $T + 1$. However, the formula values the annuity as of one period prior to the first payment.

[11]This can also be written as $C[1 - 1/(1 + r)^T]/r$

[12]We can also provide a formula for the future value of an annuity:

$$FV = C[(1 + r)^T/r - 1/r]$$

Because the annuity factor is used so often in PV calculations, we have included it in Table A.2 in the back of this book. The table gives the values of these factors for a range of interest rates, r, and maturity dates, T.

The annuity factor as expressed in the brackets of (4.13) is a complex formula. For simplification, we may from time to time refer to the annuity factor as

$$A^T_r \qquad\qquad\qquad (4.14)$$

that is, expression (4.14) stands for the present value of $1 a year for T years at an interest rate of r.

Mortgages

Mortgages are a common example of an annuity with monthly payments. To understand mortgage calculations, you need to keep in mind two institutional arrangements. First, although payments are monthly, regulations for Canadian financial institutions require that mortgage rates be quoted with semiannual compounding. Further, payments on conventional mortgages are calculated to maturity (usually after 25 years) although rate adjustments after the initial locked-in period will cause payments to change subsequently.

▪ **Example**

A financial institution is offering a $100,000 mortgage at a stated rate of 12 percent. To find the payments we first need to find the effective *monthly* rate. To do this we convert the stated semiannual rate to an equivalent annual rate.[13]

$$\text{Effective annual interest rate} = [1 + r/m]^m - 1$$
$$= [1 + .12/2]^2 - 1$$
$$= 1.062 - 1$$
$$= 12.36\%$$

Then we find the effective monthly rate used to calculate the payments.

$$\text{Stated rate} / m = (\text{Effective annual rate} + 1)^{1/m} - 1$$
$$\text{Stated rate}/ 12 = (1.1236)^{1/12} - 1$$
$$= 1.0098 - 1 = 0.98\%$$

The effective monthly rate is 0.98 percent and there are $12 \times 25 = 300$ payments so we need to find $A^{300}_{.0098}$. Since this in not in Table A.2, we use (4.13) as rearranged in footnote 11 to solve for C, the monthly payment.

$$PV = \$100,000 = C \times (1 - \text{Present value factor})/r$$
$$\$100,000 = C \times (1 - 1/1.0098^{300})/.0098$$
$$= C \times (1 - .0543)/ .0098$$
$$= C \times 96.9087$$
$$C = \$1,031.90$$

The monthly mortgage payments will be $1,031.90. ▪

---

[13]Chartered banks use 10 decimal places for all calculations. This may result in some rounding error in using this formula to check the payments on an outstanding mortgage.

■ *Example*

Earlier, we pointed out that, while mortgages are amortized over 300 months, the rate is fixed for a shorter period usually no longer than five years. Suppose the rate of 12 percent in the previous example is fixed for five years and you are wondering whether to lock in this rate or to take a lower rate of 10 percent fixed for only one year. If you chose the one-year rate, how much lower will your payments be for the first year?

The payments at 10 percent are $894.49, a reduction of $137.41 per month. If you choose to take the shorter-term mortgage with lower payments, you are betting that rates will not take a big jump over the next year leaving you with a new rate after one year much higher than 12 percent. While the mortgage formula cannot make this decision for you (it depends on risk and return discussed in Chapter 9), it does give you the risk you are facing in terms of higher monthly payments. In 1981 mortgage rates were around 20 percent! ■

Using Annuity Formulas

Our experience is that annuity formulas are not hard, but can be tricky for the beginning student. Here we present four tricks.

Trick 1: A Delayed Annuity. One of the tricks in working with annuities or perpetuities is getting the timing exactly right. This is particularly useful when an annuity or perpetuity begins at a date many periods in the future. Consider the following example.

■ *Example*

Fauzia Mohammed will receive a four-year annuity of $500 per year beginning at date 6. If the interest rate is 10 percent, what is the present value of her annuity?

This situation can be graphed as

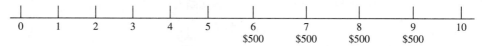

The analysis involves two steps:

1. Calculate the present value of the annuity using (4.13). This is

   Present Value of Annuity at Date 5:

$$\$500\left[\frac{1}{0.10} - \frac{1}{0.10(1.10)^4}\right] = \$500 \times A_{0.10}^4$$
$$= \$500 \times 3.1699$$
$$= \$1,584.95$$

Note that $1,584.95 represents the present value at date 5.

Students frequently think that $1,584.95 is the present value at date 6, because the annuity begins at date 6. However, our formula values the annuity as of one period prior to the first payment. This can be seen in the most typical case where the first payment occurs at date 1. The formula values the annuity as of date 0 here.

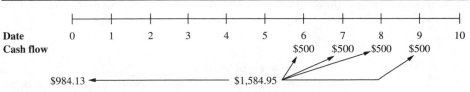

Figure 4.12
Discounting Fauzia
Mohammed's
annuity

Step One: Discount the four payments back to date 5 by using the annuity formula.
Step Two: Discount the present value at date 5 ($1,584.95) back to present value at date 0.

2. Discount the present value of the annuity back to date 0. That is

Present Value at Date 0:

$$\frac{\$1,584.95}{(1.10)^5} = \$984.13$$

Again, it is worthwhile mentioning that, because the annuity formula brings Fauzia's annuity back to date 5, the second calculation must discount over the remaining five periods. The two-step procedure is graphed in Figure 4.12.

Trick 2: Annuity in Advance. The annuity formula of (4.13) assumes that the first annuity payment begins a full period hence. This type of annuity is frequently called an *annuity in arrears.* What happens if the annuity begins today, in other words, at date 0? ▪

▪ *Example*

In a previous example, Andrea Mullings received $50,000 a year for 20 years as a prize in a lottery. In that example, she was to receive the first payment a year from the winning date. Let us now assume that the first payment occurs immediately. The total number of payments remains 20. Under this new assumption, we have a 19-date annuity with the first payment occurring at date 1—plus an extra payment at date 0. The present value is

$$\underset{\text{Payment at date 0}}{\$50,000} + \underset{\text{19-year annuity}}{\$50,000 \times A^{19}_{0.08}}$$

$$= \$50,000 + \$50,000 \times 9.6036$$
$$= \$530,180$$

The present value in this example is greater than $490,905, the present value in the earlier lottery example. This is to be expected because the annuity of the current example begins earlier. An annuity with an immediate initial payment is called an *annuity in advance.* Always remember that both formula (4.13) and Table A.2 refer to an *annuity in arrears.*

Trick 3: The Infrequent Annuity. The following example treats an annuity with payments occurring less frequently than once a year.

▪ *Example*

Alex Bourne receives an annuity of $450 payable once every two years. The annuity stretches out over 20 years. The first payment occurs at date 2, that is, two years from today. The annual interest rate is 6 percent.

The trick is to determine the interest rate over a two-year period. The interest rate over two years is

$$1.06 \times 1.06 - 1 = 12.36\%$$

That is, $100 invested over two years will yield $112.36.

What we want is the present value of a $450 annuity over 10 periods, with an interest rate of 12.36 percent per period. This is

$$\$450\left[\frac{1}{0.1236} - \frac{1}{0.1236 \times (1.1236)^{10}}\right] = \$50 \times A_{0.1236}^{10} = \$2,505.57$$

Trick 4: Equating Present Value of Two Annuities. The following example equates the present value of inflows with the present value of outflows.

■ *Example*

Jon Rabinowitz and Gila Messeri are saving for the university education of their newborn daughter, Gabrielle. They estimate that expenses will run $30,000 per year when their daughter enters university in 18 years. The annual interest rate over the next few decades will be 14 percent. How much money must they deposit in the bank each year so that their daughter will be completely supported through four years of university?

To simplify the calculations, we assume that Gabrielle is born today. Her parents will make the first of her four annual tuition payments on her 18th birthday. They will make equal bank deposits on each of her first 17 birthdays, but no deposit at date 0. This is illustrated as

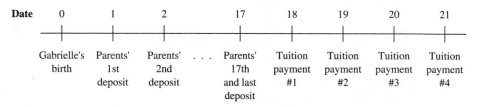

Date	0	1	2		17	18	19	20	21
	Gabrielle's birth	Parents' 1st deposit	Parents' 2nd deposit	...	Parents' 17th and last deposit	Tuition payment #1	Tuition payment #2	Tuition payment #3	Tuition payment #4

Jon and Gila will be making deposits to the bank over the next 17 years. They will be withdrawing $30,000 per year over the following four years. We can be sure they will be able to withdraw fully $30,000 per year if the present value of the deposits equals the present value of the four $30,000 withdrawals.

This calculation requires three steps. The first two determine the present value of the withdrawals. The final step determines yearly deposits that will have a present value equal to that of the withdrawals.

1. We calculate the present value of the four years at university using the annuity formula:

$$\$30,000 \times \left[\frac{1}{0.14} - \frac{1}{0.14 \times (1.14)^4}\right] = \$30,000 \times A_{0.14}^4$$
$$= \$30,000 \times 2.9137 = \$87,411$$

We assume that Gabrielle enters university on her 18th birthday.
Given our discussion in trick 1 above, $87,411 represents the present value at date 17.

2. We calculate the present value of a university education at date 0 as

$$\frac{\$87,411}{(1.14)^{17}} = \$9,422.91$$

3. Assuming that Gila Messeri and Jon Rabinowitz make deposits to the bank at the end of each of the 17 years, we calculate the annual deposit that will yield a present value of all deposits of $9,422.91 as

$$C \times A_{0.14}^{17} = \$9,422.91$$

Since

$$A_{0.14}^{17} = 6.3729$$

we find that

$$C = \frac{\$9,422.91}{6.3729} = \$1,478.59$$

Thus, deposits of $1,478.59 made at the end of each of the first 17 years and invested at 14 percent will provide enough money to make tuition payments of $30,000 over the following four years.

An alternative method would be: (1) calculate the present value of the tuition payments at Gabrielle's 18th birthday and (2) calculate annual deposits such that the future value of the deposits at her 18th birthday equals the present value of the tuition payments at that date. Although this technique can also provide the right answer, we have found that it is more likely to lead to errors. Therefore, we only equate present values in our presentation. ▪

Growing Annuity

Cash flows in business are very likely to grow over time, due either to real growth or to inflation. The growing perpetuity, which assumes an infinite number of cash flows, provides one formula to handle this growth. We now consider a **growing annuity,** which is a *finite* number of growing cash flows. Because perpetuities of any kind are rare, a formula for a growing annuity would be useful indeed. The formula is[14]

---

[14]This can be proved as follows. A growing annuity can be viewed as the difference between two growing perpetuities. Consider a growing perpetuity A, where the first payment of C occurs at date 1. Next, consider growing perpetuity B, where the first payment of $C(1 + g)^T$ is made at date $T + 1$. Both perpetuities grow at rate g. The growing annuity over T periods is the difference between annuity A and annuity B. This can be represented as:

Date	0	1	2	3	...	T	T + 1	T + 2	T + 3
Perpetuity A	C	$C \times (1 + g)$	$C \times (1 + g)^2$	...	$C \times (1 + g)^{T-1}$	$C \times (1 + g)^T$	$C \times (1 + g)^{T+1}$	$C \times (1 + g)^{T+2}$...	
Perpetuity B							$C \times (1 + g)^T$	$C \times (1 + g)^{T+1}$	$C \times (1 + g)^{T+2}$...
Annuity	C	$C \times (1 + g)$	$C \times (1 + g)^2$	...	$C \times (1 + g)^{T-1}$				

The value of perpetuity A is $\dfrac{C}{r - g}$

The value of perpetuity B is $\dfrac{C \times (1 + g)^T}{r - g} \times \dfrac{1}{(1 + r)^T}$

The difference between the two perpetuities is given by (4.15).

Formula for Present Value of Growing Annuity:

$$PV = \frac{C}{r - g}\left[1 - \left(\frac{1 + g}{1 + r}\right)^{T}\right] \tag{4.15}$$

where, as before, C is the payment to occur at the end of the first period, r is the interest rate, g is the rate of growth per period, expressed as a percentage, and T is the number of periods for the annuity.

■ *Example*

Gilles Lebouder, a second-year MBA student, has just been offered a job at $50,000 a year. He anticipates his salary increasing by 9 percent a year until his retirement in 40 years. Given an interest rate of 20 percent, what is the present value of his lifetime salary?

We simplify by assuming he will be paid his $50,000 salary exactly one year from now, and that his salary will continue to be paid in annual installments. From (4.15), the calculation is

Present value
of Gilles' $= \$50,000 \times [1/(0.20 - 0.09) - 1/(0.20 - 0.09)\,(1.09/1.20)^{40}]$
lifetime salary
                $= \$444,832$

Though the growing annuity is quite useful, it is more tedious than the other simplifying formulas. Whereas most sophisticated calculators have special programs for perpetuities, growing perpetuities, and annuities, there is no special program for growing annuities. Hence, one must calculate all the terms in (4.15) directly. ■

■ *Example*

In a previous example, Jon Rabinowitz and Gila Messeri planned to make 17 identical payments to fund the university education of their daughter, Gabrielle. Alternatively, imagine that they planned to increase their payments at 4 percent per year. What would their first payment be?

The first two steps of the previous Messeri-Rabinowitz example showed that the present value of the university costs was $9,422.91. These two steps would be the same here. However, the third step must be altered. Now we must ask, How much should their first payment be so that, if payments increase by 4 percent per year, the present value of all payments will be $9,422.91?

We set the growing annuity formula equal to $9,422.91 and solve for C:

$C[1/r - g - (1/r - g)\,(1 + g/1 + r)^{T}]$
$= C[1/0.14 - 0.04 - (1/0.14 - 0.04)\,(1.04/1.14)^{17}]$
$= \$9,422.91$

Here, $C = \$1,192.78$. Thus, the deposit on their daughter's first birthday is $1,192.78, the deposit on the second birthday is $1,240.49 (or $1.04 \times \$1,192.78$), and so on. ■

CONCEPT QUESTIONS

■ What are the formulas for perpetuity, growing perpetuity, annuity, and growing annuity?
■ What are three important points concerning the growing perpetuity formula?
■ What are four tricks concerning annuities?

What Is a Firm Worth?   4.5

Suppose you are a business appraiser who determines the value of small companies. The lesson you learn from this chapter is that the present value of a firm depends upon its future cash flows.

Let us consider the example of a firm that is expected to generate net cash flows (cash inflows minus cash outflows) of $5,000 in the first year and $2,000 for each of the next five years. The firm can be sold for $10,000 seven years from now. The owners of the firm would like to be able to make 10 percent on their investment.

The value of the firm is found by multiplying the net cash flow by the appropriate present value factor. The value of the firm is simply the sum of the present values of the individual net cash flows.

The present value of the net cash flows is given below:

End of Year	Net cash flow of the firm	Present value factor (10%)	Present value of net cash flows
1	$ 5,000	.90909	$ 4,545.45
2	2,000	.82645	1,652.90
3	2,000	.75131	1,502.62
4	2,000	.68301	1,366.02
5	2,000	.62092	1,241.84
6	2,000	.56447	1,128.94
7	10,000	.51315	5,131.58
Present value of firm			$16,569.35

We can also use the simplifying formula for an annuity to give us

$$\frac{\$5,000}{1.1} + \frac{\$2,000}{1.1} \times A_{0.10}^5 + \frac{10,000}{(1.1)^7} = \$16,569.35$$

Suppose you have the opportunity to acquire the firm for $12,000. Should you make this investment? The answer is yes because the NPV is positive.

$$\text{NPV} = \text{PV} - \text{Cost}$$
$$\$4,569.35 = \$16,569.35 - \$12,000$$

The incremental value (NPV) of acquiring the firm is $4,569.35.

Summary and Conclusions   4.6

1. Two basic concepts, *future value* and *present value,* were introduced in the beginning of this chapter. With a 10-percent interest rate, an investor with $1 today can generate a future value of $1.10 in a year, $1.21 [$1 × (1.10)^2] in two years, and so on. Conversely, present value analysis places a current value on a later cash flow. With the same 10-percent interest rate, a dollar to be received in one year has a present value of $0.909($1/1.10) in year 0. A dollar to be received in two years has a present value of $0.826 [$1/(1.10)^2].

2. One commonly expresses the interest rate as, say, 12 percent per year. However, one can speak of the interest rate as 3 percent per quarter. Although the stated annual interest rate remains 12 percent (3 percent × 4), the effective annual interest rate is 12.55 percent $[(1.03)^4 - 1]$. In other words, the compounding process increases the future value of an investment. The limiting case is continuous compounding, where funds are assumed to be reinvested every infinitesimal instant.

3. A basic quantitative technique for financial decision-making is net-present-value analysis. The net-present-value formula for an investment that generates cash flows (C_t) in future periods is

$$\text{NPV} = -C_0 + \frac{C_1}{1 + r} + \frac{C_2}{(1 + r)^2} + \ldots + \frac{C_T}{(1 + r)^T} = -C_0 + \sum_{t = 1}^{T} \frac{C_t}{(1 + r)^t}$$

The formula assumes that the cash flow at date 0 is the initial investment (a cash outflow).

4. Frequently, the actual calculation of present value is long and tedious. The computation of the present value of a long-term mortgage with monthly payments is a good example of this. We presented four simplifying formulas:

$$\text{Perpetuity: PV} = \frac{C}{r}$$

$$\text{Growing perpetuity: PV} = \frac{C}{r - g}$$

$$\text{Annuity: PV} = C\left[\frac{1}{r} - \frac{1}{r(1 + r)^T}\right]$$

$$\text{Growing annuity: PV} = C\left[\frac{1}{r - g} - \frac{1}{r - g} \times \left(\frac{1 + g}{1 + r}\right)^T\right]$$

5. We stressed a few practical considerations in the application of these formulas:

   a. The numerator in each of the formulas, C, is the cash flow to be received *one full period hence*.

   b. Cash flows are generally irregular in practice. To avoid unwieldy problems, assumptions to create more regular cash flows are made both in this textbook and in practice.

   c. A number of present value problems involve annuities (or perpetuities) beginning a few periods hence. Students should practice combining the annuity (or perpetuity) formula with the discounting formula to solve these problems.

   d. Annuities and perpetuities may have periods of every two or every n years, rather than once a year. The annuity and perpetuity formulas can easily handle such circumstances.

   e. One frequently encounters problems where the present value of one annuity must be equated with the present value of another annuity.

Key Terms

Future value 84

Compound value 84

Present value (PV) 84

Net present value (NPV) 85

Compounding 87

Simple interest 87

Compound interest 88

Discounting 92

Present value factor 92

Stated annual interest rate 95

Effective annual interest rate 96

Continuous compounding 97

Perpetuity 99

Growing perpetuity 101

Annuity 103

Annuity factor 104

Growing annuity 109

Suggested Readings

One of the best places to learn more about the mathematics of present value is the owner's manual that comes with a financial calculator. One of the best is the one that comes with the Hewlett-Packard calculators:

HP Business Consultant II: Owner's Manual, December 1989.

Other useful references are:

Texas Instruments. *Business Analyst Guidebook,* 1982.

Sharp. Business/Financial Calculator, EL-731SL, *Instruction Guide and Application Manual.*

Questions and Problems

The Multiperiod Case

4.1 Compute the future value of $1,000, annually compounded for

  a. Five years at 7 percent.

  b. Five years at 10 percent.

  c. Ten years at 7 percent.

  d. Why is the interest earned in part (*c*) not twice the amount earned in part (*a*)?

4.2 Calculate the future value of $5,000 over 12 years at a stated annual interest rate of 10 percent, compounded quarterly.

4.3 The federal government has issued a zero-coupon bond which will pay $1,000 in 25 years. The bond will have no interim coupon payments. What is the present value of the bond if the discount rate is 10 percent?

4.4 Calculate the present value of the following cash flows discounted at 10 percent.

  a. $1,000 received two years from today.

  b. $20 received one year from today.

  c. $500 received eight years from today.

4.5 It is estimated that a firm has a pension liability that will require the payment of $1 million 24 years from today. If the firm can invest in a risk-free security that has a stated annual interest rate of 6 percent, how much must the firm invest to be able to make the $1 million payment?

4.6 Would you rather receive $1,000 today or $2,000 in 10 years if the discount rate is 8 percent?

4.7 You have won the provincial lottery. Lottery officials offer you the choice of the following alternative payouts:

Alternative 1: $10,000 one year from now.
Alternative 2: $20,000 five years from now.

Which should you choose if the discount rate is
a. 0 percent?
b. 10 percent?
c. 20 percent?
d. What rate makes the options equally attractive to you?

4.8 You are selling your house. The Smiths have offered you $76,200. They will pay you immediately. The Joneses have offered you $93,750, but they cannot pay you until two years from today. The prevailing interest rate is 11 percent. Which offer should you choose?

4.9 Suppose you place $1,000 in an account at the end of each of the next four years. If the account earns 12 percent, how much will be in the account at the end of seven years? (Hint: See footnote 12.)

4.10 The Bank of Upper Canada charges 10 percent, compounded quarterly, on its personal loans. The Bank of New Brunswick charges 10.5 percent, compounded semiannually. As a potential borrower, which do you prefer?

4.11 A typical rate at a pawn shop would be 20 percent per month. Pawn brokers are legally required to report an annual percentage rate (APR). What rate should they report? What is the effective annual rate?

4.12 If you invest $10,000 today, a financial institution will pay you $18,000 at the end of 10 years. What effective annual rate does this investment offer? What continuously compounded rate does it offer?

4.13 You have the opportunity to make an investment that costs $900. If you make this investment now, you will receive $180 one year from today. You will receive $215 and $785 two and three years from today, respectively. The appropriate discount rate for this investment is 10 percent.
a. Should you make the investment?
b. What is the NPV of this opportunity?
c. If the investment costs $950, should you invest? Compute the NPV to support your answer.

4.14 Your Auntie Klara owns an auto dealership. She promised to give you $3,170 in trade-in value for your car when you graduate one year from now. Your roommate offered you $2,800 for the car now. The prevailing interest rate is 12 percent. Should you accept your roommate's offer?

4.15 Today Grushcow Inc. signed a contract to sell a capital asset for $70,000. The firm will receive payment two years from today. The asset cost $60,000 to produce.

   a. If the interest rate is 10 percent, is the firm making a profit on this item?

   b. At what interest rate will the firm break even?

Compounding Periods

4.16 What is the future value three years hence of $1,000 invested in an account with a stated annual interest rate of 8 percent under the following situations?

   a. Interest is compounded annually.

   b. Interest is compounded semiannually.

   c. Interest is compounded monthly.

   d. Interest is compounded continuously.

   e. Why does the future value increase as the compounding period shortens?

4.17 Compute the future value of $200 continuously compounded for

   a. Five years at 10 percent.

   b. Three years at 15 percent.

   c. Ten years at 12 percent.

   d. Eight years at 4 percent.

Perpetuities

4.18 The prevailing interest rate is 15 percent. What is the price of a consol bond that pays $120 annually?

Growing Perpetuities

4.19 Bunn Builders, Inc., paid a $5 dividend yesterday. If the firm raises its dividend 7 percent every year and the appropriate discount rate is 11 percent, what is the price of Bunn Builders stock?

4.20 In its most recent corporate report, Rodney's, Inc., apologized to its shareholders for not paying a dividend. The report states that management will pay a $2 dividend next year. That dividend will grow 4 percent every year thereafter. If the appropriate discount rate is 12 percent, how much are you willing to pay for a share of Rodney's, Inc.?

Annuities and Growing Annuities

4.21 Given an interest rate of 8 percent per year, what is the value at date $t = 7$ of a perpetual stream of $100 payments coming at dates $t = 12, 13, 14, \ldots$?

4.22 Should you buy an asset that will generate income of $1,200 per year for eight years? The price of the asset is $6,200 and the stated annual interest rate is 10 percent.

4.23 What is the present value of end-of-year cash flows of $2,000 per year, with the first cash flow received 3 years from today and the last one 22 years from today? Use a discount rate of 8 percent.

4.24   What is the value of a 10-year annuity that pays $300 a year? The annuity's first cash flow is at the end of year 6. The stated annual interest rate is 15 percent for years 1 through 5 and 10 percent thereafter.

4.25   You are offered the opportunity to buy a note for $12,800. The note is certain to pay $2,000 at the end of each of the next 10 years. If you buy the note, what rate of interest will you receive?

4.26   You have recently won the super jackpot in a lottery, with a payoff of $4,960,000. On reading the fine print, you discover that you have two options:

     a.   You receive $160,000 at the beginning of each year for 31 years.

     b.   You receive $1,750,000 now, but you do not have access to the full amount immediately. You are able to take $446,000 now. The remaining balance will be placed in a 30-year annuity account that pays $101,055 at the end of each year.

All payments are tax-free. Using a discount rate of 10 percent, which option should you select?

4.27   You need $25,000 five years from now. You budget to make equal payments at the end of every year into an account that pays a stated annual interest rate of 7 percent. (Hint: See footnote 12.)

     a.   What are your annual payments?

     b.   Your rich Aunt Amy died and left you $20,000. How much of it must you put into the same account as a lump sum today to meet your goal?

4.28   On December 31, Janice Vogtle bought a building for $300,000. She paid 20 percent down and took out a mortgage on the remainder for an amortization period of 15 years at a quoted rate of 11 percent. What is her monthly payment?

4.29   In the previous problem, Janice Vogtle took out a mortgage of $240,000 (80 percent of $300,000) for a 15-year amortization period. The interest rate was 11 percent locked in for five years. She is now wondering whether it would be better to extend the amortization period to 20 years and to take a rate of 10 percent locked in for only one year. While she knows that the longer amortization period on the second mortgage would make the payments lower, there is a risk that interest rates could rise giving higher payments after the first year.

     a.   How much lower will the payments be in the first year?

     b.   Suppose that Ms. Vogtle decides to take another 20-year mortgage after the first year and that the rate on this mortgage is then 14 percent. Will her payments still be lower than with the original mortgage?

     c.   How high can interest rates on 20-year mortgages rise before the payments exceed those on the original 15-year mortgage?

4.30   An entrepreneur is considering the purchase of an office in a new high-rise complex. The office is worth $333,000 and a bank is offering a mortgage for $250,000 at a quoted rate of 8 percent. If the entrepreneur's budget allows payments of $2,750 a month, how long will it take to pay off the purchase?

4.31 When Marilyn Monroe died, exhusband Joe DiMaggio vowed to place fresh flowers on her grave every Sunday as long as he lived. A bunch of fresh flowers of the quality that the former baseball player thought was appropriate for the star cost about $4 when she died in 1962. Based on actuarial tables, "Joltin' Joe" could expect to live for 30 years after the actress died. Assuming that the expected rate of inflation was 4 percent and the stated annual interest rate was 8 percent, what was the present value of this commitment?

4.32 Assume that the cost of a university education will be $20,000 per year when your child enters university 12 years from now. You presently have $10,000 to invest. What rate of interest must your investment earn to pay the cost of a four-year education for your child? For simplicity, assume the entire cost of the education must be paid when your child matriculates.

4.33 You are saving for the education of your two children.
They are two years apart in age; one will begin university in 15 years, the other will matriculate in 17 years. You estimate your children's expenses to be $21,000 per year per child. The annual interest rate is 15 percent, and it will remain 15 percent through the next 25 years. How much money must you place in an account each year to fund your children's educations? You will begin payments one year from today. You will discontinue payments when your older child enters university.

4.34 In January 1984, Richard "Goose" Gossage signed a contract to play for the San Diego Padres that guaranteed him a minimum of $9,955,000. The guaranteed payments were $875,000 in 1984, $650,000 in 1985, $800,000 in 1986, $1 million in 1987, $1 million in 1988, and $300,000 in 1989. In addition, the contract called for $5,330,000 in deferred money payable at the rate of $240,000 per year from 1990 through 2006 and then $125,000 a year from 2007 through 2016. If the relevant annual rate of interest is 9 percent and all payments are made on July 1 of each year, what would the present value of these guaranteed payments be on January 1, 1984? (Assume an interest rate of 4.4 percent per six months.) If he were to receive an equal annual salary at the end of each of the five years from 1984 through 1988, what would his equivalent annual salary be? Ignore taxes throughout this problem.

4.35 Assuming an interest rate of 10 percent, calculate the present value of the following streams of yearly payments:

   a. $1,000 per year forever, with the first payment one year from today.

   b. $500 per year forever, with the first payment two years from today.

   c. $2,420 per year forever, with the first payment three years from today.

4.36 A well-known insurance company offers a policy known as the "Estate Creator Six Pay." Typically the policy is bought by a parent or grandparent for a child at the child's birth. The details of the policy are as follows: The purchaser (say, the parent) makes the following six payments to the insurance company.

1st birthday	$730	4th birthday	$855
2nd birthday	$730	5th birthday	$855
3rd birthday	$730	6th birthday	$855

No more payments are made after the child's sixth birthday. When the child reaches age 65, he or she receives $143,723. If the opportunity cost of capital is 6 percent for the first six years and 7 percent for all subsequent years, is the policy worth buying?

4.37   Your younger brother has come to you for advice. He is about to enter university and has two options open to him. His first option is to study engineering. If he does this, his undergraduate degree would cost him $12,000 a year for four years. Having obtained this, he would need to gain two years of practical experience; in the first year he would earn $20,000, in the second year he would earn $25,000. He then would need to obtain his master's degree, which will cost $15,000 a year for two years. After that he will be fully qualified and can earn $40,000 per year for 25 years.

His other alternative is to study accounting. If he does this, he would pay $13,000 a year for four years and then he would earn $31,000 per year for 30 years.

The effort involved in the two careers is the same, so he is only interested in the earnings the jobs provide. All earnings and costs are paid at the end of the year. What advice would you give him if the applicable interest rate is 5 percent? A day later he comes back and says he took your advice, but in fact, the applicable interest rate was 6 percent. Has your brother made the right choice?

4.38   The management of Ram Research is trying to decide whether or not to undertake the following project:

Cost: $4,100.20.

After-tax cash flows: $1,000 per year for five years.

Risk level: requires a 10-percent discount rate.

Help the management make its decision by computing the NPV of the project. Should Ram Research undertake the project?

4.39   You must decide whether or not to purchase new capital equipment. The cost of the machine is $5,000. It will yield the following amounts of income. The appropriate discount rate is 10 percent.

Year	Cash flow
1	$700
2	900
3	1,000
4	1,000
5	1,000
6	1,000
7	1,250
8	1,375

Should you purchase the equipment?

4.40 You are saving for your retirement. You have decided that starting one year from today, each year you will place 2 percent of your annual salary in an account that will earn 8 percent per year. Your salary is $50,000, but it will grow at 4 percent per annum throughout your career. How much money will you have for your retirement, which will begin in 40 years?

4.41 Ms. Hops receives an offer from a large brewery for a job as a taste tester. Her base salary will be $26,000. She will receive her first annual salary payment one year from the day she begins work. In addition, she will get an immediate $5,000 bonus for joining the company. Her salary will grow 4 percent each year. Also, each year she has a 25-percent chance of receiving a bonus equal to 30 percent of her salary. Ms. Hops will work for 30 years and is exempt from taxes. What is the present value of the offer if the discount rate is 11 percent?

4.42 The MBA Publishing Company is trying to decide whether or not to revise its popular textbook, *Financial Psychoanalysis Made Simple.* It has estimated that the revision will cost $40,000. Cash flows from increased sales will be $10,000 the first year. These cash flows will increase by 8 percent per year for the next two years, and then remain stable for two more years. The book will go out of print five years from now. Assume the initial cost is paid now and all revenues are received at the end of each year. If the company requires a 10-percent return for such an investment, should it undertake the revision?

How to Value Bonds and Stocks

The previous chapter discussed the mathematics of compounding, discounting, and present value. We now use the mathematics of compounding and discounting to determine the present values of financial instruments, beginning with a discussion of how bonds are valued. Since the future cash flows of bonds are known, application of net present value techniques is fairly straightforward. The uncertainty of future cash flows makes the pricing of stocks according to NPV more difficult.

Definition and Example of a Bond 5.1

A *bond* is a certificate showing that a borrower owes a specified sum. In order to repay the money, the borrower has agreed to make interest and principal payments on designated dates. For example, imagine that Kreuger Enterprises just issued 100,000 bonds for $1,000 each carrying a coupon rate of 5 percent and a maturity of two years. Interest on the bonds is to be paid yearly. This means that

1. $100 million (or 100,000 × $1,000) has been borrowed by the firm.
2. The firm must pay interest of $5 million (or 5% × $100 million) at the end of one year.
3. The firm must pay both $5 million of interest and $100 million of principal at the end of two years.

We now consider how to value a few different types of bonds.

How to Value Bonds 5.2

Pure Discount Bonds

The **pure discount bond** is perhaps the simplest kind of bond. It promises a single payment, say $1, at a fixed future date. If the payment is one year from now, it is called a *one-year discount bond,* if it is two years from now, it is called a *two-year discount bond,* and so on. The date when the issuer of the bond makes the last payment is called the **maturity date** of the bond or just its *maturity* for short. The bond is said to mature or *expire* on the date of its final payment. The payment at maturity ($1 in this example) is termed the bond's **face value.**

Figure 5.1
Different types of
bonds: *C,* coupon
paid every six
months; *F,* face
value at year 4
(maturity for pure
discount and
coupon bonds)

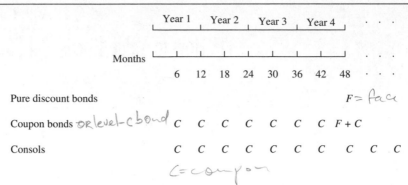

Pure discount bonds are often called *zero-coupon bonds* or *zeros* to emphasize the fact that the holder receives no cash payments until maturity. We will use the terms *zero, bullet,* and *discount* interchangably to refer to bonds that pay no coupons.

The first row of Figure 5.1 shows the pattern of cash flows from a four-year pure discount bond. Note that the face value, *F,* is paid when the bond expires in the 48th month. There are no payments of either interest or principal prior to this date.

In the previous chapter, we indicated that one discounts a future cash flow to determine its present value. The present value of a pure discount bond can easily be determined by the techniques of the previous chapter. For short, we sometimes speak of the *value* of a bond instead of its present value.

Consider a pure discount bond that pays a face value of *F* in *T* years, where the interest rate is *r* in each of the *T* years. (We also refer to this rate as the *market interest rate.*) Because the face value is the only cash flow that the bond pays, the present value of this face amount is

Value of a Pure Discount Bond:

$$PV = \frac{F}{(1 + r)^T}$$

The present value formula can produce some surprising results. Suppose that the interest rate is 10 percent. Consider a bond with a face value of $1 million that matures in 20 years. Applying the formula to this bond, its PV is given by

$$PV = \frac{\$1 \text{ million}}{(1.1)^{20}}$$
$$= \$148,644$$

or only about 15 percent of the face value.

Level-Coupon Bonds

Many bonds, however, are not of the simple, pure discount variety. Typical bonds issued by either governments or corporations offer cash payments not just at maturity, but also at regular times in between. For example, payments on Canadian government issues and Canadian corporate bonds are made every six months until the bond matures. These payments are called the **coupons** of the bond. The middle row of Figure 5.1 illustrates the case of a four-year, *level-coupon* bond: The coupon, *C,* is paid every six months and is the same throughout the life of the bond.

Note that the face value of the bond, *F,* is paid at maturity (end of year 4). *F* is sometimes called the *principal* or the *denomination.* Bonds issued in Canada typically have face values of $1,000, though this can vary with the type of bond.

As we mentioned above, the value of a bond is simply the present value of its cash flows. Therefore, the value of a level-coupon bond is merely the present value of its stream of coupon payments plus the present value of its repayment of principal. Because a level-coupon bond is just an annuity of *C* each period, together with a payment at maturity of $1,000, the value of a level-coupon bond is

Value of a Level-Coupon Bond:

$$PV = \frac{C}{1 + r} + \frac{C}{(1 + r)^2} + \cdots + \frac{C}{(1 + r)^T} + \frac{\$1,000}{(1 + r)^T}$$

where *C* is the coupon and the face value, *F,* is $1,000. The value of the bond can be rewritten as

Value of a Level-Coupon Bond:

$$PV = C \times A_r^T + \frac{\$1,000}{(1 + r)^T}$$

As mentioned in the previous chapter, A_r^T is the present value of an annuity of $1 per period for *T* periods at an interest rate per period of *r.*

▪ *Example*

Selected Government of Canada bond trading figures for June 1993 appear in Figure 5.2. Suppose an investor was interested in the CANADA 7.50 1 JUL 97. This is jargon that means the annual coupon rate is 7.5 percent.[1] The face value is $1,000, implying that the yearly coupon is $75 (7.5% × $1,000). Interest is paid each January and July, implying that the coupon every six months is $37.50 ($75/2). The face value will be paid out in July 1997, four years later. By this we mean that the purchaser obtains claims to the following cash flows:

1/94	6/94	1/95	6/95	1/96	6/96	1/97	6/97
$37.50	$37.50	$37.50	$37.50	$37.50	$37.50	$37.50	$37.50 + $1,000

If the stated annual interest rate in the market is 6.674 percent per year, what is the present value of the bond?

Our work on compounding in the previous chapter showed that the interest rate over any six-month interval is one-half of the stated annual interest rate. In the current

---

[1]The coupon rate is specific to the bond and indicates what cash flow should appear in the numerator of the NPV equation. The coupon rate does not appear in the denominator of the NPV equation.

Figure 5.2
Sample of *The Globe and Mail* bond quotation

CANADIAN BONDS

Selected quotations, with changes since the previous day, on actively traded bond issues, provided by RBC Dominion Securities. Yields are calculated to full maturity, unless marked C to indicate callable date. Price is the midpoint between final bid and ask quotations June 25, 1993.

Issuer	Coupon	Maturity	Price	Yield $ Chg	Issuer	Coupon	Maturity	Price	Yield $ Chg
GOVERNMENT OF CANADA					ONTARIO HYD	8.63	6 FEB 02	103.675	8.023 +0.270
CANADA	7.00	15 SEP 94	101.575	5.627 +0.050	ONTARIO HYD	9.00	24 JUN 02	106.025	8.043 +0.270
CANADA	7.00	15 MAR 95	101.625	5.979 +0.100	ONTARIO HYD	8.90	18 AUG 22	100.975	8.805 +0.300
CANADA	8.25	1 NOV 95	104.400	6.195 +0.100	ONTARIO	8.75	16 APR 97	105.475	7.069 +0.100
CANADA	6.00	1 FEB 96	99.300	6.294 +0.100	ONTARIO	8.00	11 MAR 03	100.075	7.986 +0.270
CANADA	6.50	1 AUG 96	100.250	6.407 +0.050	ONTARIO	9.50	13 JUL 22	107.275	8.802 +0.250
CANADA	8.25	1 MAR 97	105.150	6.637 +0.150	P E I	9.75	30 APR 02	108.175	8.415 +0.250
CANADA	7.50	1 JUL 97	102.850	6.674 +0.150	P E I	11.00	19 SEP 11	116.850	9.087 +0.200
CANADA	6.25	1 FEB 98	98.300	6.686 +0.150	QUEBEC	8.00	30 MAR 98	103.025	7.230 +0.200
CANADA	6.50	1 SEP 98	99.250	6.672 +0.150	QUEBEC	10.25	7 APR 98	111.325	7.378 +0.150
CANADA	9.50	1 OCT 98	111.250	6.901 +0.200	QUEBEC	10.25	15 OCT 01	112.900	8.079 +0.300
CANADA	9.25	1 DEC 99	111.025	7.078 +0.250	QUEBEC	9.38	16 JAN 23	104.475	8.942 +0.250
CANADA	9.75	1 JUN 01	113.425	7.469 +0.350	SASKATCHEWAN	8.13	4 FEB 97	102.250	7.395 +0.100
CANADA	9.50	1 OCT 01	111.975	7.520 +0.350	SASKATCHEWAN	9.60	4 FEB 22	104.200	9.181 +0.200
CANADA	9.75	1 DEC 01	113.950	7.482 +0.350	TORONTO MET	10.38	4 SEP 01	113.300	8.112 +0.200
CANADA	8.50	1 APR 02	106.900	7.410 +0.300	**CORPORATE**				
CANADA	10.00	1 MAY 02	115.725	7.526 +0.400	AVCO FIN	8.50	2 MAR 98	103.250	7.653 +0.250
CANADA	7.25	1 JUN 03	99.350	7.342 +0.300	BELL CANADA	9.50	15 JUN 02	109.550	7.984 +0.375
CANADA	7.50	1 DEC 03	101.330	7.314 +0.280	BELL CANADA	9.70	15 DEC 32	109.250	8.852 +0.250
CANADA	10.25	1 FEB 04	118.950	7.608 +0.300	BELL CDA ENT	7.13	1 MAY 98	99.938	7.137 +0.125
CANADA	10.00	1 JUN 08	117.050	8.018 +0.400	BELL CDA ENT	8.95	1 APR 02	105.650	8.034 +0.250
CANADA	9.50	1 JUN 10	113.250	8.051 +0.350	BC TELEPHONE	10.50	12 JUN 00	114.000	7.843 +0.250
CANADA	9.00	1 MAR 11	109.150	8.020 +0.350	BC TELEPHONE	9.65	8 APR 22	109.500	8.740 +0.250
CANADA	10.25	15 MAR 14	120.750	8.155 +0.450	BANK OF MONT	8.50	*	103.750	7.381C +0.125
CANADA	9.75	1 JUN 21	117.500	8.150 +0.400	BANK OF MONT	8.85	1 JUN 03	105.625	8.015 +0.250
CANADA	9.25	1 JUN 22	112.200	8.145 +0.350	BANK OF N S	8.10	24 MAR 03	100.375	8.041 +0.250
CANADA	8.00	1 JUN 23	100.000	7.999 +0.300	CONSUMER GAS	7.55	15 DEC 97	101.575	7.129 +0.125
PROVINCIAL					CDN UTIL	9.40	1 MAY 23	107.000	8.735 +0.375
ALBERTA	7.00	20 AUG 97	100.775	6.778 +0.150	EATN CR CARD	8.30	1 DEC 95	102.750	7.033 +0.125
ALBERTA	7.75	4 FEB 98	102.925	6.991 +0.150	IMASCO LTD	8.38	23 JUN 03	101.625	8.133 +0.250
ALBERTA	7.75	5 MAY 03	99.900	7.762 +0.240	MOLSON BREW	8.20	11 MAR 03	101.250	8.009 +0.250
B C	7.00	2 MAR 98	100.025	6.990 +0.150	MOLSON BREW	9.10	11 MAR 13	102.000	8.881 +0.250
B C	9.00	9 JAN 02	107.175	7.829 +0.270	NRTH TELECOM	7.45	10 MAR 98	101.313	7.112 +0.125
B C	7.75	16 JUN 03	99.775	7.782 +0.270	OSHAWA GROUP	8.25	30 JUN 03	101.375	8.047 +0.250
B C	8.50	23 AUG 13	100.000	8.498 +0.250	ROYAL BANK	10.50	1 MAR 02	114.500	8.131 +0.500
B C	8.75	19 AUG 22	102.075	8.554 +0.250	TELEGLOBE	8.35	20 JUN 03	101.125	8.182 +0.250
HYDRO QUEBEC	9.25	2 DEC 96	106.975	6.915 +0.100	THOMSON CORP	7.90	17 SEP 02	98.750	8.092 +0.375
HYDRO QUEBEC	10.88	25 JUL 01	116.325	8.077 +0.300	TRANSCDA PIP	9.45	20 MAR 18	106.125	8.834 +0.250
HYDRO QUEBEC	11.00	15 AUG 20	121.075	8.923 +0.300	UNION GAS	9.70	6 NOV 17	106.625	9.021 +0.250
HYDRO QUEBEC	9.63	15 JUL 22	106.975	8.947 +0.250	* 10 JUNE 02/97				
MANITOBA	6.75	24 AUG 95	101.175	6.150 +0.100					
MANITOBA	9.25	21 MAY 97	107.525	6.996 +0.100					
MANITOBA	7.88	7 APR 03	99.900	7.887 +0.270					
MANITOBA	10.50	5 MAR 31	119.300	8.741 +0.300					
NEW BRUNSWIC	7.00	17 MAR 98	99.850	7.034 +0.100					
NEW BRUNSWIC	8.38	26 AUG 02	103.250	7.867 +0.250					
NEW BRUNSWIC	8.50	28 JUN 13	99.150	8.589 +0.250					
NEWFOUNDLAND	10.13	22 NOV 14	108.225	9.234 +0.200					
NOVA SCOTIA	9.60	30 JAN 22	107.000	8.918 +0.200					
ONTARIO HYD	10.88	8 JAN 96	109.600	6.656 +0.100					
ONTARIO HYD	7.25	31 MAR 98	100.100	7.221 +0.150					
ONTARIO HYD	9.63	3 AUG 99	110.275	7.488 +0.250					

BENCHMARK INTERNATIONAL BONDS

Issuer	Coupon	Maturity	Price	Yield $ chg
U.S. Treasury	$7\frac{1}{8}$	Feb/23	105 13/32	6.70 + 12/32
British gilt	9	Oct/08	108 2/32	8.06 + 1/32
German Treuhand	$6\frac{7}{8}$	2003	101.03	6.73 -0.07
Japan #145	5.5	2002	106.84	4.410 +0.10

Source: *The Globe and Mail,* "Report on Business," June 26, 1993, p. B7. Used with permission.

example, this semiannual rate is 3.337 percent (6.674%/2). Since the coupon payment in each six-month period is $37.50, and there are eight of these six-month periods from July 1993 to July 1997, the present value of the bond is

$$PV = \frac{\$37.50}{(1.03337)} + \frac{\$37.50}{(1.03337)^2} + \ldots + \frac{\$37.50}{(1.03337)^8} + \frac{\$1,000}{(1.03337)^8}$$

$$= \$37.50 \times A_{0.0337}^8 + \$1,000/(1.03337)^8$$

$$= (\$37.50 \times 6.921) + (\$1,000 \times 0.7690)$$

$$= \$259.54 + \$769.05 = \$1,028.59$$

Traders will generally quote the bond as 102.859, indicating that it is selling at 102.859 percent of the face value of $1,000. This can be seen in Figure 5.2 in the price column for our bond. (The small difference in price between our calculations and *The Globe and Mail* listing reflects accrued interest and rounding differences.)

Here it is worthwhile to relate our example of bond pricing to the discussion of compounding in the previous chapter, where we distinguished between the stated annual interest rate and the effective annual interest rate. In particular, we pointed out that the effective annual interest rate is

$$(1 + r/m)^m - 1$$

where r is the stated annual interest rate and m is the number of compounding intervals. Since $r = 6.674\%$ and $m = 2$ (because the bond makes semiannual payments), the effective annual interest rate is

$$(1 + 0.06674/2)^2 - 1 = (1.03337)^2 - 1 = 6.785\%$$

In other words, because the bond is paying interest twice a year, the bondholder earns a 6.785-percent return when compounding is considered.[2] ∎

One final note concerning level-coupon bonds: Although our example uses government bonds, corporate bonds are identical in form. For example, Bank of Montreal has an 8.85-percent bond maturing in 2003. This means that Bank of Montreal will make semiannual payments of $44.25 (8.85%/2 × $1,000) between now and 2003 for each face value of $1,000.

Consols

Not all bonds have a final maturity date. As we mentioned in the previous chapter, consols are bonds that never stop paying a coupon, have no final maturity date, and therefore never mature. Thus, a consol is a perpetuity. In the 18th century the Bank of England issued such bonds, called *English consols.* These were bonds that the Bank of England guaranteed would pay the holder a cash flow forever! Through wars and depressions, the Bank of England continued to honour this commitment, and you can still buy such bonds in London today. The Government of Canada also once sold consols. Even though these Canada bonds were supposed to last forever and to pay their coupons forever, don't go looking for any. There is a special clause in the bond contract that gives the government the right to buy them back from the holders, and that is what the government did. Clauses like that are *call provisions;* we'll study them later.

An important current Canadian example of a consol is fixed-rate preferred stock that provides the holder a fixed dividend in perpetuity. If there were never any question that the firm would actually pay the dividend on the preferred stock, such stock would in fact be a consol.

---

[2]For an excellent discussion of how to value semiannual payments, see J. T. Lindley, B. P. Helms, and M. Haddad, "A Measurement of the Errors in Intra-Period Compounding and Bond Valuation," *The Financial Review* 22 (February 1987).

These instruments can be valued by the perpetuity formula of the previous chapter. For example, if the marketwide interest rate is 10 percent, a consol with a yearly interest payment of $50 is valued at

$$\frac{\$50}{0.10} = \$500$$

CONCEPT QUESTIONS

- Define pure discount bonds, level-coupon bonds, and consols.
- Contrast the stated interest rate and the effective annual interest rate for bonds paying semiannual interest.

5.3   Bond Concepts

We complete our discussion on bonds by considering two important concepts: the relationship between interest rates and bond prices and the concept of yield to maturity.

Interest Rates and Bond Prices

The above discussion on level-coupon bonds allows us to relate bond prices to interest rates. Consider the following example.

- *Example*

The interest rate is 10 percent. A two-year bond with a 10-percent coupon pays interest of $100 (or $1,000 × 10%). For simplicity, we assume that the interest is paid annually. The bond is priced at its face value of $1,000:

$$\$1,000 = \frac{\$100}{1.10} + \frac{\$1,000 + \$100}{(1.10)^2}$$

If the interest rate unexpectedly rises to 12 percent, the bond sells at

$$\$966.20 = \frac{\$100}{1.12} + \frac{\$1,000 + \$100}{(1.12)^2}$$

Because $966.20 is below $1,000, the bond is said to sell at a **discount.** This is a sensible result. Now that the interest rate is 12 percent, a newly issued bond with a 12-percent coupon rate will sell at $1,000. This newly issued bond will have coupon payments of $120 (or 0.12 × $1,000). Because our bond has interest payments of only $100, investors will pay less than $1,000 for it.

If interest rates fell to 8 percent, the bond would sell at

$$\$1,035.67 = \frac{\$100}{1.08} + \frac{\$1,000 + \$100}{(1.08)^2}$$

Because $1,035.67 is above $1,000, the bond is said to sell at a **premium.** ∎

Thus, we find that bond prices fall with a rise in interest rates and rise with a fall in interest rates. Furthermore, the general principle is that a level-coupon bond trades in the following ways.

1. At the face value of $1,000 if the coupon rate is equal to the marketwide interest rate.
2. At a discount if the coupon rate is below the marketwide interest rate.
3. At a premium if the coupon rate is above the marketwide interest rate.

Yield to Maturity

Let us now consider the previous example in reverse. If our bond is selling at $1,035.67, what return is a bondholder receiving? This can be answered by considering the following equation:

$$\$1,035.67 = \frac{\$100}{1 + y} + \frac{\$1,000 + \$100}{(1 + y)^2}$$

The unknown, y, is the rate of return that the holder is earning on the bond. Our earlier work implies that $y = 8\%$. Thus, traders state that the bond is yielding an 8-percent return. Equivalently, they say that the bond has a **yield to maturity** of 8 percent.

CONCEPT QUESTIONS

- What is the relationship between interest rates and bond prices?
- How does one calculate the yield to maturity on a bond?

The Present Value Formulas for Bonds

Pure Discount Bonds

$$PV = \frac{F}{(1 + r)^T}$$

Level-Coupon Bonds

$$PV = C\left[\frac{1}{r} - \frac{1}{r \times (1 + r)^T}\right] + \frac{F}{(1 + r)^T} = C \times A_r^T + \frac{F}{(1 + r)^T}$$

where F is typically $1,000 for a level-coupon bond.

Consols

$$PV = \frac{C}{r}$$

The Present Value of Common Stocks

Dividends versus Capital Gains

Our goal in this section is to value common stocks. We learned in the previous chapter that an asset's value is determined by the present value of its future cash flows. A stock provides two kinds of cash flows. First, most stocks pay dividends on a regular basis. Second, the shareholder receives the sale price when the stock is sold. Thus, in order to value common stocks, we need to answer an interesting question: Is the value of a stock equal to

1. The discounted present value of the sum of next period's dividend plus next period's stock price, or
2. The discounted present value of all future dividends?

This is the kind of question that students would love to see on a multiple-choice exam because both (1) and (2) are correct.

To see that (1) and (2) are the same, we start with an individual who will buy the stock and hold it for one year. In other words, this investor has a one-year *holding period*. In addition, the investor is willing to pay P_0 for the stock today.

$$P_0 = \frac{Div_1}{1 + r} + \frac{P_1}{1 + r} \tag{5.1}$$

Div_1 is the dividend paid at year-end and P_1 is the price at year-end. P_0 is the PV of the common stock investment. The term r in the denominator is the discount rate for the stock. It equals the interest rate when the stock is riskless. It is likely to be greater than the interest rate if the stock is risky.

That seems easy enough, but where does P_1 come from? P_1 is not pulled out of thin air. Rather, there must be a buyer at the end of year 1 who is willing to purchase the stock for P_1. This buyer determines price by

$$P_1 = \frac{Div_2}{1 + r} + \frac{P_2}{1 + r} \tag{5.2}$$

Substituting the value of P_1 from (5.2) into equation (5.1) yields

$$P_0 = \frac{1}{1 + r}\left[Div_1 + (\frac{Div_2 + P_2}{1 + r})\right] \tag{5.3}$$

We can ask a similar question for (5.3): Where does P_2 come from? An investor at the end of year 2 is willing to pay P_2 because of the dividend and stock price at year 3. This process can be repeated ad nauseam.[3] At the end, we are left with

$$P_0 = \frac{Div_1}{1 + r} + \frac{Div_2}{(1 + r)^2} + \frac{Div_3}{(1 + r)^3} + \cdots = \sum_{t=1}^{\infty} \frac{Div_t}{(1 + r)^t} \tag{5.4}$$

---

[3]This procedure reminds us of the physicist lecturing on the origins of the universe. He was approached by an elderly gentleman in the audience who disagreed with the lecture. The attendee said that the universe rests on the back of a huge turtle. When the physicist asked what the turtle rested on, the gentleman said another turtle. Anticipating the physicist's objections, the attendee said, "Don't tire yourself out, young fellow. It's turtles all the way down."

Thus, the value of a firm's common stock to the investor is equal to the present value ⟵
of all of the expected future dividends.[4]

    This is a very useful result. A common objection to applying present value
analysis to stocks is that investors are too shortsighted to care about the long-run
stream of dividends. Critics argue that an investor will generally not look past his or
her time horizon. Thus, prices in a market dominated by short-term investors will
reflect only near-term dividends. However, our discussion shows that a long-run ⟵
dividend discount model holds even when investors have short-term time horizons.
Although an investor may want to cash out early, he or she must find another investor
who is willing to buy. The price this second investor pays is dependent on dividends
after the date of purchase.

Valuation of Different Types of Stocks

The discussion to this point shows that the value of the firm is the present value of its
future dividends. How do we apply this idea in practice? Equation (5.4) represents a
very general model and is applicable regardless of whether the level of expected
dividends is growing, fluctuating, or constant. The general model can be simplified if
the firm's dividends are expected to follow any of three basic patterns: (1) zero growth,
(2) constant growth, and (3) differential growth. These cases are illustrated in Figure 5.3.

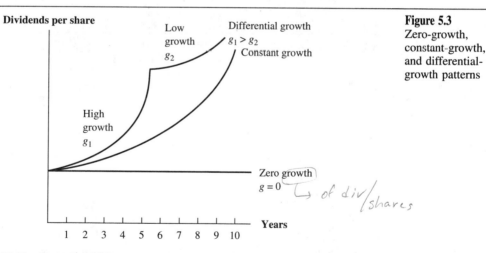

Figure 5.3
Zero-growth,
constant-growth,
and differential-
growth patterns

Dividend-growth models

Zero growth: $P_0 = \dfrac{\text{Div}}{r}$

Constant growth: $P_0 = \dfrac{\text{Div}}{r - g}$

Differential growth: $P_0 = \displaystyle\sum_{t=1}^{T} \dfrac{\text{Div}\,(1 + g_1)^t}{(1 + r)^t} + \dfrac{\dfrac{\text{Div}_{T+1}}{r - g_2}}{(1 + r)^T}$

---

[4]The dividend valuation model is often called the Gordon model in honour of Professor Myron Gordon of the University
of Toronto, its best-known developer.

Case 1 (Zero Growth)

The value of a stock with a constant dividend is given by

$$P_0 = \frac{\text{Div}_1}{1 + r} + \frac{\text{Div}_2}{(1 + r)^2} + \cdots = \frac{\text{Div}}{r}$$

Here it is assumed that $\text{Div}_1 = \text{Div}_2 = \ldots = \text{Div}$. This is just an application of the perpetuity formula of the previous chapter.

Case 2 (Constant Growth)

Dividends grow at rate g, as follows:

End of year	1	2	3	4	$\ldots$
Dividend	Div	Div$(1 + g)$	Div$(1 + g)^2$	Div$(1 + g)^3$	

Note that Div is the dividend at the end of the first period.

■ *Example*

Canadian Products will pay a dividend of $4 per share a year from now. Financial analysts believe that dividends will rise at 6 percent per year for the foreseeable future. What is the dividend per share at the end of each of the first five years?

End of year	1	2	3	4	5
Dividend	$4.00	$4x(1.06)	$4x(1.06)^2$	$4x(1.06)^3$	$4x(1.06)^4$
		= $4.24	= $4.4944	= $4.7641	= $5.0499

The value of a common stock with dividends growing at a constant rate is

$$P_0 = \frac{\text{Div}}{1 + r} + \frac{\text{Div}(1 + g)}{(1 + r)^2} + \frac{\text{Div}(1 + g)^2}{(1 + r)^3} + \frac{\text{Div}(1 + g)^3}{(1 + r)^4} + \cdots = \frac{\text{Div}}{r - g}$$

where g is the growth rate. Div is the dividend on the stock at the end of the first period. This is the formula for the present value of a growing perpetuity, which we derived in the previous chapter. ■

■ *Example*

Suppose an investor is considering the purchase of a share of the Saskatchewan Mining Company. The stock will pay a $3 dividend a year from today. This dividend is expected to grow at 10 percent per year ($g = 10\%$) for the foreseeable future. The investor thinks that the required return (r) on this stock is 15 percent, given her assessment of Saskatchewan Mining's risk. (We also refer to r as the discount rate of the stock.) What is the value of a share of Saskatchewan Mining Company's stock?

Using the constant growth formula of case 2, we assess the value to be $60:

$$\$60 = \frac{\$3}{0.15 - 0.10}$$

P_0 is quite dependent on the value of g. If g had been estimated to be 12½ percent, the value of the share would have been

$$\$120 = \frac{\$3}{0.15 - 0.125}$$

The stock price doubles (from \$60 to \$120) when g only increases 25 percent (from 10 percent to 12.5 percent). Because of P_0's dependency on g, one must maintain a healthy sense of skepticism when using this constant growth version of the dividend valuation model.

Furthermore, note that P_0 is equal to infinity when the growth rate, g, equals or exceeds the discount rate, r. Because stock prices do not grow infinitely, an estimate of g greater than r implies an error in estimation. More will be said about this later. ∎

Case 3 (Differential Growth)

In this case, an algebraic formula would be too unwieldy. Instead, we present examples.

∎ **Example**

Consider the stock of Elixir Drug Company, which has a new back rub ointment and is enjoying rapid growth. The dividend a year from today will be \$1.15. During the next four years, the dividend will grow at 15 percent per year ($g_1 = 15\%$). After that, growth (g_2) will be equal to 10 percent per year. What is the present value of the stock if the required return (r) is 15 percent?

Figure 5.4 displays the growth in the dividends. We need to apply a two-step process to discount these dividends. We first calculate the net present value of the

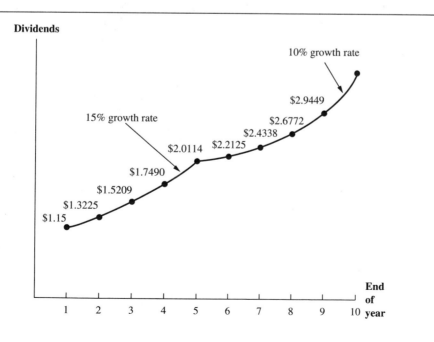

Figure 5.4
Growth in dividends for Elixir Drug Company

dividends growing at 15 percent per annum. That is, we first calculate the present value of the dividends at the end of each of the first five years. Second, we calculate the present value of the dividends beginning at the end of year 6.

Calculate Present Value of First Five Dividends   The present values of dividend payments in years 1 through 5 are

Future year	Growth rate (g_1)	Expected dividend	Present value
1	0.15	$ 1.15	$1
2	0.15	1.3225	1
3	0.15	1.5209	1
4	0.15	1.7490	1
5	0.15	2.0114	1
Years 1–5		The present value of dividends = $5	

The growing annuity formula of the previous chapter could normally be used in this step. However, note that dividends grow at 15 percent, which is also the discount rate. Since $g = r$, the growing annuity formula cannot be used in this example.

Calculate Present Value of Dividends Beginning at End of Year 6   This is the procedure for deferred perpetuities and deferred annuities that we mentioned in the previous chapter. The dividends beginning at the end of year 6 are

End of year	6	7	8	9
Dividend	$Div_5 \times (1 + g_2)$ 2.0114×1.10 = $2.2125	$Div_5 \times (1 + g_2)^2$ $2.0114 \times (1.10)^2$ = $2.4337	$Div_5 \times (1 + g_2)^3$ $2.0114 \times (1.10)^3$ = $2.6771	$Div_5 \times (1 + g_2)^4$ $2.0114 \times (1.10)^4$ = $2.9448

As stated in the previous chapter, the growing perpetuity formula calculates present value as of one year prior to the first payment. Because the payment begins at the end of year 6, the present value formula calculates present value as of the end of year 5. The price at the end of year 5 is given by

$$P_5 = \frac{Div_5}{r - g_2} = \frac{\$2.2125}{0.15 - 0.10}$$

$$= \$44.25$$

The present value of P_5 at the end of year 0 is

$$\frac{P_5}{(1 + r)^5} = \frac{\$44.25}{(1.15)^5} = \$22$$

The present value of all dividends as of the end of year 0 is $27 (or $22 + $5). ▪

5.5   Estimates of Parameters in the Dividend Discount Model

The value of the firm is a function of its growth rate, g, and its discount rate, r. How does one estimate these variables?

Where Does *g* Come From?

The previous discussion on stocks assumed that dividends grow at the rate *g*. We now want to estimate this rate of growth. Consider a business whose earnings next year are expected to be the same as earnings this year unless a *net investment* is made. This situation is likely to occur, because net investment is equal to gross, or total, investment less depreciation. A net investment of zero occurs when *total investment* equals depreciation. If total investment is equal to depreciation, the firm's physical plant is maintained, consistent with no growth in earnings.

Net investment will be positive only if some earnings are not paid out as dividends, that is, only if some earnings are retained.[5] This leads to the following equation:

$$
\begin{matrix}
\text{Earnings} \\ \text{next} \\ \text{year}
\end{matrix}
=
\begin{matrix}
\text{Earnings} \\ \text{this} \\ \text{year}
\end{matrix}
+
\underbrace{
\begin{matrix}
\text{Retained} \\ \text{earnings} \\ \text{this year}
\end{matrix}
\times
\begin{matrix}
\text{Return on} \\ \text{retained} \\ \text{earnings}
\end{matrix}
}_{\text{Increase in earnings}}
\quad (5.5)
$$

The increase in earnings is a function of both the *retained earnings* and the *return on the retained earnings.*

We now divide both sides of (5.5) by earnings this year, yielding

$$
\frac{\text{Earnings next year}}{\text{Earnings this year}} = \frac{\text{Earnings this year}}{\text{Earnings this year}} + \left(\frac{\text{Retained earnings}}{\text{Earnings this year}} \right) \times
\begin{matrix}
\text{Return on} \\ \text{retained} \\ \text{earnings}
\end{matrix}
\quad (5.6)
$$

The left-hand side of (5.6) is simply one plus the growth rate in earnings, which we write as $1 + g$.[6] The ratio of retained earnings to earnings is called the **retention ratio.** Thus, we can write

$$
1 + g = 1 + \left(\text{Retention ratio} \times \text{Return on retained earnings} \right) \quad (5.7)
$$

It is difficult for a financial analyst to determine the return to be expected on currently retained earnings, because the details on forthcoming projects are not generally public information. However, it is frequently assumed that the projects selected in the current year have an anticipated return equal to returns from projects in other years. Here, we can estimate the anticipated return on current retained earnings by the historical **return on equity (ROE).** After all, ROE is simply the return on the firm's entire equity, which is the return on the cumulation of all the firm's past projects.[7]

From (5.7), we have a simple way to estimate growth:

---

[5] We ignore the possibility of the issuance of stocks or bonds in order to raise capital. These possibilities are considered in later chapters.

[6] Previously *g* referred to growth in dividends. However, the growth rate in earnings is equal to the growth rate in dividends in this context because, as we will presently see, the ratio of dividends to earnings is held constant.

[7] Students frequently wonder whether return on equity (ROE) or return on assets (ROA) should be used here. ROA and ROE are identical in our model because debt financing is ignored. However, most real-world firms have debt. Because debt is treated in later chapters, we are not yet able to treat this issue in depth now. Suffice it to say that ROE is the appropriate rate, because both ROE for the firm as a whole and the return to equityholders from a future project are calculated after interest has been deducted.

Formula for Firm's Growth Rate:

$$g = \text{Retention ratio} \times \text{Return on retained earnings} \tag{5.8}$$

= Retention ratio × ROE

▪ Example

Trent Enterprises just reported earnings of $2 million. It plans to retain 40 percent of its earnings. The historical return on equity (ROE) was 0.16, a figure that is expected to continue into the future. How much will earnings grow over the coming year?

We first perform the calculation without reference to (5.8). Then we use (5.8) as a check.

Calculation without Reference to Equation (5.8)   The firm will retain $800,000 (or 40% × $2 million). Assuming that historical ROE is an appropriate estimate for future returns, the anticipated increase in earnings is

$800,000 × 0.16 = $128,000

The percentage growth in earnings is

$$\frac{\text{Change in earnings}}{\text{Total earnings}} = \frac{\$128{,}000}{\$2 \text{ million}} = 0.064$$

This implies that earnings in one year will be $2,128,000 (or $2,000,000 × 1.064).

Check Using Equation (5.8)   We use $g = $ Retention ratio × ROE. We have

$$g = 0.4 \times 0.16 = 0.064 \; \blacksquare$$

Where Does r Come From?

In this section, we want to estimate r, the rate used to discount the cash flows of a particular stock. There are two methods developed by academics. We present one method below but must defer the second until we give it extensive treatment in later chapters.

The first method begins with the concept that the value of a growing perpetuity is

$$P_0 = \frac{\text{Div}}{r - g}$$

Solving for r, we have

$$r = \frac{\text{Div}}{P_0} + g \tag{5.9}$$

As stated earlier, Div refers to the dividend to be received one year hence.

Thus, the discount rate can be broken into two parts. The ratio, Div/P_0, places the dividend return on a percentage basis, frequently called the *dividend yield*. The second term, g, is the growth rate of dividends.

Because information on both dividends and stock price is publicly available, the first term on the right-hand side of (5.9) can be easily calculated. The second term on the right-hand side, g, can be estimated from (5.8).

■ *Example*

Trent Enterprises, the company examined in the previous example, has 1,000,000 shares of stock outstanding. The stock is selling at $10. What is the required return on the stock?

Because the retention ratio is 40 percent, the payout ratio is 60 percent (1 − Retention ratio). The **payout ratio** is the ratio of dividends/earnings. Because earnings one year from now will be $2,128,000 (or $2,000,000 × 1.064), dividends will be $1,276,800 (or 0.60 × $2,128,000). Dividends per share will be $1.28 (or $1,276,800/ 1,000,000). Given our previous result that $g = 0.064$, we calculate r from (5.9) as follows:

$$0.192 = \frac{\$1.28}{\$10.00} + 0.064 \quad ■$$

A Healthy Sense of Skepticism

It is important to emphasize that our approach merely estimates g; it does not determine g precisely. We mentioned earlier that our estimate of g is based on a number of assumptions. For example, we assume that the return on reinvestment of future retained earnings is equal to the firm's past ROE. We assume that the future retention ratio is equal to the past retention ratio. Our estimate for g will be off if these assumptions prove to be wrong.

Unfortunately, the determination of r is highly dependent on g. In our example, if g is estimated to be 0, r equals 12.8 percent ($1.28/$10.00). If g is estimated to be 12 percent, r equals 24.8 percent ($1.28/$10.00 + 12%). Thus, one should view estimates of r with a healthy sense of skepticism.

For this reason, some financial economists generally argue that the estimation error for r for a single security is too large to be practical. Therefore, they suggest calculating the average r for an entire industry. This r would then be used to discount the dividends of a particular stock in the same industry.

One should be particularly skeptical of two polar cases when estimating r for individual securities. First, consider a firm currently paying no dividend. The stock price will be above zero because investors believe that the firm may initiate a dividend at some point or the firm may be acquired at some point. However, when a firm goes from no dividends to a positive number of dividends, the implied growth rate is *infinite*. Thus, equation (5.9) must be used with extreme caution here, if at all—a point we emphasize later in this chapter.

Second, we mentioned earlier that the value of the firm is infinite when g is equal to r. Because prices for stocks do not grow infinitely, an analyst whose estimate of g for a particular firm is equal to or above r must have made a mistake. Most likely, the analyst's high estimate for g is correct for the next few years. However, firms simply cannot maintain an abnormally high growth rate *forever*. The analyst's error was to use a short-run estimate of g in a model requiring a perpetual growth rate.

5.6

Growth Opportunities

We previously spoke of the growth rate of dividends. We now want to address the related concept of growth opportunities. Imagine a company with a level stream of earnings per share in perpetuity. The company pays all of these earnings out to shareholders as dividends. Hence,

EPS = Div

where EPS is *earnings per share* and Div is dividend per share. A company of this type is frequently called a *cash cow*.

From the perpetuity formula of the previous chapter, the value of a share of stock is

Value of a Share of Stock when Firm Acts as a Cash Cow:

$$\frac{EPS}{r} = \frac{Div}{r}$$

where r is the discount rate on the firm's stock.

The above policy of paying out all earnings as dividends may not be the optimal one. Many firms have *growth* opportunities, that is, opportunities to invest in profitable projects. Because these projects can represent a significant fraction of the firm's value, it would be foolish to forgo them in order to pay out all earnings as dividends.

While firms frequently think in terms of a *set* of growth opportunities, we focus here on only one opportunity, that is, the opportunity to invest in a single project. Suppose the firm retains the entire dividend at date 1 in order to invest in a particular capital budgeting project. The net present value *per share* of the project as of date 0 is *NPVGO*, which stands for the *net present value (per share) of the growth opportunity*.

What is the price of a share of stock at date 0 if the firm decides to take on the project at date 1? Because the per share value of the project is added to the original stock price, the stock price must now be

Stock Price after Firm Commits to New Project:

$$\frac{EPS}{r} + NPVGO \tag{5.10}$$

This, equation (5.10) indicates that the price of a share of stock can be viewed as the sum of two different items. The first term (EPS/r) is the value of the firm if it rested on its laurels, that is, if it simply distributed all earnings to the shareholders. The second term is the *additional* value if the firm retains earnings in order to fund new projects.

■ *Example*

Nova Scotia Shipping, Ltd., expects to earn $1 million per year in perpetuity if it undertakes no new investment opportunities. There are 100,000 shares outstanding, so earnings per share equal $10 (or $1,000,000/100,000). The firm will have an opportunity at date 1 to spend $1,000,000 in a new marketing campaign. The new campaign will increase earnings in every subsequent period by $210,000 (or $2.10 per share). This is a 21-percent return per year on the project. The firm's discount rate is 10 percent. What is the value per share before and after deciding to accept the marketing campaign?

The value of a share of Nova Scotia Shipping before the campaign is

Value of a Share of Nova Scotia Shipping When Firm Acts as a Cash Cow:

$$\frac{EPS}{r} = \frac{\$10}{0.1} = \$100$$

per petuity

The value of the marketing campaign as of date 1 is

Value of Marketing Campaign at Date 1:

$$-\$1,000,000 + \frac{\$210,000}{0.1} = \$1,100,000 \qquad (5.11)$$

Because the investment is made at date 1 and the first cash inflow occurs at date 2, equation (5.11) represents the value of the marketing campaign as of date 1. We determine the value at date 0 by discounting back one period as follows:

Value of Marketing Campaign at Date 0:

$$\frac{\$1,100,000}{1.1} = \$1,000,000$$

Thus, NPVGO per share is $10 (or $1,000,000/100,000).

The price per share is

$$EPS/r + NPVGO = \$100 + \$10 = \$110 \quad \blacksquare$$

The calculation can also be made on a straight net present value basis. Because all the earnings at date 1 are spent on the marketing effort, no dividends are paid to shareholders at that date. Dividends in all subsequent periods are $1,210,000 (or $1,000,000 + $210,000). In this case, $1,000,000 is the annual dividend when Nova Scotia is a cash cow. The additional contribution to the dividend from the marketing effort is $210,000. Dividends per share are $12.10 (or $1,210,000/100,000). Because these dividends start at date 2, the price per share at date 1 is $121 (or $12.10/0.1). The price per share at date 0 is $110 (or $121/1.1).

Note that value is created in this example because the project earned a 21-percent rate of return when the discount rate was only 10 percent. No value would have been created had the project earned a 10-percent rate of return—the NPVGO would have been zero. Value would have been negative had the project earned a percentage return below 10 percent—the NPVGO would be negative in that case.

Two conditions must be met in order to increase value:

1. Earnings must be retained so that projects can be funded.[8]
2. The projects must have positive net present value.

---

[8]Later in the text we discuss issuing stock or debt in order to fund projects.

Surprisingly, a number of companies seem to invest in projects known to have *negative* net present values. For example, Jensen has pointed out that, in the late 1970s, oil companies and tobacco companies were flush with cash.[9] Due to declining markets in both industries, high dividends and low investment would have been the rational action. Unfortunately, a number of companies in both industries reinvested heavily in what were widely perceived to be negative-NPVGO projects. A study by McConnell and Muscarella documents this perception.[10] They find that, during the 1970s, the stock prices of oil companies generally decreased on the days that announcements of increases in exploration and development were made.

Canada is not immune to the practice of investing in negative-NPV projects. For example, the Hibernia development has been a notorious drain on the companies involved and has been called an uneconomic project. Many resource companies have bought or developed projects that have subsequently been stopped before completion or proven unprofitable, and therefore have lowered the value of the companies.

Given that NPV analysis (such as that presented in the previous chapter) is common knowledge in business, why would managers choose projects with negative NPVs? One conjecture is that some managers enjoy controlling a large company. Because paying dividends in lieu of reinvesting earnings reduces the size of the firm, some managers find it emotionally difficult to pay high dividends.

Growth in Earnings and Dividends versus Growth Opportunities

As mentioned earlier, a firm's value increases when it invests in growth opportunities with positive NPVGOs. A firm's value falls when it selects opportunities with negative NPVGOs. However, dividends grow whether projects with positive NPVs or negative NPVs are selected. This surprising result can be explained by the following example.

∎ *Example*

Lane Supermarkets, a new firm, will earn $100,000 a year in perpetuity if it pays out all its earnings as dividends. However, the firm plans to invest 20 percent of its earnings in projects that earn 10 percent per year. The discount rate is 18 percent. An earlier formula tells us that the growth rate of dividends is

$$g = \text{Retention ratio} \times \text{Return on retained earnings} = 0.2 \times 0.10 = 2\%$$

For example, in this first year of the new policy, dividends are $80,000, calculated from $(1 - 0.2) \times \$100,000$. Dividends next year are $81,600 (or $80,000 × 1.02). Dividends the following year are $83,232 or $80,000 \times (1.02)^2$ and so on. Because dividends represent a fixed percentage of earnings, earnings must grow at 2 percent a year as well.

However, note that the policy reduces value because the rate of return on the projects of 10 percent is less than the discount rate of 18 percent. That is, the firm would have had a higher value at date 0 if it had a policy of paying all its earnings out

[9]M. C. Jensen, "Agency Costs of Free Cash Flows, Corporate Finance and Takeovers," *American Economic Review* (May 1986).

[10]J. J. McConnell and C. J. Muscarella, "Corporate Capital Expenditure Decisions and the Market Value of the Firm," *Journal of Financial Economics* 14 (1985).

as dividends. Thus, a policy of investing in projects with negative NPVs rather than paying out earnings as dividends will lead to growth in dividends and earnings, but will reduce value. ■

Dividends or Earnings: Which to Discount?

As mentioned earlier, this chapter applied the growing perpetuity formula to the valuation of stocks. In our application, we discounted dividends, not earnings. This is sensible since investors select a stock for what they can get out of it. They only get two things out of a stock: dividends and the ultimate sales price, which is determined by what future investors expect to receive in dividends.

The calculated stock price would be too high were earnings to be discounted instead of dividends. As we saw in our estimation of a firm's growth rate, only a portion of earnings goes to the shareholders as dividends. The remainder is retained to generate future dividends. In our model, retained earnings are equal to the firm's investment. To discount earnings instead of dividends would be to ignore the investment that a firm must make today in order to generate future returns.

The No-Dividend Firm

Students frequently ask the following questions: If the dividend discount model is correct, why are no-dividend stocks not selling at zero? This is a good question that addresses the goals of the firm. A firm with many growth opportunities is faced with a dilemma. The firm can pay out dividends now, or it can forgo current dividends in order to make investments that will generate even greater dividends in the future.[11] This is often a painful choice, because a strategy of dividend deferment may be optimal yet unpopular among certain shareholders.

Many firms choose to pay no dividends—and these firms sell at positive prices. Rational shareholders believe that they will either receive dividends at some point or they will receive something just as good. That is, the firm will be acquired in a merger, with the shareholders receiving either cash or shares in the acquiring firm.

Of course, the actual application of the dividend discount model is difficult for firms of this type. Clearly, the model for constant growth of dividends does not apply. Though the differential growth model can work in theory, the difficulties of estimating the date of first dividend, the growth rate of dividends after that date, and the ultimate merger price make application of the model quite difficult in reality.

Empirical evidence suggests that firms with high growth rates are likely to pay lower dividends, a result consistent with the above analysis. For example, consider McDonald's Corporation. The company started in the 1950s and grew rapidly for many years. It paid its first dividend in 1975, though it was a billion-dollar company (in both sales and market value of stockholder's equity) prior to that date. Why did it wait so long to pay a dividend? It waited because it had so many positive growth opportunities in the form of additional locations for new hamburger outlets.

---

[11]A third alternative is to issue stock so that the firm has enough cash both to pay dividends and to invest. This possibility is explored in a later chapter.

Utilities are an interesting contrast because, as a group, they have few growth opportunities. As a result, they pay out a large fraction of their earnings in dividends. For example, Canadian Utilities Limited, Utilicorp United, and Quebec-Telephone have had payout ratios of over 70 percent in many recent years.

| 5.7 | ## The Dividend Growth Model and the NPVGO Model (Advanced) |

This chapter has revealed that the price of a share of stock is the sum of its price as a cash cow plus the per share value of its growth opportunities. The Nova Scotia Shipping example illustrated this formula using only one growth opportunity. We also used the growing perpetuity formula to price a stock with a steady growth in dividends. When the formula is applied to stocks, it is typically called the *dividend growth model*. A steady growth in dividends results from a continual investment in growth opportunities, not just investment in a single opportunity. Therefore, it is worthwhile to compare the dividend growth model with the *NPVGO model* when growth occurs through continual investing.

▪ *Example*

Prairie Book Publishers has EPS of $10 at the end of the first year, a dividend-payout ratio of 40 percent, a discount rate of 16 percent, and a return on its retained earnings of 20 percent. Because the firm retains some of its earnings each year, it is selecting growth opportunities each year. This is different from Nova Scotia Shipping, which had a growth opportunity in only one year. We wish to calculate the price per share using both the dividend growth model and the NPVGO model. ▪

The Dividend Growth Model

The dividends at date 1 are $0.40 \times \$10 = \$4$ per share. The retention ratio is 0.60 (or $1 - 0.40$), implying a growth rate in dividends of 0.12 (or 0.60×0.20).

From the dividend growth model, the price of a share of stock is

$$\frac{\text{Div}}{r - g} = \frac{\$4}{0.16 - 0.12} = \$100$$

The NPVGO Model

Using the NPVGO model, it is more difficult to value a firm with growth opportunities each year (like Prairie) than a firm with growth opportunities in only one year (like Nova Scotia). In order to value according to the NPVGO model, we need to calculate on a per share basis (1) the net present value of a single growth opportunity, (2) the net present value of all growth opportunities, and (3) the stock price if the firm acts as a cash cow, that is, the value of the firm without these growth opportunities. The value of the firm is the sum of (2) + (3).

1. *Value per Share of a Single Growth Opportunity.* Out of the earnings per share of $10 at date 1, the firm retains $6 (or $0.6 \times \$10$) at that date. The firm earns

$1.20 (or $6 × 0.20) per year in perpetuity on that $6 investment. The NPV from the investment is Per Share NPV Generated from Investment at Date 1:

$$-\$6 + \frac{\$1.20}{0.16} = \$1.50 \tag{5.12}$$

That is, the firm invests $6 in order to reap $1.20 per year on the investment. The earnings are discounted at 0.16, implying a value per share from the project of $1.50. Because the investment occurs at date 1 and the first cash flow occurs at date 2, $1.50 is the value of the investment at *date 1*. In other words, the NPV from the date 1 investment has *not* yet been brought back to date 0.

2. *Value per Share of All Opportunities.* As pointed out earlier, the growth rate of earnings and dividends is 12 percent. Because retained earnings are a fixed percentage of total earnings, retained earnings must also grow at 12 percent a year. That is, retained earnings at date 2 are $6.72 (or $6 × 1.12), retained earnings at date 3 are $7.5264 [or $6 × (1.12)²], and so on.

Let's analyze the retained earnings at date 2 in more detail. Because projects will always earn 20 percent per year, the firm earns $1.344 (or $6.72 × 0.20) in each future year on the $6.72 investment at date 2.

The NPV from the investment is

NPV per Share Generated from Investment at Date 2:

$$-\$6.72 + \frac{\$1.344}{0.16} = \$1.68 \tag{5.13}$$

$1.68 is the NPV as of date 2 of the investment made at date 2. The NPV from the date 2 investment has *not* yet been brought back to date 0.

Now consider the retained earnings at date 3 in more detail. The firm earns $1.5053 (or $7.5264 × 0.20) per year on the investment of $7.5264 at date 3. The NPV from the investment is

NPV per Share Generated from Investment at Date 3:

$$-\$7.5264 + \frac{\$1.5053}{0.16} = \$1.882 \tag{5.14}$$

From (5.12), (5.13), and (5.14), the NPV per share of all of the growth opportunities, discounted back to date 0, is

$$\frac{\$1.50}{1.16} + \frac{\$1.68}{(1.16)^2} + \frac{\$1.882}{(1.16)^3} + \ldots \tag{5.15}$$

Because it has an infinite number of terms, this expression looks quite difficult to compute. However, there is an easy simplification. Note that retained earnings are growing at 12 percent per year. Because all projects earn the same rate of return per year, the NPVs in (5.12), (5.13), and (5.14) are also growing at 12 percent per year. Hence, we can rewrite (5.15) as

$$\frac{\$1.50}{1.16} + \frac{\$1.50 \times 1.12}{(1.16)^2} + \frac{\$1.50 \times (1.12)^2}{(1.16)^3} + \ldots$$

This is a growing perpetuity whose value is

$$NPVGO = \frac{\$1.50}{0.16 - 0.12} = \$37.50$$

Because the first NPV of $1.50 occurs at date 1, the NPVGO is $37.50 as of date 0. In other words, the firm's policy of investing in new projects from retained earnings has an NPV of $37.50.

3. *Value per Share if Firm Is a Cash Cow.* We now assume that the firm pays out all of its earnings as dividends. The dividends would be $10 per year in this case. Since there would be no growth, the value per share would be evaluated by the perpetuity formula:

$$\frac{Div}{r} = \frac{\$10}{0.16} = \$62.50$$

Summation

Formula (5.10) states that value per share is the value of a cash cow plus the value of the growth opportunities. This is

$$\$100 = \$62.50 + \$37.50$$

Hence, value is the same whether calculated by a discounted-dividend approach or a growth opportunities approach. The share prices from the two approaches must be equal, because the approaches are different yet equivalent methods of applying concepts of present value.

5.8 Price-Earnings Ratio

We argued earlier that one should not discount earnings in order to determine price per share. Nevertheless, financial analysts frequently relate earnings and price per share, as made evident by their heavy reliance on the price-earnings (or P/E) ratio.

Our previous discussion stated that

$$Price\ per\ share = \frac{EPS}{r} + NPVGO$$

Dividing by EPS yields

Price-earnings ratio

$$\frac{Price\ per\ share}{EPS} = \frac{1}{r} + \frac{NPVGO}{EPS}$$

The left-hand side is the formula for the price-earnings ratio. The equation shows that the P/E ratio is related to the net present value of growth opportunities. As an example, consider two firms, each having just reported earnings per share of $1. However, one firm has many valuable growth opportunities while the other firm has no growth opportunities at all. The firm with growth opportunities should sell at a higher price, because an investor is buying both current income of $1 and growth opportunities.

Suppose that the firm with growth opportunities sells for $16 and the other firm sells for $8. The $1 earnings per share number appears in the denominator of the P/E ratio for both firms. Thus, the P/E ratio is 16 for the firm with growth opportunities, but only 8 for the firm without the opportunities.

This explanation seems to hold fairly well in the real world. Electronic and other high-tech stocks generally sell at very high P/E ratios (or *multiples,* as they are often called) because they are perceived to have high growth rates. In fact, some technology stocks sell at high prices even though the companies have never earned a profit. The P/E ratios of these companies are infinite. Conversely, utilities and steel companies sell at lower multiples because of the prospects of lower growth.

Of course, the market is merely pricing *perceptions* of the future, not the future itself. We will argue later in the text that the stock market generally has realistic perceptions of a firm's prospects. However, this is not always true. In the late 1960s, many electronic firms were selling at multiples of 200 times earnings. The high perceived growth rates did not materialize, causing great declines in stock prices during the early 1970s. In earlier decades, fortunes were made in stocks like IBM and Xerox because the high growth rates were not anticipated by investors.

There are two additional factors explaining the P/E ratio. The first is the discount rate, r. The above formula shows that the P/E ratio is *negatively* related to the firm's discount rate. We have already suggested that the discount rate is positively linked to the stock's risk or variability. Thus, the P/E ratio is negatively related to the stock's risk. To see that this is a sensible result, consider two firms, A and B, behaving as cash cows. The stock market *expects* both firms to have annual earnings of $1 per share forever. However, the earnings of firm A are known with certainty while the earnings of firm B are quite variable. A rational shareholder is likely to pay more for a share of firm A because of the absence of risk. If a share of firm A sells at a higher price and both firms have the same EPS, the P/E ratio of firm A must be higher.

The second additional factor concerns the firm's choice of accounting methods. Under current accounting rules, companies are given a fair amount of leeway. For example, consider depreciation accounting where many different methods may be used. A firm's choice of depreciation method can increase or decrease its earnings in different years. Similar accounting leeway exists for construction costs (completed-contracts versus percentage-of-completion methods).

As an example, consider two identical firms: C and D. Firm C uses straight-line depreciation and reports earnings of $2 per share. Firm D uses declining-balance depreciation and reports earnings of $3 per share. The market knows that the two firms are identical and prices both at $18 per share. This price-earnings ratio is 9 (or $18/$2) for firm C and 6 (or $18/$3) for firm D. Thus, the firm with the more conservative principles has a higher P/E ratio.

This last example depends on the assumption that the market sees through differences in accounting treatments. A significant portion of the academic community believes this adhering to the hypothesis of *efficient capital markets,* a theory that we explore in great detail later in the text. Though many financial people might be more moderate in their beliefs regarding this issue, the consensus view is certainly that many of the accounting differences are seen through. Thus, the proposition that firms with conservative accountants have high P/E ratios is widely accepted.

In summary, our discussion argued that the P/E ratio is a function of three different factors. A company's ratio or multiple is likely to be high if (1) it has many growth opportunities, (2) it has low risk (reflected in a low discount rate), and (3) its accounting is conservative. While each of the three factors is important, it is our opinion that the first factor is the most important. Thus, our discussion of growth is quite relevant in understanding price-earnings multiples.

International Price-Earnings Ratios

The three factors underlying differences in P/Es among firms also help explain P/E differences between markets in different countries as well as why P/Es shift over time. For example, in the early 1990s, North American investors were puzzled by the relatively high P/E ratios in the Japanese stock market. The average P/E ratio for the Tokyo Stock Exchange was around 70, while the average U.S. or Canadian stock had a multiple of between 20 and 30. Our formula indicates that Japanese companies were perceived to have great growth opportunities. However, North American commentators frequently suggested that investors in the Japanese markets were overestimating these growth prospects. They also suggested that Japanese companies used more conservative accounting practices, thereby creating higher P/E ratios.

Consistent with the first view, by late 1993, Japanese P/E ratios had declined. At the same time, lower interest rates and improved growth opportunities flowing from expected economic recovery produced record highs on the Toronto Stock Exchange. In late 1993, the typical Canadian stock had a P/E of over 80.

CONCEPT QUESTIONS

- What are the three factors determining a firm's P/E ratio?
- How does each affect the P/E and why?

5.9   Stock Market Reporting

Financial newspapers publish information on a large number of stocks in several different markets. Figure 5.5 reproduces a small section of the stock page for the Toronto Stock Exchange (TSE) for June 23, 1993. In Figure 5.5, locate the line for Bank of Montreal. The first two numbers, $26\frac{3}{4}$ and $20\frac{3}{4}$, are the high and low prices for the last 52 weeks. Stock prices are quoted in dollars and fractions down to $\frac{1}{8}$.

The 1.12 is the annual dividend rate. Since Bank of Montreal, like most companies, pays dividends quarterly, this $1.12 is actually the last quarterly dividend multiplied by 4. So, the last cash dividend paid was $1.12 / 4 = $.28. Jumping ahead a bit, the column marked "Yield %" gives the dividend yield based on the current dividend and the closing price. For Bank of Montreal this is $1.12 / 25.50 = 4.4% as shown.

The High, Low, and Close figures are the high, low, and closing prices during the day. The "Net Chge" of "unch" (unchanged) tells us that the closing price of $25\frac{1}{2}$ per share is the same as the closing price the day before.

Figure 5.5
Sample stock market quotation from *The Financial Post*

52 Week High	52 Week Low	Stock	Div Rate	High	Low	Cls or Latest	Net Chge	Vol 100s	Yield %	P/E Ratio
153	117	BC Bancorp...............	p1.00	144	141	141	unch	15	70.9	20.1
\$17	$13\frac{3}{4}$	BC Gas..................	0.90	\$15	$14\frac{3}{4}$	$14\frac{7}{8}$	unch	450	6.1	12.8
$\$26\frac{3}{4}$	$25\frac{1}{8}$	BC Rail pf A..............	$2.31\frac{1}{4}$	$\$25\frac{7}{8}$	$25\frac{7}{8}$	$25\frac{7}{8}$	unch	z74	8.9	....
$\$11\frac{5}{8}$	$8\frac{1}{4}$	BC Sugar A...............	0.40	$\$9\frac{1}{2}$	$9\frac{1}{8}$	$9\frac{1}{8}$	$-\frac{1}{4}$	96	4.4	12.9
$\$24\frac{3}{4}$	$22\frac{5}{8}$	BC TEL \$1.70 pf...........	1.70	$\$24\frac{3}{4}$	$24\frac{3}{4}$	$24\frac{3}{4}$	$+\frac{1}{4}$	5	6.9	....
\$66	62	BC TEL \$4.75 pf...........	4.75	\$65	65	65	$+\frac{1}{4}$	3	7.3	....
\$22	$18\frac{5}{8}$	BC TELECOM Inc..........	1.20	$\$21\frac{1}{8}$	$20\frac{7}{8}$	$21\frac{1}{8}$	$+\frac{1}{4}$	1516	5.7	12.1
$\$47\frac{3}{8}$	$40\frac{3}{4}$	BCE Inc..................	2.64	\$46	$45\frac{3}{8}$	$45\frac{1}{2}$	$+\frac{1}{8}$	7571	5.8	11.4
$\$43\frac{1}{8}$	$41\frac{1}{2}$	BCE Inc ser O pf...........	v2.64	$\$42\frac{5}{8}$	$42\frac{5}{8}$	$42\frac{5}{8}$	unch	6	6.2	....
$\$6\frac{5}{8}$	300	BCE Inc wts..............	....	340	320	335	+15	830	....	....
\$39	$24\frac{1}{4}$	BCE Mobile Comm.........	....	$\$37\frac{7}{8}$	$37\frac{1}{2}$	$37\frac{7}{8}$	unch	518	....	....
$\$26\frac{5}{8}$	$24\frac{1}{2}$	BCE Place 7.375 pf.........	1.8438	$\$24\frac{1}{2}$	$24\frac{1}{2}$	$24\frac{1}{2}$	$-\frac{1}{2}$	5	7.5	....
$\$27\frac{1}{2}$	25	BCE Place 7.75 pf..........	$1.93\frac{3}{4}$	$\$25\frac{7}{8}$	$25\frac{7}{8}$	$25\frac{7}{8}$	$+\frac{1}{8}$	2	7.5	....
\$77	73	BC TEL \$5.75 pf...........	5.75	$\$76\frac{3}{4}$	$76\frac{3}{4}$	$76\frac{3}{4}$	$+1\frac{1}{2}$	1	7.5	....
10	1	BF Realty Hldgs...........	....	5	5	5	unch	553	....	....
\$12	$5\frac{1}{4}$	BGR Precious A...........	....	$\$11\frac{1}{4}$	11	11	$-\frac{1}{4}$	133	....	31.4
$\$15\frac{3}{4}$	$8\frac{3}{4}$	BII Enterprises............	p0.10	$\$15\frac{3}{4}$	$15\frac{1}{2}$	$15\frac{3}{4}$	$+\frac{1}{4}$	171	0.6	13.8
110	37	BMR Gold................	....	110	90	103	+21	10132	....	....
\$17	13	BNT Ltd	....	$\$16\frac{3}{8}$	$15\frac{3}{4}$	$16\frac{3}{8}$	$+\frac{7}{8}$	57	....	....
325	240	BRL Enterprises...........	....	300	300	300	unch	z96	....	13.6
75	18	Baca Resources A☆	....	39	39	39	−1	34	....	....
175	110	Bala Gold Inc☆	....	120	120	120	−5	7	....	....
\$9	$7\frac{7}{8}$	Ballard Power Units........	....	$\$8\frac{7}{8}$	$8\frac{3}{4}$	$8\frac{3}{4}$	$-\frac{1}{8}$	191	....	....
$\$6\frac{1}{2}$	255	Ballistic Energy☆..........	....	$\$6\frac{1}{8}$	6	$6\frac{1}{8}$	$+\frac{1}{8}$	156	....	....
$\$16\frac{1}{4}$	7	Banister Inc...............	....	\$16	$15\frac{7}{8}$	16	$-\frac{1}{8}$	55	....	
$\$26\frac{3}{4}$	$20\frac{3}{4}$	Bank of Montreal..........	1.12	$\$25\frac{3}{4}$	$25\frac{3}{8}$	$25\frac{1}{2}$	unch	12988	4.4	12.7
$\$29\frac{7}{8}$	$27\frac{1}{4}$	Bk of Mtl ser 1 pf B........	2.25	$\$29\frac{1}{2}$	$29\frac{1}{4}$	$29\frac{1}{4}$	$-\frac{1}{8}$	69	7.7	10.5
$\$29\frac{1}{2}$	$26\frac{1}{2}$	Bk of Mtl ser 4 A pf........	v2.25	$\$28\frac{3}{8}$	$28\frac{1}{4}$	$28\frac{1}{4}$	$-\frac{1}{8}$	116	8.0	....
$\$27\frac{1}{2}$	$25\frac{1}{4}$	Bk of Mtl ser 2 cl B	u1.6876	$\$27\frac{1}{2}$	$27\frac{1}{4}$	$27\frac{1}{2}$	$+\frac{1}{4}$	82	6.1	....
$\$25\frac{7}{8}$	$20\frac{1}{2}$	Bank of Nova Scotia	1.12	$\$24\frac{1}{2}$	$24\frac{1}{4}$	$24\frac{1}{2}$	$+\frac{3}{8}$	16786	4.6	
$\$22\frac{1}{2}$	20	Bk of NS FR pf............	v1.05	$\$21\frac{3}{4}$	$21\frac{1}{2}$	$21\frac{3}{4}$	unch	61	4.8	8.6
\$22	$19\frac{3}{4}$	Bk of NS ser 3 pf..........	$v1.75\frac{3}{4}$	$\$20\frac{1}{2}$	$20\frac{1}{8}$	$20\frac{1}{4}$	unch	77	8.7	....
$\$28\frac{1}{2}$	26	Bk of NS ser 4 pf..........	v2.25	$\$27\frac{1}{8}$	$26\frac{7}{8}$	$27\frac{1}{8}$	$+\frac{1}{8}$	21	8.3	....
$\$29\frac{3}{8}$	27	Bk of NS ser 5 pf..........	$2.31\frac{1}{4}$	$\$28\frac{1}{2}$	$28\frac{1}{8}$	$28\frac{1}{8}$	$-\frac{1}{4}$	42	8.2	....
$\$26\frac{3}{4}$	$24\frac{5}{8}$	Bk of NS ser 6 pf..........	$1.78\frac{3}{4}$	$\$26\frac{3}{8}$	$26\frac{1}{8}$	$26\frac{3}{8}$	$+\frac{1}{8}$	159	6.8	....

Source: *The Financial Post,* June 23, 1993, p. 25. Used with permission.

The column labelled PE (short for price/earnings or P/E ratio), is the closing price of $\$25\frac{1}{2}$ divided by annual earnings per share (based on the most recent full fiscal year). In the jargon of Bay Street, we might say that Bank of Montreal "sells for 10.5 times earnings."

The remaining column, "Vol 100s," tells how many shares traded during the reported day (in hundreds). For example, the 12988 for Bank of Montreal tells us that 1,298,800 shares changed hands. The dollar volume of transactions was on the order of $\$25.50 \times 1{,}298{,}800 = \$33$ million worth of Bank of Montreal stock.

Summary and Conclusions 5.10

In this chapter we use general present value formulas from the previous chapter to price bonds and stock.

1. Pure discount bonds and perpetuities are the polar cases of bonds. The value of a pure discount bond (also called a *zero-coupon bond* or simply a *zero*) is

$$\mathrm{PV} = \frac{F}{(1 + r)^T}$$

The value of a perpetuity (also called a *consol*) is

$$PV = \frac{C}{r}$$

2. Level-payment bonds represent an intermediate case. The coupon payments form an annuity and the principal repayment is a lump sum. The value of this type of bond is simply the sum of the values of its two parts.

3. The yield to maturity on a bond is that single rate that discounts the payments on the bond to its purchase price.

4. A stock can be valued by discounting its dividends. We mention three types of situations:

   a. The case of zero growth of dividends.

   b. The case of constant growth of dividends.

   c. The case of differential growth.

5. An estimate of the growth rate of a stock is needed for cases (4b) or (4c) above. A useful estimate of the growth rate is

   g = Retention ratio $\times$ Return on retained earnings

6. It is worthwhile to view a share of stock as the sum of its worth if the company behaves as a cash cow (the company does no investing) and the value per share of its growth opportunities. We write the value of a share as

   $$\frac{EPS}{r} + NPVGO$$

   We show that, in theory, share price must be the same whether the dividend growth model or the above formula is used.

7. From accounting, we know that earnings are divided into two parts: dividends and retained earnings. Most firms continually retain earnings in order to create future dividends. One should not discount earnings to obtain price per share since part of earnings must be reinvested. Only dividends reach the shareholders and only they should be discounted to obtain share price.

8. We suggested that a firm's price-earnings ratio is a function of three factors:

   a. The per share amount of the firm's valuable growth opportunities.

   b. The risk of the stock.

   c. The conservatism of the accounting methods used by the firm.

Key Terms

Pure discount bond 121	Maturity date 121
Face value 121	Coupons 123
Discount 126	Premium 126
Yield to maturity 127	Retention ratio 133
Return on equity (ROE) 133	Payout ratio 135

Suggested Readings

The best place to look for additional information is in investment textbooks. Some good ones are:

Z. Bodie, A. Kane, A. Marcus, S. Perrakis, and P. J. Ryan. *Investments.* 1st Canadian ed. Homewood, Ill.: Richard D. Irwin, 1993.

J. C. Francis and E. Kirzner. *Investments: Analysis and Management.* 1st Canadian ed. Toronto, Ont.: McGraw-Hill Ryerson, 1988.

J. E. Hatch and M. J. Robinson. *Investment Management in Canada.* 2nd ed. Scarborough, Ont.: Prentice Hall, 1989.

W. F. Sharpe, G. J. Alexander, and D. J. Fowler. *Investments.* 1st Canadian ed. Scarborough, Ont.: Prentice Hall, 1993.

Questions and Problems

How to Value Bonds

5.1 Price a one-year, pure discount bond that pays $1,000 at maturity to yield the following rates:

a. 6 percent

b. 9 percent

c. 11 percent

d. 15 percent

5.2 A bond with the following characteristics is available.

Principal: $1,000

Term to maturity: 20 years

Coupon rate: 8 percent

Semiannual payments

Calculate the price of the bond if the market interest rate is:

a. 8 percent

b. 10 percent

c. 6 percent

5.3 Ace Trucking has available a 6-percent, $1,000 face value 10-year bond that pays interest semiannually. If the market prices the bond to yield 10 percent, what is the price of the bond?

5.4 You have just purchased a newly issued $1,000 five-year Vanguard Company bond at par. This five-year bond pays $60 in interest semiannually. You are also considering the purchase of another Vanguard Company bond that returns $30 in semiannual interest payments and has six years remaining before it matures. This bond has a face value of $1,000.

a. What is the effective annual return on the five-year bond?

b. Assume that the rate you calculated in part (*a*) is the correct rate for the bond with six years remaining before it matures. What should you be willing to pay for that bond?

    c. How will your answer to part (*b*) change if the five-year bond pays $40 in semiannual interest but still sells for $1,000?

5.5 *a.* If the market interest rate (the required rate of return that investors demand) unexpectedly increases, what effect would you expect it to have on the prices of long-term bonds? Why?

    b. What would be the effect of the rise in the interest rate on the general level of stock prices? Why?

5.6 The appropriate discount rate for cash flows received one year from today is 7.5 percent. The appropriate discount rate for cash flows received two years from today is 11 percent. The appropriate discount rate for cash flows received three years from today is 14 percent.

    a. What is the price of a two-year, $1,000 face value bond with a 6-percent coupon?

    b. What is the yield to maturity of this bond?

5.7 Referring back to the bond quotes in Figure 5.2, calculate the price of the ONTARIO 9.50 13 JUL 22 to prove that it is 107.275 as shown.

5.8 In 1994 Quebec provincial bonds carried a higher yield than comparable Ontario bonds because of investors' uncertainty about Quebec's political future. Suppose that you were an investment manager who thought that the market was overplaying these fears. In particular, suppose that you thought that yields on Quebec bonds would fall by 50 basis points. Which bonds in Figure 5.2 would you buy or sell? Explain in words. Illustrate with a numerical example showing your potential profit.

The Present Value of Common Stock

5.9 World Wide, Ltd., is expected to pay a per share dividend of $3 next year. It also expects that this dividend will grow at a rate of 8 percent in perpetuity. What price would you expect to see for World Wide stock if the appropriate discount rate is 12 percent?

5.10 A common stock pays a current dividend of $1.00. The dividend is expected to grow at a 14-percent annual rate for the next three years; then it will grow at 5 percent in perpetuity. The appropriate discount rate is 15 percent. What is the price of this stock?

5.11 Suppose that a shareholder has just paid $50 per share for XYZ Company stock. The stock will pay a dividend of $2 per share in the upcoming year. This dividend is expected to grow at an annual rate of 10 percent for the indefinite future. The shareholder felt that the price she paid was an appropriate price, given her assessment of XYZ's risks. What is the annual required rate of return of this shareholder?

5.12 You own $100,000 worth of UOP stock. At the end of the first year you receive a dividend of $10 per share, at the end of year 2 you receive a $15 dividend, and at the end of year 3 you receive a $20 dividend. At the end of year 3 you sell the stock for $300 per share. Only ordinary (dividend) income is taxed; the rate is 28 percent. Taxes are paid at the time dividends are received. The required rate of return is 22 percent. How many shares of UOP stock do you own?

5.13   Locust Software is one of a myriad of companies selling word processing programs. Their newest—their only—program will cost $5 million to develop. First-year net cash flows will be $1.2 million. As a result of competition, profits will fall by 4 percent each year. All inflows of cash occur at year-end. If the market discount rate is 16 percent, what is the value of the company?

5.14   Whizzkids, Inc., is experiencing a period of rapid growth. Earnings and dividends are expected to grow at a rate of 18 percent during the next two years, 15 percent in the third year, and then at a constant rate of 6 percent thereafter. Whizzkids' last dividend, which has just been paid, was $1.15. If the required rate of return on the stock is 12 percent, what is the price of the stock today?

5.15   Calamity Mining Company's reserves of ore are being depleted, and its costs of recovering a declining quantity of ore are rising each year. As a result, the company's earnings are declining at the rate of 10 percent per year. If the dividend, which is about to be paid, is $5 and the required rate of return is 14 percent, what is the value of the firm's stock?

5.16   A newspaper reported last week that Bradley Enterprises earned $15 million. The report also stated that the firm's return on equity remains on its historical trend of 12 percent. Bradley retains 78 percent of its earnings. What will next year's earnings be?

5.17   Rite Bite Enterprises sells toothpicks. Gross revenues last year were $350,000 and total costs were $50,000. Rite Bite is an all-equity firm with 1 million shares outstanding. Gross sales and costs are expected to grow at 5 percent per year. Rite Bite pays no income taxes, and all earnings are paid out as dividends.

   a. If the appropriate discount rate is 15 percent and all cash flows are received at year-end, what is the price per share of Rite Bite stock?

   b. The president of Rite Bite decided to begin a program to produce toothbrushes. The project requires an immediate outlay of $400,000. In one year, another outlay of $345,000 will be needed. The year after that, net cash inflows will be $600,000. This profit level will be maintained in perpetuity. How will this project affect the price per share of stock?

5.18   Futrell Fixtures expects net cash flows of $50,000 by the end of this year. Net cash flows will grow 3 percent if the firm makes no new investments. Mike Futrell, president of the firm, can add a line of kitchen and bathroom cabinets to the business. The immediate outlay for this opportunity is $100,000 and the net cash flows from the line will begin one year from now. The cabinet business will generate $32,000 in additional net cash flows. These net cash flows will also grow at 3 percent. The firm's discount rate is 13 percent, and 200,000 shares of Futrell stock are outstanding.

   a. What is the price per share of Futrell stock without the cabinet line?

   b. What is the value of the growth opportunities that the cabinet line offers?

   c. Once Futrell adds the cabinet line, what is the price of Futrell stock?

5.19   Microhard manufactures personal computers to work with the newest generation of software. Analysts forecast a period of growth at 15 percent annually with growth later slowing to a long-term rate of 6 percent. The current dividend is $3 per share; the discount rate for stocks in this risk class is 15 percent.

    a. What is the value of a Microhard share assuming that growth at the rate of 15 percent will continue for 10 years?

    b. What is the value of a Microhard share assuming that growth will drop immediately to the long-run rate of 6 percent?

    c. Suppose that Microhard is currently trading at $150 per share. How many years of growth at 15 percent is the market predicting? How could you use your answer to decide whether to buy Microhard shares?

APPENDIX

The Term Structure of Interest Rates

Spot Rates and Yield to Maturity

In the main body of this chapter, we have assumed that the interest rate is constant over all future periods. In reality, interest rates vary through time. This occurs primarily because inflation rates are expected to differ through time.

    To illustrate, we consider two zero-coupon bonds. Bond A is a one-year bond and bond B is a two-year bond. Both have face values of $1,000. The one-year interest rate, r_1, is 8 percent. The two-year interest rate, r_2, is 10 percent. These two rates of interest are examples of spot rates. Perhaps this inequality in interest rates occurs because inflation is expected to be higher over the second year than over the first year. The two bonds are depicted in the following time chart:

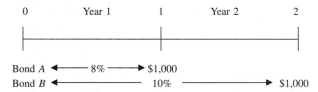

We can easily calculate the present value for bond A and bond B as

$$PV_A = \$925.93 = \frac{\$1,000}{1.08}$$

and

$$PV_B = \$826.45 = \frac{\$1,000}{(1.10)^2}$$

Of course, if PV_A and PV_B were observable and the spot rates were not, we could determine the spot rates using the PV formula, because

$$PV_A = \$925.93 = \frac{\$1,000}{(1 + r_1)} \rightarrow r_1 = 8\%$$

and

$$PV_B = \$826.45 = \frac{\$1,000}{(1 + r_2)^2} \rightarrow r_2 = 10\%$$

Now we can see how the prices of more complicated bonds are determined. Try to do the next example. It illustrates the difference between spot rates and yields to maturity.

■ *Example*

Given the spot rates, r_1 equals 8 percent and r_2 equals 10 percent, what should a 5-percent coupon, two-year bond cost? The cash flows C_1 and C_2 are illustrated in the following time chart:

The bond can be viewed as a portfolio of zero-coupon bonds with one- and two-year maturities. Therefore

$$PV = \frac{\$50}{1 + 0.08} + \frac{\$1,050}{(1 + 0.10)^2} = \$914.06 \tag{A.1}$$

We now want to calculate a single rate for the bond. We do this by solving for y in the following equation:

$$\$914.06 = \frac{\$50}{1 + y} + \frac{\$1,050}{(1 + y)^2} \tag{A.2}$$

In (A.2), y equals 9.95 percent. As mentioned in the chapter, we call y the *yield to maturity* on the bond. Solving for y for a multiyear bond is generally done by means of trial and error.[12] While this can take much time with paper and pencil, it is virtually instantaneous on a hand-held calculator.

It is worthwhile to contrast equation (A.1) and equation (A.2). In (A.1), we use the marketwide spot rates to determine the price of the bond. Once we get the bond price, we use (A.2) to calculate its yield to maturity. Because equation (A.1) employs two spot rates whereas only one appears in (A.2), we can think of yield to maturity as some sort of average of the two spot rates.[13]

Using the above spot rates, the yield to maturity of a two-year coupon bond whose coupon rate is 12 percent and PV equals $1,036.73 can be determined by

$$\$1,036.73 = \frac{\$120}{1 + r} + \frac{\$1,120}{(1 + r)^2} \rightarrow r = 9.89\%$$

As these calculations show, two bonds with the same maturity will usually have different yields to maturity if the coupons differ. ■

---

[12]The quadratic formula may be used to solve for y for a two-year bond. However, formulas generally do not apply for longer-term bonds.

[13]Yield to maturity is not a simple average of r_1, and r_2. Rather, financial economists speak of it as a time-weighted average of r_1, and r_2.

Figure 5A.1
The term structure
of interest rates

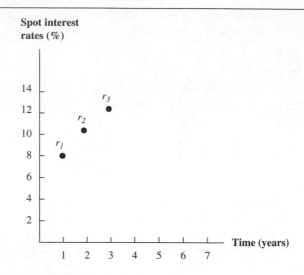

Graphing the Term Structure

The *term structure* describes the relationship of spot rates with different maturities. Figure 5A.1 graphs a particular term structure. In Figure 5A.1 the spot rates are increasing with longer maturities, that is, $r_3 > r_2 > r_1$. Graphing the term structure is easy if we can observe spot rates. Unfortunately, this can be done only if there are enough zero-coupon government bonds.

A given term structure, such as that in Figure 5A.1, exists for only a moment in time, say, 10:00 AM, July 30, 1994. Interest rates are likely to change in the next minute, so that a different (though quite similar) term structure would exist at 10:01.

CONCEPT QUESTION

■ What is the difference between a spot interest rate and the yield to maturity?

Explanations of the Term Structure

Figure 5A.1 showed one of many possible relationships between the spot rate and maturity. We now want to explore the relationship in more detail. We begin by defining a new term, the *forward rate,* and relate it to future interest rates. We also consider alternative theories of the term structure.

Definition of Forward Rate

Earlier in this appendix, we developed a two-year example where the spot rate over the first year is 8 percent and the spot rate over the two years is 10 percent. Here, an individual investing \$1 in a two-year zero-coupon bond would have \$1 $\times (1.10)^2$ in two years.

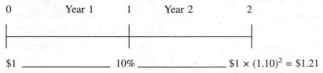

Figure 5A.2
Breakdown of a two-year spot rate into a one-year spot rate and forward rate over the second year

$1 ———————— 10% ———————— $1 × (1.10)² = $1.21

With a two-year spot rate of 10 percent, investor in two-year bond receives $1.21 at date 2.
This is the same return *as if* investor received the spot rate of 8 percent over the first year and 12.04-percent return over the second year.

$1 ——— 8% ——— $1.08 ——— 12.04% ——— $1 × 1.08 × 1.1204 = $1.21

Because both the one-year spot rate and the two-year spot rate are known at date 0, the forward rate over the second year can be calculated at date 0.

In order to pursue our discussion, it is worthwhile to rewrite[14]

$$\$1 \times (1.10)^2 = \$1 \times 1.08 \times 1.1204 \tag{A.3}$$

Equation (A.3) tells us something important about the relationship between one- and two-year rates. When an individual invests in a two-year zero-coupon bond yielding 10 percent, his wealth at the end of two years is the same as if he received an 8-percent return over the first year and a 12.04-percent return over the second year. This hypothetical rate over the second year, 12.04 percent, is called the *forward rate*. Thus, we can think of an investor with a two-year zero-coupon bond as getting the one-year spot rate of 8 percent and locking in 12.04 percent over the second year. This relationship is presented in Figure 5A.2.

More generally, if we are given spot rates, r_1 and r_2, we can always determine the forward rate, f_2, such that

$$(1 + r_2)^2 = (1 + r_1) \times (1 + f_2) \tag{A.4}$$

We solve for f_2, yielding

$$f_2 = \frac{(1 + r_2)^2}{1 + r_1} - 1 \tag{A.5}$$

If the one-year spot rate is 7 percent and the two-year spot rate is 12 percent, what is f_2?

We plug in (A.5), yielding

$$f_2 = \frac{(1.12)^2}{1.07} - 1 = 17.23\%$$

Consider an individual investing in a two-year zero-coupon bond yielding 12 percent. We say it is as if he receives 7 percent over the first year and simultaneously

---

[14]12.04 percent is equal to

$$\frac{(1.10)^2}{1.08} - 1$$

when rounding is performed after four digits.

locks in 17.23 percent over the second year. Note that both the one-year spot rate and the two-year spot rate are known at date 0. Because the forward rate is calculated from the one-year and two-year spot rates, it can be calculated at date 0 as well.

Forward rates can be calculated over later years as well. The general formula is

$$f_n = \frac{(1 + r_n)^n}{(1 + r_{n-1})^{n-1}} - 1 \qquad\qquad (A.6)$$

where f_n is the forward rate over the nth year, r_n is the n-year spot rate, and r_{n-1} is the spot rate for $n - 1$ years. ∎

■ *Example*

Assume the following set of rates:

Year	Spot rate
1	5%
2	6
3	7
4	6

What are the forward rates over each of the four years?

The forward rate over the first year is, by definition, equal to the one-year spot rate. Thus, we do not generally speak of the forward rate over the first year. The forward rates over the later years are

$$f_2 = \frac{(1.06)^2}{1.05} - 1 = 7.01\%$$

$$f_3 = \frac{(1.07)^3}{(1.06)^2} - 1 = 9.03\%$$

$$f_4 = \frac{(1.06)^4}{(1.07)^3} - 1 = 3.06\%$$

An individual investing $1 in the two-year zero-coupon bond receives $1.1236 [or $1 × (1.06)^2$] at date 2. He can be viewed as receiving the one-year spot rate of 5 percent over the first year and receiving the forward rate of 7.01 percent over the second year. Another individual investing $1 in a three-year zero-coupon bond receives $1.2250 [or $1 × (1.07)^3$] at date 3. She can be viewed as receiving the two-year spot rate of 6 percent over the first two years and receiving the forward rate of 9.03 percent over the third year. An individual investing $1 in a four-year zero-coupon bond receives $1.2625 [or $1 × (1.06)^4$] at date 4. He can be viewed as receiving the three-year spot rate of 7 percent over the first three years and receiving the forward rate of 3.06 percent over the fourth year.

Note that all of the four spot rates in this problem are known at date 0. Because the forward rates are calculated from the spot rates, they can be determined at date 0 as well. ∎

The material in this appendix is likely to be difficult for a student exposed to term structure for the first time. In brief, here is what the student should know at this point. Given equations (A.5) and (A.6), a student should be able to calculate a set of forward rates given a set of spot rates. This can simply be viewed as a mechanical computation. In addition to the calculations, a student should understand the intuition of Figure 5A.2.

We now turn to the relationship between the forward rate and the expected spot rates in the future.

Estimating the Price of a Bond at a Future Date

In the example from the body of this chapter, we considered zero-coupon bonds paying $1,000 at maturity and selling at a discount prior to maturity. We now wish to change the example slightly. Now, each bond initially sells at par so that its payment at maturity is above $1,000.[15] Keeping the spot rates at 8 percent and 10 percent, we have

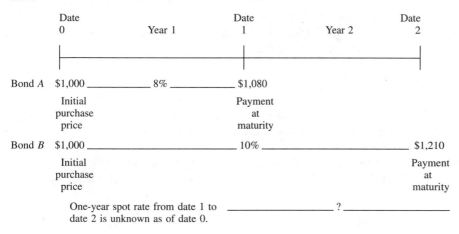

The payments at maturity are $1,080 and $1,210 for the one- and two-year zero-coupon bonds, respectively. The initial purchase price of $1,000 for each bond is determined as

$$\$1,000 = \frac{1,080}{1.08}$$

$$\$1,000 = \frac{\$1,210}{(1.10)^2}$$

We refer to the one-year bond as bond A and the two-year bond as bond B, respectively.

There will be a different one-year spot rate when date 1 arrives. This will be the spot rate from date 1 to date 2. We can also call it the spot rate over year 2. This spot rate is not known as of date 0. For example, should the rate of inflation rise between date 0 and date 1, the spot rate over year 2 would likely be high. Should the rate of inflation fall between date 0 and date 1, the spot rate over year 2 would likely be low.

Now that we have determined the price of each bond at date 0, we want to determine what the price of each bond will be at date 1. The price of the one-year bond (bond A)

---

[15]This change in assumptions simplifies our presentation but does not alter any of our conclusions.

Table 5A.1
Price of bond B at
date 1 as a
function of spot
rate over year 2

Price of bond B at date 1	Spot rate over year 2
$\$1,141.51 = \dfrac{\$1,210}{1.06}$	6%
$\$1,130.84 = \dfrac{\$1,210}{1.07}$	7%
$\$1,061.40 = \dfrac{\$1,210}{1.14}$	14%

must be $1,080 at date 1, because the payment at maturity is made then. The hard part is determining what the price of the two-year bond (bond B) will be at that time.

Suppose we find that, on date 1, the one-year spot rate from date 1 to date 2 is 6 percent. We state that this is the one-year spot rate over year 2. This means that one can invest $1,000 at date 1 and receive $1,060 (or $1,000 × 1.06) at date 2. Because one year has already passed for bond B, the bond has only one year left. Because bond B pays $1,210 at date 2, its value at date 1 is

$$\$1,141.51 = \frac{\$1,210}{1.06} \tag{A.7}$$

Note that no one knew ahead of time the price that bond B would sell for on date 1, because no one knew that the one-year spot rate over year 2 would be 6 percent.

Suppose the one-year spot rate beginning at date 1 turned out not to be 6 percent, but to be 7 percent instead. This means that one can invest $1,000 at date 1 and receive $1,070 (or $1,000 × 1.07) at date 2. In this case, the value of bond B at date 1 would be

$$\$1,130.84 = \frac{\$1,210}{1.07} \tag{A.8}$$

Finally, suppose that the one-year spot rate at date 1 turned out to be neither 6 percent nor 7 percent, but 14 percent instead. This means that one can invest $1,000 at date 1 and receive $1,140 (or $1,000 × 1.14) at date 2. In this case, the value of bond B at date 1 would be

$$\$1,061.40 = \frac{\$1,210}{1.14}$$

The above possible bond prices are represented in Table 5A.1. The price that bond B will sell for on date 1 is not known before date 1 since the one-year spot rate prevailing over year 2 is not known until date 1.

It is important to reemphasize that, although the forward rate is known at date 0, the one-year spot rate beginning at date 1 is *unknown* ahead of time. Thus, the price of bond B at date 1 is unknown ahead of time. Prior to date 1, we can speak only of the amount that bond B is *expected* to sell for on date 1. We write this as[16]

---

[16]Technically, equation (A.9) is only an approximation due to *Jensen's inequality*. That is, expected values of

$$\frac{\$1,210}{1 + \text{Spot rate}} > \frac{\$1,210}{1 + \text{Spot rate expected over year 2}}$$

However, we ignore this very minor issue in the rest of the analysis.

The Amount That Bond *B* Is Expected to Sell for on Date 1:

$$\frac{\$1,210}{1 + \text{Spot rate expected over year 2}} \tag{A.9}$$

Making two points is worthwhile now. First, because each individual is different, the expected value of bond *B* differs across individuals. Later we will speak of a consensus expected value across investors. Second, equation (A.9) represents one's forecast of the price that the bond will be selling for on date 1. The forecast is made ahead of time, that is, on date 0.

The Relationship between Forward Rate over Second Year and Spot Rate Expected over Second Year

Given a forecast of bond *B*'s price, an investor can choose one of two strategies at date 0:

1. Buy a one-year bond. Proceeds at date 1 would be

$$\$1,080 = \$1,000 \times 1.08 \tag{A.10}$$

2. Buy a two-year bond but sell at date 1. His *expected* proceeds would be

$$\frac{\$1,000 \times (1.10)^2}{1 + \text{Spot rate expected over year 2}} \tag{A.11}$$

Given our discussion of forward rates, we can rewrite (A.11) as

$$\frac{\$1,000 \times 1.08 \times 1.1204}{1 + \text{Spot rate expected over year 2}} \tag{A.12}$$

(Remember that 12.04 percent was the forward rate over year 2, f_2.)

Under what condition will the return from strategy 1 equal the expected return from strategy 2? In other words, under what condition will formula (A.10) equal formula (A.12)?

The two strategies will yield the same expected return only when

$$12.04\% = \text{Spot rate expected over year 2} \tag{A.13}$$

In other words, if the forward rate equals the expected spot rate, one would expect to earn the same return over the first year whether one invested in a one-year bond, or invested in a two-year bond but sold after one year.

The Expectations Hypothesis

Equation (A.13) seems fairly reasonable. That is, it is reasonable that investors would set interest rates in such a way that the forward rate would equal the spot rate expected by the marketplace a year from now.[17] For example, imagine that individuals in the

---

[17] Of course, each individual will have different expectations so equation (A.13) cannot hold for all individuals. However, financial economists generally speak of a consensus expectation. This is the expectation of the market as a whole.

marketplace do not concern themselves with risk. If the forward rate, f_2, is less than the spot rate expected over year 2, individuals desiring to invest for one year would always buy a one-year bond. That is, our work above shows that an individual investing in a two-year bond but planning to sell at the end of one year would expect to earn less than if he simply bought a one-year bond.

Equation (A.13) was stated for the specific case where the forward rate was 12.04 percent. We can generalize this to

Expectations Hypothesis:

$$f_2 = \text{Spot rate expected over year 2} \tag{A.14}$$

Equation (A.14) says that the forward rate over the second year is set to the spot rate that people expect to prevail over the second year. This is called the *expectations hypothesis*. It states that investors will set interest rates such that the forward rate over the second year is equal to the one-year spot rate expected over the second year.

Liquidity-Preference Hypothesis

At this point, many students think that equation (A.14) *must* hold. However, note that we developed (A.14) by assuming that investors were risk-neutral. Suppose, alternatively, that investors are adverse to risk.

Which strategy would appear more risky for an individual who wants to invest for one year:

1. Invest in a one-year bond.
2. Invest in a two-year bond but sell at the end of one year.

Strategy 1 has no risk because the investor knows that the rate of return must be r_1. Conversely, strategy 2 has much risk; the final return is dependent on what happens to interest rates.

Because strategy 2 has more risk than strategy 1, no risk-averse investor will choose strategy 2 if both strategies have the same expected return. Risk-averse investors can have no preference for one strategy over the other only when the expected return on strategy 2 is *above* the return on strategy 1. Because the two strategies have the same expected return when f_2 equals the spot rate expected over year 2, strategy 2 can only have a higher rate of return when

Liquidity-Preference Hypothesis:

$$f_2 > \text{Spot rate expected over year 2} \tag{A.15}$$

That is, in order to induce investors to hold the riskier two-year bonds, the market sets the forward rate over the second year to be above the spot rate expected over the second year. Equation (A.15) is called the *liquidity-preference hypothesis*.

We developed the entire discussion by assuming that individuals are planning to invest over one year. We pointed out that for such individuals, a two-year bond has extra risk because it must be sold prematurely. What about those individuals who want to invest for two years? (We call these people investors with a two-year *time horizon*.)

They could choose one of the following strategies:

3. Buy a two-year zero-coupon bond.

4. Buy a one-year bond. When the bond matures, they immediately buy another one-year bond.

Strategy 3 has no risk for an investor with a two-year time horizon, because the proceeds to be received at date 2 are known as of date 0. However, strategy 4 has risk since the spot rate over year 2 is unknown at date 0. It can be shown that risk-averse investors will prefer neither strategy 3 nor strategy 4 over the other when

$$f_2 < \text{Spot rate expected over year 2} \qquad \qquad \text{(A.16)}$$

Note that introducing risk aversion gives contrary predictions. Relationship (A.15) holds for a market dominated by investors with a one-year time horizon. Relationship (A.16) holds for a market dominated by investors with a two-year time horizon. Financial economists have generally argued that the time horizon of the typical investor is generally much shorter than the maturity of typical bonds in the marketplace. Thus, economists view (A.15) as the better depiction of equilibrium in the bond market with *risk-averse* investors.

However, do we have a market of risk-neutral investors or risk-averse investors? In other words, can the expectations hypothesis of equation (A.14) or the liquidity-preference hypothesis of equation (A.15) be expected to hold? As we will learn later in this book, economists view investors as being risk-averse for the most part. Yet economists are never satisfied with a casual examination of a theory's assumptions. To them, empirical evidence of a theory's predictions must be the final arbiter.

There has been a great deal of empirical evidence on the term structure of interest rates. Unfortunately (perhaps fortunately for some students), we will not be able to present the evidence in any detail. Suffice it to say that, in our opinion, the evidence supports the liquidity-preference hypothesis over the expectations hypothesis. One simple result might give students the flavour of this research. Consider an individual choosing between one of the following two strategies:

1. Invest in a one-year bond.
2'. Invest in a 20-year bond but sell at the end of one year.

(Strategy 2' is identical to strategy 2 except that a 20-year bond is substituted for a two-year bond.)

The expectations hypothesis states that the expected returns on both strategies are identical. The liquidity-preference hypothesis states that the expected return on strategy 2' should be above the expected return on strategy 1. Though no one knows what returns are actually expected over a particular time period, actual returns from the past may allow us to infer expectations. The results from January 1926 to December 1988 are illuminating. Over this time period the average yearly return on strategy 1 is 3.6 percent; it is 4.7 percent on strategy 2'.[18] This evidence is generally considered to be consistent with the liquidity-preference hypothesis and inconsistent with the expectations hypothesis.

---

[18]Taken from *SBBI 1988 Quarterly Market Report* (Chicago: Ibbotson Associates).

It is important to note that strategy 2' does not involve buying a 20-year bond and holding it to maturity. Rather, it consists of buying a 20-year bond and selling it one year later, that is, when it has become a 19-year bond. This round-trip transaction occurs 63 times in the 63-year sample from January 1926 to December 1988.

Figure 5A.3
Term structure of
interest rates, June
1993

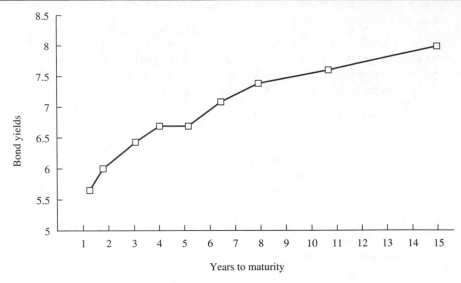

Source: *The Globe and Mail,* June 26, 1993, p. B7.

Application of Term Structure Theory

In explaining term structure theory, it was convenient to use examples of zero-coupon bonds and spot and forward rates. To see the application, we go back to coupon bonds and yields to maturity the way that actual bond data is presented in the financial press.

Figure 5A.3 shows a yield curve for Government of Canada bonds, a plot of bond yields to maturity against time to maturity. Yield curves are observed at a particular date and change shape over time. This yield curve is for June 1993.

Notice that the yield curve is ascending with the long rates above the short rates. Term structure theory gives us two reasons why the observed yield curve is ascending. Investors expect that rates will rise in the future and that there is a liquidity premium.

Now suppose you were advising a friend who was renewing a home mortgage. Suppose further that the alternatives were a one-year mortgage at 8.5 percent and a two-year mortgage at 10 percent. We know that on average, over the life of a mortgage, rolling over one-year rates will probably be cheaper because the borrower will avoid paying the liquidity premium. But we also know that this approach is riskier because the ascending yield curve for bond and mortgages suggests that investors believe that rates will rise.

Appendix Questions and Problems

5.A1 Define the forward rate.

5.A2 What is the relationship between the one-year spot rate, the two-year spot rate, and the forward rate over the second year?

5.A3 What is the expectations hypothesis?

5.A4 What is the liquidity-preference hypothesis?

5.A5. What is the difference between a spot interest rate and the yield to maturity?

6

Some Alternative Investment Rules

Chapter 4 examined the relationship between $1 today and $1 in the future. For example, a corporate project generating a set of cash flows can be valued by discounting these flows, an approach called the *net present value (NPV)* approach. While we believe that the NPV approach is the best one for evaluating capital budgeting projects, our treatment would be incomplete if we ignored alternative methods. This chapter examines these alternative methods. We first consider the NPV approach as a benchmark. Next we examine three alternatives: payback, accounting rates of return, and internal rate of return.

Why Use Net Present Value? 6.1

Before examining competitors of the NPV approach, we should ask, Why consider using NPV in the first place? Answering this question will put the rest of this chapter in a proper perspective. There are actually a number of arguments justifying the use of NPV, and you may have already seen the detailed one of Chapter 3. We now present one of the simplest justifications through an example.

- **Example**

The Alpha Corporation is considering investing in a riskless project costing $100. The project pays $107 at date 1 and has no other cash flows. The managers of the firm might contemplate one of two strategies:

1. Use $100 of corporate cash to invest in the project. The $107 will be paid as a dividend in one period.
2. Forgo the project and pay the $100 of corporate cash as a dividend today.

If strategy 2 is employed, the shareholder might deposit the dividend in the bank for one period. Because the project is riskless and lasts for one period, the shareholder would prefer strategy 1 if the bank interest rate was below 7 percent. In other words, the shareholder would prefer strategy 1 if strategy 2 produced less than $107 by the end of the year. ∎

The comparison can easily be handled by NPV analysis. If the interest rate is 6 percent, the NPV of the project is

$$\$0.94 = -\$100 + \frac{\$107}{1.06}$$

Because the NPV is positive, the project should be accepted. Of course, a bank interest rate above 7 percent would cause the project's NPV to be negative, implying that the project should be rejected.

Thus, our basic point is:

> Accepting positive NPV projects benefits the shareholders.

Although we used the simplest possible example, the results could easily be applied to more plausible situations. If the project lasted for many periods, we would calculate the NPV of the project by discounting all the cash flows. If the project were risky, we could determine the expected return on a stock whose risk is comparable to that of the project. This expected return would serve as the discount rate.

Having shown that NPV is a sensible approach, how can we tell whether alternative approaches are as good as NPV? The key to NPV is its three attributes:

1. *NPV uses cash flows.* Cash flows from a project can be used for other corporate purposes: dividend payments, other capital budgeting projects, or payments of corporate interest. By contrast, earnings are an artificial construct. While earnings are useful to accountants, they should not be used in capital budgeting because they do not represent cash.

2. *NPV uses all the cash flows of the project.* Other approaches ignore cash flows beyond a particular date; beware of these approaches.

3. *NPV discounts the cash flows properly.* Other approaches may ignore the time value of money when handling cash flows. Beware of these approaches as well.

6.2   The Payback Period Rule

Defining the Rule

One of the most popular alternatives to NPV is the **payback period rule.** Here is how the payback period rule works.

Consider a project with an initial investment of −$50,000. Cash flows are $30,000, $20,000, and $10,000 in the first three years, respectively. These flows are illustrated in Figure 6.1. A useful way of writing down investments like the preceding is with the notation

(−$50,000, $30,000, $20,000, $10,000)

The minus sign in front of the $50,000 reminds us that this is a cash outflow for the investor, and the commas between the different numbers indicate that they are received—or if they are cash outflows, that they are paid out—at different times. In this example we are assuming that the cash flows occur one year apart, with the first one occurring the moment we decide to take on the investment.

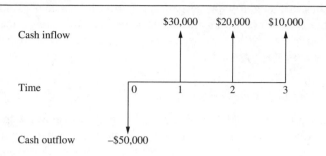

Figure 6.1
Cash flows of an
investment project

Year	A	B	C
0	−$100	−$100	−$100
1	20	50	50
2	30	30	30
3	50	20	20
4	60	60	60,000
Payback period (years)			
	3	3	3

Table 6.1
Expected cash
flows for projects
A through *C*

The firm receives cash flows of $30,000 and $20,000 in the first two years, which add up to the $50,000 original investment. This means that the firm has recovered its investment within two years. In this case two years is the *payback period* of the investment.

The payback period rule for making investment decisions is simple. A particular cutoff time, say two years, is selected. All investment projects that have payback periods of two years or less are accepted and all of those that pay off in more than two years, if at all, are rejected.

Problems with the Payback Method

There are at least three problems with the payback method. To illustrate the first two problems, we consider the three projects in Table 6.1. All three projects have the same three-year payback period, so they should all be equally attractive—right?

Actually, they are not equally attractive, as can be seen by a comparison of different *pairs* of projects.

Problem 1: Timing of Cash Flows within the Payback Period

Let us compare project *A* with project *B*. In years 1 through 3, the cash flows of project *A* rise from $20 to $50 while the cash flows of project *B* fall from $50 to $20. Because the large cash flow of $50 comes earlier with project *B,* its net present value must be higher. Nevertheless, we saw above that the payback periods of the two projects are identical. Thus, a problem with the payback period is that it does not consider the timing of the cash flows within the payback period. This shows that the payback method is inferior to NPV because, as we pointed out earlier, the NPV approach *discounts the cash flows properly.*

Problem 2: Payments after the Payback Period

Now consider projects *B* and *C*, which have identical cash flows within the payback period. However, project *C* is clearly preferred because it has the cash flow of $60,000 in the fourth year. Thus, another problem with the payback method is that it ignores all cash flows occurring after the payback period. This flaw is not present with the NPV approach because, as we pointed out earlier, the NPV approach *uses all the cash flows of the project.* The payback method forces managers to have an artificially short-term orientation, which may lead to decisions not in the shareholders' best interests.

Problem 3: Arbitrary Standard for Payback Period

We do not need to refer to Table 6.1 when considering a third problem with the payback approach. When a firm uses the NPV approach, it can go to the capital market to get the discount rate. There is no comparable guide for choosing the payback period, so the choice is arbitrary to some extent.

Managerial Perspective

The payback rule is often used by large and sophisticated companies when making relatively small decisions. The decision to build a small warehouse, for example, or to pay for a tune-up for a truck is the sort of decision that is often made by lower-level management. Typically a manager might reason that a tune-up would cost, say, $200, and if it saved $120 each year in reduced fuel costs, it would pay for itself in less than two years. On such a basis the decision would be made.

Although the treasurer of the company might not have made the decision in the same way, the company endorses such decision-making. Why would upper management condone or even encourage such retrograde activity in its employees? One answer would be that it is easy to make decisions using the payback rule. Multiply the tune-up decision into 50 such decisions a month, and the appeal of this simple rule becomes clearer.

Perhaps most important though, the payback rule also has some desirable features for managerial control. Just as important as the investment decision itself is the company's ability to evaluate the manager's decision-making ability. Under the NPV rule, a long time may pass before one can decide whether or not a decision was correct. With the payback rule we know in two years whether the manager's assessment of the cash flows was correct.

Notwithstanding all of the preceding rationale, it is not surprising to discover that as the decision grows in importance, which is to say when firms look at bigger projects, the NPV becomes the order of the day. When questions of controlling and evaluating the manager become less important than making the right investment decision, the payback period is used less frequently. For the big-ticket decisions, such as whether or not to buy a big machine, build a factory, or acquire a company, the payback rule is seldom used.

Summary of the Payback Period Rule

To summarize, the payback period is not the same as the NPV rule and is therefore conceptually wrong. With its arbitrary cutoff date and its blindness to cash flows after this date, it can lead to some flagrantly foolish decisions if it is used too literally. Nevertheless, because it is so simple, companies often use it as a screen for making the myriad of minor investment decisions they continually face.

Although this means that you should be wary of trying to change rules like the payback period when you encounter them in companies, you should probably be careful not to fall into the sloppy financial thinking they represent. After this course you would do your company a disservice if you ever used the payback period instead of the NPV when you had a choice.

CONCEPT QUESTIONS

- List the problems of the payback period rule.
- What are some advantages?

The Discounted Payback Period Rule   6.3

Aware of the pitfalls of the payback approach, some decision-makers use a variant called the **discounted payback period rule.** Under this approach, we first discount the cash flows. Then we ask how long it takes for the discounted cash flows to equal the initial investment.

For example, suppose that the discount rate is 10 percent and the cash flows on a project are given by

(−$100, $50, $50, $20)

This investment has a payback period of two years, because the investment is paid back in that time.

To compute the project's discounted payback period, we first discount each of the cash flows at the 10-percent rate. In discounted terms, then, the cash flows look like

$$(-\$100, \$50/1.1, \$50/(1.1)^2, \$20/(1.1)^3) = (-\$100, \$45.45, \$41.32, \$15.03)$$

The discounted payback period of the original investment is simply the payback period for these discounted cash flows. The payback period for the discounted cash flows is slightly less than three years since the discounted cash flows over the three years are $101.80 (or $45.45 + $41.32 + $15.03). As long as the cash flows are positive, the discounted payback period will never be smaller than the payback period, because discounting will lower the cash flows.

At first glance the discounted payback may seem like an attractive alternative, but on closer inspection we see that it has some of the same major flaws as the payback. Like payback, discounted payback first requires us to make a somewhat magical choice of an arbitrary cutoff period, and then it ignores all of the cash flows after that date.

If we have already gone to the trouble of discounting the cash flows, any small appeal to simplicity or to managerial control that payback may have, has been lost. We might just as well add up the discounted cash flows and use the NPV to make the decision. Although discounted payback looks a bit like the NPV, it is just a poor compromise between the payback method and the NPV.

6.4   The Average Accounting Return (AAR)

Defining the Rule

Another attractive and fatally flawed approach to making financial decisions is the **average accounting return (AAR).** The average accounting return is the average project earnings after taxes and depreciation, divided by the average book value of the investment during its life. In spite of its flaws, the average accounting return method is worth examining because it is used frequently in business.

■ *Example*

Consider a company that is evaluating whether or not to buy a store in a newly built mall. The purchase price is $500,000. We will assume that the store has an estimated life of five years and will need to be completely scrapped or rebuilt at the end of that time. The projected yearly sales and expense figures are shown in Table 6.2. ■

It is worth looking carefully at this table. In fact, the first step in any project assessment is a careful look at the projected cash flows. When the store starts up, it is estimated that first-year sales will be $433,333 and that, after expenses, the before-tax cash flow will be $233,333. After the first year, sales are expected to rise and expenses are expected to fall, resulting in a before-tax cash flow of $300,000. After that, competition from other stores and the loss in novelty will drop before-tax cash flow to $166,667, $100,000, and $33,333, respectively, in the next three years.

Table 6.2
Projected yearly revenue and costs for average accounting return

	Year 1	Year 2	Year 3	Year 4	Year 5
Revenue	$433,333	$450,000	$266,667	$200,000	$133,333
Expenses	200,000	150,000	100,000	100,000	100,000
Before-tax cash flow	233,333	300,000	166,667	100,000	33,333
Depreciation	100,000	100,000	100,000	100,000	100,000
Earnings before taxes	133,333	200,000	66,667	0	−66,667
Taxes $(T_c = 0.25)$*	33,333	50,000	16,667	0	−16,667
Net income	100,000	150,000	50,000	0	−50,000

$$\text{Average net income} = \frac{(\$100.000 + 150{,}000 + \$50{,}000 + \$0 - \$50{,}000)}{5} = \$50{,}000$$

$$\text{Average investment} = \frac{\$500{,}000 + \$0}{2} = \$250{,}000$$

$$\text{AAR} = \frac{\$50{,}000}{\$250{,}000} = 20\%$$

* Corporate tax rate = T_c. The tax rebate in year 5 of −$16,667 occurs if the rest of the firm is profitable. Here, the loss in the project reduces taxes of entire firm.

To compute the average accounting return on the project, we divide the average net income by the average amount invested. This can be done in three steps.

Step 1: Determining Average Net Income   The net income in any year is the net cash flow minus depreciation and taxes. Depreciation is not a cash outflow.[1] Rather, it is a charge reflecting the fact that the investment in the store becomes less valuable every year.

We assume the project has a useful life of five years, at which time it will be worthless. Because the initial investment is $500,000 and because it will be worthless in five years, we will assume that it loses value at the rate of $100,000 each year. This steady loss in value of $100,000 is called *straight-line depreciation.* We subtract both depreciation and taxes from before-tax cash flow to derive the net income, as shown in Table 6.2. The net income over the five years is $100,000 in the first year, $150,000 in year 2, $50,000 in year 3, zero in year 4, and −$50,000 in the last year. The average net income over the life of the project is therefore

Average Net Income:

[$100,000 + $150,000 + $50,000 + $0 + (−$50,000)]/5 = $50,000

Step 2: Determining Average Investment   We stated earlier that, due to depreciation, the investment in the store becomes less valuable every year. Because depreciation is $100,000 per year, the value at the end of year zero is $500,000, the value at the end of year 1 is $400,000, and so on. What is the average value of the investment over the life of the investment?

The mechanical calculation is

Average Investment:

($500,000 + $400,000 + $300,000 + $200,000 + $100,000 + $0)/6   (6.1)
= $250,000

We divide by 6 and not 5, because $500,000 is what the investment is worth at the beginning of the five years and $0 is what it is worth at the beginning of the sixth year. In other words, there are six terms in the parenthesis of equation (6.1).

Step 3: Determining AAR   The average return is simply

$$AAR = \frac{\$50,000}{\$250,000} = 20\%$$

If the firm had a targeted accounting rate of return greater than 20 percent, the project would be rejected, and if its targeted return were less than 20 percent, it would be accepted.

Analyzing the Average Accounting Return Method

By now you should be able to see what is wrong with the AAR method of making investment decisions.

---

[1]The rates of depreciation and tax used in this example are chosen for simplicity. Leasehold improvements are one of the few asset classes for which tax depreciation in Canada is straight line. We discuss these topics in detail in the Appendix to Chapter 1 and in Chapter 7.

The most important flaw in the AAR method is that it does not use the right raw materials. It uses the net income figures and the book value of the investment (from the accountant's books) to figure out whether to take the investment. Conversely, the NPV rule *uses cash flows.*

Second, AAR takes no account of timing. In the previous example, the AAR would have been the same if the $100,000 net income in the first year had occurred in the last year. However, delaying an inflow for five years would have made the investment less attractive under the NPV rule as well as by the common sense of the time value of money. That is, the NPV approach *discounts properly.*

Third, just as the payback period requires an arbitrary choice of a cutoff date, the AAR method offers no guidance on what the right targeted rate of return should be. It could be the discount rate in the market. But then again, because the AAR method is not the same as the present value method, it is not obvious that this would be the right choice.

Like the payback method, the AAR (and variations of it) is frequently used as a "backup" to discounted cash flow methods. Perhaps this is so because it is easy to calculate and uses accounting numbers readily available from the firm's accounting system.

CONCEPT QUESTIONS

- What are the three steps in calculating AAR?
- What are some flaws with the AAR approach?

6.5   The Internal Rate of Return (IRR)

Now we come to the most important alternative to the NPV approach, the internal rate of return, universally known as the IRR. The IRR is about as close as you can get to the NPV without actually being the NPV. The basic rationale behind the IRR is that it tries to find a single number that summarizes the merits of a project. That number does not depend on the interest rate that prevails in the capital market. That is why it is called the internal rate of return; the number is internal or intrinsic to the project and does not depend on anything except the cash flows of the project.

For example, consider the simple project (−$100, $110) in Figure 6.2. For a given rate, the net present value of this project can be described as

$$\text{NPV} = -\$100 + \frac{\$110}{1 + r} \tag{6.2}$$

where r is the discount rate.

What must the discount rate be to make the NPV of the project equal to zero? We begin by using an arbitrary discount rate of 0.08, which yields

$$\$1.85 = \$100 + \frac{\$110}{1.08} \tag{6.3}$$

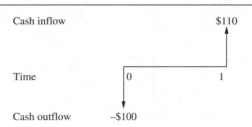

Figure 6.2
Cash flows for a
simple project

Since the NPV in equation (6.3) is positive, we now try a higher discount rate, say, 0.12. This yields

$$-\$1.79 = \$100 + \frac{\$110}{1.12} \tag{6.4}$$

Since the NPV in equation (6.4) is negative, we lower the discount rate to, say, 0.10. This yields

$$0 = -\$100 + \frac{\$110}{1.10} \tag{6.5}$$

This trial-and-error procedure tells us that the NPV of the project is zero when r equals 10 percent.[2] Thus, we say that 10 percent is the project's **internal rate of return (IRR).** In general, the IRR is the rate that causes the NPV of the project to be zero. The implication of this exercise is very simple. The firm should be equally willing to accept or reject the project if the discount rate is 10 percent. The firm should accept the project if the discount rate is below 10 percent. The firm should reject the project if the discount rate is above 10 percent.

The general investment rule is clear:

Accept the project if IRR is greater than the discount rate.
Reject the project if IRR is less than the discount rate.

We refer to this as the **basic IRR rule.** Having mastered the basics of the IRR rule, you should recognize that we used the IRR (without defining it) when we calculated the yield to maturity of a bond in Chapter 5. In fact, the yield to maturity is the bond's IRR.

Now we can try the more complicated example in Figure 6.3. As we did in equations (6.3) to (6.5), we use trial and error to calculate the internal rate of return. We try 20 percent and 30 percent, yielding

Discount rate	NPV
20%	$10.65
30	−18.39

---

[2]Of course, we could have directly solved for r in equation (6.2) after setting NPV equal to zero. However, with a long series of cash flows, one cannot generally directly solve for r. Instead, one is forced to use a trial-and-error method similar to that in equations (6.3), (6.4), and (6.5).

Figure 6.3
Cash flows for a
more complex
project than the
one in Figure 6.2

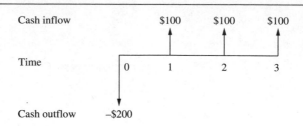

Figure 6.4
Net present value
(NPV) and
discount rates for a
relatively complex
project

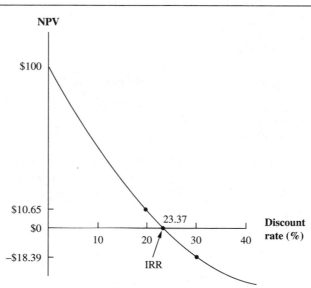

The NPV is positive for discount rates below the IRR and negative for
discount rates above the IRR.

After much more trial and error, we find that the NPV of the project is zero when the
discount rate is 23.37 percent. Thus, the IRR is 23.37 percent. With a 20-percent
discount rate the NPV is positive and we accept it. However, if the discount rate is 30
percent, we reject it.

Algebraically, IRR is the unknown in the following equation:[3]

$$0 = -\$200 + \frac{\$100}{1 + IRR} + \frac{\$100}{(1 + IRR)^2} + \frac{\$100}{(1 + IRR)^3}$$

Figure 6.4 illustrates what it means to find the IRR for a project. The figure plots the
NPV as a function of the discount rate. The curve crosses the horizontal axis at the
IRR of 23.37 percent because this is where the NPV equals zero.

---

[3]One can derive the IRR directly for a problem with an initial outflow and either one or two subsequent inflows. In the case
of two subsequent inflows, the quadratic formula is needed. In general, however, only trial and error will work for an
outflow and three or more subsequent inflows. Hand calculators calculate IRR by trial and error, though at lightning speed.

It should also be clear that the NPV is positive for discount rates below the IRR and negative for discount rates above the IRR. This means that if we accept projects like this one when the discount rate is less than the IRR, we will be accepting positive NPV projects. Thus, the IRR rule will coincide exactly with the NPV rule.

If this were all there were to it, the IRR rule would always coincide with the NPV rule. This would be a wonderful discovery because it would mean that just by computing the IRR for a project we would be able to tell where it ranks among all of the projects we are considering. For example, if the IRR rule really works, a project with an IRR of 20 percent will always be at least as good as one with an IRR of 15 percent.

But the world of finance is not so kind. Unfortunately, the IRR rule and the NPV rule are the same only for simple examples like the ones above. Several problems with the IRR occur in more complicated situations.

CONCEPT QUESTIONS

■ How does one calculate the IRR of a project?

Problems with the IRR Approach   6.6

Definition of Independent and Mutually Exclusive Projects

An **independent project** is one whose acceptance or rejection is independent of the acceptance or rejection of other projects. For example, imagine that McDonald's of Canada is considering putting a hamburger outlet in Moscow. Acceptance or rejection of this unit is likely to be unrelated to the acceptance or rejection of any other restaurant in its system. The remoteness of the outlet in question ensures that it will not pull sales away from other outlets.

Now consider the other extreme, **mutually exclusive investments.** What does it mean for two projects, A and B, to be mutually exclusive? You can accept A or you can accept B or you can reject both of them, but you cannot accept both of them. For example, A might be a decision to build an apartment building on a corner lot that you own, and B might be a decision to build a movie theater on the same lot.

We now present two general problems with the IRR approach that affect both independent and mutually exclusive projects. Next, we deal with two problems affecting mutually exclusive projects only.

Two General Problems Affecting Both Independent and Mutually Exclusive Projects

We begin our discussion with project A, which has the following cash flows:

(−$100, $130)

The IRR for project A is 30 percent. Table 6.3 provides other relevant information on the project. The relationship between NPV and the discount rate is shown for this project in Figure 6.5. As you can see, the NPV declines as the discount rate rises.

like stripping a mine.

Table 6.3 The internal rate of return and net present value

	Project A			Project B			Project C		
Dates:	0	1	2	0	1	2	0	1	2
Cash flows	−$100	$130		$100	−$130		−$100	$230	−$132
IRR		30%			30%			10%	20%
NPV @ 10%		$18.2			−$18.2				
Accept if market rate		<30%			>30%			>10%	<20%
Financing or investing		Investing			Financing			Mixture	

Figure 6.5 Net present value and discount rates for projects A, B, and C

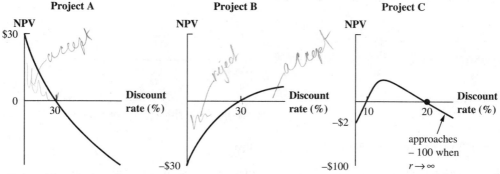

Project A has a cash outflow at date 0 followed by a cash inflow at date 1. Its NPV is negatively related to the discount rate.

Project B has a cash inflow at date 0 followed by a cash outflow at date 1. Its NPV is positively related to the discount rate.

Project C has two changes of sign in its cash flows. It has an outflow at date 0, an inflow at date 1, and an outflow at date 2. Projects with more than one change of sign can have multiple rates of return.

Problem 1: Investing or Financing?

Now consider project B, with cash flows of

($100, −$130)

These cash flows are exactly the reverse of the flows for project A. In project B, the firm receives funds first and then pays out funds later. While unusual, projects of this type do exist. For example, consider a corporation conducting a seminar where the participants pay in advance. Because large expenses are frequently incurred at the seminar date, cash inflows precede cash outflows.

Consider our trial-and-error method to calculate IRR:

$$-\$4 = +\$100 - \frac{\$130}{1.25}$$

$$\$0 = +\$100 - \frac{\$130}{1.30}$$

$$\$3.70 = +\$100 - \frac{\$130}{1.35}$$

As with project *A,* the internal rate of return is 30 percent. However, notice that the net present value is *negative* when the discount rate is *below* 30 percent. Conversely, the net present value is positive when the discount rate is above 30 percent. The decision rule is exactly the opposite of our previous result. For this type of a project, the rule is

> Accept the project when IRR is less than the discount rate.
> Reject the project when IRR is greater than the discount rate.

[handwritten: graph B when inflows are at beginning of projects]

This unusual decision rule follows from the graph of project *B* in Figure 6.5. The curve is upward sloping, implying that NPV is *positively* related to the discount rate.

The graph makes intuitive sense. Suppose that the firm wants to obtain $100 immediately. It can either (1) conduct project *B* or (2) borrow $100 from a bank. Thus, the project is actually a substitute for borrowing. In fact, because the IRR is 30 percent, taking on project *B* is tantamount to borrowing at 30 percent. If the firm can borrow from a bank at, say, only 25 percent, it should reject the project. However, if a firm can only borrow from a bank at, say, 35 percent, it should accept the project. Thus, project *B* will be accepted if and only if the discount rate is *above* the IRR.[4]

[handwritten: because to cheaper to borrow at bank]

This should be contrasted with Project *A*. If the firm has $100 of cash to invest, it can either (1) conduct project *A* or (2) lend $100 to the bank. The project is actually a substitute for lending. In fact, because the IRR is 30 percent, taking on project *A* is tantamount to lending at 30 percent. The firm should accept project *A* if the lending rate is below 30 percent. Conversely, the firm should reject project *A* if the lending rate is above 30 percent.

Because the firm initially pays out money with project *A* but initially receives money with project *B,* we refer to project *A* as an investing-type project and project *B* as a financing-type project. Investing-type projects are the norm. Because the IRR rule is reversed for a financing-type project, we view this type of project as a problem—unless it is understood properly.

Problem 2: Multiple Rates of Return

Suppose the cash flows from a project are

(−$100, $230, −$132)

Because this project has a negative cash flow, a positive cash flow, and another negative cash flow, we say that the project's cash flows exhibit two changes of sign or "flip-flops." While this pattern of cash flows might look a bit strange at first, many projects require outflows of cash after receiving some inflows. An example would be a strip-mining project. The first stage in such a project is the initial investment in excavating the mine. Profits from operating the mine are received in the second stage. The third stage involves a further investment to reclaim the land and satisfy the requirements of environmental protection legislation. Cash flows are negative at this stage.

---

[4]This paragraph implicitly assumes that the cash flows of the project are risk-free. In this way, we can treat the borrowing rate as the discount rate for a firm needing $100. With risky cash flows, another discount rate would be chosen. However, the intuition behind the decision to accept when IRR is less than the discount rate would still apply.

Projects financed by lease arrangements also produce negative cash flows followed by positive ones. We study leasing carefully in a later chapter, but for now we will give you a hint. Using leases for financing can sometimes bring substantial tax advantages. These advantages are often sufficient to make an otherwise bad investment have positive cash flows following an initial outlay. But after a while the tax advantages decline or run out. The cash flows turn negative when this occurs.

It is easy to verify that this project has not one but two IRRs: 10 percent and 20 percent.[5] In a case like this, the IRR does not make any sense. What IRR are we to use: 10 percent or 20 percent? Because there is no good reason to use one over the other, IRR simply cannot be used here.

Of course, we should not feel too worried about multiple rates of return. After all, we can always fall back on NPV. Figure 6.5 plots the NPV for this project C as a function of the different discount rates. As it shows, the NPV is zero at both 10 percent and 20 percent. Furthermore, the NPV is positive for discount rates between 10 percent and 20 percent and negative outside of this range.

This example generates multiple internal rates of return because both an inflow and an outflow occur after the initial investment. In general, these flip-flops or changes in sign produce multiple IRRs. In theory, a cash flow stream with M changes in sign can have up to M positive internal rates of return.[6] As we pointed out, projects whose cash flows change sign repeatedly can occur in business.

Are We Ever Safe from the Multiple-IRR Problem?   If the first cash flow for a project is negative—because it is the initial investment—and if all of the remaining flows are

---

[5]The calculations are

$$0 = -\$100 + \frac{\$230}{1.1} - \frac{\$132}{(1.1)^2}$$

$$= -\$100 + \$209.09 - \$109.09$$

and

$$0 = -\$100 + \frac{\$230}{1.2} - \frac{\$132}{(1.2)^2}$$

$$= -\$100 + \$191.67 - \$91.67$$

Thus, we have multiple rates of return.

[6]Readers well versed in algebra might have recognized that finding the IRR is like finding the root of a polynomial equation. For a project with cash flows of $(C_0, \ldots, C_T)$, the formula for computing the IRR requires us to find the interest rate, r, that makes

$$NPV = C_0 + C_1/(1 + r) + \ldots + C_T/(1 + r)^T = 0$$

If we let the symbol x stand for the discount factor,

$$x = 1/(1 + r)$$

then the formula for the IRR becomes

$$NPV = C_0 + C_1x + C_2x^2 + \ldots + C_Tx^T = 0$$

Finding the IRR, then, is the same as finding the roots of this polynomial equation. If a particular value x^* is a root of the equation, then, because

$$x = 1/(1 + r)$$

it follows that there is an associated IRR:

$$r^* = (1/x^*) - 1$$

From the theory of polynomials, it is well known that an nth-order polynomial has n roots. Each such root that is positive and less than 1 can have a sensible IRR associated with it. Applying Descartes' rule of signs gives the result that a stream of n cash flows can have up to M positive IRRs, where M is the number of changes of sign for the cash flows.

positive, there can be only a single, unique IRR, no matter how many periods the project lasts. This is easy to understand by using the concept of the time value of money. For example, it is easy to verify that project A in Table 6.3 has an IRR of 30 percent, because using a 30-percent discount rate gives

$$NPV = -\$100 + \$130/(1.3)$$
$$= 0$$

How do we know that this is the only IRR? Suppose that we were to try a discount rate greater than 30 percent. In computing the NPV, changing the discount rate does not change the value of the initial cash flow of −$100 because that cash flow is not discounted. But raising the discount rate can only lower the present value of the future cash flows. In other words, because the NPV is zero at 30 percent, any increase in the rate will push the NPV into the negative range. Similarly, if we try a discount rate of less than 30 percent, the overall NPV of the project will be positive. Though this example has only one positive flow, the above reasoning still implies a single, unique IRR if there are many inflows (but no outflows) after the initial investment.

If the initial cash flow is positive—and if all of the remaining flows are negative—there can only be a single, unique IRR. This result follows from reasoning similar to that above. Both these cases have only one change of sign or flip-flop in the cash flows. Thus, we are safe from multiple IRRs whenever there is only one sign change in the cash flows.

General Rules   The following chart summarizes our rules:

Flows	Number of IRRs	IRR criterion	NPV criterion
First cash flow is negative and all remaining cash flows are positive.	1	Accept if IRR $> r$ Reject if IRR $< r$	Accept if NPV > 0 Reject if NPV < 0
First cash flow is positive and all remaining cash flows are negative.	1	Accept if IRR $< r$ Reject if IRR $> r$	Accept if NPV > 0 Reject if NPV < 0
Some cash flows after first are positive and some cash flows after first are negative.	May be more than 1	No valid IRR	Accept if NPV > 0 Reject if NPV < 0

Note: IRR = Internal rate of return; r = Discount rate; and NPV = Net present value.

Note that the NPV criterion is the same for each of the three cases. In other words, NPV analysis is always appropriate. Conversely, the IRR can be used only in certain cases.

Problems Specific to Mutually Exclusive Projects

As mentioned earlier, two or more projects are mutually exclusive if the firm can, at most, accept only one of them. We now present two problems dealing with the application of the IRR approach to mutually exclusive projects. These two problems are quite similar, though logically distinct.[7]

---

[7]Another problem with IRR occurs either when long-term interest rates differ from short-term rates (that is, when the term structure of interest rates, presented in the Appendix to Chapter 5, is not flat) or when the cash flows from a project differ in risk. In these circumstances, using IRR is inappropriate because no one discount rate is applicable to all the cash flows.

The Scale Problem

A professor we know motivates class discussions on this topic with the statement: "Students, I am prepared to let one of you choose between two mutually exclusive 'business' propositions. Opportunity 1—You give me $1 now and I'll give you $1.50 back at the end of the class period. Opportunity 2—You give me $10 and I'll give you $11 back at the end of the class period. You can only choose one of the two opportunities. And you cannot choose either opportunity more than once. I'll pick the first volunteer."

Which would you choose? The correct answer is opportunity 2.[8] To see this, look at the following chart:

	Cash flow at beginning of class	Cash flow at end of class (90 minutes later)	NPV*	IRR
Opportunity 1	−$1	+$1.50	$0.50	50%
Opportunity 2	−10	+11.00	1.00	10

*We assume a zero rate of interest because the class lasted only 90 minutes. It just seemed like a lot longer.

As we have stressed earlier in the text, one should choose the opportunity with the higher NPV. This is opportunity 2 in the example. Or, as one of the professor's students explained it: "I trust the professor, so I know I'll get my money back. And I have $10 in my pocket right now so I can choose either opportunity. At the end of the class, I'll be able to play four rounds of my favorite electronic game with opportunity 2 and still have my original investment, safe and sound. The profit on opportunity 1 buys only two rounds."

We believe that this business proposition illustrates a defect with the internal rate of return criterion. The basic IRR rule says take opportunity 1, because the IRR is 50 percent. The IRR is only 10 percent for opportunity 2.

Where does IRR go wrong? The problem with IRR is that it ignores issues of scale. While opportunity 1 has a greater IRR, the investment is much smaller. In other words, the high percentage return on opportunity 1 is more than offset by the ability to earn at least a decent return on a much bigger investment under opportunity 2.[9]

Since IRR seems to be misguided here, can we adjust or correct it? We illustrate how in the next example.

■ Example

Jack and Ramona have just purchased the rights to *Corporate Finance: The Motion Picture*. They will produce this major motion picture on either a small budget or a big budget. The estimated cash flows are

	Cash flow at date 0	Cash flow at date 1	NPV @ 25%	IRR
Small budget	−$10 million	$40 million	$22 million	300%
Large budget	− 25 million	65 million	27 million	160%

---

[8] The professor uses real money here. Though many students have done poorly on the professor's exams over the years, no student ever chose opportunity 1. The professor claims that his students are "money players."

[9] A 10-percent return is more than decent over a 90-minute interval!

Because of high risk, a 25-percent discount rate is considered appropriate. Ramona wants to adopt the large budget because the NPV is higher. Jack wants to adopt the small budget because the IRR is higher. Who is right? ■

For the reasons espoused in the classroom example above, NPV is correct. Hence, Ramona is right. However, Jack is very stubborn where IRR is concerned. How can Ramona justify the large budget to Jack using the IRR approach?

This is where incremental IRR comes in. She calculates the incremental cash flows from choosing the large budget instead of the small budget as

	Cash flow at date 0 (in $ million)	Cash flow at date 1 (in $ million)
Incremental cash flows from choosing large budget instead of small budget	$-25 - (-10) = -15$	$65 - 40 = 25$

This chart shows that the incremental cash flows are −$15 million at date 0 and $25 million at date 1. Ramona calculates incremental IRR as

Not same as MIRR

Formula for Calculating the Incremental IRR:

$$0 = -\$15 \text{ million} + \frac{\$25 \text{ million}}{1 + \text{IRR}}$$

→ b/u 2 projects

IRR equals 66.67 percent in this equation. Ramona says that the **incremental IRR** is 66.67 percent. Incremental IRR is the IRR on the incremental investment from choosing the large project instead of the small project.

In addition, we can calculate the NPV of the incremental cash flows:

NPV of Incremental Cash Flows:

$$-\$15 \text{ million} + \frac{\$25 \text{ million}}{1.25} = \$5 \text{ million}$$

We know the small-budget picture would be acceptable as an independent project since its NPV is positive. We want to know whether it is beneficial to invest an additional $15 million in order to make the large-budget picture instead. In other words, is it beneficial to invest an additional $15 million in order to receive an additional $25 million next year? First, the calculations above show the NPV of the incremental investment to be positive. Second, the incremental IRR of 66.67 percent is higher than the discount rate of 25 percent. For both reasons, the incremental investment can be justified. The second reason is what Jack needed to hear to be convinced. Hence, the large-budget movie should be made.

In review, we can handle this example (or any mutually exclusive example) in one of three ways:

1. Compare the NPVs of the two choices. The NPV of the large-budget picture is greater than the NPV of the small-budget picture; that is, $27 million is greater than $22 million.

2. Compare the incremental NPV from making the large-budget picture instead of the small-budget picture. Because incremental NPV equals $5 million, we choose the large-budget picture.

3. Compare the incremental IRR to the discount rate. Because the incremental IRR is 66.67 percent and the discount rate is 25 percent, we take the large-budget picture.

All three approaches always give the same decision. However, we must not compare the IRRs of the two pictures. If we did we would make the wrong choice; that is, we would accept the small-budget picture.

One final note here. Students ask which project should be subtracted from the other in calculating incremental flows. Notice that we are subtracting the smaller project's cash flows from the bigger project's cash flows. This leaves an *outflow* at date 0. We then use the basic IRR rule on the incremental flows.[10]

The Timing Problem

Below we illustrate another, but very similar, problem with using the IRR approach to evaluate mutually exclusive projects.

■ *Example*

Suppose that the Kaufold Corporation has two alternative uses for a warehouse. It can store toxic waste containers (investment A) or electronic equipment (investment B). The cash flows are as follows:

	Year				NPV			
	0	1	2	3	@ 0%	@ 10%	@ 15%	IRR
Investment A	−$10,000	$10,000	$1,000	$ 1,000	$2,000	$669	$ 109	16.04%
Investment B	−10,000	1,000	1,000	12,000	4,000	751	−484	12.94

We find that the NPV of investment B is higher with low discount rates, and the NPV of investment A is higher with high discount rates. This is not surprising if you look closely at the cash flow patterns. The cash flows of A occur early, whereas the cash flows of B occur later. If we assume a high discount rate, we favour investment A because we are implicitly assuming that the early cash flow (for example, $10,000 in year 1) can be reinvested at that rate. Because most of investment B's cash flows occur in year 3, B's value is relatively high with low discount rates. ■

The NPVs and IRRs for both projects appear in Figure 6.6. Project A has an NPV of $2,000 at a discount rate of zero. This is calculated by simply adding up the cash flows without discounting them. Project B has an NPV of $4,000 at the zero rate. However, the NPV of project B declines more rapidly as the discount rate increases than does the NPV of project A. As stated above, this is because B's cash flows occur later. Both projects have the same NPV at a discount rate of 10.55 percent. The IRR for a project is the rate at which the NPV equals zero. Because the NPV of B declines more rapidly, B actually has a lower IRR.

---

[10]Alternatively, we could have subtracted the larger project's cash flows from the smaller project's cash flows. This would have left an *inflow* at date 0, making it necessary to use the IRR rule for financing situations. This would work but we find it more confusing.

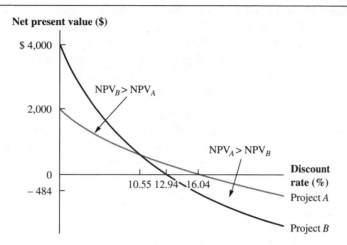

Figure 6.6
Net present value
and the internal
rate of return for
mutually exclusive
projects

As with the movie example presented above, we can select the better project with one of three different methods:

1. *Compare NPVs of the two projects.* Figure 6.6 aids our decision. If the discount rate is below 10.55 percent, one should choose project B because B has a higher NPV. If the rate is above 10.55 percent, one should choose project A because A has a higher NPV.

2. *Compare incremental IRR to discount rate.* Another way of determining that B is a better project is to subtract the cash flows of A from the cash flows of B and then to calculate the IRR. This is the incremental IRR approach we spoke of earlier.

The incremental cash flows are as follows:

						NPV of incremental cash flows		
Year:	0	1	2	3	IRR	@ 0%	@ 10%	@ 15%
B – A	0	–$9,000	0	$11,000	10.55%	$2,000	$83	–$593

This chart shows that the incremental IRR is 10.55 percent. In other words, the NPV on the incremental investment is zero when the discount rate is 10.55 percent. Thus, if the relevant discount rate is below 10.55 percent, project B is preferred to project A. If the relevant discount rate is above 10.55 percent, project A is preferred to project B.[11]

---

[11]In this example, we first showed that the NPVs of the two projects are equal when the discount rate is 10.55 percent. We next showed that the incremental IRR is also 10.55 percent. This is not a coincidence; this equality must always hold. The incremental IRR is the rate that causes the incremental cash flows to have zero NPV. The incremental cash flows have zero NPV when the two projects have the same NPV.

3. *Calculate NPV on incremental cash flows.* Finally, one could calculate the NPV on the incremental cash flows. The chart that appears with the previous method displays these NPVs. We find that the incremental NPV is positive when the discount rate is either 0 percent or 10 percent. The incremental NPV is negative if the discount rate is 15 percent. If the NPV is positive on the incremental flows, one should choose *B*. If the NPV is negative, one should choose *A*.

In summary, the same decision is reached whether one compares the NPVs of the two projects, compares the incremental IRR to the relevant discount rate, or examines the NPV of the incremental cash flows. However, as shown earlier, one should not compare the IRR of project *A* with the IRR of project *B*.

We suggested earlier that one should subtract the cash flows of the smaller project from the cash flows of the bigger project. What do we do here since the two projects have the same initial investment? Our suggestion in this case is to perform the subtraction so that the first nonzero cash flow is negative. In the Kaufold Corporation example, we achieved this by subtracting *A* from *B*. In this way, we can still use the basic IRR rule for evaluating cash flows.

These examples illustrate problems with the IRR approach in evaluating mutually exclusive projects. Both the professor–student example and the motion picture example illustrate the problem that arises when mutually exclusive projects have different initial investments. The Kaufold Corp. example illustrates the problem that arises when mutually exclusive projects have different cash flow timings. When working with mutually exclusive projects, it is not necessary to determine whether it is the scale problem or the timing problem that exists. Very likely both occur in any real world situation. Instead, the practitioner should simply use either an incremental IRR or an NPV approach.

Redeeming Qualities of the IRR

The IRR probably survives because it fills a need that the NPV does not. People seem to want a rule that summarizes the information about a project in a single rate of return. This single rate provides people with a simple way of discussing projects. For example, one manager in a firm might say to another, "Remodeling the clerical wing has a 20-percent IRR."

To their credit, however, companies that employ the IRR approach seem to understand its deficiencies. For example, companies frequently restrict managerial projections of cash flows to be negative at the beginning and strictly positive later. Perhaps, then, the ability of the IRR approach to capture a complex investment project in a single number and the ease of communicating that number explain the survival of the IRR.

A Test

To test your knowledge, consider the following two statements:

1. You must know the discount rate to compute the NPV of a project but you compute the IRR without referring to the discount rate.
2. Hence, the IRR rule is easier to apply than the NPV rule because you don't use the discount rate when applying IRR.

The first statement is true. The discount rate is needed to *compute* NPV. The IRR is *computed* by solving for the rate where the NPV is zero. No mention is made of the discount rate in the mere computation. However, the second statement is false. In order to *apply* IRR, you must compare the internal rate of return with the discount rate. Thus, the discount rate is needed for making a decision under either the NPV or IRR approach.

CONCEPT QUESTIONS

- What is the difference between independent projects and mutually exclusive projects?
- What are two problems with the IRR approach that apply to both independent and mutually exclusive projects?
- What are two additional problems applying only to mutually exclusive projects?

The Profitability Index (PI)   6.7

Another method that is used to evaluate projects is called the **profitability index (PI).** It is the ratio of the present value of the future expected cash flows *after* initial investment divided by the amount of the initial investment. The profitability index can be represented as

$$\text{Profitability index (PI)} = \frac{\text{PV of cash flows subsequent to initial investment}}{\text{Initial investment}}$$

- *Example*

Hiram Finnegan, Inc., applies a 12-percent cost of capital to two investment opportunities.

Project	Cash flows ($000,000)			PV @ 12% of cash flows subsequent to initial investment ($000,000)	Profitability index	NPV @ 12% ($000,000)
	C_0	C_1	C_2			
1	−20	70	10	70.5	3.53	50.5
2	−10	15	40	45.3	4.53	35.3 ■

For example, the profitability index is calculated for project 1 as follows. The present value of the cash flows *after* the initial investment are

$$\$70.5 = \frac{\$70}{1.12} + \frac{\$10}{(1.12)^2} \tag{6.6}$$

The profitability index is calculated by dividing the result of equation (6.6) by the initial investment of $20.[12] This yields

$$3.53 = \frac{\$70.5}{\$20}$$

---

[12]For a "borrowing" type of investment the initial cash flow is an inflow rather than an outlay. In this case, we restate the PI as the present value of the inflows divided by the present value of the outflows.

We consider three possibilities:

1. *Independent projects.* We first assume that we have two independent projects. According to the NPV criterion, both projects should be accepted since NPV is positive in each case. The NPV is positive whenever the profitability index is greater than one. Thus, the *PI decision rule* is

> Accept an independent project if PI > 1.
> Reject if PI < 1.

2. *Mutually exclusive projects.* Let us assume that you can now only accept one project. NPV analysis says accept project 1 because this project has the bigger NPV. Because project 2 has the higher PI, the profitability index leads to the wrong selection.

The problem with the profitability index for mutually exclusive projects is the same as the scale problem with the IRR that we mentioned earlier. Project 2 is smaller than project 1. Because the PI is a ratio, this index misses the fact that project 1 has a larger investment than project 2 has. Thus, like IRR, PI ignores differences of scale for mutually exclusive projects.

However, as with IRR, the flaw with the PI approach can be corrected using incremental analysis. We write the incremental cash flows after subtracting project 2 from project 1 as follows:

Project	Cash flows ($000,000)			PV @ 12% of cash flows subsequent to initial investment ($000,000)	Profitability index	NPV @ 12% ($000,000)
	C_0	C_1	C_2			
1-2	-10	55	-30	25.2	2.52	15.2

Because the profitability index on the incremental cash flows is greater than 1.0, we should choose the bigger project, that is, project 1. This is the same decision we get with the NPV approach.

3. *Capital rationing.* The two cases above implicitly assumed that the firm could always attract enough capital to make any profitable investments. Now we consider the case when a firm does not have enough capital to fund all positive NPV projects. This is the case of **capital rationing.**

Imagine that the firm has a third project, as well as the first two. Project 3 has the following cash flows:

Project	Cash flows ($000,000)			PV @ 12% of cash flows subsequent to initial investment ($000,000)	Profitability index	NPV @ 12% ($000,000)
	C_0	C_1	C_2			
3	-10	-5	60	43.4	4.34	33.4

Further, imagine that the projects of Hiram Finnegan, Inc., are independent, but the firm has only $20 million to invest. Because project 1 has an initial investment of $20 million, the firm cannot select both this project and another one. Conversely, because projects 2 and 3 have initial investments of $10 million each, both these projects can be chosen. In other words, the cash constraint forces the firm to choose either project 1 or projects 2 and 3.

What should the firm do? Individually, projects 2 and 3 have lower NPVs than project 1 has. However, when the NPVs of projects 2 and 3 are added together, they are higher than the NPV of project 1. Thus, common sense dictates that projects 2 and 3 shall be accepted.

What does our conclusion have to say about the NPV rule or the PI rule? In the case of limited funds, we cannot rank projects according to their NPVs. Instead, we should rank them according to the ratio of present value to initial investment. This is the PI rule. Both project 2 and project 3 have higher PI ratios than does project 1. Thus, they should be ranked ahead of project 1 when capital is rationed.[13]

It should be noted that the profitability index does not work if funds are also limited beyond the initial time period. For example, if heavy cash outflows elsewhere in the firm were to occur at date 1, project 3 might need to be rejected. In other words, the profitability index cannot handle capital rationing over multiple time periods.

CONCEPT QUESTIONS

- How does one calculate a project's profitability index?
- How is the profitability index applied to independent projects, mutually exclusive projects, and situations of capital rationing?

The Practice of Capital Budgeting   6.8

A number of surveys have asked large firms what types of investment criteria they actually use. Table 6.4 presents the results of one such survey of the chief financial officers of Canada's largest industrial corporations. Based on the results, the most frequently used capital budgeting technique is some form of discounted cash flow (such as NPV or IRR).

The payback period is the second most popular tool; over 60 percent of the responding firms use it, with only 19 percent using it as the primary method. Other surveys in both Canada and the United States are consistent with these results. The

	Discounted cash flow	Payback period	Average account-ing return	Other (including no method used)
Primary method	65%	19%	9%	7%
Secondary method	24	44	9	23
Total	89%	63%	18%	30%

Table 6.4
Percentage of responding firms using different types of capital budgeting

Note: The number of responding firms is 208.

Source: J. D. Blazouke, I. Carlin, and S. H. Kim, "Current Capital Budgeting Practices in Canada," *CMA Magazine,* March 1988, pp. 51–54.

---

[13]Our approach to PI ranking under capital rationing worked because the initial outlays on the two higher-ranked projects exactly used up the budget of $20 million. If some funds were left over, the PI ranking method could break down. In this case, the solution would be to consider all feasible combinations of projects within the budget and to choose the combination with the highest total NPV.

most common practice is to look at NPV or IRR along with nondiscounted cash flow criteria such as payback and AAR. Given our discussion, this is sound practice.

McCallum argues that improved capital budgeting decisions using NPV can enhance the international competitiveness of Canadian firms.

> Where capital budgeting practice is faulty, production costs inevitably get out of line with competitors'. State-of-the-art workplaces and work processes staffed by employees at the cutting edge of training and motivation are key to cost structures that enable firms to price products to capture and keep healthy market shares profitably.[14]

The use of quantitative techniques in capital budgeting varies with the industry. As one would imagine, firms that are better able to estimate cash flows precisely are more likely to use NPV. For example, estimation of cash flow in certain aspects of the oil business is quite feasible. Because of this, energy-related firms were among the first to use NPV analysis. Conversely, the flows in the motion picture business are very hard to project. The grosses of great hits like *Rocky, Star Wars, ET,* and *Fatal Attraction* were far, far greater than anyone imagined. The big failures like *Heaven's Gate* and *Howard the Duck* were unexpected as well. Consequently, NPV analysis is frowned upon in the movie business.

How does Hollywood perform capital budgeting? The information that a studio uses to accept or reject a movie idea comes from the *pitch.* An independent movie producer schedules an extremely brief meeting with a studio to pitch his or her idea for a movie. Consider the following four paragraphs of quotes concerning the pitch from the thoroughly delightful book, *Reel Power:*

> "They [studio executives] don't want to know too much," says Ron Simpson. "They want to know concept. . . . They want to know what the three-liner is, because they want it to suggest the ad campaign. They want a title. . . . They don't want to hear any esoterica. And if the meeting lasts more than five minutes, they're probably not going to do the project."

> "A guy comes in and says, 'This is my idea: *Jaws* on a spaceship,' " says writer Clay Frohman (*Under Fire*). "And they say, 'Brilliant, fantastic.' Becomes *Alien.* That is *Jaws* on a spaceship, ultimately. . . . And that's it. That's all they want to hear. Their attitude is 'Don't confuse us with the details of the story.' "

> ". . . Some high-concept stories are more appealing to the studios than others. The ideas liked best are sufficiently original that the audience will not feel it has already seen the movie, yet similar enough to past hits to reassure executives wary of anything too far-out. Thus, the frequently used shorthand: It's *Flashdance* in the country (*Footloose*) or *High Noon* in outer space (*Outland*)."

> ". . . One gambit not to use during a pitch," says executive Barbara Boyle, "is to talk about big box-office grosses your story is sure to make. Executives know as well as anyone that it's impossible to predict how much money a movie will make, and declarations to the contrary are considered pure malarkey."[15]

---

[14]J. S. McCallum, "Using Net Present Value in Capital Budgeting," *Business Quarterly,* Summer 1992, pp. 66–70.

[15]Mark Litwak, *Reel Power: The Struggle for Influence and Success in New Hollywood* (New York: William Morrow, 1986), pp. 73, 74, and 77.

Summary and Conclusions 6.9

1. In this chapter we cover different investment decision rules. We evaluate the most popular alternatives to the NPV: the payback period, the accounting rate of return, the internal rate of return, and the profitability index. In doing so, we learn more about the NPV.

2. While we find that the alternatives have some redeeming qualities, when all is said and done, they are not the NPV rule; for those of us in finance, that makes them decidedly second-rate.

3. Of the competitors to NPV, IRR must be ranked above either payback or accounting rate of return. In fact, IRR always reaches the same decision as NPV in the normal case where the initial outflows of an independent investment project are only followed by a series of inflows.

4. We classified the flaws of IRR into two types. First, we considered the general case applying to both independent and mutually exclusive projects. There appeared to be two problems here:

   a. Some projects have cash inflows followed by one or more outflows. The IRR rule is inverted here:

   One should accept when the IRR is *below* the discount rate.

   b. Some projects have a number of changes of sign in their cash flows. Here, there are likely to be multiple internal rates of return. The practitioner must use NPV here.

   Clearly, (*b*) is a bigger problem than (*a*). A new IRR criterion is called for with (*a*). No IRR criterion at all with work under (*b*).

5. Next, we considered the specific problems with the IRR for mutually exclusive projects. We showed that due to differences in either size or timing, the project with the highest IRR need not have the highest NPV. Hence, the IRR rule should not be applied. (Of course, NPV can still be applied.)

   However, we then calculated incremental cash flows. For ease of calculation, we suggested subtracting the cash flows of the smaller project from the cash flows of the larger project. In that way, the incremental initial cash flow is negative.

   One can correctly pick the better of two mutually exclusive projects in three other ways:

   a. Choose the project with the higher NPV.
   b. If the incremental IRR is greater than the discount rate, choose the bigger project.
   c. If the incremental NPV is positive, choose the bigger project.

6. We describe the capital rationing as a case where funds are limited to a fixed dollar amount. With capital rationing the profitability index can be a useful method. Of course, a manager can never go wrong by maximizing NPV.

Key Terms

Payback period rule 162

Average accounting return (AAR)
  166

Basic IRR rule 169

Mutually exclusive investments 171

Profitability index (PI) 181

Discounted payback period rule 165

Internal rate of return (IRR) 169

Independent project 171

Incremental IRR 177

Capital rationing 182

Suggested Readings

For a discussion of what capital budgeting techniques are used by large firms, see:

Harold Bierman. *Implementing Capital Budgeting Techniques.* rev. ed. The Institutional Investor Series in Finance and Financial Management Association Survey and Synthesis Series. Cambridge, Mass.: Ballinger Publishing Company, 1988.

J. D. Blazouske, I. Carlin, and S. H. Kim. "Current Capital Budgeting Practices in Canada," *CMA Magazine,* March 1988, pp. 51–54.

M. Blume, I. Friend, and R. Westerfield. *Impediments to Capital Formation.* Rodney L. White Center for Financial Research Monograph. Philadelphia: The Wharton School, University of Pennsylvania, 1980.

L. Schall and G. Sundem. "Capital Budgeting Methods and Risk: A Further Analysis." *Financial Management* (Spring 1980).

Questions and Problems

6.1 Consider the following projects:

	C_0	C_1	C_2	IRR
A	−$4,000	$2,500	$3,000	23.32%
B	− 2,000	1,200	1,500	21.65%

  a. What is the payback period for each project?

  b. How would the NPV rule rank these projects if the appropriate discount rate is 10 percent?

6.2 The annual, end-of-year, book investment accounts for the machine whose purchase your firm is considering are shown below:

	Purchase date	Year 1	Year 2	Year 3	Year 4
Gross investment	$16,000	$16,000	$16,000	$16,000	$16,000
Less: accumulated depreciation	0	4,000	8,000	12,000	16,000
Net investment	$16,000	$12,000	$ 8,000	$ 4,000	$ 0

If your firm purchases this machine, you can expect it to generate, on average, $4,500 per year in additional income.

a. What is the average accounting return for this machine?

b. What three flaws are inherent in this decision rule?

6.3 Compute the internal rate of return on a project with the following cash flows:

Time	Cash flows
0	−$100.00
1	72.00
2	57.60

6.4 Compute the internal rate of return on a project with the following cash flows:

Time	Cash flows
0	−$1,200
1	1,100
2	242

6.5 Compute the internal rate of return for the cash flows of the following two projects:

	Cash flows	
Time	A	B
0	−$200	−$150
1	200	50
2	800	100
3	−800	150

6.6 Your firm is considering the following two mutually exclusive investment projects: *can't choose both*

	Cash flows ($ thousands)			
Time:	0	1	2	3
Investment				
1	−$130	$78	$78	$ 0
2	−130	0	0	182

a. Calculate the NPV for each project at discount rates of 0 percent, 15 percent, and 25 percent and plot the NPVs in a graph similar to Figure 6.6.

b. Use your graph to find the approximate IRR for each project and verify that these are correct.

c. Now calculate the IRR on the incremental cash flows.

d. Suppose that the cost of capital is 15 percent. Show that the following three methods all give the same recommendation:

i. Comparing NPVs.

ii. Comparing the incremental IRR to the discount rate.

iii. NPV of incremental cash flows.

6.7 Suppose you are offered the following two mutually exclusive projects:

	C_0	C_1
Small	−$100	$200
Big	−10,000	15,000

   a. What are the IRRs of these two projects?

   b. If you are told only the IRRs of the projects, which would you choose?

   c. What did you ignore when you made your choice in part (*b*)?

   d. How is the problem remedied?

   e. Compute the incremental IRR for the projects.

   f. Based on your answer to part (*e*), which project should you choose?

   g. If the appropriate discount rate is 10 percent, what are the NPVs of these projects?

   h. Based on the NPV rule, which project should you choose?

6.8 Define each of the following investment rules. In your definition state the criteria for accepting or rejecting an investment under each rule.

   a. Payback period.

   b. Average accounting return.

   c. Internal rate of return.

   d. Profitability index.

   e. Net present value.

6.9 Atlantic Megaprojects has a contract to build a tunnel connecting two Atlantic provinces. The contract calls for the firm to complete the tunnel in three years with an annual cash outlay of $100 million at the end of years 1 and 2. At the end of the third year, governments will pay Atlantic Megaprojects $260 million. If it wishes, the firm can exercise an option to build the tunnel in just two years by subcontracting part of the work to a government-sponsored entity designed to create employment in the region. Under this option, Atlantic Megaprojects will make a cash payment of $220 million at the end of the first year and will receive $260 million after the second year.

   a. Suppose that Atlantic Megaprojects has a cost of capital of 15 percent. Should the firm subcontract the work?

   b. Now suppose that Atlantic Megaprojects can estimate its cost of capital only up to a range. Over what range of discount rates is subcontracting attractive?

6.10 Reconsider the three projects available to Hiram Finnegan, Inc., in Section 6.7. Suppose that projected price increases cause the period-0 cash flow for project 2 to increase from −$10 to −$20. This is the only change to the data.

   a. Recalculate the NPV and PI for project 2.

   b. Given that the total budget remains at $20 million, what is the best solution? Explain briefly.

CHAPTER 7

Net Present Value and Capital Budgeting

Previous chapters discussed the basics of capital budgeting and the net present value approach. We now want to move beyond these basics into the real world application of these techniques. We want to show you how to use discounted cash flow (DCF) analysis and net present value (NPV) in capital budgeting decisions.

In this chapter, we show how to identify the relevant cash flows of a project, including initial investment outlays, requirements for working capital, and operating cash flows. We look at the effects of depreciation and taxes. We examine the impact of inflation on interest rates and on a project's discount rate, and we show why inflation must be handled consistently in NPV analysis.

Incremental Cash Flows 7.1

Cash Flows—Not Accounting Income

You may not have thought about it, but there is a big difference between corporate finance courses and financial accounting courses. Techniques in corporate finance generally use cash flows, whereas financial accounting generally stresses income or earnings numbers. Certainly, our text has followed this tradition since our net present value techniques discounted cash flows, not earnings. When considering a single project, we discounted the cash flows that the firm receives from the project. When valuing the firm as a whole, we discounted dividends—not earnings—because dividends are the cash flows that an investor receives.

There are many differences between earnings and cash flows. In fact, much of a standard financial accounting course delineates these differences. Because we have no desire to duplicate such course material, we merely discuss one example of the differences. Consider a firm buying a building for $100,000 today. The entire $100,000 is an immediate cash outflow. However, assuming straight-line depreciation over 20 years, only $5,000 (or $100,000/20) is considered an accounting expense in the current year. Current earnings are thereby reduced only by $5,000. The remaining $95,000 is expensed over the following 19 years.

Because the seller of the property demands immediate payment, the cost of the project to the firm at date 0 is $100,000. Thus, the full $100,000 figure should be viewed as an immediate outflow for capital budgeting purposes. This is not merely our opinion but the unanimous verdict of both academics and practitioners.

In addition, it is not enough to use cash flows. In calculating the NPV of a project, only cash flows that are *incremental* to the project should be used. **Incremental cash flows** are the changes in the firm's cash flows that occur as a direct consequence of accepting the project. That is, we are interested in the difference between the cash flows of the firm with and without the project.

The use of incremental cash flows sounds easy enough, but pitfalls abound in the real world. In this section we describe how to avoid some of the pitfalls of determining incremental cash flows.

Sunk Costs

A **sunk cost** is a cost that has already occurred. Because sunk costs are in the past, they cannot be changed by the decision to accept or reject the project. Just as we "let bygones be bygones," we should ignore such costs. Sunk costs are not incremental cash outflows.

▪ *Example*

The General Milk Company is currently evaluating the NPV of establishing a line of chocolate milk. As part of the evaluation the company had paid a consulting firm $100,000 to perform a test marketing analysis. The expenditure was made last year. Is this cost relevant for the capital budgeting decision now confronting the management of General Milk Company?

The answer is no. The $100,000 is not recoverable, so the $100,000 expenditure is a sunk cost, or spilled milk. Of course, the decision to spend $100,000 for a marketing analysis was a capital budgeting decision itself and was perfectly relevant *before* it was sunk. Our point is that once the company incurred the expense, the cost became irrelevant for any future decision. ▪

Opportunity Costs

Your firm may have an asset that it is considering selling, leasing, or employing elsewhere in the business. If the asset is used in a new project, potential revenues from alternative uses are lost. These lost revenues can meaningfully be viewed as costs. They are called **opportunity costs** because, by taking the project, the firm forgoes other opportunities for using the assets.

▪ *Example*

Suppose the Pacific Trading Company has an empty warehouse in Vancouver that can be used to store a new line of electronic pinball machines. The company hopes to market the machines to affluent West Coast consumers. Should the cost of the warehouse and land be included in the costs associated with introducing a new line of electronic pinball machines?

The answer is yes. The use of a warehouse is not free; it has an opportunity cost. The cost is the cash that could be raised by the company if the decision to market the electronic pinball machines were rejected and the warehouse and land were put to some other use (or sold). If so, the NPV of the alternative uses becomes an opportunity cost of the decision to sell electronic pinball machines. ▪

Side Effects

Another difficulty in determining incremental cash flows comes from the side effects of the proposed project on other parts of the firm. The most important side effect is **erosion.** Erosion is the cash flow transferred to a new project from customers and sales of other products of the firm.

Suppose the Innovative Motors Corporation (IMC) is determining the NPV of a new convertible sports car. Some of the customers who would purchase the car are potential owners of IMC's compact sedan. Are all sales and profits from the new convertible sports car incremental?

The answer is no because some of the cash flow represents transfers from other elements of IMC's product line. This is erosion, which must be included in the NPV calculation. Without taking erosion into account, IMC might erroneously calculate the NPV of the sports car to be, say, $100 million. If IMC's managers recognized that half the customers are transfers from the sedan and that lost sedan sales have an NPV of −$150 million, they would see that the true NPV is −$50 million (or $100 million − $150 million).

deduct lost sales at other pt of sales.

CONCEPT QUESTIONS

- What are the three difficulties in determining incremental cash flows?
- Define sunk costs, opportunity costs, and side effects.

The Majestic Mulch and Compost Company: An Example   7.2

We next consider the example of a proposed investment in machinery and related items. Our example involves the Majestic Mulch and Compost Company (MMCC) and power mulching tools.

The MMCC, originally established in 1988 to make composting equipment, is now a leading producer of composters. In 1990 the company introduced "Friends of Grass," its first line of high-performance composters. The MMCC management has sought opportunities in whatever businesses seem to have some potential for cash flow. In 1993 World B. Clean, vice president of the MMCC, identified another segment of the compost market that looked promising and that he felt was not adequately served by larger manufacturers. That market was for power mulching tools, and he believed a large number of composters valued a high-performance mulcher to aid in composting. He also believed that it would be difficult for competitors to take advantage of the opportunity because of MMCC's cost advantages and because of its highly developed marketing skills.

As a result, in late 1994 MMCC decided to evaluate the marketing potential of power mulching tools. MMCC sent a questionnaire to consumers in three markets: Vancouver, Toronto, and Montreal. The results of the three questionnaires were much better than expected and supported the conclusion that the power mulching tools could achieve a 10- to 15-percent share of the market. Of course, some people at MMCC complained about the cost of the test marketing, which was $250,000. However, Clean argued that it was a sunk cost and should not be included in project evaluation.

In any case, the MMCC is now considering investing in a machine to produce power mulching tools. The power mulchers would be produced in a building owned by the firm and located outside Prince George, B.C. It is currently vacant, and has no resale value due to its location. Working with his staff, Clean is preparing an analysis of the proposed new product. He summarizes his assumptions as follows: The cost of the tool making machine is $800,000. The machine has an estimated market value at the end of eight years of $150,000. Production by year during the eight-year life of the machine is expected to be as follows: 6,000 units, 9,000 units, 12,000 units, 13,000 units, 12,000 units, 10,000 units, 8,000 units, and 6,000 units. The price of power mulchers in the first year will be $100. The power mulching tool market is highly competitive, so Clean believes that the price of power mulchers will increase only 2 percent per year, as compared to the anticipated general inflation rate of 5 percent. Conversely, the materials used to produce power mulchers are becoming more expensive. Because of this, variable production cash outflows are expected to grow 5 percent per year. First-year variable production costs will be $64 per unit, and fixed production costs will be $50,000 each year. The tax rate is 40 percent.

Net working capital is defined as the difference between current assets and current liabilities. Clean finds that the firm must maintain an investment in working capital. Like any manufacturing firm, it will purchase raw materials before production and sale, giving rise to an investment in inventory. It will maintain cash as a buffer against unforeseen expenditures. Its credit sales will generate accounts receivable. Management believes that the investment in the different items of working capital totals $40,000 in year 0, stays at 15 percent of sales at the end of each year, and falls to $0 by the project's end. In other words, the investment in working capital is completely recovered by the end of the project's life.

Projections based on these assumptions and Clean's analysis appear in Tables 7.1 through 7.4. In these tables all cash flows are assumed to occur at the *end* of the year. Because of the large amount of data in these tables, it is important to see how the tables are related. Table 7.1 shows the basic data for both investment and income. Supplementary schedules on operations and CCA, as presented in Tables 7.2 and 7.3, help explain where the numbers in Table 7.1 come from. Our goal is to obtain projections of cash flow. The data in Table 7.1 are all that is needed to calculate the relevant cash flows, as shown in Table 7.4.

An Analysis of the Project

Investments

The investment outlays required for the project are summarized in the bottom segment of Table 7.1. They consist of two parts:[1]

1. *The power mulching tool machine.* The purchase requires a cash outflow of $800,000 at year 0. The firm realizes a cash inflow when the machine is sold in year 8. These cash flows are shown in lines 9 and 10 of Table 7.1.

---

[1] If the vacant building had a resale value, this would be included as a third part to this section. Recall from section 7.1 the discussion on opportunity costs. A positive resale value would be a cash outflow in year 0.

Table 7.1 The worksheet for cash flows of the MMCC*

	Year 0	Year 1	Year 2	Year 3	Year 4	Year 5	Year 6	Year 7	Year 8
			I. Income						
(1) Sales revenues		$600,000	$918,000	$1,248,480	$1,379,570	$1,298,919	$1,104,081	$900,930	$689,211
(2) Operating costs		434,000	654,800	896,720	1,013,144	983,509	866,820	736,129	590,327
(3) CCA		80,000	144,000	115,200	92,160	73,728	58,982	47,186	37,749
(4) EBIT		86,000	119,200	236,560	274,266	241,682	178,278	117,615	61,136
(5) Taxes		34,400	47,680	94,624	109,707	96,673	71,311	47,046	24,454
(6) Net income		51,600	71,520	141,936	164,560	145,009	106,967	70,569	36,682
			II. Investments						
(7) NWC (end of year)	$ 40,000	$ 90,000	$137,700	$ 187,272	$ 206,936	$ 194,838	$ 165,612	$135,139	$ 0
(8) Change in NWC†	($ 40,000)	($ 50,000)	($ 47,700)	($ 49,572)	($ 19,664)	$ 12,098	$ 29,226	$ 30,473	$135,139
(9) Equipment†	($800,000)								
(10) Aftertax salvage									$150,000
(11) Investment cash flow	($840,000)	($ 50,000)	($ 47,700)	($ 49,572)	($ 19,664)	$ 12,098	$ 29,226	$ 30,473	$285,139

*All cash flows occur at the end of the year.

†A negative change in net working capital or equipment represents a cash outflow for the company.

Table 7.2 Operating revenues and costs of the MMCC

(1) Year	(2) Production	(3) Price*	(4) Sales revenues	(5) Cost per unit†	(6) Variable costs	(7) Fixed costs	(8) Operating costs
1	6,000	$100.00	$ 600,000	$64.00	$384,000	$50,000	$ 434,000
2	9,000	102.00	918,000	67.20	604,800	50,000	654,800
3	12,000	104.04	1,248,480	70.56	846,720	50,000	896,720
4	13,000	106.12	1,379,570	74.09	963,144	50,000	1,013,144
5	12,000	108.24	1,298,919	77.79	933,509	50,000	983,509
6	10,000	110.41	1,104,081	81.68	816,820	50,000	866,820
7	8,000	112.62	900,930	85.77	686,129	50,000	736,129
8	6,000	114.87	689,211	90.05	540,327	50,000	590,327

*Prices rise 2 percent a year.

†Unit costs rise 5 percent a year.

2. *The investment in working capital.* Required working capital appears in line
7. Working capital rises over the early years of the project as expansion
occurs. However, all working capital is assumed to be recovered at the end,
a common assumption in capital budgeting. In other words, all inventory is
sold by the end, the cash balance maintained as a buffer is liquidated, and
all accounts receivable are collected. Increases in working capital in the
early years must be funded by cash generated elsewhere in the firm. Hence,
these increases are viewed as cash *outflows.* Conversely, decreases in
working capital in the later years are viewed as cash inflows. All of these
cash flows are presented in line 8. A more complete discussion of working
capital is provided later in this section. The total cash flow from the above
two investments is shown in line 11.

[handwritten: cca capital cost allowance → depreciation for tax purposes]

[handwritten: Ucc]

Table 7.3
Annual CCA,
power mulcher
project (class 8, 20
percent rate)

Year	Beginning UCC	CCA	Ending UCC
1	$400,000	$ 80,000	$320,000
2	720,000	144,000	576,000
3	576,000	115,200	460,800
4	460,800	92,160	368,640
5	368,640	73,728	294,912
6	294,912	58,982	235,930
7	235,930	47,186	188,744
8	188,744	37,749	150,995

[handwritten notes: 800,000; 160k; 640; UCC undepreciated capital cost]

Table 7.4
Incremental cash flows for the MMCC

	Year 0	Year 1	Year 2	Year 3	Year 4	Year 5	Year 6	Year 7	Year 8
(1) Sales revenues [line 1, Table 7.1]		$600,000	$918,000	$1,248,480	$1,379,570	$1,298,919	$1,104,081	$900,930	$689,211
(2) Operating costs [line 2, Table 7.1]		434,000	654,800	896,720	1,013,144	983,509	866,820	736,129	590,327
(3) Taxes [line 5, Table 7.1]		34,400	47,680	94,624	109,707	96,673	71,311	47,046	24,454
(4) Operating cash flow [(1) – (2) – (3)]		131,600	215,520	257,136	256,720	218,737	165,949	117,755	74,430
(5) Investment cash flow	($840,000)	(50,000)	(47,700)	(49,572)	(19,664)	12,098	29,226	30,473	285,139
(6) Total project cash flow	($840,000)	$ 81,600	$167,820	$ 207,564	$ 237,056	$ 230,835	$ 195,175	$148,228	$359,570

NPV @ 4%	$ 500,135
NPV @ 10%	$ 188,042
NPV @ 15%	$ 2,280
NPV @ 20%	($137,896)

[handwritten: lost profits]

Income, Taxes, and Operating Cash Flow

Next, the determination of income and operating cash flow is presented in the top segment of Table 7.1. While we are ultimately interested in cash flow—not income—we need the income calculation in order to determine taxes. Lines 1 and 2 of Table 7.1 show sales revenues and operating costs, respectively. The projections in these lines are based on the sales revenues and operating costs computed in columns 4 and 8 of Table 7.2. The estimates of revenues and costs follow from assumptions made by the corporate planning staff at MMCC. In other words, the estimates critically depend on the fact that product prices are projected to increase at 2 percent per year and variable costs are projected to increase at 5 percent per year.

Capital cost allowance (depreciation for tax purposes and abbreviated as CCA) of the $800,000 capital investment is based on the amount allowed by Revenue Canada.[2] CCA calculations are shown in Table 7.3 and are based on a class 8, 20 percent rate. The column labelled CCA is reproduced in line 3 of Table 7.1. Earnings before interest and taxes (EBIT) is calculated in line 4 of Table 7.1. Taxes are provided in line 5 of this table, and net income is calculated in line 6.

---

[2] CCA rules are discussed in detail in the appendix to this chapter.

Project Cash Flow

Project cash flow is finally determined in Table 7.4. It consists of operating cash flow and investment cash flow. Operating cash flow is determined by subtracting operating costs and taxes from sales revenues as shown in lines 1 through 4 in Table 7.4. Adding investment cash flow from line 11 in Table 7.1 gives total project cash flow on line 6 in Table 7.4.

Net Present Value

It is possible to calculate the NPV of the MMCC power mulcher tool project from these cash flows. As can be seen at the bottom of Table 7.4, the NPV is $188,042 if 10 percent is the appropriate discount rate and −$137,896 if 20 percent is the appropriate discount rate. If the discount rate is 15.07 percent, the project will have a zero NPV. In other words, the project's internal rate of return is 15.07 percent. If the discount rate of the MMCC power mulcher tool project is above 15.07 percent, it should not be accepted because its NPV would be negative.

Which Set of Books?

It should be noted that the firm's management generally keeps two sets of books, one for Revenue Canada (called the *tax books*) and another for its annual report (called the *shareholders' books*). The tax books follow the rules of Revenue Canada. The shareholders' books follow the rules of the *Canadian Institute of Chartered Accountants (CICA)*, the governing body in accounting. The two sets of rules differ widely in certain areas. For example, deductible expenses as calculated according to CICA rules are often different from the calculations required by Revenue Canada.

Such differences result from the different purposes of the two sets of rules. CICA rules seek to represent the accounting income of the firm according to Generally Accepted Accounting Principles. Tax rules govern the calculation of corporate income tax. Because tax rules have evolved through the political process, they reflect a balance between government's desire to collect maximum revenues and its wish to promote job creation by stimulating investment. For example, CCA rules reflect the motive of economic stimulus by generally allowing faster writedowns of investment than is standard under CICA rules. The appendix gives a synopsis of the Revenue Canada rules on CCA.

Which of the two sets of rules on depreciation do we want in order to create the previous tables for MMCC? Clearly, we're interested in the Revenue Canada rules. Our purpose is to determine net cash flow, and tax payments are a cash outflow. The CICA regulations determine the calculation of accounting income, not cash flow.

A Note on Net Working Capital

The investment in net working capital is an important part of any capital budgeting analysis. While we explicitly considered net working capital in line 7 (Table 7.1) as 15 percent of sales, students may be wondering where such numbers come from. An investment in net working capital arises whenever (1) raw materials and other inventory are purchased prior to the sale of finished goods, (2) cash is kept in the project as a buffer against unexpected expenditures, and (3) credit sales are made, generating accounts receivable rather than cash. (The investment in net working capital is offset to the extent that purchases are made on credit, that is, when accounts payable are created.) This investment in net working capital represents a cash outflow, because cash generated elsewhere in the firm is tied up in the project.

To see how the investment in net working capital is built from its component parts, we focus on year 1. We see in Table 7.1 that MMCC's managers predict sales in year 1 to be $600,000 and operating costs to be $434,000. If both the sales and costs were cash transactions, the firm would receive $166,000 (or $600,000 − $434,000).

However, the managers

1. Forecast that $100,000 of the sales will be on credit, implying that cash receipts in year 1 will be only $500,000 (or $600,000 − $100,000). The accounts receivable of $100,000 will be collected in year 2.

2. Believe that they can defer payment on $40,000 of the $434,000 of costs, implying that cash disbursements will be only $394,000 (or $434,000 − $40,000). Of course, MMCC will pay off the $40,000 of accounts payable in year 2.

3. Decide that inventory of $25,000 should be left on hand at year 1 to avoid *stockouts* (that is, running out of inventory) and other contingencies.

4. Decide that cash of $5,000 should be earmarked for the project at year 1 to avoid running out of cash.

Thus, net working capital in year 1 is

$$\underset{\substack{\text{Accounts}\\\text{receivable}}}{\$100,000} - \underset{\substack{\text{Accounts}\\\text{payable}}}{\$40,000} + \underset{\text{Inventory}}{\$25,000} + \underset{\text{Cash}}{\$5,000} = \underset{\substack{\text{Net working}\\\text{capital}}}{\$90,000}$$

Because $90,000 of cash generated elsewhere in the firm must be used to offset this requirement for net working capital, MMCC's managers correctly view the investment in net working capital as a cash outflow of the project. As the project grows over time, needs for net working capital increase. Changes in net working capital from year to year represent further cash flows, as indicated by the negative numbers for the first few years of line 8 of Table 7.1. However, in the declining years of the project, net working capital is reduced—ultimately to zero. That is, accounts receivable are finally collected, the project's cash buffer is returned to the rest of the corporation, and all remaining inventory is sold off. This frees up cash in the later years, as indicated by positive numbers in years 5, 6, 7, and 8 on line 8.

Typically, corporate worksheets (such as Table 7.1) treat net working capital as a whole. The individual components of net working capital (receivables, inventory, and so on) do not generally appear in the worksheets. However, the reader should remember that the net working capital numbers in the worksheets are not pulled out of thin air. Rather, they result from a meticulous forecast of the components, just as we illustrated for year 1.

Interest Expense

It may have bothered you that interest expense was ignored in the MMCC example. After all, many projects are at least partially financed with debt, particularly a power mulcher tool machine that is likely to increase the debt capacity of the firm. As it turns out, our approach of assuming no debt financing is rather standard in the real world. Firms typically calculate a project's cash flows under the assumption that the project is only financed with equity. Any adjustments for debt financing are reflected in the discount rate, not the cash flows. The treatment of debt in capital budgeting will be covered in depth later in the text. Suffice it to say at this time that the full ramifications of debt financing are well beyond our current discussion.

CONCEPT QUESTIONS

- What are the items leading to cash flow in any year?
- Why did we determine income when NPV analysis discounts cash flows, not income?
- Why is net working capital viewed as a cash outflow?

Inflation and Capital Budgeting   7.3

Inflation is an important fact of economic life, and it must be considered in capital budgeting. We begin by considering the relationship between interest rates and *inflation*.

Interest Rates and Inflation

Suppose that the one-year interest rate that a financial institution pays is 10 percent. This means that an individual who deposits $1,000 at date 0 will get $1,100 (or $1,000 × 1.10) in one year. While 10 percent may seem like a handsome return, one can only put it in perspective after examining the rate of inflation.

Suppose that the rate of inflation is 6 percent over the year and it affects all goods equally. For example, a restaurant that charges $1.00 for a hamburger at date 0 charges $1.06 for the same hamburger at the end of the year. You can use your $1,000 to buy 1,000 hamburgers at date 0. Alternatively, if you put all of your money in the bank, you can buy 1,038 (or $1,100 / $1.06) hamburgers at date 1. Thus, you are only able to increase your hamburger consumption by 3.8 percent by lending to the bank. Since the prices of all goods rise at this 6-percent rate, lending lets you increase your consumption of any single good or any combination of goods by only 3.8 percent. Thus, 3.8 percent is what you are *really* earning through your savings account, after adjusting for inflation. Economists refer to the 3.8-percent number as the **real interest rate.** Economists refer to the 10-percent rate as the **nominal interest rate** or simply the *interest rate*. The above discussion is illustrated in Figure 7.1.

We have used an example with a specific nominal interest rate and a specific inflation rate. In general, the formula relating real and nominal cash flows can be written as

$$1 + \text{Nominal interest rate} = (1 + \text{Real interest rate}) \times (1 + \text{Inflation rate})$$

Figure 7.1
Calculation of real
rate of interest

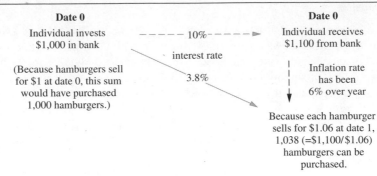

Hamburger is used as illustrative good. 1,038 hamburgers can be purchased on
date 1 instead of 1,000 hamburgers at date 0. Real interest rate = 1,038/1,000 − 1
= 3.8%.

Rearranging terms, we have

$$\text{Real interest rate} = \frac{1 + \text{Nominal interest rate}}{1 + \text{Inflation rate}} - 1 \qquad (7.1)$$

The formula indicates that the real interest rate in our example is 3.8 percent
(1.10 /1.06 − 1).

This formula determines the real interest rate precisely. The following formula is
an approximation:

$$\text{Real interest rate} \approx \text{Nominal interest rate} - \text{Inflation rate} \qquad (7.2)$$

The symbol $\approx$ indicates that the equation is approximately true. This latter formula
calculates the real rate in our example as

$$4\% = 10\% - 6\%$$

The student should be aware that, while equation (7.2) may seem more intuitive than
equation (7.1), (7.2) is only an approximation. The recent long-term real and nominal
interest rates for several countries are illustrated in Figure 7.2.[3]

Cash Flow and Inflation

The above analysis defines two types of interest rates (nominal rates and real rates) and
relates them through equation (7.1). Capital budgeting requires data on cash flows as
well as on interest rates. Like interest rates, cash flows can be expressed in either
nominal or real terms.

A cash flow is expressed in nominal terms if the actual dollars to be received (or
paid out) are given. A cash flow is expressed in real terms if the current or date 0
purchasing power of the cash flow is given.

---

[3] Chapter 31 discusses interest rate parity, which explains why nominal rates differ across countries.

Figure 7.2 Real or nominal long-term interest rates for Canada and four other countries, 1987–1993

*Deflated by rise in CPI over previous 12 months.

Sources: *Statistics Canada,* Canadian Economic Observer, June, 1993; and *The Economist* June 5, 1993.

■ *Example*

Ottawa Publishing has just purchased the rights to the next book by famed romantic novelist, Barbara Musk. Still unwritten, the book should be available to the public in four years. Currently, romantic novels sell for $10.00 in paperback. The publishers believe that inflation will be 6 percent a year over the next four years. Since romantic novels are so popular, the publishers anticipate that their prices will rise about

2 percent per year more than the inflation rate over the next four years. Not wanting to overprice, Ottawa Publishing anticipates pricing the novel at $13.60 [or $(1.08)^4 \times \$10.00$] four years from now. The firm anticipates selling 100,000 copies.

The expected cash flow in the fourth year of $1.36 million (or $13.60 \times 100,000$) is a **nominal cash flow** because the firm expects to receive $1.36 million at that time. In other words, a nominal cash flow reflects the actual dollars to be received in the future.

We determine the purchasing power of $1.36 million in four years as

$$\$1.08 \text{ million} = \frac{\$1.36 \text{ million}}{(1.06)^4}$$

The figure $1.08 million is a **real cash flow** since it is expressed in terms of date 0 purchasing power. Extending our hamburger example, the $1.36 million to be received in four years will only buy 1.08 million hamburgers because the price of a hamburger will rise from $1 to $1.26 [or $\$1 \times (1.06)^4$] over the period. ∎

∎ *Example*

Hull Booksellers, a customer of Ottawa Publishing, recently made leasehold improvements to its store for $2,000,000 to be depreciated by the straight-line method over five years. This implies yearly depreciation of $400,000 (or $2,000,000/5). Is this $400,000 figure a real or nominal quantity?

Depreciation is a *nominal quantity* because $400,000 is the actual tax deduction over each of the next four years. Depreciation becomes a real quantity if it is adjusted for purchasing power.[4] Hence, $316,837 [or $400,000/(1.06)^4$] is depreciation in the fourth year, expressed as a real quantity. ∎

Discounting: Nominal or Real?

Our previous discussion showed that interest rates can be expressed in either nominal or real terms. Similarly, cash flows can be expressed in either nominal or real terms. Given these choices, how should one express interest rates and cash flows when performing capital budgeting?

Financial practitioners correctly stress the need to maintain *consistency* between cash flows and discount rates. That is,

Nominal cash flows must be discounted at the *nominal* rate.

Real cash flows must be discounted at the *real* rate.

∎ *Example*

Shields Electric forecasts the following nominal cash flows on a particular project:

Date:	0	1	2
Cash flow	−$1,000	$600	$650

The nominal interest rate is 14 percent, and the inflation rate is forecast to be 5 percent. What is the value of the project?

---

[4] We use the word *quantity*, not *cash flow*, because it is the CCA tax shield, not the depreciation itself, that is a cash flow. Tax shields are defined later in this chapter.

Using Nominal Quantities   The NPV can be calculated as

$$\$26.47 = -\$1,000 + \frac{\$600}{1.14} + \frac{\$650}{(1.14)^2}$$

The project should be accepted.

Using Real Quantities   The real cash flows are

Date:	0	1	2
Cash flow	−$1,000	$571.43 $\left(\dfrac{\$600}{1.05}\right)$	$589.57 $\left(\dfrac{\$650}{1.05^2}\right)$

The real interest rate is 8.57143 percent (1.14/1.05 − 1).
   The NPV can be calculated as

$$\$26.47 = -\$1,000 + \frac{\$571.43}{1.0857143} + \frac{\$589.57}{(1.0857143)^2}$$

The NPV is the same when cash flows are expressed in real quantities. It must always be the case that the NPV is the same under the two different approaches.
   Because both approaches always yield the same result, which one should be used? Students will be happy to learn the following rule: Use the approach that is simpler. In the Shields Electric case, nominal quantities produce a simpler calculation because the problem gave us nominal cash flows to begin with. ∎

   In other cases it is easier to work with real cash flows. Firms will often forecast unit sales per year. They can easily convert these forecasts to real quantities by multiplying expected unit sales each year by the product price at date 0. (This assumes that the price of the product rises at exactly the rate of inflation.) Once a real discount rate is selected, NPV can easily be calculated from real quantities. In this case, nominal quantities complicate the example, because the extra step of converting all real cash flows to nominal cash flows must be taken.

CONCEPT QUESTIONS

■ What is the difference between the nominal and the real interest rate?
■ What is the difference between nominal and real cash flows?

A Capital Budgeting Simplification   7.4

Restating Operating Cash Flows

The MMCC example considered both investment outlays and operating cash flows. It is worthwhile to focus more closely on operating cash flows. In the MMCC example, we calculated operating cash flows after taxes as

Operating cash flow after taxes = Revenues − Expenses − Taxes   (7.3)

Taxes can be rewritten as

$$\text{Taxes} = T_c\,[\text{Revenues} - \text{Expenses} - \text{CCA}] \tag{7.4}$$

where T_c is the corporate tax rate. The terms in the brackets in (7.4) represent taxable income.

Substituting (7.4) for Taxes in (7.3), we can rewrite cash flow as

Operating
cash flow $= \text{Revenues} - \text{Expenses} - T_c\,[\text{Revenues} - \text{Expenses} - \text{CCA}]$
after taxes

The above equation easily simplifies into

| Operating cash flow after taxes | $=$ | Revenues $(1 - T_c)$ After-tax revenues | $-$ Expenses $(1 - T_c)$ After-tax expenses | $+$ $T_c\,\text{CCA}$ Tax shield on CCA | (7.5) |

Equation (7.5) states that operating cash flow after taxes is equal to after-tax revenues minus after-tax expenses plus the **tax shield on CCA.** Note that the coefficient on both revenues and expenses is $(1 - T_c)$ while the coefficient on CCA is T_c. As we will see, equation (7.5) is very important for at least two reasons.

First, equation (7.5) can answer the following questions on marginal contributions to cash flow:

1. How much will after-tax cash flow increase if revenues rise by $1? The formula tells us the answer must be $1 × (1 − T_c). If T_c equals 40 percent, we have $0.60 (or $1 − $0.40).
2. How much will after-tax cash flow decrease if costs rise by $1? The formula tells us the answer must be −$1 × (1 − T_c). If T_c equals 40 percent, we have −$0.60.
3. How much will after-tax cash flow increase for each dollar of CCA? The rise is $1 × T_c. Thus, a dollar of CCA produces a CCA tax shield of $1 × T_c. If T_c equals 40 percent, a dollar of CCA increases after-tax cash flow by $0.40.

Note that the coefficient of $(1 - T_c)$ applies to questions (1) and (2), but the coefficient of T_c applies to question (3).

Second, equation (7.5) can help us perform capital budgeting more efficiently. This benefit is best seen through an example.

Applying the Tax Shield Approach to the Majestic Mulch and Compost Company Project

If you look back over our analysis of MMCC you will see that most of the number crunching involved finding CCA, EBIT, and net income figures. The tax shield approach has the potential to save us considerable time. To realize that potential, we do the calculations in a different order from Table 7.4. Instead of adding the cash flow components down the columns for each year and finding the present value of the total

Table 7.5 Tax shield solution, power mulcher project

	Year 0	Year 1	Year 2	Year 3	Year 4	Year 5	Year 6	Year 7	Year 8
(1) $(R - E)(1 - T_c)$		$99,600	$157,920	$211,056	$219,856	$189,246	$142,356	$98,881	$59,331
(2) Changes in NWC	($40,000)	(50,000)	(47,700)	(49,572)	(19,664)	12,098	29,226	30,473	135,139
(3) Equipment expenditure:	(800,000)								150,000
Totals									
PV of $(R - E)(1 - T_c)$	$682,696								
PV of changes in NWC	(89,100)								
PV of equipment expenditure	(750,965)								
PV of CCA tax shield	159,649								
NPV	$2,280								

cash flows, we find the present values of each source of cash flows and add the present values. To find the present values we use a discount rate of 15 percent.

To begin, it will be helpful to define the following:

$$
\begin{aligned}
\text{OCF} &= \text{Operating cash flow} \\
R &= \text{Revenues} \\
E &= \text{Expenses (operating costs)} \\
D &= \text{Depreciation for tax purposes,[5] i.e., CCA} \\
T_c &= \text{Corporate tax rate}
\end{aligned}
$$

The first source of cash flow is $(R-E)(1-T_c)$ as shown for each year on the first line of Table 7.5. The figure for the first year is $99,600. (The numbers come from Table 7.1.)

$$
\begin{aligned}
(R - E)(1 - T_c) &= (600,000 - 434,000)(1 - .40) \\
&= 99,600
\end{aligned}
$$

Calculating the present value of the $99,600 for the first year, and adding the present values of the other $(R - E)(1 - T_c)$ figures in Table 7.5 gives a total present value for this source of $682,696 as seen in the lower part of Table 7.5.

The second term is the tax shield on CCA for the first year. Table 7.6 reproduces the first year's tax shield of $32,000 along with the corresponding tax shields for each year. The total present value of the CCA tax shield is shown as $159,649.

The changes in net working capital and equipment expenditure are the same as in Table 7.4. Their present values are shown in the lower part of Table 7.5. The NPV is the sum of the present values of the four sources of cash flow. The answer, $2,280, is identical to what we found in Table 7.4 for a discount rate of 15 percent.

Present Value of the Tax Shield on CCA

Further time savings are possible by using a formula that replaces the detailed calculation of yearly CCA. The formula is based on the idea that tax shields from CCA

---

[5] In this discussion we use the terms *depreciation* and *CCA* interchangably.

Table 7.6
PV of tax shield
on CCA

Year	CCA	.40 × CCA	PV @ 15 percent
1	$ 80,000	$32,000	$27,826
2	144,000	57,600	43,554
3	115,200	46,080	30,298
4	92,160	36,864	21,077
5	73,728	29,491	14,662
6	58,982	23,593	10,200
7	47,186	18,874	7,096
8	37,749	15,099	4,936
		PV of tax shield on CCA	$159,649

continue in perpetuity as long as there are assets remaining in the CCA class.[6] To calculate the present value of the tax shield on CCA, we first find the present value of an infinite stream of tax shields abstracting from two practical implications: the 50-percent rule for CCA and disposal of the asset. We then adjust the formula.

C = Total capital cost of the asset which is added to the pool
d = CCA rate for the asset class
T_c = Company's marginal tax rate
k = Discount rate
S = Salvage or disposal value of the asset
n = Asset life in years

We can use the growing perpetuity formula from Chapter 4 (equation 4.10) to derive the present value of the CCA tax shield. Recall that when cash flows grow at a constant rate g, the present value of the perpetuity at discount rate k is

$$PV = \frac{1\text{st payment}}{k - g}$$

Since we are temporarily ignoring the half-year rule, the growth rate in CCA payments is equal to $(-d)$, the CCA rate. Since CCA declines over time as the depreciable base (CC) reduces, the growth rate is negative. For example, in Table 7.6

$$CCA_3 = CCA_2 (1 + (-d))$$
$$= 144,000 (1 + (-.20))$$
$$= 144,000 (.8) = 115,200$$

Given the growth rate as $(-d)$, we need the first payment to complete the formula. This is the first year's tax shield calculating the CCA at rate d on the total cost of the asset added to the depreciation pool, C, and then multiplying by the tax rate, T_c.

1st payment = CdT_c

---

[6] Strictly speaking, the UCC for a class remains positive as long as there are physical assets in the class and the proceeds from disposal of assets are less than total UCC for the class.

We can now complete the formula.

$$\text{PV (CCA tax shield)} = \frac{\text{1st payment}}{k - g}$$

$$= \frac{CdT_c}{k - (-d)}$$

$$= \frac{CdT_c}{k + d}$$

The next step is to extend the formula to adjust for Revenue Canada's 50-percent rule. This rule states that a firm must add one-half of the incremental capital cost of a new project in year 1 and the other half in year 2. The result is that we now calculate present value of the tax shield in two parts. The present value of the stream starting the first year is simply one-half of the original value:

$$\text{PV of 1st half} = 1/2 \frac{CdT_c}{k + d}$$

The PV of the second half (deferred one year) is the same quantity (bracketed term below) discounted back to time zero. The total present value of the tax shield on CCA under the 50-percent rule is the sum of the two present values.

$$\text{PV tax shield on CCA} = 1/2 \, CdT_c + \frac{[1/2 \, CdT_c]}{[k + d]}(1 + k)$$

With a little algebra we can simplify the formula to

$$\text{PV} = \frac{1/2 \, CdT_c}{k + d}[1 + 1/(1 + k)] = \frac{1/2 \, CdT_c}{k + d}\left[\frac{1 + k + 1}{1 + k}\right]$$

$$= \frac{CdT_c \, [1 + .5k]}{k + d \, [1 + k]}$$

The final adjustment for salvage value begins with the present value in the salvage year, n, of future tax shields beginning in year $n + 1$.

$$\frac{SdT_c}{k + d}$$

We discount this figure back to today and subtract it to get the complete formula.[7]

$$\text{PV tax shield on CCA} = \frac{[CdT_c]}{k + d} \times \frac{[1 + .5k]}{1 + k} - \frac{SdT_c}{k + d} \times \frac{1}{(1 + k)^n} \qquad (7.6)$$

Using the first part of (7.6), the present value of the tax shield on MMCC's project is $170,932 assuming that the tax shield goes on in perpetuity.

---

[7] By not adjusting the salvage value for the 50-percent rule, we assume there will be no new investment in year n.

$$= \frac{800,000 \,(.20)\,(.40)}{.20 + .15} \times \frac{1 + .5 \times (.15)}{1 + .15}$$

$$= 182,857 \times 1.075 \times 1.15 = \$170,932$$

The adjustment for the salvage value (second part of 7.6) is

$$- \frac{150,000 \,(.20)\,(.40)}{.20 + .15} \times \frac{1}{(1 + .15)^8}$$

$$= -34,286 \times 1/(1.15)^8 = -\$11,208.$$

The present value of the tax shield on CCA is the sum of the two present values.[8]

$$\text{Present value of tax shield from CCA} = \$170,932 - \$11,208$$
$$= \$159,724.$$

Total Project Cash Flow versus Tax Shield Approach

The tax shield approach has three advantages over the total project cash flow approach:

1. Simplifying formulas such as annuities and growing annuities can be applied, where appropriate, to a cash flow source. This is not feasible for the approach we used in the first example, because cash flows from all sources were combined to determine net cash flow for a year. Because the net cash flow for each year (as in line 4 of Table 7.4) is derived from so many sources, no simplifying formula can normally be used to calculate the net present value of all the yearly cash flows.

2. The approach used in the tax shield example can discount cash flows at different rates. This is often necessary due to varying risks associated with different cash flows.

3. The approach used in the first example cannot separate real and nominal flows because cash flows from all sources are combined each year. Thus, one either must make all flows nominal or make all flows real at the start.

It is our opinion that the tax shield approach is an improvement over the total project cash flow approach. In many cases, the improvement can be substantial, because both time savings and increases in accuracy are involved. The current example appears to allow both benefits. In some situations, however, there is only a slight improvement. For example, suppose that the cash flows from each source are irregular. The tax shield method would not save time, because the cash flows from the individual sources would not fit any simplifying formula. Also, suppose one were very

---

[8] There is a slight difference between this calculation for the present value of the tax shield on CCA and what we got in Table 7.6 by adding the tax shields over the project life. The difference arises whenever the salvage value of the asset differs from its UCC. The formula solution is more accurate as it takes into account the future CCA on this difference. In this case, the asset was sold for $150,000 and had UCC of $150,995. The $995 left in the pool after eight years creates an infinite stream of CCA. At time 8, this stream has a present value of [$995(.20)(.40)]/[.20 + .15] = $227.43. At time 0, the present value of this stream at 15 percent is about $75. To get the precise estimate of the present value of the CCA tax shield, we need to add this to the approximation in Table 7.6: $159,649 + $75 = $159,724.

unsure of the appropriate discount rates. Selecting a different discount rate for each cash flow might be unnecessary.[9]

We find that real world companies use both approaches. Thus, the student should be aware of both procedures, always looking for practical situations where the latter method allows substantial benefits.

CONCEPT QUESTIONS

- What is the basic difference between the discounting approach in the total-project cash flow example and the discounting approach in the tax shield example?
- What are the benefits of using each approach?

Investments of Unequal Lives: The Equivalent Annual Cost Method

7.5

Suppose a firm must choose between two machines of unequal lives. The machines can do the same job, but they have different operating costs and will last for different time periods. A simple application of the NPV rule suggests that we should take the machine whose costs have the lower present value. This could lead to the wrong decision, though, because the lower-cost machine may need to be replaced earlier. If we are choosing between two mutually exclusive projects that have different lives, the projects must be evaluated on an equal-life basis. In other words, we must devise a method that takes into account all future replacement decisions. We first discuss the classic *replacement-chain* problem. Next, a more difficult replacement decision is examined.

Replacement Chain

- *Example*

Downtown Athletic Club must choose between two mechanical tennis ball throwers. Machine A costs less than machine B but does not last as long. The cash outflows from the two machines are

Date:	0	1	2	3	4
Machine A	$500	$120	$120	$120	
Machine B	600	100	100	100	$100

Machine A costs $500 and lasts three years. There will be maintenance expenses of $120 to be paid at the end of each of the three years. Machine B costs $600 and lasts four years. There will be maintenance expenses of $100 to be paid at the end of each of the four years. We place all costs in *real* terms, an assumption greatly simplifying

↙ at time = 0.

---

[9]One of our colleagues in accounting is particularly critical of those who employ precise methodologies in situations with vague data. He tells the story of an accountant flying over the Grand Canyon who tells his seatmate, "I'll bet you didn't know that the Grand Canyon is two billion and two years old." The seatmate says, "Well, I can understand that it's around two billion years old, but how did you come up with two billion and two?" The accountant replied, "The pilot announced that the Grand Canyon was two billion years old when I took this same flight two years ago."

the analysis. Revenues per year are assumed to be the same for both so they are ignored in the analysis. Note that all numbers in the above chart are *outflows*. ∎

To get a handle on the decision, we take the present value of the costs of each of the two machines:

$$\text{Machine } A: \$798.42 = \$500 + \frac{\$120}{1.1} + \frac{\$120}{(1.1)^2} + \frac{\$120}{(1.1)^3} \qquad (7.7)$$

$$\text{Machine } B: \$916.99 = \$600 + \frac{\$100}{1.1} + \frac{\$100}{(1.1)^2} + \frac{\$100}{(1.1)^3} + \frac{\$100}{(1.1)^4}$$

Machine B has a higher present value of outflows. A naive approach would be to select machine A because of the lower outflows. However, machine B has a longer life so perhaps its cost per year is actually lower. How might one properly adjust for the difference in useful lives when comparing the two machines? We present two methods.

1. *Matching cycles.* Suppose that we run the example for 12 years. Machine A would have four complete cycles in this case and machine B would have three, so a comparison would be appropriate. Consider machine A's second cycle. The replacement of machine A occurs at date 3. Thus, another \$500 must be paid at date 3 with the yearly maintenance cost of \$120 payable at dates 4, 5, and 6. Another cycle begins at date 6 and a final cycle begins at date 9. Our present value analysis of equation (7.7) tells us that the payments in the first cycle are equivalent to a payment of \$798.42 at date 0. Similarly, the payments from the second cycle are equivalent to a payment of \$798.42 at date 3. Carrying this out for all four cycles, the present value of all costs from machine A over 12 years is

Present Value of Costs of Machine A over 12 Years:

$$\$2,188 = \$798.42 + \frac{\$798.42}{(1.10)^3} + \frac{\$798.42}{(1.10)^6} + \frac{\$798.42}{(1.10)^9} \qquad (7.8)$$

Now consider machine B's second cycle. The replacement of machine B occurs at date 4. Thus, another \$600 must be paid at this time, with yearly maintenance costs of \$100 payable at dates 5, 6, 7, and 8. A third cycle completes the 12 years. Following our calculations for machine A, the present value of all costs from machine B over 12 years is

Present Value of Costs of Machine B over 12 Years:

$$\$1,971 = \$916.99 + \frac{\$916.99}{(1.10)^4} + \frac{\$916.99}{(1.10)^8}$$

Because both machines have complete cycles over the 12 years, a comparison of 12-year costs is appropriate. The present value of machine B's costs is lower than the present value of machine A's costs over the 12 years, implying that machine B should be chosen.

While the above approach is straightforward, it has one drawback: Sometimes the number of cycles is high, demanding an excessive amount of calculating time. For example, if machine C lasts for 7 years and machine D lasts for 11 years, these two machines must be compared over a period of 77 (7×11) years. And if machines C, D, and E are compared, where machine E has a four-year cycle, a complete set of cycles occurs over 308 ($7 \times 11 \times 4$) years. Therefore, we offer the following alternative approach.

2. *Equivalent annual cost.* Equation (7.7) showed that payments of ($500, $120, $120, $120) are equivalent to a single payment of $798.42 at date 0. We now wish to equate the single payment of $798.42 at date 0 with a three-year annuity. Using techniques of previous chapters, we have

$$\$798.42 = C \times A_{0.10}^{3}$$

$A_{0.10}^{3}$ is an annuity of $1 a year for three years, discounted at 10 percent. C is the unknown—the annuity payment per year that causes the present value of all payments to equal $798.42. Because $A_{0.10}^{3}$ equals 2.4869, C equals $321.05 (or $798.42/ 2.4869). Thus, a payment stream of ($500, $120, $120, $120) is equivalent to annuity payments of $321.05 for three years. Of course, this calculation assumes only one cycle of machine A. Use of machine A over many cycles is equivalent to annual payments of $321.05 for an indefinite period into the future. We refer to $321.05 as the *equivalent annual* cost of machine A.

Now let us turn to machine B. We calculate its equivalent annual cost from

$$\$916.99 = C \times A_{0.10}^{4}$$

Because $A_{0.10}^{4}$ equals 3.1699, C equals $916.99/3.1699 or $289.28.

The following chart facilitates a comparison of machine A with machine B.

Date:	0	1	2	3	4	5	
Machine A		$321.05	$321.05	$321.05	$321.05	$321.05	. . .
Machine B		289.28	289.28	289.28	289.28	289.28	. . .

Repeated cycles of machine A give rise to yearly payments of $321.05 for an indefinite period into the future. Repeated cycles of machine B give rise to yearly payments of $289.28 for an indefinite period into the future. Clearly, machine B is preferred to machine A.

So far, we have presented two approaches: matching cycles and equivalent annual costs. Machine B was preferred under both methods. The two approaches are simply different ways of presenting the same information so that, for problems of this type, the same machine *must* be preferred under both approaches. In other words, use whichever method is easier for you since the decision will always be the same.

Assumptions in Replacement Chains

Strictly speaking, the two approaches make sense only if the time horizon is a multiple of 12 years. However, if the time horizon is long, but not known precisely, these approaches should still be satisfactory in practice.

The problem comes in if the time horizon is short. Suppose that the Downtown Athletic Club knows that a new machine will come on the market at date 5. The machine will be incredibly cheap and virtually maintenance-free, implying that it will replace either machine A or machine B immediately. Furthermore, its cheapness implies no salvage value for either A or B.

The relevant cash flows for A and B are

Date:	0	1	2	3	4	5
Machine A	$500	$120	$120	$120 + $500	$120	$120
Machine B	600	100	100	100	100 + 600	100

Note the double cost of machine A at date 3. This occurs because machine A must be replaced at that time. However, maintenance costs still continue, because machine A remains in service until the day of its replacement. Similarly, there is a double cost of machine B at date 4.

Present values are

Present Value of Costs of Machine A:

$$\$1,331 = \$500 + \frac{\$120}{1.10} + \frac{\$120}{(1.10)^2} + \frac{\$620}{(1.10)^3} + \frac{\$120}{(1.10)^4} + \frac{\$120}{(1.10)^5}$$

Present Value of Costs of Machine B:

$$\$1,389 = \$600 + \frac{\$100}{1.10} + \frac{\$100}{(1.10)^2} + \frac{\$100}{(1.10)^3} + \frac{\$700}{(1.10)^4} + \frac{\$100}{(1.10)^5}$$

Thus, machine B is more costly. Why is machine B more costly here when it is less costly under strict replacement-chain assumptions? Machine B is hurt more than A by the termination at date 5 because B's second cycle ends at date 8 while A's second cycle ends at date 6.

One final remark: Our analysis of replacement chains applies only if one anticipates replacement. The analysis would be different if no replacement were possible. This would occur if the only company that manufactured tennis ball throwers just went out of business and no new producers are expected to enter the field. In this case, machine B would generate revenues in the fourth year whereas machine A would not. In that case, simple net present value analysis for mutually exclusive projects including both revenues and costs would be appropriate.

The General Decision to Replace

The previous analysis concerned the choice between machine A and machine B, both of which were new acquisitions. More typically, firms must decide when to replace an existing machine with a new one. The analysis is actually quite straightforward. First, calculate the *equivalent annual cost (EAC)* for the new equipment. Second, compute the yearly cost for the old equipment. This cost likely rises over time because the machine's maintenance expense should increase with age. Replacement should occur just before the cost of the old equipment exceeds the EAC on the new equipment. As with much else in finance, an example clarifies this criterion better than further explanation.

■ *Example*

Consider the situation of BIKE. BIKE is contemplating whether to replace an existing machine or to spend money overhauling it. BIKE currently pays no taxes. The replacement machine costs $9,000 now and requires maintenance of $1,000 at the end of every year for eight years. At the end of eight years it would be sold for a salvage value of $2,000. The existing machine requires increasing amounts of maintenance each year, and its salvage value falls each year, as shown:

Year	Maintenance	Salvage
Present	$ 0	$4,000
1	1,000	2,500
2	2,000	1,500
3	3,000	1,000
4	4,000	0

The existing machine can be sold for $4,000 now. If it is sold in one year, the resale price will be $2,500, and $1,000 must be spent on maintenance during the year to keep it running. The machine will last for four more years before it falls apart. If BIKE faces an opportunity cost of capital of 15 percent, when should it replace the machine? ■

Equivalent Annual Cost of New Machine

The present value of the cost of the new replacement machine is as follows:

$$\text{PV}_{\text{costs}} = \$9,000 + \$1,000 \times A^8_{0.15} - \frac{\$2,000}{(1.15)^8}$$

$$= \$9,000 + \$1,000 \times (4.4873) - \$2,000 \times (0.3269)$$

$$= \$12,833$$

Notice that the $2,000 salvage value is an inflow. It is treated as a *negative* number in the above equation because it *offsets* the cost of the machine.

The EAC of a new replacement machine equals

$$\text{PV/8-year annuity factor at } 15\% = \frac{\text{PV}}{A^8_{0.15}} = \frac{\$12,833}{4.4873} = \$2,860$$

Cost of Old Machine

The cost of keeping the existing machine one more year includes the following:

1. The opportunity cost of not selling it now ($4,000).
2. Additional maintenance ($1,000).
3. Salvage value ($2,500).

Thus, the PV of the costs of keeping the machine one more year and selling it equals

$$\$4,000 + \frac{\$1,000}{1.15} - \frac{\$2,500}{1.15} = \$2,696$$

While we normally express cash flows in terms of present value, the analysis to come is made easier if we express the cash flow in terms of its future value one year from now. This future value is

$2,696 × 1.15 = $3,100

In other words, the equivalent cost of keeping the machine for one year is $3,100 at the end of the year.

Making the Comparison

If we replace the machine immediately, we can view our annual expense as $2,860, beginning at the end of the year. This annual expense continues forever if we replace the new machine every eight years.

This cash flow stream can be written as

	Year 1	Year 2	Year 3	Year 4	...
Expenses from replacing machine immediately	$2,860	$2,860	$2,860	$2,860	...

If we replace the old machine in one year, our expense from using the old machine for that final year can be viewed as $3,100, payable at the end of the year. After replacement, we can view our annual expense as $2,860, beginning at the end of two years. This annual expense continues forever if we replace the new machine every eight years. The cash flow stream can be written as

	Year 1	Year 2	Year 3	Year 4	...
Expenses from using old machine for one year and then replacing it	$3,100	$2,860	$2,860	$2,860	...

BIKE should replace the old machine immediately in order to minimize the expense at year 1.

One caveat is in order. Perhaps the old machine's maintenance is high in the first year but drops after that. A decision to replace immediately might be premature in that case. Therefore, we need to check the cost of the old machine in future years.

The cost of keeping the existing machine a second year is

$$\text{PV of costs at time } 1 = \$2,500 + \frac{\$2,000}{1.15} - \frac{\$1,500}{1.15} = \$2,935$$

which has future value of $3,375 (or $2,935 × 1.15).

The costs of keeping the existing machine for years 3 and 4 are also greater than the EAC of buying a new machine. Thus, BIKE's decision to replace the old machine immediately still is valid.

CONCEPT QUESTIONS

- What is the equivalent annual cost method of capital budgeting?
- What assumptions must we make to use EAC? List them.

Summary and Conclusions

7.6

This chapter discusses a number of practical applications of capital budgeting.

1. Capital budgeting must be conducted on an incremental basis. This means that sunk costs must be ignored, while both opportunity costs and side effects need to be considered.

2. Inflation should be handled consistently. One approach is to express both cash flows and the discount rate in nominal terms. The other approach is to express both cash flows and the discount rate in real terms. Because either approach yields the same NPV calculation, the simpler method should be used. Which method is simpler will generally depend on the nature of the capital budgeting problem.

3. In the total-project cash flow example, we computed NPV using the following two steps:
   a. Calculate the net cash flow from all sources for each period.
   b. Calculate the NPV using the cash flows calculated above.

   In the tax shield example, we used two different steps:

   a. Calculate the present value of each source (for example, revenues and CCA tax shield).
   b. Add the present values across the different sources (including initial investment) in order to get NPV.

The second approach has three benefits. Simplifying formulas can often be used. Nominal cash flows and real cash flows can be handled in the same example. Cash flows of varying risk can be used in the same example.

Key Terms

Incremental cash flow 190

Sunk cost 190

Opportunity cost 190

Erosion 191

Net working capital 192

Real interest rate 197

Nominal interest rate 197

Nominal cash flow 200

Real cash flow 200

Tax shield on CCA 202

Suggested Readings

An examination of the capital budgeting decision is contained in:

R. Garrison, G. R. Chesley, and R. Carroll. *Managerial Accounting,* 2d Canadian ed. Homewood, Ill.: Richard D. Irwin, 1993.

H. Bierman and S. Smidt. *The Capital Budgeting Decision: Economic Analysis of Investment Projects,* 7th ed. New York: Macmillan, 1988.

An entire book devoted to replacement decisions is:

G. W. Terborgh. *Business Investment Management Machinery.* Machinery and Allied Product Institute and Council for Technological Advancement, 1967.

Questions and Problems

Incremental Cash Flows

7.1 Which of the following should be treated as incremental cash flows when computing the NPV of an investment?

   a. The reduction in the sales of the company's other products. YES

   b. The expenditure on plant and equipment. YES

   c. The cost of research and development undertaken in connection with the product during the past three years. NO, SUNK

   d. The annual CCA expense. YES

   e. Dividend payments. No, not a cost to the project.

   f. The resale value of plant and equipment at the end of the project's life. YES

   g. Salary and medical costs for production employees on leave. YES

Practical Application of NPV to Capital Budgeting (no inflation)

7.2 According to the February 7, 1983, issue of *The Sporting News,* the Kansas City Royals' designated hitter, Hal McRae, signed a three-year contract in January 1983 with the following provisions:

$400,000 signing bonus.

$250,000 salary per year for three years.

Ten years of deferred payments of $125,000 per year. (These payments begin in year 4.)

Several bonus provisions that total as much as $75,000 per year for the three years of the contract.

Assume that McRae has a 60-percent probability of receiving the bonuses each year, and that he signed the contract on January 1, 1983. (Hint: Use the expected bonuses as incremental cash flows.) Assume an effective annual interest rate of 12.36 percent, and ignore taxes. McRae's salary and bonus are paid at the end of the year. What was the present value of this contract in January when McRae signed it?

7.3 Victoria Enterprises, Inc., is evaluating alternative uses for a three-story manufacturing and warehousing building that it has purchased for $225,000. The company could continue to rent the building to the present occupants for $12,000 per year. These tenants have indicated an interest in staying in the building for at least another 15 years. Alternatively, the company could make leasehold improvements to modify the existing structure to use for its own manufacturing and warehousing needs. Victoria's production engineer feels the building could be adapted to handle one of two new product lines. The cost and revenue data for the two product alternatives follow.

	Product A	Product B
Initial cash outlay for building modifications	$ 36,000	$ 54,000
Initial cash outlay for equipment	144,000	162,000
Annual pretax cash revenues (generated for 15 years)	105,000	127,500
Annual pretax cash expenditures (generated for 15 years)	60,000	75,000

The building will be used for only 15 years for either product A or product B. After 15 years, the building will be too small for efficient production of either product line. At that time, Victoria plans to rent the building to firms similar to the current occupants. To rent the building again, Victoria will need to restore the building to its present layout. The estimated cash cost of restoring the building if product A has been undertaken is $3,750; if product B has been produced, the cash cost will be $28,125. These cash costs can be deducted for tax purposes in the year the expenditures occur.

Victoria will depreciate the original building shell (purchased for $225,000) at a CCA rate of 5 percent, regardless of which alternative it chooses. The building modifications fall into CCA class 13 and are depreciated using the straight-line method over a 15-year life. Equipment purchases for either product are in class 8 and have a CCA rate of 20 percent. The firm's tax rate is 40 percent, and its required rate of return on such investments is 12 percent.

For simplicity, assume all cash flows for a given year occur at the end of the year. The initial outlays for modifications and equipment will occur at $t = 0$, and the restoration outlays will occur at the end of year 15. Also, Victoria has other profitable ongoing operations that are sufficient to cover any losses.

Which use of the building would you recommend to management?

7.4 The Regina Wheat Company (RWC) has wheat fields that currently produce annual profits of $250,000. These fields are expected to produce average annual profits of $250,000 in real terms forever. RWC has no depreciable assets, so the annual cash flow is also $250,000. RWC is an all-equity firm with 100,000 shares outstanding. The appropriate discount rate for its stock is 15 percent. RWC has an investment opportunity with a gross present value of $600,000. The investment requires a $400,000 outlay now. RWC has no other investment opportunities. Assume that all cash flows are received at the end of each year. What is the price per share of RWC?

Advanced Applications of NPV to Capital Budgeting (with Inflation)

7.5 Smalley-Davidson Diversified Industries (SD^2I) runs a small manufacturing operation. For this year, it expects to have real net cash flows of $40,000. SD^2I is an ongoing operation, but it expects competitive pressures to erode its (inflation-adjusted) net cash flows at 4 percent per year. The appropriate real discount rate for SD^2I is 10 percent. All net cash flows are received at year-end. What is the present value of the net cash flows from SD^2I's operations?

7.6 Larry, a small restaurant owner/manager, is contemplating the purchase of a larger restaurant from its owner, who is retiring. Larry would finance the purchase by selling his existing small restaurant, taking a second mortgage on his house, selling the stocks and bonds that he owns, and, if necessary, taking out a bank loan. Because Larry would have almost all of his wealth in the restaurant, he wants a careful analysis of how much he should be willing to pay for the business. The present owner of the larger restaurant has supplied the following information from the past five years.

Year	Gross revenue	Profit
−5	$875,000	$ 62,000
−4	883,000	28,000
−3	828,000	4,400
−2	931,000	96,000
Last	998,000	103,000

As with many small businesses, the larger restaurant is structured as a sole proprietorship so no corporate taxes are deducted. The preceding figures have not been adjusted for changes in the price level. There is general agreement that the average profits for the past five years are representative of what can be expected in the future, after adjusting for inflation.

Larry is of the opinion that he could earn at least $3,000 in current dollars per month as a hired manager. Larry feels he should subtract this amount from profits when analyzing the venture. Furthermore, he is aware of statistics showing that for restaurants of this size, approximately 6 percent go out of business each year.

Larry has done some preliminary work to value the business. His analysis is as follows:

Year	Profits	Price-level factor	Profits (current dollars)	Imputed managerial wage	Net profits
−5	$ 62,000	1.28	$ 79,400	$36,000	$ 43,400
−4	28,000	1.18	33,000	36,000	−3,000
−3	4,400	1.09	4,800	36,000	−31,200
−2	96,000	1.04	99,800	36,000	63,800
Last	103,000	1.00	103,000	36,000	67,000

The average profits for the past five years, expressed in current dollars, are $28,000. Using this average profit figure, Larry produced the following figures in current dollars.

Year	Expected profits if business continues	Probability of continuing*	Risk-adjusted profits	Real discount factor 2%	Present value
Next	$28,000	1.000	$28,000	0.980	$27,400
+2	28,000	0.940	26,300	0.961	25,300
+3	28,000	0.884	24,700	0.942	23,300
+4	28,000	0.831	23,300	0.924	21,500
.	.	.	.	.	.
.	.	.	.	.	.
.	.	.	.	.	.

*Probability of the business continuing. The probability of failing in any year is 6 percent. That probability compounds over the years.

Based on these calculations, Larry has calculated that the value of the restaurant is $350,000.

a. Assume that there is indeed a 6-percent per-year probability of going out of business. Do you agree with Larry's assessment of the restaurant? In your answer, consider his treatment of inflation, his deduction of the managerial wage of $3,000 per month, and the manner in which he assessed risk.

b. What present value would you place on the revenue stream; in other words, how much would you advise Larry to be willing to pay for the restaurant?

7.7 The Biological Insect Control Corporation (BICC) has hired you as a consultant to evaluate the NPV of its proposed toad ranch. BICC plans to breed toads and sell them as ecologically desirable insect-control mechanisms. The firm anticipates that the business will continue in perpetuity. Following negligible start-up costs, BICC will incur the following nominal cash flows at the end of the year:

Revenues	$150,000
Labour costs	80,000
Other costs	40,000

The company will lease machinery for $20,000 per year. (The lease payment starts at the end of year 1.) The payments on the lease are fixed in nominal terms. Sales will increase at 5 percent per year in real terms. Labour costs will increase at 3 percent per year in real terms. Other costs will decrease at 1 percent per year in real terms. The rate of inflation is expected to be 6 percent per year. The real rate of discount for revenues and costs is 10 percent. The lease payments are risk-free; therefore, they must be discounted at the risk-free rate. The real risk-free rate is 7 percent. There are no taxes. All cash flows occur at year-end. What is the NPV of BICC's proposed toad ranch today?

7.8 You are asked to evaluate the following project for a corporation with profitable ongoing operations. The required investment on January 1 of this year is $40,000. The firm will depreciate the investment at a CCA rate of 20 percent. The firm is in the 40-percent tax bracket.

The price of the product on January 1 will be $300 per unit. That price will stay constant in real terms. Labour costs will be $12 per hour on January 1. They will increase at 2 percent per year in real terms. Energy costs will be $5 per physical unit on January 1; they will increase at 5 percent per year in real terms. The inflation rate is 10 percent. Revenue is received and costs are paid at year-end.

	Year 1	Year 2	Year 3	Year 4
Physical production, in units	100	200	200	150
Labour input, in hours	2,000	2,000	2,000	2,000
Energy input, physical units	200	200	200	200

The riskless nominal discount rate is 6 percent. The real discount rate for costs and revenues is 3 percent. Calculate the NPV of this project.

7.9 Sludge Mineral Water, Ltd.'s properties are expected to yield 50,000 cases of delicious water each year. Each case sells for $10 in real terms. Costs per case are $2 in real terms. Sales income and costs occur at year-end. Sales income is expected to rise at a real rate of 5 percent annually, while real costs are expected to rise 2 percent annually. The relevant, real discount rate is 10 percent. The corporate tax rate is 40 percent. What is Sludge worth today?

7.10 International Buckeyes is building a factory that can make 1 million buckeyes a year for five years. The factory costs $6 million. In year 1, each buckeye will sell for $3.15 in nominal terms. The price will rise 5 percent each year in real terms. During the first year, variable costs will be $0.2625 per buckeye in nominal terms and will rise by 2 percent each year in real terms. International Buckeyes will depreciate the factory at a CCA rate of 20 percent.

International Buckeyes expects to be able to sell the factory for $638,140.78 at the end of year 5 (or $500,000 in real terms). The proceeds will be invested in a new factory. The nominal discount rate for risky cash flows is 20 percent. The nominal discount rate for riskless cash flows is 11 percent. The rate of inflation is 5 percent. Cash flows, except the initial investment, occur at the end of the year. The corporate tax rate is 40 percent. What is the net present value of this project?

7.11 Majestic Mining Company is negotiating for the purchase of a new piece of equipment for its current operations. MMC wants to know the maximum price that it should be willing to pay for the equipment. That is, how high must the price be for the equipment to have an NPV of zero? You are given the following facts:

1. The new equipment would replace existing equipment that has a current market value of $20,000.

2. The new equipment would not affect revenues, but before-tax operating costs would be reduced by $10,000 per year for eight years. These savings in cost would occur at year-end.

3. The old equipment is now five years old. It is expected to last for another eight years, and to have no resale value at the end of those eight years. It was purchased for $40,000 and is being depreciated at a CCA rate of 20 percent.

4. The new equipment will be also be depreciated at a CCA rate of 20 percent. MMC expects to be able to sell the equipment for $5,000 at the end of eight years. At that time, the firm plans to reinvest in new equipment in the same CCA pool.

5. MMC has profitable ongoing operations.

6. The appropriate discount rate is 8 percent.

7.12 After extensive medical and marketing research, Pill Ltd. believes it can penetrate the pain reliever market. It can follow one of two strategies. The first is to manufacture a medication aimed at relieving headache pain. The second strategy is to make a pill designed to relieve headache and arthritis pain. Both products would be introduced at a price of $2 per package in real terms. The broader remedy would probably sell 10 million packages a year.

This is twice the sales rate for the headache-only medication. Cash costs of production in the first year are expected to be $0.95 per package in real terms for the headache-only brand. Production costs are expected to be $1.40 in real terms for the more general pill. All prices and costs are expected to rise at the general inflation rate of 6 percent.

Either strategy would require further investment in plant. The headache-only pill could be produced using equipment that would cost $9 million, last three years, and have no resale value. The machinery required to produce the broader remedy would cost $15 million and last three years. At this time the firm would be able to sell it for $3 million (in real terms). The production machinery would need to be replaced every three years at constant real costs.

Suppose that, for both projects, the firm will use a CCA rate of 20 percent. The firm faces a corporate tax rate of 40 percent. Management believes the appropriate real discount rate is 12 percent. Which pain reliever should Pill Ltd. produce?

7.13 A machine that lasts four years has the following net cash outflows: $12,000 to purchase the machine and $6,000 for the annual year-end operating cost. At the end of four years, the machine is sold for $2,000; thus, the cash flow at year 4, C_4 is only $4,000.

C_0	C_1	C_2	C_3	C_4
$12,000	$6,000	$6,000	$6,000	$4,000

The cost of capital is 6 percent. What is the present value of the costs of operating a series of such machines in perpetuity?

Replacement with Unequal Lives

7.14 BIG Industries is in need of computers. Management has narrowed the choices to the SAL 5000 and the DET 1000. It would need 10 SALs. Each SAL costs $5,000 and requires $1,000 of maintenance each year. At the end of the computer's eight-year life, BIG expects to be able to sell each one for $500. On the other hand, BIG could buy eight DETs. DETs cost $7,000 each and each machine requires $700 of maintenance every year. They last for six years and have no resale value. Whichever model BIG chooses, it will buy that model forever. Ignore tax effects, and assume that maintenance costs occur at year-end. Which model should BIG buy if the cost of capital is 10 percent?

7.15 BYO University is faced with the decision of which word processor to purchase for its typing pool. It can buy 10 Bang word processors which cost $8,000 each and have estimated annual, year-end maintenance costs of $2,000 per machine. The Bang word processors will be replaced at the end of year 4. At that time, their resale value will be zero. Alternatively, BYO could buy 11 IOU word processors to accomplish the same work. The IOU word processors would need to be replaced after three years. They cost only $5,000 each, but annual, year-end maintenance costs are $2,500 per machine. A reasonable forecast is that each IOU word processor will have a resale value of $500 at the end of three years.

The university's opportunity cost of funds for this type of investment is 14 percent. Because the university is a nonprofit institution, it does not pay taxes. It is anticipated that whichever manufacturer is chosen now will be the supplier of future machines. Would you recommend purchasing 10 Bang word processors or 11 IOU machines?

7.16 Station CJXT is considering the replacement of its old, fully depreciated sound mixer. Two new models are available. Mixer X has a cost of $216,000, a five-year expected life, and after-tax cash flow savings of $68,200 per year. Mixer Y has a cost of $345,000, a 10-year life, and after-tax cash flow of $83,400 per year. No new technological developments are expected. The cost of capital is 10 percent. Should CJXT replace the old mixer with X or Y?

7.17 Kaul Construction must choose between two pieces of equipment. Tamper A costs $7,500 and it will last five years. This tamper will require $150 of maintenance each year. Tamper B costs $9,000, but it will last seven years. Maintenance costs for tamper B are $120 per year. Kaul incurs all maintenance costs at the end of the year. The appropriate discount rate for Kaul Construction is 9 percent.

a. Which machine should Kaul purchase?

b. What assumptions are you making in your analysis for part (a)?

7.18 Philben Pharmaceutics must decide when to replace its autoclave. Philben's current autoclave will require increasing amounts of maintenance each year. The resale value of the equipment falls every year. The following table presents this data.

Year	Maintenance costs	Resale value
Today	$ 0	$900
1	200	850
2	275	775
3	325	700
4	450	600
5	500	500

Philben can purchase a new autoclave for $3,000. The new equipment will have an economic life of six years. At the end of each of those years, the equipment will require $20 of maintenance. Philben expects to be able to sell the machine for $1,200 at the end of six years. Assume that Philben will pay no taxes. The appropriate discount rate for this decision is 10 percent. When should Philben replace its current machine?

7.19 Which is better: (1) investing $10,000 in a Guaranteed Investment Certificate (GIC) for one year at 15 percent when expected inflation is 10 percent or (2) investing $10,000 in a GIC at 5 percent when expected inflation is 1 percent? In assessing these alternatives, assume that interest received is taxed at a rate of 40 percent.

7.20 A new electronic process monitor costs $140,000. This cost will be depreciated at 25 percent per year (class 9). The monitor will actually be worthless in five years. The new monitor would save us $50,000 per year before taxes in operating costs. If we require a 10-percent return, what is the NPV of the purchase? Assume a tax rate of 40 percent.

7.21 We believe we can sell 10,000 home security devices per year at $30 apiece. They cost $20 each to manufacture (variable cost). Fixed production costs will run $30,000 per year. The necessary equipment costs $150,000 to buy and will be depreciated at a 20-percent CCA rate. The equipment will have zero salvage value after the five-year life of the project. We will need to invest $40,000 in net working capital up front, but no additional net working capital investment will be necessary. The discount rate is 14 percent, and the tax rate is 43.5 percent. What do you think of the proposal?

7.22 This problem is much easier if you are working with a spreadsheet. We are contemplating the purchase of a $900,000 computer-based customer order management system. CCA on the system will be calculated at a rate of 30 percent. In five years it will be worth $330,000. We would save $500,000 before taxes per year in order processing costs, and we would reduce working capital by $220,000 (a one-time reduction). What is the DCF return on this investment? The relevant tax rate is 40 percent.

7.23 This problem is much easier if you are working with a spreadsheet. A large retailer has asked us to submit a bid for a new point-of-sale credit checking system. We would install the system in 20 stores per year for three years. We would need to purchase $250,000 worth of specialized equipment, which would be depreciated at a 25-percent rate. We would sell it in three years, at which time it should be worth about half of what we paid for it. Labour and material cost to install the system would be about $35,000 per site. Finally, we would need to invest $60,000 in working capital items. The relevant tax rate is 44 percent. What price per system should we bid if we require a 16-percent return on our investment? Try to avoid the winner's curse.

7.24 A proposed cost-saving device has an installed cost of $59,400. It is in class 9 for CCA purposes. (CCA rates are given in the tables in Appendix A at the end of this book.) It will actually function for five years, at which time it will have no value. There are no working capital consequences from the investment; the tax rate is 40 percent.

a. What must the pretax cost savings be for us to favour the investment? We require a 10-percent return. Hint: This is a variation on the problem of setting a bid price.

b. Suppose the device will be worth $11,000 in salvage (before taxes). How does this change your answer?

7.25 Klaatu Co. has recently completed a $400,000, two-year marketing study. Based on the results, Klaatu has estimated that 10,000 of its new RUR-class robots could be sold annually over the next eight years at a price of $9,615 each. Variable costs per robot are $7,400; fixed costs total $12 million per year.

Start-up costs include $40 million to build production facilities, $2.4 million in land, and $8 million in net working capital. The $40 million facility is made up of a building valued at $5 million that will belong to CCA class 3 and $35 million of manufacturing equipment (belonging to CCA class 8). (CCA rates are in Appendix A.) At the end of the project's life, the facilities (including the land) will be sold for an estimated $8.4 million, assuming the building's value will be $4 million. The value of the land is not expected to change.

Finally, start-up would also entail fully deductible expenses of $1.4 million at year zero. An ongoing, profitable business, Klaatu pays taxes at a 40-percent rate. Klaatu uses a 10-percent discount rate on projects such as this one. Should Klaatu produce the RUR-class robots?

APPENDIX

Capital Cost Allowance

Capital cost allowance (CCA) is depreciation for the purposes of taxes in Canada. Capital cost allowance is deducted in determining taxable income. Because tax law reflects various political compromises, CCA is not the same as depreciation under GAAP so there is no reason why calculation of a firm's income under tax rules has to be the same as under GAAP. For example, taxable corporate income may often be lower than accounting income because the company is allowed to use accelerated capital cost allowance rules in computing depreciation for Revenue Canada while using straight-line depreciation for GAAP reporting.[10]

CCA calculation begins by assigning every asset to a particular class. An asset's class establishes its maximum CCA rate for tax purposes. Leasehold improvements follow straight-line depreciation for CCA. For all other assets, CCA follows the declining balance method. The CCA for each year is computed by multiplying the asset's book value for tax purposes, called *undepreciated capital cost (UCC),* by the appropriate rate.

Intangible assets, such as goodwill and patents, are particularly important to knowledge-based firms like software developers and pharmaceutical companies. Such assets are not subject to CCA. Instead, intangible assets are amortized under Revenue Canada rules at an effective rate of 5.25 percent on the declining balance.

The CCA system is unique to Canada and differs in many respects from the depreciation method used in the United States. One key difference is that, in the Canadian system, the expected salvage value (what we think the asset will be worth when we dispose of it) and the actual expected economic life (how long we expect the asset to be in service) are not explicitly considered in the calculation of capital cost allowance. (Some typical CCA classes and their respective CCA rates are described in Table 7A.1.) Another unique feature of the CCA system is the concept of pooling of assets described in detail below. Calculating CCA on pools of assets rather than for each item simplifies the system.

A final difference worth noting is that, under the CCA system, Revenue Canada, not the firm, decides the allowable depreciation rate. In the United States among other countries, firms set depreciation rates. This difference can produce a disadvantage for

---

[10]Where taxable income is less than accounting income, total taxes (calculated from accounting income) are greater than current taxes (calculated from taxable income). The difference, deferred taxes for the year, is added to the deferred tax liability account on the balance sheet.

Class	Rate	Assets
3	5%	Brick buildings
6	10%	Fences and frame buildings
7	15%	Canoes and boats, ships
8	25%	Manufacturing and processing equipment
9	25%	Electrical equipment and aircraft
10	30%	Vans, trucks, tractors, and computer equipment
13	Straight-line	Leasehold improvements
16	40%	Taxicabs and rental cars
22	50%	Excavating equipment

Table 7A.1
Common CCA classes

Year	Beginning UCC	CCA	Ending UCC
1	$15,000*	$4,500	$10,500
2	25,500†	7,650	17,850
3	17,850	5,355	12,495
4	12,495	3,748	8,747
5	8,747	2,624	6,123

Table 7A.2
CCA for a van

*One-half of $30,000.
†Year 1 ending balance plus the remaining half of $30,000.

Canadian firms employing high-tech equipment which becomes obsolete at a rate faster than it is depreciable under the CCA rules.

To illustrate how capital cost allowance is calculated, suppose your firm is considering buying a van costing $30,000, including any set-up costs that must (by law) be capitalized. (No rational business would capitalize, for tax purposes, anything that could legally be expensed.) Table 7A.1 shows that vans fall in class 10 with a 30-percent CCA rate. To calculate the CCA we need to follow Revenue Canada's 50-percent rule which allows us to figure CCA on only one-half of the asset's installed cost in the first year it is put in use. Table 7A.2 shows the CCA for our van for the first five years.

As we pointed out, in calculating CCA under current tax law, the economic life and future market value of the asset are not issues. As a result, an asset's UCC can differ substantially from its actual market value. With our $30,000 van, UCC after the first year is $10,500 (or $15,000 less the first year's CCA of $4,500). The remaining UCC values are summarized in Table 7A.2. After five years, the van's undepreciated capital cost is $6,123.

Capital Cost Allowance Incentives in Practice

Since capital cost allowance is deducted in computing taxable income, larger CCA rates reduce taxes and increase cash flows. As we pointed out earlier, finance ministers sometimes tinker with the CCA rates to create incentives. For example, in the 1992 Federal Budget, the minister announced an increase in CCA rates from 20 to 25 percent for manufacturing and processing firms. The combined federal/provincial corporate tax rate for this sector is 36.5 percent.

■ *Example*

Mississauga Manufacturing was planning to acquire new processing equipment to enhance efficiency and its ability to compete with U.S. firms. The equipment had an installed cost of $1 million. How much additional tax did the new measure save Mississauga in the first year the equipment is put into use?

Under the 50-percent rule, UCC for the first year is $\frac{1}{2} \times$ $1 million = $500,000. The CCA deductions under the old and new rates are

Old rate: CCA = .25 × $500,000 = $125,000
New rate: CCA = .30 × $500,000 = $150,000

Because the firm deducts CCA in figuring taxable income, taxable income will be reduced by the incremental CCA of $25,000. With $25,000 less in taxable income, Mississauga Manufacturing's combined tax bill will drop by $25,000 × .365 = $9,125. ■

Asset Purchases and Sales

When an asset is sold, the UCC in its asset class (or pool) is reduced by what is realized on the asset or by its original cost, whichever is less. This amount is called the *adjusted cost of disposal.* Suppose that we want to sell the van in our earlier example after five years. Based on historical averages of resale prices, it's worth, say, 25 percent of the purchase price or .25 × $30,000 = $7,500. Since the $7,500 price is less than the original cost, the adjusted cost of disposal is $7,500 and the UCC in class 10 is reduced by this amount.

In this case, the $7,500 removed from the pool is $1,377 (or 7,500 − 6,123) more than the undepreciated capital cost of the van we are selling, and future CCA deductions will be reduced as the pool continues. This difference of $1,377 is called *recaptured depreciation.* On the other hand, if we sold the van for, say, $4,000, the UCC in class 10 would be reduced by $4,000 and the $2,123 excess (6,123 − 4,000) of UCC over the sale price would remain in the pool. In this case, future CCA increases as the declining balance calculations depreciate the $2,123 excess UCC to infinity.

So far, we have focused on CCA calculations for one asset. In practice, firms often buy and sell assets from a given class in the course of a year. In this case, we apply the net acquisitions rule. From the total installed cost of all acquisitions we subtract the adjusted cost of disposal of all assets in the pool. The result is net acquisitions for the asset class. If net acquisitions is positive, we apply the 50-percent rule and calculate CCA as above. If net acquisitions is negative, the 50-percent rule applies only to assets purchased.

When An Asset Pool Is Terminated

Suppose your firm decides to contract out all transport and to sell all company vehicles. If the company owns no other class 10 assets, the asset pool in this class is terminated. As before, the adjusted cost of disposal is the net sales proceeds or the total installed cost of all the pool assets, whichever is less. This adjusted cost of disposal is subtracted from the total UCC in the pool. So far, the steps are exactly the same as in our van example where the pool continued. What happens next is different. Unless the adjusted cost of disposal just happens to equal the UCC exactly, a positive or negative UCC balance remains and this has tax implications.

A positive UCC balance remains when the adjusted cost of disposal is less than UCC before the sale. In this case, the firm has a terminal loss equal to the remaining UCC. This loss is deductible from income for the year. For example, if we sell the van after two years for $10,000, then the UCC exceeds the market value by $7,850 (or 17,850 − 10,000). In this case, the terminal loss of $7,850 gives rise to a tax saving of .40 × $7,850 = $3,140. (We assume the tax rate is 40 percent.)

A negative UCC balance occurs when the adjusted cost of disposal exceeds UCC in the pool. To illustrate, return to our van example and suppose that this van is the only class 10 asset our company owns when it sells off the pool. In this case, we see that there is a $1,377 excess of adjusted cost of disposal ($7,500 − $6,123) over UCC so the final UCC balance is −$1,377.

The company must pay tax at its ordinary tax rate on this negative balance. Taxes must be paid in this case since the difference in adjusted cost of disposal and UCC is "excess" CCA recaptured when the asset is sold. We overdepreciated the asset by $7,500 − $6,123 = $1,377. Since we deducted $1,377 too much in CCA, we paid $550.80 too little in taxes, and we simply have to make up the difference.

Notice that this is not a tax on a capital gain. As a general rule, a capital gain only occurs if the market price exceeds the original cost. To illustrate a capital gain, suppose that instead of buying the van, our firm purchased a classic car for $50,000. After five years, the classic car will be sold for $75,000. In this case, the sales price exceeds the purchase price so the adjusted cost of disposal is $50,000 and UCC pool is reduced by this amount. The total negative balance left in the UCC pool is $6,123 − $50,000 = −$43,877 and this is recaptured CCA. In addition, the firm has a taxable capital gain of $75,000 − $50,000 = $25,000, the difference between the sales price and the original cost.[11]

The company must pay tax on this capital gain of $25,000. As explained in Chapter 1's appendix, at the time of writing, a corporation is taxed on 75 percent of any capital gains. Using a marginal corporate tax rate of 40 percent, the tax payable is $7,500 (or $25,000 × .75 × .40).

▪ Example

Staple Supply, Ltd., has just purchased a new computerized information system with an installed cost of $160,000. The computer is in class 10 for CCA purposes. What are the yearly capital cost allowances? Based on historical experience, we think that the system will be worth only $10,000 when we get rid of it in four years. What are the tax consequences of the sale if the company has several other computers that will still be in use in four years? Now suppose that Staple Supply will sell all its assets and wind up the company in four years. What is the total after-tax cash flow from the sale?

---

[11]This example shows that it is possible to have a recapture of CCA without closing out a pool if the UCC balance goes negative.

Year	Beginning UCC	CCA	Ending UCC
Table 7A.3 CCA for a computer system			
1	$80,000*	$24,000	$56,000
2	136,000†	40,800	95,200
3	95,200	28,560	66,640
4	66,640	19,992	46,648

*One-half of $160,000.

†Year 1 ending balance plus the remaining half of $160,000.

In Table 7A.3, at the end of year 4 the remaining balance for the specific computer system will be $46,648.[12] The pool is reduced by $10,000, but it will continue to be "depreciated." There are no tax consequences in year 4. This is only the case when the pool is active. If this is the only computer system, we close the pool and claim a terminal loss of $46,648 − $10,000 = $36,648. ∎

Appendix Questions

7A.1 What is the difference between capital cost allowance and GAAP depreciation?

7A.2 Why do governments sometimes increase CCA rates?

7A.3 Reconsider the 1992 CCA increase discussed in the incentives example. How effective do you think it was in stimulating investment? Why?

---

[12]In actuality, the capital cost allowance for the entire pool will be calculated at once, without specific identification of each computer system.

CHAPTER 8

Strategy and Analysis in Using Net Present Value

[handwritten: What it is about a project that produces a +ve NPV]

[handwritten: Corporate strategy analysis → process of asking about the sources of +ve NPV in Capital budgeting]

The previous chapter discussed how to identify the incremental cash flows involved in capital budgeting decisions. In this chapter we look more closely at what it is about a project that produces a positive net present value (NPV). The process of asking about the sources of positive NPV in capital budgeting is often referred to as *corporate strategy analysis*. We discuss corporate strategy analysis in the first part of the chapter. Next, we consider several analytical tools that help managers deal with the effects of uncertainty on incremental cash flows. The concepts of decision trees, sensitivity analysis, scenario analysis, and break-even analysis are presented.

Corporate Strategy and Positive NPV   8.1

The intuition behind discounted cash flow analysis is that a project must generate a rate of return higher than what can be earned in the capital markets. Only if this is true will a project's NPV be positive. A significant part of corporate strategy analysis is seeking investment opportunities that can produce positive NPVs.

Simple "number crunching" in a discounted cash flow analysis can sometimes erroneously lead to a positive NPV calculation. In computing discounted cash flows, it is always useful to ask, What is it about this project that produces a positive NPV? or Where does the positive NPV in capital budgeting come from? In other words, we must be able to point to the specific sources of positive increments to present value in doing discounted cash flow analysis. In general, it is sensible to assume that positive-NPV projects are hard to find and that most project proposals are "guilty until proven innocent."

Here are some ways that firms create positive NPV:

1. Be the first to introduce a new product.
2. Refine a core business to produce goods or services at lower cost than competitors.
3. Create a barrier that makes it difficult for other firms to compete effectively.
4. Introduce variations on existing products to take advantage of unsatisfied demand.
5. Create product differentiation by aggressive advertising and marketing networks.
6. Use innovation in organizational processes to do all of the above.

How to Create Positive NPV

Type of action	Examples
Introduce new product	McDonald's Canada's introduction of its fast foods into Russia
Develop core technology	The Toronto Stock Exchange's development of CATS (Computer Assisted Trading System)
Create barrier to entry	Polaroid's patent on proprietary technology for instant photographic development
Introduce variations on existing products	Corel's introduction of Corel Draw, a graphics-based software application
Create product differentiation	Coca-Cola's use of advertising: "It's the real thing"
Utilize organizational innovation	Motorola's use of "Japanese management practice," including just-in-time inventory procurement, consensus decision-making, and performance-based incentive systems

This is undoubtedly a partial list of potential sources of positive NPV. Focusing critically on such potential sources is probably the best way to avoid the *forecaster's trap* of simply extrapolating past trends as illustrated in the following example:

> In 1860, several forecasters were seconded from the financial community by the city of New York to forecast the future level of pollution caused by the use of chewing tobacco and horses. . . . In 1850, the spit level in the gutter and manure level in the middle of the road had both averaged half an inch (approximately 1 cm). By 1860, each had doubled to a level of one inch. Using this historical growth rate, the forecasters projected levels of two inches by 1870, four inches by 1880 and 1,024 inches (85 feet and 4 inches) by 1960![1]

It is also important to keep in mind that positive-NPV projects are probably not common. Our basic economic intuition should tell us that it will be harder to find positive-NPV projects in a competitive industry than in a noncompetitive industry.

Now we ask another question: How can someone find out whether a firm is obtaining positive NPV from its operating and investment activities? First, we address how share prices are related to long-term and short-term decision-making. Next we explain how managers can find clues in share price behaviour on whether they are making good decisions.

Corporate Strategy and the Stock Market

There should be a connection between the stock market and capital budgeting. If a firm invests in a project that is worth more than its cost, the project will produce positive NPV and the firm's stock price should go up. However, the popular financial press

---

[1] This apocryphal example comes from L. Kryzanowski, T. Minh-Chau, and R. Seguin, *Business Solvency Risk Analysis* (Montreal: Institute of Canadian Bankers, 1990), Chapter 5, p. 10.

frequently suggests that the best way for a firm to increase its share price is to report high short-term earnings (even if by doing so it "cooks the books").

As a consequence, it is often said that North American firms tend to reduce capital expenditures as well as research and development (R&D) to increase short-term profits and stock prices. Moreover, it is claimed that North American firms that have valid long-term goals and undertake long-term capital budgeting at the expense of short-term profits are hurt by short-sighted stock market reactions. Sometimes institutional investors are blamed for this state of affairs. In contrast, Japanese firms are said to have a long-term perspective and to make the necessary investments in research and development to provide a competitive edge.

Of course, these claims rest, in part, on the assumption that stock markets in Canada and the United States systematically overvalue short-term earnings and undervalue long-term earnings. The available evidence suggests the contrary. Johnson and Pazderka used Canadian stock market data and corporate financial data to test the market's valuation of research and development spending on firms. Their empirical results show a positive, statistically significant relationship between R&D spending and market value.[2]

In the United States, McConnell and Muscarella looked closely at the effect of corporate investment on the market value of equity.[3] They found that, for most industrial firms, announcements of increases in planned capital spending were associated with significant increases in the market value of the common stock and that announcements of decreases in capital spending had the opposite effect. The McConnell and Muscarella research suggests that the stock market does pay close attention to corporate capital spending and that it reacts positively to firms making long-term investments.

In another U.S. study, Woolridge investigated the stock market's reaction to the strategic capital spending programs of several hundred U.S. firms.[4] He looked at firms announcing joint ventures, research and development spending, new product strategies, and capital spending for expansion and modernization. He found a strong positive stock reaction to these types of announcements. This finding provides significant support for the notion that the stock market encourages managers to make long-term strategic investment decisions in order to maximize shareholders' value. It strongly opposes the viewpoint that North American markets and managers are myopic.

How Firms Can Learn about NPV from the Stock Market: The Seagram Decision to Acquire a Stake in Time Warner

Basic economic common sense tells us that the market value of a firm's outstanding shares reflects the stock market's assessment of future cash flows from the firm's

---

[2]Lewis D. Johnson and Bohumir Pazderka, "Firm Value and Investment in R&D," *Managerial and Decision Economics (January/February 1993),* pp. 15–24.

[3]John J. McConnell and Chris J. Muscarella, "Corporate Capital Expenditure Decisions and the Market Value of the Firm," *Journal of Financial Economics* (September 1985), pp. 399–422.

[4]J. Randall Woolridge, "Competitive Decline: Is a Myopic Stock Market to Blame," *Journal of Applied Corporate Finance* (Spring 1988), pp. 26–36. Another interesting study has been conducted by Su Han Chan, John Martin, and John Kensinger, "Corporate Research and Development Expenditures and Share Value," *Journal of Financial Economics* 26 (1990), pp. 255–76. They report that the share price responses to announcements of increased research and development are significantly positive, even when the firm's earnings are decreasing.

investing activities. Therefore, it is not surprising that the stock market usually reacts positively to proposed capital budgeting programs. When the market does not react positively, it is often providing a clue to a new project's NPV.

Consider the decision by Seagram Co. Ltd. to penetrate the entertainment industry.[5] On May 26, 1993, Seagram announced that it had bought a 5.7-percent stake in U.S. entertainment giant Time Warner Inc. and was intending to increase its stake to 15 percent. That day its share price closed at $38 on the TSE. The next day, Seagram fell by $\frac{7}{8}$s to 37\frac{1}{8}$. This represents a loss of $308 million to its shareholders in one day. Over the next few weeks, Seagram's share price fell to 33\frac{1}{2}$, a substantial loss of value for Seagram's shareholders.

Why would Seagram (a beverage and spirits producer) buy into Time Warner, a large entertainment company? Why did the stock market reaction suggest that the acquisition was a negative-NPV investment for Seagram? Industry watchers felt that Seagram's president was finally making his mark on the company. (That is, his interests in entertainment from a young age were being shown.) The stock market reaction reflected doubts over whether the move was desirable for Seagram. The differences in business interests between the two companies and the debt required for the purchase made investors wary. Further, Seagram's announcement of its intentions to increase its holdings of Time Warner to 15 percent may also have affected its share price. The negative reaction from the stock market suggests that Seagram's shareholders believed that the Time Warner stake was worth less than its cost to Seagram.

Overall, the evidence suggests that firms can use the stock market to help potentially short-sighted managers make positive net present value decisions. Unfortunately only a few firms use the market as effectively as they could to help them make capital budgeting decisions.

CONCEPT QUESTIONS

- What are the ways a firm can create positive-NPV projects?
- How can managers use the market to help them screen out negative-NPV projects?

8.2   Decision Trees

We have considered potential sources of value in NPV analysis. Now our interest is in coming up with estimates of NPV for a proposed project. A fundamental problem in NPV analysis is dealing with uncertain future outcomes. This section introduces the device of **decision trees** for identifying uncertain cash flows.

Imagine you are the treasurer of the Solar Electronics Corporation (SEC), and the engineering group has recently developed the technology for solar-powered jet engines. The jet engine is suitable for smaller jet aircraft designed for use as executive jets or by regional airlines. The marketing staff has proposed that SEC develop some

[5]Our discussion draws on Kevin Dougherty, "Seagram Defends Time Stake," *The Financial Post* (June 3, 1993), p. 3; and Eric Reguly, "Seagram Shares Continue to Fall on Stake in Time," *The Financial Post,* June 2, 1993.

Investment	Year 1	Year 2
Revenues		$ 6,000
Variable costs		(3,000)
Fixed costs		(1,700)
Depreciation		(300)
Pretax profit		$ 1,000
Tax ($T_c = 0.40$)		(400)
Net profit		$ 600
Cash flow		900
Initial investment costs	−$1,500	

Table 8.1
Cash flow forecasts for Solar Electronics Corporation's jet engine base case ($ millions)

Note the following assumptions: (1) Investment is depreciated in years 2 through 6 using the straight-line method for simplicity; (2) tax rate is 40 percent; and (3) the company receives no tax benefits on initial development costs.

prototypes and conduct test marketing of the engine. A corporate planning group, including representatives from production, marketing, and engineering, has recommended that the firm go ahead with the test and development phase. The planning group estimates that this preliminary phase will take a year and will cost $100 billion. Furthermore, the group believes there is a 75-percent chance that the production and marketing tests will prove successful.

Based on the company's experience in the industry, it has a fairly accurate idea of how much the development and testing expenditures will cost. Sales of jet engines, however, are subject to (1) uncertainty about the demand for business and regional air travel in the future, (2) uncertainty about future oil prices, (3) uncertainty about SEC's market share for engines, and (4) uncertainty about the demand for smaller versus larger aircraft. Future oil prices will have an impact on how rapidly businesses replace their existing fleets of less fuel-efficient aircraft such as the older Learjets.

If the initial marketing tests are *successful,* SEC can acquire some land, build a new plant, and go ahead with full-scale production. This investment phase will cost $1,500 million. Production will occur over the next five years. The preliminary cash flow projection appears in Table 8.1.[6] Should SEC decide to go ahead with investment and production on the jet engine, the NPV at a discount rate of 15 percent (in millions) is

$$NPV = -\$1,500 + \sum_{t=1}^{5} \frac{\$900}{(1.15)^t} = -\$1,500 + \$900 \times A_{0.15}^5 = \$1,517$$

Note that the NPV is calculated as of date 1, the date at which the investment of $1,500 million is made. Later we bring this number back to date 0.

If the initial marketing tests are *unsuccessful,* SEC's $1,500 million investment has an NPV of −$3,611 million. This figure is also calculated as of date 1.

---

[6]Although we use straight-line depreciation for convenience here, the appendix to Chapter 7 shows that it is realistic for finding capital cost allowance for some assets in Canada. The tax rate we use applies to manufacturing and processing companies in some provinces.

Figure 8.1
Decision tree for
SEC ($ millions)

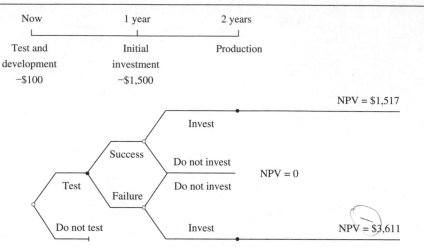

Open circles represent decision points; closed circles represent receipt of information.

Figure 8.1 displays the problem concerning the jet engine as a decision tree. If SEC decides to conduct test marketing, there is a 75-percent probability that the test marketing will be successful. If the tests are successful, the firm faces a second decision: whether to invest $1,500 million in a project that yields $1,517 million NPV or to stop. If the tests are unsuccessful, the firm faces a different decision: whether to invest $1,500 million in a project that yields –$3,611 million NPV or to stop.

As can be seen from Figure 8.1, SEC has the following two decisions to make:

1. Whether to test and develop the solar-powered jet engine.
2. Whether to invest for full-scale production following the results of the test.

One makes decisions in reverse order with decision trees. Thus, we analyze the second-stage investment of $1,500 million first. If the tests are successful, it is obvious that SEC should invest, because $1,517 million is greater than zero. Just as obviously, if the tests are unsuccessful, SEC should not invest.

Now we move back to the first stage where the decision boils down to a simple question: Should SEC invest $100 million now to obtain a 75-percent chance of $1,517 million one year later? The expected payoff evaluated at date 1 (in millions) is

Expected payoff	$=$	Probability of success	$\times$	Payoff if successful	$+$	Probability of failure	$\times$	Payoff if failure
	$=$	(0.75	$\times$	$1,517)	$+$	(0.25	$\times$	$0)
	$=$	$1,138						

The NPV of testing computed at date 0 (in millions) is

$$\text{NPV} = -\$100 + \frac{\$1,138}{1.15} = \$890$$

Thus, the firm should test the market for solar-powered jet engines.

Warning 1   We have used a discount rate of 15 percent for both the testing and the investment decisions. Perhaps a higher discount rate should have been used for the initial test-marketing decision, which is likely to be riskier than the investment decision.

Warning 2   It was assumed that, after making the initial investment to produce solar engines and then being confronted with a low demand, SEC would lose money. This worst-case scenario leads to an NPV of −$3,611 million. This is an unlikely eventuality. Instead, it is more plausible to assume that SEC would try to sell its initial investment—patents, land, buildings, machinery, and prototypes—for $1,000 million. For example, faced with low demand, suppose SEC could scrap the initial investment. In this case, it would lose $500 million of the original investment. This is much better than what would happen if it produced the solar-powered jet engines and generated a negative NPV of $3,611 million. It is difficult for decision trees to capture all of the managerial options in changing environments.

CONCEPT QUESTIONS

- What is a decision tree?
- What are two potential problems in using decision trees?

Sensitivity Analysis, Scenario Analysis, and Break-Even Analysis   8.3

One thrust of this book is that NPV analysis is a superior capital budgeting technique. In fact, because the NPV approach uses cash flows rather than profits, uses all the cash flows, and discounts the cash flows properly, it is difficult to find any theoretical fault with it. However, in our conversations with business people, we hear the phrase "a false sense of security" frequently. Managers point out that the documentation for capital budgeting proposals is often quite impressive. Cash flows are projected down to the last thousand dollars (or even the last dollar) for each year (or even each month). Opportunity costs and side effects are properly incorporated and sunk costs are ignored. When a high net present value appears at the bottom, one's temptation is to say yes to the proposal immediately. Nevertheless, the projected cash flow often goes unmet in practice, and the firm ends up with a money loser.

Sensitivity Analysis and Scenario Analysis

How can the firm get the net present value technique to live up to its potential? One approach is **sensitivity analysis** (aka *what-if analysis* and *bop analysis*[7]). This approach examines how sensitive a particular NPV calculation is to changes in underlying assumptions. We illustrate the technique with Solar Electronics' solar-powered jet engine from the previous section. As pointed out earlier, the cash flow

---

[7]*Bop* stands for *best, optimistic, pessimistic.*

forecasts for this project appear in Table 8.1. We begin by considering the assumptions underlying revenues, costs, and after-tax cash flows shown in the table.

Revenues

Sales projections for the proposed jet engine have been estimated by the marketing department as

$$\begin{array}{ccc}
\text{Number of jet} & & \text{Size of jet} \\
\text{engines sold} & = \text{Market share} \times & \text{engine market} \\
3{,}000 & = \qquad 0.30 \qquad \times & 10{,}000
\end{array}$$

$$\begin{array}{ccc}
\text{Sales revenues} & = \begin{array}{c}\text{Number of jet} \\ \text{engines sold}\end{array} \times & \begin{array}{c}\text{Price per} \\ \text{engine}\end{array} \\
\$6{,}000 \text{ million} & = \qquad 3{,}000 \qquad \times & \$2 \text{ million}
\end{array}$$

Thus, it turns out that the revenue estimates depend on three assumptions:

1. Market share
2. Size of jet engine market
3. Price per engine.

Costs

Financial analysts frequently divide costs into two types: variable and fixed. **Variable costs** change as the quantity of output changes; they are zero when production is zero. It is common to assume that variable costs are proportional to production. A typical variable cost is one that is constant per unit of output. For example, if direct labour is variable and one unit of final output requires $10 of direct labour, then 100 units of final output should require $1,000 of direct labour.

Fixed costs are not dependent on the amount of goods or services produced during the period. Fixed costs are usually measured as costs per unit of time, such as rent per month or salaries per year. Naturally, fixed costs are not fixed forever. They are only fixed over a predetermined time period.

Variable costs per unit produced have been estimated by the engineering department at $1 million. Fixed costs are $1,700 million per year. The cost breakdowns are

$$\begin{array}{ccc}
\begin{array}{c}\text{Variable} \\ \text{cost}\end{array} & = \begin{array}{c}\text{Variable cost} \\ \text{per unit}\end{array} \times & \begin{array}{c}\text{Number of jet} \\ \text{engines sold}\end{array} \\
\$3{,}000 \text{ million} & = \quad \$1 \text{ million} \quad \times & 3{,}000 \\
\text{Total cost before taxes} & = \text{Variable cost} \quad + & \text{Fixed cost} \\
\$4{,}700 \text{ million} & = \$3{,}000 \text{ million} \quad + & \$1{,}700 \text{ million}
\end{array}$$

The above estimates for market size, market share, price, variable cost, and fixed cost, as well as the estimate of initial investment, are presented in the middle column of Table 8.2. These figures represent the firm's expectations or best estimates of the different parameters. For purposes of comparison, the firm's analysts prepared both optimistic and pessimistic forecasts for the different variables. These are also provided in the table.

Variable	Pessimistic	Estimate Expected or best	Optimistic
Market size (per year)	5,000	10,000	20,000
Market share	0.2	0.3	0.5
Price	$ 1,900,000	$ 2,000,000	$ 2,200,000
Variable cost (per share)	$ 1,200,000	$ 1,000,000	$ 800,000
Fixed cost (per year)	$1,800,000,000	$1,700,000,000	$1,650,000,000
Investment	$1,900,000,000	$1,500,000,000	$1,000,000,000

Table 8.2
Different estimates for Solar Electronics' solar plane

Variable	Pessimistic	Estimate Expected or best	Optimistic
Market size (per year)*	($1,500)	$1,517	$7,551
Market share*	(494)	1,517	5,540
Price	914	1,517	2,724
Variable cost (per plane)	310	1,517	2,724
Fixed cost (per year)	1,316	1,517	1,618
Investment	1,117	1,517	2,017

Table 8.3
NPV calculations as of date 1 (in $ millions) for the solar plane using sensitivity analysis

Note: Under sensitivity analysis, one input is varied while all other inputs are assumed to meet their expectation. For example, an NPV of −$1,500 occurs when the pessimistic forecast of 5,000 is used for the market size. However, the expected forecasts from Table 8.2 are used for all other variables when −$1,500 is generated.

*We assume that the other divisions of the firm are profitable, implying that a loss on this project can offset income elsewhere in the firm. The firm reports a loss to Revenue Canada in these two cases. Thus, the loss on the project generates a tax rebate to the firm.

Standard sensitivity analysis calls for an NPV calculation for all three possibilities for a single variable, along with the expected forecast for all other variables. This procedure is illustrated in Table 8.3. For example, consider the NPV calculation of $7,551 million provided in the upper right-hand corner of this table. This occurs when the optimistic forecast of 20,000 units per year is used for market size. However, the expected forecasts from Table 8.2 are employed for all other variables when the $7,551 million figure is generated. Note that the same number, $1,517 million, appears in each row of the middle column of Table 8.3. This occurs because the expected forecast is used for the variable that was singled out, as well as for all other variables.

A table such as Table 8.3 can be used for a number of purposes. First, taken as a whole, the table can indicate whether NPV analysis should be trusted. In other words, it reduces the false sense of security we spoke of earlier. Suppose that NPV is positive when the expected forecast for each variable is used. However, further suppose that every number in the pessimistic column is wildly negative and every number in the optimistic column is wildly positive. Even a single error in this forecast greatly alters the estimate, making one leery of the net present value approach. A conservative manager might well scrap the entire NPV analysis in this case. Fortunately, this does not seem to be the case in Table 8.3, because all but two of the numbers are positive.

Managers viewing the table will likely consider NPV analysis to be useful for the solar-powered jet engine.

Second, sensitivity analysis shows where more information is needed. For example, error in the investment appears to be relatively unimportant because even under the pessimistic scenario, the NPV of $1,117 million is still highly positive. By contrast, the pessimistic forecast for market share leads to a negative NPV of −$494 million, and a pessimistic forecast for market size leads to a substantially negative NPV of −$1,500 million. Because the effect of incorrect estimates on revenues is so much greater than the effect of incorrect estimates on costs, more information on the factors determining revenues might be needed.

Unfortunately, sensitivity analysis suffers from some drawbacks. For example, sensitivity analysis may unwittingly *increase* the false sense of security among managers. Suppose all pessimistic forecasts yielded positive NPVs. A manager might feel that there is no way the project can lose money. Of course, the forecasters may simply have an optimistic view of a pessimistic forecast. To combat this, some companies do not treat optimistic and pessimistic forecasts subjectively. Rather, their pessimistic forecasts are always, say, 20 percent less than expected. Unfortunately, the cure in this case may be worse than the disease, because a deviation of a fixed percentage ignores the fact that some variables are easier to forecast than others.

In addition, sensitivity analysis treats each variable in isolation when, in reality, the different variables are likely to be related. For example, if ineffective management allows costs to get out of control, it is likely that variable costs, fixed costs, and investment will all rise above expectation at the same time. If the market is not receptive to a solar plane, both market share and price should decline together.

Managers frequently perform **scenario analysis,** a variant of sensitivity analysis, to minimize this problem. Simply put, this approach examines a number of different likely scenarios, where each scenario involves a confluence of factors. As a simple example, consider the effect of a few airline crashes. These events are likely to reduce flying in total, thereby limiting the demand for any new engines. Further, even if the crashes did not involve solar-powered aircraft, the public could become more adverse to any innovative and controversial technologies. Hence, SEC's market share might fall as well. Perhaps the cash flow calculations would look like those in Table 8.4 under the scenario of a plane crash. Given the calculations in the table, the NPV (in millions) would be $-\$2,023 = -\$1,500 - \$156 \times A_{0.15}^5$. A series of scenarios like this might illuminate issues concerning the project more effectively than would a standard application of sensitivity analysis.

Break-Even Analysis

determines the sales needed to break even

Our discussion of sensitivity analysis and scenario analysis suggests that there are many ways to examine variability in forecasts. We now present another approach, **break-even analysis.** As its name implies, this approach determines the sales needed to break even. The approach is a useful complement to sensitivity analysis, because it also sheds light on the severity of incorrect forecasts. We calculate the break-even point in terms of both accounting profit and present value.

	Year 1	Year 2
Revenues		$ 2,800
Variable costs		(1,400)
Fixed costs		(1,860)
Depreciation		(300)
Pretax profit		$ (760)
Tax $(T_c) = .40$*		304
Net profit		$ (456)
Cash flow		(156)
Initial investment costs	−$1,500	

Table 8.4
Cash flow forecast (in $ millions) under the scenario of a plane crash

Assumptions are:
  Market size, $7,000 (70 percent of expectation)
  Market share, 20% (⅔ of expectation)
  Fixed costs, $1,860 (higher than expectation)
Forecasts for all other variables are the expected forecasts as given in Table 8.2.
*Tax loss offsets income elsewhere in firm.

Table 8.5 Revenues and costs of project under different assumptions ($ millions, except unit sales)

Year 1	Years 2–6								
Initial investment	Annual unit sales	Revenues	Variable costs	Fixed costs	Depreci-ation	Taxes* $(T_c = 0.40)$	Net profits	Operating cash flows	NPV (evaluated date 1)
$1,500	$0	$0	$ 0	($1,700)	($300)	$800	($1,200)	($900)	($4,517)
1,500	1,000	2,000	(1,000)	(1,700)	(300)	400	(600)	(300)	(2,506)
1,500	3,000	6,000	(3,000)	(1,700)	(300)	(400)	600	900	1,517
1,500	10,000	20,000	(10,000)	(1,700)	(300)	(3,200)	4,800	5,100	15,596

*Loss is incurred in the first two rows. For tax purposes, this loss offsets income elsewhere in the firm.

Accounting Profit

Net profit under four different sales forecasts is

Unit sales	Net profit ($ millions)
0	−$1,200
1,000	−600
3,000	600
10,000	4,800

A more complete presentation of costs and revenues appears in Table 8.5.

We plot the revenues, costs, and profits under the different assumptions about sales in Figure 8.2. The revenue and cost curves cross at 2,000 jet planes. This is the break-even point—in other words, the point where the project generates no profits or losses. As long as sales are above 2,000 jet planes, the project will make a profit.

Figure 8.2
Break-even point
using accounting
numbers

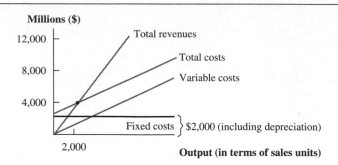

This break-even point can be calculated very easily. Because the sales price is $2 million per engine and the variable cost is $1 million per engine,[8] the after-tax difference per engine is

(Sales price − Variable cost) × (1 − T_c) = $0.60 million
($2 million − $1 million)   × (1 − 0.40)

where T_c is the corporate tax rate of 40 percent. This after-tax difference is called the **contribution margin** because it is the amount that each additional engine contributes to after-tax profit.

Fixed costs are $1,700 million and depreciation is $300 million, implying that the after-tax sum of these costs is

(Fixed costs   + Depreciation) × (1 − T_c) = $1,200 million
($1,700 million + $300 million) × (1 − 0.40)

That is, the firm incurs costs of $1,200 million, regardless of the number of sales. Because each engine contributes $0.60 million, sales must reach the following level to offset the above costs:

Accounting Profit Break-Even Point:

$$\frac{(\text{Fixed costs} + \text{Depreciation}) \times (1 - T_c)}{(\text{Sales price} - \text{Variable costs}) \times (1 - T_c)} = \frac{\$1,200 \text{ million}}{\$0.60 \text{ million}} = 2,000$$

Thus, 2,000 engines is the break-even point required for an accounting profit.

Present Value

As we have stated many times in the text, we are more interested in present value than we are in net profits. Therefore, we must calculate the present value of the cash flows. Given a discount rate of 15 percent, we have

---

[8]Though the previous section considered both optimistic and pessimistic forecasts for sales price and variable cost, break-even analysis only works with the expected or best estimates of these variables.

Unit sales	NPV ($ millions)
0	$-4,517
1,000	-2,506
3,000	1,517
10,000	15,596

These NPV calculations are reproduced in the last column of Table 8.5. We can see that the NPV is negative if SEC produces 1,000 jet engines and positive if it produces 3,000 jet engines. Obviously, the zero NPV point occurs between 1,000 and 3,000 jet engines.

The present value break-even point can be calculated very easily. The firm originally invested $1,500 million. This initial investment can be expressed as a five-year equivalent annual cost (EAC), determined by dividing the initial investment by the appropriate five-year annuity factor:

$$EAC = \frac{\text{Initial investment}}{\text{5-year annuity factor at 15\%}} = \frac{\text{Initial investment}}{A_{0.15}^5}$$

$$= \frac{\$1,500 \text{ million}}{3.3522} = \$447.5 \text{ million}$$

Note that the EAC of $447.5 million is greater than the yearly depreciation of $300 million. This must occur since the calculation of EAC implicitly assumes that the $1,500 million investment could have been invested at 15 percent; straight-line depreciation is equivalent to EAC for a zero rate of interest.

After-tax costs, regardless of output, can be viewed as

$$\underset{\text{million}}{\$1347.5} = \underset{\text{million}}{\$447.5} + \underset{\text{million}}{\$1,700} \times 0.60 - \underset{\text{million}}{\$300} \times 0.40$$

$$= EAC + \underset{\text{costs}}{\text{Fixed}} \times (1 - T_c) - \underset{\text{ation}}{\text{Depreci-}} \times T_c$$

That is, in addition to the initial investment's equivalent annual cost of $447.5 million, the firm pays fixed costs each year and receives a depreciation tax shield each year. The depreciation tax shield is written as a negative number because it offsets the costs in the equation. Because each plane contributes $0.60 million to after-tax profit, it will take the following sales to offset the above costs:

Present Value Break-Even Point: FINANCIAL

$$\frac{EAC + \text{Fixed costs} \times (1 - T_c) - \text{Depreciation} \times T_c}{(\text{Sales price} - \text{Variable costs}) \times (1 - T_c)} = \frac{\$1,347.5 \text{ million}}{\$0.60 \text{ million}}$$

$$= 2,246$$

Thus, 2,246 planes is the break-even point from the perspective of present value.

Why is the accounting break-even point different from the financial break-even point? When we use accounting profit as the basis for the break-even calculation, we subtract depreciation. Depreciation for the solar jet engines project was $300 million. If 2,000 solar jet engines are sold, SEC will generate sufficient revenues to cover the $300 million depreciation expense plus other costs. Unfortunately, at this level of sales, SEC will not cover the economic opportunity costs of the $1,500 million laid out for the investment. If we take into account that the $1,500 million could have been invested at 15 percent, the true annual cost of the investment is $447.5 million and not $300 million. Depreciation understates the true costs of recovering the initial investment. Thus, companies that break even on an accounting basis are really losing money. They are losing the opportunity cost of the initial investment.

CONCEPT QUESTIONS

- What is sensitivity analysis?
- Why is it important to perform sensitivity analysis?
- What is break-even analysis?
- Describe how sensitivity analysis interacts with break-even analysis.

8.4   Options

The analysis we have presented so far is static. Because corporations make decisions in a dynamic environment, they have options that should be considered in project valuation.

The Option to Expand

One particularly important option that we have not explicitly addressed is the option to expand. If we truly find a positive-NPV project, then there is an obvious consideration. Can we expand the project or repeat it to get an even larger NPV? Our static analysis implicitly assumes that the scale of the project is fixed.

For example, if the sales demand for a particular product were to exceed expectations greatly, we might investigate increasing production. If this is not feasible for some reason, then we could always increase cash flow by raising the price. Either way, the potential cash flow is higher than we have indicated because we have implicitly assumed that no expansion or price increase is possible. Overall, because we ignore the option to expand in our analysis, we underestimate NPV (all other things being equal).

The Option to Abandon

The option to close a facility also has value. Take the case of General Motors (GM). In 1991, GM announced plans to close 21 factories and cut 74,000 jobs by the end of 1995. Faced with low demand for its automobiles, GM decided to scrap the investment it had made in automobile manufacturing capacity and it will likely lose much of its original investment in the 21 factories (some of which are in Ontario). However, this outcome is much better than what would have resulted if GM had continued to operate these factories in a declining auto market.

Corporations frequently make changes in their plans when confronted with changing market conditions. One of the most stunning flip-flops in marketing history occurred when Coca-Cola publicly apologized for scrapping "old" Coke, a 99-year-old product. Henceforth, the company said, the "old" Coca-Cola would be revived as Coca-Cola Classic. By reviving the old Coke, the Coca-Cola Company undid an abandonment decision that had taken four-and-one-half years of planning and market research. Coke's original plan to abandon the old Coke and to replace it with new Coke was intended to break what, for several years, had been Pepsi's biggest advantage in the market: its ability to win taste contests. However, Coca-Cola's decision after two months to revive the old Coke came because of the unwillingness of a large number of consumers to go along with idea of a new Coke.

Strategic Options

Companies sometimes undertake new projects just to explore possibilities and evaluate potential future business strategies. This is a little like testing the water by sticking a toe in before diving. When McDonald's of Canada decided to open a restaurant in Moscow, strategic considerations likely dominated immediate cash flow analysis.

Since the Russian ruble was not then convertible, dollars were invested but no profits could be taken out in the foreseeable future. McDonald's strategic view was based on obtaining a potentially valuable option to spread its golden arches across the Commonwealth of Independent States from St. Petersburg to Vladivostok. In the words of McDonald's Canada executive Ron Cohen,

> If you are going to begin doing restaurant business in a country and you're looking at the long term, the last thing you want to do is offend the very people that you're there to serve. So our idea was "let's open up a ruble restaurant to serve Russians first" because that's what they want. What we want might be to generate hard currency, but we can take care of that later on.[9]

Such projects are hard to analyze using conventional discounted cash flow (DCF) because most of the benefits come in the form of strategic options (options for future related business moves). Projects that create such options may be valuable, but that value is difficult to measure. R&D, for example, is worthwhile for many firms precisely because it creates options for new products and procedures.

Other Options

Many other options present in NPV analysis should be considered. For example, implicitly we have treated proposed investments as if they were go or no-go decisions. Actually, there is a third possibility. The project can be postponed, perhaps in the hope of more favourable conditions. We call this the option to wait.

Investment decisions may trigger favourable or unfavourable tax treatment of existing assets. This can occur because, as explained in the appendix to Chapter 7, capital cost allowance calculations are based on assets in a pooled class. Tax liabilities for recaptured CCA and tax shelters from terminal losses occur only when an asset class is liquidated either by selling all the assets or by writing the undepreciated capital cost below zero. As a result, management has a potentially valuable tax option.

---

[9]P. Foster, "McDonald's Excellent Soviet Venture?" *Canadian Business,* May 1991, pp. 51-69.

Discounted Cash Flows and Options

Conventional NPV analysis discounts a project's cash flows estimated for a certain project life. The decision is whether to accept the project or reject it. In practice, our discussion showed that managers can expand or contract the scope of a project at various moments over its life. In theory, all such managerial options should be included in the project's value.

The market value of the project (M) will be the sum of the NPV of the project without options to expand or contract and the value of the managerial options (Opt):

$$M = NPV + Opt$$

▪ Example

Imagine two ways of producing Frisbees. Method A uses a conventional machine that has an active secondary market. Method B uses highly specialized machine tools for which there is no secondary market. Method B has no salvage value, but is more efficient. Method A has a salvage value, but is inefficient.

If production of Frisbees goes on until the machines employed in methods A and B are used up, the NPV of B will be greater than that of A. However, if there is some possibility that production of Frisbees will be stopped before the end of the useful life of the Frisbee-making machines, method A is better. Method A's higher value in the secondary market increases its NPV relative to B's.

Robichek and Van Horne as well as Dye and Long were among the first to recognize the abandonment value in project analysis.[10] More recently, Myers and Majd constructed a model of abandonment based on an American put option with varying dividend yields and an uncertain exercise price.[11] They present a numerical procedure for calculating abandonment value in problems similar to that of the Frisbee-making machine.

Brennan and Schwartz illustrate the value of managerial options to abandon a project in the case of a gold mine.[12] They show that a mine's value will depend on management's ability to shut it down if the price of gold falls below a certain point and to reopen it subsequently if conditions are right. They argue that valuation approaches that ignore these managerial options are likely to underestimate the value of the project substantially.

Morck, Schwartz, and Stangeland apply similar logic in valuing options to extend project life in the case of forestry resources. Depending on how rapidly trees grow and on wood prices, managers decide whether to harvest the forest or to wait for the trees to grow more.[13]

---

[10]A. Robichek and J. Van Horne, "Abandonment Value and Capital Budgeting," *Journal of Finance* (December 1967); and E. Dye and H. Long, "Abandonment Value and Capital Budgeting: Comment," *Journal of Finance* (March 1969).

[11]S. C. Myers and S. Majd, "Calculating Abandonment Value Using Option Pricing Theory," unpublished manuscript (June 1985).

[12]M. J. Brennan and E. S. Schwartz, "A New Approach to Evaluating Natural Resource Investments," *Midland Corporate Finance Journal* 3 (Spring 1985).

[13]R. Morck, E. Schwartz, and D. Stangeland, "The Valuation of Forestry Resources under Stochastic Prices and Inventories," *Journal of Financial and Quantitative Analysis* (December 1989), pp. 473–88.

There are both qualitative and quantitative approaches to adjusting for option value in capital budgeting decisions. Most firms use qualitative approaches, such as subjective judgment. However, quantitative approaches are gaining acceptance and we present further examples in Chapter 21.

Summary and Conclusions 8.5

This chapter discusses a number of practical applications of capital budgeting.

1. In Chapter 7, we observed how the net present value rule is used in capital budgeting. Here in Chapter 8, we explored the sources of positive net present value and explained what managers can do to create them.

2. Though NPV is the best capital budgeting approach conceptually, it has been criticized in practice for providing managers with a false sense of security. Sensitivity analysis calculates NPV under varying assumptions, giving managers a better feel for the project's risks. Sensitivity analysis, however, modifies only one variable at a time, while many variables are likely to vary together in the real world. Scenario analysis considers the joint movement of the different factors under different scenarios (e.g., war breaking out or oil prices skyrocketing). Finally, managers want to know how bad sales must be before a project loses money. Break-even analysis calculates the sales figure at which the project breaks even. Though break-even analysis is frequently performed on an accounting profit basis, we suggest that a net present value basis is more appropriate.

3. Discounted cash flow analysis in capital budgeting may be biased because it ignores options open to management. We discuss the option to expand and the option to abandon, strategic options, and other options.

Key Terms

Decision trees 230
Sensitivity analysis 233
Variable costs 234
Fixed costs 234

Scenario analysis 236
Break-even analysis 236
Contribution margin 238

Suggested Readings

The classic article on break-even analysis is:

U. E. Reinhart. "Breakeven Analysis for Lockheed's Tristar: An Application of Financial Theory." *Journal of Finance* (September 1977).

A trade book devoted to competitive strategy and advantage is:

M. E. Porter. *Competitive Advantage: Creating and Sustaining Superior Performance.* New York: The Free Press, 1985.

Questions and Problems

Decision Trees

8.1 The marketing manager for a growing consumer products firm is considering launching a new product. To determine consumers' interest in such a product, the manager may conduct a focus group that will cost $50,000 and has a 65-percent chance of correctly predicting the success of the product, or hire a consulting firm that will research the market at a cost of $100,000. The consulting firm boasts a correct assessment record of 85 percent. Going directly to the market with no prior testing will be the correct move 50 percent of the time. If the firm launches the product, and it is a success, the payoff will be $500,000. Which action will result in the highest expected payoff for the firm?

8.2 Tandem Bicycles is noticing a decline in sales due to the increase of lower-priced imports from the Far East. The CFO is considering a number of strategies to maintain market share. The options she sees are the following:

Price the products more aggressively, resulting in a $1.3 million decline in cash flow. With this approach, the likelihood that Tandem will lose no cash flow to the imports is 55 percent; there is a 45-percent probability that the firm will lose only $550,000 in cash flow to the imports.

Hire an Ottawa lobbyist to push for import tariffs on overseas manufacturers of bicycles. This will cost Tandem $800,000 and will have a 75-percent success rate, that is, no loss in cash flow to the importers. If the lobbyist does not succeed, Tandem Bicycles will lose $2 million in cash flow.

As the assistant to the CFO, which strategy would you recommend to your boss?

Accounting Break-Even Analysis

8.3 What is the minimum number of units that a distributor of big-screen TVs must sell in a given period to break even?

Sales price	=	$800
Variable costs	=	$100
Fixed costs	=	$200,000 (including inventory costs)
Depreciation	=	$35,000
Tax rate	=	40%

8.4 You are considering investing in a fledgling company that cultivates abalone for sale to local restaurants. The proprietor says he'll return all profits to you after covering operating costs and his salary. How many abalone must be harvested and sold in the first year of operations for you to get any payback? (Assume no depreciation.)

Price per adult abalone	=	$2.00
Variable costs	=	$0.72
Fixed costs	=	$300,000
Salaries	=	$40,000
Tax rate	=	40%

How much profit will be returned to you if he sells 300,000 abalone?

Present Value Break-Even Analysis

8.5 Using the information in the problem above, what is the present value of the break-even point if the discount rate is 17 percent, initial investment is $185,000, and the life of the project is 10 years?

8.6 The Cornchopper Company is considering the purchase of a new harvester. The company is currently involved in negotiations with the manufacturer and the parties have not come to a settlement regarding the final purchase price. The management of Cornchopper has hired you to determine the break-even purchase price of the harvester—the price that will make the NPV of the project zero. Base your analysis on the following facts:

1. The new harvester is not expected to affect revenues, but operating expenses will be reduced by $10,000 per year for 10 years.

2. The old harvester is now 5 years old, with 10 years of its scheduled life remaining. It was purchased for $45,000. It has been depreciated on a straight-line basis.

3. The old harvester has a current market value of $20,000.

4. The new harvester will be depreciated on a straight-line basis over its 10-year life.

5. The corporate tax rate is 40 percent.

6. The firm's required rate of return is 15 percent.

7. All cash flows occur at year-end. However, the initial investment, the proceeds from selling the old harvester, and any tax effects will occur immediately.

8. The expected market values of both harvesters at the end of their economic lives are zero.

Scenario Analysis

8.7 We are evaluating a project that costs $70,000, has a seven-year life, and has no salvage value. Assume that depreciation is straight-line. We require a return of 10 percent on such projects. The tax rate is 40 percent. Sales are projected at 15,000 units per year. Price per unit is $5.95, variable cost per unit is $2.63, and fixed costs are $25,000 per year.

a. Calculate the base-case cash flow and NPV. Suppose you believe that the sales projection is accurate only to within 25 percent. Evaluate the sensitivity of NPV to changes in that projection.

b. Suppose the projections given are all accurate to within 5 percent except for sales volume, which is only accurate to within 15 percent. Calculate the NPV under the best and worst cases.

8.8 You are considering a new product. It will cost $945,000 to launch, have a three-year life, and have no salvage value. Depreciation is straight-line. The required return is 20 percent, and the tax rate is 40 percent. Sales are projected at 80 units per year. Price per unit will be $35,000, variable cost per unit is $21,900, and fixed costs are $500,000 per year.

a. Based on your experience, you think that the sales, variable cost, and fixed cost projections above are probably accurate to within 10 percent. What are the upper and lower bounds for these projections? What is the base-case NPV? What are the best- and worst-case scenarios?

b. Evaluate the sensitivity of your base-case NPV to changes in fixed costs.

8.9 You are the financial analyst for a manufacturer of tennis raquets that has identified a graphite-like material that it is considering using in its raquets. Given the following information about the results of launching a new raquet, will you undertake the project? (Assumptions: Tax rate = 40 percent, Effective discount rate = 10 percent, Depreciation = $50,000 per year, and production will occur over the next three years only.)

	Estimate		
	Pessimistic	Expected	Optimistic
Market size	20,000	25,000	30,000
Market share	25%	35%	50%
Price	$ 90	$ 100	$ 115
Variable costs	$ 60	$ 55	$ 50
Fixed costs	$250,000	$200,000	$175,000
Investment	$300,000	$275,000	$250,000

8.10 What will happen to the preceding scenario if your competitor introduces a graphite composite that is even lighter than your product? What factors would this likely affect? Do an NPV analysis assuming that market size increases (due to more awareness of graphite-based raquets) to the level predicted by the optimistic scenario but your market share decreases to the pessimistic level (due to competitive forces). What does this tell you about the relative importance of market size versus market share?

8.11 We are examining a new project. In the base-case scenario we expect to sell 500 units per year at $20 net cash flow apiece for the next 10 years. In other words, annual operating cash flow is projected to be $20 × 500 = $10,000 per year. The relevant discount rate is 20 percent; initial investment is $55,000.

Refining the base-case scenario, it is likely that expected sales will be revised upward to 750 if the first year is a success and revised downward to 250 if it isn't.

There is also an option to expand the project's scale. The scale can be doubled in one year in the sense that twice as many units can be produced and sold. Naturally, expansion would only be desirable if the project is a success. This implies that if the project is a success, projected sales after expansion will be 1,500.

a. What is the base-case NPV?

b. After the first year, the project can be dismantled and sold for $40,000. If expected sales are revised based on the first year's performance, when would it make sense to abandon the investment? In other words, at what level of expected sales would it make sense to abandon the project?

c. If success and failure are equally likely, what is the NPV of the project? Consider the possibility of abandonment in answering.

d. Assuming that success and failure are equally likely, what is the value of the option to abandon in light of the revised sales forecast?

e. What is the value of the option to expand here?

PART THREE
RISK

This part of the book examines the relationship between expected return and risk for portfolios and individual assets. When capital markets are in equilibrium, they determine a trade-off between expected return and risk. The return that shareholders can expect to obtain in the capital markets is the return firms require when evaluating risky investment projects. The shareholders' required return is the firm's cost of equity capital.

Chapter 9 examines the modern history of Canadian capital markets. A central fact emerges: The return on risky assets has been higher on average than the return on risk-free assets. This fact supports the perspective we use in examining risk and return. In Chapter 9, we introduce several key intuitions of modern finance and show how they can be useful in determining a firm's cost of capital.

Chapters 10 and 11 contain more advanced discussions of risk and expected return. The chapters are self-contained and elaborate on the material in Chapter 9.

Chapter 10 shows what determines the relationship between return and risk for portfolios. The model of risk and expected return used in the chapter is called the *capital asset pricing model* (*CAPM*).

Chapter 11 examines risk and return from another perspective: the arbitrage pricing theory (APT) which yields insights that one cannot get from the CAPM. The key concept is that the total risk of individual stocks can be divided into two parts: systematic and unsystematic. The fundamental principle of diversification is that, for highly diversified portfolios, unsystematic risk disappears; only systematic risk survives.

The section on risk concludes in Chapter 12 with a discussion of estimating a firm's cost of equity capital and some of the problems involved.

CHAPTER 9

Capital Market Theory: An Overview

The previous chapters of this book presented techniques for capital budgeting with riskless cash flows. These cash flows should be discounted at the riskless rate of interest. Because most capital budgeting projects involve risky flows, a different discount rate must be used. The next four chapters are devoted to determining the discount rate for risky projects.

Past experience indicates that students find the upcoming material among the most difficult in the entire textbook. For this reason, we always teach the material by giving the results and conclusions first. By seeing where we are going ahead of time, it is easier to absorb the material when we get there. A synopsis of the four chapters follows:

1. Because our ultimate goal is to discount risky cash flows, we must first find a way to measure risk. In the current chapter, we measure the variability of a stock by the variance or standard deviation of its returns. If an individual held only *one* security, the variance or standard deviation of the security would be the appropriate measure of risk.

2. Because investors generally hold diversified portfolios, we are interested in the *contribution* of a security to the risk of the entire portfolio. Because much of an individual security's variance is neutralized in a large diversified portfolio, neither the security's variance nor its standard deviation can be viewed as its contribution to the risk of a large portfolio. Rather, this contribution is best measured by the security's *covariance* with the other securities in the portfolio. As an example, consider a stock whose returns are high when the portfolio's returns are low—and vice versa. This stock has negative covariance with the portfolio. In other words, it acts as a hedge, implying that the stock actually tends to reduce the risk of the portfolio. However, the stock could have a high variance, implying high risk for an investor holding only this security.

3. We discuss diversification and the related concept, *beta* (β) in the present chapter. The next chapter more fully develops the concept of beta. We argue that beta is the appropriate measure of a security's contribution to the risk of a large portfolio.

4. Investors will only hold a risky security if its expected return is high enough to compensate for its risk. It follows that the expected return on a security should be positively related to the security's beta. We introduce some of these ideas in the present chapter. In Chapter 10, we develop more fully the following equation:

$$\begin{matrix} \text{Expected return} \\ \text{on a security} \end{matrix} = \begin{matrix} \text{Risk-free} \\ \text{rate} \end{matrix} + \text{Beta} \times \left(\begin{matrix} \text{Expected return on} \\ \text{market portfolio} \end{matrix} - \begin{matrix} \text{Risk} \\ \text{free} \\ \text{rate} \end{matrix} \right)$$

Because the term in parentheses on the right-hand side is positive, this equation says that the expected return on a security is a positive function of its beta. This equation is frequently referred to as the *capital asset pricing model* (*CAPM*).

5. We derive the relationship between risk and return in a different manner in Chapter 11. However, many of the conclusions are quite similar. This chapter is based on *arbitrage pricing theory* (*APT*).

6. The theoretical ideas in Chapters 9, 10, and 11 are quite intellectually challenging. Fortunately, Chapter 12, which applies the theory to the selection of discount rates, is much simpler. In a world where a project has the same risk as the firm, and the firm has no debt, the expected return on the stock should serve as the project's discount rate. This expected return is taken from the capital asset pricing model, as presented above.

Because we have a long road ahead of us, the maxim that any journey begins with a single step applies here. We start with the perhaps mundane calculation of a security's return.

9.1   Returns

Dollar Returns

Suppose Canadian Atlantic Enterprises has several thousand shares of stock outstanding. You purchased some of these shares at the beginning of the year. It's now year-end, and you want to determine how well you've done on your investment.

Over the year, a company may pay cash *dividends* to its shareholders. As a shareholder in Canadian Atlantic Enterprises, you are a part owner of the company. If the company is profitable, it may choose to distribute some of its profits to shareholders. (Dividend policy is detailed in Chapter 18.)

In addition to the dividend, the other part of your return is the **capital gain** or *capital loss* on the stock arising from changes in the value of your investment. For example, consider the cash flows illustrated in Figure 9.1. The stock is selling for $37 per share. If you buy 100 shares, you have a total outlay of $3,700. Suppose that, over the year, the stock paid a dividend of $1.85 per share. By the end of the year, then, you would have received income of

Dividend = $1.85 × 100 = $185

Also the value of the stock rises to $40.33 per share by the end of the year. Your 100 shares now are worth $4,033, so you have a capital gain of

Capital gain = ($40.33 − $37) × 100 = $333

On the other hand, if the price had dropped to, say, $34.78, you would have a capital loss of

Capital loss = ($34.78 − $37) × 100 = −$222

Notice that a capital loss is the same thing as a negative capital gain.

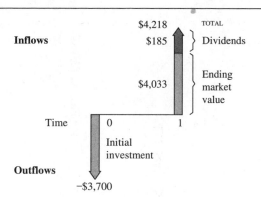

Figure 9.1
Dollar returns

The total dollar return on your investment is the sum of the dividend and the capital gain:

Total return = Dividend income + Capital gain (or loss)

In our first example, the total dollar return is thus given by

Total dollar return = $185 + 333 = $518

Notice that, if you sold the stock at the end of the year, the total amount of cash you would have would be your initial investment plus the total return. In the preceding example, then

Total cash if stock is sold = Initial investment + Total dollar return
$$= \$3,700 + 518$$
$$= \$4,218$$

As a check, notice that this is the same as the proceeds from the sale of the stock plus the dividends:

Proceeds from stock sale + Dividends = $40.33 × 100 + $185
$$= \$4,033 + 185$$
$$= \$4,218$$

Suppose you hold on to your Canadian Atlantic stock and don't sell it at the end of the year. Should you still consider the capital gain as part of your return? Isn't this only a paper gain and not really a cash flow if you don't sell it?

The answer to the first question is a strong yes; the answer to the second is an equally strong no. The capital gain is every bit as much a part of your return as the dividend, and you should certainly count it as part of your return. That you actually decided to keep the stock and not sell it or *realize* the gain in no way changes the fact that, if you want to, you could get the cash value of the stock.[1]

---

[1]After all, you could always sell the stock at year-end and immediately reinvest by buying the stock back. There is no difference between doing this and just not selling (assuming, of course, that there are no tax consequences from selling the stock). Again, the point is that whether you actually cash out or reinvest by not selling does not affect the return you earn.

Figure 9.2
Percentage returns:
Dollar return and
per-share return

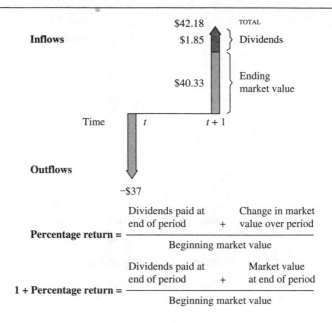

Percentage Returns

It is usually more convenient to summarize information about returns in percentage terms, rather than dollar terms, because that way your return does not depend on the amount invested. The question we want to answer is, How much do we get for each dollar we invest?

To answer this question, let P_t be the price of the stock at the beginning of the year and let D_{t+1} be the dividend paid on the stock during the year. Consider the cash flows in Figure 9.2. These are the same as those in Figure 9.1, except that we have now expressed everything on a per share basis.

In our example, the price at the beginning of the year was $37 per share and the dividend paid during the year on each share was $1.85. As we discussed in Chapter 5, expressing the dividend as a percentage of the beginning stock price results in the *dividend yield:*

Dividend yield $= D_{t+1}/P_t = \$1.85/\$37 = .05 = 5\%$

The second component of our percentage return is the capital gains yield. Recall (from Chapter 5) that this is calculated as the change in the price during the year (the capital gain) divided by the beginning price:

Capital gains yield $= (P_{t+1}-P_t)/P_t$
$$= (\$40.33 - 37)/\$37 = \$3.33/\$37 = .09 = 9\%$$

Combining these two results, we find that the *total returns* on the investment in Canadian Atlantic stock during the year, which we will label R_{t+1}, was

$$R_{t+1} = \frac{\text{Div}_{t+1}}{P_t} + \frac{(P_{t+1} - P_t)}{P_t} = 5\% + 9\% = 14\%$$

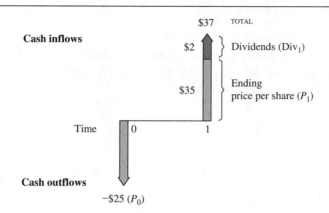

Figure 9.3
Cash flow—an investment example

From now on we will refer to returns in percentage terms.

■ *Example*

Suppose a stock begins the year with a price of $25 per share and ends with a price of $35 per share. During the year it paid a $2 dividend per share. What are its dividend yield, its capital gain, and its total return for the year? We can imagine the cash flows in Figure 9.3.

$$R_1 = \frac{Div_1}{P_0} + \frac{P_1 - P_0}{P_0}$$

$$= \frac{\$2}{\$25} + \frac{\$35 - \$25}{\$25} = \frac{\$12}{\$25}$$

$$= 8\% + 40\% = 48\%$$

Thus, the stock's dividend yield, its capital gain, and its total return are 8 percent, 40 percent, and 48 percent, respectively. ■

Suppose you had $5,000 to invest. The total dollar return you would have received on an investment in the stock is $5,000 × 1.48 = $7,400. If you know the total return on the stock, you do not need to know how many shares you would have had to purchase to figure out how much money you would have made on the $5,000 investment. You just use the total return.[2]

---

[2]Consider the stock in the previous example. We have ignored the question of when during the year you receive the dividend. Does it make a difference? To explore this question, suppose first that the dividend is paid at the very beginning of the year, and you receive it the moment after you have purchased the stock. Suppose, too, that interest rates are 10 percent, and that immediately after receiving the dividend you loan it out. What will be your total return, including the loan proceeds, at the end of the year?

Alternatively, instead of loaning out the dividend you could have reinvested it and purchased more of the stock. If that is what you do with the dividend, what will your total return be? (Warning: This does not go on forever, and when you buy more stock with the cash from the dividend on your first purchase, you are too late to get yet another dividend on the new stock.)

Finally, suppose the dividend is paid at year-end. What answer would you get for the total return? As you can see, by ignoring the question of when the dividend is paid when we calculate the return, we are implicitly assuming that it is received at the end of the year and cannot be reinvested during the year. The right way to figure out the return on a stock is to determine exactly when the dividend is received and to include the return that comes from reinvesting the dividend in the stock. This gives a pure stock return without confounding the issue by requiring knowledge of the interest rate during the year.

- What are the two parts of total return?
- Why are unrealized capital gains or losses included in the calculation of returns?
- What is the difference between a dollar return and a percentage return? Why are percentage returns more convenient?

9.2   Holding Period Returns

Investors look to capital market history as a guide to the risks and returns of alternative portfolio strategies. The data set we will use (Table 9.1) was assembled by the Alexander Group for use in advising large institutional investors. It draws on two major studies: Roger Ibbotson and Rex Sinquefield conducted a famous set of studies dealing with rates of return in U.S. financial markets. James Hatch and Robert White examined Canadian returns.[3] Our data present year-to-year historical rates of return on six important types of financial investments or asset classes:

1. *Canadian common stocks.* The common stock portfolio is based on a sample of the largest companies (in terms of total market value of outstanding stock) in Canada.[4]
2. *U.S. common stocks.* This portfolio consists of 500 of the largest U.S. companies. The full historical series is given in U.S. dollars and in Canadian dollars adjusting for shifts in exchange rates.
3. *Small stocks.* This portfolio, compiled by Burns Fry, includes the bottom fifth of stocks listed on the Toronto Stock Exchange (TSE). The ranking is by market value of equity capitalization—the price of the stock multiplied by the number of shares outstanding.
4. *Long bonds.* This a portfolio of high-quality, long-term corporate, provincial, and Government of Canada bonds.
5. *Canada Treasury bills.* This a portfolio of Treasury bills (*T-bills* for short) with a three-month maturity.
6. *Real estate.* This is a portfolio of commercial property.[5]

These returns are not adjusted for transactions costs, inflation, or taxes; thus, they are nominal, pretax returns. In addition to the year-to-year returns on these financial instruments, the year-to-year percentage change in the Statistics Canada Consumer Price Index (CPI) is also computed. This is a commonly used measure of inflation so we can calculate real returns using this as the inflation rate.

---

[3]The two classic studies are R. G. Ibbotson and R. A. Sinquefield, *Stocks, Bonds, Bills, and Inflation* (Charlottesville, Va.: Financial Analysts Research Foundation, 1982), and J. Hatch and R. White, *Canadian Stocks, Bonds, Bills, and Inflation: 1950–1983* (Charlottesville, Va.: Financial Analysts Research Foundation, 1985). Additional sources used by the Alexander Group are Burns Fry for small capitalization stocks, ScotiaMcLeod for long bonds, and Statistics Canada CANSIM for rates of exchange and inflation.

[4]From 1956 on, the TSE 300 is used. For earlier years, the Alexander Group used a sample provided by the TSE.

[5]The real estate index is the Morguard Property Index from 1972 through 1974 and the Frank Russell Property Index after 1974.

Table 9.1 Year-by-year total percentage returns, 1984−92

Year	Inflation	Canadian stock	T-bills	Long bonds	Real estate	S&P 500 (Cdn.)	S&P 500 (U.S.)	Small stocks
($ Cdn.)	($ U.S.)							
1948	8.88	12.25	0.40	−0.08	—	—	—	—
1949	1.09	23.85	0.45	5.18	—	—	—	—
1950	5.91	51.69	0.51	1.74	—	—	—	—
1951	10.66	25.44	0.71	−7.89	—	—	—	—
1952	−1.38	0.01	0.95	5.01	—	—	—	—
1953	0.00	2.56	1.54	5.00	—	—	—	—
1954	0.00	39.37	1.62	12.23	—	—	—	—
1955	0.47	27.68	1.22	0.13	—	—	—	—
1956	3.24	12.68	2.63	−8.87	—	2.35	6.53	—
1957	1.79	−20.58	3.76	7.94	—	−8.51	−10.78	—
1958	2.64	31.25	2.27	1.92	—	40.49	43.38	—
1959	1.29	4.59	4.39	−5.07	—	10.54	11.94	—
1960	1.27	1.78	3.66	12.19	—	5.15	0.48	—
1961	0.42	32.75	2.86	9.16	—	32.85	26.82	—
1962	1.67	−7.09	3.81	5.03	—	−5.77	−8.75	—
1963	1.64	15.60	3.58	4.58	—	23.19	22.65	—
1964	2.02	25.43	3.73	6.16	—	15.75	16.38	—
1965	3.16	6.68	3.79	0.05	—	12.48	12.35	—
1966	3.45	−7.07	4.89	−1.05	—	−9.32	−10.06	—
1967	4.07	18.09	4.38	−0.48	—	23.59	23.95	—
1968	3.91	22.45	6.22	2.14	—	10.28	11.08	—
1969	4.79	−0.81	6.83	−2.86	—	−8.47	−8.47	—
1970	1.31	−3.57	6.89	16.39	—	−1.98	3.98	−11.69
1971	5.16	8.01	3.86	14.84	—	13.30	14.32	15.83
1972	4.91	27.38	3.43	8.11	—	18.09	18.94	44.72
1973	9.36	0.27	4.78	1.97	35.45	−14.71	−14.80	−7.82
1974	12.30	−25.93	7.68	−4.53	19.43	−26.88	−26.49	−26.89
1975	9.52	18.48	7.05	8.02	14.06	40.79	37.27	41.00
1976	5.87	11.02	9.10	23.64	10.24	22.73	23.61	22.77
1977	9.45	10.71	7.64	9.04	14.88	0.42	−7.40	39.93
1978	8.44	29.72	7.90	4.10	11.95	15.46	6.52	44.41
1979	9.69	44.77	11.04	−2.83	13.00	16.56	18.44	46.04
1980	11.20	30.13	12.23	2.18	23.11	35.66	32.42	42.86
1981	12.20	−10.25	19.11	−2.09	26.40	−5.57	−4.91	−15.10
1982	9.23	5.54	15.27	45.82	1.19	26.03	21.58	4.55
1983	4.51	35.49	9.39	9.61	6.69	23.98	22.43	44.30
1984	3.77	−2.39	11.21	16.90	12.42	12.69	6.10	−2.33
1985	4.38	25.07	9.70	26.68	11.52	39.20	31.57	38.98
1986	4.19	8.95	9.34	17.21	12.68	16.71	18.21	12.33
1987	4.12	5.88	8.20	1.77	14.72	−1.01	5.17	−5.47
1988	3.96	11.08	8.94	11.30	16.59	6.93	16.50	5.46
1989	5.17	21.37	11.95	15.17	16.84	27.68	31.43	10.66
1990	5.00	−14.80	13.28	4.32	4.32	−3.08	−3.19	−27.32
1991	3.78	12.02	9.90	25.30	0.07	30.05	30.55	18.51
1992	2.14	−1.43	6.65	11.57	−5.54	18.43	7.68	13.01

Source: The Alexander Group.

Figure 9.4 Returns to a $1 investment, 1948–1992

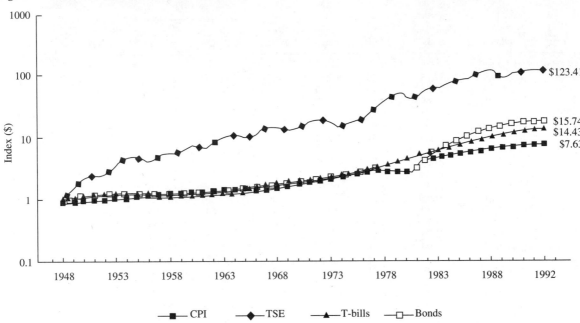

The six asset classes included cover a broad range of investments popular with Canadian individuals and financial institutions. We include U.S. stocks since Canadian investors often invest abroad—particularly in the United States.[6]

Before looking closely at the different portfolio returns, we take a look at the "big picture." Figure 9.4 shows what happened to $1 invested in three of these different portfolios at the beginning of 1948. The growth in value for each of the different portfolios over the 45-year period ending in 1992 is given separately. Notice that, to get everything on a single graph, some modification in scaling is used. As is commonly done with financial series, the vertical axis is on a logarithmic scale such that equal distances measure equal percentage changes (as opposed to equal dollar changes) in values.

Looking at Figure 9.4, we see that the common stock investments did the best overall. Every dollar invested in Canadian stocks grew to $123.41 over the 45 years.

At the other end, the T-bill portfolio grew to only $14.43. Long bonds did only slightly better with an ending value of $15.74. These values are less than impressive when we consider inflation over this period. As illustrated, the price level climbed such that $7.63 is needed just to replace the original $1.

Figure 9.4 gives the total value of a $1 investment in the Canadian stock market from 1948 through 1992. In other words, it shows what the total return would have

---

[6]Chapter 31 discusses exchange rate risk and other risks of foreign investments.

been if the dollar had been left in the stock market and if each year the dividends from the previous year had been reinvested in more stock. If R_t is the return in year t (expressed in decimals), the total you would have from year 1 to year T is the product of the returns in each of the years:

$$(1 + R_1) \times (1 + R_2)...\times (1 + R_t)...\times (1 + R_T)$$

For example, if the returns were 11 percent, -5 percent, and 9 percent in a three-year period, a \$1 investment at the beginning of the period would, at the end of the three years, be worth

$$
\begin{aligned}
(1 + R_1) \times (1 + R_2) \times (1 + R_3) &= (\$1 + 0.11) \times (\$1 - 0.05) \times (\$1 + 0.09) \\
&= \$1.11 \times \$0.95 \times \$1.09 \\
&= \$1.15
\end{aligned}
$$

Notice that 0.15 (or 15 percent) is the total return and that it includes the return from reinvesting the first-year dividends in the stock market for two more years and reinvesting the second-year dividends for the final year. The 15 percent is called a three-year **holding period return.** Table 9.1 gives annual holding period returns from 1948 to 1992. From this table you can determine holding period returns for any combination of years.

Given the historical record as discussed so far, why would any investor hold any asset class other than common stocks? A close look at Figure 9.4 provides an answer. The T-bill portfolio and the long-term bond portfolio grew more slowly than did the stock portfolio, but they also grew much more steadily. The common stocks ended up on top, but as you can see, they grew erratically at times. For example, comparing Canadian stocks with T-bills, the stocks had a smaller return than long-term government bonds in 15 years during this period.

To illustrate the variability of the different investments, we examine a few selected years in Table 9.1. For example, looking at the long-term bonds, we see the largest historical return (45.82 percent) occurred not so long ago (in 1982). This was a good year for bonds. The largest single-year return in the table is a very healthy 46.04 percent for small stocks in 1979. In the same year, T-bills returned only 11.04 percent. In contrast, the largest Treasury bill return was 19.11 percent (in 1981).

CONCEPT QUESTIONS

- With 20–20 hindsight, what was the best investment for the period 1981–82?
- Why doesn't everyone just buy common stocks as investments?
- What was the smallest return observed over the 45 years for each of these investments? When did it occur?
- How many times did large Canadian stocks (common stocks) return more than 30 percent? How many times did they return less than 20 percent?
- What was the longest winning streak (years without a negative return) for large Canadian stocks? For long-term bonds?
- How often did the T-bill portfolio have a negative return?

Figure 9.5
Frequency
distribution of
returns on
Canadian common
stocks

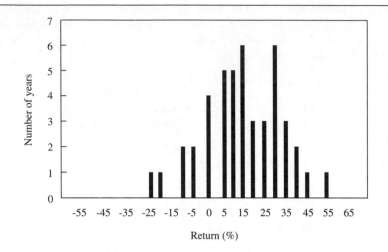

9.3   Return Statistics

The history of capital market returns is too complicated to be useful in its undigested form. To use the history we must first find some manageable ways of describing it, dramatically condensing the detailed data into a few simple statements.

This is where two important numbers summarizing the history come in. The first and most natural number we want to find is some single measure that best describes the past annual returns on the stock market. In other words, what is our best estimate of the return that an investor could have realized in a particular year over the 1948–92 period? This is the *average return*.

Figure 9.5 plots the histogram of the yearly stock market returns given in Table 9.1. This plot is the **frequency distribution** of the numbers. The height of the graph gives the number of sample observations in the range on the horizontal axis.

Given a frequency distribution like Figure 9.5's, we can calculate the **average** or **mean** of the distribution. To compute the arithmetic average of the distribution, we add up all of the values and divide the total number (45 in our case because we have 45 years of data) by T. The bar over the R is used to represent the mean, and the formula is the ordinary formula for the average:

$$\text{Mean} = \overline{R} = \frac{(R_1 + \ldots + R_T)}{T}$$

The arithmetic mean of the 45 annual returns from 1948 to 1992 is 12.58 percent.

■ *Example*

The returns on Canadian common stocks from 1989 to 1992 were (in decimals) 0.2137, −0.1480, 0.1202, and −0.0143, respectively. (These numbers are taken from Table 9.1.) The average or mean return over these four years is

$$\overline{R} = \frac{0.2137 - 0.1480 + 0.1202 - 0.0143}{4} = 0.0429 \ \blacksquare$$

■ Why are return statistics useful?

Average Stock Returns and Risk-Free Returns   9.4

Now that we have computed the average return on the stock market, it seems sensible to compare it with the returns on other securities. The most obvious comparison is with the low variability returns in the government bond market. These are free of most of the volatility we see in the stock market.

The Government of Canada borrows money by issuing bonds, which the investing public holds. As we discussed in an earlier chapter, these bonds come in many forms. The ones we'll look at here are called *Treasury bills* or *T-bills*. Once a week the government sells some bills at an auction. A typical bill is a pure discount bond that will mature in a year or less. Because the government can raise taxes to pay for the debt it incurs—a trick that many of us would like to be able to perform—this debt is virtually free of risk of default. Thus, we call this the *risk-free return* over a short time (one year or less).[7]

An interesting comparison, then, is between the virtually risk-free return on T-bills and the very risky return on common stocks. This difference between risky returns and risk-free returns is often called the *excess return on the risky asset*. It is called *excess* because it is the additional return resulting from the riskiness of common stocks, and it is interpreted as a **risk premium.**

Table 9.2 shows the average stock return, bond return, T-bill return, and inflation rate from 1948 through 1992. From this we can derive risk premiums. We can see that the average risk premiums for common stocks for the entire period was 6.39 percent (12.58% − 6.19%).

One of the most significant observations of stock market data is this long-run excess of the stock return over the risk-free return. An investor for this period was rewarded for investment in the stock market with an extra or excess return over what would have been achieved by simply investing in T-bills.

Why was there such a reward? Does it mean that it never pays to invest in T-bills and that someone who invested in them instead of in the stock market needs a course in finance? A complete answer to these questions lies at the heart of modern finance, and Chapter 10 is devoted entirely to them.

Part of the answer, however, can be found by looking more closely at Table 9.2. We see that the standard deviation of T-bills is substantially less than that of common stocks. This suggests that the risk of T-bills is below that of common stocks. Because the answer turns on the riskiness of investments in common stock, we now shift our attention to measuring this risk.

■ What is the major observation about capital markets that we will seek to explain?
■ What does the observation tell us about investors for the period from 1948 through 1992?

---

[7] A Treasury bill with a 90-day maturity is risk-free only during that particular time period.

Table 9.2 Average annual returns, 1948–1992

Investment	Average Return	Risk Premium	Standard Deviation	Distribution
Canadian common stocks	12.58%	6.39%	16.82%	
Long bonds	7.04	0.85	10.02	
Treasury bills	6.19	0.00	4.26	
Inflation	4.68		3.53	

-50%   0%   70%

9.5   Risk Statistics

The second number that we use to characterize the distribution of returns is a measure of risk. There is no universally agreed upon definition of risk. One way to think about the risk of returns on common stock is in terms of how spread out the frequency distribution in Figure 9.5 is.[8] The spread or dispersion of a distribution is a measure of how much a particular return can deviate from the mean return. If the distribution is very spread out, the returns that will occur are very uncertain. By contrast, a distribution whose returns are all within a few percentage points of each other is tight and the returns are less uncertain. The measures of risk we will discuss are variance and standard deviation.

Variance and Standard Deviation

The **variance** and its square root, the **standard deviation,** are the most common measures of variability or dispersion. We will use Var to denote the variance and SD to represent the standard deviation.

---

[8]Several condensed frequency distributions are also in the extreme right column of Table 9.2.

■ *Example*

The returns on Canadian common stocks from 1989 to 1992 were (in decimals) 0.2137, −0.1480, 0.1202, and −0.0143, respectively. The variance of this sample is computed as

$$\text{Var} = \frac{1}{T-1}[(R_1 - \overline{R})^2 + (R_2 - \overline{R})^2 + (R_3 - \overline{R})^2 + (R_4 - \overline{R})^2]$$

$$0.0250 = \frac{1}{3}[(.2137 - .0429)^2 + (.1480 - .0429)^2 + (.1202 - .0429)^2 + (-.0143 - .0429)^2]$$

$$SD = \sqrt{.0250} = .1508 = 15.80\% \quad ■$$

This formula tells us just what to do: Take each of the T individual returns $(R_1, R_2, ...)$ and subtract the average return, $\overline{R}$; square the result, and add them all up; finally, divide this total by the number of returns less one $(T-1)$. The standard deviation is always just the square root of the variance.

Using the actual stock returns in Table 9.1 for the 45-year period 1948–92 in the above formula, the resulting standard deviation of stock returns is 16.82 percent. The standard deviation is the standard statistical measure of the spread of a sample, and it will be the measure we use most of the time. Its interpretation is facilitated by a discussion of the normal distribution.

Normal Distribution and Its Implications for Standard Deviation

A large enough sample drawn from a **normal distribution** looks like the bell-shaped curve drawn in Figure 9.6. As you can see, this distribution is *symmetric* about its mean, not *skewed,* and it has a much cleaner shape than the actual distribution of yearly returns drawn in Figure 9.5.[9] Of course, if we had been able to observe stock market returns for 1,000 years, we might have filled in a lot of the jumps and jerks in Figure 9.5 and had a smoother curve.

In classical statistics, the normal distribution plays a central role, and the standard deviation is the usual way of representing the spread of a normal distribution. For the normal distribution, the probability of having a return that is above or below the mean by a certain amount depends only on the standard deviation. For example, the probability of having a return that is within one standard deviation of the mean of the distribution is approximately 0.68 or $\frac{2}{3}$, and the probability of having a return that is within two standard deviations of the mean is approximately 0.95.

The 16.82 percent standard deviation we found for stock returns from 1948 through 1992 can now be interpreted in the following way: If stock returns are roughly normally distributed, the probability that a yearly return will fall in the range −4.24 percent to +29.40 percent (12.58 percent plus or minus one standard deviation, 16.82 percent) is about 67 percent. This range is illustrated in Figure 9.6. In other words,

---

[9]Some people define risk as the possibility of obtaining a return below the average. Some measures of risk, such as semivariance, use only the negative deviations from the average return. However, for symmetric distributions, such as the normal distribution, this method of measuring downside risk is equivalent to measuring risk with deviations from the mean on both sides.

Figure 9.6
The normal
distribution

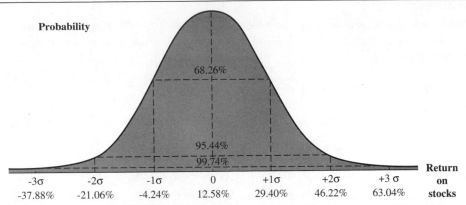

In the case of a normal distribution, there is a 68.26-percent probability that a return will be within one standard deviation of the mean. In this example, there is a 68.26-percent probability that a yearly return will be between −4.2 percent and 29.4 percent.

There is a 95.44-percent probability that a return will be within two standard deviations of the mean. In this example, there is a 95.44-percent probability that a yearly return will be between −21.1 percent and 46.2 percent.

Finally, there is a 99.74-percent probability that a return will be within three standard deviations of the mean. In this example, there is a 99.74-percent probability that a yearly return will be between −37.9 percent and 63.0 percent.

there is about one chance in three that the return will be *outside* this range. Based on historical experience and assuming that the past is a good guide to the future, investors who buy shares in large Canadian companies should expect to be outside this range in one year out of every three. This reinforces our earlier observations about stock market volatility. However, there is only a 5-percent chance (approximately) that we would end up outside the range −21.06 percent to 46.22 percent (12.58 percent plus or minus 2 × 16.82%). These points are also illustrated in Figure 9.6.

The distribution in Figure 9.6 is a theoretical distribution, sometimes called the *population*. There is no assurance that the actual distribution of observations in a given sample will produce a histogram that looks exactly like the theoretical distribution. We can see how messy the actual frequency function of historical observations is by observing Figure 9.5. If we were to keep on generating observations for a long enough period of time, however, the aberrations in the sample would disappear, and the actual historical distribution would start to look like the underlying theoretical distribution.

Our comparison illustrates how sampling error exists in any individual sample. In other words, the distribution of the sample only approximates the true distribution; we always measure the truth with some error. For example, we do not know what the true expected return was for common stocks in the 45-year history. However, we are sure that 12.58 percent is very close to it.

Further Perspective on Returns and Risk

Table 9.2 presents returns and risks for major asset classes over a reasonably long period of Canadian history. Our discussion of these data suggested that the greater the potential reward, the greater is the risk. In particular, the equity risk premium was a healthy 6 percent over this period for Canadian stocks.

Investment	Average return	Risk premium	Standard deviation
Canadian common stocks	10.79%	0.77%	17.04%
U.S. common stocks (Canadian $)	14.10	4.08	17.68
Long bonds	11.26	1.24	11.97
Treasury bills	10.02	0.00	3.17
Small Canadian stocks	14.99	4.97	23.80
Real estate	13.00	2.98	9.05
Inflation	6.91		3.13

Table 9.3
Historical returns and standard deviations, 1973–1992

Table 9.3 expands the evidence showing the average returns and standard deviations on different investments for the recent 20-year period 1973–92. Notice that we have added two new investments for which data are available for the more recent period: small Canadian stocks and real estate.

Turning first to the new asset classes, the experience of small stocks is consistent with our general conclusion about return and risk. This investment has both the highest return and the largest standard deviation in Table 9.3. On the other hand, with its relatively low standard deviation and high return, real estate appears to be an exception. However, the standard deviation (though mathematically correct) likely understates the risk for real estate. This series is based on appraised values (as opposed to market values) and so underplays the volatility of real estate returns.

Table 9.3 also presents data for the three asset classes in Table 9.2: Canadian common stock, long bonds, and Treasury bills. The difference is that, in Table 9.3, the data only span 20 recent years. Comparing the two tables uncovers some similarities and some differences. The recent period, like the longer sample, displays positive risk premiums for both long bonds and Canadian stocks. However, the risk premium for stocks is only 0.77 percent as opposed to 6.39 percent in Table 9.2. Bonds performed relatively better over the recent period and outperformed stocks marginally.

Part of this difference is likely sample-specific; Table 9.1 shows that stocks had bad years at the end of the period we chose. We would expect common stocks to have a higher risk premium than long bonds. But comparing stock risk premiums over these two periods raises a more puzzling question. Why are common stock risk premiums so high for the post–World War II period? The appendix to this chapter examines the question in detail. Here, we simply note that care must be taken in measuring and projecting historical risk premiums.

CONCEPT QUESTIONS

- Define sample estimates of variance and standard deviation.
- How does the normal distribution help us interpret standard deviation?
- Assuming that long-term bonds have an approximately normal distribution, what is the approximate probability of earning 17 percent or more in a given year? With T-bills, what is this probability?
- Real estate returns appear to be an anomaly with higher returns and lower standard deviation than common stocks in Table 9.3. What factors could explain this?

9.6

The Discount Rate for Risky Projects

We can now consider the discount rate for risky projects.

The Case Where Risk Is the Same as in the Market

Let us suppose there is a nonfinancial investment that has the same risk as the TSE 300 composite index. We will frequently call the TSE 300 the *market portfolio of risky assets.*[10] What return should we require on this investment? We should use the current expected return on the market portfolio as our discount rate because this is the return that we would give up if we took on our proposed project instead of investing in the TSE 300. As discussed earlier, financial economists frequently view the expected return on the market portfolio as

$$\text{Expected return on} \atop \text{market portfolio} = {\text{Risk-free} \atop \text{rate}} + {\text{Expected risk} \atop \text{premium}}$$

Here, the expected return on the market is expressed as the sum of the risk-free rate and the expected *risk premium.* This risk premium is simply compensation for the risk that investors in the market portfolio bear.

Because the expected return on the market portfolio consists of two parts, let us try to estimate both of them. The risk-free rate is easy to estimate. If a financial newspaper tells us that the current rate for one-year Treasury bills is 7 percent, it is quite plausible to set the risk-free rate at 7 percent. The expected risk premium is much more difficult to estimate, because expected returns on premiums are obviously not provided in the financial newspaper. Alternative methods such as surveying finance professors (or students, for that matter) would probably yield meaningless results.

Instead, we get our estimate of the risk premium from the past. Table 9.2 shows us that the average return on Canadian common stocks from 1948 to 1992 was 12.58 percent, and the average return on Canadian Treasury bills over the same period was 6.19 percent. The historical risk premium is 6.39 percent (12.58% − 6.19%). Financial economists argue that the historical risk premium is our best predictor of the expected risk premium in the future.[11] Thus, given the T-bill rate of 7 percent, they would calculate the expected return on the market as

$$\text{Expected return} \atop \text{on the market} = {\text{Current} \atop \text{risk-free rate}} + {\text{Historical} \atop \text{risk premium}}$$
$$13.39\% = 7\% + 6.39\%$$

Therefore, the discount rate on the risky, nonfinancial investment is 13.39 percent.

---

[10]Strictly speaking, the TSE 300 index is not the market portfolio because it does not include all risky assets, such as real estate. However, economists generally argue that it is an acceptable proxy for the market. In addition, it is much easier to construct than a more realistic portfolio including assets not traded in a central marketplace.

[11]Some people may not agree with this. However, if risk today is about the same as it has been over the last 45 years and individuals' distaste for risk is about the same, the historical risk premium will be a good estimate of the future risk premium.

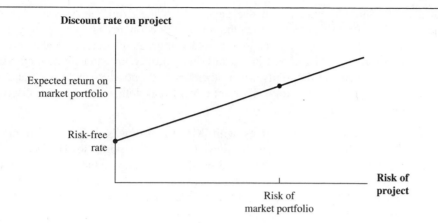

Figure 9.7
Relationship between the project's discount rate and its risk

The Case Where Risk Is Different Than in the Market

The above discussion concerned a project with risk *equal* to that of the market. How does one determine the discount rate of a project whose risk *differs* from that of the market? A possible relationship is provided in Figure 9.7, where the discount rate is positively related to the project's risk. This is plausible because (as we argued in earlier chapters) both individuals and firms demand a high expected return on a project with high risk.

In its present form, this graph is of some use; a manager could easily employ it in an *ad hoc* fashion. The manager would decide whether a project has more or less risk than the market. If the project's risk were judged to be high, the manager would choose a discount rate higher than the market's expected return. Conversely, if the project's risk were judged to be low, the manager would choose a discount rate lower than that of the market as a whole. We used the term *ad hoc* because we need to answer a question before applying the graph in a precise manner. The question is this: What is the appropriate measure of risk?

The question may surprise you, because the standard deviation of the project's return may seem the obvious choice for the project's risk measure. However, financial economists disagree. They point out that a diversified investor is not concerned with the risk of any individual asset. Rather, the investor cares about the effect of the asset on the risk of the entire portfolio.

■ *Example*

Diversified Industries is considering an investment in either a gold mining venture or a utility franchise. At a meeting of the board of directors Ms. Katherine Russell argues that the cash flows from a gold mining operation are inherently quite variable. Thus, a high discount rate should be applied to these flows. Because a typical utility is less volatile, a low discount rate is appropriate.

Another director, Mr. Zelig Breakstone, disagrees. He states that the firm itself is diversified and most of the firm's shareholders are diversified. He argues that gold prices generally rise during inflationary times, just when stock prices tend to fall. Gold prices fall in deflationary times, just when stock prices tend to rise. Thus, he argues that a gold mining venture is a hedge against both the firm's other assets and the shareholders' other investments. When the rest of the economy is doing well, gold is doing poorly—and vice versa. Because the gold venture is inherently a hedge, it does not add to the risk of a large portfolio. Conversely, utility investments do well when other assets do well and do poorly when other assets do poorly. The utility franchise adds to the risk of a large portfolio. Therefore, Mr. Breakstone wants a higher discount rate for the utility franchise. ∎

Modern portfolio theory agrees with Mr. Breakstone's logic. According to financial economists, any asset must be viewed as part of a portfolio. The asset's risk is the contribution to the variability of the portfolio. Because standard deviation and variance treat an asset in isolation, we must move to statistical measures relating one asset to another. We now turn to beta and diversification, the building blocks of modern portfolio theory.

CONCEPT QUESTION

∎ How can financial managers use the theory of capital markets to estimate the required rate of return on nonfinancial investments with the same risk as the average common stock?

9.7   Risk and Beta

Diversification

This chapter has looked closely at the historical risk and return of highly diversified portfolios typified by the TSE 300 composite index. We found that the historical standard deviation of the TSE 300 composite is around 17 percent. However, the historical standard deviations of individual common stocks are much higher than 17 percent. Table 9.4 shows estimates of standard deviation for several well-known common stocks. The table shows that the typical stock's standard deviation is much higher than that of the TSE 300 index.

The standard deviation of an individual stock differs from the standard deviation of a portfolio or an index due to the well-known phenomenon of diversification. With

Table 9.4
Standard deviations for annual returns of selected TSE companies, 1987–1991

Abitibi Price Inc.	31.87%
Bank of Montreal	21.48
Bell Canada Enterprises Inc.	11.78
Canadian Pacific Ltd.	27.71
Imperial Oil Ltd.	24.25
John Labatt Ltd.	54.39
MacMillan Bloedel Ltd.	33.60
Placer Dome Inc.	33.95
Seagram Co. Ltd.	23.90
TSE 300	18.35

Source: Calculated from the Laval Tape. This computer tape is produced by Laval University annually.

diversification, individual risky stocks can be combined in such a way that a combination of individual securities (a portfolio) is almost always less risky than any one of the individual securities. Risk elimination is possible because the returns of individual securities are not usually perfectly correlated with each other. A certain amount of risk is "diversified away."

Diversification is very effective at reducing risk. However, the risk of holding common stock cannot be completely eliminated by diversification. We have seen that the risk (measured by the standard deviation) of the TSE 300 portfolio, which includes 300 individual stocks, is still very high when compared to Canada Treasury bills. In fact, diversification makes measuring the risk of an individual security very difficult. The reason is that we are not so much interested in the standard deviation of individual securities as we are in the impact of an individual standard deviation on the risk of a portfolio.

Most individuals and institutions hold portfolios, not single securities. Conceptually, the risk of an individual security is related to how the risk of a portfolio changes when the security is added to it. It turns out that the standard deviation of an individual stock is not a good measure of this incremental risk. Therefore, the standard deviation of an individual security is not a good measure of its risk provided that most investors hold diversified portfolios.

In the next chapter we show formally that a security with a high standard deviation need not have a major impact on the standard deviation of a large portfolio. Conversely, a security with a low standard deviation may actually have a high impact on a large portfolio's standard deviation. This apparent paradox is actually the basis of the famous capital asset pricing model.

Beta

The capital asset pricing model (CAPM) shows that the risk of an individual security is well represented by its **beta** coefficient.[12] In statistical terms, the beta tells us the tendency of an individual stock to covary with the market (the TSE 300 index). A stock with a beta of 1 tends to move up and down in the same percentage as the market. Stocks with a beta coefficient less than 1 tend to move in percentage terms less than the market. Similarly, a stock with a beta higher than 1 tends to move up and down more than the market. Table 9.5 presents estimates of beta for well-known common stocks.

The expected return on a security is positively related to the security's risk, since investors will only take on extra risk if they receive extra compensation. The CAPM implies that beta, not standard deviation, is the appropriate measure of risk. This insight allows us to calculate the expected return on an individual security as follows:

$$\begin{array}{c} \text{Expected return} \\ \text{of individual} \\ \text{security} \end{array} = \begin{array}{c} \text{Current risk-} \\ \text{free rate} \end{array} + \begin{array}{c} \text{Beta of} \\ \text{a security} \end{array} \times \begin{array}{c} \text{Historical market} \\ \text{risk premium} \end{array}$$

---

[12]Statistically, beta is defined as the covariance of the return of an individual stock with the "market proxy" portfolio return divided by the variance of the market's proxy return.

Table 9.5
Beta coefficients
for selected
companies

Alcan Aluminum	1.07
Bell Canada Enterprises	0.50
B.C. Telephone	0.66
DuPont Canada	0.92
Imperial Oil	0.43
Mackenzie Financial	2.27
MacMillan Bloedel	1.46
Newbridge Networks	0.95
Royal Bank of Canada	1.25

Source: Burns Fry Limited, "Estimates of Stock
Total Return Betas" (Toronto, September 1993).

■ *Example*

Suppose the current risk-free rate is 7 percent and the historical market risk premium is 6.39 percent. If the beta of Nova Corp. is 1.12, what is its expected return? Using the CAPM, we find that the expected return for Nova Corp. is

$$= 7\% + (1.12 \times 6.39\%) = 14.16\% \ \blacksquare$$

The CAPM and beta are detailed in Chapter 10.

CONCEPT QUESTION

■ Why is a security's risk measured by its beta rather than by its standard deviation?

9.8   **Summary and Conclusions**

1. This chapter explores capital market history. Such history is useful because it tells us what to expect in the way of returns from risky assets. We summed up our study of market history with two key lessons:

   ■ Risky assets, on average, earn a risk premium. There is a reward for bearing risk.

   ■ The greater the risk from a risky investment, the greater is the required reward.

   These lessons' implications for the financial manager are discussed in the chapters ahead.

2. The statistical measures in this chapter are necessary building blocks for the next three chapters.

   ■ Standard deviation and variance measure the variability of the return on an individual security. We will argue that standard deviation and variance are appropriate measures of the risk of an individual security only if an investor's portfolio is composed exclusively of that security.

   ■ Since most investors hold portfolios, the variance (or standard deviation) is not a good measure of an individual security's risk. Beta is a better measure.

Key Terms

Capital gain 250

Holding period return 257

Frequency distribution 258

Average (mean) 258

Risk premium 259

Variance 260

Standard deviation 260

Normal distribution 261

Diversification 267

Beta 267

Suggested Readings

An important record of the performance of financial investments in Canadian capital markets can be found in:

J. E. Hatch and R. W. White. *Canadian Stocks, Bonds, Bills and Inflation: 1950–1983.* Charlottesville, Va.: Financial Analysts Research Foundation, 1985.

The corresponding study for the United States is:

R. G. Ibbotson and R. A. Sinquefield. *Stocks, Bonds, Bills and Inflation* (SBBI). Charlottesville, Va.: Financial Analysts Research Foundation, 1982. (Updated in *SBBI 1992 Yearbook.* Chicago: Ibbotson Associates.)

The problems of using sample data to estimate expected returns are described in:

M. Blume. "Unbiased Estimates of Long Run Expected Rates of Return." *Journal of the American Statistical Association* (September 1974).

R. C. Merton. "On Estimating the Expected Return on the Market: An Exploratory Investigation." *Journal of Financial Economics* 8 (December 1980).

The classic work on the statistical properties of common stock returns is:

E. F. Fama. "The Behavior of Common Stock Prices." *Journal of Business* (January 1965).

Questions and Problems

Returns

9.1 Last year, you bought 500 shares of Twedt El Dee stock at $37 per share. You have received total dividends of $1,000 during the year. Currently, Twedt El Dee stock sells for $38.

   a. How much did you earn in capital gains?

   b. What was your total dollar return?

   c. What was your percentage return?

   d. Must you sell the Twedt El Dee stock to include the capital gains in your return? Explain.

9.2 Suppose a stock had an initial price of $42 per share. During the year, the stock paid a dividend of $2.40 per share. At the end of the year, the price is $31 per share. What is the percentage return on this stock?

9.3 Lydian stock currently sells for $52 per share. You intend to buy the stock today and hold it for two years. During those two years, you expect to receive dividends at the year-ends that total $5.50 per share. Finally, you expect to sell the Lydian stock for $54.75 per share. What is your expected holding period return on Lydian stock?

9.4 Use the information from the Alexander Group provided in Table 9.1 to compute the nominal and real annual returns from 1982 to 1992 for

    a. Canadian common stock.

    b. Long-term bonds.

    c. Canada Treasury bills.

9.5 Suppose the current interest rate on Canada Treasury bills is 8.2 percent. The Alexander Group found the average return on Treasury bills from 1948 through 1992 to be 6.19 percent. The average return on common stock during the same period was 12.58 percent. Given this information, what is the current expected return on common stocks?

Average Returns, Expected Returns, and Variance

9.6 During the past seven years, the returns on a portfolio of long-term bonds were the following:

Year	Long-term bonds
−7	−2.6%
−6	−1.0
−5	43.8
−4	4.7
−3	16.4
−2	30.1
Last	19.9

    a. Calculate the average return for long-term bonds over this period.

    b. Calculate the variance and the standard deviation of the returns for long-term bonds during this period.

9.7 The following are the returns during the past seven years on a market portfolio of common stocks and on Treasury bills.

Year	Common stocks	Treasury bills
−7	32.4%	11.2%
−6	−4.9	14.7
−5	21.4	10.5
−4	22.5	8.8
−3	6.3	9.9
−2	32.2	7.7
Last	18.5	6.2

The realized risk premium is the return on the common stocks less the return on the Treasury bills.

    a. Calculate the realized risk premium of common stocks over T-bills in each year.

    b. Calculate the average risk premium of common stocks over T-bills during the period.

    c. Is it possible that this observed risk premium can be negative? Explain.

9.8 The probability that the economy will experience moderate growth next year is 0.6. The probability of a recession is 0.2, and the probability of a rapid expansion is also 0.2. If the economy falls into a recession, you can expect to receive a return on your portfolio of 5 percent. With moderate growth, your return will be 8 percent. If there is a rapid expansion, your portfolio will return 15 percent.

   a. What is your expected return?

   b. What is the standard deviation of that return?

9.9 The probability that the economy will experience moderate growth next year is 0.4. The probability of a recession is 0.3, and the probability of a rapid expansion is also 0.3. If the economy falls into a recession, you can expect to receive a return on your portfolio of 2 percent. With moderate growth your return will be 5 percent. If there is a rapid expansion, your portfolio will return 10 percent.

   a. What is your expected return?

   b. What is the standard deviation of that return?

9.10 The returns on the market and on Trebli stock are shown below for the five possible states of the economy that might prevail next year.

Economic condition	Probability	Market return	Trebli return
Rapid expansion	0.12	0.23	0.12
Moderate expansion	0.40	0.18	0.09
No growth	0.25	0.15	0.05
Moderate contraction	0.15	0.09	0.01
Serious contraction	0.08	0.03	−0.02

   a. What is the expected return on the market?

   b. What is the expected return on Trebli stock?

9.11 Four equally likely states of the economy may prevail next year. Below are the returns on the stocks of *P* and *Q* companies under each of the possible states.

State	*P* stock	*Q* stock
1	0.04	0.05
2	0.06	0.07
3	0.09	0.10
4	0.04	0.14

   a. What are the expected returns on each stock?

   b. What is the variance of the returns of each stock?

9.12 The returns on small-capitalization stocks and on the TSE 300 index of common stocks from 1971 through 1975 are tabulated below.

Year	Small-capitalization stocks	Market index of common stocks
1971	15.83%	8.01%
1972	44.72	27.38
1973	−7.82	0.27
1974	−26.89	−25.93
1975	41.00	18.48

  a. Calculate the average return for the small-capitalization stocks and the market index of common stocks.

  b. Calculate the variance and standard deviation of returns for the small-capitalization stocks and the market index of common stocks.

9.13 The following data are the returns for 1980 through 1985 on four types of capital market instruments: Canadian common stocks, small-capitalization stocks, long-term bonds, and Canada Treasury bills.

Year	Canadian common stocks	Small cap. stocks	Long-term bonds	Canada T-Bills
1980	30.13	42.86	2.18	12.23
1981	−10.25	−15.10	−2.09	19.11
1982	5.54	4.55	45.82	15.27
1983	35.49	44.30	9.61	9.39
1984	−2.39	−2.33	16.90	11.21
1985	25.07	38.98	26.68	9.70

Calculate the average return and variance for each type of security.

Expected Returns and Beta

9.14 The Alpha firm makes pneumatic equipment. Its beta is 1.2. The market risk premium is 8.5 percent, and the current risk-free rate is 6 percent. What is the expected return for the Alpha firm?

9.15 Suppose the beta for the Ramona Corporation is .80. The risk-free rate is 6 percent, and the market risk premium is 8.5 percent. What is the expected return for the Ramona Corporation?

9.16 The risk-free rate is 8 percent. The beta for the Sarah Company is 1.5, and the expected return of the market is 15 percent. What is the expected return for the Sarah Company?

APPENDIX

The Historical Market Risk Premium: The Very Long Run

The data in Chapter 9 indicate that the returns on common stock have historically been much higher than the returns on short-term government securities. This phenomenon has bothered economists, since it is difficult to justify why large numbers of rational investors purchase the lower-yielding bills and bonds.

In 1985, Mehra and Prescott published a very influential paper that showed that, for the United States, the historical returns for common stocks are far too high when compared to the rates of return on short-term government securities.[13] They pointed out that the difference in returns (frequently called the *market risk premium for equity*) implies a very high degree of risk aversion on the part of investors. Since the publication of the Mehra and Prescott research, financial economists have tried to

---

[13]Rajnish Mehra and Edward C. Prescott, "The Equity Premium: A Puzzle," *Journal of Monetary Economics* 15 (1985), pp. 145–61.

	1802–70	1871–1925	1926–90	Overall 1802–1990
Common stock	6.8	8.5	11.9	9.0
Treasury bills	5.4	4.1	3.7	4.4
Risk premium	1.4	4.4	8.4	4.6

Table 9A.1
Historical Risk
Premium

Source: Jeremy J. Seigel, "Historical Returns: The Case for Equity," working paper 10–91, Rodney L. White Center for Financial Research, Wharton School, University of Pennsylvania, Philadelphia.

explain the so-called equity risk premium puzzle. The high historical equity risk premium is especially intriguing compared to the very low historical rate of return on Treasury securities. This seems to imply behaviour that has not actually happened. For example, if people have been very risk-averse and historical borrowing rates have been low, it suggests that persons should have been willing to borrow in periods of economic uncertainty and downturn to avoid the possibility of a reduced standard of living. However, we do not observe increased borrowing in recessions.

The equity risk premium puzzle of Mehra and Prescott has been generally viewed as an unexplained paradox. However, Jeremy Seigel has shown that the historical risk premium may be substantially lower than previously realized. (See Table 9A.1.) He shows that while the risk premium averaged 8.4 percent from 1926 to 1990, it averaged only 1.4 percent from 1802 to 1870, and 4.4 percent from 1871 to 1925. It is puzzling that the trend has been rising over the past 200 years. It has been especially high since 1926. However, the key point is that, historically, the risk premium has been lower than in more recent times and we should be somewhat cautious about assumptions we make about the current risk premium.

Appendix Question

What lesson can be drawn from studying historical risk premiums dating back 200 years?

Return and Risk: The Capital Asset Pricing Model (CAPM)

The previous chapter achieved three purposes. First, it introduced the history of Canadian capital markets. Second, it presented statistics such as expected return, variance, standard deviation, and beta. Third, it presented a simplified model of the discount rate on a risky project.

However, as we pointed out in the previous chapter, the above model was *ad hoc* in nature. The next two chapters present a carefully reasoned approach to calculating the discount rate on a risky project. Chapters 10 and 11 examine the risk and the return of individual securities when these securities are part of a large portfolio. While this investigation is a necessary stepping stone to discounting projects, corporate projects are not considered here. Rather, a treatment of the appropriate discount rate for capital budgeting is reserved for Chapter 12.

The crux of the current chapter can be summarized as follows: An individual who holds one security should use expected return as the measure of the security's return. Standard deviation or variance is the proper measure of the security's risk. An individual who holds a diversified portfolio cares about the *contribution* of each security to the expected return and the risk of the portfolio. It turns out that a security's expected return is the appropriate measure of the security's contribution to the expected return on the portfolio. However, neither the security's variance nor the security's standard deviation is an appropriate measure of a security's contribution to the risk of a portfolio. The contribution of a security to the risk of a portfolio is best measured by beta.

Individual Securities   10.1

In the first part of Chapter 10 we will examine the characteristics of individual securities. In particular, we will discuss:

1. *Expected return.* This is the return that an individual expects a stock to earn over the next period. Of course, because this is only an expectation, the actual return may be either higher or lower. An individual's expectation may simply be the average return per period a security has earned in the past. Alternatively, it may be based on a detailed analysis of a firm's prospects, on some computer-based model, or on special (or inside) information.

2. *Variance and standard deviation.* There are many ways to assess the volatility of a security's return. One of the most common is variance, which is a measure of the squared deviations of a security's return from its expected return. Standard deviation, which is the square root of the variance, may be thought of as a standardized version of the variance.

3. *Covariance and correlation.* Returns on individual securities are related to one another. Covariance is a statistic measuring the interrelationship between two securities. Alternatively, this relationship can be restated in terms of the correlation between the two securities. Covariance and correlation are building blocks to an understanding of the beta coefficient.

10.2 Expected Return, Variance, and Covariance

Expected Return and Variance

Suppose financial analysts believe that there are four equally likely states of the economy: depression, recession, normal, and boom times. The returns on the Supertech Company are expected to follow the economy closely, while the returns on the Slowpoke Company are not. The return predictions are given below:

	Supertech returns R_{At}	Slowpoke returns R_{Bt}
Depression	−20%	5%
Recession	10	20
Normal	30	−12
Boom	50	9

Variance can be calculated in four steps. Calculating expected return is the first step. An additional step is needed to calculate standard deviation. (The calculations are presented in Table 10.1.)

1. Calculate the expected return:

Supertech:

$$\frac{-.20 + 0.10 + 0.30 + 0.50}{4} = 0.175 = 17.5\%$$

Slowpoke:

$$\frac{0.50 + 0.20 - 0.12 + 0.09}{4} = 0.055 = 5.5\%$$

2. For each company, calculate the deviation of each possible return from the company's expected return given above. This is presented in the third column of Table 10.1.

3. The deviations we have calculated are indications of the dispersion of returns. However, because some are positive and some are negative, it is

(1) State of economy	(2) Rate of return	(3) Deviation from expected return	(4) Squared value of deviation
	Supertech* R_{At}	(Expected return = 0.175) $(R_{At} - \overline{R}_A)$	$(R_{At} - \overline{R}_A)^2$
Depression	−0.20	−0.375 (= 0.20 − 0.175)	0.140625 [= (−0.375)²]
Recession	0.10	−0.075	0.005625
Normal	0.30	0.125	0.015625
Boom	0.50	0.325	0.105625
			0.267500
	Slowpoke† R_{Bt}	(Expected return = 0.055) $(R_{Bt} - \overline{R}_B)$	$(R_{Bt} - \overline{R}_B)^2$
Depression	0.05	−0.005 (= 0.05 − 0.055)	0.000025 [= (−0.005)²]
Recession	0.20	0.145	0.021025
Normal	−0.12	−0.175	0.030625
Boom	0.09	0.035	0.001225
			0.052900

Table 10.1 Calculating variance and standard deviation

$$*\overline{R}_A = \frac{-0.20 + 0.10 + 0.30 + 0.50}{4} = 0.175 = 17.5\%$$

$$\text{Var}(R_A) = \sigma_A^2 = \frac{0.2675}{4} = 0.066875$$

$$\text{SD}(R_A) = \sigma_A = \sqrt{0.066875} = 0.2586 = 25.86\%$$

$$†\overline{R}_B = \frac{0.05 + 0.20 - 0.12 + 0.09}{4} = 0.055 = 5.5\%$$

$$\text{Var}(R_B) = \sigma_B^2 = \frac{0.0529}{4} = 0.013225$$

$$\text{SD}(R_B) = \sigma_B = \sqrt{0.013225} = 0.1150 = 11.50\%$$

difficult to work with them in this form. For example, if we were to add up all the deviations for a single company, we would get zero as the sum.

To make the deviations more meaningful, we multiply each one by itself. Now all the numbers are positive, implying that their sum must be positive as well. The squared deviations are presented in the last column of Table 10.1.

4. For each company, calculate the average squared deviation, which is the variance:[1]

Supertech:

$$\frac{0.140625 + 0.005625 + 0.015625 + 0.015625}{4} = 0.066875$$

[1] In this example, the four states give rise to four possible outcomes for each stock. Had we used past data, the outcomes would have actually occurred. In that case, statisticians argue that the correct divisor is $N - 1$, where N is the number of observations. Thus, the denominator would be 3 (or 4 −1) in the case of past data, not 4. Note that the example in Section 9.5 involved past data and we used a divisor of $N - 1$. While this difference causes grief to both students and textbook writers, it is a minor point in practice. In the real world, samples are generally so large that using N or $N - 1$ in the denominator has virtually no effect on the calculation of variance.

Slowpoke:

$$\frac{0.000025 + 0.021025 + 0.030625 + 0.001225}{4} = 0.013225$$

Thus, the variance of Supertech is 0.066875, and the variance of Slowpoke is 0.013225.

5. Calculate standard deviation by taking the square root of the variance:

Supertech:

$$\sqrt{0.066875} = 0.2586 = 25.86\%$$

Slowpoke:

$$\sqrt{0.013225} = .1150 = 11.50\%$$

Algebraically, the formula for variance can be expressed as

$$\text{Var } (R) = \text{Expected value of } (R - \overline{R})^2$$

where $\overline{R}$ is the security's expected return and R is the actual return.

A look at the four-step calculation for variance makes it clear why it is a measure of the spread of the sample of returns. For each observation, we square the difference between the actual return and the expected return. We then take an average of these squared differences. Squaring the differences makes them all positive. If we used the differences between each return and the expected return and then averaged these differences, we would get zero because the returns that were above the mean would cancel the ones below.

However, because the variance is still expressed in squared terms, it is difficult to interpret. Standard deviation has a much simpler interpretation, which we will provide shortly. Standard deviation is simply the square root of the variance. The general formula for the standard deviation is

$$\text{SD}(R) = \sqrt{\text{Var}(R)}$$

Covariance and Correlation

The statistical estimates, variance and standard deviation, measure the variability of individual stocks. We now wish to measure the relationship between the return on one stock and the return on another. To make our discussion more precise, we need a statistical measure of the relationship between two variables. Enter **covariance** and **correlation.**

Covariance and correlation are ways of measuring whether or not two random variables are related and how. We explain these terms by extending an example presented earlier in this chapter.

▪ *Example*

We have already determined the expected returns and standard deviations for both Supertech and Slowpoke. (The expected returns are 0.175 and 0.055 for Supertech and Slowpoke, respectively. The standard deviations are 0.2586 and 0.1150, respectively.) In addition, we calculated for each firm the deviation of each possible return from the

Table 10.2 Calculating covariance and correlation

State of economy	Rate of return of Supertech R_{At}	Deviation from expected return $(R_{At} - \bar{R}_A)$	Rate of return of Slowpoke R_{Bt}	Deviation from expected return $(R_{Bt} - \bar{R}_B)$	Product of deviations $(R_{At} - \bar{R}_A) \times (R_{Bt} - \bar{R}_B)$
		(Expected return = 0.175)		(Expected return = 0.055)	
Depression	−0.20	−0.375 (= −0.20 − 0.175)	0.05	−0.005 (= 0.05 − 0.055)	0.001875 (= −0.375 × −0.005)
Recession	0.10	−0.075	0.20	0.145	−0.010875 (= −0.075 × 0.145)
Normal	0.30	0.125	−0.12	−0.175	−0.021875 (= 0.125 × −0.175)
Boom	0.50 / 0.70	0.325	0.09 / 0.22	0.035	0.011375 (= 0.325 × 0.035) / −0.0195

$$\sigma_{AB} = \text{Cov}(R_A, R_B) = \frac{-0.0195}{4} = -0.004875$$

$$\rho_{AB} = \text{Corr}(R_A, R_B) = \frac{\text{Cov}(R_A, R_B)}{\text{SD}(R_A) \times \text{SD}(R_B)} = \frac{-0.004875}{0.2586 \times 0.1150} = -0.1639$$

expected return. Using these data, covariance can be calculated in two steps. An extra step is needed to calculate correlation.

1. For each state of the economy, multiply Supertech's deviation from its expected return and Slowpoke's deviation from its expected return together. For example, Supertech's rate of return in a depression is −0.20, which is −0.375 (or −0.20 − 0.175) from its expected return. Slowpoke's rate of return in a depression is 0.05, which is −0.005 (or 0.05 − 0.055) from its expected return. Multiplying the two deviations together yields 0.001875 [or (−0.375) × (−0.005)]. The actual calculations are given in the last column of Table 10.2. This procedure can be written algebraically as

$$(R_{At} - \overline{R}_A) \times (R_{Bt} - \overline{R}_B) \tag{10.1}$$

where R_{At} and R_{Bt} are the returns on Supertech and Slowpoke in state t. $\overline{R}_A$ and $\overline{R}_B$ are the expected returns on the two securities.

2. Calculate the average value of the four states in the last column. This average is the covariance. That is,[2]

$$\sigma_{AB} = \text{Cov}(R_A, R_B) = \frac{-0.195}{4} = -0.004875 \quad \blacksquare$$

Note that we represent the covariance between Supertech and Slowpoke as either $\text{Cov}(R_A, R_B)$ or σ_{AB}. Equation (10.1) illustrates the intuition of covariance. Suppose Supertech's return is generally above its average when Slowpoke's return is above its average, and Supertech's return is generally below its average when Slowpoke's return is below its average. This is indicative of a positive dependency or a positive

---

[2]As with variance, we divide by N (4 in this example) because the four states give rise to four possible outcomes. However, had we used past data, the correct divisor would be $N - 1$ (3 in this example).

relationship between the two returns. Note that the term in equation (10.1) will be *positive* in any state where both returns are *above* their averages. In addition, (10.1) will still be *positive* in any state where both terms are *below* their averages. Thus, a positive relationship between the two returns will give rise to a positive calculation for covariance.

Conversely, suppose Supertech's return is generally above its average when Slowpoke's return is below its average, and Supertech's return is generally below its average when Slowpoke's return is above its average. This is indicative of a negative dependency or a negative relationship between the two returns. Note that the term in equation (10.1) will be *negative* in any state where one return is above its average and the other return is below its average. Thus, a negative relationship between the two returns will give rise to a negative calculation for covariance.

Finally, suppose there is no relation between the two returns. In this case, knowing whether the return on Supertech is above or below its expected return tells us nothing about the return on Slowpoke. In the covariance formula, then, there will be no tendency for the terms to be positive or negative, and on average they will tend to offset each other and cancel out. This will make the covariance zero.

Of course, even if the two returns are unrelated to each other, the covariance formula will not equal zero exactly in any actual history. This is due to sampling error; randomness alone will make the calculation positive or negative. But for a historical sample that is long enough, if the two returns are not related to each other, we should expect the formula to come close to zero.

The covariance formula seems to capture what we are looking for. If the two returns are positively related to each other, they will have a positive covariance, and if they are negatively related to each other, the covariance will be negative. Last, and very important, if they are unrelated, the covariance should be zero.

The formula for covariance can be written algebraically as

$$\sigma_{AB} = \text{Cov}(R_A, R_B) = \text{Expected value of } [(R_A - \overline{R}_A) \times (R_B - \overline{R}_B)]$$

where $\overline{R}_A$ and $\overline{R}_B$ are the expected returns for the two securities, and R_A and R_B are the actual returns. The ordering of the two variables is unimportant. That is, the covariance of A with B is equal to the covariance of B with A. This can be stated more formally as $\text{Cov}(R_A, R_B) = \text{Cov}(R_B, R_A)$ or $\sigma_{AB} = \sigma_{BA}$.

The covariance we calculated is -0.004875. A negative number like this implies that the return on one stock is likely to be above its average when the return on the other stock is below its average, and vice versa. However, the size of the number is difficult to interpret. Like the variance figure, the covariance is in squared deviation units. Until we can put it in perspective, we don't know what to make of it.

We solve the problem by computing the correlation:

3. To calculate the correlation, divide the covariance by the standard deviations of both of the two securities. For our example, we have

$$\rho_{AB} = \text{Corr}(R_A, R_B) = \frac{\text{Cov}(R_A, R_B)}{\sigma_A \times \sigma_B} = \frac{-0.004875}{0.2586 \times 0.1150} = -0.1639 \qquad (10\ .2)$$

where σ_A and σ_B are the standard deviations of Supertech and Slowpoke, respectively. Note that we represent the correlation between Supertech and Slowpoke either as $\text{Corr}(R_A, R_B)$ or ρ_{AB}. As with covariance, the ordering of the two variables is unimportant. That is, the correlation of A with B is equal to the correlation of B with A. More formally, $\text{Corr}(R_A, R_B) = \text{Corr}(R_B, R_B)$ or $\rho_{AB} = \rho_{BA}$.

Because the standard deviation is always positive, the sign of the correlation between two variables must be the same as that of the covariance between the two variables. If the correlation is positive, we say that the variables are *positively correlated;* if it is negative, we say that they are *negatively correlated;* and if it is zero, we say that they are *uncorrelated.* Furthermore, it can be proven that the correlation is always between +1 and −1. This is due to the standardizing procedure of dividing by the two standard deviations.

We can compare the correlation between different pairs of securities. For example, it turns out that the correlation between Bank of Montreal and Royal Bank of Canada is much higher than the correlation between Bank of Montreal and Northern Telecom. Hence, we can state that the first pair of securities is more interrelated than the second pair.

Figure 10.1 shows the three benchmark cases for two assets, A and B. The figure shows two assets with return correlations of +1, −1, and 0. This implies perfect positive correlation, perfect negative correlation, and no correlation, respectively. The graphs in the figure plot the separate returns on the two securities through time.

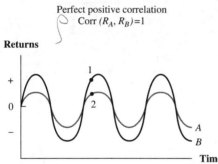

Perfect positive correlation
Corr $(R_A, R_B)=1$

Both the return on security A and the return on security B are higher than average at the same time. Both the return on security A and the return on security B are lower than average at the same time.

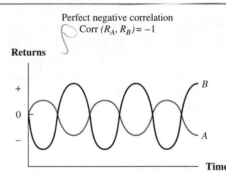

Perfect negative correlation
Corr $(R_A, R_B)= -1$

Security A has a higher-than-average return when security B has a lower-than-average return, and vice versa.

Figure 10.1
Examples of different correlation coefficients

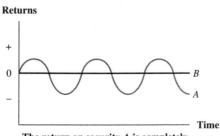

Zero correlation
Corr $(R_A, R_B)=0$

The return on security A is completely unrelated to the return on security B.

Note: The graphs in this figure plot the separate returns on the two securities through time.

Xi

10.3   The Return and Risk for Portfolios

Suppose that an investor has estimates of the expected returns and standard deviations on individual securities and the correlations between securities. How then does the investor choose the best combination or **portfolio** of securities to hold? Obviously, the investor would like a portfolio with a high expected return and a low standard deviation of return. It is therefore worthwhile to consider

1. The relationship between the expected return on individual securities and the expected return on a portfolio made up of these securities.
2. The relationship between the standard deviations of individual securities, the correlations between these securities, and the standard deviation of a portfolio made up of these securities.

The Example of Supertech and Slowpoke

In order to analyze the above two relationships, we will use the Supertech and Slowpoke example presented previously. The relevant data are as follows:[3]

Relevant Data from Example of Supertech and Slowpoke

did not take Xi into account

Item	Symbol	Value
Expected return on Supertech	$\overline{R}_{Super}$	0.175 = 17.5%
Expected return on Slowpoke	$\overline{R}_{Slow}$	0.055 = 5.5%
Variance of Supertech	σ^2_{Super}	0.066875
Variance of Slowpoke	σ^2_{Slow}	0.013225
Standard deviation of Supertech	σ_{Super}	0.2586 = 25.86%
Standard deviation of Slowpoke	σ_{Slow}	0.1150 = 11.50%
Covariance between Supertech and Slowpoke	$\sigma_{Super,Slow}$	−0.004875
Correlation between Supertech and Slowpoke	$\rho_{Super,Slow}$	−0.1639

The Expected Return on a Portfolio

The formula for expected return on a portfolio is very simple:

> The expected return on a portfolio is simply a weighted average of the expected returns on the individual securities.

---

[3]See Tables 10.1 and 10.2 for actual calculations.

■ *Example*

Consider Supertech and Slowpoke. From the box above, we find that the expected returns on these two securities are 17.5 percent and 5.5 percent, respectively.

The expected return on a portfolio of these two securities alone can be written as

Expected return on portfolio = X_{Super} (17.5%) + X_{Slow} (5.5%)

where X_{Super} is the percentage of the portfolio in Supertech and X_{Slow} is the percentage of the portfolio in Slowpoke. If the investor with $100 invests $60 in Supertech and $40 in Slowpoke, the expected return on the portfolio can be written as

Expected return on portfolio = 0.6 × 17.5% + 0.4 × 5.5% = 12.7%

Algebraically, we can write

Expected return on portfolio = $X_A R_A + X_B \overline{R}_B$ (10.3)

where X_A and X_B are the proportions of the total portfolio in the assets A and B, respectively. (Because our investor can only invest in two securities, $X_A + X_B$ must equal 1 or 100 percent.) $\overline{R}_A$ and $\overline{R}_B$ are the expected returns on the two securities. ■

Now consider two stocks, each with an expected return of 10 percent. The expected return on a portfolio composed of these two stocks must be 10 percent, regardless of the proportions of the two stocks held. This result may seem obvious at this point, but it will become important later. The result implies that you do not reduce or *dissipate* your expected return by investing in a number of securities. Rather, the expected return on your portfolio is simply a weighted average of the expected returns on the individual assets in the portfolio.

Variance and Standard Deviation of a Portfolio

The Variance

The formula for the variance of a portfolio composed of two securities, A and B, is

The Variance of the Portfolio:

$$\text{Var(portfolio)} = X_A^2 \sigma_A^2 + 2X_A X_B \sigma_{A,B} + X_B^2 \sigma_B^2 = \sigma_p^2$$ takes into account X's

Note that there are three terms on the right-hand side of the equation. The first term involves the variance of $A (\sigma_A^2)$, the second term involves the covariance between the two securities $(\sigma_{A,B})$, and the third term involves the variance of B (σ_B^2). (It should be noted that $\sigma_{A,B} = \sigma_{B,A}$. That is, the ordering of the variables is not relevant when expressing the covariance between two securities.)

The formula indicates an important point. The variance of a portfolio depends on both the variances of the individual securities and the covariance between the two securities. The variance of a security measures the variability of an individual security's return. Covariance measures the relationship between the two securities. For given variances of the individual securities, a positive relationship or covariance between the two securities increases the variance of the entire portfolio. A negative relationship or covariance between the two securities decreases the variance of the entire portfolio. This important result seems to square with common sense. If one of your securities tends to go up when the other goes down, or vice versa, your two securities are offsetting each other. You are achieving what we call a *hedge* in finance, and the risk of your entire portfolio will be low. However, if both your securities rise and fall together, you are not hedging at all. Hence, the risk of your entire portfolio will be higher.

The variance formula for our two securities, Super and Slow, is

$$\text{Var(portfolio)} = X_{Super}^2 \sigma_{Super}^2 + 2X_{Super}X_{Slow}\sigma_{Super,\,Slow} + X_{Slow}^2 \sigma_{Slow}^2 \qquad (10.4)$$

Given our earlier assumption that an individual with \$100 invests \$60 in Supertech and \$40 in Slowpoke, $X_{Super} = 0.6$ and $X_{Slow} = 0.4$. Using this assumption and the relevant data from the box above, the variance of the portfolio is

$$0.023851 = 0.36 \times 0.066875 + 2 \times [0.6 \times 0.4 \times (-0.004875)] + \qquad (10.4') $$
$$0.16 \times 0.013225$$

The Matrix Approach

Alternatively, equation (10.4) can be expressed in the following matrix format:

	Supertech	Slowpoke
Supertech	$X_{Super}^2 \sigma_{Super}^2$ $0.024075 = 0.36 \times 0.066875$	$X_{Super}X_{Slow}\sigma_{Super,Slow}$ $-0.00117 = 0.6 \times 0.4 \times (-0.004875)$
Slowpoke	$X_{Super}X_{Slow}\sigma_{Super,Slow}$ $-0.00117 = 0.6 \times 0.4 \times (-0.004875)$	$X_{Slow}^2 \sigma_{Slow}^2$ $0.002116 = 0.16 \times 0.013225$

There are four boxes in the matrix. We can add the terms in the boxes to obtain equation (10.4), the variance of a portfolio composed of the two securities. The term in the upper left-hand corner contains the variance of Supertech. The term in the lower right-hand corner contains the variance of Slowpoke. The other two boxes contain the covariance terms. These two boxes are identical, indicating why the covariance term is multiplied by 2 in equation (10.4).

At this point, students often find the box approach to be more confusing than equation (10.4). However, the box approach is easily generalized to more than two securities, a task we perform later in this chapter.

Standard Deviation of a Portfolio

Given (10.4'), we can now determine the standard deviation of the portfolio's return. This is

$$\sigma_P = \text{SD(portfolio)} = \sqrt{\text{Var(portfolio)}} = \sqrt{0.023851} = 0.1544 = 15.44\% \quad (10.5)$$

The interpretation of the standard deviation of the portfolio is the same as the interpretation of the standard deviation of an individual security. The expected return on our portfolio is 12.7 percent. A return of -2.74 percent ($12.7\% - 15.44\%$) is one standard deviation below the mean and a return of 28.14 percent ($12.7\% + 15.44\%$) is one standard deviation above the mean. If the return on the portfolio is normally distributed, a return between -2.74 percent and $+28.14$ percent occurs about 68 percent of the time.[4]

The Diversification Effect

It is instructive to compare the standard deviation of the portfolio with the standard deviation of the individual securities. The weighted average of the standard deviations of the individual securities is

$$SP = \sigma_P = \sqrt{VAR} = \sqrt{X_1 \sigma_1^2 + 2X_1 X_2 \sigma_{1,2} + 2X_2 \sigma_2^2} \qquad \left(\sigma_P = 15.44\%\right)$$

$$\text{Weighted average of standard deviations} = X_{\text{Super}}\sigma_{\text{Super}} + X_{\text{Slow}}\sigma_{\text{Slow}} \qquad (10.6)$$

$$0.2012 = 0.6 \times 0.2586 + 0.4 \times 0.115$$

One of the most important results in this chapter relates to the difference between (10.5) and (10.6). In our example, the standard deviation of the portfolio is *less* than a weighted average of the standard deviations of the individual securities.

We pointed out earlier that the expected return on the portfolio is a weighted average of the expected returns on the individual securities. Thus, we get a different type of result for the standard deviation of a portfolio than we do for the expected return on a portfolio.

It is generally argued that our result for the standard deviation of a portfolio is due to diversification. For example, Supertech and Slowpoke are slightly negatively correlated ($\rho = -0.1639$). Supertech's return is likely to be a little below average if Slowpoke's return is above average. Similarly, Supertech's return is likely to be a little above average if Slowpoke's return is below average. Thus, the standard deviation of a portfolio composed of the two securities is less than a weighted average of the standard deviations of the two securities.

The above example has negative correlation. Clearly, there will be less benefit from diversification if the two securities exhibit positive correlation. How high must the positive correlation be before all diversification benefits vanish?

To answer this question, let us rewrite (10.4) in terms of correlation rather than covariance. The covariance can be rewritten as[5]

$$\sigma_{\text{Super, Slow}} = \rho_{\text{Super, Slow}}\sigma_{\text{Super}}\sigma_{\text{Slow}} \qquad (10.7)$$

The formula states that the covariance between any two securities is simply the correlation between the two securities multiplied by the standard deviations of each. In other words, covariance incorporates both (1) the correlation between the two assets and (2) the variability of each of the two securities as measured by standard deviation.

---

[4]There are only four equally probable returns for Supertech and Slowpoke, so neither security possesses a normal distribution. Thus, probabilities would be slightly different in our example.

[5]As with covariance, the ordering of the two securities is not relevant when expressing the correlation between the two securities. That is, $\rho_{\text{Super, Slow}} = \rho_{\text{Slow, Super}}$.

From our calculations earlier in this chapter we know that the correlation between the two securities is −0.1639. Given the variances used in equation (10.4′), the standard deviations are 0.2586 and 0.115 for Supertech and Slowpoke, respectively. Thus, the variance of a portfolio can be expressed as

Variance of the portfolio's return

$$= X^2_{Super}\sigma^2_{Super} + 2X_{Super}X_{Slow}\rho_{Super, Slow}\sigma_{Super}\sigma_{Slow} + X^2_{Slow}\sigma^2_{Slow}$$

$$0.023851 = 0.36 \times 0.066875 + 2 \times 0.6 \times 0.4 \times (-0.1639) \times$$
$$0.2586 \times 0.115 + 0.16 \times 0.013225 \qquad (10.8)$$

[handwritten: SD = √VAR = 0.15443]

The middle term on the right-hand side is now written in terms of correlation, ρ, not covariance.

Suppose $\rho_{Super, Slow}$ = 1, the highest possible value for correlation. Assume all the other parameters in the example are the same. The variance of the portfolio is

Variance of the portfolio's return

$$= 0.040466 = 0.36 \times 0.066875 + 2 \times$$
$$(0.6 \times 0.4 \times 1 \times 0.2586 \times 0.115) + 0.16 \times 0.013225$$

The standard deviation is

$$\text{Standard deviation of portfolio's return} = \sqrt{0.040466} = 0.2012 = 20.12\% \qquad (10.9)$$

Note that (10.9) and (10.6) are equal. That is, the standard deviation of a portfolio's return is equal to the weighted average of the standard deviations of the individual returns when ρ = 1. Inspection of (10.8) indicates that the variance and hence the standard deviation of the portfolio must drop as the correlation drops below 1. This leads to:

> As long as ρ < 1, the standard deviation of a portfolio of two securities is less than the weighted average of the standard deviations of the individual securities.

In other words, the diversification effect applies as long as there is less than perfect correlation (as long as ρ < 1). Thus, our Supertech–Slowpoke example is a case of overkill. We illustrated diversification with an example with negative correlation. We could have illustrated diversification with an example with positive correlation—as long as it was not perfect positive correlation.

CONCEPT QUESTIONS

- What are the formulas for the expected return, variance, and standard deviation of a portfolio of two assets?
- What is the diversification effect?
- What are the highest and lowest possible values for the correlation coefficient?

The Efficient Set for Two Assets   10.4

Our results on expected returns and standard deviations are graphed in Figure 10.2. In the figure, there is a dot labeled Slowpoke and a dot labelled Supertech. Each dot represents both the expected return and the standard deviation for an individual security. As can be seen, Supertech has both a higher expected return and a higher standard deviation.

The box or "□" in the graph represents a portfolio with 60 percent invested in Supertech and 40 percent invested in Slowpoke. You will recall that we have previously calculated both the expected return and the standard deviation for this portfolio.

The choice of 60 percent in Supertech and 40 percent in Slowpoke is just one of an infinite number of portfolios that can be created. The set of portfolios is sketched by the curved line in Figure 10.3.

Consider portfolio 1. This is a portfolio composed of 90-percent Slowpoke and 10-percent Supertech. Because it is weighted so heavily toward Slowpoke, it appears close to the Slowpoke point on the graph. Portfolio 2 is higher on the curve because it is composed of 50-percent Slowpoke and 50-percent Supertech. Portfolio 3 is close to the Supertech point on the graph because it is composed of 90-percent Supertech and 10-percent Slowpoke.

There are a few important points concerning this graph.

1. We argued that the diversification effect occurs whenever the correlation between the two securities is below 1. The correlation between Supertech and Slowpoke is −0.1639. The diversification effect can be illustrated by comparison with the straight line between the Supertech point and the Slowpoke point. The straight line represents points that would have been generated had the correlation coefficient between the two securities been 1. The diversification effect is illustrated

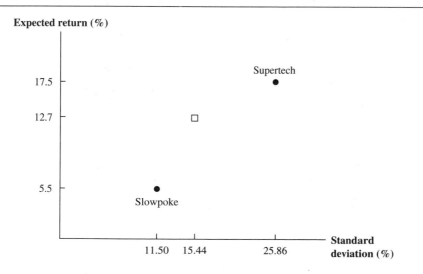

Figure 10.2
Expected return and standard deviation for (1) Supertech, (2) Slowpoke, and (3) a portfolio composed of 60 percent in Supertech and 40 percent in Slowpoke

in the figure since the curved line is always to the left of the straight line. Consider point 1'. This represents a portfolio composed of 90 percent in Slowpoke and 10 percent in Supertech if the correlation between the two were exactly 1. We argue that there is no diversification effect if ρ = 1. However, the diversification effect applies to the curved line, because point 1 has the same expected return as point 1' but has a lower standard deviation. (Points 2' and 3' are omitted to reduce the clutter in Figure 10.3.)

Though the straight line and the curved line are both represented in Figure 10.3, they do not exist simultaneously. Either ρ = −0.1639 and the curve exists or ρ = 1 and the straight line exists. In other words, though an investor can choose between different points on the curve if ρ = −0.1639, he or she cannot choose between points on the curve and points on the straight line.

2. The point MV represents the minimum variance portfolio. This is the portfolio with the lowest possible variance. By definition, this portfolio must also have the lowest possible standard deviation. (The term *minimum variance portfolio* is standard in the literature, and we will use that term. Perhaps *minimum standard*

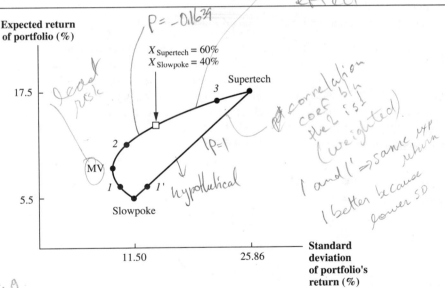

Figure 10.3
Set of portfolios composed of holdings in Supertech and Slowpoke (correlation between the two securities is −0.16)

Portfolio *1* is composed of 90-percent Slowpoke and 10-percent Supertech (ρ = −0.16).
Portfolio *2* is composed of 50-percent Slowpoke and 50-percent Supertech (ρ = −0.16).
Portfolio *3* is composed of 10-percent Slowpoke and 90-percent Supertech (ρ = −0.16).
Portfolio *1'* is composed of 90-percent Slowpoke and 10-percent Supertech (ρ = 1).
Point MV denotes the minimum variance portfolio. This is the portfolio with the lowest possible variance. By definition, the same portfolio must also have the lowest possible standard deviation.

deviation would actually be better, because standard deviation, not variance, is measured on the horizontal axis of Figure 10.3.)

3. An investor considering a portfolio of Slowpoke and Supertech faces an **opportunity set** or **feasible set** represented by the curved line in Figure 10.3. That is, the investor can achieve any point on the curve by selecting the appropriate mix between the two securities. He or she cannot achieve any points above the curve because the investor cannot increase the return on the individual securities, decrease the standard deviations of the securities, or decrease the correlation between the two securities. Neither can the investor achieve points below the curve because he or she cannot lower the returns on the individual securities, increase the standard deviations of the securities, or increase the correlation. (Of course, the investor would not want to achieve points below the curve, even if it were possible to do so.)

   Were the investor relatively tolerant of risk, he or she might choose portfolio 3. (In fact, the investor could even choose the end point by investing all his or her money in Supertech.) An investor with less tolerance for risk might choose point 2. An investor wanting as little risk as possible would choose MV, the portfolio with minimum variance or minimum standard deviation.

4. Note that the curve is backward bending between the Slowpoke point and MV. This indicates that, for a portion of the feasible set, standard deviation actually decreases as one increases expected return. Students frequently ask, "How can an increase in the proportion of the risky security, Supertech, lead to a reduction in the risk of the portfolio?"

   This surprising finding is due to the diversification effect. The returns on the two securities are negatively correlated. One security tends to go up when the other goes down. Thus, an addition of a small amount of Supertech acts as a hedge to a portfolio composed only of Slowpoke. The risk of the portfolio is reduced, implying a backward bending curve. Actually, backward bending always occurs if $\rho \leq 0$. It may or may not occur when $\rho > 0$. Of course, the curve bends backward only for a portion of its length. As one continues to increase the percentage of Supertech in the portfolio, the high standard deviation of this security eventually causes the standard deviation of the entire portfolio to rise.

5. No investor would want to hold a portfolio with an expected return below that of the minimum variance portfolio. For example, no investor would choose portfolio 1. This portfolio has less expected return but more standard deviation than the minimum variance portfolio has. We say that portfolios such as portfolio 1 are *dominated* by the minimum variance portfolio.

   Though the entire curve from Slowpoke to Supertech is called the *feasible set,* investors only consider the curve from MV to Supertech. Hence, the curve from MV to Supertech is called the **efficient set.**

   Figure 10.3 represents the opportunity set when $\rho = -0.1639$. It is worthwhile to examine Figure 10.4, which shows different curves for different correlations. As can be seen, the lower the correlation, the more bend there is in the curve. This indicates that the diversification effect rises as ρ declines. The greatest bend occurs in the limiting case where $\rho = -1$. This is perfect negative correlation. While this extreme

Figure 10.4
Opportunity sets
composed of
holdings in
Supertech and
Slowpoke

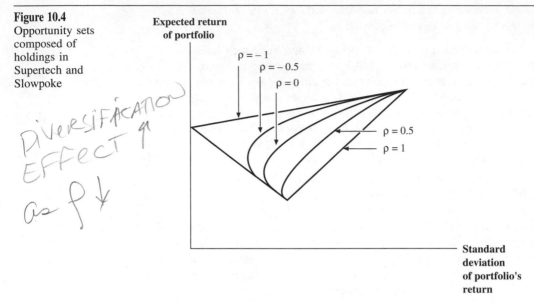

(handwritten note:) DIVERSIFACATION EFFECT ↑ as ρ ↓

Each curve represents a different correlation. The lower the correlation, the more bend in the curve.

case where $\rho = -1$ seems to fascinate students, it has little practical importance. Most pairs of securities exhibit positive correlation. Strong negative correlation, let alone perfect negative correlation, is an unlikely occurrence indeed.[6]

The graphs we examined are not mere intellectual curiosities. Rather, efficient sets can easily be calculated in the real world. As mentioned earlier, data on returns, standard deviations, and correlations are generally taken from past data, though subjective notions can be used to calculate the values of these statistics as well. Once the statistics have been determined, any one of a whole host of software packages can be purchased to generate an efficient set. However, the choice of the preferred portfolio within the efficient set is up to you. As with other important decisions like what job to choose, what house or car to buy, and how much time to allocate to this course, there is no computer program to choose the preferred portfolio.

Application to International Diversification

Research on diversification extends our discussion of historical average returns and risks in Chapter 10 to include foreign investment portfolios. It turns out that the feasible set looks like Figure 10.5 where points like U and L represent portfolios instead of individual stocks. Portfolio U represents 100-percent investment in Canadian equities and Portfolio L represents 100 percent in foreign equities. The domestic

---

[6]A major exception occurs with derivative securities. For example, the correlation between a stock and a put option on the stock is generally strongly negative. Puts will be treated later in the text.

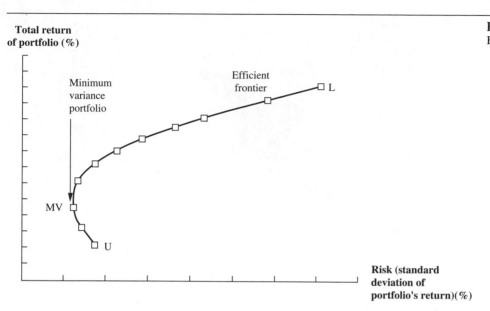

**Total return
of portfolio (%)**

Minimum
variance
portfolio

Efficient
frontier

L

MV

U

**Risk (standard
deviation of
portfolio's return)(%)**

Figure 10.5
Efficient frontier

stock portfolio is less risky than the foreign portfolio. Does this mean that Canadian portfolio managers should invest entirely in Canada?

The answer is no because the minimum variance portfolio with approximately 20-percent foreign content dominates portfolio U, the 100-percent domestic portfolio. Going from 0-percent to around 20-percent foreign content actually reduces portfolio standard deviation due the diversification effect. Increasing the foreign content beyond around 20 percent increases portfolio risk. Recognizing this point led pension managers to lobby successfully in 1992 for an increase in allowable foreign content to 20 percent.[7]

Another point worth pondering concerns the potential pitfalls of using only past data to estimate future returns. The stock markets of many foreign countries, such as Japan, had phenomenal growth in the 1980s. Thus, a graph like Figure 10.5 makes a large investment in these foreign markets seem attractive. However, abnormally high returns cannot be sustained forever, and the Japanese stock market suffered major declines in the early 1990s. To avoid the forecaster's trap inherent in blind reliance on historical returns, some subjectivity must be used when forecasting future expected returns. Scenario analysis is a useful tool here.

CONCEPT QUESTION

■ What is the relationship between the shape of the efficient set for two assets and the correlation between the two assets?

---

[7]These data come from H. S. Marmer, "International Investing: A New Canadian Perspective," *Canadian Investment Review* (Spring 1991), pp. 47–53.

Figure 10.6
The feasible set of
portfolios
constructed from
many securities

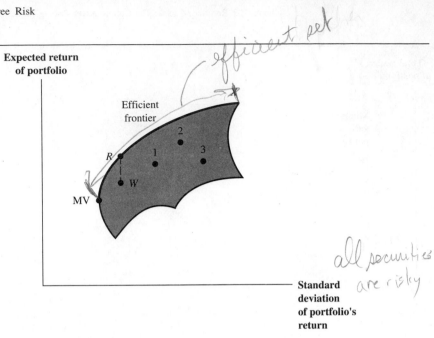

So far, Figure 10.6 is different from the earlier graphs. When only two securities
are involved, all the combinations lie on a single curve. Conversely, with many
securities the combinations cover an entire area. However, notice that an individual
will want to be somewhere on the upper edge between MV and *X*. The upper edge,

10.5   The Efficient Set for Many Securities

The previous discussion concerned two securities. We found that a simple curve
sketched out all the possible portfolios. Because investors generally hold more than
two securities, we should examine the same feasible set when more than two securities
are held. The shaded area in Figure 10.6 represents the opportunity set or feasible set
when many securities are considered. The shaded area represents all the possible
combinations of expected return and standard deviation for a portfolio. For example, in
a universe of 100 securities, point 1 might represent a portfolio of, say, 40 securities.
Point 2 might represent a portfolio of 80 securities. Point 3 might represent a different
set of 80 securities or the same 80 securities held in different proportions. Obviously,
the combinations are virtually endless. However, note that all possible combinations fit
into a confined region. No security or combination of securities can fall outside of the
shaded region. That is, no one can choose a portfolio with an expected return above
that given by the shaded region because the expected returns on individual securities
cannot be altered. Furthermore, no one can choose a portfolio with a standard
deviation below that given in the shaded area. Perhaps more surprisingly, no one can
choose an expected return below that given in the curve. In other words, the capital
markets actually prevent a self-destructive person from taking on a guaranteed loss.[8]

---

[8]Of course, someone dead set on parting with his money can do so. For example, he can trade frequently without purpose,
so that commissions more than offset the positive expected returns on the portfolio.

which we indicate in Figure 10.6 by a thick line, is called the *efficient set*. Any point below the efficient set would receive less expected return and the same standard deviation as a point on the efficient set. For example, consider R on the efficient set and W directly below it. If W contains the risk you desire, you should choose R instead in order to receive a higher expected return.

In the final analysis, Figure 10.6 is quite similar to Figure 10.3. The efficient set in Figure 10.3 runs from MV to Supertech. It contains various combinations of the securities Supertech and Slowpoke. The efficient set in Figure 10.6 runs from MV to X. It contains various combinations of many securities. The fact that a whole shaded area appears in Figure 10.6 but not in Figure 10.3 is not an important difference; no investor would choose any point below the efficient set in Figure 10.6 anyway.

We mentioned earlier that an efficient set for two securities can be traced out easily in the real world. The task becomes more difficult when additional securities are included because the number of observations grows. For example, using subjective analysis to estimate expected returns and standard deviations for, say, 100 or 500 securities may very well become overwhelming, and the difficulties with correlations may be greater still. There are almost 5,000 correlations between pairs of securities from a universe of 100 securities.

Though much of the mathematics of efficient set computation had been derived in the 1950s,[9] the high cost of computer time restricted application of the principles. In recent years, the cost has been drastically reduced and a number of software packages allow the calculation of an efficient set for portfolios of moderate size. By all accounts, these packages sell quite briskly, so that our discussion above would appear to be important in practice.

Variance and Standard Deviation in a Portfolio of Many Assets

Earlier, we calculated the formulas for variance and standard deviation in the two-asset case. Because we considered a portfolio of many assets in Figure 10.6, it is worthwhile to calculate the formulas for variance and standard deviation in the many-asset case. The formula for the variance of a portfolio of many assets can be viewed as an extension of the formula for the variance of two assets.

To develop the formula, we employ the same type of matrix that we used in the two-asset case. This matrix is displayed in Table 10.3. Assuming that there are N assets, we write the numbers 1 through N on the horizontal axis and 1 through N on the vertical axis. This creates a matrix of $N \times N = N^2$ boxes.

Consider, for example, the box with a horizontal dimension of 2 and a vertical dimension of 3. The term in the box is $X_3 X_2 \text{Cov}(R_3, R_2)$. X_3 and X_2 are the percentages of the entire portfolio that are invested in the third asset and the second asset, respectively. For example, if an individual with a portfolio of $1,000 invests $100 in the second asset, $X_2 = 10\%$ (or $100/$1,000). $\text{Cov}(R_3, R_2)$ is the covariance between the returns on the third asset and the returns on the second asset. Next, note the box with a horizontal dimension of 3 and a vertical dimension of 2. The term in the box is

---

[9]The classic is Harry Markowitz, *Portfolio Selection* (New York: John Wiley & Sons, 1959). Markowitz shared the Nobel Prize in economics in 1990 (with William Sharpe) for his work on modern portfolio theory.

Table 10.3
Matrix used to calculate the variance of a portfolio

Stock	1	2	3	...	N
1	$X_1^2\sigma_1^2$	$X_1X_2\text{Cov}(R_1,R_2)$	$X_1X_3\text{Cov}(R_1, R_3)$		$X_1X_N\text{Cov}(R_1, R_N)$
2	$X_2X_1\text{Cov}(R_2, R_1)$	$X_2^2\sigma_2^2$	$X_2X_3\text{Cov}(R_2, R_3)$		$X_2X_N\text{Cov}(R_2, R_N)$
3	$X_3X_1\text{Cov}(R_3, R_1)$	$X_3X_2\text{Cov}(R_3, R_2)$	$X_3^2\sigma_3^2$		$X_3X_N\text{Cov}(R_3, R_N)$
.					
.					
.					
N	$X_NX_1\text{Cov}(R_N, R_1)$	$X_NX_2\text{Cov}(R_N, R_2)$	$X_NX_3\text{Cov}(R_N, R_3)$		$X_N^2\sigma_N^2$

σ_i is the standard deviation of stock i.

$\text{Cov}(R_i, R_j)$ is the covariance between stock i and stock j.

Terms involving the standard deviation of a single security appear on the diagonal. Terms involving covariance between two securities appear off the diagonal.

$X_2X_3\text{Cov}(R_2, R_3)$. Because $\text{Cov}(R_3, R_2) = \text{Cov}(R_2, R_3)$, the two boxes have the same value. The second security and the third security make up one pair of stocks. In fact, every pair of stocks appears twice in the table: once in the lower left-hand side and once in the upper right-hand side.

Suppose that the vertical dimension equals the horizontal dimension. For example, the term in the box is $X_1^2\sigma_1^2$ when both dimensions are one. Here, σ_1^2 is the variance of the return on the first security.

Thus, the diagonal terms in the matrix contain the variances of the different stocks. The off-diagonal terms contain the covariances. Table 10.4 relates the numbers of diagonal and off-diagonal elements to the size of the matrix. The number of diagonal terms (number of variance terms) is always the same as the number of stocks in the portfolio. The number of off-diagonal terms (number of covariance terms) rises much faster than the number of diagonal terms. For example, a portfolio of 100 stocks has 9,900 covariance terms. Since the variance of a portfolio's returns is the sum of all the boxes, we have:

Table 10.4
Number of variance and covariance terms as a function of the number of stocks in the portfolio

Number of stocks in portfolio	Total number of terms	Number of variance terms (number of terms on diagonal)	Number of covariance terms (number of terms off diagonal)
1	1	1	0
2	4	2	2
3	9	3	6
10	100	10	90
100	10,000	100	9,900
.	.	.	.
.	.	.	.
.	.	.	.
N	N^2	N	$N_2 - N$

In a large portfolio, the number of terms involving covariance between two securities is much greater than the number of terms involving variance of a single security.

> The variance of the return on a portfolio with many securities is more dependent on the covariances between the individual securities than on the variances of the individual securities.

In a large portfolio, the number of terms involving covariance between two securities is much greater than the number of terms involving variance of a single security.

CONCEPT QUESTIONS

- What is the formula for the variance of a portfolio for many assets?
- How can the formula be expressed in terms of a box or matrix?

Diversification: An Example 10.6

The above point can be illustrated by altering the matrix in Table 10.3 slightly. Suppose that we make the following three assumptions:

1. All securities possess the same variance, which we write as $\overline{\text{var}}$. In other words, $\sigma_i^2 = \overline{\text{var}}$ for every security.

2. All covariances in Table 10.3 are the same. We represent this uniform covariance as $\overline{\text{cov}}$. In other words, $\text{Cov}(R_i, R_j) = \overline{\text{cov}}$ for every pair of securities. It can easily be shown that $\overline{\text{var}} > \overline{\text{cov}}$.

3. All securities are equally weighted in the portfolio. Because there are N assets, the weight of each asset in the portfolio is $1/N$. In other words, $X_i = 1/N$ for each security i.

Table 10.5 is the matrix of variances and covariances under these three simplifying assumptions. Note that all of the diagonal terms are identical. Similarly, all of the off-diagonal terms are identical. As with Table 10.3, the variance of the portfolio is the sum of the terms of the boxes in Table 10.5. We know that there are N diagonal terms involving variance. Similarly, there are $N \times (N - 1)$ off-diagonal terms involving covariance. Summing across all the boxes in Table 10.5, we can express the variances of the portfolio as

$$
\begin{array}{ccccccc}
\text{Variance of} \\ \text{portfolio} & = & N & \times & \left(\dfrac{1}{N^2}\right)\overline{\text{var}} & + & N(N-1) & \times & \left(\dfrac{1}{N^2}\right)\overline{\text{cov}} \\
 & & \text{Number of} & & \text{Each} & & \text{Number of} & & \text{Each} \\
 & & \text{diagonal terms} & & \text{diagonal} & & \text{off-diagonal} & & \text{off-diagonal} \\
 & & & & \text{term} & & \text{terms} & & \text{term}
\end{array}
$$

$$
= \left(\frac{1}{N}\right)\overline{\text{var}} + \left(\frac{N^2 - N}{N^2}\right)\overline{\text{cov}}
$$

$$
= \left(\frac{1}{N}\right)\overline{\text{var}} + \left(1 - \frac{1}{N}\right)\overline{\text{cov}} \tag{10.10}
$$

Table 10.5

Matrix used to calculate the variance of a portfolio*

Stock	1	2	3	. . .	N
1	$(1/N^2)\overline{\text{var}}$	$(1/N^2)\overline{\text{cov}}$	$(1/N^2)\overline{\text{cov}}$		$(1/N^2)\overline{\text{cov}}$
2	$(1/N^2)\overline{\text{cov}}$	$(1/N^2)\overline{\text{var}}$	$(1/N^2)\overline{\text{cov}}$		$(1/N^2)\overline{\text{cov}}$
3	$(1/N^2)\overline{\text{cov}}$	$(1/N^2)\overline{\text{cov}}$	$(1/N^2)\overline{\text{var}}$		$(1/N^2)\overline{\text{cov}}$
.					
.					
.					
N	$(1/N^2)\overline{\text{cov}}$	$(1/N^2)\overline{\text{cov}}$	$(1/N^2)\overline{\text{cov}}$		$(1/N^2)\overline{\text{var}}$

*When

a. All securities possess the same variance, which we represent as $\overline{\text{var}}$.

b. All pairs of securities possess the same covariance, which we represent as $\overline{\text{cov}}$ and/or changes in earnings.

c. All securities are held in the same proportion, which is $1/N$.

Equation (10.10) expresses the variance of our special portfolio as a weighted sum of the average security variance and the average covariance.[10] The intuition is confirmed when we increase the number of securities in the portfolio without limit. The variance of the portfolio becomes

$$\text{Variance of portfolio (when } N \to \infty) = \overline{\text{cov}} \qquad (10.11)$$

This occurs because (1) the weight on the variance term, $1/N$, goes to 0 as N goes to infinity and (2) the weight on the covariance term, $1 - 1/N$, goes to 1 as N goes to infinity.

Formula (10.11) provides an interesting and important result. In our special portfolio, the variances of the individual securities completely vanish as the number of securities becomes large. However, the covariance terms remain. In fact, the variance of the portfolio becomes the average covariance, $\overline{\text{cov}}$. One often hears that one should diversify. You should not put all your eggs in one basket. The effect of diversification on the risk of a portfolio can be illustrated in this example. The variances of the individual securities are diversified away, but the covariance terms cannot be diversified away.

The fact that part, but not all, of one's risk can be diversified away should be explored. Consider Mr. Smith, who brings $1,000 to the roulette table at a casino. It would be very risky if he put all his money on one spin of the wheel. For example, imagine that he put the full $1,000 on red at the table. If the wheel showed red, he would get $2,000, but if the wheel showed black, he would lose everything. Suppose, instead, he divided his money over 1,000 different spins by betting $1 at a time on red. Probability theory tells us that he could count on winning about 50 percent of the time. In other words, he could count on pretty nearly getting all his original $1,000 back.[11]

---

[10]Equation (10.10) is actually a weighted average of the variance and covariance terms because the weights, $1/N$ and $1 - 1/N$, sum to 1.

[11]This ignores the casino's cut.

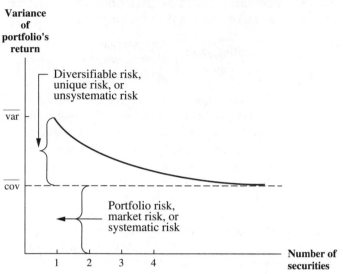

Figure 10.7
Relationship between the variance of a portfolio's return and the number of securities in the portfolio

This graph assumes
a. All securities have constant variance. $\overline{var}$.
b. All securities have constant covariance. $\overline{cov}$.
c. All securities are equally weighted in portfolio.
The variance of a portfolio drops as more securities are added to the portfolio. However, it does not drop to zero. Rather. $\overline{cov}$ serves as the floor.

Now, let's contrast this with our stock market example, which we illustrate in Figure 10.7. The variance of the portfolio with only one security is, of course, $\overline{var}$, because the variance of a portfolio with one security is the variance of the security. The variance of the portfolio drops as more securities are added, which is evidence of the diversification effect. However, unlike Mr. Smith's roulette example, the portfolio's variance can never drop to zero. Rather it reaches a floor of $\overline{cov}$, which is the covariance of each pair of securities.[12]

Because the variance of the portfolio asymptotically approaches $\overline{cov}$, each additional security continues to reduce risk. Thus, if there were neither commissions nor other transactions costs, it could be argued that one can never achieve too much diversification. However, there is a cost to diversification in the real world. Commissions per dollar invested fall as one makes larger purchases in a single stock. Unfortunately, one must buy fewer shares of each security when buying more and more different securities. Comparing the costs and benefits of diversification, Meir Statman argues that a portfolio of about 30 stocks is needed to achieve optimal diversification.[13]

---

[12]Though it is harder to show, this risk reduction effect also applies to the general case where variance and covariances are not equal.

[13]Meir Statman, "How Many Stocks Make a Diversified Portfolio?" *Journal of Financial and Quantitative Analysis* (September 1987).

We mentioned earlier that $\overline{var}$ must be greater than $\overline{cov}$. Thus, the variance of a security's return can be broken down in the following way:

$$\begin{matrix} \text{Total risk of} \\ \text{individual security} \\ (\overline{var}) \end{matrix} = \begin{matrix} \text{Portfolio risk} \\ (\overline{cov}) \end{matrix} + \begin{matrix} \text{Unsystematic or} \\ \text{diversifiable risk} \\ (\overline{var} - \overline{cov}) \end{matrix}$$

Total risk, which is $\overline{var}$ in our example, is the risk that one bears by holding one security only. *Portfolio risk* is the risk that one still bears after achieving full diversification, which is $\overline{cov}$ in our example. Portfolio risk is often called **systematic** or **market risk** as well. **Diversifiable, unique,** or **unsystematic risk** is that risk that can be diversified away in a large portfolio, which must be $(\overline{var} - \overline{cov})$ by definition.

To an individual who selects a diversified portfolio, the total risk of an individual security is not important. When considering adding a security to a diversified portfolio, the individual cares about that portion of the risk of a security that cannot be diversified away. This risk can alternatively be viewed as the *contribution* of a security to the risk of an entire portfolio. We will talk about the case where securities make different contributions to the risk of the entire portfolio.

Risk and the Sensible Investor

Having gone to all this trouble to show that unsystematic risk disappears in a well-diversified portfolio, how do we know that investors even want such portfolios? Suppose they like risk and don't want it to disappear?

We must admit that, theoretically at least, this is possible, but we will argue that it does not describe what we think of as the typical investor. Our typical investor is **risk averse.** Risk-averse behavior can be defined in many ways, but we prefer the following example: A fair gamble is one with zero expected return; a risk-averse investor would prefer to avoid fair gambles.

Why do investors choose well-diversified portfolios? Our answer is that they are risk averse, and risk-averse people avoid unnecessary risk, such as the unsystematic risk on a stock. If you do not think this is much of an answer to why investors choose well-diversified portfolios and avoid unsystematic risk, consider whether you would take on such a risk. For example, suppose you had worked all summer and had saved $5,000, which you intended to use for university expenses. Now, suppose someone came up to you and offered to flip a coin for the money: heads, you would double your money, and tails, you would lose it all.

Would you take such a bet? Perhaps you would, but the average investor would not. To induce the typical risk-averse investor to take a fair gamble, you must sweeten the pot. For example, you might need to raise the odds of winning from 50–50 to 70–30 or higher. The risk-averse investor can be induced to take fair gambles only if they are sweetened so that they become unfair to the investor's advantage.

Beyond risk aversion, the tremendous growth of mutual funds in recent years strongly suggests that investors want diversified portfolios. *Mutual funds* pool funds from individual investors, allowing them to own units in large, diversified portfolios. By holding units in different funds, individuals can achieve wide diversification across securities and markets around the world.

CONCEPT QUESTIONS

- What are the two components of the total risk of a security?
- Why doesn't diversification eliminate all risk?
- How is risk aversion defined?

Riskless Borrowing and Lending 10.7

p 291

In constructing Figure 10.6, we assume that all the securities on the efficient set are risky. Alternatively, an investor could easily combine a risky investment with an investment in a riskless or risk-free security, such as an investment in Canada Treasury bills. This is illustrated in the following example.

- *Example*

Zorana Sadiq is considering investing in the common stock of Princess Enterprises. In addition, Ms. Sadiq will either borrow or lend at the risk-free rate. The relevant parameters are

	Expected return on common stock of Princess	Guaranteed return on risk-free asset
Return	14%	10%
Standard deviation	0.20	0

Suppose Ms. Sadiq chooses to invest a total of $1,000; $350 is invested in Princess Enterprises and $650 in the risk-free asset. The expected return on her total investment is simply a weighted average of the two returns:

Expected return on portfolio
composed of one riskless $= 0.114 = 0.35 \times 0.14 + 0 + 0.65 \times 0$ (10.12)
and one risky asset

Because the expected return on the portfolio is a weighted average of the expected return on the risky asset (Princess Enterprises) and the risk-free return, the calculation is analogous to the way we treated two risky assets. In other words, equation (10.3) applies here.

Using equation (10.4), the formula for the variance of the portfolio can be written as

$$X^2_{Princess}\sigma^2_{Princess} + 2X_{Princess}X_{Risk\text{-}free}\sigma_{Princess,Risk\text{-}free} + X^2_{Risk\text{-}free}\sigma^2_{Risk\text{-}free}$$

However, by definition, the risk-free asset has no variability. Thus, both $\sigma_{Princess, Risk\text{-}free}$ and $\sigma^2_{Risk\text{-}free}$ are equal to zero, reducing the above expression to

Variance of portfolio
composed of one
riskless and one $= X^2_{Princess}\sigma^2_{Princess} = (0.35)^2 \times (0.20)^2 = 0.0049$ (10.13)
risky asset

Figure 10.8
Relationship
between expected
return and risk for
a portfolio of one
risky asset and one
riskless asset

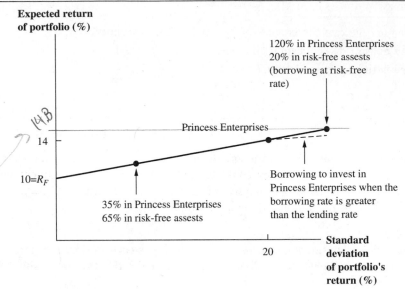

The standard deviation of the portfolio is

$$\text{Standard deviation of portfolio composed of one riskless and one risky asset} = X_{\text{Princess}}\sigma_{\text{Princess}} = 0.35 \times 0.20 = 0.07 \qquad (10.14)$$

The relationship between risk and return for one risky and one riskless asset can be seen in Figure 10.8. Ms. Sadiq's split of 35–65 percent between the two assets is represented on a *straight* line between the risk-free rate and a pure investment in Princess Enterprises. Note that, unlike the case of two risky assets, the opportunity set is straight, not curved.

Suppose that, alternatively, Ms. Sadiq borrows $200 at the risk-free rate. Combining this with her original sum of $1,000, she invests a total of $1,200 in Princess Enterprises. Her expected return would be

$$\text{Expected return on portfolio formed by borrowing to invest in risky asset} = 14.8\% = 1.20 \times 0.14 + (-0.2) \times 0.10$$

Here, she invests 120 percent of her original investment of $1,000 by borrowing 20 percent of her original investment. Note that the return of 14.8 percent is greater than the 14 percent expected return on Princess Enterprises. This occurs because she is borrowing at 10 percent to invest in a security with an expected return greater than 10 percent.

The standard deviation is

$$\text{Standard deviation of portfolio formed by borrowing to invest in risky asset} = 1.20 \times 0.2 = 0.24$$

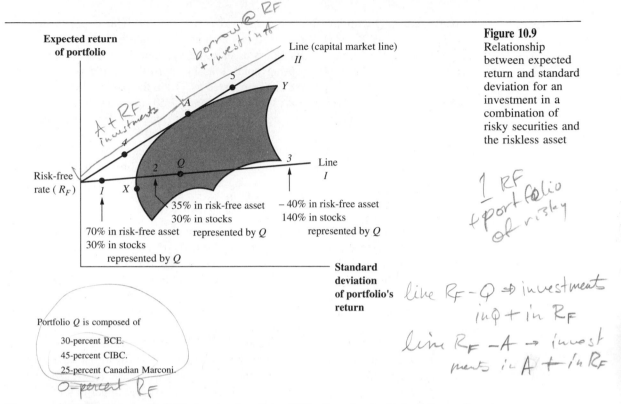

Expected return of portfolio

borrow @ RF + invest in A

Line (capital market line)
II

A + RF investments

Y

5

A

4

Risk-free rate (R_F)

X

Q

2

3

Line *I*

1

35% in risk-free asset
30% in stocks
represented by Q

70% in risk-free asset
30% in stocks
represented by Q

− 40% in risk-free asset
140% in stocks
represented by Q

Standard deviation of portfolio's return

Figure 10.9
Relationship between expected return and standard deviation for an investment in a combination of risky securities and the riskless asset

1 RF folio + portfolio of risky

like R_F − Q ⟹ investments in Q + in R_F

line R_F − A → investments in A + in R_F

Portfolio Q is composed of

30-percent BCE.

45-percent CIBC.

25-percent Canadian Marconi.

0-percent R_F

The standard deviation of 0.24 is greater than 0.20, the standard deviation of Princess Enterprises, because borrowing increases the variability of the investment. This investment also appears in Figure 10.8.

So far, we have assumed that Ms. Sadiq is able to borrow at the same rate at which she can lend.[14] Now let us consider the case where the borrowing rate is above the lending rate. The dotted line in Figure 10.8 illustrates the opportunity set for borrowing opportunities in this case. The dotted line is below the solid line because a higher borrowing rate lowers the expected return on the investment. ∎

The Optimal Portfolio

The previous section analyzed a portfolio of one riskless asset and one risky asset. In reality, an investor is likely to combine an investment in the riskless asset with a portfolio of risky assets. This is illustrated in Figure 10.9.

Consider point Q, representing a portfolio of securities. Point Q is in the interior of the feasible set of risky securities. Let us assume the point represents a portfolio of 30 percent in Bell Canada Enterprises (BCE), 45 percent in Canadian Imperial Bank of Commerce (CIBC), and 25 percent in Canadian Marconi. Individuals combining

---

[14]Surprisingly, this appears to be a decent approximation because a large number of investors are able to borrow on margin when purchasing stocks. The borrowing rate on the margin is very near the riskless rate of interest, particularly for large investors. More will be said about this in a later chapter.

investments in Q with investments in the riskless asset would achieve points along the straight line from R_F to Q. We refer to this as line I. For example, point 1 represents a portfolio of 70 percent in the riskless asset and 30 percent in stocks represented by Q. An investor with \$100 choosing point 1 as his portfolio would put \$70 in the risk-free asset and \$30 in Q. This can be restated as \$70 in the riskless asset, \$9 (or 0.3 × \$30) in BCE, \$13.50 (or 0.45 × \$30) in CIBC, and \$7.50 (or 0.25 × \$30) in Canadian Marconi. Point 2 also represents a portfolio of the risk-free asset and Q, with more (65 percent) being invested in Q.

Point 3 is obtained by borrowing to invest in Q. For example, an investor with \$100 of his or her own would borrow \$40 from the bank or broker in order to invest \$140 in Q. This can be stated as borrowing \$40 and contributing \$100 of one's own money in order to invest \$42 (or 0.3 × \$140) in BCE, \$63 (or 0.45 × \$140) in CIBC, and \$35 (or 0.25 × \$140) in Canadian Marconi.

Though any investor can obtain any point on line I, no point on the line is optimal. To see this, consider line II, a line running from R_F through A. Point A represents another portfolio of risky securities. Line II represents portfolios formed by combinations of the risk-free asset and the securities in A. Points between R_F and A are portfolios in which some money is invested in the riskless asset and the rest is placed in A. Points past A are achieved by borrowing at the riskless rate to buy more of A than one could with one's original funds alone.

As drawn, line II is tangent to the efficient set of risky securities. Whatever point an individual can obtain on line I, he or she can obtain a point with the same standard deviation and a higher expected return on line II. In fact, because line II is tangent to the efficient set, it provides the investor with the best possible opportunities. In other words, line II, which is frequently called the **capital market line,** can be viewed as the efficient set of all assets, both risky and riskless. An investor with a fair degree of risk aversion might choose a point between R_F and A, perhaps point 4. An individual with a lower degree of risk aversion might choose a point closer to A or even beyond A. For example, point 5 is achieved when an individual borrows money to increase an investment in A.

The graph illustrates an important point. With riskless borrowing and lending, the portfolio of risky assets held by any investor would always be point A. Regardless of the investor's tolerance for risk, he or she would never choose any other point on the efficient set of risky assets (represented by curve XAY) or any point in the interior of the feasible region. Rather, the investor would combine the securities of A with the riskless assets if he had high aversion to risk and would borrow the riskless asset to invest more funds in A if he or she had low aversion to risk.

This result establishes what financial economists call the **separation principle.** That is, the investor makes two separate decisions:

1. After estimating (a) the expected return and variances of individual securities and (b) the covariances between pairs of securities, the investor calculates the efficient set of risky assets, represented by curve XAY in Figure 10.9, and determines point A, the tangency between the risk-free rate and the efficient set of risky assets (curve XAY). Point A represents the portfolio of risky assets that the investor will hold. This point is determined solely from estimates of returns,

variances, and covariances. No personal characteristics, such as degree of risk aversion, are needed in this step.

2. The investor must now determine how to combine point A, the portfolio of risky assets, with the riskless asset. He or she could invest some of the funds in the riskless asset and some in portfolio A. The investor would end up at a point on the line between R_F and A in this case. Alternatively, the investor could borrow at the risk-free rate and contribute some personal funds as well, investing the sum in portfolio A. He or she would end up at a point on line II beyond A. The investor's position in the riskless asset (that is, the choice of where on the line he or she wants to be) is determined by internal characteristics, such as the investor's ability to tolerate risk.

CONCEPT QUESTIONS

- What is the formula for the standard deviation of a portfolio composed of one riskless and one risky asset?
- How does one determine the optimal portfolio among the efficient set of risky assets?

Market Equilibrium   10.8

Definition of the Market Equilibrium Portfolio

The above analysis concerns one investor. Estimates of the expected returns and variances for individual securities and the covariances between pairs of securities are unique to this individual. Other investors would obviously have different estimates of these variables. However, the estimates might not vary much because all investors would be forming expectations from the same data on past price movement and other publicly available information.

Financial economists often imagine a world where all investors possess the same estimates of expected returns, variances, and covariances. Though this can never be literally true, it can be thought of as a useful simplifying assumption in a world where investors have access to similar sources of information. This assumption is called **homogenous expectations.**[15]

If investors have homogenous expectations, Figure 10.9 would be the same for all individuals. That is, all investors would sketch out the same efficient set of risky assets because they would be working with the same inputs. This efficient set of risky assets is represented by the curve XAY. Because the same risk-free rate would apply to everyone, all investors would view point A as the portfolio of risky assets to be held.

This point A takes on great importance because all investors would purchase the risky securities that it represents. Those investors with a high degree of risk aversion

---

[15]The assumption of homogeneous expectations states that all investors have the same beliefs concerning returns, variances, and covariances. It does not say that all investors have the same aversion to risk.

might combine *A* with an investment in the riskless asset, achieving point 4, for example. Others with low aversion to risk might borrow to achieve, say, point 5. Because this is a very important conclusion, we restate it:

> In a world with homogenous expectations, all investors would hold the portfolio of risky assets represented by point *A*.

If all investors choose the same portfolio of risky assets, it is possible to determine what that portfolio is. Common sense tells us that it is a market-value weighted portfolio of all existing securities. It is the **market portfolio.**

In practice, financial economists use a broad-based index such as the Toronto Stock Exchange 300 Index (TSE 300) as a proxy for the market portfolio. Of course, all investors do not hold the same portfolio in practice. However, we know that a large number of investors hold diversified portfolios, particularly when mutual funds or pension funds are included. A broad-based index is a good proxy for the highly diversified portfolios of many investors.

Definition of Risk When Investors Hold the Market Portfolio

The previous section states that many investors hold diversified portfolios similar to broad-based indices. This result allows us to be more precise about the risk of a security in the context of a diversified portfolio.

Researchers have shown that the best measure of risk of a security in a large portfolio is the beta of the security.

$$\beta_i = \frac{\text{Cov}(R_i, R_M)}{\sigma^2(R_M)} \qquad (10.15)$$

where $\sigma^2(R_M)$ is the variance of the market. Though both $\text{Cov}(R_i, R_M)$ and β_i can be used as measures of the contribution of security to the risk of the market portfolio, β_i is much more common. The basic intuition of beta is that it measures the sensitivity of a change in the return of an individual security to the change in return of the market portfolio. One useful property is that the average beta across all securities, when weighted by the proportion of each security's market value to that of the market portfolio, is 1. That is

$$\sum_{i=1}^{N} X_i \beta_i = 1 \qquad (10.16)$$

Beta as a Measure of Responsiveness

The previous discussion shows that the beta of a security is the standardized covariance between the return on the security and the return on the market. Though this explanation is 100-percent correct, it is not likely to be 100-percent intuitively appealing to anyone other than a statistician. Luckily, there is a more intuitive explanation for beta. We present this explanation through an example.

■ *Example*

Consider the following possible returns both on the stock of Remico, Ltd., and on the market:

State	Type of economy	Return on market	Return on Remico, Ltd.
I	Bull	15%	25%
II	Bull	15	15
III	Bear	−5	−5
IV	Bear	−5	−15

Though the return on the market has only two possible outcomes (15 percent and −5 percent), the return on Remico has four possible outcomes. It is helpful to consider the expected return on a security for a given return on the market. Assuming each state is equally likely, we have

Type of economy	Return on market	Expected return on Remico
Bull	15%	$2\% = 25\% \times \frac{1}{2} + 15\% \times \frac{1}{2} = 20\%$.
Bear	−5	$-10\% = -5\% \times \frac{1}{2} + (-15\%) \times \frac{1}{2}$

Remico, Ltd., responds to market movements because its expected return is greater in bullish states than in bearish states. We now calculate exactly how responsive the security is to market movements. The market's return in a bullish economy is 20 percent [or 15% − (−5%)] greater than the market's return in a bearish economy. However, the expected return on Remico in a bullish economy is 30 percent [or 20% − (−10%)] greater than its expected return in a bearish state. Thus, Remico, Ltd., has a responsiveness coefficient of 1.5 (or 30%/20%).

This relationship appears in Figure 10.10. The returns for both Remico and the market in each state are plotted as four points. In addition, we plot the expected return on the security for each of the two possible returns on the market. These two points, which we designate by *X,* are joined by a line called the **characteristic line** of the security. The slope of the line is 1.5, the number calculated in the previous paragraph. This responsiveness coefficient of 1.5 is the beta of Remico.

The interpretation of beta from Figure 10.10 is intuitive: the graph tells us that the returns on Remico are magnified 1.5 times over those of the market. When the market does well, Remico's stock is expected to do even better. When the market does poorly, Remico's stock is expected to do even worse. Now imagine an individual with a portfolio near that of the market who is considering the addition of Remico to his portfolio. Because of Remico's *magnification factor* of 1.5, he will view this stock as contributing much to the risk of the portfolio. We showed earlier that the beta of the average security in the market is 1. Remico contributes more to the risk of a large, diversified portfolio than does an average security because Remico is more responsive to movements in the market.

Further insight can be gleaned by examining securities with negative betas. One should view these securities as either hedges or insurance policies. The security is expected to do well when the market does poorly and vice versa. Because of this,

Figure 10.10
Performance of
Remico, Ltd., and
the market
portfolio

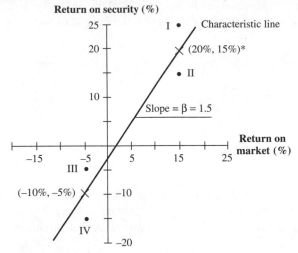

The two points marked X represent the expected return on
Remico for each possible outcome of the market portfolio.
The expected return on Remico is positively related to the return
on the market. Because the slope is 1.5, we say that Remico's
beta is 1.5. Beta measures the responsiveness of the security's
return to movement in the market.
*(20%, 15%) refers to the point where the return on the security
is 20 percent and the return on the market is 15 percent.

adding a negative beta security to a large, diversified portfolio actually reduces the risk
of the portfolio.[16]

Beta Estimation in Practice

Our example showed how to determine beta based on forecasted returns. Investment
dealers generally estimate beta using regression analysis on historical data. Students
who have studied statistics will recognize beta in Equation (10.15) as the slope
coefficient of a regression of company return (R_i) on return on a market index (R_M). In
the regression, R_i is the dependent variable and R_M is the independent variable.

A number of services sell or even give away estimates of beta for different firms.
Table 10.6 presents a page from a set of betas calculated by Burns Fry Limited. The
first column of the table is the beta estimated from monthly data over the $4\frac{1}{2}$-year
period April 1989 to September 1993. The Toronto Stock Exchange Index is used as
the market index. R^2 appears in the second column. The last column shows the number
of monthly observations used in computing the beta.

In their estimation procedure, Burns Fry analysts apparently made a number of
assumptions consistent with Canadian research on the capital asset pricing model.[17]
First, they chose monthly data, as do many financial economists. On the one hand,
statistical problems frequently arise when time intervals shorter than a month are used.

---

[16]Unfortunately, empirical evidence shows that virtually no stocks have negative betas.

[17]The suggested readings at the end of the chapter include reviews of Canadian tests of the capital asset pricing model.

Company	Beta	Percent explained by market	Number of months	
Department stores				**Table 10.6**
Hudson's Bay Co.	1.49	25.8%	54	TSE 300
Sears Canada	1.21	20.5	54	composite index:
Clothing stores				Estimates of stock
Dylex Ltd. A	1.89	15.4	54	total return betas
Reitmans (Canada) A	0.99	21.1	54	based on monthly
Specialty stores				returns, April
Canadian Tire A	0.79	14.5	54	1989–September
Gendis Inc. A	0.38	5.2	54	1993
Intl Semi-Tech A	1.28	8.3	54	
North West Company	0.85	3.8	36	
Jean Coutu Group A	0.38	3.8	54	
Hospitality				
Cara Operations A	0.88	16.8	54	
Cara Operations	0.9	15.8	54	
Four Seasons Hotels	0.79	8.7	54	
Loewen Group Inc.	0.99	17.2	54	
Banks				
Bank of Montreal	0.97	34.5	54	
Bank of Nova Scotia	1.39	44.6	54	
CIBC	1.51	51.2	54	
Laurentian Bank	0.58	12.9	54	
National Bank	1.48	41.9	54	
Royal Bank of Canada	1.25	49.4	54	
Toronto-Dominion Bank	1.03	33.3	54	

Source: Burns Fry Limited, "Estimates of Stock Total Return Betas," Toronto, 1993.

On the other hand, important information is lost when longer intervals are employed. Thus, the choice of monthly data can be viewed as a compromise.

Second, Burns Fry analysts used just under five years of data, the result of another compromise. Due to changes in production mix, production techniques, management style, and/or financial leverage, a firm's nature adjusts over time. A long time period for calculating beta implies many out-of-date observations. Conversely, a short time period leads to statistical imprecision, because few monthly observations are used.

In Table 10.6 the statistic R^2 measures the regression's "goodness of fit." R^2 is the square of the correlation coefficient, ρ, between R_i and R_M. The highest value for R^2 is 1, a situation that would occur if all points lay exactly on the characteristic line. This would be the case when the security's return is determined only by the market's return without the security having any independent variation. The R^2 is likely to approach 1 for a large portfolio of securities. For example, many widely diversified mutual funds have R^2s of 0.80 or more. The lowest possible R^2 is 0, a situation occuring when two variables are entirely unrelated to each other. Companies whose returns are pretty much independent of returns on the stock market have R^2s near zero.[18]

---

[18]Standard computer packages generally provide confidence intervals (error ranges) for beta estimates. One has greater confidence in beta estimates where the confidence interval is small. While stocks with high R^2s generally have small confidence intervals, it is the size of the confidence interval, not the R^2 itself, that is relevant here. Because expected return is related to systematic risk, the R^2 of a firm is of no concern to us once we know the firm's beta. This often surprises students trained in statistics, because R^2 is an important concept for many other purposes.

A Test

We have put these questions on past corporate finance examinations:

1. What sort of investor rationally views the variance (or standard deviation) of an individual security's return as the security's proper measure of risk?
2. What sort of investor rationally views the beta of a security as the security's proper measure of risk?

A proper answer might be something like the following:

> A rational, risk-averse investor views the variance (or standard deviation) of his or her portfolio's return as the proper measure of the risk of the portfolio. If for some reason or another the investor can hold only one security, the variance of that security's return becomes the variance of the portfolio's return. Hence, the variance of the security's return is the security's proper measure of risk.
>
> If an individual holds a diversified portfolio, he or she still views the variance (or standard deviation) of the portfolio's return as the proper measure of the risk of the portfolio. However, the investor is no longer interested in the variance of each individual security's return. Rather, he or she is interested in the *contribution* of an individual security to the variance of the portfolio.

Under the assumption of homogenous expectations, all individuals hold the market portfolio. Thus, we measure risk as the contribution of an individual security to the variance of the market portfolio. This contribution, when standardized properly, is the beta of the security. While very few investors hold the market portfolio exactly, many hold reasonably diversified portfolios. These portfolios are close enough to the market portfolio so that the beta of a security is likely to be a reasonable measure of its risk.

CONCEPT QUESTIONS

- If all investors have homogensous expectations, what portfolio of risky assets do they hold?
- What is the formula for beta?
- Why is beta the appropriate measure of risk for a single security in a large portfolio?
- What is the statistical procedure employed for calculating beta?
- Why do financial economists use monthly data when calculating beta?
- What is R^2?

10.9　Relationship between Risk and Return (CAPM)

It is commonplace to argue that the expected return on a security should be positively related to its risk. That is, individuals will hold a risky security only if its expected return compensates for its risk. This reasoning holds regardless of the measure of risk. Now consider our world where all individuals (1) have homogeneous expectations and (2) can borrow and lend at the risk-free rate. All individuals hold the market portfolio

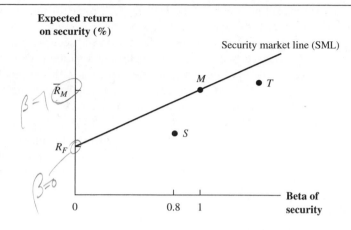

Figure 10.11
Relationship between expected return on an individual security and beta of the security

(handwritten annotations in figure: $\beta = 1$; $\beta = 0$)

(handwritten note at right: The riskier the more return is expected)

of risky securities here. We have shown that the beta of a security is the appropriate measure of risk in this context. Hence, the expected return on a security should be positively related to its beta. This is illustrated in Figure 10.11. The upward-sloping line in the figure is called the **security market line (SML).**

There are six important points associated with this figure.

1. *A beta of zero.* The expected return on a security with a beta of zero is the risk-free rate, R_F. Because a security with zero beta has no relevant risk, its expected return should equal the risk-free rate.

2. *A beta of one.* Equation (10.16) points out that the average beta across all securities, when weighted by the proportion of each security's market value to that of the market portfolio, is 1. Because the market portfolio is formed by weighting each security by its market value, the beta of the market portfolio is 1. Because all securities with the same beta have the same expected return, the expected return for any security with a beta of 1 is $\bar{R}_M$, the expected return on the market portfolio.

3. *Linearity.* The intuition behind an upward-sloping curve is clear. Because beta is the appropriate measure of risk, high-beta securities should have an expected return above that of low-beta securities. However, Figure 10.11 shows something more than an upward-sloping curve; the relationship between expected return and beta corresponds to a *straight* line.

It is easy to show that the line in Figure 10.11 is straight. To see this, consider security S with, say, a beta of 0.8. This security is represented by a point below the security market line in the figure. Any investor could duplicate the beta of security S by buying a portfolio with 20 percent in the risk-free asset and 80 percent in a security with a beta of 1. However, the homemade portfolio would itself lie on the SML. In other words, the portfolio dominates security S because the portfolio has a higher expected return and the same beta.

Now consider security T with, say, a beta greater than 1. This security is also below the SML in Figure 10.11. Any investor could duplicate the beta of security T by borrowing to invest in a security with a beta of 1. This portfolio must also lie on the SML, thereby dominating security T.

Because no one would hold either S or T, their stock prices would drop. This price adjustment would raise the expected returns on the two securities. The price adjustment would continue until the two securities lay on the security market line. The above example considered two overpriced stocks and a straight SML. Securities lying above the SML are *underpriced*. Their prices must rise until their expected returns lie on the line. If the SML is itself curved, many stocks would be mispriced. In equilibrium, all securities would be held only when prices changed so that the SML became straight. In other words, linearity would be achieved.

4. *The capital asset pricing model.* You may remember from algebra courses that a line can be described algebraically if one knows both its intercept and its slope. We can see from Figure 10.11 that the intercept of the SML is R_F. Because the expected return of any security with a beta of 1 is $\overline{R}_M$, the slope of the line is $\overline{R}_M - R_F$. This allows us to write the SML algebraically as

Capital asset pricing model:

$$
\underset{\substack{\text{Expected} \\ \text{return on} \\ \text{a security}}}{\overline{R}} = \underset{\substack{\text{Risk-} \\ \text{free} \\ \text{rate}}}{R_F} + \underset{\substack{\text{Beta} \\ \text{of the} \\ \text{security}}}{\beta} \times \underset{\substack{\text{Difference between} \\ \text{expected return} \\ \text{on market and} \\ \text{risk-free rate}}}{(\overline{R}_M - R_F)}
\qquad (10.17)
$$

According to financial economists, the above algebraic formula describing the SML is called the **capital asset pricing model (CAPM).** In words, the CAPM states that the expected return on a security depends on the security's risk relative to the risk of a market portfolio.[19] The formula can be illustrated by assuming a few special cases.

    a.   Assume $\beta = 0$. Here, $\overline{R} = R_F$; that is, the expected return on the security is equal to the risk-free rate. We argued this in point (1) above.

    b.   Assume $\beta = 1$. The equation reduces to $\overline{R} = \overline{R}_M$; that is, the expected return on the security is equal to the expected return on the market. We argued this in point (2) above.

As with any line, the line represented by equation (10.17) has both a slope and an intercept. R_F, the risk-free rate, is the intercept. Because the beta of a security is the horizontal axis, $\overline{R}_M$ less R_F is the slope. The line will be upward-sloping as long as the expected return on the market is greater than the risk-free rate. Because the market portfolio is a risky asset, theory suggests that its expected return is above the risk-free rate. In addition, the empirical evidence of the previous chapter showed that the actual return on the market portfolio over the past 45 years was well above the risk-free rate.

---

[19]Since the CAPM assumes that all investors place their wealth in the market portfolio, we can also say that the CAPM states that the expected return on a security depends on its risk relative to future wealth. An alternative version of the CAPM measures risk relative to future consumption as opposed to future wealth. Called the *consumption CAPM (CCAPM)*, this version has the merit of linking risk directly to the goal of wealth holding. For more on the CCAPM versus the CAPM, see D. Breeden, M. Gibbons, and R. Litzenberger, "Empirical Tests of the Consumption-Oriented CAPM," *Journal of Finance* 44 (June 1989), pp. 231–62.

■ *Example*

The stock of Aardvark Enterprises has a beta of 1.5; that of Zebra Enterprises has a beta of 0.7. The risk-free rate is 7 percent and the difference between the expected return on the market and the risk-free rate is 6.4 percent.[20] The expected returns on the two securities are

Expected Return for Aardvark:

$$16.45\% = 7\% + 1.5 \times 6.4\% \tag{10.18}$$

Expected Return for Zebra:

$$11.48\% = 7\% + 0.7 \times 6.4\% \quad ■$$

5. *Portfolios as well as securities.* Our discussion of the CAPM considered individual securities. Does the relationship in Figure 10.11 and equation (10.18) hold for portfolios as well?

Yes. To see this, consider a portfolio formed by investing equally in our two securities: Aardvark and Zebra. The expected return on the portfolio is

Expected Return on Portfolio:

$$13.93\% = 0.5 \times 16.45\% + 0.5 \times 11.41\% \tag{10.19}$$

The beta of the portfolio is simply a weighted average of the two securities. Thus we have

Beta of Portfolio:

$$1.1 = 0.5 \times 1.5 + 0.5 \times 0.7$$

Under the CAPM, the expected return on the portfolio is

$$14.04\% = 7\% + 1.1 \times 6.4\% \tag{10.20}$$

Because the value in (10.19) is the same as the value in (10.20), the example shows that the CAPM holds for portfolios as well as for individual securities.

6. *A potential confusion.* Students often confuse the SML in Figure 10.11 with the capital market line (line *II* in Figure 10.9). Actually, the lines are quite different. The capital market line traces the efficient set of portfolios formed from both risky assets and the riskless asset. Each point on the line represents an entire portfolio. Point *A* is a portfolio composed entirely of risky assets. Every other point on the line represents a portfolio of the securities in *A* combined with the riskless asset. The axes in Figure 10.9 are expected return of a portfolio and the standard deviation of a portfolio. Individual securities do not lie along line *II*.

The SML in Figure 10.11 relates expected return to beta. Figure 10.11 differs from Figure 10.9 in at least two ways. First, beta appears in the horizontal axis of Figure 10.11 but standard deviation appears in the horizontal axis of Figure 10.9.

---

[20]As reported in Table 9.2, the expected return on common stocks was 12.58 percent over 1948–92. The average risk-free rate over the same time interval was 6.19 percent. Thus, the average difference between the two was 6.4 percent. Financial economists use this as the best estimate of the difference to occur in the future. We will use it frequently in this text.

Second, the SML in Figure 10.11 holds both for all individual securities and for all possible portfolios, whereas line *II* (the capital market line) in Figure 10.9 holds only for efficient portfolios.

- Why is the SML a straight line?
- What is the capital asset pricing model?
- What are the differences between the capital market line and the security market line?

10.10   Summary and Conclusions

This chapter sets forth the fundamentals of modern portfolio theory. Our basic points are these:

1. This chapter shows us how to calculate the expected return and variance for individual securities, and the covariance and correlation for pairs of securities. Given these statistics, the expected return and variance for a portfolio of two securities *A* and *B* can be written as

$$\text{Expected return on portfolio} = X_A \overline{R}_A + X_B \overline{R}_B$$
$$\text{Var(portfolio)} = X_A^2 \sigma_A^2 + 2X_A X_B \sigma_{AB} + X_B^2 \sigma_B^2$$

2. In our notation, *X* stands for the proportion of a security in one's portfolio. By varying *X*, one can trace out the efficient set of portfolios. We graphed the efficient set for the two-asset case as a curve, pointing out that the degree of curvature or bend in the graph reflects the diversification effect: The lower the correlation between the two securities, the greater the bend. Without proof, we stated that the general shape of the efficient set holds in a world of many assets.

3. Just as the formula for variance in the two-asset case is computed from a 2 × 2 matrix, the variance formula is computed from an *N* × *N* matrix in the *N*-asset case. We show that, with a large number of assets, there are many more covariance terms than variance terms in the matrix. In fact, the variance terms are effectively diversified away in a large portfolio, but the covariance terms are not. Thus, a diversified portfolio can only eliminate some, but not all, of the risk of the individual securities.

4. The efficient set of risky assets we spoke of earlier can be combined with riskless borrowing and lending. In this case, a rational investor will always choose to hold the portfolio of risky securities represented by point *A* in Figure 10.9, then he or she can either borrow or lend at the riskless rate to achieve any desired point on the capital market line.

5. If (1) all investors have homogeneous expectations and (2) all investors can borrow and lend at the riskless rate, all investors will choose to hold the portfolio of risky securities represented by point *A*. They will then either borrow or lend at the riskless rate. In a world of homogeneous expectations, point *A* represents the market portfolio.

6. The contribution of a security to the risk of a large portfolio is the sum of the covariances of the security's return with the returns on the other securities in the portfolio. The contribution of a security to the risk of the market portfolio is the covariance of the security's return with the market's return. This contribution, when standardized, is called the beta. The beta of a security can also be interpreted as the responsiveness of a security's return to that of the market.

7. The CAPM states that

$$\overline{R} = R_F + \beta(\overline{R}_M - R_F)$$

In other words, the expected return on a security is positively (and linearly) related to the security's beta.

Key Terms

Covariance 278

Correlation 278

Portfolio 282

Opportunity (feasible) set 289

Efficient set 289

Systematic (market) risk 298

Diversifiable (unique) (unsystematic) risk 298

Risk averse 298

Capital market line 302

Separation principle 302

Homogeneous expectations 303

Market portfolio 304

Characteristic line 305

Security market line (SML) 309

Capital asset pricing model (CAPM) 310

Suggested Readings

The capital asset pricing model was originally published in two classic articles:

W. F. Sharpe. "Capital Asset Prices: A Theory of Market Equilibrium under Conditions of Risk." *Journal of Finance* (September 1964). (William F. Sharpe shared the Nobel Prize in economics in 1990 with Harry Markowitz for his development of CAPM.)

J. Lintner. "Security Prices, Risk and Maximal Gains from Diversification." *Journal of Finance* (December 1965).

Canadian tests of the capital asset pricing model are reviewed in current investment texts:

Z. Bodie, A. Kane, A. Marcus, S. Perrakis, and P. Ryan. *Investments,* 1st Canadian ed. Homewood, Ill.: Richard D. Irwin, 1993.

J. C. Francis and E. Kirzner. *Investments: Analysis and Management.* Toronto, Ontario: McGraw-Hill Ryerson Ltd., 1988.

J. E. Hatch and M. J. Robinson. *Investment Management in Canada,* 2d ed. Scarbough, Ontario: Prentice Hall Canada, 1989.

W. F. Sharpe, G. F. Alexander, and D. J. Fowler. *Investments,* 1st Canadian ed. Scarborough, Ontario: Prentice Hall Canada, 1993.

Questions and Problems

Expected Return, Variance, and Covariance

10.1 A portfolio consists of 20 shares of MacDonald stock, which sells for $50 per share, and 30 shares of Laurier stock, which sells for $20 per share. What are the weights of the two stocks in this portfolio?

10.2 Security F has an expected return of 10 percent and a standard deviation of 5 percent per year. Security G has an expected return of 20 percent and a standard deviation of 60 percent per year.

   a. What is the expected return on a portfolio composed 40 percent of security F and 60 percent of security G?

   b. If the correlation coefficient between the returns of G and F is 0.5, what is the covariance of returns?

Portfolios

10.3 Suppose the expected returns and variances of stocks A and B are $\overline{R}_A = 0.2$, $\overline{R}_B = 0.3$, $\sigma_A^2 = 0.1$, and $\sigma_B^2 = 0.2$, respectively.

   a. Calculate the expected return and variance of a portfolio composed of 60-percent A and 40-percent B when the correlation coefficient between the stocks is −0.5.

   b. Calculate the expected return and variance of a portfolio composed of 60-percent A and 40-percent B when the correlation coefficient between the stocks is −0.6.

   c. How does the correlation coefficient affect the variance of the portfolio?

10.4 Consider the possible rates of return that you might obtain over the next year. You can invest in stock L or stock U.

State of economy	Probability of state occurring	Stock L return if state occurs	Stock U return if state occurs
Recession	0.3	−10%	10%
Normal	0.4	20	10
Boom	0.3	50	10

   a. Determine the expected return, variance, and standard deviation for stock L.

   b. Determine the expected return, variance, and standard deviation for stock U.

   c. Determine the covariance and correlation between the returns of stock L and stock U.

   d. Determine the expected return and standard deviation of an equally weighted portfolio of stock L and stock U.

10.5 If a portfolio has a positive weight for each asset, can the expected return on the portfolio be greater than the return on the asset in the portfolio that has the highest return? Can the expected return on the portfolio be less than the return on the asset in the portfolio with the lowest return? Explain.

10.6 Your uncle in Manitoba is near retirement. A broker has advised him not to invest in gold stocks because, in her opinion, they're far too risky. She has shown your uncle evidence of how wildly the prices of gold stocks have fluctuated in the recent past. She demonstrated that the standard deviation of gold stocks is very high relative to most stocks.

Do you think the broker's advice is sound for your uncle, who is risk averse? Why or why not?

10.7 There are three securities in the market. The following chart shows their possible payoffs.

State	Probability of outcome	Return on Security 1	Return on Security 2	Return on Security 3
1	0.25	0.25	0.25	0.10
2	0.25	0.20	0.15	0.15
3	0.25	0.15	0.20	0.20
4	0.25	0.10	0.10	0.25

 a. What are the expected return and standard deviation of each security?

 b. What are the covariances and correlations between the pairs of securities?

 c. What are the expected return and standard deviation of a portfolio with half of its funds invested in security 1 and half in security 2?

 d. What are the expected return and standard deviation of a portfolio with half of its funds invested in security 1 and half in security 3?

 e. What are the expected return and standard deviation of a portfolio with half of its funds invested in security 2 and half in security 3?

 f. What do your answers in parts *(a)*, *(c)*, *(d)*, and *(e)* imply about diversification?

10.8 Suppose that there are two stocks: *A* and *B*. Suppose that their returns are independent. Stock *A* has a one-third chance of having a return of 60 percent, a one-third chance of a return of 15 percent, and a one-third chance of a return of −60 percent. Stock *B* has a one-half chance of a 40-percent return and a one-half chance of a −20-percent return.

 a. Write the list of all of the possible outcomes.

 b. What is the expected return on a portfolio with 50 percent invested in stock *A* and 50 percent invested in stock *B?*

10.9 Assume there are *N* securities in the market. The expected return of every security is 0.01. All securities also have the same variance: 0.01. The covariance between any pair of securities is 0.005.

 a. What are the expected return and variance of an equally weighted portfolio containing all *N* securities? Note: The weight of each security in the portfolio is 1/*N*.

 b. What will happen to the variance as *N* gets larger?

 c. What security characteristics are most important in the determination of the variance of a well-diversified portfolio?

10.10 Is the following statement true or false? Explain.

 The most important characteristic in determining the variance
 of a well-diversified portfolio is the variance of the individual stocks.

10.11 Briefly explain why the covariance of a security with the rest of a portfolio is a more appropriate measure of risk than the security's variance.

10.12 Comment on the following quotation from a leading investment analyst.

> Stocks that move perfectly with the market have a beta of 1. Betas get higher as volatility goes up and lower as it goes down. Thus, Northern Co., a utility whose shares have traded close to $12 for most of the past three years, has a low beta. At the other extreme, there's Canadian High Tech, which has been as high as $150 and as low as its current $75.

10.13. Assume that there are two stocks with the following characteristics. The covariance between the returns on the stocks is 0.001.

	Expected return	Standard deviation
A	0.05	0.1
B	0.10	0.2

    a. What is the expected return on the minimum variance portfolio? Hint: Find the portfolio weights X_A and X_B such that the portfolio variance is minimized. Remember that the sum of the weights must equal 1.

    b. If $Cov(R_A, R_B) = -0.02$, what are the minimum variance weights?

    c. What is the portfolio variance when $Cov(R_A, R_B) = -0.02$?

10.14 William Shakespeare's character Polonius in *Hamlet* says, "Neither a borrower nor a lender be." Under the assumptions of the CAPM, what would be the composition of Polonius's portfolio?

10.15 Securities *A, B,* and *C* have the following characteristics:

Security	E(R)	σ^2	Beta
A	10%	0.01	0.6
B	4	0.04	-0.2
C	16	0.09	1.4

    a. What is the expected return on a portfolio with equal weights?

    b. What is the beta of the same portfolio?

The CAPM

10.16 *a.* Draw the security market line for the case where the market risk premium is 5 percent and the risk-free rate is 7 percent.

    b. Suppose that an asset has a beta of −1 and an expected return of 4 percent. Plot it on the graph you drew in part (a). Is the security properly priced? If not, explain what will happen in this market.

    c. Suppose that an asset has a beta of 3 and an expected return of 20 percent. Plot it on the graph you drew in part (a). Is the security properly priced? If not, explain what will happen in this market.

10.17 A stock has a beta of 0.9. A security analyst who specializes in studying this stock expects its return to be 13 percent. Suppose the risk-free rate is 8 percent and the market-risk premium is 6 percent. Is the analyst pessimistic or optimistic about this stock relative to the market's expectations?

10.18 The expected return on a portfolio that combines the risk-free asset and the asset at the point of tangency to the efficient set is 25 percent. The expected return was calculated under the following assumptions:

The risk-free rate is 5 percent.

The expected return on the market portfolio of risky assets is 20 percent.

The standard deviation of the efficient portfolio is 4 percent.

In this environment, what expected rate of return would a security earn if it had a 0.5 correlation with the market and a standard deviation of 2 percent?

10.19 The risk-free rate is 5 percent and the market portfolio has an expected rate of return of 15 percent. The market portfolio has a standard deviation of 10 percent. Portfolio Z has a correlation coefficient with the market of −0.1 and a standard deviation of 10 percent. According to the CAPM, what is the expected rate of return on portfolio Z?

10.20 The following data have been developed for the Morgan Company:

Variance of Morgan returns = 0.62662

Variance of market returns = 0.052851

Covariance of the returns on Morgan and the market = 0.0607172

Recall that the Alexander Consulting Group's update of the Hatch and White study concluded that the market risk premium for Canadian stocks is around 6.8 percent. Suppose the expected return on Treasury bills is 6.6 percent.

a. Write the equation of the security market line.

b. What is the Morgan Company's required return?

10.21 Is the following statement true or false? Explain.
A risky security cannot have an expected return that is less than the risk-free rate because no risk-averse investor would be willing to hold this asset in equilibrium.

10.22 You have been provided the following data on the securities of three firms and the market:

Security	$\bar{R}_i$	σ_i	Corr (R_i, R_M)	Beta$_i$
Firm 1	0.15		1.0	1.5
Firm 2	0.15	0.18	0.5	
Firm 3	0.10	0.02		0.5
The market	0.10	0.04		
The risk-free asset	0.05	0		

$\bar{R}_i$ = Average returns of security i

σ_i = Standard deviation of the returns of i

Corr(R_i, R_M) = Correlation coefficient of return on asset i
with the market return

Beta$_i$ = Beta coefficient of security i

Assume the capital asset pricing model and SML are true.

a. Fill in the missing values in the table.

b. Provide an evaluation of the investment performance of the three firms.

c. What is your investment recommendation? Why?

10.23 There are two stocks in the market: stock A and stock B. The price of stock A today is $50. The price of stock A next year will be $40 if the economy is in a recession, $55 if the economy is normal, and $60 if the economy is expanding. The attendant probabilities of recession, normal times, and expansion are 0.1, 0.8, and 0.1, respectively. Stock A pays no dividend.

Assume the CAPM is true. Other information about the market includes

$$SD(R_M) = \text{Standard deviation of the market portfolio} = 0.10 = \sigma_M$$

$$SD(R_B) = \text{Standard deviation of stock } B\text{'s return} = 0.12 = \sigma_B$$

$$\overline{R}_B = \text{Expected return on stock } B = 0.09$$

$$Corr(R_A, R_M) = \text{The correlation of stock } A \text{ and the market} = 0.8$$

$$Corr(R_B, R_M) = \text{The correlation of stock } B \text{ and the market} = 0.2$$

$$Corr(R_A, R_B) = \text{The correlation of stock } A \text{ and stock} = 0.6$$

a. If you are a typical, risk-averse investor, which stock would you prefer? Why?

b. What are the expected return and standard deviation of a portfolio consisting 70 percent of stock A and 30 percent of stock B?

c. What is the beta of the portfolio in part (b)?

CHAPTER 11

An Alternative View of Risk and Return:
The Arbitrage Pricing Theory

The previous two chapters showed how variable returns on securities are. This variability is measured by variance and by standard deviation. Next, we discussed how the returns on securities are interdependent. We measured the degree of interdependence between a pair of securities by covariance and by correlation. This interdependence led to a number of interesting results. First, we showed that diversification in stocks can eliminate some, but not all, risk. By contrast, we showed that diversification in a casino can eliminate all risk. Second, the interdependence of returns led to the capital asset pricing model (CAPM). This model posits a positive (and linear) relationship between the beta of a security and its expected return.

The CAPM was developed in the early 1960s.[1] An alternative to the CAPM, called the *arbitrage pricing theory (APT),* has been developed more recently.[2] For our purposes, the differences between the two models stem from the APT's treatment of the interrelationship among the returns on securities.[3] The APT assumes that returns on securities are generated by a number of industrywide and marketwide factors. Correlation between a pair of securities occurs when these two securities are affected by the same factor or factors. By contrast, though the CAPM allows correlation among securities, it does not specify the underlying factors causing the correlation.

Both the APT and the CAPM imply a positive relationship between expected return and risk. In our (perhaps biased) opinion, the APT allows this relationship to be developed in a particularly intuitive manner. In addition, the APT views risk more generally than just as the standardized covariance or beta of a security with the market portfolio. Therefore, we offer this approach as an alternative to the CAPM.

---

[1] In particular, see Jack Treynor, "Toward a Theory of the Market Value of Risky Assets," unpublished manuscript (1961); William F. Sharpe, "Capital Asset Prices: A Theory of Market Equilibrium under Conditions of Risk," *Journal of Finance* (September 1964); and John Lintner, "The Valuation of Risky Assets and the Selection of Risky Investments in Stock Portfolios and Capital Budgets," *Review of Economics and Statistics* (February 1965).

[2] See Stephen A. Ross, "The Arbitrage Theory of Capital Asset Pricing," *Journal of Economic Theory* (December 1976).

[3] This is by no means the only difference in the assumptions of the two models. For example, the CAPM usually assumes either that the returns on assets are normally distributed or that investors have quadratic utility functions. The APT does not require either assumption. While this and other differences are quite important in research, they are not relevant to the material presented in our test.

11.1   Factor Models: Announcements, Surprises, and Expected Returns

We learned in the previous chapter how to construct portfolios and how to evaluate their returns. We now step back and examine the returns on individual securities more closely. By doing this we will find that the portfolios inherit and alter the properties of the securities they comprise.

To be concrete, let us consider the return on the stock of a company called Quebec Supply. What will determine this stock's return in, say, the coming month?

The return on any stock traded in a financial market consists of two parts. First, the *normal* or *expected return* from the stock is the part of the return that shareholders in the market predict or expect. It depends on all of the information shareholders have that bears on the stock, and it uses all of our understanding of what will influence the stock in the next month.

The second part is the *uncertain* and *risky return* on the stock. This is the portion that comes from information that will be revealed within the month. The list of such information is endless, but here are some examples:

- News about Quebec Supply's research.
- Statistics Canada figures released on the gross national product (GNP).
- Announcement of the latest federal deficit reduction plans.
- Discovery that a rival's product has been tampered with.
- News that Quebec Supply's sales figures are higher than expected.
- A sudden drop in interest rates.
- The unexpected retirement of Quebec Supply's founder and president.

A way to write the return on Quebec Supply's stock in the coming month, then, is

$$R = \overline{R} + U$$

where R is the actual total return in the month, $\overline{R}$ is the expected part of the return, and U stands for the unexpected part of the return.

Some care must be exercised in studying the effect of these and other news items on the return. For example, Statistics Canada might give us GNP or unemployment figures for this month, but how much of that is new information for shareholders? Surely, at the beginning of the month, shareholders will have some idea or forecast of what the monthly GNP will be. To the extent to which the shareholders had forecast the government's announcement, that forecast should be factored into the expected part of the return as of the beginning of the month, $\overline{R}$. On the other hand, insofar as the announcement by the government is a surprise and to the extent to which it influences the return on the stock, it will be part of U, the unanticipated part of the return.

As an example, suppose shareholders in the market had forecast that the GNP increase this month would be 0.5 percent. If GNP influences our company's stock, this forecast will be part of the information shareholders use to form the expectation, $\overline{R}$, of monthly return. If the actual announcement this month is exactly 0.5 percent, the same as the forecast, then the shareholders learned nothing new, and the announcement is not news. It is like hearing a rumour about a friend when you knew it all along. Another way of saying this is that shareholders had already discounted the announcement. This use of the word *discount* is different from that in computing present value, but the spirit is similar. When we discount a dollar in the future, we say that it is worth less to us because of the time value of money. When we discount an announcement or a news item in the future, we mean that it has less impact on the market because the market already knew much of it.

On the other hand, suppose Statistics Canada announced that the actual GNP increase during the year was 1.5 percent. Now shareholders have learned something, that the increase is one percentage point higher than they had forecast. This difference between the actual result and the forecast, one percentage point in this example, is sometimes called the *innovation* or *surprise*.

Any announcement can be broken into two parts: the anticipated or expected part and the surprise or innovation:

Announcement = Expected part + Surprise

The expected part of any announcement is part of the information the market uses to form the expectation, $\overline{R}$, of the return on the stock. The surprise is the news that influences the unanticipated return on the stock, U.

To take another example, if shareholders know in January that the president of a firm is going to resign, the official announcement in February will be fully expected and will be discounted by the market. Because the announcement was expected before February, its influence on the stock will have taken place before February. The announcement itself in February will contain no surprise, and the stock's price should not change at all at the announcement in February.

When we speak of news, then, we refer to the surprise part of any announcement and not to the portion that the market has expected and therefore has already discounted.

CONCEPT QUESTIONS

- What are the two basic parts of a return?
- Under what conditions will some news have no effect on common stock prices?

Risk: Systematic and Unsystematic   11.2

The unanticipated part of the return, that portion resulting from surprises, is the true risk of any investment. After all, if we had already got what we had expected, there would be no risk and no uncertainty.

There are important differences, though, among various sources of risk. Look at our previous list of news stories. Some of these stories are directed specifically at Quebec Supply, and some are more general. Which of the news items are of specific importance to Quebec Supply?

Announcements about interest rates or GNP are clearly important for nearly all companies, whereas the news about Quebec Supply's president, its research, its sales, or the affairs of a rival company are of specific interest to Quebec Supply. We will divide these two types of announcements and the resulting risk, then, into two components: a systematic portion, called *systematic risk,* and the remainder, which we call *specific* or *unsystematic risk.* The following definitions describe the difference:

> A *systematic risk* is any risk that affects a large number of assets, each to a greater or lesser degree.
>
> An *unsystematic risk* is a risk that specifically affects a single asset or a small group of assets.[4]

Uncertainty about general economic conditions, such as GNP, interest rates, or inflation, is an example of systematic risk. These conditions affect nearly all stocks to some degree. An unanticipated or surprise increase in inflation affects wages and the costs of the supplies that companies buy, the value of the assets that companies own, and the prices at which companies sell their products. These forces to which all companies are susceptible are the essence of systematic risk.

In contrast, the announcement of a small oil strike by a company may very well affect that company alone or a few other companies. Certainly, it is unlikely to have an effect on the world oil market. To stress that such information is unsystematic and affects only some specific companies, we sometimes call it an *idiosyncratic risk.*

The distinction between a systematic risk and an unsystematic risk is never as exact as we make it out to be. Even the most narrow and peculiar bit of news about a company ripples through the economy. It reminds us of the tale of the war that was lost because one horse lost a shoe; even a minor event may have an impact on the world. But this degree of hair-splitting should not trouble us as much. To paraphrase a judge's comment on pornography, we are not able to define systematic and unsystematic risk exactly, but we know them when we see them.

This permits us to break down the risk of Quebec Supply's stock into its two components: the systematic and the unsystematic. As is traditional, we will use the Greek epsilon, ε, to represent the unsystematic risk and write

$$R = \bar{R} + U$$
$$= \bar{R} + m + \varepsilon$$

where we have used the letter m to stand for the systematic risk. Sometimes systematic risk is referred to as *market risk.* This emphasizes the fact that m influences all assets in the market to some extent.

The important point about the way we have broken the total risk, $U,$ into its two components, m and ε, is that ε, because it is specific to the company, is unrelated to the specific risk of most other companies. For example, the unsystematic risk on Quebec Supply's stock, ε_Q, is unrelated to the unsystematic risk of Bank of Montreal's stock, ε_{BMO}. The risk that Quebec Supply's stock will go up or down because of a discovery by its research team—or its failure to discover something—probably is unrelated to any of the specific uncertainties that affect Bank of Montreal's stock.

---

[4]In the previous chapter, we briefly mentioned that unsystematic risk is risk that can be diversified away in a large portfolio. This result will also follow from the present analysis.

Using the terms of the previous chapter, this means that the unsystematic risks of Quebec Supply's stock and Bank of Montreal's stock are unrelated to each other, or uncorrelated. In the symbols of statistics,

$$\text{Corr}(\varepsilon_Q, \varepsilon_{\text{BMO}}) = 0$$

CONCEPT QUESTIONS

- Describe the difference between systematic risk and unsystematic risk.
- Why is unsystematic risk sometimes referred to as *idiosyncratic risk*?

Systematic Risk and Betas   11.3

The fact that the unsystematic parts of the returns on two companies are unrelated to each other does not mean that the systematic portions are unrelated. On the contrary, because both companies are influenced by the same systematic risks, individual companies' systematic risks and, therefore, their total returns will be related.

For example, a surprise about inflation will influence almost all companies to some extent. How sensitive is Quebec Supply's stock return to unanticipated changes in inflation? If Quebec Supply's stock tends to go up on news that inflation is exceeding expectations, we would say that it is positively related to inflation. If the stock goes down when inflation exceeds expectations and up when inflation falls short of expectations, it is negatively related. In the unusual case where a stock's return is uncorrelated with inflation surprises, inflation has no effect on it.

We capture the influence of a systematic risk like inflation on a stock by using the **beta coefficient.** The beta coefficient, β, tells us the response of the stock's return to a systematic risk. In the previous chapter, beta measured the responsiveness of a security's return to a specific risk factor, the return on the market portfolio. We used this type of responsiveness to develop the capital asset pricing model. Because we now consider many types of systematic risks, our current work can be viewed as a generalization of what we did in the previous chapter.

If a company's stock is positively related to the risk of inflation, that stock has a positive inflation beta. If it is negatively related to inflation, its inflation beta is negative, and if it is uncorrelated with inflation, its inflation beta is zero.

It is not hard to imagine stocks with positive and negative inflation betas. The stock of a company owning gold mines will probably have a positive inflation beta because an unanticipated rise in inflation is usually associated with an increase in gold prices. On the other hand, an automobile company facing stiff foreign competition might find that an increase in inflation means that the wages it pays are higher, but that it cannot raise its prices to cover the increase. This profit squeeze, as the company's expenses rise faster than its revenues, would give its stock a negative inflation beta.

Some companies that have few assets and that act as brokers—buying items in competitive markets and reselling them in other markets—might be relatively unaffected by inflation, because their costs and their revenues would rise and fall together. Their stocks would have an inflation beta of zero.

Some structure is useful at this point. Suppose we have identified three systematic risks on which we want to focus. We may believe that these three are sufficient to describe the systematic risks that influence stock returns. Three likely candidates are inflation, GNP, and interest rates. Thus, every stock will have a beta associated with each of these systematic risks: an inflation beta, a GNP beta, and an interest-rate beta. We can write the return on the stock, then, in the following form:

$$
\begin{aligned}
R &= \overline{R} + U \\
&= \overline{R} + m + \varepsilon \\
&= \overline{R} + \beta_I F_I + \beta_{GNP} F_{GNP} + \beta_r F_r + \varepsilon
\end{aligned}
$$

where we have used β_I to denote the stock's inflation beta, β_{GNP} for its GNP beta, and β_r to stand for its interest-rate beta. In the equation, F stands for a surprise, whether it be in inflation, GNP, or interest rates.

Let us go through an example to see how the surprises and the expected return add up to produce the total return, R, on a given stock. To make it more familiar, suppose that the return is over a horizon of a year and not just a month. Suppose that at the beginning of the year, inflation is forecast to be 5 percent for the year. GNP is forecast to increase by 2 percent, and interest rates are expected not to change. Suppose the stock we are looking at has the following betas:

$$
\begin{aligned}
\beta_I &= 2.0 \\
\beta_{GNP} &= 1.0 \\
\beta_r &= -1.8
\end{aligned}
$$

The magnitude of the beta describes how great an impact a systematic risk has on a stock's returns. A beta of +1 indicates that the stock's return rises and falls one for one with the systematic factor. This means, in our example, that because the stock has a GNP beta of 1, it experiences a 1-percent increase in return for every 1-percent surprise increase in GNP. If its GNP beta were −2, it would fall by 2 percent when there were an unanticipated increase of 1 percent in GNP, and it would rise by 2 percent if GNP experienced a surprise 1-percent decline.

Next let's suppose that during the year the following occurs: Inflation rises by 7 percent, GNP rises by only 1 percent, and interest rates fall by 2 percent. Lastly, suppose that we learn some good news about the company (perhaps that it's succeeding rapidly with some new business strategy) and that this unanticipated development contributes 5 percent to its return. In other words,

$$
\varepsilon = 5\%
$$

Let us assemble all of this information to find what return the stock had during the year.

First, we must determine what news or surprises took place in the systematic factors. From our information we know that

$$
\begin{aligned}
\text{Expected inflation} &= 5\% \\
\text{Expected GNP change} &= 2\% \\
\text{Expected change in interest rates} &= 0\%
\end{aligned}
$$

This means that the market had discounted these changes, and the surprises will be the difference between what actually takes place and these expectations:

F_I = Surprise in inflation

  = Actual inflation − Expected inflation

  = 7% − 5%

  = 2%

Similarly,

F_{GNP} = Surprise in GNP

  = Actual GNP − Expected GNP

  = 1% − 2%

  = −1%

and

F_r = Surprise in change in interest rates

  = Actual change − Expected change

  = −2% − 0%

  = −2%

The total effect of the systematic risks on the stock return, then, is

m = Systematic risk portion of return

  = $\beta_I F_I + \beta_{GNP} F_{GNP} + \beta_r F_r$

  = $[2 \times 2\%] + [1 \times (-1\%)] + [(-1.8) \times (-2\%)]$

  = 6.6%

Combining this with the unsystematic risk portion, the total risky portion of the return on the stock is

$m + \varepsilon = 6.6\% + 5\% = 11.6\%$

Last, if the expected return on the stock for the year is, say, 4 percent, the total return from all three components is

$R = \overline{R} + m + \varepsilon$

  = 4% + 6.6% + 5%

  = 15.6%

The model we have been looking at is called a **factor model,** and the systematic sources of risk, designated F, are called the *factors*. To be perfectly formal, a *k-factor model* is a model where each stock's return is generated by

$R = \overline{R} + \beta_1 F_1 + \beta_2 F_2 + \ldots + \beta_k F_k + \varepsilon$

where ε is specific to a particular stock and uncorrelated with the ε term for other stocks. In our preceding example, we had a three-factor model. We used inflation, GNP, and the change in interest rates as examples of systematic sources of risk (or factors). Researchers have not settled on what is the correct set of factors. Like so many other questions, this might be one of those matters that never is laid to rest.

In practice, researchers frequently use a one-factor model for returns. They do not use all of the sorts of economic factors we used previously as examples; instead, they use an index of stock market returns—like the TSE 300 or even a more broadly based index with more stocks in it—as the single factor. Using the single-factor model we can write returns as

$$R = \overline{R} + \beta(R_{TSE300} - \overline{R}_{TSE300}) + \varepsilon$$

Where there is only one factor (the returns on the TSE 300 index), we do not need to put a subscript on the beta. In this form (with minor modifications) the factor model is called a **market model.** This term is employed because the index that is used for the factor is an index of returns on the whole (stock) market. The market model is written as

$$R = \overline{R} + \beta(R_M - \overline{R}_M) + \varepsilon$$

where R_M is the return on the market portfolio.[5] The single β is called the *beta coefficient.*

CONCEPT QUESTIONS

- What is an inflation beta? A GNP beta? An interest-rate beta?
- What is the difference between a k-factor model and the market model?
- Define the beta coefficient.

11.4   Portfolios and Factor Models

Now let us see what happens to portfolios of stocks when each of the stocks follows a one-factor model. For purposes of discussion, we will take the coming one-month period and examine returns. We could have used a day, a year, or any other time period. If the period represents the time between decisions, however, we would rather it be short than long—a month is a reasonable time frame to use.

We will create portfolios from a list of N stocks, and we will use a one-factor model to capture the systematic risk. The ith stock in the list will therefore have returns

$$R_i = \overline{R}_i + \beta_i F + \varepsilon_i \qquad (11.1)$$

where we have subscripted the variables to indicate that they relate to the ith stock. Notice that the factor F is not subscripted. The factor that represents systematic risk could be a surprise in GNP, or we could use the market model and let the factor be the

---

[5]Alternatively, the market model could be written as

$$R = \alpha + \beta R_M + \varepsilon$$

Here alpha (α) is an intercept term equal to $\overline{R} - \beta \overline{R}_M$.

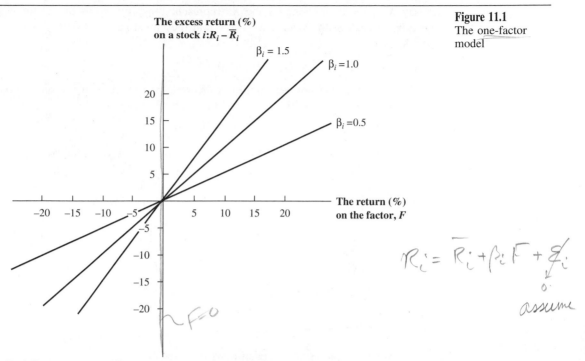

Figure 11.1
The one-factor
model

Each line represents a different security, where each security has a different beta.

difference between the TSE 300 return and what we expect that return to be, $R_{TSE\ 300} - \overline{R}_{TSE\ 300}$. In either case, the factor applies to all stocks.

The β_i is subscripted because it represents the unique way the factor influences the ith stock. To recapitulate our discussion of factor models, if β_i is zero, the returns on the ith stock are

$$R_i = \overline{R}_i + \varepsilon_i$$

In words, the ith stock's returns are unaffected by the factor, F, if β_i is zero. If β_i is positive, positive changes in the factor raise the ith stock's returns, and declines lower them. Conversely, if β_i is negative, its returns and the factor move in opposite directions.

Figure 11.1 illustrates the relationship between a stock's excess returns, $R_i - \overline{R}_i$, and the factor F for different betas, where $\beta_i > 0$. The lines in Figure 11.1 plot equation (11.1) on the assumption that there has been no unsystematic risk. That is, $\varepsilon_i = 0$. Because we are assuming positive betas, the lines slope upward, indicating that the return on the stock rises with F. Notice that, if the factor is zero ($F = 0$), the line passes through zero on the y-axis.

Now let us see what happens when we create stock portfolios where each stock follows a one-factor model. Let x_i be the proportion of security i in the portfolio. That is, if an individual with a portfolio of $100 wants $20 in TransCanada Pipelines Ltd., we say $X_{\text{TCPL}} = 20\%$. Because the Xs represent the proportions of wealth we are investing in each of the stocks, we know that they must add up to 100 percent or 1. That is,

$$X_i + X_2 + X_3 + \ldots + X_N = 1$$

We know that the portfolio return is the weighted average of the returns on the individual assets in the portfolio:

$$R_P = X_1R_1 + X_2R_2 + X_3R_3 + \ldots + X_NR_N \tag{11.2}$$

Equation (11.2) expresses the return on the portfolio as a weighted average of the returns on the individual assets. We saw from equation (11.1) that each asset's return is determined by both the factor F and the unsystematic risk of ε_i. Thus, by substituting equation (11.1) for each R_i in equation (11.2), we have

$$R_P = X_1(\overline{R}_1 + \beta_1F + \varepsilon_1) + X_2(\overline{R}_2 + \beta_2F + \varepsilon_2) + \tag{11.3}$$

(Return on stock 1)   (Return on stock 2)

$$X_3(\overline{R}_3 + \beta_3F + \varepsilon_3) + \ldots + X_N(\overline{R}_N + \beta_NF + \varepsilon_N)$$

(Return on stock 3)   (Return on stock N)

Equation (11.3) shows us that the return on a portfolio is determined by three sets of parameters:

1. The expected return on each individual security, $\overline{R}_i$.
2. The beta of each security multiplied by the factor F.
3. The unsystematic risk of each individual security, ε_i.

We express equation (11.3) in terms of these three sets of parameters as

Weighted Average of Expected Returns:

$$R_P + X_1\overline{R}_1 + X_2\overline{R}_2 + X_3\overline{R}_3 + \ldots + X_N\overline{R}_N \tag{11.4}$$

(Weighted Average of Betas)F:

$$+ (X_1\beta_1 + X_2\beta_2 + X_3\beta_3 + \ldots + X_N\beta_N)F$$

Weighted Average of Unsystematic Risks:

$$+ X_1\varepsilon_1 + X_2\varepsilon_2 + X_3\beta_3 + \ldots + X_N\varepsilon_N$$

This rather imposing equation is actually straightforward. The first row is the weighted average of each security's expected return. The items in the parentheses of the second row represent the weighted average of each security's beta. This weighted average is, in turn, multiplied by the factor F. The third row represents a weighted average of the unsystematic risks of the individual securities.

Where does uncertainty appear in equation (11.4)? There is no uncertainty in the first row because only the expected value of each security's return appears there. Uncertainty in the second row is reflected by only one item, F. That is, while we know that the expected value of F is zero, we do not know what its value will be over a particular time period. Uncertainty in the third row is reflected by each unsystematic risk, ε_i.

Portfolios and Diversification

In the previous sections of this chapter, we expressed the return on a single security in terms of our factor model. Portfolios were treated next. Because investors generally hold diversified portfolios, we now want to know what equation (11.4) looks like in a large or diversified portfolio.[6]

As it turns out, something unusual occurs to equation (11.4)—the third row actually *disappears* in a large portfolio. To see this, consider the gambler of the previous chapter who divides $1,000 by betting on red over many spins of the roulette wheel. For example, he may participate in 1,000 spins, betting $1 at a time. Though we do not know ahead of time whether a particular spin will yield red or black, we can be confident that red will win about 50 percent of the time. Ignoring the house take, the investor can be expected to end up with just about his original $1,000.

Though we are concerned with stocks, not roulette wheels, the same principle applies. Each security has its own unsystematic risk, where the surprise for one stock is unrelated to the surprise of another stock. By investing a small amount in each security, the weighted average of the unsystematic risks will be very close to zero in a large portfolio.[7]

Although the third row completely vanishes in a large portfolio, nothing unusual occurs in either row 1 or row 2. Row 1 remains a weighted average of the expected returns on the individual securities as securities are added to the portfolio. Because there is no uncertainty at all in the first row, there is no way for diversification to cause this row to vanish. The terms inside the parentheses of the second row remain a weighted average of the betas. They do not vanish, either, when securities are added. Because the factor F is unaffected when securities are added to the portfolios, the second row does not vanish.

Why does the third row vanish while the second row does not, though both rows reflect uncertainty? The key is that there are many unsystematic risks in row 3. Because these risks are independent of each other, the effect of diversification becomes stronger as we add more assets to the portfolio. The resulting portfolio becomes less and less risky, and the return becomes more certain. However, the systematic risk, F, affects all securities because it is outside the parentheses in row 2. Because one cannot avoid this factor by investing in many securities, diversification does not occur in this row.

■ *Example*

The above material can be further explained by an example similar in spirit to the diversification example of the previous chapter. We keep our one-factor model but make three specific assumptions:

1. All securities have the same expected return of 10 percent. This assumption implies that the first row of equation (11.4) must also equal 10 percent

---

[6]Technically, we can think of a large portfolio as one where an investor keeps increasing the number of securities without limit. In practice, effective diversification would occur if at least a few dozen securities were held.

[7]More precisely, we say that the weighted average of the unsystematic risk approaches zero as the number of equally weighted securities in a portfolio approaches infinity.

because this row is a weighted average of the expected returns of the individual securities.

2. All securities have a beta of 1. The sum of the terms inside parentheses in the second row of (11.4) must equal 1 because these terms are a weighted average of the individual betas. Since the terms inside the parentheses are multiplied by F, the value of the second row is $1 \times F = F$.

3. In this example, we focus on the behavior of one individual, Walter Bagehot. Being a new observer of the economic scene, Mr. Bagehot decides to hold an equally weighted portfolio. That is, the proportion of each security in his portfolio is $1/N$. ∎

We can express the return on Mr. Bagehot's portfolio as

Return on Walter Bagehot's Portfolio:

$$R_P = 10\% + \quad F + \frac{1}{N}\varepsilon_1 + \frac{1}{N}\varepsilon_2 + \frac{1}{N}\varepsilon_3 + \ldots + \frac{1}{N}\varepsilon_N \tag{11.4'}$$

From row 1 of (11.4)   From row 2 of (11.4)   From row 3 of (11.4)

We mentioned above that, as N increases without limit, row 3 of (11.4) vanishes. Thus, the return to Walter Bagehot's portfolio when the number of securities is very large is

$$R_P = 10\% + F \tag{11.4''}$$

The key to diversification is exhibited in (11.4''). The unsystematic risk of row 3 vanishes,[8] while the systematic risk of row 2 remains.

This is illustrated in Figure 11.2. Systematic risk, captured by variation in the factor, F, is not reduced through diversification. Conversely, unsystematic risk diminishes as securities are added, vanishing as the number of securities becomes infinite. Our result is analogous to the diversification example of the previous chapter. In that chapter, we said that undiversifiable or systematic risk arises from positive covariances between securities. In this chapter, we say that systematic risk arises from a common factor F. Because a common factor causes positive covariances, the arguments of the two chapters are parallel.

CONCEPT QUESTIONS

- How can the return on a portfolio be expressed in terms of a factor model?
- What risk is diversified away in a large portfolio?

---

[8]The variance of row 3 is

$$\frac{1}{N^2}\sigma_\varepsilon^2 + \frac{1}{N^2}\sigma_\varepsilon^2 + \frac{1}{N^2}\sigma_\varepsilon^2 + \ldots + \frac{1}{N^2}\sigma_\varepsilon^2 = \frac{1}{N^2}N\sigma_\varepsilon^2$$

where σ_ε^2 is the variance of each ε. This can be rewritten as σ_ε^2/N, which tends to 0 as N goes to infinity.

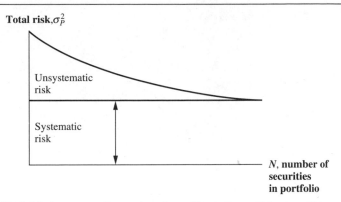

Figure 11.2
Diversification and
the portfolio risk
for an equally
weighted portfolio

Total risk decreases as the number of securities in the portfolio rises. This
drop occurs only in the unsystematic-risk component. Systematic risk is
unaffected by diversification.

Betas and Expected Returns   11.5

The Linear Relationship

We have argued many times that the expected return on a security compensates for its
risk. In the previous chapter we showed that market beta (the standardized covariance
of the security's returns with those of the market) was the appropriate measure of risk
under the assumptions of homogenous expectations and riskless borrowing and
lending. The capital asset pricing model, which posited these assumptions, implied that
the expected return on a security was positively (and linearly) related to its beta. We
will find a similar relationship between risk and return in the one-factor model of this
chapter.

   We begin by noting that the relevant risk in large and well-diversified portfolios is
all systematic because unsystematic risk is diversified away. An implication is that,
when a well-diversified shareholder considers changing holdings of a particular stock,
the security's unsystematic risk can be ignored.

   Notice that we are not claiming that stocks, like portfolios, have no unsystematic
risk. Neither are we saying that the unsystematic risk of a stock will not affect its returns.
Stocks do have unsystematic risk, and their actual returns do depend on the unsystematic
risk. Because this risk washes out in a well-diversified portfolio, however, shareholders
can ignore this unsystematic risk when they consider whether or not to add a stock to
their portfolio. Therefore, if shareholders are ignoring the unsystematic risk, only the
systematic risk of a stock can be related to its *expected* return.

   This relationship is illustrated in the security market line of Figure 11.3. Points *P,
C, A,* and *L* all lie on the line emanating from the risk-free rate of 10 percent. The
points representing each of these four assets can be created by combinations of the
risk-free rate and any of the other three assets. For example, since *A* has a beta of 2.0
and *P* has a beta of 1.0, a portfolio of 50 percent in asset *A* and 50 percent in the
riskless rate has the same beta as asset *P.* The risk-free rate is 10 percent and the

Figure 11.3
A graph of beta
and expected
return for
individual stocks
under the one
factor model

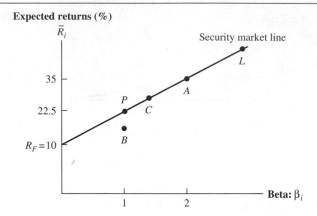

expected return on security A is 35 percent, implying that the combination's return of 22.5 percent [or $(10\% + 35\%)/ 2$] is identical to security P's expected return. Because security P has both the same beta and the same expected return as a combination of the riskless asset and security A, an individual is equally inclined to add a small amount of security P and to add a small amount of this combination to a portfolio. However, the unsystematic risk of security P need not be equal to the unsystematic risk of the combination of security A and the risk-free rate because unsystematic risk is diversified away in a large portfolio.

Of course, the potential combinations of points on the security market line are endless. One can duplicate P by combinations of the risk-free rate and either C or L (or both of them). One can duplicate C (or A or L) by borrowing at the risk-free rate to invest in P. The infinite number of points on the security market line that are not labelled can be used as well.

Now consider security B. Because its expected return is below the line, no investor would hold it. Instead, the investor would prefer security P, a combination of security A and the riskless asset or some other combination. Thus, security B's price is too high. Its price will fall in a competitive market, forcing its expected return back up to the line in equilibrium.

We know that a line can be described algebraically from two points. Because we know that the return on any zero-beta asset is R_F and the expected return on the asset is $\overline{R}_1$, it can easily be shown that

$$\overline{R} = R_F + \beta(\overline{R}_1 - R_F) \tag{11.5}$$

The Market Portfolio and the Single Factor

In the CAPM, the beta of a security measures the security's responsiveness to movements in the market portfolio. In the one-factor model of the APT, the beta of a security measures its responsiveness to the factor. We now relate the market portfolio to the single factor.

A large, diversified portfolio has no unsystematic risk because the unsystematic risks of the individual securities are diversified away. Assuming that no security has a

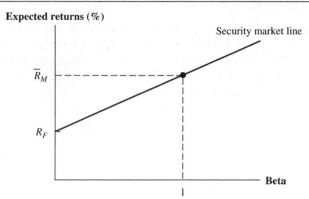

Expected returns (%)

Security market line

$\overline{R}_M$

R_F

Beta

1

Figure 11.4
A graph of beta and expected return for individual stocks under the one-factor model

The factor is scaled so that it is identical to the market portfolio.
The beta of the market portfolio is 1.

disproportionate market share, the market portfolio is fully diversified and contains no unsystematic risk.[9] In other words, the market portfolio is perfectly correlated with the single factor, implying that the market portfolio is really a scaled-up or scaled-down version of the factor. After scaling properly, we can treat the market portfolio as the factor itself.

The market portfolio, like every security or portfolio, lies on the security market line. When the market portfolio is the factor, the beta of the market portfolio is 1 by definition. This is shown in Figure 11.4. (We deleted the securities and the specific expected returns from Figure 11.3 for clarity; the two graphs are otherwise identical.) With the market portfolio as the factor, equation (11.5) becomes

$$\overline{R} = R_F + \beta(\overline{R}_M - R_F)$$

where $\overline{R}_M$ is the expected return on the market. This equation shows that the expected return on any asset, $\overline{R}$, is linearly related to the security's beta. The equation is identical to that of the CAPM, which we developed in the previous chapter.

CONCEPT QUESTION

- What is the relationship between the one-factor model and the CAPM?

The Capital Asset Pricing Model and the Arbitrage Pricing Model   11.6

The CAPM and the APT are alternative models of risk and return. It is worthwhile to consider the differences between the two models, both in terms of pedagogy and in terms of application.

---

[9]This assumption is plausible in the real world. For example, even the market value of a large company like Bell Canada Enterprises or Royal Bank of Canada is only a small fraction of the market value of the TSE 300 index.

Differences in Pedagogy

We feel that the CAPM has at least one strong advantage from the student's point of view. The derivation of the CAPM necessarily brings the reader through a discussion of efficient sets. The treatment—beginning with the case of two risky assets, moving to the case of many risky assets, and finishing when a riskless asset is added to the many risky ones—is of great intuitive value. This sort of presentation is not as easily accomplished with the APT.

However, the APT has an offsetting advantage. The model adds factors until the unsystematic risk of any security is uncorrelated with the unsystematic risk of every other security. Under this formulation, it is easily shown that (1) unsystematic risk steadily falls (and ultimately vanishes) as the number of securities in the portfolio increases but (2) the systematic risks do not decrease. This result was also shown in the CAPM, though the intuition was cloudier because the unsystematic risks could be correlated across securities.

Differences in Application

One advantage of the APT is that it can handle multiple factors while the CAPM ignores them. Although the bulk of our presentation in this chapter focused on the one-factor model, a multifactor model is probably more reflective of reality. That is, one must abstract from many marketwide and industrywide factors before the unsystematic risk of one security becomes uncorrelated with the unsystematic risks of other securities. Under this multifactor version of the APT, the relationship between risk and return can be expressed as

$$\overline{R} = R_F + (\overline{R}_1 - R_F)\beta_1 + (\overline{R}_2 - R_F)\beta_2 + \qquad\qquad (11.6)$$
$$(\overline{R}_3 - R_F)\beta_3 + \ldots + (\overline{R}_K - R_F)\beta_K$$

In this equation, β_1 stands for the security's beta with respect to the first factor, β_2 stands for the security's beta with respect to the second factor, and so on. For example, if the first factor is GNP, β_1 is the security's GNP beta. The term R_1 is the expected return on a security (or portfolio) whose beta with respect to the first factor is 1 and whose beta with respect to all other factors is zero. Because the market compensates for risk, $(\overline{R}_1 - R_F)$ will be positive in the normal case.[10] (An analogous interpretation can be given to $\overline{R}_2, \overline{R}_3$, and so on.)

The equation states that the security's expected return is related to the security's factor betas. The intuition in equation (11.6) is straightforward. Each factor represents risk that cannot be diversified away. The higher a security's beta with regard to a particular factor is, the higher is the risk that the security bears. In a rational world, the expected return on the security should compensate for this risk. The above equation states that the expected return is a summation of the risk-free rate plus the compensation for each type of risk that the security bears.

As an example, consider a classic U.S. study where the factors were monthly growth in industrial production (IP), change in expected inflation (ΔEI), unanticipated

---

[10]Actually, $(\overline{R}_i - R_F)$ could be negative in the case where factor i is perceived as a hedge of some sort.

inflation (UI), unanticipated change in the risk premium between risky bonds and default-free bonds (URP), and unanticipated change in the difference between the return on long-term government bonds and the return on short-term government bonds (UBR).[11] Using the period 1958–84, the empirical results of the study indicated that the expected monthly return on any stock, R_S, can be described as

$$R_S = 0.0041 + 0.0136\beta_{IP} - 0.0001\beta_{\Delta EI} - 0.0006\beta_{UI} +$$
$$0.0072\beta_{URP} - 0.0052\beta_{UBR}$$

Suppose a particular stock had the following betas: $\beta_{IP} = 1.1$, $\beta_{\Delta EI} = 2$, $\beta_{UI} = 3$, $\beta_{URP} = 0.1$, $\beta_{UBR} = 1.6$. The expected monthly return on that security would be

$$\overline{R}_S = 0.0041 + 0.0136 \times 1.1 - 0.0001 \times 2 -$$
$$0.0006 \times 3 + 0.0072 \times 0.1 - 0.0052 \times 1.6 = 0.0095$$

Assuming that a firm is unlevered and that one of the firm's projects has risk equivalent to that of the firm, this value of 0.0095 (i.e., .95 percent) can be used as the monthly discount rate for the project. (Because annual data is often supplied for capital budgeting purposes, the annual rate of 0.120 [or $(1.0095)^{12} - 1$] might be used instead.)

A recent Canadian study identified five similar factors:

1. The rate of growth in industrial production.
2. The changes in the slope of the term structure of interest rates (the difference between the returns on long-term and short-term Canada bonds).
3. The default risk premium for bonds (measured as the difference between the yield on long-term Canada bonds and the yield on the ScotiaMcleod corporate bond index.
4. Inflation (measured as the growth of the consumer price index).
5. The value-weighted return on the market portfolio (TSE 300).[12]

Using the period 1970–84, the empirical results of the study indicated that expected monthly returns on a sample of 100 TSE stocks could be described as a function of the risk premiums associated with these five factors.

Because many factors appear on the right side of the APT equation, the APT formulation explained expected returns in this Canadian sample more accurately than did the CAPM. However, as we mentioned earlier, one can't easily determine which are the appropriate factors. The factors in the above study were included for reasons of both common sense and convenience. They were not derived from theory.

By contrast, use of the market index in the CAPM formulation is implied by the theory of the previous chapter. We suggested in earlier chapters that the TSE 300 index mirrors stock market movements quite well. Using the Alexander Consulting Group's

[11]N. Chen, R. Roll, and S. Ross, "Economic Forces and the Stock Market," *Journal of Business* (July 1986).

[12]E. Otuteye, "How Economic Forces Explain Canadian Stock Returns," *Canadian Investment Review* (Spring 1991), pp. 93–99. An earlier Canadian study supportive of the APT is L. Kryzanowski and M. C. To, "General Factor Models and the Structure of Security Returns," *Journal of Financial and Quantitative Analysis* (March 1983), pp. 31–52.

update of the Hatch and White results, the previous chapter easily calculated expected returns on different securities from the CAPM.[13]

CONCEPT QUESTIONS

- What are the advantages and disadvantages of the CAPM and the APT?
- What conclusions can be drawn from empirical tests of APT?

11.7   Summary and Conclusions

The previous chapter presented the capital asset pricing model (CAPM). As an alternative, this chapter develops the arbitrage pricing theory (APT).

1. The APT assumes that stock returns are generated according to factor models. For example, we might describe a stock's return as

$$R = \overline{R} + \beta_I F_I + \beta_{GNP} F_{GNP} + \beta_r F_r + \varepsilon$$

The three factors F_I, F_{GNP}, and F_r represent systematic risk because these factors affect many securities. The term ε is considered unsystematic risk because it is unique to each individual security.

2. For convenience, we frequently describe a security's return according to a one-factor model:

$$R = \overline{R} + \beta F + \varepsilon$$

3. As securities are added to a portfolio, the unsystematic risks of the individual securities offset each other. A fully diversified portfolio has no unsystematic risk but still has systematic risk. This result indicates that diversification can only eliminate some, but not all, of the risk of individual securities.

4. For this reason, the expected return on a stock is positively related to its systematic risk. In a one-factor model, the systematic risk of a security is simply the beta of the CAPM. Thus, the implications of the CAPM and the one-factor APT are identical. However, each security has many risks in a multifactor model. The expected return on a security is positively related to the beta of the security with each factor.

Key Terms

Beta coefficient   323   Market model   326
Factor model   325

---

[13]Though many researchers assume that surrogates for the market portfolio are easily found, Richard Roll, "A Critique of the Asset Pricing Theory's Tests," *Journal of Financial Economics* (March 1977), argues that the absence of a universally acceptable proxy for the market portfolio seriously impairs application of the CAPM. After all, the market must include real estate, racehorses, and other assets that are not in the stock market.

Suggested Readings

Complete treatments of the APT can be found in the following articles:

S. A. Ross. "Return, Risk and Arbitrage." In Friend and Bicksler, eds. *Risk and Return in Finance.* New York: Heath Lexington, 1974.

S. A. Ross. "The Arbitrage Theory of Asset Pricing." *Journal of Economic Theory* (December 1976).

Two less technical discussions of APT are:

D. H. Bower, R. S. Bower, and D. Logue. "A Primer on Arbitrage Pricing Theory." *Midland Corporate Finance Journal* (Fall 1984).

R. Roll and S. Ross. "The Arbitrage Pricing Theory Approach to Strategic Portfolio Planning." *Financial Analysts Journal* (May/June 1984).

Discussions of Canadian tests of APT are found in:

Z. Bodie, A. Kane, A. J. Marcus, S. Perrakis, and P. J. Ryan. *Investments.* Homewood, Ill.: Irwin, 1993.

J. E. Hatch and M. J. Robinson. *Investment Management in Canada,* 2d ed. Scarborough, Ontario: Prentice Hall Canada, 1989.

E. Otuteye. "How Economic Forces Explain Canadian Stock Returns." *Canadian Investment Review* (Spring 1991).

W. F. Sharpe, G. J. Alexander, and D. J. Fowler. *Investments,* 1st Canadian ed. Scarborough, Ontario: Prentice Hall Canada, 1993.

Questions and Problems

Factor Models and Risk

11.1 You own stock in the Lewis-Striden Drug Company. Suppose you expected the following events to occur last month:

1. The government would announce that real GNP would have grown 1.2 percent during the previous quarter. The returns of Lewis-Striden are positively related to real GNP.

2. The government would announce that inflation over the previous quarter was 3.7 percent. The returns of Lewis-Striden are negatively related to inflation.

3. Interest rates would rise 2.5 percentage points. The returns of Lewis-Striden are negatively related to interest rates.

4. The president of the firm will announce his retirement. The retirement will be effective six months from the announcement day. The president is well liked; in general he is considered an asset to the firm.

5. Research data will conclusively prove the efficacy of an experimental drug. Completion of the efficacy testing means the drug will be on the market soon.

Suppose the following events actually occurred:

1. The government announced that real GNP grew 2.3 percent during the previous quarter.

2. The government announced that inflation over the previous quarter was 3.7 percent.

3. Interest rates rose 2.1 percentage points.

4. The president of the firm died suddenly of a heart attack.

5. Research results in the efficacy testing were not as strong as expected. The drug must be tested another six months and the efficacy results must be resubmitted to regulatory authorities.

6. Lab researchers had a breakthrough with another drug.

7. A competitor announced that it will begin distribution and sale of a medicine that will compete directly with one of Lewis-Striden's top-selling products.

    a. Discuss how each of the actual occurrences affects the returns on your Lewis-Striden stock.

    b. Which events represent systematic risk?

    c. Which events represent unsystematic risk?

11.2 Suppose a three-factor model is appropriate to describe the returns of a stock. Information about those three factors is presented in the following chart. Suppose this is the only information you have concerning the stock or the factors.

Factor	Beta of factor	Expected value	Actual value
GNP	0.00039	$4,416	$4,480
Inflation	−0.78	4%	5%
Interest rate	−0.36	12%	14%
Stock return		9%	

a. What is the systematic risk of the stock return?

b. What is the unsystematic risk of the stock return?

c. What is the total return on this stock?

d. Suppose unexpected bad news about the firm was announced that dampens the returns by 1.346 percentage points.

   i. What type of risk is this announcement?

   ii. What is the return on the stock?

11.3 Suppose a four-factor model is appropriate to describe the returns on a stock. Information about those four factors is presented in the following chart:

Factor	Beta of factor	Expected value	Actual value
Growth in GNP	2.04	3.5%	4.8%
Interest rates	−1.90	14.0%	15.2%
Number of competitors	−0.03	57	55
Market share growth	−1.40	2.7%	2.7%
Stock return		10.0%	

a. What is the systematic risk of the stock return?

b. What is the unsystematic risk of the stock return?

c. What is the total return on this stock?

11.4 The following three stocks are available in the market.

	Expected return	Beta
Stock A	10.5%	1.20
Stock B	13.0	0.98
Stock C	15.7	1.37
Market	14.2	1.00

Assume the market model is valid.

a. Write the market model equation for each stock.

b. What is the return on a portfolio that is 30-percent stock A, 45-percent stock B, and 25-percent stock C?

c. Suppose the return on the market is 15 percent and there are no unsystematic surprises in the returns.

i. What is the return on each stock?

ii. What is the return on the portfolio?

11.5 You are forming an equally weighted portfolio of stocks. There are many stocks that all have the same beta, 1.3. All stocks also have the same return of 8 percent. Assume a one-factor model describes the returns on each of these stocks.

a. Write the equation of the returns on your portfolio if you place only three stocks in it.

b. Write the equation of the returns on your portfolio if you place in it a very large number of stocks that all have an expected return of 8 percent and a beta of 1.3.

The APT

11.6 There are two stock markets, each driven by the same common force F with an expected value of zero and standard deviation of 10 percent. There is a large number of securities in each market; thus, you can invest in as many stocks as you wish. Due to restrictions, however, you can invest in only one of the two markets. The expected return on every security in both markets is 10 percent.

The returns for each security i in the first market are generated by the relationship

$$R_{1i} = 0.10 + 1.5F + \varepsilon_{1i}$$

where ε_{1i} is the term that measures the surprises in the returns of stock i in market 1. These surprises are normally distributed; their mean is zero. The returns for security j in the second market are generated by the relationship

$$R_{2j} = 0.10 + 0.5F + \varepsilon_{2j}$$

where ε_{2j} is the term that measures the surprises in the returns of stock j in market 2. These surprises are normally distributed; their mean is zero. The standard deviation of ε_{1i} and ε_{2j} for any two stocks, i and j, is 20 percent.

a. If the correlation between the surprises in the returns of any two stocks in the first market is zero, and if the correlation between the surprises in the returns of any two stocks in the second market is zero, in which market would a risk-averse person prefer to invest? (Note: The correlation between ε_{1i} and ε_{1j} for any i and j is zero, and the correlation between ε_{2i} and ε_{2j} for any i and j is zero.)

b. If the correlation between ε_{1i} and ε_{1j} in the first market is 0.9 and the correlation between ε_{2i} and ε_{2j} in the second market is zero, in which market would a risk-averse person prefer to invest?

c. If the correlation between ε_{1i} and ε_{1j} in the first market is zero and the correlation between ε_{2i} and ε_{2j} in the second market is 0.5, in which market would a risk-averse person prefer to invest?

d. In general, what is the relationship between the correlations of the disturbances in the two markets that would make a risk-averse person equally willing to invest in either of the two markets?

11.7 Assume that the following market model adequately describes the return-generating behavior of risky assets:

$$R_{it} = \alpha_i + \beta_i R_{Mt} + \varepsilon_{it}$$

where

R_{it} = The return for the ith asset at time t

and

R_{Mt} = The return on a portfolio containing all risky assets in some proportion, at time t

Use the following data:

Asset	β_i	$E(R_{it})$	$\text{Var}(\varepsilon_{it})$
A	0.6	10%	500
B	1.4	50	100
C	1.0	20	2,500
$\text{Var}(R_{Mt})$ =	100		

a. Assume that the only assets in this market are A, B, and C. Further assume no short selling is allowed. Calculate the variance of returns for each asset.

b. Assume short selling is allowed.

i. Calculate the variance of return of three portfolios containing an infinite number of asset types A, B, or C, respectively.

ii. Which portfolio containing an infinite number of assets (type A, B, or C) will not be held by rational investors?

iii. What equilibrium state will emerge such that no arbitrage opportunities exist? Why? Draw a graph and characterize the equilibrium algebraically.

11.8 Assume that the returns of individual securities are generated by the following two-factor model:

$$R_{it} = E(R_{it}) + \beta_{i1} F_{1t} + \beta_{i2} F_{2t}$$

R_{it} is the return for security i at time t. F_{1t} and F_{2t} are market factors with zero expectation and zero covariance. In addition, assume that there is a capital market for four securities, where each one has the following characteristics:

Security	β_1	β_2	$E(R_{it})$
1	1.0	1.5	20%
2	0.5	2.0	20
3	1.0	0.5	10
4	1.5	0.75	10

The capital market for these four assets is perfect in the sense that there are no transactions costs and short sales can take place.

a. Construct a portfolio containing (long or short) securities 1 and 2, with a return that does not depend on the market factor, F_{1t}, in any way. (Hint: Such a portfolio will have $\beta_1 = 0$.) Compute the expected return and β_2 coefficient for this portfolio.

b. Following the procedure in (a), construct a portfolio containing securities 3 and 4 with a return that does not depend on the market factor, F_{1t}. Compute the expected return and β_2 coefficient for this portfolio.

c. Consider a risk-free asset with expected return equal to 5 percent, $\beta_1 = 0$, and $\beta_2 = 0$. Describe a possible arbitrage opportunity in such detail that an investor could implement it.

d. What effect would the existence of these kinds of arbitrage opportunities have on the capital markets for these securities in the short run and long run? Graph your analysis.

CHAPTER 12

Risk, Return, and Capital Budgeting

Our text has devoted a number of chapters to net present value (NPV) analysis. We argued that a dollar to be received in the future was worth less than a dollar received today for two reasons. First, there is the simple time value of money argument in a riskless world. If you have a dollar today, you can invest it in the bank and receive more than a dollar by some future date. Second, a risky dollar is worth less than a riskless dollar. Consider a firm expecting a $1 cash flow. If actuality exceeds expectations (revenues are especially high or expenses are especially low), perhaps $1.10 or $1.20 will be received. If actuality falls short of expectations, perhaps only $0.80 or $0.90 will be received. This risk is unattractive to the typical firm.

Our work on NPV allowed us to value riskless cash flows precisely, discounting by the riskless interest rate. However, because most real world cash flows in the future are risky, business demands a procedure for discounting risky cash flows. This chapter applies the concept of net present value to risky cash flows.

We begin by reviewing previous chapters' words on NPV. We've learned that the basic NPV formula for an investment that generates cash flows (C_t) in future periods is

$$\text{NPV} = C_0 + \sum_{t=1}^{T} \frac{C_t}{(1 + r)^t}$$

For risky projects, expected incremental cash flows $\overline{C}_t$ are placed in the numerator, and the NPV formula becomes

$$\text{NPV} = C_0 + \sum_{t=1}^{T} \frac{\overline{C}_t}{(1 + r)^t}$$

In this chapter, we will show that the discount rate used to determine the NPV of a risky project can be computed from the CAPM (or APT). For example, if an all-equity firm is seeking to value a risky project, such as renovating a warehouse, the firm will determine the required return, r_S, on the project by using the SML. We call r_S the firm's **cost of equity** capital.

When firms finance with both debt and equity, the discount rate to use is the project's overall cost of capital. The overall cost of capital is a weighted average of the cost of debt and the cost of equity.

Figure 12.1
Choices of a firm
with extra cash

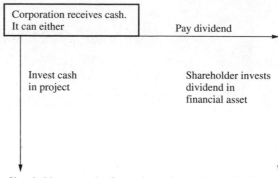

Shareholders want the firm to invest in a project only if the
expected return on the project is at least as great as that of a
financial asset of comparable risk.

12.1   The Cost of Equity Capital

Whenever a firm has extra cash, it can take one of two actions. It can pay out the cash
immediately as a dividend or the firm can invest extra cash in a project, paying out the
future cash flows of the project as dividends. Which procedure would the shareholders
prefer? If they can reinvest the dividend in a financial asset (a stock or bond) with the
same risk as that of the project, the shareholders would desire the alternative with the
higher expected return. In other words, the project should be undertaken only if its
expected return is greater than that of a financial asset of comparable risk. This is
illustrated in Figure 12.1. A very simple capital budgeting rule follows: The discount
rate of a project should be the expected return on a financial asset of comparable risk.
    From the firm's perspective, the expected return is the cost of equity capital. If we
use the CAPM for returns, the expected return on the stock will be

$$\overline{R} = r_F + \beta \times (\overline{R}_M - r_F) \quad \textit{because} \tag{12.1}$$

where $\overline{R}_M - r_F$ is the excess market return and r_F is the risk-free rate.[1]
    We now have the tools to estimate a firm's cost of equity capital. To do this, we
need to know three things:

The risk-free rate, r_F.
The market risk premium, $\overline{R}_M - r_F$.
The company beta, β_i.

▪ Example

Suppose the stock of the Quatram Company, a publisher of university textbooks, has
a beta of 1.3. The firm is 100-percent equity financed, that is, it has no debt. Quatram
is considering a number of capital budgeting projects that will double its size. Because

---

[1]Of course, we can use the k-factor APT model (Chapter 11) and estimate several beta coefficients. However, for our
purposes it is sufficient to estimate a single beta.

these new projects are similar to the firm's existing ones, the average beta on the new projects is assumed to be equal to Quatram's existing beta. The market risk premium is 8.5 percent and the risk-free rate is 7 percent. What is the appropriate discount rate for these new projects?

Now we can estimate the cost of equity r_S for Quatram as

$$r_s = 7\% + (8.5\% \times 1.3)$$
$$= 7\% + 11.05\%$$
$$= 18.05\%$$

Two key assumptions were made in this example: (1) The beta risk of the new projects is the same as the risk of the firm. (2) The firm is all-equity financed. Given these assumptions, it follows that the cash flows of the new projects should be discounted at the 18.05-percent rate. ∎

■ Example

Suppose Alpha Air Freight is an all-equity firm with a beta of 1.21. Further suppose the market risk premium is 8.5 percent, and the risk-free rate is 6 percent. We can determine the expected return on the common stock of Alpha Air Freight by using the SML of equation (12.1). We find that the expected return is

$$6\% + (1.21 \times 8.5\%) = 16.3\%$$

Because this is the return that shareholders can expect in the financial markets on a stock with a β of 1.21, it is the return they expect on Alpha Air Freight's stock.

Further suppose Alpha is evaluating the following independent projects:

Project	Project's beta (β)	Project's expected cash flows next year	Project's internal rate of return	Project's NPV when cash flows are discounted at 16.3%	Accept or reject
A	1.21	$140	40%	$20.4	Accept
B	1.21	120	20	3.2	Accept
C	1.21	110	10	-5.4	Reject

Each project initially costs $100. All projects are assumed to have the same risk as the firm as a whole. Because the cost of equity capital is 16.3 percent, projects in an all-equity firm are discounted at this rate. Projects A and B have positive NPVs, and C will have a negative NPV. Thus, only A and B will be accepted.[2] This is illustrated in Figure 12.2. ∎

---

[2]In addition to the SML, the dividend valuation model presented earlier in the text can be used to represent the firm's cost of equity capital. Using this model, the present value (P) of the firm's expected dividend payments can be expressed as

$$P = \frac{\text{Div}_1}{(1 + r_s)} + \frac{\text{Div}^2}{(1 + r_s)^2} + \ldots + \frac{\text{Div}_N}{(1 + r_s)^N} + \ldots \qquad (a)$$

where r_s is the required return of shareholders and the firm's cost of equity capital. If the dividends are expected to grow at a constant rate, g, equation (a) reduces to

$$P = \frac{\text{Div}_1}{r_s - g} \qquad (b)$$

Figure 12.2
Using the security
market line to
estimate the
risk-adjusted
discount rate for
risky projects

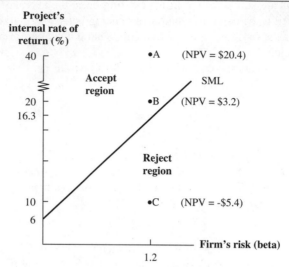

The diagonal line represents the relationship between the cost
of equity capital and the firm's beta. An all-equity firm
should accept a project whose internal rate of return is
greater than the cost of equity capital, and should reject a
project whose internal rate of return is less than the cost of
equity capital. (The above graph assumes that all projects are
as risky as the firm.)

In the previous example we assumed that the company beta was known. Of
course, beta must be estimated in the real world. We pointed out earlier that the beta
of a security is the standardized covariance of a security's return with the return on the
market portfolio. The formula for security i, first given in Chapter 10, is

$$\text{Beta of security } i = \frac{\text{Cov}(R_i, R_M)}{\text{Var}(R_M)} = \frac{\sigma_{iM}}{\sigma^2_M}$$

In words, the beta is the covariance of a security with the market, divided by the
variance of the market. Because we calculated both covariance and variance in earlier
chapters, calculating beta involves no new material.

Equation (b) can be reformulated as

$$r_S = \frac{\text{Div}_1}{P} + g \tag{c}$$

We can use equation (c) to estimate r_S. Div_1/P is the dividend yield expected over the next year. An estimate of the cost of
equity capital is determined from an estimate of Div_1/P and g.

Although there is considerable debate, many consider the dividend valuation model to be both less theoretically sound and
more difficult to apply than the SML. Hence, examples in this chapter calculate cost of equity capital using the SML
approach.

▪ *Example (Advanced)*

Suppose we sample the returns of the General Tool Company and the TSE 300 index for four years. They are tabulated as follows:

Year	General Tool Company R_G	TSE index R_M
1	−10%	−40%
2	3	−30
3	20	10
4	15	20

We can calculate beta in six steps:[3]

1. Calculate average return on each asset:

   Average Return on General Tool:

   $$\frac{-0.10 + 0.03 + 0.20 + 0.15}{4} = 0.07 \ (\text{or } 7\%)$$

   Average Return on Market Portfolio:

   $$\frac{-0.40 - 0.30 + 0.10 + 0.20}{4} = -0.10 \ (\text{or } -10\%)$$

2. For each asset, calculate the deviation of each return from the asset's average return determined above. This is presented in columns 3 and 5 of Table 12.1.

3. Multiply the deviation of General Tool's return by the deviation of the market's return. This is presented in column 6. This procedure is analogous to our calculation of covariance in an earlier chapter. The procedure will be used in the numerator of the beta calculation.

4. Calculate the squared deviation of the market's return. This is presented in column 7. This procedure is analogous to our calculation of variance in Chapter 9. The procedure will be used in the denominator of the beta calculation.

5. Take the sum of column 6 and the sum of column 7. They are

   Sum of Deviation of General Tool
   Multiplied by Deviation of Market Portfolio:

   $$0.051 + 0.008 + 0.026 + 0.024 = 0.109$$

   Sum of Squared Deviation of Market Portfolio:

   $$0.090 + 0.040 + 0.040 + 0.090 = 0.260$$

6. The beta is the sum of column 6 divided by the sum of column 7. This is

   Beta of General Tool:

   $$0.419 = \frac{0.109}{0.260} \ ▪$$

---

[3] We present these calculations as an illustration. Chapter 10 discusses beta calculation with statistical software.

Table 12.1 Calculating beta

(1) Year	(2) Rate of return on General Tool (R_G)	(3) General Tool's deviation from average return* $(R_G - \bar{R}_G)$	(4) Rate of return on market portfolio	(5) Market portfolio's deviation from average return† $(R_M - \bar{R}_M)$	(6) Deviation of General Tool multiplied by deviation of market portfolio	(7) Squared deviation of market portfolio
1	−0.10	−0.17 (−0.10 − 0.07)	−0.40	−0.30	0.051 [(−0.17) × (−0.30)]	0.090 [(−0.30) × (−0.30)]
2	0.03	−0.04	−0.30	−0.20	0.008	0.040
3	0.20	0.13	0.10	0.20	0.026	0.040
4	0.15	0.08	0.20	0.30	0.024	0.090
	Avg. = 0.07		Avg. = −0.10		Sum: 0.109	Sum: 0.260

Beta of General Tool: $0.419 = \dfrac{0.109}{0.260}$.

* Average return for General Tool is 0.07.

† Average return for market is − 0.10.

Measuring Company Betas

The basic method of measuring company betas is to estimate

$$\frac{\text{Cov }(R_{ix}, R_{Mx})}{\text{Var }(R_{Mx})}$$

Using $t = 1, 2, \ldots, T$ observations

Problems

1. Betas may vary over time.
2. The sample size may be inadequate.
3. Betas are influenced by changing financial leverage and business risk.

Solutions

1. Problems 1 and 2 (above) can be moderated by more sophisticated statistical techniques.
2. Problem 3 can be lessened by adjusting for changes in business and financial risk.
3. Look at average beta estimates of several comparable firms in the industry.

CONCEPT QUESTIONS

- How does one calculate the discount rate from the beta?
- What are the two key assumptions we used when calculating the discount rate?
- What are the six steps needed to calculate beta?

Determinants of Beta   12.2

The regression analysis approach in the previous section does not tell us where beta comes from. The beta of a stock does not come out of thin air. Rather, it is determined by the characteristics of the firm. If the firm is not traded on an exchange because it is a subsidiary of a larger firm, examining these characteristics may be the best way to estimate beta.[4] We consider three factors: the cyclical nature of revenues, operating leverage, and financial leverage.

Cyclicity of Revenues

The revenues of some firms are quite cyclical. That is, these firms do well in the expansion phase of the business cycle and do poorly in the contraction phase. Empirical evidence suggests high-tech firms, retailers, and mining firms fluctuate with the business cycle. Firms in industries such as utilities and food are less dependent upon the cycle. Because beta is the standardized covariability of a stock's return with the market's return, it is not surprising that highly cyclical stocks have high betas.

It is worthwhile to point out that cyclicality is not the same as variability. For example, a movie studio has highly variable revenues because hits and flops are not easily predictable. However, because the revenues of a studio are more dependent on the quality of its releases than on the phase of the business cycle, motion picture companies are not particularly cyclical. In other words, stocks with high standard deviations need not have high betas, a point we have stressed before.

Operating Leverage

We distinguished fixed costs from variable costs earlier in the text. At that time, we mentioned that fixed costs do not change as quantity changes. Conversely, variable costs increase as the quantity of output rises. This difference between variable costs and fixed costs allows us to define operating leverage.

■ *Example*

Consider a firm that can choose either technology A or technology B when making a particular product. The relevant differences between the two technologies are displayed below:

Technology *A*	Technology *B*
Fixed cost: $1,000/year	Fixed cost: $2,000/year
Variable cost: $8/unit	Variable cost: $6/unit
Price: $10/unit	Price: $10/unit
Contribution margin: $2 (or $10 − $8)	Contribution margin: $4 (or $10 − $6)

---

[4]An interesting example occurred in the debate over the cost of equity for Teleglobe in 1991 hearings before the Canadian Radio-Television and Telecommunications Commission. The debate was continued in C. S. Patterson, "The Cost of Equity Capital of a Non-Traded Unique Entity," in L. Booth, "Estimating the Cost of Equity Capital of a Non-Traded Unique Entity," and in C. S. Patterson, "Reply," all in *Canadian Journal of Administrative Sciences* 10 (June 1993).

Figure 12.3
Costs with two
different
technologies

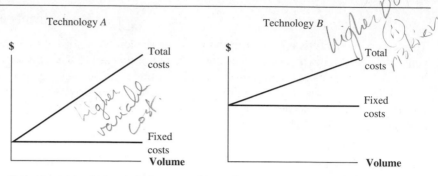

Technology A has higher variable costs and lower fixed costs than does technology B.
Technology B has higher operating leverage.

Technology *A* has lower fixed costs and higher variable costs than does technology *B*. Perhaps technology *A* involves less mechanization than does *B*. Or, the equipment in *A* may be leased whereas the equipment in *B* must be purchased. Alternatively, perhaps technology *A* involves few employees but many subcontractors, whereas *B* involves only highly skilled employees who must be retained in bad times. Because technology *B* has both lower variable costs and higher fixed costs, we say that it has higher **operating leverage.**[5]

Figure 12.3 graphs costs under both technologies. The slope of each total-cost line represents variable costs under a single technology. The slope of *A*'s line is steeper, indicating greater variable costs.

Because the two technologies are used to produce the same products, a unit price of $10 applies for both cases. We mentioned in an earlier chapter than contribution margin is the difference between price and variable cost. It measures the incremental profit from one additional unit. Because the contribution margin in *B* is greater, its technology is riskier. An unexpected sale increases profit by $2 under *A* but increases profit by $4 under *B*. Similarly, an unexpected sale cancellation reduces profit by $2 under *A* but reduces profit by $4 under *B*. This is illustrated in Figure 12.4. This figure shows the change in earnings before interest and taxes for a given change in volume. The slope of the right-hand graph is greater, indicating that technology *B* is riskier. ∎

The cyclicity of a firm's revenues is a determinant of the firm's beta. Operating leverage magnifies the effect of cyclicity on beta. As mentioned earlier, business risk is generally defined as the risk of the firm without financial leverage. Business risk depends both on the responsiveness of the firm's revenues to the business cycle and on the firm's operating leverage.

---

[5]The actual definition of operating leverage is

$$\frac{\text{Change in EBIT}}{\text{EBIT}} \times \frac{\text{Sales}}{\text{Change in sales}}$$

where EBIT is earnings before interest and taxes. That is, operating leverage measures the percentage change in EBIT for a given percentage change in sales or revenues. It can be shown that operating leverage increases as fixed costs rise and as variable costs fall.

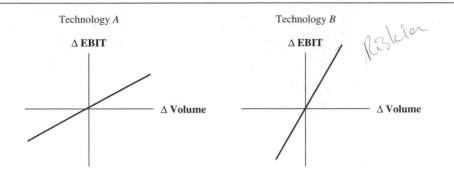

Figure 12.4
Illustration of the effect of a change in volume on the change in earnings before interest and taxes (EBIT)

While the above discussion concerns firms, it applies to projects as well. If one cannot estimate a project's beta in another way, one can examine the project's revenues and operating leverage. Those projects whose revenues appear strongly cyclical and whose operating leverage appears high are likely to have high betas. Conversely, weak cyclicity and low operating leverage implies low betas. As mentioned earlier, this approach is unfortunately qualitative in nature. Because start-up projects have little data, quantitative estimates of their betas generally are not feasible.

Financial Leverage and Beta

As suggested by their names, operating leverage and financial leverage are analogous concepts. Operating leverage refers to the firm's fixed costs of *production.* Financial leverage is the extent to which a firm relies on debt. Because a levered firm must make interest payments regardless of the firm's sales, financial leverage refers to the firm's fixed costs of *finance.*

In our discussion of beta, we have been implicitly using the firm's **equity beta.** This is the beta of the common stock of the firm. Actually, a firm has an asset beta as well as an equity beta. As the name suggests, the **asset beta** is the beta of the assets of the firm. The asset beta may also be thought of as the beta of the common stock if the firm had been financed with equity only.

Imagine an individual who owns all of the firm's debt and all of its equity. In other words, this individual owns the entire firm. What is the beta of this investor's portfolio of the firm's debt and equity?

As with any portfolio, the beta of this portfolio is a weighted average of the betas of the individual items in the portfolio. Hence, we have

$$\beta_{\text{Portfolio}} = \beta_{\text{Asset}} = \frac{\text{Debt}}{\text{Debt} + \text{Equity}} \times \beta_{\text{Debt}} + \frac{\text{Equity}}{\text{Debt} + \text{Equity}} \times \beta_{\text{Equity}} \qquad (12.2)$$

where β_{Equity} is the beta of the equity of the *levered* firm. Notice that the beta of debt is multiplied by Debt/(Debt + Equity), the percentage of debt in the capital structure. Similarly, the beta of equity is multiplied by the percentage of equity in the capital structure. Because the portfolio is the levered firm, the beta of the portfolio is equal to the beta of the levered firm. This is what we refer to as the firm's *asset beta.*

The beta of debt is very low in practice. If we make the commonplace assumption that the beta of debt is zero, we have

$$\beta_{Asset} = \frac{Equity}{Debt + Equity} \times \beta_{Equity} \qquad (12.3)$$

Because Equity/(Debt + Equity) must be below 1 for a levered firm, it follows that $\beta_{Asset} < \beta_{Equity}$. In words, the beta of the unlevered firm must be less than the beta of the equity in an otherwise identical levered firm. Rearranging the above equation, we have

$$\beta_{Equity} = \beta_{Asset}\left(1 + \frac{Debt}{Equity}\right)$$

The equity beta will always be greater than the asset beta with financial leverage.[6]

CONCEPT QUESTIONS

- What are determinants of equity betas?
- What is the difference between an asset beta and an equity beta?

12.3 Extensions of the Basic Model

The Firm versus the Project: *Vive la Différence*

We now assume that the risk of a project differs from that of the firm, while keeping the all-equity assumption. We began the chapter by pointing out that each project should be paired with a financial asset of comparable risk. If a project's beta differs from that of the firm, the project should be discounted at the rate commensurate with its own beta. This is a very important point because firms frequently speak of a *corporate discount rate.* (*Hurdle rate, cutoff rate, benchmark,* and *cost of capital* are frequently used synonymously.) Unless all projects in the corporation are of the same risk, choosing the same discount rate for all projects is incorrect.

■ *Example*

D. D. Ronnelley Co., a publishing firm, may accept a project in computer software. Noting that computer software companies have high betas, the publishing firm views the software venture as more risky than the rest of its business. It should discount the project at a rate commensurate with the risk of software companies. For example, it might use the average beta of a portfolio of publicly traded software firms. On the other hand, if all projects in D. D. Ronnelley Co. were discounted at the same rate, a bias would result. The firm would accept too many high-risk projects (software

---

[6]It can be shown that the relationship between a firm's asset beta and its equity beta with corporate taxes (see Chapter 17 for more details) is

$$\beta_{Equity} = \beta_{Asset}\left[1 + (1 - T_c)\frac{Debt}{Equity}\right]$$

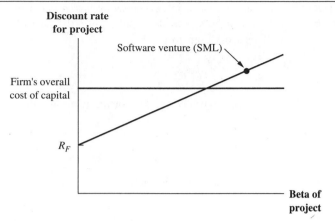

Figure 12.5
Relationship
between the firm's
cost of capital and
the security market
line

Use of a firm's cost of capital may lead to incorrect capital budgeting decisions. Projects with high risk, such as the software venture for D. D. Ronnelley Co., should be discounted at a high rate. By using the firm's cost of equity, the firm is likely to accept too many high-risk projects.

Projects with low risk should be discounted at a low rate. By using the firm's cost of capital, the firm is likely to reject too many low-risk projects.

ventures) and reject too many low-risk projects (books and magazines). This point is illustrated in Figure 12.5. ∎

The D. D. Ronnelley example assumes that the proposed project fits nicely into a particular industry, allowing the industry beta to be used. Unfortunately, many projects cannot be categorized so neatly. The beta of a new project may be greater than the beta of existing firms in the same industry because the very newness of the project likely increases its responsiveness to economywide movements. For example, a start-up computer venture may fail in a recession while Computerland, Corel, or IBM Canada will still be around. Conversely, in an economywide expansion, the venture may grow much faster than the established computer firms.

In addition, a new project may constitute its own industry. For example, do recent ventures that allow shopping by TV belong in the television industry, in the retail industry, or in an entirely new industry? We do not think the answer can easily be determined before the home shopping networks have had years of experience.

What beta should be used when an industrywide beta is not appropriate? One approach, which considers the determinants of the project's beta, was treated earlier in this chapter. Unfortunately, that approach is only qualitative in nature.

So far it was EQUITY COST OF CAPITAL

The Cost of Capital with Debt

Suppose a firm uses both debt and equity to finance its investments. If the firm pays r_B for its debt financing and r_S for its equity, what is the overall or average cost of its capital? To be concrete about this, we are asking what the firm expects to pay out to the bondholders and the shareholders for every dollar of capital that it raises from them.

(margin handwritten notes) r_S cost of EQUITY, r_B cost of debt

The cost of equity is r_S, as discussed in earlier sections. The cost of debt is the firm's borrowing rate, r_B. If a firm uses both debt and equity, the cost of capital is a weighted average of each. This works out to be

$$\frac{S}{S + B} r_S + \frac{B}{S + B} r_B$$

The weights in the formula are, respectively, the proportion of total value represented by the equity

$$\frac{S}{S + B} \quad \text{EQUITY}$$

and the proportion of total value represented by debt

$$\frac{B}{S + B} \quad \text{debt}$$

This is only natural. If the firm had issued no debt and was therefore an all-equity firm, its average cost of capital would equal its cost of equity, r_S. At the other extreme, if the firm had issued so much debt that its equity was valueless, it would be an all-debt firm, and its average cost of capital would be its cost of debt, r_B.

Of course, interest is tax deductible at the corporate level so the after-tax cost of debt is

$$\begin{array}{l} \text{Cost of debt} \\ \text{(after corporate tax)} \end{array} = r_B \times (1 - T_C)$$

Assembling these results, we get the average cost of capital (after tax) for the firm:

$$\text{Average cost of capital} = \frac{S}{S + B} \times r_S + \frac{B}{S + B} \times r_B \times (1 - T_C) \quad \text{aftertax} \tag{12.4}$$

Because the average cost of capital for a firm is a weighting of its cost of equity and its cost of debt, it is usually referred to as the **weighted average cost of capital** ($\mathbf{r_{WACC}}$). From now on we will use this term.

■ Example: Calculating WACC for Bombardier

We will illustrate the practical application of the weighted average cost of capital by calculating it for Bombardier, a large, Canadian multinational. The firm is a manufacturer of transportation equipment (including the vehicles for the Chunnel), motorized consumer products, and aerospace and defense products. Bombardier's revenue for 1991 was $2.84 billion with net income of $100 million. In this application, market values for Bombardier were observed on March 28, 1992, and we calculate the WACC for that day.[7]

---

[7]"The Markets," *Financial Post* (March 28, 1992), pp. 26–41. Other information comes from annual statements at Bombardier's year-end on January 31, 1991. When calculating the cost of capital, it is common to ignore short-term financing, such as payables and accurals. We also ignore short-term debt unless it is a permanent source of financing. As both current assets and current liabilities are ignored for our purposes, increases (or decreases) in current liabilities are netted against changes in current assets. Leases are included in long-term debt for the purposes of this analysis.

Complications arise in applying formulas in practice. As a multinational company, Bombardier does business in many countries and in many currencies; its financing reflects its multinational nature. Bombardier and its subsidiaries have issued bonds in Swiss francs, Luxembourgian francs, Belgian francs, U.S. dollars, and Canadian dollars. Ideally, we should calculate the market value of all sources of financing and determine the relative weights of each source. The difficulty of finding the market value of some nontraded bonds for Bombardier requires us to use book values for debt.[8]

To find the market value weight of equity we find the total market value of preferred and common stock. The market values are calculated as the number of shares times the share price. The figures for Bombardier, as of January 31, 1991, were 1,496,500 preferred shares and 70,721,434 common shares. Multiplying each by its price gives:

Security	Par value	Market price	Market value (millions)	Weight (%)
Debt	$547	—	$ 547	31.56
Preferred stock	37.4	$24.50	37	2.12
Class A and B common	326.4	16.25	1,149	66.32
			Total $1,733	Total 100.00

As you can see from the weights, Bombardier uses common equity and debt for the majority of its financing needs; preferred stock is almost insignificant. For this reason, we simplify the calculations by combining preferred stock with common stock for a total equity weight of 68.44 percent.

The before-tax cost of debt for Bombardier is its marginal cost of debt or the amount it would have to pay to issue debt. We estimate the cost of debt using the yield to maturity of the company's latest 10-year debt issue, 10.25 percent. To convert to an after-tax cost, we use the average tax rate for Bombardier during 1991, 16.93 percent:

$$r_B \times (1 - T_C) = 10.25\% (1 - 0.1693) = 8.51\%$$

To determine the cost of common stock for Bombardier we use the CAPM:

$$\beta = 1.18^9$$

Market risk premium $= 6.82\%^{10}$

Risk-free rate $\quad = 7.46\%$

$$r_S = r_f + \beta(\text{market risk premium})$$
$$= 7.46\% + 1.18(6.82\%)$$
$$= 15.51\%$$

---

[8]It is much more important to use the market value for the calculation of equity weights than for calculation of debt weights, as the market value of common equity may differ markedly from its book value.

[9]*Estimates of Stock Total Return Betas,* Burns Fry Limited, June 1991, p. 2.

[10]This is the risk premium from Chapter 9 for the period 1948–90. If we had used the risk premium for a more recent period starting in 1973, the cost of equity would be lower.

To find the weighted average cost of capital, we weight the cost of each source:

$$r_{WACC} = \frac{S}{(B + S)} \times r_s + \frac{B}{(B + S)} \times r_B \times (1 - T_C)$$

$$= .6632 \times 15.51\% + .3156 \times 8.51\%$$

$$= 12.97\%$$

Our analysis shows that, in March 1992, Bombardier's weighted average cost of capital was around 13 percent. ∎

∎ *Example: Capital Budgeting Application*

Suppose that Bombardier is considering taking on a warehouse renovation that is expected to cost $50 million and to yield cost savings of $12 million a year for six years.[11] Using the NPV equation and discounting the six years of expected cash flows from the renovation at the r_{WACC} of 13 percent calculated above we have[12]

$$NPV = -\$50 + \frac{\$12}{(1 + r_{WACC})} + \ldots + \frac{\$12}{(1 + r_{WACC})^6}$$

$$= -\$50 + \$12 \times A_{13}^6$$

$$= -\$50 + (12 \times 3.9975)$$

$$= -\$2.03$$

Should the firm take on the warehouse renovation? The project has a negative NPV using the firm's r_{WACC}. This means that financial markets offer superior projects in the firm's risk class. The analysis suggests that Bombardier should reject this project provided that management is convinced that the warehouse renovation carries the same risk as the firm as a whole.

But suppose, as is likely the case, that the warehouse renovation is less risky than Bombardier's typical project. Suppose further that evidence from warehousing firms supports a far lower beta of 0.50. Using this new information, we can recalculate r_S and r_{WACC} for the warehouse project:

$$r_S = r_f + \beta(\text{market risk premium})$$

$$= 7.46\% + 0.50(6.82\%)$$

$$= 10.87\%$$

$$r_{WACC} = \frac{S}{(B + S)} \times r_S + \frac{B}{(B + S)} \times r_B \times (1 - T_C)$$

$$= .6632 \times 10.87\% + .3156 \times 8.51\%$$

$$= 9.89\%$$

These revised calculations show that r_{WACC} for the warehouse project is around 10 percent.

---

[11]Our warehouse example is purely hypothetical.

[12]This discussion of WACC has been implicitly based on perpetual cash flows. However, an important paper by J. Miles and R. Ezzel, "The Weighted Average Cost of Capital, Perfect Capital Markets and Project Life: A Clarification," *Journal of Financial and Quantitative Analysis* (September 1980), shows that the WACC is appropriate even when cash flows are not perpetual.

To complete the analysis, we use the new estimate of r_{WACC} to recompute NPV for the warehouse renovation:

$$NPV = -\$50 + \frac{\$12}{(1 + r_{WACC})} + \dots + \frac{\$12}{(1 + r_{WACC})^6}$$
$$= -\$50 + \$12 \times A^6_{.10}$$
$$= -\$50 + (12 \times 4.355)$$
$$= \$2.26$$

Correcting the NPV calculations to reflect the lower risk of the warehouse renovation changes NPV from −$2.03 million to +$2.26 million. The revised analysis suggests that the firm should go ahead with this project. Our example illustrates the importance of ensuring that the cost of capital be appropriate for project risk. ∎

Summary and Conclusions   12.4

Earlier chapters on capital budgeting assumed that projects generate riskless cash flows. The appropriate discount rate in those cases is the riskless interest rate. Of course, most cash flows from real world capital budgeting projects are risky. This chapter discusses the discount rate when cash flows are risky.

1. A firm with excess cash can either pay a dividend or make a capital expenditure. Because shareholders can reinvest the dividend in risky financial assets, the expected return on a capital budgeting project should be at least as great as the expected return on a financial asset of comparable risk.

2. The expected return on any asset is dependent upon its beta. Thus, we showed how to estimate the beta of a stock. The appropriate procedure employs regression analysis on historical returns.

3. We considered the case of a project whose beta risk was equal to that of the firm. If the firm is unlevered, the discount rate on the project is equal to

$$R_F + \beta \times (\overline{R}_M - R_F)$$

where $\overline{R}_M$ is the expected return on the market portfolio and R_F is the risk-free rate. In words, the discount rate on the project is equal to the CAPM's estimate of the expected return on the security.

4. If the project's beta differs from that of the firm, the discount rate should be based on the project's beta. The project's beta can sometimes be estimated by determining the average beta of the project's industry.

5. The beta of a company is a function of a number of factors. Perhaps the three most important are

   Cyclicality of revenues.
   Operating leverage.
   Financial leverage.

6. Sometimes one should not use the average beta of the project's industry as an estimate of the beta of the project. In this case, one can estimate the project's

beta by considering the project's cyclicality of revenues and its operating leverage. This approach is qualitative in nature.

7. If a firm uses debt, the discount rate to use is the r_{WACC}. In order to calculate r_{WACC}, the cost of equity and the cost of debt applicable to a project must be estimated. Assuming a scale-enhancing project, the cost of equity can be estimated using the SML for the firm's equity. Conceptually, a dividend growth model could be used as well, though it is likely to be far less accurate in practice. In Chapter 17, three well-known approaches for incorporating debt are presented.

Key Terms

Cost of equity 343
Operating leverage 350
Equity beta 351

Asset beta 351
Weighted average cost of capital
  (r_{WACC}) 354

Suggested Readings

The following article contains a superb discussion of some of the subtleties of using WACC for project evaluation:

J. Miles and R. Ezzel. "The Weighted Average Cost of Capital, Perfect Capital Markets and Project Life: A Clarification." *Journal of Financial and Quantitative Analysis* 15 (September 1980).

An excellent article on how to use the SML in project evaluation is:

J. F. Weston. "Investment Decisions Using the Capital Asset Pricing Model." *Financial Management* (Spring 1973).

The classic papers on the stability of risk measures are

M. Blume. "On the Assessment of Risk." *Journal of Finance* (March 1971).

W. Sharpe and G. Cooper. "Risk-Return Classes of New York Stock Exchange Common Stocks 1931–1967." *Financial Analysts Journal* (March/April 1972).

An excellent treatment of practical issues is contained in:

B. Rosenberg and A. Rudd. "The Corporate Uses of Beta." In *Issues in Corporate Finance.* New York: Stern Stewart Putnam and Macklis, 1983.

Questions and Problems

Beta and the Cost of Equity

12.1 The returns for the past five years on Compli stock and the Toronto Stock Exchange 300 index are listed below.

Compli	TSE
−0.11	−0.12
0.03	0.01
0.09	0.06
0.11	0.10
0.08	0.05

a. What are the average returns on Compli stock and on the market?

b. Compute the beta of Compli stock.

12.2 The returns from the past 12 quarters on Travis Manufacturing and the market are listed below.

Travis	Market
−0.009	0.023
0.051	0.058
−0.001	−0.020
−0.045	−0.050
0.085	0.071
0.000	0.012
−0.080	−0.075
0.020	0.050
0.125	0.120
0.110	0.049
−0.100	−0.030
0.040	0.028

a. What is the beta of Travis Manufacturing stock?

b. Is Travis's beta higher or lower than the beta of the average stock?

12.3 The correlation between the returns on Fury, Inc., and the returns on the TSE 300 is 0.8756. The variance of the returns on Fury, Inc., is 0.001369, and the variance of the returns on the TSE 300 is 0.000961. What is the beta of Fury stock?

12.4 The following table lists possible rates of return on two risky assets: M and J. The table also lists their joint probabilities, that is, the probability that they will occur simultaneously.

R_M	R_J	Prob(R_M, R_J)
0.16	0.16	0.10
0.16	0.18	0.06
0.16	0.22	0.04
0.18	0.18	0.12
0.18	0.20	0.36
0.18	0.22	0.12
0.20	0.18	0.02
0.20	0.20	0.04
0.20	0.22	0.04
0.20	0.24	0.10

a. List the possible values for R_M and the probabilities that correspond to those values.

b. Compute the following items for R_M:

   i. Expected value.

   ii. Variance.

   iii. Standard deviation.

c. List the possible values for R_J and the probabilities that correspond to those values.

d. Compute the following items for R_J:

   i. Expected value.

    ii. Variance.

    iii. Standard deviation.

  e. Calculate the covariance and correlation coefficient of R_M and R_J.

  f. Assume M is the market portfolio. Calculate the beta coefficient for security J.

12.5 If you use the stock beta and the security market line to compute the discount rate for a project, what assumptions are you implicitly making?

12.6 Make Me Beautiful Cosmetics (MMBC) is evaluating a project to produce a perfume line. MMBC currently produces no body scent products. MMBC is an all-equity firm.

  a. Should MMBC use its stock beta to evaluate the project?

  b. How should MMBC compute the beta for the perfume project?

12.7 Is the discount rate for the projects of a levered firm higher or lower than the cost of equity computed using the security market line? Why? (Consider only projects that have similar risk to that of the firm.)

12.8 What factors determine the beta of a stock? Define and describe each.

Weighted Average Cost of Capital

12.9 The equity beta for Acme's Pool Supply Company is 1.5. Acme's has a debt-to-equity ratio of .50. The expected return on the market is 16 percent. The risk-free rate is 8 percent. The cost of debt capital is 8 percent. The corporate tax rate is 40 percent.

  a. What is Acme's cost of equity?

  b. What is Acme's weighted average cost of capital (WACC)?

12.10 Peach Computer Company is headquartered in Vancouver with offices in Calgary, Toronto, Ottawa, Montreal, and Halifax. The book value of Peach's outstanding debt is $10 million. Currently, the debt is trading at 90 percent of book value and is priced to yield 12 percent. The 1 million outstanding shares of Peach stock are selling for $20 per share. Peach Computer has a beta of 1.50. The current risk-free rate is 9.50 percent, and the market risk premium is 7 percent. The tax rate is 40 percent.

  a. Calculate Peach's weighted average cost of capital.

  b. Peach is considering three independent capital budgeting projects. Use the information below to analyze them. Which one(s) do you recommend and why?

Project	Life	Annual cash flows	Cost	Project beta
A	10 years	$10 million	$50 million	0.00
B	5 years	12 million	35 million	1.50
C	15 years	7 million	25 million	1.80

PART FOUR

CAPITAL STRUCTURE AND DIVIDEND POLICY

Part 2 discussed the capital budgeting decisions of the firm and argued that the objective of the firm should be to create value from these decisions. To do this, the firm must find investments with positive net present values. Here in Part 4, we concentrate on financing decisions. As with capital budgeting, the firm seeks to create value with its financing decisions. To do this, the firm must find positive-NPV financing arrangements. However, financial markets do not provide as many opportunities for positive-NPV transactions as do nonfinancial markets. We show that the sources of NPV in financing are taxes, bankruptcy costs, and agency costs.

Chapter 13 introduces the concept of efficient markets, where current market prices reflect available information. We describe several forms of efficiency: the weak form, the semistrong form, and the strong form. The chapter offers several important lessons for the corporate financial manager in understanding the logic behind efficient financial markets. The main observation is that financial managers should spend more time figuring out how to lower taxes and bankruptcy costs and less time on timing security issues and massaging the books.

In Chapter 14 we describe the basic types of long-term financing: common stock, preferred stock, and bonds. We then briefly analyze the major trends and patterns of long-term financing.

We consider the firm's overall capital structure decision in Chapters 15 and 16. In general, a firm can choose any capital structure it desires: common stock, debt, preferred stock, and so on. How should a firm choose its capital structure? Changing the capital structure changes the way the firm pays out its cash flows. Firms that borrow pay lower taxes than firms that do not. Because of corporate taxes, the value of a firm that borrows may be higher than the value of one that does not. However, with costly bankruptcy, a firm that borrows may have lower value. The combined effects of taxes and bankruptcy costs can produce an optimal capital structure.

Chapter 17 discusses capital budgeting for firms with some debt in their capital structures. It extends some of the material of Chapter 12. This chapter presents three alternative valuation methods: the weighted average cost of capital approach, the flows to equity approach, and the adjusted present value approach.

We discuss dividend policy in Chapter 18. It seems surprising that much empirical evidence and logic suggest that dividend policy does not matter. There are some good reasons for firms to pay low levels of dividends: to lower taxes and the costs of issuing new equity. However, there are also some good reasons to pay high levels of dividends: to reduce agency costs and to satisfy low-tax, high-income clienteles.

CHAPTER 13

Corporate Financing Decisions and Efficient Capital Markets

The section on value concentrated on the firm's capital budgeting decisions—the left-hand side of the balance sheet of the firm. This chapter begins our analysis of corporate financing decisions—the right-hand side of the balance sheet. We take the firm's capital budgeting decision as fixed in this section of the text.

The point of this chapter is to introduce the concept of *efficient capital markets* and its implications for corporate finance. Efficient capital markets are those in which current market prices reflect available information. This means that current market prices reflect the underlying present value of securities and there is no way to make unusual or excess profits by using the available information.

This concept has profound implications for financial managers, because market efficiency eliminates many value-enhancing strategies of firms. In an efficient market, positive-NPV opportunities cannot exist. In particular, we show that in an efficient market

1. Financial managers cannot time issues of bonds and stocks.
2. A firm can sell as many shares of stocks or bonds as it wants without fear of depressing price.
3. Stock and bond markets cannot be affected by firms artificially increasing earnings (that is, massaging the books).

Ultimately, whether or not capital markets are efficient is an empirical question. We will describe several studies examining this important issue.

Can Financing Decisions Create Value? 13.1

Earlier parts of the book show how to evaluate projects according to the net present value criterion. The real world is a competitive place where projects with positive net present value are not always easy to come by. However, through hard work or through good fortune, a firm can identify winning projects. For example, to create value from capital budgeting decisions, the firm is likely to

1. Locate an unsatisfied demand for a particular product or service.
2. Create a barrier to make it more difficult for other firms to compete.
3. Produce products or services at lower cost than competition.
4. Be the first to develop a new product.

The next five chapters concern financing decisions. Typical financing decisions include how much debt and equity to sell, what types of debt and equity to sell, and when to sell debt and equity. Just as the net present value criterion was used to evaluate capital budgeting projects, we now want to use the same criterion to evaluate financing decisions.

Though the procedure for evaluating financing decisions is identical to the procedure for evaluating projects, the results are different. It turns out that the typical firm has many more capital expenditure opportunities with positive net present values than financing opportunities with positive net present values. In fact, we later show that some plausible financial models imply that no valuable financial opportunities exist at all.

Though this dearth of profitable financing opportunities will be examined in detail later, a few remarks are in order now. We maintain that there are basically three ways to create valuable financing opportunities:

1. *Fool investors.* Assume that a firm can raise capital either by issuing stock or by issuing a more complex security, say, a combination of stock and warrants. Suppose that, in truth, 100 shares of stock are worth the same as 50 units of our complex security. If investors have a misguided, overly optimistic view of the complex security, perhaps the 50 units can be sold for more than the 100 shares of stock can. Clearly, this complex security provides a valuable financing opportunity because the firm is getting more than fair value for it.

Financial managers try to package securities to receive the greatest value. A cynic might view this as attempting to fool investors. However, empirical evidence suggests that investors cannot easily be fooled. Thus, one must be skeptical that value can easily be created.

The theory of efficient capital markets expresses this idea. In its extreme form, it says that all securities are appropriately priced at all times, implying that the market as a whole is very shrewd indeed. Thus, corporate managers should not attempt to create value by fooling investors. Instead, managers must create value in other ways.

2. *Reduce costs or increase subsidies.* We show later in the book that certain forms of financing have greater tax advantages than other forms. Clearly, a firm packaging securities to minimize taxes can increase firm value. In addition, any financing technique involves other costs. For example, investment bankers, lawyers, and accountants must be paid. A firm packaging securities to minimize these costs can also increase firm value.

Finally, any financing vehicle that provides subsidies is valuable. This last possibility is illustrated below.

■ *Example*

Suppose Mississauga Electronics Company is thinking about relocating its plant to Mexico where labour costs are lower. In the hope that it can stay in Ontario, the company has submitted an application to the province to guarantee a five-year bank term loan for $2 million. With a provincial guarantee, a chartered bank has offered to make the loan at an interest rate of 5 percent. This is an attractive rate because the normal cost of debt capital for Mississauga Electronics Company is 10 percent. What is the NPV of this potential financing transaction?

If the provincial loan guarantee is provided and the term loan is made to Mississauga Electronics Company,

$$NPV = \$2,000,000 - \left[\frac{\$100,000}{1.1} + \frac{\$100,000}{(1.1)^2} + \frac{\$100,000}{(1.1)^3} + \frac{\$100,000}{(1.1)^4} + \frac{\$2,100,000}{(1.1)^5} \right]$$

$$= \$2,000,000 - \$1,620,921$$

$$= \$379,079$$

This transaction has a positive NPV. The Mississauga Electronics Company obtains subsidized financing where the amount of the subsidy is $379,079. ∎

3. *Create a new security.* There has been a surge in financial innovation in the past two decades. For example, in a speech on financial innovation, Merton Miller asked the rhetorical question, "Can any twenty-year period in recorded history have witnessed even a tenth as much new development?"[1] Where corporations once issued only straight debt and straight common stock, they now issue zero-coupon, inflation-linked bonds, adjustable rate notes, floating rate notes, portable bonds, credit-enhanced debt securities, receivable-backed securities, convertible adjustable preferred stock, and adjustable rate convertible debt—to name just a few!

Though the advantage of each instrument is different, one general theme is that these new securities cannot easily be duplicated by combinations of existing securities.[2] Thus, a previously unsatisfied clientele may pay extra for a specialized security catering to its needs. For example, putable bonds let the purchaser sell the bond at a fixed price back to the firm. This innovation creates a price floor, allowing the investor to reduce his or her downside risk. Perhaps risk-averse investors or investors with little knowledge of the bond market would find this feature particularly attractive.

Corporations gain from developing unique securities by issuing these securities at high prices. However, we believe that the value captured by the innovator is small in the long run because the innovator usually cannot patent or copyright the idea. Soon, many firms will be issuing securities of the same kind, forcing prices down as a result.[3]

---

[1] M. Miller, "Financial Innovation: The Last Twenty Years and the Next," *Journal of Financial and Quantitative Analysis* (December 1986).

[2] Another theme is that many of these new securities are specifically designed to reduce either the investor's or the issuing corporation's taxes. This theme is part of method (2) above: Reduce costs or increase subsidies.

[3] Most financial innovations originally come from investment banks and are then sold to firms. Peter Tufano, "Financial Innovation and First-Mover Advantages," *Journal of Financial Economics* 25 (1990), pp. 213–40, looked at 58 financial innovations (including original-issue deep-discount bonds) to examine how well investment banks are compensated for developing new financial products. He finds that investment banks underwrite the lion's share of public offerings of the products they create. His study does not directly address the question of whether investment banks or corporations obtain most of the benefits of new financial products. However, it is clear that investment banks benefit substantially from creating new products.

Ray Varma and Donald Chambers, "The Role of Financial Innovation in Raising Capital," *Journal of Financial Economics* 26 (1990), pp. 289–98, look at how firms have benefited from issuing original-issue deep-discount bonds. They report no gains.

This brief introduction sets the stage for the next five chapters of the book. The rest of this chapter examines the efficient capital markets hypothesis. We show that if capital markets are efficient, corporate managers cannot create value by fooling investors. This is quite important, because managers must create value in other, perhaps more difficult ways. The following four chapters concern the costs and subsidies of various forms of financing. A discussion of new financing instruments is postponed until later chapters of the text.

CONCEPT QUESTION

- List the three ways financing decisions can create value.

13.2   A Description of Efficient Capital Markets

An efficient capital market is one in which stock prices fully reflect available information. To illustrate how an efficient market works, suppose the F-stop Camera Corporation (FCC) is attempting to develop a camera that will double the speed of the autofocusing system now available. FCC believes this research has a positive NPV. The value of the new autofocusing system will depend on demand for cameras at the time of the discovery, as well as on many other factors.

Now consider a share of stock in FCC. What determines the willingness of investors to hold shares of FCC at a particular price? One important factor is the probability that FCC will be the company to develop the new autofocusing system first. In an efficient market we would expect the price of the shares of FCC to rise if this probability increases.

Suppose a well-known engineer is hired by FCC to help develop the new autofocusing system. In an efficient market, what will happen to FCC's share price when this is announced? If the well-known scientist is paid a salary that fully reflects her contribution to the firm, the price of the stock will not necessarily change. Suppose, instead, that hiring the scientist is a positive-NPV transaction. In this case, the price of shares in FCC will increase because the market for scientists is imperfect and FCC can pay the scientist a salary below her true value to the company.

When will the increase in the price of FCC's shares take place? Assume that the hiring announcement is made in a press release on Wednesday morning. In an efficient market, the price of shares in FCC will immediately adjust to this new information. Investors should not be able to buy the stock on Wednesday afternoon and make a profit on Thursday. This would imply that it took the stock market a day to realize the implication of the FCC press release. The efficient market hypothesis predicts that the price of shares of FCC stock on Wednesday afternoon will already reflect the information contained in the Wednesday morning press release.

The **efficient market hypothesis (EMH)** has implications for investors and for firms.

- Because information is reflected in prices immediately, investors should only expect to obtain a normal rate of return. Awareness of information when it is released does an investor no good. The price adjusts before the investor has time to trade on it.

■ Firms should expect to receive the fair value for securities that they sell. *Fair* means that the price they receive for the securities they issue is the present value. Thus, valuable financing opportunities that arise from fooling investors are unavailable in efficient capital markets.

Some people spend their entire careers trying to pick stocks that will outperform the average. For any given stock, they can learn not only what has happened in the past to the stock price and dividends, but also what the company earnings have been, how much debt it owes, what taxes it pays, what businesses it is in, what market share it has for its products, how well it is doing in each of its businesses, what new investments it has planned, how sensitive it is to the economy, and so on.

If you want to learn about a given company and its stock, an enormous amount of information is available to you. The preceding list only scratches the surface; we haven't even included the information that only insiders know. **Inside information** is information possessed by people in special positions inside the company, such as the major officers of the company or people farther down in the company who might be aware of some special discovery or new development.

Not only is there a lot to know about any given company, there's also a powerful motive for doing so, the *profit motive*. If you know more about a company than other investors in the marketplace, you can profit from that knowledge by investing in the company's stock if you have good news or by selling it if you have bad news. There are other ways to use your information. If you could convince investors that you have reliable information about the fortunes of companies, you might start a newsletter and sell that information. You could even charge a varying rate depending on how fresh the information is. You could sell the monthly standard report for a subscription price of $100 per year, but for an extra $300, a subscriber could get special interim once-a-week reports. For $5,000 per year you could offer to telephone the customer as soon as you have a new idea or a new piece of information. This may sound a bit farfetched, but it's what many sellers of market information actually do.

The logical consequence of all of this information being available, studied, sold, and used in an effort to make profits from stock market trading is that the market becomes *efficient*. A market is efficient with respect to information if there is no way to make unusual or excess profits by using that information. When a market is efficient with respect to information, we say that prices *incorporate* the information. Without knowing anything special about a stock, an investor in an efficient market expects to earn an equilibrium required return from an investment, and a company expects to pay an equilibrium cost of capital.[4]

■ *Example*

Suppose Northern Telecom announces it has invented a digital switch that is 30 times faster than existing switches. The price of a share of Northern Telecom should increase immediately to a new equilibrium level.

Figure 13.1 presents three possible adjustments in stock prices. The solid line represents the path taken by the stock in an efficient market. In this case the price

---

[4]In Chapter 10 we analyze how the required return on a risky asset is determined.

Figure 13.1
Reaction of stock price to new information in efficient and inefficient markets

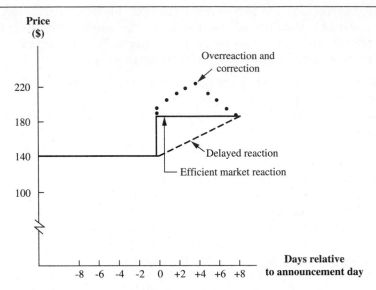

Efficient market reaction: The price instantaneously adjusts to and fully reflects new information; there is no tendency for subsequent increases and decreases.

Delayed reaction: The price partially adjusts to the new information; eight days elapse before the price completely reflects the new information.

Overreaction: The price overadjusts to the new information; there is a bubble in the price sequence.

adjusts immediately to the new information so that no further changes take place in the price of the stock. The broken line depicts a delayed reaction. Here it takes the market eight days to absorb the information fully. Finally, the dotted line illustrates an overreaction and subsequent correction back to the true price. The broken line and the dotted line show the paths that the stock price might take in an inefficient market. If the price of the stock takes several days to adjust, trading profits would be available to investors who bought at the date of the announcement and sold once the price settled back to the equilibrium.[5] ∎

CONCEPT QUESTION

∎ How do you define an efficient market?

---

[5]Now you should understand the following short story. A student was walking down the hall with his finance professor when they both saw a $20 bill on the ground. As the student bent down to pick it up, the professor shook his head slowly and, with a look of disappointment on his face, said patiently to the student, "Don't bother. If it was really there, someone else would have already picked it up."

The moral of the story reflects the logic of the efficient market hypothesis: If you think you have found a pattern in stock prices or a simple device for picking winners, you probably have not. If there were such a simple way to make money, someone else would have found it before. Furthermore, if people tried to exploit the information, their efforts would become self-defeating and the pattern would disappear.

The Different Types of Efficiency

13.3

In our previous discussion, we assumed that the market responds immediately to all available information. In actuality, certain information may affect stock prices more quickly than other information. To handle differential response rates, researchers separate information into different types. The most common classification system uses three types: information on past prices, publicly available information, and all information. The effect of these three information sets on prices is examined below.[6]

The Weak Form

Imagine a trading strategy that recommends buying a stock when it has gone up three days in a row and recommends selling a stock when it has gone down three days in a row. This strategy only uses information on past prices. It does not use any other information, such as earnings forecasts, merger announcements, or money supply figures. A capital market is said to be *weakly efficient* or to satisfy **weak-form efficiency** if it fully incorporates the information in past stock prices. Thus, the above strategy would not be able to generate profits if weak-form efficiency holds.

Often weak-form efficiency is represented mathematically as

$$P_t = P_{t-1} + \text{Expected return} + \text{Random error}_t \qquad (13.1)$$

Equation (13.1) says that the price today is equal to the sum of the last observed price plus the expected return on the stock plus a random component occurring over the interval. The last observed price could have occurred yesterday, last week, or last month, depending on one's sampling interval. The expected return is a function of a security's risk and is based on the models of risk and return in previous chapters. The random component is due to new information on the stock. It could be either positive or negative and has an expectation of zero. The random component in any one period is unrelated to the random component in any past period. Hence, this component is not predictable from past prices. If stock prices follow (13.1), they are said to follow a **random walk.**[7]

Weak-form efficiency is about the weakest type of efficiency that we would expect a financial market to display because historical price information is the easiest kind of information about a stock to acquire. If it were possible to make extraordinary profits simply by finding the patterns in the stock price movements, everyone would do it, and any profits would disappear in the scramble.

The effect of competition can be seen in Figure 13.2. Suppose the price of a stock displayed a cyclical pattern, as indicated by the wavy curve. Shrewd investors would buy at the low points, forcing those prices up. Conversely, they would sell at the high

---

[6]This is due to Harry V. Roberts, "Stock Market 'Patterns' and Financial Analysis: Methodological Suggestions," *Journal of Finance* (March 1959).

[7]For purposes of this text, the random walk can be considered synonymous with weak-form efficiency. Technically, the random walk is a slightly more restrictive hypothesis because it assumes that stock returns are identically distributed through time.

Figure 13.2
Investor behavior
tends to eliminate
cyclical patterns

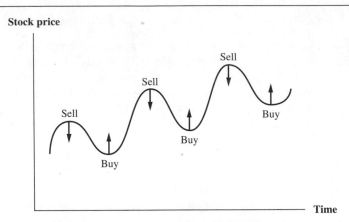

If a stock's price has followed a cyclical pattern, the pattern will be
quickly eliminated in an efficient market. A random pattern will emerge
as investors buy at the trough and sell at the peak of a cycle.

points, forcing prices down. Via competition, the cyclical regularities would be eliminated, leaving only random fluctuations.

By denying that future market movements can be predicted from past movements, we are denying the profitability of a host of techniques falling under the heading of technical analysis. Furthermore, we are denigrating the work of all of its followers, who are called *technical analysts.* The term **technical analysis,** when applied to the stock market, refers, among other things, to attempts to predict the future from the patterns of past price movements.

To get some of the flavour of technical analysis, consider two commonly used approaches. First, many technical analysts believe that stock prices are likely to follow a head-and-shoulders pattern. This is presented in the left-hand side of Figure 13.3. An analyst at point *A,* anticipating a head-and-shoulders pattern, might very well buy the stock and seek to hold it for a short-term gain. An analyst at point *B,* anticipating the completion of the pattern, would sell the stock short.

Second, other analysts believe that stocks making three tops are likely to fall in price. This pattern is presented in the right-hand side of Figure 13.3. An analyst who, at point *C,* discovers that a triple-tops pattern has occurred, might sell the stock.

At this point, one might wonder why anyone would restrict his or her information to the set of past prices. Surprisingly, many technical analysts do just that, saying that all relevant information on a security's future price movement is contained in the security's past movement. Other information is considered distracting. John Magee, one of the most renowned technical analysts, took this approach to an extreme. He reportedly worked on his stock market charts in an office with boarded-up windows. To him, weather was superfluous information that could only impede his task of stock selection.[8]

---

[8]His book (John Magee and Robert Davis Edwards, *Technical Analysis of Stock Trends,* 5th ed., Stock Trends Service, 1966) is considered by many to be the bible of technical analysis.

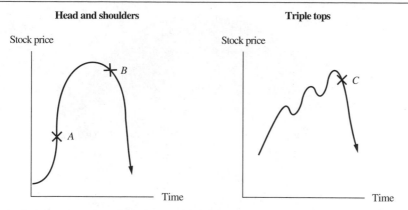

Figure 13.3
Two widely believed technical patterns

Technical analysts frequently claim that the price of a stock is likely to follow a head-and-shoulders pattern or a triple-tops pattern. According to a technical analyst, if a head-and-shoulders pattern can be identified early enough, an investor might like to buy at point *A* and sell at point *B*. A triple-tops pattern occurs when three highs are followed by a precipitous drop. If a triple-tops pattern can be identified early enough, an investor might like to sell at point *C*.

The Semistrong and Strong Forms

If weak-form efficiency is controversial, even more contentious are the two stronger types of efficiency: **semistrong-form efficiency** and **strong-form efficiency.** A market is semistrong-form efficient if prices reflect (incorporate) all publicly available information, including published accounting statements for the firm as well as historical price information. A market is strong-form efficient if prices reflect all information, public or private.

The information set of past prices is a subset of the information set of publicly available information, which in turn is a subset of all information. This is shown in Figure 13.4. Thus, strong-form efficiency implies semistrong-form efficiency, and semistrong-form efficiency implies weak-form efficiency. The distinction between semistrong-form efficiency and weak-form efficiency is that semistrong-form efficiency requires not only that the market be efficient with respect to historical price information, but also that all of the information available to the public be reflected in price.

For example, suppose that a company tried the following scheme: Whenever it observed that its stock price had risen, the company sold some shares of stock. A market that was only weak-form efficient and not semistrong-form efficient would still prevent such a scheme from generating positive NPV. According to weak-form efficiency, a recent price rise does not imply that the stock is overvalued.

As another example, suppose a company combined historical information with inside accounting information. One resulting strategy would be to buy back shares of stock before reporting that its earnings had risen. In this way, it could repurchase shares at low prices and sell them at higher prices later on. Because the company has inside information about its own earnings, this strategy is possibly profitable even if the semistrong version of the efficient market hypothesis holds.

Figure 13.4
Relationship
among three
different
information sets

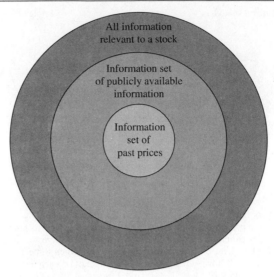

The information set of past prices is a subset of the
information set of publicly available information, which
in turn is a subset of all information. If prices reflect only
information on past prices, the market is weak-form
efficient. If prices reflect all publicly available
information, the market is semistrong-form efficient. If
prices reflect all information, both public and private, the
market is strong-form efficient.

At the furthest end of the spectrum is strong-form efficiency, which incorporates
the other two types of efficiency. This form says that anything that is pertinent to the
value of the stock and that is known to at least one investor is, in fact, fully
incorporated into the stock value. A strict believer in strong-form efficiency would
deny that an insider who knew whether a company mining operation had struck gold
could profit from that information. Such a devotee of the strong-form efficient market
hypothesis might argue that as soon as the insider tried to trade on his or her
information, the market would recognize what was happening, and the price would
shoot up before he or she could buy any of the stock. Alternatively, sometimes
believers in strong-form efficiency take the view that there are no such things as
secrets and that as soon as the gold is discovered, the secret gets out.

Are the hypotheses of semistrong-form efficiency and strong-form efficiency good
descriptions of how markets work? Expert opinion is divided here. The evidence in
support of semistrong-form efficiency is, of course, more compelling than that in
support of strong-form efficiency, and for many purposes it seems reasonable to
assume that the market is semistrong-form efficient. The extreme of strong-form
efficiency seems more difficult to accept. Before we look at the evidence on market
efficiency, we will summarize our thinking on the three versions of the efficient market
hypothesis in terms of basic economic arguments.

One reason to expect that markets are weak-form efficient is because it is so cheap
and easy to find patterns in stock prices. Anyone who can program a computer and

knows a little bit of statistics can search for such patterns. It stands to reason that if there were such patterns, people would find and exploit them, in the process causing them to disappear.

Semistrong-form efficiency, though, uses much more sophisticated information and reasoning than weak-form efficiency. An investor must be skilled at economics and statistics, and steeped in the idiosyncrasies of individual industries and companies and their products. Furthermore, to acquire and use such skills requires talent, ability, and time. In the jargon of the economist, such an effort is costly and the ability to be successful at it is probably in scarce supply.

As for strong-form efficiency, this is just farther down the road than semistrong-form efficiency. It is difficult to believe that the market is so efficient that someone with truly valuable inside information cannot prosper by using it. It is also difficult to find direct evidence concerning strong-form efficiency. What we have tends to be unfavourable to this hypothesis of market efficiency.

→ because strong means all info is incorporated in stock value

Some Common Misconceptions about the Efficient Market Hypothesis

No idea in finance has attracted as much attention as that of efficient markets, and not all of the attention has been flattering. To a certain extent this is because much of the criticism has been based on a misunderstanding of what the hypothesis does and does not say. We illustrate three misconceptions below.

The Efficacy of Dart Throwing

When the notion of market efficiency was first publicized and debated in the popular financial press, it was often characterized by the following quote: "Throwing darts at the financial page will produce a portfolio that can be expected to do as well as any managed by professional security analysts."[9] This is almost, but not quite, true.

All the efficient market hypothesis really says is that, on average, the manager will not be able to achieve an abnormal or excess return. The excess return is defined with respect to some benchmark expected return that comes from the SML. The investor must still decide how risky a portfolio he or she wants and what expected return it will normally have. A random dart thrower might wind up with all of the darts sticking into one or two high-risk stocks that deal in genetic engineering. Would you really want all of your stock investments in two such stocks? (Beware, though—a professional portfolio manager could do the same.)

The failure to understand this has often led to a confusion about market efficiency. For example, sometimes it is wrongly argued that market efficiency means that it does not matter what you do because the efficiency of the market will protect the unwary. However, as someone once remarked, "The efficient market protects the sheep from the wolves, but nothing can protect the sheep from themselves."

What efficiency does say is that the price a firm will obtain when it sells a share of its stock is a fair price in the sense that it reflects the value of that stock given the

---

[9]B. G. Malkiel, *A Random Walk down Wall Street*, 2d college ed. (New York: Norton, 1981).

information that is available about it. Shareholders need not worry that they are paying too much for a stock with a low dividend or some other characteristic, because the market has already incorporated it into the price. We sometimes say that the information has been *priced out*.

Price Fluctuations

Much of the public is skeptical of efficiency because stock prices fluctuate from day to day. However, this price movement is in no way inconsistent with efficiency, because a stock in an efficient market adjusts to new information by changing price. In fact, the absence of price movements in a changing world might suggest an inefficiency.

Shareholder Disinterest

Many laypersons are skeptical that the market price can be efficient if only a fraction of the outstanding shares changes hands on any given day. However, the number of traders in a stock on a given day is generally far fewer than the number of people following the stock. This is true because an individual will trade only when his or her appraisal of the value of the stock differs enough from the market price to justify incurring brokerage commissions and other transactions costs. Furthermore, even if the number of traders following a stock is small relative to the number of outstanding shareholders, the stock can be expected to be efficiently priced as long as a number of interested traders use the publicly available information. That is, the stock price can reflect the available information even if many shareholders never follow the stock and are not considering trading in the near future, and even if some shareholders trade with little or no information. Thus, the empirical findings suggesting that the stock market is predominantly efficient need not be surprising.

CONCEPT QUESTIONS

- How would you describe the three forms of the efficient market hypothesis?
- What could make markets inefficient?
- Does market efficiency mean you can throw darts at a *Financial Post* listing of Toronto Stock Exchange stocks to pick a portfolio?
- What does it mean to say that the price you pay for a stock is fair?

13.4   The Evidence

The record on the efficient market hypothesis is extensive, and in large measure it is reassuring to advocates of the efficiency of markets. The studies done by academics fall into broad categories. First, there is evidence as to whether changes of stock prices are predictable or random. Second are *event studies*. Third is the record of professionally managed investment firms. Fourth, there are *anomalies* (evidence contrary to the efficient market hypothesis). The final category is tests of whether insiders beat the market.

The Weak Form

The random walk hypothesis, as expressed in equation (13.1), implies that a stock's price movement in the past is unrelated to its price movement in the future. The work of Chapter 9 allows us to test this implication. In that chapter, we discussed the concept of correlation between the returns on two different stocks. For example, the correlation between the return on Stelco and the return on Dofasco is likely to be high because both stocks are in the steel industry. Conversely, the correlation between the return on Stelco and the return on the stock of, say, a European fast food chain is likely to be low.

Financial economists frequently speak of **serial correlation,** which involves only one security. This is the correlation between the current return on a security and the return on the same security over a later period. A positive coefficient of serial correlation for a particular stock indicates a tendency toward *continuation.* That is, a higher-than-average return today is likely to be followed by higher-than-average returns in the future. Similarly, a lower-than-average return today is likely to be followed by lower-than-average returns in the future.

A negative coefficient of serial correlation for a particular stock indicates a tendency toward *reversal.* A higher-than-average return today is likely to be followed by lower-than-average returns in the future and so forth. Both significantly positive and significantly negative serial correlation coefficients are indications of market inefficiencies; in either case, returns today can be used to predict future returns.

Serial correlation coefficients for stock returns near zero would be consistent with the random walk hypothesis. Thus, a current stock return that is higher than average is as likely to be followed by lower-than-average returns as by higher-than-average returns. Similarly, a current stock return that is lower than average is as likely to be followed by higher-than-average returns as by lower-than-average returns.

Figure 13.5 shows the serial correlation for daily stock price changes for two European stock markets. These coefficients indicate whether or not there are relationships between yesterday's return and today's return. For example, Germany's coefficient of 0.08 is slightly positive, implying that a higher-than-average return today makes a higher-than-average return tomorrow slightly more likely. Conversely, Belgium's coefficient is slightly negative, implying that a lower-than-average return today makes a higher-than-average return tomorrow slightly more likely.

However, correlation coefficients can, in principle, vary between -1 and 1, and the reported coefficients are quite small. A recent Canadian study, for example, found an average correlation coefficient of -0.01 for daily stock returns for TSE stocks.[10] Correlation coefficients like this one are so small relative to both estimation errors and transactions costs that the results are generally considered to be consistent with weak-form efficiency.

---

[10]Stephen R. Foerster, "The Daily and Monthly Return Behaviour of Canadian Stocks," in *Canadian Capital Markets,* Michael J. Robinson and Brian F. Smith, eds. (London, Ontario: Western Business School, 1993), pp. 1–28.

Figure 13.5
Testing the random
walk hypothesis

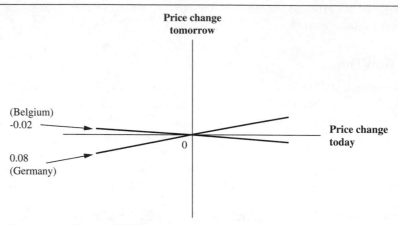

Germany's coefficient of 0.08 is slightly positive, implying that a positive return
today makes a positive return tomorrow slightly more likely. Belgium's coefficient
is negative, implying that a negative return today makes a positive return tomorrow
slightly more likely. However, the coefficients are so small relative to estimation
error and to transaction costs that the results are generally considered to be
consistent with efficient capital markets.

Source: Data from B. Solnik, "A Note on the Validity of the Random Walk for European
Stock Prices," *Journal of Finance* (December 1973).

    The weak form of the efficient market hypothesis has been tested in many other
ways as well. Our view of the literature is that the evidence, taken as a whole, is
strongly consistent with weak-form efficiency.[11]

    This finding raises an interesting thought: If price changes are truly random, why
do so many believe that prices follow patterns? The work of Harry Roberts suggests
that most people simply do not know what randomness looks like. For example,
consider Figure 13.6. The top graph was generated by computer using random
numbers and equation (13.1). Because of this, it must follow a random walk. Yet, we
have found that people examining the chart continue to see patterns. Different people
will see different patterns and will forecast different future price movements.
However, in our experience, viewers are all quite confident of the patterns they see.

    Next, consider the bottom graph, which tracks actual movements in the Dow
Jones Index. This graph may look quite nonrandom to some, suggesting weak-form
inefficiency. However, it also bears a close visual resemblance to the simulated series

---

[11]Recent, more sophisticated statistical work by Andrew Lo and Craig MacKinlay, "Stock Market Prices Do Not Follow
Random Walks: Evidence from a Simple Specification Test," *Review of Financial Studies* 1 (1988), pp. 41–66, and Jennifer
Conrad and Gautam Kaul, "Time-Variation in Expected Returns," *Journal of Business* 61 (1988), pp. 409–25, suggests that
there may be a small amount of negative autocorrelation in U.S. daily stock market returns. However, it is a very small part
of the overall variance of stock returns, and, for the most part, can be ignored.

    There is much recent evidence that expected returns on common stocks vary over time—perhaps in predictable ways.
The work of Donald Keim and Robert Stambough, "Predicting Returns in Stock and Bond Markets," *Journal of Financial
Economics* 17 (1986), and Nai-Fu Chen, "Financial Investment Opportunities and the Macroeconomy," *Journal of Finance*
46 (1991), pp. 529–54, seems to suggest that expected return can be predicted from such variables as dividend/price ratios
and default risk premiums on corporate bonds. Because these variables are likely proxies for changes in the market risk
premium, this evidence is not inconsistent with efficient markets.

A. Simulated market levels for 52 weeks

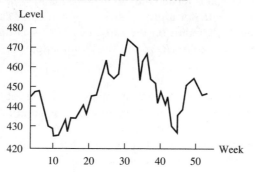

B. Friday closing levels: Dow Jones Industrial Index December 30, 1955, to December 28, 1956

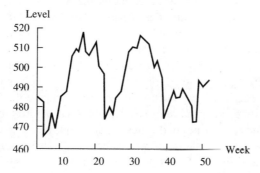

Source: H. Roberts, "Stock Market Patterns and Financial Analysis: Methodological Suggestions," *Journal of Finance* (March 1959).

Figure 13.6
Simulated and actual stock price returns

above, and statistical tests indicate that it indeed behaves like a purely random series. Thus, in our opinion, people claiming to see patterns in stock price data are probably seeing optical illusions.

The Semistrong Form

The semistrong form of the efficient market hypothesis implies that prices should reflect all publicly available information. We present two types of tests of this form.

Event Studies

A way to think of the tests of the semistrong form is to examine the following system of relationships:

Information released at time $t-1 \rightarrow \text{AR}_{t-1}$

Information released at time $t \rightarrow \text{AR}_t$

Information released at time $t + 1 \rightarrow \text{AR}_{t+1}$

where AR stands for a stock's abnormal return and where the arrows indicate that the return in any time period is related only to the information released during that period. The *abnormal return (AR)* of a given stock on a particular day can be measured by subtracting the market's return on the same day (R_m)—as measured by the market index—from the actual return (R) of the stock on that day:[12]

$$AR = R - R_m$$

According to the efficient market hypothesis, a stock's abnormal return at time t, AR_t, should reflect the release of information at the same time, t. Any information released before then, though, should have no effect on abnormal returns in this period, because all of its influence should have been felt before. In other words, an efficient market would already have incorporated previous information into prices. Because a stock's return today cannot depend on what the market does not yet know, the information that will be known only in the future cannot influence the stock's return either. Hence the arrows point in the direction that is shown, with information in any one time period affecting only that period's abnormal return. *Event studies* are statistical studies that examine whether the arrows are as shown or whether the release of information influences returns on other days.

One of the first event studies was conducted by Fama, Fisher, Jensen, and Roll, who studied 940 stock splits.[13] Figure 13.7 shows their plot of the *cumulative abnormal return (CAR)* for the stock split sample. Compare the CAR with the plots in Figure 13.1. Positive abnormal returns were observed before the stock split, probably because firms tend to split in good times. In addition, positive abnormal returns were observed around the time the split was announced. The researchers suggested that stock splits released information to the market, perhaps as signals of future dividend increases. After the split they observed no further tendency for the CAR to increase. This is consistent with efficient financial markets. Investors could not profit by buying stock on the split date, because the CAR did not continue to rise after that date.

Over the years, this type of methodology has been applied to a large number of events. Announcements of dividends, earnings, mergers, capital expenditures, and new issues of stock are a few examples of the vast literature in the area.[14] Although there are exceptions, the event study tests generally support the view that major equity markets in the United States and Canada are semistrong-form (and therefore also weak-form) efficient. In fact, the tests even tend to support the view that the market is gifted with a certain amount of foresight. By this we mean that news tends to leak out and be reflected in stock prices even before the official release of the information.

Tests of market efficiency can be found in the oddest places. The price of frozen orange juice depends to a large extent on the weather in Orlando, Florida, where many

---

[12]The abnormal return can also be measured by using the market model. In this case the abnormal return is

$$AR = R - (\alpha + \beta R_m)$$

[13]E. F. Fama, L. Fisher, M. C. Jensen, and R. Roll, "The Adjustment of Stock Prices to New Information," *International Economics Review* 10 (February 1969), pp. 1–31.

[14]In academic finance nothing is ever completely resolved, and some event studies suggest that stock market prices respond to information too slowly for the market to be efficient. For example, Lawrence Kryzanowski, "Misinformation and Regulatory Actions in the Canadian Capital Markets: Some Empirical Evidence," *Bell Journal of Economics* 9 (Fall 1978), suggests that the market does not respond properly to trading suspensions on the TSE, MSE, and VSE (Toronto, Montreal, and Vancouver stock exchanges). He found some delay in stock price responses.

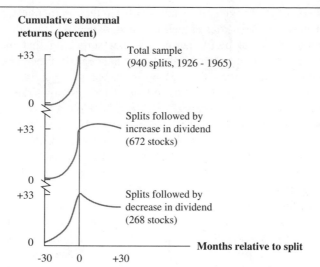

Cumulative abnormal returns (percent)

Figure 13.7
Abnormal returns for companies announcing stock splits

Cumulative abnormal returns rise prior to month of split. Very likely this occurs because splits take place in good times, that is, they take place *following* a rise in stock price. Abnormal returns are flat after month of split, a finding consistent with efficient capital markets.

Source: Redrawn from E. F. Fama, L. Fisher, M. C. Jensen, and R. Roll, "The Adjustment of Stock Prices to New Information," *International Economic Review* 10 (February 1969), pp. 1–31.

of the oranges that are frozen for juice are grown. One researcher found that he could actually use frozen orange juice prices to improve the U.S. Weather Bureau's forecast of the temperature for the following night![15] Clearly the market knows something that the weather forecasters do not.

Another group of researchers found that, as expected, stock prices generally fall on the date when the sudden death of a chief executive is announced.[16] However, the stock price generally rises for the *sudden* death of a company's founder if he's still heading the firm at the time of death. The implication is that many of these individuals have outlived their usefulness to their firms.

The Record of Mutual Funds

If the market is efficient in the semistrong form, then no matter what publicly available information mutual fund managers use to pick stocks, their average returns should be the same as those of the average investor in the market as a whole. We can test efficiency, then, by comparing the performance of these professionals with that of a market index.

---

[15]These findings are reported in Richard Roll, "Orange Juice and Weather," *American Economic Review* (December 1984).

[16]W. B. Johnson, R. P. Magee, N. J. Nagarajan, and H. A. Newman, "An Analysis of the Stock Price Reaction to Sudden Executive Deaths: Implications for the Managerial Labour Market," *Journal of Accounting and Economics* (April 1985).

As you might imagine, the studies differ in their particular samples of mutual fund performance, and they differ in their use of statistics. Because the object of the studies is to detect abnormal performance, it is not surprising that they employ different theories for determining what normal performance is. But the general conclusion of all the theories is the same—there is no evidence that the typical fund outperforms suitably selected indices. The most common indices of market performance are the Standard & Poor's (S&P) composite index in the United States and the TSE 300 index in Canada. Ignoring some small costs of trading, a big investor could achieve the index return by buying the same stocks in the same proportion as the index, that is, by *buying the index*. A small investor could achieve the same results by investing in an index fund, a mutual fund designed to have the same return and risk as the index.

The general picture that emerges from these studies is illustrated in Figure 13.8 using U.S. funds. This figure plots the average returns and betas of different mutual fund managers. The funds were divided into groups based on the managers' investment objectives. In this study, the average mutual fund manager underperformed the S&P composite index (denoted *M* in Figure 13.8).[17] Canadian studies of mutual fund performance reach the same conclusion.[18] Canadian pension fund managers also generally fail to outperform the market index.[19]

Perhaps nothing rankles successful stock market investors more than to have some professor tell them that they are not necessarily smart, just lucky. However, the view that mutual fund managers, on average, have no special ability to beat the stock market indices is largely supported by the evidence. This does not mean that no individual investor can beat the market average or that he or she lacks a special insight, only that proof seems difficult to find.

By and large, mutual fund managers rely on publicly available information. Thus, the finding that they do not outperform the market indices is consistent with semistrong-form and weak-form efficiency. This does not imply that mutual funds are

---

[17]More recent research by Gary Brinson, Randolph Hood, and Gilbert Beebower, "Determinants of Portfolio Performance," *The Financial Analysts Journal* 43 (July/August 1986), pp. 39–44, and Stephen Berkowitz, Louis Finnery, and Dennis Logue, *The Investment Performance of Corporate Pension Plans* (New York: Quorum Books, 1988), shows that, as a group, professional investors in the United States do not have superior stock and bond selection skills.

[18]A. L. Calvet and J. Lefoll, "The CAPM under Inflation and the Performance of Canadian Mutual Funds," *Journal of Business Administration* 12 (Fall 1980), pp. 279–89; Dwight Grant, "Investment Performance of Canadian Mutual Funds, 1960–1974," *Journal of Business Administration* 8 (Fall 1976), pp. 1–9; and H. L. Dhingra, "Portfolio Volatility Adjustment by Canadian Mutual Funds," *Journal of Business Finance and Accounting* 5 (Winter 1978), pp. 305–33.

[19]Vijay M. Jog, "Investment Performance of Pension Funds—A Canadian Study," *Canadian Journal of Administrative Sciences* 3 (June 1986).

When confronted with this sort of evidence, practitioners sometimes take the view that although in any given year the market indices may do very well, nevertheless some managers are able to outperform the index year after year. That may well be true, but it is not necessarily evidence against the efficient market view. Instead, it may be an example of what statisticians refer to as *survivorship bias*.

Suppose we look at a sample of the 20 largest mutual funds as of December 1994 and ask how these funds performed over the past 10 years. Would you be surprised to discover that these funds had outperformed the stock market indices? Would this constitute evidence against market efficiency?

The answer to the first question is that you should not be surprised to find that these funds had been good performers. After all, you are looking at 20 funds that survived and, since you are looking at the 20 biggest, you are looking at the funds that have thrived. It is a bit like looking at the five tallest people in a high school class and going back to when they were in grade 7 and asking how tall they were then. You wouldn't be surprised to find that, on average, they were tall then, too.

Even if mutual fund managers had no ability to pick stocks at all, if you go backward and look at the records of the 20 biggest funds today, you would still find that they were strong performers in the past. The proper way to study performance is to go back into the past, pick any sample of managers, and follow them forward in time.

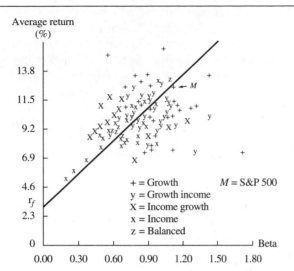

Figure 13.8
Jensen Index for mutual funds

The graph depicts average return and beta for many different mutual funds over a period from 1955 through 1964. The solid line depicts the return that a naive investor can earn from randomly selecting securities with a given beta. The evidence suggests that about half of the mutual funds outperform the line and about half underperform the line. The evidence is consistent with market efficiency.

Source: M. Jensen, "Risks, the Pricing of Capital Assets, and the Evaluation of Investment Performance," *Journal of Business* 42 (April 1969), p. 2.

bad investments for individuals. Though these funds fail to achieve better returns than some indices of the market, they do permit the investor to buy a portfolio that has a large number of stocks in it (the phrase "a well-diversified portfolio" is often used). They might also be very good at providing a variety of services such as keeping custody and records of all of the stocks.

Some Contrary Views

Although the bulk of the evidence supports the view that markets are efficient, we would not be fair if we did not note the existence of contrary results. A number of researchers have argued that the particular statistical tests that have been used are so weak that even an inefficient market would pass them. For example, some have pointed out that looking to see if prices are serially correlated is not enough; instead we should be looking at much more complicated kinds of dependence.

These arguments tend to bog down in a morass of statistics, but one particularly interesting direction suggested by these critics is the variability of stock returns. If the market is efficient, a stock's price should change with the arrival of information. The variance of stock returns, then, should be related to the amount of information. Examining this proposition, Shiller and others have unearthed some new evidence on efficiency, and much of it remains difficult to fit into our story. They conclude that the variance of stock prices is too large for efficient markets.[20]

Some of financial economics' most enigmatic empirical findings concern seasonalities. Keim has found that U.S. firms with small **market capitalizations**[21] have abnormally high returns on the first five trading days of January.[22] Jog shows that this *size effect* (also called the *small capitalization effect* or *January effect*) is international. It has been documented for Canada and in most stock exchanges around the world occurring immediately after the close of the tax year.[23] While the effect is small relative to commissions on stock purchases and sales, investors who have decided to buy small-capitalization stocks can exploit the anomaly by buying in December rather than in January.

Related research has uncovered a *weekend effect*—the returns on stocks on Friday are abnormally high and on Monday they are negative.[24] It is difficult to imagine any reasonable model of equilibrium consistent with the efficient market hypothesis that could also be consistent with the January and weekend effects.

In addition, the stock market crash of October 19, 1987, is extremely puzzling. The New York Stock Exchange (NYSE) dropped by more than 20 percent and the TSE dropped by more than 11 percent on a Monday following a weekend during which little surprising news was released. A drop of this magnitude for no apparent reason is not consistent with market efficiency. Because the crash of 1929 is still an enigma, it is doubtful that the more recent debacle will be explained anytime soon. The comments of an eminent historian in the 1970s are apt here: When asked what, in his opinion, the effect of the French Revolution of 1789 was, he replied that it was too early to tell.

Perhaps the two stock market crashes are evidence consistent with the **bubble theory** of speculative markets. That is, asset prices sometimes move wildly above their

---

[20]R. Shiller, "Do Stock Prices Move Too Much to Be Justified by Subsequent Changes in Dividends?" *American Economic Review* (June 1981).

One possible explanation is called the *fads or market overreaction hypothesis,* which argues that stock prices fluctuate around their intrinsic values as they overreact to new information. This price behaviour is also called *mean reversion* because prices revert to their means after reaching extremely high or low values. Lawrence Kryzanowski and Hao Zhang, "The Contrarian Investment Strategy Does Not Work in Canadian Markets," *Journal of Financial and Quantitative Analysis* 27 (September 1992), pp. 383–95, suggests that market overreaction, documented in the United States, does not occur in Canada. B. Espen Eckbo, "Mean Reversion in Stock Prices; a New Test with an Application to the TSE" (Financial Research Foundation of Canada, Working Paper 54, 1993), suggests that mean reversion is modest on the TSE and does not violate the efficient markets hypothesis.

[21]Market capitalization is the price per share of stock multiplied by the number of shares outstanding.

[22]D. B. Keim, "Size-Related Anomalies and Stock Return Seasonality: Further Empirical Evidence," *Journal of Financial Economics* (June 1983). See also J. Jaffe, D. Keim, and R. Westerfield, "Earnings Yields, Market Values and Stock Returns," *Journal of Finance* (March 1989). They find firms with high earnings yields and small market capitalizations have abnormally high returns.

[23]Vijay Jog, "Stock Pricing Anomalies: Canadian Experience," *Canadian Investment Review* (Fall 1988), summarizes research by Angel Berges, John McConnell, and Gary G. Schlarbaum, "The Turn-of-the-Year in Canada," *Journal of Finance* 39 (March 1984), and Seha M. Tinic, Giovanni Barone-Adesi, and Richard R. West, "Seasonality in Canadian Stock Prices: A Test of the Tax-Loss-Selling Hypothesis," *Journal of Financial and Quantitative Analysis* 21 (March 1986). Stephen R. Foerster and David C. Porter, "Calendar and Size-Based Anomalies in Canadian Stock Returns," in *Canadian Capital Markets,* Michael J. Robinson and Brian F. Smith, eds. (London, Ontario: Western Business School, 1993), pp. 133–40, supports these finding with the TSE-Western database.

[24]K. R. French, "Stock Returns and the Weekend Effect," *Journal of Financial Economics* (March 1980), documents the weekend effect in the United States. J. Jaffee and R. Westerfield, "The Week-End Effect in Common Stock Returns: The International Evidence," *Journal of Finance* (June 1985), and T. W. Chamberlain, C. S. Cheung and C. C. Y. Kwan, "Day-of-the-Week Patterns in Stock Returns: The Canadian Evidence," *Canadian Journal of Administrative Sciences* 5 (December 1988), found the effect for Canada. Stephen R. Foerster and David C. Porter, "Calendar and Size-Based Anomalies in Canadian Stock Returns," in *Canadian Capital Markets,* Michael J. Robinson and Brian F. Smith, eds. (London, Ontario: Western Business School, 1993), pp. 133–40, document the weekend effect with the TSE-Western database.

true values. Eventually prices fall back to their original level, causing great losses for investors. The 17th-century tulip craze in the Netherlands and the South Sea Bubble in England the following century are perhaps the two best-known bubbles. In the first episode, tulips rose to unheard-of prices. Example

> A single bulb of the Harlem species was exchanged for twelve acres of building ground. . . . Another variety fetched 4,600 florins, a new carriage and two grey horses, plus nine complete sets of harnesses. A bulb of the Viceroy species commanded the sum of all the following items in exchange: seventeen bushels of wheat, thirty-four bushels of rye, four fat oxen, eight fat swine, twelve fat sheep, two hogshead of wine, four tons of beer, two tons of butter, 1,000 pounds of cheese, a complete bed, a suit of clothes, and a silver drinking cup thrown in for good measure.[25]

It seems speculative fervour hit England a century later. Fantastic schemes of all types were paraded before a public eager to invest. Most of them provided good evidence for the dictums, "A sucker is born every minute," and "A fool and his money are soon parted."

According to Malkiel, "The prize, however, must surely go to the unknown soul who started 'a Company' for carrying on an undertaking of great advantage, but nobody to know what it is." The prospectus promised unheard-of rewards. At nine o'clock in the morning, when the subscription books opened, crowds of people from all walks of life practically beat down the doors in an effort to subscribe. Within five hours a thousand investors handed over their money for shares in the company. Not being greedy himself, the promoter promptly closed up shop and set off for the Continent. He was never heard from again.[26]

The Strong Form

Even the most enthusiastic adherents to the efficient market hypothesis would not be surprised to find that markets are inefficient in the strong form. After all, if an individual has information that no one else has, it is likely that he can profit from it.

One group of studies of strong-form efficiency investigates insider trading. Insiders in firms have access to information that is not generally available. But if the strong form of the efficient market hypothesis holds, they should not be able to profit by trading on their information. The Ontario Securities Commission (and its counterparts in other provinces) and the U.S. Securities and Exchange Commission require insiders in companies to reveal any trading they might do in their own company's stock. By examining the record of such trades, we can see whether they made abnormal returns. A number of studies support the view that these trades were abnormally profitable. Thus, strong-form efficiency does not seem to be substantiated by the evidence.[27]

---

[25]B. G. Malkiel, *A Random Walk down Wall Street,* College ed. (New York: Norton, 1975), pp. 31–32.

[26]Ibid.

[27]J. Jaffe, "Special Information and Insider Trading," *Journal of Business* (1974); J. E. Finnerty, "Insiders and Market Efficiency," *Journal of Finance* (1976); and H. N. Seyhun, "Insiders' Profits, Costs of Trading and Market Efficiency," *Journal of Financial Economics* (1986), study strong-form efficiency on the NYSE. Isidore Masse, Robert Hanrahan, and Joseph Kushner, "Returns to Insider Trading: The Canadian Evidence," *Canadian Journal of Administrative Sciences* 5 (September 1988); B. Espen Eckbo, "Mergers and the Market for Corporate Control: The Canadian Evidence," *Canadian Journal of Economics* 19 (May 1986); and D. J. Fowler and C. H. Rorke, "Insider Trading Profits on the Toronto Stock Exchange, 1967–1977," *Canadian Journal of Administrative Sciences* 5 (March 1988), find that insiders beat the market when trading on the TSE. Robert Heinkel and Alan Kraus, "The Effect of Insider Trading on Average Rates of Return," *Canadian Journal of Economics* 20 (August 1987), find that Vancouver Stock Exchange insiders do not clearly beat the market.

Were Japanese Stock Prices Too High?

This is the question that James M. Poterba and Kenneth R. French ask about the Japanese stock market. They show that the price-earnings ratio of the average Japanese stock was below that of the average U.S. stock in 1970 but by 1989 it was almost four times higher. This fact has frequently been used as evidence to show the cost of equity capital in Japan has been less than in the United States.

	Price-earnings ratio	
	Japan	United States
1970	9.0	18.6
1975	25.2	11.8
1980	17.9	9.6
1985	29.4	12.6
1988	54.3	12.9
1989	53.7	14.8
1990	36.6	15.9

Some have argued that the higher Japanese stock prices during the 1980s suggest that the Japanese stock market was inefficient. This may be true. However, Poterba and French show that much of the difference in Japanese and U.S. stock prices can be explained by accounting practices of the two countries. They estimate that if Japanese firms had used U.S. accounting practices, the price-earnings ratio of Japanese firms in 1988 would have been 32.1 instead of 54.3. However, they cannot explain the high run up in Japanese stock prices between 1986 and 1988 nor the 1990 collapse, which is depicted below.

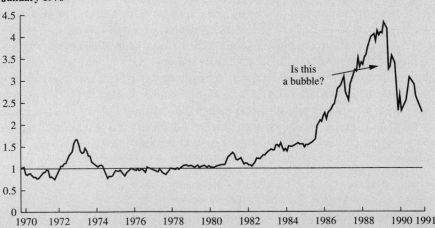

Data from Kenneth R. French and James M. Poterba, "Were Japanese Stock Prices Too High?" *Journal of Financial Economics* 29 (October 1991), pp. 337–64; and various issues of *The Wall Street Journal.*

Source: Kenneth R. French and James M. Poterba, "Were Japanese Stock Prices Too High?" *Journal of Financial Economics* 29 (October 1991), pp. 337–64.

A Case of Insider Trading in Canada

Michael DeGroote and an associate settled one of the largest insider trading cases [in April 1993]. Mr. DeGroote, who built Laidlaw over 30 years from a small trucking company into a waste management and transportation giant, resigned as an officer and director of the company in December 1990. He had sold control of Laidlaw to Canadian Pacific Ltd. two years earlier for $500 million.

Rather than a smooth transition, the first few months after Mr. DeGroote left Laidlaw have become a recurring nightmare for the company and many of those associated with it.

Laidlaw had been a favourite growth stock for investors in the 1980s, but its earnings fell apart in early 1991, shocking shareholders who believed the waste management sector was recession-proof.

Last April, Ontario securities regulators alleged that Seakist Overseas Ltd., which was based in the Channel Islands and directed by Mr. Henri Herbots, sold Laidlaw stock short using Mr. DeGrootes's money and inside knowledge as a former Laidlaw officer and director that the company was doing much worse than the investing public knew. Investors sell stock short when they expect its price to fall. Short positions give investors the right to "sell" stock they don't own at its current price and then "buy" it back in the future. If the price falls, investors can make a profit.

Mr. DeGroote lent Seakist $27 million (Canadian), at an annual interest rate of 20 percent, to run the short-selling effort, but he maintained he did not have or use inside information about Laidlaw in making the loan on an arm's-length basis.

Seakist opened an account with Midland Walwyn Capital Inc. on January 31, 1991, and, through former Midland broker, Keith Walker, sold short three million Laidlaw shares for about $61 million by March 13, when Laidlaw warned about its poor earning. The stock fell 18.6 percent in the next trading session and by March 21, Seakist had covered its short positions for $44.5 million, making a $16.5 million profit on the deal.

Mr. Herbots said he devised the short-selling plan based solely on publicly available information.

The two sides agreed to disagree on many of the facts in the settlement, with Mr. DeGroote, Mr. Herbots, and Seakist losing their trading privileges in Ontario for five years, paying $5 million to the provincial treasury and $18 million to compensate investors adversely affected by the short selling. Midland and Mr. Walker paid their total commissions from Seakist's short selling—$304,286—to the provincial treasury.

Source: Abridged from Casey Mahood, "DeGroote Faces U.S. Suit," *The Globe and Mail,"* Report on Business," September 28, 1993, p. B1. Used with permission.

CONCEPT QUESTION

- What conclusions about market efficiency can be drawn from available evidence?

13.5   Implications for Corporate Finance

Accounting and Efficient Markets

The accounting profession provides firms with a significant amount of leeway in their reporting practices. For example, companies may choose either the percentage-of-completion or the completed-contract method for construction projects. They may depreciate physical assets by either accelerated or straight-line depreciation. Financial institutions may exercise considerable judgment in setting aside loan loss provisions.

Accountants have frequently been accused of misusing this leeway in the hopes of boosting earnings and stock prices. For example, U.S. Steel (now USX Corporation) switched from straight-line to accelerated depreciation after World War II, because its high reported profits at that time attracted much government scrutiny. It switched back to straight-line depreciation in the 1960s after years of low reported earnings.

In the 1930s, Canada's largest life insurance company, Sun Life, experienced a major drop in the market value of its common stock portfolio which effectively erased the company's capital. To allow the company to remain in business, federal regulators changed the accounting rules for insurance companies to allow Sun Life to backdate the prices of its investments until the market improved.[28]

Despite such examples, accounting choice should not affect stock price provided two conditions hold. First, enough information must be provided in the annual report and other public sources so that financial analysts can construct earnings under the alternative accounting methods. This appears to be the case for many, though not necessarily all, accounting choices. Second, the market must be efficient in the semistrong form. In other words, the market must appropriately use all of this accounting information in determining the market price.

Of course, the issue of whether accounting choice affects stock price is ultimately an empirical matter.[29] A number of academic papers have addressed this issue. Kaplan and Roll found that the switch from accelerated to straight-line depreciation generally did not affect stock prices significantly.[30] Several other accounting procedures have been studied. Hong, Kaplan, and Mandelker found no evidence that the stock market was affected by the artificially higher earnings reported using the pooling method, compared to the purchase method, for reporting mergers and acquisitions.[31] Cheung found no association between security returns and inflation accounting disclosures in Canada.[32] In summary, the empirical evidence suggests that accounting changes do not fool the market.[33]

---

[28]Lawrence Kryzanowski and Gordon S. Roberts, "Capital Forbearance: A Depression-Era Case Study of Sun Life" (North York, Ontario: York University Working Paper, 1994).

[29]An excellent review of empirical literature in accounting research is in R. Mattessich, *Accounting Research in the 1980s and Its Future Relevance* (Canadian Certified General Accountants' Research Foundation, Research Monograph 17, 1991).

[30]R. S. Kaplan and R. Roll, "Investor Evaluation of Accounting Information: Some Empirical Evidence," *Journal of Business* 45 (April 1972).

[31]H. Hong, R. S. Kaplan, and G. Mandelker, "Pooling vs. Purchase: The Effects of Accounting for Mergers on Stock Prices," *Accounting Review* 53 (1978).

[32]J. K. Cheung, "Inflation Accounting Disclosures and Stock Price Adjustments: Some Canadian Results," *Accounting and Finance* 26 (November 1986).

[33]These excellent studies are slightly off the mark for our purposes. They test the hypothesis that, in aggregate, stock prices

Of course, the semistrong form of the efficient capital markets hypothesis does not imply that stock price is invariant to accounting decisions that change cash flows. In 1980, Parliament introduced the Petroleum Incentive Program (PIP), which allowed government subsidies to replace depletion allowances for exploration and development. Cheung found a significant association between abnormal returns and proxies for contracting and monitoring costs.[34]

Stock price is also likely to be affected if a company either withholds useful information or provides incorrect information that cannot be corrected based on public sources. In one rather bizarre example, a life insurance company named Equity Funding fabricated a number of its policies. Equity began the hoax by making up the names of insurance customers. To keep fooling the auditors, cash flows from other sources "became" cash flows from premiums. In addition, death reports of some of its "clients" were filed so that the life expectancy of its pool matched that of the industry as a whole. Inevitably, the scheme unravelled, but not before many investors in the stock suffered losses.[35]

In many such cases of deliberate misrepresentation, the market obtains more accurate information of its own. One example in which this did occur involved the Northland Bank. Prior to its failure in 1985, the bank used questionable accounting to cover up its exposure to bad energy loans in western Canada. According to the Estey Commission, which investigated the bank failure, "The Financial statements became gold fillings covering cavities in the assets and in the earnings of the bank." Yet research on stock prices prior to the collapse has shown that stock market investors were aware that the bank was highly risky.[36]

Timing of Issuance of Financing

In early 1994, the *Globe and Mail* reported that Bombardier Inc. was going to "take advantage of a good market" to raise $210 million with a share issue.[37] One of the most interesting phenomena of external finance is that the year-to-year variation in the use of new issues appears substantial. Some of the variations in new equity issues are explainable by corporate attempts to time new issues. Intuition suggests that corporations might try to issue more equity when they perceive stock market prices to be high. This is partially borne out. Research by Taggart on U.S. corporations and by Marsh on corporations in Great Britain seems to show that stock is more likely to be issued after stock prices have increased.[38] Cheung, Roy, and Gordon found that the price of a Canadian firm's stock plays a key role in dictating the type of long-term capital to be

---

are invariant to accounting changes. The efficient market hypothesis actually makes a stronger statement. As long as earnings can be reconstructed under alternative accounting methods, each stock should be unaffected by a change in accounting.

[34]J. K. Cheung, "The PIP Grant Accounting Controversy in Canada: A Study of the Economic Consequences of Accounting Standards," *Journal of Business Finance & Accounting* 15 (Spring 1988).

[35]Abraham J. Briloff, *More Debits than Credits* (New York: Harper & Row, 1976).

[36]R. Giammarino, E. Schwartz, and J. Zechner, "Market Valuation of Bank Assets and Deposit Insurance in Canada," *Canadian Journal of Economics* 22 (February 1989), pp. 109–26.

[37]A. Gibbon, "Bombardier to Issue Shares," *The Globe and Mail*, January 15,1994.

[38]R. A. Taggart, "A Model of Corporate Financing Decisions," *Journal of Finance* (December 1977); and P. Marsh, "The Choice between Equity and Debt: An Empirical Study," *Journal of Finance* (March 1981).

Figure 13.9
Three stock price
adjustments

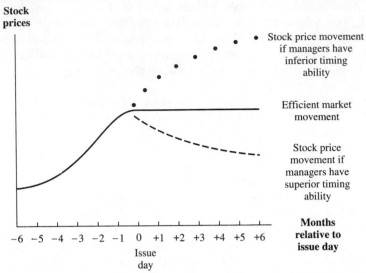

Studies show that stock is more likely to be issued after stock prices have increased.
So far no convincing evidence suggests that stock prices either increase or decrease
after the stock is issued.

raised.[39] Initial public share offerings in Canada peaked in 1987 before the Crash and
broke the 1987 record in 1993 when the TSE 300 passed its 1987 peak.[40]

The weak form of the efficient market hypothesis states that the sequence of past
stock or bond prices contains no information on the future price. Figure 13.9 shows
three possible stock price adjustments to the issuance of new stock. The evidence
suggests that financial managers have neutral timing ability. This suggests that it is
futile to try to time security issues. If by doing so financial managers are trying to
catch the market while it is high and before it goes down, they will be disappointed.

Why do corporations behave in this manner? A reasonable explanation for the
Taggart and Marsh findings is that stock prices have risen to reflect the stock market's
assessment of new corporate (positive-NPV) investment opportunities. Presumably,
the need to finance these investment opportunities necessitates the new equity issues.

Similarly, financial managers frequently do not want to issue equity when the book
value of their stock is above its market value. They feel that their stock is undervalued,
implying that the new shareholders are getting too good a deal. However, the semistrong
form of the efficient market hypothesis implies that all publicly available information,
including the book value, is properly incorporated into the market price. A stock price
below book value simply indicates a low expectation of cash flows.

By contrast, financial managers may possess private information about their firm
that the market does not have. If the special information is positive, they may choose
not to issue stock because they estimate that the current stock price is too low. However,
this private information has nothing to do with the timing issue mentioned above.
Managers could have positive information about their firm whether the stock has fallen

---

[39]J. K. Cheung, S. P. Roy, and I. Gordon, "Financing Policies of Large Canadian Corporations," *CMA Magazine,* May 1989.

[40]Doug Kelly, "IPO's Set for Value Record," *The Financial Post* (December 4, 1993), p. 17.

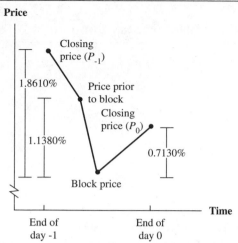

Figure 13.10
Price impacts of
block trading

Grph depicts the average price difference, expressed as a
percentage, between selected trades in the period from the
close of trading on day − 1 to the close of trading on day 0.
Day 0 is the day on which a block sale occurred. The drop
in price from a block trade and subsequent rebound is
evidence of a price-pressure effect.

Source: A. Kraus and H. R. Stoll, "Price Impacts of Block Trading on the
New York Stock Exchange," *Journal of Finance* 27 (June 1972), p. 542.

or risen in the past. Similarly, managers could have positive information whether the
stock is currently selling above or below book value. Managers in possession of such
inside information should time their security issues to take advantage of any temporary
mispricing in their debt or equity securities. However, managers are unlikely to improve
their shareholders' position by timing security issues based on *public* information such
as the past pattern of stock prices or the current market-to-book-value ratio.

Price-Pressure Effects

Suppose a firm wants to sell a large block of stock. Can it sell as many shares as it
wants without depressing the price? If capital markets are efficient, the answer should
be yes. Scholes was one of the first to examine this question empirically. He found that
the NYSE's ability to absorb large blocks of stock was virtually unlimited.[41] His
findings were surprising to practitioners because the sale of large blocks of shares is
generally believed to depress the price of a company's stock temporarily.

Subsequent researchers using more refined trade-by-trade prices found evidence
of a very small price-pressure effect on both the NYSE and the TSE. The basic price
pattern is reproduced in Figure 13.10. The price-pressure effect is less than 1 percent.[42]

---

[41]M. Scholes, "The Market for Securities: Substitution versus Price Pressure and the Effects of Information on Share
Prices," *Journal of Business* (April 1972).

[42]A. Kraus and H. R. Stoll, "Price Impacts of Block Trading on the New York Stock Exchange," *Journal of Finance* 27
(June 1972), p. 542, and Robert Holthausen, Richard Leftwich, and David Mayers, "Large-Block Transactions, the Speed
of Response, and Temporary and Permanent Stock Price Effects," *Journal of Financial Economics* 26 (1990), pp. 71–95,
conducted tests for the NYSE. Michael J. Robinson and Robert W. White, "Block Trading Price Effects: An Inter-market
Comparison" (London: University of Western Ontario, Working Paper, 1989), found that price-pressure effects were similar
for the NYSE and TSE.

Efficient Market Hypothesis: A Summary

Does Not Say
Prices are uncaused.

Investors are foolish and too stupid to be in the market.

All shares of stock have the same expected returns.

Investors should throw darts to select stocks.

There is no upward trend in stock prices.

Does Say
Prices reflect underlying value.

Financial managers cannot time stock and bond sales.

Sales of stock and bonds will not depress prices.

You cannot cook the books.

Why Doesn't Everybody Believe It?
There are optical illusions, mirages, and apparent patterns in charts of stock market returns.

The truth is less interesting.

There is evidence against efficiency:

- Seasonality.
- Insider trading.
- Excess stock price volatility.

The tests of market efficiency are weak.

Three Forms
Weak form (random walk): Prices reflect past prices; chartism (technical analysis) is useless.

Semistrong form: Prices reflect all public information; most financial analysis is useless.

Strong form: Prices reflect all that is knowable; nobody consistently makes superior profits.

Why Don't Firms Issue More Equity?

External equity as a percentage of total corporate sources of financing has historically been very low or negative. Many firms do not like to use external equity. Donaldson documented the reluctance of many corporate financial managers to use external equity as a regular source of financing.[43] He found that corporations that made use of

---

[43]G. Donaldson, *Managing Corporate Wealth* (New York: Praeger, 1984).

| | | Common stock price | | | Table 13.1 |
	Number of respondents	About right (%)	Too low (%)	Too high (%)	Market price compared to intrinsic value*
1980 survey	48	10.4%	89.6%	0%	
1984 survey	257	31.1	66.1	1.9	

*Company executives were asked, "Do you think that the market price of your stock is about right, too low, or too high compared with its intrinsic value?"

Source: M. Blume, I. Friend, and R. Westerfield, *Impediments to Capital Formation* (Philadelphia: Rodney L. White Center for Financial Research, The Wharton School, University of Pennsylvania, 1980); and M. Blume, I. Friend, and R. Westerfield, *Factors Affecting Capital Formation* (Philadelphia: Rodney L. White Center for Financial Research, The Wharton School, University of Pennsylvania, 1984).

the public equity markets did so as kind of a contingency reserve for extraordinary circumstances and outside the normal financing framework. The companies never planned to use external equity for raising cash. Some people have argued that a market inefficiency accounts for this.

Corporate managers give a number of reasons to justify why they do not issue new equity. One of the reasons is that many company executives believe that their stock is priced below true or intrinsic value (Table 13.1). This reason is inconsistent with the efficient market hypothesis, because stocks should be correctly priced under the hypothesis. In any case, it is hard to understand why a firm's stock price would be systematically below its present value. A simpler explanation is that issuance costs of new equity are much higher than those for all other forms of financing. This is true, as we shall verify in Chapter 19.

CONCEPT QUESTION

- What are three implications of the efficient market hypothesis for corporate finance?

Summary and Conclusions   13.6

1. An efficient financial market processes the information available to investors and incorporates it into the prices of securities. This has two general implications. First, in any given time period, a stock's abnormal return can depend on information or news received by the market in that period. Second, an investor who uses the same information as the market cannot expect to earn abnormal returns. In other words, systems for playing the market are doomed to fail.

2. What information does the market use to determine prices? The weakest form of the efficient market hypothesis says that the market uses the past history of prices and is therefore efficient with respect to these past prices. This implies that stock selection based on patterns of past stock price movements is not better than random stock selection.

3. A stronger theory of efficiency is semistrong-form efficiency, which argues that the market uses all publicly available information. If the market has already used all of this information and it is now reflected in the prices of stocks, investors will not be able to outperform the market by using the same information.

4. The strongest theory of efficiency, strong-form efficiency, argues that the market has available to it and uses all of the information that anybody knows about stocks, even inside information.

5. The evidence from the NYSE and TSE supports weak-form efficiency and contradicts strong-form efficiency. The weight of evidence also supports semistrong-form efficiency although there are a number of anomalies in the United States and even more in Canada. Only investors with truly superior information or ability should try to beat the market.

6. In our study of efficient markets, we stress the importance of distinguishing between the actual return on a stock and the expected return. The difference (called the *abnormal return*) comes from the release of news to the market. In the last chapter we discussed expected returns on stocks.

7. Not everybody believes the efficient market hypothesis. The boxed material on page 390 summarizes what it does and does not say.

8. Three implications of efficient markets for corporate finance are
   a. The price of a company's stock cannot be affected by a change in accounting.
   b. Financial managers cannot time issues of stocks and bonds using publicly available information.
   c. A firm can sell as many bonds or shares of stock as it desires without depressing prices significantly.

Key Terms

Suggested Readings

The concept of market efficiency is important. Classic review articles include:

E. F. Fama. "Efficient Capital Markets: A Review of Theory and Empirical Work." *Journal of Finance* (May 1970).

E. F. Fama. "Efficient Capital Markets: II." *Journal of Finance* (December 1991).

An entertaining yet informative book on efficient markets is:

B. G. Malkiel. *A Random Walk down Wall Street,* college ed. New York: Norton, 1990.

An excellent review of research on market efficiency in Canada is:

Z. Bodie, A. Kane, A. J. Marcus, S. Perrakis, and P. J. Ryan. *Investments.* Homewood, Ill.: Irwin, 1993.

Other good Canadian investments texts are:

J. E. Hatch and M. J. Robinson. *Investment Management in Canada,* 2d ed. Scarborough, Ontario: Prentice Hall Canada, 1989.

W. F. Sharpe, G. J. Alexander, and D. J. Fowler. *Investments,* 1st Canadian ed. Scarborough, Ontario: Prentice Hall Canada, 1993.

Questions and Problems

13.1 *a.* What rule should a firm follow when making financing decisions?

    b. How can firms create valuable financing opportunities?

13.2 Define the three forms of market efficiency.

13.3 Which of the following statements are true about the efficient market hypothesis?

    a. It implies perfect forecasting ability.

    b. It implies that prices reflect all available information.

    c. It implies an irrational market.

    d. It implies that prices do not fluctuate.

    e. It results from keen competition among investors.

13.4 Aerotech, an aerospace technology research firm, announced this morning that it has hired the world's most knowledgeable and prolific space researchers. Before today, Aerotech's stock had been selling for $100.

    a. What do you expect will happen to Aerotech's stock?

    b. Consider the following scenarios:

        i. The stock price jumps to $118 on the day of the announcement. In subsequent days it floats up to $123 and then falls back to $116.

        ii. The stock price jumps to $116 and remains there.

        iii. The stock price gradually climbs to $116 over the next week.

    Which scenario(s) indicate market efficiency? Which do not? Why?

13.5 When the 56-year-old founder of Gulf & Western, Inc., died of a heart attack, the stock price jumped from $18.00 a share to $20.25, a 12.5-percent increase. This is evidence of market inefficiency, because an efficient stock market would have anticipated his death and adjusted the price beforehand. Is this statement true or false? Explain.

13.6 The following announcement was just made: "Early today the Supreme Court of Canada reached a decision in the Universal Product Care case. UPC has been found guilty of polluting the environment. For the next five years, UPC must pay $2 million each year to a fund representing victims of UPC's policies." Should investors not buy UPC stock after the announcement because the decision will cause an abnormally low rate of return? Why or why not?

13.7   Sooners Investing Agency has been the hottest stock picker for the past two years. Before the rise to fame occurred, subscribers to the Sooners newsletter totaled only 200. Those subscribers beat the market consistently; they earned substantially higher returns after adjustment for risk and transaction costs. Subscriptions have now skyrocketed to 10,000. Now when Sooners recommends a stock, the stock price instantly rises several points. The subscribers now earn only a normal return when they buy a recommended stock because the price rises before anybody can act on the information. Briefly explain this phenomenon.

13.8   In a recent discussion, your broker commented that well-managed firms are not necessarily more profitable than firms with average managements. To convince you, she presented evidence from a recent study conducted by the firm for which she works. The study examined the returns on 17 small manufacturing firms that, eight years earlier, an industry magazine article had listed as the best-managed small manufacturers in the country. In the eight years since the article's publication, the 17 firms have not earned more than the market. Your broker concluded that if they were well-managed, they should have produced better-than-average returns. Do you agree with your broker?

13.9   Prospectors, Inc., is a small gold-prospecting company in Northern Ontario. Usually its searches prove fruitless; however, occasionally the prospectors find a rich vein of ore.

   a.   What pattern would you expect to observe for Prospectors' cumulative abnormal returns?

   b.   Is this a random walk? Explain.

   c.   Is this consistent with an efficient market? Explain.

13.10   You are conducting a cumulative average residual study on the effect of airline companies buying new planes. The announcement dates for the purchases of the planes were July 18 (7/18) for PWA, February 12 (2/12) for United, and October 7 (10/7) for Air Canada. Construct a cumulative abnormal return (CAR) for these stocks as a group, chart it, and explain it. All stocks have a beta of one.

PWA			United			Air Canada		
Date	Market return	Company return	Date	Market return	Company return	Date	Market return	Company return
7/12	−0.3	−0.5	2/8	−0.9	−1.1	10/1	0.5	0.3
7/13	0.0	0.2	2/9	−1.0	−1.1	10/2	0.4	0.6
7/16	0.5	0.7	2/10	0.4	0.2	10/3	1.1	1.1
7/17	−0.5	−0.3	2/11	0.6	0.8	10/6	0.1	−0.3
7/18	−2.2	1.1	2/12	−0.3	−0.1	10/7	−2.2	−0.3
7/19	−0.9	−0.7	2/15	1.1	1.2	10/8	0.5	0.5
7/20	−1.0	−1.1	2/16	0.5	0.5	10/9	−0.3	−0.2
7/23	0.7	0.5	2/17	−0.3	−0.2	10/10	0.3	0.1
7/24	0.2	0.1	2/18	0.3	0.2	10/13	0.0	−0.1

13.11 The following diagram shows the cumulative abnormal returns on the stock prices of 386 oil- and gas-exploration companies that announced oil discoveries in month 0. The sample was drawn from 1950 to 1980, and no single month had more than six announcements. Is the diagram consistent with market efficiency? Why or why not?

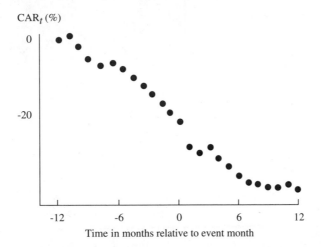

Time in months relative to event month

13.12 The following diagram represents the hypothetical results of a study of the behaviour of the stock prices of firms that lost important legal cases. Included are all firms that lost the initial court decision, even if it was later overturned on appeal. Is the diagram consistent with market efficiency? Why or why not?

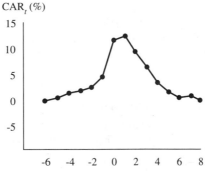

Time in months relative to event month

13.13 The following figures present the results of four cumulative average residual studies conducted to test the semistrong form of the efficient market hypothesis. Indicate in each case whether the results of the study support, reject, or are inconclusive about the hypothesis. In each figure, time 0 is the date of an event.

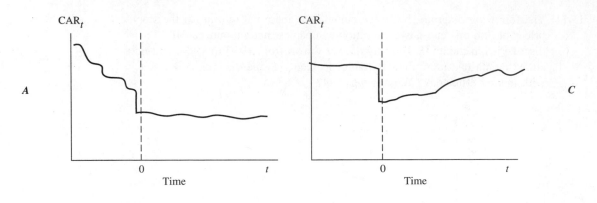

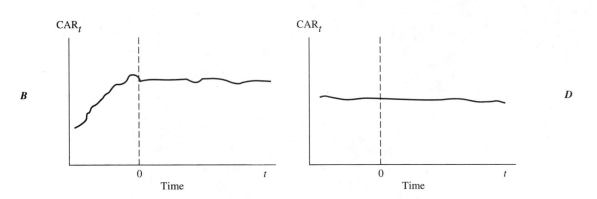

13.14 Several years ago, just before Arco purchased the firm, Kennecott Copper Corporation had large amounts of marketable securities as a consequence of receiving compensation for some overseas expropriations and other factors. For a period of time before Arco's purchase, the market value of Kennecott was actually less than the market value of the marketable securities alone. Is this evidence of market inefficiency?

13.15 Suppose the market is semistrong-form efficient. Can you expect to earn excess returns if you make trades based on

    a.   Your broker's information about record earnings for a stock?

    b.   Rumours about a merger of a firm?

    c.   Yesterday's announcement of a successful test of a new product?

13.16 Consider an efficient capital market in which a particular macroeconomic variable that influences your firm's net earnings is positively serially correlated. Would you expect price changes in your stock to be serially correlated? Why or why not?

CHAPTER 14

Long-Term Financing: An Introduction

This chapter introduces the basic sources of long-term financing: common stock, preferred stock, and long-term debt. Later chapters discuss these topics in more detail. Perhaps no other area is more perplexing to new students of finance than corporate securities such as shares of stock, bonds, and debentures. Although the concepts are simple and logical, the language is strange and unfamiliar.

The purpose of this chapter is to describe the basic features of long-term financing. We begin with a look at common stock, preferred stock, and long-term debt and then briefly consider patterns of the different kinds of long-term financing. Discussion of more complex forms of long-term finance, such as convertibles and leases, is reserved for later chapters.

Common Stock 14.1

The term **common stock** (or **common shares**) means different things to different people, but is usually applied to stock that has no special preference either in dividends or in bankruptcy. A description of the common stock of TransCanada Pipelines Limited is presented in the table below.

TransCanada Pipelines Limited, Shareholders' Equity at Book Value, 1992
(in $ thousands)

Common stock and other shareholders' equity	
Common shares, authorized unlimited, issued 176,011,944 shares	$ 791,000
Equity preferred shares, issued 12,500,000 shares	197,000
Total shares	$ 988,000
Retained earnings	825,700
Contributed surplus	269,600
Foreign exchange adjustment	14,900
Total shareholders' equity	$2,098,200

Source: Financial Post Datagroup, Datacard, 1993.

Owners of common stock in a corporation are referred to as *shareholders* or *stockholders.* They receive stock certificates for the *shares* they own. There can be a stated value on each stock certificate called the *par value,* but more typically in Canada, there is no particular par value assigned to stock.

Common shareholders are protected by *limited liability.* If the company goes bankrupt, the creditors cannot seek payment of the firm's debt from its common shareholders. On the other hand, the common shareholders are the residual claimants and almost always lose 100 percent of their investment if the firm goes bankrupt.

Authorized versus Issued Common Stock

Shares of common stock are the fundamental ownership units of the corporation. The articles of incorporation of a new corporation must state the number of shares of common stock the corporation is authorized to issue.

The board of directors of the corporation, after a vote of the shareholders, can amend the articles of incorporation to increase the number of shares authorized; there is no legal limit to the number of shares that can be authorized this way. In 1992, TransCanada Pipelines had authorized an unlimited amount of common shares, but had issued 176,011,944 shares. There is no requirement that all of the authorized shares ever be issued.

Contributed Surplus

Contributed surplus usually refers to amounts of directly contributed equity capital in excess of the par value. The contributed surplus of TransCanada Pipelines is $269.6 million. This figure indicates that the price of new shares issued by TransCanada Pipelines exceeded the par value and the difference has been entered as contributed surplus.

Retained Earnings

TransCanada Pipelines pays out around 60 percent of its net income as dividends; the rest is retained in the business and is called **retained earnings.** The cumulative amount of retained earnings (since original incorporation) was $825.7 million in 1992.

The sum of accumulated retained earnings, contributed surplus (if any), share capital, and adjustments to equity is the total shareholders' equity of the firm, which is usually referred to as the firm's **book value of equity** (or *net worth*). The book value of equity represents an accountant's measure of the amount contributed directly and indirectly to the corporation by equity investors.

To illustrate some of these definitions, suppose Western Redwood Corporation was formed in 1974 with 10,000 shares of stock issued and sold for $1 per share. By 1994, the company had been profitable and had retained profits of $100,000. Shareholders' equity of Western Redwood Corporation in 1994 is as follows:

Western Redwood Corporation Equity Accounts, 1994

Common stock (10,000 shares outstanding)	$ 10,000
Retained earnings	100,000
Total shareholders' equity	$110,000

$$\text{Book value per share} = \frac{\$110,000}{10,000} = \$11$$

Now suppose the company has profitable investment opportunities and decides to sell 10,000 shares of new stock to raise the necessary funding. The current market price is $20 per share. The table below shows the effects of the sale of stock on the balance sheet.

Western Redwood Corporation, 1994, after Sale of Stock

Common stock (20,000 shares outstanding)	$210,000
Retained earnings	100,000
Total shareholders' equity	$310,000

$$\text{Book value per share} = \frac{\$310,000}{20,000} = \$15.50$$

What happened?

1. Since 10,000 shares of new stock were issued at a book value of $20, a total of $200,000 was added to common stock.

2. The book value per share was higher than the previous book value of $11 because the market price of the new stock was higher than the book value.

Market Value, Book Value, and Replacement Value

The total book value of equity for TransCanada Pipelines in 1992 was $2,098,200,000. The company had outstanding 176,011,944 common shares and 12,500,000 equity preferred shares so that the total number of outstanding shares was 188,511,944.[1]

The book value per share was thus

$$\frac{\text{Total common shareholders' equity}}{\text{Shares outstanding}} = \frac{\$2,098,200,000}{188,511,944} = \$11.13$$

TransCanada Pipelines is a publicly owned company. Its common stock and equity preferred stock trade on the Toronto Stock Exchange (TSE) and the Montreal Stock Exchange (MSE); its common stock also trades on the New York Stock Exchange (NYSE). Thousands of shares change hands every day. Market prices of TransCanada Pipelines' common shares were between $16.00 and $18.50 per share during 1992. Thus, the market prices were above the book value.

In addition to market and book values, you may hear the term *replacement value*. This refers to the current cost of replacing the assets of the firm. Market, book, and replacement value are equal at the time when a firm purchases an asset. After that time, these values will diverge. The market–to–book-value ratio of common stock and Tobin's Q (market value of assets/replacement value of assets), introduced in the appendix to Chapter 2, are indicators of the success of the firm. A market-to-book or Tobin's Q ratio greater than 1 indicates the firm has done well with its investment decisions.

---

[1]Equity preferred shares are a Series B preferred issue that are automatically converted to common shares on August 1, 1995. The company treats these shares as identical to common shares.

Shareholders' Rights

Shareholders elect directors who, in turn, hire management to carry out their directives. Shareholders, therefore, control the corporation through the right to elect the directors; generally only shareholders have this right.

Directors are elected at an annual shareholders' meeting by a vote of those people who hold a majority of shares present and are entitled to vote. The exact mechanism for electing directors differs across companies. The two most important methods are *cumulative voting* and *straight voting.*[2]

The value of a share of common stock in a corporation is directly related to the general rights of shareholders. In addition to the right to vote for directors, shareholders usually have the following rights:

1. The right to share proportionally in dividends paid.
2. The right to share proportionally in assets remaining after liabilities have been paid in a liquidation.
3. The right to vote on matters of great importance to shareholders, such as a merger, usually decided at the annual meeting or a special meeting.
4. The right to share proportionally in any new stock sold when approved by the board of directors. Called the *preemptive right,* this right is detailed in Chapter 19.

■ *Example*

Imagine that a corporation has two shareholders: MacDonald with 25 shares and Laurier with 75 shares. Both want to be on the board of directors. Laurier does not want MacDonald to be a director. Let us assume that there are four directors to be elected and each shareholder nominates four candidates. ■

Cumulative Voting

The effect of **cumulative voting** is to permit minority participation. If cumulative voting is permitted, the total number of votes that each shareholder may cast is determined first. That number is usually calculated as the number of shares (owned or controlled) multiplied by the number of directors to be elected. Each shareholder can distribute these votes as he or she wishes over one or more candidates. MacDonald will get $25 \times 4 = 100$ votes, and Laurier is entitled to $75 \times 4 = 300$ votes. If MacDonald gives all his votes to himself, he is assured of a directorship. It is not possible for Laurier to divide 300 votes among the four candidates in such a way as to preclude MacDonald's election to the board.

In general, if there are N directors up for election, then $1/(N + 1)$ percent of the stock (plus one share) will guarantee you a seat. In our current example, this is $1/(4 + 1) = 20\%$. With cumulative voting, the more seats that are up for election at one time, the easier it is to win one.

---

[2]Outside Canada and the United States, other factors besides proportionate ownership can be important in electing directors. For example, in 1989, T. Boone Pickens, a well-known U.S. takeover specialist, acquired over 20 percent of the shares of Koito, an important auto parts manufacturer in Japan. When Pickens requested that three executives from his firm go on the Koito board, Tamotsu Aoyama, a Koito director replied, "It is necessary to build a trusting relationship first. In Japan, it is not possible to just say, 'I'm a major shareholder' and get a seat on the board right away." *The Globe and Mail* (April 27, 1989).

Straight Voting

If **straight voting** is permitted, MacDonald may cast 25 votes for each candidate and Laurier may cast 75 votes for each. As a consequence, Laurier will elect all of the candidates.

Straight voting can freeze out minority shareholders; that is the rationale for cumulative voting. But devices have been worked out to minimize its impact. One such device is to *stagger* the voting for the board of directors. Staggering permits a fraction of the directorships to come to a vote at a particular time. It has two basic effects:

1. Staggering makes it more difficult for a minority to elect a director when there is cumulative voting.
2. Staggering makes successful takeover attempts less likely by making the election of new directors more difficult.

Proxy Voting

A **proxy** is the legal grant of authority by a shareholder to someone else to vote his or her shares. For convenience, the actual voting in large public corporations usually is done by proxy.

Many companies such as BCE, Inc., have hundreds of thousands of shareholders. Shareholders can come to the annual meeting and vote in person, or they can transfer their right to vote to another party by proxy.

Obviously, management always tries to get as many proxies transferred to it as possible. However, if shareholders are not satisfied with management, an outside group of shareholders can try to obtain as many votes as possible via proxy. They can vote to replace management by adding enough directors. This is called a *proxy fight*.

Dividends

A distinctive feature of corporations is that they issue shares of stock and are authorized by law to pay dividends to the holders of those shares. **Dividends** paid to shareholders represent a return on the capital directly or indirectly contributed to the corporation by the shareholders. The payment of dividends is at the discretion of the board of directors.

Here are some important characteristics of dividends:

1. Unless a dividend is declared by the board of directors of a corporation, it is not a liability of the corporation. A corporation cannot *default* on an undeclared dividend. As a consequence, corporations cannot become *bankrupt* because of nonpayment of dividends. The amount of the dividend and even whether it is paid are decisions based on the business judgment of the board of directors.
2. The payment of dividends by the corporation is not a business expense. Dividends are not deductible for corporate tax purposes. In short, dividends are paid out of after-tax profits of the corporation.

3. Dividends received by individual shareholders are partially sheltered by a dividend tax credit discussed in detail in the Appendix to Chapter 1. Canadian corporations that own shares in other companies are permitted to exclude from taxable income 100 percent of the dividend amounts they receive from taxable Canadian corporations. The purpose of this provision is to avoid the double taxation of dividends.

Classes of Shares

Some firms have more than one class of common shares. Often, the classes are created with unequal voting rights. For example, Canadian Tire Corporation has two classes of common stock, both publicly traded. The majority of the voting common stock was distributed among offspring of the company founder and the rest held by Canadian Tire dealers, pension funds, and the general public. The nonvoting, Canadian Tire A stock is more widely held.[3]

There are many other Canadian corporations with restricted (nonvoting) stock. Such stock made up around 15 percent of the market values of TSE listed shares at the end of 1989. Nonvoting shares must receive dividends no lower than dividends on voting shares. Some companies pay a higher dividend on the nonvoting shares. In 1994, Canadian Tire's dividend rate was $.40 per share on both classes of stock.

A primary reason for creating dual classes of stock has to do with control of the firm. If such stock exists, management of a firm can raise equity capital by issuing nonvoting or limited-voting stock while maintaining control.

Lease, McConnell, and Mikkelson found the market prices of U.S. stocks with superior voting rights to be about 5-percent higher than the prices of otherwise identical stocks with inferior voting rights.[4] However, DeAngelo and DeAngelo found some evidence that the market value of differences in voting rights may be much higher when control of the firm is involved.[5] Maynes, Robinson, and White conducted a study of voting rights in Canada that reinforced the importance of control.[6]

Since it is only necessary to own 51 percent of the voting stock to control a company, nonvoting shareholders could be left out in the cold in the event of a takeover bid for the company. To protect the nonvoting shareholders, most companies have a **coattail** provision giving nonvoting shareholders the right either to vote or to convert their shares into voting shares that can be tendered to the takeover bid. In the Canadian Tire case, all Class A shareholders become entitled to vote and the coattail provision is triggered if a bid is made for "all or substantially all" of the voting shares.

The effectiveness of coattails was tested in 1986 when the Canadian Tire Dealers Association offered to buy 49 percent of the voting shares from the founding Billes

---

[3]For example, on one day in early 1994, 111,300 shares of the nonvoting stock traded and only 100 shares of the voting stock changed hands.

[4]R. C. Lease, J. J. McConnell, and W. H. Mikkelson, "The Market Value of Control in Publicly Traded Corporations," *Journal of Financial Economics* (April 1983).

[5]H. DeAngelo and L. DeAngelo, "Managerial Ownership of Voting Rights: A Study of Public Corporations with Dual Classes of Common Stock," *Journal of Financial Economics* 14 (1985).

[6]Elizabeth Maynes, Chris Robinson, and Alan White, "How Much Is a Share Vote Worth?" *Canadian Investment Review* (Spring 1990), pp. 49–56.

family. In the absence of protection, the nonvoting shareholders stood to lose substantially. The dealers bid at a large premium for the voting shares, which were trading at $40 before the bid. Nonvoting shares were priced at $14. Further, since the dealers were the principal buyers of Canadian Tire products, control of the company would have allowed them to adjust prices to benefit themselves over the nonvoting shareholders.

The key question was whether the bid triggered the coattail. The dealers and the Billes family argued that the offer was for 49 percent of the stock, not for "all or substantially all" of the voting shares. In the end the Ontario Securities Commission ruled that the offer was unfair to holders of the A shares (a view upheld in two court appeals).

As a result, investors believe that coattails have protective value but remain skeptical that they afford complete protection. In January 1994, Canadian Tire voting stock traded at a 23-percent premium over nonvoting stock.

CONCEPT QUESTIONS

- What is a company's book value?
- What rights do shareholders have?
- What is a proxy?
- Why do firms issue nonvoting shares? How are they valued?

Corporate Long-Term Debt: The Basics   14.2

Securities issued by corporations may be classified roughly as *equity* or *debt*. This distinction is basic to much of the modern theory and practice of corporate finance.

At its crudest level, debt represents something that must be repaid; it is the result of borrowing money. When corporations borrow, they contract to make regularly scheduled interest payments and to repay the original amount borrowed (that is, the *principal*). The person or firm making the loan is called a *creditor* or *lender.*

Interest versus Dividends

The corporation borrowing the money is called a *debtor* or *borrower.* The amount owed the creditor is a liability of the corporation; however, it is a liability of limited value. The corporation can legally default at any time on its liability (for example, by not paying interest) and hand over the assets to the creditors.[7] This can be a valuable option. The creditors benefit if the assets have a value greater than the value of the liability, but only foolish management would default in this circumstance. On the other hand, the corporation and the equity investors benefit if the value of the assets is less than the value of the liabilities, because equity investors are able to walk away from the liabilities and default on their payment.

---

[7] In practice, creditors can make a claim against the assets of the firm and a court will administer the legal remedy.

From a financial point of view, the main differences between debt and equity are the following:

1. Debt is not an ownership interest in the firm. Creditors do not usually have voting power. The device used by creditors to protect themselves is the loan contract (the *indenture*).

2. The corporation's payment of interest on debt is considered a cost of doing business and is fully tax deductible. Thus, interest expense is paid out to creditors before the corporate tax liability is computed. Dividends on common and preferred stock are paid to shareholders after the tax liability has been determined. Dividends are considered a return to shareholders on their contributed capital. Because interest expense can be used to reduce taxes, the government (that is, Revenue Canada) is providing a direct tax subsidy on the use of debt when compared to equity. This point is discussed in detail in the next two chapters.

3. Unpaid debt is a liability of the firm. If it is not paid, the creditors can legally claim the assets of the firm. This action may result in *liquidation* and *bankruptcy.* Thus, one of the costs of issuing debt is the possibility of *financial failure,* which does not arise when equity is issued.

Is It Debt or Equity?

Sometimes it is not clear whether a particular security is debt or equity. For example, suppose a 50-year bond is issued with interest payable solely from corporate income if and only if earned, and repayment is subordinate to all other debts of the business. Corporations are very adept at creating hybrid securities that look like equity but are called *debt.* Obviously, the distinction between debt and equity is important for tax purposes. When corporations try to create a debt security that is really equity, they are trying to obtain the tax benefits of debt while eliminating its bankruptcy costs.

Basic Features of Long-Term Debt

Long-term corporate debt usually is denominated in $1,000-units called the *principal* or *face value.* Long-term debt is a promise by the borrowing firm to repay the principal amount by a certain date, called the *maturity date.* Long-term debt almost always has a par value equal to the face value, and debt price is often expressed as a percentage of the par value. For example, it might be said that BC Telephone debt is selling at 90, which means that a bond with a par value of $1,000 can be purchased for $900. In this case, the debt is selling at a discount because the market price is less than the par value. Debt can also sell at a premium with respect to par value.

The borrower using long-term debt generally pays interest at a rate expressed as a fraction of par value. Thus, at $1,000 par value, BC Telephone's 7-percent debt means that $70 of interest is paid to holders of the debt, usually in semiannual instalments (for example, $35 on June 30 and December 31). The payment schedules are in the form of coupons that are detached from the debt certificates and sent to the company for payment.[8]

---

[8]Chapter 5 presents valuation formulas for debt.

Different Types of Debt

Typical debt securities are called *notes, debentures,* or *bonds.* In legal language, a debenture is an unsecured corporate debt, whereas a bond is secured by a mortgage on the corporate property. However, in common usage, the word *bond* is used indiscriminately and often refers to both secured and unsecured debt. A note usually refers to a short-term obligation, perhaps under seven years.

Debentures and bonds are long-term debt. *Long-term debt* is any obligation that is payable more than one year from the date it was originally issued and is sometimes called *funded debt.* Debt that is due in less than one year is unfunded and is accounted for as a current liability. Some debt is perpetual and has no specific maturity. This type of debt is referred to as a *consol.*

Repayment

Bonds can be repaid at maturity or earlier through the use of a sinking fund. A *sinking fund* is an account managed on behalf of the issuer by a bond trustee (generally a trust company) for the purpose of retiring all or part of the bonds prior to their stated maturity. The trustee retires the debt either by buying bonds in the market or by calling some of the debt. From an investor's viewpoint, a sinking fund reduces the risk that the company will be unable to repay the principal at maturity. Since it involves regular purchases, a sinking fund also improves the marketability of the bonds.

Debt may be extinguished before maturity through a *call provision* giving the firm the right to pay a specific amount (the *call price*) to *retire (extinguish)* the debt before the stated maturity date. The call price is generally higher than the par value of the debt. Debt that is callable at 105 is debt that the firm can buy back from the holder at a price of $1,050 per debenture or bond, regardless of what the market value of the debt might be. Call prices are always specified when the debt is originally issued. However, lenders are given a 5-year–to–10-year call protection period during which the debt cannot be called away.

Seniority

In general terms, **seniority** indicates preference in position over other lenders. Some debt is **subordinated.** In the event of default, holders of subordinated debt must give preference to other specified creditors. Usually, this means that the subordinated lenders will be paid off only after the specified creditors have been compensated. However, debt cannot be subordinated to equity.

Security

Security is a form of attachment to property; it provides that the property can be sold in the event of default to satisfy the debt for which security is given. A mortgage is used for security in tangible property; for example, debt can be secured by mortgages on plant and equipment. Holders of such debt have prior claim on the mortgaged assets in case of default. Debentures are not secured by a mortgage. Thus, if mortgaged property is sold in the event of default, debenture holders will obtain something only if the mortgage bondholders have been fully satisfied.

Indenture

The written agreement between the corporate debt issuer and the lender, setting forth maturity date, interest rate, and all other terms, is called an *indenture*. We treat this in detail in later chapters. For now, we note that

1. The indenture completely describes the nature of the indebtedness.
2. It lists all restrictions placed on the firm by the lenders. These restrictions are placed in *restrictive covenants*. Examples are
   a. Restrictions on further indebtedness.
   b. A maximum on the amount of dividends that can be paid.
   c. A minimum level of working capital.

CONCEPT QUESTIONS

- What is corporate debt? Describe its general features.
- Why is it sometimes difficult to tell whether a particular security is debt or equity?

14.3 Preferred Shares

Preferred shares have preference over common shares in the payment of dividends and in the distribution of corporate assets in the event of liquidation. *Preference* means that holders of the preferred shares must receive a dividend (in the case of an ongoing firm) before holders of common shares are entitled to anything. If the firm is liquidated, preferred shareholders rank behind all creditors but ahead of common shareholders.

Preferred shares are a form of equity from legal, tax, and regulatory standpoints. However, holders of preferred shares often have no voting privileges. In the 1980s, chartered banks were important issuers of preferred shares as they moved to meet higher capital requirements.

Stated Value

Preferred shares have a stated liquidating value, for example, $25 per share. The cash dividend is described in terms of dollars per share. For example, CIBC "$2.25 preferred" translates easily into a dividend yield of 9 percent of the stated $25 value.

Cumulative and Noncumulative Dividends

A preferred dividend is not like interest on a bond. The board of directors may decide not to pay the dividends on preferred shares, and their decision may have nothing to do with the current net income of the corporation.

Dividends payable on preferred shares are either *cumulative* or *noncumulative;* most are cumulative. If preferred dividends are cumulative and are not paid in a particular year, they will be carried forward as an arrearage. Usually both the cumulated (past) preferred dividends plus the current preferred dividends must be paid before the common shareholders can receive anything.

Unpaid preferred dividends are not debts of the firm. Directors elected by the common shareholders can defer preferred dividends indefinitely. However, in such cases

1. Common shareholders must also forgo dividends.

2. Holders of preferred shares are often granted voting and other rights if preferred dividends have not been paid for some time.

Because preferred shareholders receive no interest on the cumulated dividends, some have argued that firms have an incentive to delay paying preferred dividends.

Are Preferred Shares Really Debt?

A good case can be made that preferred shares are really debt in disguise, a kind of equity bond. Preferred shareholders receive a stated dividend only; and, if the corporation is liquidated, they get a stated value. Often, preferreds carry credit ratings much like bonds. Furthermore, preferred shares are sometimes convertible into common shares. Preferreds are often callable by the issuer, and the holder often has the right to sell the preferred shares back to the issuer at a set price.

In addition, in recent years, many new issues of preferred shares have had obligatory sinking funds. Such a sinking fund effectively creates a final maturity since the entire issue will ultimately be retired.

On top of all of this, preferred shares with adjustable dividends have been offered in recent years. One example is the *CARP* (*c*umulative, *a*djustable *r*ate, *p*referred). There are various types of floating rate preferred, some of which are quite innovative in the way that the dividend is determined. For example, dividends on Royal Bank of Canada First Preferred Shares Series C are set at ⅔ of the bank's average Canadian prime rate with a floor dividend of 6.67 percent per year.

For all these reasons, preferred shares seem to be a lot like debt. In comparison to debt, the yields on preferred shares can appear very low. For example, the Royal Bank has another series of preferred shares with a $2.25 stated dividend. In January 1994, the market price of the $2.25 Royal Bank preferred was about $29. This gave a yield of around 5 percent, well below the yield on Royal Bank long-term debt (about 6.875 percent at that time).[9]

Despite the apparently low yields, corporate investors have an incentive to hold preferred shares issued by other corporations as opposed to holding their debt since 100 percent of the dividends they receive are exempt from income taxes.[10] Because

---

[9]To find the yield on the Royal Bank $2.25 preferred, we must recognize that this issue is callable at $25 in around five years and so has a built-in loss reducing the dividend yield:

$$PV = \$2.25 \, A_{.05}^{5} + \$25/(1 + .05)^5 = \$29.33.$$

So the yield is around 5 percent.

[10]In the United States, the corporate dividend exclusion is only for 80 percent. I. Fooladi and G. Roberts, "On Preferred Stock," *Journal of Financial Research* 9 (Winter 1986), pp. 319–24, argue that this difference in tax law explains why Canadian firms finance much more heavily with preferred shares.

Table 14.1
Tax loophole on
preferred stock

$1000 Financing	Preferred	Debt
Issuer: Zero Tax Ltd.		
Preferred dividend/interest paid	$67.00	$100.00
Dividend tax at 40%	26.80	0.00
Tax deduction on interest	0.00	0.00
Total financing cost	$93.80	$100.00
After-tax cost	9.38%	10.00%
Purchaser: Full Tax Ltd.		
Before-tax income	$67.00	$100.00
Tax	0.00	45.00
After-tax income	$67.00	$ 55.00
After-tax yield	6.70%	5.50%

[handwritten margin notes: "67%", "10% coupon", "paydiv", "better for both"]

individual investors do not receive this tax break, most preferred shares in Canada are purchased by corporate investors.[11] Corporate investors pay a premium for preferred shares because of the tax exclusion on dividends; as a consequence, yields are low.

Preferred Shares and Taxes

Turning to the issuer's point of view, a tax loophole encourages corporations that are lightly taxed or not taxable due to losses or tax shelters, to issue preferred shares. Such low-tax companies can make little use of the tax deduction on interest. However, they can issue preferred shares and enjoy lower financing costs since preferred dividends are significantly lower than interest payments.

In 1987 the federal government attempted to close the tax loophole by introducing a tax of 40 percent of the preferred dividends to be paid by the issuer of preferred stock. The tax is refunded (through a deduction) to taxable issuers only. The effect of this and associated tax changes was to narrow but not close the loophole.

Table 14.1 shows how Zero-Tax Ltd., a corporation not paying any income taxes, can issue preferred shares attractive to Full Tax Ltd., a second corporation taxable at a combined federal and provincial rate of 45 percent. The example assumes that Zero Tax is seeking $1,000 in financing through either debt or preferred stock and that Zero Tax can issue either debt with a 10-percent coupon or preferred stock with a 6.7-percent dividend.[12]

Table 14.1 shows that with preferred shares financing, Zero Tax pays out 6.7% × $1,000 = $67.00 in dividends and 40% × $67.00 = $26.80 in tax on the dividends for a total after-tax outlay of $93.80. This represents an after-tax cost of $93.80/$1,000 = 9.38%. Debt financing is more expensive with an outlay of $100 and an after-tax yield of 10 percent. So Zero Tax is better off issuing preferred stock.

---

[11]Preferred dividends paid to individual investors qualify for the dividend tax credit.

[12]We set the preferred dividend at around two-thirds of the debt yield to reflect market prices as exemplified by the Royal Bank issue discussed earlier. Further discussion of preferred shares and taxes in Canada appears in I. Fooladi, P. A. McGraw, and G. S. Roberts, "Preferred Share Rules Freeze Out the Individual Investor," *CA Magazine* (April 11, 1988), pp. 38–41.

From the point of view of the purchaser, Full Tax Ltd., the preferred dividend is received tax-free for an after-tax yield of 6.7 percent. If it bought debt issued by Zero Tax instead, Full Tax would pay income tax of $45 for a net after-tax receipt of $55 or 5.5 percent. So again, preferred shares are better than debt.

Of course, if we change the example to make the issuer fully taxable, the after-tax cost of debt will drop to 5.5 percent, making debt financing more attractive. This reinforces our point that the tax motivation for issuing preferred shares is limited to lightly taxed companies.[13]

Beyond Taxes

For fully taxed firms, the fact that dividends are not an allowable deduction from taxable corporate income is the most serious obstacle to issuing preferred shares, but there are several reasons beyond taxes why preferreds are issued.

We can start by discussing some supply factors. First, regulated public utilities can pass the tax disadvantage of issuing preferred shares on to their customers because of the way pricing formulas are set up in regulatory environments. Consequently, a substantial amount of straight preferred shares are issued by utilities, particularly in the United States.

Second, firms issuing preferred shares can avoid the threat of bankruptcy that might otherwise exist if debt were relied on. Unpaid preferred dividends are not debts of a corporation, and preferred shareholders cannot force a corporation into bankruptcy because of unpaid dividends.

A third reason for issuing preferred shares concerns control of the firm. Since preferred shareholders often cannot vote, preferreds may be a means of raising equity without surrendering control.

On the demand side, for tax reasons discussed earlier, most preferred shares are owned by corporations. Some of the new types of adjustable-rate preferreds are ideally suited for corporations needing short-term investments for temporarily idle cash.

CONCEPT QUESTIONS

- What are preferred shares?
- Why is preferred arguably more like debt than equity?
- Why is it attractive for firms that are not paying taxes to issue preferred shares?
- What are three reasons unrelated to taxes why preferred shares are issued?

Patterns of Long-Term Financing   14.4

Grant, Webb, and Hendrick examined the relative importance of different sources of long-term financing and how these sources are used. Figures 14.1 and 14.2, drawn from their work, show how the assets and liabilities of Canadian industrial corporations evolved since 1978 and look ahead to 1998.

---

[13]L. Trigeorgis, "The Tax Hypothesis for Preferred Stock" (a paper presented at Eastern Finance Association 1994 meeting), finds that lightly taxed U.S. firms were more likely to use preferred stock financing than were fully taxed firms.

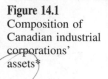

Figure 14.1
Composition of
Canadian industrial
corporations'
assets*

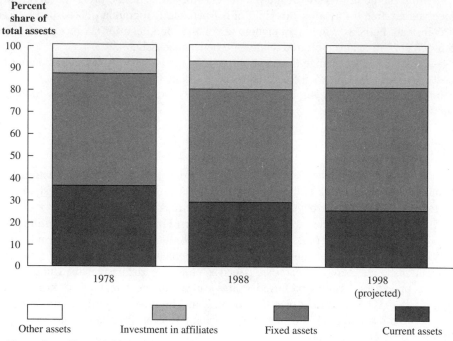

*Corporations with assets of $10 million or more.

Source: J. Grant, M. Webb, and P. Hendrick, "Financing Corporate Canada in the 1990s." *Canadian Investment Review* (Spring 1990), pp. 9–14.

Looking first at Figure 14.1's 1988 and projected 1998 assets, notice that fixed asset investment growth is predicted under the pressures of technological change and global competition. Increasing environmental consciousness will speed replacement of old equipment. Comparing fixed assets (in Figure 14.1) with shareholders' equity in Figure 14.2 shows that internally generated funds (net income less dividends plus depreciation) are not enough to finance fixed assets.[14] The "deficit" in long-term financing is made up from new common stock and long-term debt.

These data are consistent with the results of a survey by Gordon Donaldson on how firms establish long-term financing strategies.[15] He found that:

1. The first form of financing used by firms for positive-NPV projects is internally generated cash flow (net income plus depreciation minus dividends).

2. When a firm has insufficient cash flow from internal sources, it sells off part of its investment in marketable securities.

---

[14]Net income less dividends equals retained earnings and is included in shareholders' equity. Depreciation is not shown explicitly in Figure 14.1 as fixed assets are stated net of depreciation.

[15]G. G. Donaldson, *Corporate Debt Capacity: A Study of Corporate Debt Policy and Determination of Corporate Debt Capacity* (Boston: Harvard Graduate School of Business Administration, 1961). See also S. C. Myers, "The Capital Structure Puzzle," *Journal of Finance* (July 1984).

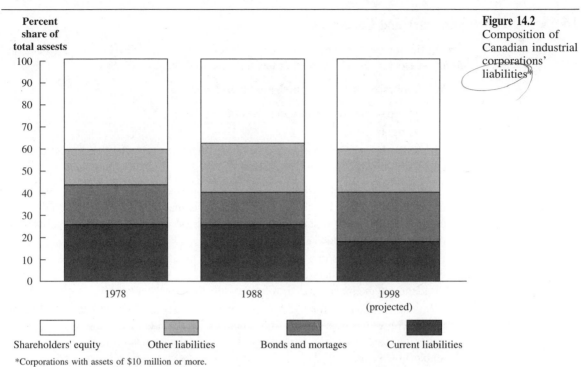

Percent
share of
total assets

Figure 14.2
Composition of
Canadian industrial
corporations'
liabilities*

Shareholders' equity   Other liabilities   Bonds and mortages   Current liabilities

*Corporations with assets of $10 million or more.

Source: J. Grant, M. Webb, and P. Hendrick, "Financing Corporate Canada in the 1990s," *Canadian Investment Review* (Spring 1990), pp. 9–14.

3. As a last resort, a firm will use externally generated cash flow. First, debt is used. Common stock is used last.

These observations, when taken together, suggest a pecking order to long-term financing strategy. At the top of the pecking order is using internally generated cash flow; at the bottom is issuing new equity.

Figure 14.2 also shows that debt-equity ratios of Canadian industrial corporations have remained relatively stable. This contrasts with increased reliance on debt financing in the United States in the 1980s. A slight decline in the proportionate use of debt financing is predicted throughout the 1990s.

Returning to Figure 14.1, notice that, in addition to fixed assets, these financing sources will likely be used for investment in affiliates. The increasing pace of globalization of markets and international competition will force companies to become larger and more international.

CONCEPT QUESTIONS

■ What are the major growth areas in assets requiring financing?

■ What are the major sources of corporate financing? What trends have emerged in recent years?

14.5   Summary and Conclusions

The basic sources of long-term financing are long-term debt, preferred stock, and common stock. This chapter describes the essential features of each.

1. We emphasize that common shareholders have

   Residual risk and return in a corporation.

   Voting rights.

   Limited liability if the corporation elects to default on its debt and must transfer some or all of the assets to the creditors.

2. Long-term debt involves contractual obligations set out in indentures. There are many kinds of debt, but the essential feature is that debt involves a stated amount that must be repaid. Interest payments on debt are considered a business expense and are tax deductible.

3. Preferred stock has some of the features of debt and some of the features of common equity. Holders of preferred stock have preference in liquidation and in dividend payments compared to holders of common equity.

4. Firms need financing for fixed assets, current assets, and investment in affiliates along with other uses. Most of the financing is provided from internally generated cash flow. The percentage mix of financing has remained relatively stable in Canada.

Key Terms

Common stock (common shares) 397

Contributed surplus 398

Retained earnings 398

Book value of equity 398

Cumulative voting 400

Straight voting 401

Proxy 401

Dividends 401

Coattail 402

Seniority 405

Subordinated (debt) 405

Preferred shares 406

Suggested Readings

Evidence on the financial structure of industrial corporations is found in:

J. Grant, M. Webb, and P. Hendrick. "Financing Corporate Canada in the 1990s." *Canadian Investment Review* (Spring 1990).

For a highly readable discussion of voting and nonvoting shares in Canada, see:

Elizabeth Maynes, Chris Robinson, and Alan White. "How Much Is a Share Vote Worth?" *Canadian Investment Review* (Spring 1990).

Questions and Problems

14.1 The Brice Co. equity accounts in 1994 are:

Common shares (1,500,000 shares outstanding)	$ 1,500,000
Retained earnings (thousands)	100,000,000
Total	$101,500,000

Suppose the company decides to issue 1,000 new common shares. The current price is $50 per share. Show the effect on the different accounts. What is the market-to-book ratio after the share issue?

14.2 In the previous question, suppose the company buys 100 of its own shares. What would happen to the accounts shown?

14.3 Which has a higher yield: preferred stock or corporate bonds? Why is there a difference? Who are the main investors in preferred stock? Why?

14.4 What are the main differences between corporate debt and equity? Why do some clever firms try to issue equity in the guise of debt? Why might preferred stock be called an equity bond?

14.5 The Babel Tower Company has $5 million of positive-NPV projects. Based on the historical pattern of long-term financing for Canadian industrial firms, what financing strategy will Babel probably use?

14.6 Ulrich Ltd.'s articles of incorporation authorize the firm to issue 500,000 shares of common stock, of which 325,000 shares have been issued at $5.60. In the quarter that ended last week, Ulrich earned net income of $260,000; 4 percent of that income was paid as a dividend. Prior to the close of the books, Ulrich had $3,545,000 in retained earnings.

a. Create the equity statement for Ulrich.

b. Create a new equity statement that reflects the sale of 25,000 authorized but unissued shares at the price of $4 per share.

14.7 The shareholders of the Unicorn Company need to elect seven new directors. There are 2 million shares outstanding. How many shares do you need to be certain that you can elect at least one director if

a. Unicorn has straight voting?

b. Unicorn has cumulative voting?

14.8 Refer to TransCanada Pipelines Limited's statement of shareholders' equity in Section 14.1.

a. Suppose that the company issues 5 million new common shares at today's market price. Prepare a new version of the table to reflect this financing. (Obtain the current price from a financial newspaper.)

b. Now suppose that instead TransCanada Pipelines buys 3 million shares. These shares are cancelled. Revise the table to reflect this change.

14.9 As an apprentice financial engineer, what new types of securities do you think might appeal to investors? What problems would have to be overcome to issue such securities?

14.10 An investor pays tax at a marginal combined federal–provincial rate of 53 percent. Long-term corporate bonds currently yield 9 percent. Because preferred shares issued by the same corporations are riskier, the investor seeks an increase in after-tax yield (for preferreds over bonds) of 1.5 percent. If a preferred share issue is as attractive as a bond issued by the same company, what dividend yield (before tax) must the preferred shares have?

CHAPTER 15

Capital Structure: Basic Concepts

Previous chapters of this book examined the capital budgeting decision. We pointed out that this decision concerns the left-hand side of the balance sheet. The previous two chapters began our discussion of the capital structure decision,[1] which deals with the right-hand side of the balance sheet.

In general, a firm can choose any capital structure that it wants. It can issue floating rate preferred stock, warrants, convertible bonds, caps, and collars. It can arrange lease financing, bond swaps, and forward contracts. Because the number of instruments is so large, the variations in capital structures are endless. We simplify the analysis by considering only common stock and straight debt in this chapter. The "bells and whistles," as they are called on Bay Street, must await later chapters of the text.

Our results in this chapter are basic. First, we discuss the capital structure decision in a world with neither taxes nor other capital market imperfections. Surprisingly, we find that the capital structure decision is a matter of indifference in this world. We next argue that there is a quirk in the Canadian tax code that subsidizes debt financing. Finally, we show that an increase in the firm's value from debt financing leads to an increase in the value of the equity.

The Capital Structure Question and the Pie Theory

15.1

How should a firm choose its debt-equity ratio? More generally, what is the best capital structure for the firm? We call our approach to the capital structure question the **pie model.** If you are wondering why we chose this name, just take a look at Figure 15.1. The pie in question is the sum of the financial claims of the firm (debt and equity in this case). We define the value of the firm to be this sum. Hence, the value of the firm, V, is

$$V = B + S \tag{15.1}$$

where B is the market value of the debt and S is the market value of the equity. Figure 15.1 presents two possible ways of slicing this pie between the stock slice and the debt

[1] It is conventional to refer to choices regarding debt and equity as *capital structure decisions*. However, the term *financial structure decisions* would be more accurate, and we use the terms interchangeably.

Figure 15.1
Two pie models of
capital structure

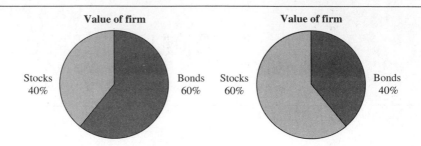

slice. If company management's goal is to make the firm as valuable as possible, then the firm should pick the debt-equity ratio that makes the pie—the total value, *V*—as big as possible.

This discussion begs two important questions:

1. Why should the shareholders in the firm care about maximizing the value of the entire firm? After all, the value of the firm is, by definition, the sum of both the debt and the equity. Instead, why should the shareholders not prefer the strategy that maximizes their interests only?

2. What is the ratio of debt to equity that maximizes the shareholders' interests?

Let us examine each of the two questions in turn.

CONCEPT QUESTION

■ What is the pie model of capital structure?

15.2   **Maximizing Firm Value versus Maximizing Shareholder Interests**

The following example illustrates that the capital structure that maximizes the value of the firm is the one that financial managers should choose for the shareholders.

■ *Example*

Suppose the market value of the J. J. Sprint Company is $1,000. The company currently has no debt, and each of J. J. Sprint's 100 shares of stock sells for $10. Further suppose that J. J. Sprint plans to borrow $500 and pay the $500 proceeds to shareholders as an extra cash dividend of $5 per share. The investments of the firm will not change as a result of this transaction. What will the value of the firm be after the proposed restructuring?

Management recognizes that, by definition, only one of three outcomes can occur from restructuring. Firm value after restructuring can be either (1) greater than the original firm value of $1,000, (2) equal to $1,000, or (3) less than $1,000. After consulting with investment bankers, management believes that restructuring will not change firm value more than $250 in either direction. Thus, it views firm values of

$1,250, $1,000, and $750 as the relevant range. The original capital structure and these three possibilities under the new capital structure are presented below.

	No debt (original capital structure)	Debt plus dividend (three possibilities after restructuring)		
		I	II	III
Debt	0	$ 500	$ 500	$500
Equity	$1,000	750	500	250
Firm value	1,000	$1,250	$1,000	$750

Of course, management recognizes that there are infinite possible outcomes. These three are to be viewed as *representative* outcomes only. We can now determine the payoff to shareholders under the three possibilities:

	Payoff to shareholders after restructuring		
	I	II	III
Capital gains	$1000-750 \to -$250$	$1000-500 \to -$500$	$1000-250 \to -$750$
Dividends	500	500	500
Net gain or loss to shareholders	$250	0	-$250

No one can be sure ahead of time which of the three outcomes will occur. However, imagine that managers believe that outcome I is most likely. They should definitely restructure the firm because the shareholders gain $250. That is, although the value of the stock declines by $250 to $750, they receive $500 in dividends. Their net gain is $250 = −$250 + $500. Also, notice that the value of the firm rises by $250.

Alternatively, imagine that managers believe that outcome III is most likely. In this case they should not restructure the firm because the shareholders expect a $250 loss. That is, the stock falls by $750 to $250 and they receive $500 in dividends. Their net loss is −$250 = −$750 + $500. Also, notice that the value of the firm falls by $250.

Finally, imagine that the managers believe that outcome II is most likely. Restructuring would not affect the shareholders' interest because the net gain to shareholders in this case is zero. Also, notice that the value of the firm is unchanged if outcome II occurs. ∎

This example explains why managers should attempt to maximize the value of the firm. In other words, it answers question (1) in section 15.1. In this example, changes in capital structure benefit the shareholders if and only if the value of the firm increases. Conversely, these changes hurt the shareholders if and only if the value of the firm decreases. This result holds generally for capital structure changes of many different types.[2] Thus, managers should choose the capital structure that they believe will have the highest firm value because this capital structure is most beneficial to the firm's shareholders.

---

[2]This result may not hold exactly in the more complex case where debt has a significant possibility of default. Issues of default are treated in the next chapter.

	Lever Company	Unlever Company
Table 15.1 Capital structure of Lever Company and Unlever Company	$V_L = ?$ $B_L = \$500$ $S_L = ?$ $r_B = 0.10$	$V_U = \$1,000 = S_U$ $B_U = 0$

S = EQUITY
B = debt

Note however that the example does not tell us which of the three outcomes is likely to occur. Thus, it does not tell us whether debt should be added to J. J. Sprint's capital structure. In other words, it does not answer question (2) in section 15.1. This second question is treated in the next section.

CONCEPT QUESTION

■ Why should financial managers choose the capital structure that maximizes the value of the firm?

15.3   ## Can an Optimal Capital Structure Be Determined?

Modigliani and Miller: Proposition I (No Taxes)

The previous section shows that the capital structure producing the highest firm value is the one most beneficial to the shareholders. In the present section, we would have liked to determine the particular capital structure that produces the highest firm value. Unfortunately, we are unable to do this. Modigliani and Miller (MM) have a convincing argument that a firm cannot change the total value of its outstanding securities by changing the proportions of its capital structure. In other words, the value of the firm is always the same under different capital structures. In still other words, no capital structure is any better or worse than any other capital structure for the firm's shareholders. This rather pessimistic result is the famous **MM Proposition I.**[3]

To see how MM Proposition I works, imagine two firms that are identical in every way except that their capital structures are different. Parameters of the two firms appear in Table 15.1. The Unlever Company has total equity, S_U, equal to \$1,000, which is the same as the total value of its assets, V_U. The Lever Company uses \$500 of debt. By definition, the value of its equity plus the value of its debt is equal to the value of the firm: $S_L + B_L = V_L$. The terms S_L and V_L are unknowns, though we will solve for them as the example progresses.

Mr. Allen is an arbitrageur. He is considering investing in 10 percent of the Unlever Company. If he does so, he will buy 10 percent of Unlever Company shares. He would pay $0.10 \, S_U = 0.10 \, V_U$ and would expect to receive 10 percent of the profits,

[3]The original paper appeared in 1958: F. Modigliani and M. Miller, "The Cost of Capital, Corporation Finance and the Theory of Investment," *American Economic Review* (June 1958).

$\tilde{Y}$ (where the tilde, $\sim$, denotes uncertainty). This is illustrated as follows:

Strategy I (buying 10 percent of Unlever Company)

Transaction	Dollar investment	Dollar return per year
Buy 0.10 of $1,000 = Buy 0.10 of V_U	$0.10 \times \$1,000 = \$100$ $= 0.10\, V_U$	$0.10\, \tilde{Y}$

Now Mr. Allen compares this to another investment: to purchase the same fraction, 0.10, of the equity of the Lever Company. The equity of the Lever Company is S_L, an unknown to us at this point. The debt, B_L, is \$500. The firm's cost of debt capital, r_B, is 0.10. (This rate is also referred to as the *interest rate on the debt* or the *return on the debt.*) Because the company pays no taxes, Mr. Allen's investment and return then would be

Strategy II (buying 10 percent of the equity of Lever Company)

Transaction	Dollar investment[4]	Dollar return per year
Buy 0.10 of S_L	$0.10\, S_L = 0.10 \times (V_L - B_L)$	$0.10 \times (\tilde{Y} - 0.10 \times \$500)$ $= 0.10\, \tilde{Y} - \$5$ $= 0.10 \times (\tilde{Y} - r_B B_L)$

Mr. Allen considers this investment a little riskier because the shares of the Lever Company are levered. He notices that his initial investment is lower. His share of the profits is also lower because of interest payments the firm must make on its debt. Thus, strategies I and II are not directly comparable.

Being an arbitrageur, he now creates another, more complex strategy.

1. He borrows $0.10\, B_L$ of debt on his own account at an interest rate of

   $r_B = 10\%$.[5]

2. Next he uses the proceeds plus his own funds to buy 10 percent of the Unlever Company, $0.10\, V_U$. (Note that $0.10\, V_U = 0.10\, S_U$.)

The strategy is illustrated as follows:

Strategy III (buying 10 percent of the equity of Unlever Company by a combination of one's own funds plus personal borrowing)

Transaction	Dollar investment	Dollar return per year
Borrow $0.10\, B_L$	$-0.10\, B_L$	$-0.10\, r_B B_L$
Buy 0.10 of V_U	$0.10\, V_U$	$0.10\, \tilde{Y}$
Total	$0.10 \times (V_U - B_L)$	$0.10 \times (\tilde{Y} - r_B B_L)$

Because Mr. Allen now borrows, his net investment of $0.10 \times (V_U - B_L)$ in strategy III is less than his net investment of $0.10\, V_U$ in strategy I. Similarly, because Mr. Allen must now pay interest, his dollar return in strategy III is less than his dollar return in strategy I.

---

[4]As mentioned earlier, the value of the firm is defined to be the sum of the value of the debt plus the value of the equity. Thus, in this example, V_L is equal to $S_L + B_L$, by definition. Rearranging, $S_L = V_L - B_L$, by definition. Hence, the dollar investment can be expressed in terms of either S_L or $V_L - B_L$.

[5]The assumption that an individual can borrow at the same interest rate as the firm is crucial for this example. Though many students believe this assumption is unrealistic, we show later that it is quite plausible in the real world.

Now let us compare strategy III with strategy II, the comparison that Modigliani–Miller use to establish their important Proposition I. Notice that the dollar returns of strategy II and strategy III are both $0.10 \times (\tilde{Y} - r_B B_L)$. Under strategy II, the arbitrageur receives his compensation as a cash dividend of 10 percent of $\tilde{Y} - r_B B_L$ from the levered firm. Under strategy III, the arbitrageur receives exactly the same compensation (10 percent of $\tilde{Y} - r_B B_L$) as a combination of a cash dividend of $0.10\,\tilde{Y}$ from the unlevered firm less an interest payment of $0.10\,r_B B_L$ on his personal borrowings. In either case, the dollar returns are identical. The costs of the two strategies are

Cost of strategy II	Cost of strategy III
$0.10 \times (V_L - B_L)$	$0.10 \times (V_U - B_L)$

Because the dollar returns on the two strategies are identical, the costs must be identical as well. The costs of the two strategies are equal only when $V_L = V_U$.[6] This proves that

MM Proposition I (no taxes):	The value of the unlevered firm is the same as the value of the levered firm, that is, $V_L = V_U$.

Though this discussion may strike you as mathematical, the intuition can be explained as follows. Suppose that our result did not hold. For example, suppose that the value of the levered firm were actually greater than the value of the unlevered firm, that is, $V_L > V_U$. Mr. Allen could borrow on his own account and invest in the stock of the Unlever Company. He would get the same dollar returns as if he had invested in the levered firm. However, his cost would be less because $V_L > V_U$. The strategy would not be unique to Mr. Allen. Given $V_L > V_U$, no rational individual would ever invest in Lever. Anyone desiring shares in Lever would get the same dollar return more cheaply by borrowing to finance a purchase of Unlever's shares. The equilibrium result would be, of course, that the value of Lever would fall and the value of Unlever would rise until $V_L = V_U$. At this point, individuals would prefer neither strategy II nor strategy III over the other.

This is perhaps the most important example in all of corporate finance. In fact, it is considered the beginning point of modern managerial finance. Before MM, the effect of leverage on the value of the firm was considered complex and convoluted. Modigliani and Miller showed a blindingly simple result: If levered firms are priced too high, rational investors will simply borrow on personal account to buy shares in unlevered firms. This substitution is often called *homemade leverage*. As long as individuals borrow (and lend) on the same terms as the firm, they can duplicate the effects of corporate leverage on their own.[7]

---

[6]Table 15.1 tells us that $V_U = \$1,000$. Hence $V_L = \$1,000$. Because $V_L = S_L + B_L$, $S_L = \$500$.

[7]If our investor held shares in Lever Company, he could lend on personal account to create cash flows identical to those from holding Unlever Company.

The above example shows that leverage does not affect the value of the firm. Since we showed earlier that shareholders' welfare is directly related to the firm's value, the example indicates that changes in capital structure cannot affect the shareholders' welfare.

CONCEPT QUESTIONS

- State MM Proposition I. What are its assumptions?
- How can a shareholder undo a firm's financial leverage?

Financial Leverage and Firm Value: An Example   15.4

The financial management of the Trans Can Corporation currently has no debt in its capital structure. The chief financial officer, Ms. Morris, is considering issuing debt to buy back some of its equity. Both its current and proposed capital structures are presented in Table 15.2. The firm's assets are $8,000,000. There are 400,000 shares of the all-equity firm, implying a market value per share of $20. The proposed debt issue is for $4,000,000, leaving $4,000,000 in equity. The interest rate is 10 percent.

Ms. Morris believes the firm's shareholders will be better off with a debt issue. To justify her conclusion, she has prepared Table 15.3, which shows both the company's current structure and its proposed structure under three different, equally probable economic scenarios.

She concludes from her analysis that

1. The effect of financial leverage depends on the company's income. If income is equal to $1,200,000, the return on equity (ROE) is higher under the proposed structure. If income is equal to $400,000, the ROE is higher under the existing structure.

This is represented in her graph, which we have reproduced as Figure 15.2. The solid line represents the case of no leverage. The line begins at the origin, indicating that earnings per share (EPS) would be zero if earnings before interest (EBI) were zero. The EPS rises in tandem with a rise in EBI.

The dotted line represents the case of $4,000,000 of debt. Here, EPS is negative if EBI is zero. This follows because $400,000 of interest must be paid regardless of the firm's profits. The slope of the dotted line (the line with debt) is steeper than the solid

	Current	Proposed
Assets	$8,000,000	$8,000,000
Debt	0	$4,000,000
Equity (market and book)	$8,000,000	$4,000,000
Interest rate	10%	10%
Market value/share	$20	$20
Shares outstanding	400,000	200,000

Table 15.2
Financial structure of Trans Can Corporation

The proposed capital structure has leverage, whereas the current structure is all equity.

Table 15.3 Alternative capital structures for Trans Can Corporation

	Current structure: no debt			Proposed structure: debt = $4,000,000		
	Recession	Expected	Expansion	Recession	Expected	Expansion
Return on assets (ROA)	5%	15%	25%	5%	15%	25%
Earnings before interest (EBI)	$400,000	$1,200,000	$2,000,000	$400,000	$1,200,000	$2,000,000
Interest	(0)	(0)	(0)	($400,000)	($400,000)	($400,000)
Earnings after interest	$400,000	$1,200,000	$2,000,000	0	$800,000	$1,600,000
Return on equity (ROE) = Net income/Equity	5%	15%	25%	0	20%	40%
Earnings per share (EPS)	$1.00	$3.00	$5.00	0	$4.00	$8.00

When EBI is high, Trans Can has higher EPS and ROE with the proposed structure than with the current structure. When EBI is low, Trans Can has lower EPS and ROE with the proposed structure. Thus, the equityholders bear more risk with the proposed structure.

Figure 15.2
Financial leverage:
EPS and EBI for
the Trans Can
Corporation

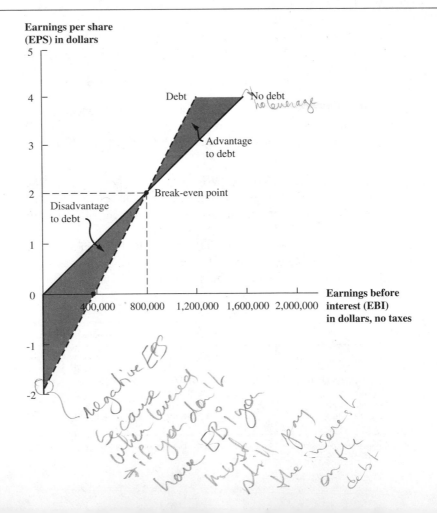

Trans Can: Proposed capital structure	Recession	Expected	Expansion
EPS	$0	$4	$8
Earnings per 100 shares	$0	$400	$800
Initial cost = 100 shares @ $20/share = $2,000			

Table 15.4
Payoff and cost to shareholders of Trans Can Corporation under the proposed structure and under the current structure with homemade leverage

Homemade leverage by shareholders of Trans Can	Recession	Expected	Expansion
Earnings per 200 shares in current Trans Can	$1 × 200 = $200	$3 × 200 = $600	$5 × 200 = $1,000
Interest at 10% on $2,000	−$200	−$200	−$200
Net	$0	$400	$800
Initial cost = 200 shares @ $20/share − $2,000 = $2,000			
Cost of stock Cost of debt			

Investor receives the same payoff whether she (1) buys shares in a levered corporation or (2) buys shares in an unlevered firm and borrows on personal account. Her initial investment is the same in either case. Thus, the firm neither helps nor hurts her by adding to capital structure.

line's slope. This occurs because the levered firm has fewer shares of stock outstanding than does the unlevered firm. Therefore, any increase in EBI leads to a greater rise in EPS for the levered firm because the earnings increase is distributed over fewer shares of stock.

Because the dotted line has a lower intercept but a steeper slope, the two lines must intersect. The *break-even* point occurs at $800,000 of EBI. If earnings before interest were $800,000, both firms would produce $2 of earnings per share. Because $800,000 is break-even, earnings above $800,000 lead to greater EPS for the levered firm. Earnings below $800,000 lead to greater EPS for the unlevered firm.

2. Because the expected income is $1,200,000, she reasons that the shareholders are better off under the proposed capital structure.

Mr. Zeldes, a financial consultant hired by the Trans Can Corporation, argues that the analysis in point (1) is correct, but the conclusion in point (2) is incorrect. He states that the shareholders of Trans Can can borrow on personal account if they want to duplicate the company's proposed financial leverage. The consultant considers an investor who would buy 100 shares of the proposed levered equity. Alternatively, the investor could buy 200 shares of the unlevered firm, partially financing his purchase by borrowing $2,000. Both the cost and the payoff from the two strategies will be the same. Thus, Mr. Zeldes concludes that Trans Can is neither helping nor hurting its shareholders by restructuring. In other words, investors aren't receiving anything from corporate leverage that they couldn't achieve on their own. His calculations are presented in Table 15.4.

His sidekick, Mr. Weiss, then stated, "This is nothing more than a discussion of the Modigliani–Miller relationship. Because individuals can create homemade leverage, there is no need for corporate leverage." He then related the story of the world's stupidest criminal. It seems someone hijacked a commercial airplane, commanding it to go to Toronto. However, Toronto was the scheduled destination anyway. Mr. Weiss concluded, "The hijacker's action neither helped nor hurt the passengers. Similarly, a change in corporate leverage can neither help nor hurt the stockholders."

A Key Assumption

The MM result hinges on the assumption that individuals can borrow as cheaply as corporations. If, alternatively, individuals can only borrow at a higher rate, one can easily show that corporations can increase firm value by borrowing.

Is this assumption of equal borrowing costs a good one? Individuals who want to buy stock and borrow can do so by establishing a margin account with a broker. Under this arrangement, the broker loans the individual a portion of the purchase price. For example, the individual might buy $10,000 of stock by investing $6,000 of personal funds and borrowing $4,000 from the broker. Should the stock be worth $9,000 on the next day, the individual's net worth or equity in the account would be $5,000 = $9,000 − $4,000.[8]

The broker fears that a sudden price drop will cause the equity in the individual's account to be negative, implying that the broker may not get the loan repaid in full. To guard against this possibility, stock exchange rules require that the individual make additional cash contributions (replenish the margin account) as the stock price falls. Because (1) the procedures for replenishing the account have developed over many years and (2) the broker holds the stock as collateral, there is little default risk to the broker.[9] In particular, if margin contributions are not made on time, the broker can sell the stock in order to satisfy the loan. Therefore, brokers generally charge low interest, with many rates being only slightly above the risk-free rate.

By contrast, corporations frequently borrow using illiquid assets (plant and equipment) as collateral. The costs to the lender of initial negotiation and ongoing supervision, as well as of working out arrangements in the event of financial distress, can be quite substantial. Thus, it is difficult to argue that individuals must borrow at higher rates than corporations can.[10]

This is, of course, the argument of MM Proposition I.

CONCEPT QUESTIONS

- Describe financial leverage.
- What is levered equity?
- How can a shareholder of Trans Can undo the company's financial leverage?

15.5   Modigliani and Miller: Proposition II (No Taxes)

At a corporate meeting where both Ms. Morris and Mr. Zeldes presented their viewpoints, a corporate officer said, "Well, maybe it does not matter whether the corporation or the individual levers—as long as some leverage takes place. Leverage benefits investors. After all, the investor's expected return rises with the amount of leverage

---

[8]We are ignoring the one-day interest charge on the loan.

[9]Had this text been published before October 19, 1987, when stock prices declined by more than 10 percent in one day, we might have used the phrase *virtually no risk* instead of *little risk*.

[10]One caveat is in order. Initial margin or borrowing is currently limited by law to 50 percent of value. Certain companies, like financial institutions, borrow over 90 percent of their firm's market value. Individuals borrowing against the stock of all-equity corporations cannot duplicate the debt of more highly levered corporations.

present." He then pointed out that, from Table 15.3, the expected return on unlevered equity is 15 percent while the expected return on levered equity is 20 percent.

Mr. Zeldes replied, "Not necessarily. Though the expected return rises with leverage, the *risk* increases as well. Note in Table 15.3 that the ROE varies only between 5 and 25 percent in the all-equity case while varying between 0 and 40 percent in the levered case. In other words, the slope in the figure is greater for the levered equity than for the unlevered equity. Therefore, the increase in expected return is merely compensation for the increase in risk." Then he stated that the 15- and 20-percent figures in Table 15.3 should be viewed as the return the market requires on unlevered and levered equity, respectively.

This type of reasoning allows us to develop **MM Proposition II.** Here, Modigliani and Miller argue that the expected return on equity is positively related to leverage, because the risk of equity increases with leverage. *also return of equity*

To develop this position, recall from Chapter 12 that the firm's weighted average cost of capital, r_{WACC}, can be written as [11]

$$\frac{B}{B + S} \times r_B + \frac{S}{B + S} \times r_S \tag{15.2}$$

where

r_B is the interest rate, also called the *cost of debt*

r_S is the expected return on equity, also called the *cost of equity* or the *required return on equity*

r_{WACC} is the firm's weighted average cost of capital

B is the value of debt

S is the value of stock or equity

Formula (15.2) is quite intuitive. It simply says that a firm's weighted average cost of capital is a weighted average of its cost of debt and its cost of equity. The weight applied to debt is the proportion of debt in the capital structure, and the weight applied to equity is the proportion of equity in the capital structure. Calculations of r_{WACC} from (15.2) for both the unlevered and the levered firm are presented in Table 15.5.

An implication of MM Propostion I is that r_{WACC} is a constant for a given firm, regardless of the capital structure.[12] For example, Table 15.5 shows that r_{WACC} for Trans Can is 15 percent, with or without leverage.

Let us now define r_0 to be the cost of capital for an all-equity firm. For the Trans Can Corp.,

$$r_0 = \frac{\text{Expected earnings to unlevered firm}}{\text{Unlevered equity}} = \frac{\$1,200,000}{\$8,000,000} = 15\%$$

As can be seen from Table 15.5, r_{WACC} is equal to r_0 for Trans Can. In fact, r_{WACC} must always equal r_0 in a world without corporate taxes.

---

[11]Since we do not have taxes here, the cost of debt is r_B, not $r_B (1 - T_C)$ as it was in Chapter 12.

[12]This statement holds in a world of no taxes. It does not hold in a world with taxes, a point to be brought out later in this chapter. (See Figure 15.6.)

Table 15.5
Cost of capital
calculations for
Trans Can

$$r_{WACC} = \frac{B}{B+S} \times r_B + \frac{S}{B+S} \times r_S$$

Unlevered
firm: $15\% = \dfrac{0}{\$8,000,000} \times 10\%* + \dfrac{\$8,000,000}{\$8,000,000} \times 15\%\dagger$

Levered
firm: $15\% = \dfrac{\$4,000,000}{\$8,000,000} \times 10\%* + \dfrac{\$4,000,000}{\$8,000,000} \times 20\%\ddagger$

*10% is the interest rate.
†From the "expected" column in Table 15.3, we learn that expected earnings
after interest are $1,200,000. From Table 15.2, we learn that equity is $8,000,000.
Thus, r_S for the unlevered firm is

$$\frac{\text{Expected earnings after interest}}{\text{Equity}} = \frac{\$1,200,000}{\$8,000,000} = 15\%$$

‡From the "expected" column in Table 15.3, we learn that expected earnings
after interest are $800,000. From Table 15.2, we learn that equity is $4,000,000.
Thus, r_S for the levered firm is

$$\frac{\text{Expected earnings after interest}}{\text{Equity}} = \frac{\$800,000}{\$4,000,000} = 20\%.$$

Proposition II states the expected return on equity in terms of leverage. The exact relationship, derived by setting $r_{WACC} = r_0$ and then rearranging (15.2), is[13]

MM Proposition II (No Taxes):

$$r_S = r_0 + \frac{B}{S}(r_0 - r_B) \tag{15.3}$$

Equation (15.3) states that the required return on equity is a linear function of the firm's debt-to-equity ratio. Examining equation (15.3), we see that if r_0 exceeds the debt rate, r_B, then the cost of equity rises with increases in the debt-equity ratio, B/S.[14]

Figure 15.3 graphs equation (15.3). As you can see, we have plotted the relation between the cost of equity, r_S, and the debt-equity ratio, B/S, as a straight line.

What we witness in equation (15.3) and illustrate in Figure 15.3 is the effect of leverage on the cost of equity. As the firm raises the debt-equity ratio, each dollar of equity is levered with additional debt. This increases the risk of equity and therefore the required return, r_S, on the equity.

---

[13]This can be derived from (15.2) by setting $r_{WACC} = r_0$ and then switching all terms to the opposite side:

$$\frac{B}{B+S} r_B + \frac{S}{B+S} r_S = r_0$$

Multiplying both sides by $(B + S)/S$ yields

$$\frac{B}{S} r_B + r_S = \frac{B+S}{S} r_0$$

We can rewrite the right-hand side as

$$\frac{B}{S} r_B + r_S = \frac{B}{S} r_0 + r_0$$

Moving $(B/S)r_B$ to the right-hand side and rearranging yields

$$r_S = r_0 + \frac{B}{S}(r_0 - r_B) \tag{15.3}$$

[14]Normally, r_0 should exceed r_B. That is, because even unlevered equity is risky, it should have an expected return greater than that on riskless debt.

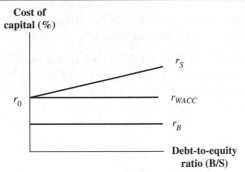

Figure 15.3
The cost of equity, the cost of debt, and the weighted average cost of capital: MM Proposition II with no corporate taxes

$$r_S = r_0 + (r_0 - r_B)B/S$$

r_S is the cost of equity.

r_B is the cost of debt.

r_0 is the cost of capital for an all-equity firm.

r_{WACC} is a firm's weighted average cost of capital. In a world with no taxes, r_{WACC} for a levered firm is equal to r_0.

The cost of equity capital, r_S, is positively related to the firm's debt-equity ratio. The firm's weighted average cost of capital, r_{WACC}, is invariant to the firm's debt-equity ratio.

Example Illustrating Proposition I and Proposition II

▪ *Example*

Luteran Motors, an all-equity firm, has an expected cash flow of $10 million per year in perpetuity. There are 10 million shares outstanding, implying expected annual cash flow of $1 per share. The cost of capital for this unlevered firm is 10 percent. The firm will soon build a new plant for $4 million. The plant is expected to generate additional cash flow of $1 million per year. These figures can be described as

Current company	New plant
Cash flow: $10 million	Initial outlay: $4 million
Number of outstanding shares: 10 million	Additional annual cash flow: $1 million

The project's net present value is

$$-\$4 \text{ million} + \frac{\$1 \text{ million}}{0.1} = \$6 \text{ million}$$

assuming that the project is discounted at the same rate as the firm as a whole. Before the market knows of the project, the *market value balance sheet* of the firm is

LUTERAN MOTORS
Balance Sheet (all equity)

Old assets: $\dfrac{\$10 \text{ million}}{0.1} = \$100$ million	Equity: $100 million (10 million shares of stock)

The value of the firm is $100 million, because the cash flows of $10 million per year are capitalized at 10 percent. A share of stock sells for $10 (or $100 million/10 million) because there are 10 million shares outstanding. ∎

The market value balance sheet is a useful tool of financial analysis. Because students are often thrown off guard by it initially, we recommend extra study here. The key is that the market value balance sheet has the same form as the balance sheet that accountants use. That is, assets are placed on the left-hand side whereas liabilities and owners' equity are placed on the right-hand side. In addition, the left-hand side and the right-hand side must be equal. The difference is in the numbers. Accountants value items in terms of historical cost (original purchase price less depreciation), whereas financial people value items in terms of market value.

The firm will either issue $4 million of equity or debt. Let us consider the effect of equity and debt financing in turn.

Share Financing

Imagine that the firm announces that, in the near future, it will raise $4 million in equity in order to build a new plant. The stock price will rise to reflect the positive net present value of the plant. According to efficient markets, the increase occurs immediately. That is, the rise occurs on the day of the announcement, not on the date of either the onset of construction of the power plant or the forthcoming stock offering. The market value balance sheet becomes

LUTERAN MOTORS
Balance Sheet
(upon announcement of equity issue to construct plant)

Old assets	$100 million	Equity	$106 million
			(10 million shares of stock)
NPV of plant:			
$-\$4 \text{ million} + \dfrac{\$1 \text{ million}}{0.1}$ = 6 million			
Total assets	$106 million		

Note that the NPV of the plant is included in the market value balance sheet. Because the new shares have not yet been issued, the number of outstanding shares remains 10 million. The price per share has now risen to $10.60 (or $106/10 million) to reflect news concerning the plant.

Shortly thereafter, $4 million of stock is floated. Because the stock is selling at $10.60 per share, 377,358 (or $4 million/$10.60) shares of stock are issued. Imagine that funds are put in the bank *temporarily* before being used to build the plant. The market value balance sheet becomes

LUTERAN MOTORS
Balance Sheet
(upon issuance of stock but before construction begins on plant)

Old assets	$100 million	Equity	$110 million
			(10,377,358 shares of stock)
NPV of plant	6 million		
Proceeds from new issue of stock	4 million		
(currently invested in bank)			
Total assets	$110 million		

The number of shares outstanding is now 10,377,358 because 377,358 new shares were issued. The price per share is $10.60 ($110,000,000/10,377,358). Note that the price has not changed. This is consistent with efficient capital markets, because stock price should only move due to new information.

Of course, the funds are placed in the bank only temporarily. Shortly after the new issue, the $4 million is given to a contractor who builds the plant. To avoid problems in discounting, we assume that the plant is built immediately. The balance sheet then becomes

LUTERAN MOTORS
Balance Sheet
(upon completion of the plant)

Old assets	$100 million	Equity	$110 million
			(10,377,358 shares of stock)
PV of plant: $\dfrac{\$1\text{ million}}{0.1}$ = 10 million			
Total assets	$110 million		

Though total assets do not change, the composition of the assets does change. The bank account has been emptied to pay the contractor. The present value of cash flows of $1 million a year from the plant are reflected as an asset worth $10 million. Because the building expenditures of $4 million have already been paid, they no longer represent a future cost. Hence, they no longer reduce the value of the plant. According to efficient capital markets, the price per share of stock remains $10.60.

Expected yearly cash flow from the firm is $11 million, $10 million of which comes from the old assets and $1 million from the new. The expected return to equityholders is

$$r_S = \frac{\$11\text{ million}}{\$110\text{ million}} = 0.10$$

Because the firm is all equity, $r_S = r_0 = 0.10$.

Debt Financing

Alternatively, imagine that the firm announces that, in the near future, it will borrow $4 million at 6 percent to build a new plant. This implies yearly interest payments of $240,000 (or $4,000,000 × 6%). Again the stock price rises immediately to reflect the positive net present value of the plant. Thus, we have

LUTERAN MOTORS
Balance Sheet
(upon announcement of debt issue to construct plant)

Old assets	$100 million	Equity	$106 million
			(10 million shares of stock)
NPV of plant:			
$-\$4\text{ million} + \dfrac{\$1\text{ million}}{0.1}$ = 6 million			
Total assets	$106 million		

The value of the firm is the same as in the equity financing case because (1) the same plant is to be built and (2) MM prove that debt financing is neither better nor worse than equity financing.

At some point, $4 million of debt is issued. As before, the funds are placed in the bank temporarily. The market value balance sheet becomes

LUTERAN MOTORS
Balance Sheet
(upon debt issuance but before construction begins on plant)

Old assets	$100 million	Debt	$ 4 million
NPV of plant	6 million	Equity	106 million
			(10 million shares of stock)
Proceeds from debt issue			
(currently invested in bank)	4 million		
Total assets	$110 million	Debt plus equity	$110 million

Note that debt appears on the right-hand side of the balance sheet. The stock price is still $10.60, in accordance with our discussion of efficient capital markets.

Finally, the contractor receives $4 million and builds the plant. The market value balance sheet becomes

LUTERAN MOTORS
Balance Sheet
(upon completion of the plant)

Old assets	$100 million	Debt	$ 4 million
PV of plant	10 million	Equity	106 million
			(10 million shares of stock)
Total assets	$110 million	Debt plus equity	$110 million

The only change here is that the bank account has been depleted to pay the contractor. The equityholders expect yearly cash flow after interest of

$$\underset{\substack{\text{Cash flow on}\\\text{old assets}}}{\$10,000,000} + \underset{\substack{\text{Cash flow on}\\\text{new assets}}}{\$1,000,000} - \underset{\substack{\text{Interest:}\\\$4 \text{ million} \times 6\%}}{\$240,000} = \$10,760,000$$

The equityholders expect to earn a return of

$$\frac{\$10,760,000}{\$106,000,000} = 10.15\%$$

This return of 10.15 percent for levered equityholders is higher than the 10 percent return for the unlevered equityholders. This result is sensible because, as we argued earlier, levered equity is riskier. In fact, the return of 10.15 percent should be exactly what MM Proposition II predicts. This prediction can be verified by plugging values into

$$r_S = r_0 + \frac{B}{S}(r_0 - r_B) \tag{15.3}$$

We obtain

$$10.15\% = 10\% + \frac{\$4,000,000}{\$106,000,000} \times (10\% - 6\%)$$

This example was useful for two reasons. First, we wanted to introduce the concept of market value balance sheets, a tool that will prove useful elsewhere in the text. Among other things, this technique allows one to calculate the price per share of a new issue of stock. Second, the example illustrates three aspects of Modigliani and Miller:

1. The example is consistent with MM Proposition I because the value of the firm is $110 million after either equity or debt financing.

2. Students are often more interested in stock price than in firm value. We show that the stock price is always $10.60, regardless of whether debt or equity financing is used.

3. The example is consistent with MM Proposition II. The expected return to equityholders rises from 10 to 10.15 percent, just as formula (15.3) states.

MM: An Interpretation

The Modigliani–Miller results indicate that managers of a firm cannot change its value by repackaging the firm's securities. Though this idea was considered revolutionary when it was originally proposed in the late 1950s, the MM model and arbitrage proof have since met with wide acclaim.[15]

MM argue that the firm's overall cost of capital cannot be reduced as debt is substituted for equity, even though debt appears to be cheaper than equity. The reason for this is that, as the firm adds debt, the remaining equity becomes more risky. As this risk rises, the cost of equity capital rises as a result. The increase in the cost of the remaining equity capital offsets the higher proportion of the firm financed by low-cost debt. In fact, MM prove that the two effects exactly offset each other, so that both the value of the firm and the firm's overall cost of capital are invariant to leverage.

MM use an interesting analogy to food. They consider a dairy farmer with two choices. Either he can sell whole milk or, by skimming, he can sell a combination of cream and low-fat milk. Though the farmer can get a high price for the cream, he gets a low price for the low-fat milk, implying no net gain. In fact, imagine that the proceeds from the whole milk strategy were less than those from the cream/low-fat milk strategy. Arbitrageurs would buy the whole milk, perform the skimming operation themselves, and resell the cream and low-fat milk separately. Competition between arbitrageurs would tend to boost the price of whole milk until proceeds from the two strategies became equal. Thus, the value of the farmer's milk is invariant with the way in which the milk is packaged.

Food found its way into this chapter earlier, when we viewed the firm as a pie.[16] MM argue that the size of the pie does not change, no matter how shareholders and bondholders divide it. MM say that a firm's capital structure is irrelevant; it is what it is by some historical accident. The theory implies that firms' debt-equity ratios could be anything. They are what they are because of whimsical and random managerial decisions about how much to borrow and how much stock to issue.

---

[15]Franco Modigliani and Merton Miller have each won the Nobel Prize in Economics, in part for their work on capital structure.

[16]Other authors have also brought food into discussions on capital structure. For example, Stewart Myers in "The Search for Optimal Capital Structure," *Midland Corporate Finance Journal* (Spring 1983), used chicken. Abstracting from the extra costs in cutting up poultry, he argues that all of the chicken parts should, in sum, sell for no more than a whole chicken.

Although scholars are always fascinated with far-reaching theories, students are perhaps more concerned with real-world applications. Do real-world managers follow MM by treating capital structure decisions with indifference? Unfortunately for the theory, virtually all companies in certain industries, such as banking, choose high debt-to-equity ratios. Conversely, companies in other industries, such as pharmaceuticals, choose low debt-to-equity ratios. In fact, almost any industry has a debt-to-equity ratio to which companies in that industry adhere. Thus, companies do not appear to be selecting their degree of leverage in a frivolous or random manner. Because of this, financial economists (including MM themselves) have argued that real world factors may have been left out of the theory.

Though many of our students have argued that individuals can only borrow at rates above the corporate borrowing rate, we disagreed with this argument earlier in the chapter. But when we look elsewhere for unrealistic assumptions in the theory, we find two:[17]

1. Taxes were ignored.
2. Bankruptcy costs and other agency costs were not considered.

We will turn to taxes shortly. Bankruptcy costs and other agency costs will be treated in the next chapter. But first, in the next box, Professor Merton Miller relates how the Modigliani–Miller results aren't easy to fully understand.

CONCEPT QUESTIONS

- Why does the expected return on equity rise with firm leverage?
- What is the exact relationship between the expected return on equity and firm leverage?
- How are market value balance sheets set up?

The Modigliani-Miller Results, in Professor Miller's Words

How difficult to summarize briefly the contribution of the [Modigliani–Miller] papers was brought home to me very clearly last October after Franco Modigliani was awarded the Nobel Prize in Economics in part—but, of course, only in part—for the work in finance. The television camera crews from our local stations in Chicago immediately descended upon me. "We understand," they said, "that you worked with Modigliani some years back in developing these M and M theorems, and we wonder if you could explain them briefly to our television viewers."

"How briefly?" I asked.

(*continued*)

---

[17]MM were aware of both of these issues, as can be seen in their original paper.

"Oh, take ten seconds," was the reply.

Ten seconds to explain the work of a lifetime! Ten seconds to describe two carefully reasoned articles, each running to more than thirty printed pages and each with sixty or so long footnotes! When they saw the look of dismay on my face, they said, "You don't have to go into details. Just give us the main points in simple, common-sense terms."

The main point of the first or cost of capital article was, in principle at least, simple enough to make. It said that in an economist's ideal world of complete and perfect capital markets and with full and symmetric information among all market participants, the total market value of all the securities issued by a firm was governed by the earning power and risk of its underlying real assets and was independent of how the mix of securities issued to finance it was divided between debt instruments and equity capital . . .

Such a summary, however, uses too many shorthanded terms and concepts, like perfect capital markets, that are rich in connotations to economists but hardly so to the general public. So I thought, instead, of an analogy that we ourselves had invoked in the original paper . . .

"Think of the firm," I said, "as a gigantic tub of whole milk. The farmer can sell the whole milk as is. Or he can separate out the cream and sell it at a considerably higher price than the whole milk would bring. (That's the analog of a firm selling low-yield and hence high-priced debt securities.) But, of course, what the farmer would have left would be skim milk with low butterfat content and that would sell for much less than whole milk. That corresponds to the levered equity. The M and M proposition says that if there were no costs of separation (and, of course, no government dairy support programs), the cream plus the skim milk would bring the same price as the whole milk."

The television people conferred among themselves and came back to inform me that it was too long, too complicated, and too academic.

"Don't you have anything simpler?" they asked. I thought of another way that the M and M proposition is presented these days, which emphasizes the notion of market completeness and stresses the role of securities as devices for "partitioning" a firm's payoffs in each possible state of the world among the group of its capital suppliers.

"Think of the firm," I said, "as a gigantic pizza, divided into quarters. If now you cut each quarter in half in eighths, the M and M proposition says that you will have more pieces but not more pizza."

Again there was a whispered conference among the camera crew, and the director came back and said, "Professor, we understand from the press release that there were two M and M propositions. Can we try the other one?" [Professor Miller tried valiantly to explain the second proposition, though this was apparently even more difficult to get across. After his attempt:]

Once again there was a whispered conversation. They shut the lights off. They folded up their equipment. They thanked me for giving them the time. They said that they'd get back to me. But I knew that I had somehow lost my chance to start a new career as a packager of economic wisdom for TV viewers in convenient ten-second bites. Some have the talent for it . . . and some just don't.

Source: GSB Chicago, University of Chicago (Autumn 1986).

Figure 15.4
Two pie models of
capital structure
under corporate
taxes

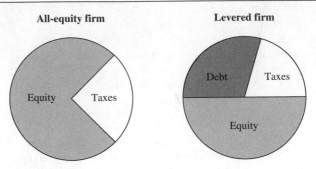

The levered firm pays less in taxes than does the all-equity firm.
Thus, sum of debt plus equity is greater for the levered firm.

15.6   Taxes

The Basic Insight

We now show that, in the presence of corporate taxes, the firm's value is positively related to its debt. The basic intuition can be seen from a pie chart, such as the one in Figure 15.4. Consider the all-equity firm on the left. Here, both equityholders and Revenue Canada have claims on the value of the firm. The value of the all-equity firm is, of course, that owned by the equityholders. The proportion going to taxes is simply a cost.

The pie on the right for the levered firm shows three claims: equityholders, debtholders, and taxes. The value of the levered firm is the sum of the value of the debt and the value of the equity. In selecting between the two capital structures in the picture, a financial manager should select the one with the higher value. Assuming that the total area is the same for both pies,[18] value is maximized for that capital structure paying the least in taxes. In other words, the manager should choose the capital structure with which Revenue Canada would be less pleased.

We will show that, due to a quirk in Canadian tax law, the proportion of the pie allocated to taxes is less for the levered firm than it is for the unlevered firm. Thus, managers should select high leverage.

The Quirk in the Tax Code

■ *Example*

The Water Products Company is evaluating two financing plans. The Water Products Company has a corporate tax rate, T_C, of 40 percent and expected earnings before interest and taxes (EBIT) of $1 million. The cost of debt, r_B, is 10 percent for both plans. Under plan I, Water Products has no debt in its capital structure. Under plan II, the company would have $4,000,000 of debt, B.

---

[18]Under the MM propositions developed earlier, the two pies should be of the same size.

The chief financial officer for Water Products makes the following calculations:

	Plan I No debt	Plan II
Earnings before interest and taxes (EBIT)	$1,000,000	$1,000,000
Interest ($r_B B$)	0	(400,000)
Earnings before taxes (EBT) = (EBIT − $r_B B$)	1,000,000	600,000
Taxes ($T_C = 0.40$)	(400,000)	(240,000)
Earnings after corporate taxes (EAT) = [(EBIT − $r_B B$) × (1 − T_C)]	600,000	360,000
Total cash flow to both shareholders and bondholders [EBIT × (1 − T_C) + $T_C r_B B$]	600,000	760,000

[handwritten margin note: HMB of debt ↓ tax shield to bond holders]

The most relevant numbers for our purposes are the two on the bottom line. Here, we see that more cash flow reaches the owners of the firm (both shareholders and bondholders) under plan II. The difference is $160,000 = $760,000 − $600,000. It does not take us long to realize the source of this difference. Revenue Canada receives less taxes under plan II ($240,000) than it does under plan I ($400,000). The difference here is $160,000 = $400,000 − $240,000.

This difference occurs because Revenue Canada handles interest differently than it does earnings going to shareholders.[19] Interest totally escapes corporate taxation, whereas earnings after interest but before corporate taxes (EBT) are taxed at the 40 percent rate. We express this relationship algebraically below.

We will assume in this discussion that all cash flows are constant (that is, perpetual without growth). If EBIT is the total cash flow of the firm before interest and taxes, and if we ignore the effect of depreciation and other items such as taxes, then the taxable income of an all-equity firm is simply EBIT.

For an all-equity firm, total taxes are

$$EBIT \times T_C$$

where T_C is the corporate tax rate. Earnings after corporate taxes are

$$EBIT \times (1 − T_C) \tag{15.4}$$

For a levered firm, taxable income is

$$EBIT − r_B B$$

Total taxes are

$$T_C \times (EBIT − r_B B)$$

Cash flow going to the shareholders is

$$EBIT − r_B B − T_C \times (EBIT − r_B B) = (EBIT − r_B B) \times (1 − T_C)$$

Cash flow going to both the shareholders and the bondholders is

$$EBIT \times (1 − T_C) + T_C r_B B \tag{15.5}$$

which quite explicitly depends on the amount of debt financing.

---

[19]Note that shareholders actually receive more under plan I ($600,000) than under plan II ($360,000). Students are often bothered by this since it seems to imply that shareholders are better off without leverage. However, remember that there are more shares outstanding in plan I than in plan II. A full-blown model would show that earnings per share are higher with leverage.

The key can be seen by comparing the difference between expressions (15.4) and (15.5). The difference, $T_C r_B B$, is the extra cash flow going to investors in the levered firm. We use the term *investors* to mean both shareholders and bondholders. It is also the extra funds not going to Revenue Canada.

Let's calculate this difference for Water Products:

$$T_C r_B B = 40\% \times 10\% \times \$4,000,000 = \$160,000$$

This is the same number that we calculated above. ∎

Value of the Tax Shield

The discussion above shows a tax advantage to debt or, equivalently, a tax disadvantage to equity. We now want to value this advantage. We previously said that the cash flow of the levered firm each period is greater than the cash flow of the unlevered firm by

$$T_C r_B B \tag{15.6}$$

Expression (15.6) is often called the *tax shield from debt.*

As long as the firm expects to be in a positive tax bracket, we can assume that the cash flow in expression (15.6) has the same risk as the interest on the debt. Thus, its value can be determined by discounting at the interest rate, r_B. Assuming that the cash flows are perpetual, the value of the tax shield is

$$\frac{T_C r_B B}{r_B} = T_C B$$

Value of the Levered Firm

We have just calculated the present value of the tax shield from debt. Our next step is to calculate the value of the levered firm. We showed above that the after-tax cash flow to the shareholders in the levered firm is

$$\text{EBIT} \times (1 - T_C) + T_C r_B B \tag{15.5}$$

The first term in expression (15.5) is the after-tax cash flow in the unlevered firm. The value of an unlevered firm (that is, a firm with no debt) is the present value of EBIT $\times (1 - T_C)$,

$$V_U = \frac{\text{EBIT} \times (1 - T_C)}{r_0}$$

where

$$V_U = \text{Present value of an unlevered firm}$$
$$\text{EBIT} \times (1 - T_C) = \text{Firm cash flows after corporate taxes}$$
$$T_C = \text{Corporate tax rate}$$
$$r_0 = \text{The cost of capital to an all-equity firm (as can be seen from}$$
$$\text{the formula, } r_0 \text{ now discounts } \textit{after-tax} \text{ cash flows)}$$

The second part of the cash flows, $T_C r_B B$, is the tax shield. To determine its value, the tax shield should be discounted at r_B.

As a consequence, we have[20]

MM Proposition I (Corporate Taxes):

$$V_L = \frac{\text{EBIT} \times (1 - T_C)}{r_0} + \frac{T_C r_B B}{r_B}$$

(15.7)

$$= V_U + T_C B$$

Equation (15.7) is **MM Proposition I under corporate taxes.** The first term in equation (15.7) is the value of the cash flows of the firm with no debt tax shield. In other words, this term is equal to V_U, the value of the all-equity firm. The value of the firm is the value of an all-equity firm plus $T_C B$, the tax rate times the value of the debt. T_C is the present value of the tax shield in the case of perpetual cash flows.[21]

The Water Products example reveals that, because the tax shield increases with the amount of debt, the firm can raise its total cash flow and its value by substituting debt for equity. We now have a clear example of why the capital structure does matter: By raising the debt-equity ratio, the firm can lower its taxes and thereby increase its total value. The strong forces that operate to maximize the value of the firm would seem to push it toward an all-debt capital structure.

▪ Example

Divided Airlines is currently an unlevered firm. It is considering a capital restructuring to allow $200 of debt. The company expects to generate $166.67 in cash flows before interest and taxes, in perpetuity. The corporate tax rate is 40 percent, implying after-tax cash flows of $100. Its cost of debt capital is 10 percent. Unlevered firms in the same industry have a cost of equity capital of 20 percent. What will the new value of Divided Airlines be?

---

[20]This relationship holds when the debt level is assumed to be constant through time. A different formula would apply if the debt-equity ratio were assumed to be a constant over time. For a deeper treatment of this point, see J. A. Miles and J. R. Ezzell, "The Weighted Average Cost of Capital, Perfect Capital Markets and Project Life," *Journal of Financial and Quantitative Analysis* (September 1980).

[21]The following example calculates the present value if we assume the debt has a finite life. Suppose the Maxwell Company has $1 million in debt with an 8-percent coupon rate. If the debt matures in two years and the cost of debt capital, r_B, is 10 percent, what is the present value of the tax shields if the corporate tax rate is 40 percent? The debt is amortized in equal installments over two years.

Year	Loan balance	Interest	Tax shield	Present value of tax shield
0	$1,000,000			
1	500,000	$80,000	0.4×$80,000	$29,090.91
2	0	40,000	0.4×$40,000	13,223.14
				$42,314.05

The present value of the tax savings is

$$\text{PV} = \frac{0.40 \times \$80,000}{1.10} + \frac{0.40 \times \$40,000}{(1.10)^2} = \$42,314.05$$

The Maxwell Company's value is higher than that of a comparable unlevered firm by $42,314.05.

Figure 15.5
The effect of
financial leverage
on firm value: MM
with corporate
taxes in the case of
Divided Airlines

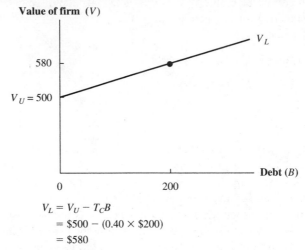

$$V_L = V_U - T_C B$$
$$= \$500 - (0.40 \times \$200)$$
$$= \$580$$

Debt reduces Divided's tax burden. As a result, the value of the firm is positively related to debt.

The value of Divided Airlines will equal[22]

$$V_L = \frac{\text{EBIT} \times (1 - T_C)}{r_0} + T_C B$$
$$= \frac{\$100}{0.20} + (0.40 \times \$200)$$
$$= \$500 + \$80$$
$$= \$580$$

Because $V_L = B + S$, the value of levered equity, S, is equal to $\$580 - \$200 = \$380$. The value of Divided Airlines as a function of leverage is shown in Figure 15.5. ∎

Expected Return and Leverage under Corporate Taxes

MM Proposition II under no taxes posits a positive relationship between the expected return on equity and leverage. This result occurs because the risk of equity increases with leverage. The same intuition also holds in a world of corporate taxes. The exact formula is[23]

---

[22]Note that, in a world with taxes, r_0 is used to discount after-tax cash flows.

[23]This relationship can be shown as follows: Given MM Proposition I under taxes, a levered firm's market value balance sheet can be written as

V_U	=	Value of unlevered firm	B	=	Debt
T_cB	=	Tax shield	S	=	Equity

The value of the unlevered firm is simply the value of the assets without benefit of leverage. The balance sheet indicates that the firm's value increases by T_cB when debt of B is added. The expected cash flow from the left-hand side of the balance sheet can be written as

$$V_U r_0 + T_C B r_B \qquad\qquad (a)$$

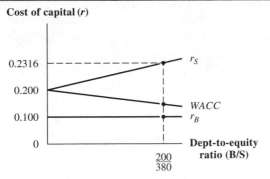

Figure 15.6
The effect of
financial leverage
on the cost of debt
and equity capital

Financial leverage adds risk to the firm's equity. As compensation, the cost of equity rises with the firm's risk.

$$r_S = r_0 + (1 - T_C)(r_0 - r_B)B/S$$

$$= 0.20 + \left(0.60 \times 0.10 \times \frac{200}{380}\right)$$

$$= 0.2316$$

MM Proposition II (Corporate Taxes):

$$r_S = r_0 + \frac{B}{S} \times (1 - T_C) \times (r_0 - r_B) \tag{15.8}$$

Applying the formula to Divided Airlines, we get

$$r_S = 0.2316 = 0.20 + \frac{200}{380} \times (1 - 0.40) \times (0.20 - 0.10)$$

This calculation is illustrated in Figure 15.6.

We can check this calculation by discounting at r_S to determine the value of the levered equity. The algebraic formula for levered equity is

$$S = \frac{(\text{EBIT} - r_B B) \times (1 - T_C)}{r_S} \tag{15.9}$$

Because assets are risky, their expected rate of return is r_0. The tax shield has the same risk as the debt, so its expected rate of return is r_B.

The expected cash to bondholders and shareholders together is

$$Sr_s + Br_B \tag{b}$$

Expression (b) reflects the fact that stock earns an expected return of r_s and debt earns the interest rate r_B.

Because all cash flows are paid out as dividends in our no-growth perpetuity model, the cash flows going into the firm equal those going to stakeholders. Hence (a) and (b) are equal:

$$Sr_S + Br_B = V_U r_0 + T_C Br_B \tag{c}$$

Dividing both sides of (c) by S, subtracting Br_B from both sides, and rearranging yields

$$r_S = \frac{V_U}{S} \times r_0 - (1 - T_c) \times \frac{B}{S} r_B \tag{d}$$

Because the value of the levered firm, V_L, equals $V_U + T_C B = B + S$, it follows that $V_U = S + (1 - T_C) \times B$. Thus, (d) can be rewritten as

$$r_S = \frac{S + (1 - T_C) \times B}{S} \times r_0 - (1 - T_c) \times \frac{B}{S} r_B \tag{e}$$

Bringing the terms involving $(1 - T_C) \times \frac{B}{S}$ together produces equation (15.8).

The numerator is the expected cash flow to levered equity after interest and taxes. The denominator is the rate at which the cash flow to equity is discounted.

For Divided Airlines we get[24]

$$\frac{(\$166.67 - 0.10 \times \$200)(1 - 0.40)}{0.2316} = \$380 \tag{15.9}$$

the same result we obtained earlier.

The Weighted Average Cost of Capital r_{WACC} and Corporate Taxes

In Chapter 12, we defined the weighted average cost of capital (with corporate taxes) as

$$r_{\text{WACC}} = \frac{B}{V_L}r_B(1 - T_C) + \frac{S}{V_L}r_S$$

For Divided Airlines,

$$r_{\text{WACC}} = \left(\frac{200}{580} \times 0.10 \times 0.60\right) + \left(\frac{380}{580} \times 0.2316\right)$$

$$= 0.1724$$

Divided Airlines has reduced its r_{WACC} from 0.20 (with no debt) to 0.1724 with reliance on debt. This result is intuitively pleasing because it suggests that, when a firm lowers its r_{WACC}, the firm's value will increase. Using the r_{WACC} approach, we can confirm that the value of Divided Airlines is $580:

$$V_L = \frac{\text{EBIT} \times (1 - T_C)}{r_{\text{WACC}}}$$

$$= \$580$$

Stock Price and Leverage under Corporate Taxes

At this point, students often believe the numbers—or at least are too intimidated to dispute them. However, they think we have asked the wrong question. "Why are we choosing to maximize the value of the firm?" they will say. "If managers are looking out for the shareholders' interest, why aren't they trying to maximize stock price?" If this question occurred to you, you have come to the right section.

Our response is twofold. First, we showed in the first section of this chapter that the capital structure that maximizes firm value is also the one that most benefits the interests of the shareholders.[25]

However, that general explanation is not always convincing to students. As a second procedure, we calculate the stock price of Divided Airlines both before and

---

[24]The calculation suffers slightly from rounding error because we only carried the discount rate, 0.2316, out to four decimal places.

[25]At that time, we pointed out that this result may not exactly hold in the more complex case where debt has a significant possibility of default. Issues of default are treated in the next chapter.

after the exchange of debt for stock. We do this by presenting a set of market value balance sheets. The market value balance sheet for the company in its all-equity form can be represented as

DIVIDED AIRLINES
Balance Sheet (all-equity firm)

Physical assets	Equity	$500
$\dfrac{166.67}{0.20} \times (1 - 0.40) = \$500$		(100 shares)

Assuming that there are 100 shares outstanding, each share is worth $5 = $500/100.

Next imagine that the company announces that, in the near future, it will issue $200 of debt to buy back $200 of stock. We know from our previous discussion that the value of the firm will rise to reflect the tax shield of debt. In efficient capital markets, the increase occurs immediately. That is, the rise occurs on the day of the announcement, not on the date of the debt-for-equity exchange. The market value balance sheet now becomes

DIVIDED AIRLINES
Balance Sheet
(upon announcement of debt issue)

Physical assets	$500	Equity	$580
Present value of tax shield	80		(100 shares)
Total assets	$580		

Note that the debt has not yet been issued. Therefore, only equity appears on the right-hand side of the balance sheet. Each share is now worth $580/100 = $5.80, implying that the shareholders have benefited by $80. The equityholders gain because they are the owners of a firm that has improved its financial policy.

The introduction of the tax shield to the balance sheet is frequently perplexing to students. Although physical assets are tangible, the ethereal nature of the tax shield bothers many students. However, remember that an asset is any item with value. The tax shield has value because it reduces the stream of future taxes. The fact that one cannot touch the shield in the way that one can touch a physical asset is a philosophical, not a financial, consideration.

At some point, the exchange of debt for equity occurs. Debt of $200 is issued, and the proceeds are used to buy back shares. How many shares of stock are repurchased? Because shares are now selling at $5.80 each, the number of shares that the firm acquires is $200/$5.80 = 34.48. This leaves 65.52 (or 100 − 34.48) shares of stock outstanding. The market value balance sheet is now

DIVIDED AIRLINES
Balance Sheet
(after exchange has taken place)

Physical assets	$500	Equity	$380
Present value of tax shield	80	(100 − 34.48 = 65.52 shares)	
		Debt	200
Total assets	$580	Debt plus equity	$580

Each share of stock is worth $380/65.52 = $5.80 after the exchange. Notice that the stock price does not change on the exchange date. As we mentioned above, the stock price moves on the date of the announcement only. Because the shareholders participating in the exchange receive a price equal to the market price per share after the exchange, they do not care whether they exchange their stock or not.

This example was provided for two reasons. First, it shows that an increase in the value of the firm from debt financing leads to an increase in the price of the stock. In fact, the shareholders capture the entire $80 tax shield. Second, we wanted to provide more work with market value balance sheets.

CONCEPT QUESTIONS

- What quirk in the tax code makes a levered firm more valuable than an otherwise identical unlevered firm?
- What is MM Proposition I under corporate taxes?
- What is MM Proposition II under corporate taxes?

15.7   Summary and Conclusions

1. We began our discussion of capital structure policy by arguing that the particular capital structure that maximizes the value of the firm is also the one that provides the most benefit to the shareholders.

2. In a world of no taxes, the famous Proposition I of Modigliani and Miller proves that the value of the firm is unaffected by the debt-to-equity ratio. In other words, financial policy is a matter of indifference in that world. The authors obtain their results by showing that either a high or a low corporate ratio of debt to equity can be offset by homemade leverage. The result hinges on the assumption that individuals can borrow at the same rate as corporations, an assumption we believe to be quite plausible.

3. MM's Proposition II in a world without taxes states

$$r_S = r_0 + \frac{B}{S}(r_0 - r_B)$$

This implies that the expected rate of return on equity (also called the *cost of equity* or the *required return on equity*) is positively related to the firm's leverage. This makes intuitive sense, because the risk of equity rises with leverage, a point illustrated by the differently sloped lines of Figure 15.2.

4. While the above work of MM is quite elegant, it does not explain the empirical findings on capital structure very well. MM imply that the capital structure decision is a matter of indifference, while the decision appears to be a weighty one in the real world. Still, learning the MM theory has been far from a waste of time. MM's arguments are a starting point; they show what does not matter and allow us to relax the assumptions so we can see exactly what does matter in the real world. To achieve real world relevance, we next considered corporate taxes.

5. In a world with corporate taxes but no bankruptcy costs, firm value is an increasing function of leverage. The formula for the value of the firm is

$$V_L = V_U + T_C B$$

Expected return on levered equity can be expressed as

$$r_S = r_0 + (1 - T_C) \times (r_0 - r_B) \times \frac{B}{S}$$

Here, value is positively related to leverage. This result implies that firms should have a capital structure almost entirely composed of debt. Because real world firms select more moderate levels of debt, the next chapter considers alternative explanations of capital structure.

Key Terms

Pie model 415

MM Proposition I 418

MM Proposition II 425

MM Proposition I (corporate taxes) 437

MM Proposition II (corporate taxes)
   438

Suggested Readings

The classic papers by Modigliani and Miller are:

F. Modigliani and M. H. Miller. "The Cost of Capital, Corporation Finance, and the Theory of Investment." *American Economic Review* (June 1958).

F. Modigliani and M. H. Miller. "Corporate Income Taxes and the Cost of Capital: A Correction." *American Economic Review* (June 1963).

Questions and Problems

Capital Structure without Taxes

15.1 Nadus Corporation and Logis Corporation are identical in every way except their capital structures. Nadus Corporation, an all-equity firm, has 5,000 shares of stock outstanding; each share sells for $20. Logis Corporation uses leverage in its capital structure. The market value of Logis Corporation's debt is $25,000. Logis's cost of debt is 12 percent. Each firm is expected to have earnings before interest of $350,000. Neither firm pays taxes.

   Suppose you want to purchase the same portion of the equity of each firm. Assume you can borrow money at 12 percent.

   a. What is the value of Nadus's stock?

   b. What is the value of Logis's stock?

   c. What will your costs and returns be if you buy 20 percent of each firm's equity?

   d. Which investment is riskier? Why?

    e. Construct an investment strategy for Nadus stock that replicates the investment returns of Logis stock.

    f. What is the value of Logis Corporation?

    g. If the value of Logis's assets is $135,000, what should you do?

15.2 Acetate, Inc., has common stock with a market value of $20 million and debt with a market value of $10 million. The cost of the debt is 14 percent. The current Treasury bill rate is 8 percent, and the expected market premium is 10 percent. The beta on Acetate's equity is 0.9.

    a. What is Acetate's debt-equity ratio?

    b. What is the firm's overall required return?

15.3 You invest $100,000 in the stock of the Liana Rope Company. To make the investment, you borrowed $75,000 from a friend at a cost of 10 percent. You expect your equity investment to return 20 percent. There are no taxes. What would your return be if you did not use leverage?

15.4 Levered, Ltd., and Unlevered, Ltd., are identical companies with identical business risk. Their earnings are perfectly correlated. Each company is expected to earn $96 million per year in perpetuity, and each company distributes all its earnings. Levered's debt has a market value of $275 million and provides a return of 8 percent. Levered's stock sells for $100 per share and there are 4.5 million outstanding shares. Unlevered has only 10 million outstanding shares worth $80 each. Unlevered has no debt. There are no taxes. Which stock is a better investment?

15.5 The Veblen Company and the Knight Company are identical in every respect except that Veblen Company is not levered. The market value of Knight Company's 6-percent bonds is $1 million. The financial statistics for the two firms appear below. Neither firm pays taxes.

	Veblen *Unlevered*	Knight *levered*
Net operating income	$ 300,000	$ 300,000
Interest on debt	0	60,000
Earnings available to common stock	$ 300,000	$ 240,000
Required return on equity	0.125	0.1400
Market value of stock	$2,400,000	$1,714,000
Market value of debt	0	1,000,000 *← 6% bond*
Market value of the firm	$2,400,000	$2,714,000
Overall required return	0.125	0.1100
Debt-equity ratio	0	0.5834

    a. An investor who is also able to borrow at 6 percent owns $10,000 worth of Knight stock. Can he increase his net return by borrowing money to buy Veblen stock? If so, show the strategy.

    b. According to Modigliani and Miller, what investors will attempt this strategy. When will the process cease?

15.6 Shades Ltd. is a Hong Kong–based corporation that sells sunglasses. The firm pays no corporate taxes, and its shareholders pay no personal income taxes.

Shades currently has 100,000 shares outstanding worth $50 each; the firm has no debt.

Consider three shareholders of Shades: Ms. A, Ms. B, and Ms. C. All three shareholders have good access to capital markets, so they can lend and borrow at 20 percent, the same rate at which the firm lends and borrows. The value of their holdings and their overall borrowing and lending positions are listed below.

	Value of Shades shares	Total borrowing	Total lending
Ms. A	$10,000	$2,000	0
Ms. B	50,000	0	$6,000
Ms. C	20,000	0	0

Shades desires a ratio of debt to total capital of 0.20. To meet that desire, suppose the firm issues $1 million in risk-free debt and uses the funds to repurchase 20,000 shares.

The three shareholders wish to keep the risk of their portfolios unchanged. Show the value of their holdings and their borrowing and lending positions after they have adjusted their portfolios.

15.7 Rayburn Manufacturing is currently an all-equity firm. The firm's equity is worth $2 million. The cost of that equity is 18 percent. Rayburn pays no taxes.

Rayburn plans to issue $400,000 in debt and to use the proceeds to repurchase stock. The cost of debt is 10 percent.

a. After Rayburn repurchases the stock, what will the firm's overall costs of capital be?

b. After the repurchase, what will the cost of equity be?

c. Explain your result in (b).

15.8 Strom, Inc., has 250,000 outstanding shares of stock that sell for $20 per share. Strom, Inc., currently has no debt. The appropriate discount rate for the firm is 15 percent. Strom's earnings last year were $750,000. The management expects that if no changes affect the assets of the firm, the earnings will remain $750,000 in perpetuity. Strom pays no taxes.

Strom plans to buy out a competitor's business at a cost of $300,000. Once added to Strom's current business, the competitor's facilities will generate earnings of $120,000 in perpetuity. The competitor has the same risk as Strom, Inc.

a. Construct the market value balance sheet for Strom before the announcement of the buyout is made.

b. Suppose Strom uses equity to fund the buyout.

　i. According to the efficient market hypothesis, what will happen to Strom's price?

　ii. Construct the market value balance sheet as it will look after the announcement.

　iii. How many shares did Strom sell?

iv. Once Strom sells the new shares of stock, how will its accounts look?

v. After the purchase is finalized, how will the market value balance sheet look?

vi. What is the return to Strom's equityholders?

c. Suppose Strom uses 10-percent debt to fund the buyout.

i. Construct the market value balance sheet as it will look after the announcement.

ii. Once Strom sells the bonds, how will its accounts look?

iii. What is the cost of equity?

iv. Explain any difference in the cost of equity between the two plans.

v. Use MM Proposition II to verify the answer in (iii).

d. Under each financing plan, what is the price of Strom stock after the buyout?

15.9 The Gulf Power Company is an electric utility that is planning to build a new conventional power plant. The company has traditionally paid out all earnings to the shareholders as dividends, and financed capital expenditures with new issues of common stock. There is no debt or preferred stock presently outstanding. Data on the company and the new power plant follow. Assume all earnings streams are perpetuities.

Company data
Current annual earnings: $27 million
Number of outstanding shares: 10 million
New power plant
Initial outlay: $20 million
Added annual earnings: $3 million

Management considers the power plant to have the same risk as existing assets. The current required rate of return on equity is 10 percent. Assume there are no taxes and no costs of bankruptcy.

a. What will the total market value of Gulf Power be if common stock is issued to finance the plant?

b. What will the total market value of the firm be if $20 million in bonds with an interest rate of 8 percent are issued to finance the plant? Assume the bonds are perpetuities.

c. Suppose Gulf Power issues the bonds. Calculate the rate of return required by shareholders after the financing has occurred and the plant has been built.

15.10 Suppose there are no taxes, no transaction costs, and no costs of financial distress. In such a world, are the following statements true, false, or uncertain? Explain your answers.

a. If a firm issues equity to repurchase some of its debt, the price of the remaining shares will rise because those shares are less risky.

b. Moderate borrowing does not significantly affect the probability of financial distress or bankruptcy. Hence, moderate borrowing will not increase the required return on equity.

15.11 *a.* List the three assumptions that lie behind the Modigliani–Miller theory.

  b. Briefly explain the effect of each upon the conclusions of the theory for the real world.

Capital Structure with Corporate Taxes

15.12 The market value of a firm with $500,000 of debt is $1,700,000. EBIT are expected to be a perpetuity. The pretax interest rate on debt is 10 percent. The company is in the 40-percent tax bracket. If the company was 100-percent equity financed, the equityholders would require a 20-percent return.

  a. What would the value of the firm be if it was financed entirely with equity?

  b. What is the net income to the shareholders of this levered firm?

15.13 An all-equity firm is subject to a 40-percent corporate tax rate. Its equityholders require a 20-percent return. The firm's initial market value is $3,500,000, and there are 175,000 shares outstanding. The firm issues $1 million of bonds at 10 percent and uses the proceeds to repurchase common stock.

  Assume there is no change in the costs of financial distress for the firm. According to MM, what is the new market value of the equity of the firm?

15.14 Streiber Publishing Company, an all-equity firm, generates perpetual earnings before interest and taxes (EBIT) of $2.5 million per year. Streiber's after-tax, all-equity discount rate is 20 percent. The company's tax rate is 40 percent.

  a. What is the value of Streiber Publishing?

  b. If Streiber adjusts its capital structure to include $600,000 of debt, what is the value of the firm?

  c. Explain any difference in your answers.

  d. What assumptions are you making when you are valuing Streiber?

15.15 Fred, Inc., is a nongrowth company in the 40-percent tax bracket. Fred's perpetual EBIT is $1.2 million per annum. The firm's pretax cost of debt is 8 percent and its interest expense per year is $200,000. Company analysts estimate that the unlevered cost of Fred's equity is 12 percent.

  a. What is the value of this firm?

  b. What does the calculation in *(a)* imply about the correct level of debt?

  c. Is the conclusion correct? Why or why not?

15.16 Green Manufacturing, Ltd., plans to announce that it will issue $2,000,000 of perpetual bonds. The bonds will have a 6-percent coupon rate. Green Manufacturing currently is an all-equity firm. The value of Green's equity is $10,000,000 and there are 500,000 shares outstanding. After the sale of the bonds, Green will maintain the new capital structure indefinitely. The expected annual pretax earnings of Green are $1,500,000. Those earnings are also expected to remain constant into the foreseeable future. Green is in the 40-percent tax bracket.

  a. What is Green's current overall required return?

b. Construct Green Manufacturing's market value balance sheet as it looks before the announcement of the debt issue.

c. What is the market value balance sheet after the announcement?

d. How many shares of stock will Green retire?

e. What will the accounts show after the restructuring has taken place?

f. What is Green's cost of equity after the capital restructuring?

15.17 The Nikko Company has perpetual EBIT of $4 million per year. The after-tax, all-equity discount rate r_0 is 15 percent. The company's tax rate is 40 percent. The cost of debt capital is 10 percent, and Nikko has $10 million of debt in its capital structure.

a. What is Nikko's value?

b. What is Nikko's r_{WACC}?

c. What is Nikko's cost of equity?

CHAPTER 16

Capital Structure: Limits to the Use of Debt

A student might ask whether the MM theory with taxes predicts the capital structures of typical firms. The answer is, unfortunately, no. The theory states that $V_L = V_U + T_C B$. One can always increase firm value by increasing leverage, implying that firms should issue maximum debt. This is inconsistent with the real world, where firms generally employ only moderate amounts of debt.

However, the MM theory tells us *where to look* when searching for the determinants of capital structure. For example, the theory ignores bankruptcy and its attendant costs. Because these costs are likely to get out of hand for a highly levered firm, the moderate leverage of most firms can now easily be explained.

In addition, the MM theory ignores personal taxes. In the real world, the *personal* tax rate on interest is higher than the *effective* personal tax rate on equity distributions. Thus, the personal tax penalties to bondholders tend to offset the tax benefits to debt at the corporate level. Even when bankruptcy costs are ignored, this idea can be shown to imply that there is an optimal amount of debt for the economy as a whole. The implications of bankruptcy costs and personal taxes are examined in this chapter.

Costs of Financial Distress 16.1

Bankruptcy Risk or Bankruptcy Cost?

As mentioned throughout the previous chapter, debt provides tax benefits to the firm. However, debt puts pressure on the firm, because interest and principal payments are obligations. If these obligations are not met, the firm may risk some sort of financial distress. The ultimate distress is *bankruptcy,* where ownership of the firm's assets is legally transferred from the shareholders to the bondholders. These debt obligations are fundamentally different from stock obligations. While shareholders like and expect dividends, they are not legally entitled to dividends in the way bondholders are legally entitled to interest and principal payments.

We show below that bankruptcy costs, or, more generally, financial distress costs, tend to offset the advantages to debt. We begin by positing a simple example of bankruptcy. All taxes are ignored to focus only on the costs of debt.

■ *Example*

The Knight Corporation plans to be in business for one more year. It forecasts a cash flow of either $100 or $50 in the coming year, each occurring with 50-percent probability. Previously issued debt requires payments of $49 of interest and principal. The Day Corporation has identical cash flow prospects but has $60 of interest and principal obligations. The cash flows of these two firms can be represented as

	Knight Corp.		Day Corp.	
	Boom times (prob. 50%)	Recession (prob. 50%)	Boom times (prob. 50%)	Recession (prob. 50%)
Cash flow	$100	$50	$100	$50
Payment of interest and principal on debt	49	49	60	50
Distribution to shareholders	$ 51	$ 1	$ 40	0

The Day Corporation will be bankrupt in a recession. Note that, under the law, corporations have limited liability. Thus, Day's bondholders will receive only $50 in a recession; they cannot get the additional $10 from the shareholders.

We assume that (1) both bondholders and shareholders are risk neutral and (2) the interest rate is 10 percent. Due to this risk neutrality, cash flows to both shareholders and bondholders are to be discounted at the 10-percent rate.[1] We can evaluate the debt, the equity, and the entire firm for both Knight and Day as follows:

$$S_{\text{KNIGHT}} = \$23.64 = \frac{\$51 \times 1/2 + \$ 1 \times 1/2}{1.10} \qquad S_{\text{DAY}} = \$18.18 = \frac{\$40 \times 1/2 + 0 \times 1/2}{1.10}$$

$$B_{\text{KNIGHT}} = \$44.54 = \frac{\$49 \times 1/2 + \$49 \times 1/2}{1.10} \qquad B_{\text{DAY}} = \$50 = \frac{\$60 \times 1/2}{1.10} + \$50 \times 1/2$$

$$V_{\text{KNIGHT}} = \$68.18 \qquad\qquad V_{\text{DAY}} = \$68.18$$

Note that the two firms have the same value, even though Day runs the risk of bankruptcy. Furthermore, notice that Day's bondholders are valuing the bonds with their eyes open. Though the promised payment of principal and interest is $60, the bondholders are willing to pay only $50. Hence, their *promised* return or yield is

$$\frac{\$60}{\$50} - 1 = 20\%$$

Day's debt can be viewed as a *junk bond,* because the probability of default is so high. As with all junk bonds, bondholders demand a high promised yield.

---

[1]Normally, one assumes that investors are averse to risk. In that case, the cost of debt capital, r_B, is less than the cost of equity capital, r_S, which rises with leverage as shown in the previous chapter. In addition, r_B may rise when the increase in leverage allows the possibility of default.

For simplicity, we assume *risk neutrality* in this example. This means that investors are indifferent to whether risk is high, low, or even absent. Here, $r_S = r_B$, because risk-neutral investors do not demand compensation for bearing risk. In addition, neither r_S nor r_B rises with leverage. Because the interest rate is 10 percent, our assumption of risk neutrality implies that $r_S = 10\%$ as well.

Though financial economists believe that investors are risk-averse, they frequently develop examples based on risk neutrality to isolate a point unrelated to risk. This is our approach, because we want to focus on bankruptcy costs—not bankruptcy risk. The same qualitative conclusions from this example can be drawn in a world of risk aversion, albeit with much more difficulty for the reader.

The Day example is not realistic because it ignores an important cash flow to be discussed below. A more realistic set of numbers might be

	DAY CORP.	
	Boom times (prob. 50%)	Recession (prob. 50%)
Earnings	$100	$50
Debt repayment	60	35
Distribution to shareholders	40	0

$$S_{DAY} = \$18.18 = \frac{\$40 \times 1/2 + 0 \times 1/2}{1.10}$$

$$B_{DAY} = \$43.18 = \frac{\$60 \times 1/2 + \$35 \times 1/2}{1.10}$$

$$V_{DAY} = \$61.36$$

Why do the bondholders receive only $35 in a recession? If cash flow is only $50, bondholders will be informed that they are not paid in full. These bondholders are likely to hire lawyers to negotiate or even to sue the company. Similarly, the firm is likely to hire lawyers to defend itself. Further costs will be incurred if the case gets to a bankruptcy court. These fees are always paid before the bondholders get paid. Thus, we are assuming that bankruptcy costs total $15 (or $50 − 35).

The value of the firm is now $61.36, an amount below the $68.18 figure calculated earlier. By comparing Day's value in a world with no bankruptcy costs against Day's value in a world with these costs, we conclude

> The possibility of bankruptcy has a negative effect on the value of the firm. However, it is not the risk of bankruptcy itself that lowers value. Rather, it is the costs associated with bankruptcy that lower value.

The explanation follows from our pie example. In a world of no bankruptcy costs, the bondholders and the shareholders share the entire pie. However, bankruptcy costs eat up some of the pie in the real world, leaving less for the shareholders and bondholders.

Because the bondholders are aware that they receive little in a recession, they pay a lower price. In this case, their promised return is

$$\frac{\$60}{\$43.18} - 1 = 39.0\%$$

The bondholders are paying a fair price if they are realistic about both the probability and the cost of bankruptcy. It is the *shareholders* who bear these future bankruptcy costs. To see this, imagine that Day Corp. was originally all equity. The shareholders want the firm to issue debt with a promised payment of $60 and use the proceeds to pay a dividend. If there had been no bankruptcy costs, our results show that bondholders would pay $50 to purchase debt with a promised payment of $60. Hence, a dividend of $50 could be paid to the shareholders. However, if bankruptcy costs exist, bondholders would only pay $43.18 for the debt. In that case, only a dividend of $43.18 could be paid to the shareholders. Because the dividend is less when bankruptcy costs exist, the shareholders are hurt by bankruptcy costs. ∎

- What does risk neutrality mean?
- Can one have bankruptcy risk without bankruptcy costs?
- Why do we say that shareholders bear bankruptcy costs?

16.2 Description of Costs

The example above showed that bankruptcy costs can lower the value of the firm. In fact, the same general result holds even if a legal bankruptcy is prevented. Thus, *financial distress costs* may be a better phrase than *bankruptcy costs*. It is worthwhile to describe these costs in more detail.

Direct Costs of Financial Distress: Legal and Administrative Costs of Liquidation or Reorganization

As mentioned earlier, lawyers are involved throughout all the stages before and during bankruptcy. With fees in the hundreds of dollars an hour, these costs can add up quickly. In addition, administrative and accounting fees can substantially add to the total bill. And, if the case goes to court, we must not forget expert witnesses. Each side may hire a number of these witnesses to testify about the fairness of a prepared settlement. Their fees can easily rival those of lawyers or accountants. (However, we personally look upon these witnesses more kindly, because they are frequently drawn from the ranks of finance professors.)

These direct costs have recently been estimated. While large in absolute amount, they are actually small as a percentage of firm value. White, Altman, and Weiss estimated the direct costs of financial distress to be about 3 percent of the market value of the firm.[2] In a study of direct financial distress costs of 20 railroad bankruptcies from 1930 to 1935, Warner found that net financial distress costs were, on average, 1 percent of the market value of the firm seven years before bankruptcy and were somewhat larger percentages as bankruptcy approached (for example, 2.5 percent of the market value of the firm three years before bankruptcy).

Warner pointed out that[3]

> It is the *expected* cost of bankruptcy that is the relevant measure of bankruptcy costs. . . . Suppose, for example, that a given railroad picks a level of debt such that bankruptcy would occur on average once every 20 years (i.e., the probability of going bankrupt is 5 percent in any given year). Assume that when bankruptcy occurs, the firm would pay a lump sum penalty equal to 3 percent of its now current market value. . . .
>
> [Then], the firm's expected cost of bankruptcy is equal to fifteen one-hundredths of one percent of its now current market value.

[2]M. J. White, "Bankruptcy Costs and the New Bankruptcy Code," *Journal of Finance* (May 1983); and E. I. Altman, "A Further Empirical Investigation of the Bankruptcy Cost Question," *Journal of Finance* (September 1984). Most recently, Lawrence A. Weiss, "Bankruptcy Resolution: Direct Costs and Violation of Priority of Claims," *Journal of Financial Economics* 27 (1990), estimates that direct costs of bankruptcy are 3.1 percent of the value of the firm. His sample is 37 New York and American Stock Exchange firms that filed for bankruptcy from 1979 to 1986.

[3]J. B. Warner, "Bankruptcy Costs: Some Evidence," *Journal of Finance* (May 1977).

Indirect Costs of Financial Distress

Impaired Ability to Conduct Business

Bankruptcy hampers conduct with customers and suppliers. Sales are frequently lost because of both fear of impaired service and loss of trust. For example, many loyal Chrysler customers switched to other manufacturers when Chrysler skirted insolvency in the 1970s. These buyers questioned whether parts and servicing would be available were Chrysler to fail. Sometimes the taint of impending bankruptcy is enough to drive customers away. For example, gamblers avoided Atlantis casino in Atlantic City after it became technically insolvent. Gamblers are a superstitious bunch. Many reasoned, If the casino itself cannot make money, how can I expect to make money there? A particularly outrageous story concerned two unrelated stores both named Mitchells. When one Mitchells declared bankruptcy, customers stayed away from both stores. In time, the second store was forced to declare bankruptcy as well.

Though these costs clearly exist, it is quite difficult to measure them. Altman has estimated that both direct and indirect costs are frequently greater than 20 percent of firm value.[4]

Agency Costs

When a firm has debt, conflicts of interest arise between shareholders and bondholders, and shareholders are tempted to pursue selfish strategies. These conflicts of interests, which are magnified when financial distress occurs, impose **agency costs** on the firm. We describe three kinds of selfish strategies that shareholders use to hurt the bondholders and help themselves. These strategies are costly because they will lower the market value of the whole firm.

Selfish Investment Strategy 1: Incentive to Take Large Risks   Firms near bankruptcy often take great chances, because they feel that they are playing with someone else's money. A good example of this occurred in the failure of two banks in Western Canada in 1985. Because they were allowed to stay in business although they were economically insolvent, the banks had nothing to lose by taking great risks. Because of these and other failures, the Canada Deposit Insurance Corporation declared a multibillion-dollar deficit in late 1993.[5]

---

[4]Altman, "A Further Empirical Investigation."

David M. Cutler and Lawrence H. Summers, "The Costs of Conflict Resolution and Financial Distress: Evidence from the Texaco-Pennzoil Litigation," *Rand Journal of Economics* 19 (1988), estimate the indirect costs of Texaco's 1987 bankruptcy to be about 9 percent of the firm's value. Steven N. Kaplan, "Campeau's Acquisition of Federated: Value Added or Destroyed," *Journal of Financial Economics* 24 (1989), finds the indirect costs of financial distress for Campeau to be very small.

A fascinating and provocative set of articles by Robert Haugen and Lemma Senbet—"The Insignificance of Bankruptcy Costs to the Theory of Optimal Capital Structure," *Journal of Finance* (May 1978); "New Perspectives on Information Asymmetry and Agency Relationships," *Journal of Financial and Quantitative Analysis* (November 1979); "Bankruptcy and Agency Costs: Their Significance to the Theory of Optimal Capital Structure," *Journal of Financial and Quantitative Analysis* (March 1988)—argues that financial distress should, at most, only slightly impair the firm's ability to conduct business. They say that customers, employees, and so on are concerned with the tenure of the firm, which is fundamentally a function of its asset characteristics. This tenure should not be dependent on the way the assets are financed. We discuss this further in Chapter 30.

[5]The same thing happened on a grander scale in the U.S. savings and loan debacle. Edward J. Kane, *The Savings and Loan Mess* (Washington, D.C.: Urban Institute Press, 1989), estimates that closing S&Ls when they first became insolvent, thus preventing them from gambling with deposits insured with taxpayers' money, would have saved half of the over U.S. $ 100 billion bill for cleaning up the industry.

To see how the incentive to take risk works, imagine a levered firm considering two mutually exclusive projects: a low-risk one and a high-risk one. There are two equally likely outcomes: recession and boom. The firm is in such dire straits that, should a recession hit, it will come near to bankruptcy with one project and actually fall into bankruptcy with the other. The cash flows for the firm if the low-risk project is taken can be described as

Low-risk project

	Probability	Value of firm	=	Stock	+	Bonds
Recession	0.5	$100	=	0	+	$100
Boom	0.5	$200	=	$100	+	$100

If recession occurs, the value of the firm will be $100, and if boom occurs, the value of the firm will be $200. The expected value of the firm is $150 (or 0.5 × $100 + 0.5 × $200).

The firm has promised to pay bondholders $100. Shareholders will obtain the difference between the total payoff and the amount paid to the bondholders. The bondholders have the prior claim on the payoffs, and the shareholders have the residual claim.

Now suppose that a riskier project can be substituted for the low-risk project. The payoffs and probabilities are as follows:

High-risk project

	Probability	Value of firm	=	Stock	+	Bonds
Recession	0.5	$ 50	=	0	+	$ 50
Boom	0.5	$240	=	$140	+	$100

The expected value of the firm is $145 (or 0.5 × $50 + 0.5 × $240), which is lower than the expected value with the low-risk project. Thus, the low-risk project would be accepted if the firm were all equity. However, note that the expected value of the stock is $70 (or 0.5 × 0 + 0.5 × $140) with the high-risk project, but only $50 (or 0.5 × 0 + 0.5 × $100) with the low-risk project. Given the firm's present levered state, shareholders will select the high-risk project.

The key is that, relative to the low-risk project, the high-risk project increases firm value in a boom and decreases firm value in a recession. The increase in value in a boom is captured by the shareholders, because the bondholders are paid in full (they receive $100) regardless of which project is accepted. Conversely, the drop in value in a recession is lost by the bondholders, because they are paid in full with the low-risk project but receive only $50 with the high-risk one. The shareholders will receive nothing in a recession anyway, whether the high-risk or low-risk project is selected. Thus, financial economists argue that shareholders expropriate value from the bondholders by selecting high-risk projects.

A story, perhaps apocryphal, illustrates this idea. It seems that Federal Express was near financial collapse within a few years of its inception. In despair the founder, Frederick Smith, took $20,000 of corporate funds to Las Vegas. He won at the gaming tables, providing enough capital to allow the firm to survive. Had he lost, the banks would simply have received $20,000 less when the firm reached bankruptcy.

	Firm without project		Firm with project		Table 16.1
	Boom	Recession	Boom	Recession	Example illustrating incentive to underinvest
Firm cash flows	$5,000	$2,400	$6,700	$4,100	
Bondholders' claim	4,000	2,400	4,000	4,000	
Shareholders' claim	1,000	0	2,700	100	

The project has positive NPV. However, much of its value is captured by bondholders. Rational managers, acting in the shareholders' interest, will reject the project.

Selfish Investment Strategy 2: Incentive toward Underinvestment   Shareholders of a firm with a significant probability of bankruptcy often find that new investment helps the bondholders at the shareholders' expense. The simplest case might be a real estate owner facing imminent bankruptcy. If he took $100,000 out of his own pocket to refurbish the building, he could increase the building's value by, say, $150,000. Though this investment has a positive net present value, he will turn it down if the increase in value cannot prevent bankruptcy. "Why," he asks, "should I use my own funds to improve the value of a building that the bank will soon repossess?"

This idea is formalized by the following simple example. Consider a firm with $4,000 of principal and interest payments due at the end of the year. It will be pulled into bankruptcy by a recession because its cash flows will be only $2,400 in that state. The firm's cash flows are presented in the left-hand side of Table 16.1. The firm could avoid bankruptcy in a recession by raising new equity to invest in a new project. The project costs $1,000 and brings in $1,700 in either state, implying a positive net present value. Clearly it would be accepted in an all-equity firm.

However, the project hurts the shareholders of the levered firm. To see this, imagine that the old shareholders contribute the $1,000 *themselves.*[6] The expected value of the shareholders' interest without the project is $500 (or 0.5 × $1,000 + 0.5 × $0). The expected value with the project is $1,400 (or 0.5 × $2,700 + 0.5 × $100). The shareholders' interest rises by only $900 (or $1,400 − $500) while costing $1,000.

The key is that the shareholders contribute the full $1,000 investment, but the shareholders and bondholders *share* the benefits. The shareholders take the entire gain if boom times occur. Conversely, the bondholders reap most of the cash flow from the project in a recession.

The discussion of selfish strategy 1 is quite similar to the discussion of selfish strategy 2. In both cases, an investment strategy for the levered firm is different from the one for the unlevered firm. Thus, leverage results in distorted investment policy. Whereas the unlevered corporation always chooses projects with positive net present value, the levered firm may deviate from this policy.

Selfish Investment Strategy 3: Milking the Property   Another strategy is to pay out extra dividends or other distributions in times of financial distress, leaving less in the firm for the bondholders. This is known as *milking the property,* a phrase taken from real

---

[6]The same qualitative results will obtain if the $1,000 is raised from new shareholders. However, the arithmetic becomes much more difficult since we must determine how many new shares are issued.

estate. Strategies 2 and 3 are very similar. In strategy 2, the firm chooses not to raise new equity. Strategy 3 goes one step further, because equity is actually withdrawn through the dividend.

Summary of Selfish Strategies

The above distortions occur only when there is a probability of bankruptcy or financial distress. Thus, these distortions *should not* affect, say, Bell Canada Enterprises (BCE) because bankruptcy is not a realistic possibility for a blue chip firm such as this. In other words, BCE's debt will be virtually risk-free, regardless of the projects it accepts. Because the distortions are related to financial distress, we included them in the earlier section "Indirect Costs of Financial Distress."

Who pays the cost of selfish investment strategies? We argue that it is ultimately the shareholders. Rational bondholders know that when financial distress is imminent, they cannot expect help from shareholders. Rather, shareholders are likely to choose investment strategies that reduce the value of the bonds. Bondholders protect themselves accordingly by raising the interest rate that they require on the bonds. Because the shareholders must pay these higher rates, they ultimately bear the costs of selfish strategies. The relationship between shareholders and bondholders is very similar to the relationship between Erroll Flynn and David Niven, good friends and movie stars in the 1930s. Niven reportedly said that the good thing about Flynn was that you knew exactly where you stood with him. When you needed his help, you could always count on him to let you down.

CONCEPT QUESTIONS

- What is the main direct cost of financial distress?
- What are the indirect costs of financial distress?
- Who pays the costs of selfish strategies?

16.3   Can Costs of Debt Be Reduced?

Each of the costs of financial distress we mentioned above is substantial in its own right. The sum of them may well affect debt financing severely. Thus, managers have an incentive to reduce these costs. We now turn to some of their methods. However, it should be mentioned at the outset that these methods can, at most, reduce the costs of debt. They cannot eliminate them entirely.

Protective Covenants

Because the shareholders must pay higher interest rates as insurance against their own selfish strategies, they frequently make arrangements with bondholders in hopes of lowering rates. These agreements, called **protective covenants,** are incorporated as part of the loan document (or *indenture*) between shareholders and bondholders. The covenants must be taken seriously since a broken covenant can lead to default. Protective covenants can be classified into two types: negative covenants and positive covenants.

A **negative covenant** limits or prohibits actions that the company may take. Here are some typical negative covenants:

1. Limitations are placed on the amount of dividends a company may pay.
2. The firm may not pledge any of its assets to other lenders.
3. The firm may not merge with another firm.
4. The firm may not sell or lease its major assets without approval by the lender.
5. The firm may not issue additional long-term debt of equal or higher seniority.

A **positive covenant** specifies an action that the company agrees to take or a condition the company must abide by. Here are some examples:

1. The company agrees to maintain its working capital at a minimum level.
2. The company must furnish periodic financial statements to the lender.
3. The company must segregate and maintain specified assets as security for the debt.

This list of covenants is not exhaustive. We have seen loan agreements with more than 30 covenants. Smith and Warner examined public issues of debt in 1975 and found that 91 percent of the bond indentures included covenants that restricted the issuance of additional debt, 23 percent restricted dividends, 39 percent restricted mergers, and 36 percent limited the sale of assets.[7]

Protective covenants should reduce the costs of bankruptcy, ultimately increasing the value of the firm. Thus, shareholders are likely to favour all reasonable covenants. To see this, consider three choices by shareholders to reduce bankruptcy costs.

1. *Issue no debt.* Because of the tax advantages to debt, this is a very costly way of avoiding conflicts.
2. *Issue debt with no restrictive and protective covenants.* In this case, the market price of debt will be much lower (and the cost of debt much higher) than would otherwise be true.
3. *Write protective and restrictive covenants into the loan contracts.* If the covenants are clearly written, the creditors may receive protection without large costs being imposed on the shareholders. They will happily accept a lower interest rate. Roberts and Viscione found that secured debt (bonds with positive covenant 3 above), carried lower yields than unsecured bonds.[8]

Thus, bond covenants, even if they are costly, can increase the value of the firm. They can be the lowest-cost solution to the shareholder–bondholder conflict. A list of typical bond covenants and their uses appears in Table 16.2.

---

[7]C. W. Smith and J. B. Warner, "On Financial Contracting: An Analysis of Bond Covenants," *Journal of Financial Economics* 7 (1979).

[8]Gordon S. Roberts and Jerry A. Viscione, "The Impact of Seniority and Security Covenants on Bond Yields," *Journal of Finance* (December 1984).

Table 16.2 Loan covenants

Covenant type	Shareholder action or firm circumstances	Reason for covenant
Financial statement signals 1. Working capital requirement 2. Interest coverage 3. Minimum net worth	As firm approaches financial distress, shareholders may want firm to make high-risk investments.	Shareholders lose value before bankruptcy; bondholders hurt much more in bankruptcy than shareholders (limited liability); bondholders hurt by *distortion of investment that leads to increases in risk.*
Restrictions on asset disposition 1. Limit dividends 2. Limit sale of assets 3. Collateral and mortgages	Shareholders attempt to transfer corporate assets to themselves.	Limits the ability of shareholders to transfer assets to themselves and to *underinvest.*
Restrictions on switching assets	Shareholders attempt to increase risk of firm.	Increased firm risk helps shareholders: bondholders hurt by *distortion of investment that leads to increases in risk.*
Dilution 1. Limit on leasing 2. Limit on further borrowing	Shareholders may attempt to issue new debt of equal or greater priority.	Restricts *dilution of the claim of existing bondholders.*

Consolidation of Debt

One reason why bankruptcy costs are so high is that different creditors (and their lawyers) fight with each other. This problem can be alleviated if one, or at most a few, lenders can shoulder the entire debt. Should financial distress occur, negotiating costs are minimized under this arrangement. In addition, bondholders can purchase stock as well. In this way, shareholders and debtholders are not pitted against each other, because they are not separate entities. This appears to be the approach in Japan where large banks generally take significant stock positions in the firms to which they lend money.[9] Debt-equity ratios in Japan are far higher than those in Canada and the United States.

CONCEPT QUESTIONS

■ How can covenants and debt consolidation reduce debt agency costs?

16.4   Integration of Tax Effects and Financial Distress Costs

Modigliani and Miller argue that the firm's value rises with leverage in the presence of corporate taxes. Because this implies that all firms should choose maximum debt, the theory does not predict the behaviour of firms in the real world. Other authors have suggested that bankruptcy and related costs reduce the value of the levered firm.

The integration of tax effects and distress costs appears in Figure 16.1. The diagonal straight line in the figure represents the value of the firm in a world with taxes

---

[9]Canadian and U.S. banks are becoming increasingly interested in taking equity options when lending to higher-risk firms. Convertible bonds (discussed in Chapter 22) include an equity option partly as a way of controlling agency costs.

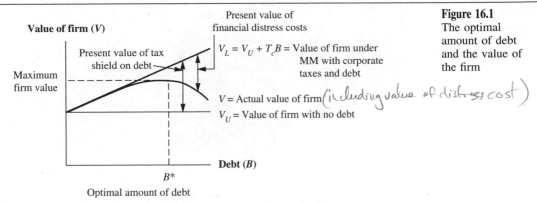

Figure 16.1
The optimal amount of debt and the value of the firm

The tax shield increases the value of the levered firm. Financial distress costs lower the value of the levered firm. The two offsetting factors produce an optimal amount of debt.

but without bankruptcy costs. The ∩-shaped curve represents the value of the firm with these costs. The ∩-shaped curve rises as the firm moves from all equity to a small amount of debt. Here, the present value of the distress costs is minimal because the probability of distress is so small. However, as more and more debt is added, the present value of these costs rises at an *increasing* rate. At some point, the increase in the present value of these costs from an additional dollar of debt equals the increase in the present value of the tax shield. This is the debt level maximizing the value of the firm; it's represented by B^* in Figure 16.1. In other words, B^* is the optimal amount of debt. Bankruptcy costs increase faster than the tax shield beyond this point, implying a reduction in firm value from further leverage.

The above discussion presents two factors that affect the degree of leverage. Unfortunately, no formula exists at this time to determine exactly the optimal debt level for a particular firm. This is because bankruptcy costs cannot be expressed in a precise way. The last section of this chapter offers some rules of thumb for selecting a debt-equity ratio in practice.

Our situation reminds one of a quote from John Maynard Keynes. He reputedly said that, although most historians would agree that Queen Elizabeth I was both a better monarch and an unhappier woman than Queen Victoria, no one has yet been able to express the statement in a precise and rigorous formula.

Pie Again

Critics of the MM theory often say that MM fails when we add such real world issues as taxes and bankruptcy costs. Taking that view, however, blinds critics to the real value of the MM theory. The pie approach offers a more constructive way of thinking about these matters and the role of capital structure.

Taxes are just another claim on the cash flows of the firm. Let G (for government and taxes) stand for the market value of the government's claim to the firm's taxes. Bankruptcy costs are another claim on the cash flows. Let us label their value with an L (for lawyers?). The cash flows to the claim L rise with the debt-equity ratio.

Figure 16.2
The pie model
with real world
factors

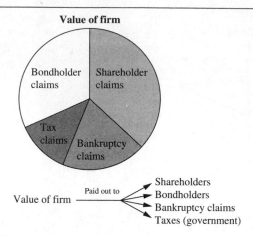

The pie theory says that all of these claims are paid from only one source, the cash flows (CF) of the firm. Algebraically, we must have

CF = Payments to shareholders

+

Payments to bondholders

+

Payments to the government

+

Payments to lawyers

+

Payments to any and all other claimants
to the cash flows of the firm

Figure 16.2 shows the new pie. No matter how many slices we take and no matter who gets them, they must still add up to the total cash flow. The value of the firm, V_T, is unaltered by the capital structure. Now, however, we must be broader in our definition of the firm's value:

$$V_T = S + B + G + L$$

We previously wrote the firm's value as

$$S + B$$

when we ignored taxes and bankruptcy costs.

Nor have we even begun to exhaust the list of financial claims to the firm's cash flows. To give an unusual example, everyone reading this book has an economic claim to the cash flows of General Motors Canada. After all, if you are injured in an accident, you might sue GM Canada. Win or lose, GM Canada will expend resources dealing with the matter. If you think this is farfetched and unimportant, ask yourself what GM Canada might be willing to pay every man, woman, and child in the country to have them promise that they would never sue the company, no matter what happened. The law does not permit such payments, but that does not mean that a value to all of those potential claims does not exist. We guess that it would run into billions of dollars, and, for GM Canada or any other company, there should be a slice of the pie labelled LS for "potential lawsuits."

This is the essence of the MM intuition and theory: V is $V(CF)$ and depends on the total cash flow of the firm. The capital structure cuts it into slices.

There is, however, an important difference between claims such as those of shareholders and bondholders on the one hand and those of government and potential litigants in lawsuits on the other. The first set of claims are **marketed claims,** and the second set are **nonmarketed claims.** One difference is that the marketed claims can be bought and sold in financial markets, and the nonmarketed claims cannot.

When we speak of the value of the firm, generally we are referring just to the value of the marketed claims, V_M, and not the value of nonmarketed claims, V_N. What we have shown is that the total value,

$$V_T = S + B + G + L$$
$$= V_M + V_N$$

is unaltered. But, as we saw, the value of the marketed claims, V_M, can change with changes in the capital structure in general and the debt-equity ratio in particular.

By the pie theory, any increase in V_M must imply an identical decrease in V_N. In an efficient market, we showed that the capital structure will be chosen to maximize the value of the marketed claims, V_M. We can equivalently think of the efficient market as working to minimize the value of the nonmarketed claims, V_N. These are taxes and bankruptcy costs in the previous example, but they also include all the other nonmarketed claims such as the LS claim.

CONCEPT QUESTIONS

- List all the claims to the firm's assets.
- Describe marketed claims and nonmarketed claims.
- How can a firm maximize the value of its marketed claims?

Shirking and Perquisites: A Note on Agency Cost of Equity   16.5

The chapter has focused on agency costs of debt so far. However, we would be remiss if we failed to consider an important agency cost of equity. A discussion of this cost of equity is contained in a well-known quote from Adam Smith:[10]

> The directors of such joint-stock companies, however, being the managers of other people's money than of their own, it cannot well be expected that they should watch over it with the same anxious vigilance with which the partners in a private copartnery frequently watch over their own. Like the stewards of a rich man, they are apt to consider attention to small matters as not for their master's honour, and very easily give themselves a dispensation from having it. Negligence and profusion, therefore, must always prevail, more or less, in the management of the affairs of such a company.

[10]Adam Smith, *The Wealth of Nations* [1776], Cannon edition (New York: Modern Library, 1937), p. 700, as quoted in M. C. Jensen and W. Meckling, "Theory of the Firm: Managerial Behavior, Agency Costs, and Ownership Structure," *Journal of Financial Economics* 3 (1978).

This elegant prose can be restated in modern vocabulary. An individual will work harder for a firm if he or she is one of its owners rather than just an employee. In addition, the individual will work harder as the owner of a larger percentage of the company. This idea has an important implication for capital structure, which we illustrate with the following example.

■ Example

Ms. Pagell is an owner-entrepreneur running a computer services firm worth $1 million. She currently owns 100 percent of the firm. Because of the need to expand, she must raise another $2 million. She can either issue $2 million of debt at 12-percent interest or issue $2 million in stock. The cash flows under the two alternatives are presented below:

	Debt issue				Stock issue			
	Cash flow	Interest	Cash flow to equity	Cash flow to Ms. Pagell (100% of equity)	Cash flow	Interest	Cash flow to equity	Cash flow to Ms. Pagell (33⅓% of equity)
6-hour days	$300,000	$240,000	$ 60,000	$ 60,000	$300,000	0	$300,000	$100,000
10-hour days	400,000	240,000	160,000	160,000	400,000	0	400,000	133,333

Like any entrepreneur, Ms. Pagell can choose the degree of intensity with which she works. In our example, she can work either 6 or 10 hours per day. With the debt issue, the extra work brings her $100,000 (or $160,000 − $60,000) more income. However, with a stock issue she retains only a one-third interest in the equity. Thus, the extra work brings her only $33,333 (or $133,333 − $100,000). Being only human, she is likely to work harder if she issues debt. In other words, she has more incentive to *shirk* if she issues equity.

In addition, she is likely to obtain more *perquisites* (a big office, a company car, more expense account meals) if she issues stock. If she is a one-third shareholder, two-thirds of these costs are paid by the other shareholders. If she is the sole owner, any additional perquisites reduce her equity stake. Thus, as the firm issues more equity, she will increase both leisure time and work-related perquisites (or *perks* for short). The leisure time and work-related amenities are called *agency costs,* because managers of the firm are agents of the shareholders. ■

This example is quite applicable to a small company considering a large stock offering. Because an owner-manager will greatly dilute his or her share in the total equity in this case, a significant drop in work intensity or a significant increase in fringe benefits is possible. Conversely, consider a large company like Royal Bank issuing shares for the umpteenth time. The typical manager has such a small percentage stake in the firm that any temptation for negligence is unlikely to change with the share issue.

Who bears the burden of these agency costs? If the new shareholders enter with their eyes open, they do not. Knowing that Ms. Pagell may work short hours, they will pay only a low price for the stock. Thus, it is the owner who is hurt by agency costs.

We saw earlier that shareholders reduce bankruptcy costs, agency cost of equity, through protective covenants. Analogously, owners try to control the agency cost of equity. Firms going public for the first time may allow monitoring by new shareholders. Owners may retain a large portion of the stock to convince new shareholders that no shirking is planned. For large firms, the monitoring role is played by the board of directors although there is considerable controversy over boards' effectiveness in this role.[11] Another common approach is to use stock options and bonuses linked to stock price performance to bring the interests of management in line with those of the shareholders. However, though these techniques may reduce the agency costs of equity, they are unlikely to eliminate them.

It is commonly suggested that leveraged buyouts (LBOs) significantly reduce the agency cost of equity. In an LBO, a purchaser (sometimes a team of existing management) buys out the shareholders at a price above the current market. In other words, the company goes private since the stock is placed in the hands of only a few people. Because the managers now own a substantial chunk of the business, they are likely to work harder than when they were simply hired hands.

Going private is one way to reduce the agency costs of equity. Another way is to increase the firm's reliance on debt. Michael Jensen has observed that the interest payments on debt can absorb excess cash flow that firms may have been tempted to spend on wasteful perquisites.[12] He argues that debt forces the firm to pay the cash flow to bondholders instead of wasting it on perquisites.

Effect of Agency Costs of Equity on Debt-Equity Financing

Before our discussion of agency costs of equity in the current section, we stated that the change in the value of the firm when debt is substituted for equity is (1) the tax shield on debt minus (2) the increase in the costs of financial distress (including the agency costs of debt). Now, the change in the value of the firm is (1) the tax shield on debt plus (2) the reduction in the agency costs of equity minus (3) the increase in the costs of financial distress (including the agency costs of debt). The optimal debt-equity ratio would be higher in a world with agency costs of equity than in a world without these costs. However, because the agency costs of debt are so significant, the costs of equity do not imply 100-percent debt financing.

CONCEPT QUESTIONS

- What are agency costs?
- Why are shirking and perquisites considered an agency cost of equity?
- How do agency costs of equity affect the firm's debt-equity ratio?

---

[11]Ronald J. Daniels, "The 'Crisis' in Canadian Corporate Governance," *Director* (Toronto: Institute of Corporate Directors, August 1993). We discuss shareholder activism in Chapter 29.

[12]Michael C. Jensen, "Agency Costs of Free Cash Flow, Corporate Finance Takeovers," *American Economic Review* 76 (1986), pp. 323–39.

16.6   ## Personal Taxes

So far in the chapter, we have considered corporate taxes only. Unfortunately, Revenue Canada does not let us off that easily. Income to individuals is taxed at federal marginal rates up to 29 percent. Combining the provincial tax rate with the federal tax rate, the marginal rates can be as high as 48 percent.[13] Furthermore, Revenue Canada offers a dividend tax credit to individuals to eliminate double taxation. The following Water Products example presents the effect of personal taxes on capital structure.

	Plan I	Plan II
Earnings before interest and taxes (EBIT)	$1,000,000	$1,000,000
Interest ($r_B B$)	0	(400,000)
Earnings before taxes (EBT = EBIT − $r_B B$)	1,000,000	600,000
Taxes ($T_C = 0.40$)	(400,000)	(240,000)
Earnings after corporate taxes	600,000	360,000
EAT = (EBIT − $r_B B$) × (1−T_c)		
Total cash flow to both shareholders and bondholders		
[EBIT × (1−T_C) + $T_C r_B B$]	$ 600,000	760,000

As presented above, this example considers corporate taxes but not personal taxes. To treat these personal taxes, we first assume that all earnings after taxes are paid out as dividends, and that both dividends and interest are taxed at the same personal rate. (We assume 36 percent.)

	Plan I	Plan II
Dividends	$ 600,000	$ 360,000
Personal taxes on dividends		
(Personal rate = 36%)	(216,000)	(129,600)
Dividends after personal taxes	$ 384,000	$ 230,400
Interest	0	$ 400,000
Taxes on interest	0	(144,000)
Interest after personal taxes	0	256,000
Total cash flow to both bondholders and shareholders		
after personal taxes	$ 384,000	$ 486,400

Total taxes paid at both corporate and personal levels are

Plan I: $400,000   + $216,000   = $616,000
          Corporate taxes   Personal taxes
                                   on dividends

Plan II: $240,000 $129,600 $144,000 = $513,600
           Corporate taxes   +   Personal taxes   +   Personal taxes
                                   on dividends   on interest

Total cash flow to all investors after personal taxes is greater under plan II. This must be the case because (1) total cash flow was higher when personal taxes were ignored and (2) all cash flows (both interest and dividends) are taxed at the same personal tax rate. Thus, the conclusion that debt increases the value of the firm still holds.

---

[13]The appendix to Chapter 1 gives more detail on taxes.

However, the analysis to this point assumed that all earnings are paid out in dividends, and the personal tax rate on dividends was the same as the personal tax rate on interest. In reality, dividends may be deferred through retention of earnings, and a dividend tax credit exists to integrate the tax system. Thus, the effective personal tax rate on distributions to shareholders is below the personal tax rate on interest.[14]

To illustrate this tax rate differential, let us assume that the effective personal tax rate on distributions to shareholders, T_S, is 10 percent and the personal tax rate on interest, T_B, is 50 percent. The cash flows for the two plans are

	Plan I	Plan II
Distributions to shareholders	$600,000	$ 360,000
Personal taxes on shareholder distributions (at 10% tax rate)	(60,000)	(36,000)
Distribution to shareholders after personal taxes	540,000	324,000
Interest	0	400,000
Taxes on interest (at 50% tax rate)	0	(200,000)
Interest after personal taxes	0	200,000
Add back shareholder distributions after personal taxes	540,000	324,000
Total cash flow to all investors after personal taxes	$540,000	$ 524,000

Total taxes paid at both personal and corporate levels are

Plan I: $400,000 + $60,000 = $460,000
Corporate taxes   Personal taxes
                      on dividends

Plan II: $240,000 $36,000 $200,000 = $476,000
Corporate taxes + Personal taxes + Personal taxes
                   on dividends   on interest

In this scenario, the total cash flows are higher under plan I than under plan II. Though the example is expressed in terms of cash flows, we would expect the value of the firm to be higher under plan I than under plan II. Which plan does Revenue Canada dislike most? Clearly, Revenue Canada dislikes plan I more because lower total taxes are paid. The increase in corporate taxes under the all-equity plan is more than offset by the decrease in personal taxes.

Interest receives a tax deduction at the corporate level. Equity distributions are taxed at a lower rate than interest at the personal level. The above examples illustrate that total tax at all levels may either increase or decrease with debt, depending on the tax rates and tax credits in effect.

The Miller Model

Valuation under Personal and Corporate Taxes

The previous example calculated *cash flows* for the two plans under personal and corporate taxes. However, we have made no attempt to determine firm value so far. It

---

[14]Positive NPV investments financed by deferring dividends will lead to capital gains also taxed at a lower rate. We discuss this in more detail in Chapter 18.

can be shown that the value of the levered firm can be expressed in terms of an unlevered firm as[15]

$$V_L = V_U + \left[\frac{1 - (1 - T_c) \times (1 - T_s)}{(1 - T_B)} \right] \times B \tag{16.1}$$

T_B is the personal tax rate on ordinary income, such as interest, and T_S is the personal tax rate on equity distributions.

If we set $T_B = T_S$, equation (16.1) simplifies to

$$V_L = V_U + T_C B \tag{16.2}$$

which is the result we calculated for a world of no personal taxes. Hence, the introduction of personal taxes does not affect our valuation formula as long as equity distributions are taxed identically to interest at the personal level.

However, the gain from leverage is reduced when $T_S < T_B$. Here, more taxes are paid at the personal level for a levered firm than for an unlevered firm. In fact, imagine that $(1 - T_C) \times (1 - T_S) = 1 - T_B$. Formula (16.1) tells us there is no gain from leverage at all! In other words, the value of the levered firm is equal to the value of the unlevered firm. The gain from leverage disappears because the lower corporate taxes for a levered firm are *exactly* offset by higher personal taxes. These results are presented in Figure 16.3.

▪ *Example*

Acme Industries anticipates a perpetual pretax earning stream of $100,000 and faces a 45-percent corporate tax rate. Investors discount the earnings stream after corporate taxes at 15 percent. The personal tax rate on equity distributions is 30 percent and the personal tax rate on interest is 47 percent. Acme currently has an all-equity capital structure but is considering borrowing $120,000 at 10 percent.

---

[15]Shareholders receive

$(EBIT - r_B B) \times (1 - T_C) \times (1 - T_S)$

Bondholders receive

$r_B B \times (1 - T_B)$

Thus, the total cash flow to all stakeholders is

$(EBIT - r_B B) \times (1 - T_C) \times (1 - T_S) + r_B B \times (1 - T_B)$

which can be rewritten as

$$EBIT \times (1 - T_C) \times (1 - T_S) + r_B B \times (1 - T_B) \times \left[\frac{1 - (1 - T_C) \times (1 - T_S)}{1 - T_B} \right] \tag{a}$$

The first term in Equation (a) is the cash flow from an unlevered firm after all taxes. The value of this stream must be V_U, the value of an unlevered firm. An individual buying a bond for B receives $r_B B \times (1 - T_B)$ after all taxes. Thus, the value of the second term in (a) must be

$$B \times \left[\frac{1 - (1 - T_C) \times (1 - T_S)}{1 - T_B} \right]$$

Therefore, the value of the stream in Equation (a), which is the value of the levered firm, must be

$$V_U + \left[\frac{1 - (1 - T_C) \times (1 - T_S)}{1 - T_B} \right] \times B$$

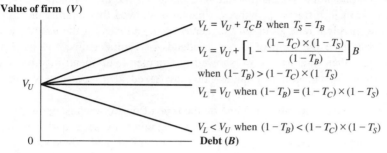

Value of firm (V)

$V_L = V_U + T_C B$ when $T_S = T_B$

$V_L = V_U + \left[1 - \dfrac{(1 - T_C) \times (1 - T_S)}{(1 - T_B)}\right] B$

when $(1 - T_B) > (1 - T_C) \times (1\ T_S)$

$V_L = V_U$ when $(1 - T_B) = (1 - T_C) \times (1 - T_S)$

$V_L < V_U$ when $(1 - T_B) < (1 - T_C) \times (1 - T_S)$

Debt (B)

Figure 16.3
Gains from
financial leverage
with both corporate
and personal taxes

T_C is the corporate tax rate.
T_B is the personal tax rate on interest.
T_S is the personal tax rate on dividends and other equity distributions.
Both personal taxes and corporate taxes are included. Bankruptcy costs and agency
costs are ignored. The effect of debt on firm value depends on T_S, T_C, and T_B.

The value of the all-equity firm is[16]

$$V_u = \frac{\$100,000 \times (1 - .45)}{0.15} = \$366,667$$

The value of the levered firm is

$$V_1 = \$366,667 + \left[\frac{1 - (1 - .45) \times (1 - .30)}{(1 - .47)}\right] \times \$120,000 = \$399,497$$

The advantage to leverage here is $\$399,497 - \$366,667 = \$32,830$. This is much smaller than the $\$54,000 = .45 \times \$120,000 = T_C \times B$, which would have been the gain in a world with no personal taxes.

Acme had previously considered the choice years earlier when $T_B = 60$ percent and $T_s = 18$ percent. Here

$$V_1 = \$366,667 + \left[\frac{1 - (1 - .45) \times (1 - .18)}{(1 - .60)}\right] \times \$120,000 = \$351,367$$

In this case the value of the levered firm, V_1 is $\$351,367$, which is *less than* the value of the unlevered firm, $V_u = \$366,667$. Hence, Acme was wise not to increase leverage years ago. Leverage causes a loss of value in this case because the personal tax rate on interest is much higher than the personal tax rate on equity distributions. In other words, the reduction in corporate taxes from leverage is more than offset by the increase in taxes from leverage at the personal level. ∎

---

[16]Alternatively, we could have said that investors discount the earnings stream after both corporate and personal taxes at $10.5\% = [15\% \times (1 - 0.30)]$:

$$V_U = \frac{\$100,000 \times (1 - .45) \times (1 - .30)}{0.105} = \$366,667$$

Which one is the most applicable to Canada? While the numbers are different for different firms in different provinces, Chapter 1 showed that interest income is taxed at the full marginal rate, around 47 percent before surtaxes for the top bracket. Equity distributions take the form of either dividends or capital gains, and both are taxed more lightly than interest. As we showed in Chapter 1, dividend income is sheltered by the dividend tax credit. Capital gains are taxed at 75 percent of the marginal tax rate.

While the exact numbers depend on the type of portfolio chosen, our first scenario for Acme is a reasonable tax scenario for Canadian investors and companies.[17] In Canada, personal taxes reduce, but do not eliminate, the advantage to corporate leverage. This result is still unrealistic. It suggests that firms should add debt, moving out on the second line from the top in Figure 16.3, until 100-percent leverage is reached. Firms do not do this. One reason is that interest on debt is not the firm's only tax shield. Investment tax credits, capital cost allowance, and depletion allowances give rise to tax shields regardless of the firm's decision on leverage. Because these other tax shields exist, increased leverage brings with it a risk that income will not be high enough to utilize the debt tax shield fully. The result is that firms will use a limited amount of debt.[18]

The results of limited tax deductibility are provided in Figure 16.4. Firm value should rise when debt is first added to the capital structure. However, as more and more debt is issued, the full deductibility of the interest becomes less likely. Firm

Figure 16.4
Value of the firm under the Miller model when interest deductibility is limited to earnings

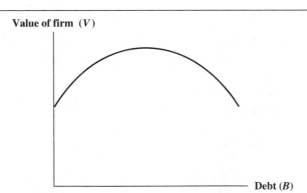

Value of firm (V)

Debt (B)

The Miller model with limited deductibility of interest leads to a ∩-shaped graph similar to the one presented in Figure 16.1. The ∩ shape in Figure 16.1 arose from the trade-off between corporate taxes and bankruptcy costs.

[17]Support for this scenario comes from M. H. Wilson, "Draft Legislation, Regulations, and Explanatory Notes Respecting Preferred Share Financing," (Ottawa: Department of Finance, April 1988).

[18]This argument was first advanced by H. DeAngelo and R. Masulis, "Optimal Capital Structure under Corporate and Personal Taxation," *Journal of Financial Economics* (March 1980), pp. 3–30. Empirical testing in Canada has so far failed to find strong support for the argument: A. H. R. Davis, "The Corporate Use of Debt Substitutes in Canada: A Test of Competing Versions of the Substitution Hypothesis," *Canadian Journal of Administrative Sciences* 11 (March 1994), pp. 105–15.

value still increases, but at a lower and lower rate. At some point, the probability of tax deductibility is low enough that an incremental dollar of debt is as costly to the firm as an incremental dollar of equity. Firm value then decreases with further leverage.

This graph looks surprisingly like the curve in Figure 16.1 where the trade-off between the tax shield and bankruptcy costs is illustrated. Thus, a key change in assumptions may explain why firms are not 100-percent debt financed under the current tax code.

CONCEPT QUESTION

- How do personal taxes change the conclusions of the Modigliani–Miller model about capital structure?

How Firms Establish Capital Structure   16.7

The theories of capital structure are among the most elegant and sophisticated in the field of finance. Financial economists should (and do!) pat themselves on the back for contributions in this area. However, the practical applications of the theories are less than fully satisfying. Consider that our work on net present value produced an exact formula for evaluating projects. Conversely, the most we can say on capital structure is provided in either Figure 16.1 or Figure 16.4; the optimal capital structure involves a trade-off between taxes and costs of debt. No exact formula is available for evaluating the optimal debt-equity ratio. For this reason, we turn to empirical evidence.

The following empirical regularities are worthwhile to consider when formulating capital structure policy:

1. *Most Canadian firms have low debt-equity ratios.* Figure 16.5 shows the trend in debt-equity ratios (measured at book values) for large industrial corporations in Canada and the United States. Notice that debt ratios in Canada are quite a bit lower. Although most corporations have debt in their capital structures, they still pay substantial taxes. Thus, it is clear that corporations have not issued debt up to the point that tax shelters have been completely used up, and we conclude that there must be limits to the amount of debt corporations can issue.

Some large corporations in the United States tested those limits in the 1980s. Use of leverage by large U.S. corporations increased substantially in the 1980s in part due to leveraged buyouts.[19] In certain well-known cases (Donald Trump and Robert Campeau creating two examples), leverage became excessive. Figure 16.5 shows that the trend toward higher leverage did not extend to Canada. Why Canadian firms use proportionately less debt is a controversial question. One possible explanation is the difference in personal taxes. In Canada, the dividend tax credit reduces personal taxes on equity distributions and reduces the tax advantage of debt financing.

---

[19]For example, Ben Bernanke, "Is There Too Much Corporate Debt?" *Business Review of the Federal Reserve Bank of Philadelphia* (September-October 1989), pp. 3–13, reports that the debt of nonfinancial corporations rose 70 percent between 1983 and 1988, more than two-thirds faster than the growth in GNP.

Figure 16.5
Canadian and U.S. debt-equity ratios for industrial corporations

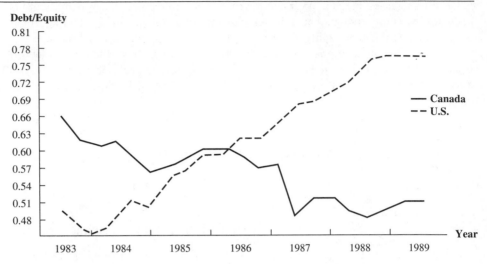

Source: J. Grant, M. Webb, and P. Hendrick, "Financing Corporate Canada in the 1990s," *Canadian Investment Review* (Spring 1990), p. 10.

2. Changes in financial leverage affect firm value. In an important study, Masulis examined the effect of announcements of changes in capital structure on stock prices.[20] Table 16.3 is an example of the type of results that Masulis obtained. The table shows the effect of announcing increases and decreases in financial leverage on abnormal returns on common stock. Notice that when firms announce an increase in leverage, there is a large increase in firm value (4.51 percent on day 0 and 3.12 percent on day 1). When they announce a decrease in leverage, there is a decrease in firm value (−2.98 percent on day 0 and −2.39 percent on day 1). These are percentages of total firm value. Several conclusions emerge from the Masulis study. First, changes in financial leverage predicted to cause a tax shield for corporate debt are associated with changes in stock price consistent with these predictions. Second, sometimes shareholders are adversely affected by a change in leverage. This suggests the firm may not be following a policy of maximizing shareholder wealth. Third, there is little evidence that bankruptcy costs have a significant effect.

3. *There are differences in the capital structures of different industries.* Table 16.4 shows Canadian debt-equity ratios for selected industries measured at book values. Clearly there are rather large differences in the use of debt among industries. Steel mills, for example, carry about twice as much debt as pharmaceutical firms.

This is consistent with our discussion of the costs of financial distress. Steel mills have large tangible assets while pharmaceutical firms carry significant intangible assets in the form of research and development. Tangible assets have lower agency costs

---

[20]Ronald Masulis, "The Effects of Capital Structure Change on Security Prices: A Study of Exchange Offers," *Journal of Financial Economics* 8 (1980).

	Increasing leverage		Decreasing leverage		**Table 16.3**
Event day	Portfolio daily returns (%)	Percentage of stock returns > 0	Portfolio daily returns (%)	Percentage of stock returns > 0	Rates of return on common stock from initial announcement of offers increasing and decreasing leverage
−10	0.38%	42.0	−0.54%	28.0	
−9	0.34	31.0	1.02	44.0	
−8	0.03	43.0	0.17	39.0	
−7	0.53	41.0	0.13	33.0	
−6	0.40	36.0	1.43	33.0	
−5	0.29	42.0	−0.43	30.0	
−4	0.16	31.0	−0.09	30.0	
−3	0.62	43.0	0.60	46.0	
−2	0.15	40.0	1.20	36.0	
−1	0.50	38.0	0.74	49.0	
0	4.51	69.0	−2.98	11.0	
1	3.12	58.0	−2.39	25.0	
2	0.00	37.0	0.06	30.0	
3	0.71	27.0	−0.60	33.0	
4	0.21	40.0	0.26	28.0	
5	0.09	34.0	0.46	32.0	
6	0.54	26.0	0.30	21.0	
7	0.15	30.0	0.31	35.0	
8	0.26	27.0	0.39	39.0	
9	0.06	39.0	−0.14	37.0	
10	0.19	37.0	−0.47	29.0	

Source: R. Masulis. "The Effects of Capital Structure Policy Change on Security Prices: A Study of Exchange Offers," *Journal of Financial Economics* 8 (1980), pp. 158–159.

since they are easier to monitor and so make better security for debt. In general, firms that have high proportions of intangible assets and growth opportunities tend to use less debt. For example, Long and Malitz found that firms heavily into advertising and research use less debt.[21] This may account for why pharmaceutical companies use very little debt. There is some evidence that firms adjust their actual debt-equity ratios toward a target ratio.[22]

We clearly have no unique formula that can establish a debt-equity ratio for all companies. We cannot state that more debt is better than less debt. However, there is evidence that firms behave as if they had target debt-equity ratios. From a theoretical perspective and from empirical research, we present three important factors in the final determination of a target debt-equity ratio:

1. *Taxes.* If a company has (and will continue to have) taxable income, an increased reliance on debt will reduce taxes paid by the company and increase taxes paid by some bondholders. If corporate tax rates are higher than bondholder tax rates, there is value from using debt.

---

[21]Michael Long and Ileen Malitz, "The Investment Financing Nexus: Some Empirical Evidence," *Midland Corporate Finance Journal* (Fall 1985).

[22]P. Marsh, "The Choice between Equity and Debt: An Empirical Study," *Journal of Finance* (March 1981); R. Taggart, "A Model of Corporate Financing Decisions," *Journal of Finance* (December 1977); and J. K. Cheung, S. P. Roy, and I. Gordon, "Financing Policies of Large Canadian Corporations," *CMA Magazine* (May 1989), pp. 26–31.

Table 16.4
Book value debt-equity ratios for selected industries in Canada, 1989

Industry	Ratio	Companies
Retail trade	2.214	85,890
Auto accessories and parts	3.048	2,929
Food stores	1.828	12,859
Gas service stations	2.576	6,878
Manufacturers	1.253	41,801
Agricultural implements	2.739	230
Cement	0.814	20
Industrial chemicals	2.041	139
Men's clothing	1.424	738
Women's clothing	1.883	1,313
Communication equipment	0.635	503
Distilleries	1.032	25
Industrial electrical equipment	0.898	223
Fish products	4.053	468
Glass and glass products	1.101	195
Motor vehicles and parts	1.149	463
Paint and varnish	0.956	131
Paper products	0.939	246
Petroleum refineries	0.985	80
Pharmaceuticals	0.686	141
Pulp and paper mills	1.446	111
Rubber products	1.202	156
Sawmills and planing mills	2.160	1,236
Soap and cleaning compounds	0.745	125
Steel and iron mills	1.389	111
Textile products	1.431	706
Wineries	0.877	41
Wood products	1.929	465
Construction	3.005	59,286
Services	2.631	120,965
Mining	1.318	7,797
Agriculture, forestry, and fishery	1.828	23,030
Agriculture	1.890	17,435
Fishing and trapping	3.206	1,550
Forestry	1.368	4,045

Source: Dun & Bradstreet, *Key Business Ratios of Canadian Businesses,* 1989.

2. *Financial distress costs.* Financial distress is costly, with or without formal bankruptcy proceedings. Firms with less certain operating income will have a greater chance of experiencing financial distress and will issue less debt. The costs of financial distress depend on the types of assets that the firm has. For example, if a firm has a large investment in land, buildings, and other tangible assets, it will have lower costs of financial distress than a firm with a large investment in research and development. Research and development typically has less resale value than land; thus, most of its value disappears in financial distress.

3. *Pecking order and financial slack.*[23] We introduced the idea of a pecking order in our discussion of the financing patterns of firms in Chapter 14. The critical assumption of the **pecking order** theory is that firms prefer internal equity (retained

---

[23]The pecking order theory is generally attributed to S. C. Myers, "The Capital Structure Puzzle," *Journal of Finance* 39 (July 1984).

earnings) over external equity (issuing new shares of stock). Two reasons can explain this:

- External equity is more costly than internal equity.
- It is hard for shareholders to price external equity accurately when managers know more about the firm than shareholders (*asymmetric information*). This can lead to shareholder reluctance to accept new equity issues.

If firms prefer internal equity over external equity, they may use less debt than is implied by theories focusing on taxes and financial distress costs. Instead, the firms will try to accumulate financial slack to reduce the chances that the firm will need to use external equity.

The pecking order theory can explain why the most profitable firms such as pharmaceuticals use less debt. More profitable firms use less debt because they have more internal equity, and internal equity comes before debt in the pecking order. The theory also explains why some firms use less debt than would otherwise seem appropriate because it allows them greater financial flexibility to avoid using costly external equity financing when the need arises. In a survey of large Canadian corporations, Cheung, Roy, and Gordon found support for the pecking order theory. Managers identified maintaining financial flexibility as the most important factor in setting the target debt ratio.[24]

In practice, firms (and lenders) also look at their industry's debt-equity ratio as a guide. This practice creates a market for Dun and Bradstreet (our source in Table 16.4), a commercial supplier of ratios to financial analysts and bankers. While looking to the industry average may strike some as a cowardly approach, it at least keeps firms from deviating far from accepted practice. After all, the existing firms in any industry are the survivors. Therefore, one should pay at least some attention to their decisions. Of course, if the entire industry is in distress, the average leverage is likely too high. For example, in 1989, the average debt-equity ratio of 3.206 for fishing and trapping was probably too high.

CONCEPT QUESTIONS

- List the empirical regularities we observe for corporate capital structure.
- What are the factors to consider in establishing a debt-equity ratio?

The Decision to Use More Debt: The Case of Campeau Corporation's Acquisition of Federated

16.8

What actually happens when a particular firm decides to use more debt?[25] Let's look at Campeau Corp.'s experiences. Campeau's increased reliance on debt in the acquisition of Federated Department Stores illustrates many important points of this chapter.

---

[24]J. K. Cheung, S. P. Roy, and I. Gordon, "Financing Policies of Large Canadian Corporations.

[25]This section draws on Steven N. Kaplan, "Campeau's Acquisition of Federated: Value Destroyed or Value Added," *Journal of Financial Economics* 25 (1989), pp. 191–212.

On May 3, 1988, after a series of acquisition events, Campeau Corp. purchased Federated Department Stores (a U.S. chain) for $8.17 billion; $7.96 billion (97 percent of the purchase) was financed with debt. In his analysis of this acquisition, Kaplan estimates that after the acquisition, Federated assets increased in value by $1.8 billion. Possible sources of increased value include tax benefits and profits from selling off assets that were undervalued on Federated's balance sheet.

However, even with this large increase in value, Federated had to file for protection under Chapter 11 of U.S. bankruptcy laws in 1990. The biggest reason why Federated filed for bankruptcy was that cash flow was not sufficient to meet the required debt service. Furthermore, Campeau did not have other assets to make up the shortfall. Kaplan argues that if Campeau had financed the acquisition with a mix of debt and equity (as opposed to 97-percent debt), Federated would not have had to file for bankruptcy: "the Federated purchase illustrates that a highly leveraged transaction can increase value, but still not be able to make its debt payments."

Benefits

First we examine benefits of Campeau's acquisition of Federated:

1. *Asset sales to more efficient managers.* After purchasing Federated, Campeau proceeded to sell many of the operating divisions. These sales of assets to other department stores and related businesses appear to have increased value. One reason is that Campeau's purchase of Federated came after the stock market crash of 1987; the stock and bond markets may have undervalued Federated. A less convincing argument why value was created is that the purchasers overpaid for the assets sold. In fact, the companies that bought assets showed good postpurchase performance. However, this potential source of value cannot be overlooked.
2. *Lower agency costs.* It is often argued that leverage reduces the agency cost of equity. The new debt from the acquisition forced managers to maximize resources and cash flow.
3. *Tax benefits.* It is well known that new debt can increase a firm's value by reducing taxes. Although Campeau retired some Federated debt with asset sales, most of the asset sales were also financed with debt, and interest tax shields were created and maintained.

Costs

Next we examine costs of the acquisition:

1. *Financial distress.* When firms such as Campeau increase their reliance on debt, they also increase the likelihood of financial distress. Financial distress can be formal bankruptcy, which happened to Federated on January 15, 1990. Bankruptcy costs include court costs (direct costs) and loss of market share (indirect costs).
2. *Financial slack.* The debt Campeau used to finance the Federated acquisition was well beyond industry norms. In fact, after the purchase, Campeau used up all of Federated's financial slack, which caused the

bankruptcy filing. One key area of concern after using up the financial slack is capital expenditures. Cuts in capital expenditures by Federated during the Campeau period may have hurt its assets' market value.

Part of Campeau's purchase of Federated can be analyzed in terms of asset sales, tax benefits, and the costs of financial distress. However, the Campeau experience shows that agency costs and financial slack are also factors in the firm's decision to use more debt.

Summary and Conclusions 16.9

1. We stated in the previous chapter that, according to theory, firms should create all-debt capital structures under corporate taxation. Because firms generally assume moderate amounts of debt in the real world, the theory presented in the previous chapter must be missing something. We point out in this chapter that costs of financial distress cause firms to restrain their issuance of debt. These costs are of two types: direct and indirect. Lawyers' and accountants' fees during the bankruptcy process are examples of direct costs. We gave four examples of indirect costs:

   Impaired ability to conduct business.
   Incentive to take on risky projects.
   Incentive toward underinvestment.
   Distribution of funds to shareholders prior to bankruptcy.

2. Because these costs are substantial and the shareholders ultimately bear them, firms have an incentive for cost reduction. We suggest three cost reduction techniques:

   Protective covenants.
   Repurchase of debt prior to bankruptcy.
   Consolidation of debt.

3. Because costs of financial distress can be reduced but not eliminated, firms will not finance entirely with debt. Figure 16.1 illustrates the relationship between firm value and debt. In the figure, firms select the debt-to-equity ratio at which firm value is maximized.

4. The results so far have ignored personal taxes. If distributions to equityholders are taxed at a lower effective personal tax rate than are interest payments, the tax advantage to debt at the corporate level is partially offset. In fact, the corporate tax advantage to debt is eliminated if

$$(1 - T_C) \times (1 - T_S) = (1 - T_B)$$

5. Miller has proposed an equilibrium model in which personal and corporate taxes are integrated. He argues that, in equilibrium,

$$r_S = r_B \times (1 - T_C)$$

In his model, firms are indifferent to whether they issue debt or issue equity. Surprisingly, this is the same conclusion that Modigliani and Miller reached in their simpler model. In addition, Miller argues that individuals in high tax brackets purchase stock while individuals in low tax brackets purchase bonds.

6. Debt-to-equity ratios vary across industries. From a theoretical perspective and from empirical research, we present three factors determining the target debt-to-equity ratio:

   a. *Taxes.* Firms with high taxable income should rely more on debt than firms with little taxable income.

   b. *Financial distress costs.* Firms for which financial distress is relatively costly should use less debt than firms that anticipate lower costs.

   c. *Pecking order.* The most profitable firms will use less debt because they have sufficient internal equity for all positive NPV projects. Some firms will accumulate financial slack to avoid using external equity.

Key Terms

Agency costs 453

Protective covenants 456

Negative covenant 457

Positive covenant 457

Marketed claims 461

Nonmarketed claims 461

Pecking order 472

Suggested Readings

Research on the stock market and capital structure is superbly summarized in:

C. Smith. "Raising Capital: Theory and Evidence." *Midland Corporate Finance Journal* (Spring 1986).

Stewart Myers's 1984 presidential address to the American Finance Association summarizes the academic insights on capital structure up to the early 1980s and the so-called static theory, and points out directions for future research:

S. Myers. "Presidential Address: The Capital Structure Puzzle." *Journal of Finance* 39 (July 1984), pp. 575–92.

An extremely influential set of articles arguing that bankruptcy costs are low are:

R. A. Haugen and L. Senbet. "The Insignificance of Bankruptcy Costs to the Theory of Optimal Capital Structure." *Journal of Finance* (May 1978).

R. A. Haugen and L. Senbet. "New Perspectives on Information Asymmetry and Agency Relationships." *Journal of Financial and Quantitative Analysis* (November 1979).

R. A. Haugen and L. Senbet. "Bankruptcy and Agency Costs: Their Significance to the Theory of Optimal Capital Structure." *Journal of Financial and Quantitative Analysis* (March 1988).

An excellent survey of various capital structure theories appears in:

Milton Harris and A. Raviv. "The Theory of Capital Structure." *Journal of Finance* (March 1991), pp. 297–355.

An interesting survey of financing policies in Canada is in:

J. K. Cheung, S. P. Roy, and I. Gordon. "Financing Policies of Large Canadian Corporations." *CMA Magazine* (May 1989), pp. 26–31.

Some Useful Formulas of Financial Structure   APPENDIX A

We start with some definitions:

$$E(EBIT) = \text{A perpetual expectation of cash operating income}$$
$$\text{before interest and taxes}$$
$$V_U = \text{Value of an unlevered firm}$$
$$V_L = \text{Value of a levered firm}$$
$$B = \text{Present value of debt}$$
$$S = \text{Present value of equity}$$
$$r_S = \text{Cost of equity}$$
$$r_B = \text{Cost of debt capital}$$
$$r_0 = \text{Cost of capital to an all-equity firm.}[26]$$

Model I (No Tax):

$$V_L = V_U = \frac{E(EBIT)}{r_0}$$

$$r_S = r_0 + (r_0 - r_B) \times \frac{B}{S}$$

Model II (Corporate tax, $T_C > 0$; No Personal Taxes, $T_S = T_B = 0$):

$$V_L = \frac{E[EBIT \times (1 - T_C)]}{r_0} + \frac{T_C r_B B}{r_B} = V_U + T_C B$$

$$r_S = r_0 + (1 - T_C) \times (r_0 - r_B) \times \frac{B}{S}$$

Model III (Corporate Tax, $T_C > 0$; Personal Tax, $T_B > 0$; $T_S > 0$):

$$V_L = V_U + \left[1 - \frac{(1 - T_C) \times (1 - T_S)}{(1 - T_B)}\right] \times B$$

---

[26]In a world of no corporate taxes, the weighted average cost of capital to a levered firm, r_{WACC} is also equal to r_0. However, with corporate taxes, r_0 is above r_{WACC} for a levered firm.

The Miller Model and the Graduated Income Tax

In our previous discussion, we assumed a flat personal income tax on interest income. In other words, we assumed that all individuals are subject to the same personal tax rate on interest income. Merton Miller derived the results of the previous section in a classic paper.[27] However, the genius of his paper was to consider the implications of personal taxes when tax rates differ across individuals.

This *graduated* income tax is consistent with the real world. For example, individuals are currently taxed at federal rates of 0, 17, 26, and 29 percent in Canada, depending on income. In addition, other entities, such as pension funds and universities, are tax-exempt.

To illustrate Miller's model with graduated taxes, we consider a world where all firms initially only issue equity. We assume that $T_C = 40$ percent and $T_S = 0.$[28] The required return on stock, r_S, is 10 percent. In addition, we posit a graduated personal income tax, where tax rates vary between 0 and 50 percent. All individuals are risk-neutral.

Now consider a courageous firm contemplating a $1,000 issue of debt. What is the interest rate that the firm can pay and still be as well off as if it issued equity? Because debt is tax deductible, the after–corporate-tax cost of debt is $(1 - T_C) \times r_B$. However, distributions to equity are not deductible at the corporate level, so the after-tax cost of equity is r_S. Thus, the firm is indifferent to whether it issues debt or equity when

$$(1 - T_C) \times r_B = r_S$$

Because $T_C = 40\%$ and $r_S = 10\%$, the firm could afford to pay a rate on debt as high as 16.67 percent.

Miller argues that those in the lowest tax brackets (tax-exempt in our example) will buy the debt because they pay the least personal tax on interest. These tax-exempt investors will be indifferent to whether they buy the stock or purchase bonds also yielding 10 percent. Thus, if this firm is the *only* one issuing debt, it can pay an interest rate well below its break-even rate of 16.67 percent.

Noticing the gain to the first firm, many other firms are likely to issue debt. However, if there are only a fixed number of tax-exempt investors, new debt issues must attract people in higher brackets. Because these individuals are taxed on interest at a higher rate than they are taxed on equity distributions, they will only buy debt if its yield is greater than 10 percent. For example, an individual in the 15-percent bracket has an interest rate after personal tax of $r_B \times (1 - 0.15)$. He will be indifferent to whether he buys bonds or stock if $r_B = 11.765\%$, because $11.765 \times 0.85 = 10\%$. Because 11.765 percent is less than the 16.67-percent rate of equation (16.3), corporations gain by issuing debt to investors in the 15-percent bracket.

Now consider investors in the 40-percent bracket. A return on bonds of 16.67 percent provides them with a $10\% = 16.67\% \times (1 - 0.40)$ interest rate after personal

---

[27]M. Miller, "Debt and Taxes," *Journal of Finance* (May 1977). Yes, this is the same Miller as in MM.

[28]The assumption that $T_S = 0$ is perhaps extreme. However, it is commonly made in the literature, justified by the investor's ability to defer realization of capital gains indefinitely. Besides, the same qualitative conclusions hold if $T_S > 0$, though the explanation would be more involved.

tax. Thus, they are indifferent to whether they earn a 16.67-percent return on bonds or a 10-percent return on stock. Miller argues that, in equilibrium, corporations will issue enough debt so that investors with personal tax brackets up to and including 40 percent will hold debt.[29] Additional debt will not be issued because the interest rate needed to attract investors in higher tax brackets is above the (16.67-percent) rate that corporations can afford to pay.

The beauty of competition is that other companies can so capitalize on someone's innovation that all value to the courageous first entrant is eliminated. According to the Miller model, firms will issue enough debt so that individuals up to and including the 40-percent bracket hold it. To induce these investors to hold bonds, the competitive interest rate becomes 16.67 percent. No firm profits from issuing debt in equilibrium. Rather, all firms are indifferent to whether they issue debt or equity in equilibrium.

Miller's work produces three results:

1. In aggregate, the corporate sector will issue just enough debt so that individuals with tax brackets equal to and below the corporate tax rate, T_C, will hold debt, and individuals with higher tax brackets will not hold debt. Thus, individuals in these higher brackets will hold stock.

2. Because people in tax brackets equal to the corporate rate hold debt, there is no gain or loss to corporate leverage. Therefore, the capital structure decision is a matter of indifference to an individual firm.[30] Though the Miller model is quite sophisticated, this conclusion is identical to that reached by MM in a world without any taxes.

3. As given in equation (16.3), the return on bonds will be higher than the return on stocks of comparable risk. (An adjustment to equation (16.3) must be made to reflect the greater risk of stocks in the real world.)

▪ Example

Consider an economy in which there are four groups of investors and no others:

Group	Marginal tax rate (%) on bonds (T_B)	Personal wealth (in $ millions)
Finance majors	50%	$1,200
Accounting majors	40	300
Marketing majors	20	150
Management majors	0	50

We assume that investors are risk-neutral and that equity income is untaxed at the personal level for all investors (i.e., $T_S = 0$). All investors can earn a tax-free return of 5.4 percent by investing in foreign real estate; therefore, this is the return on equity. The corporate tax rate is 40 percent. Interest payments are tax deductible at the corporate level and taxable at the individual level. Corporations receive a total of $120 million in cash flow before tax and interest. There are no growth opportunities, and every year is the same in perpetuity. What is the range of possible debt-equity ratios?

---

[29]All investors with $T_B < 40$ percent hold bonds. Because investors with $T_B = 40$ percent are indifferent to whether they hold stocks or bonds, only some of them are likely to choose bonds.

[30]Although capital structure is irrelevant to an individual firm, point 1 means that there will be an optimal economywide capital structure to satisfy investors facing different tax rates.

The return on equity, r_S, will be set equal to the return on foreign real estate, which is 0.054. In a Miller equilibrium, $r_S = (1 - T_C) \times r_B$. Therefore,

$$r_B = \frac{0.054}{1 - 0.40} = 0.09$$

Given the tax brackets of the different groups of investors, we would expect that finance majors would hold equity and foreign real estate, and accounting majors would be indifferent to whether they held equity or debt. Marketing and management majors would hold bonds because their personal tax rates are below 0.40. Because accounting majors are indifferent to whether they hold bonds or stocks, we must learn what happens if they invest in bonds or equity. If accounting majors use their $300 to buy bonds, $B = \$300 + \$150 + \$50 = \$500$. Then the following calculations can be made:

$$S = \frac{(\text{EBIT} - r_B B) \times (1 - T_C)}{r_S} = \frac{[\$120 - (0.09 \times \$500)] \times (1 - 0.40)}{0.054}$$

$$= \$833.33$$

$$B = \frac{r_B B}{r_B} = \$500$$

$$V_L = S + B = \$833.33 + \$500 = \$1,333.33$$

$$\frac{B}{S} = \frac{\$500}{\$833.33} = 0.600$$

If accounting majors buy stocks and foreign real estate ($B = \$150 + \$50 = \$200$),

$$S = \frac{(\text{EBIT} - r_B B) \times (1 - T_C)}{r_S} = \frac{[\$120 - (0.09 \times \$200)] \times (1 - 0.40)}{0.054}$$

$$= \$1,133.33$$

$$B = \$200$$

$$V_L = S + B = \$1,133.33 + \$200 = \$1,333.33$$

$$\frac{B}{S} = \frac{\$200}{\$1,133.33} = 0.176$$

Thus, depending on the amount of bonds held by accounting majors, the debt-equity ratio in the economy can lie in the range of 0.176 to 0.600. ∎

Questions and Problems

Capital Structure and Financial Distress

16.1 Deborah Corporation and Karen, Inc., are identical firms except that Karen, Inc., is more levered than Deborah. The companies' economists agree that the probability of a recession next year is 20 percent and the probability of a continuation of the current expansion is 80 percent. If the expansion continues, each firm will have EBIT of $2 million. If a recession occurs, each firm will have EBIT of $0.8 million. Deborah's debt obligation requires the firm to make $750,000 in payments. Because Karen carries more debt, its debt payment obligations are $1 million.

Assume that the investors in these firms are risk-neutral and that they discount the firms' cash flows at 15 percent. Assume a one-period example. Also assume there are no taxes.

a. Duane, the president of Deborah, commented to Karen's president, Hugo, that his firm has a higher value than Karen, Inc., because Deborah has less debt and, therefore, less bankruptcy risk. Is Duane correct?

b. Using the data of the two firms, prove your answer to *(a)*.

c. What might cause the firms to be valued differently?

16.2 What are the direct and indirect costs of bankruptcy? Briefly explain each.

16.3 Chrysler's financial structure in August 1983 was as follows:

Security	Number of units outstanding	Price per unit	Market value
Common stock	115,000,000	$ 26.00	$2,990,000,000
Preferred stock	10,000,000	32.50	325,000,000
Warrants	14,400,000	13.50	194,400,000
Bonds	2,000,000	650.00	1,300,000,000

Due to large losses incurred from 1978 to 1981, Chrysler had $2 billion in tax-loss carryforwards; therefore, the next $2 billion of income was free from corporate income taxes. At the time, the consensus of security analysts was that Chrysler would not have cumulative profits in excess of $2 billion over the next five years.

Most of the preferred stock was held by banks. Chrysler had agreed to retire the preferred stock over the next few years. Chrysler had to decide whether to issue debt or sell common equity to raise the funds needed to retire the preferred stock.

If you were Lee Iacocca, what would you have done? Why?

16.4 Bismarck Ltd. economists estimate that the probability of a good business environment next year equals the probability of a bad environment. Knowing that, Bismarck managers must choose between two mutually exclusive projects. Suppose the project that Bismarck chooses will be the only business it does this year. Therefore, the project's payoff will determine the value of the firm. Bismarck is obliged to make a $500 payment to its bondholders. The first project is one of low risk.

		Low-risk project						
Economy	Probability	Project payoff	Value of firm		Value of stock			Value of bonds
Bad	0.5	$500	$500	=	0	+		$500
Good	0.5	$700	$700	=	$200	+		$500

If the firm does not undertake the low-risk project, it will choose the following high-risk project:

High-risk project

Economy	Probability	Project payoff	Value of firm		Value of stock		Value of bonds
Bad	0.5	$100	$100	=	0	+	$100
Good	0.5	$800	$800	=	$300	+	$500

Which project would the shareholders prefer? Why?

16.5 Do you agree or disagree with the following statement? Explain your answer.

A firm's shareholders would never want the firm to invest in projects with negative NPVs.

16.6 What measures do shareholders undertake to minimize the costs of debt?

Capital Structure and Taxes

16.7 Fortune Enterprises (FE) is an all-equity firm that is considering issuing $13,500,000 in 10-percent debt. The firm will use the proceeds of the bond sale to repurchase equity. FE has a 100-percent payout policy. Because FE is a nongrowth firm, its earnings and debt will be perpetual. FE's income statement under each of the financial structures is:

	All equity	Debt
EBIT	$3,000,000	$3,000,000
Interest	0	1,350,000
EBT	3,000,000	1,650,000
Taxes ($T_C = 0.4$)	1,200,000	660,000
Net income	$1,800,000	$ 990,000

    a. If the personal tax rate is 30 percent, which plan offers the investors the highest cash flows? Why?

    b. Which plan should Revenue Canada prefer?

    c. Suppose shareholders demand a 20-percent return after personal taxes. What is the value of the firm under each plan?

    d. Suppose $T_S = 0.2$ and $T_B = 0.55$. What are the investors' returns under each plan?

16.8 The general expression for the value of a leveraged firm in a world in which $T_S = 0$ is

$$V_L = V_U + \left[1 - \frac{(1 - T_C)}{(1 - T_B)} \right] \times B - C(B)$$

where

V_U = Value of an unlevered firm

T_C = Effective corporate tax rate for the firm

T_B = Personal tax rate of the marginal bondholder

B = Debt level of the firm

$C(B)$ = Present value of the costs of financial distress for the firm as a function of its debt level. [Note: $C(B)$ encompasses all non–tax-related effects of leverage on the firm's value.]

Assume all investors are risk-neutral.

a. In their no-tax model, what do Modigliani and Miller assume about T_C, T_B, and $C(B)$? What do these assumptions imply about a firm's optimal debt-equity ratio?

b. In their model that includes corporate taxes, what do Modigliani and Miller assume about T_C, T_B, and $C(B)$? What do these assumptions imply about a firm's optimal debt-equity ratio?

c. Assume that Roger's Cable is certain to be able to use its interest deductions to reduce its corporate tax bill. How would Roger's Cable change in value if it issued $1 billion in debt and used the proceeds to repurchase equity? Assume that the personal tax rate on bond income is 47 percent, the corporate tax rate is 40 percent, and the costs of financial distress are zero.

d. Assume that CanX is virtually certain not to be able to use interest deductions. How would the company's value change if it added $1 of perpetual debt rather than $1 of equity? Assume that the personal tax rate on bond income is 47 percent, the corporate tax rate is 40 percent, and the costs of financial distress are zero.

e. For companies that may or may not be able to use the interest deduction, what would the change in the value of the company be from adding $1 of perpetual debt rather than $1 of equity? Assume that the personal tax rate on bond income is 47 percent, the corporate tax rate is 40 percent, and the costs of financial distress are zero. Also assume the probability of using the incremental deduction is 65 percent.

Advanced Miller Debt and Taxes

16.9 The EXES Company is assessing its present capital structure and that structure's implications for the welfare of its investors. EXES is currently financed entirely with common stock, of which 1,000 shares are outstanding. Given the risk of the underlying cash flows (EBIT) generated by EXES, investors currently require a 20-percent return on the EXES common stock. The company pays out all earnings as dividends to common stockholders.

EXES estimates that operating income may be $1,000, $2,000, or $4,200 with respective probabilities of 0.1, 0.4, and 0.5. Assume the firm's expectations about earnings will be met and that they will be unchanged in perpetuity. Also, assume that the corporate and personal tax rates are equal to zero.

a. What is the value of EXES Company?

b. The president of EXES has decided that shareholders would be better off if the company had equal proportions of debt and equity. He therefore proposes to issue $7,500 of debt at an interest rate of 10 percent. He will use the proceeds to repurchase 500 shares of common stock.

     i. What will the new value of the firm be?

     ii. What will the value of EXES's debt be?

     iii. What will the value of EXES's equity be?

c. Suppose the president's proposal is implemented.

     i. What is the required rate of return on equity?

     ii. What is the firm's overall required return?

d. Suppose the corporate tax rate is 40 percent.

     i. Use the Modigliani–Miller framework that includes taxes to find the value of the firm.

     ii. Does the presence of taxes increase or decrease the value of the firm? Why?

     iii. Verbally explain how the presence of bankruptcy costs would change the effect of taxes on the value of the firm, if at all.

e. Suppose interest income is taxed at 40 percent while the effective tax on returns to equity holders is zero. Assume that the introduction of the personal tax rate does not affect the required return on equity.

     i. What is the value of EXES in a world with personal taxes?

     ii. Under the Miller model, what will happen to the value of the firm as the tax on interest income rises?

16.10 Mueller Brewing Company has been ordered by the provincial authorities to stop polluting the Halifax Harbour. It must now spend $100 million on pollution-control equipment. The company has three alternatives for obtaining the needed $100 million.

- Sell $100 million of perpetual, taxable corporate bonds with a 20-percent coupon rate.
- Sell $100 million of perpetual pollution-control bonds with a 10-percent coupon rate. The interest on these bonds is not taxable to investors.
- Sell $100 million of common stock with a 9.5-percent current dividend yield.

Mueller Brewing Company is in the 40-percent tax bracket.

    The president of Mueller Brewing wants to sell the common stock because it has the lowest rate. Mr. Daniels, the company's treasurer, suggests bond financing because of the tax shield offered by the debt. His analysis shows that the value of the firm will increase by $r_B B T_C / r_B = $ ($100 million) $\times (0.40) = \$40$ million if Mueller issues bonds instead of equity. A newly hired financial budget analyst, Ms. Harris, argues that it does not matter which type of bond is issued. She claims that the yields will be bid up to reflect taxes, so the financing choice will not matter.

a. Comment on the analyses of the president, Mr. Daniels, and Ms. Harris.

b. Should Mueller be indifferent about which financing plan it chooses? If not, rank the three alternatives and give the benefits and costs of each.

16.11 Assume that there are three groups of investors with the following tax rates and investable funds:

Group	Investable funds (in $ millions)	Tax rate (%)
A	$375	50%
B	220	32.5
C	105	10.0

Each group requires a minimum after-tax return of 8.1 percent on any security. The only types of securities available are common stock and perpetual corporate bonds. Income from corporate bonds is subject to a personal tax, but it is deductible for corporate tax purposes. Capital gains from common stock are untaxed at the personal level. In equilibrium, common stock yields an 8.1-percent pretax return; foreign real estate also earns this rate. All funds not invested in stocks or bonds will be invested in foreign real estate. Assume the common stock and the bonds are both risk-free.

Corporate earnings before interest and taxes total $85 million each year in perpetuity. The corporate tax rate is 40 percent.

a. What is the equilibrium market rate of interest on corporate bonds, r_B?

b. In equilibrium, what is the composition of each of the groups' portfolios?

c. What is the total market value of all companies?

d. What is the total tax bill?

16.12 Consider an economy in which there are four groups of people:

Group	Marginal tax rate (%)	Wealth (in $ millions)
L	50%	$700
M	40	300
N	20	200
O	0	500

All investors can earn a tax-free return of 6 percent by investing in foreign real estate. Interest payments are taxable at the individual level, but equity income is untaxed at the personal level for all investors.

Corporations receive pretax cash flows of interest totalling $150 million. Interest payments are tax deductible at the corporate level. There are no depreciation deductions. Firms have no growth opportunities, and their plants are everlasting. The corporate tax rate is 40 percent.

a. What is the range of possible aggregate debt-equity ratios in the economy?

b. What would your answer to (a) be if the corporate tax rate is 30 percent?

CHAPTER 17

Valuation and Capital Budgeting for the Levered Firm

Instructors often structure the basic course in corporate finance around the two sides of the balance sheet. The left-hand side of the balance sheet contains assets. Chapters 4–8 treat capital budgeting, which is a decision concerning the assets of the firm. Chapters 9–12 cover the discount rate for a project, so those chapters also concern the left-hand side of the balance sheet. The right-hand side of the balance sheet contains liabilities and owner's equity. Chapters 13–16 examine the debt-versus-equity decision, which is a decision about the right-hand side of the balance sheet.

While the preceding chapters of this textbook have, for the most part, treated the capital budgeting decision separately from the capital structure decision, the two decisions are actually related. As we will see, a project of an all-equity firm might be rejected, while the same project might be accepted for a levered but otherwise identical firm. This could occur because the cost of capital frequently decreases with leverage, thereby turning some negative NPV projects into positive NPV projects.

Chapters 4 through 8 implicitly assumed that the firm is financed only with equity. The goal of this chapter is to value a project, or the firm itself, when leverage is employed. We point out that there are three standard approaches to valuation under leverage: the adjusted present value (APV) method, the flow to equity (FTE) method, and the weighted average cost of capital (WACC) method. These three approaches may seem, at first glance, to be quite different. However, we aim in this chapter to stress their similarities. For certain situations, the different approaches provide exactly the same answer. For other situations, the three approaches may provide somewhat different answers, and we discuss which method is preferred.

The three methods discussed below can be used to value either the firm as a whole or a project. The example below discusses project value, though everything we say applies to an entire firm as well.

Adjusted Present Value (APV) Approach   17.1

The **adjusted present value (APV)** method is best described by the following formula:

APV = NPV + NPVF

In words, the value of a project to a levered firm (APV) is equal to the value of the project to an unlevered firm (NPV) plus the net present value of the financing side effects (NPVF). There are four major side effects:

1. *The tax subsidy to debt.* This was discussed in Chapter 15, where we pointed out that, for perpetual debt, the value of the tax subsidy is $T_C B$. (T_C is the corporate tax rate, and B is the value of the debt.) The material on valuation under corporate taxes in Chapter 15 is actually an application of the APV approach.

2. *The costs of issuing new securities.* As we will discuss in detail in Chapter 20, investment bankers participate in the public issuance of corporate debt. These bankers must be compensated for their time and effort, a cost that lowers the value of the project.

3. *The costs of financial distress.* The possibility of financial distress, and bankruptcy in particular, arises with debt financing. As stated in the previous chapter, financial distress imposes costs, thereby lowering value.

4. *Subsidies to debt financing.* The interest rate on debt issued by the provinces and the federal government is substantially below the yield on debt issued by risky private corporations. Frequently, corporations are able to obtain loan guarantees from government, lowering their borrowing costs to a government rate. This subsidy adds value.

While each of these four side effects is important, the tax deduction to debt almost certainly has the highest dollar value in practice. For this reason, the following example considers the tax subsidy, but not the other three side effects.[1]

Consider a project of the Victoria Corporation with the following characteristics:

Sales = $500,000 per year for the indefinite future

Cash costs = 72% of sales

Initial investment = $440,000

$T_C = 40\%$

$r_0 = 20\%$, where r_0 is the cost of capital for a project of an all-equity firm

If both the project and the firm are financed with only equity, the project's cash flow is

Sales	$500,000
Cash costs	−360,000
Operating income	140,000
Corporate tax (40% tax rate)	− 56,000
Unlevered cash flow (UCF)	$ 84,000

The distinction in Chapter 4 between present value and net present value is quite important for this example. As pointed out in Chapter 4, the *present value* of a project

---

[1]The BDE example of Section 17.6 handles both flotation costs and interest subsidies.

is determined before the initial investment at date 0 is subtracted. The initial investment is subtracted for the calculation of *net* present value.

Given a discount rate of 20 percent, the present value of the project is

$$\frac{\$84,000}{.20} = \$420,000$$

The project's NPV (that is, its value to an all-equity firm) is

$$\$420,000 - \$440,000 = -\$20,000$$

Since the NPV is negative, the project would be rejected by an all-equity firm.

Now imagine that the firm finances the project with exactly $116,666.67 in debt, so that the remaining investment of $323,333.33 (or $440,000 − $116,666.67) is financed with equity. The *net* present value of the project under leverage, which we call *APV*, is

$$
\begin{aligned}
\text{APV} &= \text{NPV} &+ T_C \times B \\
\$26,666.67 &= -20,000 + .40 \times \$116,666.67
\end{aligned}
$$

That is, the value of the project when financed with some leverage is equal to the value of the project when financed with all equity plus the tax shield from the debt. Since this number is positive, the project should be accepted.

You may be wondering why we chose such a precise amount of debt. Actually, we chose it so that the ratio of debt to the present value of the project under leverage is 0.25.[2]

In this example, debt is a fixed proportion of the present value of the project, not a fixed proportion of the initial investment of $440,000. This is consistent with the goal of a target debt-to-*market*-value ratio, which we find in the real world. For example, chartered banks typically lend to real estate developers a fixed percentage of the market value of a project, not a fixed percentage of the initial investment.

CONCEPT QUESTIONS

- How is the APV method applied?
- What additional information beyond NPV does one need to calculate APV?

---

[2]That is, the present value of the project after the initial investment has been made is $466,666.67 (or $26,666.67 + $440,000). Thus, the debt-to-value ratio of the project is 0.25 (or $116,666.67/$466,666.67).

This level of debt can be calculated directly. Note that

$$
\begin{aligned}
\text{Present value of} &= \text{Present value of} &+ &\quad T_c &\times &\quad B \\
\text{levered project} &\quad \text{unlevered project} \\
V_{\text{With debt}} &= \quad\quad \$420,000 &+ &\ 0.40 \times .25 &\times &\ V_{\text{With debt}}
\end{aligned}
$$

Rearranging the last line, we have

$$V_{\text{With debt}}(1 - 0.40 \times 0.25) = \$420,000$$
$$V_{\text{With debt}} = \$466,666.67$$

Since debt is 0.25 of value, debt is $116,666.67 (or 0.25 × $466,666.67).

17.2

Flow to Equity (FTE) Approach

The **flow to equity (FTE)** approach is an alternative capital budgeting approach. The formula simply calls for discounting the cash flow from the project to the equityholders of the levered firm at the cost of equity capital, r_S. For a perpetuity, this becomes

$$\frac{\text{Cash flow from project to equityholders of the levered firm}}{r_s}$$

There are three steps to the FTE approach.

Step 1: Calculating Levered Cash Flow (LCF)[3]

Assuming an interest rate of 10 percent, the perpetual cash flow to equityholders in our example is

Sales	$500,000.00
Cash costs	−360,000.00
Interest (10% × $116,666.67)	−11,666.67
Income after interest	128,333.33
Corporate tax (.40 tax rate)	−51,333.33
Levered cash flow	$ 77,000.00

Alternatively, one can calculate levered cash flow directly from unlevered cash flow (UCF). The key here is that the difference between the cash flow that equityholders receive in an unlevered firm and the cash flow that equityholders receive in a levered firm is the after-tax interest payment. (Repayment of principal does not appear in this example, since the debt is perpetual.) One writes this algebraically as

$$UCF - LCF = (1 - T_C)r_B B$$

The term on the right-hand side of this expression is the after-tax interest payment. Thus, since cash flow to the unlevered equityholders (UCF) is $84,000 and the after-tax interest payment is $7000 [(.60) .10 × $116,666.67], cash flow to the levered equityholders (LCF) is

$$\$84,000 - \$7,000 = \$77,000$$

which is exactly the number we calculated earlier.

Step 2: Calculating r_S

The next step is to calculate the discount rate, r_s. Note that we assumed that the discount rate on unlevered equity, r_0, is .20. As we saw in Chapter 15, the formula for r_s is

$$r_S = r_0 + \frac{B}{S}(1 - T_C)(r_0 - r_B)$$

---

[3]We use the term *levered cash flow (LCF)* for simplicity. A more complete term would be *cash flow from the project to the equityholders of a levered firm.* Similarly, a more complete term for *unlevered cash flow (UCF)* would be *cash flow from the project to the equityholders of an unlevered firm.*

Note that our target debt-to-value ratio of $\frac{1}{4}$ implies a target debt-to-equity ratio of $\frac{1}{3}$. Applying the above formula to this example, we have

$$r_S = .20 + \tfrac{1}{3}(.60)(.20 - .10) = .22$$

Step 3: Valuation

The present value of the project's LCF is

$$\frac{LCF}{r_S} = \frac{\$77,000}{.22} = \$350,000$$

Since the initial investment is \$440,000 and \$116,666.67 is borrowed, the firm must advance the project \$323,333.33 (or \$440,000 − \$116,666.67) out of its own cash reserves. The *net* present value of the project is simply the difference between the present value of the project's LCF and the investment not borrowed. Thus, the NPV is

$$\$350,000.00 - \$323,333.33 = \$26,666.67$$

which is identical to the result found with the APV approach.

CONCEPT QUESTIONS

- How is the FTE method applied?
- What information is needed to calculate FTE?

Weighted Average Cost of Capital (WACC) Method   17.3

Finally, one can value a project using the **weighted average cost of capital (WACC)** method. While this method was discussed in Chapters 12 and 15, it is worthwhile to review it here. The WACC approach begins with the insight that projects of levered firms are simultaneously financed with both debt and equity. The cost of capital is a weighted average of the cost of debt and the cost of equity. As seen in Chapters 12 and 15, the cost of equity is r_S. Ignoring taxes, the cost of debt is simply the borrowing rate, r_B. However, with corporate taxes, the appropriate cost of debt is $(1 - T_C)r_B$, the after-tax cost of debt.

The formula for determining the weighted average cost of capital, r_{WACC}, is

$$r_{WACC} = \frac{S}{S + B} + r_S + \frac{B}{S + B} r_B(1 - T_C)$$

The weight for equity, $S/(S + B)$, and the weight for debt, $B/(S + B)$, are target ratios. Target ratios are generally expressed in terms of market values, not book values.

The formula calls for discounting the *unlevered* cash flow of the project (UCF) at the weighted average cost of capital, r_{WACC}. The net present value of the project can be written algebraically as

$$\sum_{t=1}^{\infty} \frac{UCF_t}{(1 + r_{WACC})^t} - \text{Initial investment}$$

If the project is a perpetuity, the net present value is

$$\frac{UCF}{r_{WACC}} - \text{Initial investment}$$

We previously stated that the target debt-to-value ratio of our project is $\frac{1}{4}$ and the corporate tax rate is .40, implying that the weighted average cost of capital is

$$r_{WACC} = \frac{3}{4} \times .22 + \frac{1}{4} \times .10(.60) = .18$$

Note that r_{WACC}, .18, is lower than the cost of equity capital for an all-equity firm, .20. This must always be the case, since debt financing provides a tax subsidy that lowers the average cost of capital.

We previously determined the UCF of the project to be $84,000, implying that the present value of the project is

$$\frac{\$84,000}{.18} = \$466,666.67$$

Since this initial investment is $440,000, the NPV of the project is

$$\$466,666.67 - \$440,000 = \$26,666.67$$

In this example, all three approaches yield the same value.

CONCEPT QUESTION

- How is the WACC method applied?

17.4   A Comparison of the APV, FTE, and WACC Approaches

Capital budgeting techniques in the early chapters of this text applied to all-equity firms. Capital budgeting for the levered firm could not be handled early in the book because the effects of debt on firm value were deferred until the previous two chapters. We learned there that debt increases firm value through tax benefits but decreases value through bankruptcy and related costs.

In the present chapter, we provide three approaches to capital budgeting for the levered firm. The adjusted present value (APV) approach first values the project on an all-equity basis. That is, the project's after-tax cash flows under all-equity financing (UCF) are placed in the numerator of the capital budgeting equation. The discount rate, assuming all-equity financing, appears in the denominator. At this point, the calculation is identical to that performed in the early chapters of this book. We then add the net present value of the debt. We point out that the net present value of the debt is likely to be the sum of four parameters: tax effects, flotation costs, bankruptcy costs, and interest subsidies.

The flow to equity (FTE) approach discounts the after-tax cash flow from a project going to the equityholders of a levered firm (LCF). LCF is the residual to equityholders after interest has been deducted. The discount rate is r_S, the cost of capital to the equityholders of a levered firm. For a firm with leverage, r_S must be greater than r_0, the cost of capital for an unlevered firm. This follows from our material in Chapter 15 showing that leverage raises the risk to the equityholders.

The last approach is the weighted average cost of capital (WACC) method. This technique calculates the project's after-tax cash flows assuming all-equity financing (UCF). The UCF is placed in the numerator of the capital budgeting equation. The denominator, r_{WACC}, is a weighted average of the cost of equity capital and the cost of debt capital. The tax advantage of debt is reflected in the denominator because the cost of debt capital is determined net of corporate tax. The numerator does not reflect debt at all.

All three approaches attempt the same task: valuation in the presence of debt financing. However, as we saw above, the approaches are markedly different in technique. Because of this, it is worthwhile to stress two points:

1. *APV versus WACC.* As stated above, both the APV and the WACC approaches use unlevered cash flows. The APV discounts these flows at r_0, yielding the value of the unlevered project. Adding the present value of the tax shield gives the value of the project under leverage. The WACC approach discounts UCF at r_{WACC}, which is lower than r_0. Thus, the APV and WACC approaches are different ways of determining the same value. While the APV approach adds a tax shield, the WACC approach lowers the denominator below r_0. Both approaches yield a value above that of the unlevered project.

2. *Entity being valued.* For both the APV and the WACC approaches, the initial investment is subtracted out in the final step ($440,000 in our example). However, for the FTE approach, only the firm's contribution to the initial investment ($323,333.33 = $440,000 − $116,666.67) is subtracted out. This occurs because, under the FTE approach, only the future cash flows to the levered equityholders (LCF) are included. Thus, since these future cash flows are reduced by interest payments, the initial investment is correspondingly reduced by debt financing.

A Suggested Guideline

The net present value of our project is exactly the same under each of the three methods. In theory, this should always be the case.[4] However, one method usually provides an easier computation than another, and, in many cases, one or more of the methods is virtually impossible computationally.

To illustrate, consider when it is best to use the WACC and FTE approaches. If the risk of a project stays constant throughout its life, it is plausible to assume that r_0 remains constant throughout the project's life. This assumption of constant risk appears to be reasonable for most real world projects. In addition, if the debt-to-value ratio remains constant over the life of the project, both r_S and r_{WACC} will remain constant as well. Under this latter assumption, either the FTE or the WACC approach is easy to apply. However, if the debt-to-value ratio varies from year to year, both

---

[4]See I. Inselbag and H. Kaufold, "A Comparison of Alternative Discounted Cash Flow Approaches to Firm Valuation" (Philadelphia: The Wharton School, University of Pennsylvania, June 1990), unpublished paper.

r_S and r_{WACC} vary from year to year as well. Using the FTE or the WACC approach when the denominator changes every year is computationally quite complex, and when computations become complex, the error rate rises. Thus, both the FTE and WACC approaches present difficulties when the debt-to-value *ratio* changes over time.

The APV approach is based on the *level* of debt in each future period. Consequently, when the debt level can be specified precisely for future periods, the APV approach is quite easy to use. However, when the debt level is uncertain, the APV approach becomes more problematic. For example, when the debt-to-value ratio is a constant, the debt level varies with the value of the project. Since the value of the project in a future year cannot be easily forecast, the level of debt cannot be easily forecast either.

Thus, we suggest the following guideline:

Use WACC or FTE if the firm's target debt-to-value *ratio* applies to the project over its life.

Use APV if the project's *level* of debt is known over the life of the project.

There are a number of situations where the APV approach is preferred. For example, in a leveraged buyout (LBO) the firm begins with a large amount of debt but rapidly pays down the debt over a number of years. Since the schedule of debt reduction in the future is known when the LBO is arranged, tax shields in every future year can be easily forecast. Thus, the APV approach is easy to use here. (This chapter's appendix shows the APV approach applied to LBOs.) By contrast, the WACC and FTE approaches are virtually impossible to apply to LBOs, since the debt-to-equity ratio cannot be expected to be constant over time. In addition, situations involving interest subsidies and flotation costs are much easier to handle with the APV approach. (The BDE example in Section 17.6 applies the APV approach to subsidies and flotation costs.) Finally, the APV approach handles the lease-versus-buy decision much more easily than does either the FTE or the WACC approach. (A full treatment of the lease-versus-buy decision appears in Chapter 23.)

The above examples are special situations. In order to see which approach is more appropriate for a typical capital budgeting situation, we must answer the following question: When managers pursue debt policy, do they think of keeping the *level* of debt fairly constant through time, or do they think of keeping the debt-equity *ratio* fairly constant through time? This is ultimately an empirical question—and one that has not been rigorously investigated. However, we believe that managers *should* think in terms of an optimal debt-equity ratio. If a project does much better than expected, both its value and its debt capacity will likely rise. A shrewd financial manager will take advantage by increasing debt. Conversely, the firm should reduce debt if the value of a project were to decline unexpectedly. Because financing is a time-consuming task, the level of debt cannot be adjusted on a day-to-day or month-to-month basis. However, the adjustment should occur over the long run.

Summing up, we recommend that the WACC and the FTE approaches, rather than the APV approach, be used in most real world situations. In addition, frequent discussions with business executives have convinced us that the WACC is by far the most widely used method in the real world. Thus, practitioners seem to agree with us that, outside of the special situations mentioned above, the APV approach is a less important method of capital budgeting.

The Three Methods of Capital Budgeting with Leverage

1. Adjusted Present Value (APV) Method

$$\sum_{t=1}^{\infty} \frac{UCF_t}{(1 + r_0)^t} + \text{Additional effects of debt} - \text{Initial investment}$$

UCF_t = The project's cash flow at date t to the equityholders of an unlevered firm

r_0 = Cost of capital for project in an unlevered firm

2. Flow to Equity (FTE) Method

$$\sum_{t=1}^{\infty} \frac{LCF_t}{(1 + r_S)^t} - (\text{Initial investment} - \text{Amount borrowed})$$

LCF_t = The project's cash flow at date t to the equityholders of a levered firm

r_S = Cost of equity capital with leverage

3. Weighted Average Cost of Capital (WACC) Method

$$\sum_{t=1}^{\infty} \frac{UCF_t}{(1 + r_{WACC})^t} - \text{Initial investment}$$

r_{WACC} = Weighted average cost of capital

Notes:

1. The middle term in the APV formula implies that the value of a project with leverage is greater than the value of the project without leverage. Since $r_{WACC} < r_0$, the WACC formula implies that the value of a project with leverage is greater than the value of the project without leverage.

2. In the FTE method, cash flow *after interest* (LCF) is used. Initial investment is reduced by *amount borrowed* as well.

Guidelines:

1. Use WACC or FTE if the firm's target debt-to-value *ratio* applies to the project over its life.

2. Use APV if the project's *level* of debt is known over the life of the project.

CONCEPT QUESTIONS

- What is the main difference between APV and WACC?
- What is the main difference between the FTE approach and the other two approaches?
- When should the APV method be used?
- When should the FTE and WACC approaches be used?

17.5   Capital Budgeting for Projects That Are Not Scale-Enhancing

In Chapter 12, we covered scale-enhancing and non–scale-enhancing projects. A scale-enhancing project is similar to the firm's existing projects (for example, a project at Ford Canada to produce automobiles). The analysis in Sections 17.1 through 17.3 can be used to value scale-enhancing projects. A somewhat different analysis is needed when a project is not scale-enhancing. This is best illustrated by an example.

■ *Example*

World-Wide Enterprises (WWE) is a large conglomerate thinking of entering the widget business, where it plans to finance projects with a debt-to-value ratio of 25 percent (or, alternatively, a debt-to-equity ratio of $\frac{1}{3}$). As a diversified conglomerate, WWE has a beta approximately equal to 1.0. However, the widget business is more risky than WWE's current operations and requires its own measure of risk. There is currently one firm in the widget industry, Alberta Widgets (AW). This firm is financed with 40-percent debt and 60-percent equity. The beta of AW's equity is 1.5.[5] AW has a borrowing rate of 12 percent, and WWE expects to borrow for its widget venture at 10 percent. The corporate tax rate for both firms is .40, the market risk premium is 8.5 percent, and the riskless interest rate is 8 percent. What is the appropriate discount rate for WWE to use for its widget venture?

As explained in Sections 17.1 through 17.3, a corporation may use one of three capital budgeting approaches: APV, FTE, or WACC. The appropriate discount rates for these three approaches are r_0, r_S, and r_{WACC}, respectively. Since AW is WWE's only competitor in widgets, we look at AW's cost of capital to calculate r_0, r_S, and r_{WACC} for WWE's widget venture. The four-step procedure below will allow us to calculate all three discount rates.

1. *Determining AW's cost of equity capital.* First, we determine AW's cost of equity capital, using the security market line (SML) of Chapter 10:

AW's Cost of Equity Capital:

$$r_S = R_F + \beta \times (\overline{R}_m - R_F)$$
$$20.75\% = 8\% + 1.5 \times 8.5$$

where $\overline{R}_M$ is the expected return on the market portfolio and R_f is the risk-free rate.

2. *Determining AW's hypothetical all-equity cost of capital.* However, we must standardize the above number in some way, since AW and WWE's widget ventures have different target debt-to-value ratios. The easiest approach is to calculate the hypothetical cost of equity capital for AW, assuming all-equity financing. This can be determined from MM's Proposition II under taxes (from Chapter 15):

[5]An alternative approach is to estimate beta for the project using projected operating and financial leverage. Cleveland Patterson, "The Cost of Equity Capital of a Non-Traded Entity: A Canadian Study," *Canadian Journal of Administrative Sciences* 10 (June 1993), pp. 116–21, applies this approach to estimate the cost of equity for Teleglobe Canada Inc. We discussed this in Chapter 12.

AW's Cost of Capital If All-Equity:

$$r_S = r_0 + \frac{B}{S}(1 - T_C)(r_0 - r_B)$$

$$20.75\% = r_0 + \frac{.4}{.6}(.60)(r_0 - 12\%)$$

In the examples of Chapter 15, the unknown in this equation was r_S.[6] However, for this example, the unknown is r_0. By solving the equation, one finds that $r_0 = .1825$. Of course, r_0 is less than r_S because the cost of equity capital would be less when the firm employs no leverage.

At this point, firms in the real world generally make the assumption that the business risk of their venture is about equal to the business risk of the firms already in the business. Applying this assumption to our problem, we assert that the hypothetical discount rate of WWE's widget venture if the venture is all-equity financed is also .1825.[7] This discount rate will be employed if WWE uses the APV approach, since the APV approach calls for r_0, the project's cost of capital in a firm with no leverage.

3. *Determining r_S for WWE's widget venture.* Alternatively, WWE might use the FTE approach, where the discount rate for levered equity is determined from

Cost of Equity Capital for WWE's Widget Venture:

$$r_S = r_0 + \frac{B}{S}(1 - T_C)(r_0 - r_B)$$

$$19.9\% = 18.25\% + \tfrac{1}{3}(.60)(18.25\% - 10\%)$$

Note that the cost of equity capital for WWE's widget venture, .199, is less than the cost of equity capital for AW, .2075. This occurs because AW has a higher debt-to-equity ratio. (As mentioned above, both firms are assumed to have the same business risk.)

4. *Determining r_{WACC} for WWE's widget venture.* Finally, WWE might use the WACC approach. The appropriate calculation here is

r_{WACC} for WWE's Widget Venture:

$$r_{\text{WACC}} = \frac{B}{S + B} r_B(1 - T_C) + \frac{S}{S + B} r_S$$

$$16.425\% = \frac{1}{4} 10\% (.60) + \frac{3}{4} \times 19.9\% \quad \blacksquare$$

CONCEPT QUESTION

- What adjustments are required in capital budgeting for projects that are not scale enhancing?

---

[6]In this example we are assuming that the debt betas for AW and WWE are zero. This assumption is not strictly correct because the cost of debt for AW and WWE is assumed to be higher than the risk-free rate. As a practical matter, most academic research suggests debt betas are very close to zero.

[7]Alternatively, a firm might assume that its venture would be somewhat riskier since it is a new entrant. Thus, the firm might select a discount rate slightly higher than .1825. Of course, no exact formula exists for adjusting the discount rate upwards.

17.6   APV Example

As mentioned above, the APV approach is effective in situations where flotation costs and subsidized financing arise. The FTE and the WACC approaches are less effective in these situations. The following is an example where the APV approach works well.

■ *Example*

Suppose BDE is considering a $30 million project that will last five years.[8] Projected operating cash flows are $9 million annually. The risk-free rate is 10 percent and the cost of equity is 20 percent. This is often called the *cost of unlevered equity* since we assume initially that the firm has no debt.

All-Equity Value

Assuming that the project is financed with 100-percent equity, its value is

$$-\$30,000,000 + \frac{\$9,000,000}{.20} \times \left[1 - \frac{1}{(1.20)^5}\right] = -\$3,084,491$$

An all-equity firm would clearly *reject* this project because the NPV is negative. And equity flotation costs (not considered yet) would only make the NPV more negative. However, debt financing may add enough value to the project to justify acceptance. We consider the effects of debt below.

Additional Effects of Debt

BDE can obtain a five-year, balloon payment loan for $22,500,000 after flotation costs. The interest rate is the risk-free cost of debt of 10 percent. The flotation costs are 1 percent of the amount raised. We look at three ways in which debt financing alters the NPV of the project.

Flotation Costs

The following formula gives us the flotation costs:

$$\$22,500,000 = (1 - .01) \times \text{Amount raised}$$

$$\text{Amount raised} = \frac{\$22,500,000}{.99} = \$22,727,273$$

So flotation costs are $227,273 and in the text we added these to the initial outlay, reducing NPV.

The APV method refines the estimate of flotation costs by recognizing that they generate a tax shield. Flotation costs are paid immediately but are deducted from taxes

---

[8]We simplify the project details by assuming the operating cash flows are an annuity. Most Canadian projects generate variable cash flows due to the CCA rules. This is handled within APV by finding the present value of each source of cash flow separately.

by amortizing over the life of the loan. In this example, the annual tax deduction for flotation costs is \$227,273 / 5 years = \$45,455. At a tax rate of 40 percent, the annual tax shield is \$45,455 × .40 = \$18,182.

To find the net flotation costs of the loan, add the present value of the tax shield to the flotation costs:

$$\text{Net flotation costs} = -\$227,273 + \frac{\$18,182}{.10} \times \left[1 - \frac{1}{(1.10)^5}\right]$$

$$= -\$227,273 + \$68,924 = -\$158,349$$

The net present value of the project after debt flotation costs but before the benefits of debt is

$$-\$3,084,491 - \$158,349 = -\$3,242,840$$

Tax Subsidy

The loan of \$22,500,000 is received at date 0. Annual interest at 10 percent is \$2,250,000. The interest cost after tax is \$1,350,000 (or \$2,250,000 × (1−.40)). The loan has a balloon payment of the full principal at the end of five years. The loan gives rise to three sets of cash flows: the loan received, the annual interest cost after taxes, and the repayment of principal. The net present value of the loan is simply the sum of three present values:

$$\text{NPV(loan)} = \begin{matrix}+\text{Amount}\\ \text{borrowed}\end{matrix} - \begin{matrix}\text{Present value}\\ \text{of after-tax}\\ \text{interest payments}\end{matrix} - \begin{matrix}\text{Present value}\\ \text{of loan}\\ \text{repayments}\end{matrix}$$

$$= +\$22,550,000 - \frac{\$1,350,000}{.10} \times \left[1 - \frac{1}{(1.10)^5}\right] - \frac{\$22,500,000}{(1.10)^5}$$

$$= +\$22,500,000 - \$5,117,562 - \$13,970,730 = \$3,411,708$$

The NPV of the loan is positive, reflecting the interest tax shield.[9]

The adjusted present value of the project with this financing is

APV	=	All-equity value	−	Flotation costs of debt	+	NPV (loan)
\$168,868	=	−\$3,084,491	−	\$158,349	+	\$3,411,708

Though we previously saw that an all-equity firm would reject the project, a firm would *accept* the project if a \$22,500,000 loan could be obtained.

Because the loan discussed above was at the market rate of 10 percent, we have considered only two of the three additional effects of debt (flotation costs and tax subsidy) so far. We now examine another loan where the third effect arises.

---

[9]The NPV (loan) must be zero in a no-tax world, because interest provides no tax shield there. To check this intuition we calculate

$$0 = +22,500,000 - \frac{\$2,250,000}{.10}\left[1 - \frac{1}{(1.10)^5}\right] - \frac{\$22,500,000}{(1.10)^5}$$

Non–Market Rate Financing

In Canada, a number of companies can obtain subsidized financing from federal or provincial governments. Suppose that the BDE project is deemed socially beneficial and a federal minister grants the firm a $22,500,000 loan at 8-percent interest. In addition, the government absorbs all flotation costs. Clearly, the company will choose this loan over the one we previously calculated. At 8-percent interest, annual interest payments are $22,500,000 × .08 = $1,800,000. After-tax payments are $1,080,000 = $1,800,000 × (1−.40). Using the equation we developed above

$$
\text{NPV(loan)} = \begin{array}{c} +\text{Amount} \\ \text{borrowed} \end{array} - \begin{array}{c} \text{Present value} \\ \text{of after-tax} \\ \text{interest payments} \end{array} - \begin{array}{c} \text{Present value} \\ \text{of loan} \\ \text{repayments} \end{array}
$$

$$
= +\$22,500,000 - \frac{\$1,080,000}{.10} \times \left[1 - \frac{1}{(1.10)^5} \right] - \frac{\$22,500,000}{(1.10)^5}
$$

$$
+\$22,500,000 - \$4,094,050 - \$13,970,730 = \$4,435,220
$$

Notice that we still discount the cash flows at 10 percent when the firm is borrowing at 8 percent. This is done because 10 percent is the fair market rate (the rate at which the firm could borrow *without* benefit of subsidization). The net present value of the subsidized loan is larger than the net present value of the earlier loan because the firm is now borrowing at the below-market rate of 8 percent. Note that the NPV (loan) calculation captures both the tax effect *and* the non–market rate effect.

The net present value of the project with subsidized debt financing is

$$
\begin{array}{ccccccc}
\text{APV} & = & \text{All-equity value} & - & \text{Flotation costs of debt} & + & \text{NPV (loan)} \\
\$1,350,729 & = & +\$3,084,491 & - & 0 & + & \$4,435,220
\end{array}
$$

Subsidized financing has enhanced the NPV substantially. The result is that the government debt subsidy program will likely achieve its result—encouraging the firm to invest in the kind of project the government wishes to encourage.

The above example illustrates the adjusted present value approach. The approach begins with the present value of a project for the all-equity firm. Next, the effects of debt are added in. The approach has much to recommend it. It is intuitively appealing because individual components are calculated separately and added together in a simple way. And, if the debt from the project can be specified precisely, the present value of the debt can be calculated precisely. ∎

CONCEPT QUESTION

- How do flotation costs and subsidized financing affect APV?

17.7   Beta and Leverage

Chapter 12 provides the formula for the relationship between the beta of the common stock and the leverage of the firm in a world without taxes:

The No-Tax Case:

$$\beta_{\text{Equity}} = \beta_{\text{Asset}}\left(1 + \frac{\text{Debt}}{\text{Equity}}\right) \qquad (17.2)$$

As pointed out in Chapter 12, this relationship holds under the assumption that the beta of debt is zero.

Since firms must pay corporate taxes in practice, it is worthwhile to provide the relationship with corporate taxes. It can be shown that the relationship between the beta of the unlevered firm and the beta of the levered equity is[10]

The Corporate-Tax Case:

$$\beta_{\text{Equity}} = \left[1 + \frac{(1 - T_C)\,\text{Debt}}{\text{Equity}}\right]\beta_{\text{Unlevered firm}} \qquad (17.3)$$

when (1) the corporation is taxed at the rate of T_C and (2) the debt has a zero beta.

Because $[1 + (1 - T_C)\text{Debt/Equity}]$ must be more than 1 for a levered firm, it follows that $\beta_{\text{Unlevered firm}} < \beta_{\text{Equity}}$. The corporate-tax case of equation (17.2) is quite similar to the no-tax case of equation (17.1), because the beta of levered equity must be greater than the beta of the unlevered firm in either case. The intuition that leverage increases the risk of equity applies in both cases.

However, notice that the two equations are not equal. It can be shown that leverage increases the equity beta less rapidly under corporate taxes. This occurs because, under taxes, leverage creates a *riskless* tax shield, thereby lowering the risk of the entire firm.

---

[10]This result holds only if the beta of debt equals zero. To see this, note that

$$V_U + T_C B = V_L = B + S \qquad (a)$$

where

V_U = Value of unlevered firm
V_L = Value of levered firm
B = Value of debt in a levered firm
S = Value of equity in a levered firm

As we stated in the text, the beta of the levered firm is a weighted average of the debt beta and the equity beta:

$$\frac{B}{B + S} \times \beta_B + \frac{S}{B + S}\beta_s$$

where β_B and β_S are the betas of the debt and the equity of the levered firm, respectively. Because $V_L = B + S$, we have

$$\frac{B}{V_L} \times \beta_B + \frac{S}{V_L} \times \beta_S \qquad (b)$$

The beta of the levered firm can also be expressed as a weighted average of the beta of the unlevered firm and the beta of the tax shield:

$$\frac{V_U}{V_U + T_C B} \times \beta_U + \frac{T_C B}{V_U + T_C B} \times \beta_B$$

where β_U is the beta of the unlevered firm. This follows from equation (a). Because $V_L = V_U + T_C B$, we have

$$\frac{V_U}{V_L} \times \beta_U + \frac{T_C B}{V_L} \times \beta_B \qquad (c)$$

We can equate equations (b) and (c) because both represent the beta of a levered firm. Equation (a) tells us that $V_U = S + (1 - T_C) \times B$. Under the assumption that $\beta_B = 0$, equating (b) and (c) and using equation (a) yields equation (17.2).

▪ *Example*

Alberta Petroleum Ltd. is considering a scale-enhancing project. The market value of the firm's debt is $100 million, and the market value of the firm's equity is $200 million. The debt is considered riskless. The corporate tax rate is 40 percent. Regression analysis indicates that the beta of the firm's equity is 2. The risk-free rate is 10 percent, and the expected market premium is 8.5 percent. What would be the project's discount rate in the hypothetical case that Alberta Petroleum is all-equity?

We can answer this question in two steps:

1. *Determining beta of a hypothetical all-equity firm.* Rearranging equation (17.2), we have

Unlevered Beta:

Unlevered Beta:

$$\frac{Equity}{Equity + (1 - T_c) \times Debt} \times \beta_{Equity} = \beta_{Unlevered\ firm} \qquad (17.3)$$

$$\frac{\$200\ million}{\$200\ million + (1 - 0.40) \times \$100\ million} \times 2 = 1.54$$

2. *Determining the discount rate.* We calculate the discount rate from the security market line (SML) as

Discount Rate:

$$r_s = R_F + \beta \times [\bar{R}_M - R_F]$$
$$23.09\% = 10\% + 1.54 \times 8.5\%$$

The Project Is Not Scale-Enhancing

Because the above example assumed that the project is scale-enhancing, we began with the beta of the firm's equity. If the project is not scale-enhancing, we could begin with the equity betas of firms in the industry of the project. For each firm, the hypothetical beta of the unlevered equity could be calculated by equation (17.3). The SML could then be used to determine the project's discount rate from the average of these betas.

CONCEPT QUESTION

▪ How is beta adjusted for leverage and corporate taxes?

17.8   ## Summary and Conclusions

Earlier chapters showed how to calculate net present value for projects of all-equity firms. We pointed out in the last two chapters that the introduction of taxes and bankruptcy costs changes a firm's financing decisions and means that rational corporations should employ some debt. Because of the benefits and costs associated with debt, the capital budgeting decision is different for levered firms than for unlevered firms. The present chapter has discussed three methods for capital budgeting by levered firms: the adjusted present value (APV), flows to equity (FTE), and weighted average cost of capital (WACC) approaches.

1. The APV formula can be written as

$$\sum_{t=1}^{\infty} \frac{UCF_t}{(1 + r_0)^t} + \begin{matrix} \text{Additional} \\ \text{effects} \\ \text{of debt} \end{matrix} - \begin{matrix} \text{Initial} \\ \text{investment} \end{matrix}$$

There are four additional effects of debt:

Tax shield from debt financing.

Flotation costs.

Bankruptcy costs.

Benefit of non–market-rate financing.

2. The FTE formula can be written as

$$\sum_{t=1}^{\infty} \frac{LCF_t}{(1 + r_s)^t} - \left(\begin{matrix} \text{Initial} \\ \text{investment} \end{matrix} - \begin{matrix} \text{Amount} \\ \text{borrowed} \end{matrix} \right)$$

3. The WACC formula can be written as

$$\sum_{t=1}^{\infty} \frac{UCF_t}{(1 + r_{WACC})^t} - \begin{matrix} \text{Initial} \\ \text{investment} \end{matrix}$$

4. Corporations frequently follow these guidelines:

   Use WACC or FTE if the firm's target debt-to-value *ratio* applies to the project over its life.

   Use APV if the project's *level* of debt is known over the life of the project.

5. The APV method is used frequently for special situations like interest subsidies, LBOs, and leases. The WACC and FTE methods are commonly used for more typical capital budgeting situations. The APV approach is a rather unimportant method for typical capital budgeting situations.

6. The beta of the equity of the firm is positively related to the leverage of the firm.

7. The beta of a project is the same as the firm's beta only in the case of scale-enhancing projects. Otherwise, one must begin with unlevered betas for firms in the same industry as the project.

Key Terms

Adjusted present value (APV) 487
Flow to equity (FTE) 490

Weighted average cost of capital (WACC) 491

Suggested Readings

The following article contains a superb discussion of some of the subtleties of using WACC for project valuation:

J. Miles and R. Ezzell. "The Weighted Average Cost of Capital, Perfect Capital Markets and Project Life: A Clarification." *Journal of Financial and Quantitative Analysis* 15 (September 1980).

This is an excellent article on how to use the SML in project valuation:

J. F. Weston. "Investment Decisions Using the Capital Asset Pricing Model." *Financial Management* (Spring 1973).

The following important article develops the adjusted present value approach:

S. Myers. "Interactions of Corporate Financing and Investment Decisions: Implications for Capital Budgeting." *Journal of Finance* (March 1974).

A fascinating article valuing leveraged buyouts in an APV framework is:

I. Inselbag and H. Kaufold. "How to Value Recapitalizations and Leveraged Buyouts." *Journal of Applied Corporate Finance* (Summer 1989).

Questions and Problems

Weighted Average Cost of Capital (WACC)

17.1 The overall firm beta for Wild Widgets Ltd. (WWI) is 0.9. WWI has a target debt-equity ratio of $\frac{1}{2}$. The expected return on the market is 16 percent, and Treasury bills are currently selling to yield 8 percent. WWI one-year bonds that carry a 7-percent coupon are selling for $972.72. The corporate tax rate is 40 percent.

    a. What is WWI's cost of equity?

    b. What is WWI's cost of debt?

    c. What is WWI's weighted average cost of capital?

17.2 Value Company has compiled the following information on its financing costs:

Type of financing	Book value	Market value	Before-tax cost
Long-term debt	$ 5,000,000	$ 2,000,000	10%
Short-term debt	5,000,000	5,000,000	8
Common stock	10,000,000	13,000,000	15
	20,000,000	20,000,000	

Value is in the 40-percent tax bracket and has a target debt-equity ratio of 100 percent. Value's managers would like to keep the market values of short-term and long-term debt equal.

    a. Calculate the weighted average cost of capital for Value Company using

       i. Book-value weights.

       ii. Market-value weights.

       iii. Target weights.

    b. Explain the differences between the WACCs. Which are the correct weights to use in the WACC calculation?

17.3 Baber Corporation's stock returns have a covariance with the market of 0.031. The standard deviation of the market returns is 0.16, and the historical market premium is 8.5 percent. Baber bonds carry a 13-percent coupon rate and are priced to yield 11 percent. The market value of the bonds is $24 million. Baber stock, of which 4 million shares are outstanding, sells for $15 per share. Baber's CFO considers the firm's current debt-equity ratio optimal. The tax rate is 40 percent, and the Treasury bill rate is 7 percent.

Baber Corp. must decide whether or not to purchase additional capital equipment. The cost of the equipment is $27.5 million. The expected cash flows from the new equipment are $9 million a year for five years. Purchasing the equipment will not change the risk level of Baber Corp. Should Baber purchase the equipment?

17.4 National Electric Company (NEC) is considering a $20 million modernization expansion project in the power systems division. Tom Edison, the company's chief financial officer, has evaluated the project; he determined that the project's after-tax cash flows will be $8 million in perpetuity. In addition, Mr. Edison has devised two possibilities for raising the necessary $20 million:

- Issue 10-year, 10-percent debt.
- Issue common stock.

NEC's cost of debt is 10 percent, and its cost of equity is 20 percent. The firm's target debt-equity ratio is 200 percent. The expansion project has the same risk as the existing business, and it will support the same amount of debt. NEC is in the 40-percent tax bracket.

Mr. Edison has advised the firm to undertake the expansion. He suggests debt to finance the project because it is cheaper and its issuance costs are lower.

a. Should NEC accept the project? Support your answer with the appropriate calculations.

b. Do you agree with Mr. Edison's opinion on the expense of the debt? Why or why not?

17.5 Referring back to Problem 17.3, Baber Corporation has chosen to purchase the additional equipment. If Baber funds the project entirely with debt, what is the firm's weighted average cost of capital? Explain your answer.

Adjusted Present Value (APV)

17.6 Honda and GM are competing to sell a fleet of cars to Hertz. For simplicity, we assume straight-line depreciation and that Hertz will dispose of the cars after five years. Hertz expects that the autos will have no salvage value. Hertz expects a fleet of 25 cars to generate $100,000 per year in pretax income. Hertz is in the 40-percent tax bracket and the firm's overall required return is 10 percent. The addition of the new fleet will not add to the risk of the firm. Treasury bills are priced to yield 6 percent.

a. What is the maximum price that Hertz should be willing to pay for the fleet of cars?

b. Suppose the price of the fleet (in Canadian dollars) is $325,000; both suppliers are charging this price. Hertz is able to issue $200,000 in debt to finance the project. The bonds can be issued at par and will carry an 8-percent interest rate. Hertz will incur no costs to issue the debt and no costs of financial distress. What is the APV of this project if Hertz uses debt to finance the auto purchase?

c. To entice Hertz to buy the cars from Honda, the Japanese government is willing to lend Hertz $200,000 at 5 percent. Now what is the maximum price that Hertz is willing to pay Honda Canada for the fleet of cars?

17.7 Peatco, Ltd., is considering a $2.1 million project that will be depreciated according to the straight-line method over the three-year life of the project. The project will generate pretax earnings of $900,000 per year, and it will not change the risk level of the firm. Peatco can obtain a three-year, 12.5-percent loan to finance the project; the bank will charge Peatco fees of 1 percent of the gross proceeds of the loan. The fee must be paid up-front, not from the loan proceeds. If Peatco financed the project with all equity, its cost of capital would be 18 percent. The tax rate is 40 percent, and the risk-free rate is 6 percent.

a. Using the APV method, determine whether or not Peatco should undertake the project.

b. After hearing that Peatco would not be initiating the project in their town, the city council voted to subsidize Peatco's loan. Under the city's proposal, Peatco will pay the same fees, but the rate on the loan will be 10 percent. Should Peatco accept the city's offer and begin the project?

17.8 MEO Foods, Inc., has made cat food for over 20 years. The company currently has a debt-equity ratio of 25 percent, borrows at a 10-percent interest rate, and is in the 40-percent tax bracket. Its shareholders require an 18-percent return.

MEO is planning to expand cat food production capacity. The equipment to be purchased would last three years and generate the following unlevered cash flows (in millions of dollars):

	Year		
0	1	2	3
−15	5	8	10

MEO has also arranged a $6 million debt issue to finance part of the expansion. Under the loan, the company would pay 10 percent annually on the outstanding balance. The firm would also make year-end principal payments of $2 million per year, completely retiring the issue at the end of the third year.

Ignoring costs of financial distress and issue costs, should MEO proceed with the expansion plan?

Combining Different Methods of Capital Budgeting

17.9 Scheschuk Inc. is an unlevered firm with expected perpetual annual before-tax cash flows of $30 million and required return on equity of 18 percent. It has 1 million shares outstanding. Scheschuk is paying tax at a marginal rate of 40 percent. The firm is planning a recapitalization under which it will issue $50 million of perpetual debt bearing a 10-percent interest rate and use the proceeds to buy back shares. Calculate the post-recapitalization share price, earnings per share, and required return on equity.

17.10 Kinedyne, Inc., has decided to divest one of its divisions. The assets of the group have the same operating risk characteristics as those of the parent firm. The capital structure for the parent has been stable at 40-percent debt/60-percent equity (in market value terms), the level determined to be optimal given the firm's assets. The required return on Kinedyne's assets is 16 percent, and the firm (like the division) borrows at a rate of 10 percent.

Sales revenue for the division is expected to remain stable indefinitely at last year's level of $19,740,000. Variable costs amount to 60 percent of sales. Annual depreciation of $1.8 million is exactly matched each year by new investment in the division's equipment. The division would be taxed at the parent's current rate of 40 percent.

a. How much is the division worth in unleveraged form?

b. If the division had the same capital structure as the parent firm, how much would it be worth?

c. At this optimal capital structure, what return will the equityholders of the division require?

d. Show that the market value of the equity of the division would be justified by the earnings to shareholders and the required return on equity.

17.11 Refer to Problem 17.10. Kinedyne has just determined that the division to be divested differs in risk from the parent firm. Firms similar to this division had an average beta of 1.75. The risk-free rate is currently 6 percent and the market risk premium is 5 percent. Rework Problem 17.10 with this new information.

The Adjusted Present Value Approach to Valuing Leveraged Buyouts

APPENDIX

Introduction

A leveraged buyout (LBO) is the acquisition by a small group of equity investors of a public or private company financed primarily with debt. The equityholders service the heavy interest and principal payments with cash from operations and/or asset sales. The shareholders generally hope to reverse the LBO within three to seven years by way of a public offering or sale of the company to another firm. A buyout is therefore likely to be successful only if the firm generates enough cash to serve the debt in the early years, and if the company is attractive to other buyers as the buyout matures.

In a leveraged buyout, the equity investors are expected to pay off outstanding principal according to a specific timetable. The owners know that the firm's debt-equity ratio will fall and can forecast the dollar amount of debt needed to finance future operations. Under these circumstances, the adjusted present value (APV) approach is more practical than the weighted average cost of capital (WACC) approach because the capital structure is changing. In this appendix, we illustrate the use of this procedure in valuing the RJR Nabisco transaction, the largest LBO in history.

The RJR Nabisco Buyout

In the summer of 1988, the price of RJR stock was hovering around $55 a share. The firm had $5 billion of debt. The firm's CEO, Ross Johnson (a transplanted Canadian), acting in concert with some other senior managers of the firm, announced a bid of $75 per share to take the firm private in a management buyout. Within days of management's offer Kohlberg Kravis and Roberts (KKR) entered the fray with a $90 bid of their own. By the end of November, KKR emerged from the ensuing bidding process with an offer of $109 a share, or $25 billion total. We now use the APV technique to analyze KKR's winning strategy.

The APV method as described in this chapter can be used to value companies as well as projects. Applied in this way, the maximum value of a levered firm (V_L) is its value as an all-equity entity (V_U) plus the discounted value of the interest tax shields from the debt its assets will support (PVTS).[11] This relation can be stated as

$$V_L = V_U + \text{PVTS}$$

$$= \sum_{t=1}^{\infty} \frac{\text{UCF}_t}{(1 + r_0)^t} + \sum_{t=1}^{\infty} \frac{T_C r_B B_{t-1}}{(1 + r_B)^t}$$

In the second part of this equation, UCF_t is the unlevered cash flow from operations for year t. Discounting these cash flows by the required return on assets, r_0, yields the all-equity value of the company. B_{t-1} represents the debt balance remaining at the end of year $(t - 1)$. Because interest in a given year is based on the debt balance remaining at the end of the previous year, the interest paid in year t is $r_B B_{t-1}$. The numerator of the second term, $T_C r_B B_{t-1}$, is therefore the tax shield for year t. We discount this series of annual tax shields using the rate at which the firm borrows, r_B.[12]

KKR planned to sell several of RJR's food divisions and operate the remaining parts of the firm more efficiently. Table 17A.1 presents KKR's projected unlevered cash flows for RJR under the buyout, adjusting for planned asset sales and operational efficiencies.

With respect to financial strategy, KKR planned a significant increase in leverage with accompanying tax benefits. Specifically, KKR issued almost $24 billion of new

---

[11]One should also deduct from this value any costs of financial distress. However, we would expect these costs to be small in the case of RJR for two reasons. As a firm in the tobacco and food industries, its cash flows are relatively stable and recession-resistant. Furthermore, the firm's assets are divisible and attractive to a number of potential buyers, allowing the firm to receive full value if disposition is required.

[12]The pretax borrowing rate, r_B, represents the appropriate discount rate for the interest tax shields when there is a precommitment to a specific debt repayment schedule under the terms of the LBO. If debt covenants require that the entire free cash flow be dedicated to debt service, the amount of debt outstanding and, therefore, the interest tax shield at any point in time are a direct function of the operating cash flows of the firm. Since the debt balance is then as risky as the cash flows, the required return on assets should be used to discount the interest tax shields.

	1989	1990	1991	1992	1993	**Table 17A.1**
Operating income	$2,620	$3,410	$3,645	$3,950	$4,310	RJR operating cash
Tax on operating income	891	1,142	1,222	1,326	1,448	flows (in $ millions)
After-tax operating income	1,729	2,268	2,423	2,624	2,862	
Add back depreciation	449	475	475	475	475	
Less capital expenditures	522	512	525	538	551	
Less change in working capital	(203)	(275)	200	225	250	
Add proceeds from asset sales	3,545	1,805				
Unlevered cash flow (UCF)	5,404	4,311	2,173	2,336	2,536	

	1989	1990	1991	1992	1993	**Table 17A.2**
Interest expenses	$3,384	$3,004	$3,111	$3,294	$3,483	Projected interest expenses and tax
Interest tax shields ($T_C = 34\%$)	1,151	1,021	1,058	1,120	1,184	shields (in $ millions)

debt to complete the buyout, raising annual interest costs to more than $3 billion.[13] Table 17A.2 presents the projected interest expense and tax shields for the transaction.

We now use the data from Tables 17A.1 and 17A.2 to calculate APV of the RJR buyout. This valuation process is presented in Table 17A.3.

The valuation presented in Table 17A.3 involves four steps.

Step 1: Calculating the present value of unlevered cash flows for 1989–93   The unlevered cash flows for 1989–93 are shown in the last line of Table 17A.1 and the first line of Table 17A.3. These flows are discounted by the required asset return, r_0, which at the time of the buyout was approximately 14 percent. The value as of the end of 1988 of the unlevered cash flows expected from 1989 through 1993 is

$$\frac{5.404}{1.14} + \frac{4.311}{1.14^2} + \frac{2.173}{1.14^3} + \frac{2.336}{1.14^4} + \frac{2.536}{1.14^5} = \$12.224 \text{ billion}$$

Step 2: Calculating the present value of the unlevered cash flows beyond 1993 (unlevered terminal value)   We assume the unlevered cash flows grow at the modest annual rate of 3 percent after 1993. These cash flows' value, as of the end of 1993, equals the following discounted value of a growing perpetuity:

$$\frac{2.536(1.03)}{.14 - .03} = \$23.746 \text{ billion}$$

---

[13]A significant portion of this debt was of the payment in kind (PIK) variety, which offers lenders additional bonds instead of cash interest. This PIK debt financing provided KKR with significant tax shields while allowing it to postpone the cash burden of debt service to future years. For simplicity of presentation, Table 17A.2 does not separately show cash versus noncash interest charges.

Table 17A.3		1989	1990	1991	1992	1993
RJR LBO valuation (in \$ millions except share data)	Unlevered cash flow (UCF)	\$ 5,404	\$4,311	\$2,173	\$2,336	\$ 2,536
	Terminal value: (3% growth after 1993)					
	Unlevered terminal value (UTV)					23,746
	Terminal value at target debt					26,654
	Tax shield in terminal value					2,908
	Interest tax shields	1,151	1,021	1,058	1,120	1,184
	PV of UCF 1989–93 at 14%	12,224				
	PV of UTV at 14%	12,333				
	Total unlevered value	24,557				
	PV of tax shields 1989–93 at 13.5%	3,877				
	PV of tax shield in TV at 13.5%	1,544				
	Total value of tax shields	5,421				
	Total value	29,978				
	Less value of assumed debt	5,000				
	Value of equity	\$24,978				
	Number of shares	229 million				
	Value per share	\$109.07				

This translates to a 1988 value of

$$\frac{23.746}{1.14^5} = \$12.333 \text{ billion}$$

As in Step 1, the discount rate is the required asset rate of 14 percent.

The total unlevered value of the firm is therefore (\$12.224 + \$12.333 =) \$24.557 billion.

To calculate the total buyout value, we must add the interest tax shields expected to be realized by debt financing.

Step 3: Calculating the present value of interest tax shields for 1989–93   Under current U.S. tax laws, every dollar of interest reduces taxes by 34 cents. The present value of the interest tax shields for the 1989–93 period can be calculated by discounting the annual tax savings at the pretax average cost of debt, which was approximately 13.5 percent. Using the tax shields from Table 17A.2, the discounted value of these tax shields is calculated as

$$\frac{1.151}{1.135} + \frac{1.021}{1.135^2} + \frac{1.058}{1.135^3} + \frac{1.120}{1.135^4} + \frac{1.184}{1.135^5} = \$3.877 \text{ billion}$$

Step 4: Calculating the present value of interest tax shields beyond 1993   Finally, we must calculate the value of tax shields associated with debt used to finance the operations of the company after 1993. We assume that debt will be reduced and maintained at 25 percent of the value of the firm from that date forward.[14] Under this assumption it is appropriate to use the WACC method to calculate a terminal value for the firm at the target capital structure. This in turn can be decomposed into an all-equity value and a value from tax shields.

If, after 1993, RJR uses 25-percent debt in its capital structure, its WACC at this target capital structure would be approximately 12.8 percent.[15] Then the levered terminal value as of the end of 1993 can be estimated as

$$\frac{2.536(1.03)}{.128 - .03} = \$26.654 \text{ billion}$$

Since the levered value of the company is the sum of the unlevered value plus the value of interest tax shields,

$$\text{Value of tax shields (end 1993)} = V_L \text{ (end 1993)} - V_U \text{ (end 1993)}$$
$$= \$26.654 \text{ billion} - 23.746 \text{ billion}$$
$$= 2.908 \text{ billion}$$

To calculate the value, as of the end of 1988, of these future tax shields, we again discount by the borrowing rate of 13.5 percent to get

$$\frac{2.908}{1.135^5} = \$1.544 \text{ billion}$$

The total value of interest tax shields therefore equals \$5.421 (or \$3.877 + \$1.544) billion.

Adding all of these components together, the total value of RJR under the buyout proposal is \$29.978 billion. Deducting the \$5 billion market value of assumed debt yields a value for equity of \$24.978 billion or \$109.07 per share.

---

[14]This 25-percent figure is consistent with the debt utilization in industries in which RJR Nabisco is involved. In fact, that was the debt–to–today-market-value ratio for RJR immediately before management's initial buyout proposal. The firm could achieve this target by 1993 if a significant portion of the convertible debt used to finance the buyout was exchanged for equity by that time. Alternatively, KKR could issue new equity (as would occur, for example, if the firm were taken public) and use the proceeds to retire some of the outstanding debt.

[15]To calculate this rate, use the weighted average cost of capital from this chapter:

$$r_{WACC} = \frac{S}{S + B}r_S + \frac{B}{S + B}r_B (1 - T_C)$$

and substitute the appropriate values for the proportions of debt and equity used, as well as their respective costs. Specifically, at the target debt-value ratio, $\frac{B}{S + B} = 25\%$, and $\frac{S}{S + B} = \left(1 - \frac{B}{S + B}\right) = 75\%$. Given this blend,

$$r_S = r_0 + \frac{B}{S}(1 - T_C)(r_0 - r_B)$$

$$= .14 + \frac{.25}{.75}(1 - .34)(.14 - .135) = .141$$

Using these findings plus the borrowing rate of 13.5 percent in r_{WACC}, we find

$$r_{WACC} = .75(.141) + .25(.135)(1 - .34) = .128$$

In fact, this value is an approximation to the true weighted average cost of capital when the market debt–value blend is constant, or when the cash flows are growing. For a detailed discussion of this issue, see Isik Inselbag and Howard Kaufold, "A Comparison of Alternative Discounted Cash Flow Approaches to Firm Valuation" (Philadelphia: The Wharton School, University of Pennsylvania, June 1990), unpublished paper.

Concluding Comments on LBO Valuation Methods

As mentioned earlier in this chapter, the WACC method is by far the most widely applied approach to capital budgeting. One could analyze an LBO and generate the results of the second section of this appendix using this technique, but it would be a much more difficult process. We have tried to show that the APV approach is the preferred way to analyze a transaction in which the capital structure is not stable over time.

Consider the WACC approach to valuing the KKR bid for RJR. One could discount the operating cash flows of RJR by a set of weighted average costs of capital and arrive at the same $30 billion total value for the company. To do this, one would need to calculate the appropriate rate for each year since the WACC rises as the buyout proceeds. This occurs because the value of the tax subsidy declines as debt principal is repaid. In other words, there is no single return that represents the cost of capital when the firm's capital structure is changing.

There is also a theoretical problem with the WACC approach to valuing a buyout. To calculate the changing WACC, one must know the market value of a firm's debt and equity. But if the debt and equity values are already known, the total market value of the company is also known. That is, one must know the value of the company to calculate the WACC. One must therefore resort to using book-value measures for debt and equity, or make assumptions about the evolution of their market values, in order to implement the WACC method.

CHAPTER 18

Dividend Policy: Why Does It Matter?

Corporations view the dividend decision as quite important because it determines what funds flow to investors and what funds are retained by the firm for reinvestment. Dividend policy can also provide information to the shareholder concerning the firm's performance.

Like capital structure, dividend policy has been the subject of extensive research, but no consensus has been reached. For this reason, all discussions of dividends are plagued by the "two-handed lawyer" problem identified by former U.S. President Truman. While discussing the legal implications of a possible presidential decision, he asked his staff to set up a meeting with a lawyer. Supposedly Truman said, "But I don't want one of those two-handed lawyers." When asked what a two-handed lawyer was, he replied. "You know, a lawyer who says, 'On the one hand I recommend you do so-and-so because of the following reasons, but on the other hand I recommend that you don't do it because of these other reasons.' "

Unfortunately, any sensible treatment of dividend policy will appear to be written by a two-handed lawyer (or, in fairness, several two-handed financial economists). On the one hand, there are many good reasons for corporations to pay high dividends, but on the other hand, there are many good reasons to pay low dividends.

We begin this chapter with a discussion of some practical aspects of dividend payments. Next, we treat dividend policy. Before delineating the pros and cons of different dividend levels, we examine a benchmark case in which the choice of the level of dividends is not important. Surprisingly, we will see that this conceptual framework is not merely an academic curiosity but instead is quite applicable to the real world. Next, we consider personal taxes—an imperfection generally inducing a low level of dividends. This is followed by reasons justifying a high dividend level. Finally, we study the initial dividend decision of the Apple Computer Company in 1987. The case provides some clues as to why firms pay dividends.

Different Types of Dividends 18.1

The term *dividend* usually refers to cash distributions of earnings. If a distribution is made from sources other than current or accumulated retained earnings, the term *distribution* rather than *dividend* is used. However, it is acceptable to refer to a distribution from earnings as a *dividend* and refer to a distribution from capital as a *liquidating dividend.* More generally, any direct payment by the corporation to the shareholders may be considered part of dividend policy.

The most common type of dividend is in the form of cash. Public companies usually pay **regular cash dividends** four times a year. Sometimes firms pay a regular cash dividend and an *extra cash dividend.* Paying a cash dividend reduces corporate cash and retained earnings shown on the balance sheet—except in the case of a liquidating dividend (where the common shares account may be reduced).[1]

Another type of dividend, paid out in shares of stock, is referred to as a **stock dividend.** It is not a true dividend, because no cash leaves the firm. Rather, a stock dividend increases the number of shares outstanding, thereby reducing the value of each share. A stock dividend is commonly expressed as a ratio; for example, with a 2-percent stock dividend, a shareholder receives one new share for every 50 currently owned.

When a firm declares a **stock split,** it increases the number of shares outstanding. For example, in a two-for-one split, each shareholder receives one additional share of stock for each share held originally, so a two-for-one stock split is equivalent to a 100-percent stock dividend. By convention, the term *stock dividend* is used for small distributions of stock, while *stock split* refers to large distributions.

After a stock split, each share is entitled to a smaller percentage of the firm's cash flow, so the stock price should fall. For example, if the managers of a firm whose stock is selling at $50 declare a 2:1 stock split, the price of a share of stock should fall to about $25.

18.2   Standard Method of Cash Dividend Payment

The decision on whether to pay a dividend rests in the hands of the board of directors of the corporation. A dividend is distributable to shareholders of record on a specific date. When a dividend has been declared, it becomes a liability of the firm and cannot be easily rescinded by the corporation. The amount of the dividend is expressed as dollars per share (*dividend per share*), as a percentage of the market price (*dividend yield*), or as a percentage of earnings per share (*dividend payout*).

The mechanics of a dividend payment can be illustrated by the example in Figure 18.1 and the following chronology:

1. **Declaration date.** On January 15 (the declaration date), the board of directors passes a resolution to pay a dividend of $1 per share on February 16 to all holders of record on January 30.

2. **Date of record.** The corporation prepares a list on January 30 of all individuals believed to be shareholders as of this date. The word *believed* is important here, because the dividend will not be paid to those individuals whose notification of purchase is received by the company after January 30.

3. **Ex-dividend date.** The procedure on the date of record would be unfair if efficient investment dealers could notify the corporation by January 30 of a trade

---

[1]Bond covenants restrict payment of liquidating dividends as we discuss in Chapter 20.

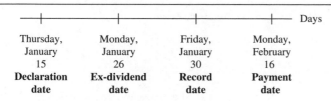

Figure 18.1
Example of
procedure for
dividend payment

1. *Declaration date:* The board of directors declares a payment of dividends.

2. *Record date:* The declared dividends are distributable to shareholders of record on a specific date.

3. *Ex-dividend date:* A share of stock becomes ex-dividend on the date the seller is entitled to keep the dividend: under TSE rules, shares are traded ex-dividend on and after the fourth business day before the record date.

4. *Payment date:* The dividend cheques are mailed to shareholders of record.

occurring on January 29, whereas the same trade might not reach the corporation until February 2 if executed by a less efficient dealer. To eliminate this problem, all investment dealers entitle shareholders to receive the dividend if they purchased the stock five business days before the date of record. The fourth day before the date of record (Monday, January 26, in our example) is called the *ex-dividend date.* Before this date the stock is said to trade *cum dividend* (Latin for "with dividend").

4. **Date of payment.** The dividend cheques are mailed to the shareholders on February 16.

Obviously, the ex-dividend date is important, because an individual purchasing the security before the ex-dividend date will receive the current dividend, whereas another individual purchasing the security on or after this date will not receive the dividend. The stock price should fall on the ex-dividend date.[2] It is worthwhile to note that this drop is an indication of efficiency, not inefficiency, because the market rationally attaches value to a cash dividend. In a world with neither taxes nor transaction costs, the stock price is expected to fall by the amount of the dividend:

Before ex-dividend date: Price = $(P + 1)$

On or after ex-dividend date: Price = P

This is illustrated in Figure 18.2.

The amount of the price drop is a matter for empirical investigation. Elton and Gruber and have argued that, due to personal taxes, the stock price should drop by less than the dividend.[3] For example, consider the case with no capital gains taxes. On the day before a stock goes ex-dividend, shareholders must decide either to buy immediately and pay tax on the forthcoming dividend, or to buy tomorrow, thereby missing the dividend. If all investors are in a 30-percent bracket for dividends and the quarterly dividend is $1, the stock price should fall by $.70 on the ex-dividend date. If

---

[2]The stock price typically falls within the first few minutes of the ex-dividend day.

[3]N. Elton and M. Gruber, "Marginal Stockholder Tax Rates and the Clientele Effect," *Review of Economics and Statistics* 52 (February 1970).

Figure 18.2
Price behaviour
around the
ex-dividend date
for a $1 cash
dividend

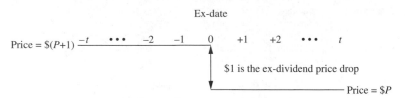

Perfect-world case

Ex-date

Price = $(P+1)

$1 is the ex-dividend price drop

Price = $P

The stock price will fall by the amount of the dividend on the ex-date (time 0). If the dividend is $1 per share, the price will be equal to P on the ex-date.

Before ex-date (−1)   Price = $(P + 1)$
Ex-date (0)   Price = P

the stock price falls by this amount on the ex-dividend date, then purchasers will receive the same return from either strategy.[4]

CONCEPT QUESTIONS

■ Describe the procedure of a dividend payment.
■ Why should the price of a stock change when it goes ex-dividend?

18.3   The Benchmark Case: An Illustration of the Irrelevance of Dividend Policy

A powerful argument can be made that dividend policy does not matter. This will be illustrated with the York Corporation, an all-equity firm in existence for 10 years. The financial managers know at the present time (date 0) that the firm will dissolve in one year (date 1). At date 0, the managers are able to forecast cash flows with perfect certainty. The managers know that the firm will receive a cash flow of $10,000 immediately and another $10,000 next year. They believe that York has no additional positive NPV projects it can use to its advantage.[5]

Current Policy: Dividends Set Equal to Cash Flow

At the present time, dividends (Div) at each date are set equal to the cash flow of $10,000. The NPV of the firm can be calculated by discounting these dividends. The firm's value can be expressed as

$$V_0 = \text{Div}_0 + \frac{\text{Div}_1}{1 + r_s}$$

[4]The situation is more complex when capital gains are considered. The individual pays capital gains taxes upon a subsequent sale. Because the price drops on the ex-dividend date, the original purchase price is higher if the purchase is made before the ex-dividend date, and the individual will reap, and pay taxes on, lower capital gains. Elton and Gruber show that the price drop is increased slightly when capital gains taxes are considered. L. D. Booth and D. J. Johnston, "The Ex-Dividend Day Behavior of Canadian Stock Prices: Tax Changes and Clientele Effects," *Journal of Finance* 39 (June 1984), find that personal taxes on dividends are the main factor in determining the price drop with a small adjustment for capital gains tax. We return to personal taxes later in the chapter.

[5]York's investment in physical assets is fixed.

where Div_0 and Div_1 are the cash flows paid out in dividends, and r_S is the discount rate. The first dividend is not discounted because it will be paid immediately.

Assuming $r_S = 10\%$, the value of the firm can be calculated by

$$\$19,090.91 = \$10,000 + \frac{\$10,000}{1.1}$$

Value of firm is the PV of all future div

If 1,000 shares are outstanding, the value of each share is

$$\$19.09 = \$10 + \frac{\$10}{1.1} \tag{18.1}$$

To simplify the example, we assume that the ex-dividend date is the same as the date of payment. After the imminent dividend is paid, the stock price will immediately fall to $9.09 (or $19.09 − $10). Several of York's board members have expressed dissatisfaction with the current dividend policy and have asked you to analyze an alternative policy.

Alternative Policy: Initial Dividend Is Greater Than Cash Flow

Another policy is for the firm to pay a dividend of $11 per share immediately, which is, of course, a total dividend of $11,000. Because the cash runoff is only $10,000, the extra $1,000 must be raised in one of a few ways. Perhaps the simplest would be to issue $1,000 of bonds or stock now (at date 0). Assume that stock is issued and the new shareholders will desire enough cash flow at date 1 to let them earn the required 10-percent return on their date 0 investment.[6] The new shareholders will demand $1,100 of the date 1 cash flow, leaving only $8,900 to the old shareholders.[7] The dividends to the old shareholders will be

	Date 0	Date 1
Aggregate dividends to old shareholders	$11,000	$8,900
Dividends per share	11.00	8.90

The present value of the dividends per share is therefore

$$\$19.09 = \$11 + \frac{\$8.90}{1.1} \tag{18.2}$$

Students often find it instructive to determine the price at which the new stock is issued. Because the new shareholders are not entitled to the immediate dividend, they would pay $8.09 (or $8.90/1.1) per share. Thus, 123.61 (or $1,000/$8.09) new shares are issued.

The Indifference Proposition

Note that the NPVs of equations (18.1) and (18.2) are equal. This leads to the initially surprising conclusion that the change in dividend policy did not affect the value of a

---

[6]The same results would occur after an issue of bonds, though the argument would be less easily resolved.

[7]Because the new shareholders buy at date 0, their first (and only) dividend is at date 1.7.

Figure 18.3
Current and
alternative
dividend policies

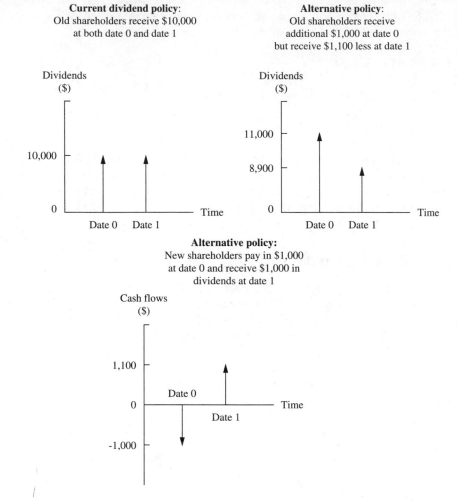

Current dividend policy:
Old shareholders receive $10,000
at both date 0 and date 1

Alternative policy:
Old shareholders receive
additional $1,000 at date 0
but receive $1,100 less at date 1

Alternative policy:
New shareholders pay in $1,000
at date 0 and receive $1,000 in
dividends at date 1

share of stock. However, upon reflection, the result seems quite sensible. The new shareholders are parting with their money at date 0 and receiving it back with the appropriate return at date 1. In other words, they are taking on a zero-NPV investment. As illustrated in Figure 18.3, old shareholders are receiving additional funds at date 0 but must pay the new shareholders their money with the appropriate return at date 1. Because the old shareholders must pay back principal plus the appropriate return, the act of issuing new stock at date 0 will neither increase nor decrease the value of the old shareholders' holdings. That is, they are giving up a zero NPV investment to the new shareholders. An increase in dividends at date 0 leads to the necessary reduction of dividends at date 1, so the value of the old shareholders' holdings remains unchanged.

This illustration is based on the pioneering work of Modigliani and Miller (MM).[8] Although our presentation is in the form of a numerical example, the MM paper proves that investors are indifferent to dividend policy in the general algebraic case. MM make the following assumptions:

1. There are neither taxes nor brokerage fees, and no single participant can affect the market price of the security through his or her trades. Economists say that perfect markets exist when these conditions are met.

2. All individuals have the same beliefs concerning future investments, profits, and dividends. As mentioned in Chapter 10, these individuals are said to have *homogenous expectations.*

3. The investment policy of the firm is set ahead of time, and is not altered by changes in dividend policy.

Homemade Dividends

To illustrate the indifference investors have toward dividend policy in our example, we used net present value equations. An alternative, and perhaps more intuitively appealing, explanation avoids the mathematics of discounted cash flows.

Suppose individual investor X prefers dividends per share of $10 at both dates 0 and 1. Would she be disappointed when informed that the firm's management is adopting the alternative dividend policy (dividends of $11 and $8.90 on the two dates, respectively)? Not necessarily, because she could easily reinvest the $1 of unneeded funds received on date 0, yielding an incremental return of $1.10 at date 1. Thus, she would receive her desired net cash flow of $11 − $1 = $10 at date 0 and $8.90 + $1.10 = $10 at date 1.

Conversely, imagine investor Z, who prefers $11 of cash flow at date 0 and $8.90 of cash flow at date 1, and who finds that management will pay dividends of $10 at both dates 0 and 1. He can sell off shares of stock at date 0 to receive the desired amount of cash flow. That is, if at date 0 he sells off shares (or fractions of shares) totalling $1, his cash flow at date 0 becomes $10 + $1 = $11. Because a sale of $1 of stock at date 0 will reduce his dividends by $1.10 at date 1, his net cash flow at date 1 will be $10 − $1.10 = $8.90.

The example illustrates how investors can make **homemade dividends.** In this instance, corporate dividend policy is being undone by a potentially dissatisfied shareholder. This homemade dividend is illustrated in Figure 18.4. Here the firm's cash flows of $10 at both date 0 and date 1 are represented by point A. This point also represents the initial dividend payout. Alternatively, as we just saw, the firm could pay out $11 at date 0 and $8.90 at date 1, a strategy represented by point B. Similarly, by either issuing new stock or buying back old stock, the managers of the firm could achieve a dividend payout represented by any point on the diagonal line.

The same diagonal line also represents the choices available to the shareholder. For example, if the shareholder receives a dividend distribution of ($11, $8.90), he or

---

[8]M. H. Miller and F. Modigliani, "Dividend Policy, Growth and the Valuation of Shares," *Journal of Business* (October 1961). Yes, this is the same MM who gave us a capital structure theory.

Figure 18.4
Homemade
dividends: A
trade-off between
dividends at date 0
and dividends at
date 1

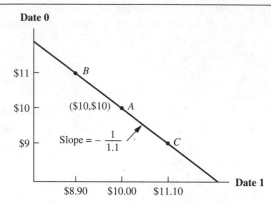

This graph illustrates both (1) how managers can vary dividend policy and (2) how individuals can undo the firm's dividend policy.

Managers varying dividend policy. A firm paying out all cash flows immediately is at point A on the graph. The firm could achieve point B by issuing stock to pay extra dividends or achieve point C by buying back old stock with some of its cash.

Individuals undoing the firm's dividend policy. Suppose the firm adopts the dividend policy represented by point B: dividends of $11 at date 0 and $8.90 at date 1. An investor can reinvest $1 of the dividends at 10 percent, which will place her at point A. Suppose, alternatively, the firm adopts the dividend policy represented by point A. An individual can sell off $1 of stock at date 0, placing him at point B. No matter what dividend policy the firm establishes, a shareholder can undo it.

she can either reinvest some of the dividends to move down and to the right on the graph or sell off shares of stock and move up and to the left.

Many corporations actually assist their shareholders in creating homemade dividend policies by offering *automatic dividend reinvestment plans* (ADPs or DRIPs). As the name suggests, with such a plan, shareholders have the option of automatically reinvesting some or all of their cash dividend in shares of stock.

Under a new-issue dividend reinvestment plan, investors buy new stock issued by the firm and receive a small discount—usually under 5 percent. This makes dividend reinvestment very attractive to investors who do not need cash flow from dividends. Since the 5-percent discount compares favourably with issue costs for new stock (which will be discussed in Chapter 19), dividend reinvestment plans are popular with large companies which periodically seek new common stock.[9]

Investment dealers also use financial engineering to create homemade dividends (or homemade capital gains). **Stripped common shares** entitle holders to receive either all the dividends from one or a group of well-known companies or an instalment receipt that packages any capital gain in the form of a call option. The option gives the investor the right to buy the underlying shares at a fixed price and so is valuable if the shares appreciate beyond that price.

The implications of Figure 18.4 can be summarized in two sentences:

1. By varying dividend policy, the managers can achieve any payout along the diagonal line in Figure 18.4.

---

[9]Reinvested dividends are still taxable.

2. Either by reinvesting excess dividends at date 0 or by selling off shares of stock at this date, any individual investor can achieve any net cash payout along the diagonal line.

Thus, because both the corporation and the individual investor can move only along the diagonal line, dividend policy in this model is irrelevant. The changes the managers make in dividend policy can be undone by an individual who, by either reinvesting dividends or selling off stock, can move to any desired point on the diagonal line.

A Test

You can test your understanding by examining these true statements:

- Dividends are relevant.
- Dividend policy is irrelevant.

The first statement follows from common sense. Clearly, investors prefer higher dividends to lower dividends at any single date if the dividend level is held constant at every other date. In other words, if the dividend per share at a given date is raised while the dividend per share for each other date is held constant, the stock price will rise. This act can be accomplished by management decisions that improve productivity, increase tax savings, or strengthen product marketing.

The second statement makes sense once we realize that dividend policy cannot raise the dividend per share at one date while holding the dividend level per share constant at all other dates. Rather, dividend policy merely establishes the trade-off between dividends at one date and dividends at another date. As we saw in Figure 18.4, an increase in date 0 dividends can be accomplished only by a decrease in date 1 dividends. The extent of the decrease is such that the present value of all dividends is not affected.

Thus, in this simple world, dividend policy does not matter. That is, managers choosing to raise or to lower the current dividend do not affect the current value of their firms. This theory is a powerful one, and the work of MM is considered a classic in modern finance. With relatively few assumptions, a rather surprising result is shown to be perfectly true.[10] Because we want to examine many real world factors ignored by MM, their work is only a starting point in this chapter's discussion of dividends. The next part of the chapter investigates these real world considerations.

Dividends and Investment Policy

The argument above shows that an increase in dividends through issuing new shares neither helps nor hurts the shareholders. Similarly, a reduction in dividends through share repurchase neither helps nor hurts shareholders.

---

[10]One of the real contributions of MM has been to shift the burden of proof. Before MM, firm value was believed to be influenced by its dividend policy. After MM, it became clear that establishing a correct dividend policy was not obvious at all.

What about reducing capital expenditures to increase dividends? Earlier chapters show that a firm should accept all positive NPV projects. To do otherwise would reduce the value of the firm. Thus, we have an important point:

> Firms should never give up a positive NPV project to increase a dividend (or to pay a dividend for the first time).

This idea was implicitly considered by Miller and Modigliani. As we pointed out, one of the assumptions underlying their dividend-irrelevance proposition was, "The investment policy of the firm is set ahead of time and is not altered by changes in dividend policy."

CONCEPT QUESTIONS

- How can an investor make homemade dividends?
- Are dividends irrelevant?
- What assumptions are needed to show that dividend policy is irrelevant?

18.4   Taxes, Issuance Costs, and Dividends

The model we used to determine the level of dividends assumed that there were no taxes, no transactions costs, and no uncertainty. It concluded that dividend policy is irrelevant. Although this model helps us to grasp some fundamentals of dividend policy, it ignores many factors that exist in reality. We begin our investigation of these real world considerations with the effect of taxes on the level of a firm's dividends.

In Canada, both dividends and capital gains are taxed at effective rates *less than* the marginal tax rate. For dividends, we showed in Chapter 1 that individual investors face a lower tax rate due to the dividend tax credit. Capital gains in the hands of individuals are taxed at 75 percent of the marginal tax rate. Since taxation only takes place when capital gains are realized, capital gains are very lightly taxed in Canada. Thus, for individual shareholders, the *effective* tax rate on dividend income is higher that the tax rate on capital gains.[11]

To facilitate our discussion of dividend policy in the presence of personal taxes, we classify firms into two groups based on whether they have sufficient cash to pay a dividend.

Firms without Sufficient Cash to Pay a Dividend

It is simplest to begin with a firm without cash owned by a single entrepreneur. If this firm should decide to pay a dividend of $100, it must raise capital. The firm might

---

[11]L. D. Booth and D. J. Johnston, "Ex-Dividend Day Behavior," found that dividends are taxed more heavily than capital gains for the marginal investor. Subsequent tax reforms have narrowed, but not eliminated this difference.

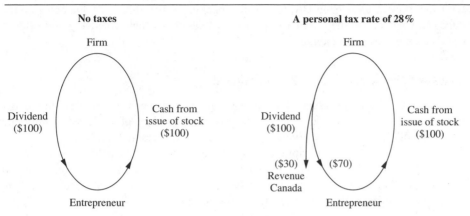

Figure 18.5
Firm issues stock in order to pay a dividend

In the no-tax case, the entrepreneur receives the $100 in dividends that he gave to the firm when purchasing stock. The entire operation is called a *wash;* in other words, it has no economic effect. With taxes, the entrepreneur still receives $100 in dividends. However, he must pay $30 in taxes to Revenue Canada. The entrepreneur loses and Revenue Canada wins when a firm issues stock to pay a dividend.

choose among a number of different stock and bond issues in order to pay the dividend. However, for simplicity, we assume that the entrepreneur contributes cash to the firm by issuing stock to himself. This transaction, diagrammed in the left-hand side of Figure 18.5, would clearly be a *wash* in a world of no taxes. Here $100 cash goes into the firm when stock is issued and is immediately paid out as a dividend. Thus, the entrepreneur neither benefits nor loses when the dividend is paid, a result consistent with Miller–Modigliani.

Now assume that dividends are taxed at 30 percent. The firm still receives $100 on issuance of stock. However, the $100 dividend is not fully credited to the entrepreneur. Instead, the dividend payment is taxed, implying that the owner receives only $70 net after tax. Thus, the entrepreneur loses $30.

Although our example is a bit simplistic, financial economists generally agree that, in a world of personal taxes, one should not issue stock to pay a dividend.

The flotation costs of issuing stock add to this effect. These costs are examined in a later chapter. Because the size of new issues can be lowered by a reduction in dividends, we have another argument in favor of a low-dividend policy.

Of course, our advice not to finance dividends through new stock issues might need to be modified somewhat in the real world. A company with a large and steady cash flow for many years in the past might be paying a regular dividend. If the cash flow unexpectedly dried up for a single year, should new stock be issued so that dividends could be continued? While our previous discussion would imply that new stock should not be issued, many managers might issue the stock anyway for practical reasons. In particular, shareholders might prefer stable dividends. Thus, managers might be forced to issue stock to achieve this stability.

There is considerable evidence that managers believe that investors, at least in certain industries, like stable dividends. For example, since its start in 1881, Bell Canada has never reduced or omitted a dividend. We will discuss theoretical and practical reasons for not cutting dividends later in the chapter. Here we note that firms

with insufficient cash generally follow the pecking order theory of financing introduced in Chapter 16; they draw on other liquid assets and debt financing and seldom
issue stock to pay a dividend.[12]

Firms with Sufficient Cash to Pay a Dividend

The previous discussion argues that, in a world with personal taxes, one should not
issue stock to pay a dividend. Does the tax disadvantage of dividends imply the
stronger policy, "Never pay dividends in a world with personal taxes"?

We argue that this prescription does not necessarily apply to firms with excess
cash. To see this, imagine a firm with $1 million in extra cash after selecting all
positive NPV projects and determining the level of prudent cash balances. The firm
might consider the following alternatives to a dividend:

1. *Select additional capital budgeting projects.* Because the firm has already taken
all the available positive NPV projects, it must invest its excess cash in
negative NPV projects. This is clearly a policy at variance with the principles of
corporate finance and represents an example of the agency costs of equity
introduced in Chapter 16. Jensen has suggested that many managers choose to take
on negative NPV projects in lieu of dividends, doing their shareholders a disservice
in the process.[13] It is frequently argued that managers who adopt negative NPV
projects are ripe for takeover, leveraged buyouts, and proxy fights.

2. *Repurchase shares.* A firm may rid itself of excess cash by repurchasing shares
of stock. In the United States, investors can treat profits on repurchased stock as
capital gains and pay lower taxes than they would if the cash were distributed as a
dividend. In Canada, funds distributed through stock repurchases may be considered
dividends for tax purposes. For this reason, share repurchases are not always an
attractive alternative to a dividend.

3. *Acquire other companies.* To avoid the payment of dividends, a firm might use
excess cash to acquire another company. This strategy has the advantage of
acquiring profitable assets. However, a firm often incurs heavy costs when it
embarks on an acquisition program. In addition, acquisitions are invariably made
above the market price. Premiums of 20 to 80 percent are not uncommon. Because
of this, a number of researchers have argued that mergers are not generally
profitable to the acquiring company, even when firms are merged for a valid
business purpose.[14] Therefore, a company making an acquisition merely to avoid a
dividend is unlikely to benefit its shareholders.

4. *Purchase financial assets.* The strategy of purchasing financial assets in lieu of a
dividend payment can be illustrated with the following example.

---

[12]U.S. evidence that firms seldom issue stock to finance a dividend is in Avner Kalay and Adam Shirat, "On the Payment
of Equity Financed Dividends" (University of Utah, working paper, 1988).

[13]M. C. Jensen, "Agency Costs of Free Cash Flows, Corporate Finance and Takeovers," *American Economic Review* (May
1986), pp. 323–29.

[14]Richard Roll, "The Hubris Hypothesis of Corporate Turnovers," *Journal of Business* (1986), pp. 197–216, explores this
idea in depth.

■ *Example*

The Regional Electric Company has $1,000 of extra cash. It can retain the cash and invest it in Treasury bills yielding 8 percent, or it can pay the cash to shareholders as a dividend. Shareholders can also invest in Treasury bills with the same yield. Suppose, realistically, that the tax rate is 44 percent on ordinary income like interest on Treasury bills for both the company and individual investors and the individual tax rate *on dividends* is 30 percent. How much cash will investors have after five years under each policy? ■

If dividends are paid now, shareholders will receive $1,000 before taxes, or $1,000 × (1 − .30) = $700 after taxes. This is the amount they will invest. If the rate on T-bills is 8 percent before taxes, then the after-tax return is 8% × (1−.44) = 4.48% per year. Thus, in five years, the shareholders will have

$$\$700 \times (1+.0448)^5 = \$871.49$$

If Regional Electric Company retains the cash, invests in Treasury bills, and pays out the proceeds five years from now, then $1,000 will be invested today. However, since the corporate tax rate is 44 percent, the after-tax return from the T-bills will be 8% × (1 − .44) = 4.48% per year. In five years, the investment will be worth

$$\$1,000 \times (1 + .0448)^5 = \$1,244.99$$

If this amount is then paid out as a dividend, the shareholders will receive (after tax)

$$\$1244.99 \times (1-.30) = \$871.49$$

In this case, dividends will be the same after tax whether the firm pays them now or later after investing in Treasury bills. The reason is that the firm invests exactly as profitably as the shareholders on their own (on an after-tax basis).[15]

This example shows that for a firm with extra cash, the dividend payout decision will depend on personal and corporate tax rates. Assuming all other things are the same, when personal tax rates are higher than corporate tax rates, a firm has incentive to reduce dividend payouts. This would have occurred if we changed our example to have the firm invest in preferred stock instead of T-bills. (Recall from Chapter 1 that corporations enjoy a 100-percent exclusion of dividends from taxable income.) However, if personal tax rates on dividends are lower than corporate tax rates (for investors in lower tax brackets or tax-exempt investors), a firm has incentive to pay out any excess cash in dividends.

Summary on Taxes

Miller and Modigliani argue that dividend policy is irrelevant in a perfect capital market. However, because dividends are taxed, the MM irrelevance principle does not necessarily hold in the presence of personal taxes.

---

[15]Personal taxes have no impact on dividend policy in our example because the dividend tax credit reduces the personal tax rate on dividends. For a detailed discussion of this *tax integration* effect, see René Huot, *Understanding Income Tax,* 1992–93 ed. (Scarborough: Carswell Thomson Professional Publishing, 1992), pp. N48–N50.

We make three points for a regime of personal taxes:

1. A firm should not issue stock to pay a dividend.
2. Managers have an incentive to seek alternative uses for funds to reduce dividends.
3. Dividend policy is not always irrelevant when we consider personal and corporate taxes.

To continue the discussion, we go back to the different tax treatment of dividends and capital gains.

CONCEPT QUESTION

■ How do personal taxes and stock issuance costs alter MM's theory that dividend policy is irrelevant?

18.5   **Expected Return, Dividends, and Personal Taxes**

The material presented so far in this chapter can properly be called a discussion of *dividend policy.* That is, it is concerned with the level of dividends chosen by the firm. A related, but distinctly different, question is, What is the relationship between the expected return on a security and its dividend yield? To answer this question, we consider a situation in which dividends are taxed at 30 percent and capital gains are not taxed at all—a scenario that is not unrealistic for many Canadian individual investors.[16] We ignore corporate taxes for the time being.

Suppose a shareholder is considering the stocks of firm G, which pays no dividend, and firm D, which pays a dividend. Firm G stock currently sells for $100; next year's price is expected to be $120. The shareholder in firm G thus expects a $20 capital gain. With no dividend, the return is $20/$100 = 20%. If capital gains are not taxed, the pretax and after-tax returns must be the same.[17]

Suppose firm D stock is expected to pay a $20 dividend next year. The stock's price is expected to be $100 after the dividend payment. If the stocks of firm G and firm D are equally risky, the market prices must be set so that their *after-tax* expected returns are equal. The after-tax return on firm D must thus be 20 percent.

What will be the price of stock in firm D? The after-tax dividend is $20 \times (1-.30) = \$14$, so our investor will have a total of $114 after taxes. At a 20-percent required rate of return (after taxes), the present value of this aftertax amount is

Present value$=\$114/1.20 = \$95.00$

---

[16]L. D. Booth and D. J. Johnston, "Ex-Dividend Day Behavior," find a "very low effective tax rate on capital gains" in the 1970s prior to the introduction of the lifetime exemption. A. Protopapadakis, "Some Indirect Evidence of Effective Capital Gains Tax Rates," *Journal of Business* (April 1983), finds that, for the United States, "the effective marginal tax rates on capital gains fluctuated between 3.4 percent and 6.6 percent between 1960 and 1978 and that capital gains are held, on average, between 24 and 31 years before they are reported" (p. 127).

[17]Under current tax law, if the shareholder in firm G does not sell the shares for a gain, it will be an unrealized capital gain, which is not taxed.

	Firm G (no dividend)	Firm D (all dividend)	
			Table 18.1
			Effect of dividend
			yield on pretax
			expected returns
Assumptions:			
Expected price at date 1	$120	$100	
Dividend at date 1 (before tax)	0	$ 20	
Dividend at date 1 (after tax)	0	$ 14	
Price at date 0	$100	(to be solved)	
Analysis:			
We solve that the price of firm D at date 0 is $95.00,* allowing us to calculate			
Capital gain	$ 20	$100 − $95 = $5	
Total gain before tax	$ 20	$20 + $5 = $25	
(both dividend			
and capital gain)			
Total percentage return (before tax)	$\dfrac{\$20}{\$100} = 0.20$	$\dfrac{\$25}{\$95} = 0.2632$	
Total gain after tax	$ 20	$14 + $5 = $19	
Total percentage return (after tax)	$\dfrac{\$20}{\$100} = 0.20$	$\dfrac{\$19}{\$95} = 0.20$	

Stocks with high dividend yields will have higher pretax expected returns than stocks with low-dividend yields. This is referred to as the *grossing up effect*.

*We solve for the price of firm D at date 0 as

$$P_0 = \frac{\$100 + \$20 \times (1 - 0.30)}{1.20} = \$95.00$$

The market price of firm D's stock thus must be $95.00.

Because the investor receives $120 from firm D at date 1 ($100 in value of stock plus $20 in dividends) before personal taxes, the expected pretax return on the security equals

$$\frac{\$120}{\$95} - 1 = 26.32\%$$

Table 18.1 shows the calculations.

This example show that the expected *pretax* return on a security with a high dividend yield is greater than the expected *pretax* return on an otherwise identical security with a low dividend yield.[18] The result is graphed in Figure 18.6. Our conclusion is consistent with efficient capital markets because much of the pretax return for a security with a high dividend yield is taxed away. One implication is that an individual in a zero tax bracket should invest in securities with high dividend yields. There is at least casual evidence that pension funds, which are not subject to taxes, select securities with high dividend yields.

Does the above example suggest that corporate managers should avoid paying dividends? One might think so at first glance, because firm G sells at a higher price at date 0 than does firm D. However, by deferring a potential $20 dividend, firm D might increase its stock price at date 0 by far less than $20. For example, this is likely to be the case if firm D's best use for its cash is to pay $20 for a company whose market

---

[18]Dividend yield is defined as

$$\frac{\text{Annual dividends per share}}{\text{Current price per share}}$$

Figure 18.6
Relationship
between expected
return and dividend
yield

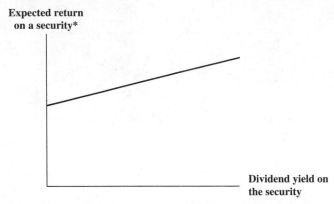

Because the tax rate on dividends at the personal level is higher than the *effective* rate on capital gains, stockholders demand higher expected returns on high-dividend stocks than on low-dividend stocks.
*Expected return includes both expected capital gain and dividend.

price is far below $20. (In the previous section we explain why managers might do this.) Moveover, our prior discussion showed that deferring dividends to purchase bonds or shares of stock is justified only when personal taxes go down by more than corporate taxes rise. Thus, our example does *not* imply that dividends should be avoided.

Some Evidence on Dividends and Taxes in Canada

Is our example showing higher pretax returns for stocks that pay dividends realistic for Canadian capital markets? Since tax laws change from budget to budget, we must be cautious in interpreting research results. Prior to 1972, capital gains were untaxed in Canada (as in our simplified example). Morgan found that stocks that paid dividends had higher pretax returns prior to 1972. From 1972 to 1977, Morgan detected no difference in pretax returns.[19]

In 1985, the lifetime exemption on capital gains was introduced. Amoako-Adu found that anticipation of this tax break for capital gains caused investors to bid up the prices of low-dividend yield stocks.[20] Subsequent budgets have reduced the size of the dividend tax credit. We suspect that from the viewpoint of individual investors, higher dividends require larger pretax returns.

Another way of measuring the effective tax rates on dividends and capital gains in Canada is to look at ex-dividend day price drops. We showed earlier that, ignoring taxes, a stock price should drop by the amount of the dividend when it goes ex-dividend. This is because the price drop offsets what investors lose by waiting to buy the stock until it goes ex-dividend. If dividends are taxed and capital gains are tax-free, the price drop should be lower, equal to the after-tax value of the dividend. However, if gains are taxed too, the price drop needs to be adjusted for the gains tax.

---

[19]I. G. Morgan, "Dividends and Stock Price Behaviour in Canada," *Journal of Business Administration* 12 (Fall 1989).

[20]Ben Amoako-Adu, "Capital Gains Tax and Equity Values: Empirical Test of Stock Price Reaction to the Introduction and Reduction of Capital Gains Tax Exemption," *Journal of Banking and Finance* 16 (1992), pp. 275–87.

An investor who waits for the stock to go ex-dividend buys at a lower price and hence has a larger capital gain when the stock is sold later.

In research designed to infer tax rates from ex-dividend day behaviour, Booth and Johnston concluded that marginal investors who set prices are taxed more heavily on dividends than on capital gains.[21] This supports our argument: Individual investors likely look for higher pretax returns on dividend-paying than on nondividend-paying stocks.[22]

C O N C E P T   Q U E S T I O N S

- What are the tax benefits of low dividends?
- Explain the relationship between a stock's dividend yield and its pretax return.

Real World Factors Favouring a High-Dividend Policy 18.6

In this section, we consider reasons why a firm might pay its shareholders higher dividends even if this means that the firm must issue more shares of stock to finance the dividend payments.

In a classic textbook, Benjamin Graham, David Dodd, and Sidney Cottle have argued that firms should generally have high dividend payouts because

1. "The discounted value of near dividends is higher than the present worth of distant dividends."

2. Between "two companies with the same general earning power and same general position in an industry, the one paying the larger dividend will almost always sell at a higher price."[23]

Two factors favouring a high dividend payout have been mentioned frequently by proponents of this view: the desire for current income and the resolution of uncertainty.

Desire for Current Income

It has been argued that many individuals desire current income. The classic example is the group of retired people and others living on a fixed income, the proverbial "widows and orphans." It is argued that this group is willing to pay a premium to get

---

[21]Booth and Johnston, "Ex-Dividend Day Behavior." Their research also showed that interlisted stocks, traded on exchanges in both the United States and Canada, tended to be priced by U.S. investors and not be affected by Canadian tax changes. J. Lakonishok and T. Vermaelen, "Tax Reforms and Ex-Dividend Day Behavior," *Journal of Finance* (September 1983), pp. 1157–58, gives a competing explanation in terms of tax arbitrage by short-term traders.

[22]U.S. evidence is mixed. On the one hand, M. Brennan, "Taxes, Market Valuation and Corporate Financial Policy," *National Tax Journal* (December 1970), and R. Litzenberger and K. Ramaswamy, "The Effect of Personal Taxes and Dividends on Capital Asset Prices: Theory and Empirical Evidence," *Journal of Financial Economics* (June 1979), found a positive association between expected pretax returns and dividend yields. On the other hand, two studies—F. Black and M. Scholes, "The Effects of Dividend Yield and Dividend Policy on Common Stock Prices and Returns," *Journal of Financial Economics* (May 1970); and M. Miller and M. Scholes, "Dividends and Taxes: Some Empirical Evidence," *Journal of Political Economy* (December 1982)—found no relationship between expected pretax returns and dividend yields.

[23]B. Graham, D. Dodd, and S. Cottle, *Security Analysis* (Homewood, Ill.: Richard D. Irwin, 1961).

a higher dividend yield. If this is true, then it lends support to the second claim by Graham, Dodd, and Cottle.

Miller and Modigliani point out that this argument is not relevant in their theoretical model. An individual preferring high current cash flow but holding low-dividend securities could easily sell off shares to provide the necessary funds. Similarly, an individual desiring a low current cash flow but holding high-dividend securities could just reinvest the dividend. This is just our homemade dividend argument again. Thus, in a world of no transaction costs, a high current dividend policy would be of no value to the shareholder.

The current income argument may have relevance in the real world as the sale of low-dividend stocks involves brokerage fees and other transaction costs. Such a sale might also trigger capital gains taxes. These direct cash expenses could be avoided by an investment in high-dividend securities. In addition, the expenditure of the shareholder's own time when selling securities and the natural (but not necessarily rational) fear of consuming out of principal might further lead many investors to buy high-dividend securities.

Even so, to put this argument in perspective, it should be remembered that financial intermediaries can perform these "repackaging" transactions for individuals at very low cost.

Uncertainty Resolution

We have just pointed out that investors with substantial current consumption needs will prefer high current dividends. In another classic treatment, Gordon has argued that a high-dividend policy also benefits shareholders because it resolves uncertainty.[24] He states that investors price a security by forecasting and discounting future dividends. Gordon then argues that forecasts of dividends to be received in the distant future have greater uncertainty than do forecasts of near-term dividends. Because investors dislike uncertainty, the stock price should be low for those companies that pay small dividends now in order to remit higher dividends at later dates.

Gordon's argument is essentially a "bird-in-hand" story. A $1 dividend in a shareholder's pocket is somehow worth more than that same $1 in a bank account held by the corporation. By now, you should see the problem with this argument. A shareholder can create a bird in hand very easily just by selling some of the stock.

Tax and Legal Benefits from High Dividends

Earlier, we saw that dividends were taxed more heavily than capital gains for individual investors. This fact is a powerful argument for a low payout. However, there are a number of other investors who do not receive unfavourable tax treatment from holding high dividend yield, rather than low dividend yield, securities.

---

[24]M. Gordon, *The Investment, Financing and Valuation of the Corporation* (Homewood, Ill.: Richard D. Irwin, 1961). This is the same Gordon who developed the dividend valuation model.

Corporate Investors

A significant tax break on dividends occurs when a corporation owns stock in another corporation. A corporate shareholder receiving either common or preferred dividends from another Canadian corporation is granted a 100-percent dividend exclusion.[25] Since the 100-percent exclusion does not apply to capital gains, this group is taxed unfavourably on capital gains.

As a result of the dividend exclusion, high dividend, low capital gains stocks may be more appropriate for corporations to hold. As we discuss elsewhere, this is why corporations hold a substantial percentage of the outstanding preferred stock in Canada. This tax advantage of dividends also leads some corporations to hold high-yielding stocks instead of long-term bonds because there is no similar tax exclusion of interest payments to corporate bondholders.

Tax-Exempt Investors

We have pointed out both the tax advantages and disadvantages of a low dividend payout. Of course, this discussion is irrelevant to those in zero tax brackets. This group includes some of the largest investors in the economy, such as pension funds, endowment funds, and trust funds.

There are some legal reasons for large institutions to favour high dividend yields. First, institutions such as pension funds and trust funds are often set up to manage money for the benefit of others. The managers of such institutions have a *fiduciary responsibility* to invest the money prudently. It has been considered imprudent in courts of law to buy stock in companies with no established dividend record.

Second, institutions such as university endowment funds and trust funds are frequently prohibited from spending any of their principal. Such institutions might therefore prefer high dividend yield stocks so they have some ability to spend. Like widows and orphans, this group thus prefers current income. Unlike widows and orphans, in terms of the amount of stock owned, this group is very large and its market share is expanding rapidly.

Overall, individual investors (for whatever reason) may have a desire for current income and may thus be willing to pay the dividend tax. In addition, some very large investors such as corporations and tax-free institutions may have a very strong preference for high dividend payouts.

Tax Arbitrage

Miller and Scholes argue that a two-step procedure can eliminate the taxes ordinarily due on investments in high-yield securities.[26] First, buy stocks with high dividend yields, borrowing enough of the purchase price so that the interest paid is equal to the dividends received. The benefit of this strategy is that no taxes would be due because dividends are taxable whereas interest is deductible. The problem with the strategy is

---

[25]For preferred stock, we assume the issuer has elected to pay the refundable withholding tax on preferred dividends.

[26]M. Miller and M. Scholes, "Dividends and Taxes," *Journal of Financial Economics* (December 1978).

that the resulting position is quite risky due to the leverage involved. Second, to offset the leverage, invest an amount equivalent to the debt already incurred in a tax-deferred account (such as a Registered Retirement Savings Plan, or RRSP). Because income in a tax-deferred account avoids taxes, no taxes are paid when the two steps are done simultaneously.

If enough investors were able to take advantage of the strategy, corporate managers would not need to view dividends as tax-disadvantaged. Lakonishok and Vermaelen find some evidence that tax arbitrage does occur in Canada but not to the extent necessary to eliminate taxes on dividends completely.[27]

CONCEPT QUESTIONS

- Why might some individual investors favour a high dividend payout?
- Why might some corporate and institutional investors prefer a high dividend payout?

18.7   A Resolution of Real World Factors?

In the previous sections, we presented some factors that favour a low-dividend policy and others that favour high dividends. Unfortunately, after years of research, no one has been able to conclude definitively which set of factors is more important. Thus, the question of dividend policy is not resolved.

A discussion of two important concepts—the information content of dividends and the clientele effect—will give the reader an appreciation of some of the relevant issues. The first topic illustrates both the importance of dividends in general and the need to distinguish between dividends and dividend policy. The second topic suggests that the dividend payout ratio may not be as important as we originally imagined.

Information Content of Dividends

To begin, we quickly review some of our earlier discussion. Previously, we examined three different positions on dividends:

1. Based on the homemade dividend argument of MM, dividend policy is irrelevant provided that future earnings are held constant.
2. Because of tax effects for individual investors, a firm's stock price may be negatively related to the current dividend when future earnings are held constant.
3. Because of the desire for current income, resolution of uncertainty, and tax effects for corporate and tax-exempt investors, a firm's stock price may be positively related to its current dividend, even when future earnings are held constant.

---

[27]Lakonishok and Vermaelen, "Tax Reforms and Ex-Dividend Day Behavior," pp. 1157–80.

What happens to stock prices when companies start paying dividends for the first time in their corporate history (or resume dividend payments after a hiatus) provides evidence on these positions. Asquith and Mullins found that stock prices rose when their sample of U.S. firms started or resumed dividends. Deshpande and Jog obtained the same result for a Canadian sample.[28]

Related evidence comes from studying the impact on stock prices when companies announce higher (or lower) dividends. A variety of tests for both Canada and the United States agree that prices move up with the announcement of higher dividends and drop when dividend cuts are announced.[29] What does this imply about any of the three positions just stated?

At first glace, the observation may seem consistent with position (3) and inconsistent with positions (1) and (2). In fact, many writers have argued this. However, other authors have countered that the observation itself is consistent with all three positions. They point out that, since companies only cut dividends with great reluctance, a dividend cut is often a signal that the firm is in trouble. Such a cut is usually not a voluntary, planned change in dividend policy. Instead, it typically signals that management does not think that the current dividend policy can be maintained. As a result, expectations of future dividends should be revised downward. The present value of expected future dividends falls and so does the stock price.

In this case, the stock price declines because the dividend cut signals the market that future dividends are expected to be lower. The fall in the stock price following the dividend signal is called the **information content effect** of the dividend change.

In the same way, dividend increases represent signals of favourable expected earnings. Because firms do not like to cut dividends, they will raise them only when future earnings and cash flow are expected to be large enough to sustain dividends at the new level. In this case, it is the expectation of good times, and not only the shareholders' affinity for current income, that raises stock price.

The information signalling theory may be restated more formally. Imagine that the stock price is unaffected or even negatively affected by the level of dividends, given that future earnings are held constant. Nevertheless, the information content effect implies that stock price may rise when dividends are raised—if dividends simultaneously cause shareholders to revise favourably their expectations of future earnings.

---

[28]P. Asquith and D. Mullins, Jr., "The Impact of Initiating Dividend Payments on Shareholder Wealth," *Journal of Business* (January 1983); S. D. Deshpande and V. M. Jog, "The Information Content of Dividend Resumptions: The Canadian Evidence," *Proceedings of the Finance Division of the Administrative Sciences Association of Canada* 7 (1986), pp. 151–72.

[29]This topic has spawned a large volume of research. Selected examples are G. Charest, "Dividend Information, Stock Returns and Market Efficiency," *Journal of Financial Economics* 6 (1978); G. Charest, "Returns to Dividend Changing Stocks on the Toronto Stock Exchange," *Journal of Business Administration* 12 (Fall 1980), pp. 1–18; R. Pettit, "Dividend Announcements, Security Performance, and Capital Market Efficiency," *Journal of Finance* (1972); J. Ahroney and I. Swary, "Quarterly Dividend and Earnings Announcements and Stockholders' Returns: An Empirical Analysis," *Journal of Finance* (March 1980); C. Kwan, "Efficient Market Tests of the Informational Content of Dividends: Critique and Extensions," *Journal of Financial and Quantitative Analysis* 16 (1981); and F. Adjaoud, "The Information Content of Dividends: A Canadian Test," *Canadian Journal of Administrative Sciences* 16 (1984), pp. 338–51.

Several theoretical models of dividend policy incorporate managerial incentives to communicate information via dividends.[30] In these models, dividends serve to signal to shareholders the firm's current and future performance. There is considerable empirical support for dividend signalling models.[31]

Dividend Signalling in Practice

A particularly dramatic example of the importance the market attaches to dividend signals involved Consolidated Edison, the largest public U.S. electric utility, in the second quarter of 1974. Faced with poor operating results and problems associated with the OPEC oil embargo, Con Ed announced after the market closed that it was omitting its regular quarterly dividend of 45 cents per share. This was somewhat surprising given Con Ed's size, prominence in the industry, and long dividend history. Also, Con Ed's earnings at that time were sufficient to pay the dividend, at least by some analysts' estimates.

The next morning, sell orders were so heavy that a market could not be established for several hours. When trading finally got started, the stock opened at about $12 per share, down from $18 the day before. In other words, Con Ed, a very large company, lost about $\frac{1}{3}$ of its market value overnight. As this case illustrates, shareholders can react very negatively to unanticipated cuts in dividends.

Canadian managers behave consistently with the theory of dividend signalling. In 1989, for example, the Bank of Montreal's earnings per share dropped from $4.89 the previous year to $.04 due to increased loan loss provisions for lesser developed country debt. Yet the annual dividend was increased slightly from $2.00 to $2.12 per share. The payout ratio skyrocketed to 5300 percent ($2.12/$.04). Management signalled the market that earnings would recover in 1990, which they did.

The Clientele Effect

In our earlier discussion, we saw that some groups (wealthy individuals, for example) have an incentive to pursue low-payout (or zero-payout) stocks. Other groups (corporations and tax-exempt investors, for example) have an incentive to pursue high-payout stocks. Companies with high payouts will thus attract one group, while low-payout companies will attract another.

---

[30]S. Bhattacharya, "Imperfect Information, Dividend Policy, and 'the Bird in the Hand' Fallacy," *Bell Journal of Economics* 10 (1979); S. Bhattacharya, "Nondissipative Signalling Structure and Dividend Policy," *Quarterly Journal of Economics* 95 (1980), p. 1; S. Ross, "The Determination of Financial Structure: The Incentive Signalling Approach," *Bell Journal of Economics* 8 (1977), p. 1; and M. Miller and K. Rock, "Dividend Policy under Asymmetric Information," *Journal of Finance* (1985).

[31]Current tests of dividend signalling are careful to distinguish this effect from another reason why stock prices should move in the same direction as dividends—the agency cost of equity. As discussed above, higher dividends could be "good news" because they restrict managers' ability to undertake negative NPV projects. Larry H. P. Lang and Robert H. Litzenberger, "Dividend Announcements: Cash Flow Signalling vs. Free Cash Flow Hypothesis?" *Journal of Financial Economics* 24 (1989); and Komlan Sedzro, "Majorations Multiformes du Dividende, Croissance et Réaction Boursière," *Fineco* 2 (1992), pp. 31–54, find support for both effects. B. Espen Eckbo and Savita Verma, "Managerial Share Ownership, Voting Power and Cash Dividend Policy," *Journal of Corporate Finance* 1 (1994), also support the importance of agency costs of equity in setting dividend policy for Canadian firms.

Groups of investors attracted to different payouts are called **clienteles,** and what we have described is a *clientele effect.* Because different groups of investors desire different levels of dividends, when a firm chooses a particular dividend policy, the only effect is to attract a particular clientele. If a firm changes its dividend policy, then it just attracts a different clientele.

This is a simple supply and demand argument. Suppose that 40 percent of all investors prefer high dividends, but only 20 percent of the firms pay high dividends. Here the high-dividend firms will be in short supply; thus, their stock prices will rise. Consequently, low-dividend firms will find it advantageous to switch policies until 40 percent of all firms have high payouts. At this point, the dividend market will be in equilibrium. Further changes in dividend policy would be pointless because all of the clienteles are satisfied. The dividend policy for any individual firm is now irrelevant.

To see if you understand the clientele effect, consider the following statement: "In spite of the theoretical argument that dividend policy is irrelevant or that firms should not pay dividends, many investors like high dividends. Therefore, a firm can boost its share price by having a higher dividend payout ratio." True or false?

The answer is false if clienteles exist. As long as enough high-dividend firms satisfy the dividend-loving investors, a firm will not be able to boost its share price by paying high dividends.

CONCEPT QUESTIONS

- How does the market react to unexpected dividend changes? What does this tell us about dividends? About dividend policy?
- What is a dividend clientele?
- All things considered, would you expect a risky firm with significant, but highly uncertain growth prospects to have a low or high dividend payout?

What We Know and Do Not Know about Dividend Policy   18.8

The Lintner Model

In 1956, Lintner suggested that managers estimate what portion of the firm's earnings is likely to be permanent and what portion of the earnings is likely to be temporary. He looked at the dividend payout patterns of firms and concluded that dividends are more likely to be raised following a permanent, rather than a temporary, increase in earnings and that firms have long-run targets for their dividend-to-earnings ratios. However, because managers need time to assess the permanence of any earnings rise, dividend changes appear to lag earnings changes by a number of periods. It follows from Lintner's analysis that the dividend-to-earnings ratio rises when a company begins a period of bad times, and the ratio falls when a company reaches a period of good times.[32]

---

[32]J. Lintner, "Distribution and Incomes of Corporations among Dividends, Retained Earnings and Taxes," *American Economic Review* (May 1956).

Lintner's work and the later work of Fama and Babiak[33] suggest that what is meant by *dividend policy* is related not only to the level of dividends but also to the change in dividends.

1. *Level of dividends.* Managers tend to think of dividend payments in terms of a proportion of income and also think investors are entitled to a "fair" share of corporate income. Corporations think in terms of a long-run target payout ratio.

2. *Change in dividends.* Managers avoid making changes in the level of dividend payments if they will have to be reversed later. Thus, the level of dividends is more stable than the level of earnings. Firms "smooth" out changes in their dividends relative to changes in their earnings.

Taken together, Lintner's observations suggest that two parameters describe dividend policy: the target payout ratio (t) and the speed of adjustment of current dividends to the target(s). Dividend changes will tend to conform to a model like the following:

$$\text{Div}_1 - \text{Div}_0 = s \times (t\text{EPS}_1 - \text{Div}_0)$$

where Div_1 and Div_0 are dividends in the next year and dividends in the current year, respectively. EPS_1 is earnings per share in the next year.

A conservative company will have a low adjustment rate; a less conservative company will have a high adjustment rate. As can be seen, if $s = 0$, $\text{Div}_1 = \text{Div}_0$, while if $s = 1$, the actual change in dividends will be equal to the target change in dividends. The level of dividends will be set by t. A firm will have a low t if it has many positive NPV projects; it will have a high t if it has few positive NPV projects relative to available cash flow.

Dividend Policy in Perspective

The knowledge of the finance profession varies across topics. For example, capital budgeting techniques are both powerful and precise. A single net present value equation can accurately determine whether a multimillion-dollar project should be accepted or rejected. The capital asset pricing model and arbitrage pricing theory provide empirically validated relationships between expected return and risk.

Conversely, the field has less knowledge of capital structure policy. Though a number of elegant theories relate firm value to the level of debt, no formula can be used to calculate the firm's optimum debt-equity ratio. Our profession is forced too frequently to employ rules of thumb, such as treating the industry's average ratio as the optimal one for the firm.

The field's knowledge of dividend policy is, perhaps, similar to its knowledge of capital structure policy. We do know that

---

[33]E. Fama and H. Babiak, "Dividend Policy: An Empirical Analysis," *Journal of the American Statistical Association* 63, no. 4 (1968).

1. Firms should never cut back on positive NPV projects to pay a dividend, with or without personal taxes.
2. Firms should never issue stock to pay a dividend in a world with personal taxes.

In addition, we know that personal taxes can encourage a policy of low dividends, and other factors can encourage a high dividend policy. However, there is no formula for calculating the optimal dividend-to-earnings ratio. Firms with many positive NPV projects relative to available cash flow should have low payout ratios. Firms with few positive NPV projects relative to available cash flow should have high payouts. There is some benefit to dividend stability, and unnecessary changes in dividend payout are avoided.

CONCEPT QUESTION

■ What factors determine dividend policy in practice?

How Firms Decide to Pay Dividends for the First Time 18.9

Perhaps the most important dividend decision a firm must make is when to pay dividends for the first time. We study the case of Apple Computer for clues to why firms pay dividends.

In 1976, two young friends, Stephen Wozniak and Steven Jobs, built the Apple I Computer in Jobs' garage in the Silicon Valley area of northern California and founded Apple Computer, Inc. The first Apple was built and sold without a monitor or keyboard. The Apple II was introduced in 1977 and was targeted at the home and educational markets as a personal computer. The Apple II was very successful—by 1980, over 130,000 units had been sold and Apple's annual revenues were $117 million. In 1980, Apple "went public" with an initial public offering (IPO) of common stock. Shortly thereafter, Wozniak left Apple and John Scully was hired from Pepsi to become president. Apple did not do well with its Lisa (1983) and Apple III computers, but the Macintosh (1984) was a huge hit—primarily in the home and educational markets. In 1985, after a widely publicized struggle for power with Scully, Jobs left to start another computer company called NeXT.

In many ways 1986 was a watershed year for Apple. By the end of 1986, Apple had annual revenues of $1.9 billion and net income of $154 million. From 1980 to 1986, its annual growth rate in net income was 53 percent. In 1986, with Mac Plus, Apple launched an aggressive effort to penetrate the expanding office computer market—the domain of its main rival IBM. However, its future prospects were not necessarily bright. Much depended on Apple's ability to do well in the business market. Competition was very intense in early 1987, and Sun Microsystems slashed the price of its least costly computer workstations to try to stop encroachment by the Apple Mac. However, Apple surprised everyone with large earnings gains in the final quarter of 1987 and by disclosing the fact that the sales on Macintosh models had increased by 41 percent.

The Pros and Cons of the Initial Dividend Decision

Pros	Cons
1. Cash dividends can underscore good results and provide support to stock price.	1. Dividends are taxed as ordinary income.
2. Dividends may attract institutional investors who prefer some return in the form of dividends. A mix of institutional and individual investors may allow a firm to raise capital at lower cost because of the ability of the firm to reach a wider market.	2. Dividends can reduce internal sources of financing. Dividends may force the firm to forgo positive NPV projects or to rely on costly external equity financing.
3. Stock price usually increases with the announcement of an initial dividend.	3. Once dividends are established, dividend cuts are hard to make without adversely affecting a firm's stock price.
4. Dividends absorb excess cash flow and may reduce agency costs that arise from conflicts between management and shareholders.	

To demonstrate its faith in its future, to underscore the recent success of the Mac, and to attract more institutional investors, on April 23, 1987, Apple declared its first ever quarterly dividend of $.12 per share. It also announced a two-for-one stock split. The stock market reacted very positively to the announcement of Apple's initial dividend. On the day of the announcements, its stock price rose $1.75. Over a four-day time span, it rose about 8 percent.

The initial dividend turned out to be a positive portent, and the next four years were good years for Apple. At the end of 1990, Apple's revenues, profits, and capital spending had achieved record highs.

	1986	1990	Growth per annum, 1986–1990
Revenues (in millions)	$1,902	$5,558	31%
Net income (in millions)	154	475	33
Capital spending (in millions)	66	223	36
Stock price	$ 20	$ 48	24
Long-term debt	0	0	0

Why do firms like Apple decide to pay dividends? There is no single answer to this question. In Apple's case, one part of the answer can be traced to Apple's attempt to "signal" the stock market about the potential growth and positive NPV prospects of its attempt to penetrate the office computer market. The payment of dividends can also "ratify" good results. Apple's initial dividend serves to convince the market that Apple's success was not temporary.

Why did Apple announce a two-for-one stock split at the same time that it announced an initial cash dividend? It is often said that a stock split without a cash dividend is like giving shareholders two $5 bills for a $10 bill. Your wallet feels thicker but you are no better off. However, a stock split accompanied by a cash dividend can amplify the positive signal and pack a more powerful message than would be true otherwise. In addition, firms sometimes split their shares, because they believe a low stock price may attract more individual investors and as a consequence increase liquidity. However, the evidence is not clear on this point, and some firms like Berkshire Hathaway disdain stock splits. (Its stock has sold as high as $8,700 a share.)

Was Apple's decision to offer an initial dividend the best decision for the company? This is an impossible question to answer precisely. However, the stock market's positive reaction and Apple's subsequent performance suggest it was a good decision. The accompanying box lists pros and cons of an initial dividend decision.

CONCEPT QUESTION

- What are the key considerations in an initial dividend decision?

Summary and Conclusions   18.10

1. The dividend decision is important because it determines the payout received by shareholders and the funds retained by the firm for investment. Dividend policy is usually reflected by the current dividend-to-earnings ratio. This is referred to as the *payout ratio*. Unfortunately, the optimal payout ratio cannot be determined quantitatively. Rather, one can only indicate qualitatively what factors lead to low- or high-dividend policies.

2. We argue that the dividend policy of the firm is irrelevant in a perfect capital market because the shareholder can effectively undo the firm's dividend strategy. If a shareholder receives a greater dividend than desired, he or she can reinvest the excess. Conversely, if the shareholder receives a smaller dividend than desired, he or she can sell off extra shares of stock. This argument is due to MM and is similar to their homemade leverage concept discussed in Chapter 15.

3. A firm should not reject positive NPV projects to increase dividend payments.

4. Although the MM argument is useful in introducing the topic of dividends, it ignores many factors in practice. We show that personal taxes and new issue costs are real world considerations that favour low dividend payout. With personal taxes and new issue costs, the firm should not issue stock to pay a dividend. However, our discussion does not imply that all firms should avoid dividends. Rather, those with high cash flow relative to positive NPV opportunities might pay dividends due to legal constraints and or to a dearth of investment opportunities.

5. The expected return on a security is positively related to its dividend yield in a world with personal taxes. This result suggests that individuals in low or zero tax brackets should consider investing in high-yielding stocks. However, the result does not imply that firms should avoid all dividends.

6. The general consensus among financial analysts is that the tax effect is the strongest argument in favour of low dividends, while the preference for current

income is the strongest argument in favour of high dividends. Unfortunately, no empirical work has determined which of these two factors dominates, perhaps because the clientele effect argues that dividend policy is quite responsive to the needs of shareholders. For example, if 40 percent of the shareholders prefer low dividends and 60 percent prefer high dividends, approximately 40 percent of companies will have a low dividend payout, and 60 percent will have a high payout. This sharply reduces the impact of an individual firm's dividend policy on its market price.

7. Research has shown that many firms appear to have a long-run target dividend payout policy. Firms that have few positive NPV projects relative to available cash flow will have high payouts. In addition, firms try to reduce the fluctuations in the level of dividends. There appears to be some value in dividend stability and smoothing.

8. The stock market reacts positively to increases in dividends (or an initial dividend payment) and negatively to decreases in dividends. This suggests that there is information content in dividend payments.

Key Terms

Regular cash dividends 514

Stock dividend 514

Stock split 514

Declaration date 514

Date of record 514

Ex-dividend date 514

Date of payment 516

Homemade dividends 519

Stripped common shares 520

Information content effect 533

Clienteles 535

Suggested Readings

The breakthrough in the theory of dividend policy is contained in:

M. Miller and F. Modigliani. "Dividend Policy, Growth and the Valuation of Shares." *Journal of Business* (October 1961).

A practitioner-oriented paper discussing what we know and do not know concerning dividend policy is:

F. Black. "The Dividend Puzzle." *Journal of Portfolio Management* (Winter 1976).

The following examine taxes and dividends in Canada:

J. Lakonishok and T. Vermaelen. "Tax Reform and Ex-Dividend Day Behavior." *Journal of Finance* 38 (September 1983).

L. D. Booth and D. J. Johnston. "The Ex-Dividend Day Behavior of Canadian Stock Prices: Tax Changes and Clientele Effects." *Journal of Finance* 39 (June 1984).

L. Booth. "The Dividend Tax Credit and Canadian Ownership Objectives." *Canadian Journal of Economics 20 (May 1987).*

I. G. Morgan. "Dividends and Stock Price Behaviour in Canada." *Journal of Business Administration* 12 (Fall 1980).

Evidence that investors regard dividend announcements as important signals appears in:

J. E. Hatch and M. J. Robinson. *Investment Management in Canada,* 2d ed. Scarborough, Ontario: Prentice Hall Canada, 1989, Chapter 14.

Questions and Problems

The Mechanics of Dividend Payouts

18.1 Identify and describe each of the following dates that are associated with a dividend payment on common stock:

> February 16
>
> February 24
>
> February 28
>
> March 14.

18.2 The Mann Company belongs to a risk class for which the appropriate discount rate is 10 percent. Mann currently has 100,000 outstanding shares selling at $100 each. The firm is contemplating the declaration of a $5 dividend at the end of the fiscal year that just began. Answer the following questions based on the Modigliani and Miller model discussed in the text.

  a. What will be the price of the stock on the ex-dividend date if the dividend is declared?

  b. What will be the price of the stock at the end of the year if the dividend is not declared?

  c. If Mann makes $2 million of new investments at the beginning of the period, earns net income of $1 million, and pays the dividend at the end of the year, how many shares of new stock must the firm issue to meet its funding needs?

  d. Is it realistic to use the MM model in the real world to value stock? Why or why not?

The Irrelevance of Dividend Policy

18.3 The growing perpetuity model expresses the value of a share of stock as the present value of the expected dividends from that stock. How can you conclude that dividend policy is irrelevant when this model is valid?

18.4 Andahl Corporation stock, of which you own 500 shares, will pay a $2 per share dividend one year from today. Two years from now Andahl will close its doors; shareholders will receive liquidating dividends of $17.5375 per share. The required rate of return on Andahl stock is 15 percent.

  a. What is the current price of Andahl stock?

  b. You prefer to receive equal amounts of money in each of the next two years. How will you accomplish this?

18.5   The net income of Novis Corporation, which has 10,000 outstanding shares and a 100-percent payout policy, is $32,000. The expected value of the firm one year hence is $1,545,600. The appropriate discount rate for Novis is 12 percent.

   a. What is the value of the firm?

   b. What is the ex-dividend price of Novis's stock if the board follows its current policy?

   c. At the dividend declaration meeting, several board members claimed that the dividend is too meager and is probably depressing Novis's price. They proposed that Novis sell enough new shares to finance a $4.25 dividend.

      i . Comment on the claim that the low dividend is depressing the stock price. Support your argument with calculations.

      ii. If the proposal is adopted, at what price will the new shares sell and how many will be sold?

Factors Influencing Dividend Policy

18.6   The University of Prince Edward Island pays no taxes on capital gains, dividend income, or interest payments. Would you expect to find low-dividend, high-growth stock in the university's portfolio? Would you expect to find bonds selling at a deep discount in the portfolio?

18.7   In their 1970 paper on dividends and taxes, Elton and Gruber reported that the ex-dividend date drop in a stock's price as a percentage of the dividend should equal the ratio of one minus the ordinary income tax rate to one minus the capital gains rate; that is,

$$\frac{P_b - P_e}{D} = \frac{1 - T_o}{1 - T_c}$$

where

   P_e = The ex-dividend stock price

   P_b = The stock price before it trades ex-dividend

   D = The amount of the dividend

   T_o = The tax rate on ordinary income

   T_c = The effective tax rate on capital gains

Note: As we pointed out in the text, the effective tax rate of capital gains is less than the actual tax rate, because these gains' realization may be postponed. Indeed, because investors could postpone their realizations indefinitely, the effective rate could be zero.

   a. If $T_o = T_c = 0$, how much will the stock's price fall?

   b. If $T_o \neq 0$ and $T_c = 0$, how much will it fall?

   c. Explain the results you found in (a) and (b).

   d. Do the results of Elton and Gruber's study imply that firms will maximize shareholder wealth by not paying dividends?

18.8 After completing its capital spending for the year, Carlson Manufacturing has $1,000 extra cash. Carlson's managers must choose between investing the cash in Treasury bonds that yield 8 percent or paying the cash out to investors who would invest in the bonds themselves.

   a. If the corporate tax rate is 40 percent, what tax rate on ordinary income would make the investors equally willing to receive the dividend and to let Carlson invest the money?

   b. Is the answer to (a) reasonable? Why or why not?

   c. Suppose the only investment choice is stock that yields 12 percent. What personal tax rate will make the shareholders indifferent to the outcome of Carlson's dividend decision?

   d. Is this a compelling argument for a low dividend payout ratio? Why or why not?

18.9 Suppose that a political advisory committee recently recommended wage and price controls to prevent the spiralling inflation that was experienced in the 1970s. Members of the investment community and several labour unions have sent the committee reports that discuss whether or not dividends should be under the controls.

   The reports from the investment community demonstrated that the value of a share of stock is equal to the discounted value of its expected dividend stream. Thus, they argued that any legislation that caps dividends will also hold down share prices, thereby increasing companies' costs of capital.

   The union reports conceded that dividend policy is important to firms that are trying to control costs. They also said that dividends are important to shareholders, but only because the dividend is the shareholders' wage. In order to be fair, the unions argued, if the government controls labour's wage, it should also control dividends.

   Discuss these arguments and explain the fallacy in them.

18.10 Deaton Co. and Grede, Inc., are in the same risk class. Shareholders expect Deaton to pay a $4 dividend next year when the stock will sell for $20. Grede has a no-dividend policy. Currently, Grede stock is selling for $20 per share. Grede shareholders expect a $4 capital gain over the next year. Capital gains are not taxed, but dividends are taxed at 25 percent.

   a. What is the current price of Deaton Co. stock?

   b. If capital gains are also taxed at 25 percent, what is the price of Deaton Co. stock?

   c. Explain the result you found in part (b).

18.11 A major Canadian corporation currently has outstanding series 4.50, nonconvertible preferred stock that pays an annual dividend of $4.50. The company has also issued 12-percent bonds that will mature in 10 years. The stock and bonds have about the same risk.

   a. The current price of the 4.50 preferred stock is $50\frac{1}{2}$. What is its dividend yield?

    b. The bonds were sold at par. What is their yield to maturity?

    c. As a financial consultant, you want to know the after-tax yields for each of these investments. The corporate tax rate is 40 percent, the personal tax rate on interest is 40 percent, and the personal tax rate on dividends is 30 percent. Compute the after-tax yields on the preferred stock and the bonds for

        i. A tax-exempt pension plan.

        ii. Another Canadian corporation.

        iii. The chairman of another Canadian corporation.

    d. Which group do you believe owns the most preferred stock?

18.12 The bird-in-the-hand argument, which states that a dividend today is safer than the uncertain prospect of a capital gain tomorrow, is often used to justify high dividend payout ratios. Explain the fallacy behind the argument.

18.13 Your aunt is in a high tax bracket and would like to minimize the tax burden of her investment portfolio. She is willing to buy and sell in order to maximize her after-tax returns and she has asked for your advice. What would you suggest she do?

18.14 In the May 4, 1981, issue of *Fortune,* an article entitled "Fresh Evidence That Dividends Don't Matter" stated,

> All told, 115 companies of the 500 [largest industrial corporations] raised their payout every year during the period 1970–1980. Investors in this . . . group would have fared somewhat better than investors in the 500 as a whole: the median total annual compound return of the 115 was 10.7% during the decade vs. 9.4% for the 500.

Is this evidence that investors prefer dividends to capital gains? Why or why not?

18.15 Last month Northern Power Company, which has been having trouble with cost overruns on a nuclear plant that it had been building, announced that it was "temporarily suspending dividend payments due to the cash flow crunch associated with its investment program." When the announcement was made, the company's stock price dropped from $28\frac{1}{2}$ to 25. What do you suspect caused the change in the stock price?

18.16 Cap Henderson owns Neotech stock because its price has been steadily rising over the past few years and he expects its performance to continue. Cap is trying to convince Rochelle Jones to purchase some Neotech stock, but she is reluctant because Neotech has never paid a dividend. She depends on steady dividends to provide her with income.

    a. What preferences are these two investors demonstrating?

    b. What argument should Cap use to convince Rochelle that Neotech stock is the stock for her?

    c. Why might Cap's argument not convince her?

18.17 If the market places the same value on $1 of dividends as on $1 of capital gains, then firms with different payout ratios will appeal to different clienteles of investors. One clientele is as good as another; therefore, a firm cannot increase its value by changing its dividend policy. Yet empirical investigations reveal a strong correlation between dividend payout ratios and other firm characteristics. For example, small, rapidly growing firms that have recently gone public almost always have payout ratios that are zero; all earnings are reinvested in the business. Explain this phenomenon if dividend policy is irrelevant.

18.18 In spite of the theoretical argument that dividend policy should be irrelevant, the fact remains that many investors like high dividends. If this preference exists, a firm can boost its share price by increasing its dividend payout ratio. Explain the fallacy in this argument.

PART FIVE

LONG-TERM FINANCING

Part 4 discussed capital structure; we determined the relationship between the firm's debt-equity ratio and the firm's value. The debt we used in Part 4 was stylized. In fact, there are many different types of debt. In Part 5 we discuss how financial managers choose the type of debt that makes the most sense, including straight debt, debt with options, and leasing.

In Chapter 14 we showed that the amount of capital spending by firms exceeds the internally generated funds. As a consequence, firms have a financial shortfall that must be covered by selling securities to the public. In Chapter 19 we describe the ways firms sell securities to the public. In general, a public issue can be sold as a general cash offer to investors at large or as a privately placed issue with a few institutions. We describe the general features of these methods.

In Chapter 20 we describe some basic features of long-term debt. This follows our discussion in Chapter 14 in which we introduced some types of long-term debt. One of the special features of most long-term bonds is that they can be called by the firm before the maturity date. We try to explain why call provisions exist. There are many types of long-term debt, including floating rate bonds, income bonds, and original-issue discount bonds. We discuss why they exist.

In Chapter 21 we describe options. First we look at the options that trade on organized exchanges. Options are contingent claims on the value of an underlying asset. Every issue of corporate securities has option features. We then present a formal model that can be used to value options. The model bears no resemblance to net present value (NPV). Our goal is to present the underlying logic of option valuation. This is important because NPV does not work well for contingent claims.

In Chapter 22 we look at bonds with special option features: bonds with warrants and bonds convertible into common stock. A warrant gives the holder a right to buy shares of common stock for cash; a convertible bond gives the holder the right to exchange it for shares of common stock. We discuss warrants and convertibles and explain why firms issue them.

Chapter 23 describes a special form of long-term debt called *leasing*. In general, a rental agreement that lasts for more than one year is a lease. Leases are a source of financing and displace debt in the balance sheet. Many silly reasons are given for leasing, and we review some of them. The major valid reason for long-term leasing is to lower taxes.

Previous chapters assume that a firm's volatility is fixed. Chapter 24 shows how firms can use financial instruments to reduce their risk. Specifically it discusses financial futures.

Issuing Equity Securities to the Public

In Chapter 14, we looked at the different types of corporate securities. This chapter examines how corporations sell equity securities to the investing public.

Issuing securities involves the corporation in a number of decisions. We briefly comment on how the majority of Canadian corporations have been deciding and on how these trends are changing in response to globalization of financial markets, deregulation, and increasing competition. The rest of the chapter explores these decisions in more depth.

Since issuing securities is a specialized activity not undertaken on a daily basis, issuing corporations generally seek assistance from an investment dealer. Depending on the type of security and the alternatives chosen, the assistance from the investment dealer may include a variety of services including advice on (1) which securities to issue, (2) how to structure and price the deal, and (3) complying with disclosure requirements set by regulators. In addition, investment dealers offer the issuer various forms of protection against receiving substantially less than the issue price or failing to sell the entire issue.

Early in the discussions with its investment dealer, the issuer decides whether to issue securities in the domestic market or in foreign markets. In 1990, Canadian corporations raised $16.7 billion in new capital, of which 72 percent was raised in domestic markets.[1] This emphasis on domestic issues held for both debt and equity issues in 1990. But, over the past decade, globalization has a brought growth in foreign debt financing by Canadian corporations with more than half of the debt raised from foreign lenders.

The new securities could be a primary market, public issue sold directly to the public with the help of an investment dealer. Once registered with provincial regulatory authorities, the newly issued securities may be traded on secondary markets (stock exchanges or over the counter).[2] In contrast, in a private placement, debt or equity (common or preferred shares) is sold directly to a small number of buyers.

Advantages for the issuer in a private placement are less stringent disclosure requirements and faster completion of the offer. Further, since the issuer is obtaining financing from a small group of knowledgeable investors, it is easier to renegotiate

---

[1] Statistics on capital markets are from B. Critchley and J. Murphy, "DS Wins Laurels Again," *Financial Post* (August 5, 1991), p. 13. The figures exclude rights offerings later discussed in detail.

[2] Primary and secondary markets are discussed in Chapter 1.

debt covenants should this become necessary. On the other hand, privately placed securities lack marketability, so they are less attractive to investors.

In a public offering of debt or equity, the investment dealer will generally act as an underwriter taking on some, or all, of the pricing risk in the new issue. The underwriter does this by buying the issue and reselling it. The underwriter takes all the pricing risk in a special type of public offering called a *bought deal.*

Instead of marketing to the general public, a corporation can sell common stock to its existing shareholders by what is called a *rights offer.* Rights offerings are usually cheaper and faster than underwritten public offerings in part because they are marketed to a narrower audience that already has shown interest in the stock. Through the 1970s, rights offerings were easily the most popular method of raising new equity in Canada.

In 1983, the Ontario Securities Commission (OSC) introduced a streamlined reporting and registration system for large companies that issue securities regularly called Prompt Offering Prospectus (POP). With deregulation and the advantages of POP, growing competition among underwriters promoted dramatic growth in the popularity of bought deals over rights offers.[3] At the close of the 1980s, the majority of equity dollars raised in Canada used POP and were bought deals.

19.1   The Public Issue

A firm issuing securities must satisfy a number of requirements set out by provincial regulations and statutes and enforced by provincial securities commissions. Regulation of the securities market in Canada is carried out by provincial commissions and through provincial securities acts. However, only five of the provinces have commissions, due in large part to an absence of exchanges in some provinces. This is in contrast to the United States, where regulation is handled by a federal body, the Securities and Exchange Commission (SEC). The regulators' goal is to promote the efficient flow of information about securities and the smooth functioning of securities markets.

All companies listed on the Toronto Stock Exchange come under the jurisdiction of the Ontario Securities Commission. The Securities Act of 1980 sets forth the provincial regulations for all new securities issues involving the province of Ontario and the Toronto Stock Exchange. The OSC administers the act. Other provinces have similar legislation and regulating bodies, but the OSC is the most noteworthy because of the TSE's scope.[4] In general terms, OSC rules seek to ensure that investors receive all material information on new issues in the form of a registration statement and prospectus.

The OSC's responsibility for efficient information flow goes beyond new issues. It continues to regulate the trading of securities after they have been issued to ensure adequate disclosure of information. Recently, the OSC broadened disclosure rules for asset transactions between related parties. An example of a *related party transaction* is

---

[3]Changes in regulations relaxed the requirement that chartered banks use only rights offerings and this also reduced their popularity.

[4]The TSE is Canada's largest stock exchange. Its dollar trading ranked seventh in the world behind Tokyo (number 1) and the NYSE (number 2) in 1991. Chapter 5 discusses equity markets in more detail.

the sale of assets by one company to a sister company controlled by the same holding company. The revised Policy 9.1 required the majority of minority shareholders to approve these and other major transactions that are not at arm's length. The OSC argued that this change is important because many Canadian companies are closely held and thus able to magnify their influence through networks of cross ownership.

Another informational role of the OSC is gathering and publishing insider reports filed by major shareholders, officers, and directors of TSE-listed firms. To ensure efficient functioning of markets, the OSC oversees the training and supervision that investment dealers provide for their personnel. It also monitors investment dealers' capital positions. Increasing market volatility and the popularity of bought deals where the dealer assumes all the price risk make capital adequacy important.

The Basic Procedure for a New Issue 19.2

There is a series of steps involved in issuing securities to the public. In general terms, the basic procedure is as follows:

1. Management's first step in issuing any securities to the public is to obtain approval from the board of directors. In some cases, the number of authorized shares of common stock must be increased. This requires a vote of the shareholders.

2. The firm must prepare and distribute copies of a preliminary **prospectus** to the OSC and to potential investors. The preliminary prospectus contains some of the financial information that will be contained in the final prospectus; it does not contain the price at which the security will be offered. The preliminary prospectus is sometimes called a **red herring,** in part because bold red letters are printed on the cover warning that the OSC has neither approved nor disapproved of the securities. The OSC studies the preliminary prospectus and notifies the company of any changes required. This process is usually completed within about two weeks.

3. Once the revised, final prospectus meets with the OSC's approval, a price is determined and a full-fledged selling effort gets under way. A final prospectus must accompany the delivery of securities or confirmation of sale, whichever comes first.

Tombstone advertisements are used by underwriters during and after the waiting period. The **tombstone** contains the name of the company whose securities are involved. It provides some information about the issue, and it lists the investment dealers (the underwriters) involved with selling the issue. Investment dealers' role in selling securities is discussed more fully below.

The investment dealers are divided into groups called *brackets* on the tombstone and prospectus. Dealers' names are listed alphabetically within each bracket. The brackets are a kind of pecking order. In general, the higher the bracket, the greater is the underwriter's prestige.

The POP System

In 1982, the SEC approved its shelf registration system designed to reduce repetitive filing requirements for large companies. In 1983, the OSC introduced the POP system with a similar goal. The five provinces with securities commissions all have compatible legislation allowing certain securities issuers prompt access to capital markets without the necessity of preparing a full preliminary and final prospectus prior to a distribution.

The POP system, accessible only by large companies, lets issuers file annual and interim financial statements regardless of whether they issue securities in a given year. To use the POP system, issuers must have been reporting for 36 months and have complied with the continuous disclosure requirements. Because the OSC has an extensive file of information on these companies, only a short prospectus is required when securities are issued. As we stated earlier, POP offerings in the form of bought deals became quite popular in the late 1980s.

In 1991, securities regulators in Canada and the SEC in the United States introduced a *Multi-Jurisdictional Disclosure System (MJDS)*. Under MJDS, large issuers in the two countries may issue securities in both countries under disclosure documents satisfactory to regulators in the home country. This is an important simplification of filing requirements for certain large Canadian companies. Together, these firms raised $12 billion (U.S.) in public offerings in the United States in 1989 and 1990. In 1991, for example, Rogers Communications Inc. completed a U.S. $270 million debt issue initiating MJDS.[5]

At the time of writing in 1994, investment dealers and the OSC were working on extending MJDS to issuers in G7 countries outside the United States. Under the proposed rules, large equity issuers with market capitalization of $3 billion or more will be allowed to sell up to 10 percent of a new equity issue in Canada based on an offering document filed in the home country. This will save the foreign company from duplicate filings and restating its financial statements to conform with Canadian Institute of Chartered Accountants (CICA) rules.[6]

CONCEPT QUESTIONS

- What are the basic procedures in selling a new issue?
- What is a preliminary prospectus?
- What is the POP system and what advantages does it offer?

19.3   The Cash Offer

If the public issue of securities is a cash offer, underwriters are usually involved. Underwriters perform the following services for corporate issuers:

1. Formulating the method used to issue the securities.
2. Pricing the new securities.
3. Selling the new securities.

---

[5]David Payne, "Accounting Watch," *Director* (September 1991), and Barry Critchley, "New Rates Open Up Cross-Border Financing," *Financial Post* (September 23, 1991), pp. 11–20.

[6]Barry Critchley, "Foreign Issuers Get New Access to Canada," *The Financial Post* (November 6, 1993), p. 32.

Typically, the underwriter buys the securities for less than the offering price and accepts the risk of not being able to sell them. Because underwriting involves risk, underwriters combine to form an underwriting group called a **syndicate** or a **banking group** to share the risk and help to sell the issue.

In a syndicate, one or more managers arrange or co-manage the offering. The lead manager typically has the responsibility for packaging and executing the deal. The other underwriters in the syndicate serve primarily to distribute the issue.

The difference between the underwriter's buying price and the offering price is called the **spread** or **discount.** It is the basic compensation received by the underwriter.

In Canada, firms often establish long-term relationships with their underwriters. With the growth in popularity of bought deals, competition among underwriters has increased. At the same time, mergers among investment dealers have reduced the number of underwriters. For example, RBC Dominion Securities (which *The Financial Post* called the leading Canadian underwriter in 1990) grew through merger with six other investment dealers and a major capital injection by the Royal Bank.[7]

Types of Underwriting

Two basic types of underwriting are involved in a cash offer: regular underwriting and a bought deal.

Regular Underwriting

With **regular underwriting** the banking group of underwriters buys the securities from the issuing firm and resells them to the public for the purchase price plus an underwriting spread. Regular underwriting includes an "out clause" which gives the banking group the option to decline the issue if the price drops dramatically. In this case, the deal is usually withdrawn. The issue might be repriced and/or reoffered at a later date. **Firm commitment underwriting** is like regular underwriting without the out clause.

A close counterpart to regular underwriting is called **best efforts underwriting.** The underwriter is legally bound to use "best efforts" to sell the securities at the agreed-upon offering price. Beyond this, the underwriter does not guarantee any particular amount of money to the issuer. This form of underwriting is more common with initial public offerings (IPOs).

Bought Deal

In a **bought deal,** the issuer sells the entire issue to one investment dealer or to a group that then attempts to resell it. As in firm commitment underwriting, the investment dealer assumes all the price risk. The dealer has usually "premarketed" the prospective issue to a few large institutional investors. Issuers in bought deals are large,

---

[7]Critchley and Murphy, "DS Wins Laurels Again."

well-known firms that qualify for the use of POP to speed up OSC filings. For these reasons, bought deals are usually executed swiftly. Bought deals are the most popular form of underwriting in Canada today.

The Investment Dealers' Association (IDA) of Canada and the OSC took another look at bought deals in 1992. Some investment dealers criticized bought deals for excluding retail investors from access to many new issues. There is also concern that the rush to premarket bought deals may prevent investment dealers from due diligence investigation.

In July 1992, the IDA released a proposal to modify equity bought deal financing. The most substantial recommendation was that a six-hour delay period should be implemented between the press release announcing a bought deal and the signing of an underwriting agreement. During this period, investment dealers could solicit expressions of interest from individual investors. The Canadian Securities Administrators (CSA) published these proposals in August 1992 and also asked for comments with regard to bought deals. In June 1993, the CSA asked for further comments on both the IDA Proposals and bought deals. A press release was issued by the CSA in October 1993 stating "that they [the CSA] are not prepared to propose any change to the bought deal financing technique at this time."[8] However, at the same time, the OSC enacted By-law 29.13 which regulates communication between the party involved in premarketing equity-bought deals and potential purchasers of the securities involved.

The Selling Period

While the issue is being sold to the public, the underwriting group agrees not to sell securities for less than the offering price until the syndicate dissolves. The principal underwriter is permitted to buy shares if the market price falls below the offering price. The purpose would be to support the market and stabilize the price from temporary downward pressure. If the issue remains unsold after a time (for example, 30 days), members can leave the group and sell their shares at whatever price the market will allow.

The Overallotment Option

Many underwriting contracts contain an *overallotment option* or *Green Shoe provision* that gives members of the underwriting group the option to purchase additional shares at the offering price less fees and commissions.[9] The stated reason for the overallotment option is to cover excess demand and oversubscriptions. The option has a short maturity (around 30 days) and is limited to about 10 percent of the original number of shares issued.

The overallotment option is a benefit to the underwriting syndicate and a cost to the issuer. If the market price of the new issue rises immediately, the overallotment option allows the underwriters to buy additional shares from the issuer and immediately resell them to the public.

---

[8]The request for comments and IDA proposals are contained in *OSC Bulletin 15* (August 7, 1993). The latest CSA bought deal press release (as of this writing) is contained in *OSC Bulletin 16* (October 1, 1993).

[9]The term *Green Shoe provision* sounds exotic, but the origin is relatively mundane. It comes from the Green Shoe Company, which once granted such an option.

Rank			Volume		Table 19.1
1990	1989		($ millions)	Number of issues	Canada's top 10 underwriters, 1990
A. Combined debt and equity					
1	1	RBC Dominion	$5,333	130	
2	3	ScotiaMcLeod	4,726	105	
3	2	Wood Gundy	4,393	113	
4	4	Merrill Lynch	2,575	39	
5	5	Burns, Fry	2,461	61	
6	8	Nesbitt, Thomson	2,286	68	
7		CS First Boston	1,801	24	
8		Union Bank of Switzerland	1,311	19	
9	10	Richardson Greenshields	1,177	46	
10	7	Gordon Capital	1,080	41	
B. Debt issues					
1	1	RBC Dominion	4,363	93	
2	2	ScotiaMcLeod	4,210	79	
3	3	Wood Gundy	3,790	86	
4	4	Merrill Lynch	2,574	38	
5	5	Burns, Fry	1,989	45	
6	6	Nesbitt, Thomson	1,826	42	
7	8	CS First Boston	1,801	24	
8	10	Union Bank of Switzerland	1,311	19	
9		Salomon Brothers	962	13	
10	9	Richardson Greenshields	858	32	
C. Equity issues					
1	1	RBC Dominion	970	37	
2	2	Gordon Capital	674	24	
3	3	Wood Gundy	603	27	
4	4	ScotiaMcLeod	516	26	
5	8	Burns, Fry	472	16	
6	6	Nesbitt, Thomson	460	26	
7	7	Trilon Securities	406	22	
8	10	Levesque, Beaubien	361	26	
9	9	Richardson Greenshields	319	14	
10	5	TD Securities	304	10	

Source: From figures in the *Financial Post*, August 5, 1991, p. 13.

Investment Dealers

Investment dealers are at the heart of new security issues. They provide advice, market the securities (after investigating the market's receptiveness to the issue), and provide a guarantee of the amount an issue will raise (with a bought deal).

Table 19.1 lists the largest underwriters in Canada based on the total dollars in securities offerings (debt and equity) managed in 1990.[10] As indicated, RBC Dominion Securities was the leading manager of underwritten public securities offerings in 1990 with 130 issues and a total of $5.3 billion managed. Parts B and C of Table 19.1 break out debt and equity issues separately. From our discussion in Chapter 14, it is not surprising that debt issues are much more common than equity issues.

---

[10]We created these tables from *The Financial Post* by using its formula that divides the total amount underwritten among members of an underwriting group with a bonus to the lead manager. Our figures include corporate and government debt and corporate equity issues.

Table 19.2 provides an international perspective by examining non-Canadian issues. Notice how U.S. underwriters dominate international equity underwritings while European and Japanese firms rank in the top four positions in the much larger international bond market. Wood Gundy ranked in the top 25 underwriters of international equities in 1991 and 1992, but no Canadian firm made the top 25 in international bond markets.

The Offering Price and Underpricing

Determining the correct offering price is an underwriter's hardest task. The issuing firm faces a potential cost if the offering price is set too high or too low. If the issue is priced below the true market price, the issuer's existing shareholders will experience an opportunity loss when they sell their shares for less than they are worth. If the issue is priced too high, it may be unsuccessful and have to be withdrawn. Of course, this is the underwriter's problem under a bought deal.

Underpricing is a fairly common occurrence and it clearly helps new shareholders earn a higher return on the shares they buy. However, to the existing shareholders of the issuing firm, underpricing is an indirect cost of issuing new securities. In the case of an IPO, underpricing reduces the proceeds received by the original owners.

The Decision to Go Public

When a private company grows to a certain size, it may consider the advantages of going public by issuing common stock through an **initial public offering (IPO.)** One important advantage is that public firms have greater access to new capital once their shares are valued on secondary markets. Further, publicly traded firms must meet OSC and other disclosure requirements that reduce information risk for potential investors. In addition, going public makes it possible for the firm's principal owners to sell some of their shares and diversify their personal portfolios while retaining control of the company.

Going public also has disadvantages. Public firms are subject to stricter disclosure and other potentially costly regulatory requirements.[11] They have to be careful to abide by OSC Policy 9.1 against self-dealing.

On balance, most large companies in Canada are public. When a firm decides to go public, it does so through an IPO.

Pricing IPOs

Because the firm has no record as a public company, pricing an IPO is a big challenge. Rotenberg summarized research on IPOs in the United States and Canada.[12] She found that firms that provide a great amount of high-quality information are able to set higher prices on their IPOs than firms that don't. Different information variables are listed in

---

[11]The boxed material on Angoss Software Corp. illustrates these disadvantages.

[12]Wendy Rotenberg, "Pricing Initial Public Equity Offerings: Who Wins, Who Loses, and Why?" *Canadian Investment Review* (Spring 1990), pp. 17–24.

	Ranking		Volume	Number
1991	Jan.–June 1992	International Equities	($ millions)	of Issues
1	1	Goldman Sachs	$ 3,077.4	37
7	2	Morgan Stanley	2,439.4	33
4	3	Lehman Brothers	1,315.0	21
5	4	Merrill Lynch	1,011.0	18
9	5	Banco Roberts	931.8	1
2	6	S.G. Warburg Group	888.0	7
3	7	Credit Suisse/CSFB Group	869.5	17
10	8	Paribas	833.5	6
—	9	J.P. Morgan Securities	745.2	4
6	10	Salomon Brothers	325.1	7
—	11	Banque Indosuez	298.3	4
—	12	Rothschild's Continuation Holdings	255.0	2
24	13	Crédit Lyonnais	239.0	2
17	14	Donaldson, Lufkin & Jenrette	224.6	6
15	15	PaineWebber	144.4	13
18	16	Baring Brothers	141.0	1
—	17	Acciones y Valores de México	133.7	2
—	18	Bear Stearns	130.1	3
—	19	Oppenheimer	120.9	3
—	20	Commerce International Merchant Bank	104.4	1
16	21	Wood Gundy	95.3	3
14	22	Skandinaviska Enskilda Bank Group	93.6	1
—	23	Den Danske Bank	82.1	2
13	24	Barclays Bank	73.4	1
—	25	Swiss Bank Corp.	73.0	2
		International bonds[*]		
3	1	Deutsche Bank	$13,627.5	53
1	2	Nomura International Group	12,057.7	53
2	3	Credit Suisse/CSFB Group	11,538.4	59
9	4	Paribas	8,856.4	39
8	5	Merrill Lynch	8,448.1	37
7	6	Union Bank of Switzerland	7,800.2	37
15	7	J.P. Morgan Securities	6,910.0	26
6	8	Goldman Sachs	6,588.3	28
11	9	Yamaichi Securities	5,994.0	44
5	10	Swiss Bank Corp.	5,795.4	46
4	11	Daiwa Securities	5,785.4	44
12	12	Nikko Securities	5,501.2	35
17	13	Crédit Lyonnais	5,236.8	19
19	14	Crédit Commercial de France	4,200.2	17
10	15	Morgan Stanley	4,175.1	18
18	16	Industrial Bank of Japan	4,096.4	15
13	17	Salomon Brothers	3,677.6	15
14	18	Dresdner Bank	2,868.7	9
28	19	Banque Nationale de Paris	2,478.5	10
—	20	Citicorp	2,442.2	11
16	21	S.G. Warburg Group	2,429.6	11
34	22	Lehman Brothers	2,310.2	16
21	23	Commerzbank	2,253.1	11
20	24	Hambros Bank	2,073.4	26
26	25	ABN Amro Bank	1,994.1	14

Table 19.2
Top 25 underwriters, 1991–1992

*This table ranks international bond underwriters in the broadest sense. It includes all Euromarket deals, as well as "foreign" bonds syndicated in domestic markets outside an issuer's home country.

Source: *Institutional Investor* (September 1992). Used with permission.

Table 19.3
What determines
subscription
prices?

Variable	Empirical evidence*
Direct disclosures	
Sales and earnings from existing operations	+ or 0
Book value of existing assets	+
Information intermediation	
High-quality (good-reputation) intermediation services	+
Signals of inside information	
Entrepreneurial ownership retention	+ or 0
Use of proceeds for risky investments	+
Stated dividend policy	0

*Expressed as positive (+), neutral (0), or negative (–).

Source: W. Rotenberg, "Pricing Initial Public Equity Offerings: Who Wins, Who Loses, and Why?" *Canadian Investment Review* (Spring, 1990), pp. 17–26.

Table 19.3. Firms that disclose past, favourable accounting information enjoy higher IPO prices. Of the accounting variables listed, book value of assets had the most impact for Canadian firms. This suggests larger firms have an advantage in going public.

A related advantage, information intermediation, links higher offering prices to firms that use auditors and underwriters with top reputations. When issuers use such top-quality (and more expensive) intermediaries, the market attaches more weight to favourable projections in their prospectuses. In other words, financial economists argue that each intermediary has a reservoir of "reputation capital."[13] Mispricing of new issues, as well as unethical dealings, are likely to reduce this reputation capital. This reputation effect may be waning as investment dealers and accounting firms become fewer, larger, and more alike through mergers.

Investors recognize that an IPO's original owners have the best information about their company's future prospects. But the owners also have an interest in maximizing the IPO price. To resolve this moral hazard problem, investors look for signals that original owners have favourable inside information. If owners believed the firm had excellent opportunities, they would retain more stock themselves. They would also use the IPO proceeds to invest in risky capital projects designed to generate positive NPVs out of the firm's opportunities. Table 19.3 shows that research on U.S. and Canadian IPOs generally supports these arguments.

So far we have discussed setting the offer price. The issue of underpricing, raised above, relates the offer price to the IPO's price after the offering period is over.

Table 19.4 draws on Rotenberg's summary of a series of studies on IPOs in the United States and Canada. For example, in the first study listed, Ibbotson found that unseasoned new equity issues in the United States typically have been offered at 11 percent below their true market value.[14] Krinsky and Rotenberg found very similar levels of underpricing for Canadian IPOs.[15] In general, these and the other studies

---

[13]The reputation effect was documented for the United States by R. Beatty and J. Ritter, "Investment Banking, Reputation and the Underpricing of Initial Public Offerings," *Journal of Financial Economics* (1986). Canadian evidence is in Rotenberg, "Pricing Initial Public Offerings."

[14]R. Ibbotson, "Price Performance of Common Stock New Issues," *Journal of Financial Economics* 2 (1975).

[15]I. Krinsky and W. Rotenberg, "The Valuation of Public Offerings," *Contemporary Accounting Research* 5, no. 2 (1985), pp. 501–15.

Sample	Sample period	Average underpricing	
120 U.S. IPOs, one randomly selected per month	1960–69	11.4%	**Table 19.4** Initial aftermarket performance: The evidence
5,000 U.S. IPOs	1960–82	18.8	
1,026 U.S. IPOs	January 1980–March 1981 hot market	48.4	
	Remainder of 1977–82	16.3	
	Subset of established firms	10.0	
1,188 U.S. IPOs	1983–87		
	74 reverse leveraged buyouts	2.0	
	1,114 IPO control sample	7.8	
1,078 U.S. IPOs	1981–85	6.2	
1,526 U.S. IPOs	1975–84	14.3	
100 Canadian IPOs	1971–83	9.0–11.5	

Source: W. Rotenberg, "Pricing Initial Public Equity Offerings: Who Wins, Who Loses, and Why," *Canadian Investment Review* (Spring 1990), pp. 17–26.

summarized in Table 19.4 found that IPOs are underpriced compared to their prices in the aftermarket immediately after the offering period. The table also shows that underpricing is cyclical. The greatest underpricing occurred in "hot market" periods when prices skyrocketed immediately after issue.

Why Does Underpricing Exist?

Based on the evidence examined, an obvious question is, Why does underpricing continue? As we discuss, there are various explanations, but, to date, there is a lack of complete agreement among researchers as to which is correct.

We present some pieces of the underpricing puzzle by stressing two important caveats to our discussion. First, the average figures presented tend to obscure the fact that much of the apparent underpricing is attributable to the smaller, more highly speculative issues. Smaller firms tend to have offering prices of less than $3 per share, and such *penny stocks* (as they are sometimes termed) can be very risky investments. Arguably, they must be significantly underpriced on average just to attract investors, and this is one explanation for the underpricing phenomenon. The impact of size is apparent in Table 19.4, where a subset of established firms showed comparatively low aftermarket performance.

The second caveat is that relatively few IPO buyers will actually get the initial high average returns observed in IPOs, and many will lose money. Although it is true that, on average, IPOs have positive initial returns, a significant fraction experiences price drops. Furthermore, when the price is too low, the issue is often *oversubscribed.* This means investors cannot buy all of the shares they want, so the underwriters allocate the shares among investors.

Consider this tale of two investors. Ms. Smarts knows precisely what companies are worth when their shares are offered. Mr. Average knows only that prices usually rise one month after the IPO. Armed with this information, Mr. Average decides to buy 1,000 shares of every IPO. Does Mr. Average actually earn an abnormally high average return across all initial offerings?

The answer is no, and at least one reason is Ms. Smarts. For example, because Ms. Smarts knows that company XYZ is underpriced, she invests all her money in its IPO.

When the issue is oversubscribed, the underwriters must allocate the shares between Ms. Smarts and Mr. Average. If they do it on a pro rata basis and if Ms. Smarts has bid for twice as many shares as Mr. Average, she will get two shares for each one Mr. Average receives. The net result is that when an issue is underpriced, Mr. Average cannot buy as much of it as he wants.

Ms. Smarts also knows that company ABC is overpriced. In this case she avoids its IPO altogether, and Mr. Average ends up with a full 1,000 shares. To summarize, Mr. Average receives fewer shares when more knowledgeable investors swarm to buy an underpriced issue, but he gets all he wants when the smart money avoids the issue.

This is called the *winner's curse,* and it explains much of the reason why IPOs have such a large average return. When the average investor wins and gets his allocation, it is because those who knew better avoided the issue. To counteract the winner's curse and to attract the average investor, underwriters underprice issues.[16]

CONCEPT QUESTIONS

- Suppose a stockbroker calls you up out of the blue and offers to sell "all the shares you want" of a new issue. Do you think the issue will be more or less underpriced than average?
- What factors determine the degree of underpricing?

19.4   New Equity Sales and the Value of the Firm

It seems reasonable to believe that new long-term financing is arranged by firms after positive net present value projects are put together. As a consequence, when the announcement of external financing is made, the firm's market value should go up. As discussed in an earlier chapter, this is precisely the opposite of what actually happens in the case of new equity financing. Asquith and Mullins, Masulis and Korwar, and Mikkelson and Partch have all found that the market value of existing U.S. equity drops on the announcement of a new issue of common stock.[17] Plausible reasons for this strange result include:

1. *Managerial information.* If management has superior information about the market value of the firm, it may know when the firm is overvalued. If it does, it will attempt to issue new shares of stock when the market value exceeds the correct value. This will benefit existing shareholders. However, the potential new shareholders are not stupid, and they will anticipate this superior information and discount it in lower market prices at the new issue date.

2. *Debt usage.* Issuing new equity may reveal that the company has too much debt or too little liquidity. One version of this argument holds that the equity issue is a

---

[16]This explanation was first suggested in K. Rock, "Why New Issues Are Underpriced," *Journal of Financial Economics* 15 (1986).

[17]P. Asquith and D . Mullins, "Equity Issues and Offering Dilution," *Journal of Financial Economics* 15 (1986); R. Masulis and A. N. Korwar, "Seasoned Equity Offerings: An Empirical Investigation," *Journal of Financial Economics* 15 (1986); and W. H. Mikkelson and M. M. Partch, "The Valuation Effects of Security Offerings and the Issuance Process," *Journal of Financial Economics* 15 (1986).

bad signal to the market. After all, if the new projects are favourable ones, why should the firm let new shareholders in on them? As you read earlier, in IPOs it is regarded as a positive signal when the original owners keep large amounts of stock for themselves. Taking this argument to the limit, the firm could just issue debt and let the existing shareholders have all the gain.

3. *Issue costs.* As we discuss next, there are substantial costs associated with selling securities.

The drop in value of the existing stock following the announcement of a new issue is an example of an indirect cost of selling securities. This drop might typically be on the order of 3 percent for an industrial corporation so, for a large company, it can be a substantial amount of money. We label this drop the abnormal return in our discussion of the costs of new issues below.

CONCEPT QUESTIONS

■ What are some possible reasons that the price of stock drops on the announcement of a new equity issue?

■ Explain why we might expect a firm with a positive NPV investment to finance it with debt instead of equity.

The Costs of Issuing Securities   19.5

Issuing securities to the public is not free, and the costs of different methods are important determinants of which method is used. These costs associated with *floating* a new issue are generically called *flotation costs*. Here we look at flotation costs associated with equity sales to the public.

The costs of selling stock fall into six categories: (1) the spread, (2) other direct expenses, (3) indirect expenses, (4) abnormal returns (discussed above), (5) underpricing, and (6) the overallotment option. We look at these costs first for United States and then for Canadian equity sales.

The costs of issuing securities	
Spread	The spread consists of direct fees paid by the issuer to the underwriting syndicate—the difference between the price the issuer receives and the offer price.
Other direct expenses	These are direct costs, incurred by the issuer, that are not part of the compensation to underwriters. These costs include filing fees, legal fees, and taxes—all reported on the prospectus.
Indirect expenses	These costs are not reported on the prospectus and include the costs of management time spent working on the new issue.
Abnormal returns	In a seasoned issue of stock, the price drops on average by 3 percent on the announcement of the issue.
Underpricing	For initial public offerings, losses arise from selling the stock below the correct value.
Overallotment (Green Shoe) option	The Green Shoe option gives the underwriters the right to buy additional shares at the offer price to cover overallotments.

Table 19.5
Flotation costs as a percentage of gross proceeds for underwritten new issues of equity by publicly traded firms, 1983

Gross proceeds ($ millions)	Direct costs reported on prospectus
$ 0–10	10.10%
10–20	7.02
20–50	4.89
50–100	3.99
100–200	3.71
200–	3.30

Source: R. Hansen, "Evaluating the Costs of a New Equity Issue," *Midland Corporate Finance Journal* 4, no. 1 (Spring 1986), p. 45.

Table 19.6
Costs of going public in Canada, 1971–83

Spread	5.96%
Other direct expenses	0.98
Underpricing (first-day trading return)	11.60
Total	18.54%

Source: I. Krinsky and W. Rotenberg, "The Valuation of Public Offerings," *Contemporary Accounting Research* 5, no. 2 (1985), pp. 501–15.

Table 19.5 reports the direct costs of new equity issues in 1983 for publicly traded U.S. firms. These are all seasoned offerings; the percentages in Table 19.5 are as reported in the prospectuses of the issuing companies. These costs only include the spread (underwriter discount) and other direct costs, including legal fees, accounting fees, printing costs, SEC registration costs, and taxes. Not included are indirect expenses, abnormal returns, underpricing, and the overallotment option.

As Table 19.5 shows, direct costs alone can be very large, particularly for smaller (less than $10 million) issues. For this group, the direct costs, as reported by the companies, averaged a little over 10 percent. This means that the company, net of costs, receives 90 percent of the proceeds of the sale on average. On a $10 million issue, this is $1 million in direct expenses—a substantial cost.

Table 19.5 only tells part of the story. For IPOs, the effective costs can be much greater because of the indirect costs. Table 19.6 reports both the direct costs of going public and the degree of underpricing based on IPOs that took place on the Toronto Stock Exchange between 1971 and 1983. These figures understate the total cost because the study did not consider indirect expenses, abnormal returns, or the overallotment option.

The total expenses of going public over these years averaged 18.54 percent. This is roughly comparable to U.S. averages for 1977–82 of 21.22 percent for firm commitment underwriting and 31.87 percent for best efforts underwriting. Comparing the two studies suggests that the U.S. costs were higher mainly due to greater underpricing.[18] Once again, we see that the costs of selling securities can be quite large.

---

[18]V. M. Jog and A. L. Riding, "Underpricing in Canadian IPOs," *Financial Analysts Journal* (November/ December 1987), pp. 48–55, report marginally lower underpricing for the same period as Table 19.6. A later study found underpricing of only 4.1 percent for Canadian IPOs for 1984–87. See J. M. Friedlan, "Understanding the IPO Market," *CGA Magazine* (March 1994), pp. 42–68.3.

Overall, three conclusions emerge from our discussion of underwriting:

1. Substantial economies of size are evident. Larger firms can raise equity more easily.
2. The cost associated with underpricing can be substantial and can exceed the direct costs.
3. The issue costs are higher for an initial public offering than for a seasoned offering.

IPOs in Practice: The Case of Air Canada

In October 1988, the Government of Canada sold 30.8 million shares of Air Canada stock in a successful partial privatization.[19] The IPO was priced at $8 per share and generated $234 million after flotation costs. The airline (government-owned since its inception as Trans-Canada Air Lines in 1937) was to remain under government majority ownership, but the government promised to refrain from taking an active role in management. At the time, the airline industry was enjoying strong growth in revenue passenger miles domestically and more moderate growth in international markets. Deregulation improved flexibility and was expected to benefit Air Canada. Net income was volatile due to fluctuating fuel prices, but had hit a high of $46 million in 1987.

The shares issued were voting shares, but non-Canadian shareholders were restricted from voting more than 25 percent of the shares. Proceeds of the issue were roughly split between retiring debt and purchase of new aircraft along with other capital expenditures. Underwriters in the top bracket were RBC Dominion Securities Inc., Wood Gundy Inc., ScotiaMcLeod Inc., Nesbitt Thomson Deacon Ltd., Richardson Greenshields of Canada Limited, Burns Fry Limited, Merrill Lynch Canada Inc., Levesque Beaubien Inc., and Pemberton Securities Inc. Twenty-seven other investment dealers also participated in the underwriting. The selling arrangement took the form of regular underwriting with the agreement containing an out clause. The underwriters also had an overallotment option up to a maximum of 10 percent of the original number of shares.

Applying the theory of underpricing to Air Canada reveals that several factors combined to moderate underpricing. Since Air Canada was relatively large, with total assets of $3.1 billion at book value in June 1988, underpricing should be more moderate than for a smaller issue. Other factors expected to moderate underpricing were availability of detailed historical financial information and inclusion of high-quality underwriters. The company's plan to use half the proceeds for capital investment in risky assets was also expected to boost the issue price.

In the actual event, the predictions of theory were accurate; immediate underpricing was not evident. The stock price declined from the issue price of $8 to a low of $7 in the month after issue. The decline was likely due to a general market drop. In January 1989, both the TSE and Air Canada turned upward and the stock rose to over $13 in June 1989. Market analysts noted that the federal government remained true to

---

[19]This section draws on two cases by the late Cecil R. Dipchand, "Air Canada (A) and (B)" (Halifax: Dalhousie University, 1990).

its promise not to interfere in the company's affairs. Debt levels were reduced to be comparable to those of large U.S. airlines while profitability was good.

In June 1989, the federal government decided to sell its remaining shares at an issue price of $12. In this case, the government benefited from market timing as the price was up by 50 percent from the initial IPO. The offering was sold in July 1989. By August 11, 1989, the price rose to a peak of $14.88. The return to investors immediately after the issue was 24 percent (or $14.88 − $12)/ $12). So in the second tranche, underpricing was significant.

To measure the effect of underpricing, suppose that the shares in the second tranche could have been sold for around 12-percent underpricing instead of 24-percent. We pick 12 percent because it is approximately the average amount of underpricing reported in Table 19.7. With 12-percent underpricing the issue price would have been $13.44 (because ($13.44 − $12)/$12 = .12). Assuming that other flotation costs had stayed the same, the government would have netted an additional $59 million (or 41 million shares × ($13.44 − $12)).

Air Canada's longer-term performance has not been as favourable. By October 1989, the price declined below the $12 offering price. In November 1994, Air Canada stock was trading at $8.00. Air Canada's longer-term performance is typical of the mixed record of IPOs.

Privatization: A Financial Innovation

Globalization of financial markets in the 1980s went hand in hand with deregulation in making privatizations attractive. Large institutional investors sought international diversification to reduce risk and enhance returns. Privatizations offered these investors shares in large, well-known companies, which underpricing made attractive. As a result, many privatizations involved record amounts.

The Government of Canada received over $700 million in the two Air Canada issues. This is impressive but substantially less than, for example, the U.S. $4.76 billion raised when British Telecom (the British-government–owned telephone company) went public in 1984. However, both of these issues pale in comparison to what NTT (Nippon Telephone and Telegraph, the Japanese telephone company) raised in 1987. In November 1987, NTT sold 1.95 million shares at a price of 2.55 million yen each. At the then-prevailing exchange rate, this was roughly U.S. $19,000 per share. The total issue amount was thus on the order of U.S. $37 billion. What is even more remarkable is that NTT had already sold 1.95 million shares in February of the same year.

More major privatizations are expected as Eastern European countries restructure their planned systems into market economies. Many enterprises in these countries will require years of restructuring after they go private. As a result, there is not likely to be much high-quality information about future prospects. The transfer to private ownership may not take the form of a sale of stock. Instead, it may be more efficient to auction the unrestructured enterprises to the highest bidder. In any event, it is certain that participants in these privatizations will carefully study the experience of Air Canada and other similar cases.[20]

---

[20]For more on privatization in Eastern Europe, see Roy C. Smith, "Privatization Programs of the 1980s: Lessons for the Treuhandstalt," working paper (New York: Salomon Brothers Center, New York University, 1990).

Table 19.7
National Power
company financial
statement before
rights offering

NATIONAL POWER COMPANY
Balance sheet

Assets		Shareholders' equity	
		Common stock	$ 5,000,000
		Retained earnings	10,000,000
Total	$15,000,000	Total	15,000,000

Income statement

Earnings before taxes	$3,333,333
Taxes (40%)	$1,333,333
Net income	$2,000,000
Earnings per share	$2
Shares outstanding	1,000,000
Market price per share	$20
Total market value	$20,000,000

CONCEPT QUESTIONS

- What are the different costs associated with security offerings?
- What lessons do we learn from studying issue costs?

Rights   19.6

When new shares of common stock are sold to the general public, the proportional ownership of existing shareholders will likely be reduced. However, if a preemptive right is contained in the firm's articles of incorporation, then the firm must first offer any new issue of common stock to existing shareholders. If the articles of incorporation do not include a preemptive right, the firm has a choice of offering the issue of common stock directly to existing shareholders or to the public. In some industries, regulatory authorities set rules concerning rights. For example, prior to the 1980 Bank Act, chartered banks were required to raise equity exclusively through rights offerings.

An issue of common stock offered to existing shareholders is called a *rights offering*. In a rights offering, each shareholder is issued one right for every share owned. The rights give the shareholder an *option* to buy a specified number of new shares from the firm at a specified price within a specified time, after which time the rights are said to expire.

The terms of the rights offering are evidenced by certificates known as *rights*. Such rights are often traded on securities exchanges or over the counter.

The Mechanics of a Rights Offering

To illustrate the various considerations a financial manager has in a rights offering, we will examine the situation faced by the National Power Company, whose abbreviated initial financial statements are given in Table 19.7.

As the table shows, National Power earns $2 million after taxes and has 1 million shares outstanding. Earnings per share are thus $2. The stock sells for $20 (10 times earnings). To fund a planned expansion, the company intends to raise $5 million of new equity funds by a rights offering.

To execute a rights offering, the financial manager of National Power must answer the following questions:

1. What should the price per share be for the new stock?
2. How many shares will have to be sold?
3. How many shares will each shareholder be allowed to buy?

Management will probably also want to ask

4. What is the likely effect of the rights offering on the per share value of the existing stock?

It turns out that these questions' answers are highly interrelated. We will get to them in just a moment.

The early stages of a rights offering are the same as for the general cash offer. The difference between a rights offering and a general cash offer lies in how the shares are sold. As discussed earlier, in a cash offer, shares are sold to retail and institutional investors through investment dealers. With a rights offer, National Power's existing shareholders are informed that they own one right for each share of stock held. National Power will then specify how many rights a shareholder needs to buy one additional share at a specified price.

To take advantage of the rights offering, shareholders must exercise the rights by filling out a subscription form and sending it, along with payment, to the firm's subscription agent. Shareholders of National Power will actually have several choices: (1) exercise and subscribe to the entitled shares, (2) sell the rights, or (3) do nothing and let the rights expire. This third course of action is inadvisable as long as the rights have value.

Number of Rights Needed to Purchase a Share

National Power wants to raise $5 million in new equity. Suppose that the subscription price is set at $10 per share. How National Power arrived at that price is something we will discuss below, but notice that the subscription price is substantially less than the current $20 per share market price.

At $10 per share, National Power will have to issue 500,000 new shares. This can be determined by dividing the total amount of funds to be raised by the subscription price:

$$\frac{\text{Number of}}{\text{new shares}} = \frac{\text{Funds to be raised}}{\text{Subscription price}} = \frac{\$5,000,000}{\$10} = 500,000 \text{ shares} \qquad (19.1)$$

Because shareholders always get one right for each share of stock they own, 1 million rights will be issued by National Power. To determine how many rights will be needed to buy one new share of stock, we can divide the number of existing outstanding shares of stock by the number of new shares:

$$\frac{\text{Number of rights}}{\text{needed to buy a}} = \frac{\text{Old shares}}{\text{New shares}} = \frac{1,000,000}{500,000} = 2 \text{ rights} \qquad (19.2)$$
share of stock

	Initial position	
Number of shares	2	
Share price	$20	
Value of holding	$40	
Terms of offer		
Subscription price	$10	
Number of rights issued	2	
Number of rights for a new share	2	
After offer		
Number of shares	3	
Value of holdings	$50	
Share price	$16.67	
Value of a right		
Old price—New price	$20 − $16.67 = $3.33	

Table 19.8
The value of rights for the individual shareholder

Thus, a shareholder will need to give up two rights plus $10 to receive a share of new stock. If all shareholders do this, National Power will raise the required $5 million.

It should be clear that the subscription price, the number of new shares, and the number of rights needed to buy a new share of stock are interrelated. For example, National Power can lower the subscription price. If so, more new shares must be issued to raise $5 million in new equity. Several alternatives are worked out here:

Subscription price	New shares	Rights needed to buy a share of stock
$20	250,000	4
10	500,000	2
5	1,000,000	1

The Value of a Right

Rights clearly have value. In the case of National Power, the right to be able to buy a share of stock worth $20 for $10 is definitely worth something.

Suppose a shareholder of National Power owns two shares of stock just before the rights offering. This situation is depicted in Table 19.8. Initially, National Power costs $20 per share, so the shareholder's total holding is worth 2 × $20 = $40. The National Power rights offer gives shareholders with two rights the opportunity to purchase one additional share for $10. The additional share does not carry a right.

The shareholder who has two shares will receive two rights. The holding of the shareholder who exercises these rights and buys the new share would increase to three shares. The total investment would be $40 +10 = $50 (the $40 initial value plus the $10 paid to the company).

The shareholder now holds three shares, all of which are identical because the new share does not have a right and the rights attached to the old shares have been exercised. Since the total cost of buying these three shares is $40 + 10 = $50, the price per share must end up at $50/3 = $16.67 (rounded to two decimal places).

Table 19.9
National Power
Company rights
offering

Initial position	
Number of shares	1 million
Share price	$20
Value of firm	$20 million
Terms of offer	
Subscription price	$10
Number of rights issued	1 million
Number of rights for a share	2
After offer	
Number of shares	1.5 million
Share price	$16.67
Value of firm	$25 million
Value of one right	$20 − $16.67 = $3.33

Table 19.9 summarizes what happens to National Power's stock price. If all shareholders exercise their rights, the number of shares will increase to 1 million + .5 million = 1.5 million. The value of the firm will increase to $20 million + 5 million = $25 million. The value of each share will thus drop to $25 million/1.5 million = $16.67 after the rights offering.

The difference between the old share price of $20 and the new share price of $16.67 reflects the fact that the old shares carried rights to subscribe to the new issue. The difference must equal the value of one right, that is, $20 − 16.67 = $3.33.

Although holding no shares of outstanding National Power stock, an investor who wants to subscribe to the new issue can do so by buying some rights. Suppose an outside investor buys two rights. This will cost $3.33 × 2 = $6.67 (accounting for previous rounding). If the investor exercises the rights at a subscription price of $10 the total cost would be $10 + 6.67 = $16.67. In return for this expenditure, the investor will receive a share of the new stock, which, as we have seen, is worth $16.67.

- **Example**

In the National Power example, suppose the subscription price was set at $8. How many shares will have to be sold? How many rights would you need to buy a new share? What is the value of a right? What will the price per share be after the rights offer?

To raise $5 million, $5 million/$8 = 625,000 shares will need to be sold. There are 1 million shares outstanding, so it will take 1 million/625,000 = 8/5 = 1.6 rights to buy a new share of stock. (You can buy five new shares for every eight you own.) After the rights offer, there will be 1.625 million shares worth $25 million all together, so the per share value is $25/1.625 = $15.38 each. The value of a right in this case is the $20 original price less the $15.38 ending price ($4.62). ▪

Theoretical Value of a Right

We can summarize the discussion with an equation for the theoretical value of a right during the rights-on period:

$$R_0 = (M_0 - S)/(N + 1)$$

$$(19.3)$$

where

M_0 = Common share price during the rights-on period

S = Subscription price

N = Number of rights required to buy one new share

We illustrate the use of Equation (19.3) by checking our answer for the value of one right in the National Power example:

$R_0 = (\$20 - 8)/(1.6 + 1) = \$4.62$

This is the same answer we got earlier.

Ex-Rights

National Power's rights have a substantial value. In addition, the rights offering will have a large impact on the market price of National Power's stock. It will drop by $3.33 on the day when the shares trade **ex-rights.**

The standard procedure for issuing rights is similar to that for paying a dividend. It begins with the firm's setting a **holder-of-record date.** Following stock exchange rules, the stock typically goes ex-rights four trading days before the holder-of-record date. If the stock is sold before the ex-rights date—rights-on, with rights, or cum rights—the new owner will receive the rights. After the ex-rights date, an investor who purchases the shares will not receive the rights.

■ *Example*

The Lagrange Point Co. has proposed a rights offering. The stock currently sells for $40 per share. Under the terms of the offer, shareholders will be allowed to buy one new share for every five that they own at a price of $25 per share. What is the value of a right? What is the ex-rights price?

You can buy five rights-on shares for 5 × $40 = $200 and then exercise the rights for another $25. Your total investment is $225, and you end up with six ex-rights shares. The ex-rights price per share is $225/6 = $37.50 per share. The rights are thus worth $40 − 37.50 = $2.50 apiece .

Using equation (19.3) we have

$R_0 = (\$40 - 25)/(5 + 1) = \$2.50$ ■

Value of Rights after Ex-Rights Date

When the stock goes ex-rights, its price drops by the value of one right. Until the rights expire, holders can buy one share at the subscription price by exercising N rights. In equation form[21]

$$M_e = M_0 - R_0 \tag{19.2}$$
$$R_e = (M_e - S)/N \tag{19.3}$$

---

[21]During the ex-rights period, a right represents a short-lived option to buy the stock. Equation 19.5 gives the minimum value of this option. The market value of rights is generally higher as explained in our discussion of options in Chapter 21.

where M_e is the common share price during the ex-rights period.

Checking the formula using this example gives

$$M_e = \$40 - 2.50 = \$37.50$$
$$R_e = (\$37.50 - 25)/5 = \$2.50$$

■ *Example*

In the previous example, suppose you could buy the rights for only $0.25 instead of the $2.50 we calculated. What could you do?

You can get rich quick, because you have found a money machine. Here is the recipe: Buy five rights for $1.25. Exercise them and pay $25 to get a new share. Your total investment to get one ex-rights share is 5 × $0.25 + $25 = $26.25. Sell the share for $37.50 and pocket the $11.25 difference. Repeat as desired. ■

A variation on this theme actually occurred in the course of a rights offering by a major Canadian chartered bank in the mid-1980s. The bank's employee stock ownership plan had promoted share ownership by tellers and clerical staff who were unfamiliar with the workings of rights offerings. When they received notification of the rights offering, many employees did not bother to respond until they were personally solicited by other, more sophisticated employees who bought the rights for a fraction of their value. We do not endorse the ethics behind such transactions. But the incident does show why it pays for everyone who owns stock to understand the workings of rights offers.

The Underwriting Arrangements

Rights offerings are typically arranged using **standby underwriting.** In standby underwriting, the issuer makes a rights offering, and the underwriter makes a firm commitment to "take up" (that is, purchase) the unsubscribed portion of the issue. The underwriter usually gets a **standby fee** and additional amounts based on the securities taken up.

Standby underwriting protects the firm against undersubscription. This can occur if investors throw away rights or if bad news causes the stock's market price to fall below the subscription price.

In practice, a small percentage (less than 10 percent) of shareholders fail to exercise valuable rights. This can probably be attributed to ignorance or vacations. Furthermore, shareholders are usually given an **oversubscription privilege,** which enables them to purchase unsubscribed shares at the subscription price. The oversubscription privilege makes it unlikely that the corporate issuer would have to turn to its underwriter for help.

Effects on Shareholders

Shareholders can exercise their rights or sell them. In either case, the shareholder will not win or lose by the rights offering. The hypothetical holder of two shares of National Power has a portfolio worth $40. If the shareholder exercises the rights, he or she ends up with three shares worth a total of $50. In other words, by spending 10, the investor's holding increases in value by $10, which means that the shareholder is neither better nor worse off.

On the other hand, if the shareholder sells the two rights for $3.33 each, he or she obtains $3.33 × 2=$6.67 and ends up with two shares worth $16.67 and the cash from selling the right:

$$
\begin{aligned}
\text{Shares held} &= 2 \times \$16.67 = \$33.33 \\
\text{Rights sold} &= 2 \times \$3.33 \ = \ \underline{6.67} \\
\text{Total} &= \hspace{3.5em} \$40.00
\end{aligned}
$$

The new $33.33 market value plus $6.67 in cash is exactly the same as the original holding of $40. Thus, shareholders cannot lose or gain from exercising or selling rights.

It is obvious that after the rights offering, the new market price of the firm's stock will be lower than it was before the rights offering. As we have seen, however, shareholders have suffered no loss because of the rights offering. The lower the subscription price, the greater is the price decline of a rights offering. It is important to emphasize that because shareholders receive rights equal in value to the price drop, the rights offering does not hurt shareholders.

There is one last issue. How do we set the subscription price in a rights offering? If you think about it, in theory, the subscription price really does not matter. It has to be below the market price of the stock for the rights to have value, but, beyond this, the price is arbitrary. In principle, it can be as low as we cared to make it as long as it is not zero.

In practice, however, the subscription price is typically 20 to 25 percent below the prevailing stock price. Once we recognize market inefficiencies and frictions, a subscription price too close to the share price may result in undersubscription due simply to market imperfections.

Cost of Rights Offerings

Until the early 1980s, rights offerings were the most popular method of raising new equity in Canada for seasoned issuers. (Obviously, rights offerings cannot be used for IPOs.) The reason was lower flotation costs from the simpler underwriting arrangements. In the late 1980s and early 1990s, with the rise of POP, bought deals replaced rights offers as the prevalent form of equity issue.

In the United States, firms use general cash offers much more often than rights offerings. This reliance on general cash offers has caused considerable debate among researchers because, as in Canada, rights offerings are usually much cheaper in terms of flotation costs . One study has found that firms making underwritten rights offers suffered substantially larger price drops than did firms making underwritten cash offers.[22] This is a hidden cost, and it may be part of the reason that underwritten rights offers are uncommon in the United States.

---

[22]Robert S. Hansen, "The Demise of the Rights Issue," *Review of Financial Studies* 1 (Fall 1988), pp. 289–309.

- How does a rights offering work?
- What questions must financial management answer in a rights offering?
- How is the value of a right determined?
- When does a rights offering affect the value of a company's shares?
- Does a rights offer cause a share price decrease? How are existing shareholders affected by a rights offer?

19.7   Hot New Issues Market on the TSE

An early 1993 headline read "New equity issues set sizzling pace." New issues, or IPOs, go through different growth stages. There may be a real boom in the number of public offerings in one year, and then a drought for four or five years. In 1992 and 1993, the new issues market broke many records. *The Globe and Mail* called it "leaving investors feeling a lot like kids in a candy store."[23] Hot new issues are often associated with a booming stock market and a strong economy. This trend held for 1993 when the TSE 300 passed its 1987 peak.

The 1993 record also included secondary issues—large blocks of stock resold by investors. In a record bought deal, the Hees-Edper group sold its 37-percent stake in Labatt to two groups of underwriters for just under $1 billion.[24]

CONCEPT QUESTION

- When you pick up a business newspaper and read about the hot new issues market, what does it mean?

19.8   Venture Capital

Previous sections of this chapter assume that the companies discussed are big enough and old enough to raise capital in the public equity markets. Of course, many firms have not reached this stage. These small, young firms may raise equity funds in the market for **venture capital.** Venture capital can be viewed as "early stage financing of new and young companies seeking to grow rapidly."[25] Such firms usually lack strong internal cash flow and the asset base to support internal financing or debt. Particularly in high-tech industries, the main assets are ideas and creative people. Following the pecking order theory, such firms seek equity financing.

Venture capital financing is tailored to the needs of this group of firms. Venture capital firms also take an active role in management and are prepared to provide

---

[23]"Torrid Cycles Drove New Issues in 1992," *The Globe and Mail* (January 4, 1993), p. B5.

[24]Erik Heinrich, "New Equity Issues Set Sizzling Pace," *The Financial Post* (March 20, 1993).

[25]S. E. Pratt, "Overview and Introduction to the Venture Capital Industry," *Guide to Venture Capital Sources,* 10th ed. (Wellesley Hills, Mass.: Venture Economics, 1987).

further financing if the firm is successful in generating growth. The venture capitalist's goal is to see the firm grow large enough to go public in an initial public offering so that the venture capital firm can "exit" with a gain. (In the case of smaller enterprises, management may buy the venture capitalist's shares.)

Stages of Venture Financing

A typical venture capital project might unfold in six stages of financing:[26]

1. *Seed-money stage.* A small amount of financing needed to prove a concept or develop a product. Marketing is not included in this stage.

2. *Start-up.* Financing for firms that started within the past year. Funds are likely to pay for marketing and product development expenditures.

3. *First-round financing.* Additional money to begin sales and manufacturing after a firm has spent its start-up funds.

4. *Second-round financing.* Funds earmarked for working capital for a firm that is currently selling its product but still losing money.

5. *Third-round financing.* Financing for a company that is at least breaking even and is contemplating an expansion. This is also known as *mezzanine financing.*

6. *Fourth-round financing.* Money provided for firms that are likely to go public within half a year. This round is also known as *bridge financing.*

The uncertainty inherent in new ventures makes venture capital more risky than investing in the equity of established firms. Venture capitalists express this risk in terms of a "two-six-two" rule. They expect that 10 venture capital investments will result in two losses, six cases of returns similar to investing in Treasury bills, and two successes with returns over 30 percent. The historical average returns on venture capital in Canada have been higher than TSE returns.

Suppliers of Financing

The Canadian venture capital industry had around $3.5 billion under management at the end of 1990.[27] Two types of private sector firms make up around two-thirds of the market in Canada. The largest category is *independent firms,* which manage venture capital funds for pension funds, individuals, and capital pools. *Venture affiliates* are funded by large parent corporations. Chartered banks, for example, participate in the venture capital market through affiliates in part as a response to criticism of their reluctance to lend to start-up ventures. Other firms, such as Bell Canada Enterprises (BCE), invest in firms developing related technological innovations.

Around one-third of venture capital activity has some government involvement. *Crown-related firms* are government-owned and include Innovation Ontario and the Venture Capital Division of the Federal Business Development Bank. Although capital

---

[26]A. V. Bruno and T. T. Tyebjee, "The Entrepreneur's Search for Capital," *Journal of Business Venturing* (Winter 1985).

[27]This section draws on material contained in the Venture Capital Industry Profile, which is published and updated by Industry, Science, and Technology Canada.

growth is important to these firms, their mandates include investing in depressed areas and targeting particular industries. *Hybrids* have a mix of government and private sector support. These firms include labour-sponsored venture capital firms and province-specific funds.

CONCEPT QUESTIONS

- What is venture capital and how does it differ from common equity issued by large corporations?
- What are the different stages for companies seeking venture capital financing?
- What are the different sources of venture capital financing?

Angoss Software Corp.—The Glare of Going Public

Lynne Stethem had a whirlwind year in 1993. Her software development company went public, opened offices overseas, made two acquisitions, and raised $2.2 million in a private placement of shares.

But fast growth in a public company puts new pressures on Ms. Stethem, 46, who now meets with investment dealers several times a month. The demands on her time are much greater than anticipated.

"Satisfying the expectations of the investment community becomes a major consideration," she says. "I wasn't prepared and had to adjust." Her company, Angoss Software Corp. (which stands for A New Generation of Software Solutions), is a study in how entrepreneurs' lives can change as their businesses seek outside funding. Ms. Stethem finds her management style under scrutiny as Angoss, like many young companies, has tapped capital markets to fuel its growth. Its shares are traded over the counter and will soon be listed on the Alberta Stock Exchange. The current price is $1.50, up from 65 cents earlier this year.

In one sense, British-born Ms. Stethem is still very much a rarity—a woman heading a software company in the male-dominated computer industry. Married with two school-aged children, she has to juggle domestic responsibilities. Ms. Stethem hopes Angoss will grow through acquisitions to $100 million in annual sales in the next four years—a goal those who work with her think is not beyond her reach.

Starting out as a systems analyst with T. Eaton Co., Ms. Stethem branched out as a computer consultant working out of her home. In 1984, she set up CS Computing Services Inc. to sell solutions for companies built around SmartWare, a practical office automation tool. In 1988, CS topped $1 million in sales.

But in 1989, SmartWare's developer was taken over by a California company and the product was allowed to languish. This presented an opportunity to Ms. Stethem, who wanted to move from consulting into software development. She signed a deal with Informix Software Inc. of Menlo Park, California, to market, develop and support SmartWare. In the process, she acquired a huge base of 500,000 business users in North America and Europe. (About 95 percent of sales are outside of Canada.)

(continued)

To pay for the acquisition, Ms. Stethem found a German company that agreed to buy part of her company, but later reneged. In desperate need of capital, she was introduced to Gornitzki Thompson & Little, a Toronto merchant banking firm that works with owner-operated businesses, in which it takes minority stakes. GTL put up bridge financing, then helped negotiate a new deal with Informix at a better price. CS Computing then merged with Eastmont Gold Mines Ltd., a shell company in which GTL had an interest, and was renamed Angoss Software Corp.

Most companies do an initial public offering of shares by filing a prospectus with a provincial securities commission. Angoss, however, engineered a reverse takeover of an inactive public company. A reverse takeover of this kind offers speed and assurance, GTL principal John Thompson says. Companies can wait so long for regulatory approval of an IPO that they have to cancel if the market turns unfavourable.

Investment dealers often lose interest in the firms they underwrite. But, GTL, with a 10 to 15 percent equity position, takes an active role in promoting Angoss and enhancing the value of its shares. Angoss is now spending $50,000 for a listing on the Alberta exchange, so that investment analysts outside Canada can follow it on their computer screens. It hopes to move to the U.S. NASDAQ market next year.

But Ms. Stethem had to do some fancy footwork when Angoss's third-quarter results showed a loss of $357,000 or 2 cents a share on revenue of $524,000. European sales are always slow in the summer, she explains, and many buyers held off acquiring the software, waiting for an upgrade that was late in arriving.

Ms. Stethem hopes to grow along the lines of Cognos, Inc., a large Ottawa-based company that shares the same market niche. But unlike Cognos, she has never received any federal funding. "We built our products and paid to build them with revenues as we went. That's why the products are so practical," she says.

Source: Ellen Roseman, "The Glare of Going Public," *The Globe and Mail* (November 29, 1993), p. B8. Used with permission.

Summary and Conclusions   19.9

This chapter looks at how corporate securities are issued.

1. The costs of issuing securities can be quite large. They are much lower (as a percentage) for larger issues.

2. For large issues, the bought deal type of underwriting is far more prevalent than regular underwriting. This is probably connected to the savings available through prompt offering prospectuses and concentrated selling efforts.

3. Direct and indirect costs of going public can be substantial. However, once a firm is public, it can raise additional capital more easily than private firms.

4. Rights offerings are cheaper than general cash offers. Even so, most new equity issues in the United States are underwritten general cash offers. In Canada, the bought deal is cheaper and dominates the new issue market.

Key Terms

Prospectus 551

Red herring 551

Tombstone 551

Syndicate (banking group) 553

Spread (discount) 553

Regular underwriting 553

Firm commitment underwriting 553

Best efforts underwriting 553

Bought deal 553

Initial public offering (IPO) 556

Ex-rights 569

Holder of record date 569

Standby underwriting 570

Standby fee 570

Oversubscription privilege 570

Venture capital 572

Suggested Readings

For further reading on underwriting in Canada and the role of the OSE, see:
Ontario Securities Commission Annual Reports.

J. Hatch and M. J. Robinson. *Investment Management in Canada,* 2d ed. Scarborough: Prentice-Hall Canada, 1989, chapters 4 and 7.

Summaries of recent research are found in:
R. Hansen. "Evaluating the Costs of a New Equity Issue." *Midland Corporate Finance Journal* (Spring 1986).

Roger G. Ibbotson, Jody L. Sindelar, and Jay R. Ritter. "Initial Public Offerings." *Journal of Applied Corporate Finance* 1 (Summer 1988).

W. Rotenberg. "Pricing Initial Public Equity Offerings: Who Wins, Who Loses and Why?" *Canadian Investment Review* (Spring 1990), pp. 17–24.

Questions and Problems

19.1 Megabucks Industries is planning to raise fresh equity capital by selling a large new issue of common stock. Megabucks is currently a publicly traded corporation, and it is trying to choose between a regular underwritten cash offer and a rights offering (not underwritten) to current shareholders. Megabucks management is interested in minimizing the selling costs and has asked you for advice on the choice of issue methods. What do you recommend and why?

19.2 Jelly Beans, Inc., is proposing a rights offering. Presently there are 100,000 outstanding shares at $25 each. There will be 10,000 new shares issued at $20.

    a. What is the value of a right?

    b. What is the ex-rights price?

    c. What is the new market value of the company?

    d. Why might a company have a rights offering rather than a cash offering?

19.3 Suppose the Newton Company has 10,000 shares of stock. Each share is worth $40, and the company's market value of equity is $400,000. Suppose the firm issues 5,000 shares of new stock at the following prices: $40, $20, $10. What will be the effect of each of the alternative offering prices on the existing price per share?

19.4 In 1993, a certain assistant professor of finance bought 12 initial public offerings of common stock . He held each for approximately one month and then sold. The investment rule he followed was to submit a purchase order for every initial public offering of oil and gas exploration companies. There were 22 of these offerings, and he submitted a purchase order for approximately $1,000 of stock for each company. With 10 of these, no shares were allocated to this assistant professor. With 5 of the 12 offerings that were purchased, fewer than the requested number of shares were allocated.

The year 1993 was very good for oil and gas exploration company owners. On average, of the 22 companies that went public, the stocks were selling for 80 percent above the offering price a month after the initial offering date. The assistant professor looked at his performance record and found the $8,400 invested in the 12 companies had grown to only $10,000, a return of only about 20 percent. (Commissions were negligible.) Did he have bad luck, or should he have expected to do worse than the average initial public offering investor? Explain.

19.5 The boxed material on the next page contains the cover page and summary of the prospectus for the initial public offering of the Pest Investigation Control Corporation (PICC), which is going public tomorrow with an initial public offering managed by investment dealer Erlanger and Ritter.

a. Assume that you know nothing about PICC other than the information contained in the prospectus. Based on your knowledge of finance, what is your prediction for the price of PICC tomorrow? Briefly explain your answer.

b. Assume that you have several thousand dollars to invest. When you get home from class tonight, you find that your stockbroker, whom you have not talked to for weeks, has left a message that PICC is going public tomorrow and that she can get you several hundred shares at the offering price if you call her back first thing in the morning. Discuss the merits of this opportunity.

19.6 Analyze the following statement: Because initial public offerings of common stock are always underpriced, an investor can make money by purchasing shares in these offerings.

19.7 Superior, Ltd., manufactures beta-blockers. (Consumers are just sick and tired of those pesky betas.) Management has concluded that additional equity financing is required to increase production capacity and that these funds are best attained through a rights offering. It has correctly concluded that, as a result of the rights offering, share price will fall from $50 to $45 ($50 being the rights-on price, $45 the ex-rights price). The company is seeking $5 million in additional funds with a per share subscription price equal to $25.

PROSPECTUS PICC
200,000 shares
PEST INVESTIGATION CONTROL CORPORATION

Of the shares being offered hereby, all 200,000 are being sold by the Pest Investigation Control Corporation, Inc. ("the Company"). Before the offering there has been no public market for the shares of PICC, and no guarantee can be given that any market will develop.

These securities have not been approved or disapproved by the OSC nor has the commission passed upon the accuracy or adequacy of this prospectus.

This is an initial public offering. The common shares are being offered, subject to prior sale, when, as, and if delivered to and accepted by the Underwriters and subject to approval of certain legal matters by their Counsel and by Counsel for the Company. The Underwriters reserve the right to withdraw, cancel, or modify such offer and to reject offers in whole or in part.

	Price to public	Underwriting discount	Proceeds to company*
Per share	$11.00	$1.10	$9.90
Total	$2,200,000	$220, 000	$1,980,000

*Before deducting expenses estimated at $27,000 payable by the company.

- -

ERLANGER AND RITTER, INVESTMENT DEALERS
April 12, 1994
Prospectus Summary

The Company The Pest Investigation Control Corporation (PICC) breeds and markets toads and tree frogs as ecologically safe insect-control mechanisms.

The Offering 200,000 shares of common stock, no par value.

Listing The company will trade over the counter.

Shares Outstanding As of March 31, 1994, 400,000 shares of common stock were outstanding. After the offering, 600,000 shares of common stock will be outstanding.

Use of Proceeds To finance expansion of inventory and receivables and general working capital, and to pay for country club memberships for certain finance professors.

How many shares were there before the offering? (Assume that the increment to the market value of the equity equals the gross proceeds from the offering.)

19.8 The Lemon Co. and the Lime Co. have announced IPOs at $5 per share. One of these is undervalued by $1, while the other is overvalued by $.50. But citrus fruits are not your specialty, so you have no way of knowing which is which. You plan on buying 100 shares of each. If an issue is underpriced, it will be rationed, and you will only get half your order. If you get 100 shares in Lemon and 100 in Lime, what will your profit be? What profit do you actually expect? What principle have you illustrated?

19.9 A publisher has announced a rights offer to raise $50 million for a new journal, *The Journal of Financial Excess*. This publication will review potential articles after the author pays a nonrefundable reviewing fee of $3,000 per page. The stock currently sells for $25 per share and there are 22 million shares outstanding.

   a. What is the maximum possible subscription price? What is the minimum?

   b. If the subscription price is set at $15 per share, how many shares must be sold? How many rights will it take to buy one share?

   c. What is the ex-rights price? What is the value of a right?

   d. Show how a shareholder with 100 shares and no desire (or money) to buy additional shares is not harmed by the rights offer.

19.10 The Peter Publishing Partnership, Inc., is considering a rights offer. The company has determined that the ex-rights price will be $20. The current price is $40 per share, and there are 10 million shares outstanding. The rights offer would raise a total of $40 million. What is the subscription price?

CHAPTER 20

Long-Term Debt

The previous chapter introduced the mechanics of new long-term financing, with an emphasis on equity. This chapter takes a closer look at long-term debt instruments.

The chapter begins with a review of the basic features of long-term debt and a description of some important aspects of publicly issued long-term bonds. We also discuss forms of long-term financing that are not publicly issued: term loans and private placement bonds. These are directly placed with lending institutions such as chartered banks and life insurance companies.

All bond agreements have protective covenants. These are restrictions on the firm that protect the bondholder. We present several types of protective covenants in this chapter.

Most publicly issued corporate bonds have call provisions, which enable a company to buy back its bonds at a predetermined call price. This chapter attempts to answer two questions about call provisions:

1. Should firms issue callable bonds?
2. When should such bonds be called?

Financial engineering has produced many different kinds of long-term bonds. We discuss zero coupon bonds, floating rate bonds, and other special types of bonds and then analyze what types of bonds are best in different circumstances.

Long-Term Debt: A Review   20.1

Long-term debt securities are promises by the issuing firm to repay principal and to pay interest on the unpaid balance. The *maturity* of a long-term debt instrument refers to the length of time the debt remains outstanding with some unpaid balance. Debt securities can be *short-term* (maturities of one year or less) or *long-term* (maturities of more than one year).[1] Short-term debt is sometimes referred to as *unfunded debt;* long-term debt is sometimes called *funded debt.*[2]

The two major forms of long-term debt are public issue and privately placed debt. We discuss public issue bonds first, and most of what we say about them holds true for

---

[1] In addition, people often refer to *intermediate-term debt,* which has a maturity of more than one year and less than three to five years.

[2] The word *funding* generally implies long-term. Thus, a firm planning to *fund* its debt requirements may be replacing short-term debt with long-term debt.

privately placed long-term debt as well. The main difference between publicly issued and privately placed debt is that private debt is directly placed with a lending institution.

There are many other attributes of long-term debt, including security, seniority, call features, sinking funds, ratings, and protective covenants. The boxed material illustrates many of these attributes.

Features of a Hypothetical Bond

Terms		Explanation
Amount of issue	$50 million	The company will issue $50 million of bonds.
Date of issue	4/15/95	The bonds will be sold on April 15, 1995.
Maturity	4/15/25	The principal will be paid in 30 years, on April 15, 2025.
Face value	$1,000	The denomination of the bonds is $1,000.
Annual coupon	8.50	Each bondholder will receive $85 per bond per year.
Offer price	100	The offer price will be 100 percent of the $1,000 face value per bond.
Yield to maturity	8.50%	If the bond is held to maturity, bondholders will receive a stated annual rate of return equal to 8.5 percent.
Coupon payment	10/15, 4/15	Coupons of $85/2 = $42.50 will be paid on October 15 and April 15.
Security	None	The bonds are debentures.
Sinking fund	Annual	The firm will make annual payments toward the sinking fund.
Call provision	Not callable before 4/15/05	The bonds have a deferred call feature.
Call price	$1,100	After 10 years, the company can buy back the bonds for $1,100 per bond.
Rating	CBRS A++	This is CBRS's highest rating. The bonds have the lowest probability of default.

20.2 The Public Issue of Bonds

The general procedures followed in a **public issue** of bonds are the same as those for stocks. The issue must be registered with the OSC and any other relevant provincial securities commissions, there must be a prospectus, and so on. The registration statement for a public issue of bonds, however, is different from the one for common stock. For bonds, the registration statement must indicate an indenture.

An **indenture** is a written agreement between the corporation (the borrower) and a trust company. It is sometimes referred to as the *deed of trust*.[3] The trust company is

---

[3]The terms *loan agreement* and *loan contract* are usually used for privately placed debt and term loans.

appointed by the corporation to represent the bondholders. The trust company must (1) be sure the terms of the indenture are obeyed, (2) manage the sinking fund, and (3) represent bondholders if the company defaults on its payments.

The typical bond indenture can be a document of several hundred pages. It generally incudes:

1. The basic terms of the bonds.
2. A description of property used as security.
3. The seniority of the bonds.
4. Details of the protective covenants.
5. The sinking fund arrangements.
6. The call provision.

Each of these is discussed below.

The Basic Terms

Bonds usually have a *face value* of $1,000. This is also called the *principal value* and it is stated on the bond certificate. In addition, the *par value* (i.e., initial accounting value) of a bond is almost always the same as the face value.

Transactions between bond buyers and bond sellers determine the market value of the bond. Actual bond market values depend on the general level of interest rates, among other factors, and need not equal the face value. Because the Canadian corporate bond market is quite illiquid, there is a good chance that it is not fully efficient. For this reason, there is likely a good payoff for investment dealers and issuers who pioneer financial engineering innovations. The bond price is quoted as a percentage of the face value. Though interest is paid only twice a year, interest *accrues* continually over the year. This is illustrated in the example below.

▪ *Example*

Suppose the Black Corporation has issued 100 bonds. The amount stated on each bond certificate is $1,000. The total face value or principal value of the bonds is $100,000. Further suppose the bonds are currently *priced* at 100, which means 100 percent of $1,000. This means that buyers and sellers are holding bonds at a price per bond of $1,000. If interest rates rise, the price of the bond might fall to, say, 97, which means 97 percent of $1,000 (or $970). ▪

Suppose the bonds have a stated interest rate of 12 percent due on January 1, 2050. The bond indenture might read:

> The bond will mature on January 1, 2050, and will be limited in aggregate principal amount to $100,000. Each bond will bear interest at the rate of 12.0 percent per annum from January 1, 1990, or from the most recent Interest Payment Date to which interest has been paid or provided for. Interest is payable semiannually on July 1 and January 1 of each year.

Suppose an investor buys the bonds on April 1. Since the last interest payment, on January 1, three months of interest at 12 percent per year would have accrued. Because interest of 12 percent a year works out to 1 percent per month, interest over the three months is 3 percent. Therefore, the buyer of the bond must pay a price of 100 percent plus the 3 percent of accrued interest ($30). On July 1, the buyer will receive an interest payment of $60. This can be viewed as the sum of the $30 he or she paid the seller plus the three months of interest, $30, for holding the bond from April 1 to July 1.

As is typical of corporate bonds, the Black bonds are registered. The indenture might read:

> Interest is payable semiannually on July 1 and January 1 of each year to the person in whose name the bond is registered at the close of business on June 15 or December 15, respectively.

This means that the company has a registrar who will record the ownership of each bond. The company will pay the interest and principal by cheque mailed directly to the address of the owner of record.

When a bond is registered with attached coupons, the bondholder must separate a coupon from the bond certificate and send it to the company registrar (paying agent). Some bonds are in **bearer** form. This means that ownership is not recorded in the company books. As with a registered bond with attached coupons, the holder of the bond certificate separates the coupon and sends it in to the company to receive payment.

There are two drawbacks to bearer bonds. First, they can be easily lost or stolen. Second, because the company does not know who owns its bonds, it cannot notify bondholders of important events. Consider, for example, Mr. and Mrs. Smith, who go to their safety deposit box and clip the coupon on their 12-percent, $1,000 bond issued by the Black Company. They send the coupon to the paying agent and feel richer. A few days later, a notice comes from the paying agent that the bond was retired and its principal paid off one year earlier. In other words, the bond no longer exists. Mr. and Mrs. Smith must forfeit one year of interest. (Of course, they can turn their bond in for $1,000.)

However, bearer bonds have the advantage of secrecy because even the issuing company does not know who the bond's owners are. The bearer form of ownership also eases transactions for investors who trade their bonds frequently.

Security

Debt securities are also classified according to the *collateral* protecting the bondholder. Collateral is a general term for the assets that are pledged as security for payment of debt. For example, *collateral trust bonds* involve a pledge of common stock held by the corporation.

■ *Example*

Suppose Railroad Holding Company owns all of the common stock of Track, Inc.; that is, Track, Inc., is a wholly owned subsidiary of the Railroad Holding Company. Railroad issues debt securities that pledge the common stock of Track, Inc., as collateral. The debts are collateral trust bonds; a trust company will hold them. If Railroad Holding Company defaults on the debt, the trust company will be able to sell the stock of Track, Inc., to satisfy Railroad's obligation. ■

Mortgage securities are secured by a mortgage on real estate or other long-term assets of the borrower.[4] The legal document that describes that mortgage is called a *mortgage-trust indenture* or *trust deed.* The mortgage can be *closed-end,* so that there is a limit as to the amount of bonds that can be issued. More frequently it is *open-end,* without limit to the amount of bonds that may be issued.

■ *Example*

Suppose the Yukon Land Company has buildings and land worth $10 million and a $4 million mortgage on these properties. If the mortgage is closed-end, the Yukon Land Company cannot issue more bonds on this property.

If the bond indenture contains no clause limiting the amount of additional bonds that can be issued, it is an open-end mortgage. In this case, the Yukon Land Company can issue additional bonds on its property, making the existing bonds riskier. For example, if additional mortgage bonds of $2 million are issued, the property has been pledged for a total of $6 million of bonds. If Yukon Land Company must liquidate its property for $4 million, the original bondholders will receive ⁴⁄₆, or 67 percent, of their investment. If the mortgage had been closed-end, they would have received 100 percent of the stated value. ■

The value of a mortgage depends on the market value of the underlying property. For this reason, mortgage bonds sometimes require that the property be properly maintained and insured. Of course, a building and equipment bought in 1914 for manufacturing slide rules might not have much value, no matter how well the company maintains it. The value of any property ultimately depends on its next best economic use. Bond indentures cannot easily insure against losses in economic value.

Sometimes mortgages are on specific property, for example, a single building. More often, blanket mortgages are used. A blanket mortgage pledges many assets owned by the company.

Some bonds represent unsecured obligations of the company. A **debenture** is an unsecured bond, where no specific pledge of property is made. Debenture holders have a claim on property not otherwise pledged: the property that remains after mortgages and collateral trusts are taken into account. Almost all public bonds issued by industrial and finance companies are debentures. However, most utility bonds are secured by a pledge of assets.

---

[4]A set of railroad cars is an example of "other long-term assets" used as security.

Seniority

In general terms, *seniority* indicates preference in position over other lenders, and debts are sometimes labelled "senior" or "junior" to indicate seniority. Some debt is *subordinated,* as in, for example, a subordinated debenture.

In the event of default, holders of subordinated debt must give preference to other special creditors. Usually, this means that the subordinated lenders are paid off from cash flow and asset sales only after the specified creditors have been compensated. However, debt cannot be subordinated to equity.

Protective Covenants

A **protective covenant** is that part of the indenture or loan agreement that limits certain actions of the borrowing company. Protective covenants can be classified into two types: negative covenants and positive covenants. A **negative covenant** limits or prohibits actions that the company may take. Here are some typical examples:

1. Limitations are placed on the amount of dividends a company may pay.
2. The firm cannot pledge any of its assets to other lenders.
3. The firm cannot merge with another firm.
4. The firm may not sell or lease its major assets without approval by the lender.
5. The firm cannot issue additional long-term debt.

A **positive covenant** specifies an action that the company agrees to take or a condition the company must abide by. Here are some examples:

1. The company agrees to maintain its working capital at a minimum level.
2. The company must furnish periodic financial statements to the lender.

The financial implications of protective covenants were treated in detail in the chapters on capital structure. In that discussion, we argued that protective covenants can benefit shareholders because, if bondholders are assured that they will be protected in times of financial stress, they will accept a lower interest rate.

The Sinking Fund

Bonds can be entirely repaid at maturity, at which time the bondholder will receive the stated value of the bond, or they can be repaid before maturity. Early repayment is more typical.

In a direct placement of debt the repayment schedule is specified in the loan contract. For public issues, the repayment takes place through the use of a sinking fund and a call provision.

A **sinking fund** is an account managed by the bond trustee for the purpose of repaying the bonds. Typically, the company makes yearly payments to the trustee. The trustee can purchase bonds in the market or can select bonds randomly using a lottery and purchase them, generally at face value. There are many different kinds of sinking fund arrangements:

> Most sinking funds start between 5 and 10 years after the initial issuance.
>
> Some sinking funds establish equal payments over the life of the bond.
>
> Most high-quality bond issues establish payments to the sinking fund that are not sufficient to redeem the entire issue. As a consequence, there is the possibility of a large *balloon* payment at maturity.

Sinking funds have two opposing effects on bondholders:

1. *Sinking funds provide extra protection to bondholders.* A firm experiencing financial difficulties would have trouble making sinking fund payments. Thus, sinking fund payments provide an early warning system to bondholders.

2. *Sinking funds give the firm an attractive option.* If bond prices fall below the face value, the firm will satisfy the sinking fund by buying bonds at the lower market prices. If bond prices rise above the face value, the firm will buy the bonds back at the lower face value.

The Call Provision

A *call provision* lets the company repurchase or *call* the entire bond issue at a predetermined price over a specified period.

Generally, the call price is above the bond's face value of $1,000. The difference between the call price and the face value is the **call premium.** For example, if the call price is 105 (that is, 105 percent of $1,000), the call premium is 50. The amount of the call premium usually becomes smaller over time. One typical arrangement is to set the call premium initially equal to the annual coupon payment and then make it decline to zero over the life of the bond.

Call provisions are not usually operative during the first few years of a bond's life. For example, a company may be prohibited from calling its bonds for the first 10 years. This is referred to as a **deferred call.** During this period, the bond is said to be **call protected.**[5]

CONCEPT QUESTIONS

- Do bearer bonds have any advantage? Why might Mr. "I Like to Keep My Affairs Private" prefer to hold bearer bonds?
- What advantages and disadvantages do bondholders derive from provisions of sinking funds?
- What is a call provision? What is the difference between the call price and the stated price?

---

[5]Many Canadian corporate bonds carry a covenant making them nonrefundable for financial advantage. Such bonds can never be called and refunded to take advantage of lower interest rates.

20.3 Bond Refunding

Replacing all or part of an issue of outstanding bonds is called bond **refunding.**
Usually, the first step in a typical bond refunding is to call the entire issue of bonds at
the call price. Bond refunding raises two questions:

1. Should firms issue callable bonds?
2. Given that callable bonds have been issued, when should the bonds be
   called?

We attempt to answer these questions in this section.

Should Firms Issue Callable Bonds?

Common sense tells us that call provisions have value. First, many publicly issued
bonds have call provisions. Second, it is obvious that a call works to the advantage of
the issuer. If interest rates fall and bond prices go up, the option to buy back the bonds
at the call price is valuable. In bond refunding, firms will typically replace the called
bonds with a new bond issue. The new bonds will have a lower coupon rate than the
called bonds.

However, bondholders will take the call provision into account when they buy the
bond. For this reason, we can expect that bondholders will demand higher interest
rates on callable bonds than on noncallable bonds. In fact, financial economists view
call provisions as being zero-sum in efficient capital markets.[6] Any expected gains to
the issuer from being allowed to refund the bond at lower rates will be offset by higher
initial interest rates. We illustrate the zero-sum aspect of callable bonds in the
following example.

▪ *Example*

Suppose Janine Intercable Company intends to issue perpetual bonds of $1,000 face
value at a 10-percent interest rate.[7] Annual coupons have been set at $100. There is an
equal chance that, by the end of the year, interest rates will either

1. Fall to $6\frac{2}{3}$ percent. If so, the bond price will increase to $1,500.
2. Increase to 20 percent. If so, the bond price will fall to $500. ▪

Noncallable Bond

Suppose the market price of the noncallable bond is the expected price it will have
next year plus the coupon, all discounted at the current 10-percent interest rate.[8] The
value of the noncallable bond is

---

[6]See A. Kraus, "An Analysis of Call Provisions and the Corporate Refunding Decision," *Midland Corporate Finance
Journal* 1 (Spring 1983), p. 1.

[7]Recall that perpetual bonds have no maturity date; their market price equals coupon/yield.

[8]We are assuming that the current price of the noncallable bonds is the expected value discounted at the risk-free rate of 10
percent. This is equivalent to assuming that the risk is unsystematic and carries no risk premium.

Value of Noncallable Bond:

$$\frac{\text{First-year coupon} + \text{Expected price at end of year}}{1 + r}$$

$$= \frac{\$100 + (0.5 \times \$1,500) + (0.5 \times \$500)}{1.10}$$

$$= \$1,000$$

Callable Bond

Now suppose the Janine Intercable Company decides to issue callable bonds. The call premium is set at $100 over par value and the bonds can be called *only* at the end of the first year.[9] In this case, the call provision will allow the company to buy back its bonds at $1,100 ($1,000 par value plus the $100 call premium). Should interest rates fall, the company will buy for $1,100 a bond that would be worth $1,500 in the absence of a call provision. Of course, if interest rates rise, Janine would not want to call the bonds for $1,100, because they are worth only $500 on the market.

Suppose rates fall and Janine calls the bonds by paying $1,100. If the firm simultaneously issues new bonds with a coupon of $100, it will bring in $1,500 (or $100/0.0667) at the 6⅔ percent interest rate. This will allow Janine to pay an extra dividend to shareholders of $400 (or $1,500 - $1,100). In other words, if rates fall from 10 percent to 6⅔ percent, exercise of the call will transfer $400 of potential bondholder gains to the shareholders.

When investors purchase callable bonds, they realize that they will forfeit their anticipated gains to shareholders if the bonds are called. As a consequence, they will not pay $1,000 for a callable bond with a coupon of $100.

How high must the coupon on the callable bond be so that it can be issued at the par value of $1,000? We can answer this in three steps.

Step 1: Determining End-of-Year Value If Interest Rates Drop　　If the interest rate drops to 6⅔ percent by the end of the year, the bond will be called for $1,100. The bondholder will receive both this amount and the annual coupon payment. If we let C represent the coupon on the callable bond, the bondholder gets the following at the end of the year:

$$\$1,100 + C$$

Step 2: Determining End-of Year Value If Interest Rates Rise　　If interest rates rise to 20 percent, the value of the bondholder's position at the end of the year is

$$\frac{C}{0.20} + C$$

That is, the perpetuity formula tells us that the bond will sell at $C/0.20$. In addition, the bondholder receives the coupon payment at the end of the year.

---

[9]Normally, bonds can be called over a period of many years. Our assumption that the bond can only be called at the end of the first year is introduced for simplicity.

Step 3: Solving for C   Because interest rates are equally likely to rise or to fall, the expected value of the bondholder's end-of-year position is

$$(\$1,100 + C) \times 0.5 + \left(\frac{C}{0.20} + C\right) \times 0.5$$

Using the current interest rate of 10 percent, we set the present value of these payments equal to par:

$$\$1,000 = \frac{(\$1,100 + C) \times 0.5 + \left(\frac{C}{0.20}\right) + C \times 0.5}{1.10}$$

C is the unknown in the equation. The equation holds if $C = \$157.14$. In other words, callable bonds can sell at par only if their coupon rate is 15.714 percent.

The Paradox Restated

If Janine issues a noncallable bond, it will only need to pay a 10-percent interest rate. By contrast, Janine must pay an interest rate of 15.7 percent on a callable bond. The interest rate differential makes an investor indifferent between the two bonds in our example. Because the return to the investor is the same with either bond, the cost of debt capital is the same to Janine with either bond. Thus, our example suggests that there is neither an advantage nor a disadvantage from issuing callable bonds.

If this analysis is correct, why are callable bonds issued in the real world? This question has vexed financial economists for a long time. We now consider four specific reasons why a company might use a call provision:

1. Superior interest rate predictions.
2. Taxes.
3. Financial flexibility for future investment opportunities.
4. Less interest rate risk.

Superior Interest Rate Forecasting

Company insiders may know more about interest rate changes on its bonds than does the investing public. For example, managers may be better informed about potential changes in the firm's credit rating. Thus, a company may prefer the call provision at a particular time because it believes that the expected fall in interest rates (the probability of a fall multiplied by the amount of the fall) is greater than the bondholders believe.

Although this is possible, there is reason to doubt that inside information is the rationale for call provisions. Suppose firms really had superior ability to predict changes that would affect them. Bondholders would infer that a company expected an improvement in its credit rating whenever it issued callable bonds. Bondholders would require an increase in the coupon rate to protect them against a call if this occurred. As a result, we would expect that there would be no financial advantage to the firm from callable bonds over noncallable bonds.

Of course, there are many non–company-specific reasons why interest rates can fall. For example, the interest rate level is connected to the anticipated inflation rate. But it is difficult to see how companies could have more information about the general level of interest rates than other participants in the bond markets.

Taxes

Call provisions may have tax advantages if the bondholder is taxed at a lower rate than the company. We have seen that callable bonds have higher coupon rates than noncallable bonds. Because the coupons provide a deductible interest expense to the corporation and are taxable income to the bondholder, the corporation will gain more than a bondholder in a low tax bracket will lose. Presumably, some of the tax saving can be passed on the bondholders in the form of a high coupon.

Future Investment Opportunities

As we have explained, bond indentures contain protective covenants that restrict a company's investment opportunities. For example, protective covenants may limit the company's ability to acquire another firm or to sell certain assets (for example, a division of the company). If the covenants are sufficiently restrictive, the cost to the shareholders in lost net present value can be large. However, if bonds are callable, the company can buy back the bonds at the call price and take advantage of a superior investment opportunity.[10]

Less Interest Rate Risk

The call provision will reduce the sensitivity of a bond's value to changes in the level of interest rates. As interest rates increase, the value of a noncallable bond will fall. Because the callable bond has a higher coupon rate, the value of a callable bond will fall less than the value of a noncallable bond. Kraus has argued that, by reducing the sensitivity of a bond's value to changes in interest rates, the call provision may reduce the risk to shareholders as well as bondholders.[11] He argues that, because the bond is a liability of the corporation, the equityholders bear risk as the bond changes value over time. Thus, it can be shown that, under certain conditions, reducing the risk of bonds through a call provision will also reduce the risk of equity.

Calling Bonds: When Does It Make Sense?

The value of the company is the value of the stock plus the value of the bonds. From the Modigliani–Miller theory and the pie model in earlier chapters, we know that firm value is unchanged by how it is divided between these two instruments. Therefore,

---

[10]This argument is from Z. Bodie and R. A. Taggart, "Future Investment Opportunities and the Value of the Call Provision on a Bond," *Journal of Finance* 33 (1978), p. 4.

[11]A. Kraus, "An Analysis of Call Provisions and the Corporate Refunding Decision," points out that the call provision will not always reduce the equity's interest rate risk. If the firm as a whole bears interest rate risk, more of this risk may be shifted from equityholders to bondholders with noncallable debt. In this case, equityholders may actually bear more risk with callable debt.

maximizing shareholder wealth means minimizing the value of the callable bonds. In a world with no transactions costs, it can be shown that the company should call its bonds whenever the callable bond value exceeds the call price. This policy minimizes the value of the callable bonds.

The preceding analysis is modified slightly by including the costs from issuing new bonds. These extra costs change the refunding rule to allow bonds to trade at prices above the call price. The objective of the company is to minimize the sum of the value of the callable bonds plus new issue costs. It has been observed that many real world firms do not call their bonds when the market value of the bonds reaches the call price. Perhaps these issue costs are the explanation.[12]

▪ *Example*

The Nipigon Lake Mining Co. has a $20 million outstanding bond issue bearing a 16 percent coupon that it issued in 1986. The bonds mature in 2001 but were callable in 1992 for a 6-percent call premium. Nipigon Lake's investment banker has assured them that up to $30 million of new nine-year bonds maturing in 2001 can be sold carrying an 11-percent coupon. To eliminate timing problems with the two issues, the new bonds will be sold a month before the old bonds are to be called. Nipigon Lake will have to pay the coupons on both issues during this month but can defray some of the cost by investing the issue at 8.5 percent, the short-term interest rate. Flotation costs for the $20 million new issue would total $1,125,000 and Nipigon Lake's marginal tax rate is 40 percent. Construct a framework to determine whether it is in Nipigon Lake's best interest to call the previous issue. ▪

In constructing a framework to analyze a refunding operation, there are three steps: cost of refunding, interest savings, and the NPV of the refunding operation. All work described here is illustrated in Table 20.1.

Cost of Refunding

The first step in this framework consists of the call premium, the flotation costs, the related tax savings, and any extra interest that must be paid or can be earned.

Call Premium

Call premium = 0.06 × ($20,000,000) = $1,200,000

Note that a call premium is not a tax-deductible expense.

Flotation Costs   Although flotation costs are a one-time expense, for tax purposes they are amortized over the life of the issue or five years, whichever is less. For Nipigon Lake, flotation costs amount to $1,125,000. This results in an annual expense for the first five years after the issue:

$1,125,000/5 = $225,000

---

[12]"Pulling the trigger" on a bond refunding extinguishes the option to wait. This option has value if rates are volatile. A. J. Kalotay, "The Sure Thing; Bond Refunding: How Operations Research Made Its Mark on Wall Street," *OR/MS Today* (April 1993), explains how this option modifies bond refunding rules.

Table 20.1 Bond refunding worksheet

	Amount before tax	Amount after tax	Time period	6.6 percent PV factor	PV
PV Cost of Refunding					
Call premium		$1,200,000	0	1.0000	$1,200,000
Flotation costs on new issue		$1,125,000	0	1.0000	1,125,000
Tax savings on new issue flotation costs		−90,000	1–5	4.1445	−373,005
Extra interest on old issue	$ 266,667	160,000	0	1.0000	160,000
Interest on short-term investment	−141,667	−85,000	0	1.0000	−85,000
Total after-tax investment					$2,026,995
Interest savings for the refunding issue: $t = 1 - 9$					
Interest on old bond	3,200,000	1,920,000			
Interest on new bond	2,200,000	1,320,000			
Net interest savings	$1,000,000	$ 600,000	1–9	6.6276	$3,976,560
NPV for refunding operation					
NPV = PV of interest savings − PV of cost refunding					$1,949,565

Flotation costs produce an annual tax shield of $90,000:

$225,000 \times (0.4) = \$90,000$

Tax Savings   The tax savings on the flotation costs are a five-year annuity and will be discounted at the after-tax cost of debt $(11\%(1-.40)=6.6\%)$. This amounts to a savings of $373,005. Therefore, the total flotation costs of issuing debt are

Flotation costs	$1,125,000
PV of tax savings	(373,005)
Total after-tax cost	$ 751,995

Additional interest   Extra interest paid on old issue totals:

$$\$20,000,000 \times (16\% \times 1/12) = \$266,667$$
After-tax interest: $266,667 \times (1 - .40) = \$160,000$

By investing the proceeds of the new issue at short-term interest rates, some of this expense can be avoided:

$$\$20,000,000 \times (8.5\% \times 1/12) = \$141,667$$
After-tax investment proceeds: $141,667 \times (1 - .40) = \$85,000$

The total additional interest is

Extra interest paid	$160,000
Extra interest earned	(85,000)
Total additional interest	$75,000

These three items amount to a total after-tax investment of

Call premium	$1,200,000
Flotation costs	751,995
Additional interest	75,000
Total investment	$2,026,995

Interest Savings on New Issue

$$\text{Interest on old bond} = \$20,000,000 \times 16\% = \$3,200,000$$
$$\text{Interest on new bond} = \$20,000,000 \times 11\% = \$2,200,000$$
$$\text{Annual savings} = \$1,000,000$$
$$\text{After-tax savings} = \$1,000,000 \times (1-.40) = \$600,000$$
$$\text{PV of annual savings over 9 years} = \$600,000 \times 6.6276 = \$3,976,560$$

NPV for the Refunding Operation

Interest savings	$3,976,560
Investment	(2,026,995)
NPV	$1,949,565

Nipigon Lake can save almost $2 million by proceeding with a call on its old bonds. The interest rates used in this example follow closely the actual interest rates during the 1980s. The example illustrates why firms would want to include a call provision when interest rates are very high.

CONCEPT QUESTIONS

- What are the advantages to a firm of having a call provision?
- What are the disadvantages to bondholders of having a call provision?

20.4   Bond Ratings

Firms frequently pay to have their debt rated. The two leading bond-rating firms in Canada are Canadian Bond Rating Service (CBRS) and Dominion Bond Rating Service (DBRS). Moody's and Standard & Poor's (S&P) are the largest U.S. bond raters; they often rate Canadian companies that raise funds in U.S. bond markets.[13] The debt ratings are an assessment of the creditworthiness of the corporate issuer. The definitions of creditworthiness used by bond-rating agencies are based on how likely the firm is to default and the protection creditors have in the event of a default.

It is important to recognize that bond ratings *only* concern the possibility of default. Bond ratings do not address the issue of interest rate risk. As a result, the price of a highly rated bond can still be volatile.

---

[13]They also rate bonds issued by the individual provinces and the federal government.

AAA	Bonds which are rated AAA are of the highest investment quality. The degree of protection afforded principal and interest is of the highest order. Earnings are relatively stable, the structure of the industry in which the company operates is very strong, and the outlook for future profitability is extremely favourable. There are few qualifying factors present which would detract from the performance of the company, and the strength of liquidity ratios is unquestioned for the industry in which the company operates.
AA	Bonds rated AA are of superior investment quality, and protection of interest and principal is considered high. In many cases, they differ from bonds rated AAA to a small degree.
A	Bonds rated A are upper-medium-grade securities. Protection of interest and principal is still substantial, but the degree of strength is less than with AA-rated companies. Companies in this category may be more susceptible to adverse economic conditions.
BBB	Bonds rated BBB are medium-grade securities. Protection of interest and principal is considered adequate, but the company may be more susceptible to economic cycles, or there may be other adversities present which reduce the strength of these bonds.
BB	Bonds rated BB are lower-medium-grade obligations and are considered mildly speculative and below average. The degree of protection afforded interest and principal is uncertain, particularly during periods of economic recession, and the size of the company may be relatively small.
B	Bonds rated B are "middle" speculative. Uncertainty exists as to the ability of the company to pay interest and principal on a continuing basis in the future, especially in periods of economic recession.
CCC	Bonds rated CCC are considered highly speculative and are in danger of default of interest and principal. The degree of adverse elements present is more severe than bonds rated B.
CC	Bonds rated CC are in default of either interest or principal, and other severe adverse elements are present.
C	C is the lowest rating provided. Bonds rated C differ from bonds rated CC with respect to the relative liquidation values.
NR	For certain companies, we may complete the editorial, yet not rate the company formally, in which case we would rate it NR, or "not rated."
High or low	In addition to the above, our ratings may be modified by the quotation "high" or "low" to indicate the relative standing within a rating classification.
Highest rating	Please note that the rating quoted at the top left of the front page of a report indicates the rating of the highest order of securities issued by the company.

Table 20.2
Descriptions of ratings used by Dominion Bond Rating Service

Source: Used with permission of Dominion Bond Rating Service.

Bond ratings are constructed from information supplied by the corporation. The rating classes and some information concerning them are shown in the accompanying table and Table 20.2.

	Investment quality bond ratings				Low-quality, speculative, and/or "junk"					
	High grade		Medium grade		Low grade		Very low grade			
Dominion Bond Rating Service	AAA	AA	A	BBB	BB	B	CCC	CC	C	N/R
Canadian Bond Rating Service	A++	A+	A	B++	B+	B	C	D	N/R	

The highest rating a firm can have is AAA or A++, and such debt is judged to be the best quality and to have the lowest degree of risk. This rating is not awarded very often; AA or A+ ratings indicate very good quality debt and are much more common. Investment grade bonds are bonds rated at least BBB. The lowest ratings are for debt that is in default. In the 1980s, a growing part of corporate borrowing has taken the form of *low-grade bonds*. These bonds are also known as either *high yield* or *junk bonds*. Low-grade bonds are corporate bonds that are rated below *investment grade* by the major rating agencies.

Bond ratings are important, because bonds with lower ratings tend to have higher interest costs. However, the most recent evidence is that bond ratings merely reflect bond risk. There is no conclusive evidence that bond ratings affect risk.[14] It is not surprising that the stock prices and bond prices of firms do not show any unusual behaviour on the days around a rating change. Because the ratings are based on publicly available information, they probably do not, in themselves, supply new information to the market.[15]

Junk Bonds

The investment community in the United States has labelled bonds with a Standard & Poor's rating of BB and below or a Moody's rating of Ba and below as **junk bonds.** These bonds are also called *high yield* or *low-grade*—we shall use all three terms interchangably. Issuance of junk bonds has grown greatly in recent years, leading to increased public interest in this form of financing.

Original-issue junk bonds have never been a major source of funds in Canadian capital markets. Their niche has been filled in part by preferred shares and, to a lesser extent, income bonds.

Table 20.3 presents data on junk bond financing from 1985 through 1991. Column 1 shows the great growth in junk bond issuance over a six-year period. Column 3 shows the default rate on junk bonds increased from 1.68 percent in 1985 to 9.01 percent in 1991. The losses experienced are shown in column 6. These losses have averaged about 3.88 percent (of par) over this six-year period.

In our opinion, the growth in junk bond financing can better be explained by the activities of one man than by a number of economic factors. While a graduate student at the University of Pennsylvania's Wharton School in the 1970s, Michael Milkin observed a large difference between the return on high yield bonds and the return on safer bonds. Believing that this difference was greater than what the extra default risk would justify, he concluded that institutional investors would benefit from purchases of junk bonds.

His later employment at Drexel Burnham Lambert allowed him to develop the junk bond market. Milkin's salesmanship simultaneously increased the demand for junk bonds among institutional investors and the supply of junk bonds among corporations. However, with the collapse of the junk bond market and with Michael Milkin's conviction for securities fraud, Drexel found it necessary to declare bankruptcy.

---

[14]M. Weinstein, "The Systematic Risk of Corporate Bonds," *Journal of Financial and Quantitative Analysis* (September 1981); J. P. Ogden, "Determinants of Relative Interest Rate Sensitivity of Corporate Bonds," *Financial Management* (Spring 1987); and F. Reilly and M. Joehnk, "The Association between Market Based Risk Measures for Bonds and Bond Ratings," *Journal of Finance* (December 1976).

[15]M. Weinstein, "The Effect of a Ratings Change Announcement on Bond Price," *Journal of Financial Economics* 5 (1977). 20.1 Junk bonds: 1985–1991.

Year	(1) Par value outstanding (in $ millions)	(2) Par value of default (in $ millions)	(3) Default rate (%)	(4) Weighted price after default	(5) Weighted coupon (%)	(6) Default loss (%)
1991	$209,400	$18,862.0	9.01%	36.0	11.59%	6.29%
1990	210,000	18,354.0	8.74	23.4	12.94	7.26
1989	201,000	8,110.3	4.03	38.3	13.40	2.76
1988	159,223	3,944.2	2.48	43.6	11.91	1.54
1987	136,952	7,485.7	5.47	75.9	12.07	1.65
1986	92,985	3,155.8	3.39	34.5	10.61	2.40
1985	59,078	992.1	1.68	45.9	13.69	1.02
Weighted average 1985–91			5.70	40.63	12.34	3.88

Table 20.3
Junk bonds, 1985–1991

Source: Edward I. Altman, "Defaults and Returns on High Yield Bonds: An Update through 1991" (1992) unpublished paper.

The junk bond market revived in 1993 with smaller issues by foreign companies and smaller U.S. issuers. This market took on increased importance when junk bonds were used to finance mergers and other corporate restructurings. While a firm can only issue a small amount of high-grade debt, the same firm can issue much more debt if low-grade financing is allowed as well. Therefore, the use of junk bonds lets acquirers effect takeovers that they could not do with only traditional bond financing techniques. Drexel was particularly successful with this technique, primarily because its huge base of institutional clients allowed it to raise large sums of money quickly.

At this time, it is not clear how the great growth in junk bond financing has altered the returns on these instruments. On the one hand, financial theory indicates that the expected return on an asset should be negatively related to its marketability.[16] Because trading volume in junk bonds has greatly increased in recent years, their marketability has risen as well. This should lower the expected return on junk bonds, thereby benefiting corporate issuers. On the other hand, the increased interest in junk bond financing by corporations (the increase in the supply of junk bonds) is likely to raise the expected returns on these assets. The net effect of these two forces is unclear.[17]

Blume and Keim find that, from 1977 to 1986, the average rate of return on low-grade bonds was higher than the average rate of return on high-grade corporate bonds, while the standard deviation of return on junk bonds was *lower.*[18] This suggests that junk bonds have attractive investment characteristics. However, because the data prior to 1977 are so sketchy, one cannot easily determine how the recent growth in the junk bond market affected these bonds' rates of return.

---

[16]For example, see Y. Amihud and H. Mendelson, "Asset Pricing and the Bid-Ask Spread," *Journal of Financial Economics* (December 1986).

[17]The actual risk of junk bonds is not known with certainty because it is not easy to measure the default rate. Paul Asquith, David W. Mullins, Jr., and Eric D. Wolff, "Original Issue High Yield Bonds: Aging Analysis of Defaults, Exchanges, and Calls," *Journal of Finance* (September 1989), show that the default rate on junk bonds can be greater than 30 percent over the life of the bond. They look at cumulative default rates and find that of all junk bonds issued in 1977 and 1978, 34 percent had defaulted by December 31, 1988. Table 20.3 shows yearly default rates. Edward I. Altman, "Setting the Record Straight on Junk Bonds: A Review of the Research on Default Rates and Returns," *Journal of Applied Corporate Finance* (Summer 1990), shows that yearly default rates of 5 percent are consistent with cumulative default rates of over 30 percent. From 1992 to 1994, the default rate on junk bonds was under 3 percent; Jacqueline Doherty, "Junk Bond Market out of the Dumps," *The Financial Post* (January 1, 1994), p. 30.

[18]M. Blume and D. Keim, "Lower Grade Bonds: Their Risk and Returns," *Financial Analysts Journal* (July-August 1987).

The recent wave of U.S. corporate mergers has often resulted in dislocations and loss of jobs. Because of junk bond financing's role in these mergers, it has come under much criticism. The social policy implications of mergers are complex, and any final judgment on them is likely to be reserved for the distant future. At any rate, junk bond financing should not be implicated too strongly in either the social benefits or the social costs of the recent wave of mergers. Perry and Taggart point out that, contrary to popular belief, this form of financing accounts for only a few percent of all mergers.[19]

CONCEPT QUESTIONS

- List and describe the different bond-rating classes.
- Why don't bond prices change when bond ratings change?

20.5   Some Different Types of Bonds

Thus far, we have considered "plain vanilla" bonds. In this section, we look at some more unusual types, the products of financial engineering: zero coupon bonds, floating rate bonds, and others.

Financial Engineering

When financial managers or their investment bankers design new securities or financial processes, their efforts are referred to as *financial engineering*.[20] Successful financial engineering reduces and controls risk and minimizes taxes. It also seeks to reduce financing costs of issuing and servicing debt as well as costs of complying with rules laid down by regulatory authorities. Financial engineering is a response to the trends we discussed in Chapter 1: globalization and deregulation and greater competition in financial markets.

When applied to debt securities, financial engineering creates exotic, hybrid securities that have many features of equity but are treated as debt. For example, suppose a corporation issues a perpetual bond with interest payable solely from corporate income if and only if earned. Whether this is really a debt is hard to judge—it is primarily a legal and semantic issue. Courts and taxing authorities would have the final say.

Obviously, the distinction between debt and equity is very important for tax purposes. So one reason that corporations try to create a debt security that is really equity is to obtain the tax benefits of debt and the bankruptcy benefits (lower agency costs) of equity.

[19]K. Perry and R. Taggart, "The Growing Role of Junk Bonds in Corporate Finance," *Journal of Applied Corporate Finance* (Spring 1988).

[20]For more on financial engineering, see John D. Finnerty, "Financial Engineering in Corporate Finance: An Overview," in *Handbook of Financial Engineering,* ed. C. W. Smith and C. W. Smithson (New York: Harper Business, 1990).

As a general rule, equity represents an ownership interest, and it is a residual claim. This means that equity holders are paid after debt holders. As a result of this, the risks and benefits associated with owning debt and equity are different. To give just one example, the maximum reward for owning a straight debt security is ultimately fixed by the amount of the loan, whereas there is no necessary upper limit to the potential reward from owning an equity interest.

Financial engineers can alter this division of claims by selling bonds with warrants attached giving bondholders options to buy stock in the firm. These warrants allow holders to participate in future rewards beyond the face value of the debt. We discuss several examples of financial engineering for debt next.

Zero Coupon Bonds

A bond that pays no coupons at all must be offered at a price that is much lower than its stated value. Such bonds are called **zero coupon bonds** or just **zeros.**[21]

Suppose the DDB Company issues a $1,000 face value five-year zero coupon bond. The initial price is set at $497. It is straightforward to check that, at this price, the bonds yield 15 percent to maturity. The total interest paid over the life of the bond is $1,000 − 497 = $503.

For tax purposes, the issuer of a zero coupon bond deducts interest every year even though no interest is actually paid. Similarly, the owner must pay taxes on interest accrued every year as well even though no interest is actually received.[22] This second tax feature makes taxable zero coupon bonds less attractive to taxable investors. However, they are still a very attractive investment for tax-exempt investors with long-term dollar-denominated liabilities, such as pension funds, because the future dollar value is known with relative certainty. Zero coupon bonds, often in the form of stripped coupons, are attractive to individual investors for tax-sheltered Registered Retirement Savings Plans (RRSPs).

Because zero coupon bonds have no intermediate coupon payments, they are quite attractive to certain investors and quite unattractive to others. For example, consider an insurance company forecasting death benefit payments of $1,000,000 five years from today. The company would like to be sure that it will have the funds to pay off the liability in five years. It could buy five-year, zero coupon bonds with a face value of $1,000,000. The company is matching assets with liabilities here, a procedure that eliminates interest rate risk. That is, regardless of the movement of interest rates, the firm's set of zeros will always be able to pay off the $1,000,000 liability.

Conversely, the firm would be at risk if it bought coupon bonds instead. For example, if it bought five-year coupon bonds, it would need to reinvest the coupon payments through to the fifth year. Because interest rates in the future are not known with certainty today, one cannot be sure if the sum of bond principal plus coupon accumulation will be worth more or less than $1,000,000 by the fifth year.

---

[21]A bond issued with a very low coupon rate (as opposed to a zero coupon rate) is an original-issue, discount (OID) bond.

[22]Calculation of yearly interest on a zero coupon bond is governed by tax law and is not necessarily the true compound interest.

Now, consider a couple saving for their child's university education in 15 years. They *expect* that, with inflation, four years of university should cost $150,000 in 15 years. Thus, they buy 15-year, zero coupon bonds with a face value of $150,000.[23] If they have forecasted inflation perfectly (and if costs keep pace with inflation), their child's tuition will be fully funded. However, if inflation rises more than expected, the tuition would be more than $150,000. Because the zero coupon bonds produce a shortfall, the child might end up working his way through school. As an alternative, the parents might have considered rolling over Treasury bills. Because the yields on Treasury bills rise and fall with the inflation rate, this simple strategy is likely to cause less risk than the strategy with zeros.

The key to these examples is the distinction between nominal and real quantities. The insurance company's liability is $1,000,000 in *nominal* dollars. Because the face value of a zero coupon bond is a nominal quantity, the purchase of zeros eliminates risk. However, it is easier to forecast university costs in real terms than in nominal terms. Thus, a zero coupon bond is a poor choice to reduce the financial risk of a child's university education.

Floating Rate Bonds

The conventional bonds discussed in this chapter have *fixed dollar obligations* because the coupon rate is set as a fixed percentage of the par value. Similarly, the principal is set equal to the par value. Under these circumstances, the coupon payment and principal are completely fixed.

With **floating rate bonds (floaters),** the coupon payments are adjustable. The adjustments are tied to the Treasury bill rate or another short-term interest rate. For example, in 1990, the Royal Bank had outstanding $250 million of floating rate notes maturing in 2083. The coupon rate was set at 0.40 percent more than the bankers' acceptance rate.

Floating rate bonds were introduced to control the risk of price fluctuations as interest rates change. The bond pricing mathematics of Chapter 5 showed that a bond with a coupon equal to the market yield is priced at par. In practice, the value of a floating rate bond depends on exactly how the coupon payment adjustments are defined. In most cases, the coupon adjusts with a lag to some base rate, so the price can deviate from par within some range. For example, suppose a coupon rate adjustment is made on June 1. The adjustment might be based on the simple average of Treasury bill yields during the previous three months. In addition, the majority of *floaters* have the following features.

1. The holder has the right to redeem his or her note at par on the coupon payment date after some specified amount of time. This is called a *put provision,* and it is discussed later.

2. The coupon rate has a floor and a ceiling, meaning that the coupon is subject to a minimum and a maximum.

---

[23] A more precise strategy would be to buy zeros maturing in years 15, 16, 17, and 18, respectively. In this way, the bonds might mature just in time to meet tuition payments. Further, taxes are ignored in this example.

Other Types of Bonds

Since bonds are financial contracts, the possible features are only limited by the imagination of the parties involved. As a result, bonds can be fairly exotic, particularly some more recent issues. We discuss a few of the more common features and types next.

Income bonds are similar to conventional bonds, except that coupon payments are dependent on company income. Specifically, coupons are paid to bondholders only if the firm's income is sufficient. In Canada, income bonds are usually issued by firms in the process of reorganization to try to overcome financial distress. The firm can skip the interest payment on an income bond without being in default. Interest paid on income bonds is not tax deductible by the issuer. Since firms in financial distress generally have little taxable income, this disadvantage is reduced. Purchasers of income bonds must pay tax on interest received.

A *convertible bond* can be swapped for a fixed number of shares of stock anytime before maturity at the holder's option. Convertibles are a debt/equity hybrid that allow the holder to profit if the issuer's stock price rises.

A *retractable bond* or *put bond* allows the holder to force the issuer to buy the bond back at a stated price. As long as the issuer remains solvent, the put feature sets a floor price for the bond. It is therefore just the reverse of the call provision. Canada Savings Bonds (CSBs) are an example of retractable bonds. Holders of CSBs may sell them back to the Bank of Canada at any time (through any financial institution) at their par value plus accrued interest. Chapters 21 and 22 detail convertible bonds, call provisions, and put provisions.

A *stripped real return bond* is a zero coupon bond with inflation protection. These bonds, issued by the Government of Canada for the first time in 1993, have their principal indexed to inflation. Investors receive a known amount in real terms. This feature is designed to make zeros more attractive to investors such as the couple saving for their child's university education in our earlier example.[24]

A given bond may have many unusual features. For example, Merrill Lynch created a popular bond called a *liquid yield option note* or LYON ("lion"). Figuratively speaking, a LYON has everything but the kitchen sink; this bond is a callable, puttable, convertible, zero coupon, subordinated note. In 1991, Rogers Communications Inc. issued the first LYON in Canada. Valuing a bond of this sort can be quite complex.

CONCEPT QUESTIONS

- Why might an income bond be attractive to a corporation with volatile cash flows? Can you think of a reason why income bonds are not more popular?
- How might a put feature affect a bond's coupon? How about a convertibility feature? Why?
- What is the attraction of a stripped real return bond?

---

[24]Barry Critchley, "Indexing Gives These Bonds a Real Return," *The Financial Post* (November 27, 1993), p. 17.

20.6   ## Direct Placement Compared to Public Issues

Earlier in this chapter, we described the mechanics of issuing debt to the public. However, a large portion of debt is privately placed. There are two basic forms of direct private long-term financing: term loans and private placements.

Term loans are direct business loans. These loans have maturities of one to five years. Most term loans are repayable during the life of the loan. The lenders include chartered banks, insurance companies, trust companies, and other lenders that specialize in corporate finance. The interest rate on a term loan may be either a fixed or floating rate.

These lenders are regulated by the Office of the Superintendent of Financial Institutions (OSFI) and, in the case of trust companies, by provincial regulators as well. Unlike the OSC in its securities regulation, OSFI does not approve each loan as it is made. Instead, it examines selected loans after they are made as it periodically inspects financial institutions. OSFI is responsible for ensuring that financial institutions have sufficient capital for the risky loans on their books. In 1985, two western banks failed, and the Canada Deposit Insurance Corporation (CDIC) paid the depositors about $700 million. A few years later, Canadian chartered banks had to write off billions in bad loans to lesser developed countries. As a result, banking regulators around the world, including OSFI, implemented stricter capital rules.

Private placements are very similar to term loans except that the maturity is longer. Unlike term loans, privately placed debt usually employs an investment dealer. The dealer facilitates the process but does not underwrite the issue. A private placement does not require a full prospectus. Instead, the firm and its investment dealer only need to draw up an offering memorandum briefly describing the issuer and the issue. Most privately placed debt is sold to *exempt purchasers*. These are large insurance companies, pension funds, and other institutions that, as sophisticated market participants, do not require the protection provided by studying a full prospectus.

The important differences between direct private long-term financing (term loans and private debt placements) and public issues of debt are

1. Registration costs are lower for direct financing. A term loan avoids the cost of OSC registration altogether. Private debt placements require an offering memorandum, but this is cheaper than preparing a full prospectus.

2. Direct placement is likely to have more restrictive covenants.

3. It is easier to renegotiate a term loan or a private placement in the event of a default. It is harder to renegotiate a public issue because hundreds of holders are usually involved.

4. Life insurance companies and pension funds dominate the private placement segment of the bond market. Chartered banks are significant participants in the term loan market.

5. The costs of distributing bonds are lower in the private market because fewer buyers are involved and the issue is not underwritten.

The interest rates on term loans and private placements are usually higher than those on an equivalent public issue. This reflects the trade-off between a higher interest rate and more flexible arrangements in the event of financial distress, as well as the lower costs and lower liquidity associated with private placements.

CONCEPT QUESTIONS

- What are the differences between private and public bond issues?
- A private placement is more likely to have restrictive covenants than is a public issue. Why?

Summary and Conclusions   20.7

This chapter describes important aspects of long-term debt financing.

1. The written agreement describing the details of the long-term debt contract is called an *indenture*. Some of the main provisions are security, repayment, protective covenants, and call provisions.

2. There are many ways that shareholders can take advantage of bondholders. Protective covenants are designed to protect bondholders from management decisions that favour shareholders at bondholders' expense.

3. Unsecured bonds are called *debentures* or *notes*. They are general claims on the company's value. Most public corporate bonds are unsecured. In contrast, utility bonds are usually secured. Mortgage bonds are secured by tangible property, and collateral trust bonds are secured by financial securities such as stocks and bonds. If the company defaults on secured bonds, the trustee can repossess the assets. This makes secured bonds more valuable.

4. Long-term bonds usually provide for repayment of principal before maturity. This is accomplished by a sinking fund. With a sinking fund, the company retires a certain number of bonds each year. A sinking fund protects bondholders because it reduces the average maturity of the bond, and its payment signals the financial condition of the company.

5. Most publicly issued bonds are callable. A callable bond is less attractive to bondholders than a noncallable bond. A callable bond can be bought back by the company at a call price that is less than the true value of the bond. As a consequence, callable bonds are priced to obtain higher stated interest rates for bondholders than noncallable bonds.

   Generally, companies should exercise the call provision whenever the bond's value is greater than the call price.

   There is no single reason for call provisions. Sensible reasons include taxes, greater flexibility, management's ability to predict interest rates, and the fact that callable bonds are less sensitive to interest rate changes.

6. There are many different types of bonds, including floating rate bonds, deep-discount bonds, and income bonds. This chapter also compares private placement with public issuance.

Key Terms

Public issue 582

Indenture 582

Bearer (bond) 584

Debenture 585

Protective covenant 586

Negative covenant 586

Positive covenant 586

Sinking fund 586

Call premium 587

Deferred call 587

Call protected 587

Refunding 588

Junk bonds 596

Zero coupon bonds (zeros) 599

Floating rate bonds (floaters) 600

Income bonds 601

Term loans 602

Private placement 602

Suggested Reading

The following provide complete coverage of bonds and the bond market:

F. J. Fabozzi, and I. Pollack, eds. *The Handbook of Fixed Income Securities,* 2d ed. Homewood, Ill.: Dow Jones-Irwin, 1987.

A. Bodie, A. Kane, A. J. Marcus, S. Perrakis, and P. J. Ryan. *Investments,* 1st Canadian ed. Burr Ridge, Ill.: Richard D. Irwin, 1993.

Questions and Problems

20.1 Raeo Corp. bonds trade at 100 today. The bonds pay semiannual interest on January 1 and July 1. The coupon on the bonds is 10 percent. How much will you pay for a Raeo bond if today is

    a. March 1?

    b. October 1?

    c. July 1?

    d. August 15?

20.2 Define the following terms:

    a. Protective covenant.

    b. Negative covenant.

    c. Positive covenant.

    d. Sinking fund.

20.3 Sinking funds have both positive and negative characteristics to the bondholders. Why?

20.4 Which of the following are characteristics of public issues, and which are characteristics of direct financing?

    a. Require OSC registration.

    b. Higher interest cost.

c. Higher fixed cost.

d. Quicker access to funds.

e. Active secondary market.

f. Easily renegotiated.

g. Lower flotation costs.

h. Require regular amortization.

i. Ease of repurchase at favourable prices.

j. High total cost to small borrowers.

k. Flexible terms.

l. Require less intensive investigation.

20.5 KIC, Inc., plans to issue $5 million of perpetual bonds. The face value of each bond is $1,000. The annual coupon on the bonds is 12 percent. Market interest rates on one-year bonds are 11 percent. With equal probability, the long-term market interest rate will be either 14 percent or 7 percent next year. Assume investors are risk-neutral.

a. If the KIC bonds are noncallable, what is the price of the bonds?

b. If the bonds are callable one year from today at $1,450, will their price be greater than or less than the price you computed in part (*a*)? Why?

20.6 Brice Manufacturing intends to issue callable, perpetual bonds. The bonds are callable at $1,250. One-year interest rates are 12 percent. There is a 60-percent probability that long-term interest rates one year from today will be 15 percent. With a 40-percent probability, long-term interest rates will be 8 percent. To simplify the firm's accounting, Brice would like to issue the bonds at par ($1,000). What must the coupon on the bonds be for Brice to be able to sell them at par?

20.7 Describe the following types of bonds:

a. Floating rate.

b. Zero coupon.

c. Income.

20.8 Ingonish Industries has decided to borrow money by issuing perpetual bonds. The face value of the bonds will be $1,000. The coupon will be 8 percent, payable annually. The one-year interest rate is 8 percent. It is known that next year there is a 65-percent chance that interest rates will decline to 6 percent, and that there is a 35-percent chance that they will rise to 9 percent.

a. What will the market value of these bonds be if they are noncallable?

b. If the company instead decides to make the bonds callable, what coupon will be demanded by the bondholders for the bonds to sell at par? Assume that the bonds can only be called in one year and that the call premium is equal to the annual coupon.

c. What will be the value of the call provision to Ingonish Industries?

20.9 Green River Electronics has $500 million of 9-percent perpetual bonds outstanding. These bonds can be called at a price of $1,090 for each $1,000 of face value. Under present market conditions, the outstanding bonds can be replaced by $500 million of 7-percent perpetual bonds. The underwriting and legal expenses of this new issue would be $80 million. What would be the net present value of this refunding? Assume that there are no taxes.

20.10 An outstanding issue of Air Canadian debentures has a call provision attached. The total principal value of the bonds is $250 million, and the bonds pay an annual coupon of $80 for each $1,000 of face value. The total cost of refunding would be 12 percent of the principal amount raised. The appropriate tax rate for the company is 40 percent. How low does the borrowing cost of Air Canadian need to drop to justify refunding with a new bond issue?

20.11 Explain how adding each of the following features would affect the price of a bond:

a. Call.

b. Retraction.

c. Conversion option.

d. Stripped coupon.

20.12 What features could be attractive to bond issuers in each of the following circumstances? Explain briefly.

a. Financial distress exists.

b. Managers have optimistic insider information.

c. Interest rates are volatile.

CHAPTER 21

Options and Corporate Finance

Options are special contractual arrangements giving the owner the right to buy or sell an asset at a fixed price anytime on or before a given date. Stock options, the most familiar type, are options to buy and sell shares of common stock. Ever since 1973, stock options have been traded on organized exchanges.

Corporate securities are very similar to stock options in several important respects. Almost every issue of corporate bonds and stocks has option features. In addition, capital structure decisions and capital budgeting decisions can be viewed in terms of options.

We start this chapter with a description of different types of publicly traded options. We identify and discuss the factors that determine their values. Next, we show how common stocks and bonds can be thought of as options on the underlying value of the firm. This leads to several new insights concerning corporate finance. For example, we show how certain corporate decisions can be viewed as options.

Options   21.1

An **option** is a contract giving its owner the right to buy or sell an asset at a fixed price on or before a given date. For example, an option on a building might give the buyer the right to buy the building for $1 million on, or anytime before, the Saturday prior to the third Wednesday in January 2010. Options are a unique type of financial contract because they give the buyer the right, but not the *obligation,* to do something. The buyer uses the option only if it is advantageous; otherwise the option can be discarded.

There is a special vocabulary associated with options. Here are some important definitions:

1. **Exercising the option.** The act of buying or selling the underlying asset via the option contract is referred to as *exercising the option.*

2. **Striking or exercise price.** The fixed price in the option contract at which the holder can buy or sell the underlying asset is called the *striking price* or *exercise price.*

3. **Expiration date.** The maturity date of the option is referred to as the *expiration date.* After this date, the option is dead.

4. **American and European options.** An American option may be exercised at any time up to and including the expiration date. A European option differs from an American option in that it can be exercised only on the expiration date.

21.2   Call Options

The most common type of option is a **call option.** A call option gives the owner the right to buy an asset at a fixed price during a particular time period. There is no restriction on the kind of asset, but the most common options traded on exchanges are on stocks and bonds. Usually the assets involved are shares of common stock.

For example, call options on Alcan stock can be purchased on the Trans Canada Options Exchange. Alcan does not issue (that is, sell) call options on its common stock. Instead, individual investors are the original buyers and sellers of these options. A representative call option on Alcan stock enables an investor to buy 100 shares of Alcan on or before October 22, 19XX, at an exercise price of $25. This is a valuable option if there is some probability that the price of Alcan common stock will exceed $25 on or before October 22, 19XX.

Virtually all stock option contracts specify that the exercise price and number of shares be adjusted for stock splits and stock dividends. To illustrate, suppose that Alcan stock was selling for $24 on the day the option was purchased. Further, suppose that the next day it split three for one. Each share would drop in price to $8, and the probability that the stock would rise over $25 per share in the near future would become very remote. To protect the option holder from such an occurrence, call options are typically adjusted for stock splits and stock dividends. In the case of a three-for-one split, the exercise price would become $8.33 (or $25/3). Furthermore, the option contract would now include 300 shares, instead of the original 100 shares.[1]

The Value of a Call Option at Expiration

What is the value of a call option contract on common stock at expiration? The answer depends on the value of the underlying stock when the option expires.

We define S_T as the market price of the underlying common stock on the expiration date, T. Of course, this price is not known prior to expiration. Suppose that a particular call option can be exercised at an exercise price of $50. If the value of the common stock at expiration, S_T, is greater than the exercise price of $50, the option will be worth the difference, $S_T - \$50$. When $S_T > \$50$, the call is said to be *in the money*.

For example, suppose that the stock price on expiration day is $60. The option holder has the right to buy the stock from the option seller for $50.[2] Because the stock is selling in the market for $60, the option holder will exercise the option, that is, buy

---

[1]No adjustment is made for the payment by Alcan of cash dividends to shareholders. This failure to adjust hurts holders of call options, though, of course, they should know the terms of option contracts before buying.

[2]We use the words *buyer, owner,* and *holder* interchangeably.

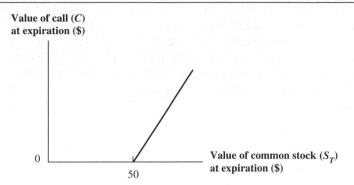

Figure 21.1
The value of a call option on the expiration date

If $S_T > \$50$, then call option value $= S_T - \$50$. If $S_T \le \$50$, then call option value $= 0$.

 A call option gives the owner the right to *buy* an asset at a fixed price during a particular time period.

the stock for $50. The holder can then sell the stock for $60 and pocket the difference of $10 (or $60 − $50).[3]

 Of course, it is also possible that the value of the common stock will turn out to be less than the exercise price. If $S_T < \$50$, the call is *out of the money*. The holder will not exercise in this case. For example, if the stock price at the expiration date is $40, no rational investor would exercise. Why pay $50 for stock worth only $40? An option holder has no obligation to exercise the call and can *walk away* from the option. As a consequence, if $S_T < \$50$ on the expiration date, the value of the call option will be 0. In this case, the value of the call option is not $S_T - \$50$, as it would be if the holder of the call option had the *obligation* to exercise the call.

 The payoff of a call option at expiration is

	Payoff on the expiration date	
	If $S_T \le \$50$	If $S_T > \$50$
Call option value	0	$S_T - \$50$

 Figure 21.1 plots the value of the call at expiration against the value of the stock. It is referred to as the *hockey stick diagram* of call option values. If $S_T < \$50$, the call is out of the money and worthless. If $S_T > \$50$, the call is in the money and rises one-for-one with increases in the stock price. Notice that the call can never have a negative value. It is a *limited liability instrument,* which means that all the holder can lose is the initial amount paid for it.

▪ Example

Suppose Mr. Optimist holds a one-year call option for 100 shares of Alcan common stock. It is a European call option and can be exercised at $25 per share. Assume that the expiration date has arrived. What is the value of the Alcan call option on the

---

[3]This example assumes that the call lets the holder purchase one share of stock at $50. In reality, a call lets the holder purchase 100 shares at $50 per share. The profit would then equal $1,000 [or ($60 − $50) × 100].

expiration date? If Alcan is selling for $30 per share, Mr. Optimist can exercise the option—purchase 100 shares of Alcan at $25 per share—and then immediately sell the shares at $30. Mr. Optimist will have made $500 (or 100 shares × $5).

Alternatively, assume that Alcan is selling for $20 per share on the expiration date. If Mr. Optimist still holds the call option, he will throw it away. The value of the Alcan call on the expiration date will be zero in this case. ■

CONCEPT QUESTIONS

- What is a call option?
- How is a call option's price related to the underlying stock price at the expiration date?

21.3 Put Options

A **put option** can be viewed as the opposite of a call option. Just as a call gives the holder the right to buy the stock at a fixed price, a put gives the holder the right to *sell* the stock for a fixed exercise price during the life of the option.

The Value of a Put Option at Expiration

The circumstances that determine the value of a put option are the opposite of those for a call option, because a put option gives the holder the right to sell shares. Let us assume that the exercise price of the put is $50. If the price, S_T, of the underlying common stock at expiration is greater than the exercise price, it would be foolish to exercise the option and sell shares at $50. In other words, the put option is worthless if $S_T > \$50$. The put is out of the money in this case. However, if $S_T < \$50$, the put is in the money. In this case, it will pay to buy shares at S_T and use the option to sell them at the exercise price of $50. For example, if the stock price at expiration is $40, the holder should buy the stock in the open market at $40. By immediately exercising, he receives $50 for the sale. His profit is $10 (or $50 − $40).

The payoff of a put option at expiration is

	Payoff on the expiration date	
	If $S_T < \$50$	If $S_T \geq \$50$
Put option value	$50 − S_T	0

Figure 21.2 plots the values of a put option for all possible values of the underlying stock. It is instructive to compare Figure 21.2 with Figure 21.1 for the call option. The call option is valuable whenever the stock is above the exercise price, and the put is valuable when the stock price is below the exercise price.

■ *Example*

In early 1992, Royal Trustco (the holding company for Royal Trust, and a member of the vast Edper-Bronfman empire) traded at over $9 per share. By early November that year, problems that eventually led to a merger with Royal Bank of Canada drove the

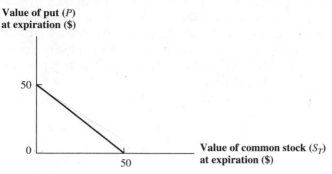

Figure 21.2
The value of a put option on the expiration date

Value of put (P)
at expiration ($)

50

0

50

Value of common stock (S_T)
at expiration ($)

If $S_T \geq \$50$, then the put option value $= 0$. If $S_T < \$50$, then the put option value $= \$50 - S_T$.
A put option gives the owner the right to *sell* an asset at a fixed price during a particular time period.

share price down to around $3. Suppose that Ms. Pessimist foresaw Royal Trustco's problems and bought puts allowing the sale of Royal Trustco shares at $5 through November 1992. At the expiration date, Ms. Pessimist exercised her puts which were then in the money. She bought 100 shares of Royal Trustco in the market for $3 per share and, on the same day, sold the shares at the exercise price of $5 per share. Her profit was $200 (or 100 shares $\times$ ($5−$3)). The value of the put contract at expiration was $200. ∎

CONCEPT QUESTIONS

- What is a put option?
- How is a put option's price related to the underlying stock price at the expiration date?

Selling Options   21.4

An investor who sells (or *writes*) a call on common stock promises to deliver the shares if required to do so by the call option holder. Notice that the seller is *obligated* to deliver if the option is exercised. The seller of a call option obtains a cash payment from the holder (or buyer) at the time the option is bought. If, at the expiration date, the price of the common stock is below the exercise price, the call option will not be exercised and the seller's liability is zero.

If, at the expiration date, the price of the common stock is greater than the exercise price, the holder will exercise the call and the seller must give the holder shares of stock in exchange for the exercise price. Here the seller loses the difference between the stock price and the exercise price. For example, assume that the stock price is $60 and the exercise price is $50. Knowing that exercise is imminent, the option seller buys stock in the open market at $60. By being obligated to sell at $50, the option seller loses $10 (or $50 − $60).

Conversely, an investor who sells a put on common stock agrees to purchase shares of common stock if the put holder should so request. The seller loses on this deal if the stock price falls below the exercise price and the holder puts the stock to the seller. For example, assume that the stock price is $40 and the exercise price is $50. The holder of the put will exercise in this case. In other words, the holder will sell the underlying stock at the exercise price of $50. This means that the seller of the put must buy the underlying stock at the exercise price of $50. Because the stock is only worth $40, the loss here is $10 (or $40 − $50).

The values of the "sell-a-call" and "sell-a-put" positions are depicted in Figure 21.3. The graph on the left-hand side of the figure shows that the seller of a call loses nothing when the stock price at expiration date is below $50. However, the seller loses a dollar for every dollar that the stock rises above $50. The graph in the center of the figure shows that the seller of a put loses nothing when the stock price at expiration date is above $50. However, the seller loses a dollar for every dollar that the stock falls below $50.

The graph also shows the value at expiration of simply buying common stock. Notice that buying the stock is the same as buying a call option on the stock with an exercise price of zero. This is not surprising. If the exercise price is 0, the call holder can buy the stock for nothing, which is really the same as owning it.

21.5   Stock Option Quotations

Now that we understand the definitions for calls and puts, let's look at the exchanges where they are traded. In the 1970s and 1980s organized trading in options grew from literally zero into some of the world's largest markets. The tremendous growth in interest in derivative securities resulted from the greatly increased volatility in financial markets we discussed in Chapter 1.[4] Exchange trading in options began in 1973 on the Chicago Board Options Exchange (CBOE). The CBOE is still the largest organized options market, and options are traded in a number of other places today, including London, Paris, Tokyo, and Hong Kong.

Option trading in Canada began in 1975 on the Montreal Exchange. Today options are traded on the Montreal, Toronto, and Vancouver exchanges and cleared through TransCanada Options Inc. (TCO). The TCO stands between option buyers and sellers. Put and call options involving stock in some of the best-known corporations in Canada are traded daily. Almost all such options are American (as opposed to European). Total volume in 1989 was $550 million, which is small relative to the size of Canadian stock markets. Continued growth in Canadian options trading is predicted as banks, pension funds, and other financial institutions gain experience with hedging techniques using derivative securities.

To illustrate how options are quoted on the TCO, Table 21.1 presents information on the options of Alcan Aluminum drawn from *The Globe and Mail.*

---

[4]Our discussion of trends in options trading draws on L. Gagnon, "Exchange-Traded Financial Derivatives in Canada: Finally off the Launching Pad," *Canadian Investment Review* (Fall 1990), pp. 63–70.

Figure 21.3 The payoffs to sellers of calls and puts, and to buyers of common stock

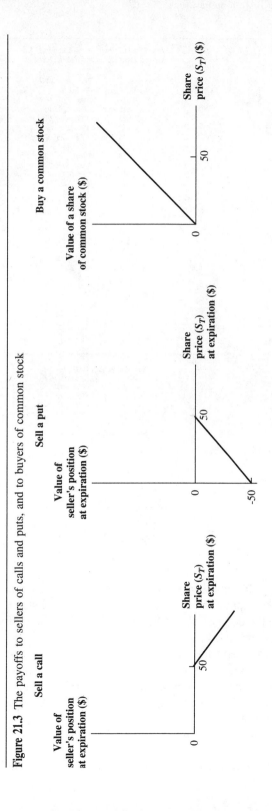

Table 21.1
Alcan Aluminum
Options

Trans Canada Options combine Montreal, Toronto and Vancouver option trading. P is a put.

Series		Bid	Ask	Last
Agnico-Eagle	C	$16 7/8		
AG $15		185	225	150
$16		85	120	100
SP $13		400	425	410
$16		180	205	185
$16	P	85	105	90
$17		120	140	135
$18		75	95	95
OC $15		290	300	290
$15	P	85	105	100
$16		215	240	205
$17		160	180	150
$17	P	160	180	155
$18		125	145	165
DC $13		475	490	485
$14		410	435	445
$16		300	325	315
$17		250	275	280
$18		205	230	200
Air Canada	C	450		
OC $4		65	80	70
JA $4		95	110	95
Alcan Alumin.	C	$26 5/8		
AG $25		160	185	180
$26		60	75	60
$28	P	120	145	125
NV $27		120	135	115
FB $25	P	85	100	95
$26		235	240	240
$27		185	200	180
Alcan Leaps 95	C	$26 5/8		
JA $20		$7 7/8	$8 5/8	
$20	P	15	55	60
$25		435	$5 1/8	
$25	P	145	195	
$30		220	270	
$30	P	415	490	
Alcan Leaps 96	C	$26 5/8		
JA $20		$9	$9 3/4	
$20	P	40	90	
$25		$5 3/4	$6 1/2	
$25	P	195	245	
$30		350	400	
$30	P	465	$5 3/8	

Source: *The Globe and Mail* (August 21, 1993), p. B16. Used with permission.

The first thing listed here is the company identifier, Alcan Alumin. This tells us that these options involve the right to buy or sell shares of stock in Alcan Aluminum. Beside the company identifier is the stock's closing price. As of the close of business (in Toronto), Alcan was selling for $26 5/8 per share.

On the next line is the expiration date for the first option. AG means the option expires in August. Four lines down is an option marked NV, meaning it expires in November. All TCO options expire on the third Friday of the expiration month.

To the right of the expiration date is the exercise (or striking) price. The Alcan Alumin. options listed here have exercise prices ranging from $25 to $28. The first two are call options; the third is a put option marked *P*. Since calls are more common, all listings are assumed to be calls unless marked *P*. The column marked *Last* gives the closing price or last traded price for the option in pennies.

The first option listed would be described as the "Alcan Alumin. $25 call." The price for this option is $1.80. If you pay the $1.80, then you have the right anytime between now and the third Friday of August to buy one share of Alcan stock for $25. Actually, trading takes place in round lots (multiples of 100 shares), so one option *contract* costs $1.80×100=$180.

The other quotations are similar. For example, the Aug $28 put option costs $1.25. If you pay $1.25×100=$125.00, then you have the right to sell 100 shares of Alcan stock at any time between now and the third Friday in August at a price of $28 per share.

LEAPS

In 1992, the Toronto and Montreal stock exchanges introduced two-year options called LEAPS (Long-term Equity AnticiPation Securities).[5] LEAPS are exactly the same as the call or put options already discussed except that they have much longer lives.

Initially, eight underlying stocks were chosen for LEAPS. However, a multitude of liquid, volatile stocks in all industries are now involved. Banking, gold, conglomerates, pipelines, telecommunications, and natural resources are some of the industries represented by LEAPS.

Table 21.1 shows quotes for Alcan LEAPS expiring in 1995 and 1996. When these quotations were made in August 1993, the Alcan LEAPS had maturities of up to three years.

Combinations of Options   21.6

Puts and calls can serve as building blocks for more complex option contracts. For example, Figure 21.4 illustrates the payoff from buying a put option on a stock and simultaneously buying the stock.

If the share price is greater than the exercise price, the put option is worthless, and the value of the combined position equals the value of the common stock. If instead the exercise price is greater than the share price, the decline in the value of the shares will be exactly offset by the rise in value of the put.

Note that the combination of buying a put and buying the underlying stock has the same *shape* in Figure 21.4 as the call purchase in Figure 21.1. Furthermore, the shape of the combination strategy in Figure 21.4 is the *mirror image* of the shape of the call sale in the upper left-hand corner of Figure 21.3. This suggests the following possibility:

> One strategy in the options market may offset another strategy, resulting in a riskless return.

This possibility is in fact true, as evidenced by the following example.

---

[5]This section draws on Bud Jorgensen, "Street Talk, Exchanges Make LEAP of Faith," *The Globe and Mail* (September 21, 1992).

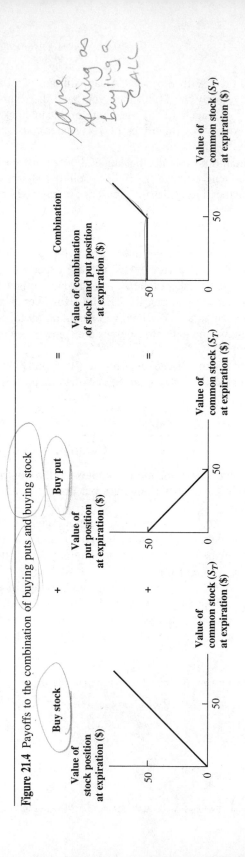

Figure 21.4 Payoffs to the combination of buying puts and buying stock

Same thing as buying a call

■ *Example*

Both the exercise price of the call and the exercise price of the put of Paper Tiger, Inc., are $55. Both options are European, so they cannot be exercised prior to expiration. The expiration date is one year from today. The stock price is currently $44. At the expiration date, the stock will be at either $58 or $34. ■

The offsetting strategy. Suppose you pursue the following strategy:

Buy the stock

Buy the put

Sell the call.

The payoffs at expiration are

	Payoffs on the expiration date	
Initial transaction	Stock price rises to $58	Stock price falls to $34
Buy a common stock	$58 ⬎	$34
Buy a put	0 (You let put expire.)	$21 = $55 − $34
Sell a call	−$ 3 = −($58 − $55)	0 (Holder lets call expire.)
Total	$55	$55

Note that, when the stock price falls, the put is in the money and the call expires without being exercised. When the stock price rises, the call is in the money and you let the put expire. The major point is that you end up with $55 in either case.

There is no risk to this strategy. While this result may bother students—or even shock some—it is actually quite intuitive. We pointed out earlier that the graph of the strategy of buying both a put and the underlying stock is the mirror image of the graph from the strategy of selling the call. Thus, combining both strategies, as we did in the example, should eliminate all risk.

The preceding payoff diagram separately valued each asset at the expiration date. Actually, a discussion of the actual exercise process may simplify things, because here the stock is always linked with an option. Consider the following strategy diagram:

	Strategies on the expiration date		
Stock price rises to $58		Stock price falls to $34	
You let put expire.	0	Call expires.	0
Call is exercised against you, obligating you to sell the stock you own. You give up stock and receive the exercise price of	$55	You choose to exercise put. That is, you sell the stock you own at the exercise price of	$55
Total	$55	Total	$55

Again, we show the riskless nature of the strategy. Regardless of the price movement of the stock, exercise entails surrendering the stock for $55.

Though we have specified the payoffs at expiration, we have ignored the earlier investment that you made. To remedy this omission, suppose that you originally pay

$44 for the stock and $7 for the put and receive $1 for selling the call.[6] In addition, the riskless interest rate is 10 percent.

You have paid

$$-\$50 = \quad -\$44 \qquad\qquad -\$7 \qquad\qquad +\$1$$

| | Stock purchase | Purchase of put | Sale of call |

Because you pay $50 today and are guaranteed $55 in one year, you are just earning the interest rate of 10 percent. Thus, the prices in this example allow no possibility of arbitrage or easy money. Conversely, if the put sold for only $6, your initial investment would be $49. You would then have a nonequilibrium return of 12.2 percent ($55/$49 − 1) over the year.

It can be proven that, in order to prevent arbitrage, the prices at the time you take on your original position must conform to the following fundamental relationship:

Put-Call Parity:

Value of stock	+	Value of put	−	Value of call	=	Present value of exercise price
$44	+	$7	−	$1	=	$50 = $\dfrac{\$55}{1.10}$

This result is called **put-call parity.** It shows that the values of a put and a call with the same exercise price and same expiration date are precisely related to each other. It holds generally, not just in the specific example we have chosen.[7]

Put-call parity has been known for at least 100 years. Legend has it that the relationship was discovered by one Russell Sage, an extremely successful U.S. businessman in the 19th century. At one point, state usury laws prohibited him from making a high interest rate loan to a customer, so he bought stock in a publicly traded company from the customer at the market price. Simultaneously, he bought a put and wrote a call on the underlying stock at fictitious prices, where the customer took the opposite side of each transaction. This provided Mr. Sage with a guaranteed rate of return on his investment, as our example would suggest. The customer, by always taking the opposite side, was effectively borrowing at this guaranteed rate. The prices of the options were set so that the rate of return to Mr. Sage was above what the usury laws allowed. Bank examiners did not prohibit this complex transaction, because they could not figure out that it was a loan in disguise.

CONCEPT QUESTION

■ What is put-call parity?

---

[6]Note that the options are both European. An American put must sell for more than $11 (or $55 − $44). That is, if the price of an American put is only $7, one would buy the put, buy the stock, and exercise immediately, generating an immediate arbitrage profit of $4 (or −$7 − $44 + $55).

[7]However, the formula is applicable only when both the put and the call are European options that have the same expiration date and the same exercise price.

Valuing Options

21.7

In the last section, we determined what options are worth on the expiration date. Now we wish to evaluate the value of options when you buy them well before expiration.[8] We begin by considering the upper and lower bounds on the value of a call.

Bounding the Value of a Call

Consider an American call that is in the money prior to expiration. For example, assume that the stock price is $60 and the exercise price is $50. In this case, the option cannot sell below $10. To see this, note the simple strategy if the option sells at, say, $9.

Date	Transaction	
Today	(1) Buy call	−$ 9
Today	(2) Exercise call, that is, buy underlying stock at exercise price	−$50
Today	(3) Sell stock at current market price	+$60
Arbitrage profit		+$ 1

The type of profit that is described in this transaction is an *arbitrage profit*. Arbitrage profits come from transactions that have no risk or cost and cannot occur regularly in normal, well-functioning financial markets.[9] The excess demand for these options would quickly force the option price up to at least $10 (or $60 − $50).[10]

In practice, the price of the option is likely to be above $10. Investors will rationally pay more than $10 because of the possibility that the stock will rise above $60 before expiration. Is there an upper boundary for the option price as well? It turns out that the upper boundary is the price of the underlying stock. That is, an option to buy common stock cannot have a greater value than the common stock itself. A call option can be used to buy common stock with a payment of an exercise price. It would be foolish to buy stock this way if the stock could be purchased directly at a lower price. The upper and lower bounds are represented in Figure 21.5.

The Factors Determining Call Option Values

The previous discussion indicated that the price of a call option must fall somewhere in the shaded region of Figure 21.5. We now determine more precisely where in the shaded region it should be. The factors that determine a call's value can be broken into two sets. The first set contains the features of the option contract. The two basic contractual features are the expiration date and the exercise price. The second set of factors affecting the call price reflects characteristics of the stock and the market.

---

[8]Our discussion in this section is of American options, because they are traded in the real world. As necessary, we will indicate differences for European calls.

[9]Paul Halpern and Stuart Turnbull, "Empirical Tests of Boundary Conditions for Toronto Stock Exchange Options," *Journal of Finance* 40 (June 1985), tested these boundary conditions for TCO options in the late 1970s when Canadian options trading was relatively new. While they detected arbitrage opportunities, it is unlikely that these persist today.

[10]Note that this lower bound is strictly true for an American option but not for a European option.

Figure 21.5
The upper and lower boundaries of call option values

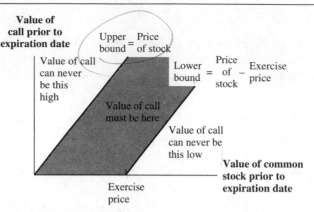

The precise option value will depend on five factors:
1. Exercise price.
2. Expiration date.
3. Stock price.
4. Risk-free interest rate.
5. Variance of the stock.

Exercise Price

It should be evident that, if all other things are held constant, the higher the exercise price, the lower the value of a call option. The value of a call option cannot be negative, however, no matter how high we set the exercise price. As long as there is some possibility that the price of the underlying asset will exceed the exercise price before the expiration date, the option will have value.

Expiration Date

The value of an American call option must be at least as great as the value of an otherwise identical option with a shorter term to expiration. Consider two American calls: One has a maturity of nine months and the other expires in six months. The nine-month call offers the same rights as the six-month call, and also has an additional three months within which these rights can be exercised. It cannot be worth less and will generally be more valuable.[11]

Stock Price

Other things being equal, the higher the stock price, the more valuable the call option will be. This is illustrated in any of our figures that plot the call price against the stock price at expiration.

---

[11]This relationship need not hold for a European call option. Consider a firm with two otherwise identical European call options: one expiring at the end of May and the other expiring a few months later. Further, assume that a *huge* dividend is paid in early June. If the first call is exercised at the end of May, its holder will receive the underlying stock. If he does not sell the stock, he will receive the large dividend shortly thereafter. However, the holder of the second call will receive the stock through exercise after the dividend is paid. Because the market knows that the holder of this option will miss the dividend, the value of the second call option could be less than the value of the first.

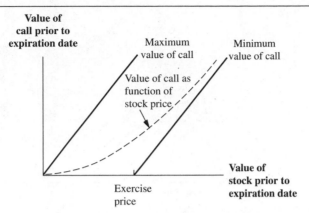

Figure 21.6
Value of a call as a
function of stock
price

The call price is positively related to the stock price. In addition,
the change in the call price for a given change in the stock price
is greater when the stock price is high than when it is low.

Now consider Figure 21.6, which shows the relationship between the call price
and the stock price prior to expiration. The curve indicates that the call price increases
as the stock price increases. Further, it can be shown that the relationship is
represented, not by a straight line, but by a *convex curve*. That is, the increase in the
call price for a given change in the stock price is greater when the stock price is high
than when the stock price is low.

The Key Factor: The Variability of the Underlying Asset

The greater the variability of the underlying asset, the more valuable the call option
will be. Consider the following example. Suppose that, just before the call expires, the
stock price will be either $100 with probability 0.5 or $80 with probability 0.5. What
will be the value of a call with an exercise price of $110? Clearly, it will be worthless
because no matter what happens to the stock, its price will always be below the
exercise price.

Now let us see what happens if the stock is more variable. Suppose that we add
$20 to the best case and take $20 away from the worst case. Now the stock has a
one-half chance of being worth $60 and a one-half chance of being worth $120. We
have spread the stock returns, but, of course, the expected value of the stock has stayed
the same:

$$(\frac{1}{2} \times \$80) + (\frac{1}{2} \times \$100) = \$90 = (\frac{1}{2} \times \$60) + (\frac{1}{2} \times \$120)$$

Notice that the call option has value now because there is a one-half chance that
the stock price will be $120, or $10 above the exercise price of $110. This illustrates
a very important point. There is a fundamental distinction between holding an option
on an underlying asset and holding the underlying asset. If investors in the marketplace
are risk-averse, a rise in the variability of the stock will decrease its market value.
However, the holder of a call receives payoffs from the positive tail of the probability
distribution. As a consequence, a rise in the variability in the underlying stock
increases the market value of the call.

Figure 21.7
Distribution of
common stock
price at expiration
for both security *A*
and security *B*,
whose options
have the same
exercise price

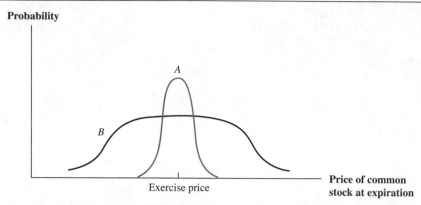

The call on stock *B* is worth more than the call on stock *A* because stock *B* is more volatile. At expiration, a call that is way in the money is more valuable than a call that is way out of the money. However, at expiration, a call way out of the money is worth zero, just as is a call only slightly out of the money.

This result can also be seen from Figure 21.7. Consider two stocks, *A* and *B,* each of which is normally distributed. For each security, the figure illustrates the probability of different stock prices on the expiration date.[12] As we see, stock *B* has more volatility than does stock *A*. This means that stock *B* has higher probability of both abnormally high returns and abnormally low returns. Let us assume that options on each of the two securities have the same exercise price. To option holders, a return much below average on stock *B* is no worse than a return only moderately below average on stock *A*. In either situation, the option expires out of the money. However, to option holders, a return much above average on stock *B* is better than a return only moderately above average on stock *A*. Because a call's price at the expiration date is the difference between the stock price and the exercise price, the value of the call on *B* at expiration will be higher in this case.

The Interest Rate

Call prices are also a function of the level of interest rates. Buyers of calls do not pay the exercise price until they exercise the option, if they do so at all. The delay of the payment is more valuable when interest rates are high, and is less valuable when interest rates are low. Thus, the value of a call is positively related to interest rates.

A Quick Discussion of Factors Determining Put Option Values

Given our extended discussion of the factors influencing a call's value, we can easily examine these factors' effect on puts. Table 21.2 summarizes the five factors

----

[12]This graph assumes that, for each security, the exercise price is equal to the expected stock price. This assumption is employed merely to facilitate the discussion. It is not needed to show the relationship between a call's value and the volatility of the underlying stock.

	Call option*	Put option*
Value of underlying asset (stock price)	+	−
Exercise price	−	+
Stock volatility	+	+
Interest rate	+	−
Time to exercise date	+	+

Table 21.2
Factors affecting American option values

* The + and − signs indicate the variables' effect on the value of the option. For example, the two +s for stock volatility indicate that an increase in volatility will increase both the value of a call and the value of a put.

influencing prices of both American calls and American puts. The effect of three factors on puts are the opposite of the effect of these three factors on calls:

1. The put's market price *decreases* as the stock price increases because puts are in the money when the stock sells below the exercise price.

2. The market value of a put with a high exercise price is *greater* than the value of an otherwise identical put with a low exercise price for the reason given in (1) above.

3. A high interest rate *adversely* affects the value of a put. The ability to sell a stock at a fixed exercise price sometime in the future is worth less if the present value of the exercise price is diminished by a high interest rate.

The effect of the other two factors on puts is the same as the effect of these factors on calls:

4. The value of an American put with a distant expiration date is greater than an otherwise identical put with an earlier expiration.[13] The longer time to maturity gives the put holder more flexibility, just as it did in the case of a call.

5. Volatility of the underlying stock increases the value of the put. The reasoning is analogous to that for a call. At expiration, a put that is deep in the money is more valuable than a put only slightly in the money. However, at expiration, a put way out of the money is worth zero, just as is a put only slightly out of the money.

■ *Example*

According to Table 21.2, when other things are held equal, increasing time to expiration raises the prices of puts and calls. Is this theory consistent with the actual option prices in Table 21.1?

We can look at time to expiration and pricing for the Alcan options. Starting with calls, all the other four factors are constant if we compare calls with the same

---

[13]Though this result must hold in the case of an American put, it need not hold for a European put.

exercise price but different expiration dates. There are two Alcan calls with a $26 exercise price:

Call		Price
AG	$26	60
FB	$26	240

As expected, the call prices increase with time to expiration. You can show the same thing with the Alcan LEAPS puts. ∎

CONCEPT QUESTIONS

- List the factors that determine the value of options.
- Why does a stock's variability affect the value of options written on it?

21.8   An Option Pricing Formula

We have explained *qualitatively* that the value of a call option is a function of five variables:

1. The current price of the underlying asset, which for stock options is the price of the shares of common stock.
2. The exercise price.
3. The time to the expiration date.
4. The variance of the underlying asset.
5. The risk-free interest rate.

It is time to replace the qualitative model with a precise option valuation model. The model we choose is the famous Black–Scholes option pricing model. You can put numbers into the Black–Scholes model and get values back.

The Black–Scholes model is represented by a rather imposing formula. A derivation of the formula is simply not possible in this textbook, as students will be happy to learn. However, some appreciation for the achievement as well as some intuitive understanding is in order.

In the early chapters of this book, we showed how to discount capital budgeting projects using the net present value formula. We also used this approach to value stocks and bonds. Why, students sometimes ask, can't the same NPV formula be used to value puts and calls? It is a good question because the earliest attempts at valuing options used NPV. Unfortunately, the attempts were simply not successful because no one could determine the appropriate discount rate. An option is generally riskier than the underlying stock, but no one knew exactly how much riskier.

Black and Scholes attacked the problem by pointing out that a strategy of borrowing to finance a stock purchase duplicates the risk of a call. Then, knowing the price of a stock already, one can determine the price of a call such that its return is identical to that of the stock-with-borrowing alternative.

We illustrate the intuition behind the Black–Scholes approach by considering a simple example where a combination of a call and a stock eliminates all risk. This example works because we let the future stock price be one of only two values. Hence, the example is called a *two-state option model.* By eliminating the possibility that the stock price can take on other values, we are able to duplicate the call exactly.

A Two-State Option Model

To find the option price, we assume a market where there can never be an arbitrage possibility. To see how it works, consider the following example. Suppose the market price of a stock is $50 and it will be either $60 or $40 at the end of the year. Further suppose that there exists a call option for 100 shares of this stock with a one-year expiration date and a $50 exercise price. Investors can borrow at 10 percent.

There are two possible trading strategies that we shall examine. The first is to buy a call on the stock, and the second is to buy 50 shares of the stock and borrow a *duplicating amount.* The duplicating amount is the amount of borrowing necessary to make the future payoffs from buying stock and borrowing the same as the future payoffs from buying a call on the stock. In our example, the duplicating amount of borrowing is $1,818. With a 10-percent interest rate, principal and interest at the end of the year total $2,000 (or $1,818 × 1.10). At the end of one year, the future payoffs are set out as follows:

	Future payoffs	
Initial transactions	If stock price is $60	If stock price is $40
1. Buy a call (100-share contract)	$100 \times (\$60 - \$50) = \$1,000$	0
2. Buy 50 shares of stock	$50 \times \$60 = \$3,000$	$50 \times \$40 = \$2,000$
Borrow $1,818	$-(\$1,818 \times 1.10) = -\$2,000$	$-\$2,000$
Total from strategy 2	$1,000	0

Note that the future payoff structure of "buy a call" is duplicated by the strategy of "buy stock" and "borrow." These two trading strategies are equivalent as far as market traders are concerned. As a consequence, the two strategies must have the same cost. The cost of purchasing 50 shares of stock while borrowing $1,818 is

$$
\begin{array}{ll}
\text{Buy 50 shares of stock} & 50 \times \$50 = \$2,500 \\
\text{Borrow \$1,818 at 10\%} & \underline{-1,818} \\
& 682
\end{array}
$$

Because the call option gives the same return, the call must be priced at $682. This is the value of the call option in a market where arbitrage profits do not exist.

Before leaving this simple example, we should comment on a remarkable feature. We found the exact value of the option without even knowing the probability that the stock would go up or down! If an optimist thought the probability of an up move was very high and a pessimist thought it was very low, they would still agree on the option value. How could that be? The answer is that the current $50 stock price already balances the views of the optimists and the pessimists. The option reflects that balance because its value depends on the stock price.

The Black–Scholes Model

The above example illustrates the duplicating strategy. Unfortunately, a strategy such as this will not work in the real world over, say, a one-year time frame, because there are many more than two possibilities for next year's stock price. However, the number of possibilities is reduced as the time period is shortened. In fact, the assumption that there are only two possibilities for the stock price over the next infinitesimal instant is quite plausible.[14]

In our opinion, the fundamental insight of Black and Scholes is to shorten the time period. They show that a specific combination of stock and borrowing can indeed duplicate a call over an infinitesimal time horizon. Because the price of the stock will change over the first instant, another combination of stock and borrowing is needed to duplicate the call over the second instant and so on. By adjusting the combination from moment to moment, they can continually duplicate the call. It may boggle the mind that a formula can (1) determine the duplicating combination at any moment and (2) value the option based on this duplicating strategy. Suffice it to say that their dynamic strategy allows them to value a call in the real world just as we showed how to value the call in the two-state model.

This is the basic intuition behind the Black–Scholes model. Because the actual derivation of their formula is, alas, far beyond the scope of this text, we simply present the formula itself. The formula is

Black–Scholes Model:

$$C = SN(d_1) - Ee^{-rt}N(d_2)$$

where

$$d_1 = [\ln(S/E) + (r + \tfrac{1}{2}\sigma^2)t]/\sqrt{\sigma^2 t}$$
$$d_2 = d_1 - \sqrt{\sigma^2 t}$$

This formula for the value of a call, C, is one of the most complex in finance. However, it involves only five parameters:

1. S = Current stock price
2. E = Exercise price of call
3. r = Continuous risk-free rate of return (annualized)
4. σ^2 = Variance (per year) of the continuous return on the stock
5. t = Time (in years) to expiration date

In addition, there is the statistical concept:

$N(d)$ = Probability that a standardized, normally distributed, random variable will be less than or equal to d

Rather than discuss the formula in its algebraic state, we illustrate with an example.

▪ *Example*

Consider Private Equipment Company (PEC). On October 4, 19X0, the PEC April $49 call option had a closing value of $4. The stock itself is selling at $50. On October 4

---

[14]A full treatment of this assumption can be found in J. Cox and M. Rubinstein, *Option Markets* (Englewood Cliffs, N.J.: Prentice Hall, 1985), chapter 5.

the option had 199 days to expiration (maturity date is April 21, 19X1). The annual risk-free interest rate is 7 percent.

The above information determines three variables directly:

1. The stock price, S, is $50.
2. The exercise price, E, is $49.
3. The risk-free rate, r, is 0.07.

In addition, the time to maturity, t, can be calculated quickly. The formula calls for t to be expressed in *years*.

4. We express the 199-day interval in years as $t = 199/365$.

In the real world, an option trader would know S and E exactly. Traders generally view Canada Treasury bills as riskless, so a current quote would be obtained for the interest rate. The trader would also know (or could count) the number of days to expiration exactly. Thus, the fraction of a year to expiration, t, could be calculated quickly. The problem comes in determining the variance of the stock's return. The formula calls for the variance measured between the purchase date of October 4 and the expiration date. Unfortunately, this represents the future, so the correct value for variance is simply not available. Instead, traders frequently estimate variance from past data, just as we calculated variance in an earlier chapter. In addition, some traders may use intuition to adjust their estimate. For example, if anticipation of an upcoming event is currently increasing the volatility of the stock, the trader might adjust the estimate of variance upward. (This problem was most severe right after the October 19, 1987, crash. The stock market was quite risky in the aftermath, so estimates using precrash data were too low.)

The above discussion was intended merely to mention the difficulties in variance estimation, not to present a solution.[15] For our purposes, we assume that a trader has come up with an estimate of variance:

5. The variance of Private Equipment Co. has been estimated to be 0.09 per year.

Using the above five parameters, we calculate the Black–Scholes value of the PEC option in three steps:

Step 1: Calculate d_1 *and* d_2. These values can be determined by a straightforward, albeit tedious, insertion of our parameters into the basic formula. We have

$$d_1 = \left[\ln\left(\frac{S}{E}\right) + (r + \tfrac{1}{2}\sigma^2)t\right] \bigg/ \sqrt{\sigma^2 t}$$

$$= \left[\ln\left(\frac{50}{49}\right) + (0.07 + \tfrac{1}{2} \times 0.09) \times \frac{199}{365}\right] \bigg/ \sqrt{0.09 \times \frac{199}{365}}$$

$$= [0.0202 + 0.0627]/0.2215 = 0.3743$$

$$d_2 = d_1 - \sqrt{\sigma^2 t}$$

$$= 0.1528$$

---

[15]A more in-depth attempt to estimate variance can be found in J. Hull, *Options, Futures and Other Derivative Securities* (Englewood Cliffs, N.J.: Prentice Hall, 1989).

Figure 21.8
Graph of
cumulative
probability

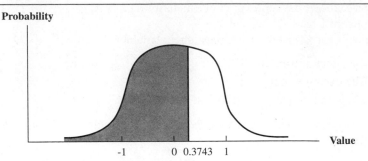

Shaded area represents cumulative probability. Because the probability is 0.6459
that a drawing from the standard normal distribution will be below 0.3743, we say
that N(0.3743) = 0.6459. That is, the cumulative probability of 0.3743 is 0.6459.

Step 2: Calculate $N(d_1)$ *and* $N(d_2)$. The values $N(d_1)$ and $N(d_2)$ can best be
understood by examining Figure 21.8. The figure shows the normal distribution with
an expected value of 0 and a standard deviation of 1. This is frequently called the
standardized normal distribution. We mentioned in an earlier chapter that the
probability that a drawing from this distribution will be between −1 and +1 (within
one standard deviation of its mean, in other words) is 68.26 percent.

Now, let us ask a different question: What is the probability that a drawing from
the standardized normal distribution will be *below* a particular value? For example, the
probability that a drawing will be below 0 is clearly 50 percent because the normal
distribution is symmetric. Using statistical terminology, we say that the **cumulative
probability** of 0 is 50 percent. Statisticians say N(0) = 50%. It turns out that

$$N(d_1) = N(0.3743) = 0.6459$$
$$N(d_2) = N(0.1528) = 0.5607$$

The first value means that there is a 64.59-percent probability that a drawing from the
standardized normal distribution will be below 0.3743. The second value means that
there is a 56.07-percent probability that a drawing from the standardized normal
distribution will be below 0.1528. More generally, $N(d)$ is the notation that a drawing
from the standardized normal distribution will be below d. In other words, $N(d)$ is the
cumulative probability of d. Note that d_1 and d_2 in our example are slightly positive,
so $N(d_1)$ and $N(d_2)$ are slightly greater than 0.50.

We can determine the cumulative probability from Table 21.3. For example,
consider $d = 0.37$. This can be found in the table as 0.3 on the vertical and 0.07 on the
horizontal. The value in the table for $d = 0.37$ is 0.1443. This value is *not* the
cumulative probability of 0.37. One must first make an adjustment to determine
cumulative probability. That is,

$$N(0.37) = 0.50 + 0.1443 = 0.6443$$
$$N(-0.37) = 0.50 - 0.1443 = 0.3557$$

Unfortunately, our table only handles two significant digits, whereas our value of
0.3743 has four significant digits. Hence, we must interpolate to find N(0.3743).
Because N(0.37) = 0.6443 and N(0.38) = 0.6480, the difference between the two

Table 21.3 Cumulative probabilities of the standard normal distribution function

d	0.00	0.01	0.02	0.03	0.04	0.05	0.06	0.07	0.08	0.09
0.0	0.0000	0.0040	0.0080	0.0120	0.0160	0.0199	0.0239	0.0279	0.0319	0.0359
0.1	0.0398	0.0438	0.0478	0.0517	0.0557	0.0596	0.0636	0.0675	0.0714	0.0753
0.2	0.0793	0.0832	0.0871	0.0910	0.0948	0.0987	0.1026	0.1064	0.1103	0.1141
0.3	0.1179	0.1217	0.1255	0.1293	0.1331	0.1368	0.1406	0.1443	0.1480	0.1517
0.4	0.1554	0.1591	0.1628	0.1664	0.1700	0.1736	0.1772	0.1808	0.1844	0.1879
0.5	0.1915	0.1950	0.1985	0.2019	0.2054	0.2088	0.2123	0.2157	0.2190	0.2224
0.6	0.2257	0.2291	0.2324	0.2357	0.2389	0.2422	0.2454	0.2486	0.2517	0.2549
0.7	0.2580	0.2611	0.2642	0.2673	0.2704	0.2734	0.2764	0.2794	0.2823	0.2852
0.8	0.2881	0.2910	0.2939	0.2967	0.2995	0.3023	0.3051	0.3078	0.3106	0.3133
0.9	0.3159	0.3186	0.3212	0.3238	0.3264	0.3289	0.3315	0.3340	0.3365	0.3389
1.0	0.3413	0.3438	0.3461	0.3485	0.3508	0.3531	0.3554	0.3577	0.3599	0.3621
1.1	0.3643	0.3665	0.3686	0.3708	0.3729	0.3749	0.3770	0.3790	0.3810	0.3830
1.2	0.3849	0.3869	0.3888	0.3907	0.3925	0.3944	0.3962	0.3980	0.3997	0.4015
1.3	0.4032	0.4049	0.4066	0.4082	0.4099	0.4115	0.4131	0.4147	0.4162	0.4177
1.4	0.4192	0.4207	0.4222	0.4236	0.4251	0.4265	0.4279	0.4292	0.4306	0.4319
1.5	0.4332	0.4345	0.4357	0.4370	0.4382	0.4394	0.4406	0.4418	0.4429	0.4441
1.6	0.4452	0.4463	0.4474	0.4484	0.4495	0.4505	0.4515	0.4525	0.4535	0.4545
1.7	0.4554	0.4564	0.4573	0.4582	0.4591	0.4599	0.4608	0.4616	0.4625	0.4633
1.8	0.4641	0.4649	0.4656	0.4664	0.4671	0.4678	0.4686	0.4693	0.4699	0.4706
1.9	0.4713	0.4719	0.4726	0.4732	0.4738	0.4744	0.4750	0.4756	0.4761	0.4767
2.0	0.4773	0.4778	0.4783	0.4788	0.4793	0.4798	0.4803	0.4808	0.4812	0.4817
2.1	0.4821	0.4826	0.4830	0.4834	0.4838	0.4842	0.4846	0.4850	0.4854	0.4857
2.2	0.4861	0.4866	0.4830	0.4871	0.4875	0.4878	0.4881	0.4884	0.4887	0.4890
2.3	0.4893	0.4896	0.4898	0.4901	0.4904	0.4906	0.4909	0.4911	0.4913	0.4916
2.4	0.4918	0.4920	0.4922	0.4925	0.4927	0.4929	9.4931	0.4932	0.4934	0.4936
2.5	0.4938	0.4940	0.4941	0.4943	0.4945	0.4946	0.4948	0.4949	0.4951	0.4952
2.6	0.4953	0.4955	0.4956	0.4957	0.4959	0.4960	0.4961	0.4962	0.4963	0.4964
2.7	0.4965	0.4966	0.4967	0.4968	0.4969	0.4970	0.4971	0.4972	0.4973	0.4974
2.8	0.4974	0.4975	0.4976	0.4977	0.4977	0.4978	0.4979	0.0479	0.4980	0.4981
2.9	0.4981	0.4982	0.4982	0.4982	0.4984	0.4984	0.4985	0.4985	0.4986	0.4986
3.0	0.4987	0.4987	0.4987	0.4988	0.4988	0.4989	0.4989	0.4989	0.4990	0.4990

$N(d)$ represents areas under the standard normal distribution function. Suppose that $d_1 = 0.24$. This table implies a cumulative probability of $0.5000 + 0.0948 = 0.5948$. If d_1 is equal to 0.2452, we must estimate the probability by interpolating between $N(0.25)$ and $N(0.24)$.

values is 0.0037 ($0.6480 - 0.6443$). Because 0.3743 is 43 percent of the way between 0.37 and 0.38, we interpolate as[16]

$$N(0.3743) = 0.6443 + 0.43 \times 0.0037 = 0.6459$$

Step 3: Calculate C. We have

$$C = S \times [N(d_1)] - Ee^{-rt} \times [N(d_2)]$$
$$= \$50 \times [N(d_1)] - \$49 \times [e^{-0.07 \times (199/365)}] \times N(d_2)$$
$$= (\$50 \times 0.6459) - (\$49 \times 0.9626 \times 0.5607)$$
$$= \$32.295 - \$26.447$$
$$= \$5.85$$

---

[16]This method is called *linear interpolation*. It is only one of a number of possible methods of interpolation.

The estimated price of $5.85 is greater than the $4 actual price, implying that the call option is underpriced. A trader believing in the Black–Scholes model would buy a call. Of course, the Black–Scholes model is fallible. Perhaps the disparity between the model's estimate and the market price reflects error in the model's estimate of variance. ■

It is no exaggeration to say that the Black–Scholes formula is among the most important contributions in finance. It allows anyone to calculate the value of an option given a few parameters. The attraction of the formula is that four of the parameters are observable: the current price of the stock, S, the exercise price, E, the interest rate, r, and the time to expiration date, t. Only one of the parameters must be estimated: the variance of return, σ^2.

To see how truly attractive this formula is, note what parameters are not needed. First, the investor's risk aversion does not affect value. The formula can be used by anyone, regardless of willingness to bear risk. Second, it does not depend on the expected return on the stock! Investors with different assessments of the stock's expected return will nevertheless agree on the call price. As in the two-state example, this is because the call depends on the stock price and that price already balances investors' divergent views.

The assumptions for the Black–Scholes model appear to be severe:

1. There are no penalties for or restrictions on short selling.
2. Transaction costs and taxes are zero.
3. The option is European.
4. The stock pays no dividends.
5. The stock price is continuous, that is, there are no jumps.
6. The market operates continuously.
7. The short-term interest rate is known and constant.
8. The stock price is "lognormally" distributed.

These assumptions are the sufficient conditions for the Black–Scholes model to be correct. However, when these assumptions do not hold, a variation of the model often works. For example, the formula can be fine-tuned to account for dividends. Empirical studies suggest that the model, particularly when fine-tuned, does a good job in computing call option value.

CONCEPT QUESTIONS

■ How does the two-state option model work?
■ What is the formula for the Black–Scholes option pricing model?

21.9 Stocks and Bonds as Options

The previous material in this chapter described, explained, and valued publicly traded options. This is important material to any finance student because much trading occurs in these listed options. The study of options has another purpose for the student of corporate finance.

You may have heard the one-liner about the elderly gentleman who was surprised to learn that he had been speaking prose all of his life. The same can be said about the corporate finance student and options. Although options were formally defined for the first time in this chapter, many corporate policies discussed earlier in the text were actually options in disguise. Though it is beyond the scope of this chapter to recast all of corporate finance in terms of options, the rest of the chapter considers three topics in which implicit options play an important role:

1. Stocks and bonds as options.
2. Capital structure decisions as options.
3. Capital budgeting decisions as options.

We begin by illustrating the implicit options in stocks and bonds through a simple example.

▪ Example

The Popov Company has been awarded the concessions at next year's Olympic Games in Antarctica. Because the firm's principals live in Antarctica and because there is no other concession business on that continent, their enterprise will disband after the games. The firm has issued debt to help finance this venture. Interest and principal due on the debt next year will be $800, at which time the debt will be paid off in full. The firm's cash flows next year are forecasted as

	Popov's cash flow schedule			
	Very successful games	Moderately successful games	Moderately unsuccessful games	Outright failure
Cash flow before interest and principal	$1,000	$850	$700	$550
Interest and principal	800	800	~~800~~ 700	~~800~~ 550
Cash flow to stockholders	$ 200	$ 50	0	0

As can be seen, the principals forecasted four equally likely scenarios. If either of the first two scenarios occurs, the bondholders will be paid in full. The extra cash flow goes to the shareholders. However, if either of the last two scenarios occurs, the bondholders will not be paid in full. Instead, they will receive the firm's entire cash flow, leaving the shareholders with nothing.

This example is similar to the bankruptcy examples presented in our chapters on capital structure. Our new insight is that the relationship between the common stock and the firm can be expressed in terms of options. We consider call options first because the intuition is easier. The put option scenario is treated next.

The Firm Expressed in Terms of Call Options

Shareholders

We now show that stock can be viewed as a call option on the firm. To illustrate this, Figure 21.9 graphs the cash flow to the shareholders as a function of the cash flow to the firm. The shareholders receive nothing if the firm's cash flows are less than $800;

Figure 21.9
Cash flow to
stockholders of
Popov Corporation
as a function of
cash flow of firm

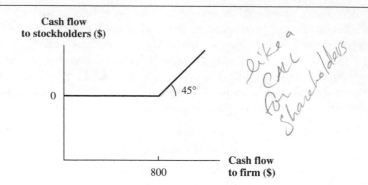

here, all of the cash flows go to the bondholders. However, the shareholders earn a dollar for every dollar that the firm receives above $800. The graph looks exactly like the call option graphs that we considered earlier in this chapter.

But what is the underlying asset upon which the stock is a call option? The underlying asset is the firm itself. That is, we can view the bondholders as owning the firm. However, the shareholders have a call option on the firm with an exercise price of $800.

If the firm's cash flow is above $800, the shareholders will choose to exercise this option. In other words, they will buy the firm from the bondholders for $800. Their net cash flow is the difference between the firm's cash flow and their $800 payment. This will be $200 (or $1,000 − $800) if the games are very successful and $50 (or $850 − $800) if the games are moderately successful.

If the value of the firm's cash flows is less than $800, the shareholders will not choose to exercise their option. Instead, they will walk away from the firm, as would any call option holder. The bondholders then receive the firm's entire cash flow.

Bondholders

What about the bondholders? Our earlier cash flow schedule showed that they get the entire cash flow of the firm if it is less than $800. Should the firm earn more than $800, the bondholders receive only $800. That is, they are entitled only to interest and principal. This schedule is graphed in Figure 21.10.

In keeping with our view that the shareholders have a call option on the firm, what does the bondholders' position consist of? The bondholders' position can be described by two claims:

1. They own the firm.
2. They have written a call against the firm with an exercise price of $800.

As we mentioned above, the shareholders walk away from the firm if cash flows are less than $800. Thus, the bondholders retain ownership in this case. However, if the cash flows are greater than $800, the shareholders exercise their option. They call the stock away from the bondholders for $800.

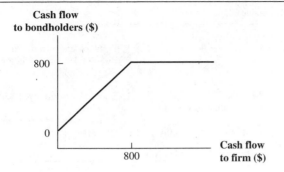

Figure 21.10
Cash flow to bondholders as a function of cash flow of firm

[handwritten note:] Bondholders have written a call against the firm w/ exercise of $800

The Firm Expressed in Terms of Put Options

The above analysis expresses the positions of the shareholders and the bondholders in terms of call options. We can now express the situation in terms of put options.

Shareholders

The shareholders' position can be expressed by three claims:

1. They own the firm.
2. They owe $800 in interest and principal to the bondholders.

If the debt were risk-free, these two claims would fully describe the shareholders' situation. However, because of the possibility of default, we have a third claim as well:

3. The shareholders own a put option on the firm with an exercise price of $800. The group of bondholders is the seller of the put.

Now consider two possibilities.

Cash Flow Is Less Than $800　Because the put has an exercise price of $800, the put is in the money. The shareholders "put" (that is, sell) the firm to the bondholders. Normally, the holder of a put receives the exercise price when the asset is sold. However, the shareholders already owe $800 to the bondholders. Thus, the debt of $800 is simply cancelled—and no money changes hands—when the stock is delivered to the bondholders. Because the shareholders give up the stock in exchange for extinguishing the debt, the shareholders end up with nothing if the cash flow is below $800.

Cash Flow Is Greater Than $800　Because the put is out of the money in this case, the shareholders do not exercise. Thus, the shareholders retain ownership of the firm but pay $800 to the bondholders as interest and principal.

Bondholders

The bondholders' position can be described by two claims:

1. The bondholders are owed $800.
2. They have sold a put option on the firm to the shareholders with an exercise price of $800.

Table 21.4	Shareholders	Bondholders
Positions of shareholders and bondholders in Popov Company in terms of calls and puts	Positions viewed in terms of call options 1. Shareholders own a call on the firm with exercise price of $800.	1. Bondholders own the firm. 2. Bondholders have sold a call on the firm to the shareholders.
	Positions viewed in terms of put options 1. Shareholders own the firm. 2. Shareholders owe $800 in interest and principal to bondholders. 3. Shareholders own a put option on the firm with exercise price of $800.	1. Bondholders are owed $800 in interest and principal. 2. Bondholders have sold a put on the firm to the shareholders.

Cash Flow Is Less Than $800   As mentioned above, the shareholders will exercise the put in this case. This means that the bondholders are obligated to pay $800 for the firm. Because they are owed $800, the two obligations offset each other. Thus, the bondholders simply end up with the firm.

Cash Flow Is Greater Than $800   Here, the shareholders do not exercise the put. Thus, the bondholders merely receive the $800 that is due them.

Expressing the bondholders' position in this way is illuminating. With a riskless default-free bond, the bondholders are owed $800. Thus, we can express the risky bond in terms of a riskless bond and a put:

$$\begin{array}{ccccc} \text{Value of} & = & \text{Value of} & - & \text{Value of} \\ \text{risky bond} & & \text{default-free bond} & & \text{put option} \end{array}$$

That is, the value of the risky bond is the value of the default-free bond less the value of the shareholders' option to sell the company for $800.

A Resolution of the Two Views

We have argued above that the positions of the shareholders and the bondholders can be viewed either in terms of calls or in terms of puts. These two viewpoints are summarized in Table 21.4. The two viewpoints can be related in terms of the put-call parity relationship discussed earlier in this chapter:

$$\begin{array}{ccccc} \text{Value of} & + & \text{Value of put} & - & \text{Value of call} & = & \text{Present value of} \\ \text{common stock} & & \text{on common stock} & & \text{on common stock} & & \text{exercise price} \end{array} \quad (21.1)$$

Using the results of this section, equation (21.1) can be rewritten as

$$\begin{array}{ccccc} \text{Value of call} & = & \text{Value of} & + & \text{Value of put} & - & \text{Value of} \\ \text{on firm} & & \text{firm} & & \text{on firm} & & \text{default-free bond} \end{array} \quad (21.2)$$

$$\underbrace{\qquad\qquad\qquad}_{\substack{\text{Shareholders'} \\ \text{position in terms} \\ \text{of call options}}} \qquad \underbrace{\qquad\qquad\qquad}_{\substack{\text{Shareholders' position} \\ \text{in terms of put options}}}$$

Going from equation (21.1) to equation (21.2) involves a few steps. First, we treat the firm, not the stock, as the underlying asset in this section. Second, the exercise price is now $800, the principal and interest on the firm's debt. Taking the present value of this amount at the riskless rate yields the value of a default-free bond. Third, the order of the terms in equation (21.1) is rearranged in equation (21.2).

Note that the left-hand side of equation (21.2) is the shareholders' position in terms of call options, as shown in Table 21.4. The right-hand side of equation (21.2) is the shareholders' position in terms of put options, as shown in the table. Thus, put-call parity shows that viewing the shareholders' position in terms of call options is equivalent to viewing the shareholders' position in terms of put options.

Now, let's rearrange terms in equation (21.2) to yield

$$
\underbrace{\begin{array}{ccc} \text{Value of} & - & \text{Value of call} \\ \text{firm} & & \text{on firm} \end{array}}_{\substack{\text{Bondholders' position in} \\ \text{terms of call options}}} = \underbrace{\begin{array}{ccc} \text{Value of} & - & \text{Value of put} \\ \text{default-free bond} & & \text{on firm} \end{array}}_{\substack{\text{Bondholders' position in} \\ \text{terms of put options}}} \qquad (21.3)
$$

The left-hand side of equation (21.3) is the bondholders' position in terms of call options, as shown in Table 21.4. The right-hand side of the equation is the bondholders' position in terms of put options, as shown in Table 21.4. Thus, put-call parity shows that viewing the bondholders' position in terms of call options is equivalent to viewing the bondholders' position in terms of put options.

A Note on Loan Guarantees

In the Popov example above, the bondholders bore the risk of default. Of course, bondholders generally ask for an interest rate that is high enough to compensate them for bearing risk. When firms experience financial distress, they can no longer attract new debt at moderate interest rates. Thus, firms experiencing distress have frequently sought loan guarantees from the government. Our framework can be used to understand these guarantees.

If the firm defaults on a guaranteed loan, the government must make up the difference. In other words, a government guarantee converts a risky bond into a riskless bond. What is the value of this guarantee?

Recall that, with option pricing,

$$
\begin{array}{ccc} \text{Value of} & = & \text{Value of} & + & \text{Value of} \\ \text{default-free bond} & & \text{risky bond} & & \text{put option} \end{array}
$$

This equation shows that the government is assuming an obligation that has a cost equal to the value of a put option.

Our analysis differs from that of either politicians or company spokespersons. They generally say that the guarantee will cost the taxpayer nothing because the guarantee enables the firm to attract debt, thereby staying solvent. However, it should be pointed out that, though solvency may be a strong possibility, it is never a certainty. Thus, at the time the guarantee is made, the government's obligation has a cost in terms of present value. To say that a guarantee costs the government nothing is like saying that a put on the stock of, say, Northern Telecom, has no value because the stock is *likely* to rise in price.

Federal and provincial governments provide guarantees for bank loans to companies whose survival is considered important to the public interest. Who benefits from a typical loan guarantee?[17]

1. If existing risky debt is guaranteed, all gains accrue to the existing bondholders or creditors. The shareholders gain nothing because the limited liability of corporations absolves the shareholders of any obligation in bankruptcy.

2. If new debt is being issued and guaranteed, the new debtholders do not gain. Rather, in a competitive market, they must accept a low interest rate because of the debt's low risk. The shareholders gain here because they are able to issue debt at a low interest rate. In addition, some of the gains accrue to the old bondholders because the firm's value is greater than would otherwise be true. Therefore, if shareholders want all the gains from loan guarantees, they should renegotiate or retire existing bonds before the guarantee is in place.

Deposit Insurance as a Loan Guarantee

When you lend money to a financial institution (by making a deposit), your loan is guaranteed (up to $60,000) by the federal government provided your institution is a member of the Canada Deposit Insurance Corporation (CDIC). As we argued above, loan guarantees are not cost-free. This point was made abundantly clear to the government when two banks collapsed in western Canada in 1985, the Principal Group collapsed in 1987, and Central Guaranty Trust collapsed in 1992.

We also pointed out that, since the put option allows a risky firm to borrow at subsidized rates, it is an asset to the shareholders. The more volatile the firm, the greater the value of the put option and the more the guarantee is worth to the shareholders. Following this logic, Giammarino, Schwartz, and Zechner modified the Black–Scholes model to value the put option in CDIC deposit insurance for Canadian banks in the mid-1980s. They found that financial markets provided early warning of bank failures as the value of the put option increased significantly before bank failure occurred. Their research also showed that, by charging the same premium for all financial institutions regardless of risk, the CDIC subsidized riskier banks and likely encouraged risk taking.[18]

U.S. taxpayers learned the same lessons about loan guarantees at far greater cost in the savings and loan collapse. The final cost to U.S. taxpayers of making good on these institutions' guaranteed deposits is unknown as this is being written, but the staggering amount seems certain to be well over $200 billion.

---

[17]A. H. Chen, M.-W. Hung, and S. C. Mazundar, "Valuation of Parent Guarantees of Subsidiary Debt: Ownership, Risk and Leverage Implications," *Pacific Basin Finance Journal* (1994), use option pricing theory to analyze the financing implications of parent loan guarantees of subsidiary debt.

[18]R. Giammarino, E. Schwartz, and J. Zechner, "Market Valuation of Bank Assets and Deposit Insurance in Canada," *Canadian Journal of Economics* (February 1989), pp. 109–27.

One result is that accountants in Canada, urged on by the auditor general, are forcing government agencies to report guarantees and other contingent liabilities in their financial statements. This may induce greater caution in extending guarantees in the first place.

CONCEPT QUESTIONS

- How can the firm be expressed in terms of call options?
- How can the firm be expressed in terms of put options?
- How does put-call parity relate these two expressions?
- Why are government loan guarantees not free? Why do such guarantees often encourage firms to increase their risk?

Capital Structure Policy and Options　　21.10

Recall our chapters on capital structure where we showed how managers, acting on behalf of the shareholders, can take advantage of bondholders. A number of these strategies can be explained in terms of options. To conserve space, we discuss only two of them. The first, selecting a high-risk project instead of a low-risk project, can be most easily explained in terms of a call option. The second, milking the firm, can be most easily understood in terms of a put option.[19]

Selecting High-Risk Projects

Imagine a levered firm considering two mutually exclusive projects: a low-risk one and a high-risk one. There are two equally likely outcomes: recession and boom. The firm is in such dire straits that, should a recession hit, it will come near to bankruptcy if the low-risk project is selected and will actually fall into bankruptcy if the high-risk project is selected. The cash flows for the firm if the low-risk project is taken can be described as

	Probability	Low-risk project Value of firm	=	Stock	+	Bonds
Recession	0.5	$400	=	0	+	$400
Boom	0.5	$800	=	$400	+	$400

If recession occurs, the value of the firm will be $400, and if boom obtains, the value of the firm will be $800. The expected value of the firm is $600 (or $0.5 \times \$400 + 0.5 \times \$800$). The firm has promised to pay the bondholders $400. Shareholders will obtain the difference between the total payoff and the amount paid to the bondholders. The

---

[19]The put-call parity relationship implies that a call option can be described as a put and vice versa. Thus, both selecting one project over another and choosing to milk the firm can be described by either a call or a put. In each case, our analysis uses the simpler approach, as the student will be happy to learn.

bondholders have the prior claim on the payoffs, and the shareholders have the residual claim.

Now suppose that a riskier project can be substituted for the low-risk project. The payoffs and probabilities are as follows:

	Probability	High-risk project Value of firm	=	Stock	+	Bonds
Recession	0.5	$ 200	=	0	+	$200
Boom	0.5	$1,000	=	$600	+	$400

The expected value of the firm is $600 (or 0.5 × $200 + 0.5 × $1,000), which is identical to the value of the firm with the low-risk project. However, note that the expected value of the stock is $300 (or 0.5 × 0 + 0.5 × $600) with the high-risk project, but only $200 (or 0.5 × 0 + 0.5 × $400) with the low-risk project. Given the firm's present levered state, shareholders will select the high-risk project.

The shareholders benefit at the expense of the bondholders when the high-risk project is accepted. The explanation is quite clear: The bondholders suffer dollar for dollar when the firm's value falls short of the $400 bond obligation. However, the bondholders' payments are capped at $400 when the firm does well.

This can be explained in terms of call options. We argued earlier in this chapter that the value of a call rises with an increase in the volatility of the underlying asset. Because the stock is a call option on the firm, a rise in the volatility of the firm increases the value of the stock. In our example, the value of the stock is higher if the high-risk project is accepted.

Table 21.4 showed that the value of a risky bond can be viewed as the difference between the value of the stock and the value of a call on the firm. Because a call's value rises with the risk of the underlying asset, the value of the bond should decline if the firm increases its risk. In our example, the bondholders are hurt when the high-risk project is accepted.

Milking the Firm

The discussion above considers the situation where the firm can choose between a high-risk and a low-risk project. The chapters on capital structure also examined the case where extra dividends and other distributions are paid out to shareholders in anticipation of financial distress. This strategy, which was previously referred to as *milking the firm,* hurts the bondholders. We can explain the option aspect of this strategy most easily by thinking in terms of puts, not calls. We stated earlier that

$$\begin{matrix} \text{Value of} \\ \text{risky bonds} \end{matrix} \quad = \quad \begin{matrix} \text{Value of} \\ \text{riskless bonds} \end{matrix} \quad - \quad \begin{matrix} \text{Value of} \\ \text{put option} \end{matrix}$$

The put option represents the ability of the shareholders to sell the firm to the bondholders in exchange for the bondholders' promised payment. Earlier in this chapter, we learned that the value of the put increases as the value of the underlying asset falls. Because the value of the firm falls when a dividend is paid, a put on the firm must rise in value when the dividend payment is announced. By the above equation, the value of the risky bonds must decrease when the put option increases in value.

The above discussion is in terms of risky bonds. Of course, a loss to the bondholders implies a benefit to the shareholders. Hence, shareholders must gain when dividends are paid during periods of financial distress.

CONCEPT QUESTION

■ How can options be used to explain strategies like selecting high-risk projects and milking the firm?

Investment in Real Projects and Options
21.11

Our discussion begins with a quick review of the material on capital budgeting presented earlier in the text. We first considered projects where forecasts for future cash flows were made at date 0. The expected cash flow in each future period was discounted at an appropriate risky rate, yielding an NPV calculation. For independent projects, a positive NPV meant acceptance and a negative NPV meant rejection.

This approach treated risk through the discount rate. We later considered decision-tree analysis, an approach that handles risk in a more sophisticated way. We pointed out that the firm will make investment and operating decisions on a project over its entire life. We value a project today, assuming that future decisions will be optimal. However, we do not yet know what these decisions will be, because much information remains to be discovered. The firm's ability to delay its investment and operating decisions until the release of information is an option. We now illustrate this option through an example.

■ *Example*

Exoff Oil Corporation is considering the purchase of an oil field in a remote northern area. The seller has listed the property for $10,000 and is eager to sell immediately. Initial drilling costs are $500,000. The firm anticipates that 10,000 barrels of oil can be extracted each year for many decades. Because the termination date is so far in the future and so hard to estimate, the firm views the cash flow stream from the oil as a perpetuity. With oil prices at $20 per barrel and extraction costs at $16 a barrel, the firm anticipates a net margin of $4 per barrel. Because the firm budgets capital in real terms, it assumes that its cash flow per barrel will always be $4. The appropriate real discount rate is 10 percent. The firm has enough tax credits from bad years in the past so that it will not need to pay taxes on any profits from the oil field. Should Exoff buy the property?

The NPV of the oil field to Exoff is

$$-\$110,000 = -\$10,000 - \$500,000 + \frac{\$4 \times 10,000}{0.10} \tag{21.4}$$

According to this analysis, Exoff should not purchase the land.

Though this approach uses the standard capital budgeting techniques of this and other textbooks, it is actually inappropriate for this situation. To see this, consider the analysis of Kirtley Thornton, a consultant to Exoff. He agrees that the price of oil is *expected* to rise at the rate of inflation. However, he points out that the next year is quite perilous for oil prices. On the one hand, OPEC is considering a long-term agreement that would raise oil prices to $35 per barrel in real terms for many years in the future. On the other hand, National Motors recently indicated that cars using a mixture of sand and water for fuel are currently being tested. Thornton argues that oil will be priced at $5 in real terms for many years, should this development prove successful. Full information on both these developments will be released in exactly one year.

Should oil prices rise to $35 a barrel, the NPV of the project would be

$$\$1,390,000 = -\$10,000 - \$500,000 + \frac{(\$35 - 16) \times 10,000}{0.10}$$

However, should oil prices fall to $5 a barrel, the NPV of the oil field will be even more negative than it is today.

Mr. Thornton makes two recommendations to Exoff's board:

1. The land should be purchased.
2. The drilling decision should be delayed until information on both OPEC's new agreement and National Motor's new automobile are developed.

He explains his recommendations to the board by first assuming that the land has already been purchased. He argues that, under this assumption, the drilling decision should be delayed. Second, he investigates his assumption that the land should have been purchased in the first place. This approach, examining the second decision (whether to drill) after assuming that the first decision (to buy the land) has been made, was also used in our earlier presentation on decision trees. Let us now work through Mr. Thornton's analysis.

Assume that the land has already been purchased. If the land has already been purchased, should drilling begin immediately? If drilling begins immediately, the NPV is −$110,000. If the drilling decision is delayed until new information is released in a year, the optimal choice can be made at that time. If oil prices drop to $5 a barrel, Exoff should not drill. Instead, the firm walks away from the project, losing nothing beyond its $10,000 purchase price for the land. If oil prices rise to $35, drilling should begin.

Mr. Thornton points out that, by delaying, the firm will only invest the $500,000 of drilling costs if oil prices rise. Thus, by delaying, the firm saves $500,000 in the case where oil prices drop. He concludes that, once the land is purchased, the drilling decision should be delayed.[20]

Should the land have been purchased in the first place? We now know that, if the land is purchased, it is optimal to defer the drilling decision until the release of information. Given that we know this optimal decision concerning drilling, should the land be purchased in the first place? Without knowing the exact probability that oil

---

[20]Actually, there are three separate effects here. First, the firm avoids drilling costs in the case of low oil prices by delaying the decision. This is the effect discussed by Mr. Thornton. Second, the present value of the $500,000 payment is less when the decision is delayed, even if drilling eventually takes place. Third, the firm loses one year of cash inflows through delay.

The first two arguments support delaying the decision. The third argument supports immediate drilling. In this example, the first argument greatly outweighs the other two arguments. Thus, Mr. Thornton avoided the second and third arguments in his presentation.

prices will rise, Mr. Thornton is nevertheless confident that the land should be purchased. The NPV of the project at $35 oil prices is $1,390,000 whereas the cost of the land is only $10,000. Kirtley believes that an oil price rise is possible, though by no means probable. Even so, he argues that the high potential return is clearly worth the risk. ∎

This example presents an approach that is similar to our decision-tree analysis of the Solar Equipment Company in a previous chapter. Our purpose here is to discuss this type of decision in an option framework. When Exoff purchases the land, it is actually purchasing a call option. That is, once the land has been purchased, the firm has an option to buy an active oil field at an exercise price of $500,000. As it turns out, one should generally not exercise a call option immediately.[21] In this case, the firm delays exercise until relevant information concerning future oil prices is released.

This section points out a serious deficiency in classical capital budgeting: net present value calculations typically ignore the flexibility that real world firms have. In our example, the standard techniques generated a negative NPV for the land purchase. Yet, by allowing the firm the option to change its investment policy according to new information, the land purchase can easily be justified.

We urge the reader to look for hidden options in projects. Because options are beneficial, managers are shortchanging their firm's projects if capital budgeting calculations ignore flexibility.

CONCEPT QUESTION

∎ Why are the hidden options in projects valuable?

Summary and Conclusions   21.12

This chapter serves as an introduction to options.

1. The most familiar options are puts and calls. These options give the holder the right to sell or buy shares of common stock at a given exercise price. American options can be exercised at any time up to and including the expiration date. European options can be exercised only on the expiration date.

2. Options can either be held in isolation or in combination. We focused on the strategy of

> Buying a put.
> Buying the stock.
> Selling a call.

---

[21]Actually, it can be shown that a call option on a stock that pays no dividend should never be exercised before expiration. However, for a dividend-paying stock, it may be optimal to exercise prior to the ex dividend date. The analogy applies to our example of an option in real assets.

The firm would receive cash flows from oil earlier if drilling begins immediately. This is equivalent to the benefit from exercising a call on a stock prematurely in order to capture the dividend. However, in our example, this dividend effect is far outweighed by the benefits from waiting.

where the put and call have both the same exercise price and the same expiration date. This strategy yields a riskless return because the gain or loss on the call precisely offsets the gain or loss on the stock-and-put combination. In equilibrium, the return on this strategy must be exactly equal to the riskless rate. From this, the put-call parity relationship was established:

$$\begin{array}{ccccccc} \text{Value of} & + & \text{Value of} & - & \text{Value of} & = & \text{Present value of} \\ \text{stock} & & \text{put} & & \text{call} & & \text{exercise price} \end{array}$$

3. The value of an option depends on five factors:

   The price of the underlying asset.

   The exercise price.

   The expiration date.

   The variability of the underlying asset.

   The interest rate on risk-free bonds.

   The Black–Scholes model can determine the intrinsic price of an option from these five factors.

4. Much of corporate financial theory can be presented in terms of options. In this chapter we pointed out that

   a. Common stock can be represented as a call option on the firm.

   b. Shareholders enhance the value of their call by increasing the risk of their firm.

   c. Milking the firm can be expressed in options.

   d. Real projects have hidden options that enhance value.

Key Terms

Option 607

Exercising the option 607

Striking or exercise price 607

Expiration date 607

American options 608

European options 608

Call option 608

Put option 610

Put-call parity 618

Standardized normal distribution 628

Cumulative probability 628

Suggested Readings

The path-breaking article on options is:

Fischer Black and Myron Scholes. "The Pricing of Options and Corporate Liabilities." *Journal of Political Economy* 81 (May–June 1973).

For a detailed discussion of options, read:

J. C. Cox and M. Rubinstein. *Options Markets.* Englewood Cliffs, N.J.: Prentice Hall, 1985. (Section 7.3 analyzes corporate securities.)

J. Hull. *Options, Futures and Other Derivative Securities.* Englewood Cliffs, N.J.: Prentice Hall, 1989.

Questions and Problems

Options: General

21.1 Define the following terms associated with options:

  a. Option.

  b. Exercise.

  c. Strike price.

  d. Expiration date.

  e. Call option.

  f. Put option.

21.2 What is the difference between American options and European options?

21.3 A call option on NAES Corporation stock currently trades for $4. The expiration date is March 18 of next year. The exercise price of the option is $78.

  a. If this is an American option, on what dates can the option be exercised?

  b. If this is a European option, on what dates can the option be exercised?

  c. Suppose the current price of NAES Corporation stock is $52. Is this option worthless?

21.4 The strike price of a call option on Chervile Cannery common stock is $50. The call sells for $7\frac{3}{8}$.

  a. What is the payoff at expiration of this call if, on the expiration date, Chervile stock sells for $64?

  b. What is the payoff at expiration of this call if, on the expiration date, Chervile stock sells for $43?

  c. Draw the payoff diagram for this option.

21.5 Puts are trading on Chervile Cannery stock. The puts sell for $4\frac{7}{8}$ each. They have a strike price of $50.

  a. What is the payoff at expiration of this put if, on the expiration date, Chervile stock sells for $64?

  b. What is the payoff at expiration of this put if, on the expiration date, Chervile stock sells for $43?

  c. Draw the payoff diagram for this option.

21.6 You hold a six-month European call option contract on Sertile stock. The exercise price of the call is $100 per share. The option will expire in moments. Assume there are no transactions costs or taxes associated with this contract.

  a. What is your profit on this contract if the stock is selling for $130?

  b. If Sertile stock is selling for $90, what will you do?

21.7 Piersol Paper Mill's common stock currently sells for $145. Both puts and calls on Piersol Paper are being traded. These options all expire eight months from today, and they have a strike price of $160. Eight months from today, Piersol Paper common stock will sell for $172 with a probability of 0.5. It will sell for $138 with a probability of 0.5. You own a put on Piersol Paper. Now, you are becoming nervous about the risk to which you are exposed.

  a. What other transactions should you make to eliminate this risk?
  b. What is the expected payoff at expiration of the strategy you developed in (a)?

21.8 Suppose you observe the following market prices:

| American Call (Strike = $100) | $8 |
| Stock | $112 |

  a. What should you do?
  b. What is your profit or loss?
  c. What do opportunities such as this imply about the lower bound on the price of American calls?
  d. What is the upper bound on the price of American calls? Explain.

21.9 List the factors that determine the value of an American call option. State how a change in each factor alters the option's value.

21.10 List the factors that determine the value of an American put option. State how a change in each factor alters the option's value.

21.11 a. If the risk of a stock increases, what is likely to happen to the price of call options on the stock? Why?
  b. If the risk of a stock increases, what is likely to happen to the price of put options on the stock? Why?

The Two-State Option Model

21.12 You bought a 100-share call contract three weeks ago. The expiration date of the calls is five weeks from today. On that date, the price of the underlying stock will be either $120 or $95. The two states are equally likely to occur. Currently, the stock sells for $96; its strike price is $112. You are able to purchase 32 shares of stock. You are able to borrow money at 10 percent per annum.

  What is the value of your call contract?

21.13 Assume only two states will exist one year from today when a call on Engel, Inc., stock expires. With equal probability, the price of Engel stock will be either $75 or $50 on that date. Today, Engel stock trades for $60. The strike price of the call is $60. The rate at which you can borrow is 9 percent.

  How much are you willing to pay for a contract of this call?

The Black–Scholes Option Model

21.14 Use the Black–Scholes model to price a call with the following characteristics:

Stock price	=	$62
Strike price	=	$70
Time to expiration	=	4 weeks
Stock price variance	=	0.35
Risk-free interest rate	=	0.05

21.15   Use the Black–Scholes model to price a call with the following
        characteristics:

Stock price	=	$110
Strike price	=	$100
Time to expiration	=	120 days
Stock price variance	=	0.20
Risk-free interest rate	=	0.05

21.16 *a.*   Use the Black–Scholes model to price a call with the following
        characteristics:

Stock price	=	$45
Strike price	=	$52
Time to expiration	=	6 months
Stock price variance	=	0.40
Risk-free interest rate	=	0.065

   b.   What does put-call parity imply the price of the corresponding put will
          be?

21.17 *a.*   Use the Black–Scholes model to price a call with the following
        characteristics:

Stock Price	=	$28
Strike price	=	$40
Time to expiration	=	6 months
Stock price variance	=	0.50
Risk-free interest rate	=	0.06

   b.   What does put-call parity imply the price of the corresponding put will
          be?

21.18   You have been asked by a client to determine the maximum price he should
        be willing to pay to purchase a Combred call. The options have an exercise
        price of $45, and they expire in 156 days. The current price of Combred
        stock is $44⅜, the annual risk-free rate is 7 percent, and the estimated rate of
        return variance of the stock is 0.0961. No dividends are expected to be
        declared over the next six months. What is the maximum price your client
        should pay?

Capital Structure and Options

21.19   It is said that the equity in a levered firm is like a call option on the
        underlying assets. Explain this statement.

Capital Budgeting and Real Options

21.20   Explain how each of the following can be understood in terms of options.

   a.   Atlantic Hydro puts off construction of a new electricity generating plant.
          Although building a plant today has a positive NPV, a new, experimental
          program to convince consumers to use less power may have a higher NPV.

   b.   In upgrading the machinery in its mine, Yukon Mining invests an extra
          $10 million to acquire the latest technology which will facilitate closing
          and reopening the mine as gold prices fluctuate.

    c. McDonald's Canada opens restaurants in Moscow selling hamburgers for rubles. But the ruble is not convertible into hard currency, so McDonald's Canada cannot repatriate its profits to Canada.

    d. A pulp mill refits to comply with new pollution control laws. The refit is designed to exceed the standards set in the current law.

In this chapter, we study two financing instruments: warrants and convertibles. A warrant gives the holder the right to buy common stock for cash. In this sense, it is very much like a call. Warrants are generally issued with privately placed bonds, though they are also packaged with new issues of common stock and preferred stock. In the case of new issues of common stock, warrants are sometimes given to investment bankers as compensation for underwriting services.

A convertible bond gives the holder the right to exchange the bond for common stock. It is therefore a mixed security blurring the traditional line between stocks and bonds. There is also convertible preferred stock.

The chapter describes the basic features of warrants and convertibles. It also discusses some of the most important questions concerning these securities:

1. How can warrants and convertibles be valued?
2. What impact do warrants and convertibles have on the value of the firm?
3. What are the differences between warrants, convertibles, and call options?
4. Why do some companies issue bonds with warrants and convertible bonds?
5. Under what circumstances are warrants and convertibles converted into common stock?

Warrants 22.1

Warrants are securities that give holders the right, but not the obligation, to buy shares of common stock directly from a company at a fixed price for a given period of time. Each warrant specifies the number of shares that the holder can buy, the exercise price, and the expiration date.

The preceding description of warrants makes it clear that they are similar to call options. The differences in contractual features between warrants and the call options that trade on the TransCanada Options Exchange are small. For example, warrants have longer maturity periods.[1] Some warrants are actually perpetual, meaning that they never expire at all.

---

[1] Warrants are usually protected against stock splits and stock dividends in the same way that call options are.

Warrants are referred to as *equity kickers* because they are usually issued in combination with privately placed bonds.[2] In most cases, warrants are attached to the bonds when issued. The loan agreement will state whether the warrants are detachable from the bond, that is, whether they can be sold separately. Usually, the warrant can be detached immediately.

Including warrants with an issue of securities makes the issue more attractive. The use of warrants is becoming increasingly popular judging by the growing numbers listed on the TSE and Toronto Futures Exchange. With the growth of financial engineering, warrant issuers are creating new varieties. Some warrant issues give investors the right to buy the issuers' bonds instead of their stock. In addition, warrants are issued on their own instead of as sweeteners in a bond issue. In 1991, the Toronto-Dominion Bank combined these features in a $2.7 million stand-alone issue. The TD warrants carry the right to purchase debentures to be issued in the future.[3]

Echo Bay Mines Ltd. of Edmonton designed an innovative financing package including gold purchase warrants with a preferred share issue. The warrants gave the holder the right to buy gold at an exercise price of U.S. $595 per ounce. When the warrants were issued in 1981, gold was trading at U.S. $500 per ounce. A further condition restricted exercise of the warrants to cases where Echo Bay met certain production levels. As a result, how much these warrants were worth depended both on how well the company was doing and on gold prices.[4]

▪ *Example*

Merger warrants are created in a leveraged buyout.[5] On November 24, 1986, Safeway, a large U.S. supermarket chain, was acquired in a leveraged buyout by the private investment firm of Kohlberg Kravis Roberts and Co. (KKR). Each share of old common stock was converted into a junior subordinated debenture (that is, a junk bond) plus a merger warrant. Each warrant gave the holder the right to purchase .279 shares of new common stock for $1.052 per warrant. To purchase one share of common stock, a holder must give up 3.584 warrants (1/.279) and pay $3.77 per share (3.584 × $1.052). This makes the exercise price of the Safeway warrants equal to $13.5117 (or 3.584 × $3.77 = $13.5117). The warrants expire on November 24, 1996.

When Safeway was acquired by KKR, it was a private firm with no publicly traded common stock or warrants. However, KKR took Safeway public on April 26, 1990, by issuing 10 million common shares in an initial public offering. On that day, several thousand warrants were traded at a closing price of $3 ⅛. The price of Safeway common stock was $12 ⅛. ▪

The relationship between the value of Safeway's warrants and its stock price is the same as the relationship between a call option and its stock price, described in the previous chapter. Figure 22.1 depicts the relationship for Safeway warrants. The lower

---

[2]Warrants are also issued with publicly distributed bonds and new issues of common and preferred shares.

[3]B. Critchley, "The Top 10 Financings: Innovative Fund-Raising in Corporate Canada for '91," *The Financial Post* (December 16, 1991), p. 15.

[4]P. P. Boyle and E. F. Kirzner, "Pricing Complex Options: Echo Bay Ltd. Gold Purchase Warrants," *Canadian Journal of Administrative Sciences* 2 (December 1985), pp. 294–306.

[5]We discuss leveraged buyouts in Appendix 17A and in Chapter 29.

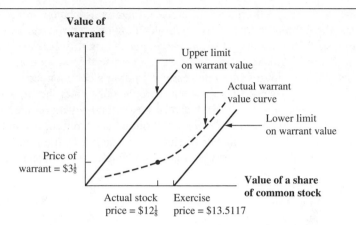

Figure 22.1
Safeway warrants
on April 26, 1990

limit on the value of the warrants is zero if Safeway's stock price is below $13.5117 per share. If the price of Safeway's common stock rises above $13.5117 per share, the lower limit is the stock price minus $13.5117. The upper limit is the price of Safeway's common stock. A warrant to buy one share of common stock cannot sell for more than the underlying common stock.

When the shares were first issued on April 26, 1990, the price of Safeway warrants was higher than the lower limit. How far the warrant price lies above the lower limit will depend on

1. The variance of Safeway's stock returns.
2. The time to the warrant's expiration date.
3. The risk-free rate of interest.
4. The stock price of Safeway.
5. The exercise price.

These are the same factors that determine the value of a call option.

The Difference between Warrants and Call Options   22.2

We saw that, from the holder's point of view, warrants are similar to call options on common stock. From the firm's point of view, however, a warrant is very different from a call option on the company's common stock. The most important difference is that call options are issued by individuals and warrants are issued by firms. When a warrant is exercised, a firm must issue new shares of stock. Each time a warrant is exercised, then, the number of shares outstanding increases.

To illustrate, suppose the Endrun Company issues a warrant giving holders the right to buy one share of common stock at $25. Further, suppose the warrant is exercised. Endrun must print one new stock certificate. In exchange for the stock certificate, it receives $25 from the holder.

In contrast, when a call option is exercised, there is no change in the number of shares outstanding. Suppose Ms. Eager holds a call option on the common stock of the Endrun Company. The call option gives Ms. Eager the right to buy one share of the common stock for $25. If Ms. Eager chooses to exercise the call option, a seller, say Mr. Swift, is obligated to give her one share of Endrun's common stock in exchange for $25. If Mr. Swift does not already own a share, he must enter the stock market and buy one. The call option is a side bet between buyers and sellers on the value of the Endrun Company's common stock. When a call option is exercised, one investor gains and the other loses. The total number of shares outstanding of the Endrun Company remains constant, and no new funds are made available to the company.

■ *Example*

To see how warrants affect the value of the firm, imagine that Mr. Canuck and Ms. America are two investors who have together purchased six ounces of platinum. At the time they bought the platinum, Mr. Canuck and Ms. America each contributed one-half of the cost, which we will assume was $3,000 for six ounces, or $500 an ounce. (They each contributed $1,500.) They incorporated, printed two share certificates, and named the firm the CA Company. Each certificate represents a one-half claim to the platinum. Mr. Canuck and Ms. America each own one certificate. They have formed a company with platinum as its only asset.

A Call Is Issued   Suppose Mr. Canuck later decides to sell to Mrs. North a call option issued on Mr. Canuck's share. The call option gives Mrs. North the right to buy Mr. Canuck's share for $1,800 within the next year. If the price of platinum rises above $600 per ounce, the firm will be worth more than $3,600 and each share will be worth more than $1,800. If Mrs. North decides to exercise her option, Mr. Canuck must turn over his stock certificate and receive $1,800.

How would the firm be affected by the exercise? The number of shares will remain the same. There will still be two shares, now owned by Ms. America and Mrs. North. If the price of platinum rises to $700 an ounce, each share will be worth $2,100 (or $4,200 / 2). If Mrs. North exercises her option at this price, she will profit by $300.

A Warrant Is Issued Instead   This story changes if a warrant is issued. Suppose that Mr. Canuck does not sell a call option to Mrs. North. Instead, Mr. Canuck and Ms. America have a shareholders' meeting. They vote that CA Company will issue a warrant and sell it to Mrs. North. The warrant will give Mrs. North the right to receive a share of the company at an exercise price of $1,800.[6] If Mrs. North decides to exercise the warrant, the firm will issue another share certificate and give it to Mrs. North in exchange for $1,800.

From Mrs. North's perspective, the call option and the warrant *seem* to be the same. The exercise prices of the warrant and the call are the same: $1,800. It is still advantageous for Mrs. North to exercise the option when the price of platinum exceeds $600 per ounce. However, we will show that Mrs. North actually makes less in the warrant situation due to dilution.

---

[6]The sale of the warrant brings cash into the firm. We assume that the sale proceeds immediately leave the firm through a cash dividend to Mr. Canuck and Ms. America. This simplifies the analysis, because the firm with warrants then has the same total value as the firm without warrants.

Value of firm if:	Price of platinum per share	
	$ 700	$ 600
No warrant		
Mr. Canuck's share	$ 2,100	$1,800
Ms. America's share	2,100	1,800
Firm	$ 4,200	$3,600
Call option		
Mr. Canuck's claim	$ 0	$1,800
Ms. America's claim	2,100	1,800
Mrs. North's claim	2,100	0
Firm	$ 4,200	$3,600
Warrant		
Mr. Canuck's share	$ 2,000	$1,800
Ms. America's share	2,000	1,800
Mrs. North's share	2,000	0
Firm	$ 6,000	$3,600

Table 22.1
Effect of call option and warrant on the CA Company

If the price of platinum is $700, the value of the firm is equal to the value of six ounces of platinum plus the excess dollars paid into the firm by Mrs. North. This amount is $4,200 + $1,800 = $6,000.

The CA Company must also consider dilution. Suppose the price of platinum increases to $700 an ounce and Mrs. North exercises her warrant. Two things will occur:

1. Mrs. North will pay $1,800 to the firm.
2. The firm will print one share certificate and give it to Mrs. North. The certificate will represent a one-third claim on the platinum of the firm.

Because Mrs. North contributes $1,800 to the firm, the value of the firm increases. It is now worth

New value of firm = Value of platinum + Contribution by Mrs. North
= $4,200   + $1,800
= $6,000

Because Mrs. North has a one-third claim on the firm's value, her share is worth $2,000 (or $6,000/3). By exercising the warrant, Mrs. North gains $2,000 − $1,800 = $200. This is illustrated in Table 22.1.

Dilution   Why does Mrs. North only gain $200 in the warrant case while gaining $300 in the call option case? The key is dilution, that is, the creation of another share. In the call option case, she contributes $1,800 and receives one of the two outstanding shares. That is, she receives a share worth $2,100 (or $\frac{1}{2} \times$ $4,200). Her gain is $300 (or $2,100 − $1,800). We rewrite this gain as

Gain on Exercise of Call:

$$\frac{\$4,200}{2} - \$1,800 = \$300 \tag{22.1}$$

In the warrant case, she contributes $1,800 and receives a newly created share. She now owns one of the three outstanding shares. Because the $1,800 remains in the firm, her share is worth $2,000 (or ($4,200 + $1,800)/3). Her gain is $200 (or $2,000 − $1,800). We rewrite this gain as

Gain on Exercise of Warrant:

$$\frac{\$4,200 + \$1,800}{2 + 1} - \$1,800 = \$200 \tag{22.2}$$

Warrants also affect accounting numbers. Warrants and (as we shall see) convertible bonds cause the number of shares to increase. This causes the firm's net income to be spread over a larger number of shares, thereby decreasing earnings per share. Firms with significant amounts of warrants and convertible issues must report earnings on a *primary* basis and a *fully diluted* basis. ■

How the Firm Can Hurt Warrant Holders

The platinum firm owned by Mr. Canuck and Ms. America has issued a warrant to Mrs. North that is *in the money* and about to expire. One way that Mr. Canuck and Ms. America can hurt Mrs. North is to pay themselves a large dividend. This could be funded by selling a substantial amount of platinum. The value of the firm would fall, and the warrant would be worth much less.

CONCEPT QUESTIONS

- What is the key difference between a warrant and a traded call option?
- Why does dilution occur when warrants are exercised?
- How can the firm hurt warrant holders?

22.3   Warrant Pricing and the Black–Scholes Model (Advanced)

We now wish to express the gains from exercising a call and a warrant in more general terms. The gain on a call can be written as

Gain from Exercising a Single Call:

$$\frac{\text{Firm's value net of debt}}{\#} - \text{Exercise price} \tag{22.3}$$

(value of a share of stock)

Equation (22.3) generalizes equation (22.1). We define the *firm's value net of debt* to be the total firm value less the value of the debt. The total firm value is $4,200 in our example and there is no debt. The # stands for the number of shares outstanding, which is 2 in our example. The ratio on the left is the value of a share of stock.

The gain on a warrant can be written as

Gain from Exercising a Single Warrant:

$$\frac{\text{Firm's value net of debt} + \text{Exercise price} \times \#_w}{\# + \#_w} - \text{Exercise price} \tag{22.4}$$

(Value of a share of stock after warrant is exercised)

Equation (22.4) generalizes (22.2). The numerator of the left-hand term is the firm's value net of debt *after* the warrant is exercised. It is the sum of the firm's value net of debt *prior* to the warrant's exercise plus the proceeds the firm receives from the exercise. The proceeds equal the product of the exercise price multiplied by the number of warrants. The number of warrants appears as $\#_w$. (Our analysis uses the plausible assumption that all warrants in the money will be exercised.) Note that $\#_w = 1$ in our numerical example. The denominator, $\# + \#_w$, is the number of shares outstanding *after* the exercise of the warrants. The ratio on the left is the value of a share of stock after exercise. By rearranging terms, equation (22.4) can be rewritten as[7]

Gain from Exercising a Single Warrant:

$$\frac{\#}{\# + \#_w} \times \left(\frac{\text{Firm's value net of debt}}{\#} - \text{Exercise price}\right) \tag{22.5}$$

(gain from a call on a firm with no warrants)

Formula (22.5) relates the gain on a warrant to the gain on a call. Note that the term within parentheses is equation (22.3). Thus, the gain from exercising a warrant is a proportion of the gain from exercising a call in a firm without warrants. The proportion $\#/(\# + \#_w)$ is the ratio of the number of shares in the firm without warrants to the number of shares after all the warrants have been exercised. This ratio must always be less than 1. Thus, the gain on a warrant must be less than the gain on an identical call in a firm without warrants. Note that $\#/(\# + \#_w) = 200/300 = \frac{2}{3}$ in our example, which explains why Mrs. North gains $300 on her call yet gains only $200 on her warrant.

Our discussion to this point implies that the Black–Scholes model must be adjusted for warrants. When a call option is issued to Mrs. North, we know that the exercise price is $1,800 and the time to expiration is one year. Though we have posited neither the price of the stock, the variance of the stock, nor the interest rate, we could easily provide these data for a real world situation. Thus, we could use the Black–Scholes model to value Mrs. North's call.

Suppose that the warrant is to be issued tomorrow to Mrs. North. We know the number of warrants to be issued, the warrant's expiration date, and the exercise price. Using our assumption that the warrant proceeds are immediately paid out as a dividend, we could use the Black–Scholes model to value the warrant. We would first calculate the value of an identical call. The warrant price is the call price multiplied by the ratio $\#/(\# + \#_w)$. As stated earlier, this ratio is $\frac{2}{3}$ in our example.

CONCEPT QUESTION

- How can the Black–Scholes model be used to value warrants?

---

[7]To derive (22.5), one should separate "Exercise price" in (22.4). This yields

$$\frac{\text{Firm's value net of debt}}{\# + \#_w} - \frac{\#}{\# + \#_w} \times \text{Exercise price}$$

By rearranging terms, one can obtain (22.5).

22.4   Convertible Bonds

A **convertible bond** is similar to a bond with warrants. The most important difference is that a bond with warrants can be separated into distinct securities, but a convertible bond cannot. A convertible bond gives the holder the right to exchange it for a given number of shares of stock at any time up to and including the maturity date of the bond.

Preferred stock can frequently be converted into common stock. A share of convertible preferred stock is the same as a convertible bond except that it has no maturity date.

■ *Example*

Brascan Limited is a large Canadian conglomerate which operates in the natural resources, consumer products, financial services, and utilities industries. Well-known companies it owns include Royal LePage, London Insurance Group, Trilon Financial, and Great Lakes Power.

During 1992, Brascan issued $250 million of 7 percent subordinated convertible debentures due in 2002. These debentures were issued for cash of $125 million and an installment receipt of $125 million due October 15, 1993. Like typical debentures, they were callable after a deferred call period (in this case, three years). Brascan bonds differed from other debentures in their convertible feature: Each bond was convertible into 50 class A shares of the common stock of Brascan at any time before maturity. The number of shares received for each bond (50 in this example) is called the **conversion ratio.**

Bond traders also speak of the **conversion price** of the bond. This is calculated as the ratio of the face value of the bond to the conversion ratio. Because the face value of each Brascan bond was $1,000, the conversion price was $20.00 (or $1,000 / 50). The bondholders of Brascan could give up bonds with a face value of $1,000 and receive 50 shares of Brascan common stock. This was equivalent to paying $20 for each share of Brascan common stock received.

When Brascan issued these convertible bonds, its common stock was trading in the range of $16 to $17 per share. The conversion price of $20 was 20 to 25 percent higher than the actual common stock price. This price difference is referred to as the **conversion premium.** It reflects the fact that the conversion option in Brascan convertible bonds was *out of the money.* This conversion premium is typical.

Convertibles are almost always protected against stock splits and stock dividends. If Brascan's common stock had been split two for one, the conversion ratio would have been increased from 50 to 100. ■

Conversion ratio, conversion price, and *conversion premium* are well-known terms in the financial community. For that reason alone, the student should master the concepts they represent. However, conversion price and conversion premium implicitly assume that the bond is selling at par. If the bond is selling at another price, the terms have little meaning. By contrast, *conversion ratio* can have a meaningful interpretation regardless of the price of the bond.

CONCEPT QUESTION

■ What are the conversion ratio, the conversion price, and the conversion premium?

The Value of Convertible Bonds

22.5

The value of a convertible bond can be described in terms of three components: straight bond value, conversion value, and option value.[8] We examine these three components below.

Straight Bond Value

The straight bond value is what the convertible bonds would sell for if they could not be converted into common stock. This value will depend on the general level of interest rates and on default risk. Suppose that straight debentures issued by Brascan had been rated BBB (high) by Dominion Bond Rating Service, and BBB (high) bonds were priced to yield 12 percent on October 2, 1993. The straight bond value of Brascan convertible bonds can be determined by discounting the coupon payment and principal amount at 12 percent:

$$
\begin{aligned}
\text{Straight bond} &= \sum_{t=1}^{9} \frac{\$70}{(1.12)^t} + \frac{\$1,000}{(1.12)^9} \\
&= \$70 \times A_{0.12}^9 + \frac{\$1,000}{(1.12)^9} \\
&= \$372.98 + 360.61 \\
&= \$733.59
\end{aligned}
$$

The straight bond value of a convertible bond is a minimum value. The price of Brascan's convertible could not have gone lower than the straight bond value. The straight bond value portion of a convertible will depend on the market's assessment of default risk. We know from previous discussions that the value of straight bonds is related to the value of the firm. The upper left-hand corner of Figure 22.2 illustrates the relationship between straight bond value and firm value. If the value of Brascan became zero, the value of the Brascan bonds would be zero. Conversely, Brascan's straight debt could be worth, at most, only the value of an equivalent risk-free bond.

Conversion Value

The value of convertible bonds depends on conversion value. **Conversion value** is what the bonds would be worth if they were immediately converted into common stock at current prices. Typically, conversion value is computed by multiplying the number of shares that will be received when the bond is converted by the current price of the common stock.

On October 2, 1993, each Brascan convertible bond could have been converted into 50 shares of Brascan common stock. Brascan common was selling for $12.63. Thus, the conversion value was 50 × $12.63 = $631.50. A convertible cannot sell for less than its conversion value. Arbitrage prevents this from happening. If Brascan's

[8]For a similar treatment see Richard Brealey, Stewart Myers, Gordon Sick, and Ronald Giammarino, *Principles of Corporate Finance*, 2d Canadian ed. (Toronto: McGraw-Hill Ryerson, 1992), chapter 22; and James C. Van Horne, *Financial Market Rates and Flows*, 2d ed. (Englewood Cliffs, N.J.: Prentice Hall, 1987), chapter 11.

Figure 22.2
The market value
of convertible
bonds

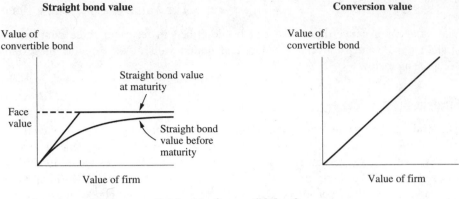

The actual value of a convertible is always higher than either its straight bond value or its conversion value.

Note: See Richard Brealey and Stewart Myers, *Principles of Corporate Finance,* 2d ed. (New York: McGraw-Hill, 1984); and James C. Van Horne, *Financial Rates and Flows,* 3d ed. (Englewood Cliffs, N.J.: Prentice Hall, 1987), chapter 11.

convertible sold for less than $631.50, investors would have bought the bonds and converted them into common stock and sold the stock. The profit would have been the difference between the value of the stock sold and the bond's conversion value.

Thus, convertible bonds have two minimum values: the straight bond value and the conversion value. The conversion value is determined by the value of the firm's underlying common stock. This is illustrated in the upper right-hand corner of Figure 22.2. As the value of common stock rises and falls, the conversion value rises and falls with it. When the value of Brascan's common stock increased by $1, the conversion value of its convertible bonds increased by $50.

Option Value

The value of a convertible bond will generally exceed both the straight bond value and the conversion value.[9] This occurs because holders of convertibles need not convert immediately. Instead, by waiting they can take advantage of whichever is greater in the

_____

[9]The most plausible exception is when conversion would provide the investor with a dividend much greater than the interest available prior to conversion. The optimal strategy here could very well be to convert immediately, implying that the market value of the bond would exactly equal the conversion value. Other exceptions occur when the firm is in default or the bondholders are forced to convert.

future: the straight bond value or the conversion value. This option to wait has value, and it raises the value over both the straight bond value and the conversion value.

When the value of the firm is low, the value of convertible bonds is most significantly influenced by their underlying value as straight debt. However, when the value of the firm is very high, the value of convertible bonds is mostly determined by their underlying conversion value. This is illustrated in the bottom portion of Figure 22.2.

The bottom portion of the figure implies that the value of a convertible bond is the maximum of its straight bond value and its conversion value, plus its option value:

$$\begin{matrix} \text{Value of} \\ \text{convertible bond} \end{matrix} = \begin{matrix} \text{The greater of (straight bond} \\ \text{value or conversion value)} \end{matrix} + \begin{matrix} \text{Option} \\ \text{value} \end{matrix}$$

■ *Example*

Suppose the Moulton Company has outstanding 1,000 shares of common stock and 100 bonds. Each bond has a face value of $1,000 at maturity. They are discount bonds and pay no coupons. At maturity each bond can be converted into 10 shares of newly issued common stock.

What circumstances will make it advantageous for holders of Moulton's convertible bonds to convert to common stock at maturity?

If the holders of the convertible bonds convert, they will receive $100 \times 10 = 1,000$ shares of common stock. Because there were already 1,000 shares, the total number of shares outstanding becomes 2,000 upon conversion. Thus, converting bondholders own 50 percent of the value of the firm, V. If they do not convert, they will receive $100,000 or V, whichever is less. The choice for the holders of Moulton's bonds is obvious. They should convert if 50 percent of V is greater than $100,000. This will be true whenever V is greater than $200,000. This is illustrated as follows:

Payoff to convertible bondholders and stockholders
of the Moulton Company

	(1) $V \leq \$100,000$	(2) $\$100,000 < V \leq \$200,000$	(3) $V > \$200,000$
Decision:	Bondholders will not convert	Bondholders will not convert	Bondholders will convert
Convertible bondholders	V	$100,000	$0.5V$
Stockholders	0	$V - \$100,000$	$0.5V$ ■

CONCEPT QUESTIONS

- What three elements make up the value of a convertible bond?
- Describe the payoff structure of convertible bonds.

Reasons for Issuing Warrants and Convertibles   22.6

The reasons for issuing convertible debt are a topic with great potential for confusion. To separate fact from fantasy, we present a rather structured argument. We first compare convertible debt with straight debt. Then we compare convertible debt with equity. For each comparison, we ask: In what situations is the firm better off with convertible debt and in what situations is it worse off?

Convertible Debt versus Straight Debt

Convertible debt pays a lower interest rate than does otherwise identical straight debt. For example, if the interest rate is 10 percent on straight debt, the interest rate on convertible debt might be 9 percent. Investors will accept a lower interest rate on a convertible because of the potential gain from conversion.

Imagine a firm that seriously considers both convertible debt and straight debt and then finally decides to issue convertibles. When will this decision benefit the firm and when will it hurt the firm? We consider two situations.

The Stock Price Later Rises So That Conversion Is Indicated

The firm clearly likes to see the stock price rise. However, it would have benefited even more had it previously issued straight debt instead of a convertible. While the firm paid out a lower interest rate than it would have with straight debt, it will be obligated to sell the convertible holders a chunk of the equity below its current market price.

The Stock Price Later Falls or Does Not Rise Enough to Justify Conversion

The firm hates to see the stock price fall. However, as long as the stock price does fall, the firm is glad that it had previously issued convertible debt instead of straight debt. This is because the interest rate on convertible debt is lower. Because conversion does not take place, our comparison of interest rates is all that is needed.

Summary

Compared to straight debt, the firm is worse off having issued convertible debt if the underlying stock subsequently does well. The firm is better off having issued convertible debt if the underlying stock subsequently does poorly. In an efficient market, one cannot predict future stock price. Thus, we cannot argue that convertibles either dominate or are dominated by straight debt.

Convertible Debt versus Common Stock

Next, imagine a firm that seriously considers both convertible debt and common stock and then finally decides to issue convertibles. When will this decision benefit the firm and when will it hurt the firm? We consider our two situations.

The Stock Price Later Rises So That Conversion Is Indicated

The firm is better off having previously issued a convertible instead of equity. To see this, consider the Brascan case. The firm could have issued stock for $16. Instead, by issuing a convertible, the firm effectively received $20 for a share upon conversion.

	If firm subsequently does poorly	If firm subsequently prospers	
Convertible bonds (CBs)	No conversion occurs because of low stock price.	Conversion occurs because of high stock price.	**Table 22.2** The cases for and against convertible bonds (CBs)
Compared to:			
Straight bonds	CBs provide cheap financing because coupon rate is lower.	CBs provide expensive financing because bonds are converted, which dilutes existing equity.	
Common stock	CBs provide expensive financing because firm could have issued common stock at high prices.	CBs provide cheap financing because firm issues stock at high prices when bonds are converted.	

The Stock Price Later Falls or Does Not Rise Enough to Justify Conversion

No firm wants to see the stock price fall. However, given that the price did fall, the firm would have been better off if it had previously issued stock instead of a convertible. The firm would have benefited by issuing stock above its later market price. That is, the firm would have received more than the subsequent worth of the stock. However, the drop in stock price did not affect the value of the convertible much because the straight bond value serves as a floor.

Summary

Compared with equity, the firm is better off having issued convertible debt if the underlying stock subsequently does well. The firm is worse off having issued convertible debt if the underlying stock subsequently does poorly. One cannot predict future stock price in an efficient market. Thus, we cannot argue that issuing convertibles is better or worse than issuing equity. The above analysis is summarized in Table 22.2.

Modigliani–Miller (MM) pointed out that, abstracting from taxes and bankruptcy costs, the firm is indifferent between issuing stock or issuing debt. The MM relationship is a quite general one. Their pedagogy could be adjusted to show that the firm is indifferent to whether it issues convertibles or issues other instruments. To conserve space (and the patience of students), we have omitted a full-blown proof of MM in a world with convertibles. However, the above results are perfectly consistent with MM. Now we turn to the real world view of convertibles.

The "Free Lunch" Story

The discussion above suggests that issuing a convertible bond is no better and no worse than issuing other instruments. Unfortunately, many corporate executives fall into the trap of arguing that issuing convertible debt is actually better than issuing alternative instruments. This is a free lunch type of explanation, of which we are quite critical.

▪ *Example*

The stock price of RW Company is $20. Suppose that this company can issue subordinated debentures at 10 percent. It can also issue convertible bonds at 6 percent with a conversion value of $800. The conversion value means that the holders can convert a convertible bond into 40 (or $800 / $20) shares of common stock.

A company treasurer who believes in free lunches might argue that convertible bonds should be issued because they represent a cheaper source of financing than either subordinated bonds or common stock. The treasurer will point out that if the company does poorly and the price does not rise above $20, the convertible bondholders will not convert the bonds into common stock. In this case, the company will have obtained debt financing at below-market rates by attaching worthless equity kickers. On the other hand, if the firm does well and the price of its common stock rises to $25 or above, convertible holders will convert. The company will issue 40 shares. The company will receive a bond with face value of $1,000 in exchange for issuing 40 shares of common stock, implying a conversion price of $25. The company will have issued common stock *de facto* at $25 per share, or 20 percent above the $20 common stock price prevailing when the convertible bonds were issued. This enables it to lower its cost of equity capital. Thus, the treasurer happily points out, regardless of whether the company does well or poorly, convertible bonds are the cheapest form of financing.

Although this argument may sound quite plausible at first glance, there is a flaw. The treasurer is comparing convertible financing *with straight debt* when the stock subsequently falls. However, the treasurer compares convertible financing *with common stock* when the stock subsequently rises. This is an unfair mixing of comparisons. By contrast, our analysis of Table 22.2 was fair, because we examined both stock increases and decreases when comparing a convertible with each alternative instrument. We found that no single alternative dominated convertible bonds in *both* up and down markets.

The "Expensive Lunch" Story

Suppose we stand the treasurer's argument on its head by comparing (1) convertible financing with straight debt when the stock rises and (2) convertible financing with equity when the stock falls.

From Table 22.2, we see that convertible debt is more expensive than straight debt when the stock subsequently rises. The firm's obligation to sell convertible holders a chunk of the equity at a below-market price more than offsets the lower interest rate on a convertible.

Also from Table 22.2, we see that convertible debt is more expensive than equity when the stock subsequently falls. Had the firm issued stock, it would have received a price higher than its subsequent worth. Therefore, the expensive lunch story implies that convertible debt is an inferior form of financing. Of course, we dismiss both the free lunch and the expensive lunch arguments.

A Reconciliation

In an efficient financial market there is neither a free lunch nor an expensive lunch. Convertible bonds can be neither cheaper nor more expensive than other instruments. A convertible bond is a package of straight debt and an option to buy common stock.

The difference between the market value of a convertible bond and the value of a straight bond is the price investors pay for the call option feature. In an efficient market this is a fair price.

In general, if a company prospers, issuing convertible bonds will turn out to be worse than issuing straight bonds and better than issuing common stock. In contrast, if a company does poorly, convertible bonds will turn out to be better than issuing straight bonds and worse than issuing common stock.

CONCEPT QUESTIONS

■ What is wrong with the simple view that it is cheaper to issue a bond with a warrant or a convertible feature because the required coupon is lower than on straight debt?
■ What is wrong with the free lunch story?
■ What is wrong with the expensive lunch story?

Why Are Warrants and Convertibles Issued?   22.7

Research on firms that issue convertible bonds shows that they are different from other firms. Here are some of the differences:

1. The bond ratings of firms using convertibles are lower than those of other firms.[10]
2. Convertibles tend to be used by smaller firms with high growth rates and more financial leverage.[11]
3. Convertibles are usually subordinated and unsecured.

The kind of company that uses convertibles provides clues to why they are issued. Sensible explanations involve matching cash flows, risk synergy, and agency costs.

Matching Cash Flows

If financing is costly, it makes sense to issue securities whose cash flows match those of the firm. A young, risky, aspiring growth firm might prefer to issue convertibles or bonds with warrants because these will have lower initial interest costs. When the firm is successful, the convertibles (or warrants) will be converted. This causes expensive dilution, but it occurs when the firm can best afford it.

---

[10]E. F. Brigham, "An Analysis of Convertible Debentures," *Journal of Finance* 21 (1966).

[11]W. H. Mikkelson, "Convertible Calls and Security Returns," *Journal of Financial Economics* 9 (September 1981), p. 3, established this result for U.S. convertible bonds. R. G. Storey and C. R. Dipchand, "Factors Related to the Conversion Record of Convertible Securities," *Journal of Financial Research* (Winter 1978), studied the conversion record in Canada over the period 1946–75. They found that 70 percent of the convertible issues were converted, suggesting that most issuers experienced growth.

Table 22.3
A hypothetical case
of the yields on
convertible bonds

	Firm risk	
	Low	High
Straight bond yield	10%	15%
Convertible bond yield	6	7

Note: The yields on straight bonds reflect the risk of default. The
yields on convertibles are not sensitive to default risk.

Risk Synergy

Another argument for convertible bonds and bonds with warrants is that they are useful when it is very costly to assess the risk of the issuing company. Suppose you are evaluating a new product offered by a start-up company. The new product is a biogenetic virus that may increase the yields of corn crops in northern climates. It may also cause cancer. This type of product is difficult to value properly. Thus, the risk of the company is very hard to determine—it may be high, or it may be low. If you could be sure the risk of the company were high, you would price the bonds for a high yield, say 15 percent. If it were low, you would price them at a lower yield, say 10 percent.

Convertible bonds and bonds with warrants can protect somewhat against mistakes of risk evaluation. Convertible bonds and bonds with warrants have two components: a straight bond and a call option on the company's underlying stock. If the company turns out to be a low-risk company, the straight bond component will have high value and the call option will have low value. However, if the company turns out to be a high-risk company, the straight bond component will have low value and the call option will have high value. This is illustrated in Table 22.3.

However, although risk has effects on value that cancel each other in convertibles and bonds with warrants, the market and the buyer nevertheless must make an assessment of the firm's potential in order to value securities. It is not clear that the effort involved is that much less than is required for a straight bond.

Agency Costs

Convertible bonds can resolve agency problems associated with raising money. In a previous chapter, we showed that a straight bond is like a risk-free bond minus a put option on the assets of the firm. This creates an incentive for creditors to force the firm into low-risk activities. In contrast, holders of common stock have incentives to adopt high-risk projects. High-risk projects with negative NPV transfer wealth from bondholders to shareholders. If these conflicts cannot be resolved, the firm may be forced to pass up profitable investment opportunities. However, because convertible bonds have an equity component, less expropriation of wealth can occur when convertible debt is issued instead of straight debt.[12] In other words, convertible bonds

---

[12]A. Barnea, R. A. Haugen, and L. Senbet, *Agency Problems and Financial Contracting,* Prentice Hall Foundations of Science Series (New York: Prentice Hall, 1985), chapter VI.

mitigate agency costs. One implication of this approach is that convertible bonds should have fewer restrictive debt covenants than do straight bonds. Casual empirical evidence seems to bear this out.

CONCEPT QUESTION

- Why do firms issue convertible bonds and bonds with warrants?

Conversion Policy   22.8

There is one aspect of convertible bonds that we have omitted so far. Firms are frequently granted a call option on the bond. The typical arrangements for calling a convertible bond are simple. When the bond is called, the holder has about 30 days to choose between

1. Converting the bond to common stock at the conversion ratio.
2. Surrendering the bond and receiving the call price in cash.

What should bondholders do? It should be clear that if the conversion value of the bond is greater than the call price, conversion is better than surrender; and if the conversion value is less than the call price, surrender is better than conversion. If the conversion value is greater than the call price, the call is said to **force conversion.**

What should financial managers do? Calling the bonds does not change the value of the firm as a whole. However, an optimal call policy can benefit the shareholders at the expense of the bondholders. Because we are speaking of dividing a pie of fixed size, the optimal call policy is very simple: Do whatever the bondholders do not want you to do.

Bondholders would love the shareholders to call the bonds when the bond's market value is below the call price. Shareholders would be giving bondholders extra value. Alternatively, should the value of the bonds rise above the call price, the bondholders would love the shareholders not to call the bonds, because bondholders would be allowed to hold onto a valuable asset.

There is only one policy left. This is the policy that maximizes shareholder value and minimizes bondholder value. This policy is

> Call the bond when its value is equal to the call price.

It is a puzzle that firms do not always call convertible bonds when the conversion value reaches the call price. Ingersoll examined the call policies of 124 firms between 1968 and 1975.[13] In most cases he found that the company waited to call the bonds

---

[13]J. Ingersoll, "An Examination of Corporate Call Policies on Convertible Bonds," *Journal of Finance* (May 1977). See also M. Harris and A. Raviv, "A Sequential Signalling Model of Convertible Debt Policy," *Journal of Finance* (December 1985). Harris and Raviv describe a signalling equilibrium that is consistent with Ingersoll's result. They show that managers with favourable information will delay calls to avoid depressing stock prices.

until the conversion value was much higher than the call price. The median company waited until the conversion value of its bonds was 44 percent higher than the call price. This is not even close to the optimal strategy.

CONCEPT QUESTIONS

■ Why will convertible bonds not be voluntarily converted to stock before expiration?

■ When should firms force conversion of convertibles? Why?

22.9　Summary and Conclusions

1. A warrant gives the holder the right to buy shares of common stock at an exercise price for a given period of time. Typically, warrants are issued in a package with privately placed bonds. Afterward, they become detached and trade separately.

2. A convertible bond is a combination of a straight bond and a call option. The holder can give up the bond in exchange for shares of stock.

3. Convertible bonds and warrants are like call options. However, there are some important differences:

   a. Warrants and convertible securities are issued by corporations. Call options are traded between individual investors.

      i. Warrants are usually issued privately and are combined with a bond. In most cases, the warrants can be detached immediately after the issue. In some cases, warrants are issued with preferred stock, with common stock, in executive compensation programs, or as stand-alone issues.

      ii. Convertibles are bonds that can be converted into common stock.

      iii. Call options are sold separately by individual investors (called *writers* of call options).

   b. Warrants and call options are exercised for cash. The holder of a warrant gives the company cash and receives new shares of the company's stock. The holder of a call option gives another individual cash in exchange for shares of stock. When someone converts a bond, it is exchanged for common stock. As a consequence, bonds with warrants and convertible bonds have different effects on corporate cash flow and capital structure.

   c. Warrants and convertibles cause dilution to the existing shareholders. When warrants are exercised and convertible bonds converted, the company must issue new shares of common stock. The percentage ownership of the existing shareholders will decline. New shares are not issued when call options are exercised.

4. Many arguments, both plausible and implausible, are given for issuing convertible bonds and bonds with warrants. One plausible rationale for such

bonds has to do with risk. Convertibles and bonds with warrants are associated with risky companies. Lenders can do several things to protect themselves from high-risk companies:

a. They can require high yields.

b. They can lend less or not at all to firms whose risk is difficult to assess.

c. They can impose severe restrictions on such debt.

Another useful way to protect against risk is to issue bonds with equity kickers. This gives the lenders the chance to benefit from risks and reduces the conflicts between bondholders and shareholders concerning risk.

5. A puzzle particularly vexes financial researchers: Convertible bonds usually have call provisions. Companies appear to delay calling convertibles until the conversion value greatly exceeds the call price. From the shareholders' standpoint, the optimal call policy would be to call the convertibles when the conversion value equals the call price.

Key Terms

Warrants 647
Convertible bond 654
Conversion ratio 654
Conversion price 654

Conversion premium 654
Conversion value 655
Force conversion 663

Suggested Readings

The following article analyzes when it is optimal to force conversion of convertible bonds:
M. Brennan and E. Schwartz. "Convertible Bonds: Valuation and Optimal Strategies for Call Conversion." *Journal of Finance* (December 1977).

Brennan examines the conventional arguments for and against convertible bonds and offers a new "risk synergy" rationale in:
M. Brennan. "The Case for Convertibles." In J. M. Stern and D. H. Chew, eds., *The Revolution in Corporate Finance.* New York: Basil Blackwell, 1986.

Storey and Dipchand assess the conversion record of convertibles in Canada in:
R. G. Storey and C. R. Dipchand. "Factors Related to the Conversion Record of Convertible Securities: The Canadian Experience, 1946–75." *Journal of Financial Research* (Winter 1978).

Courtadon and Merrick outline the basic elements of the option pricing model and then identify some applications to the design and pricing of corporate securities in:
G. R. Courtadon and J. J. Merrick. "The Option Pricing Model and the Valuation of Corporate Securities." *Midland Corporate Finance Journal* (Fall 1983).

Questions and Problems

22.1 Define

    a. Warrants.

    b. Convertibles.

Warrants

22.2 Explain why the following limits on warrant prices exist:

    a. The lower limit is zero if the stock price is below the exercise price.

    b. The lower limit is the stock price less the exercise price if the stock price is above the exercise price.

    c. The upper limit is the price of the stock.

22.3 *a.* What is the primary difference between warrants and calls?

    b. What is the implication of that difference?

22.4 Suppose the CA Company, which was discussed in the text, sells Mrs. North a warrant. Prior to the sale, the company had two shares outstanding. Mr. Canuck owned one share and Ms. America owned the other share. The assets of the firm are seven ounces of platinum, which was purchased at $500 per ounce. The exercise price of the warrant is $1,800. All funds that enter the firm are used to purchase more platinum. Mrs. North is sold the warrant moments after incorporation for $500.

    a. What is the price of CA stock before the warrant is sold?

    b. At what price for platinum will Mrs. North exercise her warrant?

    c. Suppose the price of platinum suddenly rises to $520 per ounce.

        i. What is the value of CA?

        ii. What will Mrs. North do?

        iii. What is the new price per share of CA stock?

        iv. What (if anything) did Mrs. North gain from exercise?

    d. What would Mrs. North's gain have been if Mr. Canuck had sold her a call?

    e. Why are Mrs. North's gains different with a call than with a warrant?

22.5 A warrant entitles the holder to buy four shares of common stock at $72 per share. When the market price of the stock is $70, will the market price of the warrant equal zero? Why or why not?

22.6 Hayes Manufacturing's current market value balance sheet shows the assets of the firm are $5.2 million. The market value of the debt Hayes has issued is $1.7 million. Hayes has 500,000 shares of common stock outstanding. Tomorrow, Hayes will issue 100,000 warrants. The proceeds of the issue will be used to pay the dividend that is due tomorrow. Hayes's investment banker urged Hayes to issue calls instead of warrants. The calls would be identical to the warrants. Her memo to Hayes's president noted that if calls were issued instead of warrants, they would sell for $3.50. For how much will the warrants sell?

22.7 Consider the following warrants.

> Warrant *A:* For each warrant held, one share of common stock can be purchased at an option price of $9 per share.
>
> Warrant *B:* For each warrant held, two shares of common stock can be purchased at an option price of $5 per share.

The current market price of stock *A* is $11 per share. The current market price of stock *B* is $10 per share.

a. What is the minimum value of warrant *A*?

b. What is the minimum value of warrant *B*?

Convertibles

22.8 At issuance of O'Connell Corp.'s convertible bonds, one of the two following sets of characteristics were true.

	A	B
Offering price of bond	$ 900	$1,000
Bond value (straight debt)	900	950
Conversion value	1,000	900

Which of the relationships do you believe was more likely to have prevailed? Why?

22.9 The following facts apply to a convertible security:

Conversion price	$50 share
Coupon rate	9%
Par value	$1,000
Yield on nonconvertible debenture of same quality	10%
Market price	$52/share

a. What is the minimum price at which the convertible should sell?

b. What accounts for any premium in the market price of the convertible over the value of the common stock into which it can be converted?

22.10 Ryan Home Products, Inc., issued $430,000 of 8-percent convertible debentures. Each bond is convertible into 28 shares of common stock anytime before maturity.

a. Suppose the current price of the bonds is $1,000 and the current price of Ryan common is $31.25.

   i. What is the conversion ratio?

   ii. What is the conversion price?

   iii. What is the conversion premium?

b. Suppose the current price of the bonds is $1,180 and the current price of Ryan common is $31.25.

   i. What is the conversion ratio?

   ii. What is the conversion price?

   iii. What is the conversion premium?

c. What is the conversion value of the debentures?

d. If the value of Ryan common increases $2, what will the conversion value be?

22.11   A $1,000 par convertible debenture has a conversion price for common stock of $180 per share. With the common stock selling at $60, what is the conversion value of the bond?

22.12   "Convertible bonds and warrants allow purchasers of debt to share in capital gains if the issuer's stock price rises. Therefore, a firm should issue these securities if management expects that the stock price will rise." Discuss this statement and explain why you agree or disagree.

22.13   Financial institutions sometimes take warrants or call options on the borrower's shares when making a loan. In Canada, this practice is particularly popular with Schedule 2 (foreign-owned) chartered banks. The warrants or call options can be exercised to enhance the lender's return beyond the interest paid. Why do you think that some financial institutions and borrowers prefer this blend of return over simply attaching a higher interest rate to the loan? Explain briefly.

22.14   You have been hired to value a new 30-year callable, convertible bond. The bond has a 6-percent coupon, payable annually. The conversion price is $100, and the stock currently sells for $50.12. The stock price is expected to grow at 10 percent per year. The bond is callable at $1,100, but, based on prior experience, it won't be called unless the conversion value is $1,300. The required return on this bond is 8 percent. What value would you assign?

CHAPTER 23

Leasing

From aircraft to zithers, almost any asset that can be purchased can be leased. When we take vacations or business trips, renting a car for a few days frequently seems convenient. This is an example of a short-term lease. After all, buying a car and selling it a few days later would be a great nuisance.

Corporations lease both short-term and long-term, but this chapter is primarily concerned with long-term leasing over a period of more than five years. Long-term leasing is a method of financing property, plant, and equipment. Computers and communications equipment make up the largest sector of equipment leasing in Canada. Next comes aircraft leases—big-ticket items ranging to $200 million for a 747. Leasing is popular in financing furniture and fixtures as well as manufacturing, transportation, and construction equipment.[1]

Every lease contract has two parties: the **lessee** and the **lessor.** The lessee is the user of the equipment, and the lessor is the owner. Typically, the lessee first decides on the asset needed and then negotiates a lease contract with a lessor. From the lessee's standpoint, long-term leasing is similar to buying the equipment with a secured loan. The terms of the lease contract are compared to what a banker might arrange with a secured loan. Thus, long-term leasing is a form of financing.

Many questionable advantages are claimed for long-term leasing, such as "leasing provides 100-percent financing," or "leasing conserves capital." However, the principal benefit of long-term leasing is tax reduction. Leasing allows those who need equipment, but cannot take full advantage of the tax benefits associated with ownership, to transfer the tax benefits to a party who can. If the corporate income tax were repealed, long-term leasing would decline dramatically.

Types of Leases   23.1

The Basics

A **lease** is a contractual agreement between a lessee and a lessor. The agreement establishes that the lessee has the right to use an asset and in return must make periodic payments to the lessor, the owner of the asset. The lessor is either the asset's

---

[1]L. Ramsey, "Recession Adds Reason to Lease Your Equipment," *Financial Post* (November 25, 1991), p. 20.

Figure 23.1 Buying versus leasing

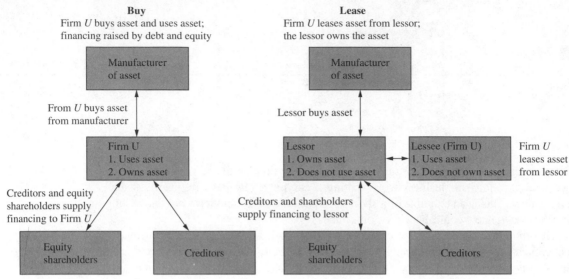

manufacturer or an independent leasing company.[2] If the lessor is an independent leasing company, it must buy the asset from a manufacturer and deliver it to the lessee.

As far as the lessee is concerned, it is the use of the asset that is important, not the ownership. The use of an asset can be obtained by a lease contract. Because the user can also buy the asset, leasing and buying involve alternative financing arrangements for the use of an asset. This is illustrated in Figure 23.1.

The example in Figure 23.1 is common in the computer industry. Firm *U,* the lessee, might be a hospital, a law firm, or any other firm that uses computers. The lessor is an independent leasing company that purchased the equipment from a manufacturer such as IBM or Apple. Leases of this type are called **direct leases.** In the figure, the lessor issued both debt and equity to finance the purchase.

Of course, a manufacturer like IBM could lease its *own* computers, though we do not show this situation in the example. Leases of this type are called **sales-type leases.** In this case, IBM would compete with the independent computer leasing company.

Operating Leases

Years ago, a lease that provided an operator along with the equipment was called an **operating lease.** Today, an operating lease (or service lease) is difficult to define precisely, but this form of leasing has several important characteristics:

---

[2]Independent of the manufacturer, the leasing company may be owned by a chartered bank. Under the current Bank Act, banks are allowed to own leasing subsidiaries but prohibited from leasing vehicles through their branch networks. This prohibition may be dropped in the future.

1. Operating leases are usually not fully amortized. This means that the payments required under the terms of the lease are not enough to recover the full cost of the asset for the lessor. This occurs because the term or life of the operating lease is usually less than the economic life of the asset. Thus, the lessor must expect to recover the costs of the asset by renewing the lease or by selling the asset for its residual value.

2. Operating leases usually require the lessor to maintain and insure the leased assets.

3. Perhaps the most interesting feature of an operating lease is the cancellation option. This option gives the lessee the right to cancel the lease contract before the expiration date. If the option to cancel is exercised, the lessee must return the equipment to the lessor. The value of a cancellation clause depends on whether future technological and/or economic conditions are likely to make the value of the asset to the lessee less than the value of the future lease payments under the lease.

To leasing practitioners, these characteristics constitute an operating lease. However, accountants use the term in a slightly different way, as we will see shortly.

Financial Leases

Financial leases are the exact opposite of operating leases, as is seen from their important characteristics:

1. Financial leases do not provide for maintenance or service by the lessor.
2. Financial leases are fully amortized.
3. The lessee usually has a right to renew the lease on expiration.
4. Generally, financial leases cannot be cancelled. In other words, the lessee must make all payments or face the risk of bankruptcy.

The characteristics of a financial lease (particularly the fact that it is fully amortized) make it very similar to debt financing, so the name is a sensible one. Two special types of financial leases are the **sale and lease-back** arrangement and the leveraged lease.

Sale and Lease-Back

A sale and lease-back occurs when a company sells an asset it owns to another firm and immediately leases it back. In a sale and lease-back, two things happen:

1. The lessee receives cash from the sale of the asset.
2. The lessee makes periodic lease payments, thereby retaining use of the asset.

For example, in January 1989, Air Canada arranged a sale and lease-back of four Boeing 767-200ER aircraft. The purchaser was a Canadian financial institution and the transaction proceeds were $260 million. Further examples include Canadian universities and hospitals that set up sale lease-back deals for library books and medical equipment.[3] With a sale and lease-back, the lessee may have the option to repurchase the leased assets at the end of the lease.

Leveraged Leases

A **leveraged lease** is a three-sided arrangement among the lessee, the lessor, and the lenders:

1. As in other leases, the lessee uses the assets and makes periodic lease payments.
2. As in other leases, the lessor purchases the assets, delivers them to the lessee, and collects the lease payments. However, the lessor puts up no more than 40 to 50 percent of the purchase price.
3. The lenders supply the remaining financing and receive interest payments from the lessor. Thus, the arrangement on the right-hand side of Figure 23.1 would be a leveraged lease if the bulk of the financing were supplied by creditors.

The lenders in a leveraged lease typically use a nonrecourse loan. This means that the lessor is not obligated to the lender in case of a default. However, the lender is protected in two ways:

1. The lender has a first lien on the asset.
2. In the event of loan default, the lease payments are made directly to the lender.

The lessor puts up only part of the funds but gets the lease payments and all of the tax benefits of ownership. Lease payments are used to service the nonrecourse loan. The lessee benefits because, in a competitive market, the lease payment is lowered when the lessor saves taxes.

CONCEPT QUESTIONS

- What are the differences between an operating lease and a financial lease?
- What is a sale and lease-back agreement?
- How does a leveraged lease work?

23.2   Accounting and Leasing

Before 1979, leasing was frequently called **off–balance-sheet financing.** As the name implies, a firm could arrange to use an asset through a lease without disclosing the existence of the lease contract on the balance sheet. Lessees only had to report information on leasing activity in the footnotes of their financial statements.

---

[3]Tax law changes subsequently restricted sale and lease-backs and heavy equipment and aircraft leasing in Canada; we discuss this later. "Report on Business," *The Globe and Mail* (January 9, 1989), p. B2; B. Critchley and B. Baxter, "Why the SLB Ban?" *The Financial Post* (April 28, 1989), p. B6; and G. Athanassakos and M. Klatt, "Lease or Buy? How Recent Tax Changes Have Affected the Decision," *Canadian Tax Journal* 41 (1993), pp. 444–53.

1. Initial balance sheet (the company buys a $100,000 truck with debt)				**Table 23.1**
Truck	$100,000	Debt	$100,000	Leasing and the
Other assets	100,000	Equity	100,000	balance sheet
Total assets	$200,000	Total debt plus equity	$200,000	

2. Operating lease (the company has an operating lease for the truck)			
Truck	$0	Debt	$0
Other assets	100,000	Equity	100,000
Total assets	$100,000	Total debt plus equity	$100,000

3. Capital (financial) lease (the company has a capital lease for the truck)			
Assets under capital lease	$100,000	Obligations under capital lease	$100,000
Other assets	100,000	Equity	100,000
Total assets	$200,000	Total debt plus equity	$200,000

In the first case, a $100,000 truck is purchased with debt. In the second case, an operating lease is used; no balance sheet entries are created. In the third case, a capital (financial) lease is used; the lease payments are capitalized as a liability, and the leased truck appears as an asset.

Of course, this meant that firms could acquire the use of a substantial number of assets and incur a substantial long-term financial commitment through financial leases yet not disclose the impact of these arrangements in their financial statements. Operating leases, being cancelable at little or no penalty, do not involve any significant financial commitment. So operating leases did not generate much concern about complete disclosure. As a result, the accounting profession wanted to distinguish clearly between operating and financial leases to ensure that the impact of financial leases was included in the financial statements.

In 1979, the Canadian Institute of Chartered Accountants implemented new rules for lease accounting (CICA 3065). The basic idea is that all financial leases (called *capital leases* in CICA 3065) must be "capitalized." This requirement means that the present value of the lease payments must be calculated and reported along with debt and other liabilities on the right-hand side of the lessee's balance sheet.[4] The same amount must be shown as an asset on the left-hand side of the balance sheet. Operating leases are not disclosed on the balance sheet. Exactly what constitutes a financial or operating lease for accounting purposes is discussed below.

The accounting implications of CICA 3065 are illustrated in Table 23.1. Imagine a firm that has $100,000 in assets and no debt, implying that the equity is also $100,000. The firm needs a truck costing $100,000 that it can lease or buy. The top of the table shows the balance sheet assuming that the firm borrows the money and buys the truck.

If the firm leases the truck, then one of two things will happen. If the lease is an operating lease, then the balance sheet will look like the one in the center of the table. In this case, neither the asset (the truck) nor the liability (the lease payments) appear. If the lease is a capital (financial) lease, then the balance sheet would look like the one at the bottom of the table, where the truck is shown as an asset and the present value of the lease payments is shown as a liability.

---

[4]The income statement is also affected. The asset created is amortized over the lease life and reported income is adjusted downward.

For accounting purposes, a lease is declared to be a financial lease, and must therefore be disclosed, if at least one of the following criteria is met:

1. The lease transfers ownership of the property to the lessee by the end of the term of the lease.
2. The lessee has an option to purchase the asset at a price below fair market value (bargain purchase price option) when the lease expires.
3. The lease term is 75 percent or more of the estimated economic life of the asset.
4. The present value of the lease payments is at least 90 percent of the asset's fair market value at the start of the lease.

A firm might be tempted to try to cook the books by taking advantage of the somewhat arbitrary distinction between operating leases and capital leases. Suppose a trucking firm wants to lease the $100,000 truck in our example in Table 23.1. The truck is expected to last for 15 years. A (perhaps unethical) financial manager could try to negotiate a lease contract for 10 years with lease payments having a present value of $89,000. These terms would get around criteria 3 and 4. If criteria 1 and 2 are similarly circumvented, the arrangement would be an operating lease and would not show up on the balance sheet.

Does this sort of gimmickry pay? The semistrong form of the efficient capital markets hypothesis implies that stock prices reflect all publicly available information. As we discussed earlier in this text, the empirical evidence generally supports this form of the hypothesis. Though operating leases do not appear in the firm's balance sheet, information on these leases must be disclosed elsewhere in the annual report. All this suggests that attempts to keep leases off the balance sheet will not affect stock price in an efficient capital market.

CONCEPT QUESTIONS

- Define the terms *capital lease* and *operating lease*.
- How are capital leases reported in a firm's financial statements?

23.3   Taxes, Revenue Canada, and Leases

The lessee can deduct lease payments for income tax purposes if the lease is qualified by Revenue Canada. The tax shields associated with lease payments are critical to the economic viability of a lease, so Revenue Canada guidelines are an important consideration. Tax rules on leasing have changed considerably in the past few years and further changes may occur. The discussion that follows summarizes the rules in force at the time of writing.

Essentially, Revenue Canada requires that a lease be primarily for business purposes and not merely for tax avoidance. In particular, Revenue Canada is on the lookout for leases that are really conditional sales agreements in disguise. The reason is that, in a lease, the lessee gets a tax deduction on the full lease payment. In a conditional sales agreement, only the interest portion of the payment is deductible. If Revenue Canada detects one or more of the following, the lease will be disallowed:[5]

1. The lessee automatically acquires title to the property after payment of a specified amount in the form of rentals.
2. The lessee is required to buy the property from the lessor during or at the termination of the lease.
3. The lessee has the right during or at the expiration of the lease to acquire the property at a price less than fair market value.

These rules also apply to sale and lease-back agreements. Revenue Canada auditors will rule that a sale and lease-back is really a secured loan if they find one of the above clauses in the agreement.

Once leases are qualified for tax purposes, lessors still must be aware of further tax regulations limiting their use of CCA tax shields on leased assets. Current regulations allow lessors to deduct CCA from leasing income only. Any unused CCA tax shields cannot be passed along to other companies owned by the same parent holding company.

In addition, the 1989 Federal Budget introduced rules to reduce the tax advantages of sale and lease-backs. The new rules place strict limits on a lessor's CCA write-offs on expensive assets such as aircraft. The 1989 Budget also practically ended sale and lease-backs by nonprofit institutions such as universities and hospitals.

CONCEPT QUESTIONS

- Why is Revenue Canada concerned about leasing?
- What are some standards Revenue Canada uses in evaluating a lease?

The Cash Flows of Financial Leasing   23.4

To begin our analysis of the leasing decision, we need to identify the relevant cash flows. The first part of this section illustrates how this is done. A key point, and one to watch for, is that taxes are a very important consideration in a lease analysis.

The Incremental Cash Flows

Consider the business decision facing TransCanada Distributors, a distribution firm which runs a fleet of company cars for its sales staff. Business has been expanding and the firm needs 50 more cars to provide basic transportation in support of sales. The type of car required can be purchased wholesale for $10,000. TransCanada has determined that each car can be expected to generate $6,000 per year in added sales for the next five years.

---

[5]Note that Revenue Canada's tax rules are different from the CICA's accounting rules. For more details on these conditions, see Revenue Canada Interpretation Bulletin IT233R (1983) and updates.

Table 23.2
Tax shield on CCA
for car

Year	UCC	CCA	Tax shield
0	$5,000	$2,000	$ 800
1	8,000	3,200	1,280
2	4,800	1,920	768
3	2,880	1,152	461
4	1,728	691	276
5	1,037		415

TransCanada has a corporate tax rate (combined federal and provincial) of 40 percent. The cars would qualify for a CCA rate of 40 percent (as rental cars) and, due to the hard-driving habits of TransCanada's sales staff, the cars would have no residual value after five years. Financial Lease Co. has offered to lease the cars to TransCanada for lease payments of $2,500 per year for each car over the five-year period. Lease payments are made at the beginning of the year. With the lease, TransCanada would remain responsible for maintenance, insurance, and operating expenses.

Susan Smart, a recently hired MBA, has been asked to compare the direct incremental cash flows from leasing the cars to the cash flows associated with buying them. The first thing she realizes is that, because TransCanada will have the cars either way, the $6,000 saving will be realized whether the cars are leased or purchased. Thus, this cost saving and any other operating costs or revenues can be ignored in the analysis because they are not incremental.

Upon reflection, Ms. Smart concludes that there are only three important cash flow differences between financial leasing and buying.[6]

1. If the cars are leased, TransCanada must make a lease payment of $2,500 each year. However, lease payments are fully tax deductible, so there is a tax shield of $1,000 on each lease payment. The after-tax lease payment is $2,500 − $1,000 = $1,500. This is a cost of leasing instead of buying.[7]

2. If the cars are leased, TransCanada does not own them and cannot depreciate them for tax purposes.

Table 23.2 shows the CCA and undepreciated capital cost (UCC) schedule for one car. Notice that Revenue Canada's half-year rule means that the eligible UCC is only $5,000 when the car is put in use in period 0. Table 23.2 also shows the tax shield on CCA for each year. For example, in period zero, the tax shield is $2,000 × .40 = $800. The tax shields for years 1 through 4 are calculated in the same way. In year 5, the car is scrapped for a zero salvage value. We assume that the asset pool is closed at this time, so there is a tax shield on the terminal loss of $1,037 × .40 = $415.[8] All these tax shields are lost to TransCanada if it leases so they are a cost of leasing.

---

[6]There is fourth consequence that we do not discuss here. If the car has a nontrivial salvage value and we lease, we give up that salvage value. This is another cost of leasing instead of buying.

[7]Lease payments are made at the beginning of the year as shown in Table 23.3. Firms pay taxes later, but our analysis ignores this difference for simplicity.

[8]If the pool were continued, the remaining UCC of $1,037 would be depreciated to infinity as explained in the Appendix to Chapter 1.

	Year					
	0	1	2	3	4	5
Investment	$10,000					
Lease payment	−2,500	−$ 2,500	−$2,500	−$2,500	−$2,500	
Payment shield	1,000	1,000	1,000	1,000	1,000	
Forgone tax shield	−800	−1,280	−768	−461	−276	−$415
Total cash flow	$ 7,700	−$ 2,780	−$2,268	−$1,961	−$1,776	−$415

Table 23.3
Incremental cash flows for TransCanada from leasing one car instead of buying

3. If the cars are leased, TransCanada does not have to spend $10,000 apiece today to buy them. This is a benefit to leasing.

The cash flows from leasing instead of buying are summarized in Table 23.3. Notice that the car's cost shows up with a positive sign in year 0, reflecting the fact that TransCanada *saves* $7,700 by leasing instead of buying. We could have expressed the cash flows from the purchase relative to the cash flows from leasing. These cash flows would be

	Year					
	0	1	2	3	4	5
Net cash flows from purchase alternative relative to lease alternative	−$7,700	$2,780	$2,268	$1,961	$1,776	$415

Of course, the cash flows here are the opposite of those in the bottom line of Table 23.3. Depending on our purpose, we may look at either the purchase relative to the lease or vice versa. Students should become comfortable with either viewpoint.

Now that we have the cash flows, we can make our decision by discounting the flows properly. However, because the discount rate is tricky, we take a detour in the next section before moving back to the TransCanada case. There we show that cash flows in the lease-versus-buy decision should be discounted at the after-tax interest rate—the after-tax cost of debt capital.

CONCEPT QUESTIONS

- What are the cash flow consequences of leasing instead of buying?
- Explain why the $7,700 in Table 23.3 has a positive sign.

A Detour on Discounting and Debt Capacity with Corporate Taxes 23.5

The analysis of leases is difficult, so both financial practitioners and academics have made conceptual errors. These errors revolve around taxes. We hope to avoid their mistakes by beginning with the simplest type of example, a loan for one year. Though this example is unrelated to our lease-versus-buy situation, principles developed here will apply directly to lease–buy analysis.

Table 23.4
Lending and borrowing in a world with corporate taxes (with 11-percent interest rate and 42-percent corporate tax rate)

	Date 0	Date 1
Lending example		
Lend −$100		Receive +$100.00 of principal
		Receive +$ 11.00 of interest
	6.6% lending rate	Pay −$ 4.40 (= −0.42 × $11) in taxes
		+$106.60
	After-tax lending rate is 6.6%.	
Borrowing example		
Borrow +$100		Pay −$100.00 of principal
		Pay −$ 11.00 of interest
	6.6% borrowing rate	Receive +$ 4.40 (= 0.42 × $11) as a tax rebate
		−$106.60
	After-tax borrowing rate is 6.6%.	

General principle: In a world with corporate taxes, riskless cash flows should be discounted at the after-tax interest rate.

Present Value of Riskless Cash Flows

Consider a corporation that lends $100 for a year. If the interest rate is 11 percent, the firm will receive $111 at the end of the year. Of this amount, $11 is interest and the remaining $100 is the original principal. A corporate tax rate of 40 percent implies taxes on the interest of $4.40 (or 0.40 × $11). Thus, the firm ends up with $106.60 (or $111 − $4.40) after taxes on a $100 investment.

Now, consider a company that borrows $100 for a year. With an 11-percent interest rate, the firm must pay $111 to the bank at the end of the year. However, the borrowing firm can take the $11 of interest as a tax deduction. The corporation pays $4.40 (or 0.40 × $11) less in taxes than it would have paid had it not borrowed the money at all. Thus, considering this reduction in taxes, the firm must pay $106.60 (or $111 − $4.40) on a $100 loan. The cash flows from both lending and borrowing are displayed in Table 23.4.

The above two paragraphs show a very important result: The firm is indifferent between receiving $100 today or $106.60 next year. If it received $100 today, it could lend it out, thereby receiving $106.60 after corporate taxes at the end of the year. Conversely, if it knows today that it will receive $106.60 at the end of the year, it could borrow $100 today. The after-tax interest and principal payments on the loan would be paid with the $106.60 that the firm will receive at the end of the year. Because of the interchangability illustrated above, we say that a payment of $106.60 next year has a present value of $100. Because $100 = $106.60/1.066, a riskless cash flow should be discounted at the after-tax interest rate of 0.066 [or 0.11 × (1 − 0.40)].

Our discussion considers a specific example. The general principle is

> In a world with corporate taxes, the firm should discount riskless cash flows at the after-tax riskless rate of interest.

Optimal Debt Level and Riskless Cash Flows (Advanced)

In addition, our simple example can illustrate a related point concerning the optimal debt level. Consider a firm that has just determined that the current level of debt in its capital structure is optimal. Immediately following that determination, the firm is surprised to learn that it will receive a guaranteed payment of $106.60 in one year from, say, a tax-exempt government lottery. This future windfall is an asset that, like any asset, should raise the firm's optimal debt level. How much does this payment raise the firm's optimal level?

Our analysis above implies that the firm's optimal debt level must be $100 more than it previously was. That is, the firm could borrow $100 today, perhaps paying the entire amount out as a dividend. It would owe the bank $111 at the end of the year. However, because it receives a tax rebate of $4.40 (or 0.40 × $11), its net repayment will be $106.60. Thus, its borrowing of $100 today is fully offset by next year's government lottery proceeds of $106.60. In other words, the lottery proceeds act as an irrevocable trust that can service the increased debt. Note that we need not know the optimal debt level before the lottery was announced. We are merely saying that, whatever this prelottery optimal level was, the optimal debt level is $100 more after the lottery announcement.

Of course, this is just one example. The general principle is[9]

> In a world with corporate taxes, one determines the increase in the firm's optimal debt level by discounting a future guaranteed after-tax inflow at the after-tax riskless interest rate.

Conversely, suppose that a second and unrelated firm is surprised to learn that it must pay $106.60 next year to the government for back taxes. Clearly, this additional liability impinges on the second firm's debt capacity. By the same reasoning, it follows that the second firm's optimal debt level must be lowered by exactly $100.

CONCEPT QUESTION

- How should one discount a riskless cash flow?

NPV Analysis of the Lease-versus-Buy Decision   23.6

The detour leads to a simple method for evaluating leases: discount all cash flows at the after-tax interest rate. From the bottom line of Table 23.3, TransCanada's incremental cash flows from leasing versus purchasing are

---

[9]This principle holds for riskless or guaranteed cash flows only. Unfortunately, there is no easy formula for determining the increase in optimal debt level from a *risky* cash flow.

	Year					
	0	1	2	3	4	5
Net cash flows from lease alternative relative to purchase alternative	$7,700	−$2,780	−$2,268	−$1,961	−$1,776	−$415

Let us assume that TransCanada can either borrow or lend at the 11-percent interest rate. If the corporate tax rate is 40 percent, the correct discount rate is the after-tax rate of 6.6 percent we used earlier [11% × (1 − 10.40)]. When 6.6 percent is used to compute the NPV of the lease, we have

$$NPV = 7,7000 - \frac{2,780}{(1.066)} - \frac{2,268}{(1.066)^2} - \frac{1,961}{(1.066)^3} - \frac{1,776}{(1,066)^4} - \frac{415}{(1.066)^5} = -\$199 \tag{23.1}$$

Because the net present value of the incremental cash flows from leasing relative to purchasing is negative, TransCanada prefers to purchase.

Equation (23.1) is the correct approach to lease-versus-buy analysis. However, students are often bothered by two things. First, they question whether the cash flows in Table 23.3 are truly riskless. We examine this issue next. Second, they feel that this approach lacks intuition. We address this concern a little later.

The Discount Rate

Because we discounted at the after-tax riskless rate of interest, we have implicitly assumed that the cash flows in the TransCanada example are riskless. Is this appropriate?

A lease payment is like the debt service on a secured bond issued by the lessee, and the discount rate should be approximately the same as the interest rate on such debt. In general, this rate will be slightly higher than the riskless rate considered in the previous section. The various tax shields could be somewhat riskier than the lease payments for two reasons. First, the value of the CCA tax benefits depends on TransCanada's ability to generate enough taxable income to use them. Second, the corporate tax rate may change. For these two reasons, a firm might be justified in discounting the CCA tax benefits at a rate higher than that used for the lease payments. However, our experience is that, in practice, companies discount both the CCA shield and lease payments at the same rate. This implies that financial practitioners view the above two risks as minor. We adopt the pragmatic convention of discounting the two flows at the same rate—the after-tax interest rate on secured debt issued by the lessee.

At this point some students still ask the question, Why not use r_{WACC} as the discount rate in lease-versus-buy analysis? But r_{WACC} should not be used for lease analysis because the cash flows are more like debt-service cash flows than operating cash flows, so the risk is much less. The discount rate should reflect the risk of the incremental cash flows.

Assets		Liabilities		
Initial situation				
Current	$ 50,000	Debt	$ 60,000	
Fixed	50,000	Equity	40,000	
Total	100,000	Total	100,000	
Buy with secured loan				
Current	$ 50,000	Debt	$ 66,000	
Fixed	50,000	Equity	44,000	
Machine	10,000			
Total	110,000	Total	110,000	
Lease				
Current	$ 50,000	Lease	$ 10,000	
Fixed	50,000	Debt	56,000	
Machine	10,000	Equity	44,000	
Total	110,000	Total	110,000	

Table 23.5
Debt displacement elsewhere in the firm when a lease is instituted

This example shows that leases reduce the level of debt elsewhere in the firm. Though the example illustrates a point, it is not meant to show a *precise* method for calculating debt displacement.

Debt Displacement and Lease Valuation   23.7

The Basic Concept of Debt Displacement (Advanced)

The previous analysis allows one to calculate the right answer in a simple manner. Although simplicity is an important benefit, the analysis has little intuitive appeal. To remedy this, we hope to make lease–buy analysis more intuitive by considering the issue of debt displacement.

A firm that purchases equipment will generally issue debt to finance the purchase and the debt becomes a liability of the firm. A lessee incurs a liability equal to the present value of all future lease payments. This comparison suggests that leases displace debt. The balance sheets in Table 23.5 illustrate how leasing might affect debt.

Suppose a firm initially has $100,000 of assets and a 150-percent optimal debt-equity ratio. The firm's debt is $60,000, and its equity is $40,000. Suppose the firm must use a new $10,000 machine. The firm has two alternatives:

1. *The firm can purchase the machine.* If it does, it will finance the purchase with a secured loan and with equity. The debt capacity of the machine is assumed to be the same as for the firm as a whole.

2. *The firm can lease the asset and get 100-percent financing.* That is, the present value of the future lease payments will be $10,000.

If the firm finances the machine with both secured debt and new equity, its debt will increase by $6,000 and its equity by $4,000. Its optimal debt-equity ratio of 150 percent will be maintained.

Conversely, consider the lease alternative. Because the lessee views the lease payment as a liability, the lessee thinks in terms of a *liability-to-equity* ratio, not just a debt-to-equity ratio. As mentioned above, the present value of the lease liability is $10,000. If the leasing firm is to maintain a liability-to-equity ratio of 150 percent, debt elsewhere in the firm must fall by $4,000 when the lease is instituted. Because debt must be repurchased, net liabilities only rise by $6,000 (or $10,000 − $4,000) when $10,000 of assets are placed under lease.[10]

Debt displacement is a hidden cost of leasing. If a firm leases, it will not use as much regular debt as it would otherwise. The benefits of debt capacity will be lost, particularly the lower taxes associated with interest expense.

Optimal Debt Level in the TransCanada Example (Advanced)

The previous section showed that leasing displaces debt. Though the section illustrated a point, it was not meant to show the precise method for calculating debt displacement. Below, we describe the precise method for calculating the difference in optimal debt levels between purchase and lease in the TransCanada example.

From the last line of Table 23.3, we know that the cash flows from the *purchase* alternative relative to the cash flows from the lease alternative are[11]

	Year					
	0	1	2	3	4	5
Net cash flows from purchase alternative relative to lease alternative	−$7,700	$2,780	$2,268	$1,961	$1,776	$415

An increase in the optimal debt level at year 0 occurs because the firm learns at that time of guaranteed cash flows beginning at year 1. Our detour on discounting and debt capacity taught us to calculate this increased debt level by discounting the future riskless cash inflows at the after-tax interest rate. Thus, the additional debt level of the purchase alternative relative to the lease alternative is

$$\text{Increase in optimal debt level from purchase alternative} = \$7,899.42 = \frac{\$2,780}{(1.066)} + \frac{\$2,268}{(1.066)^2} + \frac{\$1,961}{(1.066)^3} + \frac{\$1,776}{(1.066)^4} + \frac{\$415}{(1.066)^5}$$

That is, whatever the optimal amount of debt under the lease alternative, the optimal amount of debt will be $7,899.42 higher under the purchase alternative.

This result can be stated in another way. Imagine there are two identical firms except that one firm purchases a corporate car and the other leases it. From Table 23.3, we know that the purchasing firm generates more cash flow after taxes in each of the five years than does the leasing firm. Further, imagine that the same bank lends money to both firms. The bank should lend the purchasing firm more money because it has a greater cash flow each period. How much extra money should the bank lend the

---

[10]In practice, growing firms generally will not repurchase debt when instituting a lease. Rather, they will issue less debt in the future than they would have without the lease.

[11]The last line of Table 23.3 presents the cash flows from the lease alternative relative to the purchase alternative. As pointed out earlier, our cash flows are now reversed because we are now presenting the cash flows from the purchase alternative relative to the lease alternative.

Table 23.6 Calculation of increase in optimal debt level if TransCanada purchases instead of leases

	Year					
	0	1	2	3	4	5
Outstanding balance of loan	$7,899.42	$5,640.78*	$3,745.07	$2,031.24	$ 389.31	$ 0.00
Interest		868.94	620.49	411.96	223.44	42.82
Tax deduction on interest		347.57	248.19	164.78	89.37	17.13
After-tax interest expenses		$ 521.36	$ 372.29	$ 247.17	$ 134.06	$ 25.69
Extra cash that purchasing firm generates over leasing firm (from Table 23.3)		2,780.00	2,268.00	1,961.00	1,776.00	415.00
Repayment of loan		$2,258.64†	$1,895.71	$1,713.83	$1,641.94	$389.31

*$5,640.78=$7,899.42–$2,258.64
†$2,258.64=$2,780.00–$521.36

purchasing firm so that the incremental loan can be paid off by the extra cash flows shown in Table 23.3? The answer is exactly $7,899.42, the increase in the optimal debt level we calculated earlier.

To see this, Table 23.6 works through the example on a year-by-year basis. Because the purchasing firm borrows $7,899 more at year 0 than does the leasing firm, the purchasing firm will pay interest of $868.94 (or $7,899.42 × 0.11) at year 1 on the additional debt. The interest allows the firm to reduce its taxes by $347.57 (or $868.94 × 0.40), leaving an after-tax interest expense of $521.36 (or $868.94 – 347.57) at year 1.

We know from Table 23.3 that the purchasing firm generates $2,780 more cash at year 1 than does the leasing firm. Because the purchasing firm has the extra $2,780 coming in at year 1 but must pay interest on its loan, how much of the loan can the firm repay at year 1 and still have the same cash flow as the leasing firm has? The purchasing firm can repay $2,258.64 of the loan at year 1 and still have the same net cash flow that the leasing firm has. After the repayment, the purchasing firm will have a remaining balance of $5,640.78 (or $7,899.42 – $2,258.64) at year 1. For each of the five years, this sequence of cash flows is displayed in Table 23.6. The outstanding balance goes to zero over the five years. Thus, the cash flows shown at the bottom of Table 23.3, which represent the extra cash from purchasing instead of leasing, fully amortize the loan of $7,899.42.

Our analysis of debt capacity has two purposes. First, we want to show the additional debt capacity from purchasing and we just completed this task. Second, we want to determine whether or not the lease is preferred to the purchase. This decision rule follows easily from our discussion. By leasing the equipment and having $7,899.42 less debt than under the purchase alternative, the firm has exactly the same cash flow in years 1 to 5 that it would have through a levered purchase. Thus, we can ignore cash flows beginning in year 1 when comparing the lease alternative with the purchase-with-debt alternative. However, the cash flows differ between the alternatives at year 0. These differences are

1. *The purchase cost at year 0 of $7,700 is avoided by leasing.* This should be viewed as a cash inflow under the leasing alternative.

2. *The firm borrows $7,899 less at year 0 under the lease alternative than it can under the purchase alternative.* This should be viewed as a cash outflow under the leasing alternative.

Because the firm borrows $7,899 less by leasing but saves only $7,700 on the equipment, the lease alternative requires an extra cash outflow at year 0 relative to the purchase alternative of −$199 (or $7,700 − $7,899). Because cash flows in later years from leasing are identical to those from purchasing with debt, the firm should purchase.

This conclusion can be expressed another way by looking at the cash flows of the purchase alternative relative to those from the lease. Point 2 means that these incremental cash flows can service a loan of $7,899. However, buying instead of leasing requires an outlay of only $7,700 in year 0. Therefore, buying instead of leasing generates a surplus in year 0 (NPV) of $199.

This is exactly the same answer we got earlier in this chapter when we discounted all cash flows at the after-tax interest rate. Of course, this is no coincidence because the increase in the optimal debt level is also determined by discounting all flows at the after-tax interest rate. The accompanying box presents both methods. (The numbers in the box are in terms of the NPV of the lease relative to the purchase. Thus, a negative NPV indicates that the purchase alternative should be taken.)

Two Methods for Calculating Net Present Value of Lease Relative to Purchase

Method 1: Discount all cash flows at the after-tax interest rate

$$-\$199 = \$7,700 - \text{PV (cash flows) at } 6.6\%$$
$$= \$7,700 - \$7,899$$

Method 2: Compare the purchase price with the reduction in optimal debt level under the leasing alternative

$$-\$199 = \$7,700 - \$7,899$$

$$\underset{\text{price}}{\text{Purchase}} - \underset{\begin{array}{c}\text{optimal debt}\\\text{level if leasing}\end{array}}{\text{Reduction in}}$$

Note: Because we are calculating the NPV of the lease relative to the purchase, a negative value indicates that the purchase alternative is preferred.

23.8   Does Leasing Ever Pay? The Base Case

We previously looked at the lease-versus-buy decision from the perspective of the potential lessee, TransCanada Industries. We now turn things around and look at the lease from the perspective of the lessor, Financial Leasing. The cash flows associated

			Year			
	0	1	2	3	4	5
Investment	−$10,000					
Lease payment	2,500	$ 2,500	$ 2,500	$ 2,500	$ 2,500	
Payment shield	−1,000	−1,000	−1,000	−1,000	−1,000	
Forgone tax shield	800	1,280	768	461	276	$415
Total cash flow	−$ 7,700	$ 2,780	$ 2,268	$ 1,961	$ 1,776	$415
NPV	$ 199					

Table 23.7
Cash flows to the lessor

with the lease from the lessor's perspective are shown in Table 23.7. First, the lessor must buy each car for $10,000, so there is a $10,000 outflow today. Next, Financial Leasing depreciates the machine at a CCA rate of 40 percent to obtain the CCA tax shields shown. Finally, the lessor receives a lease payment of $2,500 each year on which it pays taxes at a 40-percent tax rate. The after-tax lease payment received is $1,500.

Now examine the total cash flows to Financial Leasing, as displayed in the bottom line of Table 23.7. Readers with a healthy memory will notice something very interesting. These cash flows are exactly the opposite of those of TransCanada, as displayed in the bottom line of Table 23.3. Readers with a healthy sense of skepticism may be thinking something very interesting: "If the cash flows of the lessor are exactly the opposite of those of the lessee, the combined cash flow of the two parties must be zero each year. Thus, there does not seem to be any joint benefit to this lease. Because the net present value to the lessee was −$199, the NPV to the lessor must be $199. The joint NPV is $0 (or −$199 + 199). There does not appear to be any way for the NPV of both the lessor and the lessee to be positive at the same time. Because one party would inevitably lose money, the leasing deal could never fly."

This is one of the most important results of leasing. Though Table 23.7 concerns one particular leasing deal, the principle can be generalized. As long as (1) both parties are subject to the same interest and tax rates and (2) transaction costs are ignored, there can be no leasing deal that benefits both parties. However, there is a lease payment for which both parties would calculate an NPV of zero. For that lease payment, TransCanada would be indifferent to whether it leased or bought, and Financial Leasing would be indifferent to whether it leased or not. To find the indifference lease payment, we rerun our leasing spreadsheet from Table 23.7, setting the NPV of leasing equal to zero. Table 23.8 shows that the indifference lease payment is $2,425.

A student with a healthy sense of skepticism might say, "This textbook appears to be arguing that leasing is not beneficial. Yet, we know that leasing occurs frequently in the real world. Maybe, just maybe, the textbook is wrong." Although we will not admit to being wrong (what textbook would!), we freely admit to being incomplete at this point. The next section considers factors that create benefits to leasing.

Table 23.8
Indifference lease
payments

	Year					
	0	1	2	3	4	5
Investment	$10,000					
Lease payment	−2,425	−$ 2,425	−$2,425	−$2,425	−$2,425	
Payment shield	969	969	969	969	969	
Forgone tax shield	−800	−1,280	−768	−461	−276	−$415
Total cash flow	$ 7,745	−$ 2,735	−$2,223	−$1,916	−$1,731	−$415
NPV	$ 0					

23.9

Reasons for Leasing

Proponents of leasing make many claims about why firms should lease assets rather than buy them. Some of the reasons given to support leasing are good, and some are not. We discuss here the reasons for leasing we think are good and some that we think are not so good.

Good Reasons for Leasing

If leasing is a good choice, it is because one or more of the following is true:

1. Taxes may be reduced by leasing.
2. The lease contract may reduce certain types of uncertainty.
3. Transactions costs can be higher for buying an asset and financing it with debt or equity than for leasing the asset.

Tax Advantages

By far the most important reason for long-term leasing is tax avoidance. If the corporate income tax were repealed, long-term leasing would become much less important. A lease contract is not a zero sum game between the lessee and lessor when their effective tax rates differ. In this case, the lease can be structured so that both sides benefit. Any tax benefits from leasing can be split between the two firms by setting the lease payments at the appropriate level, and the shareholders of both firms will benefit from this tax transfer arrangement. The loser will be Revenue Canada.

This works because a lease contract swaps two sets of tax shields. The lessor obtains the CCA tax shields due to ownership. The lessee receives the tax shield on lease payments made. In a full-payout lease, the total dollar amounts of the two sets of tax shields may be roughly the same, but the critical difference is the timing. CCA tax shields are accelerated deductions reducing the tax burden in early years. Lease payments, on the other hand, reduce taxes by the same amount in every year. As a result, the ownership tax shields often have a greater present value provided the firm is fully taxed.

The basic logic behind structuring a leasing deal makes a firm in a high tax bracket want to act as the lessor. Low-tax (or untaxed) firms will be lessees, because they will not be able to use the tax advantages of ownership, such as CCA and debt financing. These ownership tax shields are worth less to the lessee in this case because the lessee faces a lower tax rate or may not have enough taxable income to absorb the accelerated tax shields in the early years.

Overall, less tax is paid by the lessee and lessor combined and this tax savings occurs sooner rather than later. The lessor gains on the tax side; the lessee may lose but the amount of any loss is less than the lessor gains. To make the lease attractive, the lessor must pass on some of the tax savings in the form of lower lease payments. In the end, the lessor gains by keeping part of the tax savings, the lessee gains through a lower lease payment, and Revenue Canada pays for both gains through a reduction in tax revenue.

To see how this would work in practice, recall the example of Section 23.8 and the situation of Financial Leasing. The value of the lease it proposed to TransCanada was $199. However, the value of the lease to TransCanada was exactly the opposite, −$199. Since the lessor's gains came at the expense of the lessee, no deal could be arranged. However, if TransCanada paid no taxes and the lease payments were reduced to $2,437 from $2,500, both Financial Leasing and TransCanada would find there is positive NPV in leasing.

To see this, we can rework Table 23.7 with a zero tax rate. This would occur when TransCanada has enough alternate tax shields to reduce taxable income to zero for the foreseeable future.[12] In this case, notice that the cash flows from leasing are simply the lease payments of $2,437 because no CCA tax shield is lost and the lease payment is not tax deductible. The cash flows from leasing are thus:

			Year			
	0	1	2	3	4	5
Cost of car	$10,000					
Lease payment	−2,437	−$2,437	−$2,437	−$2,437	−$2,437	0
Cash flow	$ 7,563	−$2,437	−$2,437	−$2,437	−$2,437	0

The value of the lease for TransCanada is

$$NPV = \$7,563 - \$2,437 \times (1 - 1/1.11^4)/.11$$
$$= \$2.34$$

which is positive. Notice that the discount rate here is 11 percent because TransCanada pays no taxes; in other words, this is both the pretax and after-tax rate.

From Table 23.9, the value of the lease to Financial Leasing can be worked out as +$32.

As a consequence of different tax rates, the lessee (TransCanada) gains $2.34, and the lessor (Financial Leasing) gains $32.00. Revenue Canada loses. What this example shows is that the lessor and the lessee can gain if their tax rates are different. The lease contract allows the lessor to take advantage of the CCA and interest tax shields that cannot be used by the lessee. Revenue Canada will experience a net loss of tax revenue, and some of the tax gains to the lessor are passed on to the lessee in the form of lower lease payments.

---

[12]Strictly speaking, the UCC of the cars would be carried on the books until the firm is able to claim CCA. However, the present value of this deferred CCA tax shield would be low, so for the sake of simplicity, we ignore it here.

Table 23.9
Revised cash flows
to lessor

	Year					
	0	1	2	3	4	5
Cost of car	−$10,000					
Lease payment	2,437	$2,437	$2,437	$2,437	$2,437	
Payment shield	−974	−974	−974	−974	−974	
CCA tax shield	800	1,280	768	461	276	$415
Total cash flow	−$ 7,738	$2,742	$2,230	$1,923	$1,739	$415
NPV lessor	$ 32					

A Reduction of Uncertainty

We have noted that the lessee does not own the property when the lease expires. The value of the property at this time is called the *residual value* and belongs to the lessor. When the lease contract is signed, there may be substantial uncertainty as to what the residual value of the asset will be. Thus, under a lease contract, this residual risk is borne by the lessor. Conversely, the user bears this risk when purchasing.

It is common sense that the party best able to bear a particular risk should do so. If the user firm has little risk aversion, it will not suffer by purchasing. However, if it is highly averse to risk, the user should find a third-party lessor more capable of assuming this burden.

This latter situation frequently arises when the user is a small or newly formed firm. Because the risk of the entire firm is likely to be quite high and because the principal shareholders are likely to be undiversified, the firm desires to minimize risk wherever possible. A potential lessor (such as a large, publicly held financial institution) is far more capable of bearing the risk. Conversely, this situation is unlikely when the user is a blue chip corporation. That potential lessee is more able to bear risk.

Transactions Costs

The costs of changing an asset's ownership are generally greater than the costs of writing a lease agreement. Consider the choice that confronts a person who lives in Vancouver but must do business in Toronto for two days. Renting a hotel room for two nights is clearly cheaper than buying a condominium for two days and then selling it.

Unfortunately, leases generate agency costs as well. For example, the lessee might misuse or overuse the asset, since the lessee has no interest in the asset's residual value. This cost will be implicitly paid by the lessee through a high lease payment. Although the lessor can reduce these agency costs through monitoring, monitoring itself is costly.

Thus, leasing is most beneficial when the transaction costs of purchase and resale outweigh the agency costs and monitoring costs of a lease. Flath argues that this occurs in short-term leases but not in long-term leases.[13]

---

[13]D. Flath, "The Economics of Short Term Leasing," *Economic Inquiry* 18 (April 1980).

Bad Reasons for Leasing

Leasing and Accounting Income

In Section 23.2 ("Accounting and Leasing"), we pointed out that a firm's balance sheet shows fewer liabilities with an operating lease than with either a capitalized lease or a purchase financed with debt. We indicated that a firm desiring to project a strong balance sheet might select an operating lease. In addition, the firm's return on assets (ROA) is generally higher with an operating lease than with either a capitalized lease or a purchase. To see this, we examine, in turn, the numerator and denominator of the ROA formula.

With an operating lease, lease payments are treated as an expense. If the asset is purchased, both capital cost allowance and interest charges are expenses. At least in the early part of the asset's life, the yearly lease payment is generally less than the sum of yearly capital cost allowance and yearly interest. Thus, accounting income, the numerator of the ROA formula, is higher with an operating lease than with a purchase. Because accounting expenses with a capitalized lease are analogous to CCA and interest if the asset is purchased, accounting income does not increase when a lease is capitalized.

In addition, leased assets do not appear on the balance sheet with an operating lease. Thus, the total asset value of a firm, the denominator of the ROA formula, is smaller with an operating lease than it is with either a purchase or a capitalized lease. These two effects cause the firm's ROA to be higher with an operating lease than with either a purchase or a capitalized lease.

Of course, in an efficient capital market, accounting information cannot be used to fool investors. It is unlikely, then, that leasing's impact on accounting numbers should create value for the firm. Savvy investors should be able to see through attempts by management to improve the firm's financial statements.

One Hundred–Percent Financing

It is often claimed that leasing provides 100-percent financing, while secured equipment loans require an initial down payment. However, we argued earlier that leases tend to displace debt elsewhere in the firm. Our earlier analysis suggests that leases do not permit a greater level of total liabilities than do purchases with borrowing.

Other Reasons

There are, of course, many special reasons for some companies to find advantages in leasing. For example, leasing may be used to circumvent capital expenditure control systems set up by bureaucratic firms.

Leasing Decisions in Practice

The reduction-of-uncertainty motive for leasing is the one that is most often cited by corporations. For example, computers have a way of becoming technologically outdated very quickly, and computers are very commonly leased instead of purchased.

In a recent U.S. survey, 82 percent of the responding firms cited the risk of obsolescence as an important reason for leasing, whereas only 57 percent cited the potential for cheaper financing.[14]

Yet, cheaper financing based on shifting tax shields is an important motive for leasing. One piece of evidence is Canadian lessors' strong reaction to 1989 changes in tax laws restricting sale and lease-backs. Further evidence comes from a study by Dipchand, Gudikunst, and Roberts analyzing decisions taken by Canadian railroads to lease rolling stock. They examined 20 lease contracts and found that, in 17 cases, leasing provided cheaper financing than debt.[15]

CONCEPT QUESTION

- Summarize the good and bad arguments for leasing.

23.10   Some Unanswered Questions

Our analysis suggests that the primary advantage of long-term leasing results from the differential tax rates of the lessor and the lessee. Other valid reasons for leasing are lower contracting costs and risk reduction. There are several questions our analysis has not specifically answered.

Are the Uses of Leases and of Debt Complementary?

Ang and Peterson find that firms with high debt tend to lease frequently as well.[16] This result should not be puzzling. The corporate attributes that support high debt capacity may also make leasing advantageous. Thus, even though leasing displaces debt (that is, leasing and borrowing are substitutes) for an individual firm, high debt and extensive leasing can go hand in hand.

Why Are Leases Offered by Both Manufacturers and Third-Party Lessors?

The offsetting effects of taxes can explain why both manufacturers and third-party lessors offer leases:

1. For manufacturer lessors, the basis for determining capital cost allowance is the manufacturer's cost. For third-party lessors, the basis is the sales price that the lessor paid to the manufacturer. Because the sales price is generally greater than the manufacturer's cost, this is an advantage to third-party lessors.

---

[14]T. K. Mukherjee, "A Survey of Corporate Leasing Analysis," *Financial Management* 20 (Autumn 1991), pp. 96–107.

[15]C. R. Dipchand, A. C. Gudikunst, and G. S. Roberts, "An Empirical Analysis of Canadian Railroad Leases," *Journal of Financial Research* 3 (Spring 1980), pp. 57–67.

[16]J. Ang and P. P. Peterson, "The Leasing Puzzle," *Journal of Finance* 39 (September 1984).

2. However, the manufacturer must recognize a profit for tax purposes when selling the asset to the third-party lessor. The manufacturer's profit for some equipment can be deferred if the manufacturer becomes the lessor. This provides an incentive for manufacturers to lease.

Why Are Some Assets Leased More Commonly Than Others?

Certain assets appear to be leased more frequently than others. Smith and Wakeman have looked at nontax incentives affecting leasing.[17] Their analysis suggests that asset and firm characteristics are important in the lease-or-buy decision:

1. The more sensitive is the value of an asset to use and maintenance decisions, the more likely it is that the asset will be purchased instead of leased. Ownership provides a better incentive to minimize maintenance costs than does leasing.

2. Price discrimination opportunities may be important. Leasing may be a way of circumventing laws against charging too *low* a price.

Summary and Conclusions 23.11

A large fraction of equipment is leased rather than purchased. This chapter describes the institutional arrangements surrounding leases and shows how to evaluate leases financially.

1. Leases can be separated into two types: financial and operating. Financial leases are generally longer-term, fully amortized, and not cancelable. In effect, the lessor obtains economic but not legal ownership. Operating leases are usually shorter-term, partially amortized, and cancelable and can be likened to a rental agreement.

2. When a firm purchases an asset with debt, both the asset and the liability appear on the firm's balance sheet. If a lease meets at least one of a number of criteria, it must be capitalized. This means that the present value of the lease appears as both an asset and a liability. A lease escapes capitalization if it does not meet any of these criteria. Leases not meeting the criteria are called *operating leases,* though the accountant's definition differs somewhat from the practitioner's definition. Operating leases do not appear on the balance sheet. For cosmetic reasons, many firms prefer that an asset be called *operating.*

3. Firms generally lease for tax purposes. To protect its interests, Revenue Canada allows financial arrangements to be classified as leases only if a number of criteria are met.

4. We showed that risk-free cash flows should be discounted at the after-tax, risk-free rate. Because both lease payments and CCA tax shields are nearly

---

[17]C. W. Smith, Jr., and L. M. Wakeman, "Determinants of Corporate Leasing Policy," *Journal of Finance* (July 1985).

riskless, all relevant cash flows in the lease–buy decision should be discounted at a rate near this after-tax rate. We use the practical convention of discounting at the after-tax interest rate on the lessee's secured debt.

5. Though this method is simple, it lacks certain intuitive appeal. In an optional section, we present an alternative, more intuitively appealing method. Relative to a lease, a purchase generates debt capacity. This increase in debt capacity can be calculated by discounting the difference between the cash flows of the purchase and the cash flows of the lease using the after-tax interest rate. The increase in debt capacity from a purchase is compared to the extra outflow at year 0 from a purchase.

6. If the lessor is in the same tax bracket as the lessee, the cash flows to the lessor are exactly the opposite of the cash flows to the lessee. Thus, the value of the lease to the lessee plus the value of the lease to the lessor must be zero. While this suggests that leases can never fly, there are actually at least three good reasons for leasing:

   a. Differences in tax brackets between lessor and lessee.

   b. Shift of risk bearing to the lessor.

   c. Minimization of transaction costs.

   We also document a number of bad reasons for leasing.

Key Terms

Lessee 669

Lessor 669

Lease 669

Direct lease 670

Sales-type lease 670

Operating lease 670

Sale and lease-backs 671

Financial lease 671

Leveraged lease 672

Off–balance-sheet financing 672

Debt displacement 682

Suggested Readings

A classic article on lease valuation is:

S. Myers, D. A. Dill, and A. J. Bautista. "Valuation of Financial Lease Contracts." *Journal of Finance* (June 1976).

A good review and discussion of leasing is contained in:

C. W. Smith, Jr., and L. M. Wakeman. "Determinations of Corporate Leasing Policy." *Journal of Finance* (July 1985).

The survey evidence mentioned in this chapter is from:

Tarun K. Mukherjee. "A Survey of Corporate Leasing Analysis." *Financial Management* (Autumn 1991).

Questions and Problems

23.1 Discuss the validity of each of the following statements:

a. Leasing reduces risk and can reduce a firm's cost of capital.

b. Leasing provides 100-percent financing.

c. Firms that do a large amount of leasing will not do much borrowing.

d. If the tax advantages of leasing were eliminated, leasing would disappear.

Use the following information to work the next six problems:

You work for a nuclear research laboratory that is contemplating leasing a diagnostic scanner. (Leasing is a common with expensive, high-tech equipment.) The scanner costs $540,000 and qualifies for a 30-percent CCA rate. Because of radiation contamination, the scanner will be completely valueless in four years. You can lease it for $160,000 per year for four years.

23.2 Assume that the tax rate is 40 percent. You can borrow at 10 percent pretax. Should you lease or buy?

23.3 What are the cash flows from the lease from the lessor's viewpoint? Assume a 40-percent tax bracket.

23.4 What would the lease payment have to be for both lessor and lessee to be indifferent to the lease?

23.5 Assume that your company does not contemplate paying taxes for the next several years. What are the cash flows from leasing in this case?

23.6 Combining the information in Questions 23.3 and 23.5, over what range of lease payments will the lease be profitable for both parties?

23.7 Rework Problem 23.2 assuming that the scanner qualifies for a special CCA rate of 50 percent per year.

23.8 An asset costs $86.87. The CCA rate for this asset is 20 percent. The asset's useful life is two years. It will have no salvage value. The corporate tax rate on ordinary income is 40 percent. The interest rate on risk-free cash flows is 10 percent.

a. What set of lease payments will make the lessee and the lessor equally well off?

b. Show the general condition that will make the value of a lease to the lessor the negative of the value to the lessee.

c. Assume that the lessee pays no taxes and the lessor is in the 40-percent tax bracket. For what range of lease payments does the lease have a positive NPV for both parties?

23.9 High electricity costs have made Farmer Corporation's chicken-plucking machine economically worthless. There are only two machines available to replace it.

The International Plucking Machine (IPM) model is available only on a lease basis. The annual, end-of-year payments are $2,100 for five years. This machine will save Farmer $6,000 per year through reductions in electricity costs in each of the five years.

As an alternative, Farmer can purchase a more energy-efficient machine from Basic Machine Corporation (BMC) for $15,000. This machine will save $9,000 per year in electricity costs. Farmer's bank has offered to finance the machine with a $15,000 loan. The interest rate on the loan will be 10 percent on the remaining balance with five annual principal payments of $3,000.

Farmer has a target debt-to-asset ratio of 67 percent. As a small business, Farmer is in the 40-percent combined federal–provincial tax bracket. After five years, both machines are worthless. CCA for chicken-plucking machines is at the rate of 30 percent. The savings that Farmer will enjoy are known with certainty, because Farmer has a long-term chicken purchase agreement with Kanes Food Products, Inc., and a four-year backlog of orders.

a. Should Farmer lease the IPM machine or purchase the more efficient BMC machine?

b. Does your answer depend on the form of financing for direct purchase?

c. How much debt is displaced by this lease?

23.10 Tollufson Corporation has decided to purchase a new machine that costs $3,000. The machine will be worthless after three years. CCA for this type of machine is 40 percent. Tollufson is in the 40-percent combined tax bracket. The Royal Canadian Bank has offered Tollufson a three-year loan for $3,000. The repayment schedule is three yearly principal repayments of $1,000 and an interest charge of 14 percent on the outstanding balance of the loan at the beginning of each year. Fourteen percent is the marketwide rate of interest. Both principal repayments and interest are due at the end of each year.

York Leasing Corporation offers to lease the same machine to Tollufson. Lease payments of $1,200 per year are due at the end of each of the three years of the lease.

a. Should Tollufson lease the machine or buy it with bank financing?

b. What is the annual lease payment that will make Tollufson indifferent to whether it leases the machine or purchases it?

APPENDIX   # APV Approach to Leasing

A box appearing earlier in this chapter showed two methods for calculating the NPV of the lease relative to the purchase:

1. Discount all cash flows at the after-tax interest rate.

2. Compare the purchase price with the reduction in the optimal debt level under the leasing alternative.

Surprisingly (and perhaps unfortunately) there is still another method. We feel compelled to present this third method, because it has important links with the adjusted present value (APV) approach discussed in Chapter 17. We illustrate this approach using the TransCanada Distributors example developed in Table 23.3.

In a previous chapter, we learned that the APV of any project can be expressed as

APV = All-equity value + Additional effects of debt

In other words, the adjusted present value of a project is the sum of the net present value of the project when financed by all equity plus the additional effects from debt financing. In the context of the lease-versus-buy decision, the APV method can be expressed as

$$
\begin{array}{ccc}
\text{Adjusted present value} & & \text{Net present value of the} \\
\text{of the lease relative} & = & \text{lease relative to the purchase} \\
\text{to the purchase} & & \text{when purchase is financed} \\
& & \text{by all equity}
\end{array}
-
\begin{array}{c}
\text{Additional effects} \\
\text{when purchase is financed} \\
\text{with some debt}
\end{array}
$$

All-Equity Value

From Chapter 17, we know that the all-equity value is simply the NPV of the cash flows discounted at the *pretax* interest rate. For the TransCanada example from Table 23.3, this value is

$$
\$505.68 = \$7,700 - \left[\frac{\$2,780}{(1.11)} + \frac{\$2,268}{(1.11)^2} + \frac{\$1,961}{(1.11)^3} + \frac{\$1,776}{(1.11)^4} + \frac{\$415}{(1.11)^5} \right]
$$

This calculation is identical to method 1 in the earlier box except that we are now discounting at the pretax interest rate. The calculation shows that the lease is preferred over the purchase by $505.68 if the purchase is financed by all equity. Because debt financing generates a tax subsidy, it is not surprising that the lease alternative would be preferred by over $500 over the purchase alternative if debt were not allowed.

Additional Effects of Debt

We learned earlier in the text that the interest tax shield in any year is the interest multiplied by the corporate tax rate. Taking the interest in each of the five years from Table 23.6, the present value of the interest tax shield is

$$
\$704.02 = .40 \left[\frac{\$868.89}{(1.11)} + \frac{\$620.44}{(1.11)^2} + \frac{\$411.91}{(1.11)^3} + \frac{\$223.38}{(1.11)^4} + \frac{\$42.77}{(1.11)^5} \right]
$$

This tax shield must be subtracted from the NPV of the lease because it represents interest deductions not available under the lease alternative. The adjusted present value of the lease relative to the purchase is

$$
-\$199 = \$504.68 - \$704.02
$$

This value is the same as our calculations from the previous two approaches, implying that all three approaches are equivalent. The accompanying box presents the APV approach.

Which approach is easiest to calculate? The first approach is easiest because one need only discount the cash flows at the after-tax interest rate. Though the second and third approaches look easy, the extra step of calculating the increased debt capacity is needed for both of them.

Which approach is most intuitive? Our experience is that students generally find the third method the most intuitive. This is probably because they have already learned the APV method from Chapter 17. The second method is generally straightforward for those students who have a good understanding of the increased-debt-level concept. However, the first method seems to have the least intuitive appeal because it is merely a mechanical approach.

Which approach should the practitioner use? The practitioner should use the simplest approach, which is the first. We include the others only for intuitive appeal.

A Third Method for Calculating Net Present Value of Lease Relative to Purchase*

Method 3: Calculate APV
All-Equity Values

$$\$505.68 = \$7,700 - \left[\frac{\$2,780}{(1.11)} + \frac{\$2,268}{(1.11)^2} + \frac{\$1,961}{(1.11)^3} + \frac{\$1,776}{(1.11)^4} + \frac{\$415}{(1.11)^5}\right]$$

Additional effects of debt:†

$$\$704.02 = .40\left[\frac{\$868.89}{(1.11)} + \frac{\$620.44}{(1.11)^2} + \frac{\$411.91}{(1.11)^3} + \frac{\$223.38}{(1.11)^4} + \frac{\$42.77}{(1.11)^5}\right]$$

APV $= -\$199 = \$504.68 - \$704.02$

*Because we are calculating the NPV of the lease relative to the purchase, a negative value indicates that the purchase alternative is preferred. (The first two methods are shown in the earlier box appearing in this chapter.)
†The firm misses the interest deductions if it leases. Because we are calculating the NPV of the lease relative to the purchase, the additional effect of debt is subtracted.

A central point in finance is that risk is undesirable. In our chapters on risk and return, we pointed out that individuals would choose risky securities only if the expected return compensated for the risk. Similarly, a firm will accept a risky capital budgeting project only if the internal rate of return on the project is high enough.

We focus on risk in this chapter, though we examine it in a manner slightly different from past chapters. In the capital budgeting decision of earlier chapters, the firm considered the risk of a project before deciding to accept or reject it. In its analysis, the firm treated the project's risk as *unchangeable*. Now we ask, What can the firm do to reduce the risk of either a project or the firm as a whole? The answer is **hedging.** Hedging offsets risk by a set of transactions in the financial markets.

We begin our discussion on hedging by considering forward contracts. Next, we look at a slightly more sophisticated financial instrument, futures contracts. Hedging for companies facing inventory risk is discussed next. Our hedging examples involve agricultural and metallurgical futures contracts. We complete the chapter by considering interest rate risk. Hedging through interest rate futures contracts and through duration matching of assets and liabilities is examined.

Forward Contracts 24.1

We can begin our discussion of hedging by considering forward contracts. You have probably been dealing in forward contracts your whole life without knowing it. To illustrate, suppose you walk into a bookstore on, say, February 1 to buy the best-seller, *Eating Habits of the Rich and Famous*. The cashier tells you that the book is currently sold out but he takes your phone number, saying that he will reorder it for you. He says the book will cost $10.00. If you agree on February 1 to pick up and pay $10.00 for the book when called, you and the cashier have engaged in a **forward contract.** That is, you have agreed both to pay for the book and to pick it up when the bookstore notifies you. Since you are agreeing to buy the book at a later date, you are *buying* a forward contract on February 1. In commodity parlance, you will be **taking delivery** when you pick up the book. The book is called the **deliverable instrument** or **delivery vehicle.**

The cashier, acting on behalf of the bookstore, is selling a forward contract. (Alternatively, we say that he is writing a forward contract.) The bookstore has agreed to turn the book over to you at the predetermined price of $10.00 as soon as it arrives. The act of turning the book over to you is called **making delivery.** Table 24.1

Table 24.1
Illustration of book
purchase as a
forward contract

February 1	Date when book arrives
Buyer agrees to 1. Pay the purchase price of $10.00. 2. Receive book when book arrives.	Buyer 1. Pays purchase price of $10.00. 2. Receives book.
Seller agrees to 1. Give up book. 2. Accept payment of $10.00 when book arrives.	Seller 1. Gives up book. 2. Accepts payment of $10.00.

Note that cash does not change hands on February 1. Cash changes hands when the book arrives.

illustrates the book purchase. Note that the agreement takes place on February 1. The price is set and the conditions for sale are set at that time. In this case, the sale will occur when the book arrives. In other cases, an exact date of sale would be given. However, *no* cash changes hands on February 1; cash changes hands only when the book arrives.

Though forward contracts may have seemed exotic to you before you began this chapter, you can see that they are quite commonplace. Forward contracts occur frequently in business. Every time a firm orders an item that cannot be delivered immediately, a forward contract takes place. Sometimes, particularly when the order is small, an oral agreement will suffice. Other times, particularly when the order is larger, a written agreement is necessary.

Note that a forward contract is not an option. Both the buyer and the seller are obligated to perform under the terms of the contract. In contrast, the buyer of an option *chooses* whether or not to exercise the option.

A forward contract should be contrasted with a **cash transaction,** that is, a transaction where exchange is immediate. Had the book been on the bookstore's shelf, your purchase of it would have been a cash transaction.

CONCEPT QUESTIONS

- What is a forward contract?
- Give examples of forward contracts in your life.

24.2   Futures Contracts

A variant of the forward contract takes place on financial exchanges. Contracts on exchanges are usually called **futures contracts.** For example, consider Table 24.2, which provides data on trading in wheat for Friday, October 8, 1993. The first detail to notice is "WHEAT 5000 bu, cents per bushel"; 5,000 bushels is the contract size for wheat futures on the Chicago Board of Trade. The quotes listed are in U.S. funds at cents per bushel. We build our example around the December 93 futures contract in the first row of the table. The first trade of the day, or open price, in the contract was for $3.2150 per bushel. The price reached a high of $3.23 and a low of $3.21 during the day. The last trade was at $3.22. In other words, the contract *closed* or *settled* at

Mth.	Open	High	Low	Settle	Chg.	Opint
WHEAT 5000 bu, cents per bushel						
Dec93	321½	323	321	322	−½	35000
Mar94	325½	327¼	325	326¼		18515
May94	321	323¼	321	321¾	+¾	1875
Jul94	309½	311¾	309½	311¼	+1¼	4846
Sep94	316	316	316	316	+1	26
Dec94	323¾	323¾	323¾	323¾	−¼	34

Table 24.2
Wheat Futures Contracts, Friday, October 3, 1993

Source: "Report on Business," *The Globe and Mail* (October 9, 1993), p. B17. Used with permission.

$3.22. The price decreased ½ cent per bushel during the day, indicating that the price closed the previous day at $3.2250 (or $3.22 + $0.0050). The open interest indicates (Opint) that the number of *contracts outstanding* at the close of October 8 was 35,000.

To gain perspective on futures contracts, we consider a similar forward contract first. Suppose you wrote a *forward* contract for December wheat at $3.22. From our discussion on forward contracts, this would mean that you agree to turn over a set number of wheat bushels for $3.22 per bushel on some specified date through to December.

A futures contract differs somewhat from a forward contract. The first difference involves terminology: a seller of a futures contract is said to be *short* the contract and the buyer is *long*. Three other features distinguish a futures contract from a forward contract. First, the seller can choose to deliver the wheat on any day through the delivery month, that is, the month of December. This gives the seller leeway that he would not have with a forward contract. When the seller decides to deliver, he notifies the exchange clearinghouse. The clearinghouse then notifies an individual who bought a December wheat contract to stand ready to accept delivery within the next few days. Though each exchange selects the buyer in a different way, the buyer is generally chosen in a random fashion. Because there are so many buyers at any one time, the buyer selected by the clearinghouse to take delivery almost certainly did not originally buy the contract from the seller now making delivery. In practice, over 95 percent of futures contracts are not settled through delivery. Most are offset by other contracts before the delivery date.

Second, futures contracts are traded on an exchange, but forward contracts are generally traded off an exchange. For this reason, there is generally a liquid market in futures contracts. A buyer can net out a futures position with a sale. A seller can net out a futures position with a purchase. This procedure is analogous to the *netting out* process in the options markets. However, the buyer of an options contract can also walk away from the contract by not exercising it. If a buyer of a futures contract does not subsequently sell the contract, the buyer must take delivery.

Third, and most important, the prices of futures contracts are **marked to the market** on a daily basis. That is, suppose that the price falls to $3.20 on the following Monday's close. Because all buyers lost two cents per bushel on that day, they each must turn over the two cents per bushel to their brokers within 24 hours, who subsequently remit the proceeds to the clearinghouse. Because all sellers gained two cents per bushel on that day, they each receive two cents per bushel from their brokers.

Their brokers are subsequently compensated by the clearinghouse. Because there is a buyer for every seller, the clearinghouse must break even every day.

Now suppose that the price rises to $3.27 on the close of the following Tuesday. Each buyer receives seven cents ($3.27 − $3.20) per bushel and each seller must pay seven cents per bushel. Finally, suppose that, on Tuesday, a seller notifies her broker of her intention to deliver.[1] The delivery price will be $3.27, which is Tuesday's close.

There are clearly many cash flows in futures contracts. However, after all the dust settles, the *net price* must be the price at which the buyer bought originally. That is, an individual buying at Friday's closing price of $3.22 and being called to take delivery on Tuesday, pays two cents per bushel on Monday, receives seven cents per bushel on Tuesday, and takes delivery at $3.27. This buyer's net outflow per bushel is −$3.22 (or −$0.02 + $0.07 − $3.27), which is the price contracted on Thursday. (Our analysis ignores the time value of money.) Conversely, an individual selling at Friday's closing price of $3.22 and notifying his broker concerning delivery the following Tuesday, receives two cents per bushel on Monday, pays seven cents per bushel on Tuesday, and makes delivery at $3.27. His net inflow per bushel is $3.22 (or $0.02 − $0.07 + $3.27), which is the price at which he contracted on Friday.

These details are presented in the adjacent box. For simplicity, we assumed that the buyer and seller who initially transact on Friday's close meet in the delivery process.[2] The point in the example is that the buyer's net payment of $3.22 per bushel is the same as if this buyer purchased a forward contract for $3.22. Similarly, the seller's net receipt of $3.22 per bushel is the same as if he sold a forward contract for $3.22 per bushel. The only difference is the timing of the cash flows. The buyer of a forward contract knows that he will make a single payment of $3.22 on the expiration date. He will not need to worry about any other cash flows in the interim. On the other hand, though the cash flows to the buyer of a futures contract will net to exactly $3.22 as well, the pattern of cash flows is not known ahead of time.

The mark-to-the-market provision on futures contracts has two related effects. The first concerns differences in net present value. For example, a large price drop immediately following purchase means an immediate cash outflow for the buyer of a futures contract. Though the net outflow of $3.22 is still the same as under a forward contract, the present value of the cash outflows is greater to the buyer of a futures contract. Of course, the present value of the cash outflows is less to the buyer of a futures contract if a price rise followed purchase.[3] Though this effect could be substantial in certain theoretical circumstances, it appears to be of quite limited importance in the real world.[4]

Second, the firm must have extra liquidity to handle a sudden outflow prior to expiration. This added risk may make the futures contract less attractive.

Students frequently ask, "Why in the world would managers of the commodity exchanges ruin perfectly good contracts with these bizarre mark-to-the-market provi-

---

[1]She will deliver on Thursday, two days later.

[2]As pointed out earlier, this is actually very unlikely to occur in the real world.

[3]The direction is reversed for the seller of a futures contract. However, the general point that the net present value of cash flows may differ between forward and futures contracts holds for sellers as well.

[4]See J. C. Cox, J. E. Ingersoll, and S. A. Ross, "The Relationship between Forward and Future Prices," *Journal of Financial Economics* (1981).

Illustration of Example Involving Marking to Market in Futures Contracts

Both buyer and seller originally transact at Friday's closing price. Delivery takes place at Tuesday's closing price.*

	Friday, October 8	Monday, October 11	Tuesday, October 12	Delivery (Notification given by seller on Tuesday)
Closing price:	$3.22	$3.20	$3.27	
BUYER	Buyer purchases futures contract at closing price of $3.22/bushel.	Buyer must pay two cents/bushel to clearinghouse within one business day.	Buyer receives seven cents/ bushel from clear- inghouse within one business day.	Buyer pays $3.27/ bushel and re- ceives grain.

Buyer's net payment of −$3.22 (or −$0.02 + $0.07 − $3.27) is the same as if buyer purchased a forward contract for $3.22/bushel.

SELLER	Seller sells fu- tures contract at closing price of $3.22/bushel.	Seller receives two cents/bushel from clearing- house within one business day.	Seller pays seven cents/bushel to clearinghouse within one busi- ness day.	Seller receives $3.27/bushel and delivers grain within one busi- ness day.

Seller's net receipts of $3.22 (or $0.02 − $0.07 + $3.27) are the same as if seller sold a forward contract for $3.22/bushel.

*For simplicity, we assume that buyer and seller both (1) initially transact at the same time and (2) meet in delivery process. This is actually very unlikely to occur in the real world because the clearinghouse assigns the buyer to take delivery in a random manner.

sions?" Actually, the reason is a very good one. Consider the forward contract of Table 24.1 concerning the bookstore. Suppose that the public quickly loses interest in *Eating Habits of the Rich and Famous.* By the time the bookstore calls the buyer, other stores may have dropped the price of the book to $6.00. Because the forward contract was for $10.00, the buyer has an incentive not to take delivery on the forward contract. Conversely, should the book become a hot item selling at $15.00, the bookstore may simply not call the buyer.

As indicated, forward contracts have a very big flaw. Whichever way the price of the deliverable instrument moves, one party has an incentive to default. There are many cases where defaults have occurred. One famous case concerned Coca-Cola. When the company began in the early 20th century, Coca-Cola made an agreement to supply its bottlers and distributors with cola syrup at a constant price *forever*. Of course, subsequent inflation would have caused Coca-Cola to lose large sums of money had it honoured the contract. After much legal effort, Coke and its bottlers put an *inflation escalator clause* in the contract. Another famous case concerned Westing-house. It seems the firm had promised to deliver uranium to certain utilities at a fixed

Table 24.3
Futures contracts
listed in *The Globe
and Mail*

Contract	Contract size	Exchange*
Agricultural (grain and oilseeds):		
Corn	5,000 bushels	CBT
Oats	5,000 bushels	CBT, Minneapolis
Soybeans	5,000 bushels	CBT
Soybean meal	100 tons	CBT
Soybean oil	60,000 lbs.	CBT
Wheat	5,000 bushels	CBT
Wheat	5,000 bushels	KC
Wheat	5,000 bushels	Minneapolis
White wheat	1,000 bushels	Minneapolis
Barley	20 metric tons	WPG
Flaxseed	20 metric tons	WPG
Canola	20 metric tons	WPG
Wheat	20 metric tons	WPG
Rye	20 metric tons	WPG
Oats	20 metric tons	WPG
Western barley	20 metric tons	WPG
Agricultural (livestock and meat):		
Cattle (feeder)	50,000 lbs.	CME
Cattle (live)	40,000 lbs.	CME
Hogs	40,000 lbs.	CME
Pork bellies	40,000 lbs.	CME
Agricultural (food, fiber, and wood):		
Cocoa	10 metric tons	CSCE
Coffee	37,500 lbs.	CSCE
Cotton	50,000 lbs.	CTN
Orange juice	15,000 lbs.	CTN
Sugar (world)	112,000 lbs.	CSCE
Sugar (domestic)	112,000 lbs.	CSCE
Lumber	160,000 board feet	CME
Metals and petroleum:		
Copper (standard)	25,000 lbs.	CMX
Gold	100 troy oz.	CMX
Platinum	50 troy oz.	NYM
Palladium	100 troy oz.	NYM

price. The price of uranium skyrocketed in the 1970s, making Westinghouse lose money on every shipment. Westinghouse defaulted on its agreement. The utilities took Westinghouse to court but did not recover anything near what Westinghouse owed them.

The mark-to-the-market provisions minimize the chance of default on a futures contract. If the price rises, the seller has an incentive to default on a forward contract. However, after paying the clearinghouse, the seller of a futures contract has little reason to default. If the price falls, the same argument can be made for the buyer. Because changes in the value of the underlying asset are recognized daily, there is no accumulation of loss, and the incentive to default is reduced.

Because of this default issue, forward contracts generally involve individuals and institutions who know and can trust each other. But as W. C. Fields said, "Trust everybody, but cut the cards." Lawyers earn a handsome living writing supposedly

Contract	Contract size	Exchange*	**Table 24.3**
			(concluded)

Contract	Contract size	Exchange*
Metals and petroleum: (concluded)		
Silver	5,000 troy oz.	CMX
Liquid propane	42,000 U.S. gal.	NYM
Natural gas	10,000 mmbtu	NYM
Crude oil (light sweet)	1,000 barrels	NYM
Heating oil no. 2	42,000 gallons	NYM
Gas oil	100 metric tons	IPEL
Gasoline unleaded	42,000 gallons	NYM
Financial:		
British pound	62,500 pounds	IMM
Australian dollar	100,000 dollars	IMM
Canadian dollar	100,000 dollars	IMM
Japanese yen	12.5 million yen	IMM
Swiss franc	125,000 francs	IMM
German mark	125,000 marks	IMM
3-month bankers acceptances	$1 million	Montreal Futures
1-month bankers acceptances	$3 million	Montreal Futures
Government of Canada bond	$100,000	Montreal Futures
Eurodollar	$1 million	IMM
U.S. Dollar Index	500 times index	FINEX
CRB Index	500 times index	NYFE
Treasury bonds	$100,000	CBT
90-day T-Bills	$1 million	CME
5-year Treasury notes	$100,000	CBT
5-year Treasury notes	$100,000	FINEX
Treasury bonds	$50,000	MCE
Treasury bonds	$1 million	IMM
Financial indexes:		
Municipal bonds	1,000 times Bond Buyer Index	CBT
S&P 500 Index	500 times index	CME
NYSE Composite	500 times index	NYFE
Kansas City Value Line Index	500 times index	KC
Nikkei Index	5 times index	CME
Toronto 35	$500 times index	Toronto Futures

*CBT: Chicago Board of Trade; KC: Kansas City; WPG: Winnipeg; CME: Chicago Merchantile Exchange; CSCE: Coffee, Sugar, and Cocoa Exchange; CTN: New York Cotton Exchange; CMX: Commodity Exchange in New York; NYM: New York Merchantile; IPEL: International Petroleum Exchange of London; IMM: International Monetary Market in Chicago; FINEX: Financial Instrument Exchange in New York; NYFE: New York Futures Exchange.

air-tight forward contracts, even among friends. The genius of the mark-to-the-market system is that it can prevent default where it is most likely to occur—among investors who do not know each other. Textbooks on futures contracts from one or two decades ago usually included a statement such as "No major default has ever occurred on the commodity exchanges." No textbook published after the Hunt Brothers defaulted on silver contracts in the 1970s can make that claim. Nevertheless, the extremely low default rate in futures contracts is truly impressive.

Futures contracts are traded in three areas: agricultural commodities, metals and petroleum, and financial assets. The extensive array of futures contracts is listed in Table 24.3.

- What is a futures contract?
- How is a futures contract related to a forward contract?
- Why do exchanges require futures contracts to be marked to market?

24.3   Hedging

Now that we have determined how futures contracts work, we turn to hedging. There are two types of hedges: long and short. We discuss the short hedge first.

▪ Example

In June, Mike Oleschuk, a Saskatchewan farmer, anticipates a harvest of 50,000 bushels of wheat at the end of September. He has two alternatives:

1. *Write futures contracts against his anticipated harvest.* The September wheat contract on the Winnipeg Commodity Exchange is trading at $3.75 a bushel on June 1. He executes the following transaction:

Date of transaction	Transaction	Price per bushel
June 1	Write 10 September futures contracts	$3.75

   He notes that transportation costs to the designated delivery point in Winnipeg are 30 cents/bushel. Thus, his net price per bushel is $3.45 = $3.75 − $0.30.

2. *Harvest the wheat without writing a futures contract.* Alternatively, Mr. Oleschuk could have harvested the wheat without benefit of a futures contract. The risk would be quite great here since no one knows what the cash price in September will be. If prices rise, he will profit. Conversely, he will lose if prices fall.

We say that strategy 2 is an unhedged position because there is no attempt to use the futures markets to reduce risk. Conversely, strategy 1 involves a hedge. That is, a position in the futures market offsets the risk of a position in the physical (that is, in the actual) commodity.

Though hedging may seem quite sensible to you, it should be mentioned that not everyone hedges. Mr. Oleschuk might reject hedging for at least two reasons.

First, he may simply be uninformed about hedging. Not everyone in business understands the hedging concept. Some executives do not want to use futures markets for hedging their inventories because they feel that the risks are too great.[5] However, we disagree. While there are large price fluctuations in these markets, hedging actually reduces the risk that an individual holding inventories bears.

---

[5]B. Kalymon, *Global Innovation and the Impact on Canada's Financial Markets* (Toronto: Wiley, 1989), chapter 1, found that many Canadian managers expressed this view when hedging markets were relatively new.

Second, Mr. Oleschuk may have a special insight or some special information that commodity prices will rise. He would not be wise to lock in a price of $3.75 if he expects the cash price in September to be well above this price.

Strategy 1 is called a **short hedge,** because Mr. Oleschuk reduces his risk by taking a short position in a futures contract. The short hedge is very common in business. It occurs whenever someone either anticipates receiving inventory or is holding inventory. Mr. Oleschuk was anticipating the harvest of grain. A manufacturer of soybean meal and oil may hold large quantities of raw soybeans, which are already paid for. However, the price to be received for meal and oil is not known because no one knows what the market price will be when the meal and oil are produced. The manufacturer may write futures contracts in meal and oil to lock in a sales price.

An oil company may hold large inventories of petroleum to be processed into heating oil. The firm could sell futures contracts in heating oil in order to lock in the sales price. A mortgage banker may assemble mortgages slowly before selling them in bulk to a financial institution. Movements of interest rates affect the value of the mortgages during the time they are in inventory. The mortgage banker could sell Government of Canada bond futures contracts in order to offset this interest rate risk. (This last example is treated later in this chapter.) ∎

■ *Example*

On April 1, Alberta Chemical agreed to sell petrochemicals to the Canadian government in the future. The delivery dates and the prices have been determined. Because oil is a basic ingredient of the production process, Alberta Chemical will need to have large quantities of oil on hand. The firm can get the oil in one of two ways:

1. *Buy the oil as the firm needs it.* This is an unhedged position because, as of April 1, the firm does not know the prices it will later have to pay for the oil. Oil is quite a volatile commodity, so Alberta Chemical is bearing a good bit of risk. The key to this risk-bearing is that the sales price to the Canadian government has already been fixed. Thus, Alberta Chemical cannot pass on increased costs to the consumer.

2. *Buy futures contracts.*[6] The firm can buy futures contracts with expiration months corresponding to the dates on which inventory is needed. A futures contract locks in the purchase price to Alberta Chemical. Because there is a crude oil futures contract for every month, selecting the correct futures contract is not difficult. Many other commodities have only five contracts per year, frequently necessitating buying contracts one month away from the month of production.

As mentioned earlier, Alberta Chemical is interested in hedging the risk of fluctuating oil prices because it cannot pass any cost increases on to the consumer. Suppose, alternatively, that Alberta Chemical were not selling petrochemicals on fixed contract to the Canadian government. Instead, imagine that the petrochemicals were to be sold to private industry at currently prevailing prices. The price of petrochemicals

---

[6]Alternatively, the firm could buy the oil on April 1 and store it. This would eliminate the risk of price movement, because the firm's oil costs would be fixed upon the immediate purchase. However, this strategy is often inferior to strategy 2 because storage costs often exceed the difference between the futures contract quoted on April 1 and the April 1 cash price.

should move directly with oil prices, because oil is a major component. Because cost increases are likely to be passed on to the consumer, Alberta Chemical would probably not want to hedge in this case. Instead, the firm is likely to choose strategy 1, buying oil as it is needed. If oil prices increase between April 1 and September 1, Alberta Chemical will, of course, find that its inputs have become quite costly. However, in a competitive market, its revenues are likely to rise as well.

Strategy 2 is called a **long hedge** because one takes a long position in a futures contract to reduce risk. In other words, one takes a long position in the futures market. In general, a firm institutes a long hedge when it is committed to a fixed sales price. One class of situations involves actual written contracts with customers, such as Alberta Chemical had with the Canadian government. Alternatively, a firm may find that it cannot easily pass on costs to consumers or does not want to pass on these costs.

For example, a group of students opened a small meat market called What's Your Beef near the University of Pennsylvania in the late 1970s.[7] You may recall that this was a time of volatile consumer prices, especially food prices. Knowing that their fellow students were particularly budget-conscious, the owners vowed to keep food prices constant, regardless of price movements in either direction. They accomplished this by purchasing futures contracts in various agricultural commodities. ∎

CONCEPT QUESTIONS

- Define *short* and *long hedges*.
- Under what circumstances is each of the two hedges used?

24.4   Interest Rate Futures Contracts

In this section, we consider interest rate futures contracts. Our examples deal with futures contracts on Government of Canada bonds because of their high popularity. We first price Canada bonds and Canada bond forward contracts. Differences between futures and forward contracts are explored. We then provide hedging examples using Canada government bond (CGB) futures traded on the Montreal Futures Exchange.

Pricing of Government of Canada Bonds

As explained in Chapter 5, a Canadian Government bond pays semiannual interest over its life. In addition, the face value of the bond is paid at maturity. Consider a 20-year, 8-percent coupon bond that was issued on March 1. The first payment is to occur in six months, that is, on September 1. The value of the bond can be determined as

Pricing of a Canadian Government Bond:

$$P_{CGB} = \frac{\$40}{1 + r_1} + \frac{\$40}{(1 + r_2)^2} + \ldots + \frac{\$40}{(1 + r_{39})^{39}} + \frac{\$1,040}{(1 + r_{40})^{40}} \tag{24.1}$$

[7]Ordinarily, an unusual firm name in this textbook is a tip-off that it is fictional. This, however, is a true story.

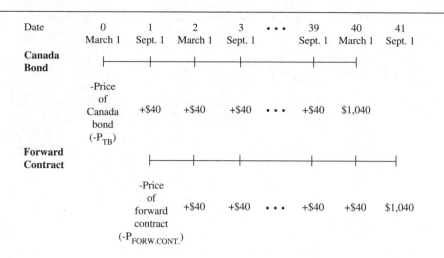

Figure 24.1
Cash flows for both a Canada bond and a forward contract on a Canada bond

Because this 8-percent coupon bond pays interest of $80 a year, the semiannual coupon is $40. Principal is paid at maturity along with the last semiannual coupon. The price of the Canadian Government bond, P_{CGB} is determined by discounting each payment at the appropriate spot rate. Because the payments are semiannual, each spot rate is expressed in semiannual terms. That is, imagine a flat term structure where the effective annual yield is 12 percent for all maturities. Because each spot rate, r, is expressed in semiannual terms, each spot rate is $\sqrt{1.12} - 1 = 5.83\%$. Because coupon payments occur every six months, there are 40 spot rates over the 20-year period.

Pricing of Forward Contracts

Now, imagine a *forward* contract where, on March 1, you agree to buy a new 20-year, 8-percent coupon, Canada bond in six months, that is, on September 1. As with typical forward contracts, you will pay for the bond on September 1, not March 1. The cash flows from both the Canada bond issued on March 1 and the forward contract that you purchase on March 1 are presented in Figure 24.1. The cash flows on the Canada bond begin exactly six months earlier than do the cash flows on the forward contract. The bond is purchased with cash on March 1 (date 0). The first coupon payment occurs on September 1 (date 1). The last coupon payment occurs at date 40, along with the face value of $1,000. The forward contract compels you to pay $P_{FORW.CONT.}$, the price of the forward contract, on September 1 (date 1). You receive a new Canada bond at that time. The first coupon payment from the bond you receive occurs on March 1 of the following year (date 2). The last coupon payment occurs at date 41, along with the face value of $1,000.

Given the 40 spot rates, equation (24.1) showed how to price a Canada bond. How does one price the forward contract on a Canada bond? Just as we saw earlier in the text that net present value analysis is used to price bonds, we will now show that net present value analysis can be used to price forward contracts. Given the cash flows for the forward contract in Figure 24.1, the price of the forward contract must satisfy the following equation:

$$\frac{P_{\text{FORW.CONT.}}}{1 + r_1} = \frac{\$40}{(1 + r_2)^2} + \frac{\$40}{(1 + r_3)^3} + \ldots + \frac{\$40}{(1 + r_{40})^{40}} + \frac{\$1,040}{(1 + r_{41})^{41}} \qquad (24.2)$$

The right-hand side of equation (24.2) discounts all the cash flows from the delivery instrument (the Canada bond issued on September 1) back to date 0 (March 1). Because the first cash flow occurs at date 2 (March 1 of the subsequent year), it is discounted by $1/(1 + r_2)^2$. The last cash flow of $1,040 occurs at date 41, so it is discounted by $1/(1 + r_{41})^{41}$. The left-hand side represents the cost of the forward contract as of date 0. Because the actual payment occurs at date 1, it is discounted by $1/(1 + r_1)$.

Students often ask, "Why are we discounting everything back to date 0, when we are actually paying for the forward contract on September 1?" The answer is simply that we apply the same techniques to equation (24.2) that we apply to all capital budgeting problems; we want to put everything in today's (date 0's) dollars. Given that the spot rates are known in the marketplace, traders should have no more trouble pricing a forward contract by equation (24.2) than they would have pricing a bond by equation (24.1).

Forward contracts are similar to the underlying bonds themselves. If the entire term structure of interest rates unexpectedly shifts upward on March 2, the Canada bond issued the previous day should fall in value. This can be seen from equation (24.1). A rise in each of the spot rates lowers the present value of each of the coupon payments. Hence, the value of the bond must fall. Conversely, a fall in the term structure of interest rates increases the value of the bond.

The same relationship holds with forward contracts, as can be seen from rewriting equation (24.2) as

$$P_{\text{FORW.CONT.}} = \frac{\$40 \times (1 + r_1)}{(1 + r_2)^2} + \frac{\$40 \times (1 + r_1)}{(1 + r_3)^3} + $$
$$\ldots + \frac{\$40 \times (1 + r_1)}{(1 + r_{40})^{40}} + \frac{\$1,040 \times (1 + r_1)}{(1 + r_{41})^{41}} \qquad (24.3)$$

We went from (24.2) to (24.3) by multiplying both the left- and the right-hand sides by $(1 + r_1)$. If the entire term structure of interest rates unexpectedly shifts upward on March 2, the first term on the right-hand side of equation (24.3) should fall in value.[8] That is, both r_1 and r_2 will rise an equal amount. However, r_2 enters as a *squared* term, $1/(1 + r_2)^2$, so an increase in r_2 more than offsets the increase in r_1. As we move further to the right, an increase in any spot rate, r_i more than offsets an increase in r_1. Here, r_i enters as the ith power, $1/(1 + r_i)^i$. Thus, as long as the entire term structure shifts upward an equal amount on March 2, the value of a forward contract must fall on that date. Conversely, as long as the entire term structure shifts downward an equal amount on March 2, the value of a forward contract must rise.

---

[8]We are assuming that each spot rate shifts by the same amount. For example, suppose that, on March 1, $r_1 = 5\%$, $r_2 = 5.4\%$, and $r_3 = 5.8\%$. Assuming that all rates increase by ½ percent on March 2, r_1 becomes 5.5 percent (5% + ½%), r_2 becomes 5.9 percent, and r_3 becomes 6.3 percent.

Government of Canada bond (CGB) $100,000; pts of 100%.									**Table 24.4**
Season					Settle		Open		Listing for Government of
High	Low	Month	High	Low	price	Change	interest		Canada bond
112.56	108.82	Dec	112.80	111.20	112.56	+	1.1816166		(CGB) futures

Estimated volume: 3,431
Previous day's volume: 3,316
Previous day's open interest: 16,166

Source: "Report on Business," *The Globe and Mail* (October 9, 1993), p. B6. Used with permission.

Futures Contracts

Our discussion so far has concerned a forward contract in Canada bonds, that is, a forward contract where the deliverable instrument is a Canada bond. What about a futures contract on such a bond?[9] We stated earlier that futures contracts and forward contracts are quite similar, though there are a few differences between the two.

First, futures contracts are generally traded on exchanges, whereas forward contracts are not traded on an exchange. In this case, the Canada bond futures contract is traded on the Montreal Futures Exchange. Table 24.4 shows a listing for CGB futures. The terminology is similar to what we presented earlier for wheat futures. For the bond futures contract, the delivery month is December 1993. The delivery vehicle is a CGB with maturity between 6.5 and 10 years and the face value is $100,000. The listing shows that the settle (closing) price for the futures contract was $112.56 per $100 of par value. Open interest shows that 16,166 contracts were outstanding at this time.

Second, futures contracts generally allow the seller a period of time in which to deliver, whereas forward contracts generally call for delivery on a particular day. The seller of a Canada bond futures contract can choose to deliver on any business day during the delivery month.[10] Third, futures contracts are subject to the mark-to-the-market convention, whereas forward contracts are not. Traders in Canada bond futures contracts must adhere to this convention. Fourth, there is generally a liquid market for futures contracts allowing contracts to be quickly netted out. That is, a buyer can sell a futures contract at any time and a seller can buy back a futures contract at any time. On the other hand, because forward markets are generally quite illiquid, traders cannot easily net out their positions. The popularity of the Canada bond futures contract has produced a reasonably liquid market and positions of some size can be netted out quite easily.

Our discussion is not intended to be an exhaustive list of differences between forward contracts and futures contracts on Canada bonds. Rather, it is intended to show that the two types of contracts share fundamental characteristics. Though there are differences, the two instruments should be viewed as variations of the same species, not different species. Thus, the pricing equation of (24.3), which is exact for the forward contract, should be a decent approximation for the futures contract.

---

[9]Futures contracts on bonds are also called *interest rate futures contracts*.

[10]Delivery occurs two days after the seller notifies the clearinghouse of the intention to deliver.

Hedging in Interest Rate Futures

Now that we have covered the basic institutional details of bond futures, we are ready for examples of hedging. Our examples feature bond futures rather than forward contracts because the greater liquidity of futures, discussed above, makes them better suited for hedging.

■ *Example*

Peter James is a mortgage officer for a small trust company. On March 1, he made a commitment to lend $1 million on May 1 in a mortgage on a piece of commercial property. The loan is a seven-year mortgage at 12-percent, the going interest rate on mortgages at the time. Thus, the mortgage is made at par. Though the borrower would not use the term, we could say that Mr. James is buying a forward contract on a mortgage. That is, he agrees on March 1 to give $1 million to the borrower on May 1 in exchange for principal and interest every month for the next seven years.

Like many small mortgage lenders, Peter James has no intention of keeping the $1 million loan on his trust company's balance sheet. Rather, he intends to sell the mortgage to an insurance company. Thus, the insurance company will actually lend the funds and will receive principal and interest over the next seven years. Mr. James sets April 30 as a deadline for making the sale because the borrowers expect the funds on the following day.

Suppose that Mr. James sells the mortgage to the Great Saskatchewan Life Insurance Company on April 15. What price will the insurance company pay for the mortgage?

You may think that the insurance company will obviously pay $1 million. However, suppose interest rates have risen above 12 percent by April 15. The insurance company will buy the mortgage at a discount. For example, suppose the insurance company agrees to pay only $940,000 for the mortgage. Because the mortgage banker agreed to loan a full $1 million to the borrower, the difference of $60,000 (or $1 million − $940,000) represents a loss to the trust company.

Alternatively, suppose that interest rates fall below 12 percent by April 15. The mortgage can be sold at a premium under this scenario. If the insurance company buys the mortgage at $1.05 million, the mortgage banker will have made an unexpected profit of $50,000 (or $1.05 million − $1 million).

Because Peter James cannot forecast interest rates, this risk is something that he would like to avoid. The risk is summarized in Table 24.5.

Seeing the interest rate risk, students at this point may ask, "What does the mortgage banker get out of this loan to offset his risk-bearing?" Mr. James wants to sell the mortgage to the insurance company so that he can get two fees. The first is an *origination fee,* which is paid to the mortgage banker from the insurance company on April 15, that is, on the date the loan is sold. An industry standard in certain locales is 1 percent of the value of the loan, that is, $10,000 (or 1% × $1 million). In addition, Mr. James will act as a collection agent for the insurance company. For this service, he will receive a small portion of the outstanding balance of the loan each month.

Though Mr. James will earn profitable fees on the loan, he bears interest rate risk. He loses money if interest rates rise after March 1, and he profits if interest rates fall after March 1. To hedge this risk, he writes June Government of Canada bond futures

Mortgage interest rate on April 15	Above 12%	Below 12%	**Table 24.5** Effects of changing interest rate on Peter James, mortgage banker
Sale price to Great Saskatchewan Life Insurance Company	Below $1 million (We assume $940,000.)	Above $1 million (We assume $1.05 million.)	
Effect on mortgage banker	He loses because he must loan full $1 million to borrowers.	He gains because he loans only $1 million to borrowers.	
Dollar gain or loss	Loss of $60,000 (or $1 million − $940,000)	Gain of $50,000 (or $1.05 million − $1 million)	

The interest rate on March 1, the date when the loan agreement was made with the borrowers, was 12 percent. April 15 is the date the mortgages were sold to Great Saskatchewan Life Insurance Company.

	Cash markets	Futures markets	**Table 24.6** Illustration of hedging strategy for Peter James, mortgage banker
March 1	Mortgage banker makes forward contract to loan $1 million at 12 percent for 20 years. The loans are to be funded on May 1. No cash changes hands on March 1.	Mortgage banker writes 10 June Government of Canada bond futures contracts.	
April 15	Loans are sold to Great Saskatchewan Life Insurance Company. Mortgage banker will receive sale price from Saskatchewan on the May 1 funding date.	Mortgage banker buys back all the futures contracts.	
If interest rates rise:	Loans are sold at a price below $1 million. Mortgage banker *loses* because he receives less than the $1 million he must give to borrowers.	Each futures contract is bought back at a price below the sales price, resulting in *profit*. Mortgage banker's profit in futures market offsets loss in cash market.	
If interest rates fall:	Loans are sold at a price above $1 million. Mortgage banker *gains* because he receives more than the $1 million he must give to borrowers.	Each futures contract is bought back at a price above the sales price, resulting in *loss*. Mortgage banker's loss in futures market offsets gain in cash market.	

contracts on March 1. As with mortgages, Government of Canada bond futures contracts fall in value if interest rates rise. Because he *writes* the contract, he makes money on these contracts if they fall in value. Therefore, with an interest rate rise, the loss he endures in the mortgages is offset by his gain in the futures market.

In the opposite case, Government of Canada bond futures contracts rise in value if interest rates fall. Because he writes the contracts, he suffers losses on them when rates fall. With an interest rate fall, the profit he makes on the mortgages is offset by the loss he suffers in the futures markets. ∎

The details of this hedging transaction are presented in Table 24.6. The column on the left is labelled "Cash markets," because the deal in the mortgage market is transacted off an exchange. The column on the right shows the offsetting transactions in the futures markets. Consider the first row. The mortgage banker enters into a forward contract on March 1. He simultaneously writes Government of Canada bond futures contracts. Ten contracts are written because the deliverable instrument on each contract is $100,000 of Government of Canada bonds. The total is $1 million (or 10 × $100,000), which is equal to the value of the mortgages. Mr. James would prefer to write May Government of Canada bond futures contracts. Here, Government of Canada bonds would be delivered on the futures contract during the same month that the loan is funded. Because there is no May Government of Canada bond futures contract, Mr. James achieves the closest match through a June contract.[11]

If held to maturity, the June contract would obligate the mortgage banker to deliver Government of Canada bonds in June. Interest rate risk ends in the cash market when the loans are sold. Interest rate risk must be terminated in the futures market at that time. Thus, Mr. James nets out his position in the futures contract as soon as the loan is sold to Great Saskatchewan Life Insurance.

Risk is clearly reduced via an offsetting transaction in the futures market. However, is risk totally eliminated? The answer would be yes if losses in the cash markets were exactly offset in the futures markets and vice versa. This is unlikely to happen because mortgages and Government of Canada bonds are not identical instruments. First, mortgages may have different maturities than Government of Canada bonds. Second, Government of Canada bonds have a different payment stream than do mortgages. Principal is only paid at maturity on Government of Canada bonds, whereas principal is paid every month on mortgages. Because mortgages pay principal continuously, these instruments have a shorter *effective* time to maturity than do Government of Canada bonds of equal maturity.[12] Third, mortgages have default risk whereas Government of Canada bonds do not. The term structure applicable to instruments with default risk may change even when the term structure for risk-free assets remains constant. Fourth, mortgages may be paid off early and hence have a shorter *expected maturity* than Canada bonds of equal maturity.

Because mortgages and Government of Canada bonds are not identical instruments, they are not identically affected by interest rates.[13] If Canada bonds are less volatile than mortgages, a financial consultant may advise Mr. James to write more than 10 Government of Canada bond futures contracts. Conversely, if these bonds are more volatile, the consultant may state that fewer than 10 futures contracts are indicated. An optimal ratio of futures contracts to mortgages will reduce risk as much as possible. However, because the price movements of mortgages and Government of Canada bonds are not perfectly correlated, Mr. James' hedging strategy cannot eliminate all risk.

The strategy we described is called a *short hedge* because Mr. James sells futures contracts in order to reduce risk. Though it involves an interest rate futures contract,

---

[11]The Government of Canada bond futures contract is by no means the only instrument available to use for hedging. In Canada, there are also futures on bankers acceptances, which are short-term paper. These futures can be used to hedge interest rate risk in the same way that Government of Canada bond futures are used. As well, the expiration months vary with the instrument.

[12]Alternatively, we can say that mortgages have shorter duration than do Government of Canada bonds of equal maturity. A precise definition of duration is provided later in this chapter.

[13]In formal terminology, this type of risk is called *basis risk*. When Mr. James heges mortgages with Government of Canada bond futures, he is said to be cross-hedging his position, because he is not using identical instruments.

	Cash markets	Future markets
March 1	Nadia Comeau decides to purchase $25 million in long-term bonds over the next three months.	Pension fund manager buys 250 G of C bond futures contracts.
April 15	Pension fund manager purchases $25 million in long-term Canada bonds.	Pension fund manager sells all futures contracts.
If interest rates rise:	Pension fund manager gains because the price of bonds will have fallen.	Futures contract is sold at a price below purchase price, resulting in loss. Pension fund manager's loss in futures market offsets gain in cash market.
If interest rates fall:	Pension fund manager loses because the price of bonds will have risen.	Futures contract is sold at a price above purchase price, resulting in gain. Pension fund manager's gain in futures market offsets loss in cash market.

Table 24.7
Illustration of futures hedge for Nadia Comeau, pension fund manager

this short hedge is analogous to short hedges in agricultural and metallurgical futures contracts. We argued at the beginning of this chapter that individuals and firms institute short hedges to offset inventory price fluctuation. Once Mr. James makes a contract to lend money, the mortgage effectively becomes his inventory. He writes a futures contract to offset the price fluctuation of his inventory.

We now consider an example of a long hedge.

■ *Example*

Canada Wide Ltd. is a large conglomerate with thousands of employees. Nadia Comeau manages the firm's pension fund. In the next three months, Canada Wide's pension fund is expecting to purchase $25 million in long-term Government of Canada bonds because the pension fund managers have been selling securities for the past month, and they feel that they have too much cash on hand. Ms. Comeau's pension fund group faces problems similar to those facing Mr. James' firm. However, in this case, we will be dealing with a long hedge instead of a short hedge.

As with Mr. James, changing interest rates will affect Ms. Comeau. If interest rates fall before she purchases the long-term Canada bonds, the price of the bonds will increase, and she will be paying more than was expected. Conversely, if interest rates rise, the price of long-term Canada bonds will fall, and the bonds can be purchased for less than expected.

The details are provided in the left-hand column of Table 24.7. Like Mr. James, Ms. Comeau finds the risk excessive. Therefore, she offsets her decision to purchase bonds with a transaction in the futures markets. Because she loses in the cash market when interest rates fall, she buys futures contracts to reduce the risk. When interest rates fall, the value of her futures contracts increases. The gain in the futures market offsets the loss in the cash market. Conversely, she gains in the cash markets when interest rates rise. The value of her futures contracts decreases when interest rates rise, offsetting her gain. ■

We call this a *long hedge* because Ms. Comeau offsets risk in the cash markets by buying a futures contract. Though it involves an interest rate futures contract, this long hedge is analogous to long hedges in agricultural and metallurgical futures contracts. We argued at the beginning of this chapter that individuals and firms institute long hedges when their finished goods are to be sold at a fixed price. Once Ms. Comeau makes the decision to purchase Government of Canada bonds, she has the ability to fix her purchase price. She buys a futures contract to offset the price fluctuation of the bonds.

CONCEPT QUESTIONS

- How are forward contracts on bonds priced?
- What are the differences between forward contracts on bonds and futures contracts on bonds?
- Give examples of hedging with futures contracts on bonds.

24.5   Duration Hedging

The prior section concerned the risk of interest rate changes. We now wish to explore this risk in a more precise manner. In particular, we want to show that the concept of duration is a prime determinant of interest rate risk. We begin by considering the effect of interest rate movements on bond prices.

The Case of Zero Coupon Bonds

Suppose that interest rates are 10 percent across all maturities. A one-year, pure discount bond pays $110 at maturity. A five-year, pure discount bond pays $161.05 at maturity. Both of these bonds are worth $100, as given by[14]

Value of One-Year, Pure Discount Bond:

$$\$100 = \frac{\$110}{1.10}$$

Value of Five-Year, Pure Discount Bond:

$$\$100 = \frac{\$161.05}{(1.10)^5}$$

Which bond value will change more when interest rates move? To find out, we calculate the values of these bonds when interest rates are either 8 or 12 percent. The results are presented in Table 24.8. As can be seen, the five-year bond has greater price swings than does the one-year bond. That is, both bonds are worth $100 when interest rates are 10 percent. The five-year bond is worth more than the one-year bond when interest rates are 8 percent and worth less than the one-year bond when interest rates are 12 percent. We state that the five-year bond is subject to greater price volatility. This point, which was mentioned in passing in an earlier section of the chapter, is not difficult to understand. The interest rate term in the denominator, $1 + r$, is taken to the fifth power

---

[14]Alternatively, we could have chosen bonds that pay $100 at maturity. Their values would be $90.91. (or $100/1.10) and $62.09 [or $100/(1.10)^5]. However, our comparisons to come are made easier if both have the same initial price.

Interest rate	1-year pure discount bond	5-year pure discount bond
8%	$101.85 = $\dfrac{\$110}{1.08}$	$109.61 = $\dfrac{\$161.05}{(1.08)^5}$
10%	$100.00 = $\dfrac{\$110}{1.10}$	$100.00 = $\dfrac{\$161.05}{(1.10)^5}$
12%	$98.21 = $\dfrac{\$110}{1.12}$	$91.38 = $\dfrac{\$161.05}{(1.12)^5}$

Table 24.8
Value of a pure discount bond as a function of interest rate

For a given interest rate change, a five-year, pure discount bond fluctuates more in price than does a one-year, pure discount bond.

for a five-year bond and only to the first power for the one-year bond. Thus, the effect of a changing interest rate is magnified for the five-year bond. The general rule is:

> The percentage price changes in long-term pure discount bonds are greater than the percentage price changes in short-term pure discount bonds.

The Case of Two Bonds with the Same Maturity but with Different Coupons

The previous example concerned pure discount bonds of different maturities. We now want to see the effect of different coupons on price volatility. To abstract from the effect of differing maturities, we consider two bonds with the same maturity but with different coupons.

Consider a five-year, 10-percent coupon bond and a five-year, 1-percent coupon bond. When interest rates are 10 percent, the bonds are priced at

Value of Five-Year, 10-Percent Coupon Bond:

$$\$100 = \frac{\$10}{1.10} + \frac{\$10}{(1.10)^2} + \frac{\$10}{(1.10)^3} + \frac{\$10}{(1.10)^4} + \frac{\$110}{(1.10)^5}$$

Value of Five-Year, 1-Percent Coupon Bond:

$$\$65.88 = \frac{\$1}{1.10} + \frac{\$1}{(1.10)^2} + \frac{\$1}{(1.10)^3} + \frac{\$1}{(1.10)^4} + \frac{\$101}{(1.10)^5}$$

Which bond value will experience greater change in percentage terms if interest rates change?[15] To find out, we calculate the values of these bonds when interest rates are either 8 or 12 percent. The results are presented in Table 24.9. As we would expect, the 10-percent coupon bond always sells for more than the 1-percent coupon bond. Also, as we would expect, each bond is worth more when the interest rate is 8 percent than when the interest rate is 12 percent.

---

[15]The bonds are at different prices initially. Thus, we are concerned with percentage price changes, not absolute price changes.

Table 24.9
Value of coupon
bonds at different
interest rates

Interest rate

5-year, 10% coupon bond

8%
$$\$107.99 = \frac{\$10}{1.08} + \frac{\$10}{(1.08)^2} + \frac{\$10}{(1.08)^3} + \frac{\$10}{(1.08)^4} + \frac{\$110}{(1.08)^5}$$

10%
$$\$100.00 = \frac{\$10}{1.10} + \frac{\$10}{(1.10)^2} + \frac{\$10}{(1.10)^3} + \frac{\$10}{(1.10)^4} + \frac{\$110}{(1.10)^5}$$

12%
$$\$92.79 = \frac{\$10}{1.12} + \frac{\$10}{(1.12)^2} + \frac{\$10}{(1.12)^3} + \frac{\$10}{(1.12)^4} + \frac{\$110}{(1.12)^5}$$

5-year, 1% coupon bond

8%
$$\$72.05 = \frac{\$1}{1.08} + \frac{\$1}{(1.08)^2} + \frac{\$1}{(1.08)^3} + \frac{\$1}{(1.08)^4} + \frac{\$101}{(1.08)^5}$$

10%
$$\$65.88 = \frac{\$1}{1.10} + \frac{\$1}{(1.10)^2} + \frac{\$1}{(1.10)^3} + \frac{\$1}{(1.10)^4} + \frac{\$101}{(1.10)^5}$$

12%
$$\$60.35 = \frac{\$1}{1.12} + \frac{\$1}{(1.12)^2} + \frac{\$1}{(1.12)^3} + \frac{\$1}{(1.12)^4} + \frac{\$101}{(1.12)^5}$$

We calculate percentage price changes for both bonds as the interest rate changes from 10 to 8 percent and from 10 to 12 percent. These percentage price changes are

	10% coupon bond	1% coupon bond
Interest rate changes from 10% to 8%	$7.99\% = \dfrac{\$107.99}{\$100} - 1$	$9.37\% = \dfrac{\$72.05}{\$65.88} - 1$
Interest rate changes from 10% to 12%	$-7.21\% = \dfrac{\$92.79}{\$100} - 1$	$-8.39\% = \dfrac{\$60.35}{\$65.88} - 1$

As can be seen, the 1-percent coupon bond has a greater percentage price increase than does the 10-percent coupon bond when the interest rate falls. Similarly, the 1-percent coupon bond has a greater percentage price decrease than does the 10-percent coupon bond when the interest rate rises. Thus, we say that the percentage price changes on the 1-percent coupon bond are greater than are the percentage price changes on the 10-percent coupon bond.

Duration

The question, of course, is "Why?" We can answer this question only after we have explored a concept called **duration.** We begin by noticing that any coupon bond is actually a combination of pure discount bonds. For example, the five-year, 10-percent coupon bond is made up of five pure discount bonds:

1. A pure discount bond paying $10 at the end of year 1.
2. A pure discount bond paying $10 at the end of year 2.
3. A pure discount bond paying $10 at the end of year 3.
4. A pure discount bond paying $10 at the end of year 4.
5. A pure discount bond paying $110 at the end of year 5.

Similarly, the five-year, 1-percent coupon bond is made up of five pure discount bonds. Because the price volatility of a pure discount bond is determined by its maturity, we would like to determine the average maturity of the five pure discount bonds that make up a five-year coupon bond. This leads us to the concept of duration.

We calculate average maturity in three steps. For the 10-percent coupon bond, we

1. *Calculate present value of each payment.* We do this as

Year	Payment	Present value of payment by discounting at 10%
1	$ 10	$ 9.091
2	10	8.264
3	10	7.513
4	10	6.830
5	110	68.302
		$100.00

2. *Express the present value of each payment in relative terms.* We calculate the relative value of a single payment as the ratio of the present value of the payment to the value of the bond. The value of the bond is $100. We have

Year	Payment	Present value of payment	Relative value =	$\dfrac{\text{Present value of payment}}{\text{Value of bond}}$
1	$10	$9.091	$9.091/$100 =	0.09091
2	10	8.264		0.08264
3	10	7.513		0.07513
4	10	6.830		0.06830
5	110	68.302		0.68302
		$100.00		1.0

The bulk of the relative value, 68.302 percent, occurs at year 5 because the principal is paid back at that time.

3. *Weight the maturity of each payment by its relative value.* We have

$$4.1699 \text{ years} = 1 \text{ year} \times 0.09091 + 2 \text{ years} \times 0.08264 + 3 \text{ years} \times 0.07513 + 4 \text{ years} \times 0.06830 + 5 \text{ years} \times 0.68302$$

There are many ways to calculate the average maturity of a bond. We have calculated it by weighting the maturity of each payment by the percentage of total present value received at that maturity. We find that the *effective* maturity of the bond is 4.1699 years. *Duration* is a commonly used word for effective maturity. Thus, the bond's duration is 4.1699 years. Note that duration is expressed in units of time.[16]

---

[16]The mathematical formula for duration is

$$\text{Duration} = \frac{PV(C_1)1 + PV(C_2)2 + \ldots + PV(C_T)t}{PV}$$

and

$$PV = PV(C_1) + PV(C_2) + \ldots + PV(C_T)$$

$$PV(C_T) = \frac{C_T}{(1 + r)^T}$$

where C_T is the cash to be received at time T and r is the current discount rate.

   Also note that in the above numerical example we discounted each payment by the interest rate of 10 percent. This was done because we wanted to calculate the duration of the bond before a change in the interest rate occurred. After a change in the rate to, say, 8 or 12 percent, all three of our steps would need to reflect the new interest rate. In other words, the duration of a bond is a function of the current interest rate.

Because the five-year, 10-percent coupon bond has a duration of 4.1699 years, its percentage price fluctuations should be the same as those of a zero-coupon bond with a duration of 4.1699 years.[17] It turns out that the five-year, 1-percent coupon bond has a duration of 4.8742 years. Because the 1-percent coupon bond has a higher duration than the 10-percent bond, the 1-percent coupon bond should be subject to greater price fluctuations. This is exactly what we found earlier. In general, we say

> The percentage price changes of a bond with high duration are greater than the percentage price changes of a bond with low duration.

A final question: Why does the 1-percent bond have a greater duration than the 10-percent bond, even though they have the same five-year maturity? As mentioned earlier, duration is an average of the maturity of the bond's cash flows, weighted by the present value of each cash flow. The 1-percent coupon bond receives only $1 in each of the first four years. Thus, the weights applied to years 1 through 4 in the duration formula will be low. Conversely, the 10-percent coupon bond receives $10 in each of the first four years. The weights applied to years 1 through 4 in the duration formula will be higher.

Matching Liabilities with Assets

Earlier in this chapter we argued that firms can hedge risk by trading in futures. Because some firms are subject to interest rate risk, we showed how they can hedge with interest rate futures contracts. Firms may also hedge interest rate risk by matching liabilities with assets. This approach follows from our discussion of duration.

■ *Example*

The Colonist Bank of Canada has the following market value balance sheet:

THE COLONIST BANK OF CANADA
Market Value Balance Sheet

	Market value	Duration
Assets		
Overnight money	$ 35 million	0
Accounts-receivable–backed loans	500 million	3 months
Inventory loans	275 million	6 months
Industrial loans	40 million	2 years
Mortgages	150 million	14.8 years
	$1,000 million	
Liabilities and Owners' Equity		
Chequing and savings accounts	$400 million	0
Certificates of deposit	300 million	1 year
Long-term financing	200 million	10 years
Equity	100 million	
	$1,000 million	

---

[17]Actually, this relationship only holds exactly in the case of a one-time shift in a flat yield curve, where the change in the spot rate is identical for all different maturities.

The bank has $1,000 million of assets and $900 million of liabilities. Its equity is the difference between the two: $100 million (or $1,000 million − $900 million). Both the market value and the duration of each individual item are provided in the balance sheet. Both overnight money and chequing and savings accounts have a duration of zero. This is because the interest paid on these instruments adjusts immediately to changing interest rates in the economy.

The bank's executives think that interest rates are likely to be volatile in the coming months. Because they do not know in which direction rates will move, they are worried that their bank is vulnerable to changing rates. They call in a consultant, Robert Charest, to determine hedging strategy.

Mr. Charest first calculates the duration of the assets and the duration of the liabilities.[18]

Duration of Assets:

$$2.56 \text{ years} = 0 \text{ years} \times \frac{\$35 \text{ million}}{\$1,000 \text{ million}} + \frac{1}{4} \text{ year} \times \frac{\$500 \text{ million}}{\$1,000 \text{ million}}$$

$$+ \frac{1}{2} \text{ year} \times \frac{\$275 \text{ million}}{\$1,000 \text{ million}} + 2 \text{ years} \times \frac{\$40 \text{ million}}{\$1,000 \text{ million}}$$

$$+ 14.8 \text{ years} \times \frac{\$150 \text{ million}}{\$1,000 \text{ million}} \qquad (24.4)$$

Duration of Liabilities:

$$2.56 \text{ year} = 0 \text{ years} \times \frac{\$400 \text{ million}}{\$900 \text{ million}} + 1 \text{ year} \times \frac{\$300 \text{ million}}{\$900 \text{ million}}$$

$$+ 10 \text{ years} \times \frac{\$200 \text{ million}}{\$900 \text{ million}} \qquad (24.5)$$

The duration of the assets, 2.56 years, equals the duration of the liabilities. Because of this, Mr. Charest argues that the firm is immune to interest rate risk.

Just to be on the safe side, the bank calls in a second consultant, Gail Ellert. Ms. Ellert argues that it is incorrect simply to match durations, because assets total $1,000 million and liabilities total only $900 million. If both assets and liabilities have the same duration, the price change on a dollar of assets should be equal to the price change on a dollar of liabilities. However, the total price change will be greater for assets than for liabilities, because there are more assets than liabilities. The firm will be immune from interest rate risk only when the duration of the liabilities is greater than the duration of the assets. Ms. Ellert states that the following relationship must hold if the bank is to be **immunized,** that is, immune to interest rate risk:

$$\begin{matrix} \text{Duration of} \\ \text{assets} \end{matrix} \times \begin{matrix} \text{Market value of} \\ \text{assets} \end{matrix} = \begin{matrix} \text{Duration of} \\ \text{liabilities} \end{matrix} \times \begin{matrix} \text{Market value} \\ \text{of liabilities} \end{matrix} \qquad (24.6)$$

She says that the bank should not equate the duration of the liabilities with the duration of the assets. Rather, using equation (24.6), the bank should match the duration of the liabilities to the duration of the assets. She suggests two ways to achieve this match.

---

[18]Note that the duration of a group of items is an average of the durations of the individual items, weighted by the market value of each item. This is a simplifying step that greatly increases duration's practicality.

1. *Increase the duration of the liabilities without changing the duration of the assets.* Ms. Ellert argues that the duration of the liabilities could be increased to

$$\frac{\text{Duration of}}{\text{assets}} \times \frac{\text{Market value of assets}}{\text{Market value of liabilities}}$$

$$= 2.56 \text{ years} \times \frac{\$1,000 \text{ million}}{\$900 \text{ million}}$$

$$= 2.84 \text{ years}$$

Equation (24.5) then becomes

$$2.56 \times \$1 \text{ billion} = 2.84 \times \$900 \text{ million}$$

2. *Decrease the duration of the assets without changing the duration of the liabilities.* Alternatively, Ms. Ellert points out that the duration of the assets could be decreased to

$$\frac{\text{Duration of}}{\text{liabilities}} \times \frac{\text{Market value of liabilities}}{\text{Market value of assets}}$$

$$= 2.56 \text{ years} \times \frac{\$900 \text{ million}}{\$1,000 \text{ million}}$$

$$= 2.30 \text{ years}$$

Equation (24.6) then becomes

$$2.30 \times \$1 \text{ billion} = 2.56 \times \$900 \text{ million}$$

Though we agree with Ms. Ellert's analysis, the bank's current mismatch was small anyway. ∎

Duration in Practice

Huge mismatches have occurred between the durations of assets and liabilities of financial institutions. Probably the most famous example occurred in the United States savings and loan (S&L) industry. S&Ls invested large portions of their assets in mortgages. The durations of these mortgages were over 10 years. Many of the funds available for mortgage lending were financed by short-term credit, especially savings accounts. The duration of such instruments is quite small. A thrift institution in this situation faced major interest rate risk, because any increase in interest rates greatly reduced the value of the mortgages. Because an interest rate rise only reduced the value of the liabilities slightly, the equity of the firm fell. As interest rates rose over much of the 1960s and 1970s, many S&Ls found that the market value of their equity turned negative. Allowed to stay in business by regulators, these "zombie thrifts" increased the eventual clean-up costs by engaging in risky investments.[19]

Duration and the accompanying immunization strategies are useful in other areas of finance. For example, many firms establish pension funds to meet obligations to

---

[19]This behavior is a good example of a selfish investment strategy from Chapter 16. Firms near bankruptcy often take great chances, because they feel that they are playing with someone else's money. In this case, deposit insurance allowed S&Ls to play with taxpayers' money. The example also illustrates our discussion of deposit insurance as a put option in Chapter 21.

retirees. If the assets of a pension fund are invested in bonds and other fixed-income securities, the duration of the assets can be computed. Similarly, the firm views the obligations to retirees as analogous to interest payments on debt. The duration of these liabilities can be calculated as well. The manager of a pension fund could choose pension assets so that the duration of the assets is matched with the duration of the liabilities. In this way, changing interest rates would not affect the net worth of the pension fund.

Life insurance companies receiving premiums today are legally obligated to provide death benefits in the future. Actuaries view these future benefits as analogous to interest and principal payments of fixed-income securities. The duration of these expected benefits can be calculated. Insurance companies frequently invest in bonds where the duration of the bonds is matched to the duration of the future death benefits.

The business of a leasing company is quite simple. The firm issues debt to purchase assets, which are then leased. The lease payments have a duration, as does the debt. Leasing companies frequently structure debt financing so that the duration of the debt matches the duration of the lease. If the firm did not do this, the market value of its equity could be eliminated by a sudden change in interest rates.

Bond managers for mutual funds and pension funds routinely calculate the duration of their portfolios. Applying the basic duration principle that bond price volatility is higher for bonds with high durations, fund managers lengthen duration when they predict that falling interest rates will boost bond prices. When they expect rates to rise, managers shorten duration to shield portfolios against losses. Research on duration concludes that duration strategies have been effective in controlling interest rate risk in Canadian bond portfolios.[20]

CONCEPT QUESTIONS

- What is duration?
- How is the concept of duration used to reduce interest rate risk?

Summary and Conclusions 24.6

1. Firms hedge to reduce risk. This chapter introduces a number of hedging strategies.
2. A forward contract is an agreement by two parties to sell an item for cash at a later date. The price is set at the time the agreement is signed. However, cash changes hands on the date of delivery. Forward contracts are generally not traded on organized exchanges.
3. Futures contracts are also agreements for future delivery. They have certain advantages, such as liquidity, that forward contracts do not. An unusual feature of futures contracts is the mark-to-the-market convention. If the price of a futures contract drops on a particular day, every buyer of the contract must pay

[20]I. J. Fooladi and G. S. Roberts, "How Effective Are Duration-Based Bond Strategies in Canada?" *Canadian Investment Review* (Spring 1989), pp. 57–62.

money to the clearinghouse. Every seller of the contract receives money from the clearinghouse. Everything is reversed if the price rises. The mark-to-the-market convention is designed to prevent defaults on futures contracts.

4. We divided hedges into two types: short hedges and long hedges. An individual or firm selling a futures contract to reduce risk is instituting a short hedge. Short hedges are generally appropriate for holders of inventory. An individual or firm that buys a futures contract to reduce risk is instituting a long hedge. Long hedges are typically used by firms with contracts to sell finished goods at a fixed price.

5. An interest rate futures contract employs a bond or other interest-sensitive security as the deliverable instrument. Because of their popularity, we worked with Government of Canada bond futures contracts, showing that they can be priced using the same type of net present value analysis that is used to price Government of Canada bonds themselves.

6. Many firms are faced with interest rate risk. They can reduce this risk by hedging with interest rate futures contracts. As with other commodities, a short hedge involves the sale of a futures contract. Firms that are committed to buying mortgages or other bonds are likely to institute short hedges. A long hedge involves the purchase of a futures contract. Firms that have agreed to sell mortgages or other bonds at a fixed price are likely to institute long hedges.

7. Duration measures the average maturity of all the cash flows in a bond. Bonds with high duration have high price variability. Firms frequently try to match the duration of their assets with the duration of their liabilities.

Key Terms

Hedging 697

Forward contract 697

Taking delivery 697

Deliverable instrument
  (delivery vehicle) 697

Making delivery 697

Cash transaction 698

Futures contract 698

Marked to the market 699

Short hedge 705

Long hedge 706

Duration 716

Immunized 719

Suggested Readings

Two useful books on futures are:

R. W. Kolb. *Understanding Futures Markets.* Glenview, Ill.: Scott Foresman, 1988.

J. Hull. *Options, Futures and Other Derivative Securities.* Englewood Cliffs, N.J.: Prentice Hall, 1989.

For more on duration and immunization, see:

G. O. Bierwag. *Duration Analysis.* Cambridge, Mass.: Ballinger, 1987.

Questions and Problems

Futures and Forward Contracts

24.1 Define
  a. Forward contract.
  b. Futures contract.

24.2 Explain the three ways in which futures contracts and forward contracts differ.

24.3 Closing prices for wheat futures contracts are

January 15	$6.03
January 16	6.08
January 17	6.12
January 18	6.10
January 19	5.98

  a. Say you bought one contract at $6.00 at the opening of trading on January
       15. Then on January 18 you receive from your broker a notice of delivery
       on that day.
       i. What is the delivery price?
       ii. What price did you pay for wheat?
       iii. List the cash flows associated with this contract.

  b. Suppose on January 19 you receive from your broker a notice of delivery
       on that day.
       i. What is the delivery price?
       ii. What price did you pay for wheat?
       iii. List the cash flows associated with this contract.

24.4 a. How is a short hedge created?
  b. In what type of situation is a short hedge a wise strategy?
  c. How is a long hedge created?
  d. In what type of situation is a long hedge a wise strategy?

24.5 A classmate of yours recently entered the import/export business. During a
       visit with him last week, he said to you, "If you play the game right, this is
       the safest business in the world. By hedging all my transactions in the foreign
       exchange futures market, I eliminate all risk." Do you agree with your
       friend's assessment of hedging? Why or why not?

24.6 This morning you agreed to buy a three-year Government of Canada bond six
       months from today. The bond carries an 8-percent coupon rate and has a
       $1,000 face. The expected spot rates of interest for the life of the bond are
       listed below. These rates are semiannual rates.

Time from today	Semiannual rate (%)
6 months	0.048
12 months	0.050
18 months	0.052
24 months	0.055
30 months	0.057
36 months	0.060
42 months	0.061

  a. How much should you have paid for this forward contract?

  b. Suppose that shortly after you purchased the forward contract, all semiannual rates increased 20 basis points; that is, the six-month rate increased from 0.048 to 0.050.

   i. State what you expect will happen to the value of the forward contract

   ii. What is the value of the forward contract?

24.7 After reading the text's example about Peter James, the mortgage banker, you decide to enter the business. You begin small; you agree to provide $200,000 to an old university roommate to finance the purchase of her home. The loan is a 10-year loan and has a 10-percent interest rate. Ten percent is the current market rate of interest. For ease of computation, assume the mortgage payments are made annually. Your former roommate needs the money four months from today. You do not have $200,000, but you intend to sell the mortgage to South American Life. The president of South American is also an old friend, so you know with certainty that he will buy the mortgage. Unfortunately, he is unavailable to meet with you until three months from today.

  a. What is your former roommate's mortgage payment?

  b. What is the most significant risk you face in this deal?

  c. How can you hedge this risk?

24.8 Refer to question 24.7. There are Government of Canada bond futures available for four months from now. A single contract is for $100,000 of Government of Canada bonds.

  a. Suppose between today and your meeting with the president of South American, the market rate of interest rises to 12 percent.

   i. How much is South American's president willing to pay you for the mortgage?

   ii. What happened to the value of the Government of Canada bond futures contract?

   iii. What is your net gain or loss if you wrote a futures contract?

  b. Suppose that between today and your meeting with the president of South American, the market rate of interest falls to 9 percent.

   i. How much is South American's president willing to pay you for the mortgage?

   ii. What happened to the value of the Government of Canada bond futures contract?

   iii. What is your net gain or loss if you wrote a futures contract?

Duration

24.9 Available are three zero-coupon, $1,000 face value bonds. All of these bonds are initially priced using a 12-percent interest rate. Bond *A* matures one year from today, bond *B* matures four years from today, and bond *C* matures nine years from today.

  a. What is the current price of each bond?

b. If the market rate of interest rises to 14 percent, what are the prices of these bonds?

c. Which bond experienced the greatest percentage change in price?

24.10 Consider two four-year bonds. Each bond has a $1,000 face value. Bond *A*'s coupon rate is 7 percent, while bond *B*'s coupon rate is 11 percent.

a. What is the price of each bond when the market rate of interest is 10 percent?

b. What is the price of each bond when the market rate of interest is 7 percent?

c. Which bond experienced the greatest percentage change in price?

d. Explain your result in (*c*).

24.11 Calculate the duration of a five-year, $1,000 face value bond with a 9-percent coupon rate, selling at par.

24.12 Calculate the duration of a four-year, $1,000 face value bond with a 9-percent coupon rate, selling at par.

24.13 Calculate the duration of a four-year, $1,000 face value bond with a 6-percent coupon rate, selling at par.

24.14 The following balance sheet is for Etobicoke Community Bank.

	Market value	Duration
Assets		
Cash	$ 43 million	0
Accounts receivable loans	615 million	4 months
Short-term loans	345 million	9 months
Long-term loans	55 million	5 years
Mortgages	197 million	15 years
Liabilities and Equity		
Chequing and savings deposits	$490 million	0
Certificates of deposit	370 million	18 months
Long-term financing	250 million	10 years
Equity	145 million	

a. What is the duration of Etobicoke's assets?

b. What is the duration of Etobicoke's liabilities?

c. Is Etobicoke Community Bank immune to interest rate risk?

24.15 Refer to the previous problem. To what values must the durations of Etobicoke Community Bank change to make the bank immune to interest rate risk if

a. Only the durations of the liabilities change?

b. Only the durations of the assets change?

24.16 Why do portfolio managers use duration instead of maturity as a measure of a bond's price volatility?

24.17 You are managing a bond portfolio by placing bets on your interest rate forecasts. You think that rates have bottomed and are likely to rise. The average duration of your portfolio is 4.5 years. Which bonds are more attractive for new purchases: those with a 10-year duration or 3-year duration? Explain.

PART SIX

FINANCIAL PLANNING AND SHORT-TERM FINANCE

Financial planning establishes the blueprint for change in a firm. It is necessary because (1) it includes putting forth the goals of the firm to motivate the organization and to provide benchmarks for performance measurement, (2) the financing and investment decisions of the firm are not independent and their interaction must be identified, and (3) in an uncertain world, the firm must anticipate changing conditions and surprises.

Most of Chapter 25 is devoted to long-term financial planning. Long-term financial planning incorporates decisions such as capital budgeting, capital structure, and dividend policy. These decisions involve investment opportunities and financing arrangements that go beyond one year. An important part of Chapter 25 is the discussion of building corporate financial models. Here we introduce the concept of sustainable growth and show that a firm's growth rate depends on its spending characteristics (profit margin and asset turnover) and financial policies (dividend policy and capital structure).

In Chapter 26 we introduce short-term financial planning, which involves short-lived assets and liabilities. We discuss two aspects of short-term financial planning: (1) the size of the firm's investment in current assets, such as cash, accounts receivable, and inventory, and (2) how to finance short-term assets. We describe the primary tool for short-term financial planning, the cash budget. It incorporates the short-term financial goals of the firm and tells the financial manager the amount of necessary short-term financing.

In Chapter 27 we describe the management of a firm's investment in cash. The chapter divides cash management into three separate areas:

1. Determining the appropriate target cash balance.
2. Collecting and disbursing cash.
3. Investing the excess cash in marketable securities.

Chapter 28 describes what is involved when a firm makes the decision to grant credit to its customers. This decision involves three types of analysis:

1. A firm must decide on the conditions under which it sells its goods and services for credit. These conditions are the terms of the sale.
2. Before granting credit, the firm must analyze the risk that the customer will not pay; this is called *credit analysis*.
3. After credit is extended, the firm must determine how to collect its cash.

CHAPTER 25

Corporate Financial Models and Long-Term Planning

Financial planning establishes guidelines for change in the firm. They should include (1) an identification of the firm's financial goals, (2) an analysis of the differences between these goals and the current financial status of the firm, and (3) a statement of the actions needed for the firm to achieve its financial goals. In other words, as one member of GM's board was heard to say, "Planning is a process that, at best, helps the firm avoid stumbling into the future backwards."

The basic policy elements of financial planning have been put forth in various chapters in this book. They comprise (1) the investment opportunities the firm elects to undertake, (2) the degree of financial leverage the firm chooses to employ, and (3) the amount of cash the firm thinks is necessary and appropriate to pay shareholders. These are the financial policies that the firm must decide upon for its growth and profitability.

Almost all firms use an explicit, companywide growth rate as a major component of their long-run financial planning. There are direct connections between the growth that a company can achieve and its financial policy. One purpose of this chapter is to look at the financial aspects of strategic decisions.

The chapter first describes what is usually meant by corporate financial planning. Mostly we talk about long-term financial planning. Short-term financial planning is discussed in the next chapter. We examine what the firm can accomplish by developing a long-term financial plan. This enables us to make an important point: Investment and financing decisions frequently interact. The different interactions of investment and financing decisions can be analyzed in the planning model.

Finally, financial planning forces the corporation to think about goals. A goal frequently espoused by corporations is growth. Indeed, one of the consequences of accepting positive NPV projects is growth. We show how financial planning models can be used to understand better how growth is achieved.

What Is Corporate Financial Planning?   25.1

Financial planning formulates the method by which financial goals are to be achieved. It has two dimensions: a time frame and a level of aggregation.

A financial plan is a statement of what is to be done in a future time. The GM board member was right on target when he explained the virtues of financial planning.

Most decisions have long lead times, which means they take a long time to implement. In an uncertain world, this requires that decisions be made far in advance of their implementation. If a firm wants to build a factory in 1995, it may need to line up contractors in 1993. It is sometimes useful to think of the future as having a short run and a long run. The short run, in practice, is usually the coming 12 months. Initially, we focus our attention on financial planning over the long run, which is usually taken to be a two-year–to–five-year period of time.

Financial plans are compiled from the capital budgeting analyses of each of a firm's projects. In effect, the smaller investment proposals of each operational unit are added up and treated as a big project. This process is called **aggregation.**

Financial plans always entail alternative sets of assumptions. For example, suppose a company has two separate divisions: one for consumer products and one for gas turbine engines. The financial planning process might require each division to prepare three alternative business plans for the next three years:

1. *A worst case.* This plan would require making the worst possible assumptions about the company's products and the state of the economy. It could mean divestiture and liquidation.

2. *A normal case.* This plan would require making most likely assumptions about the company and the economy.

3. *A best case.* Each division would be required to work out a case based on the most optimistic assumptions. It could involve new products and expansion.

Because the company is likely to spend a lot of time preparing proposals on different scenarios that will become the basis for the company's financial plan, it seems reasonable to ask what the planning process will accomplish:

1. *Interactions.* The financial plan must make explicit the linkages between investment proposals for the different operating activities of the firm and the financing choices available to the firm. IBM's 15-percent growth target goes hand in hand with its financing program.

2. *Options.* The financial plan provides the opportunity for the firm to work through various investment and financing options. The firm addresses questions of what financing arrangements are optimal, and evaluates options of closing plants or marketing new products.

3. *Feasibility.* The different plans must fit into the overall corporate objective of maximizing shareholder wealth.

4. *Avoiding surprises.* Financial planning should identify what may happen in the future if certain events take place. Thus, one of the purposes of financial planning is to avoid surprises.

CONCEPT QUESTIONS

- What are the two dimensions of the financial planning process?
- Why should firms draw up financial plans?

A Financial Planning Model: The Ingredients 25.2

Just as companies differ in size and products, financial plans are not the same for all companies. However, there are some common elements:

1. **Sales forecast.** All financial plans require a sales forecast. Perfectly accurate sales forecasts are not possible, because sales depend on the uncertain future state of the economy. Firms can get help from forecasters and consultants specializing in macroeconomic and industry projections.

2. **Pro forma statements.** The financial plan will have a forecast balance sheet, an income statement, and a sources-and-uses statement. These are called *pro forma statements* or *pro formas.*

3. **Asset requirements.** The plan will describe projected capital spending. In addition, it will discuss the proposed uses of net working capital.

4. **Financial requirements.** The plan will include a section on financing arrangements. This part of the plan should discuss dividend policy and debt policy. Sometimes firms will expect to raise equity by selling new shares of stock. In this case, the plan must consider what kinds of securities must be sold and what methods of issuance are most appropriate.

5. **Plug.** Suppose a financial planner assumes that sales, costs, and net income will rise at a particular rate, g_1. Further suppose that the planner desires assets and liabilities to grow at a different rate, g_2. These two different growth rates may be incompatible unless a third variable is also adjusted. For example, compatibility may only be reached if common stock outstanding grows at a different rate, g_3. In this example, we treat the growth in outstanding stock as the *plug* variable. That is, the growth rate in outstanding stock is chosen to make the growth rate in income statement items consistent with the growth rate in balance sheet items. Surprisingly, even if the income statement items grow at the *same* rate as the balance sheet items, consistency might be achieved only if outstanding stock grows at a different rate.

   Of course, the growth rate in outstanding stock need not be the plug variable. One could have income statement items grow at g_1, and assets, long-term debt, and outstanding stock grow at g_2. In this case, compatibility between g_1 and g_2 might be achieved by letting short-term debt grow at a rate of g_3.

6. **Economic assumptions.** The plan must explicitly state the economic environment that the firm expects will prevail over the life of the plan. Among the economic assumptions that must be made is the level of interest rates.

■ *Example*

The Canadian Computerfield Corporation's 19X1 financial statements are as follows:

Income Statement 19X1			Balance Sheet Year-End 19X1			
Sales	$1,000		Assets	$500	Debt	$250
Costs	(800)				Equity	$250
Net income	$ 200		Total	$500	Total	$500

In 19X1, Canadian Computerfield's profit margin is 20 percent, and it has never paid a dividend. Its debt-equity ratio is 1. This is also the firm's *target* debt-equity ratio. Unless otherwise stated, the financial planners at Canadian Computerfield assume that all variables are tied directly to sales and that current relationships are optimal.

Suppose that sales increase by 20 percent from 19X1 to 19X2. Because the planners would then also forecast a 20-percent increase in costs, the pro forma income statement would be

Income Statement
19X2

Sales	$1,200
Costs	(960)
Net income	$ 240

The assumption that all variables will grow by 20 percent will enable us to construct the pro forma balance sheet as well:

Balance Sheet
Year-End, 19X2

Assets	$600	Debt	$300
		Equity	300
Total	$600	Total	600

Now we must reconcile these two pro formas. How, for example, can net income be equal to $240 and equity increase by only $50? The answer is that Canadian Computerfield must have paid a dividend or repurchased common shares equal to $190. In this case dividends are the plug variable.

Suppose Canadian Computerfield does not pay a dividend and does not repurchase its own common shares. With these assumptions, Canadian Computerfield's equity will grow to $490 and debt must be retired to keep total assets equal to $600. In this case the debt-to-equity ratio is the plug variable. This example shows the interaction of sales growth and financial policy. The next example focuses on the need for external funds. It identifies a six-step procedure for constructing the pro forma balance sheet. ∎

■ *Example*

The St. Lawrence Corporation is thinking of acquiring a new machine. With this new machine the company expects sales to increase from $20 million to $22 million—10 percent growth. The corporation believes that its assets and liabilities vary directly with its level of sales. Its profit margin on sales is 10 percent, and its dividend payout ratio is 50 percent.

The company's current balance sheet (reflecting the purchase of the new machine) is as follows:

Current Balance Sheet		**Pro Forma Balance Sheet**	
			Explanation
Current assets	$ 6,000,000	$ 6,600,000	30% of sales
Fixed assets	24,000,000	26,400,000	120% of sales
Total assets	$30,000,000	$33,000,000	150% of sales

Current Balance Sheet		Pro Forma Balance Sheet	
Short-term debt	$10,000,000	$11,000,000	50% of sales
Long-term debt	6,000,000	6,600,000	30% of sales
Common stock	4,000,000	4,000,000	Constant
Retained earnings	10,000,000	11,100,000	Net income
Total financing	$30,000,000	$32,700,000	
		$ 300,000	Funds needed (the difference between total assets and total financing)

From this information we can determine the pro forma balance sheet, which is on the right-hand side. The change in retained earnings will be

$$\text{Net income} \quad - \quad \text{Dividends} \quad = \quad \frac{\text{Change in}}{\text{retained earnings}}$$

$$(0.10 \times \$22 \text{ million}) - (0.5 \times 0.10 \times \$22 \text{ million}) = \$1.1 \text{ million}$$

In this example the plug variable is new shares of stock. The company must issue $300,000 of new stock. The equation that can be used to determine if external funds are needed is

External Funds Needed (EFN):

$$\left(\frac{\text{Assets}}{\text{Sales}}\right) \times \Delta\text{Sales} - \left(\frac{\text{Debt}}{\text{Sales}}\right) \times \Delta\text{Sales} - (p \times \text{Projected sales}) \times (1 - d)$$

$$= (1.5 \times \$2 \text{ million}) - (0.80 \times \$2 \text{ million}) - (0.10 \times \$22 \text{ million}) \times 0.5$$

$$= \$1.4 \text{ million} \qquad\qquad\qquad - \$1.1 \text{ million}$$

$$= \$0.3 \text{ million}$$

where

$$\frac{\text{Assets}}{\text{Sales}} = 1.5$$

$$\frac{\text{Debt}}{\text{Sales}} = 0.8$$

p = Net profit margin = 0.10

d = Dividend payout ratio = 0.5

ΔSales = Projected change in sales

The steps in the estimation of the pro forma balance sheet for the St. Lawrence Corporation and the external funds needed (EFN) are as follows:

1. Express balance sheet items that vary with sales as a percentage of sales.
2. Multiply the percentages determined in step (1) by projected sales to obtain the amounts for the future period.
3. Where no percentage applies, simply insert the previous balance sheet figure in the future period.
4. Compute projected retained earnings as follows:

$$\frac{\text{Projected}}{\text{retained earnings}} = \frac{\text{Present}}{\text{retained earnings}} + \frac{\text{Projected}}{\text{net income}} - \frac{\text{Cash}}{\text{dividends}}$$

5. Add the asset accounts to determine projected assets. Next, add the liabilities and equity accounts to determine the total financing; any difference is the *shortfall*. This equals EFN.
6. Use the plug to fill EFN. ∎

CONCEPT QUESTION

∎ What is the logic underlying a financial planning model?

25.3   What Determines Growth?

Firms frequently make growth forecasts an explicit part of financial planning. Donaldson finds that many firms state corporate goals in terms of growth rates.[1] This may seem puzzling in the light of our previous emphasis on maximizing the firm's value as the central goal of management. One way to reconcile the difference is to think of growth as an intermediate goal that leads to higher value. Rappaport correctly points out that, in applying the NPV approach, growth should not be a goal but must be a consequence of decisions that maximize NPV.[2] In fact, if the firm is willing to accept negative NPV projects just to grow in size, growth will probably make the shareholders (but perhaps not the managers) worse off.

Donaldson also concludes that most major industrial companies are very reluctant to use external equity as a regular part of their financial planning. Many small firms and start-up operations simply do not have access to new external equity financing. To illustrate the linkages between the ability of a firm to grow and its financial policy when the firm does not issue equity, we can make some planning assumptions that are consistent with the financial policy of the Peace River Corporation.

1. The firm's assets will grow in proportion to its sales.
2. Net income is a constant proportion of its sales.
3. The firm has a given dividend payout policy and a given debt-equity ratio.
4. The firm will not change the number of outstanding shares of stock.

There is only one growth rate that is consistent with the preceding assumptions. In effect, with these assumptions, growth has been made a plug variable. To see this, recall that a change in assets must always be equal to a change in debt plus a change in equity:

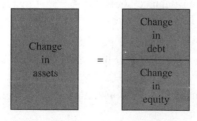

---

[1]G. Donaldson, *Managing Corporation Wealth: The Operations of a Comprehensive Financial Goals System* (New York: Praeger, 1984).

[2]A. Rappaport, *Creating Shareholder Value: The New Standard for Business Performance* (New York: Free Press, 1986).

Now we can write the conditions that ensure this equality and solve for the growth rate that will give it to us.

The variables used in this demonstration are

T = The ratio of total assets to sales

p = The net profit margin on sales

d = The dividend payout ratio

L = The debt-equity ratio

S_0 = Sales this year

ΔS = The change in sales $(S_1 - S_0 = \Delta S)$

RE = Retained earnings = Net income $\times$ Retention ratio = $S_1 \times p \times (1 - d)$

NI = Net income = $S_1 \times p$

If the firm is to increase sales by ΔS during the year, it must increase assets by $T\Delta S$. The firm is assumed not to be able to change the number of shares of stock outstanding, so the equity financing must come from retained earnings. Retained earnings will depend on next year's sales, the payout ratio, and the profit margin. The amount of borrowing will depend on the amount of retained earnings and the debt-equity ratio.

New equity: $S_1 \times p \times (1 - d)$

plus

Borrowing: $[S_1 \times p \times (1 - d)] \times L$

equals

Capital spending: $T\Delta S$

Moving things around a little gives

$$T\Delta S = [S_1 \times p \times (1 - d)] + [S_1 \times p \times (1 - d) \times L]$$

and

$$\frac{\Delta S}{S_0} = \frac{p \times (1 - d) \times (1 + L)}{T - [p \times (1 - d) \times (1 + L)]} = \text{Growth rate in sales} \qquad (25.1)$$

This is the growth-rate equation. Given the profit margin (p), the payout ratio (d), the debt-equity ratio (L), and the asset-requirement ratio (T), the growth rate can be determined.[3] It is the only growth possible with the preset values for the four variables. Higgins has referred to this growth rate as the firm's **sustainable growth rate.**[4]

---

[3] This is approximately equal to the rate of return on equity (ROE) multiplied by the retention rate (RR): ROE × RR. This expression is only precisely equal to equation (25.1) above in continuous time; otherwise it is an approximation. More precisely,

$$\text{Growth rate in sales} = \frac{\text{ROE} \times \text{RR}}{1 - (\text{ROE} \times \text{RR})}$$

[4] R. C. Higgins, "Sustainable Growth under Inflation," *Financial Management* (Autumn 1981). The definition of sustainable growth was popularized by the Boston Consulting Group and others.

Table 25.1
Current financial
statement: The
Peace River
Corporation (in
$ thousands)

Income Statement

	This year
Net sales (*S*)	$10,000
Cost of sales	7,000
Earnings before taxes and interest	3,000
Interest expense	500
Earnings before taxes	2,500
Taxes	850
Net income (NI)	$ 1,650

Sources and Uses of Cash

Sources:	
Net income (NI)	$ 1,650
Depreciation	500
Operating cash flow	2,150
Borrowing	455
New stock issue	0
Total sources	$ 2,605
Uses:	
Increase in net working capital	455
Capital spending	955
Dividends	1,195
Total uses	$ 2,605

Balance Sheet

	This year	Last year	Change
Assets			
Net working capital	$ 5,000	$4,545	$ 455
Fixed assets	5,000	4,545	455
Total assets	$10,000	$9,090	$ 910
Liabilities and shareholders' equity			
Debt	$ 5,000	$4,545	$ 455
Equity	5,000	4,545	455
Total liabilities and shareholders' equity	$10,000	$9,090	$ 910

▪ *Example*

Table 25.1 shows the current income statement, the sources and uses of funds statement, and the balance sheet for the Peace River Corporation. Net income for the corporation was 16.5 percent ($1,650/$10,000) of sales revenue. The company paid out 72.4 percent ($1,195/$1,650) of its net income in dividends. The interest rate on debt was 10 percent, and the long-term debt was 50 percent ($5,000/$10,000) of assets. (Notice that, for simplicity, we use the single term *net working capital* in Table 25.1, instead of separating current assets from current liabilities.) Peace River's assets grew at the rate of 10 percent ($910/$9,090). In addition, sales grew at 10 percent, though this increase is not shown in Table 25.1.

    The cash flow generated by Peace River was enough not only to pay a dividend but also to increase net working capital and fixed assets by $455 each. The company did not issue any shares of stock during the year. Its debt-equity ratio and dividend payout ratio remained constant throughout the year.

The sustainable growth rate for the Peace River Corporation is 10 percent, or

$$\frac{0.165 \times 0.276 \times 2}{1 - (0.165 \times 0.276 \times 2)} = 0.1$$

However, suppose its desired growth rate was 20 percent. It is possible for Peace River's desired growth to exceed its sustainable growth if Peace River is able to issue new shares of stock. A firm can do several things to increase its sustainable growth rate as seen from the Peace River example:

1. Sell new shares of stock.
2. Increase its reliance on debt.
3. Reduce its dividend payout ratio.
4. Increase profit margins.
5. Decrease its asset requirement ratio. ∎

Now we can see the use of a financial planning model to test the feasibility of the planned growth rate. If sales are to grow at a rate higher than the sustainable growth rate, the firm must improve operating performance, increase financial leverage, decrease dividends, or sell new shares. Of course, the planned rates of growth should be the result of a complete NPV-based planning process.

Determinants of Growth and Canadian Practice

As we described early in this chapter, one of the primary benefits to financial planning is to ensure internal consistency among the firm's various goals. The sustainable growth rate captures this element nicely. For this reason, sustainable growth is included in the Fast™ and Turbofast™ software used by commercial lenders at several Canadian chartered banks in analyzing their accounts. One major bank has engaged consultants to conduct seminars on sustainable growth for its small and midsized loan customers.

Also, we now see how a financial planning model can be used to test the feasibility of a planned growth rate. If sales are to grow at a rate higher than the sustainable growth rate, the firm must increase profit margins, increase total asset turnover, increase financial leverage, increase earnings retention, or sell new shares.

At the other extreme, suppose the firm is losing money (has a negative profit margin) or is paying out more than 100 percent of earnings in dividends so that the retention rate $(1 - d)$ is negative. In each of these cases, the negative sustainable growth rate signals the rate at which sales and assets must shrink. Firms can achieve negative growth by selling off assets and closing divisions. The cash generated by selling assets is often used to pay down excessive debt taken on earlier to fund rapid expansion. Campeau and Edper are examples of Canadian firms that have had to undergo this painful deleveraging process.

CONCEPT QUESTIONS

- When are the goals of growth and value maximization in conflict, and when are they aligned?
- What are the determinants of growth?

25.4   Some Caveats on Financial Planning Models

Financial planning models suffer from a great deal of criticism. We present two commonly voiced attacks below.

First, financial planning models do not indicate which financial policies are the best. For example, our model could not tell us whether Peace River's decision to issue new equity to achieve a higher growth rate raises the NPV of the firm.

Second, financial planning models are too simple. In reality, costs are not always proportional to sales, assets need not be a fixed percentage of sales, and capital budgeting involves a sequence of decisions over time. These assumptions are generally not incorporated into financial plans.

Financial planning models are necessary to assist in planning the future investment and financial decisions of the firm. Without some sort of long-term financial plan, the firm may find itself adrift in a sea of change without a rudder for guidance. But, because of the assumptions and the abstractions from reality necessary in the construction of the financial plan, we also think that they should carry the label:

> Let the user beware!

25.5   Summary and Conclusions

Financial planning forces the firm to think about and forecast the future. It involves

1. Building a corporate financial model.
2. Describing different scenarios of future development from worst to best cases.
3. Using the models to construct pro forma financial statements.
4. Running the model under different scenarios (conducting sensitivity analysis).
5. Examining the financial implications of ultimate strategic plans.

Corporate financial planning should not become a purely mechanical activity. If it does, it will probably focus on the wrong things. In particular, plans are formulated all too often in terms of a growth target with an explicit linkage to creation of value. Nonetheless, the alternative to financial planning is stumbling into the future.

Key Terms

Aggregation 730	Financial requirements 731
Sales forecast 731	Plug 731
Pro forma statements 731	Economic assumptions 731
Asset requirements 731	Sustainable growth rate 735

Suggested Readings

Approaches to building a financial planning model are contained in:

W. T. Carleton and C. L. Dick, Jr. "Financial Policy Models: Theory and Practice." *Journal of Financial and Quantitative Analysis* 8 (1973).

J. C. Francis and D. R. Rowell. "A Simultaneous-Equation Model of the Firm for Financial Analysis and Planning." *Financial Management* (Spring 1978).

S. C. Myers and G. A. Pogue. "A Programming Approach to Corporate Financial Management." *Journal of Finance* 29 (May 1974).

J. M. Warren and J. R. Shelton. "A Simultaneous-Equation Approach to Financial Planning." *Journal of Finance* (December 1971).

Two textbooks treating financial planning are:

C. F. Lee. *Financial Analysis and Planning: Theory and Application.* Reading, Mass.: Addison-Wesley, 1985.

J. A. Viscione. *Financial Analysis: Tools and Concepts.* New York; National Association of Credit Management, 1984.

For a critical discussion of sustainable growth, see:

A. Rappaport. *Creating Shareholder Value: The New Standard for Business Performance.* New York: Free Press, 1986.

Questions and Problems

Financial Forecasting

25.1 After examining patterns from recent years, management found the following regression-estimated relationships between some company balance sheets and income statement accounts and sales:

$$CA = 0.5 \text{ million} + 0.25\,S$$
$$FA = 1.0 \text{ million} + 0.50\,S$$
$$CL = 0.1 \text{ million} + 0.10\,S$$
$$NP = 0.0 \text{ million} + 0.02\,S$$

where

CA = Current assets
FA = Fixed assets
CL = Current liabilities
NP = Net profit after taxes
S = Sales

The company's sales for last year were $10 million. The year-end balance sheet is shown below:

Current assets	$3,000,000	Current liabilities	$1,100,000
Fixed assets	6,000,000	Bonds	2,500,000
		Common stock	2,000,000
		Retained earnings	3,400,000
Total	$9,000,000	Total	$9,000,000

Management further found that the company's sales bear a relationship to GNP:

$$S = 0.00001 \times GNP$$

The forecast of GNP for next year is $3.135 trillion. The firm pays out 40 percent of net profits after taxes in dividends.

Create a pro forma balance sheet for this firm.

Sustainable Growth

25.2 The Farah Company has determined that the following will be true next year:

T = Ratio of total assets to sales = 1
P = Net profit margin on sales = 5%
d = Dividend payout ratio = 50%
L = Debt-equity ratio = 1

a. What is Farah's sustainable growth rate in sales?
b. Can Farah's actual growth rate in sales be different from its sustainable growth rate? Why or why not?
c. How can Farah change its sustainable growth?

25.3 The Optimal Scam Company would like to see its sales grow at 20 percent for the foreseeable future. Its financial statements for the current year are presented below.

Income Statement ($ millions)		Balance Sheet ($ millions)	
Sales	$32.00	Current assets	$16
Costs	28.97	Fixed assets	16
Gross profit	3.03	Total assets	$32
Taxes	1.03		
Net income	$2.00	Current debt	10
		Long-term debt	4
Dividends	$1.40	Total debt	$14
Retained earnings	$0.60	Common stock	14
		Retained earnings	4
		Total liabilities and equity	$32

The current financial policy of the Optimal Scam Company includes

Dividend payout ratio (d) = 70%
Debt-to-equity ratio (L) = 77.78%
Net profit margin (P) = 6.25%
Assets-sales ratio (T) = 1

a. Determine Optimal Scam's need for external funds next year.
b. Construct a pro forma balance sheet for Optimal Scam.

    c. Calculate the sustainable growth rate for the Optimal Scam Company.

    d. How can Optimal Scam change its financial policy to achieve its growth objective?

25.4 The Lower Canada Company does not want to grow. The company's financial management believes it has no positive NPV projects. The company's operating financial characteristics are

        Profit margin = 10%

        Assets-sales ratio = 150%

        Debt-equity ratio = 100%

        Dividend payout ratio = 50%

    a. Calculate the sustainable growth rate for the Lower Canada Company.

    b. How can the Lower Canada Company achieve its stated growth goal?

25.5 Your firm recently hired a new MBA. She insists that your firm is incorrectly computing its sustainable growth rate. Your firm computes the sustainable growth rate using the formula

$$\frac{P \times (1 - d) \times (1 + L)}{T - P \times (1 - d) \times (1 + L)}$$

    P = Net profit margin on sales

    d = Dividend payout ratio

    L = Debt-equity ratio

    T = Ratio of total assets to sales

Your new employee claims that the correct formula is

$$\frac{ROE\,(1 - d)}{ROE - (1 - d)}$$

where ROE is net profit divided by net worth. Is your new employee correct?

NPV versus Growth

25.6 Throughout this text, you have learned that financial managers should select positive net present value projects. How does this project selection criterion relate to financial planning models?

CHAPTER 26

Short-Term Finance and Planning

Up to now we have described many of the decisions of long-term finance: capital budgeting, dividend policy, and capital structure. This chapter introduces short-term finance. Short-term finance is an analysis of decisions that (1) affect current assets and current liabilities, and (2) will frequently have an impact on the firm within a year.

The term *net working capital* is often associated with short-term financial decision-making. Net working capital is the difference between current assets and current liabilities. The focus of short-term finance on net working capital seems to suggest that it is an accounting subject. However, making net working capital decisions still relies on cash flow and net present value.

There is no universally accepted definition of short-term finance. The most important difference between short-term and long-term finance is the timing of cash flows. Short-term financial decisions involve cash inflows and outflows within a year or less. For example, a short-term financial decision is involved when a firm orders raw materials, pays in cash, and anticipates selling finished goods in one year for cash, as illustrated in Figure 26.1. A long-term financial decision is involved when a firm purchases a special machine that will reduce operating costs over the next five years, as illustrated in Figure 26.2.

Here are some questions of short-term finance:

1. What is a reasonable level of cash to keep on hand (in a bank) to pay bills?

2. How much raw material should be ordered?

3. How much credit should be extended to customers?

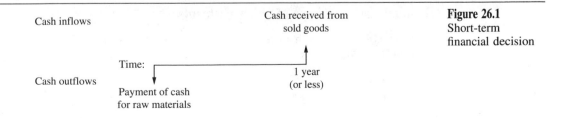

Figure 26.1
Short-term
financial decision

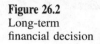

Figure 26.2
Long-term
financial decision

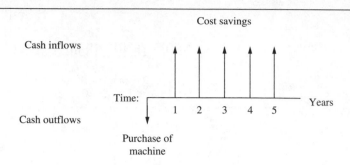

This chapter introduces the basic elements of short-term financial decisions. First, we describe the short-term operating activities of the firm, and then we identify alternative short-term financial policies. Finally, we outline the basic elements in a short-term financial plan and describe short-term financing instruments.

26.1   Tracing Cash and Net Working Capital

In this section we trace the components of cash and net working capital as they change from one year to the next. Our goal is to describe the short-term operating activities of the firm and their impact on cash and working capital.

Current assets are cash and other assets that are expected to be converted to cash within the year. Current assets are presented in the balance sheet in order of their accounting **liquidity**—the ease with which they can be converted to cash at a fair price and the time it takes to do so. Table 26.1 gives the balance sheet and income statement of the Tradewinds Manufacturing Corporation for 19X2 and 19X1. The four major items found in the current asset section of the Tradewinds balance sheet are cash, marketable securities, accounts receivable, and inventories.

As a counterpart to their investment in current assets, firms use several kinds of short-term debt called *current liabilities*. Current liabilities are obligations that are expected to require cash payment within one year or within the operating cycle, whichever is shorter.[1] The three major items found as current liabilities are accounts payable; accrued wages, taxes, and other expenses payable; and notes payable.

26.2   Defining Cash in Terms of Other Elements

Now we will define cash in terms of the other elements of the balance sheet. The balance sheet equation is

$$\frac{\text{Net working}}{\text{capital}} + \frac{\text{Fixed}}{\text{assets}} = \frac{\text{Long-term}}{\text{debt}} + \text{Equity} \qquad (26.1)$$

---

[1]As we will learn in this chapter, the operating cycle begins when inventory is received and ends when cash is collected from the sale of the inventory.

Table 26.1
Financial
statements

TRADEWINDS MANUFACTURING CORPORATION
December 31, 19X2, and December 31, 19X1

Balance Sheet	19X2	19X1
Assets		
Current assets:		
Cash..	$500,000	$500,000
Marketable securities (at cost)	500,000	450,000
Accounts receivable less allowance for bad debts...............	2,000,000	1,600,000
Inventories......................................	3,000,000	2,000,000
Total current assets	6,000,000	4,550,000
Fixed assets (property, plant, and equipment):		
Land......................................	450,000	450,000
Building	4,000,000	4,000,000
Machinery	1,500,000	800,000
Office equipment......................................	50,000	50,000
Less: Accumulated depreciation	2,000,000	1,700,000
Net fixed assets	4,000,000	3,600,000
Prepayments and deferred charges	400,000	300,000
Intangibles	100,000	100,000
Total assets......................................	$10,500,000	$8,550,000
Liabilities		
Current liabilities:		
Accounts payable......................................	$1,000,000	$750,000
Notes Payable	1,500,000	500,000
Accrued expenses payable	250,000	225,000
Taxes payable	250,000	225,000
Total current liabilities	3,000,000	1,700,000
Long-term liabilities:		
First mortgage bonds, 5% interest, due 2025...................	3,000,000	3,000,000
Deferred taxes	600,000	600,000
Total liabilities......................................	$6,600,000	$5,300,000
Stockholders' Equity		
Common stock, $5 par value each: authorized,	1,500,000	1,500,000
issued, and outstanding 300,000 shares		
Capital surplus......................................	500,000	500,000
Accumulated retained earnings......................................	1,900,000	1,250,000
Total stockholders' equity	3,900,000	3,250,000
Total liabilities and stockholders' equity	$10,500,000	$8,550,000
Consolidated Income Statement		
Net sales......................................	$11,500,000	$10,700,000
Cost of sales and operating expenses:		
Cost of goods sold......................................	8,200,000	7,684,000
Depreciation......................................	300,000	275,000
Selling and administration expenses............................	1,400,000	1,325,000
Operating profit	1,600,000	1,416,000
Other income:		
Dividends and interest......................................	50,000	50,000
Total income from operations............................	1,650,000	1,466,000
Less: Interest on bonds and other liabilities...................	300,000	150,000
Income before provision for income tax	1,350,000	1,316,000
Provision for income tax......................................	610,000	600,000
Net profit	$740,000	$716,000
Dividends paid out	$90,000	$132,000
Retained earnings	$650,000	$584,000

Net working capital is cash plus the other elements of net working capital; that is,

$$\text{Net working capital} = \text{Cash} + \text{Other current assets} - \text{Current liabilities} \qquad (26.2)$$

Substituting equation (26.2) into (26.1) yields

$$\text{Cash} + \text{Other current assets} - \text{Current liabilities} = \text{Long-term debt} + \text{Equity} - \text{Fixed assets} \qquad (26.3)$$

Rearranging, we find that

$$\text{Cash} = \text{Long-term debt} + \text{Equity} - \text{Net working capital (excluding cash)} - \text{Fixed assets} \qquad (26.4)$$

The natural interpretation of equation (26.4) is that increasing long-term debt and equity and decreasing fixed assets and net working capital (excluding cash) will increase cash to the firm.

The Sources and Uses of Cash Statement

From the right-hand side of equation (26.4), we can see that an increase in long-term debt or equity leads to an increase in cash. Moreover, a decrease in net working capital or fixed assets leads to a decrease in cash. In addition, the sum of net income and depreciation increases cash, whereas dividend payments decrease cash.[2] This reasoning allows an accountant to create a sources and uses of cash statement, which shows all the transactions that affect a firm's cash position.

Let us trace the changes in cash for Tradewinds during the year. Notice that Tradewinds' cash balance remained constant during 19X2, even though cash flow from operations was $1.04 million (net income plus depreciation). Why did cash remain the same? The answer is simply that the sources of cash were equal to the uses of cash. From the firm's sources and uses of cash statement (Table 26.2), we find that Tradewinds generated cash as shown below:

1. It generated cash flow from operations of $1.04 million.
2. It increased its accounts payable by $250,000. This is the same as increasing borrowing from suppliers.
3. It increased its borrowing from banks by $1 million. This shows up as an increase in notes payable.
4. It increased accrued expenses by $25,000.
5. It increased taxes payable by $25,000, in effect borrowing from Revenue Canada.

---

[2] Depreciation is really not a source of cash; it is added back as a correction because it was originally a noncash deduction from net income.

TRADEWINDS MANUFACTURING CORPORATION Sources and Uses of Cash (in $ thousands)		Table 26.2 Sources and uses of cash statement
Source of cash:		
Cash flow from operations:		
Net income	$ 740	
Depreciation	300	
Total cash flow from operations	1,040	
Decrease in net working capital:		
Increase in accounts payable	250	
Increase in notes payable	1,000	
Increase in accrued expenses	25	
Increase in taxes payable	25	
Total sources of cash	2,340	
Uses of cash:		
Increase in fixed assets	700	
Increase in prepayments	100	
Dividends	90	
Increase in net working capital:		
Investment in inventory	1,000	
Increase in accounts receivable	400	
Increase in marketable securities	50	
Total uses of cash	2,340	
Change in cash balance	0	

Tradewinds used cash for the following purposes:

1. It invested $700,000 in fixed assets.
2. It increased prepayments by $100,000.
3. It paid a $90,000 dividend.
4. It invested in inventory worth $1 million.
5. It lent its customers additional money. Hence, accounts receivable increased by $400,000.
6. It purchased $50,000 worth of marketable securities.

This example illustrates the difference between a firm's cash position on the balance sheet and cash flows from operations.

CONCEPT QUESTIONS

- What is the difference between net working capital and cash?
- Will net working capital always increase when cash increases?
- List the potential uses of cash.
- List the potential sources of cash.

Figure 26.3
Cash flow time
line and the
short-term
operating activities
of a typical
manufacturing firm

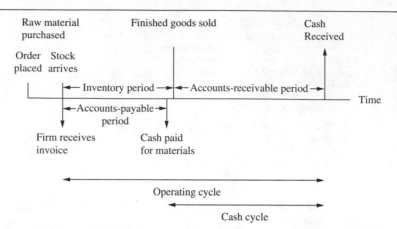

The *operating cycle* is the time period from the arrival of stock until the receipt of
cash. (Sometimes the operating cycle is defined to include the time from placement
of the order until arrival of the stock.) The *cash cycle* begins when cash is paid for
materials and ends when cash is collected from receivables.

26.3   The Operating Cycle and the Cash Cycle

Short-term finance is concerned with the firm's **short-run operating activities.** A
typical manufacturing firm's short-run operating activities consist of a sequence of
events and decisions:

Events	Decisions
1. Buying raw materials	1. How much inventory to order?
2. Paying cash for purchases	2. To borrow, or draw down cash balance?
3. Manufacturing the product	3. What choice of production technology?
4. Selling the product	4. To offer cash terms or credit terms to customers?
5. Collecting cash	5. How to collect cash?

These activities create patterns of cash inflows and cash outflows that are both
unsynchronized and uncertain. They are unsynchronized because the payment of cash
for raw materials does not happen at the same time as the receipt of cash from selling
the product. They are uncertain because future sales and costs are not known with
certainty.

Figure 26.3 depicts the short-term operating activities and cash flows for a typical
manufacturing firm along the **cash flow time line.** The **operating cycle** is the time
interval between the arrival of inventory stock and the date when cash is collected
from receivables. The **cash cycle** begins when cash is paid for materials and ends
when cash is collected from receivables. The cash flow time line consists of an
operating cycle and a cash cycle. The need for short-term financial decision-making is
suggested by the gap between the cash inflows and cash outflows. This is related to the
lengths of the operating cycle and the accounts payable period. This gap can be filled
either by borrowing or by holding a liquidity reserve for marketable securities. The
gap can be shortened by changing the inventory, receivable, and payable periods. Now
we take a closer look at the operating cycle.

The length of the operating cycle is equal to the sum of the lengths of the inventory and accounts receivable periods. The *inventory period* is the length of time required to order, produce, and sell a product. The *accounts receivable period* is the length of time required to collect cash receipts.

The *cash cycle* is the time between cash disbursement and cash collection. It can be thought of as the operating cycle less the accounts payable period:

Cash cycle = Operating cycle − Accounts payable period

The *accounts payable period* is the length of time the firm is able to delay payment on the purchase of various resources, such as wages and raw materials.

In practice, the inventory period, the accounts receivable period, and the accounts payable period are measured by days in inventory, days in receivables, and days in payables, respectively. We illustrate how the operating cycle and the cash cycle can be measured in the following example.

■ *Example*

Tradewinds Manufacturing is a diversified manufacturing firm with the balance sheet and income statement shown in Table 26.1 for 19X1 and 19X2. The operating cycle and the cash cycle can be determined for Tradewinds after calculating the appropriate ratios for inventory, receivables, and payables. Consider inventory first:

$$\frac{\text{Average}}{\text{inventory}} = \frac{\$3 \text{ million} + \$2 \text{ million}}{2} = \$2.5 \text{ million}$$

The terms in the numerator are the ending inventory in the second and first years, respectively.

We next calculate the inventory turnover ratio:

$$\frac{\text{Inventory}}{\text{turnover ratio}} = \frac{\text{Cost of goods sold}}{\text{Average inventory}} = \frac{\$8.2 \text{ million}}{\$2.5 \text{ million}} = 3.3$$

This implies that the inventory cycle occurs 3.3 times a year. Finally, we calculate days in inventory:

$$\frac{\text{Days in}}{\text{inventory}} = \frac{365}{3.3} = 110.6 \text{ days}$$

Our calculation implies that the inventory cycle is slightly more than 110 days. We perform analogous calculations for receivables and payables:[3]

$$\frac{\text{Average}}{\substack{\text{accounts}\\\text{receivable}}} = \frac{\$2.0 \text{ million} + \$1.6 \text{ million}}{2} = \$1.8 \text{ million}$$

$$\frac{\text{Average}}{\substack{\text{receivable}\\\text{turnover}}} = \frac{\text{Credit sales}}{\substack{\text{Average accounts}\\\text{receivable}}} = \frac{\$11.5 \text{ million}}{\$1.8 \text{ million}} = 6.4$$

---

[3]We assume that Tradewinds Manufacturing makes no cash sales.

$$\text{Days in receivable} = \frac{365}{6.4} = 57 \text{ days}$$

$$\text{Average payables} = \frac{\$1.0 \text{ million} + \$0.75 \text{ million}}{2} = \$0.875 \text{ million}$$

$$\text{Accounts payable deferral period} = \frac{\text{Cost of goods sold}}{\text{Average payables}} = \frac{\$8.2 \text{ million}}{\$0.875 \text{ million}} = 9.4$$

$$\text{Days in payables} = \frac{365}{9.4} = 38.8 \text{ days}$$

These calculations allow us to determine both the operating cycle and the cash cycle:

$$\text{Operating cycle} = \text{Days in inventory} + \text{Days in receivables}$$
$$= 110.6 \text{ days} + 57 \text{ days} = 167.6 \text{ days}$$

$$\text{Cash cycle} = \text{Operating cycle} - \text{Days in payables}$$
$$= 167.6 \text{ days} - 38.8 \text{ days} = 128.8 \text{ days} \quad \blacksquare$$

The need for short-term financial decision-making is suggested by the gap between the cash inflows and cash outflows. This is related to the lengths of the operating cycles and accounts payable period. This gap can be filled either by borrowing or by holding a liquidity reserve in the form of marketable securities. The gap can be shortened by changing the inventory, receivable, and payable periods. We now take a closer look at this aspect of short-term financial policy.

CONCEPT QUESTIONS

- What does it mean to say that a firm has an inventory turnover ratio of four?
- Describe the operating cycle and cash cycle. What are the differences between them?

26.4   Some Aspects of Short-Term Financial Policy

The policy that a firm adopts for short-term finance will be composed of at least two elements:

1. *The size of the firm's investment in current assets.* This is usually measured relative to the firm's level of total operating revenues. A flexible or accommodative short-term financial policy would maintain a high ratio of current assets to sales. A restrictive short-term financial policy would entail a low ratio of current assets to sales.

2. *The financing of current assets.* This is measured as the proportion of short-term debt to long-term debt. A restrictive short-term financial policy means a high proportion of short-term debt relative to long-term financing, and a flexible policy means less short-term debt and more long-term debt.

The Size of the Firm's Investment in Current Assets

Flexible short-term financial policies include

1. Keeping large balances of cash and marketable securities.
2. Making large investments in inventory.
3. Granting liberal credit terms, which result in a high level of accounts receivable.

Restrictive short-term financial policies are

1. Keeping low cash balances and no investment in marketable securities.
2. Making small investments in inventory.
3. Allowing no credit sales and no accounts receivable.

Determining the optimal investment level in short-term assets requires an identification of the different costs of alternative short-term financing policies. The objective is to trade off the cost of restrictive policies against those of the flexible ones to arrive at the best compromise.

Current asset holdings are highest with a flexible short-term financial policy and lowest with a restrictive policy. Thus, flexible short-term financial policies are costly in that they require higher cash outflows to finance cash and marketable securities, inventory, and accounts receivable. However, future cash inflows are highest with a flexible policy. Sales are stimulated by the use of a credit policy that provides liberal financing to customers. A large amount of inventory on hand ("on the shelf") provides a quick delivery service to customers and increases sales.[4] In addition, the firm can probably charge higher prices for the quick delivery service and the liberal credit terms of flexible policies. A flexible policy also may result in fewer production stoppages because of inventory shortages.[5]

Managing current assets can be thought of as involving a trade-off between costs that rise with the level of investment and costs that fall with the level of investment. Costs that rise with the level of investment in current assets are called **carrying costs.** Costs that fall with increases in the level of investment in current assets are called **shortage costs.**

Carrying costs are generally of two types. First, because the rate of return on current assets is low compared with that of other assets, there is an opportunity cost. Second, there is the cost of maintaining the economic value of the item. The cost of warehousing inventory is an example.

Shortage costs are incurred when the investment in current assets is low. If a firm runs out of cash, it will be forced to sell marketable securities. If a firm runs out of cash and cannot readily sell marketable securities, it may need to borrow or default on an obligation. (This general situation is called a *cash-out*). If a firm has no inventory (a *stock-out*) or if it cannot extend credit to its customers, it will lose business.

There are two kinds of shortage costs:

1. *Trading or order costs.* Order costs are the costs of placing an order for more cash (*brokerage costs*) or more inventory (*production set-up costs*).

---

[4]This is true of some types of finished goods.

[5]This is true of inventory of raw material but not of finished goods.

2. *Costs related to safety reserves.* These are costs of lost sales, lost customer goodwill, and disruption of production schedules.

Figure 26.4 illustrates the basic nature of carrying costs.

The total costs of investing in current assets are determined by adding the carrying costs and the shortage costs. The minimum point on the total cost curve (CA*) reflects the optimal balance of current assets. The curve is generally quite flat at the optimum, and it is difficult, if not impossible, to find the precise optimal balance of shortage and carrying costs. Usually we are content with a choice near the optimum.

If carrying costs are low or shortage costs are high, the optimal policy calls for substantial current assets. In other words, the optimal policy is a flexible one. This is illustrated in the middle graph of Figure 26.4

If carrying costs are high or shortage costs are low, the optimal policy is a restrictive one. That is, the optimal policy calls for modest current assets. This is illustrated in the bottom graph of the figure.

Alternative Financing Policies for Current Assets

In the previous section we examined the level of investment in current assets. Now we turn to the level of current liabilities, assuming the investment in current assets is optimal.

An Ideal Model

In an ideal economy, short-term assets can always be financed with short-term debt, and long-term assets can be financed with long-term debt and equity. In this economy, net working capital is always zero.

Imagine the simple case of a grain elevator operator. Grain elevator operators buy crops after harvest, store them, and sell them during the year. They have high inventories of grain after the harvest and end with low inventories just before the next harvest.

Bank loans with maturities of less than one year are used to finance the purchase of grain. These loans are paid with the proceeds from the sale of grain.

The situation is shown in Figure 26.5. Long-term assets are assumed to grow over time, whereas current assets increase at the end of the harvest and then decline during the year. Short-term assets end at zero just before the next harvest. These assets are financed by short-term debt, and long-term assets are financed with long-term debt and equity. Net working capital—current assets minus current liabilities—is always zero.

Different Strategies in Financing Current Assets

Current assets cannot be expected to drop to zero in the real world because a long-term rising level of sales will result in some permanent investment in current assets. A growing firm can be thought of as having both a permanent requirement for current assets and one for long-term assets. This total asset requirement will exhibit balances over time reflecting (1) a secular growth trend, (2) a seasonal variation around the trend, and (3) unpredictable day-to-day and month-to-month fluctuations. This is

Financing policy

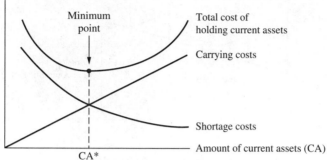

Flexible policy

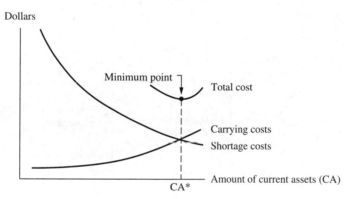

Restrictive policy

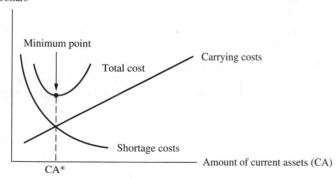

Figure 26.4
Carrying costs and
shortage costs

Carrying costs increase with the level of investment in current assets. They
include both opportunity costs and the costs of maintaining the asset's
economic value. *Shortage costs* decrease with increases in the level of
investment in current assets. They include trading costs and the costs of
running out of the current asset (for example, being short of cash).

*The optimal amount of current assets. This point minimizes costs.

Figure 26.5
Financing policy
for an idealized
economy

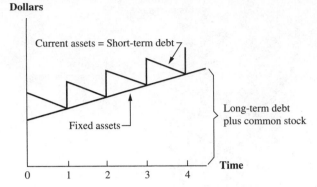

In an ideal world, net working capital is always zero because
short-term assets are financed by short-term debt.

Figure 26.6
The total asset
requirement over
time

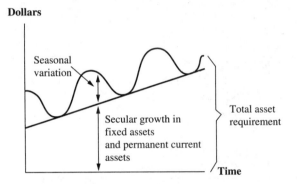

depicted in Figure 26.6. (We have not tried to show the unpredictable day-to-day and
month-to-month variations in the total asset requirement.)

Now, let us look at how this asset requirement is financed. First, consider the
strategy (strategy F in Figure 26.7) where long-term financing covers more than the
total asset requirement, even at seasonal peaks. The firm will have excess cash
available for investment in marketable securities when the total asset requirement falls
from peaks. Because this approach implies chronic short-term cash surpluses and a
large investment in net working capital, it is considered a flexible strategy.

When long-term financing does not cover the total asset requirement, the firm
must borrow short-term to make up the deficit. This restrictive strategy is labelled
strategy R in Figure 26.7.

Which Is Better?

Which is the more appropriate amount of short-term borrowing? There is no definitive
answer. Several considerations must be included in a proper analysis:

1. *Cash reserves.* The flexible financing strategy implies surplus cash and little
   short-term borrowing. This strategy reduces the probability that a firm will

Figure 26.7
Alternative
asset-financing
policies

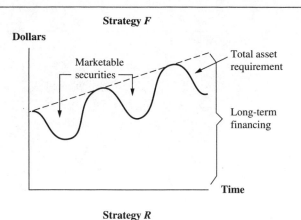

Strategy F

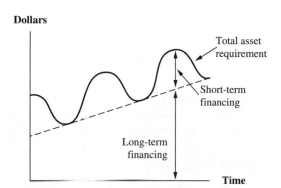

Strategy R

Strategy *F* always implies a short-term cash surplus and a
large investment in cash and marketable securities.
Strategy *R* uses long-term financing for secular asset
requirements only, and short-term borrowing for seasonal
variations.

experience financial distress. Firms may not need to worry as much about
meeting recurring, short-run obligations. However, investments in cash and
marketable securities are zero–net-present-value investments at best.

2. *Maturity hedging.* Most firms finance inventories with short-term bank
   loans, but pay for fixed assets with long-term financing. Firms tend to avoid
   financing long-lived assets with short-term borrowing. This type of maturity
   mismatching would necessitate frequent refinancing and is inherently risky
   because short-term interest rates are more volatile than longer rates.

   Maturity mismatching also produces rollover risk, the risk that renewed
   short-term financing may not be available. A recent example is the financial
   distress faced in 1992 by Olympia & York (O&Y), a real estate
   development firm privately owned by the Reichmann family of Toronto.
   O&Y's main assets were office towers including First Canadian Place in
   Toronto and Canary Wharf outside London, England. Financing for these
   long-term assets was short-term bank loans and commercial paper. In early

Table 26.3		1989	1984	1979
Current assets and current liabilities as percentages of total assets for Canadian firms, 1979–1989	**Current assets:**			
	Cash and marketable securities	5.0%	6.5%	7.2%
	Accounts receivable	14.8	16.9	19.3
	Inventory	15.1	20.2	23.7
	Other	1.1	0.8	0.8
	Total current assets	36.0%	44.4%	51.0%
	Current liabilities:			
	Short-term debt	8.1%	6.6%	7.0%
	Accounts payable	13.8	16.7	18.4
	Income tax payable	0.6	1.2	1.9
	Current portion of long-term debt	0.7	0.7	0.6
	Other	1.1	1.1	1.4
	Total current liabilities	24.3%	26.3%	29.3%

Source: *Industrial Corporations Financial Statistics* (Ottawa: Statistics Canada, 1992). Used with permission.

1992, investor fears about real estate prospects prevented O&Y from rolling over its commercial paper. The crisis pushed O&Y into financial distress and eventually into bankruptcy.

3. *Term structure.* Short-term interest rates are normally lower than long-term interest rates. This implies that, on average, it is more costly to rely on long-term borrowing than on short-term borrowing.

Current Assets and Liabilities in Practice

Table 26.3 shows that current assets made up 36 percent of all assets for Canadian industrial firms in 1989. Short-term financial management deals with a significant portion of the balance sheet for this sample of large firms. For small firms, especially in the retailing and service sectors, current assets make up an even larger portion of total assets.

The table also reveals a decrease in current assets over the 1980s. This suggests that Canadian firms are now managing current assets more closely. In the language of the previous section (as illustrated in Figures 26.4 through 26.7), Canadian industrial firms are moving away from flexible policies and toward a more restrictive approach to current assets. One important reason is that management is applying new techniques such as just-in-time inventory and on-line cash management.

Current liabilities are also declining as a percentage of total assets according to Table 26.3. Firms are practicing maturity hedging as they match lower current liabilities with decreased current assets. In addition to these differences over time, there are differences between industries in policies on current assets and liabilities.

The cash cycle is longer in some industries than in others, while various products and industry practices require different levels of inventory and receivables. This is why we saw in Chapter 2 that industry average ratios are not the same. For example, the aircraft industry carries more than five times as much inventory as printing and publishing carries. Does this mean that aircraft manufacturers are less efficient? Most likely the higher inventory consists of airplanes under construction. Because building planes takes more time than most printing processes, it makes sense that aircraft manufacturers carry higher inventories than printing and publishing firms.

- What keeps the real world from being an ideal one where net working capital can always be zero?
- What considerations determine the optimal compromise between flexible and restrictive net working capital policies?

Cash Budgeting 26.5

The **cash budget** is a primary tool of short-run financial planning. It allows the financial manager to identify short-term financing needs (and opportunities). It will tell the manager the required borrowing in the short term. It is a way of identifying the cash flow gap on the cash flow time line. The idea of the cash budget is simple: It records estimates of cash receipts and disbursements. We illustrate cash budgeting with the following example of Fun Toys.

■ *Example*

All of Fun Toys' cash inflows come from the sale of toys. Cash budgeting for Fun Toys starts with a sales forecast for the next year, by quarter:

	Quarter			
	First	Second	Third	Fourth
Sales (in $ millions)	$100	$200	$150	$100

Fun Toys' fiscal year starts on July 1. Fun Toys' sales are seasonal and are usually very high in the second quarter, due to Christmas sales. But Fun Toys sells to department stores on credit, and sales do not generate cash immediately. Instead, cash comes later from collections on accounts receivable. Fun Toys has a 90-day collection period, and 100 percent of sales are collected the following quarter. In other words,

Collections = Last quarter's sales

This relationship implies that

$$\text{Accounts receivable at end of last quarter} = \text{Last quarter's sales} \tag{26.5}$$

We assume that sales in the fourth quarter of the previous fiscal year were $100 million. From equation (26.5), we know that accounts receivable at the end of the fourth quarter of the previous fiscal year were $100 million and collections in the first quarter of the current fiscal year are $100 million.

The first quarter sales of the current fiscal year of $100 million are added to the accounts receivable, but $100 million of collections are subtracted. Therefore, Fun Toys ended the first quarter with accounts receivable of $100 million. The basic relation is

$$\text{Ending accounts receivable} = \text{Starting accounts receivable} + \text{Sales} - \text{Collections}$$

Table 26.4
Sources of cash (in
$ millions)

	Quarter			
	First	Second	Third	Fourth
Sales	$100	$200	$150	$100
Cash collections	100	100	200	150
Starting receivables	100	100	200	150
Ending receivables	100	200	150	100

Table 26.5
Disbursement of
cash (in $ millions)

	Quarter			
	First	Second	Third	Fourth
Sales	$100	$200	$150	$100
Purchases	100	75	50	50
Uses of cash				
Payments of accounts payable	50	100	75	50
Wages, taxes, and other expenses	20	40	30	20
Capital expenditures	0	0	0	100
Long-term financing expenses: interest and dividends	10	10	10	10
Total uses of cash	80	150	115	180

Table 26.4 shows cash collections for Fun Toys for the next four quarters. Though collections are the only source of cash here, this need not always be the case. Other sources of cash could include sales of assets, investment income, and long-term financing. ∎

Cash Outflow

Next, we consider the cash disbursements. They can be put into four basic categories, as shown in Table 26.5.

1. *Payments of accounts payable.* These are payments for goods or services, such as raw materials. These payments will generally be made after purchases. Purchases will depend on the sales forecast. In the case of Fun Toys, assume that

   Payments = Last quarter's purchases
   Purchases = 1 / 2 of next quarter's sales forecast

2. *Wages, taxes, and other expenses.* This category includes all other normal costs of doing business that require actual expenditures. Depreciation, for example, is often thought of as a normal cost of business, but it requires no cash outflow.

3. *Capital expenditures.* These are payments of cash for long-lived assets. Fun Toys plans a major capital expenditure in the fourth quarter.

		Quarter			
	First	Second	Third	Fourth	
Total cash receipts	$100	$100	$200	$150	
Total cash disbursements	80	150	115	180	
Net cash flow	20	(50)	85	(30)	
Cumulative excess cash balance	20	(30)	55	25	
Minimum cash balance	5	5	5	5	
Cumulative finance surplus (deficit) requirement	15	(35)	50	20	

Table 26.6
The cash balance
(in $ millions)

4. *Long-term financing.* This category includes interest and principal payments on long-term outstanding debt and dividend payments to shareholders.

The total forecasted outflow appears in the last line of Table 26.5.

The Cash Balance

The net cash balance appears in Table 26.6, and a large net cash outflow is forecast in the second quarter. This large outflow is not caused by an inability to earn a profit. Rather, it results from delayed collections on sales. This results in a cumulative cash shortfall of $30 million in the second quarter.

Fun Toys had established a minimum operating cash balance equal to $5 million to facilitate transactions and to protect against unexpected contingencies. This means that it has a cash shortfall in the second quarter equal to $35 million.

CONCEPT QUESTIONS

■ How would you conduct a sensitivity analysis for Fun Toys' net cash balance?

■ What could you learn from such an analysis?

The Short-Term Financial Plan   26.6

Short-Term Planning and Risk

The short-term financial plan represents Fun Toys' "best guess" for the future. Large firms go beyond the "best guess" to ask "what if" questions using scenario analysis, sensitivity analysis, and simulation. We introduced these techniques in Chapter 8's discussion of project analysis. They are tools for assessing the degree of forecasting risk and identifying those components that are most critical to a financial plan's success or failure.

Recall that scenario analysis involves varying the base case plan to create several others: a best case, worst case, and so on. Each will produce different financing needs to give the financial manager a first look at risk.

Sensitivity analysis is a variation on scenario analysis that is useful in pinpointing areas where forecasting risk is especially severe. The basic idea of sensitivity analysis is to freeze all variables except one and then see how sensitive our estimate of financing needs is to changes in that one variable. If our projected financing turns out to be very sensitive to, say, sales, then we know that extra effort in refining the sales forecast will pay off.

Since the original financial plan was almost surely developed on a computer spreadsheet, scenario and sensitivity analysis are quite straightforward and widely used.

Simulation analysis combines features of scenario and sensitivity analysis, varying all variables over a range of outcomes simultaneously. Simulation analysis yields a probability distribution of financing needs.

Air Canada uses simulation analysis in forecasting its cash needs. The simulation is useful in capturing the variability of cash flow components in Canada's airline industry. Bad weather, for example, causes delays and cancelled flights with unpredictable dislocation payments to travellers and crew overtime. This and other risks are reflected in a probability distribution of cash needs, giving the treasurer better information for planning borrowing needs.

Short-Term Borrowing

Fun Toys has a short-term financing problem. It cannot meet the forecast cash outflows in the second quarter from internal sources. Its financing options include (1) unsecured bank borrowing, (2) secured borrowing, and (3) other sources.

Operating Loans

The most common way to finance a temporary cash deficit is to arrange a short-term, **operating loan** from a chartered bank. This is an agreement under which a firm is authorized to borrow up to a specified amount for a given period, usually one year (much like a credit card)[6] Operating loans can be either unsecured or secured by collateral. Large corporations with excellent credit ratings usually structure the facility as an unsecured line of credit. Because unsecured credit lines are backed only by projections of future cash flows, bankers offer this "cash flow" lending only to top-drawer credits.

Short-term lines of credit are classified as either *committed* or *noncommitted*. The latter is an informal arrangement. Committed lines of credit are more formal, legal arrangements and usually involve a commitment fee paid by the firm to the bank. (Usually the fee is on the order of 0.25 percent of the total committed funds per year.) A firm that pays a commitment fee for a committed line of credit is essentially buying insurance to guarantee that the bank cannot back out of the arrangement (absent some material change in the borrower's status).

---

[6]Descriptions of bank loans draw on L. Wynant and J. Hatch, *Banks and Small Business Borrowers* (London: University of Western Ontario, 1990).

Factor	Percentage of mentions
1. Economic environment	
Opportunities and risks	6.1%
2. Industry environment	
Competitive conditions, prospects, and risks	40.4
3. Client's marketing activities	
Strategies, strengths, and weaknesses	30.8
4. Firm's operations management	
Strengths and weaknesses	59.5
5. Client's financial resources, skills, and performance	
Financial management expertise	44.9
Historical or future profitability	84.8
Future cash flows	41.6
Future financing needs (beyond the current year)	20.5
6. Management capabilities and character	
Strengths and weaknesses	79.6
Length of ownership of the firm	95.1
Past management experience relevant to the business	57.1
7. Collateral security and the firm's net worth position	97.7
8. Borrower's past relationship with bank	65.3

Table 26.7

Factors mentioned in the credit files (1, 539 cases)

Source: Larry Wynant and James Hatch, *Banks and Small Business Borrowers* (London: University of Western Ontario, 1990), p. 136.

Compensating the Bank   The interest rate on an operating loan is typically set equal to the bank's prime lending rate plus an additional percentage, and the rate will usually float. For example, suppose that the prime rate is 7 percent when the loan is initiated and the loan is at prime plus 1.5 percent. The original rate charged the borrower is 8.5 percent. If after, say, 125 days, prime increases to 7.5 percent, the company's borrowing rate goes up to 9 percent and interest charges are adjusted accordingly.

The premium charged over prime will reflect the banker's assessment of the borrower's risk. Table 26.7 lists factors bankers use in assessing risk in loans to small business. Notice that risks related to management appear most often since poor management is considered the major risk with small business. There is a trend among bankers to look more closely at industry and economic risk factors. A similar set of risk factors applies to loans to large corporations.

Banks are in the business of lending mainly to low-risk borrowers. For this reason, bankers generally prefer to decline risky business loans that would require an interest rate above prime plus 3 percent. Many of the loan requests that banks turn down are from small businesses, especially start-ups. Around 60 percent of these "turn-downs" find financing elsewhere. Federal government agencies that assist small business include the Federal Business Development Bank and the Small Businesses Loans Act Program. The Atlantic Canada Opportunities Agency (ACOA) and the Western Economic Development Program are federal programs that assist businesses in their regions. Provincial programs also exist.

In addition to charging interest, banks also levy fees for account activity and loan management. Small businesses may also pay application fees to cover the costs of

Table 26.8
Loan conditions
for approved bank
credits in the credit
file sample (1,382
cases)

Condition	Percentage of cases*
Postponement of shareholder claims	39.8%
Life insurance on key principals	39.4
Fire insurance on company premises	35.7
Accounts receivable and inventory reporting	27.8
Limits on withdrawals and dividends	11.9
Limits on capital expenditures	10.5
Maintenance of minimum working capital levels	2.9
Restrictions on further debt	2.5
Restrictions on disposal of company assets	1.7
Maintenance of minimum cash balances	0.9
Other conditions	6.2

*Adds to more than 100 percent because of multiple responses.
Source: Larry Wynant and James Hatch, *Banks and Small Business Borrowers*
(London: University of Western Ontario, 1990), p. 173.

processing loan applications. Fees are becoming increasingly important in bank compensation.[7] Fees and other details of any short-term business lending arrangements are highly negotiable. Banks will generally work with firms to design a package of fees and interest.

Letters of Credit

A **letter of credit** is a common arrangement in international finance. With a letter of credit, the bank issuing the letter promises to make a loan if certain conditions are met. Typically, the letter guarantees payment on a shipment of goods provided that the goods arrive as promised. A letter of credit can be revocable (subject to cancellation) or irrevocable (not subject to cancellation if the specified conditions are met).

Secured Loans

Banks and other financial institutions often require *security* for a loan. Security for short-term loans usually consists of accounts receivable or inventories. Table 26.7 shows that collateral security is a factor in virtually every small business loan. In addition, banks routinely limit risk through loan conditions called **covenants.** Table 26.8 lists common covenants in Canadian small business loans. You can see that bankers expect to have a detailed knowledge of their clients' businesses.

Under **accounts receivable financing,** receivables are either *assigned* or *factored.* Under assignment, the lender not only has a lien on the receivables but also has recourse to the borrower. Factoring involves the sale of accounts receivable. The

---

[7]U.S. banks sometimes require that the firm keep some account of money on deposit. This is called a **compensating balance.** A compensating balance is some of the firm's money kept by the bank in low-interest or non–interest-bearing accounts. By leaving these funds with the bank and receiving no interest, the firm further increases the effective interest rate earned by the bank on the line of credit, thereby compensating the bank.

purchaser, who is called a *factor,* must then collect on the receivables. The factor assumes the full risk of default on bad accounts.

Financial engineers have come up with a new approach to receivables financing. When a large corporation like Sears Canada, Ltd., *securitized* receivables, it sold them to Sears Canada Receivables Trust (SCRT), a wholly owned subsidiary. SCRT issued debentures and commercial paper backed by a diversified portfolio of receivables. Since receivables are liquid, SCRT debt is less risky than lending to Sears Canada and the company hopes to benefit through interest savings.[8]

As the name implies, an **inventory loan** uses inventory as collateral. Some common types of inventory loans are

1. *Blanket inventory lien.* The blanket inventory lien gives the lender a lien against all the borrower's inventories.
2. *Trust receipt.* Under this arrangement, the borrower holds the inventory in trust for the lender. The document acknowledging the loan is called the *trust receipt.* Proceeds from the sale of inventory are remitted immediately to the lender.
3. *Field warehouse financing.* In field warehouse financing, a public warehouse company supervises the inventory for the lender.

When a firm purchases supplies on credit, the increase in accounts payable is a source of funds and automatic financing. As compared with bank financing, **trade credit** has the advantage of arising automatically from the firm's business. It does not require a formal financing agreement with covenants that may restrict the borrower's business activities. Suppliers offer credit to remain competitive; in many industries, the terms of credit include a cash discount for paying within a certain period.

Other Sources

There are a variety of other sources of short-term funds employed by corporations. The most important of these are the issuance of **commercial paper** and financing through **banker's acceptances.**

Commercial paper consists of short-term notes issued by large and highly rated firms. Firms issuing commercial paper in Canada generally have borrowing needs over $20 million. Rating agencies, the Dominion Bond Rating Service, and the Canadian Bond Rating Service discussed in Chapter 20 rate commercial paper similarly to bonds. Typically, these notes are of short maturity, ranging from 30 to 90 days with some maturities up to 365 days. Commercial paper is offered in denominations of $100,000 and up. Because the firm issues paper directly and because it usually backs the issue with a special bank line of credit, the interest rate the firm obtains is below the rate a bank would charge for a direct loan (usually by around 1 percent). Another advantage is that commercial paper offers the issuer flexibility in tailoring the maturity and size of the borrowing.

---

[8]M. Evans, "Sears Securitizes Some of Its Assets," *Financial Post* (November 19, 1991).

Banker's acceptances are a variant on commercial paper. When a bank "accepts" paper, it charges a stamping fee in return for a guarantee of the paper's principal and interest. Stamping fees vary from .20 percent to .75 percent. Banker's acceptances are more widely used than commercial paper in Canada because Canadian chartered banks enjoy stronger credit ratings than all but the largest corporations.[9] The main buyers of banker's acceptances and commercial paper are institutions including mutual funds, insurance companies, and banks.[10]

A disadvantage of borrowing through banker's acceptances or commercial paper is the risk that the market might temporarily dry up when it comes time to "roll over" the paper.

CONCEPT QUESTIONS

- What are the two basic forms of short-term financing?
- Describe two types of secured loans.

26.7   **Summary and Conclusions**

1. This chapter introduces the management of short-term finance. Short-term finance involves short-lived assets and liabilities. We trace and examine the short-term sources and uses of cash as they appear on the firm's financial statements. We see how current assets and current liabilities arise in the short-term operating activities and the cash cycle of the firm. From an accounting perspective, short-term finance involves net working capital.

2. Managing short-term cash flows involves the minimization of costs. The two major costs are carrying costs (the interest and related costs incurred by overinvesting in short-term assets such as cash) and shortage costs (the cost of running out of short-term assets). The objective of managing short-term finance and of short-term financial planning is to find the optimal trade-off between these two costs.

3. In an ideal economy, the firm could perfectly predict its short-term uses and sources of cash, and net working capital could be kept at zero. In the real world, net working capital provides a buffer that lets the firm meet its ongoing obligations. The financial manager seeks the optimal level of each of the current assets.

4. The financial manager can use the cash budget to identify short-term financial needs. The cash budget tells the manager what borrowing is required or what lending will be possible in the short run. The firm has available to it a number of possible ways of acquiring funds to meet short-term shortfalls, including unsecured and secured loans.

---

[9]The reverse situation prevails in the United States.

[10]Our discussion of commercial paper and banker's acceptances draws on "The Canadian Commercial Paper Market: Myth and Reality," *Canadian Treasury Management Review* (March–April 1991), and D. Hogarth, "Quick Money Peps Poor Balance Sheets," *Financial Post* (December 17, 1990).

Key Terms

Liquidity 744	Operating loan 760
Short-run operating activities 748	Letter of credit 762
Cash flow time line 748	Covenant 762
Operating cycle 748	Accounts receivable financing 762
Cash cycle 748	Inventory loan 763
Carrying costs 751	Trade credit 763
Shortage costs 751	Commercial paper 763
Cash budget 757	Banker's acceptance 763

Suggested Readings

Books that describe working capital management include:

G. W. Gallinger and P. B. Healey. *Liquidity Analysis and Management.* Reading, Mass.: Addison-Wesley, 1987.

N. C. Hill and W. L. Sartoris. *Short-Term Financial Management.* New York: Macmillan, 1988.

J. G. Kahl and K. Parkinson. *Current Asset Management: Cash, Credit and Inventory.* New York: John Wiley & Sons, 1984.

J. Vander Weide and S. F. Maier. *Managing Corporate Liquidity: An Introduction to Working Capital Management.* New York: John Wiley & Sons, 1985.

Questions and Problems

Tracing Cash

26.1 Indicate whether the following corporate actions increase, decrease, or cause no change to cash.
   a. Cash is paid for raw materials purchased for inventory.
   b. A dividend is paid.
   c. Merchandise is sold on credit.
   d. Common stock is issued.
   e. Raw material is purchased for inventory on credit.
   f. A piece of machinery is purchased and paid for with long-term debt.
   g. Payments for previous sales are collected.
   h. Accumulated depreciation is increased.
   i. Merchandise is sold for cash.
   j. Payment is made for a previous purchase.
   k. A short-term bank loan is received.
   l. A dividend is paid with funds received from a sale of common stock.

    m. Allowance for bad debts is decreased.

    n. A piece of office equipment is purchased and paid for with a short-term note.

    o. Marketable securities are purchased with retained earnings.

    p. Last year's taxes are paid.

    q. This year's tax liability is increased.

    r. Interest on long-term debt is paid.

26.2 Below are the 19X6 balance sheet and income statement for Country Kettles, Inc. Use this information to construct a sources and uses of cash statement.

COUNTRY KETTLES, INC.
Balance Sheet
December 31, 19X6

	19X6	19X5
Assets		
Cash	$ 42,000	$ 35,000
Accounts receivable	94,250	84,500
Inventory	78,750	75,000
Property, plant, equipment	181,475	168,750
Less: Accumulated depreciation	61,475	56,250
Total assets	$335,000	$307,000
Liabilities and Equity		
Accounts payable	$ 60,500	$ 55,000
Accrued expenses	5,150	8,450
Long-term debt	15,000	30,000
Common stock	28,000	25,000
Retained earnings	226,350	188,550
Total liabilities and equity	$335,000	$307,000

COUNTRY KETTLES, INC.
Income Statement
19X6

Net sales	$765,000
Cost of goods sold	459,000
Sales, general, and administrative costs	91,800
Advertising	26,775
Rent	45,000
Depreciation	5,225
Profit before taxes	137,200
Taxes	68,600
Net profit	$ 68,600
Dividends	$ 30,800
Retained earnings	$ 37,800

26.3 The 19X6 balance sheet and income statement for the S/B Corporation follow. Use them to construct a sources and uses of cash statement.

S/B CORPORATION
Balance Sheet
December 31, 19X6
(in $ thousands)

	19X6	19X5
Assets		
Cash	$ 388	$ 375
Accounts receivable	1,470	1,219
Inventories	2,663	2,777
Net fixed assets	9,314	9,225
Total assets	$13,835	$13,596
Liabilities and Equity		
Accounts payable	$ 282	$ 259
Bank loan payable	1,300	924
Taxes payable	(33)	99
Accrued expenses payable	95	106
Mortgage	4,000	4,000
Common stock	4,000	4,000
Retained earnings	4,191	4,208
Total liabilities and equity	$13,835	$13,596

S/B CORPORATION
Income Statement
19X6
(in $ thousands)

Net sales	$1,030
Cost of goods sold:	
Materials	652
Overhead	64
Depreciation	50
Gross profit	264
Selling and administrative costs	98
Profit before taxes	166
Taxes	83
Net profit	$ 83
Dividends paid	$ 100

The Operating Cycle and Cost Cycle

26.4 Define:
   a. Operating cycle.
   b. Cash cycle.
   c. Accounts payable period.

26.5 Indicate whether the following company actions increase, decrease, or cause no change to the cash cycle and the operating cycle.
   a. The use of discounts offered by suppliers is decreased.
   b. More finished goods are being produced for order instead of for inventory.
   c. A greater percentage of raw materials purchases is paid for with cash.

    d. The terms of discounts offered to customers are made more favourable for the customers.

    e. A larger than usual amount of raw materials is purchased as a result of a price decline.

    f. An increased number of customers pays with cash instead of credit.

Short-Term Financial Policy

26.6 *a.* Define flexible short-term financing.
      b. Define restrictive short-term financing.
      c. When is flexible short-term financing optimal?
      d. When is restrictive short-term financing optimal?

26.7 What are the costs of shortages? Describe them.

26.8 NWT Compressor and St. John's Pneumatic are competing manufacturing firms. Their financial statements are printed below.

NWT COMPRESSOR
Balance Sheet
December 31, 19X2

	19X2	19X1
Assets		
Cash	$ 13,862	$ 16,339
Net accounts receivable	23,887	25,778
Inventory	54,867	43,287
Total current assets	92,616	85,404
Fixed assets:		
Plant, property, and equipment	101,543	99,615
Less: Accumulated depreciation	34,331	31,957
Net fixed assets	$ 67,212	$ 67,658
Prepaid expenses	1,914	1,791
Other assets	13,052	13,138
Total assets	$174,794	$167,991
Liabilities and Equity		
Current liabilities:		
Accounts payable	$ 6,494	$ 4,893
Notes payable	10,483	11,617
Accrued expenses	7,422	7,227
Other taxes payable	9,924	8,460
Total current liabilities	34,323	32,197
Long-term debt	22,036	22,036
Total liabilities	56,359	54,233
Equity:		
Common stock	38,000	38,000
Paid-in capital	12,000	12,000
Retained earnings	68,435	63,758
Total equity	118,435	113,758
Total liabilities and equity	$174,794	$167,991

NWT COMPRESSOR
Income Statement
19X2

Income:	
Sales	$162,749
Other income	1,002
Total income	163,751
Operating expenses:	
Cost of goods sold	103,570
Selling and administrative expenses	28,495
Depreciation	2,274
Total expenses	134,339
Pretax earnings	29,412
Taxes	14,890
Net earnings	$ 14,522
Dividends	$ 9,845
Retained earnings	$ 4,677

ST. JOHN'S PNEUMATIC
Balance Sheet
December 31, 19X2

	19X2	19X1
Assets		
Cash	$ 5,794	$ 3,307
Net accounts receivable	26,177	22,133
Inventory	46,463	44,661
Total current assets	78,434	70,101
Fixed assets:		
Plant, property, and equipment	31,842	31,116
Less: Accumulated depreciation	19,297	18,143
Net fixed assets	12,545	12,973
Prepaid expenses	763	688
Other assets	1,601	1,385
Total assets	$93,343	$85,147
Liabilities and Equity		
Current liabilities:		
Accounts payable	$ 6,008	$ 5,019
Bank loans	3,722	645
Accrued expenses	4,254	3,295
Other taxes payable	5,688	4,951
Total current liabilities	19,672	13,910
Equity:		
Common stock	20,576	20,576
Paid-in capital	5,624	5,624
Retained earnings	48,598	46,164
Less: Treasury stock	1,127	1,127
Total equity	73,671	71,237
Total liabilities and equity	$93,343	$85,147

ST. JOHN'S PNEUMATIC
Income Statement
19X2

Income:	
Sales	$91,374
Other income	1,067
Total income......................................	92,441
Operating expenses:	
Cost of goods sold	59,042
Selling and administrative expenses	18,068
Depreciation	1,154
Total expenses....................................	78,264
Pretax earnings..	14,177
Taxes...	6,838
Net earnings	$ 7,339
Dividends	$ 4,905
Retained earnings	$ 2,434

    a. How are the current assets of each firm financed?

    b. Which firm has the larger investment in current assets? Why?

    c. Which firm is more likely to incur carrying costs, and which is more likely to incur shortage costs? Why?

26.9 In an ideal economy, net working capital is always zero. Why might net working capital be greater than zero in the real world?

The Cash Budget

26.10 The following is the sales budget for the Smithe and Wreston Company for the first quarter of 19X1.

	January	February	March
Sales budget	$90,000	$100,000	$120,000

The aging of credit sales is

Thirty percent collected in the month of sale.

Forty percent collected in the month after sale.

The accounts receivable balance at the end of the previous quarter is $36,000. Of that amount, $30,000 is uncollected December sales.

    a. Compute the sales for December.

    b. Compute the cash collections from sales for each month from January through March.

26.11 Here are some important figures from the budget of the Pine Mulch Company for the second quarter of 19X5.

	April	May	June
Credit sales	$160,000	$140,000	$192,000
Credit purchases	68,000	64,000	80,000
Cash disbursements:			
Wages, taxes, and expenses	8,000	7,000	8,400
Interest	3,000	3,000	3,000
Equipment purchases	50,000		4,000

The company predicts that 10 percent of its sales will never be collected; 50 percent of its sales will be collected in the month of the sale; the rest of its sales will be collected in the following month. Purchases on trade accounts will be paid in the month following the purchase. In March 19X2 the sales were $180,000.

Use this information to complete the following cash budget:

	April	May	June
Beginning cash balance	$200,000		
Cash receipts:			
Cash collections from credit sales			
Total cash available			
Cash disbursements:			
Pay credit purchases	$65,000		
Wages, taxes, and expenses			
Interest			
Equipment purchases			
Total cash disbursed			
Ending cash balance			

The typical large Canadian corporation holds around 3 percent of its assets in highly liquid form—just over 1 percent in cash and the rest in marketable securities.[1] Since cash earns no interest, why would a corporation hold cash? It would seem more sensible to put cash into marketable securities, such as Treasury bills, to earn some investment income. Of course, one reason Canadian companies hold cash is to pay for goods and services. They might prefer to pay their employees in Canada Treasury bills, but the minimum denomination of Treasury bills is $10,000! The firm must use cash because cash is more divisible than Treasury bills.[2]

This chapter is about how firms manage cash. The basic objective in cash management is to keep the investment in cash as low as possible while still operating the firm's activities efficiently and effectively. The chapter separates cash management into three steps:

1. Determining the appropriate target cash balance.
2. Collecting and disbursing cash efficiently.
3. Investing excess cash in marketable securities.

Determining the appropriate target cash balance involves an assessment of the trade-off between the benefit and cost of liquidity. The benefit of holding cash is the convenience in liquidity it gives the firm. The cost of holding cash is the interest income that the firm could have received from investing in Treasury bills and other marketable securities. If the firm has achieved its target cash balance, the value it gets from the liquidity provided by its cash will be exactly equal to the value forgone in interest on an equivalent holding of Treasury bills. In other words, a firm should increase its holding of cash until the net present value from doing so is zero. The incremental liquidity value of cash should decline as more of it is held.

After the optimal amount of liquidity is determined, the firm must establish procedures so that cash is collected and disbursed as efficiently as possible.

Firms must invest temporarily idle cash in short-term marketable securities. These securities can be bought and sold in the *money market.* Money market securities have very little risk of default and are highly marketable.

---

[1] *Industrial Corporations Financial Statistics* (Ottawa: Statistics Canada, 1990). Figures are for industrial firms with assets over $10 million.

[2] Cash is liquid. One property of liquidity is divisibility, that is, how easily an asset can be divided into parts.

27.1 Reasons for Holding Cash

John Maynard Keynes, in his great work, *The General Theory of Employment, Interest and Money,* identified three reasons why liquidity is important: the precautionary motive, the speculative motive, and the transactions motive.

The **speculative motive** is the need to hold cash in order to be able to take advantage of bargain purchases that might arise, attractive interest rates, and (in the case of international firms) favourable exchange rate fluctuations. For most firms, reserve borrowing ability and marketable securities can be used to satisfy speculative motives. Thus, for a modern firm, there might be a speculative motive for liquidity, but not necessarily for cash per se.

This is also true, to a lesser extent, for precautionary motives. The **precautionary motive** is the need for a safety supply to act as a financial reserve. Once again, there probably is a precautionary motive for liquidity. However, given that the value of money market instruments is relatively certain and that instruments such as T-bills are extremely liquid, there is no real need to hold substantial amounts of cash for precautionary purposes.

Cash is needed to satisfy the **transactions motive,** the need to have cash on hand to pay bills. Transaction-related needs come from the normal disbursement and collection activities of the firm. The disbursement of cash includes the payment of wages and salaries, trade debts, taxes, and dividends.

Cash is collected from sales, the selling of assets, and new financing. The cash inflows (*collections*) and outflows (*disbursements*) are not perfectly synchronized, and some level of cash holdings is necessary to serve as a buffer. Perfect liquidity is the characteristic of cash that allows it to satisfy the transactions motive.

As electronic data interchange (EDI) and other high-speed, "paperless" payment mechanisms continue to develop, even the transactions demand for cash may all but disappear. Even if it does, however, there will still be a demand for liquidity and a need to manage it efficiently.

CONCEPT QUESTIONS

- What is the transactions motive, and how does it lead firms to hold cash?
- What is the cost to firms of holding excess cash?

27.2 Determining the Target Cash Balance

The **target cash balance** involves a trade-off between the opportunity costs of holding too much cash and the trading costs of holding too little. Figure 27.1 presents the problem graphically. If a firm tries to keep its cash holdings too low, it will find itself selling marketable securities (and perhaps later buying marketable securities to replace those sold) more frequently than if the cash balance were higher. Thus, trading costs will tend to fall as the cash balance becomes larger. In contrast, the opportunity costs of holding cash rise as the cash holdings rise. At point C^* in Figure 27.1, the sum of both costs, depicted as the total cost curve, is at a minimum. This is the target or optimal cash balance.

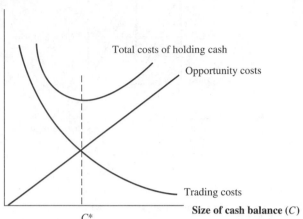

**Cost in dollars
of holding cash**

Total costs of holding cash

Opportunity costs

Trading costs

Size of cash balance (C)

C^*

Figure 27.1
Costs of holding
cash

Trading costs are increased when the firm must sell securities to establish
a cash balance. Opportunity costs are increased when there is a cash
balance because there is no return to cash.
*Optimal size of cash balance.

The Baumol Model

William Baumol was the first to provide a formal model of cash management
incorporating opportunity costs and trading costs.[3] His model can be used to establish
the target cash balance.

Suppose the Golden Socks Corporation began week 0 with a cash balance of $C =$
$1.2 million, and outflows exceed inflows by $600,000 per week. Its cash balance will
drop to zero at the end of week 2, and its average cash balance will be $C/2 = $1.2
million/2 = $600,000 over the two-week period. At the end of week 2, Golden Socks
must replace its cash either by selling marketable securities or by borrowing. Figure
27.2 shows this situation.

If C were set higher (say, at $2.4 million), cash would last four weeks before the
firm would need to sell marketable securities, but the firm's average cash balance
would increase to $1.2 million (from $600,000). If C were set at $600,000, cash would
run out in one week and the firm would need to replenish cash more frequently, but its
average cash balance would fall from $600,000 to $300,000.

Because transactions costs (for example, the brokerage costs of selling marketable
securities) must be incurred whenever cash is replenished, establishing large initial
cash balances will lower the trading costs connected with cash management. However,
the larger the average cash balance, the greater the opportunity cost (the return that
could have been earned on marketable securities).

---

[3]W. S. Baumol, "The Transactions Demand for Cash: An Inventory Theoretic Approach," *Quarterly Journal of Economics*
66 (November 1952).

Figure 27.2
Cash balances for
the Golden Socks
Corporation

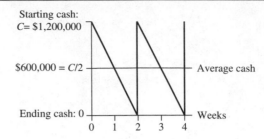

The Golden Socks Corporation begins week 0 with
cash of $1,200,000. The balance drops to zero by the
second week. The average cash balance is $C/2 =$
$1,200,000/2 = $600,000 over the period.

To solve this problem, Golden Socks needs to know three things:

F = The fixed cost of selling securities to replenish cash

T = The total amount of new cash needed for transactions purposes over the
relevant planning period, say, one year

K = The opportunity cost of holding cash (the interest rate on marketable
securities)

With this information, Golden Socks can determine the total costs of any
particular cash balance policy. It can then determine the optimal cash balance policy.

The Opportunity Costs

The total opportunity costs of cash balances, in dollars, must be equal to the average
cash balance multiplied by the interest rate:

Opportunity costs ($) = $(C/2) \times K$

The opportunity costs of various alternatives are given here:

Initial cash balance	Average cash balance	Opportunity costs ($K = 0.10$)
C	$C/2$	$(C/2) \times K$
$4,800,000	$2,400,000	$240,000
2,400,000	1,200,000	120,000
1,200,000	600,000	60,000
600,000	300,000	30,000
300,000	150,000	15,000

The Trading Costs

Total trading costs can be determined by calculating the number of times that Golden
Socks must sell marketable securities during the year. The total amount of cash
disbursement during the year is $600,000 × 52 weeks = $31.2 million. If the initial

cash balance is set at $1.2 million, Golden Socks will sell $1.2 million of marketable securities every two weeks. Thus, trading costs are given by

$$\frac{\$31.2 \text{ million}}{\$1.2 \text{ million}} \times F = 26F$$

The general formula is

Trading costs ($) = $(T/C) \times F$

A schedule of alternative trading costs follows:

Total disbursements during relevant period	Initial cash balance	Trading costs ($F = \$1,000$)
T	C	$(T/C) \times F$
$31,200,000	$4,800,000	$ 6,500
31,200,000	2,400,000	13,000
31,200,000	1,200,000	26,000
31,200,000	600,000	52,000
31,200,000	300,000	104,000

The Total Cost

The total cost of cash balances consists of the opportunity costs plus the trading costs:

Total cost = Opportunity costs + Trading costs
= $(C/2) \times K$ + $(T/C) \times F$

Cash balance	Total cost	=	Opportunity costs	Trading costs
$4,800,000	$246,500		$240,000	$ 6,500
2,400,000	133,000		120,000	13,000
1,200,000	86,000		60,000	26,000
600,000	82,000		30,000	52,000
300,000	119,000		15,000	104,000

The Solution

We can see from the preceding schedule that a $600,000 cash balance results in the lowest total cost ($82,000) of the possibilities presented. But what about $700,000, $500,000, or other possibilities? To determine minimum total costs precisely, Golden Socks must equate the marginal reduction in trading costs as balances rise with the marginal increase in opportunity costs associated with cash balance increases. The target cash balance should be the point where the two offset each other. This can be calculated by using either numerical iteration or calculus.

Recall that the total cost equation is

Total cost (TC) = $(C/2) \times K + (T/C) \times F$

If we differentiate the TC equation with respect to cash balance and set the derivative equal to zero, we will find that

$$\frac{dTC}{dC} = \frac{K}{2} - \frac{TF}{C^2} = 0$$

Marginal total cost	=	Marginal opportunity costs	+	Marginal trading costs[4]

The solution for the general cash balance, C^*, is obtained by solving this equation for C:

$$\left(\frac{K}{2} = \frac{TF}{C^2}\right)$$

$$C^* = \sqrt{2TF/K}$$

If $F = \$1,000$, $T = \$31,200,000$, and $K = 0.10$, then $C^* = \$789,936.71$. Given the value of C^*, opportunity costs are

$$(C^*/2) \times K = \frac{\$789,936.71}{2} \times 0.10 = \$39,496.84$$

Trading costs are

$$(T/C^*) \times F = \frac{\$31,200,000}{\$789,936.71} \times \$1,000 = \$39,496.84$$

Hence, total costs are

$$\$39,496.84 + \$39,496.84 = \$78,993.68$$

Limitations

The Baumol model represents an important contribution to cash management. The limitations of the model include the following:

1. *The model assumes the firm has a constant disbursement rate.* In practice, disbursements can be only partially managed, because due dates differ and costs cannot be predicted with certainty.

2. *The model assumes there are no cash receipts during the projected period.* In fact, most firms experience both cash inflows and outflows on a daily basis.

3. *No safety stock is allowed for.* Firms will probably want to hold a safety stock of cash designed to reduce the possibility of a cash shortage or *cash-out*. However, to the extent that firms can sell marketable securities or borrow in a few hours, the need for a safety stock is minimai.

---

[4]Marginal trading costs are negative because trading costs are *reduced* when C is increased.

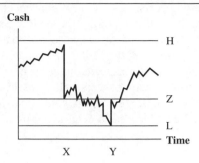

Cash

H

Z

L

Time

X   Y

Figure 27.3
The Miller–Orr
model

H is the upper control limit; *L* is the lower
control limit. The target cash balance is *Z*.
As long as cash is between *L* and *H*, no
transaction is made.

The Baumol model is possibly the simplest and most stripped-down, sensible model for determining the optimal cash position. Its chief weakness is that it assumes discrete, certain cash flows. We next discuss a model designed to deal with uncertainty.

The Miller–Orr Model

Merton Miller and Daniel Orr developed a cash balance model to deal with cash inflows and outflows that fluctuate randomly from day to day.[5] In the Miller–Orr model, both cash inflows and cash outflows are included. The model assumes that the distribution of daily net cash inflows (cash inflow minus cash outflow) is normally distributed. On each day the net cash flow could be the expected value or some higher or lower value. We will assume that the expected net cash flow is zero.

Figure 27.3 shows how the Miller–Orr model works. The model operates in terms of upper (*H*) and lower (*L*) control limits, and a target cash balance (*Z*). The firm allows its cash balance to wander randomly within the lower and upper limits. As long as the cash balance is between *H* and *L*, the firm makes no transaction. When the cash balance reaches *H*, such as at point *X*, then the firm buys $H - Z$ units (or dollars) of marketable securities. This action will decrease the cash balance to *Z*. In the same way, when cash balances fall to *L*, such as at point *Y* (the lower limit), the firm should sell $Z - L$ securities and increase the cash balance to *Z*. In both situations, cash balances return to *Z*. Management sets the lower limit, *L*, depending on how much risk of a cash shortfall the firm is willing to tolerate.

Like the Baumol model, the Miller–Orr model depends on trading costs and opportunity costs. The cost per transaction of buying and selling marketable securities, *F*, is assumed to be fixed. The percentage opportunity cost per period of holding cash, *K*, is the daily interest rate on marketable securities. Unlike the Baumol model, the number of transactions per period is a random variable that varies from period to period, depending on the pattern of cash inflows and outflows.

---

[5]M. H. Miller and D. Orr, "A Model of the Demand for Money by Firms," *Quarterly Journal of Economics* (August 1966).

As a consequence, trading costs per period are dependent on the expected number of transactions in marketable securities during the period. Similarly, the opportunity costs of holding cash are a function of the expected cash balance per period.

Given L, which is set by the firm, the Miller–Orr model solves for the target cash balance (Z), and the upper limit (H). Expected total costs of the cash balance return policy (Z, H) are equal to the sum of expected transactions costs and expected opportunity costs. The values of Z (the return point) and H (the upper limit) that minimize the expected total cost have been determined by Miller and Orr:

$$Z^* = \sqrt[3]{3F\sigma^2/4K} + L$$
$$H^* = 3Z^* - 2L$$

where * denotes optimal values, and σ^2 is the variance of net daily cash flows.

The average cash balance in the Miller–Orr model is

$$\text{Average cash balance} = \frac{4Z - L}{3}$$

■ *Example*

To clarify the Miller–Orr model, suppose that $F = \$1,000$, the interest rate is 10 percent annually, and the standard deviation of daily net cash flows is $2,000. The daily opportunity cost, K, is

$$(1 + K)^{365} - 1.0 = 0.10$$

$$1 + K = \sqrt[365]{1.10} = 1.000261$$

$$K = 0.000261$$

The variance of daily net cash flows is

$$\sigma^2 = (2,000)^2 = 4,000,000$$

Let us assume that $L = 0$:

$$Z^* = \sqrt[3]{(3 \times \$1,000 \times 4,000,000) / (4 \times 0.000261)} + 0$$
$$= \sqrt[3]{\$11,493,900,000,000} = \$22,568$$
$$H^* = 3 \times \$22,568 = \$67,704$$
$$\text{Average cash balance} = \frac{4 \times \$22,568}{3} = \$30,091 \ \blacksquare$$

Implications of the Miller–Orr Model

To use the Miller–Orr model, the manager must do four things:

1. Set the lower control limit for the cash balance. This lower limit can be related to a minimum safety margin decided on by management.
2. Estimate the standard deviation of daily cash flows.
3. Determine the interest rate.
4. Estimate the trading costs of buying and selling marketable securities.

These four steps allow the upper limit and return point to be computed. Miller and Orr tested their model using nine months of data for cash balances for a large industrial firm. The model was able to produce average daily cash balances much lower than the averages actually obtained by the firm.[6]

The Miller–Orr model clarifies the issues of cash management. First, the model shows that the best return point, Z^*, is positively related to trading costs, F, and negatively related to K, the daily interest rate on marketable securities. These relationships are consistent with and analogous to the Baumol model and are useful in explaining the evolution of computerized cash management techniques.

High interest rates (prime rate over 22 percent) in the early 1980s caused the cost of idle cash to skyrocket. In response, large corporations and banks invested in applying computer and communications technologies to cash management. The result was lower trading costs. With systems in place, banks are now able to offer cash management products to smaller customers.

Second, the Miller–Orr model shows that the best return point and the average cash balance are positively related to the variability of cash flows. That is, firms whose cash flows are subject to greater uncertainty should maintain a larger average cash balance.

Third, the Miller–Orr model illustrates the importance of operations research applications in finance. Beyond cash management applications, control models have been applied to evaluate real investment decisions such as firm entry into a new market.[7]

Other Factors Influencing the Target Cash Balance

Borrowing

In our previous examples, the firm obtains cash by selling marketable securities. Another alternative is to borrow cash. Borrowing introduces additional considerations to cash management.

1. Borrowing is likely to be more expensive than selling marketable securities because the interest rate on a loan is likely to be higher than the return on marketable securities.

2. The need to borrow will depend on management's desire to hold low cash balances. A firm is more likely to need to borrow to cover an unexpected cash outflow, the greater its cash flow variability and the lower its investment in marketable securities.

Relative Costs

For large firms, the trading costs of buying and selling securities are very small when compared to the opportunity costs of holding cash. For example, suppose a firm has

---

[6]D. Mullins and R. Hamonoff discuss tests of the Miller–Orr model in "Applications of Inventory Cash Management Models," in *Modern Developments in Financial Management,* ed. S. C. Myers (New York: Praeger, 1976). They show that the model works very well when compared to the actual cash balances of several firms. However, simple rules of thumb do as good a job as the Miller–Orr model.

[7]The models are also useful in analyzing monetary policy; A. H. Chen and S. C. Mazundar, "An Instantaneous Control Model of Bank Reserves and Federal Funds Management," *Journal of Banking and Finance* 16 (December 1992), pp. 1073–95.

$1 million in cash that won't be needed for 24 hours. Should the firm invest the money or leave it sitting?

Suppose the firm can invest the money overnight at the call money rate. To do this the treasurer arranges through a chartered bank to lend funds for 24 hours to an investment dealer. Suppose that the firm can do this at an annualized rate of 7.75 percent per year. The daily rate in this case is about two basis points (.02 percent or .0002).

The daily return earned on $1 million is thus 0.0002 × $1 million = $200. In most cases, the order cost would be much less than this. For example, following up on our earlier point about technology and cash management, large corporations buy and sell securities daily on terminals similar to automated bank machines so they are unlikely to leave substantial amounts of cash idle.

CONCEPT QUESTIONS

- What is a target cash balance?
- What are the strengths and weaknesses of the Baumol model and the Miller–Orr model?

27.3   ## Managing the Collection and Disbursement of Cash

A firm's cash balance as reported in its financial statements (*book cash* or *ledger cash*) is not the same thing as the balance shown in its bank account (*bank cash* or *collected bank cash*). The difference between bank cash and book cash is called **float** and represents the net effect of cheques in the process of collection.

▪ *Example*

Imagine that General Mechanics, Inc. (GMI), currently has $100,000 on deposit with its bank. It purchases some raw materials, paying its vendors with a cheque written on July 8 for $100,000. The company's books (that is, ledger balances) are changed to show the $100,000 reduction in the cash balance. But the firm's bank will not find out about this cheque until it has been deposited at the vendor's bank and has been presented to the firm's bank for payment on, say, July 15. Until the cheque's presentation, the firm's bank cash is greater than its book cash, and it has *positive float.*

Position Prior to July 8:

Float = Firm's bank cash − Firm's book cash
  = $100,000 − $100,000
  = 0

Position from July 8 through July 14:

Disbursement float = Firm's bank cash − Firm's book cash
      = $100,000 − 0
      = $100,000

During the period of time that the cheque is *outstanding,* GMI has a balance with the bank of $100,000. Cheques written by the firm generate *disbursement float,* causing an immediate decrease in book cash but no immediate change in bank cash. ▪

■ *Example*

Imagine that GMI receives a cheque from a customer for $100,000. Assume, as before, that the company has $100,000 deposited at its bank and has a *neutral float position.* It processes the cheque through the bookkeeping department and increases its book balance by $100,000 to $200,000. However, the additional cash is not available to GMI until the cheque is deposited in the firm's bank. This will occur on, say, October 9, the next day. In the meantime, the cash position at GMI will reflect a collection float of $100,000.

Position Prior to November 8:

Float = Firm's bank cash − Firm's book cash
       = $100,000 − $100,000
       = 0

Position from November 8 to November 9:

Collection float = Firm's bank cash − Firm's book cash
                 = $100,000 − $200,000
                 = −$100,000 ■

Cheques received by the firm represent *collection float,* which increases book cash immediately but does not immediately change bank cash. The firm is helped by disbursement float and is hurt by collection float. The sum of disbursement float and collection float is *net float.*

A firm should be more concerned with net float and bank cash than with book cash. If a financial manager knows that a cheque will not clear for several days, he or she will be able to keep a lower cash balance at the bank. Good float management can generate a great deal of money. For example, the average daily sales of Exxon are about $248 million. If Exxon speeds up the collection process or slows down the disbursement process by one day, it frees up $248 million, which can be invested in marketable securities. With an interest rate of 10 percent, this represents overnight interest of approximately $68,000 [or ($248 million/365) × $0.10].

Float management involves controlling the collection and disbursement of cash. The objective in cash collection is to reduce the lag between the time customers pay their bills and the time the cheques are collected. The objective in cash disbursement is to slow down payments, thereby increasing the time between when cheques are written and when cheques are presented. Of course, to the extent that the firm succeeds in doing this, the customers and suppliers lose money, and the trade-off is the effect on the firm's relationship with them.

Collection float can be broken down into three parts: mail float, in-house processing float, and availability float:

1. *Mail float* is the time during which cheques are trapped in the postal system.
2. *In-house processing float* is the time it takes the receiver of a cheque to process the payment and deposit it in a bank for collection.
3. *Availability float* refers to the time required to clear a cheque through the banking system. In the Canadian banking system, availability float cannot exceed one day and is often zero, so this is the least important part.

■ *Example*

A cheque for $1,000 is mailed by a customer on Monday, September 1. Because of mail, processing, and clearing delays, it is not credited as available cash in the firm's bank until the following Monday, seven days later. The float for this cheque is

Float = $1,000 × 7 days = $7,000

Another cheque for $7,000 is mailed on September 1. It is available on the next day. The float for this cheque is

Float = $7,000 × 1 day = $7,000

The measurement of float depends on the time lag and the dollars involved. The cost of float is an opportunity cost, because the cash is unavailable for use during the time cheques are tied up in the collection process. The cost of float can be determined by (1) estimating the average daily receipts, (2) calculating the average delay in obtaining the receipts, and (3) discounting the average daily receipts by the *delay-adjusted cost of capital*. ■

■ *Example*

Suppose that Concepts, Inc., received two items each month:

	Amount	Number of days delay	Float
Item 1	$5,000,000	× 3 =	$15,000,000
Item 2	3,000,000	× 5 =	15,000,000
Total	$8,000,000		$30,000,000

The average daily float over the month is equal to

Average Daily Float:

$$\frac{\text{Total float}}{\text{Total days}} = \frac{\$30,000,000}{30} = \$1,000,000$$

Another procedure that can be used to calculate average daily float is to determine average daily receipts and multiply by the average daily delay.

Average Daily Receipts:

$$\frac{\text{Total receipts}}{\text{Total days}} = \frac{\$8,000,000}{30} = \$266,666.67$$

$$\begin{aligned}\text{Weighted} \\ \text{average delay}\end{aligned} = (5/8) \times 3 + (3/8) \times 5$$

$$= 1.875 + 1.875 = 3.75 \text{ days}$$

$$\begin{aligned}\text{Average} \\ \text{daily float}\end{aligned} = \text{Average daily receipts} \times \text{Weighted average delay}$$

$$= \$266,666.67 \times 3.75 = \$1,000,000$$

■ *Example*

Suppose Concepts, Inc., has average daily receipts of $266,667. The float results in this amount being delayed 3.75 days. The present value of the dealyed cash flow is

$$V = \frac{\$266,667}{1 + r_B}$$

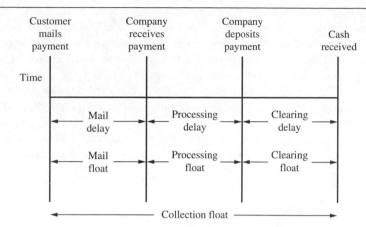

Figure 27.4
The cash collection process

where r_B is the cost of debt capital for Concepts, adjusted to the relevant time frame. Suppose the annual cost of debt capital is 10 percent. Then

$$r_B = 0.1 \times (3.75/365) = 0.00103$$

and

$$V = \frac{\$266,667}{1 + 0.00103} = \$266,392.62$$

Thus, the net present value of the delay float is $266,392.62 − $266,667 = −$274.38 per day. For a year, this is −$274.38 × 365 = −$100,148.70. ∎

Accelerating Collections

Based on our discussion above, we depict the basic parts of the cash collection process in Figure 27.4. The total time in this process is made up of mailing time, cheque-processing time, and the bank's cheque-clearing time. The amount of time that cash spends in each part of the cash collection process depends on where the firm's customers are located and how efficient the firm is at collecting cash.

Coordinating the firm's efforts in all areas is its cash flow information system. Tracking payments through the system and providing the cash manager with up-to-date daily cash balances and investment rates are its key tasks. Chartered banks offer cash information systems that all but put the bank on the manager's desk.[8] Linking the manager's terminal with the bank's on-line, real time system, the system gives the manager access to account balances and transactions plus information on money market rates. It is open $15\frac{1}{2}$ hours a day from 7:30 A.M. through 11 P.M. Toronto time. The system also allows the manager to transfer funds and make money market investments.

---

[8] Our discussion of cash management systems is based on D. W. Rogers, "Work Smart, Not Hard: A Treasurer's Guide to Electronic Banking," *Canadian Treasury Management Review* (January-February 1988), pp. 5–7; and on materials provided by a Big Six chartered bank.

Since it is the corporate equivalent of a bank machine, the cash management system has security features to prevent unauthorized use.[9] Different passwords allow access to each level of authority. For example, a receivables clerk could have access to deposit activity files but not to payroll. Some systems use **smart cards** for security. A smart card looks like a credit card but contains a computer chip that can be programmed to grant access to certain files only. The card must be inserted into an access device attached to a personal computer and provides another safeguard in addition to a password.

We next discuss several techniques used to accelerate collections and reduce collection time: systems to expedite mailing and cheque processing as well as concentration banking.

Over-the-Counter Collections

In an over-the-counter system, customers pay in person at field offices or stores. Most large retailers, utilities, and many other firms receive some payments this way. Because the payments are made at a company location, there is no mail delay. The manager of the field location is responsible for ensuring that cheques and cash collected are deposited promptly and for reporting daily deposit amounts to the head office.

As an alternative to over-the-counter collections, a company may instruct customers to mail cheques to a collection point address on its invoices. By distributing the collection points locally throughout its market area, the company can reduce mail time below what it would take if all payments were mailed to its head office. If the collection points are field offices, the next steps are the same as for over-the-counter collection. A popular alternative, lockboxes, contracts out the collection points to a bank.

Lockboxes

Lockboxes are special post office boxes set up to intercept accounts receivable payments.

Figure 27.5 illustrates a lockbox system. The collection process is started by having business and retail customers mail their cheques to a post office box instead of sending them to the firm. The lockbox is maintained at a local bank branch. Large corporations may maintain a number of lockboxes, one in each significant market area. The location depends on a trade-off between bank fees and savings on mailing time.

In the typical lockbox system, the local bank branch collects the lockbox cheques from the post office daily. The bank deposits the cheques directly to the firm's account. Details of the operation are recorded (in some computer-usable form) and sent to the firm.

A lockbox system reduces mailing time because cheques are received at a nearby post office instead of at corporate headquarters. Lockboxes also reduce the processing time because the corporation does not have to open the envelopes and deposit cheques for collection. In all, a bank lockbox should enable a firm to get its receipts processed, deposited, and cleared faster than if it were to receive cheques at its headquarters and deliver them itself to the bank for deposit and clearing.

---

[9]The bank machine comparison is literally true for commercial (midsized) customers of one bank that allows them to use its bank machines as a lower-cost alternative to direct computer links to the firm's office.

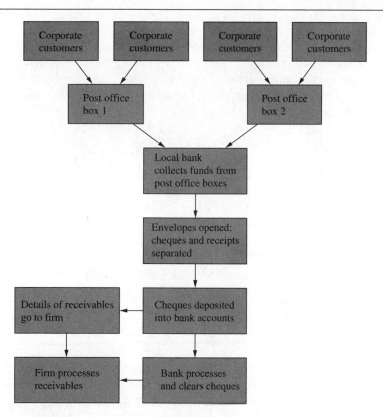

Figure 27.5
Overview of
lockbox processing

The flow starts when a corporate customer mails remittances to a post office box number instead of to the corporation. Several times a day the bank collects the lockbox receipts from the post office. The cheques are then put into the company bank accounts.

Electronic Collection Systems

Over-the-counter and lockbox systems are standard ways to reduce mail and processing float time. They are used by almost all large firms in Canada that can benefit from them. Newer approaches focus on reducing float virtually to zero by replacing cheques with electronic funds transfer. Examples used in Canada include preauthorized payments, point-of-sales transfers, and electronic trade payables. We discuss the first two here and the third later when we look at disbursement systems.[10]

Pre-authorized payments are paperless transfers of contractual or installment payments from the customer's account directly to the firm's. Common applications are mortgage payments and installment payments for insurance, rent, and cable TV. This system eliminates all paperwork in invoices as well as in deposit and reconciliation of

---

[10]These systems are part of the system of electronic data interchange (EDI) in which firms conduct all transactions with suppliers and customers electronically. EDI is at the heart of just-in-time inventory systems used in Canadian manufacturing firms.

cheques. There is no mail or processing float. The system is presently limited mainly to annuity payments, but the technology could handle any payments.

Point-of-sales systems use **debit cards** to transfer funds directly from a customer's bank account to a retailer's. A debit card works like a bank machine (ATM) card with a personal identification number (PIN) for security. Unlike with a credit card, the funds are transferred immediately. Point-of-sales systems are now in use in major centres in Canada.

Cash Concentration

Using lockboxes or other collection systems helps firms collect cheques from customers and rapidly deposit them. But the job is not finished yet since those systems give the firm cash at a number of widely dispersed branches. Until it is concentrated in a central account, the cash is of little use to the firm for paying bills, reducing loans, or investing.

With a **concentration banking** system, sales receipts are processed at field sales offices and bank branches providing lockbox services; they are then deposited locally. Surplus funds are transferred from the various local branches to a single, central concentration account. This process is illustrated in Figure 27.6, where concentration accounts are combined with over-the-counter collection and lockboxes in a total cash management system.

Large firms in Canada may manage collections across the country through one chartered bank. Chartered banks offer a concentrator account which automatically electronically transfers deposits at any branch in Canada to the firm's concentration account. These funds receive **same day value.** This means that the firm has immediate use of the funds even though it takes 24 hours for a cheque to clear in Canada. If the concentration involves branches of more than one bank, electronic transfers will take place between banks.

Once the funds are in the concentration account, the bank can make automatic transfers to pay down the firm's credit line or, if there is a surplus, to an investment account. Transfers are made in units of minimum size agreed in advance. A common practice is in units of $5,000. Midsized firms lacking money market expertise may invest in bank accounts at competitive interest rates. The largest firms are able to purchase money market instruments electronically.

Controlling Disbursements

Accelerating collections is one method of cash management; slowing down disbursements is another. This can be a sensitive area—some practices exist that we do not recommend. For example, some small firms that are short of working capital make disbursements on the "squeaky wheel principle." Payables invoices are processed prior to their due dates and cheques printed. When the cheques are ready, the firm's controller puts them all in a desk drawer. As suppliers phone and ask for their money, the cheques come out of the drawer and go into the mail! We do not recommend the desk drawer method because it is bad for supplier relations and borders on being unethical.

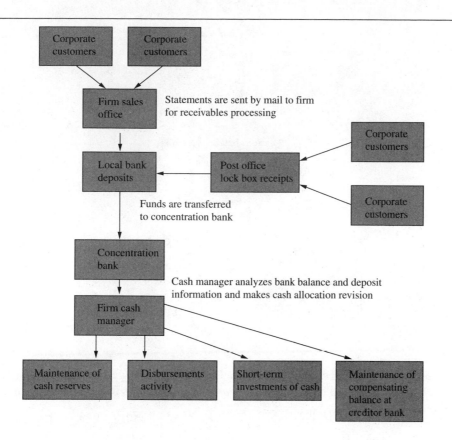

Figure 27.6
Lockboxes and concentration banks in a cash management system

Ethical and Legal Questions

The cash manager must work with collected bank cash balances and not the firm's book balance (which reflects cheques that have been deposited but not collected). If this is not done, a cash manager could be drawing on uncollected cash as a source for making short-term investments. Most banks charge a penalty rate for the use of uncollected funds. The issue is minor in Canada since there can be a maximum of only one day's deposit float. In the United States, however, smaller banks' accounting and control procedures may not be accurate enough to make them fully aware of the use of uncollected funds. This raises some ethical and legal questions for firms doing business across the border.

For example, in May 1985, Robert Fomon, chairman of E.F. Hutton (a large New York investment bank), pleaded guilty to 2,000 charges of mail and wire fraud in connection with a scheme the firm had operated from 1980 to 1982. E.F. Hutton employees wrote cheques totalling hundreds of millions of dollars against uncollected cash. The proceeds were then invested in short-term money market assets. This type of systematic overdrafting of accounts (sometimes called *cheque kiting*) is neither legal nor ethical—and is apparently not widespread among corporations.

Figure 27.7
Zero-balance
accounts

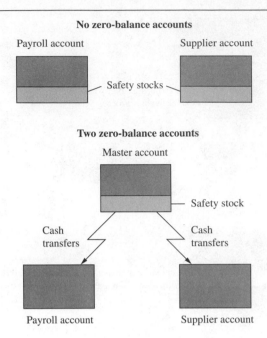

For its part, E.F. Hutton paid a $2 million fine, reimbursed the government (the U.S. Dept. of Justice) $750,000, and reserved an additional $8 million for restitution to defrauded banks.

Controlling Disbursements in Practice

As we have seen, float in terms of slowing down payments comes from mail delivery, cheque-processing time, and collection of funds. As we just showed, in the United States, disbursement float can be increased by writing a cheque on a geographically distant bank. Because there are significant ethical (and legal) issues associated with deliberately delaying disbursements in these and similar ways, such strategies appear to be disappearing. In Canada, banks provide same day availability so the temptation is easy to resist.

For these reasons, the goal is to control rather than simply to delay disbursements. A treasurer should try to pay payables on the last day appropriate for net terms or a discount.[11] The traditional way is to write a cheque and mail it timed to arrive on the due date. With the cash management system we described earlier, the payment can be programmed today for electronic transfer on the future due date. This eliminates paper along with guesswork about mail times.

The electronic payment is likely to come from a disbursement account, kept separate from the concentration account to ease accounting and control. Firms keep separate accounts for payroll, vendor disbursements, customer refunds, and so on. This makes it easy for the bank to provide each cost or profit centre with its own statement.

---

[11]We discuss credit terms in depth in Chapter 28.

Firms use **zero-balance accounts** to avoid carrying extra balances in each disbursement account. With a zero-balance account, the firm, in cooperation with its bank, transfers in just enough funds to cover cheques presented that day. Figure 27.7 illustrates how such a system might work. In this case, the firm maintains two disbursement accounts: one for suppliers and one for payroll. As shown, if the firm does not use zero-balance accounts, then each of these accounts must have a safety stock of cash to meet unanticipated demands. If the firm does use zero-balance accounts, then it can keep one safety stock in a master account and transfer in the funds to the two subsidiary accounts as needed. The key is that the total amount of cash held as a buffer is smaller under the zero-balance arrangement, thereby freeing up cash to be used elsewhere.

CONCEPT QUESTIONS

- Describe collection and disbursement float.
- What are lockboxes? Concentration banking? Zero-balance accounts?
- How do computer and communications technologies aid in cash management by large corporations?

Investing Idle Cash   27.4

If a firm has a temporary cash surplus, it can invest in short-term, or money market, securities. Short-term financial assets that trade in the money market have maturities of one year or less. Most large firms manage their own short-term financial assets, transacting through banks and investment dealers.

Some smaller firms use money market funds that invest in short-term financial assets for a management fee. The management fee is compensation for the professional expertise and diversification provided by the fund manager. Canadian chartered banks compete with money market funds offering arrangements in which the bank takes all excess available funds at the close of each business day and invests them for the firm.

Temporary Cash Surpluses

Firms may have temporary cash surpluses for the financing of seasonal or cyclical activities or for financing of planned or possible expenditures.

Some firms have a predictable cash flow pattern with surplus cash flows during part of the year and deficit cash flows the rest of the year. For example, Toys "R" Us, a retail toy firm, has a seasonal cash flow pattern influenced by Christmas. A firm such as Toys "R" Us may buy marketable securities when surplus cash flows occur and sell marketable securities when deficits occur. Of course, bank loans are another short-term financing device. The use of bank loans and marketable securities to meet temporary financing needs is illustrated in Figure 27.8. In this case, the firm is following a compromise working capital policy in the sense we discussed in the previous chapter.

Firms frequently accumulate temporary investments in marketable securities to provide the cash for a plant construction program, dividend payment, and other large

Figure 27.8
Seasonal cash
demands

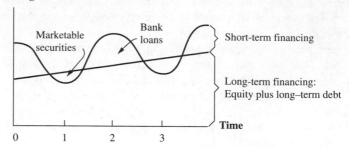

Time 1: A surplus cash flow exists. Seasonal demand for investing is low. The
surplus cash flow is invested in short-term marketable securities.
Time 2: A deficit cash flow exists. Seasonal demand for investing is high. The
financial deficit is financed by selling marketable securities and by bank borrowing.

expenditures. Thus, firms may issue bonds and common shares before the cash is
needed, investing the proceeds in short-term marketable securities and then selling the
securities to finance the expenditures. Also, firms may face the possibility of having to
make a large cash outlay and may build up cash surpluses against such a contingency.

For example, on December 31, 1981, U.S. Steel (now USX Corporation) had $1.5
billion invested in marketable securities. This represented more than 11 percent of the
total assets of U.S. Steel. This balance had been built up to finance a merger with
Marathon Oil that was completed in March 1982.

Characteristics of Short-Term Securities

Given that a firm has some temporarily idle cash, there are a variety of short-term
securities available for investing. Their most important characteristics are maturity,
default risk, marketability, and taxability.

Maturity

Maturity refers to the time period over which interest and principal payments are
made. For a given change in the level of interest rates, the prices of longer-maturity
securities will change more than those for shorter-maturity securities. As a consequence, firms that invest in long-term securities are accepting greater risk than firms
that invest in securities with short-term maturities. This type of risk is usually called
interest-rate risk. Most firms limit their investments in marketable securities to those
maturing in less than 90 days. Of course, the expected return on securities with
short-term maturities is usually less than the expected return on securities with longer
maturities.

▪ *Example*

Suppose you are the treasurer of a firm with $10 million needed to make a major
capital investment after 90 days. You have decided to invest in Government of Canada

Figure 27.9 Money market quotations

MONEY RATES

ADMINISTERED RATES		Commercial Paper (R-1 Low)		Dealers commercial paper:	months, 3.375-3.50; 6 months, 3.4375-
Bank of Canada	4.51%	1-month	4.48%	30-180 days: 3.10-3.36	3.5625; 1 year, 3.625-3.75
Canadian prime	5.75%	2-month	4.49%	Commercial paper by finance	London Interbank Offered Rate: 3
MONEY MARKET RATES		3-month	4.49%	company: 30-270 days: 3.10-3.29	months, 3.50; 6 months, 3.5625; 1
(for transactions		Call money	4.62%	Bankers acceptances dealer indi-	year, 3.75
of $1-million or more)		**Supplied by Dow Jones**		cations: 30 days, 3.10; 60 days, 3.36;	Treasury Bill auction results: av-
3-mo. T-bill(when-issued)	4.30%	**Telerate Canada**		90 days, 3.36; 120 days, 3.36; 150	erage discount rate: 3-month as of
1-month treasury bills	4.28%	**UNITED STATES**		days, 3.36; 180 days, 3.36	Nov. 1: 3.11; 6-month as of Nov. 1:
2-month treasury bills	4.29%	NEW YORK (AP) — Money rates for		Certificates of Deposit Primary: 30	3.25
3-month treasury bills	4.262%	Tuesday as reported by Telerate Sys-		days, 2.52; 90 days, 2.64; 180 days,	Treasury Bill, annualized rate on
6-month treasury bills	4.428%	tems Inc:		2.70	weekly average basis, yield adjusted
1-year treasury bills	4.747%	Telerate interest rate index: 3.310		Certificates of Deposit by dealer:	for constant maturity, 1-year, as of
10-year Canada bonds	6.84%	Prime Rate: 6.00		30 days, 3.12; 60 days, 3.40; 90 days,	Nov. 1: 3.46
30-year Canada bonds	7.53%	Discount Rate: 3.00		3.40; 120 days, 3.40; 150 days, 3.40;	Treasury Bill market rate, 1-year:
1-month banker's accept.	4.34%	Broker call loan rate: 5.00		180 days, 3.45	3.44-3.42
2-month banker's accept.	4.36%	Federal funds market rate:		Eurodollar rates: Overnight, 3-	Treasury Bond market rate, 30-
3-month banker's accept.	4.36%	High 3.0625, low 3, last 3		3.125; 1 month, 3.0625-3.1875; 3	year: 6.07

Source: *The Globe and Mail* (November 3, 1993), p. B21. Used with permission.

obligations to eliminate all possible default risk. The newspaper (or your computer screen) lists securities and rates (Figure 27.9). The safest investment is three-month Treasury bills yielding 4.30 percent. Because this matches the maturity of the investment with the planned holding period, there is no interest rate risk. After three months, the Treasury bills will mature for a certain future cash flow of $10 million.[12]

If instead you invest in 10-year Canada bonds, the expected return will be higher, 6.84 percent, but so will the risk. If interest rates rise over the next three months, the bond will drop in price. The resulting capital loss will reduce the yield, possibly below the 4.30 percent on Treasury bills. ∎

Default Risk

Default risk refers to the probability that interest and principal will not be paid in the promised amounts on the due dates. In Chapter 20, we observed that bond rating agencies, such as the Dominion Bond Rating Service (DBRS) and the Canadian Bond Rating Service (CBRS), compile and publish ratings of various corporate and public securities. These ratings are connected to default risk. Of course, some securities have negligible default risk, such as Canada Treasury bills. Given the purposes of investing idle corporate cash, firms typically avoid investing in marketable securities with significant default risk.

Small variations in default risk are reflected in the rates in Figure 27.9. For example, look at the rates on three alternative 90-day (three-month) investments. Since the maturities are the same, they differ only in default risk. In increasing order of default risk the securities are Treasury bills (4.30 percent yield), banker's acceptances (4.36 percent yield), and commercial paper (4.49 percent yield). All three are unsecured paper. Treasury bills (the least risky) are backed by the credit of the

---

[12]Treasury bills are sold on a discount basis so the future cash flow includes principal and interest.

Government of Canada. Commercial paper (the most risky) is backed by the credit of the issuing large corporation. Banker's acceptances are a slightly less risky variation on commercial paper guaranteed by a chartered bank as well as by the issuing corporation.

Marketability

Marketability refers to how easy it is to convert an asset to cash. Sometimes marketability is referred to as *liquidity*. It has two characteristics:

1. *No price-pressure effect.* If an asset can be sold in large amounts without changing the market price, it is marketable. Price-pressure effects are those that come about when the price of an asset must be lowered to facilitate the sale.
2. *Time.* If an asset can be sold quickly at the existing market price, it is marketable. In contrast, a Renoir painting or antique desk appraised at $1 million will likely sell for much less if the owner must sell quickly on short notice.

In general, marketability is the ability to sell an asset for its face market value quickly and in large amounts. Perhaps the most marketable of all securities are Canada Treasury bills.

Taxability

Interest earned on money market securities is subject to federal and provincial corporate income taxes. Capital gains and dividends on common and preferred shares are taxed more lightly, but these long-term investments are subject to significant price fluctuations; most managers consider them too risky for the marketable securities portfolio.

One exception is the strategy of **dividend capture.** Under this strategy, portfolio managers purchase high-grade preferred stock or blue chip common stock just prior to a dividend payment. They hold the stock only long enough to receive the dividend. In this way, firms willing to tolerate price risk for a short period can benefit from the dividend exclusion allowing corporations to receive dividends tax-free from other Canadian corporations.

To mitigate price risk and to make their firms' preferred shares more attractive to managers seeking to capture dividends, financial engineers have invented various forms of floating rate preferred shares. The idea is to make the dividends adjust to changes in market yields, keeping the price of the preferred share near par.[13]

Some Different Types of Money Market Securities

The money market securities listed in Figure 27.9 are generally highly marketable and short-term. They usually have low risk of default. These securities are issued by the

---

[13]Since there is some lag in adjustment, the price can move away from the par value somewhat. Also, since all preferred shares bear some default risk, the floating rate does not protect investors from price declines arising from the downgrading of the issuer's credit rating.

federal government (for example, Treasury bills), domestic and foreign banks (for example, certificates of deposit), and business corporations (for example, commercial paper). There are many types in all, and we only illustrate a few of the most common here.

Treasury bills are obligations of the federal government that mature in three months, six months, or one year. They are sold at weekly auctions and traded actively over the counter by banks and investment dealers.

Commercial paper refers to short-term securities issued by finance companies, banks, and corporations. Typically, commercial paper is unsecured.[14] Maturities range from a few weeks to three months. There is no active secondary market in commercial paper. As a consequence, the marketability is low; however, firms that issue commercial paper will often repurchase it directly before maturity. The default risk of commercial paper depends on the financial strength of the issuer. DBRS and CBRS publish quality ratings for commercial paper. These ratings are similar to the bond ratings we discussed in Chapter 20.

As explained earlier, *banker's acceptances* are a form of corporate paper stamped by a chartered bank that adds its guarantee of principal and interest.

Certificates of deposit (CDs) are short-term loans to chartered banks. Rates quoted are for CDs in excess of $100,000. There are active markets in CDs of 3-month, 6-month, 9-month, and 12-month maturities, particularly in the United States.

Dollar swaps are foreign currency deposits that will be converted or swapped back into Canadian dollars at a predetermined rate by chartered banks. They allow the Canadian treasurer to place funds in major money markets outside Canada without incurring foreign exchange risk.

Our brief look at money markets illustrates the challenges and opportunities for treasurers in the 1990s. Securitization has produced dramatic growth in banker's acceptances and commercial paper. Currency swaps are a financial engineering product driven by globalization of financial markets.

CONCEPT QUESTIONS

- Why do firms find themselves with idle cash?
- What are some types of money market securities?

Summary and Conclusions 27.5

1. A firm holds cash to conduct transactions and to compensate banks for the various services they render.

2. The optimal amount of cash for a firm to hold depends on the opportunity cost of holding cash and the uncertainty of future cash inflows and outflows. The Baumol model and the Miller–Orr model are two transactions models that provide rough guidelines for determining the optimal cash position.

---

[14]Commercial paper and banker's acceptances are sources of short-term financing for their issuers. We discussed them in more detail in Chapter 26.

3. The firm can make use of a variety of procedures to manage the collection and disbursement of cash in such a way as to speed up the collection of cash and slow down payments. Some methods to speed up collection are lockboxes, concentration banking, and electronic collection systems.

4. Because of seasonal and cyclical activities, to help finance planned expenditures, or as a reserve for unanticipated needs, firms temporarily find themselves with cash surpluses. The money market offers a variety of possible vehicles for parking this idle cash.

Key Terms

Speculative motive 774

Precautionary motive 774

Transactions motive 774

Target cash balance 774

Float 782

Smart card 786

Lockbox 786

Debit card 788

Concentration banking 788

Same day value 788

Zero-balance account 791

Dividend capture 794

Suggested Readings

A good source on cash management practices is:

N. C. Hill, and W. L. Sartoris. *Short-Term Financial Management.* New York: Macmillan, 1988, chapters 6–10.

To keep up with Canadian practices, consult the following periodical:

Canadian Treasury Management Review (Toronto: Royal Bank of Canada).

Questions and Problems

The Cash Balance

27.1 Indicate whether the following actions increase, decrease, or cause no change in a company's optimal cash balance:

    a. Interest rates paid on money market securities rise.

    b. Commissions charged by brokers increase.

    c. The cost of borrowing decreases.

    d. The firm's credit rating declines.

    e. Direct fees for banking services are established.

27.2 Explain how current trends in financial markets (discussed in Chapter 1) are changing the practice of cash management in Canada.

27.3 A company's weekly average cash balances are

Week 1	$24,000
Week 2	34,000
Week 3	10,000
Week 4	15,000

If the annual interest rate is 12 percent, what return can be earned on the average cash balances?

Cash Balance Models

27.4 The Casablanca Piano Company is currently holding $800,000 in cash. It projects that, over the next year, its cash outflows will exceed its cash inflows by $345,000 per month. Each time securities are bought or sold through a broker, the company pays a fee of $500. The annual interest rate on money market securities is 7 percent.

  a. How much of this cash should be retained and how much should be used to increase the company's holdings of marketable securities?

  b. After the initial investment of excess cash, how many times during the next 12 months will securities be sold?

27.5 The variance of the daily net cash flows for the Tseneg Asian Import Company is $1.44 million. The opportunity cost to the firm of holding cash is 8 percent per year. The fixed cost of buying and selling securities is $600 per transaction. What should the target cash level and upper limit be, if the tolerable lower limit has been established at $20,000?

Lockbox System

27.6 Garden Groves, Inc., a Manitoba-based company, has determined that a majority of its customers are located in the Winnipeg area. Therefore, it is considering using a lockbox system offered by a bank branch located in Winnipeg. The bank has estimated that use of the system will reduce collection float by three days. Based on the following information, should the lockbox system be adopted?

  Average number of payments per day: 150.

  Average value of payment: $15,000.

  Fixed annual lockbox fee: $80,000.

  Variable lockbox fee: $0.50/transaction.

  Annual interest rate on money market securities: 7.5%.

27.7 A large British Columbia lumber producer, Salisbury Stakes, Inc., is planning to use a lockbox system to speed collections from customers in the western provinces. A Saskatoon area bank branch will provide this service for an annual fee of $15,000 plus $0.25 per transaction. The estimated reduction in collection and processing time is two days. Treasury bills are currently yielding 6 percent per year.

If the average customer payment in this region is $4,500, how many customers each day, on average, must use the system to make it profitable?

Float

27.8 Each business day, on average, a company writes cheques totalling $12,000 to pay its suppliers. The usual clearing time for these cheques is five days. Each day, the company receives payments from its customers in the form of cheques totalling $15,000. The cash from the payments is available to the firm after one day.

Calculate the company's disbursement float, collection float, and net float. How would these values change if the collected funds were available the same day instead of after one day?

27.9 It takes the Herman Company about seven days to receive and deposit cheques from customers. The top management of the Herman Company is considering a lockbox system. It is expected that the lockbox system will reduce float time to four days. Average daily collections are $100,000. The marketwide interest rate is 12 percent.

  a. What would the reduction in outstanding cash balances be as a result of implementing the lockbox system?

  b. What is the return that could be earned on these savings?

  c. What is the maximum monthly charge the Herman Company should pay for this lockbox system?

When a firm sells goods and services, it can (1) be paid in cash immediately or (2) wait for a time to be paid, that is, extend credit to customers. Granting credit is investing in a customer, an investment tied to the sale of a product or service. This chapter examines the firm's decision to grant credit.

An account receivable is created when credit is granted. These receivables include credit granted to other firms, called *trade credit,* and credit granted to consumers, called *consumer credit.* About 15 percent of all the assets of Canadian industrial firms are in the form of accounts receivable. For retail firms, the figure is much higher.

The investment in accounts receivable for any firm depends on both the amount of credit sales and the average collection period. For example, if a firm's daily credit sales are $1,000 and its average collection period is 30 days, its accounts receivable will be $30,000. Thus, a firm's investment in accounts receivable depends on factors influencing credit sales and collection. A firm's credit policy affects these factors.

The following are the components of credit policy:

1. **Terms of the sale.** A firm must decide on certain conditions when selling its goods and services for credit. The terms of sale may specify the credit period, the cash discount, and the type of credit instrument.

2. **Credit analysis.** When granting credit, a firm tries to distinguish between customers who will pay and those who will not. Firms use a number of devices and procedures to determine the probability that customers will pay.

3. **Collection policy.** Firms that grant credit must establish a policy for collecting the cash when it becomes due.

This chapter discusses each of the components of credit policy that make up the decision to grant credit.

In some ways, the decision to grant credit is connected to the cash collection process described in the previous chapter. This is illustrated with a cash flow diagram in Figure 28.1.

The typical sequence of events when a firm grants credit is (1) the credit sale is made, (2) the customer sends a cheque to the firm, (3) the firm deposits the cheque, and (4) the firm's account is credited for the amount of the cheque.

Figure 28.1
The cash flows of
granting credit

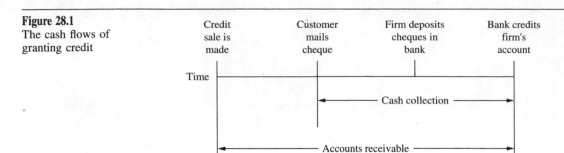

28.1   ## Terms of the Sale

The terms of sale refer to the period for which credit is granted, the cash discount, and
the type of credit instrument. Within a given industry, the terms of sale are usually
fairly standard, but across industries these terms vary quite a bit. In many cases, the
terms of sale are remarkably archaic and literally date to previous centuries. Organized
systems of trade credit that resemble current practice can be easily traced to the great
fairs of medieval Europe, and they almost surely existed long before then.

Why Trade Credit Exists

Set aside the venerable history of trade credit for a moment and ask yourself why it
should exist.[1] It is quite easy to imagine that all sales could be for cash and, from the
firm's viewpoint, this would get rid of receivables' carrying costs and collection costs.
Bad debts would be zero (assuming that the firm was careful to accept no counterfeit
money).

Imagine this cash-only economy in the context of perfectly competitive product
and financial markets. Competition would force companies to lower their prices to
pass the savings from immediate collections on to customers. Any company that then
chose to grant credit to its customers would have to raise its prices accordingly to
survive. If a purchaser needed financing over the operating cycle, it could borrow from
a bank or the money market. In this, "perfect markets" environment, it would make no
difference to the seller or the buyer whether credit were granted.

But, in practice, firms spend significant resources setting credit policy and
managing its implementation. So deviations from perfect markets—market
imperfections—must explain why trade credit exists. We look briefly at several
imperfections and how trade credit helps to overcome them.

In practice, buyers and sellers have imperfect information. Buyers lack perfect
information on the quality of the product. For this reason, the buyer may prefer credit
terms that give time to return the product if it is defective or unsuitable. When the

---

[1]Our discussion of trade credit draws on N. C. Hill and W. S. Sartoris, *Short-Term Financial Management* (New York:
Macmillan, 1988), chapter 14.

seller offers credit, it "signals" potential customers that the product is of high quality and likely to provide satisfaction.[2]

In addition, in practice, any firm granting credit lacks perfect information on the creditworthiness of the borrower. Although it is costly for a bank or other third-party lender to acquire this information, a seller that has been granting trade credit to a purchaser likely has it already. Further, the seller may have superior information on the resale value of the product serving as collateral. These information advantages may allow the seller to offer more attractive, more flexible credit terms and to be more liberal in authorizing credit.

Finally, perfect markets have zero transactions costs but, in reality, it is costly to set up a bank borrowing facility or to borrow in money markets. We discussed some of the costs in Chapter 26. It may be cheaper to utilize credit from the seller.

The Basic Form

Suppose a customer is granted credit with terms of 2/10, net 30. This means that the customer has 30 days from the invoice date within which to pay. (An **invoice** is a bill written by a seller of goods or services and submitted to the buyer. The invoice date is usually the same as the shipping date.) In addition, a cash discount of 2 percent from the stated sales price is to be given if payment is made in 10 days. If the stated terms are net 60, the customer has 60 days from the invoice date to pay and no discount is offered for early payment.

When sales are seasonal, a firm might use seasonal dating. O. M. Scott and Sons is a manufacturer of lawn and garden products with a seasonal dating policy that is tied to the growing season. Payments for winter shipments of fertilizer might be due in the spring or summer. A firm offering 3/10, net 60, May 1 dating, is making the effective invoice date May 1. The stated amount must be paid on June 30, regardless of when the sale is made. The cash discount of 3 percent can be taken until May 10.

Credit Period

Credit periods vary among different industries. For example, a jewelry store may sell diamond engagement rings for 5/30, net 4 months. A food wholesaler, selling fresh fruit and produce, might use net 7.[3] Generally a firm must consider three factors in setting a credit period:

1. *The probability that the customer will not pay.* A firm whose customers are in high-risk businesses may find itself offering restrictive credit terms.

2. *The size of the account.* If the account is small, the credit period will be shorter. Small accounts are more costly to manage, and customers are less important.

---

[2]This use of signalling is very similar to dividend signalling discussed in Chapter 18. There, corporations signalled the quality of projected cash flows by maintaining dividends even when earnings were down.

[3]From T. Beckman and R. Bartels, *Credits and Collections: Management and Theory,* 8th ed. (New York: McGraw-Hill, 1969).

Figure 28.2
Cash flows for
different credit
terms

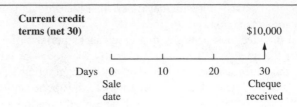

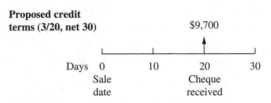

Current situation: Customers usually pay 30 days from the
sale date and receive no discount.
Proposed situation: Customer will pay 20 days from the sale
date at a 3-percent discount from the $10,000 purchase price.

3. *The extent to which the goods are perishable.* If the collateral values of the
goods are low and cannot be sustained for a long period, less credit will be
granted.

Lengthening the credit period effectively reduces the price paid by the customer.
Generally this increases sales.

Cash Discounts

Cash discounts are often part of the terms of sale. One reason they are offered is to
speed up the collection of receivables. The firm must balance this against the cost of
the discount.

▪ *Example*

Edward Manalt, the chief financial officer of Charlottetown Grocers, is considering the
request of the company's largest customer, who wants to take a 3-percent discount for
payment within 20 days on a $10,000 purchase. In other words, the customer intends
to pay $9,700 [or $10,000 × (1 − 0.03)]. Normally, this customer pays in 30 days with
no discount. The cost of debt capital for Charlottetown is 10 percent. Edward has
worked out the cash flow implications illustrated in Figure 28.2. He assumes that the
time required to cash the cheque when the firm receives it is the same under both credit
arrangements. He has calculated the present value of the two proposals:

Current Policy:

$$PV = \frac{\$10,000}{(1 + .10)^{30/365}} = \$9,921.97$$

Proposed Policy:

$$PV = \frac{\$9,700}{(1 + .10)^{20/365}} = \$9,649.46$$

**Current credit
terms (net 30)**

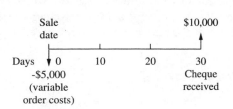

**Proposed credit
terms (3/20, net 30)**

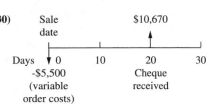

Figure 28.3
Cash flows for
different credit
terms: The impact
of new sales and
costs

His calculation shows that granting the discount would cost the Charlottetown firm $272.50 (or $9,921.97 − $9,649.47) in present value. Consequently, Charlottetown is better off with the current credit arrangement.[4] ∎

In the example, we implicitly assumed that granting credit had no side effects. However, the decision to grant credit may generate higher sales and involve a different cost structure. The next example illustrates the impact of changes in the level of sales and costs in the credit decision.

∎ *Example*

Suppose that Charlottetown Grocers has variable costs of $0.50 per $1 of sales. If offered a discount of 3 percent, customers will increase the order size by 10 percent. This new information is shown in Figure 28.3. That is, the customer will increase the order size to $11,000 and, with the 3-percent discount, will remit $10,670 [or $11,000 × (1 − 0.03)] to Charlottetown in 20 days. It will cost more to fill the larger order because variable costs are $5,500. The net present values are worked out here:

Current Policy

$$NPV = -\$5,000 + \frac{\$10,000}{(1.10)^{30/365}} = \$4,921.97$$

Proposed Policy:

$$NPV = -\$5,500 + \frac{\$10,670}{(1.10)^{20/365}} = \$5,114.42$$

---

[4]We can reinforce this division by calculating a *customer's* rate of return from taking the discount if it were offered. With the cash discount, a customer pays $9,700 instead of $10,000. By passing on the discount, the customer takes a loan for 20 days and pays 3/97 = 3.09% more for the order. By adopting the policy, the customer takes 365/20 = 18.25 loans per year. By investing, say, one dollar at 3.09 percent per period for 18.25 periods, the customer receives a future value at the end of one year of $(1.0309)^{18.25}=1.7426$—a return of 74.26 percent annually.

Now it is clear that the firm is better off with the proposed credit policy. This increase is the net effect of several different factors including the larger initial costs, the earlier receipt of the cash inflows, the increased sales level, and the discount. ∎

Credit Instruments

Most credit is offered on *open account*. This means that the only formal **credit instrument** is the invoice, which is sent with the shipment of goods, and which the customer signs as evidence that the goods have been received. Afterward, the firm and its customers record the exchange on their books.

When the order is large or the firm anticipates a problem in collections, it may require that the customer sign a *promissory note* or IOU. Promissory notes can prevent future controversies about the existence of a credit agreement.

However, promissory notes are signed after delivery of the goods. One way to obtain a credit commitment from a customer before the goods are delivered is through the use of a *commercial draft*. The selling firm typically writes a commercial draft calling for the customer to pay a specific amount by a specified date. The draft is then sent to the customer's bank with the shipping invoices. The bank has the buyer sign the draft before turning over the invoices. The goods can then be shipped to the buyer. If immediate payment is required, it is called a *sight draft*. Here, funds must be turned over to the bank before the goods are shipped.

Frequently, even the signed draft is not enough for the seller. In this case, the seller might demand that the banker pay for the goods, and collect the money from the customer. When the banker agrees to do so in writing, the document is called a *banker's acceptance*. That is, the banker *accepts* responsibility for payment. Because banks generally are well-known and well-respected institutions, the banker's acceptance becomes a liquid instrument. In other words, the seller can then sell (*discount*) the banker's acceptance in the secondary market.

A firm can also use a *conditional sales contract* as a credit instrument. This is an arrangement where the firm retains legal ownership of the goods until the customer has completed payment. Conditional sales contracts usually are paid off in installments and have interest costs built into them.

CONCEPT QUESTIONS

- What considerations enter into the determination of the terms of sale?
- Explain the design of common credit instruments.

28.2   ## The Decision to Grant Credit: Risk and Information

Locust Industries has been in existence for two years. It is one of several successful firms that develop computer programs. The present financial managers have set out two alternative credit strategies: The firm can offer credit, or the firm can refuse credit.

Suppose Locust has determined that, if it offers no credit to its customers, it can sell its existing computer software for $50 per program. It estimates that the costs to produce a typical computer program are equal to $20 per unit.

The alternative is to offer credit. In this case, customers of Locust will pay one period later. With some probability, Locust has determined that if it offers credit, it can charge higher prices and expect higher sales.

Strategy 1: Refuse credit. If Locust refuses to grant credit, cash flows will not be delayed, and period 0 net cash flows, NCF, will be

$$P_0 Q_0 - C_0 Q_0 = \text{NCF}$$

The subscripts denote the time when the cash flows are incurred, where

P_0 = Price per unit received at time 0
C_0 = Cost per unit incurred at time 0
Q_0 = Quantity sold at time 0

The net cash flows at period 1 are zero, and the net present value to Locust of refusing credit will simply be the period 0 net cash flow:

$$\text{NPV} = \text{NCF}$$

For example, if credit is not granted and $Q_0 = 100$, the NPV can be calculated as

$$\$50 \times 100 - \$20 \times 100 = \$3,000$$

Strategy 2: Offer credit. Alternatively, let us assume that Locust grants credit to all customers for one period. The factors that influence the decision are listed below.

	Strategy 1: Refuse credit	Strategy 2: Offer credit
Price per unit	$P_0 = \$50$	$P_0' = \$50$
Quantity sold	$Q_0 = 100$	$Q_0' = 200$
Cost per unit	$C_0 = \$20$	$C_0' = \$25$
Probability of payment	$h = 1$	$h = 0.90$
Credit period	0	1 period
Discount rate	0	$r_B = 0.01$

The prime (') denotes the variables under the second strategy. If the firm offers credit and the new customers pay, the firm will receive revenues of $P_0' Q_0'$ one period hence, but its costs, $C_0' Q_0'$, are incurred in period 0. If new customers do not pay, the firm incurs costs $C_0' Q_0'$ and receives no revenues. The probability that customers will pay, is 0.90 in the example. Quantity sold is higher with credit, because new customers are attracted. The cost per unit is also higher with credit because of the costs of operating a credit policy.

The expected cash flows for each policy are set out as follows:

	Expected cash flows	
	Time 0	Time 1
Refuse credit	$P_0 Q_0 - C_0 Q_0$	0
Offer credit	$- C_0' Q_0'$	$h \times P_0' Q_0'$

Note that granting credit produces delayed expected cash inflows equal to $h \times P_0'Q_0'$. The costs are incurred immediately and require no discounting. The net present value if credit is offered is

$$\text{NPV (offer)} = \frac{h \times P_0'Q_0'}{1 + r_B} - C_0'Q_0'$$

$$= \frac{0.9 \times \$50 \times 200}{1.01} - \$5,000 = \$3,910.89$$

Locust Software's decision should be to adopt the proposed credit policy. The NPV of granting credit is higher than that of refusing credit. This decision is very sensitive to the probability of payment. If it turns out that the probability of payment is 81 percent, Locust Software is indifferent to whether it grants credit or not. In this case the NPV of granting credit is $3,000, which we previously found to be the NPV of not granting credit:

$$\$3,000 = h \times \frac{\$50 \times 200}{1.01} - \$5,000$$

$$\$8,000 = h \times \frac{\$50 \times 200}{1.01}$$

$$h = 80.8\%$$

The decision to grant credit depends on four factors:

1. The delayed revenues from granting credit, $P_0'Q_0'$.
2. The immediate costs of granting credit, $C_0'Q_0$.
3. The probability of payment, h.
4. The appropriate required rate of return for delayed cash flows, r_B.

The Value of New Information about Credit Risk

Obtaining a better estimate of the probability that a customer will default can lead to a better decision. How can a firm determine when to acquire new information about the creditworthiness of its customers?

It may be sensible for Locust Software to determine which of its customers are most likely not to pay. The overall probability of nonpayment is 10 percent. But credit checks by an independent firm show that 90 percent of Locust's customers (computer stores) have been profitable over the past five years and that these customers have never defaulted on payments. The less profitable customers are much more likely to default. In fact, 100 percent of the less profitable customers have defaulted on previous obligations.

Locust would like to avoid offering credit to the deadbeats. Consider its projected number of customers per year of $Q_0' = 200$ if credit is granted. Of these customers, 180 have been profitable over the past five years and have never defaulted on past obligations. The remaining 20 have not been profitable. Locust Software expects that all of these less profitable customers will default. This information is set out in a table:

Type of customer	Number	Probability of nonpayment	Expected number of defaults
Profitable	180	0	0
Less profitable	20	100%	20
Total customers	200	10%	20

The NPV of granting credit to the customers who default is

$$\frac{hP_0'Q_0'}{1 + r_B} - C_0'Q_0' = \frac{0 \times \$50 \times 20}{1.01} - \$25 \times 20 = -\$500$$

(the cost of providing them with the software). If Locust can identify these customers without cost, it would certainly deny them credit.

In fact, it actually costs Locust $3 per customer to figure out whether a customer has been profitable over the past five years. The expected payoff of the credit check on its 200 customers is then

$$\begin{array}{ccc} \text{Gain from not} & \text{Cost of} & \\ \text{extending credit} & - & \text{credit checks} \\ \$500 & - & \$3 \times 200 = -\$100 \end{array}$$

For Locust, credit is not worth checking. It would need to pay $600 to avoid a $500 loss.

Future Sales

Up to this point, Locust has not considered the possibility that offering credit will permanently increase the level of sales in future periods (beyond next month). In addition, payment and nonpayment patterns in the current period will provide credit information that is useful for the next period. These two factors should be analyzed.

In the case of Locust, there is a 90-percent probability that the customer will pay in period 1. But, if payment is made, there will be another sale in period 2. The probability that the customer will pay in period 2, if the customer has paid in period 1, is 100 percent. Locust can refuse to offer credit in period 2 to customers that have refused to pay in period 1. This is diagrammed in Figure 28.4.

CONCEPT QUESTION

■ List the factors that influence the decision to grant credit.

Optimal Credit Policy   28.3

So far we have discussed how to compute net present value for two alternative credit policies. However, we have not discussed the optimal amount of credit. At the optimal amount of credit, the incremental cash flows from increased sales are exactly equal to the carrying costs from the increase in accounts receivable.

Figure 28.4
Future sales and
the credit decision

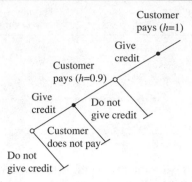

There is a 90-percent probability that a
customer will pay in period 1. However,
if payment is made, there will be another
sale in period 2. The probability that the
customer will pay in period 2 is 100
percent— if the customer has paid in
period 1.

Consider a firm that does not currently grant credit. This firm has no bad debts, no credit department, and relatively few customers. Now consider another firm that grants credit. This firm has lots of customers, a credit department, and a bad-debt expense.

It is useful to think of the decision to grant credit in terms of carrying costs and opportunity costs:

1. *Carrying costs* are the costs associated with granting credit and making an investment in receivables. Carrying costs include the delay in receiving cash, the losses from bad debts, and the costs of managing credit.

2. *Opportunity costs* are the lost sales from refusing to offer credit. These costs drop as credit is granted.

We represent these costs in Figure 28.5.

The sum of the carrying costs and the opportunity costs of a particular credit policy is called the *total credit cost curve*. A point is identified as the minimum of the total credit cost curve. If the firm extends more credit than the minimum, the additional net cash flow from new customers will not cover the carrying costs of the higher investment in receivables.

The concept of optimal credit policy in the context of modern principles of finance should be somewhat analogous to the concept of the optimal capital structure discussed earlier in the text. In perfect financial markets, there should be no optimal credit policy. Alternative amounts of credit for a firm should not affect the value of the firm. Thus, the decision to grant credit would be a matter of indifference to financial managers.

Just as with optimal capital structure, we could expect taxes, bankruptcy costs, and agency costs to be important in determining an optimal credit policy in a world of imperfect financial markets. For example, customers in high tax brackets would be better off borrowing and taking advantage of cash discounts offered by firms than would customers in low tax brackets. Corporations in low tax brackets would be less

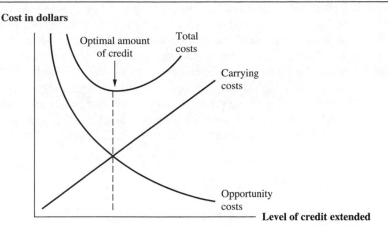

Figure 28.5
The costs of granting credit

Carrying costs are the cash flows that must be incurred when credit is granted. They are positively related to the amount of credit extended.
Opportunity costs are the lost sales from refusing credit. These costs drop when credit is granted.

able to offer credit, because borrowing would be relatively more expensive than for firms in high tax brackets.

The optimal credit policy depends on characteristics of particular firms. Assuming that the firm has more flexibility in its credit policy than in the prices it charges, firms with excess capacity, low variable operating costs, high tax brackets, and repeat customers should extend credit more liberally than others.

Organizing the Credit Function

Firms that run strictly internal credit operations are self-insured against default risk. An alternative is to buy credit insurance through an insurance company. The insurance company offers coverage up to a pre-set dollar limit for accounts. As you would expect, accounts with a higher credit rating merit higher insurance limits. Exporters may qualify for credit insurance through the Export Development Corporation, a crown corporation of the federal government.

Large corporations commonly extend credit through a wholly owned subsidiary called a *captive finance company* instead of a credit department. General Motors, for example, finances its dealers and car buyers through General Motors Acceptance Corporation (GMAC). Consumer and dealer receivables are the assets of GMAC and they are financed largely through commercial paper. Setting up the credit function as a separate legal entity has potential advantages in facilitating borrowing against receivables. Since they are segregated on the balance sheet of a captive, the receivables may make better collateral. As a result, the captive may be able to carry more debt and save on borrowing costs.[5]

---

[5]The trend toward securitization of receivables through wholly owned subsidiaries discussed in Chapter 27 is supporting evidence. This somewhat controversial view of finance captives comes from G. S. Roberts and J. A. Viscione, "Captive Finance Subsidiaries and the M-Form Hypothesis," *Bell Journal of Economics* (Spring 1981), pp. 285–95.

A related issue in credit administration, whether through a finance captive or in-house, is the importance of having a set of written credit policies on credit terms, the information needed for credit analysis, collection procedures, and the monitoring of receivables.[6] Having clearly stated policies helps to control possible conflicts between the credit department and salespeople. For example, during the 1991–1992 recession, some Canadian companies tightened their credit-granting rules to offset the higher probability of customer bankruptcy. Other companies eased credit to promote sales and to provide flexibility for regular customers. The decision depends on the considerations we analyzed earlier. Either way, sales and credit have to work together.

CONCEPT QUESTION

- Why do many large U.S. and Canadian corporations form captive finance subsidiaries?

28.4   Credit Analysis

When granting credit, a firm tries to distinguish between customers who will pay and those who will not pay. There are a number of sources of information for determining creditworthiness.

Credit Information

Information commonly used to assess creditworthiness includes the following:

1. *Financial statements.* A firm can ask a customer to supply financial statement information such as balance sheets and income statements. Minimum standards and rules of thumb based on financial ratios like the ones we discussed in the Appendix to Chapter 2 can then be used as a basis for extending or refusing credit.

2. *Credit reports on customer's payment history with other firms.* Several organizations sell information on the credit strength and credit history of business firms. Dun & Bradstreet Canada provides subscribers with a credit reference book and credit reports on individual firms. Ratings and information are available for a huge number of firms, including very small ones. Creditel of Canada also provides credit reporting and has the capability to send reports electronically.

3. *Banks.* Banks will generally provide some assistance to their business customers in providing information on the creditworthiness of other firms.

4. *The customer's payment history with the firm.* The most obvious way to obtain information about the likelihood of a customer's not paying is to examine whether the customer paid up in the past and how much trouble collecting turned out to be.

---

[6]Our discussion draws on "A Written Credit Policy Can Overcome a Host of Potential Problems," Joint Venture Supplement, *Financial Post* (June 20, 1991).

Credit Evaluation and Scoring

There are no magical formulas for assessing the probability that a customer will not pay. In very general terms, the classic *five C's of credit* are the basic factors to be evaluated:

1. *Character.* The customer's willingness to meet credit obligations.
2. *Capacity.* The customer's ability to meet credit obligations out of operating cash flows.
3. *Capital.* The customer's financial reserves.
4. *Collateral.* A pledged asset in the case of default.
5. *Conditions.* General economic conditions in the customer's line of business.

Credit scoring refers to the process of (1) calculating a numerical rating for a customer based on information collected and (2) then granting or refusing credit based on the result. For example, a firm might rate a customer on a scale of 1 (very poor) to 10 (very good) on each of the five C's of credit using all the information available about the customer. A credit score could then be calculated based on the total. From experience, a firm might choose to grant credit only to customers with a score of more than, say, 30 out of a possible 50 points.

Financial institutions have developed elaborate statistical models for credit scoring. This approach has the advantage of being objective as compared to scoring based on judgments on the five C's. Usually, all legally relevant and observable characteristics of a large pool of customers are studied to find their historic relation to default rates. Based on the results, it is possible to determine the variables that best predict whether or not a customer will pay; then a credit score based on those variables is calculated.

Computerized scoring models employ a statistical technique called **multiple discriminant analysis (MDA)** to predict which customers will be good or bad accounts.[7] Similar to regression analysis, MDA chooses a set of variables that best discriminates between good and bad credits with hindsight in a sample whose outcomes are known. The variables are then used to classify new applications that come in. For consumer credit, for example, these variables include length of time in current job, monthly income, whether the customer's home is owned or rented, and other financial obligations. For business customers, financial ratios are the relevant variables.

To illustrate how MDA works without getting into the derivation, suppose only two ratios explain whether a business customer is creditworthy: sales/total assets (total asset turnover) and EBIT/total assets. What MDA does is draw a line to separate good (G) from bad (B) accounts as shown in Figure 28.6. The equation for the line is

$$\text{Score} = Z = 0.4 \times [\text{Sales/Total assets}] + 3.0 \times \text{EBIT/Total assets} \qquad (28.1)$$

For example, suppose Locust Software has a credit application from Kiwi Computers. Kiwi's financial statements reveal sales/total assets of 1.8 and EBIT/total assets of 0.16. We can calculate Kiwi's score as

$$Z = 0.4 \times 1.8 + 3.0 \times 0.16 = 1.2$$

---

[7]Our discussion draws on Hill and Sartoris, *Short-Term Financial Management,* chapter 14; and L. Kryzanowski et al., *Business Solvency Risk Analysis* (Montreal: Institute of Canadian Bankers, 1990), chapter 6.

Figure 28.6
Credit scoring with multiple discriminant analysis

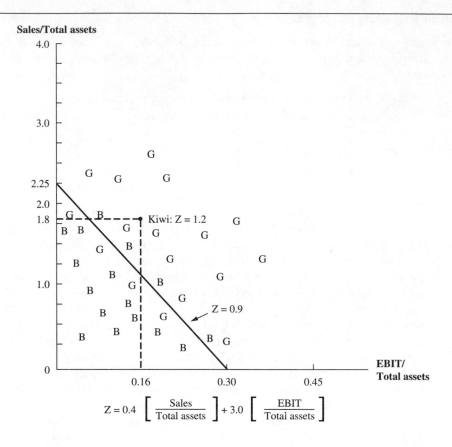

$$Z = 0.4 \left[\frac{\text{Sales}}{\text{Total assets}} \right] + 3.0 \left[\frac{\text{EBIT}}{\text{Totai assets}} \right]$$

The line in Figure 28.6 is drawn at a cutoff score of .90. Since Kiwi's score is higher, it lies above the line and the model predicts it will be a good account. The decision rule is to grant credit to all accounts with scores over 0.9, that is, to all accounts above the line.

To test scoring models' track record, researchers have compared their predictions with the actual outcomes. If the models were perfect, all good accounts would be above the line and all bad accounts below it. As you can see in Figure 28.6, the model does a reasonable job, but there are some errors. For this reason, firms using scoring models assign scores near the line to a "gray area" for further investigation.

As you might expect, statistical scoring models work best when there is a large sample of similar credit applicants. Research on scoring models bears this out: The models are most useful in consumer credit.

Because credit-scoring models and procedures determine who is and who is not creditworthy, it is not surprising that they have been the subject of government regulation. In particular, the kinds of background and demographic information that can be used in the credit decision are limited. For example, suppose a consumer applicant was formerly bankrupt but had discharged all obligations. After a waiting period which varies from province to province, this information cannot be used in the credit decision.

Credit scoring is used for business customers by Canadian chartered banks. Lenders in Canadian banks and other credit analysts have access to scoring results on a popular financial analysis package called TURBOFAST™. Scoring for small business loans is a particularly promising application because the technique offers the advantages of objective analysis without taking more of the lending officer's time than could be justified for a small account.

CONCEPT QUESTIONS

- What is credit analysis?
- What are the five C's of credit?
- What are credit scoring models and how are they used?

Collection Policy 28.5

Collection refers to obtaining payment of past-due accounts. The credit manager keeps a record of payment experience with each customer.

Average Collection Period

Acme Compact Disc Players sells 100,000 compact disc players a year at $300 each. All sales are for credit with terms of 2/20, net 60.

Suppose that 80 percent of Acme customers take the discounts and pay on day 20; the rest pay on day 60. The **average collection period (ACP)** measures the average amount of time required to collect an account receivable. The ACP for Acme is 28 days:

$$0.8 \times 20 \text{ days} + 0.2 \times 60 \text{ days} = 28 \text{ days}$$

(The average collection period is frequently referred to as *days' sales outstanding* or *days in receivables.*)

Of course, this is an idealized example where customers pay on either one of two dates. In reality, payments arrive in a random fashion, so that the average collection period must be calculated differently.

To determine the ACP in the real world, firms first calculate average daily sales. The **average daily sales (ADS)** equal annual sales divided by 365. The ADS of Acme are

$$\text{Average daily sales} = \frac{\$300 \times 100,000}{365 \text{ days}} = \$82,192$$

If receivables today are $2,301,376, the average collection period is

$$
\begin{aligned}
\text{Average collection period} &= \frac{\text{Accounts receivable}}{\text{Average daily sales}} \\
&= \frac{\$2,301,376}{\$82,192} \\
&= 28 \text{ days}
\end{aligned}
$$

In practice, firms observe sales and receivables on a daily basis. Consequently, an average collection period can be computed and compared to the stated credit terms. For example, suppose Acme had computed its ACP at 40 days for several weeks, versus its credit terms of 2/20, net 60. With a 40-day ACP, some customers are paying later than usual. It may be that some accounts are overdue.

However, firms with seasonal sales will often find the *calculated* ACP changing during the year, making the ACP a somewhat flawed tool. This occurs because receivables are low before the selling season and high after the season. Thus, firms may keep track of seasonal movement in the ACP over past years. In this way, they can compare the ACP for today's date with the average ACP for that date in previous years. To supplement the information in the ACP, the credit manager may make up a schedule of aging of receivables.

Aging Schedule

The **aging schedule** tabulates receivables by age of account. In the following schedule, 75 percent of the accounts are on time, but a significant number are more than 60 days past due. This signifies that some customers are in arrears.

Aging schedule

Age of account	Percentage of total value of accounts receivable
0–20 days	50
21–60 days	25
61–80 days	20
Over 80 days	5
	100

The aging schedule changes during the year. To avoid confusion, the aging schedule is often augmented by the payments pattern. The *payments pattern* describes the lagged collection pattern of receivables. Like a mortality table that describes the probability that a 23-year-old will live to be 24, the payments pattern describes the probability that a 67-day-old account will still be unpaid when it is 68 days old.

Collection Effort

The firm usually employs a sequence of procedures for customers that are overdue. It

1. Sends a delinquency letter informing the customer of the past-due status of the account.
2. Makes a telephone call to the customer.
3. Employs a collection agency.
4. Takes legal action against the customer.

At times, a firm may refuse to grant additional credit to customers until arrearages are paid. This may antagonize a normally good customer, and it points to a potential conflict of interest between the collections department and the sales department.

One last point should be stressed. We have presented the elements of credit policy as though they were somewhat independent of each other. In fact, they are closely interrelated. For example, the optimal credit policy is not independent of collection and monitoring policies. A tighter collection policy can reduce the probability of default and this in turn can raise the NPV of a more liberal credit policy.

CONCEPT QUESTION

■ What tools can a manager use to analyze a collection policy?

Other Aspects of Credit Policy 28.6

Factoring

A *factor* is an independent company that acts as "an outside credit department" for the client. It checks the credit of new customers, authorizes credit, and handles collection and bookkeeping. As the accounts are collected, the factor pays the client the face amount of the invoice less a 1- or 2-percent discount.[8] If any accounts are late, the factor still pays the selling firm on an average maturity date determined in advance. The legal arrangement is that the factor purchases the accounts receivable from the firm. Thus, factoring provides insurance against bad debts since any bad accounts are the factor's problem.

Factoring in Canada is conducted by independent firms whose main customers are small businesses. Factoring is popular with manufacturers of retail goods—especially in the apparel business—because it allows outside professionals to handle the headaches of credit.

What we have described so far is *maturity factoring* and does not involve a formal financing arrangement. What factoring does is remove receivables from the balance sheet and so, indirectly, it reduces the need for financing. It may also reduce the costs associated with granting credit. Since factors do business with many firms, they may be able to achieve scale economies, reduce risks through diversification, and carry more clout in collection.

Firms financing their receivables through a chartered bank may also use the services of a factor to improve the receivables' collateral value. In this case, the factor buys the receivables and assigns them to the bank. This is called maturity factoring with assignment of equity. Or, the factor will provide an advance on the receivables and charge interest at prime plus 2.5 to 3 percent. In this case of advance factoring, the factor is providing financing as well as other services.

Credit Management in Practice

CO-OP Atlantic is a groceries and fuel distributor located in Moncton, N.B.[9] Its credit manager, Gary Steeves, is responsible for monitoring and collecting over $450 million in receivables annually. CO-OP's customers include large grocery stores with balances

---

[8]Our discussion of factoring draws on D. Reidy, "Factoring Smooths Banking Relationships," *Profit* (November 1991); and S. Horvitch, "Busy Days for Factoring Firms," *Financial Post* (February 15, 1991).

[9]This section draws on "High Technology Systems Boost Productivity and Bring New Efficiency to Credit Management," Joint Venture Supplement, *Financial Post* (June 20, 1991).

over $1 million as well as several thousand small accounts with balances around $1,000. By installing a computerized system, CO-OP has reduced its average collection period by two days with a savings (NPV) of millions. The system improved monitoring of receivables and credit granting analysis. It also saved on labour costs in processing receivables documentation.

To make monitoring easy, treasury credit staff call up customer information from a central database. For example, in the home fuel division, aging schedules are used to identify overdue accounts that require authorization by an analyst before further deliveries can be made. Under the old manual system, this information was not available. The system also provides collections staff with a daily list of accounts due for a telephone call with a complete history of each account.

Credit analysis centres around an early warning system examining the solvency risk of existing and new commercial accounts. The software scores the accounts based on financial ratios. By mechanizing the analysis, CO-OP can now score all its large commercial accounts. Under the manual system, detailed financial analysis was done on an exception basis and often came too late.

CO-OP achieved these gains in monitoring and analysis without adding any staff in the credit department. The department has the same number of people as it did in 1981, when sales were half the present level. Steeves estimates that automation saved the company over $100,000 in additional wages.

CONCEPT QUESTION

- What services do factors provide?

28.7   Summary and Conclusions

1. The three components of a firm's credit policy are the terms of sale, the credit analysis, and the collection policies.
2. The terms of sale describe the amount and period of time for which credit is granted and the type of credit instrument.
3. The decision to grant credit is a straightforward NPV decision, and can be improved by additional information about the payment characteristics of the customers. Additional information about the customers' probability of defaulting is valuable, but this value must be traded off against the expense of acquiring the information.
4. The optimal amount of credit the firm offers is a function of the competitive conditions in which it finds itself. These conditions will determine the carrying costs associated with granting credit and the opportunity costs of the lost sales from refusing to offer credit. The optimal credit policy minimizes the sum of these two costs.
5. We have seen that knowledge of the probability that customers will default is valuable. To enhance its ability to assess customers' default probability, a firm can score credit. This relates the default probability to observable characteristics of customers.

6. The collection policy is the method of dealing with past-due accounts. The first step is to analyze the average collection period and to prepare an aging schedule that relates the age of accounts to the proportion of the accounts receivable they represent. The next step is to decide on the collection method and to evaluate the possibility of factoring, that is, selling the overdue accounts.

Key Terms

Terms of the sale 799

Credit analysis 799

Collection policy 799

Invoice 801

Credit period 801

Cash discount 802

Credit instrument 804

Credit scoring 811

Multiple discriminant analysis (MDA) 811

Average collection period (ACP) 813

Average daily sales (ADS) 813

Aging schedule 814

Factoring 815

Suggested Readings

An excellent textbook on short-term financial management is:

N. C. Hill and W. L. Sartoris. *Short-Term Financial Management.* New York: Macmillan, 1988.

Information on credit management in Canada is available from:

The Canadian Institute of Credit and Financial Management in Mississauga, Ontario.

Our treatment of the credit decision owes much to:

H. Bierman, Jr., and W. H. Hausman. "The Credit Granting Decision." *Management Science* 16 (April 1970).

Questions and Problems

Credit Terms

28.1 The North County Publishing Company has provided the following data:

> Annual credit sales: $10 million.
>
> Average collection period: 60 days.
>
> Terms: net 30.
>
> Interest rate: 10%.

North County Publishing proposes to offer a discount policy of 2/10, net 30. It anticipates that 50 percent of its customers will take advantage of this new policy. As a result, the collection period will be reduced to 30 days. Should the North County Publishing Company offer the new credit terms?

28.2 Mike and Martin Hardware Company sells on credit terms of net 45. Its accounts are on average 45 days past due. If annual credit sales are $5 million, what is the company's balance in accounts receivable?

28.3 The Tropeland Company has provided the following information:

> Annual credit sales: $30 million.
>
> Collection period: 60 days.
>
> Terms: net 30.
>
> Interest rate: 12%.

The company is considering offering terms of 4/10, net 30. It anticipates that 50 percent of its customers will take advantage of the discount. The collection period is expected to decrease by one month. Should the new credit policy be adopted?

The Decision to Grant Credit

28.4 Berkshire Sports, Inc., operates a mail-order running shoe business. Management is considering dropping its policy of no credit. The credit policy under consideration by Berkshire follows:

	No credit	Credit
Price per unit	$35	$40
Cost per unit	$25	$32
Quantity sold	2,000	3,000
Probability of payment	100%	85%
Credit period	0	1
Discount rate	0	3%

a. Should Berkshire offer credit to its customers?

b. What must the probability of payment be before Berkshire would adopt the policy?

28.5 The Fort St. John Corporation (FSJ), a manufacturer of high-quality stuffed animals, does not extend credit to its customers. A study has shown that, by offering credit, the company can increase sales from the current 750 units to 1,000 units. The cost per unit, however, will increase from $43 to $45, reflecting the expense of managing accounts receivable. The current price of a toy is $48. The probability of a customer making a payment on a credit sale is 92 percent, and the appropriate discount rate is 2.7 percent.

How much should FSJ increase the price to make offering credit an attractive strategy?

28.6 The Silver Spokes Bicycle Shop has decided to offer credit to its customers during the spring selling season. Sales are expected to be 300 cycles. A cycle's average cost to the shop is $240. The owner knows that only 95 percent of the customers will be able to make their payments. To identify the remaining 5 percent, she is considering subscribing to a credit agency. The initial charge for this service is $500, with an additional charge of $4 per individual report. Should she subscribe to the agency?

Investment in Receivables

28.7 Ancaster Electronics sells 85,000 personal stereos each year at a price per unit of $55. All sales are on credit; the terms are 3/15, net 40. The discount is taken by 40 percent of the customers. What is the investment in accounts receivable?

In reaction to a competitor, Ancaster Electronics is considering changing its credit terms to 5/15, net 40, to preserve its sales level. Describe qualitatively how this policy change will affect the investment in accounts receivable.

28.8 The Moose Jaw Company has monthly credit sales of $600,000. The average collection period is 90 days. The cost of production is 70 percent of the selling price. What is the Moose Jaw Company's average investment in accounts receivable?

In Part 7 we discuss three special topics: mergers and acquisitions, financial distress, and international corporate finance.

Chapter 29 describes the corporate finance of mergers and acquisitions. The acquisition of one firm by another is a capital budgeting decision. Here the basic principles of NPV analysis apply; that is, a firm should be acquired if it generates positive NPV to the shareholders of the acquiring firm. Chapter 29 tells how to value an acquisition candidate. However, the NPV of an acquisition candidate is more difficult to determine than that of a typical investment project because of complex accounting, tax, and legal effects.

Chapter 30 discusses what happens when a firm experiences financial distress. Financial distress is a special circumstance when a firm's cash flow falls below its contractually required payments. Financial restructuring involving private workouts or formal bankruptcy usually follows financial distress.

Our last chapter concerns international corporate finance. Many firms have significant foreign operations and must consider special financial factors that do not directly affect purely domestic firms. These factors include foreign exchange rates, interest rates that vary from country to country, and complex accounting, legal, and tax rules.

CHAPTER 29

Mergers and Acquisitions

There is no more dramatic or controversial activity in corporate finance than the acquisition of one firm by another or the merger of two firms. It is the stuff of which reporters' dreams are made, and, occasionally, it is an embarrassing source of scandal.

The acquisition of one firm by another is, of course, an investment made under uncertainty. The basic principle of valuation applies: A firm should be acquired if it generates a positive net present value to the shareholders of the acquiring firm. However, because the NPV of an acquisition candidate is very difficult to determine, mergers and acquisitions are interesting topics in their own right. Here are some of the special features of this area of finance:

1. The benefits from acquisitions are called *synergies*. It is hard to estimate synergies using discounted cash flow techniques.

2. There are complex accounting, tax, and legal effects when one firm is acquired by another.

3. Acquisitions are an important control device of shareholders. It appears that some acquisitions are a consequence of an underlying conflict between the interests of management and of shareholders. Agreeing to be acquired by another firm is one way that shareholders can remove managers.

4. Acquisition analysis frequently focuses on the total value of the firms involved. But usually an acquisition will affect the relative values of stocks and bonds as well as their total value.

5. Mergers and acquisitions sometimes involve unfriendly transactions. Thus, when one firm attempts to acquire another, it does not always involve quiet negotiations. The sought-after firm may use defensive tactics, including poison pills, greenmail, and white knights (which we discuss later).

This chapter starts by introducing the basic legal, accounting, and tax aspects of acquisitions. The chapter next discusses how to determine the NPV of an acquisition candidate—the difference between the synergy from the merger and the premium to be paid. We consider the following types of synergy: (1) revenue enhancement, (2) cost reduction, (3) lower taxes, and (4) lower cost of capital. The premium paid for an acquisition is the price paid minus the market value of the acquisition prior to the merger. The premium depends on whether cash or securities are used to finance the offer price.

29.1   The Basic Forms of Acquisitions

There are three basic legal procedures that one firm can use to acquire another firm: (1) merger or consolidation, (2) acquisition of stock, and (3) acquisition of assets.

Although these forms are different from a legal standpoint, the financial press frequently does not distinguish among them. To make the terminology more confusing, both the Canadian and Ontario Business Corporation Acts refer to combinations of firms as **amalgamations.** In our discussion, we use the term *merger* regardless of the actual form of the acquisition.

In our discussion, we will frequently refer to the acquiring firm as the **bidder**. This is the company that makes an offer to distribute cash or securities to obtain the stock or assets of another company. The firm that is sought (and perhaps acquired) is often called the *target firm*. The cash or securities offered to the target firm are the *consideration* in the acquisition.

Merger or Consolidation

A **merger** refers to the absorption of one firm by another. The acquiring firm retains its name and identity, and acquires all of the assets and liabilities of the acquired firm. After a merger, the acquired firm ceases to exist as a separate business entity.

A **consolidation** is the same as a merger except that an entirely new firm is created. In a consolidation, both the acquiring firm and the acquired firm terminate their previous legal existence and become part of the new firm. In a consolidation, the distinction between the acquiring and the acquired firm is not important. However, the rules for mergers and consolidations are basically the same. Acquisitions by merger and consolidation result in combinations of the assets and liabilities of acquired and acquiring firms.

▪ *Example*

Suppose firm A acquires firm B in a merger. Further, suppose firm B shareholders are given one share of firm A's stock in exchange for two shares of firm B's stock. From a legal standpoint, firm A's shareholders are not directly affected by the merger. However, firm B's shares cease to exist. In a consolidation, the shareholders of firm A and firm B exchange their shares for the shares of a new firm (firm C). Because the differences between mergers and consolidations are minor for our purposes, we shall refer to both types of reorganizations as *mergers*.

There are some advantages and some disadvantages to using a merger to acquire a firm:

1. A merger is legally straightforward and does not cost as much as other forms of acquisition. It avoids the necessity of transferring title of each individual asset of the acquired firm to the acquiring firm.

2. A primary disadvantage is that a merger must be approved by a vote of the shareholders of each firm.[1] Typically, two-thirds (or even more) of the share

---

[1]As we discuss later, obtaining majority assent is less of a problem in Canada than in the United States because fewer Canadian corporations are widely held.

votes are required for approval. Obtaining the necessary votes can be time-consuming and difficult. Furthermore, as we discuss in greater detail below, the cooperation of the target firm's existing management is almost a necessity for a merger. This cooperation may not be easily or cheaply obtained.

Acquisition of Stock

A second way to acquire another firm is to purchase the firm's voting stock in exchange for cash, shares of stock, or other securities. This process will often start as a private offer from the management of one firm to another. At some point the offer is taken directly to the target firm's shareholders through a tender offer. A **tender offer** is a public offer to buy shares made by one firm directly to the shareholders of another firm.

If the shareholders choose to accept the offer, they tender their shares by exchanging them for cash or securities (or both), depending on the offer. A tender offer is frequently contingent on the bidder's obtaining some percentage of the total voting shares. If not enough shares are tendered, then the offer might be withdrawn or reformulated.

The takeover bid is communicated to the target firm's shareholders by public announcements such as newspaper advertisements. Takeover bids may be either by **circular bid** mailed directly to the target's shareholders or by **stock exchange bid** (through the facilities of the TSE or other exchange). In either case, Ontario securities law requires that the bidder mail a notice of the proposed share purchase to shareholders. Furthermore, the management of the target firm must also respond to the bid, including its recommendation to accept or to reject the bid. In the case of a circular bid, the response must be mailed to shareholders. If the bid is made through a stock exchange, the response is through a press release.

The following are factors involved in choosing between an acquisition of stock and a merger:

- In an acquisition of stock, no shareholder meetings must be held and no vote is required. If the shareholders of the target firm do not like the offer, they are not required to accept it and they will not tender their shares.

- In an acquisition of stock, the bidding firm can deal directly with the shareholders of a target firm by using a tender offer. The target firm's management and board of directors can be bypassed.

- Acquisition of stock is often unfriendly and is used in an effort to circumvent the target firm's management, which is usually actively resisting acquisition. Resistance by the target firm's management often makes the cost of acquisition by stock higher than the cost by merger.

- Sometimes a minority of shareholders will hold out in a tender offer, and thus the target firm cannot be completely absorbed.

- Complete absorption of one firm by another requires a merger. Many acquisitions of stock end with a formal merger later.

Acquisition of Assets

One firm can acquire another by buying all of its assets. A formal vote of the shareholders of the selling firm is required. This approach to acquisition will avoid the potential problem of having minority shareholders, which can occur in an acquisition of stock. But, acquisition of assets involves a costly legal process of transferring title.

A Classification Scheme

Financial analysts typically classify acquisitions into three types:

1. *Horizontal acquisition*. This is an acquisition of a firm in the same industry as the acquiring firm. The firms compete with each other in their product market.
2. *Vertical acquisition*. A vertical acquisition involves firms at different stages of the production process. The acquisition by an airline company of a travel agency would be a vertical acquisition.
3. *Conglomerate acquisition*. The acquiring firm and the acquired firm are not related to each other. The acquisition of Federated Department Stores by Campeau Corporation, a real estate company, was considered a conglomerate acquisition. Later we discuss this acquisition in detail.

A Note on Takeovers

Takeover is a general and imprecise term referring to the transfer of control of a firm from one group of shareholders to another.[2] The bidder offers to pay cash or securities to obtain the stock or assets of another company. If the offer is accepted, the target firm will give up control over its stock or assets to the bidder in exchange for the *consideration*—its stock, its debt, or cash.

For example, when a bidding firm acquires a target firm, the right to control the operating activities of the target firm is transferred to a newly elected board of directors of the acquiring firm. This is a takeover by acquisition.

Takeovers can occur by acquisition, proxy contests, and going-private transactions. Thus, as shown in Figure 29.1, takeovers encompass a broader set of activities than acquisitions.

If a takeover is achieved by acquisition, it will be by merger, tender offer for shares of stock, or purchase of assets. In mergers and tender offers, the acquiring firm buys the voting common stock of the acquired firm.

Takeovers can occur with *proxy contests* in which a group of shareholders attempts to gain controlling seats on the board of directors by voting in new directors. A *proxy* authorizes the proxy holder to vote on all matters in a shareholders' meeting. In a proxy contest, proxies from the rest of the shareholders are solicited by an insurgent group of shareholders.

In **going-private transactions**, all of the equity shares of a public firm are purchased by a small group of investors. Usually, the group includes members of

---

[2]*Control* may be defined as having a majority vote on the board of directors.

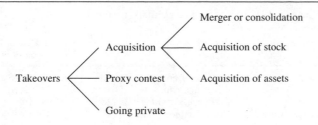

Figure 29.1
Varieties of takeovers

incumbent management and some outside investors. Such transactions have come to be known generically as **leveraged buyouts (LBOs)** because a large percentage of the money needed to buy up the stock is usually borrowed. Such transactions are also termed *management buyouts* (MBOs) when existing management is heavily involved. The shares of the firm are delisted from stock exchanges and no longer can be purchased in the open market.

LBOs were common in the late 1980s, and some recent ones have been quite large. As this is written, the largest acquisition in history (and possibly the single largest private transaction ever of any kind) is the 1989 LBO of RJR Nabisco, the U.S. tobacco and food products giant. The acquisition price in that buyout was an astonishing U.S. $25 billion. In that LBO, as with most of the large ones, much of the financing came from junk bond sales. (See Chapter 20 for a discussion of junk bonds.)

The 1980s saw a large number of mergers, acquisitions, and LBOs, many of them involving very familiar companies. In fact, the largest such transactions ever all took place in the 1980s. Table 29.1 lists the 20 largest mergers in Canada between 1979 and 1989. While lagging behind RJR Nabisco, Campeau Corporation (the largest merger on the Canadian list) ranks number 7 in the top 20 U.S. mergers for the same period.[3] Another significant trend is foreign involvement. Three of the top 20 mergers involved Canadian firms buying U.S. companies, while six featured foreign firms acquiring Canadian assets.

CONCEPT QUESTIONS

- What is a merger? How does a merger differ from other forms of acquisition?
- What is a takeover?

The Tax Forms of Acquisitions 29.2

If one firm buys another firm, the transaction may be taxable or tax-free. In a *taxable acquisition,* the shareholders of the target firm are considered to have sold their shares, and they will have capital gains or losses that will be taxed. In a *tax-free acquisition,* since the acquisition is considered an exchange instead of a sale, no capital gain or loss occurs.

---

[3]W. Adams and J. W. Brock, *Dangerous Pursuits* (New York: Pantheon, 1989), p. 14.

Table 29.1 Twenty largest mergers in Canada, 1979–1989, ranked by market value in 1989

Rank	Purchase price (in $ million)	Acquiring company	Acquired or merged company	Date of acquisition	Percentage of stock acquired
1	$6,600*	Campeau Corp.	Federated Department Stores, Cincinnati, Ohio	1988	100%
2	4,133	Dome Petroleum Ltd.	Hudson's Bay Oil & Gas Ltd.	1981	100
3	5,500	Amoco Petroleum Corp., Chicago, Illinois	Dome Petroleum Ltd.	1988	100
4	5,004*	Campeau Corp.	Allied Stores Corp., New York	1986	100
5	4,960	Imperial Oil Ltd.	Texaco Canada Ltd.	1989	100
6	3,091*	Seagram Co.	Du Pont, Wilmington, Delaware	1981	20
7	3,000†	Gulf Canada Corp.	Hiram Walker Resources Ltd.	1986	70
8	2,850	Olympia & York Dev.	Gulf Canada Ltd.	1985	60
9	2,600†	Allied Lyons PLC, UK	Hiram Walker–Gooderham & Worts	1986	51
10	2,570	Imasco Ltd.	Genstar Corp.	1986	100
11	2,600	JMB Realty Corp., Chicago, Illinois	Cadillac Fairview	1987	100
12	1,496	Petro-Canada	Pacific Petroleums Ltd.	1979	100
13	2,600	Stone Container, Chicago, Illinois	Consolidated-Bathurst Ltd.	1989	100
14	1,600	Canada Dev. Corp.	Aquitaine Co. of Canada	1981	100
15	2,200	Noranda Inc., Trelleborg AG, Sweden	Falconbridge Ltd.	1989	100
16	1,453	Petro-Canada	Petrotina Canada Ltd.	1981	100
17	1,167	Consumers' Gas Co.	Hiram Walker–Gooderham & Worts	1980	100
18	1,421	Canadian Pacific Ltd.	CP Enterprises Ltd.	1985	30
19	1,100	CP Enterprises Ltd.	Canadian International Paper	1981	100
20	1,635	Houston Industries Inc., Houston, Texas	U.S. Cable Assets, Rogers Communications Inc.	1989	100

*Converted from $ U.S.
† Original purchase price.
Source: *Financial Post 500* (Summer 1990).

Determinants of Tax Status

The general requirements for tax-free status are that (1) the acquisition involves two Canadian corporations subject to corporate income tax, and (2) there be a continuity of equity interest. In other words, the shareholders in the target firm must retain an equity interest in the bidder.

The specific requirements for a tax-free acquisition depend on the legal form of the acquisition, but, in general, if the buying firm offers the selling firm cash for its equity, it will be a taxable acquisition. If shares of stock are offered, it will be a tax-free acquisition.

In a tax-free acquisition, the selling shareholders are considered to have exchanged their old shares for new ones of equal value, and no capital gains or losses are experienced.

Taxable versus Tax-Free Acquisitions

There are two factors to consider when comparing a tax-free acquisition and a taxable acquisition: the capital gains effect and the write-up effect. The *capital gains effect* refers to the fact that the target firm's shareholders may have to pay capital gains taxes in a taxable acquisition. They may demand a higher price as compensation, thereby increasing the cost of the merger. This is a cost of a taxable acquisition.

The bidder's shareholders may be willing to pay this cost because the bidder enjoys a *write-up effect* in a taxable acquisition. The tax status of an acquisition also affects the appraised value of the assets of the selling firm. In a taxable acquisition, the assets of the selling firm are revalued or "written up" from their historic book value to their estimated current market value. This is the write-up effect, and it is important because the depreciation expense on the acquired firm's assets can be increased in taxable acquisitions. Remember that an increase in depreciation is a noncash expense, but it has the desirable effect of reducing taxes.

CONCEPT QUESTIONS

- What factors influence the choice between a taxable and a tax-free acquisition?
- What is the write-up effect in a taxable acquisition?

Accounting for Acquisitions   29.3

Earlier in this text we mentioned that firms keep two distinct sets of books: the shareholders' books and the tax books. The previous section concerned the effect of acquisitions on the tax books. We now consider the shareholders' books. When one firm acquires another firm, the acquisition will be treated as either a purchase or a pooling of interests on the shareholders' books.

The Purchase Method

The **purchase method** of reporting acquisitions requires that the assets of the acquired firm be reported at their fair market value on the books of the acquiring firm. This allows the acquiring firm to establish a new cost basis for the acquired assets.

In a purchase, an accounting entry called *goodwill* is created. **Goodwill** is the excess of the purchase price over the sum of the values of the individual assets acquired.

- *Example*

Suppose firm A acquires firm B, creating a new firm, AB. Firm A's and firm B's financial positions at the date of the acquisition are shown in Table 29.2. The book value of firm B on the date of the acquisition is $10 million. This is the sum of $8 million in buildings and $2 million in cash. However, an appraiser states that the sum of the fair market values of the individual buildings is $14 million. With $2 million in cash, the sum of the market values of the individual assets in firm B is $16 million. This represents the value to be received if the firm is liquidated by selling off the individual assets separately.

However, the whole is often worth more than the sum of the parts in business. Firm A pays $19 million in cash for firm B. This difference of $3 million (or $19 million − $16 million) is goodwill. It represents the increase in value by keeping the

Table 29.2
Accounting for
acquisitions:
Purchase (in $
millions)

Firm A					Firm B			
Cash	$ 4	Equity	$20		Cash	$ 2	Equity	$10
Land	16				Land	0		
Buildings	0				Buildings	8		
Total	$20		$20		Total	$10		$10

Firm AB			
Cash	$6	Debt	$19
Land	16	Equity	20
Buildings	14		
Goodwill	3		
Total	$39		$39

When the purchase method is used, the assets of the acquired firm (firm B) appear in the combined firm's books at their fair market value.

firm intact as an ongoing business. Firm A issued $19 million in new debt to finance the acquisition. The last balance sheet in Table 29.2 shows what happens under purchase accounting.

1. The total assets of firm AB increase to $39 million. The buildings of firm B appear in the new balance sheet at their current market value. That is, the market value of the assets of the acquired firm become part of the book value of the new firm. However, the assets of the acquiring firm (firm A) remain at their old book value. They are not revalued upward when the new firm is created.

2. The excess of the purchase price over the sum of the fair market values of the individual assets acquired is $3 million. ∎

Pooling of Interests

Under a **pooling of interests**, the assets of the new firm are valued at the same level at which they were carried on the books of the acquired and acquiring firms. Using the previous example, assume that, to acquire firm B, firm A issues common stock with a market value of $19 million. Table 29.3 illustrates this merger.

The new firm is owned jointly by all the shareholders of the previously separate firms. The total assets and the total equity are unchanged by the acquisition. No goodwill is created. Furthermore, the $19 million used to acquire firm B does not appear in Table 29.3.

Purchase or Pooling of Interests: A Comparison

One important difference between purchase and pooling of interests accounting is goodwill. A firm may prefer pooling because it does not involve goodwill. Some firms do not like goodwill because the original amount must be amortized over a period of years (not to exceed 40 years).

The goodwill amortization expense must be deducted from reported income. This is a noncash deduction, of course, but, unlike depreciation, it is not tax-deductible. As

Firm A				Firm B				**Table 29.3**
Cash	$ 4	Equity	$20	Cash	$ 2	Equity	$10	Accounting for acquisitions:
Land	16			Land	0			Pooling of interests
Buildings	0			Buildings	8			(in $ millions)
Total	$20		$20	Total	$10		$10	

Firm AB			
Cash	$6	Equity	$30
Land	16		
Buildings	8		
Total	$30		$30

In a pooling of interests, the assets appear in the combined firm's books at the same value that they had in each separate firm's books prior to the merger.

a result of this expense, purchase accounting will usually result in lower reported income than pooling of interests accounting. Also, purchase accounting may result in a larger book value for total assets (because of the write-up in asset values). The combination of lower reported income and larger book value from purchase accounting has an unfavourable impact on accounting-based performance measures, such as return on assets (ROA) and return on equity (ROE).

Purchase accounting does not, in itself, affect taxes. The tax status of a merger is determined by Revenue Canada. Because the amount of tax-deductible expense is not directly affected by the method of acquisition accounting, cash flows are not affected, and the NPV of the acquisition should be the same whether pooling or purchase accounting is used. Not surprisingly, there doesn't appear to be any evidence suggesting that acquiring firms create more value under one method than under the other.

CONCEPT QUESTION

- What is the difference between purchase accounting and pooling-of-interests accounting?

Determining the Synergy from an Acquisition   29.4

Suppose firm A is contemplating acquiring firm B. The value of firm A is V_A and the value of firm B is V_B. (It is reasonable to assume that, for public companies, V_A and V_B can be determined by observing the market prices of the outstanding securities.) The difference between the value of the combined firm (V_{AB}) and the sum of the values of the firms as separate entities is the *synergy* from the acquisition:

$$\text{Synergy} = V_{AB} - (V_A + V_B)$$

The acquiring firm must generally pay a premium for the acquired firm. For example, if stock of the target is selling for $50, the acquirer might need to pay $60 a share, implying a premium of $10 or 20 percent. Firm A will want to determine the synergy before entering into negotiations with firm B on the premium.

The synergy of an acquisition can be determined from the usual discounted cash flow model:

$$\text{Synergy} = \sum_{t=1}^{T} \frac{\Delta CF_t}{(1 + r)^t}$$

where ΔCF_t is the difference between the cash flows at date t of the combined firm and the sum of the cash flows of the two separate firms. In other words, ΔCF_t is the incremental cash flow at date t from the merger. The term r is the risk-adjusted discount rate appropriate for the incremental cash flows. This is generally considered to be the required rate of return on the equity of the target.

From the chapters on capital budgeting we know that the incremental cash flows can be separated into four parts:

$$\Delta CF_t = \Delta Rev_t - \Delta Costs_t - \Delta Taxes_t - \Delta \text{Capital requirements}_t$$

where ΔRev_t is the incremental revenue of the acquisition, $\Delta Costs_t$ is the incremental costs of the acquisition, $\Delta Taxes_t$ is the incremental acquisition taxes, and $\Delta Capital$ requirements$_t$ is the incremental new investment required in working capital and fixed assets.

29.5   Sources of Synergy from Acquisitions

It follows from our classification of incremental cash flows that the possible sources of synergy fall into four basic categories: revenue enhancement, cost reduction, lower taxes, and lower cost of capital.

Revenue Enhancement

One important reason for acquisitions is that a combined firm may generate greater revenues than two separate firms. Increased revenues may come from marketing gains, strategic benefits, and market power.

Marketing Gains

It is frequently claimed that mergers and acquisitions can produce greater operating revenues from improved marketing. Improvements can be made in:

1. Previously ineffective media programming and advertising efforts.
2. A weak existing distribution network.
3. An unbalanced product mix.

Strategic Benefits

Some acquisitions promise a *strategic* advantage.[4] This is an opportunity to take advantage of the competitive environment if certain situations materialize. In this

---

[4]For a discussion of the financial side of strategic planning, see S. C. Myers, "Finance Theory and Finance Strategy," *Interfaces* 14 (January-February 1984), p. 1.

regard, a strategic benefit is more like an option than like a standard investment opportunity. For example, imagine that a sewing machine company acquired a computer company. The firm would be well positioned if technological advances allowed computer-driven sewing machines in the future. Michael Porter has used the word *beachhead* in his description of the process of entering a new industry to exploit perceived opportunities.[5] The beachhead is used to spawn new opportunities based on *intangible* relationships. He views Procter & Gamble's initial acquisition of the Charmin Paper Company as a beachhead that allowed Procter & Gamble to develop a highly interrelated cluster of paper products: disposable diapers, paper towels, feminine hygiene products, and bathroom tissue.

Market or Monopoly Power

One firm may acquire another to increase its market share and market power. Profits can be enhanced through higher prices and reduced competition for customers. In theory, such mergers are controlled by law. In practice, however, horizontal mergers are far more common in Canada than in the United States due to weaker legal restrictions against combinations of competitors that might limit market competition.[6]

The empirical evidence does not suggest that increased market power is a significant reason for mergers. If monopoly power is increased through an acquisition, all firms in the industry should benefit as the price of the industry's product is increased. However, Stillman's and Eckbo's examinations of merger announcement effects on the share prices of firms that compete with the merger target indicate that this is not the case.[7] They find no consistent tendency for the share prices of rivals to increase, so the Stillman–Eckbo data do not support the monopoly power theory.

Cost Reduction

One of the most basic reasons to merge is that a combined firm may operate more efficiently than two separate firms. A merger or acquisition can increase a firm's operating efficiency in several different ways: economies of scale, economies of vertical integration, complementary resources, and elimination of inefficient management.

Economies of Scale

If the average cost of production falls while the level of production increases, there is said to be an economy of scale. Figure 29.2 illustrates that economies of scale result while the firm grows to its optimal size. Beyond this size, diseconomies of scale occur. In other words, average cost increases with further firm growth. The phrase *spreading overhead* is frequently used in connection with economies of scale from horizontal

---

[5]M. Porter, *Competitive Advantage* (New York: Free Press, 1985).

[6]From the mid-1950s to the mid-1980s, only one merger in Canada was blocked under the Combines Investigation Act. In the same period, U.S. antitrust laws "prevented several hundred horizontal mergers" according to B. E. Eckbo, "Mergers and the Market for Corporate Control: The Canadian Evidence," *Canadian Journal of Economics* (May 1986), pp. 236–60.

[7]R. Stillman, "Examining Antitrust Policy toward Horizontal Mergers," *Journal of Financial Economics* 11 (April 1983); and E. B. Eckbo, "Horizontal Mergers, Collusion and Stockholder Wealth," *Journal of Financial Economics* 11 (April 1983).

Figure 29.2
Economies of scale
and the optimal
size of the firm

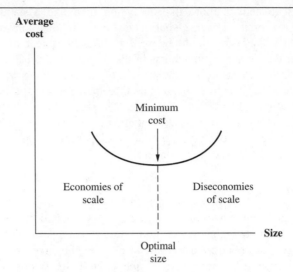

mergers. This refers to the sharing of central facilities such as corporate headquarters, top management, and a large mainframe computer.

Economies of Vertical Integration

Operating economies can be gained from vertical as well as horizontal combinations. The main purpose of vertical acquisitions is to make coordination of closely related operating activities easier. This is probably the reason why most forest product firms that cut timber also own sawmills and hauling equipment. Economies from vertical integration probably explain why most airline companies own airplanes; it also may explain why some airline companies have purchased hotels and car rental companies.

Technology transfers are another reason for vertical integration. Consider the merger of General Motors and Hughes Aircraft in 1985. An automobile manufacturer might well acquire an advanced electronics firm if the special technology of the electronics firm can improve the quality of the automobile.

Complementary Resources

Some firms acquire others to make better use of existing resources or to provide the missing ingredient for success. Think of a ski equipment store that could merge with a tennis equipment store to produce more even sales over both the winter and summer seasons—and better use of store capacity.

Elimination of Inefficient Management

There are firms whose value could be increased with a change in management. For example, Jensen and Ruback argue that acquisitions can occur because of changing technology or market conditions that require a restructuring of the corporation.[8] Incumbent managers in some cases do not understand changing conditions. They have trouble abandoning strategies and styles they have spent years formulating.

The oil industry is an example of managerial inefficiency cited by Jensen. In the late 1970s, changes in the oil industry included reduced expectations of the future price of oil, increased exploration and development costs, and increased real interest rates. As a result of these changes, substantial reductions in exploration and development were called for. However, many oil company managers were unable to downsize their firms. For example, a study by McConnell and Muscarella reports that the stock prices of oil companies tended to drop upon announcements of increases in exploration and development expenditures in the period 1975–81.[9]

Acquiring companies sought out oil firms in order to reduce the investment levels of these oil companies.[10] For example, T. Boone Pickens of Mesa Petroleum perceived the changes taking place in the oil industry and attempted to buy several oil companies: Unocal, Phillips, and Getty. The results of these attempted acquisitions were reduced expenditures on exploration and development and huge gains to the shareholders of the affected firms.

Perks consumption by top management is another inefficiency that may be eliminated by acquisition. For example, Ross Johnson (former CEO of RJR Nabisco) is described as "a relentlessly cheerful rogue who reveled in all the apartments, country-club memberships, jets, Jaguars, and scotch his corporate treasuries could afford."[11]

Mergers and acquisitions can be viewed as part of the labour market for top management. Jensen and Ruback have used the phrase *market for corporate control*, in which alternative management teams compete for the rights to manage corporate activities.

The Negative Side of Takeovers

While most financial analysts would likely agree that competition for corporate control can enhance efficiency, there is concern over whether the cost is too high. Critics of takeovers (and especially of LBOs) are concerned that social costs are not counted when the post-takeover search for efficiency gains leads to plant closures and layoffs. When plants close or move, workers and equipment can be turned to other uses only at some cost to society. For example, taxpayers may need to subsidize retraining and relocation programs for workers or tax incentives for investment. In an extreme case, suppose a mine is closed down in a rural area where there is no other large employer. All capital goods that cannot be moved may become worthless.

---

[8]M. C. Jensen and R. S. Ruback, "The Market for Corporate Control: The Scientific Evidence," *Journal of Financial Economics* 11 (April 1983); and M. C. Jensen, "Agency Costs of Free Cash Flow, Corporate Finance and Takeovers," *American Economic Review* (May 1986).

[9]J. J. McConnell and C. J. Muscarella, "Corporate Capital Expenditure Decisions and the Market Value of the Firm," *Journal of Financial Economics* 14 (1985).

[10]More than 26 percent of the total valuation of all takeover transactions involved a selling firm in the oil and gas industry from 1981 to 1984 [W. T. Grimm, *Mergerstat Review* (1985), p. 41].

[11]B. Burroughs, "Barbarians in Retreat," *Vanity Fair* (March 1993), p. 226.

Critics of takeovers argue that they reduce trust between management and labour, thus reducing efficiency and increasing costs. They point to Japan, Germany, and Korea (where there are few takeovers) as examples of more efficient economies. They argue that, as an alternative to takeovers, a strong board of outside directors could maximize management's efficiency.[12]

Evidence on Market Power and Efficiency Gains

Most of the evidence on merger gains is measured in terms of returns to shareholders. We discuss this later to see who gains in mergers. To attribute any gains from mergers to specific advantages like market share requires an industrial organization approach. A recent study of Canadian mergers in the 1970s found that gains occurred in market share, productivity, or profitability. This suggests that revenue enhancement and cost reduction are valid reasons at least for some mergers.[13]

Tax Gains

Tax gains often are a powerful incentive for acquisitions. Possible tax gains from an acquisition include

1. The use of tax losses.
2. The use of unused debt capacity.
3. The use of surplus funds.
4. The ability to write up the value of depreciable assets.

Net Operating Losses

Firms that lose money on a pretax basis will not pay taxes. Such firms can end up with tax losses that they cannot use. These tax losses are referred to as *NOL* (an acronym for *net operating losses*).

A firm with net operating losses may be an attractive merger partner for a firm with significant tax liabilities. Absent any other effects, the combined firm will have a lower tax bill than the two firms considered separately. This is a good example of how a firm can be more valuable merged than standing alone. For example, tax savings made possible by Dome Petroleum's large losses were an important attraction to Amoco when it bought Dome in 1988. Table 29.1 shows this was the third largest merger in Canada between 1979 and 1989.

There is an important qualification to our NOL discussion. Canadian tax laws permit firms that experience periods of profit and losses to even things out through loss carry-back and carry-forward provisions. A firm that has been profitable in the past but has a loss in the current year can obtain refunds of income taxes paid in the three previous years. After that, losses can be carried forward for up to seven years. Thus, a

---

[12]This section draws on C. Robinson's arguments in C. Robinson versus W. Block, "Are Corporate Takeovers Good or Bad? A Debate," *Canadian Investment Review* (Fall 1991), pp. 53–60; and on a piece by the late W. S. Allen, "Relegating Corporate Takeovers to the 'Campeaust' Heap: A Proposal," *Canadian Investment Review* (Spring 1990), pp. 71–76.

[13]Inefficiencies in real goods markets explain why it is sometimes cheaper to acquire resources and strategic links through mergers. J. R. Baldwin and P. K. Gorecki, "Mergers and the Competitive Process," Working Paper, Statistics Canada, 1990.

merger to exploit unused tax shields must offer tax savings over and above what can be accomplished by firms via carry-overs.

Unused Debt Capacity

Some firms do not use as much debt as they are able. This makes them potential acquisition candidates. Adding debt can provide important tax savings, and many acquisitions are financed with debt. The acquiring company can deduct interest payments on the newly created debt and reduce taxes.[14]

Surplus Funds

Another quirk in the tax laws involves surplus funds. Consider a firm that has *free cash flow*—cash flow available after all taxes have been paid and after all positive net present value projects have been financed.

In this situation, aside from purchasing fixed income securities, the firm has several ways to spend the free cash flow, including

1. Pay dividends.
2. Buy back its own shares.
3. Acquire shares in another firm.

We discussed the first two options in Chapter 18 and showed that an extra dividend will increase the income tax paid by some investors. And, under Revenue Canada regulations, share repurchase seldom reduces the taxes paid by shareholders when compared to paying dividends.

To avoid these problems, the firm can buy another firm. This avoids the tax problem associated with paying a dividend. Of course, if the purchase is a negative-NPV investment, this action exemplifies inefficient management and may make the bidder into a target.

Asset Write-ups

We have previously observed that, in a taxable acquisition, the assets of the acquired firm can be revalued. If the value of the assets is increased, tax deductions for depreciation will be a gain.

The Cost of Capital

The cost of capital can often be reduced when two firms merge because the costs of issuing securities are subject to economies of scale. As we observed in earlier chapters, the costs of issuing both debt and equity are much lower for larger issues than for smaller issues.

CONCEPT QUESTIONS

■ What are sources of possible synergy in acquisitions?

---

[14]While unused debt capacity can be a valid reason for a merger, hindsight shows that many mergers in the 1980s overused debt financing. We discuss this in more detail later.

29.6   Calculating the Value of the Firm after an Acquisition

Now that we have listed the possible sources of synergy from a merger, we examine how to value these sources. Consider two firms. Gamble, Inc., manufactures and markets soaps and cosmetics. The firm has a reputation for its ability to attract, develop, and keep talented people and has successfully introduced several major products in the past two years. It would like to enter the over-the-counter drug market to round out its product line. Shapiro, Inc., is a well-known maker of cold remedies. Al Shapiro, the great-grandson of the founder of Shapiro, Inc., became chairman of the firm last year. Unfortunately, Al knows nothing about cold remedies, and as a consequence Shapiro, Inc., has had lackluster financial performance. For the most recent year, pretax cash flow fell by 15 percent. The firm's stock price is at an all-time low.

The financial management of Gamble finds Shapiro an attractive candidate. It believes that the cash flows from the combined firms would be far greater than what each firm would have alone. The anticipated cash flows and present values from the acquisition are shown in Table 29.4. The increased cash flows (CF_t) come from three benefits.

1. *Tax gains*. If Gamble acquires Shapiro, Gamble will be able to use some tax-loss carry-forwards to reduce its tax liability. The additional cash flows from tax gains should be discounted at the cost of debt capital because they can be determined with very little uncertainty. The financial management of Gamble estimates that the acquisition will reduce taxes by $1 million per year in perpetuity. The relevant discount rate is 5 percent, and the present value of the tax reduction is $20 million.

2. *Operating efficiencies*. The financial management of Gamble has determined that Gamble can take advantage of some of the unused production capacity of Shapiro. At times, Gamble has been operating at full capacity with a large backlog of orders. Shapiro's manufacturing facilities, with a little reconfiguration, can be used to produce Gamble's soaps. Thus, more soaps and cold remedies can be produced without adding to the combined firm's capacity and cost. These operating efficiencies will increase after-tax cash flows by $1.5 million per year. Using Shapiro's discount rate and assuming perpetual gains, the PV of the unused capacity is determined to be $10 million.

Table 29.4 Acquisition of Shapiro, Inc., by Gamble, Inc.		Net cash flow per year (perpetual)	Discount rate	Value
	Gamble, Inc.	$10.0 million	0.10	$100 million
	Shapiro, Inc.	4.5 million	0.15	30 million*
	Benefits from acquisition:	5.5 million	0.122	45 million
	Strategic fit	3.0 million	0.20	15 million
	Tax shelters	1.0 million	0.05	20 million
	Operating efficiencies	1.5 million	0.15	10 million
	Gamble–Shapiro	20.0 million	0.114	175 million

*The market value of Shapiro's outstanding common stock is $30 million; 1 million shares are outstanding.

3. *Strategic fit*. The financial management of Gamble has determined that the acquisition of Shapiro will give Gamble a strategic advantage. The management of Gamble believes that the addition of the Shapiro Bac-Rub ointment for sore backs to its existing product mix will give it a better chance to launch successful new skin care cosmetics if these markets develop in the future. Management of Gamble estimates that there is a 50-percent probability that $6 million in after-tax cash flow can be generated with the new skin care products. These opportunities are contingent on factors that cannot be easily quantified. Because of the lack of precision here, the managers decided to use a high discount rate. Gamble chooses a 20-percent rate, and it estimates that the present value of the strategic factors is $15 million (or 0.50 × $6 million/0.20).

Avoiding Mistakes

The Gamble–Shapiro illustration is very simple and straightforward. It is deceptive because the incremental cash flows have already been determined. In practice, an analyst must estimate these cash flows and determine the proper discount rate. Valuing the benefits of a potential acquisition is harder than valuing benefits for standard capital budgeting projects. Many mistakes can be made. Here are some general rules:

1. *Do not ignore market values*. In many cases it is very difficult to estimate values using discounted cash flows. Because of this, an expert business appraiser should know the market prices of comparable opportunities. In an efficient market, prices should reflect value. Because the market value of Shapiro is $30 million, we use this estimate of Shapiro's current value.

2. *Estimate only incremental cash flows*. Only incremental cash flows from an acquisition will add value to the acquiring firm. Thus, it is important to estimate the cash flows that are incremental to the acquisition.

3. *Use the correct discount rate*. The discount rate should be the required rate of return for the incremental cash flows associated with the acquisition.[15] It should reflect the risk associated with the *use* of funds, not their *source*. It would be a mistake for Gamble to use its own cost of capital to value the cash flows from Shapiro.

4. *If Gamble and Shapiro combine, there will be transactions costs*. These will include fees to investment bankers, legal fees, and disclosure requirements.

A Cost to Shareholders from Reduction in Risk   29.7

The previous section discussed gains to the firm from a merger. In a firm with debt, these gains are likely to be shared by both bondholders and shareholders. We now consider how a merger could benefit the bondholders at the expense of the shareholders.

---

[15]Recall that the required rate of return is sometimes referred to as the *cost of capital* or the *opportunity cost of capital*.

Table 29.5
Stock-swap mergers

	NPV			Market value
	State 1	State 2	State 3	
Base case: two all-equity firms before merger				
Firm *A*	$80	$50	$25	$60
Firm *B*	$50	$40	$15	$40
Probability	0.5	0.3	0.2	
After merger*				
Firm *AB*	$130	$90	$40	$100
Firm *A*, equity and risky debt before merger				
Firm *B*, all-equity before merger				
Firm *A*	$80	$50	$25	$60
Debt	$40	$40	$25	$37
Equity	$40	$10	$0	$23
Firm *B*	$50	$40	$15	$40
After merger†				
Firm *AB*	$130	$90	$40	$100
Debt	$40	$40	$40	$40
Equity	$90	$50	$0	$60

Value of debt rises after merger. Value of original stock in acquiring firm falls correspondingly.

*Shareholders in *B* receive stock value of $40. Therefore, shareholders of *A* have a value of $100 − $40 = $60 and are *indifferent to merger.*

†Because firm *B*'s shareholders receive stock in firm *A* worth $40, original shareholders in firm *A* have stock worth $20 (or $60 − $40). Gains and losses from merger are
    $20 − $23 = −$3: Therefore, shareholders of *A* lose $3.
    $40 − $37 = $3: Therefore, bondholders of *A* gain $3.

When two firms merge, the variability of their combined values is usually lower than if the firms remained separate entities. The variability of firm values can fall if the values of the two firms are less than perfectly correlated. The resulting reduction in the cost of borrowing will make the creditors better off than before because the probability of financial distress is reduced by the merger.

Unfortunately, the shareholders are likely to be worse off. The gains to creditors are at the expense of the shareholders if the total value of the firm does not change. The relationship among the value of the merged firm, debt capacity, and risk is very complicated. We now consider two examples.

The Base Case

Consider a base case where two all-equity firms merge. Table 29.5 gives the net present values of firm *A* and firm *B* in three possible states of the economy: prosperity, average, and depression. The market value of firm *A* is $60, and the market value of firm *B* is $40. The market value of each firm is the weighted average of the values in each of the three states. For example, the value of firm *A* is

$$\$60 = \$80 \times 0.5 + \$50 \times 0.3 + \$25 \times 0.2$$

The values in each of the three states for firm *A* are $80, $50, and $25, respectively. The probabilities of each of the three states occurring are 0.5, 0.3, and 0.2, respectively.

When firm A merges with firm B, the combined firm AB will have a market value of $100. There is no synergy from this merger, and consequently the value of firm AB is the sum of the values of firm A and firm B. Shareholders of B receive stock with a value of $40, and therefore shareholders of A have a value of $100 − $40 = $60. Thus, shareholders of A and B are indifferent to the proposed merger.

The Case Where One Firm Has Debt

Alternatively, imagine firm A has some debt and some equity outstanding before the merger.[16] Firm B is an all-equity firm. Firm A will default on its debt in state 3 because the net present value of firm A in this state is $25, and the value of the debt claim is $40. As a consequence, the full value of the debt claim cannot be paid by firm A. The creditors take this into account, and the value of the debt is $37 (or $40 × 0.5 + $40 × 0.3 + $25 × 0.2).

Though default occurs without a merger, no default occurs with a merger. To see this, notice that, when the two firms are separate, firm B does not guarantee firm A's debt. That is, if firm A defaults on its debt, firm B does not help the bondholders of firm A. However, after the merger, the bondholders can draw on the cash flows from both A and B. When one of the divisions of the combined firm fails, creditors can be paid from the profits of the other division. This mutual guarantee, which is called the *coinsurance effect*, makes the debt less risky and more valuable than before.

The bonds are worth $40 after the merger. Thus, the bondholders of AB gain $3 (or $40 − $37) from the merger.

The shareholders of firm A lose $3 (or $20 − $23) from the merger. That is, firm A's stock is worth $23 prior to the merger. The stock is worth $60 after the merger. However, shareholders in firm B receive $40 of stock in firm A. Hence, those individuals who were shareholders in firm A prior to the merger have stock worth only $20 (or $60 − $40) after the merger.

There is no net benefit to the firm as a whole. The bondholders gain the coinsurance effect, and the shareholders lose the coinsurance effect. Some general conclusions emerge from the preceding analysis.

1. Bondholders in the aggregate will usually be helped by mergers and acquisitions. The size of the gain to bondholders depends on the reduction of bankruptcy risk after the combination. That is, the less risky the combined firm is, the greater are the gains to bondholders.
2. Shareholders of the acquiring firm will be hurt by the amount that bondholders gain.
3. The conclusions apply to mergers and acquisitions where no synergy is present. In the case of synergistic combinations, much depends on the size of the synergy.

---

[16]This example was provided by David Babbel.

How Can Shareholders Reduce Their Losses from the Coinsurance Effect?

The coinsurance effect allows some mergers to increase bondholder values by reducing shareholder values. However, there are at least two ways that shareholders can reduce or eliminate the coinsurance effect. First, the shareholders in firm *A* could retire its debt *before* the merger announcement date and reissue an equal amount of debt after the merger. Because debt is retired at the low, premerger price, this type of refinancing transaction can neutralize the coinsurance effect to the bondholders.

Also, note that the debt capacity of the combined firm is likely to increase because the acquisition reduces the probability of financial distress. Thus, the shareholders' second alternative is simply to issue more debt after the merger. An increase in debt following the merger will have two effects, even without the prior action of debt retirement. The interest deduction from new corporate debt raises firm value. In addition, an increase in debt after merger raises the probability of financial distress, thereby reducing or eliminating the bondholders' gain from the coinsurance effect.

CONCEPT QUESTION

- How is the distribution of merger gains complicated if one of the firms has debt outstanding?

29.8   Two "Bad" Reasons for Mergers

Earnings Growth

An acquisition can create the appearance of earnings growth, which may fool investors into thinking that the firm is worth more than it really is. Suppose Global Resources, Ltd., acquires Regional Enterprises. The financial positions of Global and Regional before the acquisition are shown in Table 29.6. Regional has had very poor earnings growth and sells at a price-earnings ratio much lower than that of Global. The merger creates no additional value. If the market is smart, it will realize that the combined firm is worth the sum of the values of the separate firms. In this case, the market value of the combined firm will be $3,500, which is equal to the sum of the values of the separate firms before the merger.

At these values, Global will acquire Regional by exchanging 40 of its shares for 100 Regional shares, so that Global will have 140 shares outstanding after the merger.[17] Because the stock price of Global is unchanged by the merger, the price-earnings ratio must fall. This is true because the market is smart and recognizes that the total market value has not been altered by the merger. This scenario is represented by the third column of Table 29.6.

Let us now consider the possibility that the market is fooled. One can see from Table 29.6 that the acquisition enables Global to increase its earnings per share from $1 to $1.43. If the market is fooled, it might mistake the 43-percent increase in

---

[17]This ratio implies a fair exchange because a share of Regional is selling for 40 percent ($10/$25) of the price of a share of Global.

	Global Resources before merger	Regional Enterprises before merger	Global Resources after merger	
			The market is "smart"	The market is "fooled"
Earnings per share	$1.00	$1.00	$1.43	$1.43
Price per share	$25.00	$10.00	$25.00	$35.71
Price-earnings ratio	25	10	17.5	25
Number of shares	100	100	140	140
Total earnings	$100.00	$100.00	$200.00	$200.00
Total value	$2,500.00	$1,000.00	$3,500.00	$5,000.00

Table 29.6 Financial positions of Global Resources and Regional Enterprises

Exchange ratio: 1 share in Global for 2.5 shares in Regional.

earnings per share for true growth. In this case, the price-earnings ratio of Global may not fall after the merger. Suppose the price-earnings ratio of Global remains equal to 25. The total value of the combined firm will increase to $5,000 (or 25 × $200), and the stock price per share of Global will increase to $35.71 (or $5,000/140). This is reflected in the last column of Table 29.6.

This is earnings growth magic. Like all good magic, it is just illusion. For it to work, the shareholders of Global and Regional must receive something for nothing. This is highly unlikely in an efficient market.

Diversification

Diversification often is mentioned as a benefit of one firm's acquiring another. For example, U.S. Steel included diversification as a benefit in its acquisition of Marathon Oil Company, a merger that ranked in size just behind Campeau's purchase of Federated Department Stores. In 1982 U.S. Steel was a cash-rich company. (Over 20 percent of its assets were in the form of cash and marketable securities.) It is not uncommon to see firms with surplus cash articulating a need for diversification.

However, we argue that diversification, by itself, cannot produce increases in value. To see why, recall that a business's variability of return can be separated into two parts: (1) what is specific to the business and called *unsystematic* and (2) what is *systematic* because it is common to all businesses.

Systematic variability cannot be eliminated by diversification, so mergers will not eliminate this risk at all. In contrast, unsystematic risk can be diversified away through mergers. However, the investor does not need widely diversified companies such as Canadian Pacific Enterprises and Imasco to eliminate unsystematic risk. Shareholders can diversify more easily than corporations by simply purchasing common stock in different corporations. For example, the shareholders of U.S. Steel could have purchased shares in Marathon if they believed there would be diversification gains in doing so. Thus, diversification through conglomerate merger may not benefit shareholders.[18]

---

[18]Recent evidence suggests that diversification can actually hurt shareholders. Randall Mork, Andrei Shleifer, and Robert W. Vishney, "Do Managerial Objectives Drive Bad Acquisitions," *Journal of Finance* 45 (1990), pp. 31–48, show that shareholders did poorly in firms that diversified by acquisition in the 1980s.

Diversification can produce gains to the acquiring firm only if two things are true:

1. Diversification decreases the unsystematic variability at lower costs than investors could via adjustments to personal portfolios. This seems very unlikely.
2. Diversification reduces risk and thereby increases debt capacity. This possibility was mentioned earlier in the chapter.

CONCEPT QUESTIONS

- Why can a merger create the appearance of earnings growth?
- Why is diversification generally a poor motive for a merger?

29.9   The NPV of a Merger

Firms typically use NPV analysis when making acquisitions.[19] The analysis is relatively straightforward when the consideration is cash. The analysis becomes more complex when the consideration is stock.

Cash

Suppose firm A and firm B have values as separate entities of $500 and $100, respectively. They are both all-equity firms. If firm A acquires firm B, the merged firm AB will have a combined value of $700 due to synergies of $100. The board of firm B has indicated that it will sell firm B if it is offered $150 in cash.

Should firm A acquire firm B? Assuming that firm A finances the acquisition out of its own retained earnings, its value after the acquisition is [20]

$$\begin{array}{ccc} \text{Value of} & & \\ \text{firm } A \text{ after} & = & \text{Value of} \quad - \quad \text{Cash} \\ \text{the acquisition} & & \text{combined firm} \quad\quad \text{paid} \\ & = & \$700 \quad\quad - \quad \$150 \\ & = & \$550 \end{array}$$

Because firm A was worth $500 prior to the acquisition, the NPV to firm A's shareholders is

$$\$50 = \$550 - \$500 \tag{29.1}$$

Assuming that there are 25 shares in firm A, each share of the firm is worth $20 (or $500/25) prior to the merger and $22 (or $550/25) after the merger. These calculations are displayed in the first and third columns of Table 29.7. Looking at the rise in stock price, we conclude that firm A should make the acquisition.

---

[19]The NPV framework for evaluating mergers can be found in S. C. Myers, "A Framework for Evaluating Mergers," in *Modern Developments in Financial Management*, S. C. Myers ed. (New York: Praeger, 1976).

[20]The analysis will be essentially the same if new stock is issued. However, it will differ if new debt is issued to fund the acquisition because of the tax shield to debt. An adjusted present value (APV) approach would be necessary here.

	Before acquisition		After acquisition: Firm A		
	(1)	(2)	(3)	(4) Common stock:† Exchange ratio (0.75:1)	(5) Common stock:† Exchange ratio (0.6819:1)
	Firm A	Firm B	Cash*		
Market value (V_A, V_B)	$500	$100	$550	$700	$700
Number of shares	25	10	25	32.5	31.819
Price per share	$ 20	$ 10	$ 22	$ 21.54	$ 22

Table 29.7
Cost of acquisition: Cash versus common stock

*Value of firm A after acquisition—cash:
$$V_A = V_{AB} - \text{Cash}$$
$$\$550 = \$700 - \$150$$

†Value of firm A after acquisition—common stock:
$$V_A = V_{AB}$$
$$\$700 = \$700$$

We spoke earlier of both the synergy and the premium of a merger. We can also value the NPV of a merger to the acquirer as

$$\text{NPV of a merger to acquirer} = \text{Synergy} - \text{Premium}$$

Because the value of the combined firm is $700 and the premerger values of A and B were $500 and $100, respectively, the synergy is $100 [or $700 − ($500 + $100)]. The premium is $50 (or $150 − $100). Thus, the NPV of the merger to the acquirer is

$$\text{NPV of merger to firm } A = \$100 - \$50 = \$50$$

One *caveat* is in order. This textbook has consistently argued that the market value of a firm is the best estimate of its true value. However, we must adjust our analysis when discussing mergers. If the true price of firm A *without the merger* is $500, the market value of firm A may actually be above $500 when merger negotiations take place. This occurs because the market price reflects the possibility that the merger will occur. For example, if the probability is 60 percent that the merger will take place, the market price of firm A will be

Market value of firm A with merger	×	Probability of merger	+	Market value of firm A without merger	×	Probability of no merger
$530 = 550	×	0.60	+	$500	×	0.40

The managers would underestimate the NPV from merger in equation (29.1) if the market price of firm A is used. Thus, managers are faced with the difficult task of valuing their own firm without the acquisition.

Common Stock

Of course, firm A could purchase firm B with common stock instead of cash. Unfortunately, the analysis is not as straightforward here. In order to handle this scenario, we need to know how many shares are outstanding in firm B. We assume that there are 10 shares outstanding, as indicated in column 2 of Table 29.7.

Suppose firm A exchanges 7.5 of its shares for the entire 10 shares of firm B. We call this an exchange ratio of 0.75:1. The value of each share of firm A's stock before the acquisition is $20. Because $7.5 \times \$20 = \$150$, this exchange *appears* to be the equivalent of purchasing firm B in cash for $150.

This is incorrect: The true cost is greater than $150. To see this, note that firm A has 32.5 (or 25 + 7.5) shares outstanding after the merger. Firm B shareholders own 23 percent (7.5/32.5) of the combined firm. Their holdings are valued at $161 (or 23% × $700). Because these shareholders receive stock in firm A worth $161, the cost of the merger to firm A's shareholders must be $161, not $150.

This result is shown in column 4 of Table 29.7. The value of each share of firm A's stock after a stock-for-stock transaction is only $21.54 (or $700/32.5). We found out earlier that the value of each share is $22 after a cash-for-stock transaction. The difference is that the cost of the stock-for-stock transaction to firm A is higher.

This nonintuitive result occurs because the exchange ratio of 7.5 shares of firm A for 10 shares of firm B was based on the *premerger* prices of the two firms. However, since the stock of firm A rises after the merger, firm B shareholders receive more than $150 in firm A stock.

What should the exchange ratio be so that firm B shareholders receive only $150 of firm A's stock? We begin by defining α, the proportion of the shares in the combined firm that firm B's shareholders own. Because the combined firm's value is $700, the value of firm B shareholders after the merger is

Value of Firm B Shareholders after Merger:

$$\alpha \times \$700$$

Setting $\alpha \times \$700 = \$150$, we find that $\alpha = 21.43\%$. In other words, firm B's shareholders will receive stock worth $150 if they receive 21.43 percent of the firm after merger.

Now we determine the number of shares issued to firm B's shareholders. The proportion, α, that firm B's shareholders have in the combined firm can be expressed as

$$\alpha = \frac{\text{New shares issued}}{\text{Old shares + New shares issued}} = \frac{\text{New shares issued}}{25 + \text{New shares issued}}$$

Plugging our value of α into the equation yields

$$0.2143 = \frac{\text{New shares issued}}{25 + \text{New shares issued}}$$

Solving for the unknown, we have

New shares = 6.819 shares

Total shares outstanding after the merger is 31.819 (or 25 + 6.819). Because 6.819 shares of firm A are exchanged for 10 shares of firm B, the exchange ratio is 0.6819:1.

Results at the exchange ratio of 0.6819:1 are displayed in column 5 of Table 29.7. Each share of common stock is worth $22, exactly what it is worth in the stock-for-cash transaction. Thus, given that the board of firm B will sell its firm for $150, this is the fair exchange ratio, not the ratio of 0.75:1 used earlier.

Cash versus Common Stock

Whether to finance an acquisition by cash or by shares of stock is an important decision.[21] The choice depends on several factors:

1. *Overvaluation.* If in the opinion of management the acquiring firm's stock is overvalued, using shares of stock can be less costly than using cash.
2. *Taxes.* Acquisition by cash usually results in a taxable transaction. Acquisition by exchanging stock is tax-free.
3. *Sharing gains.* If cash is used to finance an acquisition, the selling firm's shareholders receive a fixed price. In the event of a hugely successful merger, they will not participate in any additional gains. Of course, if the acquisition is not a success, the losses will not be shared and shareholders of the acquiring firm will be worse off than if stock were used.

CONCEPT QUESTION

- In an efficient market with no tax effects, should an acquiring firm use cash or stock?

Defensive Tactics   29.10

Target firm managers frequently resist takeover attempts. Resistance usually starts with press releases and mailings to shareholders presenting management's viewpoint. It can eventually lead to legal action and solicitation of competing bids. Managerial action to defeat a takeover attempt may make target shareholders better off if it elicits a higher offer premium from the bidding firm or another firm. Of course, management resistance may simply reflect pursuit of self-interest at the expense of shareholders; the target firm's managers may resist a takeover in order to preserve their jobs. In this section, we describe various defensive tactics that have been used by target firm managements to resist unfriendly takeover attempts.

The Control Block and the Corporate Charter

If one individual or group owns 51 percent of a company's stock, this **control block** makes a hostile takeover virtually impossible. In the extreme, one interest may own all the stock. Examples are privately owned companies like Irving Oil and Crown corporations like Ontario Hydro. Many Canadian companies are subsidiaries of foreign corporations that own control blocks. Many domestically owned companies have controlling shareholders.[22]

---

[21]All-cash transactions are much more common than all-stock transactions. In 1985, only about 10 percent of U.S. acquisitions were financed by all stock. (See *Mergers and Acquisitions*, "Almanac and Review: 1985." In the 1980s, mergers in Canada were also mostly for cash.

[22]Important exceptions are chartered banks. As we stated in Chapter 1, the Bank Act prohibits any one interest from owning more than 10 percent of the shares.

Table 29.8
Ownership makeup
of the top 100
corporations

	Canada	United States
Widely held	15	73
Control block	50	25
Privately owned	28	2
Government-owned	7	0

Source: D.H. Thain and D.S.R. Leighton, "Ownership Structure and the Board," *Canadian Investment Review* (Fall 1991), pp. 61–66.

As a result, control blocks are typical in Canada although they are the exception in the United States. Table 29.8 shows that only 15 percent of the top 100 corporations in Canada were widely held in 1989 versus 73 percent for the United States.[23] One important implication is that minority shareholders need protection in Canada. One key group of minority shareholders are pension funds and other institutional investors. They are becoming increasingly vocal in opposing defensive tactics that are seen to be entrenching management at the expense of shareholders. We will discuss several examples below.

For widely held companies, the corporate charter establishes the conditions that allow for a takeover. The *corporate charter* refers to the articles of incorporation and corporate bylaws that establish the governance rules of the firm. Firms can amend corporate charters to make acquisitions more difficult. For example, usually two-thirds of the shareholders of record must approve a merger. Firms can make it more difficult to be acquired by changing this to a higher percentage. This is called a *supermajority amendment*.

Another device is to stagger the election of the board members. This makes it more difficult to elect a new board of directors quickly. In examining samples of U.S. adopting firms, DeAngelo and Rice, and Linn and McConnell, found that antitakeover amendments to corporate charters had no adverse effect on stock prices.[24]

Repurchase/Standstill Agreements

Managers may arrange a *targeted repurchase* to forestall a takeover attempt. In a targeted repurchase, a firm buys back its own stock from a potential bidder, usually at a substantial premium. These premiums can be thought of as payments to potential bidders to delay or stop unfriendly takeover attempts. Critics of such payments label them *greenmail*.

In addition, managers of target firms may simultaneously negotiate standstill agreements. *Standstill agreements* are contracts under which the bidding firm agrees to limit its holdings of another firm. These agreements usually lead to cessation of takeover attempts, and announcements of such agreements have had a negative effect on stock prices.

[23]The list of top 100 corporations in Canada is from *Financial Post 500*. The U.S. corporations list comes from *Fortune 500*. The table is from D. H. Thain and D. S. R. Leighton, "Ownership Structure and the Board," *Canadian Investment Review* (Fall 1991), pp. 61–66.

[24]H. DeAngelo and E. M. Rice, "Antitakeover Charter Amendments and Stockholder Wealth," *Journal of Financial Economics* 11 (April 1983); and S. G. Linn and J. J. McConnell, "An Empirical Investigation of the Impact of Antitakeover Amendments on Common Stock Prices," *Journal of Financial Economics* 11 (April 1983).

■ *Example*

In summer 1985, Bay Street rumours abounded that Southam Inc., a major newspaper chain, was a takeover target.[25] The rumours proved true as, on August 25, 1985, Southam signed a standstill agreement with Torstar Corporation. No greenmail was paid, but the agreement took Southam "out of play" as a takeover target.

On the next day of trading, Southam's stock price dropped by $3.75 from $17.75 to $14.00. Eckbo analyzed this event and found that over 80 percent of the price change was caused by the announcement of the standstill agreement. Apparently, the pre-announcement price included a takeover premium that disappeared when the standstill agreement became public.

Exclusionary Offers and Nonvoting Stock

An *exclusionary offer* is the opposite of a targeted repurchase. Here, the firm makes a tender offer for a given amount of its own shares while excluding targeted shareholders.

A well-known example occurred in 1986 when the Canadian Tire Dealers Association offered to buy 49 percent of the company's voting shares from the founding Billes family. The dealers' bid was at $169 per share for voting shares trading at $40 before the bid. The nonvoting shares were priced at $14. Further, since the dealers were the principal buyers of Canadian Tire products, control of the company would have allowed them to adjust prices to benefit themselves over the nonvoting shareholders.

The offer was voided by the Ontario Securities Commission and it appears that any future exclusionary offers are likely to be viewed as an illegal form of discrimination against one group of shareholders.

Going Private and Leveraged Buyouts

Going private refers to what happens when the publicly owned stock in a firm is purchased by a private group, often composed of existing management. As a consequence, the firm's stock is taken off the market (if it is an exchange-traded stock, it is delisted) and is no longer traded. Thus, in going-private transactions, shareholders of publicly held firms are forced to accept cash for their shares.

Going-private transactions are frequently *leveraged buyouts (LBOs)*. One result of going private is that takeovers via tender offer can no longer occur since there are no publicly held shares.

In this sense, an LBO can be a takeover defense. However, it is only a defense for management. From shareholders' point of view, an LBO is a takeover because they are bought out. From the viewpoint of management, an LBO is a risky defense. In the RJR Nabisco LBO, F. Ross Johnson (CEO and transplanted Canadian) inadvertently put the company "in play" with a plan to go private. In the end, Johnson was outbid by the

---

[25]Our example comes from B. Espen Eckbo, "Anatomy of a Takeover Defense: The Southam–Torstar Standstill Agreement," *Canadian Investment Review* (Fall 1991), pp. 73–78.

Wall Street firm of Kohlberg, Kravis and Roberts (KKR), which paid U.S. $25 billion for RJR Nabisco.[26]

The selling shareholders are invariably paid a premium above market price in an LBO, just as they are in a merger.[27] As with a merger, the acquirer profits only if the synergy created is greater than the premium. Synergy is quite plausible in a merger of *two* firms. (We delineated a number of types of synergy earlier in this chapter.) However, it is much harder to explain synergy in an LBO, because only *one* firm is involved.

There are generally two reasons given for the ability of an LBO to create value. First, the extra debt provides a tax deduction, which, as earlier chapters suggested, increases firm value. Most LBOs are on firms with stable earnings and with low to moderate debt. The LBO may simply increase the firm's debt to its optimum level.

Second, the LBO usually turns the previous managers into owners, thereby increasing their incentive to work hard. The increase in debt is a further incentive because managers must earn more than the debt service to obtain any profit for themselves.

Though it is easy to value the additional tax shields from an LBO, it is quite difficult to value the gains from increased efficiency. Nevertheless, this increased efficiency is considered to be at least as important as the tax shield in explaining the LBO phenomenon.[28]

LBOs to Date: The Record

Since the mid-1980s, ongoing experience with LBOs has revealed some weaknesses in both the concept and the financing vehicle—junk bonds. One of the first large LBOs in the United States was Revco for $1.3 billion in 1986. Less than two years later, the company filed for bankruptcy. The failure was caused by overambitious sales growth predictions combined with a lack of funds to refurbish dilapidated stores.

Further, LBOs sometimes lead to spinoffs of assets to pay down debt. For example, Nova Corp. bought Polysar Energy & Chemical Company for U.S. $2.3 billion in 1988. To pay down the debt used to finance the deal, Nova sold off $500 million in assets.[29]

Problems facing LBOs in the early 1990s are exemplified in the trials of Robert Campeau whose real estate company took over Allied Stores in 1986 and then Federated Department Stores in 1988.[30] Table 21.1 shows that these takeovers ranked high in the Canadian list for the 1980s. The Allied takeover for $5 billion was number 4 and the Federated purchase at $6.6 billion number 1.

---

[26]A fascinating and highly readable account of the RJR Nabisco LBO is in B. Burroughs and J. Helyar, *Barbarians at the Gate: The Fall of RJR Nabisco* (New York: Harper Perennial, 1990).

[27]H. DeAngelo, L. DeAngelo, and E. M. Rice, "Going Private: Minority Freezeouts and Shareholder Wealth," *Journal of Law and Economics* 27 (1984). They show that the premiums paid to existing shareholders in LBOs and other going-private transactions are about the same as in interfirm acquisitions.

[28]For the academic community's view of LBOs, see "A Discussion of Corporate Restructuring," *Midland Corporate Finance Journal* (Summer 1984), which features a roundtable discussion by a number of prominent university professors.

[29]Our discussion of LBOs and junk bonds draws on J. Cazzin, "The Road to Decline," *Macleans* (January 29, 1990); and V. Ross, "Campeau Battles to the End," *The Globe and Mail* (January 29, 1992), p. 1.

[30]The appendix to this chapter presents the takeover in detail.

Campeau was correct that Federated Department Stores' assets were undervalued at the pretakeover share price of $33, but hindsight shows that the $73.50 per share takeover price was too high. Further, the deal was overleveraged with 97-percent debt financing. With either a lower purchase price or lower leverage, the deal might have survived.[31]

Despite an injection of $300 million from Olympia & York Developments Ltd. (then owned by the Reichmann family of Toronto), Campeau had to default on its bank loans. As a result, the National Bank of Canada took over 35 percent of Campeau's voting stock in January 1990. Shortly after, Allied and Federated filed for bankruptcy protection in the United States. Over the next year, Campeau sold just under $2 billion in Canadian real estate to try to reduce its debt to manageable levels in order to survive.[32] In January 1991, Campeau Corp.'s name was changed to Candev with a 65-percent control block in the hands of Olympia & York. Robert Campeau lost his seat on the board and all but 2 percent of the company's stock.

Problems with Campeau and other LBOs reflected on high-yield or junk bonds used heavily to finance them. For example, when Allied and Federated sought bankruptcy protection in 1990, Campeau junk bonds that had a face value of $1,000 sold for $110.

Only around 100 junk bond issues have appeared in the Canadian market as most Canadian takeovers have been financed with bank loans. LBO problems also affected banks that provided loans to finance them. But Canadian banks have remained sound, avoiding the LBO-related problems faced by some U.S. banks and S&Ls.[33]

Poison Pills and Share Rights Plans

A **poison pill** is a tactic designed to repel would-be suitors. The term comes from the world of espionage. Agents are supposed to bite a pill of cyanide rather than permit capture. Presumably, this prevents enemy interrogators from learning important secrets. In the equally colourful world of corporate finance, a poison pill is a financial device designed to make it impossible for a firm to be acquired without management's consent—unless the buyer is willing to commit financial suicide.

In recent years, many of the largest U.S. and Canadian firms have adopted poison pill provisions of one form or another, often calling them **share rights plans (SRPs)** or something similar. Table 29.9 lists poison pills in Canadian firms in early 1990. The table also shows the "trigger" level (discussed below) and the TSE weight for the company's stock. In 1990, firms with a poison pill made up just under 20 percent of the TSE market value.

SRPs differ quite a bit in detail from company to company; we will describe a kind of generic approach here. In general, when a company adopts an SRP, it distributes share rights to its existing shareholders. These rights allow shareholders to buy shares of stock (or preferred stock) at some fixed price. The rights issued with an SRP have a number of unusual features. First, the exercise or subscription price on the

---

[31]S. N. Kaplan, "Campeau's Acquisition of Federated: Value Destroyed or Value Added?" *Journal of Financial Economics* (December 1989), pp. 189–212.

[32]S. Horvitch, "Campeau 'Selling Itself' to Survive," *Financial Post* (July 1, 1991), p. 22.

[33]J. McNish, "Scotiabank Scores on U.S. Loans," *Globe and Mail* (November 29, 1993), p. B1.

Table 29.9
Poison pills in
Canada: Current
status

Name	Date	Trigger percent	TSE weight
Inco	Oct. 3/88	20%	1.83%
Pegasus	Dec. 2/88	10	0.2
Agnico-Eagle	May 10/89	20	0.14
Aur*	Jul. 20/89	15	0.14
Turbo	Jul. 27/89	20.5	0.05
Numac*	Jul. 28/89	10	0.08
Falconbridge*	Sept. 2/89	15	N.A.
Dominion Textile	Aug. 9/89	20	0.27
Finning	Sept. 4/89	15	0.21
Canada Packers	Oct. 2/89	10	0.35
Maclean Hunter	Oct. 24/89	10	0.99
Sherritt Gordon	Nov. 26/89	20	0.14
Dofasco	Nov. 26/89	10	0.89
Canadian Pacific	Dec. 6/89	10	4.55
Alcan	Dec. 15/89	20	3.35
Placer Dome	Jan. 5/90	15	2.76
Nowsco Well	Jan. 5/90	15	0.14
Franco Nevada	Jan. 15/90	N.A.	0.67
Moore Corp.	Jan. 18/90	15	1.74
Southam	Feb. 2/90	15	0.62
United Coin Mines	Feb. 5/90	N.A.	N.A.
Total weight			19.12%

*Not implemented.

N.A.—Not available.

Source: P. Halpern, "Poison Pills: Whose Interest Do They Serve?" *Canadian Investment Review* (Spring 1990), pp. 57–66.

right is usually set high enough so the rights are well out of the money, meaning that the purchase price is much higher than the current stock price. The rights will often be good for 10 years, and the purchase or exercise price is usually a reasonable estimate of what the stock will be worth at that time.

In addition, unlike ordinary stock rights, these rights cannot be exercised immediately, and cannot be bought and sold separately from the stock. Also, they can be cancelled by management at any time—redeemed (bought back) for a penny apiece or some similarly trivial amount.

Typically, the rights will be triggered when someone acquires 20 percent of the common stock or otherwise announces a tender offer. This means that the rights become exercisable, they can be bought and sold separately from the stock, and they are not easily cancelled or redeemed. When the rights are triggered, they can be exercised. Since they are out of the money, it takes a *flip-over provision* to make exercise attractive. The flip-over provision is the "poison" in the pill. In the event of a merger, the holder of a right can pay the exercise price and receive common stock in the merged firm worth twice the exercise price. In other words, holders of the right can buy stock in the merged firm at half price.

The rights issued in connection with an SRP are poison pills because anyone trying to force a merger triggers the rights. When this happens, all the target firm's shareholders can effectively buy stock in the merged firm at half price. This greatly increases the cost of the merger to the bidder because the target firm's shareholders end up with a much larger percentage of the merged firm.

Notice that the flip-over provision does not prevent someone from acquiring control of a firm by purchasing a majority interest. It just acts to prevent a complete merger of the two firms. Even so, this inability to combine can have serious tax and other implications for the buyer.

The intention of a poison pill is to force a bidder to negotiate with management. Frequently, merger offers are made with the contingency that the rights are cancelled by the target firm. Poison pills have been heavily criticized for helping to entrench management. Supporting this view, U.S. studies have found evidence of negative share price reactions when poison pills are introduced. So far, the Canadian evidence is mixed.[34]

Other Defensive Devices

As corporate takeovers become more common, other colorful terms have become popular.

- **Golden parachutes**. Some target firms provide compensation to top-level management if a takeover occurs. This can be viewed as a payment to management to make it less concerned for its own welfare and more interested in shareholders when considering a takeover bid. Alternatively, the payment can be seen as an attempt to enrich management at the shareholders' expense.

- **Crown jewels**. Firms often sell major assets—crown jewels—when faced with a takeover threat. This is sometimes referred to as the *scorched earth strategy*.

- **White knight**. Target firms sometimes seek a competing bid from a friendly bidder—a white knight—who promises to maintain the jobs of existing management and to refrain from selling off the target's assets.

- *Example*

On March 30, 1994, shareholders in Maclean Hunter tendered over 93 percent of the firm's shares to bidder Rogers Communications.[35] At $17.50 per share, the total bid was worth $3.1 billion, making it the largest ever in the communications industry; it is tied at number 6 with Seagram's bid for Dupont in Table 29.1's rankings of Canada's largest mergers. Figure 29.3 shows features of the two firms and makes apparent that synergies and scale economies are important factors in this deal. Strategic positioning to develop opportunities along the information highway likely also came into play.

Before accepting Rogers' final bid, Maclean Hunter's board of directors explored takeover defences. They considered the white knight defence by stating that time was

---

[34] Detailed discussion of poison pills in Canada appears in P. Halpern, "Poison Pills: Whose Interest Do They Serve?" *Canadian Investment Review* (Spring 1990).

[35] Our discussion draws on J. Partridge, H. Enchin, and B. Jorgensen, "Rogers Adamant on Bid Price," *The Globe and Mail* (February 12, 1994), p. B1; and J. Partridge, "Rogers Takeover Bid over the Top," *The Globe and Mail* (April 1, 1994), p. B1.

Figure 29.3
Features of Rogers
Communications
Inc. and Maclean
Hunter Inc.

Rogers Communications Inc.

BUSINESS

- Owns and operates the largest cable television business in Canada with 15 systems.
- 16 radio stations.
- Cellular telephone network
- Video rental stores
- Multilingual television station in Toronto
- Cable television home shopping network.
- One of two major shareholders in Unitel Communications.

FINANCIAL

Nine months 1993
Revenue: $980.5-million
Loss: $123.7-million

EMPLOYEES

7,000 in 1993.

SHARE PRICE

52-week high: $25.62
52-week low: $16.12
Yesterday: $23, up $1.50

Maclean Hunter Inc.

BUSINESS

- Cable television represents 70 per cent of company's income with 35 systems.
- Publishes 200 periodicals in 10 countries.
- Holds a controlling interest in the Toronto Sun Publishing.
- 21 radio stations
- Radio paging
- Business forms
- Commercial printing
- Consumer and trade shows

FINANCIAL

1993
Revenue: $1.7-billion
Profit: $56.6-million

EMPLOYEES

12,000 in 1993.

SHARE PRICE

52-week high: $18.75
52-week low: $10.87
Yesterday: $17.37, up $0.37

Source: *The Globe & Mail* (February 12, 1994), p. B1. Used with permission.

needed to allow competing bids. Maclean Hunter also publicly considered the possibility of selling the firm's prized U.S. cable assets—its crown jewels. Maclean Hunter has a poison pill plan and, in this case, it served its purpose, forcing Rogers to negotiate with management. When Maclean Hunter's board approved the offer, it agreed to waive the poison pill provision.

CONCEPT QUESTION

■ What can a firm do to make a takeover less likely?

29.11   Some Evidence on Acquisitions

One of the most controversial issues surrounding our subject is whether mergers and acquisitions benefit shareholders.

Takeover technique	Target	Bidder
Tender offer	30%	4%
Merger	20	0
Proxy contest	8	NA

Table 29.10
Stock price changes in successful U.S. corporate takeovers

NA = Not applicable.
Source: Modified from Michael C. Jensen and Richard S. Ruback,
"The Market for Corporate Control: The Scientific Evidence,"
Journal of Financial Economics 11 (April 1983), pp. 7–8. © Elsevier
Science Publishers B.V. (North-Holland).

	Target	Bidder
1,930 mergers, 1964–83*	9%	3%
119 mergers, 1963–82†	23	11
173 going-private transactions, 1977–89‡	25	NA
Minority buyouts	27	
Noncontrolling bidder	24	

Table 29.11
Abnormal returns in successful Canadian mergers

NA = Not applicable
*From B. Espen Eckbo, "Mergers and the Market for Corporate Control:
The Canadian Evidence," *Canadian Journal of Economics* (May 1986),
pp. 236–60. The test for bidders excluded firms involved in multiple
mergers.
†From A.L. Calvet and J. Lefoll, "Information Asymmetry and Wealth
Effect of Canadian Corporate Acquisitions," *Financial Review* (November
1987), pp. 415–31.
‡Modified from B. Amoako-Adu and B. Smith, "How Do Shareholders
Fare in Minority Buyouts?" *Canadian Investment Review* (Fall 1991),
pp. 79–88.

Do Acquisitions Benefit Shareholders?

Much research has attempted to estimate the effect of mergers and takeovers on stock prices of the bidding and target firms. These studies are called *event studies* because they estimate abnormal stock price changes on and around the offer announcement date (the event). Abnormal returns are usually defined as the difference between actual stock returns and a market index, to take account of the influence of marketwide effects on the returns of individual securities.

Table 29.10 summarizes the results of numerous studies that look at the effects of merger and tender offers on stock prices in the United States. Table 29.11 shows highpoints of three studies on mergers in Canada. Both tables are relevant since firms from one country often purchase companies in the other.

The tables show that shareholders of target companies in successful takeovers gain substantially. Starting with U.S. takeovers in Table 29.10, when the takeover is accomplished by merger, the gains are 20 percent; when the takeover is via tender offer, the gains are 30 percent.

The Canadian studies did not distinguish among tender offers, mergers, and proxy contests in looking at target returns. The first study found a gain of just over 9 percent, more modest than for the United States. The other studies found that target firm shareholders in going-private transactions enjoyed an abnormal return of 23 to 25 percent, a figure consistent with U.S. results in Table 29.10.

The Canadian study of going-private transactions also looked at whether minority shareholders suffer. You can see from Table 29.11 that the answer is no. Returns to minority shareholders hardly differ from returns occurring when firms went private with no majority shareholder.

For both countries, these gains are a reflection of the merger premium that is typically paid by the acquiring firm. These gains are excess returns, that is, returns over and above what the shareholders would normally have earned.

The shareholders of bidding firms do not fare as well. According to the U.S. studies summarized in Table 29.10, bidders experience gains of 4 percent in tender offers, but this gain is about zero in mergers. Canadian research places bidders' gains in a range of 3 to 11 percent.

What conclusions can be drawn from Tables 29.10 and 29.11? First, the evidence strongly suggests that shareholders of successful target firms achieve substantial gains from takeovers. The gains appear to be larger in tender offers than in mergers. This may reflect the fact that takeovers sometimes start with a friendly merger proposal from the bidder to the management of the target firm. If management rejects the offer, the bidding firm may take the offer directly to the shareholders with a tender offer. As a consequence, tender offers are frequently unfriendly.

Also, the target firm's management may actively oppose the offer with defensive tactics. This often leads to the bidding firm's raising the tender offer; on average, friendly mergers may be arranged at lower premiums than unfriendly tender offers.

The second conclusion we can draw is that shareholders of bidding firms earn significantly less from takeovers. The balance is more even for Canadian mergers than for U.S. ones. This may be because there is less competition among bidders in Canada. Two reasons for this are that the Canadian capital market is smaller, and there are federal government agencies to review foreign investments.[36]

In fact, studies have found that acquiring firms actually lose value in many mergers. These findings are a puzzle, and there are a variety of explanations:

1. Anticipated merger gains may not have been completely achieved, and shareholders thus experienced losses. This can happen if managers of bidding firms tend to overestimate the gains from acquisition, as we saw happened to Campeau Corp.

2. The bidding firms are often much larger than the target firms. Thus, even though dollar gains to the bidder may be similar to dollar gains earned by the target firm's shareholders, the percentage gains will be much lower.[37]

3. Another possible explanation for the low returns to bidding firms' shareholders in takeovers is simply that management may not be acting in shareholders' interest when it attempts to acquire other firms. Perhaps it is attempting to increase the firm's size even if this reduces its value per share.

---

[36]Halpern, "Poison Pills," p. 66; and A. L. Calvet and J. Lefoll, "Information Asymmetry," p. 432.

[37]This factor cannot explain the imbalance in returns in the first Canadian study in Table 29.11. In this sample, bidder and target firms were about the same size.

4. The market for takeovers may be sufficiently competitive that the NPV of acquiring is zero because the prices paid in acquisitions fully reflect the value of the acquired firms. In other words, the sellers capture all of the gain.

5. Finally, announcement of a takeover may not convey much new information to the market about the bidding firm. This can occur because firms frequently announce intentions to engage in merger "programs" long before they announce specific acquisitions. In this case, the bidding firm's stock price may already reflect anticipated gains from mergers.

CONCEPT QUESTION

■ What does the evidence say about the distribution of benefits of mergers and acquisitions?

Summary and Conclusions 29.12

1. One firm can acquire another in several different ways. The three legal forms of acquisition are merger and consolidation, acquisition of stock, and acquisition of assets. Mergers and consolidations are the least costly to arrange from a legal standpoint, but they require a vote of approval by the shareholders. Acquisition by stock does not require a shareholder vote and is usually done via a tender offer. However, it is difficult to obtain 100-percent control with a tender offer. Acquisition of assets is comparatively costly because it requires more difficult transfer of asset ownership.

2. Mergers and acquisitions require an understanding of complicated tax and accounting rules. Mergers and acquisitions can be taxable or tax-free transactions. In a taxable transaction, each selling shareholder must pay taxes on the stock's capital appreciation. Should the acquiring firm elect to write up the assets, additional tax implications arise. However, acquiring firms do not generally elect to write up the assets for tax purposes. The selling shareholders do not pay taxes at the time of a tax-free acquisition.

   Accounting for mergers and acquisitions involves a choice of the purchase method or the pooling-of-interests method. The choice between these two methods does not affect after-tax cash flows of the combined firm. However, most financial managers prefer the pooling-of-interests method, because net income of the combined firm under this method is higher than it is under the purchase method.

3. The synergy from an acquisition is defined as the value of the combined firm (V_{AB}) less the value of the two firms as separate entities (V_A and V_B):

$$\text{Synergy} = V_{AB} - (V_A + V_B)$$

   The shareholders of the acquiring firm will gain if the synergy from the merger is greater than the premium.

4. The possible benefits of an acquisition come from

   a. Revenue enhancement.

      b. Cost reduction.

      c. Lower taxes.

      d. Lower cost of capital.

In addition, the reduction in risk from a merger may actually help bondholders and hurt shareholders.

5. Some of the most colourful language of finance stems from defensive tactics in acquisition battles. *Poison pills, golden parachutes, crown jewels, white knights,* and *greenmail* are terms that describe various antitakeover tactics discussed in this chapter.

6. The empirical research on mergers and acquisitions is extensive. Its basic conclusions are that, on average, the shareholders of acquired firms fare very well, while the shareholders of acquiring firms do not gain much.

Key Terms

Amalgamation 824	Purchase method 829
Bidder 824	Goodwill 829
Merger 824	Pooling of interests 830
Consolidation 824	Control block 847
Tender offer 825	Poison pill 851
Circular bid 825	Share rights plan (SRP) 851
Stock exchange bid 825	Golden parachute 853
Going-private transaction 826	Crown jewels 853
Leveraged buyout (LBO) 827	White knight 853

Suggested Readings

How to quantify the value from mergers and acquisitions is covered in:

A. Rappaport. *Creating Shareholder Value: The New Standard for Business Performance.* New York: Free Press, 1986, chapter 9.

Good articles on mergers and acquisitions appear in:

J. M. Stein and D. H. Chew, eds. *The Revolution in Corporate Finance.* New York: Basil Blackwell, 1986.

"A Symposium on the Market for Corporate Control: The Scientific Evidence." *Journal of Financial Economics* (April 1983).

"A Symposium on the Distribution of Power among Corporate Managers, Shareholders and Directors." *Journal of Financial Economics* (January/March 1988).

Canadian Investment Review, Fall 1991 issue.

Two fascinating paperbacks on LBOs are:

C. Bruck. *The Predator's Ball: The Inside Story of Drexel Burnham, and the Rise of the Junk Bond Raiders.* New York: Penguin Books, 1989.

B. Burroughs and J. Helyar. *Barbarians at the Gate: The Fall of RJR Nabisco.* New York: Harper Perennial, 1991.

Questions and Problems

Accounting for Acquisitions

29.1 The Lager Brewing Corporation has acquired the Moncton Pretzel Company in a vertical merger. Lager Brewing has issued $300,000 in new long-term debt to pay for its purchase ($300,000 being the purchase price). Construct the balance sheet for the new corporation if the merger is treated as a purchase for accounting purposes. The balance sheets shown here represent the assets of both firms at their true market values. Assume these market values are also the book values.

LAGER BREWING
Balance sheet
(in $ thousands)

Current assets	$400	Current liabilities	$200
Other assets	100	Long-term debt	100
Net fixed assets	500	Equity	700
Total	$1,000	Total	$1,000

MONCTON PRETZEL
Balance sheet
(in $ thousands)

Current assets	$80	Current liabilities	$80
Other assets	40	Equity	120
Net fixed assets	80		
Total	$200	Total	$200

29.2 Suppose the balance sheet for Moncton Pretzel in Problem 29.1 shows the assets at their book value and not at their market value of $240,000. Construct the balance sheet for the new corporation. Again, treat the transaction as a purchase.

Earnings Growth

29.3 Refer to the Global Resources example in section 29.8 of the text.

Suppose that instead of 40 shares, Global exchanges 100 of its shares for the 100 shares of Regional. The new Global Resources will now have 200 shares outstanding and earnings of $200. Assume the market is smart.

a. Calculate Global's value after the merger.

b. Calculate Global's earnings per share.

c. Calculate Global's price per share.

d. Redo your answers to (a), (b), and (c), if the market is fooled.

29.4 Coldran Aviation has voted in favour of being bought out by Arcadia Financial Corporation. Information about each company is presented below.

	Arcadia Financial	Coldran Aviation
Price-earnings ratio	16	10.8
Number of shares	100,000	50,000
Earnings	$225,000	$100,000

Shareholders in Coldran Aviation will receive six-tenths of a share of Arcadia for each share they hold.

a. How will the earnings per share (EPS) for these shareholders be changed?

b. How will EPS changes affect the original Arcadia shareholders?

Valuation

29.5 Fly-by-Night Couriers is analyzing the possible acquisition of Flash-in-the-Pan Restaurants. Neither firm has debt. The forecasts of Fly-by-Night show that the purchase would increase its annual after-tax cash flow by $600,000 indefinitely. The current market value of Flash-in-the-Pan is $20 million. The current market value of Fly-by-Night is $35 million. The appropriate discount rate for the incremental cash flows is 8 percent.

a. What is the synergy from the merger?

b. What is the value of Flash-in-the-Pan to Fly-by-Night?
   Fly-by-Night is trying to decide whether it should offer 25 percent of its stock or $15 million in cash to Flash-in-the-Pan.

c. What is the cost to Fly-by-Night of each alternative?

d. What is the NPV to Fly-by-Night of each alternative?

e. Which alternative should Fly-by-Night use?

29.6 St. John's Manufacturing is considering making an offer to purchase Newfoundland Industries. The treasurer of St. John's has collected the following information:

	St. John's	Newfoundland
Price-earnings ratio	15	12
Number of shares	1,000,000	250,000
Earnings	$1,000,000	$750,000

The treasurer also knows that securities analysts expect the earnings and dividends (currently $1.80 per share) of St. John's to grow at a constant rate of 5 percent each year. Her research indicates, however, that the acquisition would provide St. John's with some economies of scale that would improve this growth rate to 7 percent per year.

a. What is the value of Newfoundland to St. John's?

b. If St. John's offers $40 in cash for each outstanding share of Newfoundland, what would the NPV of the acquisition be?

c. If instead St. John's were to offer 600,000 of its shares in exchange for the outstanding stock of Newfoundland, what would the NPV of the acquisition be?

d. Should the acquisition be attempted, and, if so, should it be a cash or stock offer?

e. St. John's management thinks that 7-percent growth is too optimistic and that 6-percent growth is more realistic. How does this change your previous answers?

29.7 Company *A* is contemplating acquiring company *B*. Company *B*'s projected revenues, costs, and required investments appear in the accompanying table.

The table also shows sources for financing company B's investments if B is acquired by A. The table incorporates the following information:

- Company B will immediately increase its leverage with a $110 million loan, which would be followed by a $150 million dividend to company A. (This operation will increase the debt-to-equity ratio of company B from 1/3 to 1/1.)
- Company A will use $50 million of tax-loss carry-forwards available from the firm's other operations. The terminal, total value of company B is estimated to be $900 million in five years, and the projected level of debt then is $300 million.
- The risk-free rate and the expected rate of return on the market portfolio are 6 percent and 14 percent, respectively. Company A analysts estimate the weighted average cost of capital for their company to be 10 percent. The borrowing rate for both companies is 8 percent. The beta coefficient for the stock of company B (at its current capital structure) is estimated to be 1.25.
- The board of directors of company A is presented with an offer for $68.75 per share of company B, or a total of $550 million for the 8 million shares outstanding.

Evaluate this proposal. The accompanying table may help you.

Projections for company B if acquired by company A (in $ millions)

	Year 1	Year 2	Year 3	Year 4	Year 5
Sales	800	900	1,000	1,125	1,250
Production costs	562	630	700	790	875
Depreciation	75	80	82	83	83
Other expenses	80	90	100	113	125
EBIT	83	100	118	139	167
Interest	19	22	24	25	27
EBT	64	78	94	114	140
Taxes	32	39	47	57	70
Net income	32	39	47	57	70
Investments:					
Net working capital	20	25	25	30	30
Net fixed assets	15	25	18	12	7
Total	35	50	43	42	37
Sources of financing:					
Net debt financing	35	16	16	15	12
Profit retention	0	34	27	27	25
Total	35	50	43	42	37

Cash flows—Company A						
	Year 0	Year 1	Year 2	Year 3	Year 4	Year 5
Acquisition of B	—					
Dividends from B	150	—	—	—	—	—
Tax loss carry-forwards			25	25		—
Terminal value	—	—	—	—	—	—
Total	—	—	—	—	—	—

Risk Shifting

29.8 The Chocolate Ice Cream Company and the Vanilla Ice Cream Company have agreed to merge and form Fudge Swirl Consolidated. The two companies are exactly alike except for being located in different towns. The end-of-period value of each firm is determined by the weather, as shown.

Weather	Probability	Value
Rainy	0.1	$100,000
Warm	0.4	200,000
Hot	0.5	400,000

Because the towns are separated by a mountain range, their weather conditions are independent of each other. Furthermore, each company has an outstanding debt claim of $200,000. Assume that no premiums are paid in the merger.

a. What is the distribution of joint values?

b. What is the distribution of end-of-period debt values and stock values after the merger?

c. Show that the value of the combined firm is the sum of the individual values.

d. Show that the bondholders are better off and the shareholders are worse off in the combined firm than they would have been if the firms remained separate.

29.9 Upper Canada Hydro, a public utility, provides electricity to the province of Ontario. Recent events at its Quickering Nuclear Station have been discouraging. Several shareholders have expressed concern over last year's financial statements.

Income statement last year (in $ millions)		Balance sheet end of year (in $ millions)	
Revenue	$110	Assets	$400
Fuel	50	Debt	300
Other expenses	30	Equity	100
Interest	30		
Net income	$0		

Recently, a wealthy group of individuals has offered to purchase one half of Upper Canada's assets at fair market value. Management recommends that this offer be accepted because "We believe our expertise in the energy industry can be better exploited by Upper Canada if we sell our electricity generating and transmission assets and enter the telecommunications business. Although telecommunications is a riskier business than providing electricity as a public utility, it is also potentially very profitable."

    Should the management approve this transaction? Why or why not?

Reasons for Mergers

29.10 Indicate whether you think the following claims regarding takeovers are true or false. Briefly explain your answers.

a. By merging competitors, takeovers have created monopolies that will raise product prices, reduce production, and harm consumers.

b. Managers act in their own interest at times and, in reality, may not be answerable to shareholders. Takeovers may reflect runaway management.

c. In an efficient market, takeovers would not occur because market price would reflect the true value of corporations. Thus, bidding firms would not be justified in paying premiums above market prices for target firms.

d. Traders and institutional investors, having extremely short time horizons, are influenced by their perceptions of what other market traders will be thinking of stock prospects; they do not value takeovers based on fundamental factors. Thus, they will sell shares in target firms despite the true value of the firms.

e. Mergers are a way of avoiding taxes because they allow the acquiring firm to write up the value of the assets of the acquired firm.

f. Acquisitions analysis frequently focuses on the total value of the firms involved. An acquisition, however, will usually affect relative values of stocks and bonds as well as their total value.

Campeau Corp.'s Acquisition of Federated Department Stores

APPENDIX

Campeau Corp.'s 1988 takeover of Federated (the largest U.S. department store conglomerate) for a total purchase consideration of $6.6 billion is one of the biggest takeovers in U.S. corporate history. Although well-known in Canada, Campeau was unknown on Wall Street before his purchase of Allied Stores at the end of 1986. Allied Stores (a department and specialty store conglomerate similar to Federated) cost Campeau $4.1 billion.

Brief Description of the Acquisition

In summer 1987, approximately six months after his purchase of Allied Stores, Campeau commissioned the First Boston Corporation (which had been heavily involved in the Allied deal) to prepare a research analysis of Federated. In early October, Campeau began to purchase shares of Federated through a dummy corporation. Through the end of 1987, Campeau continued to work out plans to launch a bid for Federated. These actions were the prelude to one of the largest acquisitions ever.

On January 25, 1988, Campeau made a bid of $47 per share for all 90 million outstanding shares of Federated Department Stores. Before the announcement, Federated stock traded for about $36 per share on the New York Stock Exchange. Campeau's bid price was widely regarded as too low, and it was expected that the Federated board would reject the offer. On Monday, January 25, 1988, Federated's shares shot up immediately to the $49 range for a one-day increase in share price of more than 35 percent. The market reacted to Campeau's offer by bidding Campeau's common stock to $17¾, which was down $¼ from the previous trading day. The data suggest that the market viewed Campeau's bid as low and unlikely to be accepted. The dramatic response of Federated's share price was very likely caused by anticipation of more bidding.

On February 3, Campeau offered to raise his bid to $61 per share for all of Federated's shares. On February 4, Federated's directors unanimously rejected Campeau's $47 offer. Lack of sufficient financing was cited as one key reason for the rejection. By this time, Federated's share price had increased to $56¼. The market had not priced Federated's shares at $61 because it was not confident about Campeau's financing ability. On February 8, Federated's share price closed at $59⅛ on expectations of the entry of fresh bidders.

On February 16, Campeau increased his bid to $66 a share; however, Federated's board rejected this proposal. Around this time, R.H. Macy & Co. expressed an interest in merging with Federated. Although it was not publicly released, Macy and Federated signed a confidentiality arrangement, and Macy received secret Federated growth forecasts. Federated's shares closed at $63¾ on February 16, but then fell to $61¾ on February 17. This was due to the rejection of Campeau's offer combined with market speculation that the company would attempt an internal restructuring or leveraged recapitalization.

In order to aid in financing the takeover, Campeau decided to sell one of Allied Stores' major divisions. By Friday, February 26, it appeared that Campeau and Federated had come to a friendly agreement for a takeover at $68 per share, and negotiations began. Federated's share price closed at $64.50 on February 26.

Over the weekend, Macy contacted Federated and made a revised offer. On February 29, Federated announced that it was considering a surprise offer. And by March 2, Federated's directors accepted Macy's merger proposal. Macy's offer was $73.80 per share for 80 percent of Federated's shares. Federated's share price closed at $67.75 on March 1.

After Federated accepted the Macy offer, Campeau vowed to persevere, and he created a two-tiered offer of $75 a share for 80 percent of Federated and $44 a share for the remaining balance. On March 14, Macy increased the cash portion of its offer at the expense of the securities portion. As well, the three companies went to court on March 14. Campeau wanted Federated's poison pill thrown out, and Macy wanted Campeau's bid to remain open. Federal Court Judge Leonard Sand issued no ruling, but stated that the bids must remain open for three business days after any decision was made.

On March 15, Campeau made a one-tier, all-cash bid of $68 per share for all of Federated's shares. Three days later, Judge Sand ruled that Federated's poison pill was valid, but Campeau's bid could close on March 25. In response, Campeau increased his bid to a two-tiered offer worth $73 a share on March 22. Federated's share price closed at $69.25 on March 22.

Over the next week, numerous bids were tendered by Campeau and Macy. The auction finally ended on April 1. The settlement price paid by Campeau for all of Federated's shares was $73.50 in cash. The completion of the bidding war was announced on April 3.

Conclusion

The text above summarizes several studies showing that significant positive abnormal returns are earned for the target shareholders in takeover activity. In this case, we saw that Federated's share price increased from approximately $36 on January 22, 1988, to

$69¼ on March 22, 1988. The final price paid for each share, as announced on April 3, 1988, was $73.50.

Kaplan shows that Campeau paid a premium of around $1.6 billion for Federated's assets.[38] These results support the notion that the real winners in takeover battles are (1) the shareholders of target firms and (2) those traders who identify undervalued firms that will become takeover targets, buy their stock before bidding begins, and hold it until just after the last bid is made.

As we noted, Campeau did not fare as well as the target shareholders. On January 15, 1990, both Allied and Federated applied for protection under Chapter 11 of the U.S. Federal Bankruptcy Code. Campeau Corp. was closed down and its name changed; and as of this writing, Robert Campeau is still being sued for unpaid personal loans that he allegedly took out of the corporation.

Chronology of the Events in the Acquisition of Federated Department Stores

- *January 1988*—Rumours circulate that a bid for Federated is imminent. Campeau quietly buys 130,000 shares on the open market at prices near U.S. $37 each for a total of $4.8 million. Donald Trump, a New York takeover raider, announces an interest in the company.[39]

- *January 23*—Federated's board strengthens the company's poison pill takeover defence.

- *January 25*—Campeau bids $47 a share or $4.25 billion.

- *January 26*—Edward Finkelstein, chief executive of Macy, telephones Howard Goldfeder, Federated's chairman, to offer advice about the Campeau offer. (No specific plans or proposals were discussed, according to takeover documents.)

- *February 3*—Robert Campeau writes Federated's board, offering to raise his bid to $61 a share or $5.51 billion.

- *February 4*—Federated directors unanimously reject Campeau's official $47 offer.

- *February 11*—Olympia & York agrees to buy up to $260 million of Campeau convertible debentures to help finance the takeover. If exercised, conversion would reduce Mr. Campeau's voting stake from 77 percent to about 50.

- *February 14*—Macy contacts Federated to explore the possibility of a merger of the two retailing giants.

- *February 15*—Federated says it is negotiating with a number of parties, but because none of the other parties are identified publicly, it appears for a time that Campeau is bidding against phantoms. Macy signs a confidentiality agreement and obtains secret Federated internal growth forecasts.

---

[38]Kaplan, "Campeau's Acquisition of Federated"; and S. N. Kaplan, "Campeau's Acquisition of Federated: Post-Bankruptcy Results," *Journal of Financial Economics 35* (February 1994), pp. 123–36.

[39]The events from January to March 22, 1988, are from "Quiet Buying Gave Early Hint of Fight for Federated," *The Globe and Mail* (March 23, 1988).

- *February 16*—Federated directors reject a Campeau proposal for $66 a share or $5.97 billion.
- *February 22*—Macy representatives orally propose to Federated an acquisition for $50 in cash and $11 in securities for each share.
- *February 25*—Campeau agrees to sell the Brooks Brothers division of Allied Stores Corp. to Marks and Spencer PLC. Of the $770 million in proceeds, $220 million would be used to finance the Federated takeover.
- *February 26*—Federated and Campeau start negotiations for a friendly takeover at $68 a share or $6.15 billion.
- *February 27*—Macy contacts Federated to make a revised offer. As Federated drafts a takeover agreement with Campeau, it secretly begins talks with Macy. Over this weekend, the Campeau forces work feverishly to complete an agreement.
- *February 29*—In the early hours of the day, Federated's advisors ask for copies of the agreement with Campeau for distribution to Federated's directors. Campeau advisors believe they have won the fight.

  At midmorning, Federated announces it is considering a surprise offer from an unnamed party, later identified as Macy. Mr. Finkelstein, Macy's chief, makes a presentation to the Federated board.
- *March 1*—Federated's board continues meeting in New York to study offers from Macy and Campeau. At the last minute, Campeau's advisors tell the directors they would be willing to recommend increasing their offer to $69.50 a share.
- *March 2*—Federated's directors accept a merger proposal from Macy, which would buy 80 percent of Federated for $74.50 a share and exchange the balance for securities in a firm to be formed from the merger of the two retailing giants.

  Campeau vows to fight on and changes its offer. The new deal is $75 a share for 80 percent of Federated, to be followed by a merger offering $44 a share for the balance.
- *March 4*—Campeau says it has arranged to sell two of Federated's divisions to May Department Stores Co. for about $1.5 billion if the takeover succeeds.
- *March 14*—Macy sweetens the cash portion of its bid by about $200 million, raising the purchase price to $77.35 a share from $74.50. But the improvement comes at the expense of the securities to be issued as part of the deal.

  All three companies battle late that night in a New York courtroom before Federal Court Judge Leonard Sand. Campeau wants Federated's poison pill thrown out. Macy wants the judge to extend the period Campeau's bid must remain open. The judge issues no rulings, but declares the bids must remain open for three business days after any decision.
- *March 15*—Campeau writes an angry letter to Federated's directors, announcing that he is willing to make a one-tier, all-cash bid at $68 a share. He asks to meet the Federated board as Mr. Finkelstein has been allowed to do, but is rebuffed.

- *March 18*—Judge Sand rules that Federated's poison pill defence is valid, which means Campeau will likely have to raise its bid. But the judge also decides that Campeau's revised bid is not a new offer and can close March 25, an advantage over Macy's April 4 expiry date.
- *March 22*—Campeau sweetens its bid by $450 million to a two-tier blended offer worth $73 a share, with a cash bid of $82 for the first 80 percent.
- *April 3*—The completion of the Federated takeover is announced with Campeau's agreement to pay $73.50 in cash per share.

Suggested Readings

For an excellent, easily readable discussion of the Campeau story, see:

J. Rothchild. *Going for Broke—How Robert Campeau Bankrupted the Retail Industry, Jolted the Junk Bond Market, and Brought the Booming Eighties to a Crashing Halt.* Toronto: Simon & Schuster, 1991.

Detailed clinical studies of Campeau's acquisition of Federated appear in:

S. N. Kaplan. "Campeau's Acquisition of Federated: Value Destroyed or Value Added." *Journal of Financial Economics* 25 (December 1989), pp. 191–212.

S.N. Kaplan. "Campeau's Acquisition of Federated: Post-Bankruptcy Results." *Journal of Financial Economics* 35 (February 1994), pp. 123–36.

This chapter discusses financial distress, private workouts, and bankruptcy. A firm that does not generate enough cash flow to pay interest or other contractually required payments will experience financial distress. If it defaults on a required payment, a firm may be forced to liquidate its assets. More often, a defaulting firm will reorganize its financial structure. Financial restructuring involves replacing old financial claims with new ones; it takes place with private workouts or legal bankruptcy. Private workouts are voluntary arrangements to restructure a company's debt, such as postponing a payment or reducing the size of the payment. Sometimes a private workout is not possible and formal bankruptcy is required.

What Is Financial Distress? 30.1

Financial distress is surprisingly hard to define precisely—partly because of the variety of events befalling firms under financial distress. The list of events is almost endless. Examples include

Dividend reductions.

Plant closings.

Losses.

Layoffs.

CEO resignations.

Plummeting stock prices.

Financial distress occurs when a firm's operating cash flows are not sufficient to satisfy current obligations (such as trade credits or interest expenses) and the firm is forced to take corrective action.[1] Financial distress may lead a firm to default on a contract, and it may involve financial restructuring between the firm, its creditors, and its equity investors. Usually the firm is forced to take actions that it would not have taken if it had sufficient cash flow.

---

[1] This definition is close to the one used by Karen Wruck, "Financial Distress: Reorganization and Organization Efficiency," *Journal of Financial Economics* 27 (1990), p. 425.

Figure 30.1
Insolvency

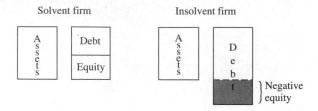

A. Stock-based insolvency

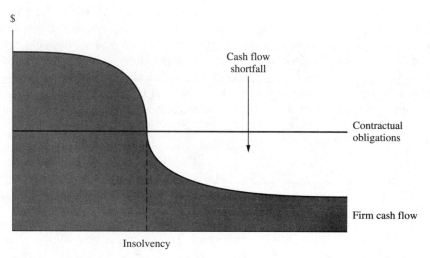

B. Flow-based insolvency

Stock-based insolvency occurs when the value of the assets of a firm are less than the value of the debts. This implies negative equity. Flow-based insolvency occurs when firm cash flows are insufficient to cover contractually required payments.

Our definition of financial distress can be expanded somewhat by linking it to insolvency. *Insolvency* is defined in *Black's Law Dictionary* as[2]

> Inability to pay one's debts; lack of means of paying one's debts. Such a condition of [one's] assets and liability that the former made immediately available would be insufficient to discharge the latter.

This definition has two general themes: stocks and flows.[3] These two ways of thinking about insolvency are depicted in Figure 30.1. *Stock-based insolvency* occurs when a firm has negative net worth, so the value of its assets is less than the value of

---

[2]*Black's Law Dictionary,* 5th ed. (St. Paul, Minn.: West, 1979), p. 716.

[3]Edward Altman was one of the first to distinguish between stock-based insolvency and flow-based insolvency. See Edward Altman, *Corporate Financial Distress: A Complete Guide to Predicting, Avoiding and Dealing with Bankruptcy* (New York: John Wiley & Sons, 1983).

its debts. *Flow-based insolvency* occurs when operating cash flow is insufficient to meet current obligations. Flow-based insolvency refers to the inability to pay one's debts.

The two kinds of insolvency usually occur together, but this is not always the case. For example, a firm that had no current obligations could remain in business even if its debt exceeded its assets. Such a firm would be solvent according to the flow-based measure but insolvent by the stock-based measure. When this occurs, firms often resort to creative accounting to hide their stock-based insolvency and increase their risk to try to increase the value of assets. This represents an agency cost of debt as we discussed in Chapter 16.

CONCEPT QUESTIONS

- Describe financial distress.
- What are stock-based and flow-based insolvency?

What Happens in Financial Distress? 30.2

In early 1993, Royal Trustco Ltd., which controlled Canada's second largest trust operation, experienced financial distress. It lost a substantial amount of money in 1992 and was forced to sell some of its international operations at fire-sale prices. By early 1993, a plummeting stock price and further losses culminated in an agreement for Royal Trustco to sell its Canadian and European operations to the Royal Bank. This is one way of handling financial distress.

Firms deal with financial distress in many ways such as

1. Selling major assets.
2. Merging with another firm.
3. Reducing capital spending as well as research and development.
4. Issuing new securities.
5. Negotiating with banks and other creditors.
6. Exchanging equity for debt.
7. Filing for bankruptcy.

Items (1), (2), and (3) concern the firm's assets. Items (4), (5), (6), and (7) involve the right-hand side of the firm's balance sheet and are examples of financial restructuring. Financial distress may involve both asset restructuring and financial restructuring— changes on both sides of the balance sheet.

Some firms may actually benefit from financial distress by restructuring their assets. In 1992, Olympia & York's decision to seek court protection allowed the company to restructure its assets and avoid formal bankruptcy liquidation. Olympia & York's cash flow was not sufficient to cover required payments, and it emerged from court protection as solely a property management company; previously, it was in many different lines of business. This example shows that, for some firms, financial distress may bring about new organizational forms and new operating strategies. However, in this chapter we focus on financial restructuring.

Figure 30.2
What happens in
financial distress

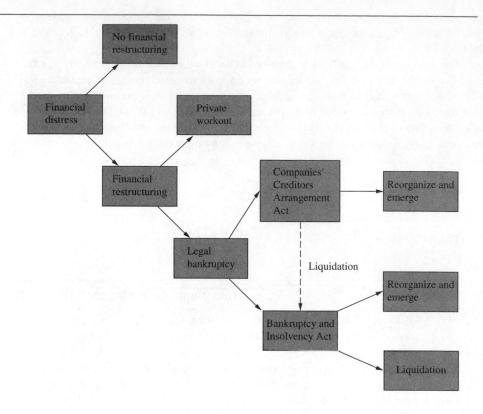

Figure 30.2 shows how firms move through financial distress in Canada. Previously, most legal bankruptcies in this country ended with liquidation. However, new changes to the bankruptcy process are encouraging restructurings, reorganizations, and private workouts.

Financial distress can serve as a firm's "early warning" system for trouble. Firms with more debt will experience financial distress earlier than firms with less debt. However, firms that experience financial distress earlier will have more time for private workouts and reorganization. Firms with low leverage will experience financial distress later and, in many instances, be forced to liquidate.

CONCEPT QUESTIONS

- Why doesn't financial distress always cause firms to die?
- What is a benefit of financial distress?

30.3   Bankruptcy Liquidation and Reorganization

Firms that cannot or choose not to make contractually required payments to creditors have two basic options: liquidation or reorganization. **Liquidation** means termination of the firm as a going concern, and it involves selling off the assets of the firm. The proceeds, net of selling costs, are distributed to creditors in order of established priority. **Reorganization** is the option of keeping the firm a going concern; it often involves issuing new securities to replace old ones. Liquidation or reorganization is the result of a bankruptcy proceeding. Which occurs depends on whether the firm is worth more "dead" or "alive."

Liquidation and reorganization are covered under the Bankruptcy and Insolvency Act (1993); reorganization is also covered under the Companies' Creditors Arrangement Act. In late 1992, after intense criticism of the inherent difficulties of reorganization under the old law, the federal government introduced wide-ranging changes to the Bankruptcy and Insolvency Act to make it "debtor friendly." The changes have met with mixed reviews, but most industry experts agree that the changes facilitate corporate restructurings.[4]

Bankruptcy Liquidation

Liquidation occurs when the court directs sale of all assets of the firm. The following sequence of events is typical.

1. A petition is filed in a federal court. Corporations may file a voluntary petition, or involuntary petitions may be filed against the corporation by creditors. Creditors must give 10 days notice before filing a petition.

2. A trustee-in-bankruptcy is elected by the creditors to take over the assets of the debtor corporation. The trustee will attempt to liquidate the assets.

3. When the assets are liquidated, after payment of the bankruptcy administration costs, the proceeds are distributed among the creditors.

4. If any assets remain, after expenses and payments to creditors, they are distributed to the shareholders.

The distribution of the proceeds of the liquidation occurs according to the following priority. (The higher a claim is on this list, the more likely it is to be paid. In many of these categories, there are various limitations and qualifications that we omit for the sake of brevity.[5])

1. Administrative expenses associated with the bankruptcy.

2. Other expenses arising after the filing of an involuntary bankruptcy petition but before the appointment of a trustee.

3. Wages, salaries, and commissions.

4. Municipal tax claims.

5. Rent.

6. Claims resulting from employee injuries that are not covered by workers' compensation.

7. Unsecured creditors.

8. Preferred shareholders.

9. Common shareholders.

---

[4]P. P. Farkas, "What's Really Wrong with Our Bankruptcy Act?" *CA Magazine* (June 1991), pp. 39–40.

[5]Our discussion draws on R. Klapstein, *Legal Aspects of Financial Counselling* (Montreal: Institute of Canadian Bankers, 1994), chapter 16.

Three qualifications to this list are in order. The first concerns unpaid federal source deductions such as income tax and unemployment insurance premiums. These funds are beyond the grasp of the bankruptcy trustee and must be paid to the government ahead of any payments to the claimants on our list. (Provincial source deductions have the same status only if the bankrupt company had kept them in a separate bank account.) The second qualification concerns secured creditors. Such creditors are entitled to the proceeds from the sale of the security and are outside this ordering. However, if the secured property is liquidated and provides insufficient cash to cover the amount owed, the secured creditors join with unsecured creditors in dividing the remaining liquidated value. In contrast, if the secured property is liquidated for proceeds greater than the secured claim, the net proceeds are used to pay unsecured creditors and others.

▪ *Example*

The B. O. Drug Company is to be liquidated. Its liquidating value is $2.5 million. Bonds worth $1.5 million are secured by a mortgage on the B. O. Drug Company corporate headquarters building, which is sold for $1 million; $200,000 is used to cover administrative costs and other claims (including unpaid wages, pension benefits, consumer claims, and taxes). The amount available to pay secured and unsecured creditors is $2.5 million. This is less than the amount of unpaid debt of $4 million. Following our list of priorities, all creditors must be paid before shareholders, and the mortgage bondholders have first claim on the $1 million obtained from the sale of the headquarters building.

The trustee has proposed the following distribution:

Type of claim	Prior claim	Cash received under liquidation
Bonds (secured by mortgage)	$ 1,500,000	$1,500,000
Subordinated debentures	2,500,000	1,000,000
Common shareholders	10,000,000	0
Total	$14,000,000	$2,500,000

Calculation of the distribution

Cash received from sale of assets available for distribution	$2,500,000
Cash paid to secured bondholders on sale of mortgaged property	1,000,000
Available to bond and debenture holders	$1,500,000
Total claims remaining ($4,000,000 less payment of $1,000,000 on secured bonds)	3,000,000

Distribution of remaining $1,500,000 to cover total remaining claims of $3,000,000

Type of claim remaining	Claim on liquidation proceeds	Cash received
Bonds	$ 500,000	$ 500,000
Debentures	2,500,000	1,000,000
Total	$3,000,000	$1,500,000 ▪

The third qualification is that, in reality, courts have a great deal of freedom in deciding what actually happens and who actually gets what in the event of bankruptcy. As a result, the priority set out above is not always followed.

The 1988 restructuring of Dome Petroleum is an example. Declining oil prices in 1986 found Dome already in difficulties after a series of earlier debt reschedulings. Dome's board believed that if the company went into bankruptcy, secured creditors could force disposal of assets at fire-sale prices, producing losses for unsecured creditors and shareholders. One estimate obtained at the time projected that unsecured creditors would receive, at best, 15 cents per dollar of debt under liquidation. As a result, the board sought and received court and regulatory approval for sale of the company as a going concern to Amoco Canada. Unsecured creditors eventually received 45 cents on the dollar.

Bankruptcy Reorganization

The general objective of corporate reorganization is to plan to restructure the corporation with some provision for repayment of creditors. The new provisions introduced to the Bankruptcy and Insolvency Act in 1992 were intended to facilitate the corporate reorganization process. Here is a typical sequence of events:

1. A voluntary petition can be filed by the corporation, or an involuntary petition can be filed by creditors. Under the new legislation, creditors must provide the insolvent company with 10 days notice before filing the petition.
2. A federal judge either approves or denies the petition. If the petition is approved, a time for filing proofs of claims is set. A debtor files a notice of intention to make a proposal (reorganization plan), and a stay of proceedings of 30 days is effected against all creditors. A further 21 days is added until the creditors meet to vote on the proposal. The court can add a maximum of five months to the stay period.
3. In almost all cases, the corporation (the "debtor in possession") continues to run the business. While the stay of proceedings is in effect, the new legislation has included several safeguards intended to prevent the collapse of the business.
4. The corporation is required to submit a proposal, which is the reorganization plan.
5. Creditors and shareholders are divided into classes. A class of creditors accepts the plan if a majority of the class (in dollars or in number) agrees. The secured creditors must vote before the unsecured creditors. The debtor decides on the classes of secured creditors, and can force proposals on uncooperative creditors.
6. After acceptance by creditors, the plan is confirmed by the court.
7. Payments in cash, property, and securities are made to creditors and shareholders. The plan may provide for the issuance of new securities.

■ *Example*

Suppose B. O. Drug Co. decides to reorganize under the Bankruptcy and Insolvency Act. Generally, senior claims are honoured in full before various other claims receive anything. Assume that the "going concern" value of B. O. Drug Co. is $3 million and that its balance sheet is as shown:

Assets	$3,000,000
Liabilities	
Mortgage bonds	1,500,000
Subordinated debentures	2,500,000
Shareholders' equity	−1,000,000

The firm has proposed the following reorganization plan:

Old security	Old claim	New claim with reorganization plan
Mortgage bonds	$1,500,000	$1,500,000
Subordinated debentures	2,500,000	1,500,000

and a distribution of new securities under new claim with reorganization plan:

Old security	Receives under proposed reorganization plan
Mortgage bonds	$1,000,000 in 9% senior debentures
	$500,000 in 11% subordinated debentures
Debentures	$1,000,000 in 8% preferred stock
	$500,000 in common stock

The corporation may wish to allow the old shareholders to retain some participation in the firm. Needless to say, this may lead to protests by the holders of unsecured debt. ∎

Companies' Creditors Arrangement Act

The Companies' Creditors Arrangement Act (CCAA)—federal legislation originally enacted during the 1930s—allows for the reorganization and continuation of insolvent businesses.[6] Some important differences between the CCAA and the Bankruptcy and Insolvency Act are

1. The Bankruptcy and Insolvency Act is primarily restricted to dealing with unsecured creditors, but the CCAA can deal with any or all creditors.
2. The CCAA is a brief statute that is silent on the framework for proceeding with an arrangement (reorganization plan). Therefore, a series of court orders must be used to develop an appropriate framework.
3. When a company applies for protection under the CCAA, there is no provision for the debtor to be placed in bankruptcy for failing to carry out the agreed-upon terms.

In the 1980s, the CCAA became a popular statute for major reorganizations. The advantage that it gives debtors in dealing with secured creditors makes this statute invaluable for certain corporate restructurings. Later in the chapter we will look at this statute's use in the reorganization of Olympia & York.

---

[6]An excellent description of the CCAA is provided in E. B. Leonard, *Guide to Commercial Insolvency in Canada* (Toronto: Butterworths Canada, 1988), pp. 20-1 to 20-6.

Agreements to Avoid Bankruptcy

When a firm defaults on an obligation, it may still be able to avoid bankruptcy. Because the legal process of bankruptcy can be lengthy and expensive, it is often in everyone's best interest to devise a *private workout* that avoids a bankruptcy filing. Much of the time, creditors can work with the management of a company that has defaulted on a loan contract. Voluntary arrangements to restructure the company's debt can be and often are made. This may involve *extension,* which postpones the date of payment, or *composition,* which involves a reduced payment.

CONCEPT QUESTIONS

- What is bankruptcy?
- What is the difference between liquidation and reorganization?
- What is the Companies' Creditors Arrangement Act?

Current Issues in Financial Distress   30.4

In this section we examine two important tactics in financial distress: private workouts and prepackaged bankruptcies. Prevalent in the United States, it is expected that these responses to financial distress will grow in importance in Canada under the new legislation. For this reason, this section relates U.S. experience to the new Canadian law.

Private Workout or Bankruptcy: Which Is Best?

A firm that defaults on its debt payments will need to restructure its financial claims. The firm will have two choices: formal bankruptcy or **private workout.** The previous section described two types of formal bankruptcies: liquidation and reorganization. This section compares private workouts with bankruptcy reorganizations. Both types of financial restructuring involve exchanging new financial claims for old financial claims. Usually senior debt is replaced with junior debt, and debt is replaced with equity. Much recent academic research in the United States has described what happens in private workouts and formal bankruptcies.[7]

- Historically, one-half of financial restructurings have been private, but recently formal bankruptcy has dominated.
- Firms that emerge from private workouts experience stock price increases that are much greater than those for firms emerging from formal bankruptcies.
- The direct costs of private workouts are only about 10 percent of the costs of formal bankruptcies.
- Top management usually loses pay and sometimes jobs in both private workouts and formal bankruptcies.

---

[7]For example, see Stuart Gilson, "Managing Default: Some Evidence on How Firms Choose between Workouts and Bankruptcy," *Journal of Applied Corporate Finance* (Summer 1991); and Stuart C. Gilson, Kose John; and Larry N. P. Lang, "Troubled Debt Restructuring: An Empirical Study of Private Reorganization of Firms in Defaults," *Journal of Financial Economics* 27 (1990).

These facts, when taken together, seem to suggest that a private workout is much better than a formal bankruptcy. In Canada, the new Bankruptcy and Insolvency Act has added increased costs and time commitments to the formal bankruptcy proceedings. Therefore, direct negotiations (private workouts) between creditors and debtors can be expected to increase. In some cases, however, formal bankruptcy is the better alternative.

Holdouts

Bankruptcy is usually better for equity investors than for creditors because equity investors can usually hold out for a better deal in bankruptcy. The priority of claims, which favours creditors over equity investors, is usually violated in formal bankruptcies. One recent study found that in 81 percent of recent U.S. bankruptcies, equity investors obtained some compensation.[8]

Complexity

A firm with a complicated capital structure will have more trouble putting together a private workout. Firms with secured creditors and trade creditors will usually use formal bankruptcy because it is too difficult to reach an agreement with many different types of creditors.

Lack of Information

There is an inherent conflict of interest between equity investors and creditors, and the conflict is accentuated when both have incomplete information about the circumstances of financial distress. When a firm initially experiences a cash flow shortfall, it may not know whether the shortfall is permanent or temporary. If the shortfall is permanent, creditors will push for a formal reorganization or liquidation. However, if the cash flow shortfall is temporary, formal reorganization or liquidation may not be necessary and equity investors will take this viewpoint. This conflict of interest cannot easily be resolved.

These last two points are especially important. They suggest that financial distress will be more expensive if complexity is high and information is incomplete. Complexity and lack of information make cheap workouts less likely.

Prepackaged Bankruptcy

On October 1, 1986, the Crystal Oil Company filed for protection from its creditors under Chapter 11 of the U.S. Bankruptcy Code.[9] Given the firm's heavy indebtedness, perhaps the outcome was not very surprising. However, less than three months later, Crystal Oil came out of bankruptcy with a different capital structure. This surprised

---

[8]Lawrence A. Weiss, "Bankruptcy Dissolution: Direct Costs and Violation of Priority and Claims," *Journal of Financial Economics* 23 (1990).

[9]Chapter 11 is the U.S. version of the reorganization laws in Canada.

many people because, traditionally, bankruptcy has been very costly and it often takes many years to emerge from it. Crystal Oil avoided a lengthy bankruptcy by negotiating a reorganization plan with its creditors several months before the bankruptcy filing date.[10]

This new reorganization arrangement has been called **prepackaged bankruptcy.** Prepackaged bankruptcy is a combination of private workout and legal bankruptcy. In prepackaged bankruptcy, the firm and most of its creditors agree to private reorganization outside formal bankruptcy. After the private reorganization is put together, the firm files a formal bankruptcy.

Prepackaged bankruptcy arrangements require that most creditors reach agreement privately. Prepackaged bankruptcy does not seem to work when there are thousands of reluctant trade creditors, such as in the case of retail trading firms.

The main benefit of prepackaged bankruptcy is that it forces holdouts to accept a bankruptcy reorganization. If a large fraction of a firm's creditors can agree privately to a reorganization plan, the holdout problem may be avoided. This makes a reorganization plan in formal bankruptcy easier to put together.[11]

CONCEPT QUESTIONS

- What are two ways a firm can restructure its finances?
- Why do firms use formal bankruptcy?
- What is prepackaged bankruptcy?
- What is the main benefit of prepackaged bankruptcy?

The Decision to Seek Court Protection: The Case of Olympia & York   30.5

Olympia & York (O&Y) was one of the largest companies in Canada. Privately held by the powerful Reichmann family, Olympia & York Developments was best known for its real estate development projects. The company was also involved in ownership of real estate, energy, natural resources, financial services, and beverage companies. Outside of Canada, O&Y was the largest landowner in Manhattan, New York, and owner of the Canary Wharf project in London, England.

On May 14, 1992, O&Y filed for court protection in Canada under the Companies' Creditors Arrangement Act. At the same time, several O&Y affiliates filed for Chapter 11 bankruptcy protection in the United States. Finally, on May 27, O&Y also filed for court protection in the U.K. due to an inability to meet payments on the Canary Wharf project.

The recession of the early 1990s led to a major decline in real estate prices and an increase in vacancy rates. O&Y (a highly leveraged company) could not service its

---

[10]John McConnell and Henri Servaes, "The Economics of Prepackaged Bankruptcy," *Journal of Applied Corporate Finance* (Summer 1991), describes prepackaged bankruptcy and the Crystal Oil Company.

[11]The original reorganization plan of Crystal Oil was accepted by the public creditors, but it was not accepted by the secured creditors. During bankruptcy a slightly revised plan was "crammed down" on the secured creditors. A bankruptcy court can force creditors to participate in a reorganization if it can be shown that the plan is "fair and equitable."

debt because of a lack of cash flow. Here is a brief summary of the decision to file for protection and the events following.

1. In the late 1980s, O&Y embarked upon numerous real estate developments. As the largest landowner in the world, O&Y undertook large projects in North America and Europe.

2. The 1990s recession led to a liquidity crisis for O&Y, and the company could not service its debt.

3. In May 1992, O&Y filed for court protection in Canada, the United States, and the U.K.

4. Court protection allowed O&Y some breathing room, as its assets were not touchable by creditors until a formal restructuring plan had been presented.[12] In the United States and Canada, $8.6 billion of debt was immediately frozen from servicing. In the U.K., $7.7 billion of debt was frozen.

5. After numerous deadline extensions and a difficult eight months, O&Y presented a restructuring plan to creditors (over 100 in total) in Canada; it was approved on January 25, 1993. At the time of writing, O&Y was still attempting to save some U.S. properties from Chapter 11. In the U.K., a buyer for the Canary Wharf project was being sought.

6. The acceptance of the Canadian restructuring plan resulted in O&Y's emerging as a small property management company, and the company was significantly downsized.

Costs of the O&Y restructuring include

1. *Direct costs of restructuring.* Formal protection can be expensive and time consuming. O&Y was under court protection in Canada for eight months, and was still negotiating in the United States and the U.K. when this was written. The first six months of restructuring were estimated to cost O&Y $20 million. Fees include

Legal fees	$5.75 million
Accounting fees	2.65 million
Costs of financial advisors	8.50 million

These fees are for O&Y alone and do not go beyond the first six months of restructuring. Creditors will also be paying huge legal fees; for example, one bank estimated its total legal bill to be $7 million.[13]

2. *Indirect costs of restructuring.* There are many indirect costs of financial distress, including management distraction, loss of customers, and loss of reputation. Indirect costs may occur whether or not formal bankruptcy is declared.

3. *Costs of a complicated financial structure.* Firms such as O&Y that have bank loans, senior subordinated debt, and junior subordinated debt with many different creditors will have a difficult time getting all claimholders to agree to an out-of-court settlement. It is axiomatic that the more complicated a firm's financial

---

[12]As we stated in Section 30.3, the CCAA can apply to all creditors, which was important for O&Y.

[13]These fees were derived from "O&Y's Restructuring Bill to Reach $20M: Report," *The Globe and Mail* (June 20, 1992).

structure, the more difficult it will be to work out private arrangements to avoid bankruptcy. Conflicts between managers, shareholders, and creditors make reaching a private agreement difficult. There is a tendency for each group to try to gain value at the expense of the others.

CONCEPT QUESTIONS

- Was O&Y's insolvency stock-based or flow-based?
- What are some costs of the O&Y bankruptcy?

Summary and Conclusions   30.6

This chapter examines what happens when firms experience financial distress.

1. Financial distress occurs when a firm's operating cash flow is not sufficient to cover contractual obligations. Financially distressed firms are often forced to take corrective actions and to undergo financial restructuring. Financial restructuring involves exchanging new financial claims for old ones.

2. Financial restructuring can be accomplished with a private workout or formal bankruptcy. Financial restructuring can involve liquidation or reorganization. However, liquidation is becoming less common in Canada.

3. Two important tactics in restructuring are private workouts and prepackaged bankruptcies. Both are expected to increase in Canada with the advent of "debtor friendly" legislation.

4. In the example of Olympia & York's filing for court protection to avoid bankruptcy proceedings, we see how a complicated financial structure can make it hard to achieve agreement among creditors.

Key Terms

Financial distress 869   Private workout 877
Liquidation 872   Prepackaged bankruptcy 879
Reorganization 873

Suggested Readings

An excellent book on financial distress by a leading authority is:

Edward A. Altman. *Corporate Financial Distress: A Complete Guide to Predicting, Avoiding and Dealing with Bankruptcy.* New York: John Wiley & Sons, 1983.

Many recent academic articles on financial distress appear in:

Michael Jensen and Richard Rubeck, eds. "Symposium on the Structure and Governance of Enterprise, Part II." *Journal of Financial Economics* 27 (1990). Articles by Lawrence Weiss,

Stuart G. Gilson, Kose John, Larry N. P. Lang, Steven Kaplan, David Reishus, Frank Easterbrook, and Karen H. Wruck appear.

Canadian statutes regarding bankruptcy and insolvency are found in:

L. W. Houlden and C. H. Morawetz. *The Annotated Bankruptcy and Insolvency Act 1993.* Scarsborough, Ontario: Carswell, 1992.

Questions and Problems

General Questions

30.1 Define financial distress using the stock-based and flow-based approaches. Explain how a company could be insolvent under one measure but not the other.

30.2 Why do so many firms file for legal bankruptcy when private workouts are so much less expensive?

30.3 What are some benefits of financial distress?

Bankruptcy

30.4 When the Beacon Computer Company (BCC) filed for bankruptcy liquidation under the Canadian Bankruptcy and Insolvency Act, it had the following balance sheet:

Liquidating value	Claims	
Net realizable assets $5,000	Trade credit	$ 1,000
	Secured notes (by a mortgage)	1,000
	Senior debenture	3,000
	Junior debenture	1,000
	Equity	(1,000)

As a trustee, what distribution of liquidating value do you propose?

30.5 When the Master Printing Company filed for bankruptcy reorganization under the Canadian Bankruptcy and Insolvency Act, it had the following balance sheet:

Assets	Claims	
Going concern value $15,000	Mortgage bonds	$10,000
	Senior debenture	6,000
	Junior debenture	4,000
	Equity	(5,000)

As a trustee, what reorganization plan would you accept?

30.6 The A&Z Real Estate Company is to be liquidated. The book value of its assets is $20 billion. Bonds with a face value of $7 billion are secured by a mortgage on the company's flagship building. A&Z has subordinated debentures outstanding in the amount of $11 billion; shareholders' equity has a book value of $2 billion; $300 million is used to cover administrative costs and other claims (including unpaid wages, pension benefits, legal fees, and taxes).

The company has a liquidating value of $10 billion. Of this amount, $5 billion represents the proceeds from the sale of the flagship building.

As the trustee in bankruptcy, you wish to follow the bankruptcy law strictly. What is your proposed distribution?

30.7 Now suppose that the A&Z Real Estate Company in Problem 30.6 wishes to reorganize instead of liquidating. In this case the company has a going concern value of $13 billion. What proposal would you recommend? How does this proposal differ from your solution in the case of liquidation? Explain briefly.

CHAPTER 31

International Corporate Finance

Canada has an open economy linked very closely by a free trade agreement to its largest trading partner, the United States. There are also important economic and financial ties to Mexico, Europe, the Pacific Rim, and other major economies worldwide.

Corporations that have significant foreign operations are often referred to as *international corporations* or *multinationals*. International corporations must consider many financial factors that do not directly affect purely domestic firms. These include foreign exchange rates, different interest rates from country to country, complex accounting methods for foreign operations, foreign tax rates, and foreign government intervention. These topics are also of interest to many smaller Canadian businesses.

Smaller corporations do not qualify as multinationals in the league of Alcan or McCain, but their financial managers must know how to manage foreign exchange risk.

The basic principles of corporate finance apply to international corporations. Like domestic companies, international ones seek to (1) invest in projects that create more value for the shareholders than they cost and (2) arrange financing that raises cash at the lowest possible cost. That is, the net present value principle holds for both foreign and domestic operations. However, it is usually more complicated to apply the NPV principle to foreign operations.

Perhaps the most important complication of international finance is foreign exchange. The foreign exchange markets provide information and opportunities for an international corporation when it undertakes capital budgeting and financing decisions. The relationship among foreign exchange, interest rates, and inflation is defined by the basic theories of exchange rates: purchasing power parity, interest rate parity, and the expectations theory.

Typically, international financing decisions involve a choice of three basic approaches:

1. Export domestic cash to the foreign operations.
2. Borrow in the country where the investment is located.
3. Borrow in a third country.

We will discuss the merits of each approach.

31.1   **Terminology**

A common buzzword across all business school subjects is *globalization*. The first step in learning about the globalization of financial markets is to conquer the new vocabulary. Here are some of the most common terms used in international finance and in this chapter:

1. A **Belgian dentist** is a stereotype of the traditional Eurobond (see below) investor. This self-employed professional (a dentist, for instance) must report income, has a disdain for tax authorities, and likes to invest in foreign currencies. Anonymous-bearer Eurobonds fit the bill nicely for this type of investor because they are unregistered and so are untraceable. Such individual investors do not mind paying a premium for Eurobonds, because the bonds effectively are issued on a tax-free basis.

2. The **cross rate** is the exchange rate between two foreign currencies, generally neither of which is the U.S. dollar. The U.S. dollar, however, is used as an interim step in determining the cross rate. For example, if an investor wants to sell Canadian dollars and buy Swiss francs, he would sell Canadian dollars against U.S. dollars and then buy francs with those U.S. dollars. So, although the transaction is designed to be Canadian dollars for francs, the U.S. dollar's exchange rate serves as a benchmark.

3. **Eurobonds** are bonds denominated in a particular currency and issued simultaneously in the bond markets of several European countries. For many international companies and governments, they have become an important way to raise capital. Eurobonds are issued outside the restrictions that apply to domestic offerings and are typically syndicated in London. Trading can and does take place anywhere there is a buyer and a seller.

4. **Eurocurrency** is money deposited in a financial centre outside of the country whose currency is involved. For instance, Eurodollars—the most widely used Eurocurrency—are U.S. dollars deposited in banks outside the United States.

5. **Foreign bonds,** unlike Eurobonds, are issued in a single country and are usually denominated in that country's currency. Often, the country in which these bonds are issued will draw distinctions between them and bonds issued by domestic issuers, including different tax laws, restrictions on the amount issued, or tougher disclosure rules.

    Foreign bonds often are nicknamed for the country where they are issued: Yankee bonds (United States), Samurai bonds (Japan), Rembrandt bonds (the Netherlands), and Bulldog bonds (Britain). Partly because of tougher regulations and disclosure requirements, the foreign bond market has not grown in past years with the vigour of the Eurobond market. A substantial portion of all foreign bonds are issued in Switzerland.

6. **Gilts,** technically, are British and Irish government securities, although the term also includes issues of local British authorities and some overseas public sector offerings.

7. The **London Interbank Offered Rate (LIBOR)** is the rate that most international banks charge one another for loans of Eurodollars overnight in the London market. LIBOR is a cornerstone in the pricing of money market issues and

other short-term debt issues by both governments and corporate borrowers. Less creditworthy issuers will often borrow at a rate above LIBOR.

8. There are two basic kinds of **swaps:** interest rate and currency. An interest rate swap occurs when two parties exchange debt with a floating rate payment for debt with a fixed-rate payment, or vice versa. Currency swaps are agreements to deliver one currency against another currency. Often both types of swaps are used in the same transaction when debt denominated in different currencies is swapped.

9. **Export Development Corporation (EDC)** is a federal Crown corporation with a mandate to promote Canadian exports. EDC provides long-term financing for foreign companies that purchase Canadian exports. To qualify for EDC support, exporters must produce or market goods with a minimum Canadian content of 60 percent.

Other government programs to support exports include the federal Programme for Export Market Development (PEMD), which reimburses part of the costs of developing export markets and a variety of provincial programs.

CONCEPT QUESTION

■ What is the difference between a Eurobond and a foreign bond?

Foreign Exchange Markets and Exchange Rates   31.2

The **foreign exchange market** is undoubtedly the world's largest financial market. It is the market where one country's currency is traded for another's. Most of the trading takes place in a few currencies: the U.S. dollar ($), German deutsche mark (DM), British pound sterling (£), Japanese yen (¥), Swiss franc (SF), and French franc (FF).

The foreign exchange market is an over-the-counter market. There is no single location where traders get together. Instead, traders are located in the major banks around the world. They communicate using computer terminals, telephones, and other telecommunication devices. One element in the communications network for foreign transactions is the *Society for Worldwide Interbank Financial Telecommunications* (*SWIFT*), a Belgian not-for-profit cooperative. A bank in Toronto, the centre of Canada's foreign exchange trading, can send messages to a bank in London via SWIFT's regional processing centres. The connections are through data transmission lines.

The many different types of participants in the foreign exchange market include

1. Importers who convert their domestic currency to foreign currency to pay for goods from foreign countries.
2. Exporters who receive foreign currency and may want to convert to the domestic currency.
3. Portfolio managers who buy and sell foreign stocks and bonds.
4. Foreign exchange brokers who match buy and sell orders.
5. Traders who make the market in foreign exchange.
6. Speculators who try to profit from changes in exchange rates.

Exchange Rates

An **exchange rate** is simply the price of one country's currency expressed in terms of another country's currency. In practice, almost all trading of currencies worldwide takes place in terms of the U.S. dollar.

Table 31.1 reproduces exchange rate quotations as they appear in *The Globe and Mail.* Notice that the rates were supplied by the Bank of Montreal, part of the over-the-counter foreign exchange market. Because of the heavy volume of transactions in U.S. dollars, U.S./Canada rates appear at the top of Table 31.1. The first column (labeled "$1 U.S. in Cdn $") gives the number of Canadian dollars it takes to buy one unit of foreign currency. For example, the U.S./Canada spot rate is quoted at 1.3333, which means that you can buy one U.S. dollar today with 1.3333 Canadian dollars.[1]

The second column in the U.S./Canada section shows the indirect exchange rate. This is the amount of U.S. currency per Canadian dollar. The U.S./Canada spot rate is quoted here at 0.7500, so you can get 0.7500 U.S. dollars for one Canadian dollar. Naturally, this second exchange rate is just the reciprocal of the first one, $1/.7500 = 1.3333$.

The rest of Table 31.1 shows exchange rates for other foreign currencies. Notice that the most important currencies are listed first: British pounds, German marks, and Japanese yen. In this part of the table, the first column, labeled "Cdn. $ per unit," gives the price of one unit of the foreign currency in Canadian dollars, the same as in the Canada/U.S. section. For example, you can buy one British pound for $1.9886 Canadian. The second column in this part of the table repeats the price of one unit of foreign currency in U.S. dollars. You can buy the same one British pound for U.S. $1.4915.

There are two reasons for quoting all foreign currencies in terms of the U.S. dollar. First, it reduces the number of possible cross-currency quotes. For example, with five major currencies, there would potentially be 10 exchange rates. Second, it makes **triangular arbitrage** more difficult. If all currencies were traded against each other, it would make inconsistencies more likely. That is, the exchange rate of the British pound against the Canadian dollar would be compared to the exchange rate between the U.S. dollar and the Canadian dollar. This implies a particular rate between the British pound and the U.S. dollar to prevent triangular arbitrage.

▪ *Example*

What if the pound traded for DM4 in Frankfurt and U.S. $1.60 in London? If the U.S. dollar traded for DM2 in Frankfurt, there would be a triangular arbitrage opportunity. Starting with U.S. $1.60, a trader could purchase £1 in London. This pound could then be used to buy DM4 in Frankfurt. With the U.S. dollar trading at DM2, the DM4 could then be traded for U.S. $2 in Frankfurt as illustrated in Figure 31.1. The net gain from going around this "triangle" would be (in U.S. dollars) $2.00 − $1.60 = $0.40. Imagine what the return would be on an initial $1 billion U.S. purchase. ▪

---

[1] The spot rate is for immediate trading. Forward rates are for future transactions and are discussed in detail later. When we write *today,* we refer to the date the rates were quoted.

FOREIGN EXCHANGE

Table 31.1
Exchange rate
quotations

Mid-market rates in Toronto at noon, Dec. 29, 1993. Prepared by the Bank of Montreal Treasury Group.

		$1 U.S. in Cdn.$ =	$1 Cdn. in U.S.$ =
U.S./Canada spot		1.3333	0.7500
1 month forward		1.3340	0.7496
2 months forward		1.3346	0.7493
3 months forward		1.3351	0.7490
6 months forward		1.3373	0.7478
12 months forward		1.3403	0.7461
3 years forward		1.3458	0.7431
5 years forward		1.3688	0.7306
7 years forward		1.4068	0.7108
10 years forward		1.4733	0.6787
Canadian dollar	High	1.2403	0.8063
in 1993:	Low	1.3480	0.7418
	Average	1.2907	0.7748

Country	Currency	Cdn.$ per unit	U.S. $ per unit
Britain	Pound	1.9886	1.4915
1 month forward		1.9862	1.4889
2 months forward		1.9843	1.4868
3 months forward		1.9817	1.4843
6 months forward		1.9776	1.4788
12 months forward		1.9738	1.4727
Germany	Mark	0.7763	0.5822
1 month forward		0.7746	0.5807
3 months forward		1.7722	0.5784
6 months forward		0.7702	0.5760
12 months forward		0.7697	0.5743
Japan	Yen	0.011950	0.008963
1 month forward		0.011966	0.008970
3 months forward		0.012004	0.008991
6 months forward		0.012081	0.009034
12 months forward		0.012254	0.009143
Algeria	Dinar	0.0674	0.0505
Antigua, Grenada and St. Lucia	E.C. Dollar	0.4947	0.3711
Argentina	Peso	1.33437	1.00080
Australia	Dollar	0.8997	0.6748
Austria	Schilling	0.11083	0.08313
Bahamas	Dollar	1.3333	1.0000
Barbados	Dollar	0.6629	0.4972
Belgium	Franc	0.03731	0.02798
Bermuda	Dollar	1.3333	1.0000
Brazil	Cruzeiro	0.00428	0.00321
Bulgaria	Lev	0.0505	0.0379
Chile	Peso	0.003101	0.002326
China	Renminbi	0.2295	0.1721
Cyprus	Pound	2.6066	1.9550
Czech Rep.	Koruna	0.0452	0.0339
Denmark	Krone	0.1988	0.1491
Egypt	Pound	0.3953	0.2965
Fiji	Dollar	0.8733	0.6550

Country	Currency	Cdn.$ per unit	U.S. $ per unit
Finland	Markka	0.2330	0.1747
France	Franc	0.2282	0.1712
Greece	Drachma	0.00541	0.00406
Hong Kong	Dollar	0.1727	0.1295
Hungary	Forint	0.01338	0.01004
Iceland	Krona	0.01856	0.01392
India	Rupee	0.04289	0.03217
Indonesia	Rupiah	0.000632	0.000474
Ireland	Punt	1.9046	1.4285
Israel	N. Shekel	0.4468	0.3351
Italy	Lira	0.000787	0.000590
Jamaica	Dollar	0.04678	0.03509
Jordon	Dinar	1.8966	1.4225
Lebanon	Pound	0.000779	0.000584
Luxembourg	Franc	0.03731	0.02798
Malaysia	Ringgit	0.5047	0.3785
Mexico	N Peso	0.4296	0.3222
Netherlands	Guilder	0.6924	0.5193
New Zealand	Dollar	0.7446	0.5585
Norway	Krone	0.1794	0.1346
Pakistan	Rupee	0.04447	0.03336
Philippines	Peso	0.04808	0.03606
Poland	Zloty	0.0000634	0.0000475
Portugal	Escudo	0.00765	0.00574
Romania	Leu	0.0010	0.0008
Russia	Ruble	0.001069	0.000802
Saudi Arabia	Riyal	0.3555	0.2666
Singapore	Dollar	0.8325	0.6244
Slovakia	Koruna	0.0409	0.0307
South Africa	Rand	0.3939	0.2954
South Korea	Won	0.001650	0.001237
Spain	Peseta	0.00944	0.00708
Sudan	Dinar	0.1026	0.0769
Sweden	Krona	0.1610	0.1208
Switzerland	Franc	0.9157	0.6868
Taiwan	Dollar	0.0504	0.0370
Thailand	Baht	0.0525	0.0394
Trinidad, Tobago	Dollar	0.2415	0.1812
Turkey	Lira	0.0000934	0.0000701
Venezuela	Bolivar	0.01276	0.00957
Zambia	Kwacha	0.002319	0.001739
European Currency Unit		1.5041	1.1281
Special Drawing Right		1.8414	1.3811

The U.S. dollar closed at $1.3347 in terms of Canadian funds, up $0.0084 from Friday. The pound sterling closed at $1.9714, down $0.0227.

In New York, the Canadian dollar closed down $0.0048 at $0.7492, in terms of U.S. funds. The pound sterling was down $0.0265 to $1.4770.

Source: *The Globe and Mail* (December 30, 1993), p. B8. Used with permission.

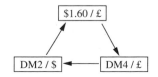

Figure 31.1
Triangular
arbitrage

Types of Transactions

Three types of trades take place in the foreign exchange market: spot, forward, and swap. **Spot trades** involve an agreement on the exchange rate today for settlement in two days. The rate is called the **spot exchange rate. Forward trades** involve an agreement on exchange rates today for settlement in the future. The rate is called the **forward exchange rate.** As seen in Table 31.1, maturities for forward trades range from one month to 10 years. A swap is the sale (purchase) of a foreign currency with a simultaneous agreement to repurchase (resell) it sometime in the future. The difference between the sale price and the repurchase price is called the **swap rate.**

■ *Example*

On October 11, bank *A* pays Canadian dollars to bank *B*'s account at a Toronto bank and *A* receives pounds sterling in its account at a bank in London. On November 11, as agreed on October 11, the transaction is reversed. *A* pays the sterling back to *B*, while *B* pays back the dollars to *A*. This is a swap. In effect, *A* has borrowed pounds sterling while giving up the use of Canadian dollars to *B*. ■

CONCEPT QUESTION

- What are the three kinds of foreign exchange transactions?

31.3

The Law of One Price and Purchasing Power Parity

What determines the level of the spot exchange rate? One answer is the **law of one price (LOP).** The law of one price says that a commodity will cost the same regardless of the country in which it is purchased. More formally, let $S_£(t)$ be the spot exchange rate, that is, the number of Canadian dollars needed to purchase a British pound at time t.[2] Let $P^{CDN}(t)$ and $P^{UK}(t)$ be the current Canadian and British prices of a particular commodity, say, apples. The law of one price says that

$$P^{CDN}(t) = S_£(t)\, P^{UK}(t)$$

for apples.

The rationale behind LOP is similar to that of triangular arbitrage. If LOP did not hold, arbitrage would be possible by moving apples from one country to another. For example, suppose that apples in Toronto are selling for $4 per bushel, while in London the price is £2.50 per bushel. Then the law of one price implies that

$$\$4 = S_£(t) \times £2.50$$

and

$$S_£(t) = \$1.60/£$$

That is, the spot exchange rate implied by the LOP is $1.60 per pound.

---

[2]Throughout this chapter, we quote foreign exchange in direct terms.

Suppose instead that the actual exchange rate is $2.00 per pound. Starting with $4, a trader could buy a bushel of apples in Toronto, ship it to London, and sell it there for £2.50. The pounds sterling could then be converted into dollars at the exchange rate, $2/£, yielding a total of $5 for a $1 (or $5 − $4) gain.

The rationale of the LOP is that if the exchange rate is not $1.60/£ but is instead, say, $2/£, then forces would be set in motion to change the rate and/or the price of apples. In our example, tons of apples would be flying from Toronto to London. Thus, demand for apples in Toronto would raise the dollar price for apples there, and the supply in London would lower the pound sterling price. The apple traders converting pounds sterling into dollars, that is, supplying pounds sterling and demanding Canadian dollars, would also put pressure on the exchange rate to drop from $2/£.

As you can see, for the LOP to be strictly true, three assumptions are needed:

1. The transactions cost of trading apples—shipping, insurance, wastage, and so on—must be zero.

2. No barriers to trading apples, such as tariffs or taxes, can exist.

3. Finally, an apple in Toronto must be identical to an apple in London. It won't do for you to send red apples to London if the English eat only green apples.

Given the reality that transactions costs are not zero and that the other conditions are rarely exactly met, the LOP is really applicable only to traded goods, and then only to very uniform ones. The LOP does not imply that a Mercedes costs the same as a Ford or that a nuclear power plant in France costs the same as one in Ontario. In the case of the cars, they are not identical. In the case of the power plants, even if they were identical, they are expensive and very difficult to ship.

Because consumers purchase many goods, economists refer to **purchasing power parity (PPP),** the idea that the exchange rate adjusts so that a *market basket* of goods costs the same regardless of the country in which it is purchased. In addition, a relative version of purchasing power parity has evolved. **Relative purchasing power parity (RPPP)** says that the rate of change in the price level of commodities in one country relative to the rate of change in the price level in another determines the rate of change of the exchange rate between the two countries. Formally,

$$\frac{P^{CDN}(t+1)}{P^{CDN}(t)} = \frac{S_£(t+1)}{S_£(t)} \times \frac{P^{UK}(t+1)}{P^{UK}(t)}$$

$$1 + \begin{matrix} CDN \\ \text{inflation rate} \end{matrix} = \left(1 + \begin{matrix} \text{Change in foreign} \\ \text{exchange rate} \end{matrix}\right) \times \left(1 + \begin{matrix} \text{British} \\ \text{inflation rate} \end{matrix}\right)$$

This states that the rate of inflation in Canada relative to that in the U.K. determines the rate of change in the value of the dollar relative to that of the pound during the interval t to $t + 1$. It is common to write Π_{CDN} as the rate of inflation in Canada. $1 + \Pi_{CDN}$ is equal to $P^{CDN}(t + 1)/P^{CDN}(t)$. Similarly, Π_{UK} is the rate of inflation in Great Britain. $1 + \Pi_{UK}$ is equal to $P^{UK}(t + 1)/P^{UK}(t)$.

Using Π to represent the rate of inflation, the above equation can be rearranged as

$$\frac{1 + \Pi_{CDN}}{1 + \Pi_{UK}} = \frac{S_£(t + 1)}{S_£(t)} \tag{31.1}$$

We can rewrite this in an approximate form as

$$\Pi_{CDN} \approx \Pi_{UK} + \frac{\dot{S}_£}{S_£}$$

where $\dot{S}_£/S_£$ now stands for the rate of change in the dollars-per-pound exchange rate.

As an example, suppose that inflation in France during the year is equal to 4 percent and inflation in Canada is equal to 10 percent. Then, according to RPPP, the price of the French franc in terms of the Canadian dollar should rise; that is, the Canadian dollar declines in value in terms of the French franc. Using our approximation, the dollars-per-franc exchange rate should rise by

$$\frac{\dot{S}_{FF}}{S_{FF}} \approx \Pi_{CDN} - \Pi_F$$
$$= 10\% - 4\%$$
$$= 6\%$$

where $\dot{S}_{FF}/S_{FF}$ stands for the rate of change in the dollars-per-franc exchange rate. That is, if the French franc is worth \$0.20 at the beginning of the period, it should be worth approximately \$0.212 (or \$0.20 × 1.06) at the end of the period.

RPPP says that the change in the ratio of domestic commodity prices of two countries must be matched in the exchange rate. This version of the law of one price suggests that, to estimate changes in the spot rate of exchange, it is necessary to estimate the differences in relative inflation rates. In other words, we can express our formula in expectational terms as

$$E\left(\frac{\dot{S}_{FF}}{S_{FF}}\right) = E(\Pi_{CDN}) - E(\Pi_F)$$

If we expect the Canadian inflation rate to exceed the French inflation rate, we should expect the dollar price of French francs to rise, which is the same as saying that the dollar is expected to fall against the franc.

The more exact relationship of equation (31.1) can be expressed in expectational terms as

$$\frac{E(1 + \Pi_{CDN})}{E(1 + \Pi_{UK})} = \frac{E(S_£(t + 1))}{S_£(t)} \qquad (31.2)$$

CONCEPT QUESTIONS

- What is the law of one price? What is purchasing power parity?
- What is the relationship between inflation and exchange rate movements?

31.4 Interest Rates and Exchange Rates: Interest Rate Parity

The forward exchange rate and the spot exchange rate are tied together by the same sort of arbitrage that underlies the law of one price. To explain the link, we begin with some useful terminology. If forward exchange rates are greater than the spot exchange rate in a particular currency, the forward foreign currency is said to be at a *premium*. (This implies the domestic currency is at a discount.) If the values of forward exchange rates are less than the spot exchange rate, the forward rate on foreign currency is at a discount.

For example, in Table 31.1, the spot U.S. dollar rate is U.S. $0.75 = $1.00 CDN, and the one-month forward U.S. dollar is U.S. $0.7496 = $1.00 CDN. Because fewer U.S. dollars are needed to buy a Canadian dollar at the forward rate than are needed to buy at the spot rate, the U.S. dollar is more valuable in the forward market than in the spot market. This means that the one-month forward U.S. dollar is at a premium. Of course, the forward standing of the U.S. dollar must be opposite that of the Canadian dollar. In this example, the Canadian dollar is at a discount because its forward value is less than the spot value. Forward exchange is quoted in terms of the premium or discount that is to be added onto the spot rate.

Whether forward rates are at a premium or a discount when compared to a domestic currency depends on the relative interest rates in the foreign and domestic currency markets. The **interest rate parity theorem** states that, if interest rates are higher domestically than in a particular foreign country, the foreign country's currency will be selling at a premium in the forward market; and if interest rates are lower domestically, the foreign currency will be selling at a discount in the forward market.

We need some notation to develop the interest rate parity theorem. Let $S(0)$ be the current domestic currency price of spot foreign exchange (current time is denoted by 0). If the domestic currency is the Canadian dollar and the foreign currency is the DM, we might observe $S(0) = \$0.40/DM$. $S(0)$ is in direct terms. Let $F(0,1)$ be the current domestic currency price of forward exchange for a contract that matures in one month. Thus, the contract is for forward exchange one month hence. Let i and i^* be the yearly rates of interest paid on Eurocurrency deposits denominated in the domestic (i) and foreign (i^*) currencies, respectively. Of course, the maturity of the deposits can be chosen to coincide with the maturity of the forward contract.

Now consider a trader who has access to the interbank market in foreign exchange and Eurocurrency deposits. Suppose the trader has some dollars to invest for one month. The trader can make a dollar loan or a DM loan. The annual interest rate is 10 percent in deutsche marks and 6 percent in dollars. Which is better?

The Dollar Investment

Given an annual interest rate of 6 percent, the one-month rate of interest is 0.5 percent, ignoring compounding. If the trader invests $1 million now, the trader will get $1 million × 1.005 = $1.005 million at the end of the month. Here is an illustration:

Time 0	Time 1
Lend 1 unit of dollars	Obtain $1 + i \times (1/12)$ units of domestic currency
$1,000,000	$1,000,000 × (1 + 0.005) = $1,005,000

The DM Investment

The current spot rate is $0.40/DM. This means the trader can currently obtain $1 million/0.40 = DM2.5 million. The rate of interest on one-year DM loans is 10 percent.

For one month, the interest rate is 0.10/12 = 0.0083. Thus, at the end of one month the trader will obtain DM2.5 million × 1.0083 = DM2,520,750. Of course, if the trader wants dollars at the end of the month, the trader must convert the DM back into dollars. The trader can fix the exchange rate for one-month conversion. Suppose the one-month forward is $0.39869/DM. Then the trader can sell deutsche marks forward. This will ensure that the trader gets DM2,520,750 × 0.39869 = $1.005 million at the end of the month. The general relationships are set forth here:

Time 0	Time 1
Purchase 1 unit $[1/S(0)]$ of foreign exchange	Deposit matures and pays $[1/S(0)] \times [1 + i \times (1/12)]$ units of foreign exchange
DM2,500,000	DM2,500,000 × 1.0083 = DM2,520,750
Sell forward $[1/S(0)] \times [1 + i^* \times (1/12)]$ units of forward exchange at the forward rate $F(0,1)$	Deliver foreign exchange in fulfillment of forward contract, receiving
	$[1/S(0)] \times [1 + i^* \times (1/12)] \times [F(0,1)]$
	DM2,500,000 × 1.0083 × 0.39869 = $1,005,000

In our example, the investments earned exactly the same rate of return and $1 + i \times (1/12) = [1/S(0)] \times [1 + i^* \times (1/12)] \times [F(0,1)]$. In competitive financial markets, this must be true for risk-free investments. When the trader makes the DM loan, the interest rate is higher. But the return is the same because the DM must be sold forward at a lower price than it can be exchanged for initially. If the domestic interest rate were different from the covered foreign interest rate, the trader would have arbitrage opportunities.

To summarize, to prevent arbitrage possibilities from existing, we must have equality of the Canadian interest rate and covered foreign interest rates:

$$1 + i = \frac{1}{S(0)} \times (1 + i^*) \times F(0,1)$$

or

$$\frac{1 + i}{1 + i^*} = \frac{F(0,1)}{S(0)} \tag{31.3}$$

The last equation is the famous interest rate parity theorem. It relates the forward exchange rate and the spot exchange rate to interest rate differentials. Notice that, if $i > i^*$, the spot rate (expressed as dollars per unit of foreign currency) will be less than the forward rate.

■ *Example*

Let the spot rate $S(0) = \$0.40/DM$ and the one-year forward rate $F(0,1) = \$0.42/DM$. Let the one-year rates on Euro-Canadian dollar deposits and Euro-DM deposits be, respectively, $i = 11.3\%$ and $i^* = 6\%$. Then, comparing the return on domestic borrowing with the return on covered foreign lending,

$$\$(1 + i) = \$(1 + 0.113) = \$1.113$$
$$\$[1/S(0)] \times (1 + i^*) \times F(0,1) = \$(1/0.40) \times (1 + 0.06) \times \$0.42 = \$1.113$$

For each dollar borrowed domestically, a trader must repay $1.113. The return from using the $1.00 to buy spot foreign exchange, placing the deposit at the foreign rate of interest, and selling the total return forward would be $1.113. These two amounts are equal, so it would not be worth anyone's time to try to exploit the difference. In this case, interest parity can be said to hold. ∎

The Forward Discount and Expected Spot Rates

A close connection exists between forward exchange rates and expected spot rates. A trader's buy and sell decisions in today's forward market are based on the trader's market expectation of the future spot rate. In fact, if traders were completely indifferent to risk, the forward rate of exchange would depend solely on expectations about the future spot rate. For example, suppose the one-year forward rate on DM is $0.40/DM [that is, $F(0,1) = \$0.40/DM$]. This must mean that traders expect the spot rate to be $0.40/DM in one-year [$E(S(1)) = \$0.40/DM$]. If they thought it would be higher, there would be an arbitrage opportunity. Traders would buy DM forward at the low price and sell deutsche marks one year later at the expected higher price. This implies that the forward rate of exchange is equal to the expected spot, or (in general terms)

$$F(0,1) = E[S(1)]$$

and

$$\frac{F(0,1)}{S(0)} = \frac{E[S(1)]}{S(0)} \tag{31.4}$$

An equilibrium is achieved only when the forward discount (or premium) equals the expected change in the spot exchange rate.

Exchange Rate Risk

Exchange rate risk is the natural consequence of international operations in a world where foreign currency values move up and down. International firms usually enter into some contracts that require payments in different currencies. For example, suppose that the treasurer of an international firm knows that, one month from today, the firm must pay £2 million for goods it will receive in England. The current exchange rate is $1.50/£, and if that rate prevails in one month, the dollar cost of the goods to the firm will be $1.50/£ × £2 million = $3 million. The treasurer in this case is obligated to pay pounds in one month. (Alternatively, we say that he is *short* in pounds.) A net short or long position of this type can be very risky. If, during the month, the pound rises to $2/£, the treasurer must pay $2/£ × £2 million = $4 million, an extra $1 million.

This is the essence of foreign exchange risk. The treasurer may want to hedge his position. When forward markets exist, the most convenient means of hedging is the purchase or sale of forward contracts. In this example, the treasurer may want to consider buying £2 million one month forward. If the one-month forward rate quoted today is also $1.50/£, the treasurer will fulfill the contract by exchanging $3 million for £2 million in one month. The £2 million he receives from the contract can then be used to pay for the goods. By hedging today, he fixes the outflow one month from now to exactly $3 million.

Should the treasurer hedge or speculate? There are two reasons why the treasurer should hedge:

1. In an efficient foreign exchange market, speculation is a zero-NPV activity. Unless the treasurer has special information, nothing will be gained from foreign exchange speculation.

2. The costs of hedging are not large. The treasurer can use forward contracts to hedge, and if the forward rate is equal to the expected spot, the costs of hedging are negligible. Of course, there are ways to hedge foreign exchange risk other than with forward contracts. For example, the treasurer can borrow dollars, buy pounds sterling in the spot market today, and lend them for one month in London. By the interest rate parity theorem, this will be the same as buying the pounds sterling forward.

More Advanced Short-Term Hedges

Currency swaps, currency options, and other financially engineered products are taking considerable business away from the forward exchange market.[3] A **currency swap** is an arrangement among a borrower, a second borrower (called a *counterparty*), and a bank. The borrower and the counterparty each raise funds in a different currency and then swap liabilities. The bank guarantees the borrower's and counterparty's credit as in a banker's acceptance. The result is that the borrower obtains funds in the desired currency at a lower rate than for direct borrowing.

For example, in 1986, the federal government of Canada made an 80 billion–yen bond issue and swapped part of it into U.S. dollars. The interest rate was six-month LIBOR and the ending liability was in U.S. dollars, not yen. The interest cost turned out to be 54 basis points below the cost of direct borrowing in the United States.

Currency options are similar to options on stock (discussed in Chapter 21) except the exercise price is an exchange rate. They are exchange traded in the United States with exercise prices in various currencies including the Canadian dollar. Currency options can be exercised at any time prior to maturity. In the jargon of options, they are **American options.** A call option on the Canadian dollar gives the holder the right, but not the obligation, to buy C$ at a fixed exercise price in U.S.$. The call increases in value as the C$ exchange rate in U.S.$ rises. A put option allows the holder to sell C$ at the exercise price. A put becomes more valuable when the C$ declines against the U.S.$.

The basic idea behind hedging with options is to take an options position opposite to the cash position. For this reason, hedge analysis starts by looking at the unhedged position of the business. For example, suppose an exporter expects to collect receivables totalling U.S. $1 million in 30 days. Suppose the present C$ exchange rate is U.S. $.75. If the rate remains at 75 cents, the exporter will receive U.S. $1 million/.75 = $1,333,333 CDN after 30 days. The exporter is at risk if the exchange rate rises so that the U.S. $1 million will buy fewer Canadian dollars. For example, if

---

[3]Our discussion of currency swaps in practice draws on B. Critchley, "Explosion of New Products Cuts Foreign Currency Risk," *Financial Post* (September 14, 1987).

the exchange rate rises to .77, the exporter will receive only U.S. $1 million/.77 = $1,298,701 CDN. The loss of $34,632 comes out of profits.

Since the exporter loses if the exchange rate rises, buying call options is an appropriate hedge. Calls on the C$ will increase in value if the exchange rate rises. The profit on the calls will help offset the loss on exchange. To implement this strategy, the exporter will likely seek expert advice on how many calls to buy and, more generally, the relative cost of hedging with options versus with forwards.

The Hedging Decision in Practice

Hedging the exchange rate for the U.S. dollar is important for the Toronto Blue Jays.[4] When they won the World Series for the second consecutive year in 1993, the Blue Jays had the highest payroll in major league baseball—U.S. $48.3 million. Players' contracts are negotiated in U.S. dollars and paid over the baseball season. The team receives some revenues in U.S. dollars from television contracts and gate receipts for games on the road, but the majority of its income—receipts at the SkyDome and Canadian television contracts—is in Canadian dollars. As a result, the team is exposed to currency losses if the Canadian dollar falls. According to one estimate, the Jays lose $800,000 (Canadian) for every one-cent drop in the Canadian dollar.

Blue Jays management has used both forward contracts and currency options to hedge its exposure. At the time of writing at the start of the baseball season of 1994, management was tracking the results of its earlier decision not to hedge. As the Canadian dollar fell from around U.S. 80 cents in 1993 to under 73 cents, locking in the exchange rate looked more and more attractive. As the risk of a player's strike loomed large, the ideal hedge would have been with options, because options would have allowed the Jays to get out of the hedge when payroll obligations ceased.

CONCEPT QUESTIONS

- What is the interest rate parity theorem?
- Why is the forward rate related to the expected future spot rate?
- How can one offset foreign exchange risk through a transaction in the forward markets?
- How can firms hedge using currency swaps or currency options?

International Capital Budgeting 31.5

Kihlstrom Equipment, a Canadian-based international company, is evaluating an investment in France. Kihlstrom's exports of drill bits have increased to such an extent that it is considering operating a plant in France. The project will cost FF20 million; it is expected to produce cash flows of FF8 million a year for the next three years. The current spot exchange rate for French francs is $S(0) = \$0.20/FF$. How should Kihlstrom calculate the net present value of the projects in Canadian dollars?

---

[4]Our discussion is based on L. Millson, "Jays Fortunes Ride on Shaky Canuck Buck," *Globe and Mail* (April 8, 1994), p. A12.

Table 31.2
Net present value
of foreign cash
flows: Kihlstrom
Equipment

	End of year			
	0	1	2	3
Incremental cash flows (CF_{FF}) (FF millions)	−20	8	8	8
Foreign exchange rate ($/FF)	0.15	0.145	0.14	0.135
Foreign exchange rate conversion	−20 × 0.15	8 × 0.145	8 × 0.14	8 × 0.135
Incremental cash flows ($ millions)	−3	1.16	1.12	1.08

NPV at 15% = −$0.43 million.

Although the investment is made abroad, this does not alter Kihlstrom's NPV criterion. The firm must identify incremental cash flows and discount them at the appropriate cost of capital. After making the required discounted cash flow calculations, Kihlstrom should undertake projects with positive NPVs. However, two major factors complicate such international NPV calculations: foreign exchange conversion and repatriation of funds.

Foreign Exchange Conversion

The simplest way for Kihlstrom to calculate the NPV of the investment is to convert all French-franc cash flows to Canadian dollars. This involves a three-step process:

Step 1. Estimate future cash flows in French francs.
Step 2. Convert to Canadian dollars at the predicted exchange rate.
Step 3. Calculate NPV using the cost of capital in Canadian dollars.

In Table 31.2 we apply these three steps to Kihlstrom's French investment. Notice here that Kihlstrom's French-franc cash flows were converted to dollars by multiplying the foreign cash flows by the predicted foreign exchange rate.

How might Kihlstrom predict future exchange rates? Using the theory of efficient markets, Kihlstrom could calculate NPV using the foreign exchange market's implicit predictions. To discover these predictions, Kihlstrom can use the basic foreign exchange relationships described in earlier sections of this chapter.

Kihlstrom begins by obtaining publicly available information on exchange rates and interest rates:

Exchange rate: $S_{FF}(0)$ = $0.15/FF (i.e., one French franc can be purchased for $0.15)

Interest rate in Canada: i_{CDN} = 8%
Interest rate in France: i_F = 12%

Using (31.2), (31.3), and (31.4), Kihlstrom can calculate the following set of relationships:

$$\frac{E(1 + \Pi_{CDN})}{E(1 + \Pi_F)} = \frac{E(S_{FF}(1))}{S_{FF}(0)} = \frac{F_{FF}(0,1)}{S_{FF}(0)} = \frac{1 + i_{CDN}}{1 + i_F} \quad (31.5)$$

Relative purchasing power parity

Forward rate related to expected spot rate

Interest rate parity

(31.2)   (31.4)   (31.3)

From the left, the first equality follows from relative purchasing power parity. The expected inflation rates in the two countries determine the expected movement in the spot rate, expressed earlier in equation (31.2). The equality between the second and third terms is a consequence of our discussion on forward rates and expected spot rates, expressed earlier in (31.4). The last equality is interest rate parity, which appeared earlier in (31.3).

We now compare the left-hand term to the right-hand term. We have

$$\frac{1 + i_{CDN}}{1 + i_F} = \frac{E(1 + \Pi_{CDN})}{E(1 + \Pi_F)}$$

$$\frac{1.08}{1.12} = \frac{E(1 + \Pi_{CDN})}{E(1 + \Pi_F)}$$

If the expected inflation rate in Canada is 8 percent, it follows that the expected inflation rate in France is 12 percent:

$$\frac{1.08}{1.12} = \frac{1.08}{E(1 + \Pi_F)}$$

$$E(\Pi_F) = 12\%$$

Using relative purchasing power parity, Kihlstrom can compute the expected spot exchange rate in one year:

$$\frac{E(1 + \Pi_{CDN})}{E(1 + \Pi_F)} = \frac{E[S_{FF}(1)]}{S_{FF}(0)}$$

$$\frac{1.08}{1.12} = \frac{E[S_{FF}(1)]}{0.15}$$

which implies $E[S_{FF}(1)] = 0.145$. The exchange rate expected at the end of year 2 is obtained from

$$0.15 \times \left(\frac{1.08}{1.12}\right)^2 = 0.14$$

For year 3, the expected exchange rate is obtained from

$$0.15 \times \left(\frac{1.08}{1.12}\right)^3 = 0.135$$

Finally, the NPV of the project is computed:

$$NPV = \sum_{t=0}^{3} \frac{CF_{FF}(t) \times E[S_{FF}(t)]}{(1+r^*)^t}$$

where $CF_{FF}(t)$ refers to the French francs forecasted to be received in each of the next three years. The discount rate we use is Kihlstrom's Canadian cost of capital. We do not use the Canadian risk-free rate of 8 percent because Kihlstrom's project is risky; a risk-adjusted discount rate must be used. Because the NPV at 15 percent is −$430,000, Kihlstrom should not invest in a subsidiary in France.

In this example, we used the foreign exchange market's implicit forecast of future exchange rates. Why not use management's own forecast of foreign exchange rates in the calculations? Suppose that the financial management of Kihlstrom feels optimistic about the French franc. If its forecasts are sufficiently optimistic and they are used, Kihlstrom's investment in a French subsidiary will generate a positive NPV. But, in general, it is a good idea to separate the economic prospects of an investment from the foreign exchange prospects, and it is unwise to use the latter projections in the NPV calculation. If Kihlstrom wishes to speculate on an increase in the French franc relative to the Canadian dollar, the best way to do this is to buy French francs in the forward foreign exchange market. By using the forward exchange rates implicit in the domestic and foreign interest rates, the firm is using the actual dollar flows that it could, in principle, lock in today by borrowing in the foreign currency. This makes the foreign cash flows equivalent to domestic cash flows.

Unremitted Cash Flows

The previous example assumed that all after-tax cash flows from the foreign investment were remitted to the parent firm. The remittance decision is similar to the dividend decision for a purely domestic firm. Substantial differences can exist between the cash flows of a project and the amount that is actually remitted to the parent firm. Of course, the net present value of a project will not be changed by deferred remittance if the unremitted cash flows are reinvested at a rate of return equal (as adjusted for exchange rates) to the domestic cost of capital.

A foreign subsidiary can remit funds to a parent in many ways, including

1. Dividends.
2. Management fees for central services.
3. Royalties on the use of trade names and patents.

International firms must pay special attention to remittance for two reasons. First, there may be present and future exchange controls. Many governments are sensitive to the charge of being exploited by foreign firms. Therefore, governments are tempted to limit the ability of international firms to remit cash flows. Funds that cannot be remitted are sometimes said to be blocked.

Another reason is taxes. It is always necessary to determine what taxes must be paid on profits generated in a foreign country. International firms must usually pay foreign taxes on their foreign profits. The total taxes paid by an international firm may be a function of the time of remittance. For example, Kihlstrom's French subsidiary would need to pay taxes in France on the profits it earns in France. Kihlstrom will also pay taxes on dividends it remits to Canada. In most cases, Kihlstrom can offset the payment of foreign taxes against the Canadian tax liability. Thus, if the French corporate income tax is 40 percent, Kihlstrom will not be liable for additional Canadian taxes.

The Cost of Capital for International Firms

An important question for firms with international investments is whether or not the required return for international projects should be different from that of similar domestic projects. The answer to this question depends on

1. Segmentation of the international financial market.
2. Foreign political risk of expropriation, foreign exchange controls, and taxes.

Lower Cost of Capital from International Diversification

Suppose barriers prevented shareholders in Canada from holding foreign securities; the financial markets of different countries would be segmented. Further suppose that firms in Canada were not subject to the same barriers. In such a case, a firm engaging in international investing could provide indirect diversification for Canadian shareholders that they could not achieve by investing within Canada. This could lead to the lowering of the risk premium on international projects.

Alternatively, if there were no barriers to international investing, shareholders could obtain the benefit of international diversification for themselves by buying foreign securities. In this case, the project cost of capital for a firm in Canada would not depend on whether the project were in Canada or in a foreign country.

To resolve this issue, researchers have compared the variances of purely domestic and international stock portfolios. The result is that internationally diversified portfolios have lower variance; firms can benefit from a lower cost of capital for international projects that provide diversification services for the firms' shareholders.[5] In practice, holding foreign securities involves substantial expenses. These expenses include taxes, the costs of obtaining information, and trading costs. This implies that although Canadian investors are free to hold foreign securities, they will not be perfectly internationally diversified.

Financial engineering is aiding investors in avoiding some of these costs. As a result, as investors diversify globally, the cost of capital advantage to firms will likely decline.

An *index participation* (*IP*) is a current example of a financially engineered vehicle for international diversification.[6] An IP on the Standard & Poor's 500 Index, for example, gives an investor an asset that will track this well-known U.S. market index. IPs are highly liquid, thus reducing trading costs. Information costs are also reduced since the holder need not research each of the 500 individual stocks that make up the index.

International diversification for Canadian investors is being made easier by the lowering of an important barrier. In 1992, the maximum allowable foreign holding for pension funds and RRSPs was doubled from 10 to 20 percent. Increased demand fueled the development of global mutual funds and related new products to exploit this opportunity.

Foreign Political Risks

Firms may determine that international investments inherently involve more political risk than domestic investments. This extra risk may offset the gains from international diversification. Firms may increase the discount rate to allow for the risk of expropriation and foreign exchange remittance controls.

Political risk can be hedged in several ways, particularly when confiscation or nationalization is a concern. The use of local financing, perhaps from the government of the foreign country in question, reduces the possible loss because the company can

---

[5] B. H. Solnik, "Why Not Diversify Internationally Rather Than Domestically?" *Financial Analysts Journal* (July–August 1974).

[6] G. Axford and Y. Lin, "Surprise! Currency Risk Improves International Investment," *Canadian Treasury Management Review,* Royal Bank of Canada (March–April 1990).

refuse to pay on the debt in the event of unfavourable political activities. Structuring the operation such that it requires significant parent company involvement to function is another way some firms try to reduce political risk.

Some companies avoid the implicit threats in the methods just discussed by simply trying to be "good corporate citizens" in the host country. This approach is an international application of the view of the corporation as responsible to shareholders and stakeholders that we presented in Chapter 1.

CONCEPT QUESTIONS

- What problems do international projects pose for the use of net present value techniques?
- How is international capital budgeting affected by growing investor interest in international diversification?

31.6   International Financing Decisions

An international firm can finance foreign projects in three basic ways:

1. It can raise cash in the home country and export it to finance the foreign project.
2. It can raise cash by borrowing in the foreign country where the project is located.
3. It can borrow in a third country where the cost of debt is lowest.

If a Canadian firm raises cash for its foreign projects by borrowing in Canada, it faces exchange rate risk. If the foreign currency depreciates, the Canadian parent firm will experience an exchange rate loss when the foreign cash flow is remitted to Canada. Of course, the Canadian firm may sell foreign exchange forward to hedge this risk. However, for many currencies, it is difficult to sell forward contracts beyond one year.

Firms may borrow in the country where the foreign project is located. This is the usual way of hedging long-term foreign exchange risk up to the amount borrowed. Any residual (equity) would not be hedged. Thus, if Kihlstrom Equipment wishes to invest FF20 million in France, it may attempt to raise much of the cash in France. Toyota took this approach and financed assembly plants in the United States in U.S. dollars during the early 1970s. Volkswagen also built plants in the United States, but financed them in DM. During the late 1970s, the U.S. dollar dropped against both the yen and DM. Toyota was unaffected on the financing side, but Volkswagen faced increased costs, putting it at a disadvantage in selling low-end cars.

Another alternative is to find a country where interest rates are low. This approach, however, is not as simple as it seems as shown by the following example.

▪ Example: The Halifax–Dartmouth Bridge Commission

The two bridges spanning the Halifax Harbour are the responsibility of the Halifax–Dartmouth Bridge Commission.[7] In 1969, the commission, then chaired by A. Murray

---

[7]Our example is based on J. Myrden, "Bridges of Debt," *Halifax Chronicle Herald* (January 18, 1992), p. C1.

MacKay, decided to combine $3 million in outstanding debt from building the MacDonald Bridge in the mid-1950s with new borrowings for the MacKay Bridge built in 1970 for $39 million.

Because Canadian interest rates were high in 1970, the commission decided to borrow in DM. This left the commission exposed because its revenues (bridge tolls) were in Canadian dollars. When the DM rose in the 1970s, the outstanding principal rose far beyond the initial cost of the bridges. A refinancing in Swiss francs experienced the same problem. Only in 1991 was the debt converted to Canadian dollars and stabilized. ∎

The example shows that foreign interest rates may be lower because of lower expected foreign inflation which will likely cause appreciation of the foreign currency. Thus, financial managers must be careful to look beyond nominal interest rates to real interest rates.

Short-Term and Medium-Term Financing

In raising short-term and medium-term cash, Canadian international firms have a choice between borrowing from a chartered bank at the Canadian rate or borrowing Euro-Canadian (or other Eurocurrency) from a bank outside Canada through the Eurocurrency market.

Eurocurrency markets are the **Eurobanks** that make loans and accept deposits in foreign currencies. Most Eurocurrency trading involves the borrowing and lending of time deposits at Eurobanks. For example, suppose the Bank of Nova Scotia receives a 30-day Eurodollar deposit from McCain in London. The BNS then makes a U.S.-dollar–denominated loan to the Bank of Tokyo. Ultimately, the Bank of Tokyo makes a loan to a Japanese importer with invoices to pay in the United States. As our example shows, the Eurocurrency market is not a retail market. The customers are large corporations, banks, and governments.

One important characteristic of the Eurocurrency market is that loans are made on a floating rate basis. The interest rates are set at a fixed margin above the London Interbank Offered Rate (LIBOR) for the given period and currency involved. For example, if LIBOR is 8 percent and the margin is 0.5 percent for Eurodollar loans in a certain risk class, called a *tier,* the Eurodollar borrower will pay an interest rate of 8.5 percent. Eurodollar loans have maturities ranging up to 10 years.

Securitization and globalization have produced alternatives to borrowing from a Eurobank. Under a **note issuance facility (NIF),** a large borrower issues short-term notes with maturities of three to six months usually but ranging to one year.[8] Banks may underwrite NIFs or sell them to investors. In the latter case, where banks simply act as an agent, the Euronotes issued are called *Euro-commercial paper* (*ECP*). ECP is similar to domestic commercial paper but, because the Eurocredit market is not regulated, ECP offers improved flexibility in available maturities and tax avoidance.

The drive to escape regulation (part of the regulatory dialectic introduced in Chapter 1) explains the attraction and growth of the Euromarkets. Eurocurrency

---

[8]Our discussion of NIFs draws on A. L. Melnik and S. E. Plaut, *The Short-Term Eurocredit Market* (New York: New York University, Salomon Center, 1991).

markets developed to allow borrowers and banks to operate without regulation and taxes. They offer borrowers an opportunity to tap large amounts of short-term funds quickly and at competitive rates. As banking regulations (for example, capital rules) become tighter, alternatives to bank borrowing, such as NIFs, are growing and sharing the Euromarket with banks.

International Bond Markets

Trading in international bonds is over-the-counter and takes place in loosely connected individual markets. These individual markets are closely tied to the corresponding domestic bond markets. International bonds can be divided into two main types: foreign bonds and Eurobonds.

Foreign Bonds

Foreign bonds are issued by foreign borrowers in a particular country's domestic bond market. They are often nicknamed for the country of issuance. They are denominated in the country's domestic currency. For example, suppose a Swiss watch company issues U.S.-dollar–denominated bonds in the United States. These foreign bonds would be called *Yankee bonds*. Like all foreign bonds issued in the United States, Yankee bonds must be registered under the Securities Act of 1933. Yankee bonds are usually rated by a bond-rating agency such as Standard & Poor's Corporation. Many Yankee bonds are listed on the New York Stock Exchange.

Many foreign bonds, such as Yankee bonds, are registered. This makes them less attractive to Belgian dentists, investors having a disdain for tax authorities. For obvious reasons, these traders like the Eurobond market better than the foreign bond market. Registered bonds have an ownership name assigned to the bond's serial number. The transfer of ownership of a registered bond can take place only via legal transfer of the registered name. Transfer agents (for example, banks) are required.

Eurobonds

Eurobonds are denominated in a particular currency and are issued simultaneously in the bond markets of several countries. The prefix *Euro* means that the bonds are issued outside the countries in whose currencies they are denominated. Most Eurobonds are bearer bonds. Ownership is established by possession of the bond.

Most issues of Eurobonds are arranged by underwriting. However, some Eurobonds are privately placed.[9] A public issue with underwriting is similar to the public debt sold in domestic bond markets. The borrower sells its bonds to a group of managing banks. Managing banks, in turn, sell the bonds to other banks. The other banks are divided into two groups: underwriters and sellers. The underwriters and sellers sell the bonds to dealers and fund investors. The managing banks also serve as underwriters and sellers. Underwriters usually sell Eurobonds on a firm commitment basis. That is, they are committed to buy the bonds at a prenegotiated price and attempt to sell them at a higher price in the market. Eurobonds appear as straight bonds,

---

[9]In general, the issue costs are lower in private placements, as compared to public issues, and the yields are higher.

floating rate notes, convertible bonds, zero coupon bonds, mortgage backed bonds, and dual currency bonds.[10]

■ *Example*

A Canadian firm makes an offering of $500 million of floating rate notes. The notes are offered in London. They mature in 2020 and have semiannual interest of 0.5 percent above the six-month London Interbank Offered Rate. When the bonds are issued, the six-month LIBOR is 10 percent. Thus, in the first six months the Canadian firm will pay interest (at the annual rate) of 10% + 0.5% = 10.5%. ■

CONCEPT QUESTIONS

■ What are the three ways firms can finance foreign projects?
■ What sources of financing are available?

International Capital Structure   31.7

There is no general agreement on capital structure differences among countries. Rutterford has studied the differences, and her results suggest that Japanese firms depend heavily on debt whereas U.S. and U.K. firms have more equity.[11] Rutterford argues that tax factors do not appear to explain these differences. Agency costs are one possible answer. For example, in both Japan and Germany there is a closer relationship between banks and client firms (which may reduce the agency costs of issuing debt) than in the United States.

Kester's results, however, are not consistent with those of Rutterford.[12] He shows that Japanese manufacturing is not as highly leveraged as previously thought. On a market-value basis there appear to be no national differences in leverage between the United States and Japan after controlling for attributes of firms and industries.

Reporting Foreign Operations   31.8

When a Canadian company calculates its accounting net income and EPS for some period, it must "translate" everything into Canadian dollars. This can create problems for accountants when there are significant foreign operations. In particular, two issues arise:

1. What is the appropriate exchange rate to use for translating each balance sheet account?
2. How should balance sheet accounting gains and losses from foreign currency translation be handled?

---

[10]There is a small but growing international equity market. International equities are stock issues underwritten and distributed to a mix of investors without regard to national borders. Our definition of international equity encompasses two basic types: those issues that have been internationally syndicated and distributed outside all national exchanges (termed *Euroequities*) and those that are issued by underwriters in domestic markets other than their own.

[11]J. Rutterford, "An International Perspective on Capital Structure," *Midland Corporate Finance Journal* 3 (Fall 1985), p. 3.

[12]W. C. Kester, "Capital and Ownership Structure: A Comparison of United States and Japanese Manufacturing Corporations," *Financial Management* (Spring 1986).

To illustrate the accounting problem, suppose we started a small foreign subsidiary in Lilliputia a year ago. The local currency is the gulliver, abbreviated GL. At the beginning of the year, the exchange rate was GL 2 = $1CDN. The balance sheet in gullivers looked like this:

Assets	GL 1,000	Liabilities	GL 500
		Equity	500

At 2 gullivers to the dollar, the beginning balance sheet in dollars was

Assets	$500	Liabilities	$250
		Equity	250

Lilliputia is a quiet place, and nothing at all happened during the year. As a result, net income was zero (before consideration of exchange rate changes). However, the exchange rate did change to 4 gullivers = $1 purely because the Lilliputian inflation rate is much higher than the Canadian inflation rate.

Since nothing happened, the accounting ending balance sheet in gullivers is the same as the beginning one. However, if we convert to dollars at the new exchange rate, we get

Assets	$250	Liabilities	$125
		Equity	125

Notice that the value of the equity has gone down by $125, even though net income was exactly zero. Despite the fact that absolutely nothing really happened, there is a $125 accounting loss. How to handle this $125 loss has been a controversial accounting question.

One obvious and consistent approach is simply to report the loss on the parent company's income statement. During periods of volatile exchange rates, this kind of treatment can dramatically impact an international company's reported EPS. This is purely an accounting phenomenon, but, even so, such fluctuations are disliked by financial managers.

The current, compromise approach to translation gains and losses is based on rules set out in Canadian Institute of Chartered Accountants (CICA) 1650. The rules divide a firm's foreign subsidiaries into two categories: integrated and self-sustaining. For the most part, the rules require that all assets and liabilities be translated from the subsidiary's currency into the parent's currency using the exchange rate that currently prevails.[13] Since Canadian accountants consolidate the financial statements of sub-

---

[13]The rules also define the current exchange rate differently for the types of subsidiaries. An integrated subsidiary uses the exchange rate observed on the last day of its fiscal year. For a self-sustaining subsidiary, the exchange rate prescribed is the average rate over the year. For detailed discussion of CICA 1650, see A. Davis and G. Pinches, *Canadian Financial Management*, 2d ed. (New York: HarperCollins, 1991), pp. 684–86.

sidiaries owned over 50 percent by the parent firm, translation gains and losses are reflected on the income statement of the parent company.

For a self-sustaining subsidiary, any translation gains and losses that occur are accumulated in a special account within the shareholders' equity section of the parent company's balance sheet. This account might be labeled something like "unrealized foreign exchange gains (losses)." These gains and losses are not reported on the income statement. As a result, the impact of translation gains and losses will not be recognized explicitly in net income until the underlying assets and liabilities are sold or otherwise liquidated.

CONCEPT QUESTION

- What issues arise when reporting foreign operations?

Summary and Conclusions 31.9

The international firm has a more complicated life than the purely domestic firm. Management must understand the connection between interest rates, foreign currency exchange rates, and inflation, and it must become aware of a large number of different financial market regulations and tax systems.

1. This chapter describes some fundamental theories of international finance:

    The purchasing power parity theorem (law of one price).
    The expectations theory of exchange rates.
    The interest rate parity theorem.

2. The purchasing power parity theorem states that $1 should have the same purchasing power in each country. This means that an apple costs the same whether you buy it in Toronto or in Tokyo. One version of the purchasing power parity theorem states that the change in exchange rates between the currencies of two countries is connected to the inflation rates in the countries' commodity prices.

3. The expectations theory of exchange rates states that the forward rate of exchange is equal to the expected spot rate.

4. The interest rate parity theorem states that the interest rate differential between two countries will be equal to the difference between the forward exchange rate and the spot exchange rate. This equality must prevail to prevent arbitrageurs from devising get-rich-quick strategies. The equality requires the rate of return on risk-free investments in Canada to be the same as that in other countries.

    Of course, in practice the purchasing power parity theorem and the interest rate parity theorem cannot work perfectly. Government regulations and taxes prevent this. However, there is much empirical work and intuition that suggests that these theories describe international financial markets in an approximate way.

5. The chapter also describes some of the problems of international capital budgeting. The net present value rule is still the appropriate way to choose projects, but the main problem is to choose the correct cost of capital. We argue that it should be equal to the rate that shareholders can expect to earn on a portfolio of domestic and foreign securities. This rate should be about the same as for a portfolio of domestic securities. However, two adjustments may be necessary:

    a. The cost of capital of an international firm may be *lower* than that of a domestic counterpart because of the benefits of international diversification.

    b. The cost of capital of an international firm may be *higher* because of the extra risks of international investment.

6. We briefly describe international financial markets. International firms may want to consider borrowing in the local financial market or in the Eurocurrency and Eurobond markets. The interest rates are likely to appear different in these markets. Thus, international firms must be careful to consider differences in taxes and government regulations.

Key Terms

Belgian dentist 886

Cross rate 886

Eurobonds 886

Eurocurrency 886

Foreign bonds 886

Gilts 886

London Interbank Offered Rate (LIBOR) 886

Swaps 887

Export Development Corporation (EDC) 887

Foreign exchange market 887

Exchange rate 888

Triangular arbitrage 888

Spot trades 890

Spot exchange rate 890

Forward trades 890

Forward exchange rate 890

Swap rate 890

Law of one price (LOP) 890

Purchasing power parity (PPP) 891

Relative purchasing power parity (RPPP) 891

Interest rate parity theorem 893

Currency swap 896

American options 896

Eurobanks 903

Note issuance facility (NIF) 903

Suggested Readings

The following are useful books on the modern theory of international markets:

J. O. Grabbe. *International Financial Markets.* New York: Elsevier, 1986.

M. Levi. *International Finance.* New York: McGraw-Hill, 1983.

These two articles describe capital budgeting for international projects:

D. R. Lessard. "Evaluating Foreign Projects: An Adjusted Present Value Approach." In *International Financial Management,* ed. D. R. Lessard. Boston: Warren, Gorham & Lamont, 1979.

A. C. Shapiro. "Capital Budgeting for the Multinational Corporation." *Financial Management* (Spring 1978).

For an up-to-date discussion of short- and intermediate-term Euromarkets, see:

A. L. Melnik and S. E. Plaut. *The Short-Term Eurocredit Market.* New York: New York University, Salomon Center, 1991.

Questions and Problems

Some Basics

31.1 Use Table 31.1 to answer the following questions:

    a. What is the quote in direct terms for the British pound sterling and the Canadian dollar on spot exchange? What is it in indirect terms for the West German mark and the Canadian dollar?

    b. Is the Japanese yen at a premium or a discount to the Canadian dollar in the forward markets?

    c. To which type of foreign exchange participants would the forward prices of the Japanese yen be important? Why? What types of transactions might these participants use to cover their exposed risk in the foreign exchange markets?

    d. Suppose you are a British exporter of watches. If you are to be paid in Canadian dollars three months from now for a shipment worth $100,000 made to Canada, how many British pounds would you receive if you locked in the price today with a forward contract? Would you buy or sell the dollar forward?

    e. Calculate the U.K. pound/German deutsche mark cross rate for spot exchange in terms of the U.S. dollar. Do the same for the yen–Swiss franc cross rate.

    f. In the text a swap transaction is described. Why might both banks profit from the use of such a mutual agreement?

The Law of One Price and Purchasing Power Parity

31.2 Are the following statements true or false? Explain.

    a. If Japan's general price index rises faster than Canada's (assuming that there are zero transactions costs, that no barriers to trade exist, and that products are identical in both countries), we would expect the yen to appreciate with respect to the dollar.

    b. Suppose you are a French wine exporter who receives all payments in foreign currency. The French government undertakes an expansionary monetary policy. If it is certain that the result will be higher inflation in France than in other countries, you would be wise to use forward markets to protect yourself against future losses resulting from the deterioration of the value of the French franc.

c. If you could accurately estimate differences in relative inflation between two countries over a long period of time (and other participants in the market were unable to do so), you could successfully speculate in spot currency markets.

31.3 a. The treasurer of a major Canadian firm has $5 million to invest for three months. The annual interest rate in Canada is 12 percent. The interest rate in the United Kingdom is 9 percent. The spot rate of exchange is $2/£, and the three-month forward rate is $2.015/£. Barring transactions costs, in which country would the treasurer want to invest the company's capital if she can fix the exchange rate three months hence through a forward contract?

b. The spot rate of foreign exchange between Canada and the United Kingdom at time t is $1.50/£. If the interest rate is 13 percent in Canada and 8 percent in the United Kingdom, what would you expect the one-year forward rate to be if no immediate arbitrage opportunities existed?

c. If you are an exporter who must make payments in foreign currency three months after receiving each shipment and you predict that the domestic currency will appreciate in value over this period, is there any value in hedging your currency exposure?

International Capital Budgeting

31.4 a. Suppose it is your task to evaluate two different investments in new subsidiaries for your company, one in your own country and the other in a foreign country. You calculate the cash flows of both projects to be identical after exchange rate differences. Under what circumstances might you choose to invest in the foreign subsidiary? Give an example of a country where certain factors might influence you to alter this decision and invest at home.

b. Suppose Kihlstrom Equipment decides to make another investment in Germany. The project cost DM10 million and is expected to produce cash flows of DM4 million in year 1 and DM3 million in each of years 2 and 3. The current spot exchange rate is $0.5/DM1, and the current risk-free rate in Canada is 11.3 percent, compared to that in Germany of 6 percent. The appropriate discount rate for the project is estimated to be 15 percent, the Canadian cost of capital for the company. In addition, the subsidiary can be sold at the end of three years for an estimated DM2.1 million. What is the NPV of the project?

c. An investment in a foreign subsidiary is estimated to have a positive NPV, after the discount rate used in the calculations is adjusted for political risk and any advantages from diversification. Does this mean the project is acceptable? Why or why not?

   d. If a Canadian firm raises funds for a foreign subsidiary, would you expect disadvantages to borrowing in Canada? Why or why not? If so, how would you overcome this problem?

International Capital Markets

31.5 *a.* What is a Euroyen?

   b. If financial markets are perfectly competitive and the Euro–Canadian dollar rate is above that offered in the Canadian loan market, you would immediately want to borrow money in Canada and invest it in Eurodollars. True or false? Explain.

   c. What distinguishes a Eurobond from a foreign bond? Which particular feature makes the Eurobond more popular than the foreign bond?

   d. How would you describe a bond issued by a Canadian firm in the United States with payments denominated in U.S. dollars?

Mathematical Tables

Table A.1 Present value of $1 to be received after T periods $= 1/(1 + r)^r$

	Interest rate								
Period	1%	2%	3%	4%	5%	6%	7%	8%	9%
1	0.9901	0.9804	0.9709	0.9615	0.9524	0.9434	0.9346	0.9259	0.9174
2	0.9803	0.9612	0.9426	0.9246	0.9070	0.8900	0.8734	0.8573	0.8417
3	0.9706	0.9423	0.9151	0.8890	0.8638	0.8396	0.8163	0.7938	0.7722
4	0.9610	0.9238	0.8885	0.8548	0.8227	0.7921	0.7629	0.7350	0.7084
5	0.9515	0.9057	0.8626	0.8219	0.7835	0.7473	0.7130	0.6806	0.6499
6	0.9420	0.8880	0.8375	0.7903	0.7462	0.7050	0.6663	0.6302	0.5963
7	0.9327	0.8706	0.8131	0.7599	0.7107	0.6651	0.6227	0.5835	0.5470
8	0.9235	0.8535	0.7894	0.7307	0.6768	0.6274	0.5820	0.5403	0.5019
9	0.9143	0.8368	0.7664	0.7026	0.6446	0.5919	0.5439	0.5002	0.4604
10	0.9053	0.8203	0.7441	0.6756	0.6139	0.5584	0.5083	0.4632	0.4224
11	0.8963	0.8043	0.7224	0.6496	0.5847	0.5268	0.4751	0.4289	0.3875
12	0.8874	0.7885	0.7014	0.6246	0.5568	0.4970	0.4440	0.3971	0.3555
13	0.8787	0.7730	0.6810	0.6006	0.5303	0.4688	0.4150	0.3677	0.3262
14	0.8700	0.7579	0.6611	0.5775	0.5051	0.4423	0.3878	0.3405	0.2992
15	0.8613	0.7430	0.6419	0.5553	0.4810	0.4173	0.3624	0.3152	0.2745
16	0.8528	0.7284	0.6232	0.5339	0.4581	0.3936	0.3387	0.2919	0.2519
17	0.8444	0.7142	0.6050	0.5134	0.4363	0.3714	0.3166	0.2703	0.2311
18	0.8360	0.7002	0.5874	0.4936	0.4155	0.3503	0.2959	0.2502	0.2120
19	0.8277	0.6864	0.5703	0.4746	0.3957	0.3305	0.2765	0.2317	0.1945
20	0.8195	0.6730	0.5537	0.4564	0.3769	0.3118	0.2584	0.2145	0.1784
21	0.8114	0.6598	0.5375	0.4388	0.3589	0.2942	0.2415	0.1987	0.1637
22	0.8034	0.6468	0.5219	0.4220	0.3418	0.2775	0.2257	0.1839	0.1502
23	0.7954	0.6342	0.5067	0.4057	0.3256	0.2618	0.2109	0.1703	0.1378
24	0.7876	0.6217	0.4919	0.3901	0.3101	0.2470	0.1971	0.1577	0.1264
25	0.7798	0.6095	0.4776	0.3751	0.2953	0.2330	0.1842	0.1460	0.1160
30	0.7419	0.5521	0.4120	0.3083	0.2314	0.1741	0.1314	0.0994	0.0754
40	0.6717	0.4529	0.3066	0.2083	0.1420	0.0972	0.0668	0.0460	0.0318
50	0.6080	0.3715	0.2281	0.1407	0.0872	0.0543	0.0339	0.0213	0.0134

*The factor is zero to four decimal places.

					Interest rate					
10%	12%	14%	15%	16%	18%	20%	24%	28%	32%	36%
0.9091	0.8929	0.8772	0.8696	0.8621	0.8475	0.8333	0.8065	0.7813	0.7576	0.7353
0.8264	0.7972	0.7695	0.7561	0.7432	0.7182	0.6944	0.6504	0.6104	0.5739	0.5407
0.7513	0.7118	0.6750	0.6575	0.6407	0.6086	0.5787	0.5245	0.4768	0.4348	0.3975
0.6830	0.6355	0.5921	0.5718	0.5523	0.5158	0.4823	0.4230	0.3725	0.3294	0.2923
0.6209	0.5674	0.5194	0.4972	0.4761	0.4371	0.4019	0.3411	0.2910	0.2495	0.2149
0.5645	0.5066	0.4556	0.4323	0.4104	0.3704	0.3349	0.2751	0.2274	0.1890	0.1580
0.5132	0.4523	0.3996	0.3759	0.3538	0.3139	0.2791	0.2218	0.1776	0.1432	0.1162
0.4665	0.4039	0.3506	0.3269	0.3050	0.2660	0.2326	0.1789	0.1388	0.1085	0.0854
0.4241	0.3606	0.3075	0.2843	0.2630	0.2255	0.1938	0.1443	0.1084	0.0822	0.0628
0.3855	0.3220	0.2697	0.2472	0.2267	0.1911	0.1615	0.1164	0.0847	0.0623	0.0462
0.3505	0.2875	0.2366	0.2149	0.1954	0.1619	0.1346	0.0938	0.0662	0.0472	0.0340
0.3186	0.2567	0.2076	0.1869	0.1685	0.1372	0.1122	0.0757	0.0517	0.0357	0.0250
0.2897	0.2292	0.1821	0.1625	0.1452	0.1163	0.0935	0.0610	0.0404	0.0271	0.0184
0.2633	0.2046	0.1597	0.1413	0.1252	0.0985	0.0779	0.0492	0.0316	0.0205	0.0135
0.2394	0.1827	0.1401	0.1229	0.1079	0.0835	0.0649	0.0397	0.0247	0.0155	0.0099
0.2176	0.1631	0.1229	0.1069	0.0930	0.0708	0.0541	0.0320	0.0193	0.0118	0.0073
0.1978	0.1456	0.1078	0.0929	0.0802	0.0600	0.0451	0.0258	0.0150	0.0089	0.0054
0.1799	0.1300	0.0946	0.0808	0.0691	0.0508	0.0376	0.0208	0.0118	0.0068	0.0039
0.1635	0.1161	0.0829	0.0703	0.0596	0.0431	0.0313	0.0168	0.0092	0.0051	0.0029
0.1486	0.1037	0.0728	0.0611	0.0514	0.0365	0.0261	0.0135	0.0072	0.0039	0.0021
0.1351	0.0926	0.0638	0.0531	0.0443	0.0309	0.0217	0.0109	0.0056	0.0029	0.0016
0.1228	0.0826	0.0560	0.0462	0.0382	0.0262	0.0181	0.0088	0.0044	0.0022	0.0012
0.1117	0.0738	0.0491	0.0402	0.0329	0.0222	0.0151	0.0071	0.0034	0.0017	0.0008
0.1015	0.0659	0.0431	0.0349	0.0284	0.0188	0.0126	0.0057	0.0027	0.0013	0.0006
0.0923	0.0588	0.0378	0.0304	0.0245	0.0160	0.0105	0.0046	0.0021	0.0010	0.0005
0.0573	0.0334	0.0196	0.0151	0.0116	0.0070	0.0042	0.0016	0.0006	0.0002	0.0001
0.0221	0.0107	0.0053	0.0037	0.0026	0.0013	0.0007	0.0002	0.0001	*	*
0.0085	0.0035	0.0014	0.0009	0.0006	0.0003	0.0001	*	*	*	*

Table A.2 Present value of an annuity of $1 per period for T periods $= [1 - 1/(1 + r)^T]/r$

Number of periods	Interest rate								
	1%	2%	3%	4%	5%	6%	7%	8%	9%
1	0.9901	0.9804	0.9709	0.9615	0.9524	0.9434	0.9346	0.9259	0.9174
2	1.9704	1.9416	1.9135	1.8861	1.8594	1.8334	1.8080	1.7833	1.7591
3	2.9410	2.8839	2.8286	2.7751	2.7232	2.6730	2.6243	2.5771	2.5313
4	3.9020	3.8077	3.7171	3.6299	3.5460	3.4651	3.3872	3.3121	3.2397
5	4.8534	4.7135	4.5797	4.4518	4.3295	4.2124	4.1002	3.9927	3.8897
6	5.7955	5.6014	5.4172	5.2421	5.0757	4.9173	4.7665	4.6229	4.4859
7	6.7282	6.4720	6.2303	6.0021	5.7864	5.5824	5.3893	5.2064	5.0330
8	7.6517	7.3255	7.0197	6.7327	6.4632	6.2098	5.9713	5.7466	5.5348
9	8.5660	8.1622	7.7861	7.4353	7.1078	6.8017	6.5152	6.2469	5.9952
10	9.4713	8.9826	8.5302	8.1109	7.7217	7.3601	7.0236	6.7101	6.4177
11	10.3676	9.7868	9.2526	8.7605	8.3064	7.8869	7.4987	7.1390	6.8052
12	11.2551	10.5753	9.9540	9.3851	8.8633	8.3838	7.9427	7.5361	7.1607
13	12.1337	11.3484	10.6350	9.9856	9.3936	8.8527	8.3577	7.9038	7.4869
14	13.0037	12.1062	11.2961	10.5631	9.8986	9.2950	8.7455	8.2442	7.7862
15	13.8651	12.8493	11.9379	11.1184	10.3797	9.7122	9.1079	8.5595	8.0607
16	14.7179	13.5777	12.5611	11.6523	10.8378	10.1059	9.4466	8.8514	8.3126
17	15.5623	14.2919	13.1661	12.1657	11.2741	10.4773	9.7632	9.1216	8.5436
18	16.3983	14.9920	13.7535	12.6593	11.6896	10.8276	10.0591	9.3719	8.7556
19	17.2260	15.6785	14.3238	13.1339	12.0853	11.1581	10.3356	9.6036	8.9501
20	18.0456	16.3514	14.8775	13.5903	12.4622	11.4699	10.5940	9.8181	9.1285
21	18.8570	17.0112	15.4150	14.0292	12.8212	11.7641	10.8355	10.0168	9.2922
22	19.6604	17.6580	15.9369	14.4511	13.1630	12.0416	11.0612	10.2007	9.4424
23	20.4558	18.2922	16.4436	14.8568	13.4886	12.3034	11.2722	10.3741	9.5802
24	21.2434	18.9139	16.9355	15.2470	13.7986	12.5504	11.4693	10.5288	9.7066
25	22.0232	19.5235	17.4131	15.6221	14.0939	12.7834	11.6536	10.6748	9.8226
30	25.8077	22.3965	19.6004	17.2920	15.3725	13.7648	12.4090	11.2578	10.2737
40	32.8347	27.3555	23.1148	19.7928	17.1591	15.0463	13.3317	11.9246	10.7574
50	39.1961	31.4236	25.7298	21.4822	18.2559	15.7619	13.8007	12.2335	10.9617

Interest rate

10%	12%	14%	15%	16%	18%	20%	24%	28%	32%
0.9091	0.8929	0.8772	0.8696	0.8621	0.8475	0.8333	0.8065	0.7813	0.7576
1.7355	1.6901	1.6467	1.6257	1.6052	1.5656	1.5278	1.4568	1.3916	1.3315
2.4869	2.4018	2.3216	2.2832	2.2459	2.1743	2.1065	1.9813	1.8684	1.7663
3.1699	3.0373	2.9137	2.8550	2.7982	2.6901	2.5887	2.4043	2.2410	2.0957
3.7908	3.6048	3.4331	3.3522	3.2743	3.1272	2.9906	2.7454	2.5320	2.3452
4.3553	4.1114	3.8887	3.7845	3.6847	3.4976	3.3255	3.0205	2.7594	2.5342
4.8684	4.5638	4.2883	4.1604	4.0386	3.8115	3.6046	3.2423	2.9370	2.6775
5.3349	4.9676	4.6389	4.4873	4.3436	4.0776	3.8372	3.4212	3.0758	2.7860
5.7590	5.3282	4.9464	4.7716	4.6065	4.3030	4.0310	3.5655	3.1842	2.8681
6.1446	5.6502	5.2161	5.0188	4.8332	4.4941	4.1925	3.6819	3.2689	2.9304
6.4951	5.9377	5.4527	5.2337	5.0286	4.6560	4.3271	3.7757	3.3351	2.9776
6.8137	6.1944	5.6603	5.4206	5.1971	4.7932	4.4392	3.8514	3.3868	3.0133
7.1034	6.4235	5.8424	5.5831	5.3423	4.9095	4.5327	3.9124	3.4272	3.0404
7.3667	6.6282	6.0021	5.7245	5.4675	5.0081	4.6106	3.9616	3.4587	3.0609
7.6061	6.8109	6.1422	5.8474	5.5755	5.0916	4.6755	4.0013	3.4834	3.0764
7.8237	6.9740	6.2651	5.9542	5.6685	5.1624	4.7296	4.0333	3.5026	3.0882
8.0216	7.1196	6.3729	6.0472	5.7487	5.2223	4.7746	4.0591	3.5177	3.0971
8.2014	7.2497	6.4674	6.1280	5.8178	5.2732	4.8122	4.0799	3.5294	3.1039
8.3649	7.3658	6.5504	6.1982	5.8775	5.3162	4.8435	4.0967	3.5386	3.1090
8.5136	7.4694	6.6231	6.2593	5.9288	5.3527	4.8696	4.1103	3.5458	3.1129
8.6487	7.5620	6.6870	6.3125	5.9731	5.3837	4.8913	4.1212	3.5514	3.1158
8.7715	7.6446	6.7429	6.3587	6.0113	5.4099	4.9094	4.1300	3.5558	3.1180
8.8832	7.7184	6.7921	6.3988	6.0442	5.4321	4.9245	4.1371	3.5592	3.1197
8.9847	7.7843	6.8351	6.4338	6.0726	5.4509	4.9371	4.1428	3.5619	3.1210
9.0770	7.8431	6.8729	6.4641	6.0971	5.4669	4.9476	4.1474	3.5640	3.1220
9.4269	8.0552	7.0027	6.5660	6.1772	5.5168	4.9789	4.1601	3.5693	3.1242
9.7791	8.2438	7.1050	6.6418	6.2335	5.5482	4.9966	4.1659	3.5712	3.1250
9.9148	8.3045	7.1327	6.6605	6.2463	5.5541	4.9995	4.1666	3.5714	3.1250

Table A.3 Future value of $1 at the end of T periods $= (1 + r)^T$

Period	| Interest rate								
	1%	2%	3%	4%	5%	6%	7%	8%	9%
1	1.0100	1.0200	1.0300	1.0400	1.0500	1.0600	1.0700	1.0800	1.0900
2	1.0201	1.0404	1.0609	1.0816	1.1025	1.1236	1.1449	1.1664	1.1881
3	1.0303	1.0612	1.0927	1.1249	1.1576	1.1910	1.2250	1.2597	1.2950
4	1.0406	1.0824	1.1255	1.1699	1.2155	1.2625	1.3108	1.3605	1.4116
5	1.0510	1.1041	1.1593	1.2167	1.2763	1.3382	1.4026	1.4693	1.5386
6	1.0615	1.1262	1.1941	1.2653	1.3401	1.4185	1.5007	1.5869	1.6771
7	1.0721	1.1487	1.2299	1.3159	1.4071	1.5036	1.6058	1.7138	1.8280
8	1.0829	1.1717	1.2668	1.3686	1.4775	1.5938	1.7182	1.8509	1.9926
9	1.0937	1.1951	1.3048	1.4233	1.5513	1.6895	1.8385	1.9990	2.1719
10	1.1046	1.2190	1.3439	1.4802	1.6289	1.7908	1.9672	2.1589	2.3674
11	1.1157	1.2434	1.3842	1.5395	1.7103	1.8983	2.1049	2.3316	2.5804
12	1.1268	1.2682	1.4258	1.6010	1.7959	2.0122	2.2522	2.5182	2.8127
13	1.1381	1.2936	1.4685	1.6651	1.8856	2.1329	2.4098	2.7196	3.0658
14	1.1495	1.3195	1.5126	1.7317	1.9799	2.2609	2.5785	2.9372	3.3417
15	1.1610	1.3459	1.5580	1.8009	1.0789	2.3966	2.7590	3.1722	3.6425
16	1.1726	1.3728	1.6047	1.8730	2.1829	2.5404	2.9522	3.4259	3.9703
17	1.1843	1.4002	1.6528	1.9479	2.2920	2.6928	3.1588	3.7000	4.3276
18	1.1961	1.4282	1.7024	2.0258	2.4066	2.8543	3.3799	3.9960	4.7171
19	1.2081	1.4568	1.7535	2.1068	2.5270	3.0256	3.6165	4.3157	5.1417
20	1.2202	1.4859	1.8061	2.1911	2.6533	3.2071	3.8697	4.6610	5.6044
21	1.2324	1.5157	1.8603	2.2788	2.7860	3.3996	4.1406	5.0338	6.1088
22	1.2447	1.5460	1.9161	2.3699	2.9253	3.6035	4.4304	5.4365	6.6586
23	1.2572	1.5769	1.9736	2.4647	3.0715	3.8197	4.7405	5.8715	7.2579
24	1.2697	1.6084	2.0328	2.5633	3.2251	4.0489	5.0724	6.3412	7.9111
25	1.2824	1.6406	2.0938	2.6658	3.3864	4.2919	5.4274	6.8485	8.6231
30	1.3478	1.8114	2.4273	3.2434	4.3219	5.7435	7.6123	10.063	13.268
40	1.4889	2.2080	3.2620	4.8010	7.0400	10.286	14.974	21.725	31.409
50	1.6446	2.6916	4.3839	7.1067	11.467	18.420	29.457	46.902	74.358
60	1.8167	3.2810	5.8916	10.520	18.679	32.988	57.946	101.26	176.03

*FVIF < 99,999.

					Interest rate					
10%	12%	14%	15%	16%	18%	20%	24%	28%	32%	36%
1.1000	1.1200	1.1400	1.1500	1.1600	1.1800	1.2000	1.2400	1.2800	1.3200	1.3600
1.2100	1.2544	1.2996	1.3225	1.3456	1.3924	1.4400	1.5376	1.6384	1.7424	1.8496
1.3310	1.4049	1.4815	1.5209	1.5609	1.6430	1.7280	1.9066	2.0972	2.3000	2.5155
1.4641	1.5735	1.6890	1.7490	1.8106	1.9388	2.0736	2.3642	2.6844	3.0360	3.4210
1.6105	1.7623	1.9254	2.0114	2.1003	2.2878	2.4883	2.9316	3.4360	4.0075	4.6526
1.7716	1.9738	2.1950	2.3131	2.4364	2.6996	2.9860	3.6352	4.3980	5.2899	6.3275
1.9487	2.2107	2.5023	2.6600	2.8262	3.1855	3.5832	4.5077	5.6295	6.9826	8.6054
2.1436	2.4760	2.8526	3.0590	3.2784	3.7589	4.2998	5.5895	7.2058	9.2170	11.703
2.3579	2.7731	3.2519	3.5179	3.8030	4.4355	5.1598	6.9310	9.2234	12.166	15.917
2.5937	3.1058	3.7072	4.0456	4.4114	5.2338	6.1917	8.5944	11.806	16.060	21.647
2.8531	3.4785	4.2262	4.6524	5.1173	6.1759	7.4301	10.657	15.112	21.199	29.439
3.1384	3.8960	4.8179	5.3503	5.9360	7.2876	8.9161	13.215	19.343	27.983	40.037
3.4523	4.3635	5.4924	6.1528	6.8858	8.5994	10.699	16.386	24.759	36.937	54.451
3.7975	4.8871	6.2613	7.0757	7.9875	10.147	12.839	20.319	31.691	48.757	74.053
4.1772	5.4736	7.1379	8.1371	9.2655	11.974	15.407	25.196	40.565	64.359	100.71
4.5950	6.1304	8.1372	9.3576	10.748	14.129	18.488	31.243	51.923	84.954	136.97
5.0545	6.8660	9.2765	10.761	12.468	16.672	22.186	38.741	66.461	112.14	186.28
5.5599	7.6900	10.575	12.375	14.463	19.673	26.623	48.039	85.071	148.02	253.34
6.1159	8.6128	12.056	14.232	16.777	23.214	31.948	59.568	108.89	195.39	344.54
6.7275	9.6463	13.743	16.367	19.461	27.393	38.338	73.864	139.38	257.92	468.57
7.4002	10.804	15.668	18.822	22.574	32.324	46.005	91.592	178.41	340.45	637.26
8.1403	12.100	17.861	21.645	26.186	38.142	55.206	113.57	228.36	449.39	866.67
8.9543	13.552	20.362	24.891	30.376	45.008	66.247	140.83	292.30	593.20	1178.7
9.8497	15.179	23.212	28.625	35.236	53.109	79.497	174.63	374.14	783.02	1603.0
10.835	17.000	26.462	32.919	40.874	62.669	95.396	216.54	478.90	1033.6	2180.1
17.449	29.960	50.950	66.212	85.850	143.37	237.38	634.82	1645.5	4142.1	10143.
45.259	93.051	188.88	267.86	378.72	750.38	1469.8	5455.9	19427.	66521.	*
117.39	289.00	700.23	1083.7	1670.7	3927.4	9100.4	46890.	*	*	*
304.48	897.60	2595.9	4384.0	7370.2	20555.	56348.	*	*	*	*

Table A.4 Sum of annuity of $1 per period for T periods $= \{[(1 + r)^T - 1]/r\}$

Number of periods	Interest rate								
	1%	2%	3%	4%	5%	6%	7%	8%	9%
1	1.0000	1.0000	1.0000	1.0000	1.0000	1.0000	1.0000	1.0000	1.0000
2	2.0100	2.0200	2.0300	2.0400	2.0500	2.0600	2.0700	2.0800	2.0900
3	3.0301	3.0604	3.0909	3.1216	3,1525	3.1836	3.2149	3.2464	3.2781
4	4.0604	4.1216	4.1836	4.2465	4.3101	4.3746	4.4399	4.5061	4.5731
5	5.1010	5.2040	5.3091	5.4163	5.5256	5.6371	5.7507	5.8666	5.9847
6	6.1520	6.3081	6.4684	6.6330	6.8019	6.9753	7.1533	7.3359	7.5233
7	7.2135	7.4343	7.6625	7.8983	8.1420	8.3938	8.6540	8.9228	9.2004
8	8.2857	8.5830	8.8932	9.2142	9.5491	9.8975	10.260	10.637	11.028
9	9.3685	9.7546	10.159	10.583	11.027	11.491	11.978	12.488	13.021
10	10.462	10.950	11.464	12.006	12.578	13.181	13.816	14.487	15.193
11	11.567	12.169	12.808	13.486	14.207	14.972	15.784	16.645	17.560
12	12.683	13.412	14.192	15.026	15.917	16.870	17.888	18.977	20.141
13	13.809	14.680	15.618	16.627	17.713	18.882	20.141	21.495	22.953
14	14.947	15.974	17.086	18.292	19.599	21.015	22.550	24.215	26.019
15	16.097	17.293	18.599	20.024	21.579	23.276	25.129	27.152	29.361
16	17.258	18.639	20.157	21.825	23.657	25.673	27.888	30.324	33.003
17	18.430	20.012	21.762	23.698	25.840	28.213	30.840	33.750	36.974
18	19.615	21.412	23.414	25.645	28.132	30.906	33.999	37.450	41.301
19	20.811	22.841	25.117	27.671	30.539	33.760	37.379	41.446	46.018
20	22.019	24.297	26.870	29.778	33.066	36.786	40.995	45.762	51.160
21	23.239	25.783	28.676	31.969	35.719	39.993	44.865	50.423	56.765
22	24.472	27.299	30.537	34.248	38.505	43.392	49.006	55.457	62.873
23	25.716	28.845	32.453	36.618	41.430	46.996	53.436	60.893	69.532
24	26.973	30.422	34.426	39.083	44.502	50.816	58.177	66.765	76.790
25	28.243	32.030	36.459	41.646	47.727	54.865	63.249	73.106	84.701
30	34.785	40.568	47.575	56.085	66.439	79.058	94.461	113.28	136.31
40	48.886	60.402	75.401	95.026	120.80	154.76	199.64	259.06	337.88
50	64.463	84.579	112.80	152.67	209.35	290.34	406.53	573.77	815.08
60	81.670	114.05	163.05	237.99	353.58	533.13	813.52	1253.2	1944.8

*FVIFA < 99,999.

					Interest rate					
10%	12%	14%	15%	16%	18%	20%	24%	28%	32%	36%
1.0000	1.0000	1.0000	1.0000	1.0000	1.0000	1.0000	1.0000	1.0000	1.0000	1.0000
2.1000	2.1200	2.1400	2.1500	2.1600	2.1800	2.2000	2.2400	2.2800	2.3200	2.3600
3.3100	3.3744	3.4396	3.4725	3.5056	3.5724	3.6400	3.7776	3.9184	4.0624	4.2096
4.6410	4.7793	4.9211	4.9934	5.0665	5.2154	5.3680	5.6842	6.0156	6.3624	6.7251
6.1051	6.3528	6.6101	6.7424	6.8771	7.1542	7.4416	8.0484	8.6999	9.3983	10.146
7.7156	8.1152	8.5355	8.7537	8.9775	9.4420	9.9299	10.980	12.136	13.406	14.799
9.4872	10.089	10.730	11.067	11.414	12.142	12.916	14.615	16.534	18.696	21.126
11.436	12.300	13.233	13.727	14.240	15.327	16.499	19.123	22.163	25.678	29.732
13.579	14.776	16.085	16.786	17.519	19.086	20.799	24.712	29.369	34.895	41.435
15.937	17.549	19.337	20.304	21.321	23.521	25.959	31.643	38.593	47.062	57.352
18.531	20.655	23.045	24.349	25.733	28.755	32.150	40.238	50.398	63.122	78.998
21.384	24.133	27.271	29.002	30.850	34.931	39.581	50.895	65.510	84.320	108.44
24.523	28.029	32.089	34.352	36.786	42.219	48.497	64.110	84.853	112.30	148.47
27.975	32.393	37.581	40.505	43.672	50.818	59.196	80.496	109.61	149.24	202.93
31.772	37.280	43.842	47.580	51.660	60.965	72.035	100.82	141.30	198.00	276.98
35.950	42.753	50.980	55.717	60.925	72.939	87.442	126.01	181.87	262.36	377.69
40.545	48.884	59.118	65.075	71.673	87.068	105.93	157.25	233.79	347.31	514.66
45.599	55.750	68.394	75.836	84.141	103.74	128.12	195.99	300.25	459.45	700.94
51.159	63.440	78.969	88.212	98.603	123.41	154.74	244.03	385.32	607.47	954.28
57.275	72.052	91.025	102.44	115.38	146.63	186.69	303.60	494.21	802.86	1298.8
64.002	81.699	104.77	118.81	134.84	174.02	225.03	377.46	633.59	1060.8	1767.4
71.403	92.503	120.44	137.63	157.41	206.34	271.03	469.06	812.00	1401.2	2404.7
79.543	104.60	138.30	159.28	183.60	244.49	326.24	582.63	1040.4	1850.6	3271.3
88.497	118.16	158.66	184.17	213.98	289.49	392.48	723.46	1332.7	2443.8	4450.0
98.347	133.33	181.87	212.79	249.21	342.60	471.98	898.09	1706.8	3226.8	6053.0
164.49	241.33	356.79	434.75	530.31	790.95	1181.9	2640.9	5873.2	12941.	28172.3
442.59	767.09	1342.0	1779.1	2360.8	4163.2	7343.9	22729.	69377.	*	*
1163.9	2400.0	4994.5	7217.7	10436.	21813.	45497.	*	*	*	*
3034.8	7471.6	18535.	29220.	46058.	*	*	*	*	*	*

Table A.5 Future value of $1 with a continuously compounded rate r for T periods: Values of e^{rT}

Period (T)	\multicolumn{10}{c}{Continuously compounded rate (r)}
	1%	2%	3%	4%	5%	6%	7%	8%	9%	10%
1	1.0101	1.0202	1.0305	1.0408	1.0513	1.0618	1.0725	1.0833	1.0942	1.1052
2	1.0202	1.0408	1.0618	1.0833	1.1052	1.1275	1.1503	1.1735	1.1972	1.2214
3	1.0305	1.0618	1.0942	1.1275	1.1618	1.1972	1.2337	1.2712	1.3100	1.3499
4	1.0408	1.0833	1.1275	1.1735	1.2214	1.2712	1.3231	1.3771	1.4333	1.4918
5	1.0513	1.1052	1.1618	1.2214	1.2840	1.3499	1.4191	1.4918	1.5683	1.6487
6	1.0618	1.1275	1.1972	1.2712	1.3499	1.4333	1.5220	1.6161	1.7160	1.8221
7	1.0725	1.1503	1.2337	1.3231	1.4191	1.5220	1.6323	1.7507	1.8776	2.0138
8	1.0833	1.1735	1.2712	1.3771	1.4918	1.6161	1.7507	1.8965	2.0544	2.2255
9	1.0942	1.1972	1.3100	1.4333	1.5683	1.7160	1.8776	2.0544	2.2479	2.4596
10	1.1052	1.2214	1.3499	1.4918	1.6487	1.8221	2.0138	2.2255	2.4596	2.7183
11	1.1163	1.2461	1.3910	1.5527	1.7333	1.9348	2.1598	2.4109	2.6912	3.0042
12	1.1275	1.2712	1.4333	1.6161	1.8221	2.0544	2.3164	2.6117	2.9447	3.3201
13	1.1388	1.2969	1.4770	1.6820	1.9155	2.1815	2.4843	2.8292	3.2220	3.6693
14	1.1503	1.3231	1.5220	1.7507	2.0138	2.3164	2.6645	3.0649	3.5254	4.0552
15	1.1618	1.3499	1.5683	1.8221	2.1170	2.4596	2.8577	3.3201	3.8574	4.4817
16	1.1735	1.3771	1.6161	1.8965	2.2255	2.6117	3.0649	3.5966	4.2207	4.9530
17	1.1853	1.4049	1.6653	1.9739	2.3396	2.7732	3.2871	3.8962	4.6182	5.4739
18	1.1972	1.4333	1.7160	2.0544	2.4596	2.9447	3.5254	4.2207	5.0531	6.0496
19	1.2092	1.4623	1.7683	2.1383	2.5857	3.1268	3.7810	4.5722	5.5290	6.6859
20	1.2214	1.4918	1.8221	2.2255	2.7183	3.3201	4.0552	4.9530	6.0496	7.3891
21	1.2337	1.5220	1.8776	2.3164	2.8577	3.5254	4.3492	5.3656	6.6194	8.1662
22	1.2461	1.5527	1.9348	2.4109	3.0042	3.7434	4.6646	5.8124	7.2427	9.0250
23	1.2586	1.5841	1.9937	2.5093	3.1582	3.9749	5.0028	6.2965	7.9248	9.9742
24	1.2712	1.6161	2.0544	2.6117	3.3201	4.2207	5.3656	6.8210	8.6711	11.0232
25	1.2840	1.6487	2.1170	2.7183	3.4903	4.4817	5.7546	7.3891	9.4877	12.1825
30	1.3499	1.8221	2.4596	3.3204	4.4817	6.0496	8.1662	11.0232	14.8797	20.0855
35	1.4191	2.0138	2.8577	4.0552	5.7546	8.1662	11.5883	16.4446	23.3361	33.1155
40	1.4918	2.2255	3.3201	4.9530	7.3891	11.0232	16.4446	24.5235	36.5982	54.5982
45	1.5683	2.4596	3.8574	6.0496	9.4877	14.8797	23.3361	36.5982	57.3975	90.0171
50	1.6487	2.7183	4.4817	7.3891	12.1825	20.0855	33.1155	54.5982	90.0171	148.4132
55	1.7333	3.0042	5.2070	9.0250	15.6426	27.1126	46.9931	81.4509	141.1750	244.6919
60	1.8221	3.3201	6.0496	11.0232	20.0855	36.5982	66.6863	121.5104	221.4064	403.4288

Continuously compounded rate (r)

11%	12%	13%	14%	15%	16%	17%	18%	19%	20%	21%
1.1163	1.1275	1.1388	1.1503	1.1618	1.1735	1.1853	1.1972	1.2092	1.2214	1.2337
1.2461	1.2712	1.2969	1.3231	1.3499	1.3771	1.4049	1.4333	1.4623	1.4918	1.5220
1.3910	1.4333	1.4770	1.5220	1.5683	1.6161	1.6653	1.7160	1.7683	1.8221	1.8776
1.5527	1.6161	1.6820	1.7507	1.8221	1.8965	1.9739	2.0544	2.1383	2.2255	2.3164
1.7333	1.8221	1.9155	2.0138	2.1170	2.2255	2.3396	2.4596	2.5857	2.7183	2.8577
1.9348	2.0544	2.1815	2.3164	2.4596	2.6117	2.7732	2.9447	3.1268	3.3201	3.5254
2.1598	2.3164	2.4843	2.6645	2.8577	3.0649	3.2871	3.5254	3.7810	4.0552	4.3492
2.4109	2.6117	2.8292	3.0649	3.3201	3.5966	3.8962	4.2207	4.5722	4.9530	5.3656
2.6912	2.9447	3.2220	3.5254	3.8574	4.2207	4.6182	5.0531	5.5290	6.0496	6.6194
3.0042	3.3201	3.6693	4.0552	4.4817	4.9530	5.4739	6.0496	6.6859	7.3891	8.1662
3.3535	3.7434	4.1787	4.6646	5.2070	5.8124	6.4883	7.2427	8.0849	9.0250	10.0744
3.7434	6.2207	4.7588	5.3656	6.0496	6.8210	7.6906	8.6711	9.7767	11.0232	12.4286
4.1787	4.7588	5.4195	6.1719	7.0287	8.0045	9.1157	10.3812	11.8224	13.4637	15.3329
4.6646	5.3656	6.1719	7.0993	8.1662	9.3933	10.8049	12.4286	14.2963	16.4446	18.9158
5.2070	6.0496	7.0287	8.1662	9.4877	11.0232	12.8071	14.8797	17.2878	20.0855	23.3361
5.8124	6.8210	8.0045	9.3933	11.0232	12.9358	15.1803	17.8143	20.9052	24.5325	28.7892
6.4883	7.6906	9.1157	10.8049	12.8071	15.1803	17.9933	21.3276	25.2797	29.9641	35.5166
7.2427	8.6711	10.3812	12.4286	14.8797	17.8143	21.3276	25.5337	30.5694	36.5982	43.8160
8.0849	9.7767	11.8224	14.2963	17.2878	20.9052	25.2797	30.5694	36.9661	44.7012	54.0549
9.0250	11.0232	13.4637	16.4446	20.0855	24.5325	29.9641	36.5982	44.7012	54.5982	66.6863
10.0744	12.4286	15.3329	18.9158	23.3361	27.7892	35.5166	43.8160	54.0549	66.6863	82.2695
11.2459	14.0132	17.4615	21.7584	27.1126	33.7844	42.0980	52.4573	65.3659	81.4509	101.4940
12.5535	15.7998	19.8857	25.0281	31.5004	39.6464	49.8990	62.8028	79.0436	99.4843	125.2110
14.0132	17.8143	22.6464	28.7892	36.5982	46.5255	59.1455	75.1886	95.5835	121.5104	154.4700
15.6426	20.0855	25.7903	33.1155	42.5211	54.5982	70.1054	90.0171	115.5843	148.4132	190.5663
27.1126	36.5982	49.4024	66.6863	90.0171	121.5104	164.0219	221.4064	298.8674	403.4288	544.5719
46.9931	66.6863	94.6324	134.2898	190.5663	270.4264	383.7533	544.5719	772.7843	1096.633	1556.197
81.4509	121.5104	181.2722	270.4264	403.4288	601.8450	897.8473	1339.431	1998.196	2980.958	4447.067
141.1750	221.4064	347.2344	544.5719	854.0588	1339.431	2100.646	3294.468	5166.754	8103.084	12708.17
244.6919	403.4288	665.1416	1096.633	1808.042	2980.958	4914.769	8103.084	13359.73	22026.47	36315.50
424.1130	735.0952	1274.106	2208.348	3827.626	6634.244	11498.82	19930.37	34544.37	59874.14	103777.0
735.0952	1339.431	2440.602	4447.067	8103.084	14764.78	26903.19	49020.80	89321.72	162754.8	296558.6

Table A.5 (*continued*) Future value of $1 with a continuously compounded rate r for T periods: Values of e^{rT}

Continuously compounded rate (r)

Period (T)	22%	23%	24%	25%	26%	27%	28%
1	1.2461	1.2586	1.2712	1.2840	1.2969	1.3100	1.3231
2	1.5527	1.5841	1.6161	1.6487	1.6820	1.7160	1.7507
3	1.9348	1.9937	2.0544	2.1170	2.1815	2.2479	2.3164
4	2.4109	2.5093	2.6117	2.7183	2.8292	2.9447	3.0649
5	3.0042	3.1582	3.3201	3.4903	3.6693	3.8574	4.0552
6	3.7434	3.9749	4.2207	4.4817	4.7588	5.0531	5.3656
7	4.6646	5.0028	5.3656	5.7546	6.1719	6.6194	7.0993
8	5.8124	6.2965	6.8210	7.3891	8.0045	8.6711	9.3933
9	7.2427	7.9248	8.6711	9.4877	10.3812	11.3589	12.4286
10	9.0250	9.9742	11.0232	12.1825	13.4637	14.8797	16.4446
11	11.2459	12.5535	14.0132	15.6426	17.4615	19.4919	21.7584
12	14.0132	15.7998	17.8143	20.0855	22.6464	25.5337	28.7892
13	17.4615	19.8857	22.6464	25.7903	29.3708	33.4483	38.0918
14	21.7584	25.0281	28.7892	33.1155	38.0918	43.8160	50.4004
15	27.1126	31.5004	36.5982	42.5211	49.4024	57.3975	66.6863
16	33.7844	39.6464	46.5255	54.5982	64.0715	75.1886	88.2347
17	42.0980	49.8990	59.1455	70.1054	83.0963	98.4944	116.7459
18	52.4573	62.8028	75.1886	90.0171	107.7701	129.0242	154.4700
19	65.3659	79.0436	95.5835	115.5843	139.7702	169.0171	204.3839
20	81.4509	99.4843	121.5104	148.4132	181.2722	221.4064	270.4264
21	101.4940	125.2110	154.4700	190.5663	235.0974	290.0345	357.8092
22	126.4694	157.5905	196.3699	244.6919	304.9049	379.9349	473.4281
23	157.5905	198.3434	249.6350	314.1907	395.4404	497.7013	626.4068
24	196.3699	249.6350	317.3483	403.4288	512.8585	651.9709	828.8175
25	244.6919	314.1907	403.4288	518.0128	665.1416	854.0588	1096.633
30	735.0952	992.2747	1339.431	1808.042	2440.602	3294.468	4447.067
35	2208.348	3133.795	4447.067	6310.688	8955.293	12708.17	18033.74
40	6634.244	9897.129	14764.78	22026.47	32859.63	49020.80	73130.44
45	19930.37	31257.04	49020.80	76879.92	120571.7	189094.1	296558.6
50	59874.14	98715.77	162754.8	268337.3	442413.4	729416.4	1202604
55	179871.9	311763.4	540364.9	936589.2	1623346	2813669	4876801
60	540364.9	984609.1	1794075	3269017	5956538	10853520	19776403

Table A.6 Present value of $1 with a continuous discount rate r for T periods: Values of e^{-rT}

Period (T)	Continuous discount rate (r)						
	1%	2%	3%	4%	5%	6%	7%
1	0.9900	0.9802	0.9704	0.9608	0.9512	0.9418	0.9324
2	0.9802	0.9608	0.9418	0.9231	0.9048	0.8869	0.8694
3	0.9704	0.9418	0.9139	0.8869	0.8607	0.8353	0.8106
4	0.9608	0.9231	0.8869	0.8521	0.8187	0.7866	0.7558
5	0.9512	0.9048	0.8607	0.8187	0.7788	0.7408	0.7047
6	0.9418	0.8869	0.8353	0.7866	0.7408	0.6977	0.6570
7	0.9324	0.8694	0.8106	0.7558	0.7047	0.6570	0.6126
8	0.9231	0.8521	0.7866	0.7261	0.6703	0.6188	0.5712
9	0.9139	0.8353	0.7634	0.6977	0.6376	0.5827	0.5326
10	0.9048	0.8187	0.7408	0.6703	0.6065	0.5488	0.4966
11	0.8958	0.8025	0.7189	0.6440	0.5769	0.5169	0.4630
12	0.8869	0.7866	0.6977	0.6188	0.5488	0.4868	0.4317
13	0.8781	0.7711	0.6771	0.5945	0.5220	0.4584	0.4025
14	0.8694	0.7558	0.6570	0.5712	0.4966	0.4317	0.3753
15	0.8607	0.7408	0.6376	0.5488	0.4724	0.4066	0.3499
16	0.8521	0.7261	0.6188	0.5273	0.4493	0.3829	0.3263
17	0.8437	0.7118	0.6005	0.5066	0.4274	0.3606	0.3042
18	0.8353	0.6977	0.5827	0.4868	0.4066	0.3396	0.2837
19	0.8270	0.6839	0.5655	0.4677	0.3867	0.3198	0.2645
20	0.8187	0.6703	0.5488	0.4493	0.3679	0.3012	0.2466
21	0.8106	0.6570	0.5326	0.4317	0.3499	0.2837	0.2299
22	0.8025	0.6440	0.5169	0.4148	0.3329	0.2671	0.2144
23	0.7945	0.6313	0.5016	0.3985	0.3166	0.2516	0.1999
24	0.7866	0.6188	0.4868	0.3829	0.3012	0.2369	0.1864
25	0.7788	0.6065	0.4724	0.3679	0.2865	0.2231	0.1738
30	0.7408	0.5488	0.4066	0.3012	0.2231	0.1653	0.1225
35	0.7047	0.4966	0.3499	0.2466	0.1738	0.1225	0.0863
40	0.6703	0.4493	0.3012	0.2019	0.1353	0.0907	0.0608
45	0.6376	0.4066	0.2592	0.1653	0.1054	0.0672	0.0429
50	0.6065	0.3679	0.2231	0.1353	0.0821	0.0498	0.0302
55	0.5769	0.3329	0.1920	0.1108	0.0639	0.0369	0.0213
60	0.5488	0.3012	0.1653	0.0907	0.0498	0.0273	0.0150

Table A.6 (*continued*) Present value of $1 with a continuous discount rate r for T periods: Values of e^{-rT}

Continuous discount rate (r)

Period (T)	8%	9%	10%	11%	12%	13%	14%	15%	16%	17%
1	0.9231	0.9139	0.9048	0.8958	0.8869	0.8781	0.8694	0.8607	0.8521	0.8437
2	0.8521	0.8353	0.8187	0.8025	0.7866	0.7711	0.7558	0.7408	0.7261	0.7118
3	0.7866	0.7634	0.7408	0.7189	0.6977	0.6771	0.6570	0.6376	0.6188	0.6005
4	0.7261	0.6977	0.6703	0.6440	0.6188	0.5945	0.5712	0.5488	0.5273	0.5066
5	0.6703	0.6376	0.6065	0.5769	0.5488	0.5220	0.4966	0.4724	0.4493	0.4274
6	0.6188	0.5827	0.5488	0.5169	0.4868	0.4584	0.4317	0.4066	0.3829	0.3606
7	0.5712	0.5326	0.4966	0.4630	0.4317	0.4025	0.3753	0.3499	0.3263	0.3042
8	0.5273	0.4868	0.4493	0.4148	0.3829	0.3535	0.3263	0.3012	0.2780	0.2567
9	0.4868	0.4449	0.4066	0.3716	0.3396	0.3104	0.2837	0.2592	0.2369	0.2165
10	0.4493	0.4066	0.3679	0.3329	0.3012	0.2725	0.2466	0.2231	0.2019	0.1827
11	0.4148	0.3716	0.3329	0.2982	0.2671	0.2393	0.2144	0.1920	0.1720	0.1541
12	0.3829	0.3396	0.3012	0.2671	0.2369	0.2101	0.1864	0.1653	0.1466	0.1300
13	0.3535	0.3104	0.2725	0.2393	0.2101	0.1845	0.1620	0.1423	0.1249	0.1097
14	0.3263	0.2837	0.2466	0.2144	0.1864	0.1620	0.1409	0.1225	0.1065	0.0926
15	0.3012	0.2592	0.2231	0.1920	0.1653	0.1423	0.1225	0.1054	0.0907	0.0781
16	0.2780	0.2369	0.2019	0.1720	0.1466	0.1249	0.1065	0.0907	0.0773	0.0659
17	0.2567	0.2165	0.1827	0.1541	0.1300	0.1097	0.0926	0.0781	0.0659	0.0556
18	0.2369	0.1979	0.1653	0.1381	0.1153	0.0963	0.0805	0.0672	0.0561	0.0469
19	0.2187	0.1809	0.1496	0.1237	0.1023	0.0846	0.0699	0.0578	0.0478	0.0396
20	0.2019	0.1653	0.1353	0.1108	0.0907	0.0743	0.0608	0.0498	0.0408	0.0334
21	0.1864	0.1511	0.1225	0.0993	0.0805	0.0652	0.0529	0.0429	0.0347	0.0282
22	0.1720	0.1381	0.1108	0.0889	0.0714	0.0573	0.0460	0.0369	0.0296	0.0238
23	0.1588	0.1262	0.1003	0.0797	0.0633	0.0503	0.0400	0.0317	0.0252	0.0200
24	0.1466	0.1153	0.0907	0.0714	0.0561	0.0442	0.0347	0.0273	0.0215	0.0169
25	0.1353	0.1054	0.0821	0.0639	0.0498	0.0388	0.0302	0.0235	0.0183	0.0143
30	0.0907	0.0672	0.0498	0.0369	0.0273	0.0202	0.0150	0.0111	0.0082	0.0061
35	0.0608	0.0429	0.0302	0.0213	0.0150	0.0106	0.0074	0.0052	0.0037	0.0026
40	0.0408	0.0273	0.0183	0.0123	0.0082	0.0055	0.0037	0.0025	0.0017	0.0011
45	0.0273	0.0174	0.0111	0.0071	0.0045	0.0029	0.0018	0.0012	0.0007	0.0005
50	0.0183	0.0111	0.0067	0.0041	0.0025	0.0015	0.0009	0.0006	0.0003	0.0002
55	0.0123	0.0071	0.0041	0.0024	0.0014	0.0008	0.0005	0.0003	0.0002	0.0001
60	0.0082	0.0045	0.0025	0.0014	0.0007	0.0004	0.0002	0.0001	0.0001	0.0000

				Continuous discount rate (r)						
18%	19%	20%	21%	22%	23%	24%	25%	26%	27%	28%
0.8353	0.8270	0.8187	0.8106	0.0825	0.7945	0.7866	0.7788	0.7711	0.7634	0.7558
0.6977	0.6839	0.6703	0.6570	0.6440	0.6313	0.6188	0.6065	0.5945	0.5827	0.5712
0.5827	0.5655	0.5488	0.5326	0.5169	0.5016	0.4868	0.4724	0.4584	0.4449	0.4317
0.4868	0.4677	0.4493	0.4317	0.4148	0.3985	0.3829	0.3679	0.3535	0.3396	0.3263
0.4066	0.3867	0.3679	0.3499	0.3329	0.3166	0.3012	0.2865	0.2725	0.2592	0.2466
0.3396	0.3198	0.3012	0.2837	0.2671	0.2516	0.2369	0.2231	0.2101	0.1979	0.1864
0.2837	0.2645	0.2466	0.2299	0.2144	0.1999	0.1864	0.1738	0.1620	0.1511	0.1409
0.2369	0.2187	0.2019	0.1864	0.1720	0.1588	0.1466	0.1353	0.1249	0.1153	0.1065
0.1979	0.1809	0.1653	0.1511	0.1381	0.1262	0.1153	0.1054	0.0963	0.0880	0.0805
0.1653	0.1496	0.1353	0.1225	0.1108	0.1003	0.0907	0.0821	0.0743	0.0672	0.0608
0.1381	0.1237	0.1108	0.0993	0.0889	0.0797	0.0714	0.0639	0.0573	0.0513	0.0460
0.1153	0.1023	0.0907	0.0805	0.0714	0.0633	0.0561	0.0498	0.0442	0.0392	0.0347
0.0963	0.0846	0.0743	0.0652	0.0573	0.0503	0.0442	0.0388	0.0340	0.0299	0.0263
0.0805	0.0699	0.0608	0.0529	0.0460	0.0400	0.0347	0.0302	0.0263	0.0228	0.0198
0.0672	0.0578	0.0498	0.0429	0.0369	0.0317	0.0273	0.0235	0.0202	0.0174	0.0150
0.0561	0.0478	0.0408	0.0347	0.0296	0.0252	0.0215	0.0183	0.0156	0.0133	0.0113
0.0469	0.0396	0.0334	0.0282	0.0238	0.0200	0.0169	0.0143	0.0120	0.0102	0.0086
0.0392	0.0327	0.0273	0.0228	0.0191	0.0159	0.0133	0.0111	0.0093	0.0078	0.0065
0.0327	0.0271	0.0224	0.0185	0.0153	0.0127	0.0105	0.0087	0.0072	0.0059	0.0049
0.0273	0.0224	0.0183	0.0150	0.0123	0.0101	0.0082	0.0067	0.0055	0.0045	0.0037
0.0228	0.0185	0.0150	0.0122	0.0099	0.0080	0.0065	0.0052	0.0043	0.0034	0.0028
0.0191	0.0153	0.0123	0.0099	0.0079	0.0063	0.0051	0.0041	0.0033	0.0026	0.0021
0.0159	0.0127	0.0101	0.0080	0.0063	0.0050	0.0040	0.0032	0.0025	0.0020	0.0016
0.0133	0.0105	0.0082	0.0065	0.0051	0.0040	0.0032	0.0025	0.0019	0.0015	0.0012
0.0111	0.0087	0.0067	0.0052	0.0041	0.0032	0.0025	0.0019	0.0015	0.0012	0.0009
0.0045	0.0033	0.0025	0.0018	0.0014	0.0010	0.0007	0.0006	0.0004	0.0003	0.0002
0.0018	0.0013	0.0009	0.0006	0.0005	0.0003	0.0002	0.0002	0.0001	0.0001	0.0001
0.0007	0.0005	0.0003	0.0002	0.0002	0.0001	0.0001	0.0000	0.0000	0.0000	0.0000
0.0003	0.0002	0.0001	0.0001	0.0001	0.0000	0.0000	0.0000	0.0000	0.0000	0.0000
0.0001	0.0001	0.0000	0.0000	0.0000	0.0000	0.0000	0.0000	0.0000	0.0000	0.0000
0.0001	0.0000	0.0000	0.0000	0.0000	0.0000	0.0000	0.0000	0.0000	0.0000	0.0000
0.0000	0.0000	0.0000	0.0000	0.0000	0.0000	0.0000	0.0000	0.0000	0.0000	0.0000

Table A.6. (*concluded*) Present value of $1 with a continuous discount rate r for T periods: Values of e^{-rT}

Period (T)	Continuous discount rate (r)						
	29%	30%	31%	32%	33%	34%	35%
1	0.7483	0.7408	0.7334	0.7261	0.7189	0.7188	0.7047
2	0.5599	0.5488	0.5379	0.5273	0.5169	0.5066	0.4966
3	0.4190	0.4066	0.3946	0.3829	0.3716	0.3606	0.3499
4	0.3135	0.3012	0.2894	0.2780	0.2671	0.2567	0.2466
5	0.2346	0.2231	0.2122	0.2019	0.1920	0.1827	0.1738
6	0.1755	0.1653	0.1557	0.1466	0.1381	0.1300	0.1225
7	0.1313	0.1225	0.1142	0.1065	0.0993	0.0926	0.0863
8	0.0983	0.0907	0.0837	0.0773	0.0714	0.0659	0.0608
9	0.0735	0.0672	0.0614	0.0561	0.0513	0.0469	0.0429
10	0.0550	0.0498	0.0450	0.0408	0.0369	0.0334	0.0302
11	0.0412	0.0369	0.0330	0.0296	0.0265	0.0238	0.0213
12	0.0308	0.0273	0.0242	0.0215	0.0191	0.0169	0.0150
13	0.0231	0.0202	0.0178	0.0156	0.0137	0.0120	0.0106
14	0.0172	0.0150	0.0130	0.0113	0.0099	0.0086	0.0074
15	0.0129	0.0111	0.0096	0.0082	0.0071	0.0061	0.0052
16	0.0097	0.0082	0.0070	0.0060	0.0051	0.0043	0.0037
17	0.0072	0.0061	0.0051	0.0043	0.0037	0.0031	0.0026
18	0.0054	0.0045	0.0038	0.0032	0.0026	0.0022	0.0018
19	0.0040	0.0033	0.0028	0.0023	0.0019	0.0016	0.0013
20	0.0030	0.0025	0.0020	0.0017	0.0014	0.0011	0.0009
21	0.0023	0.0018	0.0015	0.0012	0.0010	0.0008	0.0006
22	0.0017	0.0014	0.0011	0.0009	0.0007	0.0006	0.0005
23	0.0013	0.0010	0.0008	0.0006	0.0005	0.0004	0.0003
24	0.0009	0.0007	0.0006	0.0005	0.0004	0.0003	0.0002
25	0.0007	0.0006	0.0004	0.0003	0.0003	0.0002	0.0002
30	0.0002	0.0001	0.0001	0.0001	0.0001	0.0000	0.0000
35	0.0000	0.0000	0.0000	0.0000	0.0000	0.0000	0.0000
40	0.0000	0.0000	0.0000	0.0000	0.0000	0.0000	0.0000
45	0.0000	0.0000	0.0000	0.0000	0.0000	0.0000	0.0000
50	0.0000	0.0000	0.0000	0.0000	0.0000	0.0000	0.0000
55	0.0000	0.0000	0.0000	0.0000	0.0000	0.0000	0.0000
60	0.0000	0.0000	0.0000	0.0000	0.0000	0.0000	0.0000

Chapter 2

2.1   Total assets = $128,000
Common stock = $107,000

2.2 Common stock = $110,000,000
         RE = $ 22,000,000

2.6 *a.* $400,000

    b. $300,000

    c. $180,000

    d. $380,000

2.7 Total cash flow to investors = ($5,000)

Chapter 3

3.1 $65,000

3.2 $73,600

3.9 *a.* $11 million

    b. *ii.* $11 million − $5 million × 1.1

         = $5.5 million

Chapter 4

4.1 *a.* $1,402.55

    b. $1,610.51

    c. $1,967.15

4.3 $92.30

4.5 $246,978.55

4.7 *a.* $PV_1 = \$10,000$ $PV_2 = \$20,000$

    b. $PV_1 = \$9,090.91$ $PV_2 = \$12,418.43$

    c. $PV_1 = \$8,333.33$ $PV_2 = \$8,037.55$

    d. $r = 18,921\%$

4.9 $6,714.61

    APR = 240%

    EAR = 791.61%

4.13 *a.* $PV = \$931.10$

     b. $NPV = \$ 31.10$

     c. $NPV = -\$ 18.90$

4.15 *a.* NPV = Profit = −$2,148.70

     b. $r = 8.012\%$

4.16 *a.* $1.259.71

     b. $1,265.32

     c. $1,270.24

     d. $1,271.25

4.19 P = $133.75

4.21 $PV_7 = \$918.79$

4.23 PV = $16,834.88

4.25 $r = 9.0648\%$

4.28 $c = \$2.691.18$

4.30 $T = 139$ months

4.31 PV = $3,730.65

4.33 Payment = $2,544.80

4.37   Engineer NPV = $352,533
      Accountant NPV = $345,958

Chapter 5

5.1 *a.* $943.40

    b. 917.43

    c. $900.90

    d. $869.57

5.3 P = $750.76

5.7 P = $1,072.78

5.9 P = $75

5.11 $r = 14\%$

5.13 $1,000,000

5.15 P = $23.75

Chapter 6

6.1   *a.*   Payback for A = 1.5 years
            Payback for B = 1.53 years

       b. NPV_A = \$752.07
            NPV_B = \$330.58

6.2   *a.*   56.25%

6.4   IRR = 10%

6.5   For Project A: IRR_1 = 0%
                   IRR_2 = 100%
     For Project B: IRR = 36.1944%

6.7   *a.* IRR_S = 100%; IRR_B = 50%

       e.   IRR = 49.49%

       g. NPV_S = \$82; NPV_B = \$3,636

6.9   *a.*   NPV contract   = \$8.383 million
            NPV subcontract = \$5.293 million
            NPV incremental = −\$3.09 million

       b. IRR_1 = 21.13%; IRR_2 = 78.87%

Chapter 7

7.2 $E(\text{Salary})$ = \$295,000
            PV = \$1,594,825.68

7.4   NPVGO = \$2.00
            P_O = \$18.67

7.8   NPV = \$21,568.55

7.9   PV = \$5,250,000

7.12   Headache only: NPV = \$278,668
          Headache and arthritis: NPV = −\$1,804,421

7.15   Bang EAC = \$47,456
          IOU EAC = \$49,592

7.17   Tamper A EAC = \$2,078.17
          Tamper B EAC = \$1,908.20

Chapter 8

8.3   336

Chapter 9

9.1   *a.*   \$1 per share

       b.   \$1,500

       c.   8.11%

9.3   15.865%

9.5 $E(R)$ = 14.59%

9.7   *b.*   8.49%

9.9   *a.* $E(R)$ = 5.6%

       b.   Standard deviation = 3.137%

9.10   *a.* $\bar{R}_M$ = 0.153

       b. $\bar{R}_T$ = 0.0628

9.12   *a.* $\bar{R}_S$ = 13.368%; $\bar{R}_M$ = 5.642%

       b. σ_S = 0.309118; σ_M = 0.204243

Chapter 10

10.2   *a.* $\bar{R}_p$ = 0.16

       b. σ_p = 0.3704

10.4   *a.* $\bar{R}_L$ = 0.20; σ = 0.2324

       b. $\bar{R}_U$ = 0.10; σ = 0

10.8   *b.* $E(R)$ = 7.5%

10.15   *a.* $E(R_p)$ = 10%

       b. β_p = 0.6

10.18 $E(R_M) - R_f$ = 15%
          $E(R_p) - R_f$ = 20%
               β_p = 1.33
             $\sigma(R_m)$ = 3%
             $E(R_S)$ = 10%

10.20   *a.* $\bar{R}_i$ = 6.6% + β_i(6.8%)

       b. β_S = 1.1488; $\bar{R}_S$ = 14.41%

10.23   *a.* $\sigma(R_A)$ = 0.0980; β_A = 0.784;
              β_B = 0.24

       b. R_p = 0.083; σ_p = 0.0947

       c. β_p = 0.621

Chapter 11

11.3   *a.* M = 0.372

       b.   Unsystematic risk = 0.06

       c. R = 10.432%

11.4   *a.* R_A = 10.5 + 1.2 × $(R_M - 14.2)$ + ε_A
            R_B = 13.0 + 0.98 × $(R_M - 14.2)$ + ε_B
            R_C = 15.7 + 1.37 × $(R_M - 14.2)$ + ε_C

       b. R_p = 12.925 + 1.1435 × $(R_M - 14.2)$ +
              $0.30\varepsilon_A + 0.45\varepsilon_B + 0.25\varepsilon_C$

       c. R_p = 13.8398%

11.7   *a.* σ_A^2 = 536; σ_B^2 = 296; σ_C^2 = 2,600

       b. σ_A^2 = 36; σ_B^2 = 196; σ_C^2 = 100

Chapter 12

12.2   *a.* $\bar{R}_T$ = 0.01633; β_T = 1.14036

12.4 *b.* *i.* $\bar{R}_M = 0.18$
    iii. $\sigma_M = 0.01265$
  d. *i.* $\bar{R}_J = 0.2$
    ii. $\sigma_J^2 = 0.00048$
  e. Corr $(R_M, R_J) = 0.635$
  f. $\beta_J = 1.1$

Chapter 14

14.1 Common shares   = $51,500
           Total = $151,500
  Market/Book ratio = 0.825
14.2 Common shares   = $51,500
           Total = $146,500

Chapter 15

15.1 *a.* $100,000
  b. $S = V - \$25,000$
  c. Costs: Nadus = $20,000
           Logis = $0.20 \times (V - \$25,000)$
      Returns: Nadus = $70,000
           Logis = $69,400
  f. $V = \$100,000$
15.3 12.5%
15.7 *a.* 18%
  b. $r_s = 20\%$
15.9 *a.* Value = $300 million
  b. Value = $300 million
  c. r_S 10.14%
15.12 *a.* $V_U = \$1,500,000$
  b. $270,000
15.13 $2,900,000
15.15 *a.* $V = \$7,000,000$

Chapter 16

16.7 *a.* Total cash flow to stakeholders:
      Equity plan = $1,260,000
        Debt plan = $1,638,000
  b.   Taxes (Debt) = $1,362,000
     Taxes (Equity) = $1,740,000
  c. $V_U = \$ 6,300,000$
     $V_L = \$11,700,000$
  d. Total cash flow to stakeholders:
      Equity plan = $1,440,000
        Debt plan = $1,399,500

16.9 *a.* $V = \$15,000$
  b. *i.* $V = 15,000$
    ii. $B = \$7,500$
    iii. $S = \$7,500$
  c. *i.* $r_s = 30\%$
    ii. $r_o = 20\%$
  d. *i.* $V_u = \$9,000$; $V_L = \$12,000$
  e. *i.* $V_L = \$9,000$
    ii. $V_L = \$6,500$
16.12 *a.* Debt/Equity range: ⅞ to 2
  b. Equilibrium interest rate = 8.57%
    Debt/Equity = 0.667

Chapter 17

17.1 *a.* $r_s = 17.361$
  b. $r_B = 10\%$, pre-tax
    After-tax cost of debt = 6.6%
  c. 13.77%
17.2 *a.* *i.* WACC = .102
    ii. WACC = .1155
    iii. WACC = .102
17.3 $\beta_S = 1.21$; $r_S = 17.293\%$
  $V = \$84,000,000$; WACC = 14.238%
  NPV = $3.222 million
17.6 *a.* $I = \$343,052$
  b. *B/C* NPV = $11,968.66
    APV = $37,522
  c. $I = \$403,272.87$

Chapter 18

18.4 *a.* $P = \$15$
  b. Each year you receive $4,613.37
18.5 *a.* Value = $1,412,000
  b. Ex-dividend price = $138
  c. *ii.* P = $136.95
       Number of shares sold = 76.67
18.10 *a.* $P_0 = \$19.17$
  b. $P_0 = \$20.00$
18.11 *a.* 0.0891
  b. 11%

  c.

	Preferred Stock	Debt
i.	8.91%	12.00%
ii.	8.91%	7.20%
iii.	6.24%	7.20%

Chapter 19

19.3   At $40, $P = \$40.00$
At $20, $P = \$33.33$
At $10, $P = \$30.00$

19.9   *a.*   Max = $25; Min = Anything > $0
b.   3,333,333 shares
c. $M_e = \$23.68$; $R_o = \$1.32$
d.   After: $2,500; Before: $2,500

19.10 $S = \$3.33$

Chapter 20

20.5   *a.* $P = \$1,266.41$
20.6   Coupon rate = 12.4%
20.8   *a.* $V_{NC} = \$1,164.61$
b. $C = \$77.63$
c. 130.12
20.9   NPV = $17,857,143
20.10   Borrowing cost $\leq 7.46\%$

Chapter 21

21.4   *a.* $14
b.   0
21.5   *a.*   0
b. $7
21.12 $0.5974
21.14 $C = \$1.61$
21.15 $C = \$17.58$
21.17   *a.* $C = \$2.50$
b. $P = \$13.35$
21.18 $C = \$3.87$

Chapter 22

22.4   *a.* $1,750
b. $514.29
c.   *i.* $3,640
iii. $5,440/3 = \$1,813.33$
iv.   Gain = $13.33
d. $20
22.6 $2.92
22.7   *a.* $2
b. $10
22.9   *a.* $1,040
22.11 $333.33

Chapter 23

23.2   Lease vs. buy NPV = $12,485
23.4 $L = \$165,665.67$
23.6   Min L = $147,018; Max L = $158,263
23.8   *a.* $L = \$15.98$
c. $L = \$16.22$
23.9   *a.*   Lease vs. buy NPV = −$2,748
b. $17,748

Chapter 24

24.3   *a.*   *i.* $6.10
ii. $6.00
b.   *i.* $5.98
ii. $6.00
24.7   *a.* $C = \$32,548.91$
24.9   *a.* $A = \$892.86$; $B = \$635.52$; $C = \$360.61$
b. $A = \$877.19$; $B = \$592.08$; $C = \$307.51$
c. $A = 1.755\%$; $B = 6.835\%$; $C = 14.725\%$
24.11   4.2399 years
24.13   3.6730 years
24.14   *a.*   2.943 years
b.   2.752 years
24.15   *a.*   3.327 years
b.   2.434 years

Chapter 25

25.2   *a.*   5.26%
25.4   *a.*   7.14%
b.   Increase dividend payout ratio to $d = 1$.

Chapter 26

26.2   Total sources = $82,325
26.3   Total sources = $646,000
26.10   *a.* $S = \$42,857$
b.   January = $44,143
February = $66,000
March = $76,000

Chapter 27

27.3 $2,631.62
27.4   *a.*   Retain $243,193 in cash.
b.   17 times

27.5 $Z^* = \$34,536$
$H = \$63,608$

27.6 Reduction in float = \$6,750,000
Cost of lockbox = \$107,375

27.7 $N = 33.43$

27.8 Net float = \$45,000

Chapter 28

28.1 PV(Old) = \$26,948.12
$T = 50$ days (for customers not taking the discount)

28.2 \$1,232,876.71

28.3 PV(New) = \$29,110,225.07

28.4 *a.* NPV(Credit) = \$3,029.13
b. 99.57%

28.7 Accounts receivable = \$384,247

Chapter 29

29.3 *a.* \$3,500
b. \$1
c. \$17.50

29.5 *a.* \$7,500,000
b. V = \$27,500,000
c. Cash: \$15,000,000
Stock: \$15,625,000

29.6 $r = 10.25\%$

29.7 NPV = $-\$21.2$

29.8 *a.* Prob (Joint value = \$200,000) = 0.01
Prob (Joint value = \$600,000) = 0.40
b. Prob (Debt value = \$300,000) = 0.08
Prob (Debt value = \$400,000) = 0.91
Prob (Stock value = \$0) = 0.25
c. Value of each company = \$290,000
d. Total debt value before merger = \$380,000
Total debt value after merger = \$390,000

Chapter 31

31.1 *a.* In direct terms, \$1.9886/£
In indirect terms, DM \$1.2882/\$
e. £0.3903/DM
¥76.6261/SF

31.3 *a.* Investment in U.K.: \$5,150,843.75
Investment in Canada: \$5,150,000
b. \$1.57/£

31.4 *b.* $E[\$/DM(1)] = \$0.525/DM$
$E[\$/DM(3)] = \$0.5788/DM$
NPV   = \$17,582

AAR Average accounting return.

ACRS Accelerated cost recovery system.

APT Arbitrage pricing theory.

Absolute priority rule (APR) Establishes priority of claims under liquidation.

Accounting insolvency Total liabilities exceed total assets. A firm with negative net worth is insolvent on the books.

Accounting liquidity The ease and quickness with which assets can be converted to cash.

Accounts payable Money the firm owes to suppliers.

Accounts receivable Money owed to the firm by customers.

Accounts receivable financing A secured short-term loan that involves either the assigning of receivables or the factoring of receivables. Under assignment, the lender has a lien on the receivables and recourse to the borrower. Factoring involves the sale of accounts receivable. Then the purchaser, called the *factor,* must collect on the receivables.

Accounts receivable turnover Credit sales divided by average accounts receivable.

Additions to net working capital Component of cash flow of firm, along with operating cash flow and capital spending.

Adjusted present value (APV) Base case net present value of a project's operating cash flows plus present value of any financing benefits.

Advance commitment A promise to sell an asset before the seller has lined up purchase of the asset. This seller can offset risk by purchasing a futures contract to fix the sales price.

Agency costs Costs of conflicts of interest among stockholders, bondholders, and managers. Agency costs are the costs of resolving these conflicts. They include the costs of providing managers with an incentive to maximize shareholder wealth and then monitoring their behavior, and the cost of protecting bondholders from shareholders. Agency costs are borne by stockholders.

Agency theory The theory of the relationship between principals and agents. It involves the nature of the costs of resolving conflicts of interest between principals and agents.

Aggregation Process in corporate financial planning whereby the smaller investment proposals of each of the firm's operational units are added up and in effect treated as a big picture.

Aging schedule A compilation of accounts receivable by the age of account.

American Depository Receipt (ADR) A security issued in the United States to represent shares of a foreign stock, enabling that stock to be traded in the United States.

American options Options contracts that may be exercised anytime up to the expiration date. A European option may be exercised only on the expiration date.

Amortization Repayment of a loan in installments.

Angels Individuals providing venture capital.

Annualized holding-period return The annual rate of return that, when compounded T times, would have given the same T-period holding return as actually occurred from period 1 to period T.

Annuity A level stream of equal dollar payments that lasts for a fixed time. An example of an annuity is the coupon part of a bond with level annual payments.

Annuity factor The term used to calculate the present value of the stream of level payments for a fixed period.

Annuity in advance An annuity with an immediate initial payment.

Annuity in arrears An annuity with a first payment one full period hence, rather than immediately. That is, the first payment occurs on date 1 rather than on date 0.

Appraisal rights Rights of shareholders of an acquired firm that allow them to demand that their shares be purchased at a fair value by the acquiring firm.

Arbitrage Buying an asset in one market at a lower price and simultaneously selling an identical asset in another market at a higher price. This is done with no cost or risk.

Arbitrage pricing theory (APT) An equilibrium asset pricing theory that is derived from a factor model by using diversification and arbitrage. It shows that the expected return on any risky asset is a linear combination of various factors.

Arithmetic average The sum of the values observed divided by the total number of observations—sometimes referred to as the *mean.*

Asset requirements A common element of a financial plan that describes projected capital spending and the proposed use of net working capital.

Assets Anything that a firm owns.

Auction market A market where all traders in a certain good meet at one place to buy or sell an asset. The NYSE is an example.

Autocorrelation The correlation of a variable with itself over successive time intervals.

Availability float Refers to the time required to clear a check through the banking system.

Average (mean) The average of the observations in a frequency distribution.

Average accounting return (AAR) The average project earnings after taxes and depreciation divided by the average book value of the investment during its life.

Average collection period Average amount of time required to collect an account receivable. Also referred to as *days sales outstanding.*

Average cost of capital A firm's required payout to the bondholders and the stockholders expressed as a percentage of capital contributed to the firm. Average cost of capital is computed by dividing the total required cost of capital by the total amount of contributed capital.

Average daily sales Annual sales divided by 365 days.

Balance sheet A statement showing a firm's accounting value on a particular date. It reflects the equation, Assets ≡ Liabilities + Stockholders' equity.

Balloon payment Large final payment, as when a loan is repaid in installments.

Banker's acceptance Agreement by a bank to pay a given sum of money at a future date.

Bankruptcy State of being unable to pay debts. Thus the ownership of the firm's assets is transferred from the stockholders to the bondholders.

Bankruptcy costs See **Financial distress costs.**

Bargain-purchase-price option Gives lessee the option to purchase the asset at a price below fair market value when the lease expires.

Basic IRR rule Accept the project if IRR is greater than the discount rate; reject the project if IRR is less than the discount rate.

Bearer bond A bond issued without record of the owner's name. Whoever holds the bond (the bearer) is the owner.

Belgian Dentist Stereotype of the traditional European investor as a professional who must report income, has a disdain for tax authorities, and likes to invest in foreign currencies.

Beta A measure of the sensitivity of a security's return to movements in an underlying factor. It is a measured systematic risk.

Best efforts underwriting An offering in which an underwriter agrees to distribute as much of the offering as possible and to return any unsold shares to the issuer.

Bidder A firm or person that has made an offer to take over another firm.

Black-Scholes call pricing equation An exact formula for the price of a call option. The formula requires five variables: the risk-free interest rate, the variance of the underlying stock, the exercise price, the price of the underlying stock, and the time to expiration.

Blanket inventory lien A secured loan that gives the lender a lien against all the borrower's inventories.

Bond A long-term debt of a firm. In common usage, the term *bond* often refers to both secured and unsecured debt.

Book cash A firm's cash balance as reported in its financial statements. Also called *ledger cash.*

Book value of equity Per-share accounting equity value of a firm. Total accounting equity divided by the number of outstanding shares.

Borrow To obtain or receive money on loan with the promise or understanding of returning it or its equivalent.

Bought deal One underwriter buys securities from an issuing firm and sells them directly to a small number of investors.

Break-even analysis Analysis of the level of sales at which a project would make zero profit.

Bubble theory (of speculative markets) Security prices sometimes move wildly above their true values.

Business failure A business that has terminated with a loss to creditors.

Business risk The risk that the firm's stockholders bear if the firm is financed only with equity.

Buying the index Purchasing the stocks in the Standard & Poor's 500 in the same proportion as the index to achieve the same return.

CAPM Capital asset pricing model.

CAR Cumulative abnormal return.

CICA Canadian Institute of Chartered Accountants.

Call option The right—but not the obligation—to buy a fixed number of shares of stock at a stated price within a specified time.

Call premium The price of a call option on common stock.

Call price of a bond Amount at which a firm has the right to repurchase its bonds or debentures before the stated maturity date. The call price is always set at equal to or more than the par value.

Call protected Describes a bond that is not allowed to be called, usually for a certain early period in the life of the bond.

Call provision A written agreement between an issuing corporation and its bondholders that gives the corporation the option to redeem the bond at a specified price before the maturity date.

Callable Refers to a bond that is subject to be repurchased at a stated call price before maturity.

Canada bond or note Debt obligations of the Government of Canada that make semiannual coupon payments and are sold at or near par value in denominations of $1,000 or more. They have original maturities of more than one year.

Capital asset pricing model (CAPM) An equilibrium asset pricing theory that shows that equilibrium rates of expected return on all risky assets are a function of their covariance with the market portfolio.

Capital budgeting Planning and managing expenditures for long-lived assets.

Capital gain The positive change in the value of an asset. A negative capital gain is a capital loss.

Capital market line The efficient set of all assets, both risky and riskless, that provides the investor with the best possible opportunities.

Capital markets Financial markets for long-term debt and for equity shares.

Capital rationing The case where funds are limited to a fixed dollar amount and must be allocated among competing projects.

Capital structure The mix of the various debt and equity capital maintained by a firm. Also called *financial structure*. The composition of a corporation's securities used to finance its investment activities; the relative proportions of short-term debt, long-term debt, and owners' equity.

Capital surplus Amounts of directly contributed equity capital in excess of the par value.

Carrying costs Costs that increase with increases in the level of investment in current assets.

Carrying value Book value.

Cash budget A forecast of cash receipts and disbursements expected by a firm in the coming year. It is a short-term financial planning tool.

Cash cow A company that pays out all earnings per share to stockholders as dividends.

Cash cycle In general, the time between cash disbursement and cash collection. In net working capital management, it can be thought of as the operating cycle less the accounts payable payment period.

Cash discount Discount given for a cash purchase. One reason a cash discount may be offered is to speed up the collection of receivables.

Cash flow Cash generated by the firm and paid to creditors and shareholders. It can be classified as (1) cash flow from operations, (2) cash flow from changes in fixed assets, and (3) cash flow from changes in net working capital.

Cash flow after interest and taxes Net income plus depreciation.

Cash flow time line Line depicting the operating activities and cash flows for a firm over a particular period.

Cash offer A public equity issue that is sold to all interested investors.

Cash transaction A transaction where exchange is immediate, as contrasted to a forward contract, which calls for future delivery of an asset at an agreed-upon price.

Cashout Refers to situation where a firm runs out of cash and cannot readily sell marketable securities.

Certificates of deposit Short-term loans to commercial banks.

Change in net working capital Difference between net working capital from one period to another.

Changes in fixed assets Component of cash flow that equals sales of fixed assets minus the acquisition of fixed assets.

Characteristic line The line relating the expected return on a security to different returns on the market.

Clearing The exchanging of checks and balancing of accounts between banks.

Clientele effect Argument that stocks attract clienteles based on dividend yield or taxes. For example, a tax clientele effect is induced by the difference in tax treatment of dividend income and capital gains income; high-tax-bracket individuals tend to prefer low-dividend yields.

Coinsurance effect Refers to the fact that the merger of two firms decreases the probability of default on either's debt.

Collateral Assets that are pledged as security for payment of debt.

Collateral trust bond A bond secured by a pledge of common stock held by the corporation.

Collection float An increase in book cash with no immediate change in bank cash, generated by checks deposited by the firm that have not cleared.

Collection policy Procedures followed by a firm in attempting to collect accounts receivable.

Commercial draft Demand for payment.

Commercial paper Short-term, unsecured promissory notes issued by corporations with a high credit standing. Their maturity ranges up to 270 days.

Common equity Book value.

Common stock Equity claims held by the "residual owners" of the firm, who are the last to receive any distribution of earnings or assets.

Compensating balance Deposit that the firm keeps with the bank in a low-interest or non-interest-bearing account to compensate banks for bank loans or services.

Competitive offer Method of selecting an investment banker for a new issue by offering the securities to the underwriter bidding highest.

Composition Voluntary arrangement to restructure a firm's debt, under which payment is reduced.

Compound interest Interest that is earned both on the initial principal and on interest earned on the initial principal in previous periods. The interest earned in one period becomes in effect part of the principal in a following period.

Compound value Value of a sum after investing it over one or more periods. Also called *future value*.

Compounding Process of reinvesting each interest payment to earn more interest. Compounding is based on the idea that interest itself becomes principal and therefore also earns interest in subsequent periods.

Concentration banking The use of geographically dispersed collection centers to speed up the collection of accounts receivable.

Conditional sales contract An arrangement whereby the firm retains legal ownership of the goods until the customer has completed payment.

Conflict between bondholders and stockholders These two groups may have interests in the corporation that conflict. Sources of conflict include dividends, dilution, distortion of investment, and underinvestment. Protective covenants work to resolve these conflicts.

Conglomerate acquisition Acquisition in which the acquired firm and the acquiring firm are not related, unlike a horizontal or vertical acquisition.

Consol A bond that carries a promise to pay a coupon forever; it has no final maturity date and therefore never matures.

Consolidation A merger in which an entirely new firm is created.

Consumer credit Credit granted to consumers. Trade credit is credit granted to other firms.

Contingent claim Claim whose value is directly dependent on, or is contingent on, the value of its underlying assets. For example, the debt and equity securities issued by a firm derive their value from the total value of the firm.

Contingent pension liability Under ERISA, the firm is liable to the plan participants for up to 30 percent of the net worth of the firm.

Continuous compounding Interest compounded continuously, every instant, rather than at fixed intervals.

Contribution margin Amount that each additional product, such as a jet engine, contributes to after–tax profit of the whole project: (Sales price − Variable cost) $\times (1 - T_c)$, where T_c is the corporate tax rate.

Control block An interest controlling 50 percent of outstanding votes plus one; thereby it may decide the fate of the firm.

Conversion premium Difference between the conversion price and the current stock price divided by the current stock price.

Conversion price The amount of par value exchangeable for one share of common stock. This term really refers to the stock price and means the dollar amount of the bond's par value that is exchangeable for one share of stock.

Conversion ratio The number of shares per $1,000 bond (or debenture) that a bondholder would receive if the bond were converted into shares of stock.

Conversion value What a convertible bond would be worth if it were immediately converted into the common stock at the current price.

Convertible bond A bond that may be converted into another form of security, typically common stock, at the option of the holder at a specified price for a specified period of time.

Corporation Form of business organization that is created as a distinct "legal person" composed of one or more actual individuals or legal entities. Primary advantages of a corporation include limited liability, ease of ownership transfer, and perpetual succession.

Correlation A standardized statistical measure of the dependence of two random variables. It is defined as the covariance divided by the standard deviations of two variables.

Cost of equity The required return on the company's common stock in capital markets. It is also called the *equityholders' required rate of return* because it is what equityholders can expect to obtain in a capital market. It is a cost from a firm's perspective.

Coupon The stated interest on a debt instrument.

Covariance A statistical measure of the degree to which random variables move together.

Credit analysis The process of determining whether a credit applicant meets the firm's standards and what amount of credit the applicant should receive.

Credit instrument Device by which a firm offers credit, such as an invoice, a promissory note, or a conditional sales contract.

Credit periods Time allowed a credit purchaser to remit the full payment for credit purchases.

Credit scoring Determining the probability of default when granting customers credit.

Creditor Person or institution that holds the debt issued by a firm or individual.

Cross rate The exchange rate between two foreign currencies, neither of which is generally the U.S. dollar.

Crown jewels An antitakeover tactic in which major assets—the crown jewels—are sold by a firm when faced with a takeover threat.

Cum dividend With dividend.

Cumulative abnormal return (CAR) Sum of differences between the expected return on a stock and the actual return that comes from the release of news to the market.

Cumulative dividend Dividend on preferred stock that takes priority over dividend payments on common stock. Dividends may not be paid on the common stock until all past dividends on the preferred stock have been paid.

Cumulative probability The probability that a drawing from the standardized normal distribution will be below a particular value.

Cumulative voting A procedure whereby a shareholder may cast all of his or her votes for one member of the board of directors.

Current asset Asset that is in the form of cash or that is expected to be converted into cash in the next 12 months, such as inventory.

Current liabilities Obligations that are expected to require cash payment within one year or the operating period.

Current ratio Total current assets divided by total current liabilities. Used to measure short-term solvency of a firm.

Date of payment Date that dividend checks are mailed.

Date of record Date on which holders of record in a firm's stock ledger are designated as the recipients of either dividends or stock rights.

Dates convention Treating cash flows as being received on exact dates—date 0, date 1, and so forth—as opposed to the end-of-year convention.

Days in receivables Average collection period.

Days sales outstanding Average collection period.

De facto Existing in actual fact although not by official recognition.

Dealer market A market where traders specializing in particular commodities buy and sell assets for their own account. The OTC market is an example.

Debenture An unsecured bond, usually with maturity of 15 years or more. A debt obligation backed by the general credit of the issuing corporation.

Debt Loan agreement that is a liability of the firm. An obligation to repay a specified amount at a particular time.

Debt capacity Ability to borrow. The amount a firm can borrow up to the point where the firm value no longer increases.

Debt displacement The amount of borrowing that leasing displaces. Firms that do a lot of leasing will be forced to cut back on borrowing.

Debt ratio Total debt divided by total assets.

Debt service Interest payments plus repayments of principal to creditors, that is, retirement of debt.

Decision trees A graphical representation of alternative sequential decisions and the possible outcomes of those decisions.

Declaration date Date on which the board of directors passes a resolution to pay a dividend of a specified amount to all qualified holders of record on a specified date.

Dedicated capital Total par value (number of shares issued multiplied by the par value of each share). Also called *dedicated value.*

Deed of trust Indenture.

Deep-discount bond A bond issued with a very low coupon or no coupon and selling at a price far below par value. When the bond has no coupon, it is also called a *pure-discount* or *original-issue-discount* bond.

Default risk The chance that interest or principal will not be paid on the due date and in the promised amount.

Defeasance A debt-restructuring tool that enables a firm to remove debt from its balance sheet by establishing an irrevocable trust that will generate future cash flows sufficient to service the decreased debt.

Deferred call A provision that prohibits the company from calling the bond before a certain date. During this period the bond is said to be *call protected.*

Deferred nominal life annuity A monthly fixed-dollar payment beginning at retirement age. It is nominal because the payment is fixed in dollar amount at any particular time, up to and including retirement.

Deferred taxes Noncash expense.

Deficit The amount by which a sum of money is less than the required amount; an excess of liabilities over assets, of losses over profits, or of expenditure over income.

Deliverable instrument The asset in a forward contract that will be delivered in the future at an agreed-upon price.

Denomination Face value or principal of a bond.

Depreciation A noncash expense, such as the cost of plant or equipment, charged against earnings to write off the cost of an asset during its estimated useful life.

Dilution Loss in existing shareholders' value. There are several kinds of dilution: (1) dilution of ownership, (2) dilution of market value, and (3) dilution of book value and earnings, as with warrants and convertible issues. Firms with significant amounts of warrants or convertible issues outstanding are required to report earnings on a "fully diluted" basis.

Direct lease Lease under which a lessor buys equipment from a manufacturer and leases it to a lessee.

Disbursement float A decrease in book cash but no immediate change in bank cash, generated by checks written by the firm.

Discount If a bond is selling below its face value, it is said to sell at a discount.

Discount rate Rate used to calculate the present value of future cash flows.

Discounted payback period rule An investment decision rule in which the cash flows are discounted at an interest rate and the payback rule is applied on these discounted cash flows.

Discounting Calculating the present value of a future amount. The process is the opposite of compounding.

Distribution A type of dividend paid by a firm to its owners from sources other than current or accumulated retained earnings.

Diversifiable (unique) (unsystematic) risk A risk that specifically affects a single asset or a small group of assets.

Diversification Process of combining assets so that the portfolio is always less risky than any one of the individual assets.

Dividend Payment made by a firm to its owners, either in cash or on stock. Also called the "income component" on the return of an investment in stock.

Dividend growth model A model wherein dividends are assumed to be at a constant rate in perpetuity.

Dividend payout Amount of cash paid to shareholders expressed as a percentage of earnings per share.

Dividend yield Dividends per share of common stock divided by market price per share.

Dividends per share Amount of cash paid to shareholders expressed as dollars per share.

Double-declining balance depreciation Method of accelerated depreciation.

DuPont system of financial control Highlights the fact that return on assets (ROA) can be expressed in terms of the profit margin and asset turnover.

Duration The weighted average time of an asset's cash flows. The weights are determined by present value factors.

EAC Equivalent annual cost.

EBIT Earnings before interest and taxes.

EMH Efficient market hypothesis.

Economic assumptions Economic environment in which the firm expects to reside over the life of the financial plan.

Effective annual interest rate The interest rate as if it were compounded once per time period rather than several times per period.

Efficient market hypothesis (EMH) The prices of securities fully reflect available information. Investors buying bonds and stocks in an efficient market should expect to obtain an equilibrium rate of return. Firms should expect to receive the "fair" value (present value) for the securities they sell.

Efficient set Graph representing a set of portfolios that maximize expected return at each level of portfolio risk.

End-of-year convention Treating cash flows as if they occur at the end of a year (or, alternatively, at the end of a period), as opposed to the dates convention. Under the end-of-year convention, the end of year 0 is the present, the end of year 1 occurs one period hence, and so on.

Equilibrium rate of interest The interest rate that clears the market. Also called *market-clearing interest rate*.

Equity Ownership interest of common and preferred stockholders in a corporation. Also, total assets minus total liabilities, or net worth.

Equity beta Systematic risk of a firm's stock decomposed into contributions of risk from assets and financial leverage.

Equity kicker Used to refer to warrants because they usually are issued in combination with privately placed bonds.

Equity share Ownership interest.

Equivalent annual cost (EAC) The net present value of cost divided by an annuity factor that has the same life as the investment.

Equivalent loan The amount of the loan that makes leasing equivalent to buying with debt financing in terms of debt capacity reduction.

Erosion Cash flow amount transferred to a new project from customers and sales of other products of the firm.

Eurobanks Banks that make loans and accept deposits in foreign currencies.

Eurobonds International bonds sold primarily in countries other than the country in whose currency the issue is denominated.

Eurocurrency Money deposited in a financial center outside of the country whose currency is involved.

Eurodollar A dollar deposited in a bank outside the United States.

Eurodollar CD Deposit of dollars with foreign banks.

European Currency Unit (ECU) An index of foreign exchange consisting of about 10 European currencies, originally devised in 1979.

European option An option contract that may be exercised only on the expiration date. An American option may be exercised anytime up to the expiration date.

Event study A statistical study that examines how the release of information affects prices at a particular time.

Ex-rights or ex-dividend Phrases used to indicate that a stock is selling without a recently declared right or dividend. The ex-rights or ex-dividend date is generally four business days before the date of record.

Exchange rate Price of one country's currency for another's.

Exclusionary self-tender The firm makes a tender offer for a given amount of its own stock while excluding targeted stockholders.

Ex-dividend date Date four business days before the date of record for a security. An individual purchasing stock before its ex-dividend date will receive the current dividend.

Exercise price Price at which the holder of an option can buy (in the case of a call option) or sell (in the case of a put option) the underlying stock. Also called the *striking price*.

Exercising the option The act of buying or selling the underlying asset via the option contract.

Expectations hypothesis (of interest rates) Theory that forward interest rates are unbiased estimates of expected future interest rates.

Expected return Average of possible returns weighted by their probability.

Expiration date Maturity date of an option.

Export Development Corporation (EDC) Federal Crown corporation that promotes Canadian exports by making loans to foreign purchasers.

Extension Voluntary arrangements to restructure a firm's debt, under which the payment date is postponed.

Extinguish Retire or pay off debt.

Face value The value of a bond that appears on its face. Also referred to as *par value* or *principal*.

Factor A financial institution that buys a firm's accounts receivables and collects the debt.

Factor model A model in which each stock's return is generated by common factors, called the *systematic sources of risk.*

Factoring Sale of a firm's accounts receivable to a financial institution known as a *factor.*

Fair market value Amount at which common stock would change hands between a willing buyer and a willing seller, both having knowledge of the relevant facts. Also called *market price.*

Feasible set Opportunity set.

Field warehouse financing A form of inventory loan in which a public warehouse company acts as a control agent to supervise the inventory for the lender.

Financial Accounting Standards Board (FASB) The governing body in accounting in the United States.

Financial distress Events preceding and including bankruptcy, such as violation of loan contracts.

Financial distress costs Legal and administrative costs of liquidation or reorganization (direct costs); an impaired ability to do business and an incentive toward selfish strategies such as taking large risks, underinvesting, and milking the property (indirect costs).

Financial intermediaries Institutions that provide the market function of matching borrowers and lenders or traders. Financial institutions may be categorized as depository, contractual savings, and investment-type.

Financial lease Long-term noncancelable lease, generally requiring the lessee to pay all maintenance costs.

Financial leverage Extent to which a firm relies on debt. Financial leverage is measured by the ratio of long-term debt to long-term debt plus equity.

Financial markets Markets that deal with cash flows over time, where the savings of lenders are allocated to the financing needs of borrowers.

Financial requirements In the financial plan, financing arrangements that are necessary to meet the overall corporate objective.

Financial risk The additional risk that the firm's stockholders bear when the firm is financed with debt as well as equity.

Firm commitment underwriting An underwriting in which an investment banking firm commits to buy the entire issue and assumes all financial responsibility for any unsold shares.

Firm's net value of debt Total firm value minus value of debt.

First principle of investment decision making An investment project is worth undertaking only if it increases the range of choices in the financial markets. To do this, it must be at least as desirable as what is available to shareholders in the financial markets.

Fixed asset Long-lived property owned by a firm that is used by a firm in the production of its income. Tangible fixed assets include real estate, plant, and equipment. Intangible fixed assets include patents, trademarks, and customer recognition.

Fixed costs A cost that is fixed in total for a given period of time and for given volume levels. It is not dependent on the amount of goods or services produced during the period.

Fixed-dollar obligations Conventional bonds for which the coupon rate is set as a fixed percentage of the par value.

Flat benefit formula Method used to determine a participant's benefits in a defined benefit plan by multiplying months of service by a flat monthly benefit.

Float The difference between bank cash and book cash. Float represents the net effect of checks in the process of collection, or clearing. *Positive float* means the firm's bank cash is greater than its book cash until the check's presentation. Checks written by the firm generate *disbursement float,* causing an immediate decrease in book cash but no change in bank cash. In *neutral float position,* bank cash equals book cash. Checks written by the firm represent *collection float,* which increases book cash immediately but does not immediately change bank cash. The sum of disbursement float and collection float is *net float.*

Floaters Floating-rate bonds.

Floating-rate bond A debt obligation with an adjustable coupon payment.

Flow to equity (FTE) An alternative budgeting approach. A projects' cash flow to equity holders (of the levered firm) are discounted at the cost of equity capital.

Force conversion If the conversion value of a convertible is greater than the call price, the call can be used to force conversion.

Foreign bonds An international bond issued by foreign borrowers in another nation's capital market and traditionally denominated in that nation's currency.

Foreign exchange market Market in which arrangements are made today for future exchange of major currencies; used to hedge against major swings in foreign exchange rates.

Forward contract An arrangement calling for future delivery of an asset at an agreed-upon price.

Forward exchange rate A future day's exchange rate between two major currencies.

Forward trades Agreements to buy or sell based on exchange rates established today for settlement in the future.

Frequency distribution The organization of data to show how often certain values or ranges of values occur.

Fully diluted See **Dilution.**

Funded debt Long-term debt.

Future value Value of a sum after investing it over one or more periods. Also called *compound value.*

Futures contract Obliges traders to purchase or sell an asset at an agreed-upon price on a specified future date. The long position is held by the trader who commits to purchase. The short position is held by the trader who commits to sell. Futures differ from forward contracts in their standardization, exchange trading, margin requirements, and daily settling (marking to market).

GAAP Generally Accepted Accounting Principles.

General cash offer A public issue of a security that is sold to all interest investors, rather than only to existing shareholders.

General partnership Form of business organization in which all partners agree to provide some portion of the work and cash and to share profits and losses. Each partner is liable for the debts of the partnership.

Generally Accepted Accounting Principles (GAAP) A common set of accounting concepts, standards, and procedures by which financial statements are prepared.

Geometric mean Annualized holding-period return.

Gilts British and Irish government securities.

Going-private transaction Publicly owned stock in a firm is replaced with complete equity ownership by a private group. The shares are delisted from stock exchanges and can no longer be purchased in the open market.

Golden parachutes Compensation paid to top-level management by a target firm if a takeover occurs.

Goodwill The excess of the purchase price over the sum of the fair market values of the individual assets acquired.

Greenmail Payments to potential bidders to cease unfriendly takeover attempts.

Green-shoe provision A contract provision that gives the underwriter the option to purchase additional shares at the offering price to cover overallotments.

Growing annuity A finite number of growing annual cash flows.

Growing perpetuity A constant stream of cash flows without end that is expected to rise indefinitely. For example, cash flows to the landlord of an apartment building might be expected to rise a certain percentage each year.

Growth opportunity Opportunity to invest in profitable projects.

Hedging Taking a position in two or more securities that are negatively correlated (taking opposite trading positions) to reduce risk.

High-yield bond Junk bond.

Holder of record date The date on which holders of record in a firm's stock ledger are designated as the recipients of either dividends or stock rights. Also called *date of record.*

Holding period Length of time that an individual holds a security.

Holding period return The rate of return over a given period.

Homemade dividends An individual investor can undo corporate dividend policy by reinvesting excess dividends or selling off shares of stock to receive a desired cash flow.

Homemade leverage Idea that as long as individuals borrow (and lend) on the same terms as the firm, they can duplicate the effects of corporate leverage on their own. Thus, if levered firms are priced too high, rational investors will simply borrow on personal accounts to buy shares in unlevered firms.

Homogeneous expectations Idea that all individuals have the same beliefs concerning future investments, profits, and dividends.

Horizontal acquisition Merger between two companies producing similar goods or services.

IPO Initial public offering.

IRR Internal rate of return.

Idiosyncratic risk An unsystematic risk.

Immunized Immune to interest-rate risk.

In the money Describes an option whose exercise would produce profits. *Out of the money* describes an option whose exercise would not be profitable.

Income bonds Bonds on which the payment of income is contingent on sufficient earnings. Income bonds are commonly used during the reorganization of a failed or failing business.

Income statement Financial report that summarizes a firm's performance over a specified time period.

Incremental cash flow Difference between the firm's cash flow with and without a project.

Incremental IRR IRR on the incremental investment from choosing a large project instead of a smaller project.

Indenture Written agreement between the corporate debt issuer and the lender, setting forth maturity date, interest rate, and other terms.

Independent project A project whose acceptance or rejection is independent of the acceptance or rejection of other projects.

Inflation An increase in the amount of money in circulation, resulting in a fall in its value and rise in prices.

Inflation-escalator clause A clause in a contract providing for increases or decreases in inflation based on fluctuations in the cost of living, production costs, etc.

Information content effect The rise in the stock price following the dividend signal.

In-house processing float Refers to the time it takes the receiver of a check to process the payment and deposit it in a bank for collection.

Initial public offering (IPO) The original sale of a company's securities to the public. Also called an *unseasoned new issue*.

Inside information Nonpublic knowledge about a corporation possessed by people in special positions inside a firm.

Instruments Financial securities, such as money market instruments or capital market instruments.

Interest coverage ratio Earnings before interest and taxes divided by interest expense. Used to measure a firm's ability to pay interest.

Interest on interest Interest earned on reinvestment of each interest payment on money invested.

Interest rate The price paid for borrowing money. It is the rate of exchange of present consumption forfuture consumption, or the price of current dollars in terms of future dollars.

Interest rate on debt The firm's cost of debt capital. Also called *return on the debt*.

Interest rate parity theorem The interest rate differential between two countries will be equal to the difference between the forward-exchange rate and the spot-exchange rate.

Interest rate risk The chance that a change in the interest rate will result in a change in the value of a security.

Interest subsidy A firm's deduction of the interest payments on its debt from its earnings before it calculates its tax bill under current tax law.

Internal financing Net income plus depreciation minus dividends. Internal financing comes from internally generated cash flow.

Internal rate of return (IRR) A discount rate at which the net present value of an investment is zero. The IRR is a method of evaluating capital expenditure proposals.

Inventory A current asset, composed of raw materials to be used in production, work in process, and finished goods.

Inventory loan A secured short-term loan to purchase inventory. The three basic forms are a blanket inventory lien, a trust receipt, and field warehouse financing.

Inventory turnover ratio Ratio of annual sales to average inventory that measures how quickly inventory is produced and sold.

Investment bankers Financial intermediaries who perform a variety of services, including aiding in the sale of securities, facilitating mergers and other corporate reorganizations, acting as brokers to both individual and institutional clients, and trading for their own accounts.

Investment grade bond Debt that is rated BBB and above by Standard & Poor's or Baa and above by Moody's.

Invoice Bill written by a seller of goods or services and submitted to the purchaser.

Irrelevance result The MM theorem that a firm's capital structure is irrelevant to the firm's value.

Junk bond A speculative grade bond, rated Ba or lower by Moody's, or BB or lower by Standard & Poor's, or an unrated bond. Also called a *high-yield* or *low-grade* bond.

LBO Leveraged buyout.

LIBOR See **London Interbank Offered Rate.**

Law of one price (LOP) A commodity will cost the same regardless of what currency is used to purchase it.

Lease A contractual arrangement to grant the use of specific fixed assets for a specified time in exchange for payment, usually in the form of rent. An operating lease is generally a short-term cancelable arrangement, whereas a financial, or capital, lease is a long-term noncancelable agreement.

Ledger cash A firm's cash balance as reported in its financial statements. Also called *book cash.*

Legal bankruptcy A legal proceeding for liquidating or reorganizing a business.

Lend To provide money temporarily on the condition that it or its equivalent will be returned, often with an interest fee.

Lessee One that receives the use of assets under a lease.

Lessor One that conveys the use of assets under a lease.

Letter of comment A communication to the firm from the U.S. Securities and Exchange Commission or the Ontario Securities Commission that suggests changes to a registration statement.

Level-coupon bond Bond with a stream of coupon payments that are the same throughout the life of the bond.

Leveraged buyout (LBO) Takeover of a company by using borrowed funds, usually by a group including some member of existing management.

Leveraged equity Stock in a firm that relies on financial leverage. Holders of leveraged equity face the benefits and costs of using debt.

Leveraged lease Tax-oriented leasing arrangement that involves one or more third-party lenders.

Liabilities Debts of the firm in the form of financial claims on a firm's assets.

Limited partnership Form of business organization that permits the liability of some partners to be limited by the amount of cash contributed to the partnership.

Limited-liability instrument A security, such as a call option, in which all the holder can lose is the initial amount put into it.

Line of credit A *noncommitted* line of credit is an informal agreement that allows firms to borrow up to a previously specified limit without going through the normal paperwork. A *committed* line of credit is a formal legal arrangement and usually involves a commitment fee paid by the firm to the bank.

Lintner's observations John Lintner's work (1956) suggested that dividend policy is related to a target level of dividends and the speed of adjustment of change in dividends.

Liquidating dividend Payment by a firm to its owners from capital rather than from earnings.

Liquidation Termination of the firm as a going concern. Liquidation involves selling the assets of the firm for salvage value. The proceeds, net of transaction costs, are distributed to creditors in order of established priority.

Liquidity Refers to the ease and quickness of converting assets to cash. Also called *marketability.*

Liquidity-preference hypothesis Theory that the forward rate exceeds expected future interest rates.

Lockbox Post office box set up to intercept accounts receivable payments. Lockboxes are the most widely used device to speed up collection of cash.

London Interbank Offered Rate (LIBOR) Rate the most creditworthy banks charge one another for large loans of Eurodollars overnight in the London market.

Long hedge Protecting the future cost of a purchase by purchasing a futures contract to protect against changes in the price of an asset.

Long run A period of time in which all costs are variable.

Long-term debt An obligation having a maturity of more than one year from the date it was issued. Also called *funded debt.*

Low-grade bond Junk bond.

MM Proposition I (corporate taxes) A proposition of Modigliani and Miller (MM) stating that by raising the debt-equity ratio, a firm can lower its taxes and thereby increase its total value. Capital structure does matter.

MM Proposition I (no taxes) A proposition of Modigliani and Miller (MM) stating that a firm cannot change the total value of its outstanding securities by changing its capital structure proportions. Also called an *irrelevance result.*

MM Proposition II A proposition of Modigliani and Miller (MM) stating that the cost of equity is a linear function of the firm's debt-equity ratio.

Mail float Refers to the part of the collection and disbursement process where checks are trapped in the postal system.

Make a market The obligation of a specialist to offer to buy and sell shares of assigned stocks. It is assumed that this makes the market liquid because the specialist assumes the role of a buyer for investors if they wish to sell, and assumes the role of a seller if they wish to buy.

Making delivery Refers to the seller's actually turning over to the buyer the asset agreed upon in a forward contract.

Marked to the market The daily settlement of obligations on futures positions.

Market capitalization Price per share of stock multiplied by the number of shares outstanding.

Market clearing Total demand for loans by borrowers equals total supply of loans from lenders. The market clears at the equilibrium rate of interest.

Market model A one-factor model for returns where the index that is used for the factor is an index of the returns on the whole market.

Market portfolio In concept, a value-weighted index of all securities. In practice, it is an index, such as the S&P 500, that describes the return of the entire value of the stock market, or at least the stocks that make up the index. A market portfolio represents the average investor's return.

Market price The current amount at which a security is trading in a market.

Market risk Systematic risk. This term emphasizes the fact that systematic risk influences to some extent all assets in the market.

Market value The price at which willing buyers and sellers trade a firm's assets.

Market-to-book (M/B) ratio Market price per share of common stock divided by book value per share.

Marketability Refers to the ease and quickness of converting an asset to cash. Also called *liquidity*.

Marketed claims Claims that can be bought and sold in financial markets, such as those of stockholders and bondholders.

Maturity date The date on which the last payment on a bond is due.

Mean The average of the observations in a frequency distribution.

Merger Combination of two or more companies.

Minimum variance portfolio The portfolio of risky assets with the lowest possible variance. By definition, this portfolio must also have the lowest possible standard deviation.

Money markets Financial markets for debt securities that pay off in the short term (usually less than one year).

Money purchase plan A defined benefit contribution plan in which the participant contributes some part and the firm contributes at the same or a different rate. Also called an *individual account plan.*

Mortgage securities A debt obligation secured by a mortgage on the real property of the borrower.

Multiple rates of return More than one rate of return from the same project that make the net present value of the project equal to zero. This situation arises when the IRR method is used for a project in which negative cash flows follow positive ones.

Multiples Another name for price-earnings ratios.

Mutually exclusive investments Investment decisions in which the acceptance of a project precludes the acceptance of one or more alternative projects.

NPV Net present value.

NPVGO model A model valuing the firm in which net present value of new investment opportunities is explicitly examined. NPVGO stands for net present value of growth opportunities.

Negative covenant Part of the indenture or loan agreement that limits or prohibits actions that the company may take.

Negotiated offer The issuing firm negotiates a deal with one underwriter to offer a new issue rather than taking competitive bidding.

Net cash balance Beginning cash balance plus cash receipts minus cash disbursements.

Net float Sum of disbursement float and collection float.

Net investment Gross, or total, investment minus depreciation.

Net operating losses (NOL) Losses that a firm can take advantage of to reduce taxes.

Net present value (NPV) rule The present value of future cash returns, discounted at the appropriate market interest rate, minus the present value of the cost of the investment.

Net working capital Current assets minus current liabilities.

Netting out To get or bring in as a net; to clear as profit.

Neutral flat position See **Float.**

Nominal cash flow A cash flow expressed in nominal terms if the actual dollars to be received (or paid out) are given.

Nominal interest rate Interest rate unadjusted for inflation.

Noncash items Expenses against revenue that do not directly affect cash flow, such as depreciation and deferred taxes.

Nonmarketed claims Claims that cannot be easily bought and sold in the financial markets, such as those of the government and litigants in lawsuits.

Normal annuity form The manner in which retirement benefits are paid out.

Normal distribution Symmetric bell-shaped frequency distribution that can be defined by its mean and standard deviation.

Note Unsecured debt, usually with maturity of less than 15 years.

OSC Ontario Securities Commission.

Odd lot Stock trading unit of less than 100 shares.

Off-balance-sheet financing Financing that is not shown as a liability on a company's balance sheet.

One-factor APT A special case of the arbitrage pricing theory that is derived from the one-factor model by using diversification and arbitrage. It shows the expected return on any risky asset is a linear function of a single factor. The CAPM can be expressed as one-factor APT in which a single factor is the market portfolio.

Open account A credit account for which the only formal instrument of credit is the invoice.

Operating activities Sequence of events and decisions that create the firm's cash inflows and cash outflows. These activities include buying and paying for raw materials, manufacturing and selling a product, and collecting cash.

Operating cash flow Earnings before interest and depreciation minus taxes. It measures the cash generated from operations, not counting capital spending or working capital requirements.

Operating cycle The time interval between the arrival of inventory stock and the date when cash is collected from receivables.

Operating lease Type of lease in which the period of contract is less than the life of the equipment and the lessor pays all maintenance and servicing costs.

Operating leverage The degree to which a company's costs of operation are fixed as opposed to variable. A firm with high operating costs, when compared to a firm with a low operating leverage, has relatively larger changes in EBIT with respect to a change in the sales revenue.

Opportunity cost Most valuable alternative that is given up. The rate of return used in NPV computation is an opportunity interest rate.

Opportunity (feasible) set The possible expected return; standard deviation pairs of all portfolios that can be constructed from a given set of assets. Also called a *feasible set.*

Option A right—but not an obligation—to buy or sell underlying assets at a fixed price during a specified time period.

Original-issue-discount bond A bond issued with a discount from par value. Also called a *deep-discount* or *pure-discount* bond.

Out of the money Describes an option whose exercise would not be profitable. *In the money* describes an option whose exercise would produce profits.

Oversubscribed issue Investors are not able to buy all the shares they want, so underwriters must allocate the shares among investors. This occurs when a new issue is underpriced.

Oversubscription privilege Allows shareholders to purchase unsubscribed shares in a rights offering at the subscription price.

Over-the-counter (OTC) market An informal network of brokers and dealers who negotiate sales of securities (not a formal exchange).

Par value The nominal or face value of stocks or bonds. For stock, it is a relatively unimportant value except for bookkeeping purposes.

Partnership Form of business organization in which two or more co-owners form a business. In a general partnership each partner is liable for the debts of the partnership. Limited partnership permits some partners to have limited liability.

Payback period rule An investment decision rule that states that all investment projects with payback periods equal to or less than a particular cutoff period are accepted, and all of those that pay off in more than the particular cutoff period are rejected. The payback period is the number of years required for a firm to recover its initial investment required by a project from the cash flow it generates.

Payments pattern Describes the lagged collection pattern of receivables (for instance the probability that a 72-day-old account will still be unpaid when it is 73 days old).

Payout ratio Proportion of net income paid out in cash dividends.

Pecking order in long-term financing Hierarchy of long-term financing strategies, in which using internally generated cash is at the top and issuing new equity is at the bottom.

Perfect markets Perfectly competitive financial markets.

Perfectly competitive financial markets Markets in which no trader has power to change the price of goods or services. Perfect markets are characterized by the following conditions: (1) Trading is costless, and access to the financial markets is free. (2) Information about borrowing and lending opportunities is freely available. (3) There are many traders, and no single trader can have a significant impact on market prices.

Performance shares Shares of stock given to managers on the basis of performance as measured by earnings per share and similar criteria—a control device used by shareholders to tie management to the self-interest of shareholders.

Perpetuity A constant stream of cash flows without end. A British consol is an example.

Perquisites Management amenities such as a big office, a company car, or expense-account meals. "Perks" are agency costs of equity, because managers of the firm are agents of the stockholders.

Pie model A model of a firm's debt-equity ratio. It graphically depicts slices of "pie" that represent the value of the firm in the capital markets.

Plug A variable that handles financial slack in the financial plan.

Poison pill Strategy by a takeover target company to make a stock less appealing to a company that wishes to acquire it.

Pooling of interests Accounting method of reporting acquisitions under which the balance sheets of the two companies are simply added together item by item.

Portfolio Combined holding of more than one stock, bond, real estate asset, or other asset by an investor.

Portfolio variance Weighted sum of the covariances and variances of the assets in a portfolio.

Positive covenant Part of the indenture or loan agreement that specifies an action that the company must abide by.

Positive float See **Float.**

Post Particular place on the floor of an exchange where transactions in stocks listed on the exchange occur.

Preemptive right The right to share proportionally in any new stock sold.

Preferred stock A type of stock whose holders are given certain priority over common stockholders in the payment of dividends. Usually the dividend rate is fixed at the time of issue. Preferred stockholders normally do not receive voting rights.

Premium If a bond is selling above its face value, it is said to sell at a premium.

Prepackaged bankruptcy A combination of private workout and legal bankruptcy. A private reorganization is prepackaged and then the firm files for formal bankruptcy.

Present value The value of a future cash steam discounted at the appropriate market interest rate.

Present value factor Factor used to calculate an estimate of the present value of an amount to be received in a future period.

Price takers Individuals who respond to rates and prices by acting as if they have no influence on them.

Price-to-earnings (P/E) ratio Current market price of common stock divided by current annual earnings per share.

Priced out Means the market has already incorporated information, such as a low dividend, into the price of a stock.

Primary market Where new issues of securities are offered to the public.

Principal The value of a bond that must be repaid at maturity. Also called the face value or par value.

Principle of diversification Highly diversified portfolios will have negligible unsystematic risk. In other words, unsystematic risks disappear in portfolios, and only systematic risks survive.

Private placement The sale of a bond or other security directly to a limited number of investors.

Private workout Financial restructuring agreement that does not involve formal, legal bankruptcy.

Pro forma statements Projected income statements, balance sheets, and sources-and-uses statements for future years.

Profit margin Profits divided by total operating revenue. The net profit margin (net income divided by total operating revenue) and the gross profit margin (earnings before interest and taxes divided by the total operating revenue) reflect the firm's ability to produce a good or service at a high or low cost.

Profitability index (PI) A method used to evaluate projects. It is the ratio of the present value of the future expected cash flows after initial investment divided by the amount of the initial investment.

Promissory note Written promise to pay.

Prospectus The legal document that must be given to every investor who contemplates purchasing registered securities in an offering. It describes the details of the company and the particular offering.

Protective covenants Parts of the indenture or loan agreement that limit certain actions a company takes during the term of the loan to protect the lender's interest.

Proxy A grant of authority by the shareholder to transfer his or her voting rights to someone else.

Proxy contest Attempt to gain control of a firm by soliciting a sufficient number of stockholder votes to replace the existing management.

Public issue Sale of securities to the public.

Purchase accounting Method of reporting acquisitions requiring that the assets of the acquired firm be reported at their fair market value on the books of the acquiring firm.

Purchase method A method of accounting for acquisitions in which the assets of the acquired firm are reported at their fair market value in the financial statements of the acquiring firm, allowing for the creation of goodwill.

Purchasing power parity (PPP) Idea that the exchange rate adjusts to keep purchasing power constant among currencies.

Pure discount bond Bonds that pay no coupons and only pay back face value at maturity. Also referred to as "bullets" and "zeros."

Put option The right to sell a specified number of shares of stock at a stated price on or before a specified time.

Put provision Gives holder of a floating-rate bond the right to redeem his or her note at par on the coupon payment date.

Put-call parity The value of a call equals the value of buying the stock plus buying the put plus borrowing at the risk-free rate.

Q ratio or Tobin's Q ratio Market value of firm's assets divided by replacement value of firm's assets.

Quick assets Current assets minus inventories.

Quick ratio Quick assets (current assets minus inventories) divided by total current liabilities. Used to measure short-term solvency of a firm.

R squared (R^2 Square of the correlation coefficient proportion of the variability explained by the linear model.

Random walk Theory that stock price changes from day to day are at random; the changes are independent of each other and have the same probability distribution.

Real cash flow A cash flow is expressed in real terms if the current, or date 0, purchasing power of the cash flow is given.

Real interest rate Interest rate expressed in terms of real goods; that is, the nominal interest rate minus the expected inflation rate.

Receivables turnover ratio Total operating revenues divided by average receivables. Used to measure how effectively a firm is managing its accounts receivable.

Red herring First document released by an underwriter of a new issue to prospective investors.

Refunding The process of replacing outstanding bonds, typically to issue new securities at a lower interest rate than those replaced.

Registration statement The registration that discloses all the pertinent information concerning the corporation that wants to make the offering. The statement is filed with the U.S. Securities and Exchange Commission.

Regular cash dividends Cash payments by firm to its shareholders, usually four times a year.

Regular underwriting The purchase of securities from the issuing company by an investment banker for resale to the public.

Regulation A The securities regulation that exempts small public offerings (those valued at less than $1.5 million) from most registration requirements.

Relative purchasing power parity (RPPP) Idea that the rate of change in the price level of commodities in one country relative to the price level in another determines the rate of change of the exchange rate between the two countries' currencies.

Reorganization Financial restructuring of a failed firm. Both the firm's asset structure and its financial structure are changed to reflect their true value, and claims are settled.

Replacement value Current cost of replacing the firm's assets.

Replacement-chain problem Idea that future replacement decisions must be taken into account in selecting among projects.

Repurchase agreement (repos) Short-term, often overnight, sales of government securities with an agreement to repurchase the securities at a slightly higher price.

Repurchase of stock Device to pay cash to firm's shareholders that provides more preferable tax treatment for shareholders than dividends. Treasury stock is the name given to previously issued stock that has been repurchased by the firm.

Residual dividend approach An approach that suggests that a firm pay dividends if and only if acceptable investment opportunities for those funds are currently unavailable.

Residual losses Lost wealth of the shareholders due to divergent behavior of the managers.

Residual value Usually refers to the value of a lessor's property at the time the lease expires.

Restrictive covenants Provisions that place constraints on the operations of borrowers, such as restrictions on working capital, fixed assets, future borrowing, and payment of dividend.

Retained earnings Earnings not paid out as dividends.

Retention ratio Retained earnings divided by net income.

Return Profit on capital investment or securities.

Return on assets (ROA) Income divided by average total assets.

Return on equity (ROE) Net income after interest and taxes divided by average common stockholders' equity.

Reverse split The procedure whereby the number of outstanding stock shares is reduced; for example, two outstanding shares are combined to create only one.

Rights offer An offering that gives a current shareholder the opportunity to maintain a proportionate interest in the company before the shares are offered to the public.

Risk averse A risk-averse investor will consider risky portfolios only if they provide compensation for risk via a risk premium.

Risk class A partition of the universal set of risk measures so that projects that are in the same risk class can be comparable.

Risk premium The excess return on the risky asset that is the difference between expected return on risky assets and the return on risk-free assets.

Round lot Common stock trading unit of 100 shares or multiples of 100 shares.

S&P 500 Standard & Poor's Composite Index.

SEC U.S. Securities and Exchange Commission.

SML Security market line.

SMP Security market plane.

Safe harbor lease A lease to transfer tax benefits of ownership (depreciation and debt tax shield) from the lessee, if the lessee could not use them, to a lessor that could.

Sale and lease-back An arrangement whereby a firm sells its existing assets to a financial company, which then leases them back to the firm. This is often done to generate cash.

Sales forecast A key input to the firm's financial planning process. External sales forecasts are based on historical experience, statistical analysis, and consideration of various macroeconomic factors; internal sales forecasts are obtained from internal sources.

Sales-type lease An arrangement whereby a firm leases its own equipment, such as IBM leasing its own computers, thereby competing with an independent leasing company.

Scale enhancing Describes a project that is in the same risk class as the whole firm.

Scenario analysis Analysis of the effect of different scenarios on the project, with each scenario involving a confluence of factors.

Seasoned new issue A new issue of stock after the company's securities have previously been issued. A seasoned new issue of common stock can be made by using a cash offer or a rights offer.

Secondary markets Already-existing securities are bought and sold on the exchanges or in the over-the-counter market.

Security market line (SML) A straight line that shows the equilibrium relationship between systematic risk and expected rates of return for individual securities. According to the SML, the excess return on a risky asset is equal to the excess return on the market portfolio multiplied by the beta coefficient.

Security market plane (SMP) A plane that shows the equilibrium relationship between expected return and the beta coefficient of more than one factor.

Semistrong-form efficiency Theory that the market is efficient with respect to all publicly available information.

Seniority The order of repayment. In the event of bankruptcy, senior debt must be repaid before subordinated debt receives any payment.

Sensitivity analysis Analysis of the effect on the project when there is some change in critical variables such as sales and costs.

Separation principle The principle that portfolio choice can be separated into two independent tasks: (1) determination of the optimal risky portfolio, which is a purely technical problem, and (2) the personal choice of the best mix of the risky portfolio and the risk-free asset.

Separation theorem The value of an investment to an individual is not dependent on consumption preferences. All investors will want to accept or reject the same investment projects by using the NPV rule, regardless of personal preference.

Serial correlation Correlation between the current return on a security and the return on the same security over a later period.

Serial covariance The covariance between a variable and the lagged value of the variable; the same as *autocovariance.*

Set-of-contracts viewpoint View of the corporation as a set of contracting relationships among individuals who have conflicting objectives, such as shareholders and managers. The corporation is a legal contrivance that serves as the nexus for the contracting relationships.

Share rights plan (SRP) Provisions allowing existing shareholders to purchase stock at some fixed price if an outside takeover bid occurs, designed to discourage hostile takeover attempts.

Shareholder Holder of equity shares. The terms *shareholders* and *stockholders* usually refer to owners of common stock in a corporation.

Shelf life Number of days it takes to get goods purchased and sold, or days in inventory.

Shelf registration An SEC procedure that allows a firm to file a master registration statement summarizing planned financing for a two-year period, and then file short statements when the firm wishes to sell any of the approved master statement securities during the period.

Shirking The tendency to do less work when the return is smaller. Owners may have more incentive to shirk if they issue equity as opposed to debt, because they retain less ownership interest in the company and therefore may receive a smaller return. Thus, shirking is considered an agency cost of equity.

Short hedge Protecting the value of an asset held by selling a futures contract.

Short run That period of time in which certain equipment, resources, and commitments of them are fixed.

Short sale Sale of a security that an investor doesn't own but has instead borrowed.

Short-run operating activities Events and decisions concerning the short-term finance of a firm, such as how much inventory to order and whether to offer cash terms or credit terms to customers.

Short-term debt An obligation having a maturity of one year or less from the date it was issued. Also called *unfunded debt.*

Short-term tax exempts Short-term securities issued by states, municipalities, local housing agencies, and urban renewal agencies.

Shortage costs Costs that fall with increases in the level of investment in current assets.

Side effects Effects of a proposed project on other parts of the firm.

Sight draft A commercial draft demanding immediate payment.

Signaling approach Approach to the determination of optimal capital structure asserting that insiders in a firm have information that the market does not; therefore the choice of capital structure by insiders can signal information to outsiders and change the value of the firm. This theory is also called the *asymmetric information approach.*

Simple interest Interest calculated by considering only the original principal amount.

Sinking fund An account managed by the bond trustee for the purpose of repaying the bonds.

Sole proprietorship A business owned by a single individual. The sole proprietorship pays no corporate income tax but has unlimited liability for business debts and obligations.

Spot exchange rate Exchange rate between two currencies for immediate delivery.

Spot interest rate Interest rate fixed today on a loan that is made today.

Spot trades Agreements today on the exchange rates, for settlement in two days.

Spread The gap between the interest rate a bank pays on deposits and the interest rate it charges on loans.

Spread Compensation to the underwriter, determined by the difference between the underwriter's buying price and offering price (underwriting).

Spread underwriting Difference between the underwriter's buying price and the offering price. The spread is a fee for the service of the underwriting syndicate.

Spreadsheet A computer program that organizes numerical data into rows and columns on a terminal screen, for calculating and making adjustments based on new data.

Stakeholders Both stockholders and bondholders.

Stand-alone principle Investment principle that states a firm should accept or reject a project by comparing it with securities in the same risk class.

Standard deviation The positive square root of the variance. This is the standard statistical measure of the spread of a sample.

Standardized normal distribution A normal distribution with an expected value of 0 and a standard deviation of 1.

Standby fee Amount paid to an underwriter who agrees to purchase any stock that is not subscribed to the public investor in a rights offering.

Standby underwriting An agreement whereby an underwriter agrees to purchase any stock that is not purchased by the public investor.

Standstill agreement Contract in which the bidding firm in a takeover attempt agrees to limit its holdings of another firm.

Stated annual interest rate The interest rate expressed as a percentage per annum, by which interest payment is determined.

Static theory of capital structure Theory that the firm's capital structure is determined by a tradeoff of the value of tax shields against the costs of bankruptcy.

Stock dividend Payment of a dividend in the form of stock rather than cash. A stock dividend comes from treasury stock, increasing the number of shares outstanding, and reduces the value of each share.

Stock split The increase in the number of outstanding shares of stock while making no change in shareholders' equity.

Stockholder Holder of equity shares in a firm. The terms *stockholders* and *shareholders* usually refer to owners of common stock.

Stockholders' books Set of books kept by firm management for its annual report that follows Canadian Institute of Chartered Accountants rules. The tax books follow the Revenue Canada rules.

Stockholders' equity The residual claims that stockholders have against a firm's assets, calculated by subtracting total liabilities from total assets; also called *net worth.*

Stockout Running out of inventory.

Straight voting A shareholder may cast all of his or her votes for each candidate for the board of directors.

Straight-line depreciation A method of depreciation whereby each year the firm depreciates a constant proportion of the initial investment less salvage value.

Striking price Price at which the put option or call option can be exercised. Also called the *exercise price.*

Strong-form efficiency Theory that the market is efficient with respect to all available information, public or private.

Subordinated debt Debt whose holders have a claim on the firm's assets only after senior debtholder's claims have been satisfied.

Subscription price Price that existing shareholders are allowed to pay for a share of stock in a rights offering.

Sum-of-the-year's-digits depreciation Method of accelerated depreciation.

Sunk cost A cost that has already occurred and cannot be removed. Because sunk costs are in the past, such costs should be ignored when deciding whether to accept or reject a project.

Super-majority amendment A defensive tactic that requires 80 percent of shareholders to approve a merger.

Surplus funds Cash flow available after payment of taxes in the project.

Sustainable growth rate The only growth rate possible with preset values for four variables: profit margin, payout ratio, debt-equity ratio, and asset utilization ratio, if the firm issues no new equity.

Swap rate The difference between the sale (purchase) price and the price to repurchase (resell) it in a swap.

Swaps Exchanges between two securities or currencies. One type of swap involves the sale (or purchase) of a foreign currency with a simultaneous agreement to repurchase (or sell) it.

Sweep account Account in which the bank takes all excess available funds at the close of each business day and invests them for the firm.

Syndicate A group of investment banking companies that agree to cooperate in a joint venture to underwrite an offering of securities for resale to the public.

Systematic Common to all businesses.

Systematic (market) risk Any risk that affects a large number of assets, each to a greater or lesser degree.

Systematic risk principle Only the systematic portion of risk matters in large, well-diversified portfolios. Thus, the expected returns must be related only to systematic risks.

T-bill Treasury bill.

T-period holding-period return The percentage return over the T-year period an investment lasts.

Takeover General term referring to transfer of control of a firm from one group of shareholders to another.

Taking delivery Refers to the buyer's actually assuming possession from the seller of the asset agreed upon in a forward contract.

Target cash balance Optimal amount of cash for a firm to hold, considering the trade-off between the opportunity costs of holding too much cash and the trading costs of holding too little.

Target firm A firm that is the object of a takeover by another firm.

Target payout ratio A firm's long-run dividend-to-earnings ratio. The firm's policy is to attempt to pay out a certain percentage of earnings, but it pays a stated dollar dividend and adjusts it to the target as increases in earnings occur.

Targeted repurchase The firm buys back its own stock from a potential bidder, usually at a substantial premium, to forestall a takeover attempt.

Tax books Set of books kept by firm management for Revenue Canada that follows Revenue Canada rules. The stockholders' books follow Canadian Institute of Chartered Accountants rules.

Tax-free acquisition An acquisition in which the selling shareholders are considered to have exchanged their old shares for new ones of equal value, and in which they have experienced no capital gains or losses.

Tax shield on CCA Portion of an investment that can be deducted from taxable income.

Taxable acquisition An acquisition in which shareholders of the acquired firm will realize capital gains or losses that will be taxed.

Taxable income Gross income less a set of deductions.

Technical analysis Research to identify mispriced securities that focuses on recurrent and predictable stock price patterns.

Technical insolvency Default on a legal obligation of the firm. For example, technical inventory occurs when a firm doesn't pay a bill.

Tender offer Public offer to buy shares of a target firm.

Term loan Direct business loan of, typically, one to five years.

Terms of the sale Conditions on which a firm proposes to sell its goods and services for cash or credit.

Time value of money Price or value put on time. Time value of money reflects the opportunity cost of investing at a risk-free rate. The certainty of having a given sum of money today is worth more than the certainty of having an equal sum at a later date because money can be put to profitable use during the intervening time.

Tobin's Q Market value of assets divided by replacement value of assets. A Tobin's Q ratio greater than 1 indicates the firm has done well with its investment decisions.

Tombstone An advertisement that announces a public offering of securities. It identifies the issuer, the type of security, the underwriters, and where additional information is available.

Total asset-turnover ratio Total operating revenue divided by average total assets. Used to measure how effectively a firm is managing its assets.

Total cash flow of the firm Total cash inflow minus total cash outflow.

Trade acceptance Written demand that has been accepted by a firm to pay a given sum of money at a future date.

Trade credit Credit granted to other firms.

Trading costs Costs of selling marketable securities and borrowing.

Trading range Price range between highest and lowest prices at which a security is traded.

Transactions motive A reason for holding cash that arises from normal disbursement and collection activities of the firm.

Treasury bill Short-term discount debt maturing in less than one year. T-bills are issued weekly by the federal government and are virtually risk free.

Treasury stock Shares of stock that have been issued and then repurchased by a firm.

Triangular arbitrage Striking offsetting deals among three markets simultaneously to obtain an arbitrage profit.

Trust receipt A device by which the borrower holds the inventory in "trust" for the lender.

Underpricing Issuing of securities below the fair market value.

Underwriter An investment firm that buys an issue of security from the firm and resells it to the investors.

Unfunded debt Short-term debt.

Unit benefit formula Method used to determine a participant's benefits in a defined benefit plan by multiplying years of service by the percentage of salary.

Unseasoned new issue Initial public offering (IPO).

Unsystematic What is specific to a firm.

Unsystematic risk See **Diversifiable** risk.

VA principle Value additivity principle.

Value additivity (VA) principle In an efficient market the value of the sum of two cash flows is the sum of the values of the individual cash flows.

Variable cost A cost that varies directly with volume and is zero when production is zero.

Variance of the probability distribution The expected value of squared deviation from the expected return.

Venture capital Early-stage financing of young companies seeking to grow rapidly.

Vertical acquisition Acquisition in which the acquired firm and the acquiring firm are at different steps in the production process.

WACC Weighted average cost of capital.

Waiting period Time during which the U.S. Securities and Exchange Commission or the Ontario Securities Commission studies a firm's registration statement. During this time the firm may distribute a preliminary prospectus.

Warrant Security that gives the holder the right—but not the obligation—to buy shares of common stock directly from a company at a fixed price for a given time period.

Wash Gains equal losses.

Weak-form efficiency Theory that the market is efficient with respect to historical price information.

Weighted average cost of capital (WACC) The average cost of capital on the firm's existing projects and activities. The weighted average cost of capital for the firm is calculated by weighting the cost of each source of funds by its proportion of the total market value of the firm. It is calculated on a before- and after-tax basis.

Weighted average maturity A measure of the level of interest-rate risk calculated by weighting cash flows by the time to receipt and multiplying by the fraction of total present value represented by the cash flow at that time.

White Knight A takeover defense in which the management seems to be a friendly bidder.

Winner's curse The average investor wins—that is, gets the desired allocation of a new issue—because those who knew better avoided the issue.

Wire transfer An electronic transfer of funds from one bank to another that eliminates the mailing and check-clearing times associated with other cash-transfer methods.

Yankee bonds Foreign bonds issued in the United States by foreign banks and corporations.

Yield to maturity The discount rate that equates the present value of interest payments and redemption value with the present price of the bond.

Zero-balance account (ZBA) A checking account in which a zero balance is maintained by transfers of funds from a master account in an amount only large enough to cover checks presented.

Zero coupon bonds Bonds that make no coupon payments and thus are initially priced at a deep discount.

INDEX